HANDBOOK OF
SOCIAL FUNCTIONING
IN SCHIZOPHRENIA

Related Titles of Interest

Treatment Resistance: A Guide for Practitioners
Salvatore Cullari
ISBN: 0-205-15572-3

Schizophrenia from a Neurocognitive Perspective: Probing the Impenetrable Darkness
Michael Foster Green
ISBN: 0-205-18477-4

The Clinician's Handbook: Integrated Diagnostics, Assessment, and Intervention in Adult and Adolescent Psychopathology, Fourth Edition
Robert G. Meyer and Sarah E. Deitsch
ISBN: 0-205-17181-8

Case Studies in Abnormal Behavior, Third Edition
Robert G. Meyer and Yvonne Hardaway Osborne
ISBN: 0-205-18755-2

Behavioral Family Therapy for Psychiatric Disorders
Kim T. Mueser and Shirley M. Glynn
ISBN: 0-205-16653-9

From Behavior Theory to Behavior Therapy
Joseph J. Plaud and Georg H. Eifert (Editors)
ISBN: 0-205-17477-9

For more information or to purchase a book, please call 1-800-278-3525.

HANDBOOK OF SOCIAL FUNCTIONING IN SCHIZOPHRENIA

Edited by

Kim T. Mueser

Department of Psychiatry, Dartmouth Medical School

Nicholas Tarrier

University of Manchester, England

Allyn and Bacon
Boston   London   Toronto   Sydney   Tokyo   Singapore

Series editor: Carla F. Daves
Series editorial assistant: Susan Hutchinson
Manufacturing buyer: Suzanne Lareau
Marketing manager: Joyce Nilsen
Advertising manager: Anne Morrison

Copyright © 1998 by Allyn & Bacon
A Viacom Company
Needham Heights, MA 02194

Internet: www.abacon.com
America Online: keyword: College Online

Library of Congress Cataloging-in-Publication Data

Handbook of social functioning in schizophrenia / edited by Kim T.
  Mueser, Nicholas Tarrier.
      p.   cm.
   Includes bibliographical references and index.
   ISBN 0-205-16444-7
    1. Schizophrenia—Social aspects.   I. Mueser, Kim Tornvall.
  II. Tarrier, Nicholas.
  616.89'82—dc21   97-27797
                           CIP

Printed in the United States of America

10 9 8 7 6 5 4 3 2 1   02 01 00 99 98

We dedicate this book to all the patients with schizophrenia and their families whose resolute courage in the face of hardship has been a vital source of our inspiration and commitment to improving the quality of their lives.

CONTENTS

PREFACE

This book explores social functioning in schizophrenia spectrum disorders. *Social functioning* or *social adjustment* are general terms used to refer to the ability of individuals to meet societally defined roles such as homemaker, worker, student, spouse, family member, or friend. In addition, individuals' satisfaction with their ability to meet these roles, their ability to care for themselves, and the extent of their leisure and recreational activities are often subsumed under the rubric of social functioning.

Social functioning is of critical importance to schizophrenia for at least four reasons: (1) impaired social functioning has long been recognized to be characteristic of schizophrenia; (2) problems in social functioning are often included among criteria for the diagnosis of schizophrenia; (3) social functioning is a potent predictor of outcome; and (4) social functioning is a primary target of many rehabilitation programs for schizophrenia. We briefly discuss each of these reasons below.

Since the earliest descriptions of schizophrenia, impairments in social functioning have been noted as central to the disorder. For example, Kraepelin (1919/1971) wrote:

> Very striking and profound damage occurs as a rule in the emotional life of our patients. The most important of these changes is their *emotional dulness.* The disorders of attention which have already been mentioned might be essentially connected with the loss of interest, the loss of inner sympathy, with the giving way of those emotional main-springs which move us to exert our mental powers, to accomplish our tasks, to follow trains of thought. The singular indifference of the patients towards their former emotional relations, the extinction of affection for relatives and friends, of satisfaction in their work and vocation, in recreation and pleasures, is not seldom the first and most striking symptom of the onset of disease. The patients have no real joy in life, "no human feelings"; to them "nothing matters, everything is the same"; they feel "no grief and

no joy," "their heart is not in what they say." (pp. 32–33).

> Another phenomenon of emotional dementia is the *disappearance of delicacy of feeling.* The patients have no longer any regard for their surroundings; they do not suit their behaviour to the situation in which they are, they conduct themselves in a free and easy way, laugh on serious occasions, are rude and impertinent towards their superiors, challenge them to duels, lost their deportment and personal dignity; they go about in untidy and dirty clothes, unwashed, unkempt, go with a lighted cigar into church, speak familiarly to strangers, decorate themselves with gay ribbons. The feeling of disgust and of shame is also gone. (p. 34)

Similarly, Bleuler (1911/1950) observed:

> Even in the less severe forms of the illness, indifference seems to be the external sign of their state; an indifference to everything—to friends and relations, to vocation or enjoyment, to duties or rights, to good fortune or to bad. (p. 40)

> Intercourse with other people is not disturbed merely by the schizophrenics' irritability and their peculiarities. In their autism they can comport themselves in a crowded work-room as if they were alone; everything which concerns the others does not exist for them. . . . They have turned their backs on the world, and seek to protect themselves from all influences coming from the outside. . . . Should schizophrenics have to have relations with others, they assume quite a peculiar form. Sometimes patients are obtrusive. . . . At other times they comport themselves very disdainfully, curtly, rudely. . . . Such are cases that are still capable of acting and having relations with people. However, when autism gets the upper hand, it creates a complete isolation around the sick psyche. (pp. 93–94)

Although Kraepelin and Bleuler described poor social functioning in schizophrenia as stemming from more basic impairments of the illness, such as the loss of emotions, attentional problems, and autism, modern diagnostic systems have emphasized the importance of social impairments to the diagnosis of the illness. For example, the DSM series (American Psychiatric Association, 1980, 1987, 1994) has required impairment in social functioning as a necessary criterion for the diagnosis of schizophrenia:

> *Social/occupational dysfunction:* For a significant portion of the time since the onset of the disturbance, one or more major areas of functioning such as work, interpersonal relations, or self-care are markedly below the level achieved prior to the onset (or when the onset is in childhood or adolescence, failure to achieve expected level of interpersonal, academic, or occupational achievement). (American Psychiatric Association, 1994, p. 285)

Thus, poor social functioning is currently recognized as a hallmark of schizophrenia, not just a common ancillary symptom.

Social impairments are not only a defining part of schizophrenia, but also predictive of the long-term outcome of the disorder. Over the past several decades, abundant evidence has accumulated demonstrating that premorbid social functioning (Bailer, Bräuer, & Rey, 1996; Zigler & Glick, 1986) and social adjustment after the onset of schizophrenia (Johnstone, MacMillan, Frith, Benn, & Crow, 1990; Jonsson & Nyman, 1991; Perlick, Stastny, Mattis, & Teresi, 1992; Rajkumar & Thara, 1989; Sullivan, Marder, Liberman, Donahoe, & Mintz, 1990) are strong predictors of both social and nonsocial outcomes. The prognostic value of poor social functioning in schizophrenia provides further evidence of its centrality to the disorder.

Finally, improving the social functioning of patients with schizophrenia has become a major priority of psychosocial treatment programs, such as social skills training, family intervention, and vocational rehabilitation. Several factors have contributed to the strong focus of these programs on social adjustment. First, the discovery in the 1950s of neuroleptic medications rendered many patients amenable to psychosocial treatments who previously were unable to participate in such interventions. Second, despite the beneficial effects of neuroleptics on lowering symptom severity and forestalling relapses, even under optimal conditions these medications usually have limited effects on social adjustment, indicating a need for interventions that target these areas of functioning. Third, the prognostic significance of social functioning in schizophrenia suggests that interventions that are successful in

improving social adjustment may have positive effects on the long-term outcome of the disorder.

Although impairments in social functioning are widely accepted to be of crucial importance to understanding and treating schizophrenia, few volumes have focused on summarizing the progress made in this area. This book is aimed at exploring social functioning in schizophrenia, including recent advances in the measurement of social adjustment and related concepts, developmental course, clinical and demographic correlates, social functioning in specific subgroups of patients, and the effects of psychosocial and pharmacological treatments on social adjustment. Because of the complexity of schizophrenia and the tremendous growth in our understanding of the illness, we have selected a wide range of topics related to social functioning for this book, with a particular emphasis on reviewing recent research in this area.

Schizophrenia is a severe mental illness that challenges patients, families, and clinicians alike. Impoverished social functioning is one of the core features of this disease that merits special attention. We believe this book will provide a useful synthesis of our current understanding of social functioning in schizophrenia. Considering the progress made in recent years in understanding and improving social functioning in schizophrenia, we are optimistic that continued work will further enhance the quality of lives of patients with this illness and their loved ones.

REFERENCES

American Psychiatric Association. (1980). *Diagnostic and statistical manual of mental disorders* (3rd ed.). Washington, DC: Author.

American Psychiatric Association. (1987). *Diagnostic and statistical manual of mental disorders* (3rd ed.–rev.). Washington, DC: Author.

American Psychiatric Association. (1994). *Diagnostic and statistical manual of mental disorders* (4th ed.). Washington, DC: Author.

Bailer, J., Bräuer, W., & Rey, E.-R. (1996). Premorbid adjustment as predictor of outcome in schizophrenia: Results of a prospective study. *Acta Psychiatric Scandinavia, 93,* 368–377.

Bleuler, E. (1950). *Dementia praecox or the group of schizophrenias* (J. Zinkin, Trans.). New York: International Universities Press. (Original work published in 1911)

Johnstone, E. C., MacMillan, J. F., Frith, C. D., Benn, D. K., & Crow, T. J. (1990). Further investigation of the predictors of outcome following first schizophrenic episodes. *British Journal of Psychiatry, 157,* 182–189.

Jonsson, H., & Nyman, A. K. (1991). Predicting long-term out-come in schizophrenia. *Acta Psychiatric Scandinavia, 83,* 342–346.

Kraepelin, E. (1971). *Dementia praecox and paraphrenia* (R. M. Barclay, Trans.) New York: Robert E. Kreiger. (Original work published in 1919)

Perlick, D., Stastny, P., Mattis, S., & Teresi, J. (1992). Contribu-tion of family, cognitive, and clinical dimensions to long-term outcome in schizophrenia. *Schizophrenia Research, 6,* 257–265.

Rajkumar, S., & Thara, R. (1989). Factors affecting relapse in schizophrenia. *Schizophrenia Research, 2,* 403–409.

Sullivan, G., Marder, S. R., Liberman, R. P., Donahoe, C. P., & Mintz, J. (1990). Social skills and relapse history in outpatient schizophrenics. *Psychiatry, 53,* 340–345.

Zigler, E., & Glick, M. (1986). *A developmental approach to adult psychopathology.* New York: Wiley.

ACKNOWLEDGMENTS

We are indebted to our many colleagues, support staff, patients, and relatives whose collaboration made this volume possible. We would also like to acknowledge the expertise, help, and encouragement of our former editor, Mylan Jaixen, our current editor, Carla Daves, and her assistant, Sue Hutchinson, for their assistance in completing this volume. Our appreciation goes to the following reviewers for their comments on the manuscript: Nina R. Schooler, University of Pittsburgh School of Medicine, and Paul Stuve, Fulton State Hospital, Fulton, MO. Finally, we would like to thank our families, Rachel, Jacob, Anna, Benjamin, Christine, Laura, Faye, and Alex.

ABOUT THE EDITORS
AND CONTRIBUTORS

ABOUT THE EDITORS

Kim T. Mueser, is a licensed clinical psychologist and a Professor in the Departments of Psychiatry and Community and Family Medicine at the Dartmouth Medical School in Hanover, New Hampshire. Dr. Mueser received his Ph.D. in clinical psychology from the University of Illinois at Chicago in 1984 and completed his psychology internship training at Camarillo State Hospital in California in 1985. He was on the faculty of the Psychiatry Department at the Medical College of Pennsylvania in Philadelphia from 1985 until 1994, where he was an Assistant Professor and then Associate Professor of Psychiatry. In 1994 Dr. Mueser moved to Dartmouth Medical School. Dr. Mueser's clinical and research interests include the assessment of social functioning and psychiatric rehabilitation of schizophrenia and other severe mental illnesses. He has lectured widely on the treatment of severe mental illness, both nationally and internationally, including topics such as family intervention, social skills training, and treatment of dual disorders (mental illness and substance abuse). He has published over 100 articles in journals and numerous book chapters, and he has co-authored several books, including *Social Skills Training for Psychiatric Patients* (with Robert P. Liberman and William T. DeRisi), *Behavioral Family Therapy for Psychiatric Disorders* (with Shirley M. Glynn), *Coping With Schizophrenia: A Guide for Families* (with Susan Gingerich), and *Social Skills Training for Schizophrenia: A step-by-step guide* (with Alan S. Bellack, Susan Gingerich, & Julie Agresta). Dr. Mueser is on the editorial board of several journals, including *Behavior Therapy* and *Behavior Modification*. Dr. Mueser is a member of several professional organizations, including the American Psychological Association, the Association for the Advancement of Behavior Therapy, and the American Association of Applied and Preventive Psychology.

Nicholas Tarrier is professor of clinical psychology in the Department of Clinical Psychology, School of Psychiatry and Behavioural Sciences, University of Manchester, UK. He received his Ph.D. from the Institute of Psychiatry, London, and carried out his professional training in clinical psychology at the University of Manchester. He also has a MSc in Experimental Psychology from Sussex University and a First Class Honours degree in Zoology from Nottingham University. He has been involved in research into schizophrenia since 1974 and has developed and evaluated a number of psychosocial and psychological interventions with this group of patients. He co-authored and co-edited several books including *Families of Schizophrenic Patients: A Cognitive Behavioural Intervention* (with C. Barrowclough) and over 100 journal papers and book chapters. He is a Fellow of the British Psychological Society and Honorary Fellow and a Past Chair of the British Association for Behavioural and Cognitive Psychotherapy.

ABOUT THE CONTRIBUTORS

Christine Barrowclough is Reader in Clinical Psychology, Department of Clinical Psychology, School of Psychiatry and Behavioural Sciences, University of Manchester, UK.

Deborah R. Becker is a rehabilitation specialist and a Research Associate at the New Hampshire–Dartmouth

Psychiatric Research Center, Department of Community and Family Medicine, Dartmouth Medical School. She has been the project director for several vocational research studies and provides consultation and training on vocational rehabilitation for people with severe mental illness. Becker was educated at Macalester College and Kent State University. She has worked in positions of direct service and administration in community support programs for people with severe mental illness.

Alan S. Bellack received his Ph.D. from the Pennsylvania State University in 1970. He currently is Professor of Psychiatry and Director of the Division of Psychology at the University of Maryland School of Medicine. He is a past president of the Association for Advancement of Behavior Therapy, and a Diplomate of the American Board of Behavior Therapy and the American Board of Professional Psychology. He was the first recipient of the American Psychological Foundation Gralnick Award for his lifetime research on psychosocial aspects of schizophrenia. Dr. Bellack is co-author or co-editor of 27 books and has published over 125 journal articles. He received an NIMH Merit Award and has had continuous funding from NIMH for over 20 years for his work on schizophrenia, depression, and social skills training. He is editor and founder of the journals *Behavior Modification* and *Clinical Psychology Review,* and he serves on the editorial boards of nine other journals.

Max Birchwood is Professor of Clinical Psychology at All Saints Hospital, University of Birmingham, Birmingham, UK.

Jack J. Blanchard earned his Ph.D. in clinical psychology from the State University of New York at Stony Brook in 1991. After completing an NIMH Post-doctoral Fellowship at the Medical College of Pennsylvania, he then joined the faculty at the Medical College, eventually serving as director of the Psychology Internship Program. Currently Dr. Blanchard is Assistant Professor of Psychology and Psychiatry at the University of New Mexico. His research interests involve schizophrenia with an emphasis on the interplay among the emotional, social, and neuropsychological deficits of this disorder.

Gary R. Bond is a Professor of Psychology and Director of the Doctoral Program in Clinical Rehabilitation Psychology at Indiana University Purdue University Indianapolis, where he has been since 1983. Bond received his doctorate in psychology from the University of Chicago in 1975. In 1979, he assumed a research position at Thresholds, a psychiatric rehabilitation agency in Chicago. Since that time he has been conducting evaluation studies of case management and employment programs for people with severe and persistent mental illness. His research includes studies identifying critical ingredients of effective rehabilitation programs. He is currently collaborating on several projects to evaluate supported employment strategies for persons with severe psychiatric disabilities. Other currently funded research includes a project to train mental health consumers to work as human service providers. His publications include over 90 journal articles and book chapters, and he has received 5 national research awards.

Mary F. Brunette is Assistant Professor of Psychiatry at Dartmouth Medical School, Research Trainee at the New Hampshire-Dartmouth Psychiatric Research Center, and Clinical Associate at Dartmouth Hitchcock Medical Center. She went to medical school at Oregon Health Sciences University and completed her psychiatry residency at Dartmouth Hitchcock Medical Center. Her research interests include women's mental health, co-occurring substance use disorder and severe mental illness, and HIV prevention in people with severe mental illness.

Linda Clare is Research Associate at the Applied Psychology Unit, Cambridge University, Cambridge, UK.

John H. Coverdale is an Associate Professor in the Department of Psychiatry and Behavioural Science, School of Medicine and Health Sciences, University of Auckland, New Zealand, and holds adjunct status at Baylor College of Medicine, Houston, Texas. He has published widely on topics including the family planning needs and STD risk behaviors of psychiatric patients, physician–patient sexual contact, psychiatric ethics, the management of mental illness during pregnancy, and medical education.

Patrick W. Corrigan is an Associate Professor of Psychiatry at the University of Chicago, where he directs the Center for Psychiatric Rehabilitation. The center is a clinical, research, and training program dedicated to persons with severe mental illness and their families. Dr. Corrigan is also principal investigator and director of the Illinois Staff Training Institute, a research and training program that investigates educational and organizational models of human resource development in mental health. He is a prolific researcher, having written four books and more than 100 articles. Recently, Dr. Corrigan was named editor of a new journal called *Psychiatric Rehabilitation Skills,* which describes psychosocial interventions that target disease and discrimination factors affecting the course of severe mental illness.

Tom K. J. Craig is Professor of Psychiatry at St. Thomas's Medical School, UMDS, London, UK.

Larry Davidson is an Assistant Professor in the Department of Psychiatry of the Yale University School of Medicine and Assistant Director for Program Development and Coordinator of psychology training for the Division of Outpatient Services of the Connecticut Mental Health Center in New Haven, Connecticut.

Robert E. Drake is a Professor of Psychiatry and Community and Family Medicine at Dartmouth Medical School. He also directs the New Hampshire–Dartmouth Psychiatric Research Center, a multidisciplinary mental health services research group that provides a public–academic liaison between state mental health authorities in New Hampshire and other states and researchers at Dartmouth Medical School, Dartmouth College, and other universities. Drake was educated at Princeton, Duke, and Harvard Universities. He spent 10 years as a practicing community psychiatrist. His major research interests concern the long-term course of severe mental illness, co-occurring severe mental illness and substance use disorder, and vocational rehabilitation for people with severe mental illness.

Amerigo Farina is Professor Emeritus in the Department of Psychology at the University of Connecticut. His teaching and research have focused on the role of interpersonal factors in psychopathology. He has studied how society both responds to and affects mental disorders. The negative impact of society's stigmatization of those who have suffered a mental problem has been of particular interest to him.

Lorraine S. Garratt is a Research Associate in the Department of Psychiatry of the Western Psychiatric Institute and Clinic and the University of Pittsburgh School of Medicine. After graduating with a B.A. in Psychology from Princeton University in 1993, she earned a master's degree in biostatistics from the School of Public Health at the University of Pittsburgh. Ms. Garratt's research interests include gender differences in normal and psychiatric populations, and she has contributed to research on gender differences in symptomatology, social functioning, and cognition in schizophrenia.

Shirley M. Glynn received her Ph.D. in clinical/social psychology from the University of Illinois at Chicago in 1985. She is currently a Clinical Research Psychologist at the West Los Angeles VA Medical Center and an Assistant Research Psychologist in the Department of Psychiatry and Biobehavioral Sciences at UCLA. Her professional work has emphasized designing and evaluating psychosocial interventions for serious psychiatric illnesses, including schizophrenia and chronic PTSD, in randomized controlled clinical trials.

Michael F. Green is professor in residence at the Department of Psychiatry and Biobehavioral Sciences, UCLA-Neuropsychiatric Institute, Los Angeles, California.

Henry Grunebaum is a Clinical Professor of Psychiatry at the Harvard Medical School and Director of the Family Division at the Cambridge Hospital, Cambridge, Massachusetts. He as had a long-standing interest in the problems of psychotic mothers and the development of their children, and initiated the first family planning services for mental patients in the United States. He is the author of numerous articles, and his books, co-authored and edited, deal with the subjects of mentally ill mothers and their children, family and couples therapy, community psychiatry, and the relationship among mothers, their daughters, and their own mothers.

Gretchen L. Haas is an Associate Professor of Psychiatry and Director of the Family and Psychosocial Studies Program at the University of Pittsburgh School of Medicine. Dr. Haas received her B.A. in psychology from Cornell University and her doctorate degree in clinical psychology from Wayne State University in Detroit, Michigan. She was awarded funding by the National Institute of Mental Health (NIMH) to conduct a longitudinal study of sex differences in first-episode and chronic schizophrenia. Her pioneering work in this area focuses on the identification of sex differences in clinical, psychosocial, and neurocognitive functioning in schizophrenia. Since moving to the University of Pittsburgh, where she joined the faculty of the Department of Psychiatry and the Center for Neurosciences of Mental Disorders—Schizophrenia, Dr. Haas has pursued investigations of the premorbid phase of first-episode schizophrenia, including examination of psychosocial and neurocognitive factors related to sex differences in age at onset of schizophrenia.

Karl E. Haglund is a medical student Research Fellow and third-year medical student at the Yale University School of Medicine in New Haven, Connecticut.

Courtenay Harding is an Associate Professor of Psychiatry and the Associate Director of the Programs for Public Psychiatry at the University of Colorado School of Medicine. She is also the Director of the Mental Health Program at the Western Interstate Commission for Higher Education, which serves the 15 western states for public policy, research/evaluation, and workforce training. Her research has included two three-decade studies of schizophrenia and other psychotic disorders and the longest study of deinstitutionalized patients in the United States.

Jonathan S. E. Hellewell was Lecturer is Psychiatry, University of Manchester, UK, and is now Medical Advisor with Zeneca Pharmaceuticals, UK.

Peter Huxley is Professor of Psychiatric Social Work, School of Psychiatry and Behavioural Sciences, University of Manchester, UK.

Eve C. Johnstone is Professor of Psychiatry, University of Edinburgh, UK.

Andrew B. Keller is the Assistant Deputy Director of MHCD, the Public Mental Health Authority for Denver, Colorado, and a Senior Fellow in public psychology at the University of Colorado Health Sciences Center. His management duties and research interests center on policy considerations related to capitation and service system reforms, as well as service system design and delivery for adults and children with serious mental illnesses and emotional disorders. His clinical interests focus on traumatized children and their families.

Robert S. Kern is an Assistant Professor in the Department of Psychiatry and Biobehavioral Sciences, UCLA-Neuropsychiatric Institute, Los Angeles, California.

Alex Kopelowicz is an Assistant Professor of Psychiatry at the UCLA School of Medicine and Medical Director of the San Fernando Mental Health Center, a community mental health center operated by the Los Angeles County Department of Psychiatry. Dr. Kopelowicz received his undergraduate degree from Haverford College in 1984 and his medical degree from the University of Medicine and Dentistry in New Jersey in 1988. Dr. Kopelowicz, who is bilingual and bicultural, has written a number of articles and book chapters on biobehavioral treatment and psychiatric rehabilitation techniques and is a frequent lecturer on the local, state, national, and international levels.

Anthony F. Lehman is a Professor of Psychiatry and Director of the Center for Mental Health Services Research at the University of Maryland. His clinical, teaching, and research activities have focused on serving persons with severe and persistent mental illnesses. Much of his research has examined outcomes, in particular assessing quality of life. He has also studied the effects of substance use disorders among persons with mental illnesses on diagnosis and outcomes. In addition to writing numerous scientific articles, Dr. Lehman is co-author of *Work-*

ing with Families of the Mentally Ill (with K. F. Berheim) and *Double Jeopardy: Chronic Mental Illness and Substance Use Disorders* (with Anthony F. Lehman & Lisa B. Dixon). Currently he is principal investigator for the Schizophrenia Patient Outcomes Research Team, funded by the Agency for Health Care Policy and Research and the National Institute of Mental Health. He is also principal investigator on the Maryland Employment Demonstration Project for Persons with Psychiatric Disabilities, funded by the Center for Mental Health Services, and co-principal investigator on the NIMH-funded Center for Research on Services for Severe Mental Illnesses and the Maryland Medicaid Patterns of Care and Outcomes Study, also funded by NIMH. Dr. Lehman received the American Psychiatric Association's Senior Award for Research Development for Mental Health Services in 1994. He has been cited by the National Alliance for the Mentally Ill as an Exemplary Psychiatrist and has been named in *Best Doctors in America* for the past three years.

Robert P. Liberman is a Professor of Psychiatry at the UCLA School of Medicine and Director of the UCLA Clinical Research Center for Schizophrenia and Psychiatric Rehabilitation. Dr. Liberman is one of the pioneers in the field of psychiatric rehabilitation, having started his work in the early 1970s at the Camarillo State Hospital in California. Dr. Liberman is the author of numerous articles, book chapters, and books in the areas of psychiatric rehabilitation, social skills training, and behavior therapy. His Social and Independent Living Skills modules, a training package designed to teach seriously mentally ill individuals how to effectively live with their illness, has been translated into a dozen languages.

Massimo Moscarelli is Consultant Psychiatrist, Association for Research into Costs and Assessments in Psychiatry, via Daniele Crespi 7, 20123 Milan, Italy.

Craig S. Neumann is an Assistant Professor of Psychology at the University of North Texas in Denton, Texas. He received his Ph.D. in clinical psychology from the University of Kansas in 1994. His research interests include the origins of neuropsychological deficits and the determinants of psychopathology.

Catherine Panzarella earned her Ph.D. in clinical psychology from Temple University in 1990. She is currently an Assistant Professor in the Department of Clinical and Health Psychology at Allegheny University of the Health Sciences in Philadelphia, Pennsylvania. Her current research interests include the contribution of interpersonal factors to the development and maintenance of psychopathology.

David L. Penn is Assistant Professor of Psychology at Louisiana State University. His primary research interests are in the investigation of social–cognitive processes in schizophrenia. Dr. Penn also has interest in the variables that contribute to stigmatization of individuals with schizophrenia, with an eye toward developing strategies to combat negative attitudes toward these individuals.

J. Meg Racenstein is an advanced doctoral student in clinical psychology at the Illinois Institute of Technology, Institute of Psychology. Her research involves studies of individuals with schizophrenia, substance abuse, dual diagnosis, and treatment efficacy. Clinical interests include chronic mental illness and family intervention.

Eugenia T. Randolph is an Assistant Research Sociologist in the Department of Psychiatry and Behavioral Sciences at UCLA and Research Sociologist at the West Los Angeles Veterans Administration Medical Center. Her primary research interests are in schizophrenia and post-traumatic stress disorder (PTSD). Her current research focuses on testing the efficacy of individual and family treatment modalities for PTSD and the influence of family factors in chronic psychiatric disorders.

Robert Sandler qualified in medicine in Cape Town in 1976, obtained postgraduate qualifications in psychiatry and worked as a specialist psychiatrist in South Africa before obtaining a Nuffield Postgraduate Fellowship in 1986. He held this in the Department of Pharmacology in the University of Oxford under the supervision of Professor David Smith. He obtained his D Phil from the University of Oxford in 1990. He thereafter resumed work as a psychiatrist requiring to retrain and obtain the MRC Psych in order to practice in the United Kingdom. He worked as a lecturer in psychiatry at the University of Edinburgh 1992–1996 and is currently acting as consultant psychiatrist at the Argyll and Bute Hospital, Lochgilphead, Scotland.

Mark Schade is Implementation Coordinator and Program Director of the Social Learning Program at Austin State Hospital, Austin, Texas. He has co-authored several articles and book chapters on skills training and psychosocial rehabilitation with schizophrenic patients.

Jack E. Scott is a Research Assistant Professor in the Department of Psychiatry at the University of Maryland at Baltimore. His research interests include recovery processes in individuals with severe mental illnesses and co-occurring substance use disorders, quality of life, and mental health services for persons with HIV/AIDS. For the past five years, Dr. Scott has served as project manager and co-investigator on the Schizophrenia Patient Outcomes Research Team (PORT) Project, a five-year project jointly funded by the Agency for Health Care Policy and Research and the National Institute of Mental Health.

Geoff Shepard is Director of Research, The Sainsbury Centre for Mental Health, London, UK.

David Stayner is a Postdoctoral Associate in the Department of Psychiatry of the Yale University School of Medicine and project director for the Partnership Project, a peer support program for individuals with psychiatric disabilities, of the Consultation Center of the Connecticut Mental Health Center in New Haven, Connecticut.

Elaine F. Walker is the Samuel Candler Dobbs Professor of Psychology at Emory University in Atlanta, Georgia. She received her Ph.D. from the University of Missouri in 1979. Her primary area of research interest is psychopathology, particularly the neurodevelopmental origins of schizophrenia.

Jane F. Whittaker is Clinical Tutor in Child and Adolescent Psychiatry, School of Psychiatry and Behavioural Sciences, University of Manchester, UK.

Til Wykes is Reader in Clinical Psychology, Institute of Psychiatry, London, UK.

CHAPTER 1

SOCIAL FUNCTIONING IN THE COMMUNITY

Jack E. Scott
Anthony F. Lehman

Disturbances in functional status are a prominent aspect of schizophrenia and a major contributor to the poor quality of life of many persons with this disorder. Social withdrawal and an inability to fulfill social roles are heightened during acute phases of illness but typically persist after acute symptoms abate (Bellack, Morrison, Mueser, Wade, & Sayers, 1990). Moreover, research indicates that impaired functional status constitutes a dimension of outcomes relatively independent of the defining positive and negative symptoms of schizophrenia (Strauss, Kokes, Klorman, & Sacksteder, 1977; Peralta, Cuesta, & de Leon, 1994).

The concept of functional status is complex and encompasses several dimensions. These range from basic brain neurocognitive functions (such as memory and the ability to make abstract associations) to basic activities of daily living (such as bathing and grooming) to more complex social behaviors (such as work, parenting, and social affiliation in everyday life). This chapter focuses on this last dimension, so-called social functioning. Social functioning is related to more basic brain functions and activities of daily living as well as other psychological dimensions (such as depression) and environmental conditions (such as the job or housing markets). Also, a distinction is commonly made between functional status and handicap. The former refers to lost functions within the individual, whereas the latter refers to a loss of participation in usual social roles and activities that results from the interaction of the individual who has an impairment with an environment that may or may not accommodate for that impairment. Whether a functional impairment results in a social handicap depends heavily on the environment in which a person lives. As will be seen in this review of measures of social functioning, these terms are often blurred in their usage so that measures of social function frequently include measures of basic daily living activities and do not distinguish between functional impairments and social handicaps.

The central importance of social functioning in schizophrenia and other severe mental illnesses has fueled efforts to develop rehabilitation interventions to help persons recover or achieve fuller functioning in the community. Interest in this aspect of the illness has also been fueled by recent advances in the pharmacotherapy of schizophrenia. Conventional antipsychotic medications have helped many patients move from the hospital to the community, but generally have been disappointing in their capacity to otherwise alter the functional impairments due to schizophrenia (Dixon, Lehman, & Levine, 1995). The advent of newer antipsychotic agents (e.g., clozapine, olanzapine, sertindole, quetapine, and ziprazidone) has been accompanied by new claims and hopes that these innovations will have a greater impact on functional impairments. Whether this is the case remains to be seen. The need to assess impaired social functioning and the variety of therapeutic efforts currently available or under development to improve functioning require good methods for assessing and monitoring social functioning.

Between 1975 and 1996, at least 16 literature reviews and chapters have been published that have described and compared measures for the assessment of social functioning in psychiatric patients (including the chronically mentally ill). These reviews have discussed over 65 instruments (although many of these are not well suited for use with persons with severe and persistent mental illnesses). These reviews show that several instruments have been used repeatedly in research on individuals with severe and persistent mental illnesses and have been reviewed so frequently that they are acknowledged as standards in the field. Among these we would include the Katz Adjustment Scale (Katz & Lyerly, 1963); the Personal Adjustment and Roles Scale (PARS) (Ellsworth, Foster, Childers, Arthur, & Kroeker, 1968); the Social Adjustment Scale-II (Schooler, Hogarty, & Weissman, 1979); the Social Behavior Assessment Schedule (Platt, Weyman, Hirsch, & Hewett 1980); the Standardized Interview to Assess Social Maladjustment (SIASM) (Clare & Cairns, 1978); and the Structured and Scaled Interview to Assess Maladjustment (SSIAM) (Gurland, Yorkston, Stone, Frank, & Fleiss 1972). There are established data on the reliability and validity of each of these instruments.

During the past 15 years, however, several instruments have emerged that incorporate newer approaches to assessment. These newer instruments have not been widely disseminated in the research and clinical practitioner communities, yet they may deserve further consideration and exploration in future work. This chapter reviews 16 instruments published since 1981, and discusses several issues concerning the assessment of social functioning in community settings.

METHODOLOGY

This chapter covers instruments published in the literature between 1981 and 1996. To identify previous literature reviews and research publications that described social functioning measures applicable to persons with schizophrenia, we conducted computerized searches of the PSYCHLIT and MEDLINE bibliographic databases between 1981 and 1996. In addition to this bibliographic search, we reviewed the bibliographies of the following literature reviews: Weissman (1975); Platt (1981); Weissman, Sholomskas, and John (1981); Katschnig (1983); Kane, Kane, and Arnold (1985); Platt (1986); Wallace (1986); Green and Gracely (1987); Linn (1988); Wing (1989); Wykes and Hurry (1991); Cook (1992); Goldman, Skodol, and Lave (1992); Vaccaro, Pitts, & Wallace (1992); Phelan, Wykes, and Goldman (1994); and de Jong, van der Lubbe, and Wiersma (1996).

Using these sources, we identified papers and chapters that described various social functioning measures and tests of their psychometric properties. We established the following six criteria for inclusion of a social functioning measure in this review: the instrument was designed for use with patients with psychotic disorders; it can be used in community-based settings; data are available on the instrument's reliability *and* validity; the instrument assesses multiple domains of social functioning; it has not been reviewed extensively in the previous reviews listed above; and it has been developed since the early 1980s. The application of these criteria resulted in the final set of 16 measures.

These 16 measures include the Community Competence Scale; the Role Activity Performance Scale; the Social Dysfunction Index; the Medical Research Council's Needs for Care Assessment; the Cardinal Needs Schedule; the Camberwell Assessment of Needs; the Independent Living Skills Survey; the Missouri Level of Care; Needs and Resources Assessment Interview; the Social Functioning Scale; the Multnomah Community Ability Scale; CPC Level of Functioning Assessment, The Disability Rating Form; St. Louis Inventory of Community Living Skills; the Assessment of Interpersonal Problem-Solving Skills; and the Social Problem-Solving Assessment Battery. Key attributes of these measures are summarized in Table 1.1. The titles of some of these measures refer to other constructs, in particular, "needs" and "level of care." They are included here because their contents in fact focus on social functioning in order to define needs for services. As such they are potentially useful measures of social

Table 1.1. Content Areas Covered by Measures of Social Functioning

MEASURE	TYPE	LENGTH	AREAS OF FUNCTIONAL STATUS
Assessment of Interpersonal Problem-Solving Skills	Role play	30–60 min	Problem identification, goal description, processing, content of role play, performance, overall score
Camberwell Assessment of Needs	Semistructured interview	25 min	Accommodations, food, household skills, self-care, occupation, physical health, psychotic symptoms, knowledge about condition and treatment, psychological distress, safety to self, safety to others, alcohol, drugs, company of others, intimate relationships, sexual expression, child care, basic education, use of telephone, transport, money, welfare benefits
Cardinal Needs Schedule	Semistructured interview	60 min	Psychotic symptoms, underactivity, side-effects, dangerous or destructive behavior, organic symptoms, physical illness, neurotic symptoms, socially embarrassing behavior, domestic skills, money and own affairs, transportation and amenities, education, occupation, hygiene, dressing
Community Competence Scale	Semistructured interview	60–90 min	Judgment, emergencies and acquiring money, compensation for incapacities, money management, communication, care of medical needs, adequate memory, satisfactory living arrangements, proper diet, mobility, sensation, motivation, personal hygiene, household maintenance, use of transportation, verbal–math skills, social adjustment, dangerous behavior
Community Psychiatric Clinic Level of Functioning Assessment	Rating form	10–20 min	Self-care, vision and hearing, mobility and chronic medical illness, community living, interpersonal relations, dangerous behavior, mood disturbance, psychotic symptoms, substance abuse
Disability Rating Form	Rating form	5–10 min	Activities of daily living, social functioning, concentration and task performance, adaptation to change, impulse control
Independent Living Skills Survey	Self-administered questionnaire	20–30 min	Eating habits, grooming skills, domestic activities, food preparation skills, health maintenance skills, economic skills, use of public transportation, leisure activities, job-seeking skills
Missouri Level of Care	Self-administered questionnaire	Not stated	Community skills, self-care skills, nuisance behaviors, sociability, skilled nursing care needs, proclivity for violent behavior, control of anger
Multnomah Community Ability Scale	Rating form	5–10 min	Physical health, intellectual functioning, thought processes, mood abnormality, response to stress and anxiety, ability to manage money, independence in daily living, acceptance of illness, social acceptability, social interest, social effectiveness, social network, meaningful activity, medication compliance, cooperation with treatment providers, alcohol/drug abuse, impulse control

Continued

3

Table 1.1. *Continued*

MEASURE	TYPE	LENGTH	AREAS OF FUNCTIONAL STATUS
Medical Research Council's Needs for Care Assessment	Semistructured interview	3–5 hours	Positive psychotic symptoms, underactivity, side effects from medications, neurotic symptoms, organic brain disorder, physical disorder, violence to self or others, embarrassing behavior, distress, personal cleanliness, household shopping, cooking or buying meals, household chores, use of public transportation, use of public amenities, basic literacy and arithmetic skills, occupational skills, social interaction skills, management of money, management of household affairs
Needs and Resources Assessment Interview	Self-administered questionnaire	Not stated	Housing, physical health, teeth, mental health, income and finances, education, job status, friends, family, leisure time, spiritual life, legal problems, drug-related problems
Role Activity Performance Scale	Semistructured interview	60–90 min	Work/work equivalent, education, home management, family of origin and extended family relationships, mate relationship, parenting, social relationships, leisure activities, self-management, health care, hygiene and appearance, rehabilitation
Social Dysfunction Index	Semistructured interview	30–40 min	Public self-presentation, independent living, occupational functioning, family relationships, important relations with others outside family of origin, leisure and recreational activities, health maintenance, communications, insight and expectations
Social Functioning Scale	Self-administered questionnaire	Not stated	Social engagement/withdrawal, interpersonal behavior, prosocial behavior, recreation, independence– competence, independence–performance, employment/occupation
Social Problem-Solving Assessment Battery	Role play	3–5 hours	Role-Play Test, Response Generation Test, Response Evaluation Test
St. Louis Inventory of Community Living Skills	Rating form	10–15 min	Personal hygiene, grooming, dress skills, self-care, communications, safety, time management, money management, leisure activities, clothing maintenance, meal preparation, sexuality, use of resources, problem solving, health practices, physical impairments

4

functioning with the more explicit purpose of defining needs.

RESULTS

The 16 measures can be classified into four broad categories: interviews; self-administered questionnaires; rating forms; and role-play tests.

Interviews

Six interview-based measures of social functioning were found. These instruments include three social functioning measures (the Community Competence Scale, the Role Activity Performance Scale, and the Social Dysfunction Index) and three needs assessment protocols, which are largely interview-based (the Medical Research Council's Needs for Care Assessment, the Cardinal Needs Schedule, and the Camberwell Assessment of Needs).

Community Competence Scale

Description of Instrument. The Community Competence Scale (CCS) (Searight, Oliver, & Grisso, 1983) was originally developed for assessment of the personal and social competence of the elderly. It was revised subsequently for use with the deinstitutionalized mentally ill. The CCS is a 124-item interview that includes 18 subscales: Judgment, Emergencies and Acquiring Money, Compensate for Incapacities, Manage Money, Communication, Care of Medical Needs, Adequate Memory, Satisfactory Living Arrangements, Proper Diet, Mobility, Sensation, Motivation, Personal Hygiene, Maintain Household, Utilize Transportation, Verbal–Math Skills, Social Adjustment, and Dangerousness. The number of items within each subscale varies, ranging from 4 for Sensation to 20 for Communication. There are two types of items. Most (75) items require the subject to actually perform a task or provide factual information and are scored 0–1. The remaining 49 items require the subject to provide a response requiring judgment or reasoning; these are scored 0, 1, or 2 depending on the quality of the response. Some items require apparatus such as a telephone, blank checks and money orders, a telephone book, an envelope, and play money. There are scoring guidelines. The instrument was designed for use as a preplacement community placement decision-making tool. The assessment is conducted by a trained interviewer and requires approximately 60 to 90 minutes to administer.

A brief version of the CCS is mentioned in Searight et al. (1983) and described more completely in Oliver and Searight (1988), Oliver, Dripps, and Grisson (1988), and Searight and Goldberg (1991). This 50-item version consists of 5 subscales: Communication, Verbal–Math Skills, Proper Diet, Emergencies, and Utilize Transportation. The brief version requires 20 to 40 minutes to administer. A 42-item scale (the Community Placement Scale) derived from the CCS with slightly modified content is described by Oliver et al. (1988).

Reliability. The initial reliability study (Searight et al. 1983) in psychiatric patients included a sample of 27 subjects recruited from board-and-care homes (n = 15) and apartment residents (n = 12). Eleven of these subjects were tested again after a one-week interval. The stability coefficient for the boarding home subjects was .94 and for the apartment residents was .98. Overall, test–retest was .94. Only two subscales exhibited coefficients less than .60: Proper Diet and Sensation. Cronbach's alpha was .97. Although the authors note the limitations of a small sample of 27 to establish reliability, no subsequent data on reliability among psychiatric patients are presented.

Validity. Several types of validity studies have been reported. Searight et al. (1983) reported an analysis of discriminant validity (classifying subjects as boarding home residents versus apartment residents). Searight, Oliver, and Grisso (1986) compared CCS scores with the Social Competence Scale (SCS) and hospitalization data (criterion validity) for 52 subjects residing in urban boarding homes, rural boarding homes, and apartments. The CCS and the SCS were moderately correlated, and the CCS score and duration of hospitalization prior to community placement were significantly and negatively correlated. CCS scores again discriminated successfully between apartment residents and boarding home residents (78.9% classification with age and diagnosis in discriminant function). CCS scores also significantly differentiated subjects by diagnosis. Patients with affective disorders and personality disorders scored significantly higher than patients with schizophrenia, who scored significantly higher than patients with mental retardation or organic impairment. CCS scores did not differ significantly by gender, differed marginally by race, and correlated significantly and negatively with age.

Role Activity Performance Scale

Description of Instrument. The Role Activity Performance Scale (RAPS) (Good-Ellis, Fine, Spencer, & DeVittis, 1987) is a semistructured interview originally developed for use in a study of inpatient family intervention for patients with schizophrenia where it was used to assess social functioning during the 18 months preceding admission. However, the instrument can also be used in an outpatient setting. The RAPS is a rating instrument and is designed to be administered by a trained occupational therapist. It measures functional skills in 12 areas: work/work equivalent, education, home management, family of origin and extended family relationships, mate relationship, parenting, social relationships, leisure activities, self-management, health care, hygiene and appearance, and rehabilitation treatment settings. Each area consists of 8 to 16 questions. The interviewer completes a rating scale in each of the functional areas. Ratings can range from 1 to 6 and an operational definition is provided for each of the points on the scale. If the subject's functioning falls between points, this can be indicated by use of a plus or minus sign. Within each area, interview questions first elicit background information about the place of the role in the respondent's life and long-term functioning history; the role environment and actual responsibilities during the time period under study; difficulties in functioning and changes in functioning throughout the time period; how the subject copes with and adapts to difficulties; and the subject's and others' assessments of how the subject performed in the role. The assessment integrates data from several sources, including the interview with the subject, information from significant others, and information from the medical record and the different members of the clinical team. The full interview requires approximately 60 to 90 minutes to administer.

An important feature of this instrument is that functioning is broken out by specific time segments during which performance was consistent (e.g., by month) so that changes in different domains can be plotted over time. Segments can be combined in a weighted average to produce an overall performance rating for each role over the entire period. In addition, the duration of the total time period assessed can be set to whatever length is needed by the specific research or clinical application.

The rating system provides an overall score as well as a summary of the average score within each area, the best and worst functioning level within each area, and the number of changes in functioning within each area occurring over the study period. A primary role score can be derived based on work, education, and home management.

Reliability. Interrater reliability was tested across two pairs of raters for 30 subjects; intraclass correlation coefficients across all subscales were greater than .82, and the primary role score and weighted and unweighted total scores were .98.

Validity. Validity was tested in three ways: review of the instrument by experts in occupational therapy (OT); tests of discrimination between a sample of schizophrenic patients and a sample of patients with major affective disorders; comparison with other standardized measures of social functioning (Katz, SAS-II, GAS, DSM-III Axis V, and Levels of Functioning Scale). The RAPS did differentiate between the two patient groups and correlated significantly with appropriate subscales from the indicated tests.

Social Dysfunction Index

Description of Instrument. The Social Dysfunction Index (SDI) (Munroe-Blum, Collins, McCleary, & Nuttall, 1996) is a semistructured interview developed for clinical assessment and planning and research studies on social functioning and therapeutic response in evaluations of psychosocial interventions and drug treatment. The interview examines dysfunction during the past 30 days in nine areas: public self (behavior, appearance, and social presentation); independent living; occupational functioning; family relationships; important relationships with others outside the family of origin; community, leisure, and recreational activities; health maintenance activities; communications; and insight and expectations (a broad measure of locus of control and learned helplessness). Within each domain, several areas of social functioning are examined. The interview protocol contains a number of probes related to these areas. Information from the interview is used in completing a set of 27 items (three items for each of the nine domains). Within each domain, the first item is a rating of the degree of dysfunction within the past month (ranging from 0 to 3). The second item is the number of specific areas of dysfunction within the domain (scored on a scale from 0 to 3). There are specific anchors for completing the ratings on these first two items. The third item within each component is a rating of satisfaction with the patient's functioning (scored 0 or 1). Overall dysfunction is calculated as a percentage of total possible score for the 27 items. Separate scores for each domain are calculated from the first two items within the domain. A total satisfaction score can be calculated by summing the nine domain-specific satisfaction items and dividing by nine. The interview can be conducted with patients, relatives, or mental health care providers, and requires an average of 40 minutes to complete.

Reliability. Data on the internal consistency of the SDI are provided from a sample of 113 subjects (Munroe-Blum et al., 1996); the mean interitem correlation was reported as −.13 and ranged from −.23 to .94. Coefficient alpha of .80 was obtained for this sample. To assess interrater reliability, four raters completed the SDI for 16 subjects. An intraclass correlation coefficient of .96 was obtained for the SDI.

Validity. Several small-scale validity studies have been completed by the authors with this measure (Munroe-Blum et al., 1996). A principal components factor analysis (with oblique rotation) was conducted from the responses of 113 patients. Nine factors accounting for 72% of the variance were extracted. Seven of these factors corresponded to unique SDI domains. Family relationships, occupational functioning, health maintenance, independent living, and insight/expectations items emerged as unique factors, whereas the other important relationships and community/leisure/recreation items loaded together and the public presentation of self and communications items loaded together. Two final factors reflected satisfaction with various domains. Several construct validity analyses were performed as well. These showed that patients who lived in independent living arrangements exhibited less social dysfunction than those living in boarding homes, patients who were employed exhibited less dysfunction than those who were unemployed, and dysfunction was independent of age and education. SDI scores were also shown to be significantly correlated with scores obtained from the Global Assessment Scale (−.51), the Social Adjustment Scale-II (.49), and the Social Behavior Assessment Scale disturbed behavior subscale (.41) and the social role performance subscale (.30). Criterion validity was assessed by correlating SDI scores with several existing measures of social functioning.

Medical Research Council's Needs for Care Assessment

Description of Instrument. The Medical Research Council's Needs for Care Assessment (MRC-NCA) (Brewin, Wing, Mangen, Brugha, & MacCarthy, 1987) is described as a comprehensive system for patient needs assessment developed during the mid-1980s for assessing needs for the care of severely mentally ill persons in either an inpatient or community-based service setting. The full-scale MRC-NCA incorporates several standardized instruments as part of the overall assessment procedure. These include the Present State Examination, the Social Behavioral Schedule, the Mini-Mental Status Examination, the Abnormal Involuntary Movements Scale, a test of educational attainment, and a medical status questionnaire. In addition to these data gathered directly from interviews with the patient, the MRC-NCA protocol collates information from medical chart data, contacts with relatives, and clinician or treatment team knowledge of the patient.

The protocol is organized around assessments of three basic components: *social functioning, interventions,* and *need status.* The assessment of social functioning incorporates the Social Behavioral Schedule, although the more recent revision (Brewin & Wing, 1993) now uses the REHAB interview. A total of 20 areas of social functioning are assessed, including positive psychotic symptoms, underactivity, side effects from medications, neurotic symptoms, organic brain disorder, physical disorder, violence to self/others, embarrassing behavior, distress, personal cleanliness, household shopping, cooking or buying meals, household chores, use of public transport, use of public amenities, basic literacy and arithmetic skills, occupational skills, social interaction skills, management of money, and the management of household affairs (paying bills, organizing repairs).

The assessment of interventions involves the development of a taxonomy of interventions appropriate for each of the 9 categories of symptoms and behaviors and 11 categories of personal and social skills. Each intervention is rated on a 7-point scale that reflects its actual or potential effectiveness in alleviating the specific problem and its appropriateness and acceptability to the patient.

The assessment of need status involves consideration of the current level of functioning for each of the 20 categories and the ratings of actual/potential effectiveness for the available intervention(s). Need status is defined as a primary or a secondary classification. The primary classification includes no need, met need, and unmet need. The secondary classification includes overprovision, future need, and lack of performance. Need for care in a given domain is considered present when (1) a patient's functioning falls below or threatens to fall below some minimum specified level, and (2) this is due to some remediable or potentially remediable cause. A need is considered met when it has attracted some at least partly effective intervention and when no other interventions of greater potential effectiveness exist. A need is considered unmet when it has attracted only partly effective or no intervention and when other interventions of greater potential effectiveness exist. Overprovision is rated when one or more interventions is assessed as superfluous. Future need signals that the patient has fallen below minimum functioning but cannot receive any appropriate intervention due to incapacitating symptoms or other priorities for intervention. Lack of performance arises when a patient is known to possess a specific social skill, is not receiving any intervention for that skill, but fails to exercise that skill.

Brewin and Wing (1993) note that a revised version of the MRC-NCA was issued in 1989. This revision differs from the 1987 version in several ways: the total number of areas of functioning was reduced from 21 to 20 through deletion of the item on decision making; the revised version permits ratings of met need and future need for the same item; and a fourth primary status is introduced—no meetable need—which describes situations in which disablement exists but no action is appropriate or feasible. This reference provides a recent update on the use of the instrument in the UK and Europe.

The need to administer and score these and the requirement for involving a treatment team in the assessment process mean that the MRC-NCA is a time-consuming process. It generally takes between 3.5 and 5.5 hours to complete.

Reliability.   Brewin et al. (1987) report data on interrater reliability from a sample of 16 long-term patients in a day care setting; two interviewers completed needs assessments on these patients on the basis of an interview with the same staff respondent. From a total of 336 judgments (classified as no need, met need, and unmet need) the two interviewers agreed on classification of each judgment 98% of the time, although 60 of the judgments had to be excluded because they required more information than was available at the time. Thus, one staff member is unlikely to be able to provide all of the information required to complete this protocol. Van Haaster, Lesage, Cyr, and Toupin, (1994) examined the reliability of a French translation of the instrument with short-term and long-term patients in Montreal. Restricting their analysis to items in which primary need was met or unmet, the study compared two independent judges' ratings on data from 33 patients; agreement between judges was 96%.

Validity.   Brewin et al. (1987) report some initial studies of validity. In terms of face validity, the authors describe a review of the instrument by 50 rehabilitation specialists who rated the clinical importance of specific functioning areas; the majority of skills were rated as essential or fairly important by at least 80% of the respondents. The specialist sample (mostly clinical psychologists) rated the "usefulness" of the interventions specified for the areas of functioning. Brewin et al. (1988) describes a study of 145 long-term psychiatric patients in day hospitals and day centers in Camberwell. Patterns of overprovision (of psychotropic medication and shelter) and underprovision (of skills training) of interventions were found to vary by treatment setting. Wainwright, Holloway, and Brugha (1988) adapted the protocol for use by a single investigator (rather than a team) and found similar numbers of problems per patient and levels of unmet need to those reported in Brewin et al. (1988). Two studies raised issues that suggest the protocol may not be appropriate for use in certain patient populations. Pryce et al. (1993) encountered problems in the use of the protocol with psychiatric inpatients, reporting that 9 of the 11 social skills areas were applicable to only two-thirds of their sample. Hogg and Marshall (1992) questioned the value of the information produced from the protocol in their study of the needs of homeless mentally ill patients residing in hostels.

Cardinal Needs Schedule

Description of Instrument.   A further revision of the MRC-NCA instrument was introduced in Marshall, Hogg, Gath, and Lockwood (1995). This revision (now called the Cardinal Needs Schedule) incorporates three new features: the assessment procedures are simplified and shortened; ratings of need now include views of patients and their caregivers; and needs are identified in a manner that is more concise and easier to interpret (five categories are used rather than nine). In addition, the standardized assessments conducted as part of the overall procedure have been changed. These now include the Manchester Scale; REHAB behavioral assessment; a short additional information questionnaire; a brief client interview; and a computerized rating assessment completed by clinical staff. The patient remains an important source of information for the assessment of functioning, but the protocol permits integration of additional information from relatives and other caregivers. The authors strongly encourage interviewing a range of respondents about the patient. The Cardinal Needs Schedule requires approximately 60 minutes to complete.

The Cardinal Needs Schedule incorporates a new and more systematic framework for eliciting clinical judgment of need for care based on three criteria: the cooperation criterion (the patient is willing to accept help for a problem); the carer stress criterion (the problem causes considerable stress, anxiety, frustration, or inconvenience to those who care for the patient); the severity criterion (the problem endangers the health or safety of the patient or the safety of other people). These criteria are applied as relevant across the 15 functioning areas assessed in the procedure.

The final output of the Cardinal Needs Schedule consists of "needs for care" and "placement failures." A need for care means that a patient has a cardinal problem for which there exists at least one suitable intervention that has not been given a recent trial, and a placement failure means that a patient has a cardinal problem for which all suitable interventions have already been offered. Both of these outputs provide a direct mechanism for evaluating the extent to which the psychiatric service has not delivered suitable interventions.

Marshall et al. (1995) note that the Cardinal Needs Schedule now assesses 15 areas of functioning: psychotic symptoms, underactivity, side effects, dangerous or destructive behavior, organic symptoms, physical illness, neurotic symptoms, socially embarrassing behavior, domestic skills, money and own affairs, transportation and amenities, education, occupation, hygiene, and dressing.

Reliability. Marshall et al. (1995) reported a study of interrater reliability for the Cardinal Needs Schedule based on a small inpatient sample. This study found that, in general, the interrater reliability of the Cardinal Needs Schedule is acceptable, but in two areas it is questionable (underactivity and hygiene and dressing). In a one-week test–retest reliability study, percentage agreement for the 15 CNS areas was between 87% and 100%.

Validity. Marshall et al. (1995) administered the Cardinal Needs Schedule and the Lehman Quality of Life Interview to a sample of 80 patients with severe mental illness (SMI); a significant negative correlation (−.36) existed between needs for care and quality of life.

Camberwell Assessment of Needs

Description of Instrument. The Camberwell Assessment of Needs (CAN) instrument was developed as a needs assessment procedure, although it is used for research purposes as well. The CAN assesses 22 areas of social func-

tioning using a structured interview format. These areas include: accommodations, food, household skills, self-care, occupation, physical health, psychotic symptoms, information about condition and its treatment, psychological distress, safety to self, safety to others, alcohol, drugs, company of others, intimate relationships, sexual expression, child care, basic education, use of telephone, transport, money, and welfare benefits. There are two versions: one for use by clinicians (CAN-C) and one for use by researchers (CAN-R). The two versions each contain four sections and are identical for the first three sections, differing only in the fourth. The average time required to complete the assessment is about 25 minutes.

The first section of the interview establishes whether a need exists by asking about current difficulties in each area. Patients' responses are rated on a 3-point scale where 0 = No serious problem; 1 = No serious problem or moderate problem because a continuing intervention is being provided (met need); 2 = Current serious problem (unmet need). Section 2 asks about how much help the patient receives from friends, relatives, and/or other informal caregivers. Section 3 focuses on how much help the patient is now receiving from local service providers. Levels of help in these two sections are rated on a 4-point scale: 0 = None; 1 = Low; 2 = Moderate; 3 = High. Guidelines provide descriptive information to rate each of these levels.

In the CAN-C, Section 4 records the views of the respondent about the type of assistance that individual believes is needed and outlines a care plan. In the CAN-R, Section 4 records whether the respondent is getting the most appropriate form of help and whether the respondent is satisfied with the help received.

The CAN is now being disseminated widely, with 13 European translations in preparation. A PC software version (Windows-compatible) is available. The authors are developing versions suitable for use with the elderly and with persons having learning disabilities.

Reliability. Phelan et al. (1995) report tests of interrater reliability and test–retest reliability (after one week) based on a sample of 60 patients. A high level of agreement existed for interrater reliability (> .90); for test–retest reliability (Section 1), a moderate correlation existed (> .70). On some items, test–retest correlations were low (especially on physical health, psychological distress, drugs, telephone, and money). Because Sections 2 and 3 were completed only if a current problem was reported, there were fewer cases to examine. Interrater reliability was found to be moderate, and test–retest reliability was low, suggesting some instability. In a second study of interrater reliability, Hansson, Bjorkman, and Svensson (1995) reported results with a Swedish-language version: an agreement of > .90 was found for each of the 22 areas for Section 1; agreement was > .80 for all areas in Section 2 and > .90 for 12 of the 22 areas; in Section 3, agreement was > .90 for 8 areas, > .80 for 11 areas, and > .70 for 3 areas; on the adequacy of the help received, agreement was > .90 for 20 areas and low in only one (.66).

Validity.   Phelan et al. (1995) reported on a study of consensual and content validity conducted through a survey of 50 experienced mental health professionals and 59 respondents with SMI. Results from these two surveys were used to fine-tune the instrument. To assess construct validity, the CAN was compared with the Global Assessment of Functioning, (GAF) (to approximate a global rating). A subset of the CAN areas were aggregated to form a global index (household skills, self-care, psychotic symptoms, psychological distress, risk of self-harm, danger to others, social contact). This index correlated strongly and significantly with the GAF (−.51).

Self-Administered Questionnaires

Four self-administered questionnaires are described in this section: the Independent Living Skills Survey, the Missouri Level of Care, the Needs and Resources Assessment Interview, and the Social Functioning Scale.

Independent Living Skills Survey

Description of Instrument.   The Independent Living Skills Survey (ILSS) (Wallace, Kochanowicz, & Wallace, 1985) was developed to assess the community living skills of chronically mentally ill patients living with significant others or in residential care facilities. The ILSS is a questionnaire comprised of 112 items that describe specific behaviors that define nine skill areas, including eating habits, grooming skills, domestic activities, food preparation skills, health maintenance skills, economic skills, use of public transportation, leisure activities, and job-seeking skills. Each item is rated on a 6-point scale for the preceding month (rating points include Never, Sometimes, Often, Usually, Always, and No opportunity to perform). There is an additional 5-point scale that measures the degree to which each behavior is a problem (Never a problem, Occasionally a problem, Sometimes a problem, Frequently a problem, and Always a problem). Originally, the ILSS was designed to be completed by a significant

other or a residential care home operator; however, a patient self-report version has now been developed (Cyr, Toupin, Lesage, & Valiquette, 1994). This version requires between 20 and 30 minutes to complete.

Reliability.   Wallace (1986) reports on a limited reliability study. Operators of 59 family-care homes completed the ILSS on one patient with chronic schizophrenia from each facility. Coefficient alphas for the nine skill areas ranged from .67 to .84; split-half reliabilities ranged from .63 to .89. Three of the areas (eating habits, food preparation skills, and job-seeking skills) had lower reliability due to restricted variance (e.g., few patients were allowed to prepare their own meals). Cyr et al. (1994) reported reliability data on the self-report version (translated into French) in a French sample. Coefficient alphas for the nine scales ranged from .47 to .93 (average was .69). The lowest coefficient was for leisure activities, while the highest was found for job-seeking skills. Test–retest correlations ranged from .48 to .85 with a mean of .67 for all scales (time interval not described).

Validity.   Wallace (1986) reported on concurrent validity by assessing patients with the Nurses Observation Scale for Inpatient Evaluation (NOSIE-30) and the Motality, Affect, Communication, Cooperation-II (MACC-II); moderate correlations were found with the communication and the cooperation scales on the MACC-II, and with the positive factors on the NOSIE-30. Cyr et al. (1994) compared the ILSS self-report version with the NOSIE–30 and the Social Adjustment Scale II (SAS-II), with similar results. The self-report version discriminated between patients living in different types of sheltered homes, between psychotic patients living alone and those living with families, and between patients with schizophrenia and other diagnoses.

Missouri Level of Care

Description of Instrument.   The Missouri Level of Care (MLC) (Massey, Pokorny, & Kramer, 1989) is a self-administered questionnaire designed to assess social functioning and produce placement recommendations within the Missouri community placement program. The 79 items cover seven subscales: community skills, self-care skills, nuisance behaviors, sociability, skilled nursing care needs, proclivity for violent behavior, and control of anger. No information is provided on the length of time required to complete the questionnaire.

Reliability. Coefficient alpha (internal consistency) ranged from .79 to .98 in an initial sample of 1,295 cases and from .77 to .98 in a second sample of 985 cases.

Validity. A factor analytic study of the questionnaire identified seven factors corresponding to the above subscales that together explained about 55% of variance; 73 of the 79 items loaded on these factors. Conceptually, the questionnaire is described as similar to a community placement questionnaire developed by Oliver et al. (1988) (the CCC).

Needs and Resources Assessment Interview

Description of Instrument. The Needs and Resources Assessment Interview (NRAI) (Corrigan, Buican, & McCracken, 1995) is a needs assessment protocol developed for use with outpatients (SMI) in psychiatric rehabilitation settings. The NRAI is designed to be a self-administered questionnaire although it can also be conducted as an interview. It combines open-ended and standardized questions to assess four dimensions of social disablement. The instrument assesses 13 domains, including housing, physical health, teeth, mental health, income and finances, education, job status, friends, family, leisure time, spiritual life, legal problems, and drug-related problems. For each domain, subjects are asked (1) to list specific needs relative to the domain; (2) to list specific resources needed to meet these needs; (3) to rate overall satisfaction with their functioning for each domain; and (4) to rate the importance of each need. No information is presented on the amount of time needed to complete the assessment.

Reliability. Internal consistency (using Cronbach's alpha) was reasonably high (.66 to .81). Test–retest reliability over a one-week period ranged from .71 to .86.

Validity. The Needs and Resources subscales were significantly associated (.60), and the Needs and Importance subscales were also significantly associated (.68). Satisfaction with functioning was relatively independent of these three subscales. Construct validity was assessed by comparing the NRAI with the GAF. The Needs subscale was not significantly associated with GAF score, but was found to be significantly associated with the size of the social support network (.49), as was the Resource scale (.43). Total satisfaction score was significantly associated with the score on the Lehman Quality of Life measure (.79). Needs were associated with depression on the Brief Psychiatric Rating Scale (BPRS) (.33). The Impor-

tance scale was not associated significantly with the GAF, the BPRS, the social support network measure, or the quality of life measure. The authors note that subjects seemed to have difficulty discriminating between the importance of individual needs, rating most as very important.

Social Functioning Scale

Description of Instrument. The Social Functioning Scale (SFS) (Birchwood, Smith, Cochrane, Wetton, & Copestake, 1990) is an 81-item self-administered questionnaire that can be completed by patients, relatives, or clinicians. Developed for assessment of social role and behavioral functioning in persons with schizophrenia in the community, the instrument was first used in studies on family interventions with schizophrenia. The SFS assesses social functioning in seven areas: social engagement/withdrawal, interpersonal behavior, pro-social behavior, recreation, independence–competence, independence–performance; and employment/occupation. Scores are derived for each area and for the total. No information is provided on the length of time required to complete the questionnaire.

Reliability. Coefficient alpha for the seven scales (and total score) ranged from .69 to .87. Interrater reliability ranged from .69 to .96. A comparison of external rater and patient ratings ranged from .62 to .99. Item-total correlations ranged from .30 to .71.

Validity. Construct validity was assessed using an alpha factor analytic model; a single factor was identified, which accounted for 57% of the variance. Criterion validity was assessed by comparing a sample of patients with schizophrenia with "normal" individuals from the community who had no psychiatric disorder; SFS scales distinguished significantly between these groups. SFS scales were also shown to be moderately and significantly negatively correlated with positive symptoms, and positively correlated with negative symptoms. Other studies (evaluations of family interventions) showed that the SFS is sensitive to changes over time (Barrowclough & Tarrier, 1990).

General Rating Instruments

Four global rating scales have been included in this section: the Multnomah Community Ability Scale, the Community Psychiatric Clinic Level of Functioning

Assessment, the Disability Rating Form, and the St. Louis Inventory of Community Living Skills.

Multnomah Community Ability Scale

Description of Instrument. The Multnomah Community Ability Scale (CAS) (Barker et al. 1994a & b) is a 17-item rating scale developed for use with patients with chronic mental illness living in the community. The CAS was designed to serve as a one page form to be completed by case managers or other frontline community mental health workers. The 17 items address the following areas: physical health, intellectual functioning, thought processes, mood abnormality, response to stress and anxiety, ability to manage money, independence in daily living, acceptance of illness, social acceptability, social interest, social effectiveness, social network, meaningful activity, medication compliance, cooperation with treatment providers, alcohol and drug abuse, and impulse control. The 17 items use 5-point rating scales, and a brief training manual contains anchors for ratings for each item. A total score is calculated by summing the ratings across all items; three levels of disability are described (low, medium, and high). In addition, four subscales can be formed by summing the ratings for individual items; these include Interference with Functioning, Adjustment to Living, Social Competence, and Behavioral Problems. The one-page rating form takes approximately 5 to 10 minutes to complete by a case manager or other mental health worker who knows the patient well. The training manual contains separate statistical norms for male patients aged 18–34, 35–50, and 51–91; and female patients aged 18–34, 35–50, and 51–91. A training video is also available. This instrument has proved very popular since its introduction, and it currently is in use as an assessment tool and outcome measure in many community mental health agencies.

Reliability. The authors state that the total CAS score has interrater reliability of .85 and test–retest reliability of .83 (Barker et al., 1994a). Individual items with an intraclass correlation of .60 or better included intellectual functioning, thought processes, independence in daily life, acceptance of illness, social acceptability, social effectiveness, cooperation with treatment providers, alcohol/drug abuse, the four subscales, and the total scale score. Items with intraclass correlations of .50 to .59 included mood abnormality, response to stress and anxiety, ability to manage money, and social interest. Items with intraclass correlations of less than .50 included physical health, social network, social participation, medication

compliance, and impulse control. Test–retest reliability was tested at two agencies over a two-week period and a one-month period with good results. Internal consistency (Cronbach's alpha) was computed at .90.

Validity. A factor analysis of 240 questionnaires identified four factors that corresponded with the four subscales. Other analyses of validity included a comparison with a global assessment made by rating clinicians; the correlation was −.78. Correlations with several "criterion" variables were computed; CAS items correlate highly with measures of outpatient Community Mental Health Clinic service use and state hospital utilization.

Community Psychiatric Clinic Level of Functioning Assessment

Description of Instrument. The Community Psychiatric Clinic Level of Functioning Assessment (CPC-LOFA) (Uehara, Smukler, & Newman, 1994) was developed as a tool to identify physical, social, and psychological functioning among mental health consumers (including those with schizophrenia) in public mental health care delivery systems. The CPC-LOFA is a 53-item rating instrument derived from the Specific Level of Functioning (SLOF) scale. The CPC-LOFA is used as part of the Level of Need–Care Assessment (LONCA) system, which links identified needs with service interventions. The CPC-LOFA is based on an earlier instrument developed by Schneider and Struening (1983). The modifications include greater specificity in the descriptive anchors used, the addition of specific items that tap symptoms such as psychotic symptoms, mood disturbance, and alcohol/drug use. The rating instructions were also rewritten to require raters to rate the average behavioral and skill levels of consumers against the functioning of the average non-mentally-ill individual of similar age, gender, and race. Ratings are made on three 5-point Likert scales. There are nine domains that address physical functioning (self-care, vision/hearing, mobility and chronic medical illness), social functioning (community living, interpersonal relations); and psychological functioning (dangerous behavior, mood disturbance, psychotic symptoms, substance abuse). The time required to complete this assessment is between 10 and 20 minutes.

Reliability. Interrater and test–retest (after one week) reliability was assessed using a sample of 598 outpatients (43 for interrater study) with various diagnoses (60% schizophrenia). On an item-by-item analysis, intra-class correlation coefficients (ICCs) ranged from .31 to .94, with 80% of the correlations > .60. Coefficient alpha for the entire instrument is .95.

Validity.   Construct validity was assessed through a factor analytic study of all items except those related to occupational functioning. Nine factors were identified (as reported under domains). Concurrent validity was assessed through comparison of scores on LOFA scales with the Ohio Level of Functioning Scale, the GAF, and a substance use scale. Scores on the physical, social, and psychological functioning domains of the LOFA correlated significantly with the GAF and the Basic Living Skills scale from the Ohio Level of Functioning Scale. There were also moderate correlations between the LOFA substance abuse scale and the substance use scale.

Disability Rating Form

Description of Instrument.   The Disability Rating Form (DRF) (Hoyle, Nietzel, Guthrie, Baker-Prewitt, & Heine, 1992) was developed on a sample of adult patients with severe mental illnesses in two rural areas of Kentucky. The DRF is a 5-item global rating form adapted from the New Jersey Functional Assessment Scales. Items consist of a global rating on a 5-point scale for each of five domains: activities of daily living, social functioning, concentration and task performance, adaptation to change, and impulse control. Rating points are anchored by explicit behavioral descriptors of the extent of disability. Following each rating of the severity of disability, the rater completes a second item that elicits data on the *duration* of time during which the patient has experienced this level of disability. The instrument is completed by a therapist or other clinician who knows the patient well. The instrument requires about 5 to 10 minutes to complete. The authors note that because the DRF produces a series of general ratings (rather than behavioral ratings), there is reason to question whether the instrument will be sensitive to change in disability status. Although the authors state that they believe the measure does not confound symptoms with social functioning, the presence of impulse control indicates that both constructs are being assessed.

Reliability.   Item-total score reliabilities and test–retest reliability are reported in Hoyle et al. (1992). Coefficient alpha was .86 for Time 1 and .87 for Time 2 ratings. Therapist DRF ratings were stable over a 2 to 4 month period.

Validity.   The results from a confirmatory factor analysis are reported, and these support a single factor model. Preliminary discriminant validity data based on comparison of DRF ratings by diagnosis and duration suggest that disability ratings differentiated between diagnostic groups; results were less clear for duration, but this may have reflected a preponderance of subjects with disability that exceeded two years. No comparisons presented with other measures.

St. Louis Inventory of Community Living Skills

Description of Instrument.   The St. Louis Inventory of Community Living Skills (SLICLS) (Evenson & Boyd, 1993) is a needs assessment instrument developed for use with SMI patients in various community settings, including outpatient programs and nursing homes. It was developed as a brief measure that could be used for level-of-care placement decisions in Missouri and was specifically developed as a briefer alternative to the Missouri Level of Care (MLC) instrument. The rater (usually a mental health clinician) rates the patient's current level of functioning in 15 areas using a 7-point scale, which ranges from 1 = Few or no skills to 7 = Self-sufficient, very adequate skills. A 16th nonscored item is a brief checklist of physical impairments. The 15 areas include personal hygiene, grooming, dress skills, self-care, communications, safety, handling time, handling money, leisure activities, clothing maintenance, meal preparation, sexuality, use of resources, problem solving, and health practices. The authors note that the rating form requires only a "few minutes" to complete.

Reliability.   Evenson and Boyd (1993) reported a study of interrater reliability in which the intraclass correlation coefficient for two raters was .83. Coefficient alpha was .91. Fitz and Evenson (1995) reported on the interrater reliability of the SLICLS in a sample of 60 patients in three community settings in which subjects were each rated by two independent raters. The intraclass correlation coefficient for two raters it was .85. Coefficient alpha was .97.

Validity.   Fitz and Evenson (1995) examined the discriminant validity and construct validity of the SLICLS. They found that the SLICLS successfully differentiated between clients at three types of community residences. They also examined correlations of the SLICLS with the

Missouri Level of Care instrument; SLICLS scores correlated significantly with MLC subscales of self-care, behavior, and community living skills. The SLICLS also correlated with a social worker's estimate of the best level of placement (r = .77).

Role-Play Assessments

Two newer role-play tests are discussed here: the Assessment of Interpersonal Problem-Solving Skills and the Social Problem-Solving Assessment Battery.

Assessment of Interpersonal Problem-Solving Skills

Description of Instrument. The Assessment of Interpersonal Problem-Solving Skills (AIPSS) (Donahoe et al., 1990) is a videotaped role-play test of social skills based on Wallace's three-stage model of receiving, processing, and sending skills. Patients are shown a series of 14 role-play vignettes involving an interpersonal problem; they are instructed to identify the problem in the vignette, describe a solution that minimizes negative consequences, and role-play this solution for the examiner. The AIPSS contains six scales: Identification (does examinee describe the problem correctly); Description (examinee correctly identifies the goal of the principal character and the obstacle he/she faces); Processing (what the respondent says he/she would say or do if in the pictured situation); Content (of role play) (the likelihood that the examinee's solution would solve the problem while minimizing negative consequence); Performance (how polished the role play is); and Overall score (how effective the role play is considering both content and performance). At least two scoring systems are available: a general scoring procedure that involves summing across the problem scene scores and dividing by the maximum possible score for that scale, and a specific procedure in which the item score for a particular subscale is used to derive a total score for that scale only if there is "quality" output from an item on the same scene at a previous RPS stage. The protocol requires administration by an experienced, trained rater. The protocol requires approximately 30 to 60 minutes to administer and score.

Reliability. Test–retest reliability was computed for a sample of nine outpatients with schizophrenia over a two-week interval; correlations ranged from .46 to .77 for the general scoring method and from .56 to .84 for the specific scoring method. Interrater reliability was found to be adequate; there were no significant differences in scale scores derived from two independent raters.

Validity. Donahoe et al. (1990) reported an examination of the conditional probabilities of obtaining a particular score for one stage given a specific score on an earlier stage. Examination of these probabilities partially supported the receiving-processing-sending skills (RPS) model on which the AIPSS is based. Moderately significant correlations existed between sending skills scales and IQ on the Shipley-Hartford test, but not between receiving or processing skill scales. Sullivan, Marder, Liberman, Donahoe, and Mitz (1990) compared AIPSS scores for 19 patients with schizophrenia who were enrolled in an ongoing study of maintenance antipsychotic medications; of these 19 subjects, 10 had been randomly assigned to a standard dose treatment and 9 to a low dose treatment. Seven subjects had experienced a "symptom exacerbation" prior to testing with the AIPSS, whereas the remaining 12 had not. Exacerbators scored significantly lower on all six AIPSS scales than nonexacerbators. Two AIPSS scores (receiving and processing) were significantly correlated with a Strauss-Carpenter cluster score that reliably predicted poor prognosis in several earlier studies; three AIPSS scale scores were significantly correlated with the SAS-II global social leisure score. The authors note that an examination of the AIPSS subscale scores and the timing of the exacerbation shows a highly significant curvilinear relationship between these variables; they suggest that this may show that the AIPSS is measuring a long-term residual effect, with the greatest social skills deficit occurring in the year following exacerbation.

Social Problem-Solving Assessment Battery

Description of Instrument. The Social Problem Solving and Assessment Battery (SPSAB) (Sayers, Bellack, Wade, Bennett, & Fong, 1995) is a role-play test developed for use in assessing social skill and problem-solving ability in chronic psychiatric patient populations in community settings. The authors state that their goal was to develop an empirical method for assessing major components of real-world social problem solving. To that end, their assessment seeks to evaluate ". . . the cognitive and behavioral skills that enable individuals to identify social problems, to generate response alternatives, to evaluate the effectiveness of others' as well as one's own responses, and to carry out effective interactions" (p. 270). An important aspect of the development of this assessment was the involvement of patients, providers, and family members in identifying problems that challenge individuals with schizophrenia at several stages. For example, patients, providers, and family members were asked to describe problem situations, which later became the basis for the role plays. Once an initial set of unduplicated interpersonal problem situations had been identified, a sample of 20 patients was asked to rate both the difficulty and the relevance/familiarity of a subset of 30 problem situations that could be classified into one of four categories (asking for help, assertion, compromise, and conversation initiation). The final set of problems included those that were rated as at least moderately difficult by a majority of patients, and as somewhat familiar to them. Because none of the "asking for help" situations met these criteria, this category was dropped. A total of 12 problem situations met the difficulty and familiarity criteria for inclusion in the final instrument. A sample of community volunteers (employees of the medical center where the instrument was developed) was used to construct a rating system for the role-play task.

The battery contains three assessments that tap different aspects of the functional ability to solve problems: a Role-Play Test (RPT), a Response Generation Test (RGT), and a Response Evaluation Test (RET). Role plays (a total of six) involve the use of a confederate and are videotaped. The RGT is a test of the subject's ability to identify problems and propose solutions. It is based on six videotaped interchanges between two individuals who portray a conflict or problem. The RET consists of an audiotape of 12 dyadic interactions, 6 depicting effective behavior and 6 depicting ineffective behavior. The subject listens to the taped exchange, identifies the target individual whose behavior is to be rated, and then rates the behavior on a 5-point Likert scale (Effective–Ineffective). The dependent measure for the RET is a difference score subtracting the mean rating of the ineffective scenes from the mean rating of the effective scenes (higher scores reflect greater sensitivity to differences between effective and ineffective social problem-solving behavior). This battery requires a trained rater to complete with the patient. Typical duration for the assessment is not described; however, in Sayers et al. (1995) the assessment was completed over two consecutive days.

Reliability. Sayers et al. (1995) reported the results of preliminary tests of the reliability of the SPSAB based on a sample of 24 patients with schizophrenia, 17 patients with bipolar disorder, and a nonpsychiatric control group (n = 19). Interrater reliability (using intraclass correlation coefficients) for the ratings of role-play behavior (RPT) ranged from .54 to .85; only the Social Norm Violations category was found to be less than .60 (ICC = .54). Interrater reliability for the six RGT categories ranged from .22 (Hostility) to .91 (Work). The low reliability for the Hostility category was attributed to the very low frequency of its occurrence within the sample.

Validity. The same study also sought to validate the empirically derived RPT rating system by correlating the ratings of the primary research rater with ratings obtained from community volunteers. All but two of the categories (Focused and Negative Behaviors) were significantly and positively correlated, with correlations ranging from .28 to .48. Bellack, Sayers, Mueser, and Bennett (1994) reported additional results from this study. Patients with schizophrenia exhibited significantly poorer performance in each of the three problem-solving domains assessed by the SPSAB when compared with nonpsychiatric controls. This study also showed that there were few significant relationships between symptomatology and social problem-solving ability (although there was a slight relationship between negative symptoms and the ability to implement solutions on the RPT). Of note was the finding that the bipolar patients were at least as impaired (and sometimes more so) on all measures as the schizophrenic patients.

DISCUSSION

The 16 instruments reviewed above provide a range of measures for social functioning that are appropriate for use with patients with severe mental illnesses (including schizophrenia). Few of these instruments were developed explicitly for schizophrenia (although any of them could be used with schizophrenic patients). Initial data on reliability and validity are available for each instrument, although more extensive studies are clearly warranted. In general, these instruments appear to be promising measures for which further investigation seems warranted.

There are several issues related to the assessment of social functioning in schizophrenia that we wish to highlight. These include the variability of social functioning in schizophrenia, concerns about the use of self-administered questionnaires, and issues posed by special populations.

Variability of Social Functioning in Schizophrenia

Social functioning in schizophrenia tends to vary among patients and within patients at different points in time (as well as in different stages of illness). For these reasons, two desirable characteristics in measures of social functioning for patients with schizophrenia would be sensitivity to change and incorporation of time as a dimension in the instrument. Because most of these instruments have been developed fairly recently, their sensitivity to change has not been well established. This represents an important area for further investigative work. One development we find interesting is the incorporation of time as a specific dimension of the assessment process. One example of how this can be done is the Role Activity Performance Scale, which tracks changes in social functioning across specific domains by month, so that a record can be compiled that relates changes in each domain over time.

The Use of Self-Administered Questionnaires

Although the use of self-administered questionnaires provides an attractive option for rapid data collection with patients with schizophrenia, there are several issues that should be addressed by future research. Data on the comprehensibility and the reading level needed for successful completion of these instruments should be provided. For patients with schizophrenia, neuropsychological deficits and impairments may interfere with the ability to complete these instruments, and studies should be conducted to establish the effects of neuropsychological variables on the validity of self-administered questionnaires for these patients.

Special Populations

The reliability and validity of measures of social functioning in special populations of patients with schizophrenia should be examined also. In particular, we recommend that studies be conducted to examine the psychometric properties of instruments among homeless patients, substance abusing patients, elderly patients, and higher-functioning patients. Each of these groups poses special problems for measurement (as noted in some of the studies cited earlier), and it will be important to establish whether existing measures can be used for these groups, whether these measures will require modification, or whether new measures will need to be developed.

Matching Measures to Assessment Goals and Capacities

As presented, the measures reviewed vary considerably in their scope, complexity, and administration demands. This variability requires that a prospective user exercise considerable forethought to ensure that specific assessment goals are met and to avoid costly and unnecessary data collection.

First, one must determine which aspects of social functioning are most salient to a given application. For some purposes what is needed is an overall measure that combines functioning across domains into a single aggregate score. In selecting such a measure, one must make sure that the domains aggregated are the ones of most concern. An aggregate score combining basic activities of daily living, money management, and capacity to use transportation may be quite different from one that combines ratings of parenting, marital, and vocational functioning. For other purposes, an aggregate score may be less useful than measures of functioning in specific domains. In short, care should be taken to select a measure with the appropriate content.

The use to which the assessment of social functioning will be put must also be considered. If the assessment is to be used for service planning, some of the measures specifically keyed to needs assessment may be the most useful. If the assessment is to be used for the evaluation of services, the more general questionnaires may be a better fit. The setting and resources available to conduct the assessment will determine the feasibility and utility of a measure. Settings in which patients spend considerable time and in which staff have extended exposure to patients lend themselves well to rating forms that require deeper, more extensive knowledge of the patient's functioning. Examples of these include the various needs assessment scales and the Multnomah Community Ability Scale. In these settings, the various role-play assessments may also be feasible and desirable. Conversely, the structured questionnaires and interviews will be more feasible in situations in which the assessor has little or no prior knowledge or exposure to the respondent. Costs and staffing requirements will govern these decisions.

Validity

Because of its complexity, social functioning is a difficult concept to measure validly. Ideally social functioning should be measured by direct observation of a person's functioning over time in his or her natural environment. This is rarely feasible, and none of the measures reviewed attempt this. The measures rely on various techniques: patient self-report (either by questionnaire or interview), judgments of others with varying levels of knowledge about the patient, and direct observation of artificial role plays. Each of these methods carries certain biases that will threaten validity, although for each of the measures reviewed, some validity data have been presented. To the extent possible, measures that consider multiple perspectives on the respondent's functioning (for example, self-report and observation over time) may offer the most promise.

REFERENCES

Barker, S., Barron, N., McFarland, B. H., & Bigelow, D. A. (1994a). A Community Ability Scale for chronically mentally ill consumers: Part I. Reliability and validity. *Community Mental Health Journal, 30,* 363–383.

Barker, S., Barron, N., McFarland, B. H., Bigelow, D. A., & Carnahan, T. (1994b). A Community Ability Scale for chronically mentally ill consumers: Part II. Applications. *Community Mental Health Journal, 30,* 459–472.

Bellack, A. S., Morrison, R. L., Mueser, K. T., Wade, J. H., & Sayers, S. L. (1990). Role play for assessing the social competence of psychiatric patients. *Psychological Assessment, 2,* 248–255.

Bellack, A. S., Sayers, M., Mueser, K. T., & Bennett, M. (1994). Evaluation of problem solving in schizophrenia. *Journal of Abnormal Psychology, 103,* 371–378.

Birchwood, M., Smith, J., Cochrane, R. Wetton, S., & Copestake, S. (1990). The Social Functioning Scale: The development and validation of a new scale of social adjustment for use in family intervention programmes with schizophrenic patients. *British Journal of Psychiatry, 157,* 853–859.

Brewin, C. R., & Wing, J. K. (1993). The MRC Needs for Care Assessment: Progress and controversies. *Psychological Medicine, 22,* 837–841.

Brewin, C. R., Wing, J. K., Mangen, S. P., Brugha, T. S., & MacCarthy, B. (1987). Principles and practice of measuring need in the long-term mentally ill: The MRC Needs for Care Assessment. *Psychological Medicine, 17,* 971–981.

Brewin, C. R., Wing, J. K., Mangen, S., Brugha, T., MacCarthy, B., & Lesage, A. (1988). Needs for care among long-term mentally ill: A report from the Camberwell High Contact study. *Psychological Medicine, 18,* 457–468.

Clare, A. W., & Cairns, V. E. (1978). Design, development and use of a standardized interview to assess social maladjustment and dysfunction in community studies. *Psychological Medicine, 8,* 589–604.

Cook, J. A. (1992). *Outcome assessment in psychiatric rehabilitation services for persons with severe and persistent mental illness.* Prepared for the National Institute of Mental Health, Contract No. 91MF23474902D.

Corrigan, P. W., Buican, B., & McCracken, S. (1995). The Needs and Resources Assessment Interview for severely mentally ill adults. *Psychiatric Services, 46,* 504–505.

Cyr, M., Toupin, J., Lesage, A. D., & Valiquette, C. A. M. (1994). Assessment of independent living skills for psychotic patients: Further validity and reliability. *Journal of Nervous and Mental Disease, 182,* 91–97.

de Jong, A., van der Lubbe, P. M., & Wiersma, D. (1996). Social dysfunctioning in rehabilitation: Classification and assessment. In M. Moscarelli, A. Rupp, & N. Sartorius (Eds.). *Handbook of mental health economics and policy, Volume I* (pp. 27–38). London: Wiley.

Dixon, L. B., Lehman, A. F., & Levine, J. (1995). Conventional antipsychotic medications for schizophrenia. *Schizophrenia Bulletin, 21,* 567–578.

Donahoe, C. P., Carter, M. J., Bloem, W. D., Hirsch, G. L., Laasi, N., & Wallace, C. J. (1990). Assessment of interpersonal problem-solving skills. *Psychiatry, 53,* 329–339.

Ellsworth, R. B., Foster, L., Childers, B., Arthur, G., & Kroeker, D. (1968). Hospital and community adjustment as perceived by psychiatric patients, their families, and staff. *Journal of Consulting and Clinical Psychology, 32,* 1–41.

Evenson, R. C., & Boyd, M. A. (1993). The St. Louis Inventory of Community Living Skills. *Psychosocial Rehabilitation Journal, 17,* 93–99.

Fitz, D., & Evenson, R. C. (1995). A validity study of the St. Louis Inventory of Community Living Skills. *Community Mental Health Journal, 31,* 369–377.

Goldman, H. H., Skodol, A. E., & Lave, T. R. (1992). Revising Axis V for DSM-IV: A review of measures of social functioning. *American Journal of Psychiatry, 149,* 1148–1156.

Good-Ellis, M. A., Fine, S. B., Spencer, J. H., & DiVittis, A. (1987). Developing a Role Activity Performance Scale. *American Journal of Occupational Therapy, 41,* 232–241.

Green, R. S., & Gracely, E. J. (1987). Selecting a rating scale for evaluating services to the chronically mentally ill. *Community Mental Health Journal, 23,* 91–102.

Gurland, B. J., Yorkston, N. J., Stone, A. R., Frank, J. D., & Fleiss, J. L. (1972). The Structured and Scaled Interview to Assess Maladjustment (SSIAM) I. Description, rationale and development. *Archives of General Psychiatry, 27,* 259–264.

Hansson, L., Bjorkman, T., & Svensson, B. (1995). The assessment of needs in psychiatric patients: Inter-rater reliability of the Swedish version of the Camberwell Assessment of Needs instrument and results from a cross-sectional study. *Acta Psychiatrica Scandinavia, 92,* 285–291.

Hogg, L. I., & Marshall, M. (1992). Can we measure need in the homeless mentally ill? Using the MRC Needs for Care in hostels for the homeless. *Psychological Medicine, 22,* 1027–1034.

Hoyle, R. H., Nietzel, M. T., Guthrie, P. R., Baker-Prewitt, J. L., & Heine, R. (1992). The Disability Rating Form: A brief schedule for rating disability associated with severe mental illness. *Psychosocial Rehabilitation Journal, 16,* 77–94.

Kane, R. A., Kane, R. L., & Arnold, S. (1985). *Measuring social functioning in mental health studies: Concepts and instruments* (Series DN No. 5, USDHHS Publication No. ADM 85–1384). Washington, DC: U.S. Government Printing Office.

Katschnig, H. (1983). Methods for measuring social adjustment. In T. Helgason (Ed.), *Methodology in evaluation of psychiatric treatment* (pp. 205–218). Cambridge: Cambridge University Press.

Katz, M. M., & Lyerly, S. B. (1963). Methods for measuring adjustment and social behavior in the community: 1. Rationale, description, discriminative validity and scale development. *Psychological Reports, 13,* 503–535.

Linn, M. W. (1988). A critical review of scales used to evaluate social and interpersonal adjustment in the community. *Psychopharmacology Bulletin, 24,* 615–621.

Marshall, M., Hogg, L. I., Gath, D. H., & Lockwood, A. (1995). The Cardinal Needs Schedule: A modified version of the MRC Needs for Care Assessment Schedule. *Psychological Medicine, 25,* 603–617.

Massey, O. T., Pokorny, L. J., & Kramer, B. H. (1989). The development of factor-based level of functioning scales from a level of care instrument. *Journal of Clinical Psychology, 45,* 903–909.

Munroe-Blum, H., Collins, E., McCleary, L., & Nuttall, S. (1996). The Social Dysfunction Index (SDI) for patients with schizophrenia and related disorders. *Schizophrenia Research, 20,* 211–219.

Oliver, J. M., Dripps, B. J., & Grisson, J. T. (1988). The Community Placement Scale: An adaptation of the Community Competence Scale for placement of the deinstitutionalized mentally ill. *Journal of Clinical Psychology, 44,* 375–384.

Oliver, J. M., & Searight, H. R. (1988). The Community Competence Scale: A preliminary short form for residential placement of deinstitutionalized psychiatric patients. *Adult Foster Care Journal, 2,* 176–188.

Peralta, V., Cuesta, M. J., & de Leon, J. (1994). An empirical analysis of latent structures underlying schizophrenic symptoms: A four-syndrome model. *Biological Psychiatry, 36,* 726–736.

Phelan, M., Slade, M., Thornicroft, G., Dunn, G., Holloway, F., Wykes, T., Strathdee, G., Loftus, L., McCrone, P., & Hayward, P. (1995). The Camberwell Assessment of Need: The validity and reliability of an instrument to assess the needs of people with severe mental illness. *British Journal of Psychiatry, 167,* 589–595.

Phelan, M., Wykes, T., & Goldman, H. (1994). Global function scales. *Social Psychiatry and Psychiatric Epidemiology, 29,* 205–211.

Platt, S. (1981). Social adjustment as a criterion of treatment success: Just what are we measuring? *Psychiatry, 44,* 95–112.

Platt, S. (1986). Evaluating social functioning. A critical review of scales and their underlying concepts. In P. B. Bradley, & S. R. Hirsch (Eds.), *The psychopharmacology and treatment of schizophrenia* (pp. 263–285). London: Oxford University Press.

Platt, S., Weyman, A., Hirsch, S., & Hewitt, S. (1980). The Social Behavior Assessment Schedule (SBAS): Rationale, contents, scoring, and reliability of a new interview schedule. *Social Psychiatry, 15,* 43–55.

Pryce, I. G., Griffiths, R. D., Gentry, R. M., Hughes, I. C. T., Montague, L. R., Watkins, S. E., Champney-Smith, J., & McLackland, B. M. (1993). How important is the assessment of social skills in current long-stay inpatients? *British Journal of Psychiatry, 162,* 498–502.

Sayers, M. D., Bellack, A. S., Wade, J. H., Bennett, M. E., & Fong, P. (1995). An empirical method for assessing social problem solving in schizophrenia. *Behavior Modification, 19,* 267–289.

Schooler, N., Hogarty, G., & Weissman, M. M. (1979). Social Adjustment Scale-II (SAS-II). In W. A. Hargreaves, C. C. Attkisson, & J. E. Sorenson (Eds.), *Resource materials for community mental health program evaluators* (USDHEW Publication No. ADM 79–328). Washington, DC: U.S. Government Printing Office.

Searight, H. R., & Goldberg, M. A. (1991). The Community Competence Scale as a measure of daily functional living skills. *Journal of Mental Health Administration, 18,* 128–134.

Searight, H. R., Oliver, J. M., & Grisso, J. T. (1983). The Community Competence Scale: Preliminary reliability and validity. *American Journal of Community Psychology, 11,* 609–613.

Searight, H. R., Oliver, J. M., & Grisso, J. T. (1986). The Community Competence Scale in the placement of the deinstitutionalized mentally ill. *American Journal of Community Psychology, 14,* 291–301.

Strauss, J. S., Kokes, R. F., Klorman, R., & Sacksteder, J. L. (1977). Premorbid adjustment in schizophrenia: Concepts, measures, and implications: I. The concept of premorbid adjustment. *Schizophrenia Bulletin, 3,* 182–185.

Sullivan, G., Marder, S. R., Liberman, R. P., Donahoe, C. P., & Mintz, J. (1990). Social skills and relapse history in outpatient schizophrenics. *Psychiatry, 53,* 340–345.

Uehara, E. S., Smukler, M., & Newman, F. L. (1994). Linking resource use to consumer level of need: Field test of the Level of Need-Care Assessment (LONCA) method. *Journal of Consulting and Clinical Psychology, 62,* 695–709.

Vaccaro, J. V., Pitts, D. B., & Wallace, C. J. (1992). Functional assessment. In R. P. Liberman (Ed.), *Handbook of psychiatric rehabilitation* (pp. 78–94). New York: Macmillan.

van Haaster, I., Lesage, A. D., Cyr, M., & Toupin, J. (1994). Further reliability and validity studies with the Needs for Care Assessment schedule. *Psychological Medicine, 24,* 215–222.

Wainwright, T., Holloway, F., & Brugha, T. S. (1988). Day care in an inner city. In A. Lavender, & F. Holloway (Eds.), *Community care in practice: Services for the continuing care client* (pp. 72–79). Chichester: Wiley.

Wallace, C. J. (1986). Functional assessment in rehabilitation. *Schizophrenia Bulletin, 12,* 604–630.

Wallace, C. J., Kochanowicz, N., & Wallace, J. (1985). *Independent Living Skills Survey.* Mental Health Clinical Research Center for the Study of Schizophrenia, West Los Angeles VA Medical Center (Brentwood Division).

Weissman, M. M. (1975). The assessment of social adjustment: A review of techniques. *Archives of General Psychiatry, 32,* 357–365.

Weissman, M. M., Sholomskas, D., and John, K. (1981). The assessment of social adjustment—an update. *Archives of General Psychiatry, 38,* 1250–1258.

Wing, J. K., (1989). The measurement of 'social disablement'—The MRC social behaviour and social role performance schedules. *Social Psychiatry and Psychiatric Epidemiology, 24,* 173–178.

Wykes, T., & Hurry, J. (1991). Social behavior and psychiatric disorders. In P. E. Bebbington (Ed.), *Social psychiatry: Theory, methodology and practice* (pp. 183–209). New Brunswick: TRANSACTION.

CHAPTER 2

SOCIAL FUNCTIONING IN RESIDENTIAL AND INSTITUTIONAL SETTINGS

Til Wykes

This chapter not only discusses social functioning in those patients with schizophrenia who require residential or institutional support, but also investigates the relationship between environments and the deficits observed. The investigation draws on information from studies of the effects of environments on normal populations as well as that from studies of patients with schizophrenia. An evaluation of the rather disparate evidence on institutionalization, which fueled the closure of mental hospitals around the world, is provided. Finally, the case for the importance of social functioning assessment in the provision of residential care is made and a brief review of the most appropriate instruments is given as a guide.

BACKGROUND

The diagnosis of schizophrenia carries with it the notion of some social dysfunction at least when the person is in an acute episode of the disorder. Some diagnostic systems even use deterioration in social functioning as part of the definition of the active, prodromal, and resid-

ual phases of the disorder (American Psychiatric Association, 1994). Social functioning problems occur in a variety of areas, including work, social relationships, and self-care. Clearly in an acute phase of the disorder when perceptual distortions such as hallucinations are experienced and when the person's model of the world includes delusional material, this must affect perceptions of social cues. In addition, people with schizophrenia are also deficient at providing social cues, especially in their language and nonverbal skills (Corrigan, Wallace, & Green, 1992; Wykes & Leff 1982). Later if the disorder takes a chronic course, patients may develop more long-lasting deficits in social functioning despite the absence of symptomatic behavior.

But people with schizophrenia can react in a variety of ways even when the form of the disorder is the same. Some seem able to continue fulfilling social relationships, whereas others withdraw completely from the world. Differences can occur not only between people, but also in the same person at different times in their life. Recent studies using computerized life charts have shown that when there is a strict adherence to a longitudinal design, a broad range of outcomes exist for chronic patients. Harding and colleagues (1987a, 1987b) have now followed up 269 severely disabled chronic schizophrenic patients over 32 years. They have explored the myth of continuous poor functioning. In their study some patients had windows of good functioning in their lives that lasted for varying periods of time. Similarly in a follow-up study in the United Kingdom in a semirural community, 58% of patients who were first admissions had good outcome with little or no impairment despite the fact that a number had experienced recurrent episodes (Watt, Katz, & Shepherd, 1983).

Harding and colleagues explain the illusion of continual poor functioning in several ways. First, clinicians have a great deal more contact with those people who show little improvement or who deteriorate over time. The estimates suggest that clinicians are in contact with the group that does not recover 64 times as often as the intermittently recovered group. Second, clinicians have been taught to expect that chronic severely disabled patients are unlikely to improve very much in the future. Third, the research designs adopted have not been truly longitudinal. Often patients are contacted several times, but their functioning over only a small time is assessed. If life history measures are taken, then a different pattern emerges with functioning in different areas of a patient's life changing at different times and at different rates. The notion of schizophrenia as a disorder that entails continued poor life functioning is therefore not supported by longitudinal or epidemiological data.

The elaborate relationship between social functioning deficits and the diagnosis of schizophrenia is described in detail elsewhere in this handbook. The explanations include causality, vulnerability, predictability, and reactivity. However, this chapter will concentrate on the relationships between institutional and residential environments and social functioning that may lead to more understanding of schizophrenia. Apart from its theoretical interest, clinicians are interested for pragmatic reasons because the level of social functioning will have a direct bearing on the treatment and rehabilitation plans for a patient. Levels of functioning are highly correlated with the level of psychiatric support (Wykes, Sturt, & Creer, 1982) and therefore have a strong association with the economic costs of the disorder within the health and welfare system.

In summary, deficits in social functioning are associated with schizophrenia. They may be prodromal symptoms signaling the onset of the disorder, they may accompany the acute phases of the disorder, and they may remain or develop into chronic disabilities following remission of an acute phase (Wing, 1980). They are critical in determining treatment and rehabilitation and contribute to the economic costs of the disorder. Before discussing the interplay between social functioning and the environment, we need to define both social functioning and residential and institutional care.

SOCIAL FUNCTIONING

Social functioning encompasses most, if not all, human behaviors and for the purposes of this chapter has been divided into three layers: social attainments, social roles, and instrumental behavior. *Social attainments* are easily identifiable global measures that mark life achievements, such as having a job or being married. Information about the highest level of achievement can indicate previous competence, for example, that the person has been acceptable as a marital partner. These attainments need to be viewed within the context of the social and economic conditions in the period under consideration. For instance, in the United Kingdom during the Second World War women were encouraged to take paid work and to leave their children at nurseries, whereas in the following decade the position reversed and women were encouraged to remain at home with their children. Levels of unemployment affect the probability of getting a job and this, too, needs to be kept in mind when making assessments of prior competence. The interpretation of employment history therefore depends on gender as well as the economic conditions in the decades when employment was likely. In summary, the presence of attainments does provide information on competence, but the absence of such achievements does not necessarily indicate the absence of competency but must be weighed together with other prevailing social and economic factors.

The next level of social functioning is *social roles*, which provides more detail on functioning within particular roles, such as not only whether the person has children but whether he or she can adequately care for them. Again the social and cultural context must affect our expectation of the functioning in roles. For example, our expectations of a man in his 60s who has young children will not be the same as those of a man in his 30s. These expectations will be further complicated if we know the social class and ethnic origin of the two men. This layer of detail provides information on functioning in both current and past roles, but for patients who are in residential and institutional settings, the scope for carrying out some roles is reduced. This is known as role attrition. The environment may therefore interfere with our perceptions of the role functioning potential of people in residential care.

The final level of social functioning is *instrumental behavior*, which provides more detail about functioning in particular roles. For example, the skills necessary for social interaction, such as initiating conversation or responding to others, can be divided. This analysis can be continued to provide even finer detail, such as whether gestures, tone of voice, and pauses are used appropriately.

Which level of assessment is most appropriate for patients in residential or institutional settings depends on why the data are being collected. General data on social attainments will provide a framework for comparison with the general population, but they will not provide adequate information for assessing the individual residents' needs or for planning programs of rehabilitation. This leaves the two other levels, social roles and instrumental behavior. A comparison between the ratings on these two scales of patients in one large U.K. psychiatric hospital was carried by Sturt and Wykes (1987). They showed that social role measures of functioning were affected not only by the rate of attrition for those roles but also by floor effects (i.e., role functioning in many patients was very low, so the ratings showed little variability). However, a measure of instrumental functioning allowed more variable ratings and was able to define clearly a range of functioning in this group.

Although the levels of description of social functioning can be defined within these levels, especially in role performance and instrumental behavior, turning these descriptions into adequate measuring instruments is problematic. To define a decrement in performance one must define normal behavior, but this is not easy to do. One possibility is to define social functioning in terms of ideal functioning, but this does have its drawbacks. Apart from the fact that cultural mores change over time, a further complication is that not many "normal" people live up to the expectations of such ideal functioning. One clear example of this is a measure of social functioning called the Self-Care Measurement Schedule (Barnes & Benjamin, 1987). This schedule includes eating a meal in bed and not going shopping as items that contribute to a deviant behavior score. Although I consider myself reasonably "normal," I have certainly scored on both these items in the past month. But I do not consider myself to be deviant!

Other possibilities for a definition of normal functioning might include using the variety of responses from different groups on a measurement schedule to produce a profile of responses from which to draw up a statistical normal curve. This would then allow deviations from the average to be measured. Cultural and social expectations complicated by pure demographic characteristics such as age and sex complicate the identification of ideal functioning, making it necessary to provide many different norms, which could change within a decade as social expectations alter.

A more useful approach is to turn the problem on its head and to define not ideal functioning but levels of disability. These levels, unlike those for normal or ideal functioning, would be ones below which the majority of the population would not score but which would provide discrimination between people who have serious and those who have minor social functioning disability. This schema has generally been adopted in studies of social functioning especially in relation to the evaluation of treatments and services for patients with schizophrenia. It provides the most unambiguous and culture-free definition. It is quite easy to provide continuous checks on the definition by evaluating whether people not disabled by serious illnesses score on any of the items on the assessment schedule. This is the approach adopted in the development of many schedules of the instrumental functioning type, such as the Social Behavior Schedule (Wykes & Sturt, 1986) and REHAB (Baker & Hall, 1988).

RESIDENTIAL AND INSTITUTIONAL SETTINGS

Residential and institutional settings in the context of this book are ones that provide care for patients with psychiatric disorders and in addition provide some shelter from the community. Institutions are a subset of residential settings distinguished mainly by the rules that regulate the behavior of both the patients and the staff. In fact, in several dictionaries the word *institution* is defined by "law, custom and practice." These rules do not take account of the individuals who live in the institution, rather they are or were developed for the benefit of the institution or its administrators. Sometimes the rules may have lost their original meaning but continue to be incorporated into the depersonalized routine. Many rules provide little opportunity to practice normal social roles.

The above definition and description compares poorly with the reasons for setting up such institutions. More than 100 years ago the trustees of the Willard Asylum for the insane in western New York explained the purpose of their new institution.

. . . It would be a home for those people who have neither home nor friends, and who are without the means financially or capacity intellectually to provide for themselves, with intellect shattered, minds darkened, living amid delusions, a constant prey to unrest, haunted by wild imagining. They now have in their sole misfortune a safe refuge, kindly care, constant watching, and are as comfortable as their circumstances will allow. (Cited in Bassuk & Gerson, 1978, p. 53)

The subsequent failure to maintain or improve institutions with that purpose probably reflects economic, political, and administrative realities over the subsequent century. Despite progressive social policies, conditions similar to the worst institutions of 50 years ago still exist today. One recent example being in the State Mental Hospital on the island of Leros in Greece (Bouras, Webb, Clifford, Papadatos, & Zouni, 1992).

King and Raynes (1968a) developed measures of the practices within these large institutions. They, too, decided that administrative realities do affect the way in which practices develop. A large organization often reacts by establishing a hierarchical management structure, which removes some responsibility and much of the power from individuals at lower levels in the hierarchy (King & Raynes, 1968b). But not all large establishments develop institutional rather than client-oriented practices and not all small ones are prevented by their size from becoming impersonal institutions. In one study of community care, the most restrictive environment was found to be a small, privately run residential home in a wealthy suburban area. This community home was even more restrictive than an acute hospital ward (Wykes et al., 1982). Clients were allowed out only in groups of four or five people. There was little privacy for bathing (i.e., no locks on the bathroom), and no flexibility was permitted in the general rules for individuals.

The notion that patients should spend as little time in a hospital as possible is not a new one. Staff have been energetically discharging patients from large mental hospitals for many decades, although the term *community care* was not coined until the 1960s. Surveys of patients (e.g., Wing & Brown, 1970) had reported that even those people who had been in a hospital for some time could be moved directly to community services. However, others needed some form of social rehabilitation before being transferred. There was even some optimism that we might be able to dispense with beds in long-term psychiatric care altogether, given the new pharmacological and social treatments for schizophrenia that had become available in

that decade. However, it soon became obvious to clinicians that the initial optimism had to be tempered. Many patients were identified who could not be transferred into the community unless other supportive services were provided, such as day care and sheltered housing. Surveys of hospitals in the 1970s (Mann & Cree, 1976b; Mann & Sproule, 1972) revealed that there was even a group of people who were accumulating in hospitals, despite the advantages of all the new medical and social care. This group of patients became known as the "new" long stay. Although some studies have advocated drastically reducing the number and length of admissions to psychiatric hospital, few have advocated the closure of all psychiatric beds.

Because patients exhibit a variety of handicaps and disabilities, the residential settings available need to provide a range of levels of support. At the least-supported end of the spectrum is housing designated specifically for patients with psychiatric difficulties where patients live alone but are visited at regular intervals by carers from the psychiatric services. The next general level is the group home where several people with psychiatric problems live together supported by psychiatric care workers. Usually the people in the group home have been prepared for this lifestyle when they were long-term inpatients. Living together does not mean that all household tasks are shared. At the next level there are more highly supported hostels where meals are provided and where there is often a supervisor on the premises at night.

In addition to the community residences is an establishment falling in between the hospital ward and the community. These settings are known as "new" long-stay hostels. The first was opened at the Maudsley Hospital in the late 1970s and was followed (too slowly) by three other examples. These were literally "wards in house." They were staffed by nurses but offered many of the opportunities of a normal home.

Patients in a Residential or Institutional Setting

In the past a great majority of patients suffering from schizophrenia in industrialized countries were admitted to a hospital. A proportion were detained for long periods. In the United Kingdom many mental hospitals were built outside of main towns and were relatively independent of the outside world. Some had farms attached to them and provided for the work, leisure, and social life of the patients who lived there. There was a wide variation in the quality of care these hospitals provided.

Economic and social pressures over the past 30 years have led to government policy changes about the site of long-term psychiatric care and the development of care in the community. This has led to the reduction in the number and size of psychiatric hospitals around the world. The process has been known as deinstitutionalization. The re-provision of the services provided by large hospitals has as a priority the shelter of these individuals, so there has been a great increase in the type and availability of houses, flats, group homes, and hostels in the community. Although patients with schizophrenia may have somewhere to live when they leave the hospital, they may not have anything to do during the day.

Just as for most of the population, the choices of where to live are varied. One can live with family or friends, in one's own home or someone else's home, in a city or the countryside. But these choices depend on being able to maintain certain levels of functioning, so that bills are paid and the shopping brought home. For some patients with schizophrenia even these tasks are too difficult, and they need the continued support of psychiatric services to prevent gross deterioration. For this subgroup of patients with schizophrenia the most optimal outcome is to be provided with continued psychiatric care, which is titrated to provide the "minimum therapeutic dose of psychiatric support" for maximizing potential functioning (Birley, 1974). For some patients this means that they will be provided with outpatient care, for others home visits by a community psychiatric nurse, and for others the asylum and the care of a hospital is needed either in the short or long term. These needs for care may fluctuate over time and require a flexible, responsive psychiatric service.

A crude estimate of the numbers of patients with a chronic course of schizophrenia who are in touch with hospital services, living in hostels or group homes, or attending day centers can be derived from psychiatric case registers. For Camberwell, a deprived inner urban area of London, the prevalence of psychiatric disorder is about 170 per 100,000 population (Wing, 1983), and other more recent estimates have suggested that the need for high-dependency care (24-hour staffed accommodation) is between 50 and 60 per 100,000 population (Wing & Furlong, 1986; Clifford, Charman, Webb, & Best, 1991). The majority of these patients will have diagnoses of schizophrenia. This figure, of course, excludes the group of people "living rough" who are thought to contain a number who are suffering from schizophrenia. About 40% of these patients were recommended for long-term hospital

placement (Clifford et al., 1991), possibly in hospital hostels. The remaining people in the high-dependency group were judged to be able to move to highly supported accommodations in the community. The main difficulty with this recommendation is that there are few of these places available (Audit Commission, 1986).

The provision of a variety of settings should (if there are enough) allow some appropriate matching of setting and level of patient dependency. Cross-sectional studies have shown that this is possible. Wykes et al. (1982) carried out a study of community care facilities and discovered that there were differences in the social behavior of residents of residential services depending on the level of support they were providing (see Figure 2.1). Group homes had the least disabled and hostels had the most disabled people. This result was replicated in Australia using a different measure of social performance (Andrews, Teeson, Stewart, & Hoult, 1990). Similarly in comparisons of "new" long-stay inpatients and hostel residents, the long-stay inpatients receiving the highest level of care were significantly more socially disabled (Wykes & Wing, 1992). But the matching is not absolute, and there is variability of disability within each type of residential setting.

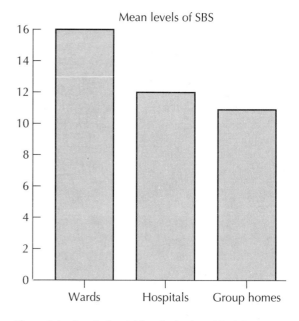

Figure 2.1.   Level of social functioning in residential care

Source: Wykes, Sturt, & Creer (1982).

SOCIAL BEHAVIOR AND INSTITUTIONAL PRACTICES

Institutional practices undoubtedly have an effect on human beings. Social expectations can increase or decrease the range of behaviors that are shown and can sometimes change behavior markedly. In 1973 social psychologists carried out a remarkable experiment on the effects of social roles and environments on social behavior (Haney, Banks, & Zimbardo, 1973). The basement at Stanford University was converted to a sham prison. Twenty-one volunteer students who had been assessed as emotionally stable were chosen by the researchers to act as either warders or prisoners. To make it as realistic as possible, the research participants were "arrested" at their homes by the local police and brought to the prison where they were stripped and showered before being dressed in prison uniforms. The "warders" wore uniforms, too, which reflected their status. They also had mirrored sunglasses, batons, and whistles. The experiment had been planned to last two weeks, but it was stopped after only a few days because of the increasing psychological brutality of the "warders." They were not allowed to use physical violence, but they introduced rules, such as making it a privilege to go to the toilet. Five of the prisoners had to be released from the study, because they began to show psychological disturbances such as anxiety and depression.

A number of factors affected behavior in this study, the main one being role expectation. The "warders" were not the only ones who took on their roles; the "prisoners" did too. They expected to be helpless and at the guards' mercy and rapidly became depressed and dependent.

Another factor is the process of deindividuation. This refers to the loss of personal identity, so that individuals merge into a mob. The uniforms, mirrored sunglasses, and so on all contributed toward the identification of the group. Johnson and Downing (1979) in a further investigation of the effects of this role association asked groups of women to give shocks to a stooge participant. The real research subjects were dressed either in their own clothes, in nurse uniforms, or in a sort of "Ku Klux Klan" outfit. It was suggested that the wearing of a uniform would increase deindividuation by role association. There was some support for this hypothesis, but fortunately the participants dressed in nurse uniforms gave the smallest shocks of all the groups.

Although there is much critical debate about the potency of deindividuation (see Prentice-Dunn & Rogers, 1982), people in a crowd are likely to act more cruelly and impulsively than they would if they were on their own. A follow-up study designed by Zimbardo to investigate different ways of preventing the cruelty produced by the Stanford prison experiment (e.g., prior staff training) was never allowed because of the ethical problems associated with such experiments. But as far as we known the people who took part in the original study did not show long-term adverse effects to the traumatic conditions they were subjected to, witnessed, or took part in so the roles and institutions only produced a temporary change in behavior.

It is not just the short-term studies of student populations that lead us to the conclusion that institutions with their potent role expectations can affect our behavior. Descriptions of life in a concentration camp compels readers to accept that both guards and inmates can react to conditions that permit persecution in ways in which most people can hardly contemplate.

The evidence of the effects of institutions on the long-term course of social development is mixed. The results of long-term follow-up studies of children adopted from deprived environments (institutions or the streets) show that about three quarters do quite well in adulthood (Tizard, 1991). Some more recent evidence suggests that subtle differences might still exist at adolescence, but these were certainly not overwhelming (Hodges & Tizard, 1989). That there are increased risks of psychological disturbances in children who are exposed to environmental poverty is clear, but these relationships may be extremely complicated. A continuation of the effects into adulthood probably depends on the presence of other adverse experiences or choices made by the individual throughout life (Rutter, 1993).

Although the word *institution* has become synonymous with poor regimes within psychiatry, in other areas institutions may change people's behavior for the better. These good institutions include schools and religious organizations, which are both usually either tolerated or valued because society approves of, or is indifferent to, their goals.

In summary, institutions can change behavior for the good or ill, permanently and temporarily, but what we need to consider as part of this chapter is how much they are responsible for the behavioral changes seen in patients who are diagnosed as having schizophrenia.

A Model of Social Disability in Patients with Schizophrenia

To investigate the relationship between social behavior and institutional practices in a theoretical framework, we first need to consider a model of the development of handicap in patients with schizophrenia. The one that has had the most influence was developed by Wing (1978). He characterized these difficulties in social functioning as being made up of intrinsic impairments, social disadvantages, and adverse self-attitudes.

Intrinsic impairments are those that underlie the disorder and are biological or psychosocial. Many existed prior to the onset of the disorder, such as the cognitive factors that in high-risk groups (those with a parent or close relative with schizophrenia) are predictive of membership of the high-risk group and whose severity is predictive of those people who later develop the disorder. But they can also include factors that may be shared by many others, such as low intelligence and being physically disabled. In some versions of the model, symptomatology is included. The positive symptoms of schizophrenia—such as hallucinations, delusions, or perceptual distortions—that are pathognomonic of the disorder are also included as well as negative symptoms such as social withdrawal, inactivity, and poverty of thought of speech. In addition the affective symptoms of anxiety or depression can affect both the level of the disability produced by primary handicaps as well as the severity of other symptoms.

Social disadvantages, such as poverty or homelessness either before or after the onset of schizophrenia, can lead to the development of an unnecessary degree of social disablement. Any adverse responses to the person with schizophrenia by family or friends following the onset of the disorder also fall into this category.

Adverse self-attitudes, such as an individual's attitude to the impairment of schizophrenia or to the social disadvantage, can add a further layer of disablement. This secondary disability can be so severe as to sometimes be indistinguishable from the underlying impairment. For example, some patients become so apathetic that they lose all initiative. At its extreme it is known as institutionalism. In its milder forms, adverse self-attitudes may mean a loss of confidence in using skills that are unimpaired. All three factors—intrinsic impairments, social disadvantages, and adverse self-attitudes—contribute to the degree of social impairment.

Institutions may therefore interfere with social disability by changing the primary handicaps of the patients and producing positive as well as negative symptomatic behavior. It may also act to increase secondary handicaps by removing the patients from their normal social contacts and by preventing them from continuing to practice skills and also allow further development of adverse attitudes and hopelessness about the disorder.

Social Behaviors of People with Schizophrenia in Institutions and Residential Settings

Behaviors can be divided into those that are socially inappropriate and those that are part of a syndrome of social withdrawal. But all people with schizophrenia are unique, and although they share some general features it is usual for the category "other problematic behaviors" to be the most frequent in the long-term population. Table 2.1 shows the percentage of people in one hospital survey who show problems in social functioning as scored on (Social Behavior Scale Wykes & Sturt, 1986). All the problems scored on SBS are observable behaviors. For example, depression is only scored if the person cries or exhibits a depressed countenance, not just if the person

Table 2.1. Level of Behavior Problems in Patients with Schizophrenia

Attention seeking	21%
Acting on delusions	25%
Incoherent speech	18%
Severe concentration problems	14%
Depression	14%
Socially unacceptable behavior (e.g., poor table manners)	11%
Hostility toward others	18%
Poor personal hygiene	36%
Difficulties initiating conversation	25%
Laughing and talking to self	32%
Odd or inappropriate conversation	42%
Other behaviors that impede living in the community	36%
Overactivity	14%
Panic attacks and phobias	24%
Posturing and mannerisms	32%
Inappropriate sexual behavior toward others	4%
Slowness	21%
Problems of social mixing	39%
Suicidal behavior	7%
Underactivity	14%
Destructive behavior toward property	7%

Source: Data taken from an original sample described in Wykes and Sturt (1986).

says they are depressed. This is therefore a conservative estimate of the difficulties in this sample.

No one in the sample scored on more than 11 problem areas, which suggests a wide variability on the behavior profiles, and two people did not score at all even though they were currently attending supportive day care and living in a hostel. The four highest categories of problem behaviors are odd or inappropriate conversation, problems of social mixing, personal hygiene, and other behaviors. Poor personal hygiene and odd conversation can dramatically affect the opportunities for social interaction in the community. The category of social mixing refers to the ability of the patients to respond appropriately in the community. "Other behaviors" consisted of a range of problems such as eating problems (either too much or too little), stealing, and suspiciousness. None of these individual items was a problem for more than 5% of the population.

At least one of the potential difficulties that prevents normal social interaction (e.g., ability to initiate conversations, responding appropriately, odd or inappropriate conversation, incoherent speech) was exhibited by 86% of the sample (i.e., the majority exhibited behaviors that prevented normal social functioning).

Institutions and the Social Behavior of Patients with Schizophrenia

Types of Studies and Their Problems

There are problems in investigating how much institutions affect social behavior in any group of patients but particularly so if the patients are diagnosed as having schizophrenia, in which a change in social behavior is at the core of the diagnosis. There are several ways in which it can be explored although the results are all subject to some caveats.

First, one can compare patients who have been exposed to institutions with those who have not been exposed. Most of these studies are cross-sectional or short-term prospective studies comparing the social behavior of patients in the same or different countries who are exposed to different sorts regimes. For studies carried out in the same country, unless they are randomized trials, there is no certainty that those who are exposed to institutions for a long time were the same initially as those who have had little exposure. This is because the patients who spend a large proportion of their time in a hospital may be more aggressive, have fewer social supports, or have poorer

premorbid histories. Diagnostic variations over time will also complicate our understanding of the effects.

When comparisons are made between different countries, assumptions have to be made that diagnostic practices, social support, and history of service availability across countries are similar. This is apart from any assumptions about the effects of culture on the manifestation of the disorder itself.

The other type of study is longitudinal and either investigates the same patients over time or compares cohorts of patients who have been exposed to different environments. But over time many changes occur not only in the environment provided but also in other treatment practices, such as medication. These extra-environment changes could account for the observed variations in behavior. One further problem is that a selected sample of patients is investigated. Those who have good social supports such as a marriage are more likely to be discharged and are therefore less likely to be included. The study will then only provide information on a subset of those with schizophrenia.

All prospective studies must also take into account the natural history of the disorder. Now more studies suggest that patients with a diagnosis of schizophrenia have a number of possible courses affected by symptomatic, occupational, interpersonal, and motivational factors at each stage (Strauss et al., 1985). However, despite the heterogeneity progressive deterioration clearly is not a characteristic of schizophrenia in general. Deterioration tends to be a phenomenon of the earlier 5 to 10 years followed by a plateau, termed *end states* by Bleuler (1978). Acute relapses may interrupt the plateau phase but usually resolve back to approximately the earlier level and improvement may occur in even the very long term (Miller & Cohen, 1987). This general phasic course will interfere with the identification of the environmental changes. For example, if there is exposure to poor environments initially, then the effects may be difficult to eradicate in the more reactive stage (i.e., it may have more permanent effects than either in other groups or in later stages of the disorder). Further changes in the environment after this initial toxic phase may then have little dramatic effect on the overall course of the disorder.

One must also consider the length of time that patients are exposed to institutionalizing environments. A short-term incarceration may produce only temporary effects. On the other hand, many years isolated with little social stimulation would surely affect most people in some way.

One of the first to suggest that a relationship may exist between service provision and psychiatric disorder was Gruenberg (1967). He showed that empirically defined behaviors that correlated with social withdrawal and hostility had reduced over time, both in frequency and in duration. He argued that this reduction was due to the reorganization of psychiatric services, which resulted in shorter hospital stays.

Social Behavior and Environmental Poverty

The major work on the effects of institutions on patients with schizophrenia was carried out by Wing and Brown (1970) in three large psychiatric hospitals in the United Kingdom between 1960 and 1968. They compared the practices of these hospitals with each other and related these differences to the social behavior of the resident patients. They did not find the tyrannical regimes discussed by Goffman (1968); rather they found a variety of levels of social deprivation where benign neglect alternated with an authoritarian concentration on patient hygiene. Patients were given little responsibility for their own care, and on one ward staff even combed every patient's hair once (and once only) every day. A brief quote from their description of Kerry ward will provide a flavor of the poverty of the environments that could be found during their study in the 1960s. This was a ward with the highest level of restrictions and contained 100 women who had lived in the hospital for a median of 14 years.

> The ward was on the first floor of the main hospital building with no ready access to the grounds. Its door was always locked. Practically the whole of the patients' lives was spent within the ward. There was little contact with the rest of the hospital and practically none with the world outside. . . . The hospital had extensive and attractive grounds, a hospital shop and a cinema; and there was work available for some patients. . . . But on Kerry ward only five patients were allowed to leave without the supervision of a nurse and only one worked elsewhere in the hospital. . . . Nurses took groups of patients for walks but these were irregular and brief and at the time of the survey no outing had taken place for some time.
> Movement around the ward was also restricted. Storerooms were locked (to keep them tidy) and washrooms except at mealtimes. The dormitories were locked during the day to prevent patients from going to bed too early (pp. 132–133)

Wing and Brown (1970) go on to describe the routine of the day, which involved a fixed timetable of dressing, washing, and eating. Clothes were given out from the hospital laundry by size rather than ownership, hair was combed by the staff, and everyone was bathed once a week. Patients had little to identify their individuality. They had few possessions and anyway there was nowhere to put anything even if they had had any. There was no evidence of tyranny; rather staff seemed to indulge in practices in order to provide some order to the working day. This then is a stringent test of the effects of poor environments on the social behavior of patients.

On other wards, such as Downswood Villa, movement was relatively unrestricted. Meetings were held between staff and patients to discuss problems and the rules on the ward. The kitchen was locked at eight o'clock when the day staff went off duty. All the patients went into the hospital grounds and some went to the nearby village. So even when institutions had poor reputations for the care, there were still islands of good practice.

Wing and Brown (1970) found significant correlations between the severity of what they describe as the "clinical poverty syndrome" (made up of poverty of speech, flatness of affect, and social withdrawal) with a range of indices of social poverty in these hospitals (correlations ranged from .32 to .66). The relationship between environmental poverty and the positive symptoms of schizophrenia (hallucinations, delusions, etc.) was not so consistent (correlations ranged from .09 to .36). This study not only was cross-sectional but also included a longitudinal prospective component. In this latter part, they measured the changes in behavior over time as the environments improved or deteriorated. They found that an improvement in the social environment was always accompanied by an overall reduction in social withdrawal and that clinical and social deterioration also always occurred together. However, not all patients did improve with changes in the social environment and some in fact deteriorated, but this will be discussed later in this chapter.

Curson, Pantelis, Ward, and Barnes (1992) replicated the three hospitals study and showed only a weak correlation between clinical poverty and poverty of the social environment. However, there were fewer patients in the new study who fell into the severe impairment category perhaps because of treatment or diagnosis changes. Fortunately, there were also less extreme examples of environmental poverty and therefore less variation in the hospital environment than in the previous study. Both these factors could account for the different results.

Social Behavior and Length of Hospitalization

As well as relating the poverty of environments to social behavior and symptoms, Wing and Brown (1970) also found a relationship between length of hospital stay and the current clinical poverty syndrome. But the relationship between environmental poverty and the clinical poverty remained even when length of stay had been controlled. This suggests that some effects of the environment are independent of the time spent in that poor environment.

Since this seminal work a number of studies have reported that length of hospital stay was not correlated with current clinical state. For example, Johnstone, Owen, Gold, Crow, and McMillan (1981) found that when the total samples of inpatients and outpatients were compared, outpatients showed significantly less impairment in terms of negative features and cognitive function. But when they used a procedure to match the two groups, they eliminated the differences in negative symptoms but not that in cognitive functioning. The authors suggested that their initial results could have lead to the conclusion that hospital care had contributed to the increased negative features in the hospital group, but this effect was eliminated by their matching procedure. But the conclusion of no effect of environment is also problematic, because patients in long-term hospital care seem to be selected on the basis of their intrinsic impairments. For this group of patients the institutional regime of a large mental hospital may have little effect on the end state. Their matching procedure, however, is somewhat problematic because it excluded more than half the patients who had longer illnesses, and the final inpatient sample was much less disabled than typical hospital populations (Abramson & Brenner, 1978).

Others, too, have noted high levels of social withdrawal and disability in patients who have not spent many years in a hospital and had had the opportunity of new medical and social treatments. These patients had been in a hospital between one and four years and are known as the "new" long-stay patients (Mann & Sproule, 1972; Mann & Cree, 1976a; Wykes, 1982).

Mathai and Gopinath (1985) compared patients with schizophrenia who were outpatients, day patients, or inpatients of two hospitals. They claimed that they found no evidence of the relationship between an environmental measure and ratings on the Wing Ward behavior rating scale. However, the samples were small and no information is provided about the inclusion or exclusion criteria. The social behavior scores are only provided as summaries not as divided into the positive and negative components. In the original three hospitals study, there was only a relationship between the negative symptoms and the poverty of environments.

Comparisons of Social Behavior in Different Psychiatric Services

Randomized control trials comparing hospital based with community treatments measure changes in symptoms, satisfaction, and social behavior up to two years after entering the programs. All studies of this type, irrespective of the intervention and the group of patients (acute versus chronic, first admission only, etc.), show reductions in hospital admission rates and time spent in a hospital for the community-treated group. But many do not show improvements in either symptoms or social behavior of the community-treated group over the group given traditional hospital-based care (e.g., Creed et al., 1991; Marks et al., 1994; Burns, Raftery, Beadsmore, McGuigan & Dickson, 1993; Merson et al., 1992). This result may be due to the measuring instruments adopted in these studies (i.e., they use social role functioning measures, which are less likely to change over the period of the study). The effects of providing treatment in two different environments may be subtle especially in the first few years. These subtle changes are unlikely to be identified by changes in social roles, and instrumental functioning measures would be more suitable. The changes, especially in the longer-term patient groups, are also less likely to respond in the short periods investigated in these studies.

However, two community care studies have shown differences between hospital-based and community-based treatments (Stein & Test, 1980; Hoult & Reynolds, 1994), but in these studies the community group had many sorts of treatments that differed from the traditional hospital-based treatment, including more contact with a professional carer. This element of social contact alone could account for the social behavior differences rather than the effect of the opportunities provided by the different environments.

Novel residential settings that care for the "new" long stay (i.e., those who seem to have developed clinical poverty early in their psychiatric career) have been evaluated. Two of these evaluations produced positive results. Patients who were transferred to the new settings improved their social behavior initially and the time spent doing nothing compared with similar patients who remained in a typical hospital ward (Wykes, 1982). The improvements, however, did not seem to continue, and although some behavior problems reduced other behaviors became problematic. These "hospital hostels" provided homelike atmospheres, less restrictions than on a ward, and more opportunities to use local facilities. They also produced better management practices in that staff were more client centered than in hospital wards. The staff felt more involved with the treatment procedures, and they began to set up wider-ranging rehabilitation programs (see Garety & Morris, 1984). But not all the hospital hostels were a success, and clearly some were able to accept patients with more disruptive behaviors than others. The first hospital hostel had the best outcome and accepted all patients referred on the basis of the time spent in a hospital and sent fewer patients back to the referring ward. But this hostel was in close proximity to the hospital (it was actually on the hospital site). There was professional backup available if necessary, and although this was rarely used it gave the nurses confidence in dealing with disruptive and difficult behaviors. The distance between the hostel and the hospital base was inversely correlated with the level of exclusions from that care. So, with some reservations, it is possible to provide severely disabled patients with less restrictive care offering more opportunities to practice skills, but measurable effects on social behavior occur within a short time after admission and from then onward take some considerable time to change.

The interpretation of these disparate results is clearly complicated by the changing admission and diagnostic criteria and the availability of treatments especially in the early stages of the disorder. But they do suggest that time within an environment is not crucial to the development of the clinical poverty syndrome in patients diagnosed with schizophrenia. However, to conclude, as many authors have, that these results suggest that institutionalism does not occur would be incorrect.

Longitudinal studies of changes in environments, such as providing more choice and access to services by moving from an institution (psychiatric hospital) to the community, is usually measured over a relatively short time,

perhaps 2 to 3 years. Many of these studies of reprovision have shown little change over this time in behavior although there are some minor improvements in the social networks of these patients (Anderson et al., 1993). But a recent study found that symptomatic and social functioning effects were only measurable after the person had been living continuously in the community for at least 3 years (Wykes, 1994). These patients were similar to those in the Curson et al. (1992) study. There were fewer severely disabled than in the original three hospitals study, but in this case the environments were very different not perhaps in the restrictiveness but in the opportunities that the new community environments could offer.

Deterioration Following Environmental Improvements

Not all patients improve their functioning when they are transferred to settings that have more opportunities. Wing and Brown (1970) noted that when environmental poverty was decreased some of their patients deteriorated. Francis, Vessey, and Lowe (1994) reported on the behavior of a total hospital population over the period when the hospital closed and patients were transferred to community settings. Using time-series analyses of individual data sets, they did not detect any significant behavior changes in the majority of patients. However, approximately 20% did show improvements and 12% showed behavioral deterioration. No variables were found to discriminate the deteriorated from the remaining group.

In a recent series of studies following up patients who have moved into the community (from one of the original three hospitals), patients who had cognitive disabilities were found in settings with higher levels of support and were less likely to be transferred to less dependent care. But if they were transferred, they were likely to deteriorate (Wykes, Katz, Sturt & Hemsley, 1992; Wykes & Dunn, 1992; Wykes, 1994). The patients in the longer-stay settings with cognitive disabilities could not be distinguished from those who did not have such disabilities on the basis of the chronicity of disorder, their current mental state, or their social behavior. Few variables, apart from cognitive deficit, were significant predictors for the group of patients who had a diagnosis of schizophrenia. This in itself suggests that perhaps for some patients their clinical poverty was due not to the institution but to their intrinsic impairments. However, this leaves a number of other patients who did not show response processing difficulties but who still showed high levels of negative symptoms and social withdrawal. It is this group that might be the most affected by their environment and be prone to institutionalism.

Cognitive factors, not symptomatic factors, were also found by Johnstone, Owens, Frith, and Leary (1991) to differentiate those patients who remained in a hospital and those who were attending outpatient care. Breier, Schreiber, Dyer, and Pickar (1991) also showed that cognitive deficits measured by neuropsychological tests of frontal lobe functioning significantly correlated with outcome levels of negative symptoms and social functioning even when hospitalization was controlled.

Further recent data also support the view that cognitive deficits may be important in the process of rehabilitation. Mueser, Bellack, Douglas, and Wade (1991) have shown that memory problems are associated with the severity of social skills problems and interfere with the rehabilitation of these skills. Hoffman and Satel (1993) also found that memory problems interfered with a program of language therapy for patients with diagnoses of schizophrenia. The relationship between basic cognitive deficits and social functioning outcome has not yet been defined adequately although Morrison and Bellack (1987) have suggested that some cognitive deficits may produce some basic distortions in the interpretation of social information. The person's response to these distortions could be to communicate inappropriately or to reduce responding (i.e., produce more negative symptoms such as poverty of speech).

Studies reported by Wallace (1984) suggest that certain subgroups of patients with schizophrenia show lower rates of social responding, sensitivity to social reward, and poorer processing of social information. These patients also show deficient personal functioning prior to the onset of the original episode of schizophrenia. In other words, their deficits were obvious prior to onset and their first experience of hospital admission.

Patients who had information-processing deficits and were transferred to the community were at a disadvantage in the studies reported by Wykes and colleagues (e.g., Wykes, Sturt, & Katz, 1990); Wykes, 1994). These patients did not improve; on the contrary, they deteriorated just as some patients in the three hospitals study deteriorated after there was an increase in social stimulation on the wards. Other studies have also noted this effect of "overstimulation" (e.g., Brown & Birley, 1968). This led to the notion that the best outcome was to provide the optimal environment. But perhaps patients with cognitive deficits seek environments that reduce their need to process information. These environments would be predictable and would reduce the need of the patient to make choices. These are just the sort of environments that are provided by the old mental hospitals or asylums.

The process of institutionalism has therefore been complicated by the presence of two groups. The first group consists of people with schizophrenia who have cognitive deficits who may be less responsive to institutionalism. The second group includes patients who do not show such profound deficits and are therefore more likely to be affected adversely by the low stimulation and poor individual choice provided by institutions. But, patients with deficits are more likely to respond poorly to environments that have high processing demands such as those that are part of the community care spectrum of settings.

Concluding that the cognitive deficit subgroup should be allowed to live in low stimulation wards in institutions, however, would be wrong. Living in the community is what people with schizophrenia want to do, and their satisfaction with services is the most consistent result in the community care literature. What these data do suggest is a way of identifying a possible core deficit in schizophrenia that prevents further progress. This deficit may be described as a vulnerability factor in schizophrenia, but this does not necessarily mean that it is refractory or that new approaches to information-processing skills could not be found to overcome some of the disability produced. What is needed is a new rehabilitation focus for these deficits as suggested by Kern and Green, (Chapter 21), which may help these patients achieve their maximum potential and quality of life.

Influences of Staff Behavior

Hospitals and residential facilities for patients with schizophrenia rely on staff to provide the vital support necessary for alleviating distress and for improving the quality of life of severely disabled patients. The way in which roles may affect staff has been discussed, but other specific factors in the behavior of staff toward patients also could have a detrimental effect. These factors are especially important when there is continuity of staff within a small service and when the key worker system promotes long-term relationships between staff and particular clients.

The first major effect staff can have on patients is via their expressed emotion (EE). This was initially developed as a way of measuring family life (Brown, Birley, & Wing 1972). It is detected from interviews and consists of five main components: critical comments, hostility, positive remarks, emotional overinvolvement, and warmth. The first three components are now known to predict relapse in patients with schizophrenia (see Kuipers, 1994, for a review and Chapter 3 for details of its effects). In summary if the number of critical comments in a short interview are greater or equal to six, then there is a higher chance of a relapse. The relapse rates over a number of studies and across cultures show that they are approximately 21% for low EE groups and 48% for high EE groups.

Recently these notions have begun to be investigated in carers rather than families. After all, many patients do not live with their families, but they see some staff almost every day. A series of studies have now shown that staff emit a range of EE attitudes. In the first study, over 40% of key workers had a high rating about at least one of their key patients (Moore, 1992). A study in Italy showed that no relationship existed between staff EE and family EE, showing that the patients themselves did not reliably predict a high EE response in carers (Beltz et al., 1991).

Similar outcome results have been obtained in studies of EE in families. For example, in a prospective study of two hostels, one of which was characterized by staff with high EE attitudes and one by low EE attitudes, patients in the former had poorer outcomes (Ball, Moore, & Kuipers, 1992).

There is little work on the development of such potentially destructive attitudes in staff, but in an unpublished study of staff who had been assaulted, Cottle, Kuipers, and Murray, (1992) found a raised incidence of EE toward the assailant and raised anxiety in the subsequent month. In a further study, a content analysis of the staff's major criticisms showed that socially embarrassing or difficult behavior and the clinical poverty syndrome were often cited (Moore, Kuipers, & Bull, 1992). Although there does not seem to be a stereotypical patient who attracts high levels of criticism, certain profiles of social behaviors will increase the probability of a high EE response in staff.

The effect of patients on the behavior of others was graphically described by Morgan (1977). To study whether there was an abnormality of diurnal rhythm in patients with schizophrenia, he went with two chronically disabled patients with diagnoses of schizophrenia into an isolation bunker for 3 weeks. In the bunker they were completely cut off from the outside world, so that they did not know whether it was day or night. On entering the

bunker Morgan's expectation was that there would be a sharing of domestic chores, but this was not the case as the quote below illustrates.

> It was difficult to have any flexible arrangement for doing the kind of jobs that healthy people would have shared on a spontaneous rota. Whenever I did any small thing that was conventionally theirs, their subsequent hesitation suggested that they thought I might want to take it over completely. . . . Yet in a strange way, the patients were very easy to live with . . . the sort of behaviour that leads healthy people to get on each others nerves in such a situation had been eliminated. I noticed first that they kept out of my way, but I noticed later that they were equally careful to keep out of each other's way and avoid body contact. It was made very plain to me . . . that custodial care is the outcome of a two way process. The view that it is provided by staff alone to unwilling or passive patients is an oversimplification. My patients deliberately (if non-verbally) asked for the ingredients of custodial care, such as direction, over-protection and under-estimation. I found it quite natural to collaborate with them in supplying what they wanted and practically impossible to refrain and raise my expectation when what they wanted and practically impossible to refrain and raise my expectation when what this then received was repeated disappointment. This experience further increased the respect I had for the skill and technique of the modern mental nurse, who can rise above this level. (Morgan p. 508, 1977)

These two factors—EE and the responsiveness of staff to patient dependency—clearly affect the social milieu of residential and institutional settings in a way that may be detrimental to the social functioning of the residents. Training for staff to prevent the latter is part of professional qualifications, although as more untrained staff are involved in residential care the quality of the staff input must be closely monitored. Training packages are currently being developed to help staff overcome or evade high EE (Kuipers, 1994).

Social Functioning Assessments in Residential Settings

The process of developing assessments to measure the level of social functioning has been categorized by Wing (1989) into the following:

1. to understand and differentiate among the causes of social disablement,
2. to devise ways of preventing or reducing the impact of these causes,

3. to design services that will identify people in need and provide them with effective, acceptable, and economic help.

The role that the assessment of social functioning has played in relating behavior to environmental demand and its association with rehabilitation programs has been discussed in some detail. This section will concentrate on the role of social functioning assessments in the design of appropriate residential services.

As services change and evolve, especially toward more care in the community, there is a need to plan for the future patient population needs. Using the normative data from cross-sectional studies of community services, one can suggest levels of service provision based on measures of the global functioning of patients. However, these general surveys provide no information on which individuals would benefit from which services as there is wide variability in the acceptability of patients into specific facilities. For instance, a patient may only have one problem, such as violence to others, whereas another may have numerous social functioning problems that do not include violence. But despite the level of disability, the patient with many problems would probably be more easily placed in the community.

The same assessment instruments can therefore be used to provide profiles of patient populations as well as an individual profile of the pattern of problems. But even this individual pattern gives little guidance to the specific rehabilitation program the patient may be offered. To design specific packages of care, Brewin et al. (1988) devised the Needs for Care Schedule based on earlier work on the needs of people living in the community (Wykes, Sturt, & Creer, 1982). The final detailed schedule assesses the social functioning of patients using a modified form of SBS and a list of needs for care, such as the need for sheltered housing or day care. This then enables the appropriate package of care to be devised.

Measuring instruments have been designed to cover the three areas discussed at the beginning of this chapter: social attainments, social roles, and instrumental behavior. The sort of measuring instrument adopted will depend on the question to be answered and the availability of resources to collect data. Social attainment data only provide historical context and are probably of little use in determining the residential status of either individuals or populations. However, social role functioning and instrumental functioning are important, and the severity of the disability of the population will determine which sort of

schedule should be used. Those patients who are severely disabled and who require residential care will usually require the detail provided by instrumental functioning schedules. Instrumental functioning schedules such as REHAB (Baker & Hall, 1988), SBS (Wykes & Sturt, 1986), and Life Skills Profile (Rosen, Hadzi-Pavlovic, & Parker, 1989) have all been used in predicting levels of supervised accommodation as well as the Needs for Care schedule (e.g., Pryce et al., 1993).

As well as predicting individual programs and population needs for residential care, social functioning assessments are also essential in monitoring the quality of care of residential settings over time. All residential settings should provide as a minimum the maintenance of current functioning, and those that fail this simple test need further investigation.

Keeping staff morale high when they are working with severely disabled patients who do not show many changes over time is sometimes difficult. Social assessments, especially those that are detailed and that will pick up subtle changes that are hard to notice during the working day, can provide staff with some essential positive reinforcement to aid morale and enthusiasm for the long rehabilitation process.

In the next section a few examples will be provided of appropriate methods for the assessment of social functioning in residential settings (i.e., for those populations of patients who are more severely disabled). This will not be a comprehensive list, and others will be described in subsequent chapters. Anyone who requires more detail on the numerous tools available should refer to the following reviews: Wallace (1986); Weissman (1975); Weissman, Scholomkas, and John (1981); Kane, Kane, and Arnold (1985); Beels, Gutworth, Berkeley, & Streuening (1984); Anthony and Farkas (1982); Platt (1986). However, the reader must be prepared to be disappointed with the material in such reviews as the criticisms of most assessments are often quite damning. Hall (1980) in a review of 29 ward rating scales for the severely disabled population only found two that he though were acceptable rating instruments.

Social Functioning Assessment Instruments for Use in Residential Settings

Table 2.2 provides an overview of instruments that have reasonable reliability and validity and that have been used in studies of community residential facilities. More

Table 2.2. Social Role and Instrumental Behavior Rating Scales

NAME	AREAS ASSESSED
Katz Adjustment Scale	Symptoms and expected activities
Rehabilitation Evaluation of Hall & Baker (REHAB)	General and deviant behavior
Social Behavior Schedule	Instrumental behaviors
Morningside Rehabilitation Status Scale	Symptoms, social roles, and deviant behavior
Life Skills Profile	Social roles and deviant behavior
Social Functioning Scale	Social roles
Social Behavior Assessment Scales	Eight roles
Global Assessment Scale	Symptoms and behavior combined in a single scale

detail of more frequently used schedules is provided below.

Social Behavior Schedule

The Social Behavior Schedule (SBS; Wykes & Sturt, 1986) contains 21 areas of problematic behavior almost all scored on a 5-point scale. Although they are generally rated on a 5-point scale to provide sensitivity to change, one can produce overall scores for the scale and individual severe or mild and severe problem scores for each item. The scale was designed to be completed by a rater following an interview with a key staff member, but it has now been shown that it can be used by staff members themselves and completed from information from relatives. The areas were determined by staff judgments of which problems would prevent transfer to less supported settings. These were tested in a hospital and community sample, and in all but one area, sexually inappropriate behavior, at least 5% of the population scored as having some difficulty on each item. Sexually inappropriate behavior was included because although it did not occur frequently it was felt by staff to be a vital area that would prevent transfer to the community. There are good reliability and validity data on the scale, which has now been used in many other studies and clinical settings (e.g., Vazquez Morejon & Jimenez-Garcia, 1989; Creed et al., 1991). The scale is also sensitive to changes in behavior

over time (Wykes, 1982). Norms are available for comparison. Overall scores of mild or severe problems can be derived. Pantelis, Taylor, and Campbell (1991) identified nine items that could produce the three syndromes suggested by Liddle (1987). The same authors found that symptom measures on these syndromes showed high correlations with the factors derived from SBS.

Social Functioning Scale

The Social Functioning Scale (SFS; Birchwood, Smith, Cochrane, Wetton, & Copestake 1990) was designed like the SBS to provide information vital to the community tenure of individuals with schizophrenia. It covers basic areas of functioning: social engagement, interpersonal behavior, prosocial activities, recreation, independence, and employment, which informants score as present or absent. The scale also differentiates between lack of performance and lack of competence in relation to skills necessary for independent living. Reliability and validity information is provided. The scale is also sensitive to change (Barrowclough & Tarrier, 1990), and scores can be compared with normative data.

REHAB

REHAB (Baker & Hall, 1988) was devised to monitor patients' rehabilitation outcome. It is divided into two main sections—a 16-item general behavior scale and a 7-item deviant behavior scale. The general behavior scale is divided further into 5 factors. Good reliability and validity data are available, and the scale is sensitive to change. Norms are available.

Life Skills Profile

The Life Skills Profile (Rosen et al., 1989) contains 39 items, which should be rated by two independent raters and the mean of the two ratings taken as the judgment. It was designed to measure functioning during periods of relative stability. The schedule consists of five scales: self-care, nonturbulence (offensive behavior, violence to others), social contact, communication, and responsibility (e.g., unreliable about taking medication). Each item is scored on a 4-point scale. There are good reliability and validity data available. The main difference between this scale and others in this area is that there are no items that measure symptomatic behavior.

Social Behavior
Assessment Scales

There are a number of separate parts to the Social Behavior Assessment scales (Platt, Weyman, & Hirsch,
1983), which can be used independently. The two main
social functioning scales are B and C. The B scale contains 66 questions relating to 22 types of behaviors, and C
has 48 items on social role performance. This is perhaps
the most comprehensive scale but unfortunately this
means it is lengthy for most clinical uses.

CONCLUSION

Patients with schizophrenia have social functioning
problems. In the past it was thought that some of this disability was due to the environments to which people with
diagnoses of schizophrenia were subjected. However,
even in the work of Wing and Brown (1970) the possibility of these social functioning problems being part of the
disorder was suggested. Wing and Brown actually characterized institutionalism not as those negative features
still seen in patients with schizophrenia wherever they live
(e.g., Johnstone et al., 1991) but as the indifferent attitude
to discharge. A reappraisal of the evidence suggests that
there are effects of environments that are subtle and may
be differentially related to the presence of other cognitive
deficits.

Because there are effects of different environments on
behavior (for good or ill), we must maintain appropriate
environments for people with schizophrenia. None of the
evidence suggests that we should return to the institutional
settings of the past. Rather it points to the need for providing havens in the community that improve the quality
of life of our patients. That is what users are demanding
and what (if they are allowed) health service professionals would wish to provide. The assessment of social functioning is an integral part of this endeavor. If we are to discover the links between environments and social behavior
in patients with schizophrenia and to discover new ways
of improving functioning, we must improve the subtlety
of our assessments not only of functioning but also of environmental demands.

REFERENCES

Abramson, D., & Brenner, D. (1978). *A study of "old long-stay"*
patients in Goodmayes Hospital. Final report of work carried
out during tenure of a DHSS grant 1976–78. London: DHSS.

Afflect, J., & McGuire, R. (1984). The measurement of psychiatric rehabilitation status. A review of needs and a new scale.
British Journal of Psychiatry, 145, 517–525.

American Psychiatric Association. (1994). *Diagnostic and statistical manual of mental disorders* (4th ed.). Washington, DC:
Author.

Anderson, J., Dayson, D., Willis, W., Gooch, C., Margolius, O.,
O'Driscoll, C., & Leff, J. (1993). Clinical and social outcomes
of long-stay psychiatric patients after one year in the community. *British Journal of Psychiatry Supplement, 19,* 45–56.

Andrews, G., Teeson, M., Stewart, G., & Hoult, J. (1990). Follow-up of community placement of chronic mentally ill in
New South Wales. *Hospital & Community Psychiatry, 41,*
184–188.

Anthony, W. A., & Farkas, M. A. (1982). A client outcome planning model for assessing psychiatric rehabilitation interventions. *Schizophrenia Bulletin, 8,* 13–38.

Audit Commission. (1986). *Making a reality of community care.*
London: HMSO.

Baker, R., & Hall, J. (1988). REHAB: A new assessment instrument for chronic psychiatric patients. *Schizophrenia Bulletin,
14,* 97–111.

Ball, R. A., Moore, E., & Kuipers, L. (1992). EE in community
care facilities: A comparison of patient outcome in a 9 month
follow-up of two residential hostels. *Social Psychiatry and
Psychiatric Epidemiology, 27,* 35–39.

Barnes, D., & Benjamin, S. (1987). The self-care assessment
schedule SCAS-1. The purpose and construction of a new assessment of self-care behaviors. *Journal of Psychometric Research, 31,* 191–202.

Barrowclough, C., & Tarrier, N. (1990). Social functioning in
schizophrenic patients: I. The effects of EE and family intervention. *Social Psychiatry and Psychiatric Epidemiology, 25,*
125–129.

Bassuk, E., & Gerson, S. (1978). Deinstitutionalization and mental health services. *American Journal of Psychiatry, 238,*
46–53.

Beels, C. C., Gutworth, L., Berkeley, J., & Struening, E. (1984).
Measurements of social support in schizophrenia. *Schizophrenia Bulletin, 10,* 399–411.

Beltz, J., Bertrando, P., Clerici, M., Albertini, E., Merat, O., &
Cazullo, C. (1991). Emotiva Espresso and schizophrenia: dai
failian agli operatori psichiatrici. Symposium of Expressed
Emotion in Latin Based Languages, Barcelona, Spain.

Birchwood, M., & Smith, J. (1990). Relatives and patients as
partners in the management of schizophrenia. *Psychological
Rehabilitation Journal, 13,* 27–30.

Birchwood M., Smith, J., Cochrane, R., Wetton S., and Copestake S. (1990). The Social Functional Scale. The development
and validation of a new scale for social adjustment for use in
family intervention programmes with schizophrenic patients.
British Journal of Psychiatry, 157, 853–859.

Birley, J. (1974). A housing association for psychiatric patients.
Psychiatric Quarterly, 48, 568–571.

Bleuler, M. (1978). *The schizophrenia disorders: Long-term patient and family studies.* New Haven: Yale University Press.

Bouras, N., Webb, Y., Clifford, P., Papadatos, Y., & Zouni, M. (1992). A needs survey among patients in Leros asylum. *British Journal of Psychiatry, 161,* 75–79.

Breier A., Schreiber J., Dyer, J., & Pickar, D. (1991). National Institute of Mental Health longitudinal study of chronic schizophrenia. Prognosis and predictors of outcome. *Archives of General Psychiatry, 48,* 239–246.

Brewin, C., Wing, J., Mangen, S., Brugha, T., MacCarthy, B., & Lesage, A. (1988). Needs for care among the long-term mentally ill: A report from the Camberwell High Contact Survey. *Psychological Medicine, 18,* 457–468.

Brown, G., & Birley, J. (1968). Crises and life changes and the onset of schizophrenia. *Journal of Health and Social Behaviour, 9,* 203–214.

Brown, G., Birley, J., & Wing, J. K. (1972). Influence of family life on the course of psychiatric disorder: A replication. *British Journal of Psychiatry, 121,* 241–258.

Burns, T., Raftery, J., Beadsmoore, A., McGuigan, S., & Dickson, M. (1993). A controlled trial of home based acute psychiatric services: II. Treatment patterns and costs. *British Journal of Psychiatry, 163,* 55–61.

Clifford, P., Charman, A., Webb, Y., & Best, S. (1991). Planning for community care: Long stay populations of hospitals scheduled for rundown or closure. *British Journal of Psychiatry, 158,* 190–196.

Corrigan, P., Wallace, C., & Green, M. (1992). Deficits in social schemata in schizophrenia. *Schizophrenia Research, 8,* 129–135.

Cottle, M., Kuipers, L., & Murray, G. (1992). *Expressed Emotion attributions and coping in staff victims of violence.* Unpublished MSc thesis, Institute of Psychiatry, London.

Creed, F., Black, D., Anthony, P., Osborn, M., Thomas, P., & Tormenson, B. (1991). Randomised control trial of day-patients vs. in-patients' psychiatric treatment. *British Medical Journal, 300,* 1033–1037.

Curson, D. A., Pantelis, C., Ward, J., & Barnes, T. R. E. (1992). Institutionalism and schizophrenia thirty years on: Clinical poverty and the social environment in three British mental hospitals in 1960 compared with a fourth in 1990. *British Journal of Psychiatry, 160,* 230–241.

Endicott, J., Spitzer, R., Fleiss, J., & Cohen, J. (1976). The Global Assessment Scale. *Archives of General Psychiatry, 33,* 776–771.

Francis, V., Vesey, P., & Lowe, G. (1994). The closure of a long stay psychiatric hospital: A longitudinal study of patients behaviour. *Social Psychiatry and Psychiatric Epidemiology, 29,* 184–189.

Garety, P., & Morris, I. (1984). A new unit for long stay psychiatric patients: Organization attitudes and quality of care. *Psychological Medicine, 14,* 183–192.

Goffman, E. (1968). *Asylums: Essays on the social situation of mental patients and other inmates.* Harmondsworth: Penguin.

Gruenberg, E. (1967). The social breakdown syndrome—Some origins. *American Journal of Psychiatry, 123,* 12–20.

Hall, J. (1980). Ward rating scales for long-stay patients: A review. *Psychological Medicine, 10,* 277–288.

Hall, J., & Baker, R. (1984). *REHAB: Users manual for rehabilitation evaluation.* Aberdeen: Vine Publishing.

Haney, C., Banks, W., & Zimbardo, P. (1973). Interpersonal dynamics in a simulated prison. *International Journal of Criminology and Penology, 1,* 69–79.

Harding, C., Brooks, G., Ashkinaga, T., Strauss, J., & Breier, A. (1987b). The Vermont longitudinal study of persons with severe mental illness I: Methodology, study sample and overall status 32 years later. *American Journal of Psychiatry, 144,* 718–736.

Harding, C., Zubin, J., & Strauss, J. (1987a). Chronicity in schizophrenia: Fact, partial fact or artifact. *Hospital & Community Psychiatry, 38,* 477–486.

Hodges, J., & Tizard, B. (1989). Social and family relationships of ex-institutional adolescents. *Journal of Child Psychology and Psychiatry, 30,* 77–97.

Hoffman, R., & Satel, S. (1993). Language therapy for schizophrenic patients with persistent "voices." *British Journal of Psychiatry, 162,* 755–758.

Hoult, J., & Reynolds, I. (1994). Schizophrenia: A comparative trail of community orientated and hospital orientated psychiatric care. *Acta Psychiatrica Scandinavica, 69(5),* 359–372.

Johnson, R. D., & Downing, L. E. (1979). Deindividuation and valence of cues: Effects on prosocial and antisocial behaviour. *Journal of Personality and Social Psychology, 37,* 1532–1538.

Johnstone, E. C., Owens, D. G., Frith, C. D., & Leary, J. (1991). Clinical findings. Abnormalities of the mental state and movement disorder and their correlates. *British Journal of Psychiatry, 159,* 21–25.

Johnstone, E. C., Owens, D. G. C., Gold, A., Crow, T. J., & McMillan, J. F. (1981). Institutionalism and the defects of schizophrenia. *British Journal of Psychiatry, 139,* 195–203.

Kane, R., Kane, R. L., & Arnold, S. (1985). *Measuring social functioning in mental health studies: Concepts and instruments* (DHSS Publication No. ADM 85–1384). Washington, D.C.: U.S. Government Printing Office.

Katz, M., & Lyerly, S. (1963). Methods for measuring adjustment and social behaviour in the community: I Rationale, description, discriminative ability and scale development. *Psychological Reports, 13,* 502–535.

King, R. D., & Raynes, N. (1968a). An operational measure of inmate management in residential institutions. *Social Science and Medicine, 2,* 41.

King, R. D., & Raynes, N. (1968b). Patterns of institutional care for the severely subnormal. *American Journal of Mental Deficiency, 72,* 700.

Kuipers, L. (1994). The measurement of expressed emotion: Its influence on research and clinical practice. *International Review of Psychiatry, 6,* 187–199.

Liddle, P. F. (1987). The symptoms of chronic schizophrenia: A re-examination of the positive–negative dichotomy. *British Journal of Psychiatry, 151,* 145–151.

Mann, S. A., & Cree, W. (1976b). 'New' long stay psychiatric patients: A national sample of fifteen mental hospitals in England and Wales 1972–3. *Psychological Medicine, 6,* 603–616.

Mann, S. A., & Sproule, J. (1972). Reasons for a six months stay. In J. K. Wing & A. Hailey (Eds.), *Evaluating a community psychiatric service. The Camberwell Register 1964–1971* (pp. 233–45). London: Oxford University Press.

Marks, I. M., Connolly, J., Muijen, J., Audini, B., McNamee, G., & Lawrence, R. (1994). Home-based versus hospital-based care for people with serious mental illness. *British Journal of Psychiatry, 165,* 179–194.

Mathai, P., & Gopinath, P. (1985). Deficits of chronic schizophrenia in relation to long term hospitalization. *British Journal of Psychiatry, 148,* 509–516.

Merson, S., Tyrer, P., Onyett, S., Lack, S., Birkett, P., Lynch, S., & Johnson, T. (1992). Early interventions in psychiatric emergencies. *Lancet, 339,* 1311–1314.

Miller, L. E., & Cohen, D. G. (Eds.). (1987). *Schizophrenia and aging.* New York: Guilford.

Moore, E. (1992). *Care of the long-term mentally ill: EE in staff patient relationships.* Unpublished PhD thesis, London University.

Moore, E., Ball, R. A. & Kuipers, L. (1992). Expressed Emotion in staff working with the long-term adult mentally ill. *British Journal of Psychiatry, 161,* 802–808.

Moore, E., Kuipers, L., & Ball, R. (1992). Staff patient relationships in the case of the long-term mentally ill: A content analysis of EE interviews. *Social Psychiatry and Psychiatric Epidemiology, 27,* 28–34.

Morgan, R. (1977). Three weeks in isolation with two chronic schizophrenic patients. *British Journal of Psychiatry, 131,* 504–513.

Morrison, R., & Bellack, A. (1987). Social functioning of schizophrenia patients: Clinical and research issues. *Schizophrenia Bulletin, 13,* 715–725.

Mueser, K., Bellack, A., Douglas, M., & Wade, J. (1991). Prediction of social skill acquisition in schizophrenic and major affective disorder patients from memory and symptomatology. *Psychiatric Research, 37,* 281–296.

Pantelis, C., Taylor, J., & Campbell, P. G. (1991). The Camden Schizophrenia Surveys: Symptoms and syndromes in schizophrenia. *Biological Psychiatry, 29,* 646S.

Platt, S. (1986). Evaluating social functioning. A critical review of scales and their underlying concepts. In P. B. Bradley & S. R. Hirsch (Eds.), *The psychopharmocology of schizophrenia* (pp. 263–285). London: Oxford University Press.

Platt, S., Weyman, A., & Hirsch, S. (1983). *Social Behaviour Assessment Schedule (SBAS)* (3rd ed.). NFER, Windsor, Berks.

Prentice-Dunn, S., & Rogers, R. (1982). Effects of public and private self-awareness on deindividuation and aggression. *Journal of Personality and Social Psychology, 43,* 503–513.

Pryce, I., Griffiths, R., Gentry, R., Hughes, I., Montague, L., Watkins, S., Champney-Smith, J., & McLackland, B. (1993). How important is the assessment of social skills in current long stay in-patients? An evaluation of clinical response to needs for assessment, treatment and care in a long stay psychiatric in-patient population. *British Journal of Psychiatry, 162,* 498–502.

Rosen, A., Hadzi-Pavlovic, D., & Parker, G. (1989). The Life Skills Profile: A measure assessing function and disability in schizophrenia. *Schizophrenia Bulletin, 15,* 325–337.

Rutter, M. (1993). Resilience: Some conceptual issues. *Journal of Adolescent Health, 14,* 626–631.

Stein, L. J., & Test, M. A. (1980). Alternative to mental hospital treatment. 1. Conceptual model, treatment program and clinical evaluation. *Archives General Psychiatry, 37,* 392–397.

Strauss, J. S., Hafez, H., Liberman, P., & Harding, C. (1985). The course of psychiatric disorders: Longitudinal principles. *American Journal of Psychiatry, 142,* 289–296.

Sturt, E., & Wykes. T. (1987). Assessment schedules for chronic psychiatric patients. *Psychological Medicine, 17,* 485–493.

Tizard, B. (1991). Intercountry adoption: A review of the evidence. *Journal of Child Psychology and Psychiatry, 32,* 743–756.

Vazquez Morejon, A. J., & Jimenez-Garcia, R. (1989). Behaviour disorders and schizophrenia: A study using the SBS (Social Behaviour Schedule) in the Ecija District. *Actas-Luso Espana Neurologia Psiquiatria Ciencia Afines, 17,* 281–293.

Wallace, C. J. (1984). Community and interpersonal functioning in the course of schizophrenia disorders. *Schizophrenia Bulletin, 10,* 233–257.

Wallace, C. J. (1986). Functional assessment in rehabilitation. *Schizophrenia Bulletin, 12,* 604–630.

Watt, D., Katz, M., & Shepherd, M. (1983). The natural history of schizophrenia: A 5-year prospective follow-up of a representative sample of schizophrenics by means of a standardised clinical and social assessment. *Psychological Medicine, 13,* 663–670.

Weissman, M. Sholomkas, D., & John, R. (1981). The assessment of social adjustment by patient self-report. *Archives of General Psychiatry, 32,* 357–365.

Weissman, M. (1975). The assessment of social adjustment: An update. *Archives General Psychiatry, 38,* 1250–1258.

Wing, J. (1978). *Reasoning about madness.* London: Oxford University Press.

Wing, J. K. (1980). Innovations in social psychiatry. *Psychological Medicine, 10,* 219–230.

Wing, J. K. (1983). Schizophrenia. In R. N. Watts & D. H. Bennett (Eds.), *Theory and practice of rehabilitation* (pp. 45–64). Chichester: Wiley.

Wing, J. K. (1989). The measurement of "Social Disablement." The MRC Social Behaviour and Social Role Performance Schedules. *Social Psychiatry and Psychiatric Epidemiology, 24,* 173–178.

Wing, J. K., & Brown, G. (1970). *Institutionalism and schizophrenia*. London: Cambridge University Press.

Wing, J. K., & Furlong, R. (1986). A haven for the severely disabled within the context of a comprehensive psychiatric community service. *British Journal of Psychiatry, 149*, 440–457.

Wykes, T. (1982). A hostel ward for new long-stay patients. *Psychological Medicine Monograph Supplement, 2*, 59–97.

Wykes, T., Sturt, E., & Creer, C. (1982). Practices of day and residential units in relation to the social behaviour of attenders. *Psychological Medicine Monograph Supplement, 2*, 15–27.

Wykes, T. (1994). Predicting symptomatic and behavioural outcomes of community care. *British Journal of Psychiatry*, 486–492.

Wykes, T., & Dunn, G. (1992). Cognitive deficit and the prediction of rehabilitation success in a chronic psychiatric group. *Psychological Medicine, 22*, 389–398.

Wykes, T., Katz, R., Sturt, E. & Hemsley, D. (1992). Abnormalities of response processing in a chronic psychiatric group: A possible predictor of rehabilitation success. *British Journal of Psychiatry, 160*, 244–252.

Wykes, T., & Sturt, E. (1986). The measurement of social behaviour in psychiatric patients: An assessment of the reliability and validity of SBS. *British Journal of Psychiatry, 148*, 1–11.

Wykes, T., & Wing, J. K. (1992). The size and nature of the problem. In K. Woof (Ed.), *Residential needs for severely disabled psychiatric patients: The case for hospital hostels*. London: HMSO.

Wykes, T., Sturt, E. & Katz, R. (1990). The prediction of rehabilitation success after three years: The use of social, symptom and cognitive variables. *British Journal of Psychiatry, 157*, 865–870.

CHAPTER 3

SOCIAL ADJUSTMENT OF PATIENTS LIVING AT HOME

Linda Clare
Max Birchwood

A significant proportion of people with a diagnosis of schizophrenia are likely to live at home with their families. In the West, this is one outcome of the increasing focus on community-based services and reduction in long-stay hospital provision. In many other cultures, the family has traditionally been viewed as the main source of care and continues to fulfill this function (Karno & Jenkins 1990). The typical onset in early adulthood and the damaging effects of the illness in terms of employment make reliance on the parental family particularly likely. "Home" can mean a variety of things, but most research and clinical reports relate to families in which parents support an offspring with schizophrenia (Bennun & Lucas, 1990); relatively little information is available regarding people with schizophrenia living with spouses or, indeed, on their own. Another form of care in a home setting is that provided in foster homes (e.g. Linn, Klett, & Caffey, 1980).

In this chapter we summarize available evidence about the number of patients remaining with their families and how this changes with time. We also discuss the influ-

ences that are brought to bear affecting the social adjustment of patients living at home, including relatives' own social functioning, disordered family relationships, and their reciprocal impact on the patient. We discuss the notion that social adjustment has no absolute frame of reference, but must be viewed relative to socially valued roles and goals that have cultural underpinnings. We argue that this is an absolutely essential frame of reference when determining what is a *deficit* and what is a *need*. The chapter concludes with a view of recommended measures appropriate to the family context.

SOCIAL ADJUSTMENT IN THE HOME CONTENT

Follow-up studies in the United Kingdom suggest that perhaps 60 to 70% of people with schizophrenia return to live with their families (Goldman, 1980). Johnstone, Owens, Gold, Crow, and MacMillan (1984) attempted to follow up 120 patients with schizophrenia who had been discharged from Shenley Hospital between 1970 and

1974; of the 66 patients living in the community who were both traced and willing to be interviewed, 26 lived with parents or relatives, 23 lived with a spouse, and 17 lived alone. The Scottish Schizophrenia Research Group (SSRG; 1988) documented the living situation of 49 patients admitted with a first episode of psychosis and given a diagnosis of schizophrenia; 65% lived with their parents, 13% with a spouse, 13% with another relative, and 9% in other circumstances. Forty-one of the patients were followed up after 12 months, at which time 46% lived with their parents, 10% with a spouse, 20% with another relative, 17% alone, and 7% in other circumstances.

When these studies have investigated social adjustment, serious difficulties were reported, including limited social networks and prominent social withdrawal (Johnstone et al., 1984; McCreadie & Barron, 1984). Among chronic patients there was significant impairment in adjustment and role functioning; for example, McCreadie and Barron reported that according to self-report and relatives' reports, using the Social Adjustment Scale (Self-Report), 39% had no friends or had met none within the past 2 weeks, 34% had not gone out socially at all in the past 2 weeks, and 52% had spent no time engaging in interests other than watching television. Unemployment was common and well above average for the community as a whole; 41 patients (62% of the sample) followed up by Johnstone et al. (1984) were not in full-time employment, and out of 14 patients whose role was described as "housewife," 10 were said to be "ineffective" in fulfilling the demands of this role. McCreadie and Barron (1984) reported a 73% unemployment rate among their sample of 82 chronic patients. At 12-month follow-up, 51% of first-episode patients were unemployed, compared with 21% at admission (SSRG, 1988). Unfortunately this study did not attempt to measure patients' social adjustment in other ways, focusing instead on psychotic symptoms, a common limitation of research in this area.

Birchwood (1983) found that 70% of families of first-episode patients experienced disturbed behavior in their relative, which was "severe" in 15% of cases. Behavior seen as problematic included withdrawal, impaired self-care and domestic skills, and aggression, as well as positive symptoms. Gibbons, Horn, Powell, and Gibbons (1984) found that more than 75% of patients living at home played little part in household tasks and engaged in leisure activities on a very limited basis. Hewitt (1983) asked relatives of 39 patients attending a day hospital to assess behavior of the patients, the majority of whom were male and living in the parental home. Approximately one-third of the patients were said to exhibit "socially embarrassing" behavior such as poor mixing, lack of conversation, shouting or swearing at others, and poor self-care; relatives did not always view these behaviors as problematic within the family context. However, it appears this was a relatively stable group.

Outcome in terms of social adjustment appears to be more favorable in non-Western, nonindustrial cultural contexts, where differing expectations and explanatory models may promote better adjustment. A 5-year follow-up study of 66 patients in Sri Lanka (Waxler, 1979) found that all were living with their families. Fifty percent were considered to display "normal" social adjustment with 58% performing a normal role within the home, and 45% had been able to work continuously over the 5-year period. El-Islam (1982) reported better social adjustment at one-year follow-up in patients living within extended families than in patients living within nuclear families. The patients in extended families participated in social contact and religious practice to a greater extent and were more active in personal care. However, he does comment that this may apply more to male than female patients, for whom the expectations within the extended family may be less helpful.

Although some social environments and cultural contexts may facilitate greater social adjustment than others, many patients and families face major difficulties in this respect. Attempts to understand the key variables influencing outcomes in the home setting have focused on two main areas, expressed emotion and coping, each of which are influenced by culture and gender. We will consider the contribution of each of these in turn before proceeding to a discussion of the practicalities of assessment.

Factors Affecting Social Functioning at Home

Culture and Gender

A high score on a scale of social functioning represents something that most people would value or covet. Like height and weight, such concepts have universal validity and value. It is the term *value* that betrays the cultural relativism of the social adjustment concept; the goals and roles that are inherent in the concept will show wide cultural variation. The most striking contrast is between countries of the Asian subcontinent and the Western cultures. Western cultures value autonomy and individual advancement, and leaving home "to make your way in the world" is a value widely expressed, finding expression in the proliferation of nuclear family structures. Thus, for example, the Social Functioning Scale (SFS; Birchwood, Smith, Cochrane, Wetton, & Copestake, 1990) contains scales of independence in both competence and performance, and is a clear expression of this value. In the Indian subcontinent and among immigrants to the United Kingdom from India, leaving home "to set up on our own" tends to run against the cultural norm where extended or functionally joined families are the rule.

Remaining in the parental home might be regarded as a poor outcome in the West but quite acceptable in Eastern cultures, and indeed a valued outcome. This has implications for other familiar components of social adjustment. Friendships and engagement in extra-familial social networks are strong Western values seen as vital for maintaining well-being (e.g., Brown & Harris, 1978), and again in some social functioning scales items include the number of social contacts *outside* the immediate family, whereas in some cultures a greater family orientation in social contacts is seen. Recreation which tends to be highly represented in social functioning schedules, is another concept less well understood in many Eastern cultures.

Social functioning should therefore be considered and measured only in relation to valued goals and roles. These vary by culture, but also within culture, such as by class or caste, gender, and age. Members of a particular cultural group make such intuitive judgments when evaluating an individual's social functioning; thus, in defining needs based on, for example, scores in an inventory, the expressed needs as well as the normative ones defined by the inventory need to be assessed directly.

The family support service described by Smith and Birchwood (1990) in Birmingham, United Kingdom, included many families of South Asian origin. The deficiencies in social functioning available from the Social Functioning Scale Birchwood, et al. (1990) were in many instances entirely rejected as expressed needs because of the conflict with cultural values; for example, a young Indian male was seen to have low scores in the performance of independence skills and in recreational activities, but these were, however, rejected as areas of need by himself and his family.

Individuals who remain at home following the onset of schizophrenia will, in the West, tend to be those more disabled by their illness or where kinship loyalty is greatest. Given that this is a reality and a choice for many, by what

yardstick should their social functioning be measured and their needs defined? We have taken the conservative view that social functioning should be measured relative to the population of patients remaining at home, as this will set a more realistic baseline (Birchwood et al., 1990).

There will be cultural difficulties in the proportion of families remaining at home. Table 3.1 shows data from a study by Birchwood, Cochrane, MacMillan, and Copestake (1992) in which a sample of 130 first-episode schizophrenics were followed up for 12 months. The figures document the proportion of patients remaining with their families after 12 months in three cultural groups: blacks, whites, and South Asians.

Whereas only 42% of black patients remained with their families, fully 96% of Asian patients had done so compared with 53% of whites. The study pointed to a selective attrition of patients leaving white homes who were generally more able to obtain jobs or function reasonably independently, leaving behind on the whole a more dependent and disabled group. Clearly comparing cultural groups in the home context on standard measures is fraught with difficulty, and in general patients remaining at home are likely to be more disabled. We believe it is important to standardize social functioning measures relative to the group remaining at home, while also providing a point of comparison with community norms and different cultural groups.

Expressed Emotion

A key concept in research and clinical work with families has been that of expressed emotion (EE) and its relationship with outcome. EE is most commonly assessed using the Camberwell Family Interview (Leff, Kuipers, Berkowitz, & Sturgeon, 1985; Vaughn & Leff, 1976). Relatives are described as showing high or low EE on the basis of a frequency count of critical comments about the

Table 3.1. Living Circumstances of Three Ethnic Groups in the United Kingdom 12 Months After First Admission[a]

	WHITE BRITISH %	ASIAN BRITISH %	BLACK BRITISH %
Living with family	70.2	90	31.6
Living alone	21.3	2.1	54.3

[a] From Birchwood et al., 1992.

patient and global ratings of hostility toward, and emotional overinvolvement (EOI) with, the patient. For a family to be classified as high EE, only one relative need score sufficiently highly on these measures.

The main focus of interest has been on EE as a predictor of relapse. Kavanagh (1992) notes that there is considerable support for the usefulness of EE as a predictor of relapse over a 9-to 12-month period following an acute episode. Parker and Hadzi-Pavlovic (1990) report an analysis of aggregated data from 12 studies published between 1962 and 1988, which showed that patients living with families rated as high EE are 3.7 times more likely to relapse than those who do not. However, some published studies do not show this effect at all, and in those that do, the predictive strength of EE appears to have waned over time. Discussing their naturalistic prospective study, which did not support the predictive value of EE, McCreadie and Philips (1988) comment that explanations for the differing results could include the use of different diagnostic criteria, varying sample characteristics such as degree of chronicity, the operation of other relevant variables such as the effect of social problems or stressful life events, and the presence of protective factors such as the greater stability and continuity that exists within a rural community. This last point links to the cultural variation in outcome, with EE failing to predict outcome in studies conducted in non-Western cultures (Leff et al., 1990); high EE families are less commonly found in these societies, where greater tolerance and acceptance is demonstrated by families in rural, nonindustrial communities.

Given that the overall balance of evidence favors the predictive utility of the EE concept, at least in industrialized societies, it is important to consider what mechanisms have been adduced to account for its effects. EE has been seen as linked to negative emotional responses by relatives and an emotional climate that stimulates increased disturbance in the patient. Mediating factors in relatives may include their attributions regarding the patients' behavior; high EE relatives are more likely to attribute the patient's behavior to personal factors such as laziness (Berkowitz, Shavit, & Leff, 1990), and consequently to respond in a hostile manner (Leff et al., 1990). Limited knowledge about the medical model of the disorder may increase this tendency toward misattribution. Low EE relatives, in contrast, seem to understand that the patient's behavior is due to illness, have lower expectations, respond calmly and tolerantly, and tend to be more

adaptable and flexible (Vaughn, 1986). Relatives' own emotional responses to the illness, particularly grief and loss, are also likely to affect their interactions with the patient and may fuel hostile or critical attitudes (Miller, Dworkin, Ward, & Barone, 1990). Relatives' difficult emotions may lead to intolerance and inflexibility, unpredictability and inconsistency, or attempts to control or coerce the patient (e.g., MacCarthy, Hemsley, Shrank-Fernandez, Kuipers, & Katz, 1986). This in turn can have a strong impact on patients who are having difficulty with information processing or who may be preoccupied with thoughts and beliefs connected with control (Vaughn, 1986).

Perhaps one of the main limitations of the EE research, however, is a limited understanding of what actually happens in interactions between relative and patients; there is a lack of study using direct observation. This is particularly important when consideration is given to the relationship with social functioning. Since the initial study by Brown, Monck, Carstairs, and Wing (1962), such methods have been conspicuous by their absence, at least as far as families coping with schizophrenia are concerned. Consequently there is no clear model of the high EE family interior. (Kavanagh, 1992). A number of studies demonstrate that the components of EE form a risk factor in a range of conditions. These include depression (Hooley, 1986) and physical conditions such as rheumatoid arthritis (Manne & Zautra, 1989).

The concept of EE itself has a number of limitations. It is usually treated as a global measure, yet it appears there is little correlation between the three main components, criticism, hostility, and EOI (Kavanagh, 1992). Different studies emphasize the contribution of one or another component to relapse; for example, MacMillan, Gold, Crow, Johnson, and Johnstone (1986) reported a strong link with criticism, whereas Leff et al. (1990) found hostility to be most relevant. Another difficulty is the focus on negative emotions and responses; some early studies investigated positive responses, but more recently these have been excluded from consideration (Kavanagh, 1992) although their presence may mitigate negative reactions. Brown, Birley, and Wing (1972) found that warmth was related to positive outcome. Furthermore, use of the EE concept involves a straightforward dichotomous classification of families as high EE or low EE and an assumption that low EE status is a positive attribute. This is problematic (Kuipers & Bebbington, 1988). Some researchers have commented that, although low EE may indicate successful coping, it could also indicate that the relative has become disengaged or detached from the patient and is coping by fostering patients' withdrawal (Birchwood & Smith, 1987; Birchwood & Cochrane, 1990).

Another debate, fueled perhaps by the use of this dichotomous and categorical classification, has concerned the status of EE as a trait or state variable (Birchwood, 1992). The observation that high EE families may change to a low EE rating over time, in the absence of any intervention, suggests that EE level is not a fixed characteristic. EE is now generally viewed not as a trait, but as a characteristic that develops over time (Birchwood & Smith, 1987; Tarrier, 1991) and as a "snapshot" of the stress present in a given relationship at a given time (Lam, 1991). This has opened the possibility of adopting an interactional model that places relatives' responses in the context of their attempts to cope with the patient's disturbed behavior and social difficulty (Birchwood & Smith, 1987). Response styles develop and change over time through the transactions between relative and patient. Kavanagh (1992) outlines an interactive model of EE and its role in relapse, involving the behavior and reactions of patient and relative, the attributions each makes about these, and the repertoire of coping skills available to each. The whole cycle is embedded in the context of the quality of family relationships over time and the past history of these relationships. Positive effects can also be explained within this model; for example, social support may moderate the strain imposed by the illness, whereas pleasant experiences may offset negative emotional reactions. As well as acknowledging the interactional nature of EE, this model has the advantage of incorporating the effects of other factors, such as life events, thus going some way to meet the need for a more complex, circular explanation than that offered by the early EE studies.

A further comment on the EE concept relates to the intervention studies. These will not be considered in detail here, but it is important to note that while there is considerable evidence for the effectiveness of psychosocial family interventions in improving the course of schizophrenia (Kavanagh, 1992; Lan, 1991; Bennun & Lucas, 1990), the lack of a clear model of the interior of the high EE family means that a range of differing approaches have been adopted (Lam, 1991). While some common factors can be identified, the precise mechanisms of change in these interventions remain unclear. In particular, it is not clear that the interventions exert their influence on relapse exclusively by means of change in EE status; some studies note improvements in outcome, or changes in measures such as attributional style or coping skills, without change in EE status (e.g., Hogarty et al., 1986; Bennun & Lucas, 1990; Berkowitz et al., 1990).

Clinically, therefore, the EE concept appears in general to have some limited usefulness (Smith & Birchwood, 1990). It is not a satisfactory basis for clinical assessment and may lack reliability because it is not stable over time. It can focus attention away from the needs of relatives and the stresses and burdens they face in caring for the patient, and it can have pejorative connotations in terms of how the family is viewed, because even if the issue of what caused the illness is side-stepped, the high EE family is seen as possibly "causing" the patient's relapse. Perhaps one of the most important limitations, from the point of view of the topic with which we are concerned in this chapter, is the focus on relapse and positive symptoms adopted by the EE research. Studies have generally not considered social functioning as an outcome measure, even though this may have greater day-to-day relevance to the lives of the majority of patients and families and may relate more closely to stress, burden, and coping. It may well be, for example, that if EE was defined in terms of its ability to predict social outcome, a very different classification and set of processes may be discerned.

EE and social functioning. There is some evidence available regarding the relationship between EE and social adjustment. Early studies showed that patients living in high EE households were at less risk of relapse if they had limited face-to-face contact with their relatives, and it was suggested that social withdrawal could be an adaptive response to high EE relatives (Vaughn & Leff, 1979). Patients seldom avoid low EE relatives, but are much more likely to withdraw in high EE households (Vaughn, 1986). Kavanagh (1992) notes that the relationship between low face-to-face contact and lower rates of relapse is probably confounded with the patient's level of social functioning and with the benefits that both patient and relative may derive from being involved in other activities outside the home. He suggests that since hostility and coercion by relatives is linked to both relapse and withdrawal by patients, sequences of high EE behavior by relatives and withdrawal by patients may be important for both relapse risk and social functioning. It has also been suggested that some low EE relatives may detach themselves emotionally from patients and thereby promote social withdrawal.

Barrowclough and Tarrier (1990) reported that high EE ratings in relatives were associated with lower social functioning in the patient as measured by the Social Functioning Scale (Birchwood et al., 1990); in particular, lowered social functioning was related to hostility. Brown et al. (1972) found that high EE environments were associated with lower social functioning in the patient during the preceding 2 years, and Hogarty et al. (1988) found that patients living in low EE families showed better social functioning over a 2-year follow-up period. In contrast, Otsuka, Nakane, and Ohta (1994) found no significant differences in social functioning between patients living with high EE relatives and patients living with low EE relatives; however, relatives' assessment of the patient's social adjustment varied considerably, with high EE relatives rating the patient's social adjustment less favorably. This was interpreted as showing that they had unreasonably high expectations of what the patient should be achieving and a negative view of the patient's involvement in leisure activities; these factors were seen as contributing to the high EE rating. Size and quality of parents' own social networks does not appear to be linked to EE status (Anderson, Hogarty, Bayer, & Needleman, 1984), although parents' social networks do decrease as the duration of illness increases.

Smith, Birchwood, Cochrane, and George (1993) explicitly compared patients from high and low EE families on their standardized measure of social functioning (Table 3.2). This confirms previous findings that patients from high EE families have a lower level of social functioning, amounting to one standard deviation on the SFS. This difference was apparent on all scales of the SFS (social contacts, independence, recreation, and social activities). It is difficult to determine the direction of causality. The concept of the EE as a state variable (Birchwood & Smith, 1987; Schreiber, Brier, & Pickar, 1995) rather than a trait characteristic raises the possibility of *bidirectional* influences in line with the possibilities outlined at the beginning of this section. Indeed the family intervention study of Barrowclough and Tarrier (1992) found that reductions in relatives' expressed emotion were linked with improvements in social functioning, as a result of their intervention program, although not to the level of patients from low EE families (cf. Smith et al., 1993); in their program reductions in EE were achieved by direct attempts to improve the functioning of the patient and by improving the communication and coping of relatives.

The concept of EE as a "thermometer" of ongoing transactions between patient and carer is important, since this argues that the dynamics rest in part on perceived deficiencies in the patient's functioning that attract, for example, criticism as a remediating maneuver once it is known to be linked to relatives', subjective and objective burden (Smith et al., 1993).

Stress, Burden, and Coping: Interactions with Social Functioning

The tendency during the 1960s to view families as the cause of schizophrenia, and the subsequent focus on EE, largely precluded any real attempt to understand the burden and stress faced by families caring for a relative with schizophrenia. Services made little attempt to assist families (Creer & Wing, 1974), and families were rightly suspicious of services. Only recently has the extent of family burden been acknowledged, leading to attempts to address this in terms of service provision. At the same time, the increasing emphasis on community care has tended to increase the burden on families. Family burden remains a relatively underresearched area (Fadden, Bebbington, & Kuipers, 1987).

Social adjustment of the patient is an important factor in relation to burden, since "one person's poor social performance is another person's burden" (Kuipers & Bebbington, 1985). Perceptions of both social performance and burden depend on the family's expectations and values, which may, as we have discussed, differ widely within as well as between cultures. Thus there can be a discrepancy between objective burden, in terms of specific costs or changes in lifestyle, and subjective dissatisfaction. Stress and burden are, however, related to the degree of behavioral disturbance and social impairment shown by the patient, indicating that social functioning and adjustment have an important influence on the perceived level of stress and burden reported by relatives (Smith et al., 1992).

Sources of stress and burden for families are many and varied (Birchwood & Smith, 1987; Fadden et al., 1987). There may be severe disruption to roles within the family, and tension or loss of cohesion may develop as a result of disagreements about how to understand and manage the individual. Difficulties in the patient's relationship with other family members may lead to rejection; equally, parents may become overprotective and the needs of siblings may be ignored. Relatives may find themselves increasingly isolated, with limitations on social and leisure activities arising where relatives feel guilty about attending to their own needs when their relative is suffering, fear

Table 3.2. Distribution of SFS Scores for Patients Living with High and Low EE Relatives

| Score | LOW EE RELATIVES (N=19) | | | HIGH EE RELATIVES (N = 30) | | | SCHIZOPHRENIC SAMPLE[a] (n = 334) | COMMUNITY SAMPLE[a] (n = 100) |
	FIRST EPISODE (n = 5)	READMISSION (n = 11)	TOTAL[b] (n = 16)	FIRST EPISODE (n = 14)	READMISSION (n = 14)	TOTAL[b] (n = 28)		
	n (%)	n (%)	n (%)	n (%)	n (%)	n (%)	(%)	(%)
<96	0 (0%)	1 (9%)	1 (6%)	4 (29%)	4 (29%)	8 (29%)	26.6%	1.0%
96–105	1 (20%)	4 (36%)	5 (31%)	3 (21%)	4 (29%)	7 (25%)	30.0%	6.0%
106–115	2 (40%)	5 (46%)	7 (44%)	6 (43%)	5 (36%)	11 (39%)	29.0%	19.0%
>115	2 (40%)	1 (9%)	3 (19%)	1 (7%)	1 (7%)	2 (7%)	14.4%	74.0%

[a] Birchwood et al. (1990).
[b] Missing data: low EE (n = 3), high EE (n = 2).

45

what will happen if the person is left alone, or anticipate adverse reactions due to social stigma. Practical problems such as financial difficulties can have a severe impact, especially where employment is sacrificed in order to care for the patient, and the long-term goals of other family members may be drastically altered. Relatives also have to deal with their own emotional reactions to the illness, including anger, grief, and loss. Finally, responding to problem behavior, whether associated with positive or negative symptoms, represents a major source of stress. Behavior driven by positive symptoms can be very difficult to cope with, especially where some element of aggression is involved, but it is the behavior resulting from negative symptoms that often causes the most conflict (e.g., Creer & Wing, 1974), perhaps because it is harder to attribute these symptoms to the illness as opposed to, say, laziness or selfishness, and therefore harder to make allowances for them. The family's beliefs about schizophrenia also influence stress and coping, and in this respect stereotypical images presented by the media can have a negative effect, for example, reinforcing the erroneous belief that all people with severe mental illness are liable to become violent.

The stress of caring may directly affect the physical and mental well-being of the carer as relatives struggle to cope with disturbed behavior in the context of attempting to deal with their own emotional reactions to the illness. One study using the General Health Questionnaire (GHQ-28) found that relatives of first-episode patients show high levels of distress; on the admission 77% were classified as suffering psychological distress, and 40% remained in this category after 12 months—twice the population norm for the United Kingdom (SSRG, 1988). This study also noted that relatives' own social functioning, as recorded by the Social Adjustment Scale Self-Report, was poorer than that of a general community sample and remained so at follow-up. This was attributed by the authors to the stress of the patient becoming ill; the level of both positive and negative symptoms in the patients correlated with relatives' level of distress.

Recent work has attempted to describe the coping styles of families caring for a relative with schizophrenia. Birchwood and Cochrane (1990) found that families tend to employ particular coping styles fairly consistently. Coping strategies include coercion, avoidance, collusion, indifference, and reassurance, and disorganized or constructive styles of responding can be observed. Coping styles adopted by families do appear to be associated with the patient's social adjustment. For example, where patients' social functioning is poor, relatives are more likely to use coercive responses; this style of responding is in turn linked to higher rates of relapse. It is not possible to determine the direction of any causal relationships between family coping styles and patients' behavior; however, as we have already indicated, it is more helpful to think in terms of a reciprocal relationship between the two factors developing over time and rooted in the family interactions prior to the onset of illness.

A review of the factors seen as particularly relevant to outcome for patients living at home with their family indicates the complexity of the variables in operation and the need for interactional models that allow for reciprocal effects and incorporate a temporal dimension. It follows from this that the assessment of patients in the family context requires a full acknowledgment of this complexity and that a broad-based approach is essential.

Conclusion

The social functioning of patients living at home is influenced by factors operating at a number of levels. First, *the concept of social dysfunction* is not absolute but relative to valued goals and roles, which must be assessed when choosing a measurement instrument and when determining need. Second, *cultural differences*, both between cultures and within cultural groups, will affect the propensity of patients and families to continue living together and, since there is evidence of selective attrition of the better functioning patients in some groups, this will give the erroneous impression of greater disability. Third, there is evidence of a link between the *well-being of the family unit*, as shown by indices such as stress, burden, coping, and EE, and the social behavior of the patient. These are not fixed but ones which can unfold and reciprocally influence one another over time. Finally, the *availability of services* such as day care can reduce time spent at home and relieve family burden and, depending on the quality of the service, may directly serve to promote or limit social behavior.

ASSESSMENT OF THE FAMILY CONTEXT

In assessing the social adjustment of patients living at home, as we have shown, a particularly broad-based approach will be required to evaluate not just the patient's individual functioning but also the family context. An understanding of the family context will involve an assessment of the following areas:

1. The impact on the family of the patient's needs, disabilities, behavior, and symptoms in terms of burden, stress, emotional distress, and needs for support.
2. The impact of the family environment on the patient in terms of the family's coping skills, styles of responding, beliefs and attributions, and knowledge about the illness.
3. Problems facing the family as a whole in terms of their social and financial circumstances.
4. The values and expectations of the family and patient that will be influenced by the social and cultural norms to which they adhere.

The purpose of assessment must be borne in mind. If assessment is a precursor to a family-based intervention, then assessment will be crucial in laying the basis for partnership with the family in tackling their needs and difficulties (Smith & Birchwood, 1990). Meeting some of the family member's needs may help the patient, just as meeting some of the patient's needs may help the family; therefore, engagement of both patient and relatives is important. Assessment of needs will form the basis for a joint negotiation of the goals of any subsequent intervention.

Assessment of the Patient

In setting out a framework for assessment of the patient's functioning, a number of conceptual models may be relevant. One useful medical model distinguishes among pathology (internal etiological factors), impairment (symptoms resulting from pathology), disability (restrictions on functioning resulting from impairment), and handicap (social disadvantage resulting from disability). In assessing patients with schizophrenia, the emphasis has generally been more on assessment of impairment in terms of psychotic symptoms than on assessment of disability. While it is important to be aware of symptoms, it is also important to make a distinct assessment of the level of functional disability. This may be a more stable and enduring aspect of the illness than the level of positive and negative symptoms (Heinrichs, Hanlon, & Carpenter, 1984).

The limitations of this model lie in its focus on disability and deficit. A counterbalance is provided by the normalization approach; this is more commonly associated with learning disability, but may equally well be applied to working with people who have a mental illness. Such an approach advocates an overall awareness of the person in context. This would focus on developing an understanding of the person's life experiences, interests, achievements, skills and preferences; the family context; the nature and quality of social relationships, current lifestyle, involvement with services, and impact of the illness on their life and social functioning; and what expectations they have about themselves and their future. This implies an emphasis on evaluating the person's quality of life.

Where the purpose of assessment is the identification of rehabilitation goals, it makes sense to synthesize these two models and adopt a broad-based constructional approach based on an identification of the person's strengths and needs. It is important to attempt to understand what the person is capable of as well as his or her current level of performance, and the reasons for any discrepancy between the two.

Key areas to be covered in assessing social functioning include:

1. Living skills, such as self-care, domestic skills, budgeting, and ability to use public transport and community facilities;
2. Interpersonal skills, such as the ability to converse and interact appropriately with family members, friends, and other contacts; and
3. Social engagement, including social networks, frequency of social contact, quality of relationships, and involvement in activities.

In addition, the factors underpinning these will be relevant. These factors may include positive and negative symptoms, depression, or cognitive impairments in areas such as memory, attention, and problem solving. Literacy and numeracy should also be assessed. The function of observed deficits needs to be considered in relation to the course of the illness and risk of relapse, as this will have implications for intervention; for example, social withdrawal may be an adaptive means of coping with positive symptoms, or a maladaptive response to loss of confidence and feelings of being stigmatized.

No one scale can capture all the relevant information, and the precise angle to be taken will be determined in part by the purpose of the assessment. However, a wide range of factors must be considered, and it will often be appropriate to use a battery of measures to elicit the required details, as well as direct observation and semi-structured interviews.

Assessment Measures

This section presents brief details of a selection of relevant measures covering the important dimensions of assessment of social functioning in the family context.

General Family Assessment

Relatives Assessment Inverview (Barrowclough & Tarrier, 1992). This structured interview schedule is a modified version of the Camberwell Family Interview, adapted for clinical rather than research use. It elicits information about the patient's psychiatric history, behavior, and perceived social functioning, including withdrawal, self-care, performance of household tasks, budgeting, interests, and activities. It elicits information about the relatives' responses to the patient, including beliefs, feelings, and behavior; about the perceived impact of the illness; about helpful and unhelpful attempts to cope; and about areas of difficulty and tensions in the family. Relatives are asked directly about their emotional responses to the patient. Although this is not a formal assessment of EE, examples of criticism, hostility, and EOI can be noted.

Relatives' Burden and Distress

Family Questionnaire (Barrowclough & Tarrier, 1992). This is a 50-item checklist of problem behaviors, attitudes, or responses, for example, is unclean and untidy, swears or is rude to people, thinks other people are against him/her, talks nonsense when spoken to. Relatives are asked to rate on a 5-point scale the frequency of occurrence of each behavior, the extent to which this bothers them, and how well they feel able to control and cope with the behavior in question. The questionnaire gives an overview of the perceived problems faced by the family in interacting with the patient and can be used as a outcome measure or as a repeated measure of change.

General Health Questionnaire (GHQ), (Goldberg, 1978). Psychological distress may be evaluated by standard measures such as the General Health Questionnaire. This consists of a checklist of symptoms, and respondents are asked to rate changes in severity on a 5-point scale with the aim of determining "careness." Versions of varying lengths are available.

A thorough review of 21 scales for the assessment of burden and their suitability for research and/or clinical use is provided by Schene, Tessler, and Gamache (1994).

Relatives' Knowledge and Beliefs about Schizophrenia

Knowledge about Schizophrenia Interview (Barrowclough & Tarrier, 1992). This interview schedule elicits understanding of the diagnosis, symptoms, course, and prognosis of the illness, attributions about symptoms, beliefs about causes of the problem, knowledge about medication, and views on management of the disorder. Detailed scoring criteria are provided.

The Knowledge Questionnaire (Birchwood & Smith, 1987). This multiple-choice questionnaire assess knowledge about the illness, etiology, and treatment.

Assessment of the Patient's Social Functioning

Several important characteristics of a scale designed to measure social functioning have been identified by Birchwood et al. (1990) and by Rosen, Hadzi-Pavlovic, and Parker (1989), and may be summarized as follows:

- As well as providing a comprehensive overview, it should be possible to compare scores on different subscales so as to elicit both strengths and needs.
- It should allow the identification of key areas of need and provide a starting point for designing rehabilitation programs.
- Items should focus on single, observable behaviors.
- Norms for a population comparable in terms of age, sex, and social disadvantage should be available; ratings should not depend on normative value judgments.
- The scale should be sensitive to the likely level of impairment and to changes in functioning.
- It should be possible for both professionals and nonprofessionals to use the scale; raters should not require special training to complete it.
- The results should be presented in a format that makes sense to professionals and service users.
- Appropriate levels of reliability and validity should be demonstrated.

Social Functioning Scale (Birchwood et al., 1990). This scale is designed to assess areas of functioning that are important to living in the community in terms of "normative" rather than "expressed" need. Its use is primarily clinical; it provides a detailed assessment of strengths and needs as a basis for planning intervention strategies. It requires ratings of observable behaviors rather than subjective normative judgments, and in relation to skills of independent living it makes the important distinction between competence and performance, providing a separate assessment of each. It is completed on the basis of information provided by a relative and the patient. The scale covers seven areas of functioning: social withdrawal, interpersonal functioning, prosocial activities, recreation, level of independence (competence), level of dependence (performance), and employment. Satisfactory levels of reliability and validity are reported, and norms are provided for patients living at home together with a matched sample of people without schizophrenia (their siblings). It has been used extensively in family intervention studies in the United Kingdom (e.g., Barrowclough & Tarrier, 1992) and permits comparison between scales to determine patients' strengths and weaknesses.

Life Skills Profile (Rosen et al., 1989; Parker, Rosen, Emdur, & Hadzi-Pavlovic, 1991). The profile may be completed by a professional rater who knows the patient well or by a relative. It is a 39-item measure designed to assess level of functioning and disability in patients with schizophrenia for use in clinical and research settings. Observable behaviors are assessed on a 4-point scale. These fall into five categories: self-care, nonturbulence, social contact, communication, and responsibility. Reliability and validity are discussed.

WHO Psychiatric Disability Assessment Schedule (DAS; World Health Organization, 1984). The DAS is primarily a research instrument. The assessment is made by a professional on the basis of the relative's report and information from case notes, plus an interview with the patient if this is possible. It is acknowledged that the ratings are based on the clinical judgment of a trained interviewer; the patient's behavior is evaluated in comparison to the presumed functioning of an average individual of the same age, sex, and sociocultural background. Ratings are made on a 6-point scale ranging from no dysfunction to maximum dysfunction. The areas of functioning covered are as follows: overall behavior (including self-care, activity, and withdrawal), social role performance, patient in hospital (if relevant), modifying factors, and global evaluation.

Personal Functioning Scale (Barrowclough & Tarrier, 1992). This structured interview conducted with a relative elicits an account of the patient's functioning over the past month in four areas: general household activities, general sociability and manner, activities outside the family, and overall behavior. Global ratings using a 5-point scale are made by the interviewer on the basis of the relative's account, in terms of level of activity (the amount of time spent on the activity or frequency of engaging in the activity), change in level of functioning in comparison to the previous month, and relative's satisfaction with the current level of activity.

Conclusion

In this chapter we have argued that there are special influences affecting the social functioning of patients living at home. These include the cultural context and its value base; the way in which the family has adjusted to the development of the psychosis, including the notion of kinship loyalty; the availability of support and services; coping; burden; and EE. The assessment of social functioning in this enmeshed social context must take into account felt or expressed needs of patients and carers, the complexity of family transactions that influence social functioning, and families' knowledge and use of services. Changing social behavior within the family context requires an awareness of these multiple influences and values in addition to the straightforward assessment of social deficit.

REFERENCES

Anderson, C. M., Hogarty, G., Bayer, T., & Needleman, R. (1984). Expressed emotion and social networks of parents of schizophrenic patients. *British Journal of Psychiatry, 144,* 247–255.

Barrowclough, C., & Tarrier, N. (1990). Social functioning in schizophrenic patients: I. The effects of expressed emotion and family intervention. *Social Psychiatry and Psychiatric Epidemiology, 25,* 125–129.

Barrowclough, C., & Tarrier, N. (1992). Families of schizophrenic patients: Cognitive behavioral intervention. London, Chapman-Hall.

Bennun, I., & Lucas, R. (1990). Using the partner in the psychosocial treatment of schizophrenia: A multiple single case design. *British Journal of Clinical Psychology, 29,* 1185–1292.

Berkowitz, R., Shavit, N., & Leff, J. P. (1990). Educating relatives of psychiatric patients. *Social Psychiatry and Psychiatric Epidemiology, 25,* 216–220.

Birchwood, M. (1983). *Family coping behavior and the course of schizophrenia: A two-year follow-up study*. Unpublished Ph.D. thesis, University of Birmingham.

Birchwood, M. (1992). Family factors in psychiatry. *Current Opinion in Psychiatry, 5,* 295–299.

Birchwood, M., & Cochrane, R. (1990). Families coping with schizophrenia: Coping styles, their origins and correlates. *Psychological Medicine, 20,* 857–865.

Birchwood, M., Cochrane, R., MacMillan, J. F., & Copestake, S. (1992). The influence of ethnicity and family structure on relapse in first episode schizophrenia. *British Journal of Psychiatry, 161,* 783–789.

Birchwood, M., & Smith, J. (1987). Schizophrenia and the family. In J. Orford (Ed.), *Coping with disorder in the family* (pp. 35–61). London: Croom Helm.

Birchwood, M., Smith, J., Cochrane, R., Wetton, S., & Copestake, S. (1990). The Social Functioning Scale: The development and validation of a new scale of social adjustment for use in the family intervention with schizophrenic patients. *British Journal of Psychiatry, 157,* 853–859.

Brown, G. W., Birley, J. L. T., & Wing, J. K. (1972). Influence of family life on the course of schizophrenic disorders: A replication. *British Journal of Psychiatry, 121,* 241–258.

Brown, G. W., & Harris, T. O. (1978). *Social origins of depression.* London: Tavistock.

Brown, G. W., Monck, E. M., Carstairs, G. M., & Wing, J. K. (1962). The influence of family life on the course of schizophrenic illness. *British Journal of Preventative Social Medicine, 16,* 55–68.

Creer, C., & Wing, J. K. (1974). *Schizophrenia at home.* Surbiton: National Schizophrenia Fellowship.

Doane, J. A., Falloon, I. R., Goldstein, M. J., & Mintz, J. (1985). Parental affective style and the treatment of schizophrenia: Predicting course of illness and social functioning. *Archives of General Psychiatry, 42,* 34–42.

El-Islam, M. F. (1982). Rehabilitation of schizophrenics by the extended family. *Acta Psychiatrica Scandinavica, 65(2),* 112–119.

Fadden, G., Bebbington, P., & Kuipers, L. (1987). The burden of care: The impact of functional psychiatric illness on the patient's family. *British Journal of Psychiatry, 150,* 285–292.

Gibbons, J. S., Horn, S. H., Powell, J. M., & Gibbons, J. L. (1984). Schizophrenic patients and their families: A survey in a psychiatric service based in a District General Hospital Unit. *British Journal of Psychiatry, 144,* 70–77.

Goldberg, D. (1978). *Manual of the General Health Questionnaire.* Windsor: NFER.

Goldman, H. (1980). The post-hospital mental patient and family therapy: Prospects and populations. *Journal of Marital and Family Therapy, 6,* 447–452.

Goldstein, M. J., & Doane, J. A. (1982). Family factors in the onset, course and treatment of schizophrenia spectrum disorders. *Journal of Nervous and Mental Disease, 170,* 692–700.

Heinrichs, D. W., Hanlon, T. E., & Carpenter, W. T. (1984). The Quality of Life Scale: An instrument for rating the schizophrenic deficit syndrome. *Schizophrenia Bulletin, 10,* 388–398.

Hewitt, K. E. (1983). The behavior of schizophrenic day patients at home: An assessment by relatives. *Psychological Medicine, 13,* 885–889.

Hogarty, G. E., Anderson, C. M., Reiss, D. J., Kornblith, S. J., Greebwald, D. P., Javana, C. D., & Madonia, M. J. (1986). Family psycho-education, social skills training and maintenance chemotherapy in the aftercare treatment of schizophrenia: I. One year effects of a controlled study on relapse and expressed emotion. *Archives of General Psychiatry, 43,* 633–642.

Hogarty, G. E., McEvoy, J. P., Munetz, M., Di Barry, A. L., Bartone, P., Cather, R., Cooley, S. J., Ulrichm, R. F., Carter, M., & Madonia, M. J. (1988). Dose of fluphenazine, familial expressed emotion and outcome in schizophrenia. *Archives of General Psychiatry, 45,* 797–805.

Hooley, J. M. (1986). Expressed emotion and depression: Interactions between patients and high versus low-expressed-emotion spouses. *Journal of Abnormal Psychology, 95,* 237–246.

Karno, M., and Jenkins, J. K. (1990). Expressed emotion and schizophrenic outcome among Mexican-American families. *Journal of Nervous and Mental Disease, 175,* 143–151.

Johnsone, E. C., Owens, D. G. C., Gold, A., Crow, T. J., & MacMillan, J. F. (1984). Schizophrenic patients discharged from hospital: A follow up study. *British Journal of Psychiatry, 145,* 586–590.

Kavanagh, D. (1992). Recent developments in expressed emotion and schizophrenia. *British Journal of Psychiatry, 160,* 601–620.

Kuipers, L., & Bebbington, P. (1985). Relatives as a resource in the management of functional illness. *British Journal of Psychiatry, 147,* 465–470.

Kuipers, L., & Bebbington, P. (1988). Expressed emotion research in schizophrenia: Theoretical and clinical implications. *Psychological Medicine, 18,* 893–909.

Lam, D. (1991). Psychosocial family intervention in schizophrenia: A review of empirical studies. *Psychological Medicine, 21,* 423–441.

Leff, J., Kuipers, L., Berkowitz, R., & Sturgeon, D. (1985). A controlled trial of suicidal intervention in the families of schizophrenic patients; two year follow up. *British Journal of Psychiatry, 146,* 594–600.

Leff, J. P., Wig, N. N., Bedi, H., Menon, D. K., Juipers, L., Korten, A., Ernberg, G., Day, R., Sartorius, N., & Jablensky, A. (1990). Relatives expressed emotion and the course of schizophrenia in Chandigarh: A two year follow up of a first contact sample. *British Journal of Psychiatry, 156,* 351–356.

Linn, M. W., Klett, J., & Caffey, E. M. (1980). Foster home characteristics and psychiatric patient outcome: The wisdom of Geel confirmed. *Archives of General Psychiatry, 37,* 129–132.

MacCarthy, B., Hemsley, D., Shrank-Fernandez, C., Kuipers, L., & Katz, R. (1986). Unpredictability as a correlate of expressed emotion in the relatives of schizophrenics. *British Journal of Psychiatry, 148*, 727–731.

MacMillan, J. F., Gold, A., Crow, T. J., Johnson, A. C., & Johnstone, E. C. (1986). The Northwick Park study of first episodes of schizophrenia IV. Expressed emotion and relapse. *British Journal of Psychiatry, 148*, 133–143.

Manne, S. L., & Zautra, A. T. (1989). Spouse criticism and support, their association with coping and psychological adjustment among women with rheumatoid arthritis. *Journal of Personality and Social Psychology, 56(4)*, 608–617.

McCreadie, R. G., & Barron, E. T. (1984). The Nithsdale schizophrenia survey IV. Social adjustment by self-report. *British Journal of Psychiatry, 144*, 547–550.

McCreadie, R. G., & Philips, K. (1988). The Nithsdale schizophrenia survey VII. Does relatives' high expressed emotion predict relapse? *British Journal of Psychiatry, 152*, 477–481.

Miller, F., Dworkin, J., Ward, M., & Barone, D. (1990). A preliminary study of unresolved grief in families of seriously mentally ill patients. *Hospital and Community Psychiatry, 41*, 1321–1325.

Otska, T., Nakane, Y., & Ohta, Y. (1994). Symptoms and social adjustment of schizophrenic patients as evaluated by family members. *Acta Psychiatrica Scandinavica, 89*, 111–116.

Parker, G., & Hadzi-Pavlovic, D. (1990). Expressed emotion as a predictor of schizophrenic relapse: An analysis of aggregated data. *Psychological Medicine, 20*, 961–965.

Parker, G., Rosen, A., Emdur, N., & Hadzi-Pavlovic, D. (1991). The Life Skills Profile: Psychometric properties of a measure assessing function and disability in schizophrenia. *Acta Psychiatrica Scandinavica, 83*, 145–152.

Rosen, A., Hadzi-Pavlovic, D., & Parker, G. (1989). The Life Skills Profile: A measure assessing function and disability in schizophrenia. *Schizophrenia Bulletin, 15*, 325–337.

Schene, A. H., Tessler, R. C., & Gamache, G. M. (1994). Instruments measuring family of caregiver burden in severe mental illness. *Social Psychiatry and Psychiatric Epidemiology, 29*, 228–240.

Schreiber, J., Brier, A., & Pickar, D. (1995). Expressed emotion: Trait or state? *British Journal of Psychiatry, 166*, 647–649.

Scottish Schizophrenia Research Group. (1988). The Scottish first episode schizophrenia study: V. One year follow up. *British Journal of Psychiatry, 152*, 470–476.

Smith, J., & Birchwood, M. (1990). Relatives and patients as partners in the management of schizophrenia—The development of a service model. *British Journal of Psychiatry, 156*, 654–660.

Smith, J. Birchwood, M. Cochrane, R. and George, S. (1993). The needs of high and low expressed emotion families. *Social Psychiatry and Psychiatric Epidemiology, 28*, 11–16.

Tarrier, N. (1991). Familial factors in psychiatry. *Current Opinion in Psychiatry, 4*, 320–323.

Vaughn, C. (1986). Patterns of emotional response in the families of schizophrenic patients. In M. J. Goldstein et al. (Eds.), *Treatment of schizophrenia*. Berlin: Springer-Verlag.

Vaughn, C. E., & Leff, J. P. (1976). The influence of family and social factors on the course of psychiatric illness. *British Journal of Psychiatry, 129*, 125–137.

Vaughn, C., & Leff, J. P. (1979). The influence of family and social factors on the course of psychiatric illness: A comparison of schizophrenic and depressed neurotic patients. *British Journal of Psychiatry, 129*, 125–137.

Waxler, N. E. (1979). Is outcome for schizophrenia better in nonindustrial societies? The case of Sri Lanka. *Journal of Nervous and Mental Disease, 167(30)*, 144–158.

World Health Organization. (1984). *WHO Psychiatric Disability Assessment Schedule (WHO/DAS)*. Geneva: Author.

CHAPTER 4

QUALITY OF LIFE

Peter Huxley

The World Health Organization (WHO; 1993) has defined quality of life as "an individual's perception of their position in life in the context of the culture and value systems in which they live and in relation to their goals, expectations, standards and concerns. It is a broad ranging concept incorporating in a complex way the person's physical health, psychological state, level of independence, social relationships, personal beliefs and the relationship to salient features of the environment." Quality of life (QOL), then, can encompass, potentially, all aspects of an individual's existence (Torrance, 1987; Fitzpatrick et al., 1992), but according to the WHO definition, is essentially a subjective concept. There is, however, a longstanding debate about the nature of QOL. At the heart of this debate is the extent to which QOL should be regarded as including both success in obtaining certain prerequisite external or material circumstances (objective quality of life) (McCall, 1975) as well as "the sense of well-being and satisfaction experienced by people under their current life conditions" (Lehman, 1983b, p. 143) (subjective quality of life).

In this chapter I will review the potential relevance of QOL in work with schizophrenia sufferers. I will then consider the relationship between societal and individual conceptions of quality of life, and the relationship between objective and subjective indicators of well-being. Next, I will review a number of the available scales and consider issues of reliability and validity. Finally, I will conclude by comparing social functioning and QOL measurement and by examining the results of using QOL assessment in service evaluation and some of the issues that this raises.

I have been influenced to a considerable extent by the work undertaken in Manchester and Lancashire in the United Kingdom and Boulder, Colorado, in the United States, in the development and use of the Lancashire Quality of Life Profile (LQOLP). From time to time, I will use the development of the LQOLP to illustrate some of the points I wish to make. The results of this work have been published as Quality of Life and Mental Health Services (Oliver, Huxley, Bridges, & Mohamad, 1996).

RELEVANCE OF QUALITY OF LIFE IN WORK WITH SCHIZOPHRENIA SUFFERERS

Tantam (1988) has pointed out that traditional health outcomes may not be useful in mental health services. Mortality is low (although higher than the normal population in some groups of schizophrenia sufferers), and the disability levels produced by the same impairments varies from person to person. The effects of illness may vary according to subjective responses and social factors, which may enhance or restrict the impact of the illness. For a substantial proportion of schizophrenia sufferers (perhaps as many as one-third) the impact of the illness on social functioning is so severe that it is perhaps more appropriate to abandon symptomatic improvement and the restoration of full functioning as the ultimate goals of care and treatment. In such instances it is perhaps better to talk of maintenance of the client's circumstances rather than improvement. Maintaining a client's quality of life is a realistic objective for service providers and one that is acceptable to many patients. Baker and Intagliata (1982) have suggested that QOL measures can be used to demonstrate maintenance as well as change. However, if improvement is the aim, then QOL measures can also help to ensure that the focus of treatment and social care remains on individual improvement. QOL measures are regarded positively by both carers and patients, and compliance rates with interviews, and reinterviews, is high. In our research experience we have found that schizophrenic patients value the quality of life assessment because, in contrast to many if not most other assessments, it covers topics of major significance to them. Similar impressions have been reported in respect of QOL assessment procedures applied to other illnesses such as asthma and diabetes (Meadows & McColl, 1993).

Psychiatric services involve a variety of professionals with divergent, sometimes opposing views. Under such circumstances, the means of evaluation can easily become controversial and a source of disagreement and professional rivalry. Because of their potential breadth, quality of life measures cover many different areas of professional competence and therefore tend to be generally acceptable to different professional groups and hence facilitate teamwork.

Brief QOL measures that are operationally acceptable and take relatively little time to complete are more acceptable to service providers than long research instruments. An operationally acceptable measure of QOL may help to overcome worker (and management) resistance to service evaluation.

SOCIETAL VIEWS OF QOL: SOCIAL INDICATORS

Interest in QOL measurement began in the United States, during the 1950s (Flanagan, 1982). The Eisenhower Commission identified a variety of social and environmental influences on the determination of national goals (President's Commission on National Goals, 1960). Dann (1984) points out that this was followed by a number of national government research programs, which aimed to inform social policy development. In the 1950s and early 1960s the statistics that were collected covered economic indicators such as income level, savings levels, production, and sales figures (Campbell, 1976). Economic activity was thought to be the main driving force of societal well-being. A linear relationship was assumed between economic growth and improvement in the welfare of the nation. However, economic measures were inadequate reflections of the life quality of the nation, and alternative measures known as *social indicators* were adopted during the 1960s. Campbell (1976) has pointed out that these statistics (which were collected largely by statutory agencies) did not use individualized responses. These indicators became known as objective social indicators. Although they were an improvement over economic indicators as an assessment of the state of the nation's well-being, they still did not make a direct assessment of individual well-being. Milbrath (1978, 1979) suggests that judgments about environmental quality are essentially subjective judgments and that it is environmental conditions that need to be measured objectively. This distinction has been used by researchers investigating the quality of life of people with schizophrenia (Malm, May, & Dencker, 1981; Skantze, Malm, Dencker, May, & Corrigan, 1992).

A major problem with economic and objective social indicators is that changes in economic circumstances and changes in work patterns, family patterns, or crime statistics are not necessarily reflected in the way individuals view their quality of life. In fact rises in material well-being could be accompanied by a general decline in satisfaction levels. This might be due to the difference between the socially mediated expectations of participation in the greater wealth that is available and the perceived lack of material possessions experienced by the individual. A good deal of sociological theorizing of the 1960s was preoccupied with this type of theoretical position.

The outcome of this debate has been the recognition that subjective and objective aspects of well-being need to be treated separately. For the investigation of the objective circumstances one needs to assess social indicators, and for the investigation of individual perceptions one needs to assess subjective well-being (Zautra & Goodheart, 1979).

Subjective Well-being Indicators

A great number of studies have reported on subjective well-being in clinical and normal populations (Andrews & Withey, 1976; Bradburn, 1969; Cantril, 1965; Campbell Converse, & Rogers, 1976; and Gurin, Veroff, & Field, 1960). Diener (1984) was forced to conclude, even 10 years ago, that there were too many studies of subjective well-being to be reviewed in one article. The situation has become even more complicated in the recent past. A WHO (1993) review identified 1,520 publications with "quality of life" keyword references for 1992 and 1,570 for 1993. In spite of this exponential growth in QOL publications, Meltzer and Bond (1994) could only find 20 studies in a Medline search from 1987 to 1993 that considered quality of life in schizophrenia.

A useful distinction has been made between two different aspects of subjective well-being that Lawton (1984) describes as "perceived quality of life" and "psychological well being." Perceived quality of life is a measure of satisfaction and can be described as the set of evaluations that a person makes about each major domain of his or her life. Psychological well-being is more global and less clearly tied to the separate domains of everyday life. "Psychological well-being is a subjective sense of overall satisfaction and positive mental health that is commonly thought to be the best indicator of unobservable constructs such as self-esteem and ego strength" (Lawton, 1984). This distinction seems to be worthwhile, and researchers (e.g., Baker & Intagliata, 1982; Bigelow, Brodsky, Stewart, & Olson, 1982; Oliver et al., 1995) have incorporated separate measures of the latter within their QOL inventories.

Employing an empirical approach to perceived quality of life, Flanagan (1982) developed a comprehensive list of life domains based on a survey of the behavior and experience of adult Americans using a technique known as *critical incident technique*. A critical incident refers to something that happens that materially affects the QOL of the individual concerned. About 6,500 critical incidents were collected, and they were classified into 15 major areas, which were then collapsed into 5 life domains: physical and material well-being; relations with other people; social, community, and civic activities; personal development and fulfillment; and recreation. Other writers who have applied QOL assessment to schizophrenic subjects (e.g., Lehman, Ward, & Linn, 1982; Thapa & Rowland, 1989; Simpson, Hyde, & Faragher, 1989; Oliver, 1991; Huxley & Warner, 1992) have used somewhat greater numbers of life domains: living arrangements, family relations, social relations, leisure, work, law and safety, health, finances, religion, sense of hope, and purpose (Lawton, 1984). Boevink Wolf, van Nieuwenhuizen, and Schene (1994) have used *concept mapping* with mental health professionals, patients and significant others, which produced nine life domains similar to these.

Relationship Between Subjective and Objective Well-being

An important theoretical and practical question concerns the relationship between objective indicators and subjective indicators of well-being. Several life domains have a weak relationship between objective experience and subjective appraisal of these circumstances in the normal population (Strack, Argyle, & Schwarz, 1991). Among these are race (Campbell et al., 1976), age (Stock, Okun, Haring, & Witter, 1983), and sex (Andrews & Withey, 1976). However, other variables have a strong positive relationship between subjective well-being and objective well being. Among these are income levels (Larson, 1978); unemployment (Bradburn, 1969; Campbell et al., 1976); friendship (Rhodes, 1980); and self-reported health (Campbell et al., 1976; Larson, 1978; Moum, 1992). Education (Campbell, 1981) and religion (McClure & Loden, 1982) also show significant but less pronounced influences. Subjective well-being is also strongly associated with psychological variables such as self-esteem (Anderson, 1977; Campbell et al., 1976) and locus of control (Anderson, 1977).

The association of subjective and objective conditions is not widely appreciated. Recent research suggests that there is an even stronger association between objective and subjective measures than was previously thought. Cunningham (1985) has established that in larger and more homogeneous samples, the association between social indicators and the way that individuals perceive their lives is quite high, with social indicators accounting for 40% to 50% of the variance subjective appraisals, a finding mirrored by research in Manchester (Oliver et al., 1995).

Nevertheless, some authors continue to support the identification of quality of life with subjective well-being (e.g., Dalkey & Rourke, 1972; WHO, 1993). However, as the evidence above indicates many aspects of subjective well-being are closely linked to, and in some circumstances determined by, external rather than internal factors. There seem to me to be a number of fundamental drawbacks to defining QOL in purely subjective terms. Malm et al., (1981) has summarized two of the main dangers. First, he says, ignoring the environmental dimensions of life quality "may lead to failure to distinguish the privileged from the disadvantaged and so prove a convenient excuse for inaction" (Malm et al., 1981, p. 477). Second, such a definition "ignores mental abnormality by a tacit assumption that happiness and dissatisfaction are never pathological" (Malm et al., 1981, p. 477). He is right to raise the question of the association between psychopathology and life quality, which is complex, and research findings are far from conclusive. Lehman's (1983b) conclusion was that while symptoms certainly influenced subjective-well being they did not determine it. However, it may be worthwhile making a number of further points about the measurement of subjective well-being in schizophrenic subjects on the basis of our own research experience.

PROBLEMS OF MEASUREMENT IN THE SCHIZOPHRENIC SUBJECT

Whether the patient is in the community or in hospital, there are problems in the assessment of quality of life, particularly with regards to the reliability of subjective ratings. Severe forms of psychopathology affect the cognitive processes involved in the perception and evaluation of personal experiences. When working with severely ill people this needs to be taken into account, and greater importance may have to be given to objective assessments made by staff and independent assessors.

In a study by Mechenzie (personal communication) an association was found between the degree of negative phenomena experienced by patients and whether the assessor rated their responses to the subjective assessments of different life domains as reliable. In essence the investigators found that patients with high scores for negative phenomena as assessed by the Psychological Impairment Rating Scale were more likely to have been rated as unreliable informants (Bridges, Huxley, & Oliver, 1994). Peo-

ple with the most severe cognitive impairments may not be suitable subjects to provide self-report assessments. However, Meltzer and Bond (1994) have suggested that QOL can successfully be used to show improvements in treatment-resistant long-term patients receiving Clozaril.

An interesting study by Lowe (in press) examined field dependency (Parkes, 1981, 1982) in relation to quality of life assessment using the LQOLP. Field independent individuals are thought to be intellectually analytical, be perceptually discriminating, and have a better sense of separate identity. Field dependent individuals have a global or holistic mode of perception, tend to be influenced by others in making judgments, and appear to be more willing to disclose information about themselves. For instance, they are less able to distinguish emotions such as anxiety, depression, and irritability than are field independent people (Parkes, 1981). The correlations between ratings of life domains should, accordingly, be higher in field dependent subjects. However, in normal subjects, Lowe found that field dependent subjects' life domain ratings were correlated more highly with global well-being in only 4 out of 10 domains. Moreover, in the intercorrelations between life domains only two significant associations (at the .001 level) emerged for the field independent group but four in the field dependent group. However, three of the four (and four additional items significant at the .01 level) involved the relationship between the health domain and other domains. Although this is not consistent with the hypothesis, it does show that field dependent and field independent subjects do have different patterns of perception of quality of life domains. This work needs to be replicated with schizophrenic subjects to see whether they show a tendency toward less differentiated thinking in respect of their quality of life.

In all the studies in which the LQOLP has been used, the rate at which patients with schizophrenia have had to be excluded because they were unable to give satisfactory responses has been extremely low. The number who have refused because they have felt unable to understand or to use the 7-point subjective well-being scale has been tiny. To make the conceptualization of the responses on the 7-point scale more concrete, a "faces" version has been used occasionally (Baker & Intagliata, 1982; Corten, Mercier, & Pelc (1992). Another indicator of the subject's subjective response to the assessment itself is given by the rate at which subsequent interviews have been refused. In general, agreement for a further assessment has never been lower than 95% and is usually around 98%. In the author's personal experience consent has been refused only twice in hundreds of applications over a 5-year period.

To assume that people suffering from schizophrenia are inherently less able to judge their subjective well-being is clearly a mistake. It is evident, though, that the schizophrenia sufferer at the height of an episode of illness, or who has significant brain damage, or who is completely uncommunicative, will not be able to make a reliable or valid subjective judgment. In this respect, quality of life assessment is like any other measure of social functioning, and only observational methods or independent clinical assessments can perform any better with subjects who have these severe conditions.

QUALITY OF LIFE MEASURES FOR SCHIZOPHRENIA

A number of bibliographies of instruments that are currently being used as quality of life measures within health care research have become available (e.g., WHO, 1993). Some authors seem to equate quality of life assessment with the assessment of health status. This narrow focus may be inappropriate for the assessment of schizophrenic patients, because their needs cover a wider range than health status alone. Bowling (1991) reviewed this literature and confirmed that there is a tendency to employ measures that neglect aspects of quality of life, such as subjective well-being, life satisfaction, and general welfare, as measured through the range of social indicators. In an effort to limit the scope of the concept (and of measures of it), there has been a growing interest in confining attention to health-related quality of life (Bowling & Wright, 1993). This does not solve all the problems; for instance, quality of life definitions used by elderly people are composed of many things other than health status (Farquhar, 1993); social networks are of importance to the individual's quality of life but are said to be beyond the scope of health professionals; and single health indicators are regarded as too gross and insensitive to assess change in status (Jenkinson & Ruta, 1993).

The Nottingham Health Profile is sometimes regarded as an indicator of quality of life. It is a self-administered questionnaire, is cheap to administer, brief, easy to score, valid and reliable, sensitive to changes, and general enough to be used for various conditions (McEwen, 1983). It involves an individual evaluation of the level of impairment and disability, and the degree to which a person estimates his or her condition causes functional problems in six areas: physical mobility, pain, sleep, energy,

social isolation, and emotional reactions. It is, therefore, clearly a measure of health status and not a measure of QOL as defined above, including objective as well as subjective assessments. Oliver et al. (1996) have argued that "it is recommended overenthusiastically for a broad range of uses in evaluation of medical and social interventions, surveys, outcome measures and the like for the purposes of identifying needs, developing social policy for the allocation of resources, etc. It does not relate to most life domains and it is not a measure of perceived life satisfaction but of satisfaction only with health." (p. 37).

Similar criticisms, from the point of view of the assessment of the quality of life of schizophrenic patients, can be leveled at the SF-36 (Ware & Sherbourne, 1992; Ware, Snow, Kosinski, & Gandek, 1993). The SF-36 is a generic measure of health status consisting of eight multi-item scales: physical functioning, role limitations due to physical problems, social functioning, bodily pain, general mental health, role limitation due to emotional problems, vitality, and general health perceptions. One can see immediately that in terms of the range of problems and needs faced by schizophrenia sufferers these scales do not cover an adequate range; nor do they adequately reflect the range of life domains that a non-health-related profile would require. In addition, a study of the use of the SF-36 with schizophrenic subjects (Jarema, Konieczynska, Jakubiak, Golwczak, & Meder, 1994) showed that the patients' ratings about their own health were not significantly related to Brief Psychiatric Rating Scale (BPRS) score.

Partly as a result of problems with generic measures many condition-specific QOL measures have been developed (too many to mention here, but see, for example, Aaronson, 1990; Isaac, Wood-Dauphinee, Ernst, & Shennib, 1993; Spitzer & Dobson, 1981). Among the other prominent measures that are probably inadequate for mental health professionals wishing to assess the QOL of schizophrenic subjects are the WHOQOL, which is entirely subjective, health-related, and generic (Caria, 1994), and the EuroQOL (Brazier, Jones, & Kind, 1993), which is also generic, and health-related, and will require standardized valuations of life domains by large groups of schizophrenia sufferers before it can be used in practice.

Although a generic measure that can permit comparison across cultures and conditions has many attractions, particularly for comparative research, these advantages are, in my view, outweighed by the disadvantages in range of content (being too closely identified with health assessment) and a lack of specificity in respect of social domains. The assessment of the quality of life of mentally ill people, for whom domains such as meaningful employment and social integration are of great significance, must be much wider than an assessment of health-related QOL. If the scope of the instrument is limited by a failure to attend to the social aspects of QOL (whether these are objective or subjectively assessed), then it is not likely to be useful in studies of schizophrenia. As Shepherd (1988) said, "whatever the biological substrate to the disorder, personal and social factors play an important part in determining its course and outcome" (p. 226). Warner (1994) recently reiterated, "It is not only biological, genetic or psychological factors which determine the distribution and course of schizophrenia. We should be prepared to expand our concern with social factors beyond family dynamics and socioeconomic status" (p. xi).

Bigelow and his colleagues in Oregon (1982) described a program impact monitoring system (PIMS), which used quality of life as an outcome assessment tool for evaluating the performance of community mental health support service delivery. They tried to integrate quality of life and role theory focusing on social adaptation. They chose to include a measure of self-esteem (the Rosenberg scale). The original questionnaire was a self-report form (Bigelow, Olsen, Smoyer, & Stewart, 1991a), and this was followed by an interviewer version (Bigelow, Gareau, & Young, 1991b). The latter version is semistructured and allows for a great deal of interviewer discretion; however, it is 34 pages long and contains 141 questions. It is more suitable for research purposes than for routine use as an instrument to evaluate or monitor client progress in an operational context. The self-report version is 32 pages long with 40 pages of guidelines.

Baker and Intagliata (1982) developed a quality of life assessment for the evaluation of the community support system in New York State. They distinguish between psychological well-being, for which they used Bradburn's Affect Balance Scale (1969) and the life-domain approach, for which they use the "faces" version of the Andrews and Withey 7-point scale (Andrews & Withey, 1976).

van Nieuwenhuizen and Schene (1994) reviewed 36 instruments in current use. They examined the instruments in terms of reliability, validity, and operational utility, as well as conceptual integration. They narrowed the field to four instruments (the LQOLP, the SF-36, Lehman's instrument, and that of Bigelow) and decided that for research and operational purposes the LQOLP was the most satisfactory for use with schizophrenic patients and others in community settings. This degree of sophisticated independent corroboration provides some support for use of the LQOLP to illustrate methodological issues.

METHODOLOGICAL ISSUES: RELIABILITY AND VALIDITY

Instruments designed to measure quality of life should be valid, reliable, and sensitive to change (Cox et al., 1992). Russel and Jones (1993) have argued that two particular aspects of the measures of quality of life—test–retest reliability and the reliability of scale scores—are of most significance. I will begin with these issues and then examine some aspects of validity using results from our application of the LQOLP in over 1,500 cases.

Test–Retest Reliability

Part of the quality of life interview, the 7-point life satisfaction scale (LSS) is administered in respect of global well-being both pre- and postinterview. Typically, data derived from this test–retest of a subjective QOL measure gathered both by academic researchers and practitioners in many work settings (from community mental health teams in the United Kingdom; from physically disabled individuals in the United Kingdom; and from surveys of a Community Mental Health Center (CMHC) and a general health center in the United States; full details are provided in Oliver et al., 1996) has proved stable, revealing little systematic bias. The test–retest correlations from these data sets were strong (Pearson r = .60 to .78) with no evidence of systematic bias in mean score pre- or postinterview differences (t = 1.7 to −1.7; P = N.S.).

Reliability of Scale Scores

Perceived quality of life is assessed in nine domains (Andrews & Withey, 1976), and through the use of the affect balance or mental health scale (Bradburn, 1969) and the self-esteem scale (Rosenberg, 1965). Reliability was tested by means of internal consistency and split-half methods. Perceived quality of life (the twenty-six 7-point items rated from "could not be better" to "could not be worse"—the LSS) in the life domains produced stable results. Although the mean interitem correlations were low (.19) due to the different nature of individual questions, Cronbach's alphas (.86) and Guttman split-half coefficients (.82) showed acceptable levels of reliability. Subsequent assessment of these domain scores for internal consistency (Horst, 1954) showed that nearly all domains produced acceptable levels of consistency in different countries (U.K. data, .72 to .89; U.S. data, .65 to .83; German data, .68 to .82). Low internal consistency appears to occur when either the sample is particularly heterogenous in that domain or when the questions used within the domain are dissimilar (further work is continuing to explore this matter).

The Affect Balance Scale contains two 5-item components: negative affect (restlessness, boredom, depression, loneliness, and upset) and positive affect (accomplishment, success, pride, interest, and high spirits). Negative affect produced less sound evidence for reliability. Analysis produced a mean interitem correlation for the negative affect scale of .32, a Cronbach's alpha of .70, but a Guttman split-half coefficient of .64. Positive affect was generally the stronger of the two with a .37 interitem correlation, an alpha coefficient of .75, and a split-half coefficient of .70.

The Self-Esteem Scale also has two 5-item scales: positive self-esteem (high self-worth, good qualities, ability, positive attitude, and self-satisfaction) and negative self-esteem (failure, lack of pride, lack of self-respect, uselessness, and low self-worth). For negative self-esteem, the mean interitem correlation was .45, the alpha coefficient was .80, and the split-half coefficient was .76.

In our later work, an overall pattern of adequacy emerged among the measures with internal consistency and split-half measures only infrequently falling below .7 and frequently being above .8. These reliabilities were sustained in an analysis of more than 1,400 cases drawn from several different phases of our research.

Construct Validity

The bivariate correlations between three subjective global well-being measures (Cantril's ladder, the average score for the LSS pre- and postinterview, the happiness scale) and two psychological well-being items (the Affect Balance and the Self Esteem Scales) are all significant and range in strength (in different studies) from .35 to .57.

These correlations are similar to those reported for the normal population by Andrews and Withey (1976), from two surveys of 1,118 and 1,072 respondents. For instance, their Global Well-Being Scale was related to the 3-point happiness scale at .39 (in the LQOLP it was .35); to a 7-point satisfaction scale at .46 (in the LQOLP it was slightly higher .57); and to the affect balance scale at .32 (LQOLP .56).

Content Validity

In a small-scale investigation into content validity, 25 mental health professionals were asked to identify the most important life domains for their personal life satisfaction. The list of life domains were then classified by independent mental health professionals into similar types. No reference to the Lancashire Quality of Life Profile was made to either group prior to the exercise. The cluster of domains produced through this exercise encompassed all of those contained in the LQOLP, and more importantly did not produce any substantial areas that fell outside the domains used in the profile.

Furthermore, when the domain areas were rated for importance, this rating was not correlated with global well-being or with the domain scores. Domain scores were significantly correlated (p = .03) with the global well-being rating. It appears from this admittedly small-scale exercise that the importance of a domain is a separate entity from the subjective well-being experienced by the subjects in that domain, and the importance ratings make no contribution to the subjects' global well-being. This finding needs to be replicated on a much larger sample of subjects.

Criterion Validity

As mentioned above, there are no external absolute standards against which the measures can be tested. Lehman (1983b) suggested that global well-being serves as an independent criterion measure for other quality of life variables and proposed a model for analysis. He reported the results of a multiple regression analysis of personal characteristics, objective and subjective QOL on global well-being measures designed to establish the utility of his model. As we have reported elsewhere (Oliver et al., 1996), a duplication of his analysis on our samples gives strikingly similar results. A three-stage hierarchical regression analysis was performed using the LSS scores that were common to both U.S. and U.K. studies as the dependent variable. In the first stage of analysis the dependent variables were regressed against personal characteristics alone. The second step was to enter personal characteristics plus objective well-being variable sets. The final stage was to enter personal characteristics plus objective well-being sets plus subjective well-being sets. Other global well-being measures were not included to avoid possible multicollinearity.

The results showed that personal characteristics account for small amounts of variance as shown in r^2 values (0 to 4%). The addition of objective measures to the model accounts for substantially more variance (19 to 47%). Subjective well-being also adds something to the explanation of variance (18 to 35%). The total amount of variance ultimately accounted for by the questionnaire is between 63 and 69%. The findings derived from the U.K. studies were slightly more impressive in this respect than those reported by Lehman, which explained 58% of the variance of the LSS.

THE RELATIONSHIP BETWEEN QOL AND SOCIAL FUNCTIONING

The number of studies in which social functioning measures and quality of life measures have been administered together appears to be very limited but is growing. Arns and Linney (1995) briefly review the literature and conclude that while there is some evidence for an association between patient skill levels and better residential and vocational outcomes "little empirical work has explored the relationship between functional skills and subjective client outcomes." (p. 260). The best indicators of future vocational performance appear to be work skill ratings made in a sheltered environment (Anthony & Jansen, 1984). Arns and Linney (1995) were unable to find any studies that related skill levels to self-esteem. Some studies have reported positive relationships between global estimates of functioning and global well-being measures (Baker & Intagliata, 1982; Sullivan, Wells, & Leake, 1992), whereas others (Shadish et al., 1985) failed to find any association between nurses' ratings of patient skills and patient ratings of well-being. Franklin et al. (1986) found that patient ratings of daily living skills were positively related to satisfaction ratings in a number of life domains including housing, social relations, and work.

In a cross-sectional evaluation of three psychosocial rehabilitation programs, Arns and Linney (1995) confirmed the finding that better social functioning was associated with residential and vocational status, but not to self-esteem or life satisfaction ($n = 99$). As they observe, prospective longitudinal studies are required to determine the direction of the relationship. Jerrell and Ridgely (1995) have reported one such study with follow-up over 18 months, but the patients ($n = 147$) were not exclusively schizophrenia sufferers, but dually diagnosed patients, with one or more episodes of institutional care, poor social circumstances, or inappropriate social behavior. Interviewer ratings reported significant improvement over time in work productivity, independent living, and social contacts. Changes in the patient's subjective satisfaction rating showed similar improvement, but only reached sig-

nificance in respect to work. Interrelationships between social functioning measures and quality of life ratings are not reported.

In view of the paucity of published work, we have included some more detailed results from a study in progress in the United Kingdom, in order to explore the relationship between two established measures, the LQOLP and the Social Functioning Scale (SFS) (Birchwood, Smith, & Cochrane, 1990). In a study of 100 patients (over half of whom are schizophrenia sufferers) resident in the community and cared for by a community team, the SFS and LQOLP were both administered. In addition to the nine life domains referred to earlier, the LQOLP data includes a measure of affect (two items) and self-concept (two items), and five global well-being scales. The LQOLP domain items were produced by factor analyzing a much larger set of items and then using only those which captured significant amounts of variance. Many of the LQOLP items can be regarded, therefore, as objective indicators rather than detailed domain assessments. The development of the LQOLP for use in operational services demanded this abbreviated construction. To illustrate this point we compared some of the LQOLP objective indicators with the SFS subscores hoping to observe meaningful and understandable associations. The SFS has 94 items and only 10 were directly duplicated in the LQOLP, which suggests that the two questionnaires were produced to address different conceptual constructs.

The analysis did produce meaningful results. Whether the respondent went out shopping (LQOLP) was associated with higher prosocial activity scores and higher independence scores in both competence and performance (SFS). Similarly, going for a ride in a bus or car (other than to work) was also associated with the same three subscores as well as with better functioning in recreation. Having another family member in the home was associated with less social withdrawal and better functioning in recreation, and both independence subscales. In some cases—for example, employment—concurrent validity was demonstrated in that the employed cases, according to the LQOLP assessment, had significantly higher employment functioning scores than on the SFS.

Of the global measures of well-being on the LQOLP, only 3 out of 35 associations with the SFS subscores were significant. Greater happiness was associated with greater independence–competence; the worker rating of overall QOL was significantly associated with the patient having greater interpersonal skills; and overall subjective well-being was associated with a lower score on employment.

This latter finding is perhaps explicable in schizophrenia sufferers. For self-concept/self-esteem, there were 14 possible associations and none reached significance—a finding that is entirely consistent with the literature reviewed above. In contrast, 4 of the 14 relationships (29%) between the SFS subsections and the affect balance scale of the LQOLP were significant (three of them at the .01 level). A higher positive affect score was associated with better functioning in interpersonal relationships, prosocial activity, recreation, and independence–performance.

For the major life domains and the SFS subsections (a possible 63 associations) there were only three significant results (5%). As one might expect (since there were directly comparable questions on both instruments), well-being in leisure was associated with better recreational functioning. Greater well-being in health was associated with a better prosocial activity score, and better functioning in independence–performance.

In summary, meaningful associations emerged where the questionnaires covered similar items, but the amount of overall overlap was low. The SFS looks in considerable detail at the microfunctioning of patients in each subsection, whereas the LQOLP, if it looks at the same areas, does so in much less detail and uses indicators (which, in the present study are significantly and appropriately associated with social functioning subscores). As an outcome measure for social interventions in the subsections of the SFS, the SFS is clearly going to be a superior instrument. The subsections contain more detail and there is therefore likely to be greater variance in responses. The more crude indicators used in the LQOLP do change over time, but there are fewer of them and they almost certainly will be less sensitive.

At the same time, the SFS is not synonymous with a measurement of life quality. The concept of QOL embodied in the LQOLP encompasses affect and self-concept, and the former is certainly important in social functioning, where a reciprocal relationship probably exists. It is probably reasonable to conclude, from the results of the single study cited here, that social functioning and QOL can be related (through positive affect in many cases), but for the most part they remain conceptually distinct. One might argue that conceptually, social functioning lies somewhere between objective (material) circumstances and the individual's subjective appreciation of his or her circumstances (Arns & Linney, 1995). Capacity to perform (or function) is partly dependent on internal and external resources, so, as we have seen above, affect and material circumstances are both directly (and indirectly) related to an individual's level of social functioning in different life domains. One might go on to argue that a complete assessment of life quality should assess material and subjective well-being and social functioning as well. What appears to be required in the future is multidimensional and multivariate modeling, preferably with longitudinal data, to establish the causal processes at work among social functioning, objective circumstances, and subjective well-being.

QOL MEASURES IN USE IN RESEARCH AND EVALUATION OF SERVICES FOR SCHIZOPHRENIA SUFFERERS

Improvement in the patient's quality of life through the processes of resettlement and integration into the community has been at the heart of the effort to deinstitutionalize mental health services (Rosenfield, 1987) (see also Bachrach, 1975; Beiser, Shore, Peters, & Tatum, 1985; Lamb, 1981; Levine, 1987; Stein & Test, 1978). Perhaps self-evidently, the quality of life of resettled ex-patients tends to increase immediately after resettlement (e.g., MacDonald, Sibbald, & Hoare, 1988). Similar pictures of improved quality of life following hospital discharge have been found in the United Kingdom in studies of resettlement in England (Simpson et al., 1989) and Scotland (MacGilip, 1991). In the United States, Okin, Dolnick, and Pearsall (1983) reported a study of 31 patients resettled into community residences using a repeated measures design in which the patients were reevaluated on three occasions at 8-month intervals. Significant positive changes in quality of life measures were found, and no patients needed readmission.

Lehman reported on the quality of life of resettled patients in Los Angeles (Lehman et al., 1982; Lehman, 1983a; Lehman, 1983b; Lehman, Possidente, & Hawker, 1986). He and his colleagues studied 278 patients in 30 board-and-care residences in the Los Angeles area. They described the circumstances of these discharged patients in terms of their quality of life using the domains that have been incorporated into the LQOLP. The patients were shown to be much less satisfied with life conditions than the general population in most life areas. Baker and Intagliata (1982) studied the quality of life of 118 discharged chronic psychiatric patients in receipt of two community support services (CSS) in New York State, one voluntary and one state funded. Data were gathered by interviews and case managers' ratings. They used the life domain model of quality of life employed by Lehman and included a measure of psychological well-being (the

Affect Balance Scale; Bradburn, 1969), which has been widely used in previous work (Andrews & Withey, 1976; Baier, 1974; Beiser, 1974; Berkman, 1971).

Simpson et al. (1989) used an earlier version of the LQOLP in a study of long-term patients in different types of homes in the community and hospital settings. There was an overall tendency for the QOL to be better in group homes, with higher levels of global well-being, subjective satisfaction with the living situation, total social contacts, finances, and comfort. For the long-stay patients on the acute wards, the situation was not so good, although there were higher levels of cohesion, objective leisure, and subjective satisfaction with the living situation. However, the hospital wards had the highest levels of victimization, a finding also reported elsewhere (Lehman et al., 1986). The hostel-ward residents' environment was socially cohesive and comfortable, had a higher level of total social contacts, and appeared to be the safest. However, residents of the hostel ward were disadvantaged financially as they were officially inpatients and therefore entitled only to meager state benefit payments (Simpson et al., 1989).

Corten, Mercier, and Pelc (1992) have used satisfaction with life domains as part of a study of psychosocial rehabilitation in Belgium and Canada. Sixty-seven of their subjects suffered from schizophrenia. A principal components analysis, carried out on 120 subjects, produced five factors that accounted for 45% of the variance. The first factor represented high satisfaction in various domains and good health; the second reflected social roles and self-actualization. Schizophrenic subjects had lower levels of satisfaction and required more assistance in performing daily activities.

Oliver et al. (1996) report on the development of the LQOLP and its use in a number of different mental health settings in the United Kingdom and the United States; these include the independent residential sector, a clubhouse psychosocial rehabilitation service, a case management team, community support services, and rehabilitation services.

CURRENT AND FUTURE ISSUES IN QUALITY OF LIFE ASSESSMENT IN MENTAL HEALTH SERVICE EVALUATION

A number of issues arise in connection with the use of quality of life assessments of patients in community treatment programs. The first of these also applies to assessments in general. This is that community treatment services may take some time to show an impact on ser-

vice users, especially those who have enduring problems, substance abuse, assaultive behaviors, and so on. This is a well-known phenomenon in case management research where the impact may not show for up to 2 years and can be contrasted with the short-term improvements seen in drug trials (Meltzer & Bond, 1994). A controlled study of clubhouse users (Huxley, Warner, & Berg, 1995) shows that the reduction in the patients' use of other treatment services only begins to be dramatic after about 18 months. One must allow for the possibility that programs failing to show an impact over time may well be impotent interventions!

The second issue is that the impact of community programs may be different for different patient groups and that using diagnostic criteria alone to distinguish groups of patients may not isolate those with different QOL profiles; for example, it is just as possible that patients who differ in their dependency levels have different QOL profiles. Service evaluations will have to disaggregate patients groups on social as well as clinical dimensions in order to be able to demonstrate effects that might otherwise be masked by these differences.

The third issue is called the specificity of effects. This can be illustrated by examining an article by Barry, Crosby, and Bogg (1993) who as part of a resettlement research program studied multiple baseline QOL of patients who remained in hospital, three times over a period of 9 months. In this paper they bemoan the lack of association between objective and subjective assessment (where the objective circumstances were low and the authors thought the subjective ratings were higher than they should be). However, their own data show that the patients' subjective ratings were responsive to the immediate environment around them and responded in a meaningful way to the changes that took place. The only real intervention during the 9 months of the study was the integration of two wards of patients as deinstitutionalization removed so many patients that care had to be reorganized within the hospital. There was a (significant) deterioration in the QOL objective scores for living situation and safety. Although not significant there was a corresponding decrease in subjective satisfaction with the living situation.

Previous work (Bridges et al., 1994; Huxley et al., in press; Oliver et al., 1996) suggests a specificity of effects. In addition, Shern and his colleagues (1994) have shown a pattern of results from the Colorado treatment outcome study that lends weight to the specificity of effects argument. In their study, the results of the QOL assessment revealed that vocational services had an impact on finance, social and leisure activity, and family relations, whereas case management had an impact on safety and living situation.

Specificity of effects has also been observed in case management services, according to a recent report in the United Kingdom. Housing and social functioning were found to have improved in projects that focused on rehabilitation, and mental health was found to have improved in those that focused primarily on treatment (Audit Commission, 1994). Moreover, it is my belief that only a significant and potent intervention of some substance is likely to have an effect, and this effect is most likely to occur within one life domain—the one targeted—or possibly a closely related domain. Further research is required to examine this hypothesis. Another potentially fruitful area may be a reexamination of life event research. Major adverse life events could be said to be rapid deteriorations in the objective QOL of the patient. An associated decline in subjective well-being might be an intervening variable between the event and relapse. Cases in which events are not accompanied by a decline in subjective well-being may be less likely to relapse. Subjective well-being responses to adverse life events could be used as a detector of resilience to adverse circumstances. Research into this proposition might assist us in the identification of client characteristics that are positively associated with social functioning.

CONCLUSION

The development of QOL assessments for use with schizophrenic patients has been described and methodological issues have been considered. The brief review of the development and use of QOL scales in mental health and our experience with the LQOLP lead us to propose a number of operational uses to which quality of life assessment is well-suited (see Oliver et al., 1996).

Quality of life assessments put the actual needs derived from individual patient assessment at the center of service provision and care planning. Quality of life assessments can be a useful way to monitor patient progress when improvement is unlikely, or where it is achieved over a long period.

Quality of life assessment brings together information of many different types and offers a mutually acceptable common base of information for health and social care professionals by focusing on the total life circumstances of the individual.

The feedback from the quality of life profile can be used in clinical practice. Graphic feedback of the LQOLP

profile was well received by schizophrenia sufferers in a study in Boulder, Colorado. This type of feedback might be useful in helping clients to achieve personal goals. Another possible clinical use is in the collection of QOL data from clients and the use of these data in the supervision of junior staff or trainees.

Quality of life interviews are generally well received by clients. They assist in opening discussion, engaging sufferers in the process of care and treatment, and keeping their interest and cooperation over long periods.

Finally, as Meltzer and Bond (1994) suggest: "QOL research can have a very beneficial effect and provide a unique source of data to permit both policy makers and researchers to assess the ability of current therapies to ameliorate the course of schizophrenia." (p. 9).

REFERENCES

Aaronson, N. C. (1990). Quality of life research in cancer clinical trials: A need for common rules and language. *Oncology, 4,* 59–66.

Anderson, M. R. (1977). A study of the relationship between life satisfaction and self-concept, locus of control, satisfaction with primary relationships and work satisfaction. *Dissertation Abstracts International, 38,* 2638–2639a. (University Microfilms No. 77–25, 214)

Andrews, F., & Withey, S. B. (1976). *Social indicators of well-being: Americans perceptions of life quality.* New York: Plenum Press.

Anthony, W. A., & Jansen, M. A. (1984). Predicting the vocational capacity of the chronically mentally ill. *American Psychologist, 39,* 537–544.

Arns, P. G., & Linney, J. A. (1995). Relating functional skills of severely mentally ill clients to subjective and societal benefits. *Psychiatric Services, 46(3),* 260–265.

Audit Commission. (1994). *Finding a place: A review of mental health services for adults.* London: Author.

Bachrach, L. L., (1975). *Deinstitutionalization: An analytical review and sociological perspective.* Washington, DC: U.S. Department of Health, Education and Welfare.

Baier, K. (1974). Towards a definition of "quality of life." In R. O. Clarke & P. C. List (Eds.), *Environmental spectrum: Social and economic views of the quality of life* (pp. 27–38). New York: Van Nostrand.

Baker, F., & Intagliata, J. (1982). Quality of life in the evaluation of community support systems. *Evaluation and Program Planning, 5,* 69–79.

Barry, M., Crosby, C., & Bogg, J. (1993). Methodological issues in evaluating the quality of life of long-stay psychiatric patients. *Journal of Mental Health, 2,* 43–56.

Beiser, M. (1974). Components and correlates of mental well-being. *Journal of Health and Social Behavior, 15,* 320–327.

Beiser, M., Shore, J. H., Peters, R., & Tatum, E. (1985). Does community care for the mentally ill make a difference? A tale of two cities. *American Journal of Psychiatry, 142*, 1047–1052.

Berkman, P. L. (1971). Life stress and psychological well-being: A replication of Langner's analysis in the midtown Manhattan study. *Journal of Health and Social Behavior, 12*, 35–45.

Bigelow, D. A., Brodsky, G., Stewart, L., & Olson, M. (1982). The concept and measurement of quality of life as a dependent variable in evaluation of mental health services. In P. J. Stahler & W. R. Tash (Eds.), *Innovative approaches to mental health evaluation* (pp. 345–366). New York: Academic Press.

Bigelow, D. A., Olsen, M. M., Smoyer, S., & Stewart, L. (1991a). *Quality of life questionnaire: Respondent self-report version.* Portland: Western Mental Health Research Center, Oregon Health Sciences University.

Bigelow, D. A., Gareau, M. J. G., & Young, D. J. (1991b). *Quality of life questionnaire: Interviewer rating version.* Portland: Western Mental Health Research Center, Oregon Health Sciences University.

Birchwood, M., Smith, J., Cochrane, R., Wetton, S., & Copestake, S. (1990). The Social Functioning Scale: The development and validation of a scale of social adjustment for use in family intervention programs with schizophrenic patients. *British Journal of Psychiatry, 157*, 853–59.

Boevink, W. A., Wolf, J. R. L. M., van Nieuwenhuizen, C., & Schene, A. (1994, June). *The use of concept mapping to explore the quality of life concept of the chronically mentally ill bottom up.* Paper presented at the First International European Network for Mental Health Service Evaluation (ENMESH) Conference, Amsterdam, Netherlands.

Bowling, A. (1991). *Measuring health: A review of quality of life measurement scales.* Milton Keynes: Open University Press.

Bowling, A., & Wright, S. (1993). Society for Social Medicine workshop on *"Health-Related Quality of Life." Quality of Life Newsletter, 7–8*, 10–11.

Bradburn, N. (1969). *The structure of psychological well-being.* Chicago: Aldine.

Brazier, J., Jones, N., & Kind, P. (1993). Testing the validity of the EuroQOL and comparing it with the SF-36 health survey questionnaire. *Quality of Life Research, 2*, 169–180.

Bridges, K., Huxley, P. J., & Oliver, J. P. J. (1994). Psychiatric rehabilitation: Redefined for the 1990s. *International Journal of Social Psychiatry, 40*, 1–16.

Campbell, A. (1976). Subjective measures of well-being. *American Psychologist, 31*, 117–124.

Campbell, A. (1981). *The sense of well-being in America: Recent patterns and trends.* New York: McGraw-Hill.

Campbell, A., Converse, P., & Rogers, W. L. (1976). *The quality of American life: Perceptions, evaluations and satisfactions.* New York: Russel Sage.

Cantril, H. (1965). *The pattern of human concerns.* New Brunswick, NJ: Rutgers University Press.

Caria, A. (1994, June). *The development of the WHO QOL instrument: The WHOQOL.* Paper presented at the First International European Network for Mental Health Service Evaluation (ENMESH) Conference, Amsterdam, Netherlands.

Corten, P., Mercier, C., & Pelc, I. (1992). *"Quality of Life": Clinical model for assessment of rehabilitation treatment in psychiatry.* QUAVISUPT Project, Brussels, Belgium.

Cox, D. R., Fitzpatrick, R., Fletcher, A. E., Gore, S. M., Spiegelhalter, D. J. & Jones, D. R. (1992). Quality of life assessment; Can we keep it simple? *Journal of Royal Statistical Society, 155*, 353–393.

Cunningham, J. K. (1985). Reexamining the apparent lack of covariance between objects and satisfactions (Quality of Life, Attitudes). *Dissertation Abstracts International, 46(08B).*

Dalkey, N. C., & Rourke, D. L. (1972). *The Delphi procedure and rating quality of life factors.* Unpublished doctoral thesis, University of California at Los Angeles.

Dann, G. (1984). *The quality of life in Barbados.* London: Macmillan.

Diener, E. (1984). Subjective well-being. *Psychological Bulletin, 95*, 542–575.

Farquhar, M. (1993). Lay definitions of health-related quality of life. *Quality of Life Newsletter, 7–8*, 10.

Fitzpatrick, R., Fletcher, A., Gore, S., Jones, D., Spiegelhalter, D., & Cox. D. (1992). Quality of life measures in health care. I: Applications and issues in assessment. *British Medical Journal, 305*, 1074–1077.

Flanagan, J. C. (1982). Measurement of quality of life: Current state of the art. *Archives of Physical Medicine and Rehabilitation, 63*, 56–59.

Franklin, J. L., Simmons, J., Solovitz, B., Clemons, J. R., & Miller, G. E. (1986). Assessing quality of life of the mentally ill: A three dimensional model. *Evaluation and the Health Professions, 9*, 376–388.

Gurin, G., Veroff, J., & Field, S. (1960). *Americans view their mental health.* New York: Basic Books.

Horst, A. P. (1954). The estimation of immediate retest reliability. *Educational and Psychological Measurement, 14*, 702–706.

Huxley, P. J., & Warner, R. (1992). Case management, quality of life, and satisfaction with services of long term psychiatric patients. *Hospital and Community Psychiatry, 43(8)*, 799–802.

Huxley, P. J., Warner, R., & Berg, T. (1995). *A controlled evaluation of the impact of clubhouse membership on quality of life and treatment utilization.* Manuscript submitted for publication.

Isaac, L., Wood-Dauphinee, S., Ernst, P., & Shennib, H. (1993). Assessment of quality of life in lung transplant patients: Development of a type specification to supplement the SF-36. *Quality of Life Newsletter, 7–8*, 6–7.

Jarema, M., Konieczynska, Z., Jakubiak, A., Golwczak, M., & Meder, J. (1994). First results of quality of life evaluation in treated schizophrenic patients. *Quality of Life Newsletter, 10–11*, 8.

Jenkinson, C., & Ruta, D. (1993). Measurement issues. *Quality of Life Newsletter, 7–8*, 10.

Jerrell, J. M., & Ridgely, M. S. (1995). Evaluating changes in symptoms and functioning of dually diagnosed clients in specialized treatment. *Psychiatric Services, 46*, 233–238.

Lamb, H. R. (1981). What did we really expect from deinstitutionalization? *Hospital and Community Psychiatry, 32*, 105–109.

Larson, R. (1978). Thirty years of research on the subjective well-being of older Americans. *Journal of Gerontology, 33*, 109–125.

Lawton, M. P. (1984). The varieties of well-being. In C. Z. Maltatesta & C. E. Izard (Eds.), *Emotion in adult development*, (pp. 39–47). Beverly Hills: Sage.

Lehman, A. F. (1983a). The well-being of chronic mental patients: Assessing their quality of life. *Archives of General Psychiatry, 40*, 369–373.

Lehman, A. F. (1983b). The effects of psychiatric symptoms on quality of life assessments among the chronic mentally ill. *Evaluation and Programme Planning, 6*, 143–151.

Lehman, A. F., Possidente, S., & Hawker, F. (1986). The quality of life of chronic patients in a state hospital and in community residences. *Hospital and Community Psychiatry, 37*, 901–907.

Lehman, A. F., Ward, N. C., & Linn, L. S. (1982). Chronic mental patients: The quality of life issue. *American Journal of Psychiatry, 139*, 1271–1276.

Levine, S. (1987). The changing terrains of medical sociology: Emergent concern with quality of life. *Journal of Health and Social Behavior, 28*, 1–6.

Lowe, L. (in press). Quality of life assessment in relation to field dependency. *Social Work and Social Sciences Review*.

Malm, U., May, P. R. A., & Dencker, S. J. (1981). Evaluation of the quality of life of the schizophrenic outpatient: A checklist. *Schizophrenia Bulletin, 7*, 477–487.

MacDonald, L., Sibbald, B., & Hoare, C. (1988). Measuring patient satisfaction with life in a long-stay psychiatric hospital. *International Journal of Social Psychiatry, 34*, 292–304.

MacGilip, D. (1991). A quality of life study of discharged long-term psychiatric patients. *Journal of Advanced Nursing, 16*, 1206–1215.

McCall, S. (1975). Quality of life. *Social Indicator Research, 2*, 229–248.

McClure, R. F., & Loden, M. (1982). Religious activity, denomination membership and life satisfaction. *Psychology, a Quarterly Journal of Human Behavior, 19*, 12–17.

McEwen, J. (1983). The Nottingham health profile: A measure of perceived health. In G. Teeling-Smith (Ed.), *Measuring the social benefits of medicine* (pp. 75–85). London: Office of Health Economics.

Meadows, K., & McColl, E. (1993). Outcome measurement in practice. *Quality of Life Newsletter, 7–8*, 11.

Meltzer, H. Y., & Bond, D. B. (1994). Quality of life in schizophrenia: Importance for psychopharmacology research and practice. *Quality of Life Newsletter, 9*, 8–9.

Milbrath, L. W. (1978). Indicators of environmental quality. In *Indicators of environmental quality of life* (Publication SS-CH-38, Reports and Papers in the Social Sciences.) Paris: UNESCO, 32–56.

Milbrath, L. W. (1979). Policy relevant to quality of life research. *Annals of the American Association of Political and Social Scientists, 444*, 32–45.

Moum, T. (1992). Self-assessed health among Norwegian adults. *Social Science and Medicine, 35*, 935–947.

Okin, R. L., Dolnick, J. A., & Pearsall, D. T. (1983). Patients' perspectives on community alternatives to hospitalization: A follow-up study. *American Journal of Psychiatry, 140*, 1460–1464.

Oliver, J. P. J. (1991). The social care directive: Development of a quality of life profile for use in community services for the mentally ill. *Social Work and Social Sciences Review, 3*, 5–45.

Oliver J. P. J., Huxley, P. J., Bridges, K., & Mohamad, H. (1996). *Quality of life and mental health services*. London: Routledge.

Parkes, K. R. (1981). Field dependence and differentiation of affective states. *British Journal of Psychiatry, 139*, 52–58.

Parkes, K. R. (1982). Field dependence and the factor structure of the General Health Questionnaire in normal subjects. *British Journal of Psychiatry, 140*, 392–400.

President's Commission on National Goals. (1960). *Goals for Americans*. New York: Columbia University, The American Assembly.

Rhodes, A. A. (1980). The correlates of life satisfaction in a sample of older Americans from a rural area. *Dissertation Abstracts International, 41*, 1958–9a. (University Microfilms No. 80–26,072).

Rosenberg, M. (1965). *Society and the adolescent self-image*. Princeton: Princeton University Press.

Rosenfield, S. (1987). Services organization and quality of life among the seriously mentally ill. In D. Mechanic (Ed.), *Improving mental health services: What the social sciences can tell us*, (pp. 42–52). San Francisco: Jossey Bass.

Russel, I., & Jones, N. (1993). Statistical issues. *Quality of Life Newsletter, 7–8*, 11.

Shadish, W. R., Orwin, R. G., & Silber, B. G. (1985). The subjective well-being of mental patients in nursing homes. *Evaluation and Program Planning, 8*, 239–250.

Shepherd, G. (1988). The contribution of psychological interventions to the treatment and management of schizophrenia. In P. Bebbington & P. McGuffin (Eds.), *Schizophrenia: The major issues* (pp. 251–266). London: Heinemann.

Shern, D., Wilson, N., Coen, S., & Ellis, R. H. (1994). Client outcomes II: Longitudinal client data from the Colorado Treatment Outcome study. *The Milbank Quarterly, 71*, 123–148.

Simpson, C. J., Hyde, C. E., & Faragher, E. B. (1989). The chronically mentally ill in community facilities: A study of quality of life. *British Journal of Psychiatry, 154*, 77–82.

Skantze, K., Malm, U., Dencker, S. J., May, P. R. A., & Corrigan, P. (1992). Comparison of quality of life with standard of living in schizophrenic outpatients. *British Journal of Psychiatry, 161*, 797–801.

Spitzer, W. O., & Dobson, A. J. (1981). Measuring the quality of life of cancer patients. *Journal of Chronic Diseases, 34*, 585–597.

Stein, L. I., & Test, M. A. (1978). Training in community living:

Research design and results. In L. I. Stein & M. A. Test (Eds.), *Alternatives to mental hospital treatment* (pp. 57–74). New York: Plenum Press.

Stock, W. A., Okun, M. A., Haring, M. J., & Witter, R. A. (1983). Age and subjective well-being: A meta-analysis. In R. J. Light, (Ed.), *Evaluation studies: Review annual* (pp. 279–302). Beverly Hills: Sage.

Strack, F., Argyle, J., & Schwarz, N. (Eds). (1991). *Subjective well-being—An interdisciplinary approach.* Oxford: German Press.

Sullivan, G., Wells, K. B., & Leake, B. (1992). Clinical factors associated with better quality of life in a seriously mentally ill population. *Hospital and Community Psychiatry, 43,* 794–798.

Tantam, D. (1988). Review article: Quality of life and the chronically mentally ill. *International Journal of Social Psychiatry, 34,* 243–247.

Thapa, K., & Rowland, L. A. (1989). Quality of life perspectives in long-term care: Staff and patient perceptions. *Acta Psychiatrica Scandinavica, 80,* 267–271.

Torrance, G. W. (1987). Utility approach to measuring health-related quality of life. *Journal of Chronic Diseases, 40,* 607–617.

van Nieuwenhuizen, C., & Schene, A. (1994, June). Assessment of quality of life of the chronically mentally ill: A comparison between caregivers and their patients. Paper presented at the First International European Network for Mental Health Service Evaluation (ENMESH) Conference, Amsterdam, Netherlands.

Ware, J. A., & Sherbourne, C. D. (1992). The MOS 36-item Short-Form Health Survey (SF–36). I: Conceptual framework and item selection. *Medical Care, 30,* 473–483.

Ware, J. A., Snow, K. K., Kosinski, M., & Gandek, B. (1993). *SF-36 Health Survey Manual and Interpretation Guide.* Boston, MA: New England Medical Center.

Warner, R. (1994). *Recovery from schizophrenia: Psychiatry and political economy.* London: Routledge.

World Health Organization. (1993). WHOQOL: *Study protocol.* Geneva: Author.

Zautra, A., & Goodheart, D. (1979). Quality of life indicators: A review of the literature. *Community Mental Health Review, 4,* 2–10.

CHAPTER 5

PSYCHOPATHOLOGY AND SOCIAL FUNCTIONING IN SCHIZOPHRENIA

Shirley M. Glynn

To some, just posing the question of whether psychopathology limits social functioning in persons with schizophrenia may seem hopelessly naive. A slow, intractable deterioration in mental abilities and social functioning, conveyed in the label *dementia praecox* (Kraepelin, 1919/1971), was once thought to be the predominant illness course. Certainly, anyone who has passed by a disheveled, unkempt, obviously psychotic man mumbling to himself on a city street would likely conclude that the person's symptoms have prohibited him in some way from being able to make enough money to keep a roof over his head and live a satisfying life. Similarly, many mental health professionals interact with highly paranoid people who are unable to tolerate the interpersonal contact required to build friendships and romantic relationships.

Nevertheless, many clinicians are also acquainted with persons with schizophrenia who are able to hold down jobs, keep house well, and maintain long-standing friendships. Contrary to the Kraepelinian view, illness is not

destiny. Over the course of the illness, persons with schizophrenia evidence a wide range of psychosocial functioning, significant recovery is possible (and perhaps likely) (Ciompi, 1980; Harding, Brooks, Ashikakga, Strauss, & Brier, 1987), and the experience of psychiatric symptoms is only one of a myriad of variables influencing social adjustment.

The objective of this chapter is to examine carefully the association of psychiatric symptoms and social functioning among persons with schizophrenia and schizoaffective disorder. First, the prevailing scientific model of psychopathology in schizophrenia will be outlined and updated. Second, the literature on the association between schizophrenic symptoms, as derived from these models, and concurrent social functioning will be reviewed. Third, the literature on the utility of schizophrenic symptoms in predicting subsequent social functioning months or even years after the psychopathology assessment will be detailed. Fourth, findings on the relation of nonschizophrenic symptoms, such as depression and anxiety, to social functioning in persons with schizophrenia will be presented. Finally, areas of potential research interest will be described.

THE TWO SYNDROME MODEL OF PSYCHOPATHOLOGY IN SCHIZOPHRENIA

There are no pathognomonic symptoms of schizophrenia; that is, there is no symptom (or set of symptoms) that is found only in schizophrenia and no other mental disorder. To most observers, the most discernable indicants of schizophrenia are the presence of psychotic symptoms such as hallucinations or delusions. Most persons with the illness eventually report the presence of hallucinations (i.e., false sensory perceptions) such as hearing voices or seeing unusual visions, and/or delusions (false convictions that others do not share), such as the belief that they are famous or that they are being persecuted by others. Hallucinations and delusions are classified as "positive" symptoms of schizophrenia, as their very presence is suggestive of the diagnosis. These symptoms are thought to reflect functional abnormalities in the brain, especially in the neurotransmitter system (see Crow, 1980, 1985). Adequate doses of neuroleptic medication usually reduce or eliminate positive symptoms in individuals with schizophrenia (Kane & Marder, 1993). Thus, during much of the duration of the illness, most persons with schizophrenia will have few, if any, positive symptoms. Unfortunately, a substantial minority of persons with the illness, perhaps as much as 25 to 30%, will continue to experience positive symptoms even when they take adequate doses of antipsychotic medications as prescribed (Davis, 1975; Kane & Marder, 1993).

There is another set of schizophrenic symptoms that is at least as prevalent and debilitating as positive symptoms. These are labeled "negative" symptoms and are operationalized as a reduction in capacities or behaviors typically found in persons without the illness (Strauss, Carpenter, & Bartko, 1974). These symptoms include poverty of speech (alogia), inability to feel pleasure or intimacy (anhedonia/asociality), expressing little or no emotion (flat affect), impersistence and lack of energy and motivation (anergia, amotivation), and attentional impairment. Although they are frequently less recognized as integral to schizophrenia in modern times, when the initial notions of the disorder were conceived in the early 1900s, a predominance of negative symptoms was conceptual-

ized as the core aspect of the illness. Positive symptoms such as hallucinations and delusions were thought of as more ancillary (Bleuler, 1911/1950).

If the patient is at least somewhat forthcoming about his or her thoughts and internal experiences, positive symptoms can be reliably assessed on a number of available instruments. Accurately identifying and measuring negative symptoms can be more complicated, however, as a result of the many potential confounding factors. For example, antipsychotic medications can cause side effects such as akinesia, which yields a masklike face that may appear topographically similar to the negative symptom of affective flattening (Prosser et al., 1987). Similarly, the desire to withdraw from others to reduce paranoia may appear to be asociality, but it may actually reflect fear of, rather than indifference to, social contact (Strauss, Rakefeldt, Harding, & Lieberman, 1989). Thus, careful attention to the type of symptom, its severity, and its likely cause are important in accurately assessing negative symptoms.

A topic of special concern involves discriminating negative symptoms from depression (Barnes, Liddle, Curson, & Patel, 1989; Carpenter, Heinrichs, & Wagmen, 1988; Crow, 1985; Johnstone, 1989). Upon cursory examination, it would seem that the psychomotor retardation and social isolation found in depression might appear similar to the negative symptoms of anergia and asociality. However, a number of reports have now established that depressive affect can be reliably distinguished from negative symptoms based on a thorough clinical interview, with special attention paid to discriminating sad emotion from a general lack of feeling (Goldman, Tandon, Liberzon, & Greden, 1992; Kulhara et al., 1989; Lindenmayer & Kay, 1989; McKenna, Lund, & Mortimer, 1989; Newcomer, Faustman, Yeh, & Csernansky, 1990).

When negative symptoms endure and do not reflect medication side effects or attempts to cope with positive symptoms, they have been labeled the *deficit* form of schizophrenia (see Carpenter et al., 1988). These enduring symptoms have been hypothesized to reflect some defect in brain structure, although the exact nature of this abnormality is still to be determined (Andreasen, 1982a, 1982b; Andreasen, Flaum, Swayze, Tyrrell, & Arndt, 1990; Crow, 1985); there is some suggestion that traditional neuroleptic medications are less effective in reducing negative symptoms, as compared with positive (Arndt, Andreasen, Flaum, Miller, & Nopolous, 1995). Some of the most valuable benefits of the newer novel antipsychotic medications such as risperidone and clozapine are their effects on negative symptoms (Kane & Marder, 1993).

A fundamental feature of schizophrenia is symptom diversity. Two persons may each be diagnosed with the disorder, and yet share no symptoms. In an effort to try to organize clinical and research efforts within such a heterogeneous framework, many authors have suggested that there may be subtypes of schizophrenia that can be reliably and validly diagnosed. Over the years, many different nosologies of schizophrenia subtypes have been proposed and then discarded: reactive versus process, acute versus chronic, paranoid versus nonparanoid. These subtypes have been thought to have different symptom profiles, distinct etiologies, and contrasting clinical and social outcomes.

The issue of whether positive and negative symptoms fit this typology framework of schizophrenia has attracted great research interest in the past 15 years or so. The primary research question has been: Are constellations of positive and negative symptoms better conceptualized as independent "types" of schizophrenia, as proposed by Andreasen and colleagues (Andreasen 1982a, 1982b), or as potentially co-occurring dimensions of the illness, as suggested by Crow (1980, 1985)? That is, can most individuals with the disorder be classified as having primarily a positive or negative symptom subtype, or do all the symptoms vary independently, such that a person may evidence a high level of positive and negative symptoms simultaneously?

Many investigators have examined this positive–negative typology question using a similar research design (Jorgensen & Jensen, 1990; Lenzenweger, Dworkin, & Wethington, 1989; Mosscarrlli et al., 1987). Typically, a sample of well-diagnosed individuals with schizophrenia is assessed using a variety of scales designed to measure either positive or negative symptoms or both. A number of semistructured clinical interviews are available for this purpose, including the Scale for the Assessment of Positive Symptoms (SAPS; Andreasen, 1984), the Scale for the Assessment of Negative Symptoms (SANS; Andreasen, 1983), the Brief Psychiatric Rating Scale (BPRS; Overall & Gorham, 1962), the Positive and Negative Symptom Scale (PANSS; Kay, Fiszbein, & Opler, 1987), the Comprehensive Psychiatric Rating Scale (CPRS; Asberg, Perris, Schalling, & Sedvall, 1978), the Negative Symptom Rating Scale (NSRS; Iager, Kirch, & Wyatt, 1985), and the Quality of Life Scale (QLS; Heinrichs, Hanlon, & Carpenter, 1984). These instruments are widely available, and assessors can be trained to use them

reliably, although the relative strengths and weaknesses of each of the scales is a matter of debate (see, for example, Kay, 1991, and Sommers, 1985).

Using data collected on these scales, most investigators first have conducted factor analyses (usually, but not always, using principal components techniques), seeking a two-factor solution. Inherent in this factor analytic strategy is the conceptualization of symptoms as dimensions. These analyses have tended to yield both a positive and negative symptom factor solution, supporting the validity of the two constructs.

Attempts to develop some heuristic to classify patients (rather than symptoms) as either positive or negative have been less successful (see, for example, Breier et al., 1987; Guelfi, Faustman, & Csernansky, 1989; Andreasen et al., 1990). Although a variety of decision rules have been generated and tested, most samples are still primarily composed of patients who do not exhibit primarily positive or negative symptoms. Patients may have extreme scores on both dimensions or low levels on both.

With the overall failure of the typology scheme, some investigators have recently reconsidered the allocation of symptoms to positive or negative dimensions and have conducted new factor analyses, permitting more than two factors to emerge. A remarkable consistency of results has been reported across studies (Andreasen, Arndt, Miller, Flaum, & Nopolous, 1995; Brekke, DeBonis, & Graham, 1994; Goldman, Tandon, Liberzon, Goodson, & Greden, 1991; Kay, 1991; Liddle, 1987; Schuldberg, Quinlan, Morgenstern, & Glazer, 1990). In brief, while the negative symptom factor is stable, there appear to be two other types of symptoms. Hallucinations and delusions load on one positive factor, whereas formal thought disorder and bizarre behavior load on a separate disorganized symptom factor.

To reflect this evolution in thinking, many of the traditional schizophrenia symptom rating scales are being revised. For example, Andreasen and colleagues have reconsidered their assignment of symptoms to categories on the SAPS and SANS. When evaluated as specific items, poverty of content of speech and inappropriate affect loaded on the disorganized, rather than negative, factor. Attentional impairments loaded modestly on all three factors, suggesting some lack of specificity of this symptom (Miller, Arndt, & Andreasen, 1993). The SAPS and SANS items are being modified accordingly (Andreasen et al., 1995).

Prior to reviewing the published research on psychopathology and social functioning, a discussion of some of the measurement difficulties inherent in this task is merited. The conceptual distinctions among positive symptoms, disorganized symptoms, and social functioning are relatively easy to draw. However, the overlap in items ostensibly assessing either negative symptoms or social behavior and adjustment on the widely used scales raises significant concerns regarding the validity and independence of the two constructs (Dworkin, 1992). For example, although these instruments are primarily intended to assess psychopathology, rather than role functioning, both the SANS and the QLS include items on work performance (as a measure of impersistence and amotivation) and frequency of social contact (as a measure of asociality). It is thus not altogether surprising that the QLS is used in some studies as a baseline measure of psychopathology (Mueser, Douglas, Bellack, & Morrison, 1991) and in other studies as a outcome measure of social functioning (Mueser, Bellack, Morrison, & Wixted, 1990). Many clinical researchers in schizophrenic psychopathology have highlighted this concern about the validity of the assessment of negative symptoms (see, for example, Crow, 1985; Dworkin, 1992; Kay 1991), but there is of yet no consensus on how to best handle this issue of redundancy, and the research described below has not addressed this issue in any rigorous manner. Thus, interpretations of the significant results, particularly as they pertain to negative symptoms and impaired role functioning, must be made with caution.

THE RELATION OF SCHIZOPHRENIC SYMPTOMS AND CONCURRENT SOCIAL FUNCTIONING

As reflected as long ago as the application of the term *dementia praecox* to schizophrenia, and as recently as the inclusion of deterioration in social functioning as a requisite diagnostic criterion in DSM-IV (American Psychiatric Association [APA], 1994), clinicians and researchers in schizophrenia have posited that symptoms and social functioning are intertwined. However, it is only in the past 25 years that this hypothesized relation has been subjected to rigorous empirical evaluation. As has been noted in other chapters of this book, a significant limiting factor in the development of this area of inquiry has been a paucity of reliable, valid, standardized measures that can be used to quantify social functioning.

Fortunately, the methodology available to study the relation of psychopathology and social functioning has evolved since the early 1970s. The simultaneous creation of psychometrically sound scales to assess both psychopathology and social adjustment, and the development of powerful statistical techniques, have permitted more informative investigations of the questions of interest posed in this chapter. The research designs used in these studies are typically one of two types. Most incorporate a comprehensive assessment of psychopathology using such scales as the BPRS, PANSS, CPRS, NSRS, SAPS, and/or SANS in a sample of medicated, well-diagnosed individuals with schizophrenia and a concurrent assessment of social adjustment, typically using semistructured interviews such as the Social Adjustment Scale (SAS-II; Schooler, Hogarty, & Weissman, 1979), the role functioning items from the QLS, or the Disability Assessment Scale (DAS; Jablensy, Schwartz, & Tomov, 1980). A second, less prevalent, strategy involves a more thorough assessment of the relation of overall psychopathology to a single area of social functioning, such as work or social activity. In either case, symptomatology is typically dimensionally operationalized in these studies, with few studies attempting to subtype patients into positive or negative categories. The primary statistical analyses use regression techniques to determine whether there is a significant association between any of the psychopathology scales and social functioning. The most compelling of these studies attempt to test more expanded models of predictors of social functioning by including one or two other theoretically interesting variables, such as premorbid functioning or level of social skills, which also might be hypothesized to account for some variance in social functioning.

Considered together, the published research in this area supports the hypothesis that there is a modest, but statistically significant relation between at least some measures of psychopathology and concurrent social functioning. Further, the results suggest that, when separate constellations of symptoms are evaluated, negative symptoms tend to have the strongest relation with social functioning. Bellack, Mueser, and colleagues have most systematically examined the relation of psychopathology and concurrent social functioning. In a series of papers, these investigators evaluated the relation of premorbid adjustment, social skills as measured in a role play, psychopathology as measured on the BPRS and SANS, and social adjustment as assessed on the SAS-II and QLS. Their mixed-diagnosis inpatient sample included 57 persons with schizophrenia and 16 with schizoaffective disorder. These authors found a significant positive relation between premorbid adjustment and current level of social skill ($r = .34$), a significant positive relation between social skills and social adjustment ($r = .60$), a significant negative relation between social skills and psychopathology ($r = -.30$), and a significant negative relationship between global psychopathology and social adjustment ($r = -.64$) (Mueser et al., 1990). These investigators then conducted a more fine-grained analysis of the relation of specific types of psychopathology and social functioning in discrete domains (Bellack, Morrison, Wixted, & Mueser, 1990). Of a total of 54, there were 39 (72%) nonsignificant relations (alpha set at .01 to protect against Type I errors) between BPRS scales and social adjustment scales. However, the BPRS thought disorder, activation, hostility, and global subscale scores were all significantly associated with poor interpersonal relations and intrapsychic deficits as measured on the QLS and social/leisure functioning on the SAS. Overall, the average correlation between the BPRS psychopathology subscales and the QLS and SAS social adjustment subscales was .25, which would not be statistically significant at $p < .01$, given their sample size. As expected, the investigators found a stronger pattern of results with SANS negative symptoms, where 73% of the correlations between the five SANS symptom categories and the nine social adjustment categories (four on the QLS and five on the SAS) were statistically significant at the $p < .01$ level. The average correlation between SANS symptom and social adjustment measure was .44, which would be significant at the $p < .01$ level, given the sample size.

Appelo et al. (1992) similarly investigated the relation of positive and negative symptoms, social skill, and social adjustment in a sample of 39 inpatients with schizophrenia. These investigators reported that positive symptoms ($r = -.53$), as assessed on the CPRS, and negative symptoms ($r = -.56$), as assessed on the SANS, were both significantly related to ward social adjustment, as measured on the Rehabilitation Evaluation of Hall and Baker (REHAB; Baker & Hall, 1988). In contrast to Mueser et al. (1990), these authors found that social skills, as rated in a role-play test, were independent of psychopathology; however, they were significantly related to social adjustment.

More recently, investigators have expanded use of the positive–negative symptom dichotomy to include the third dimension of schizophrenic psychopathology—disorganized symptoms, including formal thought disorder and bizarre behavior—in their studies of social functioning. Liddle (1987) evaluated the symptoms (using the

Comprehensive Assessment of Symptoms and History [CASH; Andreasen 1985] and the Present State Exam [PSE; Wing, Cooper, & Sartorious, 1974]) and social functioning (using selected items from the SANS) of 40 individuals (both inpatients and outpatients) with schizophrenia. He reported that both the negative symptom factor and the disorganization factor were significantly related to domains of social functioning. Negative symptoms were significantly related to physical anergia ($r = -.52$), recreational deficits ($r = -.29$), and impaired relationships with friends and peers ($r = -.35$). Disorganized symptoms were significantly related to poor grooming and hygiene ($r = -.56$), impersistence at work ($r = -.38$), lack of intimacy ($r = -.31$), and social inattentiveness ($r = -.39$). Positive symptoms were not significantly related to any of the social functioning items (all $ps > -18$).

Brekke, DeBonis, and Graham (1994) examined the association among the three symptom dimensions (assessed on the BPRS augmented with selected items to assess alogia, anhedonia, and avolition) and social functioning, assessed on the Community Adjustment Form (CAF; Test et al., 1991). Similar to the Liddle results above, negative and disorganized symptoms were more related to social adjustment than were positive symptoms. Negative symptoms were significantly related to days worked ($r = -.29$), quantity ($r = -.17$), frequency ($r = -.18$) and quality of friendships ($r = -.39$), social satisfaction ($r = -.24$), and social competence ($r = -.55$). Disorganized symptoms were significantly related to days worked ($r = -.22$), quality of friendships ($r = -.33$), social satisfaction ($r = -.19$), and social competence ($r = -.42$). Positive symptoms were significantly related to quality of friendships ($r = -.28$) and social satisfaction ($r = -.18$).

Palacios-Araus et al. (1995) used the SANS and SAPS to assess the three dimensions of psychopathology among a sample of 111 inpatients with schizophrenia. Social functioning was assessed using the DAS. Negative symptoms were significantly related to 70% of the social functioning items (e.g., self-care, use of free time, interpersonal relationships outside the house), positive symptoms were significantly related to 30% of the items, and disorganized symptoms were significantly related to 20%.

In spite of the plausible interpretation of the results of the aforementioned studies that there is at least a modest relation between concurrent psychopathology and social functioning, some null results have been reported. For example, Halford and Hayes (1995) tested the associations of social skill (as demonstrated in a roleplay), positive symptoms (as assessed on the BPRS thinking disturbance subscale), and social functioning (as assessed on the QLS, self-report diaries of time use, and the Social Situation Questionnaire [Bryant & Trower, 1974], a measure of social anxiety). The investigators found that social skills were significantly related to social functioning ($r = .45$), but positive symptomatology was not ($r = .04$). The authors note that they were using a well-stabilized sample of outpatients with little overt psychosis, so the failure to find a relation between symptoms and social functioning may reflect constrained variance on the BPRS psychoticism subscale. In addition, they did not present data on negative symptoms, which may have been more informative.

Three recent studies have examined the relation of psychopathology and a single facet of social functioning—either work or social contacts. Each used samples of outpatients with schizophrenia and found, that, in comparison to other symptom dimensions, negative symptoms were most related to functional impairments. Massel et al. (1990) evaluated the relation of BPRS subscale scores and performance over a 15-day period in a sheltered workshop setting. Here, vocational functioning was an actual measure of observable behaviors (e.g., attendance, punctuality, amount accomplished) rather than a self-report. The strongest correlate of poor work performance in the sample of 55 (both inpatients and outpatients) male veterans with schizophrenia was emotional withdrawal ($r = -.35$), which is a negative symptom. Other significant predictors included suspiciousness ($r = -.33$), hostility ($r = -.30$), and delusions ($r = -.29$).

Glynn et al. (1992) examined the relation of BPRS subscales and SANS items to work functioning as assessed on the SAS-II in a sample of 41 male veterans. Again, negative symptoms were much more likely to be associated with work functioning. Eight of 12 correlations between SANS items and work functioning were statistically significant (rs between $-.26$ and $-.49$). Only one BPRS symptom factor had any relation to work function; depression and anxiety in this sample were associated with *better* work functioning ($r = .29$).

Finally, Hamilton Ponzoha, Cutler, and Weigel (1989) examined the social relationships of 40 male veterans with schizophrenia and found that negative symptoms (as assessed on the NSRS and the SANS) were associated with smaller networks ($r = -.64$), fewer shared activities with friends and acquaintances ($r = -.52$), less support from friends and acquaintances ($r = -.53$), reduced reciprocity with friends and acquaintances ($r = -.52$), and less fre-

quency of contacts with friends and acquaintances ($r = -.56$). Positive symptoms were not significantly related to any of the social network variables.

In summary, there appears to be at least a modest relation between negative symptoms and concurrent social functioning, and a slightly weaker (but still often statistically significant) relation between both disorganized symptoms and positive symptoms and social functioning. Extrapolating from the literature presented above, it seems that approximately 15 to 20% of the variance in social functioning is shared with negative symptoms, and 10 to 15% with positive symptoms. These associations hold across diverse samples and many instruments and are likely independent of current level of social skill. Given these findings, the next question of interest is "Does psychopathology continue to predict follow-up social functioning months or years later?"

THE PREDICTION OF SOCIAL FUNCTIONING OUTCOMES FROM SCHIZOPHRENIC SYMPTOMS

The rise of the deinstitutionalization movement in the treatment of serious psychiatric disorders highlighted the importance of social functioning as a relevant rehabilitation variable. When patients spent most of their lives residing in hospitals or other supervised settings, or were sheltered in families in which little autonomy was required, the assessment, prediction, and enhancement of social functioning in persons with schizophrenia and other disorders had little relevance. The advent and wide administration of antipsychotic medications in the 1950s, and the subsequent focus on community reentry in the 1960s and 1970s, brought the issue of social functioning in the community to the foreground. Successful community adaptation requires more than the elimination of psychotic symptoms. No longer hearing voices or surrendering the belief that someone is in control of one's body does not immediately render one an adequate breadwinner or capable of fulfilling interpersonal relationships. Actual adaptive functioning is required.

Concurrent with an emphasis on community treatment in the late 1960s and early 1970s, research interest became focused on identifying characteristics that might presage a better outcome in schizophrenia. One line of inquiry was directed at identifying *environmental* characteristics, such as relative's low level of expressed emotion, that were associated with a more benign illness course (e.g., Brown,

Birley, & Wing, 1972; Brown, Carstairs, & Topping, 1958; Vaughn & Leff, 1976). A second line of investigation attempted to isolate *treatment* variables, such as mediation compliance, that predicted fewer psychotic exacerbations (Davis, 1975). A final line of investigation involved identifying *patient* characteristics, such as premorbid competence and current level of symptomatology, which predicted later social adjustment (e.g., Strauss & Carpenter, 1972; 1974a,b 1977). The overarching question driving this research field was, now that patients are going home after briefer hospital stays, what factors facilitate community tenure?

The typical design used in these prospective studies involved the collection of baseline data on a wide array of variables, including symptoms, psychiatric history, and past and current level of social functioning. Subjects were then followed for a period of time ranging from 6 months to 5 years, and the utility of these variables in predicting subsequent outcome was evaluated. Outcome at the follow-up point(s) was typically operationalized as having two components: (1) clinical outcomes (e.g., number of days hospitalized during the follow-up period and current level of symptoms) and (2) social outcomes (e.g., a gross measure of employment and social contacts) (Strauss & Carpenter, 1972). The researchers often integrated measures of premorbid functioning, family history, level of symptoms, and treatment response to generate a significant composite predictor of outcome (e.g., the Strauss-Carpenter Prognostic Scale [Strauss & Carpenter, 1974b]).

Viewed in hindsight 10 or 20 years later, it is clear that the early literature in this area had significant limitations. Many of these studies did not assess symptoms comprehensively or report findings with the specificity required to determine whether psychopathology independently predicted social outcomes. Diagnostic groups were often combined (e.g., Pietzker & Gaebel, 1987), and many researchers focused primarily on whether subjects meeting different schizophrenia diagnostic system criteria had disparate outcomes (e.g., Endicott, Nee, Cohen, Fleiss, & Simon, 1986; Strauss & Carpenter, 1974a). Statistical analyses and research designs were often unsatisfying (Pogue-Geile, 1989). For example, in their study on the relation of 67 specific baseline symptoms and 5-year outcome in the Washington University cohort of the International Pilot Study of Schizophrenia, Carpenter, Bartko, Strauss, and Hawk (1978) used only univariate statistical tests. They found one statistically significant predictor (i.e., "restricted affect") and never discussed data inter-

pretation problems resulting from inflated alpha levels. Finally, extended follow-up studies expanding the positive–negative symptom classification to include the putative third dimension—disorganized behavior—have not yet been published. Thus, while there are have been many published reports of social outcome in schizophrenia, relatively few of them can illuminate the questions of interest here.

More rigorously designed studies on the influence of initial psychopathology on social outcomes in persons with schizophrenia suggest that (1) outcome social functioning is often poor, (2) initial symptoms do modestly predict later impairments in social functioning, and (3) both initial positive and negative symptoms have a pernicious relation to subsequent social adjustment. Pogue-Geile and Harrow (1984, 1985) have conducted a series of examinations on predictors of outcome among a mixed sample of inpatients treated in the Chicago Follow-up Study. In contrast to examining the predictive value of baseline symptoms, these investigators reported the concurrent relations of symptoms and social functioning at 1.5-year follow-up (Pogue-Geile & Harrow, 1984), and then the prediction of 5-year outcome from 2.5-year follow-up data in the schizophrenic subsample ($n = 39$) (Pogue-Geile & Harrow, 1985). At 1.5-year follow-up, the negative symptom total score, as measured on Brief Rating Schedule of the Psychiatric Assessment Interview (Carpenter, Sacks, Strauss, Bartko, & Rayner, 1976) was correlated with current work ($r = -.29$) and social ($r = -.27$) functioning; the positive symptom total correlated only with work ($r = .-27$), but not social ($r = .01$) functioning. In their subsequent 5-year follow-up, the 2.5-year negative symptom total score continued to predict poor instrumental work outcomes ($r = -.33$) but not social outcomes ($r = .04$); comparable data on positive symptoms were not provided.

Biehl, Maurer, Schubart, Krumm, and Jung (1986) conducted a 2-, 3-, and 5-year follow-up on a cohort of 70 first-admission patients with schizophrenia in Germany. The investigators were interested in the longitudinal course and predictors of social disability, symptoms, and use of medical services. Negative symptoms and social disability 6 months after the initial episode were significant predictors of 2- 3-, and 5-year social outcomes (as measured on the DAS). Duration of acute psychotic symptoms assessed on the PSE in the first 6 months, the variable most approximating a traditional definition of positive symptoms, was not predictive of social outcomes at any of the subsequent time points.

Other studies highlighting the importance of negative symptoms in predicting subsequent social functioning include that of Prudo and Blum (1987). These investigators examined predictor and outcome relations in the London cohort ($n = 100$) of the WHO International Pilot Study of Schizophrenia. Patients were dichotomized as having good or bad social outcomes at the 5-year follow-up, based on their occupational performance, their interpersonal relations, and their residence status. Thirty-three percent of the sample had poor social outcomes. Not surprisingly, in a stepwise multiple regression, baseline social functioning was the best predictor of social outcome at follow-up, but level of negative symptoms, as assessed on an expanded PSE, also entered into the equation as a significant predictor. Baseline positive symptoms did not.

Öhman et al. (1989) evaluated the relation of electrodermal psychophysiological reactivity, premorbid adjustment, and symptomatology, as assessed on the CPRS, as predictors of 2-year outcome in a sample of 37 persons with schizophrenia or schizophreniform disorder. Classification in the "good social functioning" category required having at least a part-time job and some social contact with others. In contrast to the Prudo and Blum study, only 7 (19%) patients had good social outcomes. Poor social outcome patients exhibited marginally more severe symptoms at baseline, with the most robust discriminative items being "lack of appropriate emotion," "withdrawn," and "blank spells." They also exhibited a longer duration of illness at baseline, deviant premorbid behavior, and electrodermal abnormalities.

Vocational adjustment may be especially susceptible to the influence of negative symptoms. For example, in their study of predictors of 2-year outcome among persons with a first episode of schizophrenia, Johnstone, Macmillan, Frith, Benn, and Crow (1990) reported that 55% of the sample had poor work outcome (operationalized as unemployment or working at a lesser level than when first ill). Baseline relatives' report of the patient "being withdrawn" for the year prior to the break was related to poor work outcome. The only other significant predictors were pretreatment duration of illness, the patient failing to have at least one friend, the patient's inability to manage money, and nurses' judgments regarding lack of suitability for home visits on the weekend during the index admission.

Similarly, Lysaker and Bell (1995) recently reported on predictors of work performance in their sample of male veterans with schizophrenia participating in a supported employment program. Veterans were employed in competitive positions, but had access to work-support counseling groups. Subjects were administered the PANSS prior to being placed in a position, and work performance was assessed biweekly for a 6-month period. Subjects with prominent negative symptoms demonstrated poorer work performance, social skills, and presentation during the 6-month trial. In spite of the intervention and the opportunity to develop more skill with the passage of time, neither predominantly negative nor nonnegative patients showed evidence of improved work functioning during the study period.

Phase of illness may also play a role in understanding the predictive value of baseline levels of symptoms on subsequent social adjustment. Lindenmayer, Kay, and Friedman (1986) reported that baseline negative symptoms portended a good social outcome in a sample of 19 young *acute* schizophrenia subjects at 2-year follow-up. Initial symptoms were assessed using the PANSS, and clinical and social outcomes were evaluated using the Strauss-Carpenter Outcome Scale. Negative symptoms were *positively* related to subsequent quality of social relationships ($r = .48$), quantity ($r = .73$) and quality of useful work ($r = .61$), and fullness of life ($r = .59$); positive symptoms were not significant predictors of any social or clinical variable. At the time of 2-year follow-up, psychopathology was again assessed and the expected inverse relations between negative symptoms and work functioning were obtained. This reversal of findings raises the possibility that negative symptoms during an acute admission are somewhat different from those experienced in the chronic form of the illness, as hypothesized by Carpenter et al. (1988). These findings highlight the need for attention to be paid to the notion of *enduring* negative symptoms, as operationalized in the deficit form of schizophrenia, if we are to truly understand the influence of these symptoms on social functioning.

Kay and colleagues then revisited the same research issues in a sample of 46 *chronic* patients with schizophrenia. Kay and Murrill (1990) evaluated outcome 1 to 4 years (mean 2.7) after a comprehensive inpatient assessment similar to that conducted in the Lindenmayer et al. (1986) study described above. In stepwise multiple regression equations, high levels of baseline negative symptoms accounted for about 6% of the variance in poor work functioning (both in quantify and quality of work) at follow-up. High levels of positive symptoms also predicted subsequent poor quantities of useful work, accounting for 2.8% of the variance. Poor social functioning was predicted by initial high levels of inappropriate affect. In a finding reminiscent of the Glynn et al. (1992) results reported above, high levels of baseline depression were associated with better work functioning at follow-up, accounting for 5 to 10% of the variance of the measures.

Bland, Parker, and Orn (1978) followed up 88 Canadian first-admission patients with schizophrenia 10 years later. Outcome social adjustment (primarily a measure of friends and social contacts) and economic productivity (work pattern) were assessed on a scale developed by the investigators. High levels of confusion during the index admission, but not emotional blunting, entered into stepwise multiple regression equations predicting both poor social adjustment and economic adequacy 10 years later. Interestingly, baseline depression was *positively* correlated with subsequent social adjustment.

Breier, Schreiber, Dyer, and Pickar (1991) reported long-term follow-up (2 to 12 years—mean 6 years) on a cohort of 58 young schizophrenic and schizoaffective patients who were hospitalized at National Institute of Mental Health. The primary baseline symptom measures used were positive and negative symptom indices on the BPRS. At follow-up, social outcomes were poor. Sixty-six percent of the sample was unemployed, and 50% had minimal or no social contacts. Contemporaneous assessments of psychopathology and social functioning taken at the follow-up assessment established that both current negative symptoms and positive symptoms were correlated with frequency of social contact, quantity of work, and ability to meet own needs, with rs ranging from $-.36$ to $-.60$ (all significant at $p < .01$), and the correlations with negative symptoms to social functioning being slightly higher than those of positive symptoms and symptom functioning. Among medicated patients, initial negative symptoms predicted poor follow-up work functioning ($r = -.41$) but not social functioning ($r = -.22$); initial positive symptoms predicted both poor work ($r = -.49$) and social ($r = -.30$) outcomes. A subsequent stepwise multiple regression revealed that initial positive symptoms accounted for most of the variance in the social outcome variables; initial negative symptoms did not enter into the equation after positive symptoms had been entered. Interestingly, initial symptom measures taken when patients were in a drug-free state did not correlate with subsequent follow-up. The investigators interpret this null result to suggest that symptom patterns in medicated patients include some variance attributable to treatment responsivity, and that prior treatment response is an important predictor of subsequent treatment response. The authors suggest that one reason for the relatively weak negative

symptoms results here may be the failure to use a comprehensive negative symptom measure in the initial assessment package.

In summary, even over a follow-up period of several years, baseline symptoms continue to predict subsequent social functioning. The relative strength of positive and negative symptoms in predicting outcomes is unclear. Confounds resulting from phase of illness and measurement difficulties may be a factor in these discrepant results. Nevertheless, an estimate that approximately 10% of the variance in social functioning is predicted by either the positive or negative symptom cluster would be supported by the available literature.

DO OTHER SYMPTOMS PLAY A ROLE IN SOCIAL FUNCTIONING IN SCHIZOPHRENIA?

Persons with schizophrenia are, of course, more than just a constellation of positive, negative, and disorganized symptoms. The experience of a serious psychiatric illness has a profound impact on the life circumstances and aspirations of the person with the disorder and those who care about him or her. A diagnosis of schizophrenia does not protect one from all the other types of psychopathology prevalent in those experiencing serious, chronic illness, whether physical or mental. Thus, the high rates of concurrent depression, anxiety, and substance abuse in persons with schizophrenia must also be acknowledged. Unfortunately, the influence of other psychopathology on social outcomes in schizophrenia has not been well studied. While an excess of schizophrenic symptoms portends poorly for social outcomes, a modest level of depression or anxiety may have a beneficial impact, as noted in the Glynn et al. (1992), Lysker and Bell (1995), and Kay and Murril (1990) studies described above. In the light of the societal impediments to successful vocational achievement for the disabled, it may be that unemployed persons with schizophrenia must be experiencing a significant level of internal distress to be motivated to confront these painful realities.

While empirical information on the role of social anxiety in schizophrenia is lacking, both Heinssen and Glass (1990) and Penn, Hope, Spaulding, and Kucera (1994) raise the hypothesis that poor social functioning in schizophrenia may reflect a performance, rather than skills, deficit. They posit that the performance deficit underlying poor social adjustment may result from social anxiety, and this hypothesis is supported in the work of Westermeyer and Harrow (1987) who conducted extensive clinical interviews on vocational difficulties in 125 participants of their follow-up study on outcomes in serious psychiatric illness. Based on the interviews, reasons for poor work performance could be reliably classified into four categories. The first two categories—flagrant florid psychopathology and the effects of deficit or negative symptoms—are consistent with the previous themes of this chapter. However, the other two categories—external environmental factors such as stigma and lack of job opportunities and negative self-attitudes, fear of failure, and fear of social relationships—are not inherent symptoms of psychosis. These impediments to successful social adjustment may raise critical challenges for a substantial proportion of schizophrenic patients; the issue of the relation of nonpsychotic symptomatology to social adjustment in schizophrenia clearly merits more empirical and clinical attention.

SOME RESEARCH QUESTIONS TO BE ADDRESSED

While the above review supports the hypothesis that psychopathology is associated with both current and future social functioning, there are many empirical questions still to be addressed. First, phase of illness has been ignored in most studies, and yet the results of Kay and colleagues suggest that this variable may be critical. Certainly, it makes logical sense that the relation of psychopathology and social functioning may differ between persons who are first ill and those who have been ill for many years. At a most basic level, individuals experiencing their first break may still have access to vocational or social opportunities, such as the potential return to college, a job, or a marriage, that are lost with subsequent exacerbations. Mintz, Mintz, Arruda, and Hwang (1992) reported, in their recent study of recovery from major depression, that it is *repeated* relapse that gradually impedes vocational adjustment; such a pattern is likley in schizophrenia as well.

A further complication may result for symptom status at the time of the testing. Some studies have evaluated (presumably stabilized) outpatients whereas others have used (presumably exacerbated) inpatients and others have used mixed samples. Given the brief nature of most positive symptom exacerbations in this age of assertive neuroleptic treatment, examining the relation of social functioning and psychopathology during a "flare-up" would seem to convey less useful information than examining re-

lations in more stabilized persons, where the duration of the symptoms may actually influence ongoing social functioning.

A final, paramount area of concern involves identifying the mechanism by which psychopathology influences social functioning. The results discussed in this chapter are correlational and, of course, correlation does not imply causation. If symptoms do result in an actual decline in social adjustment, the manner in which this deterioration occurs has yet to be specified. Does preoccupation with psychotic symptoms cause social skills to atrophy over time, causing people to lose their friends and their ability to meet job tasks? Do psychosocial losses accrue over time, providing people with fewer and fewer opportunities to "pick themselves up by their bootstraps"? Are there unspecified third variables, such as the availability of disability compensation, which serve as the mediating variables between psychotic symptoms and social adjustment? There are many questions still to be resolved; only by resolving some of these issues will we be able to help improve social adjustment among those with serious psychiatric illness.

REFERENCES

American Psychiatric Association (1994). *Diagnostic and statistical manual of mental disorders*, 4th Ed. Washington, DC: Author.

Andreasen, N. C. (1982a). Negative symptoms in schizophrenia: Definition and reliability. *Archives of General Psychiatry, 39*, 784–788.

Andreasen, N. C. (1982b). Negative versus positive schizophrenia: Definition and validation. *Archives of General Psychiatry, 39*, 789–794.

Andreasen, N. C. (1983). *The Scale for the Assessment of Negative Symptoms (SANS)*. Iowa City: University of Iowa.

Andreasen, N. C. (1984). *The Scale for the Assessment of Positive Symptoms (SAPS)*. Iowa City: University of Iowa.

Andreasen, N. C. (1985). *Comprehensive Assessment of Symptoms and History (CASH)*. Iowa City: University of Iowa.

Andreasen, N. C., Arndt, S., Miller, D., Flaum, M., & Nopoulos, P. (1995). Correlational studies of the scale for the assessment of negative symptoms and the scale for the assessment of positive symptoms: An overview and update. *Psychopathology, 28*, 7–17.

Andreasen, N. C., Flaum, M., Swayze, V. W., Tyrrell, G., & Arndt, S. (1990). Positive and negatives symptoms in schizophrenia. A critical reappraisal. *Archives of General Psychiatry, 47*, 615–621.

Appelo, M. T., Woonings, F. M. J., Van Nieuwenhuizen, C. J., Emmelkamp, P. M. G., Slooff, C. J., & Louwerens, J. W.

(1992). Specific skills and social competence in schizophrenia. *Acta Psychiatrica Scandinavia, 85,* 419–422.

Arndt, S., Andreasen, N. C., Flaum, M., Miller, D., & Nopoulos, P. (1995). A longitudinal study of symptom dimensions in schizophrenia. Prediction and patterns of change. *Archives of General Psychiatry, 52,* 352–360.

Asberg, M., Perris, C., Schalling, D., & Sedvall, G. (1978). The CPRS—development and applications of a psychiatric rating scale. *Acta Psychiatrica Scandinavia, 271,* 5–27.

Baker, R., & Hall, J. N. (1988). REHAB: A new assessment instrument for chronic psychiatric patients. *Schizophrenia Bulletin, 14,* 97–110.

Barnes, T. R. E., Liddle, P. F., Curson, D. A., & Patel, M. (1989). Negative symptoms, tardive dyskinesia and depression in chronic schizophrenia. *British Journal of Psychiatry, 155,* 99–103.

Bellack, A. S., Morrison, R. L., Wixted, J. T., & Mueser, K. T. (1990). An analysis of social competence in schizophrenia. *British Journal of Psychiatry, 156,* 809–818.

Biehl, H., Maurer, K., Schubart, S., Krumm, B., & Jung, E. (1986). Prediction of outcome and utilization of medical services in a prospective study of first onset schizophrenics: Results of a prospective 5-year follow-up study. *European Archives of Psychiatry and Neurological Sciences, 236,* 139–147.

Bland, R. C., Parker, J. H., & Orn, H. (1978). Prognosis in schizophrenia. Prognostic predictors and outcome. *Archives of General Psychiatry, 35,* 72–77.

Bleuler E. (1950). *Dementia Praecox of the Group of Schizophrenias* (J. Zinkin, Trans.). New York: International Universities Press. (Original work published in 1911.)

Breier, A., Wolkowitz, O. M., Doran, A. R., Roy, A., Boronow, J., Hommer, D. W., & Pickar, D. (1987). Neuroleptic responsivity of negative and positive symptoms in schizophrenia. *American Journal of Psychiatry, 144,* 1549–1555.

Breier, A., Schreiber, J. L., Dyer, J., & Pickar, D. (1991). National Institute of Mental Health Longitudinal Study of Chronic Schizophrenia. Prognosis and predictors of outcome. *Archives of General Psychiatry, 48,* 239–246.

Brekke, J. S., DeBonis, J. A., & Graham, J. W. (1994). A latent structure analysis of the positive and negative symptoms in schizophrenia. *Comprehensive Psychiatry, 35,* 252–259.

Brown, C. W., Birley, J. L. T., & Wing, J. K. (1972). Influence of family life on the course of schizophrenic disorders: A replication. *British Journal of Psychiatry, 121,* 241–258.

Brown, G. W., Carstairs, G. M., & Topping, G. (1958). Influence of family life on the course of schizophrenic disorders: A replication. *British Journal of Psychiatry, 121,* 241–258.

Bryant, B., & Trower, P. E. (1974). Social difficulty in a student sample. *British Journal of Educational Psychology, 44,* 13–21.

Carpenter, W. T., Bartko, J. J., Strauss, J. S., & Hawk, A. B. (1978). Signs and symptoms as predictors of outcome: A report from the international pilot study of schizophrenia. *American Journal of Psychiatry, 135,* 940–944.

Carpenter, W. T., Heinrichs, D. W., & Wagman, M. I. (1988). Deficit and nondeficit forms of schizophrenia: The concept. *American Journal of Psychiatry, 145,* 578–583.

Carpenter, W. T., Sacks, M. H., Strauss, J. S., Bartko, J. J., & Rayner, J. (1976). Evaluating signs and symptoms: Comparisons of structured interview and clinical approaches. *British Journal of Psychiatry, 128,* 397–403.

Ciompi, L. (1980). Catamnestic long-term study on the course of life and aging of schizophrenics. *Schizophrenia Bulletin, 6,* 606–618.

Crow, T. J. (1980). Molecular pathology of schizophrenia: More than one dimension of pathology? *British Medical Journal, 280,* 66–68.

Crow, T. J. (1985). The two-syndrome concept: Origins and current status. *Schizophrenia Bulletin, 11,* 471–485.

Davis, J. M. (1975). Overview: Maintenance therapy in psychiatry: I. Schizophrenia. *American Journal of Psychiatry, 132,* 1237–1245.

Dworkin, R. H. (1992). Affective deficits and social deficits in schizophrenia: What's what? *Schizophrenia Bulletin, 18,* 59–64.

Endicott, J., Nee, J., Cohen, J., Fleiss, J. L., & Simon, R. (1986). Diagnosis of schizophrenia. Prediction of short-term outcome. *Archives of General Psychiatry, 43,* 13–19.

Goldman, R. S., Tandon, R., Liberzon, I., Goodson, J., & Greden, J. F. (1991). Stability of positive and negative symptom constructs during neuroleptic treatment in schizophrenia. *Psychopathology, 24,* 247–252.

Goldman, R. S., Tandon, R. Liberzon, I., & Greden, J. F. (1992). Measurement of depression and negative symptoms in schizophrenia. *Psychopathology, 25,* 49–56.

Glynn, S. M., Randolph, E. T., Eth, S., Paz, G. G., Leong, G. B., Shaner, A. L., & Van Vort, W. (1992). Schizophrenic symptoms, work adjustment, and behavioral family therapy. *Rehabilitation Psychology, 37,* 323–338.

Guelfi, G. P., Faustman, W. O., & Csernansky, J. G. (1989). Independence of positive and negative symptoms in a population of schizophrenic patients. *Journal of Nervous and Mental Disease, 177,* 285–290.

Halford, W. K., & Hayes, R. L. (1995). Social skills in schizophrenia: Assessing the relationship between social skills, psychopathology and community functioning. *Social Psychiatry and Epidemiology, 30,* 14–19.

Hamilton, N. G., Ponzoha, C. A., Cutler, D. L., & Weigel, R. M. (1989). Social networks and negative versus positive symptoms of schizophrenia. *Schizophrenia Bulletin, 15,* 625–633.

Harding, C. M., Brooks, G. W., Ashikakga, T., Strauss, J., & Brier, A. (1987). The Vermont longitudinal study of persons with severe mental illness, II: Long-term outcome of subjects who retrospectively met DSM-III criteria for schizophrenia. *American Journal of Psychiatry, 144,* 727–735.

Heinrichs, D. W., Hanlon, T. E., & Carpenter, W. T. (1984). The Quality of Life Scale: An instrument for rating the schizophrenic deficit syndrome. *Schizophrenia Bulletin, 10,* 388–396.

Heinssen, R. K. & Glass, C. R. (1990). Social skills, social anxiety, and cognitive factors in schizophrenia. In H. Leitenberg (Ed.), *Handbook of social and evaluation anxiety* (pp. 325–355). New York: Plenum.

Iager, A. C., Kirch, D. C., & Wyatt, R. J. (1985). A negative symptom rating scale. *Psychiatry Research, 16,* 27–36.

Jablensky, A., Schwartz, R., & Tomov, T. (1980). World Health Organization collaborative study on impairments and disabilities associated with the schizophrenic disorders. A preliminary communication: Objectives and methods. *Acta Psychiatrica Scandinavia, 62,* 285.

Johnstone, E. C. (1989). The assessment of negative and positive features in schizophrenia. *British Journal of Psychiatry, 155,* 41–44.

Johnstone, E. C., Macmillan, J. F., Frith, C. D., Benn, D. K., & Crow, T. J. (1990). Further investigation of the predictors of outcome following first schizophrenics episodes. *British Journal of Psychiatry, 157,* 182–189.

Jorgensen, P., & Jensen, J. (1990). A dimensional approach to severe delusional psychoses. *Psychopathology, 23,* 9–14.

Kane, J. M., & Marder, S. R. (1993). Psychopharmacologic treatment of schizophrenia. *Schizophrenia Bulletin, 19,* 287–302.

Kay, S. R. (1991). *Positive and negative syndromes in schizophrenia: assessment and research.* New York: Brunner/Mazel.

Kay, S. R., Fiszbein, A., & Opler, L. A. (1987). The Positive and Negative Syndrome Scale (PANSS) for schizophrenia. *Schizophrenia Bulletin, 13,* 261–276.

Kay, S. R., & Murrill, L. M. (1990). Predicting outcome of schizophrenia: Significance of symptom profiles and outcome dimensions. *Comprehensive Psychiatry, 31,* 91–102.

Kraepelin, E. (1971). *Dementia Praecox and Paraphrenia* (R. M. Barclay, Trans.). Huntington, NY: Krieger. (Original work published 1919).

Kulhara, P., Avasthi, A., Chadda, R., Chandiramani, K., Mattoo, S. K., Kota, S. K., & Joseph, S. (1989). Negative and depressive symptoms in schizophrenia. *British Journal of Psychiatry, 154,* 207–211.

Lenzenweger, M. F., Dworkin, R. H., & Wethington, E. (1989). Models of positive and negative symptoms in schizophrenia: An empirical evaluation of latent structures. *Journal of Abnormal Psychology, 98,* 62–70.

Liddle, P. F. (1987). The symptoms of chronic schizophrenia. A reexamination of the positive–negative dichotomy. *British Journal of Psychiatry, 151,* 145–151.

Lindenmayer, J. P., & Kay, S. R . (1989). Depression, affect and negative symptoms in schizophrenia. *British Journal of Psychiatry, 155,* 108–114.

Lindenmayer, J. P., Kay, S. R., & Friedman, C. (1986). Negative and positive schizophrenic syndromes after the acute phase: A prospective follow-up. *Comprehensive Psychiatry, 27,* 276–286.

Lysaker, P., & Bell, M. (1995). Negative symptoms and vocational impairment in schizophrenia: Repeated measurements of work performance over six months. *Acta Psychiatrica Scandinavia, 91,* 205–208.

Massel, H., Liberman, R., Mintz, J., Jacobs, H., Rush, T., Giannini, C., & Zarate, R. (1990). Evaluating the capacity to work of the mentally ill. *Psychiatry, 53,* 31–43.

McKenna, P. J., Lund, C. E., & Mortimer, A. M. (1989). Negative symptoms: Relationship to other schizophrenic symptom classes. *British Journal of Psychiatry, 155,* 104–107.

Miller, D. D., Arndt, S., & Andreasen, N. C. (1993). Alogia, attentional impairment, and inappropriate affect: Their status in the dimensions of schizophrenia. *Comprehensive Psychiatry, 34,* 221–226.

Mintz, J., Mintz, L.I., Arruda, M. J., & Hwang, S. S. (1992). Treatments of depression and the functional capacity to work. *Archives of General Psychiatry, 49,* 761–768.

Moscarelli, M., Maffei, C., Cesana, B. M., Boato, P., Farma, T., Grilli, A., Lingiardi, V., & Cazzullo, C. L. (1987). An international perspective on assessment of negative and positive symptoms in schizophrenia. *American Journal of Psychiatry, 144,* 1595–1598.

Mueser, K. T., Bellack, A. S., Morrison, R. L., & Wixted, J. T. (1990). Social competence in schizophrenia: Premorbid adjustment, social skill, and domains of functioning. *Journal of Psychiatry Research, 24,* 51–63.

Mueser, K. T., Douglas, M. S., Bellack, A. S., & Morrison, R. L. (1991). Assessment of enduring deficit and negative symptom subtypes in schizophrenia. *Schizophrenia Bulletin, 17,* 565–582.

Newcomer, J. W., Faustman, W. O., Yeh, W. & Csernansky, J. G. (1990). Distinguishing depression and negative symptoms in unmedicated patients with schizophrenia. *Psychiatry Research, 31,* 243–250.

Öhman, A., Öhlund, L. S., Alm, T., Wieselgren, I., Öst, L., & Lindström, L. H. (1989). Electrodermal nonresponding, premorbid adjustment, and symptomatology as predictors of long-term social functioning in schizophrenics. *Journal of Abnormal Psychology, 98,* 426–435.

Overall, J. E., & Gorham, D. R. (1962). Brief psychiatric rating scale. *Psychological Reports, 10,* 799–912.

Palacios-Araus, L., Herran, A., Sandoya, M., Gonzalez, H. E., Vazquez-Barquero, J. L., & Diez-Manrique, J. F. (1995). Analysis of positive and negative symptoms in schizophrenia. A study from a population of long-term outpatients. *Acta Psychiatry Scandinavia, 92,* 178–182.

Penn, D. L., Hope, D. A., Spaulding, W., & Kucera, J. (1994). Social anxiety in schizophrenia. *Schizophrenia Research, 11,* 277–284.

Pietzker, A., & Gaebel, W. (1987). Prospective study of course in illness in schizophrenia: Part 1. Outcome at 1 year. *Schizophrenia Bulletin, 13,* 287–297.

Pogue-Geile, M. F. (1989). The prognostic significance of negative symptoms in schizophrenia. *British Journal of Psychiatry, 155,* 123–127.

Pogue-Geile, M. F., & Harrow, M. (1984). Negative and positive symptoms in schizophrenia and depression: A follow-up. *Schizophrenia Bulletin, 10,* 371–387.

Pogue-Geile, M. F., & Harrow, M. (1985). Negative symptoms

in schizophrenia: Their longitudinal course and prognostic importance. *Schizophrenia Bulletin, 11,* 427–439.

Prosser, E. S., Csernansky, J. G., Kaplan, J., Thiemann, S., Becker, T. J., & Hollister, L. E. (1987). Depression, parkinsonian symptoms, and negative symptoms in schizophrenics treated with neuroleptics. *Journal of Nervous and Mental Disease, 175,* 100–105.

Prudo, R., & Blum, H. M. (1987). Five-year outcome and prognosis in schizophrenia: A report from the London Field Research Centre of the International Pilot Study of Schizophrenia. *British Journal of Psychiatry, 150,* 345–354.

Schooler, N., Hogarty, G., & Weissman, M. (1979). Social Adjustment Scale II (SAS-II). In W. A. Hargreaves, C. C. Atkisson, & J. E. Sorenson (Eds.), *Resource materials for community mental health program evaluators* (pp. 290–303). Rockville, MD: Department of Health, Education, and Welfare.

Schuldberg, D., Quinlan, D. M., Morgenstern, H., & Glazer, W. (1990). Positive and negative symptoms in chronic psychiatric outpatients: Reliability, stability, and factor structure. *Journal of Consulting and Clinical Psychology, 2,* 262–268.

Sommers, A. A. (1985). "Negative Symptoms": Conceptual and methodological problems. *Schizophrenia Bulletin, 11,* 364–379.

Strauss, J. S., & Carpenter, W. T. (1977). The prediction of outcome in schizophrenia: III. Five-year outcome and its predictors. *Archives of General Psychiatry, 34,* 159–163.

Strauss, J. S., Carpenter, W. T., & Bartko, J. J. (1974). The diagnosis and understanding of schizophrenia: II. Speculations on the processes that underlie schizophrenic symptoms and signs. *Schizophrenia Bulletin, 1,* 61–76.

Strauss, J. S., & Carpenter, W. T. (1972). The prediction of outcome in schizophrenia. Characteristics of outcome. *Archives of General Psychiatry, 27,* 739–746.

Strauss, J. S., & Carpenter, W. T. (1974a). Characteristic symptoms and outcome in schizophrenia. *Archives of General Psychiatry, 30,* 429–434.

Strauss, J. S., & Carpenter, W. T. (1974b). The prediction of outcome in schizophrenia: II. Relationships between predictor and outcome variables: A report from the WHO International Pilot Study of Schizophrenia. *Archives of General Psychiatry, 31,* 37–42.

Strauss, J. S., Rakefeldt, J., Harding, C. M., & Lieberman, P. (1989). Psychological and social aspects of negative symptoms. *British Journal of Psychiatry, 155,* 120–132.

Test, M. A., Knoedler, W. H., Allness, D. J., Burke, S. S., Brown, R. L., & Wallisch, L.S. (1991). Long-term community care through an assertive continuous treatment team. In C. Tamminga and S. Schultz (Eds.), *Advances in neuropsychiatry and psychopharmacology. Vol 1. Schizophrenia research* (pp. 239–246). New York: Raven.

Vaughn, C. E., & Leff, J. (1976). The influence of family and social factors on the course of psychiatric illness. *British Journal of Psychiatry, 129,* 125–137.

Westermeyer, J. F., & Harrow, M. (1987). Factors associated with work impairments in schizophrenic and nonschizophrenic patients. In R. R. Grinker Sr. & M. Harrow (Eds.), *Clinical research in schizophrenia: A multidimensional approach* (pp. 280–298). Springfield, IL: Charles C. Thomas.

Wing, J. K., Cooper, J. E., & Sartorius, N. (1974). *The measurement and classification of psychiatric symptoms.* Cambridge: Cambridge University Press.

CHAPTER 6

SOCIAL SKILLS AND SOCIAL FUNCTIONING

Kim T. Mueser
Alan S. Bellack

Social impairments have long been recognized to be a core feature of schizophrenia. The importance of poor social functioning in schizophrenia is reflected by the fact that most diagnostic systems require problems in social functioning, such as poor interpersonal relationships, inability to work or meet other role expectations, and impoverished self-care skills, in order to diagnose the illness (e.g., American Psychiatric Association, 1994). Despite recognition of the poor social functioning in schizophrenia, it was only in the 1960s and 1970s that systematic efforts were mounted to systematically improve the social behavior of persons with schizophrenia (e.g., Ayllon & Azrin, 1968; Hersen & Bellack, 1976).

One concept that has been useful in the development of interventions designed to improve social functioning of persons with schizophrenia has been the social skills construct. *Social skills* can be broadly understood to be those behaviors that are hypothesized to be critical for successful social interactions. Focused attention on the assessment and modification of social skills has lead to a paradigm for understanding how specific behaviors influence social adjustment. In this chapter, we review the theoretical and empirical basis of the social skills model of social functioning in schizophrenia. Specifically, we first discuss the definition and measurement of social skills. Next, we describe two models that have served as heuristics in guiding research on social skill in schizophrenia, the social skills model and the stress-vulnerability-coping skills model. Then, we review research on the prevalence and temporal stability of social skill deficits in schizophrenia, followed by the relationship between social skills and social functioning. We then consider the relationships between social skill, symptomatology, social perception, cognitive impairment, problem solving, and gender. We conclude with a summary of the support for the skills model and recommendations for future directions for research in this area. Clinical strategies and research on social skills training are reviewed in Chapter 19.

DEFINITIONS OF SOCIAL SKILL

A variety of definitions of social skill have been proposed, varying from rather broad, generic definitions to more precise, descriptive definitions. For example,

Liberman, DeRisi, and Mueser (1989) offer a broad definition of social skill as "all the behaviors that help us to communicate our emotions and needs accurately and allow us to achieve our interpersonal goals" (p. 3). Alternatively, Hersen and Bellack (1977) provide a more specific definition of social skills as the

> ability to express both positive and negative feelings in the interpersonal context without suffering consequent loss of reinforcement. Such skill is demonstrated in a large variety of interpersonal contexts and involves the coordinated delivery of appropriate verbal and nonverbal responses. In addition, the socially skilled individual is attuned to the realities of the situation and is aware when he is likely to be reinforced for his efforts. (p. 512)

Trower, Bryant, and Argyle (1978) define social *un*skillfulness in a way much the opposite of Hersen and Bellack's definition of social skill:

> A person can be regarded as socially inadequate if he is unable to affect the behaviour and feelings of others in the way that he intends and society accepts. Such a person will appear annoying, unforthcoming, uninteresting, cold, destructive, bad-tempered, isolated or inept, and will generally be unrewarding to others. (p. 2)

The Hersen and Bellack (1977) definition is the most explicit in specifying the importance of social perception skills, such as the ability to perceive relevant situational parameters, as an important ingredient in successful social interactions. Both the Liberman et al. (1989) and Hersen and Bellack (1977) definitions refer to an individual's ability to use specific behaviors to achieve socially oriented goals. Finally, all three definitions allude to social skills as involving the ability to elicit favorable responses from the individual's social environment. In general, there is a broad consensus across clinicians and researchers that the behavioral dimension of social skills can be conceptualized in terms of specific component behaviors and that teaching these behaviors is a major focus of social skills training.

Components of Social Skill

The components of social skill can be roughly divided into four areas: nonverbal skills, paralinguistic elements, verbal content, and interactive balance. *Nonverbal skills* refer to behaviors such as eye contact, facial expression, use of gestures, and body orientation that, in combination, convey important information about an individual's mood and level of engagement during an interaction. *Paralinguistic elements* are the specific qualities of an individual's speech, such as voice tone, loudness, inflection, pitch, and rate of speech that, similar to nonverbal skills, are vital to communicating affect and a sense of involvement during social interactions. *Verbal content* is the specific choice of words and phrasing, independent of the manner or style in which it is said. Finally, *interactive balance* refers to the skills necessary for maintaining a satisfactory give-and-take during a conversation. For example, the latency of response after one person stops speaking and another begins, the relative amount of time that each speaker talks, and the use of minimal verbal encouragers (e.g., "uh-huh," "I see") in combination determine the ease and satisfaction of conversing with someone.

Each of the broad component areas has an influence on the effectiveness of social behavior. People who have poor nonverbal and paralinguistic skills may be ineffective at achieving their needs even if their verbal content and interactive balance are appropriate. For example, someone who avoids eye contact and says in a meek voice "I don't like it when you change the TV channel in the middle of my program" is unlikely to get his or her message across and be taken seriously, compared with another who conveys this verbal message with good eye contact and in a clearly audible, forceful voice tone. On the other hand, if verbal content is inappropriate, the communicator is also unlikely to achieve his or her goals, either due to violation of social norms (e.g., assuming undue familiarity with the other person), or unclear or psychotic speech. Last, poor interactive balance (i.e., very long pauses between conversational turns) may simply make the person awkward or unrewarding to converse with, resulting in prematurely terminated conversations or avoidance of the person altogether.

Assessment of Social Skill

A variety of different techniques have been used to assess the social skills of patients with schizophrenia (Bellack, 1979, 1983; Liberman, 1982; Mueser & Sayers, 1992). Different methods include role-play assessments, naturalistic observations, and the reports of self and significant others.

Role-Play Tests

The most widely used strategy for assessing social skills is the use of *role-play tests*. Role plays are simulated interactions involving the subject and another individual who plays the role of the partner during the interaction. When conducting a role-play test, the subject is informed about of the situation, his or her goal in the role-play, and the role played by the other person (e.g., friend, parent). Subjects are instructed to act as they naturally would if such a situation actually occurred. For assessment purposes (rather than in the context of social skills training) role-plays are usually audiotaped or videotaped and rated later on a variety of dimensions of social skill.

Some role-play tests are relatively brief and highly structured in order to standardize the situation across different subjects. Such assessments typically involved one to three verbal exchanges between the subject and the confederate in the role-play. A role-play test will consist of a variety of brief interactions, involving situations such as initiating conversations, expressing positive feelings, and assertiveness. An advantage of brief, highly structured role-play assessments is that the performance of different subjects is easier to compare because the confederate's responses to the subject are very similar. A limitation to brief role-play scenarios is that these short interactions may not be an accurate reflection of most social interactions in the "real world."

An alternative strategy to brief, highly structured role-plays of social skill is to conduct more open-ended assessments with less explicit scripting for the confederate. An example of such an assessment is the Conversation Probe, in which subjects are engaged in a relatively unstructured conversation that extends for several minutes (Torgrud & Holborn, 1992). These open-ended role-plays may be more generalizable to naturalistic interactions, although by their very nature they are more difficult to standardize across subjects.

Role-play assessments of social skill have a number of advantages over other assessment strategies. First, because they can be audiotaped or videotaped and later rated on specific dimensions of social skill, a more in-depth evaluation of specific social skill assets and deficits can be conducted than based on live observations or reports. Second, role-play assessments are convenient because they do not require access to patients in their natural environment, in contrast to other assessment procedures. Third, role-playing can be integrated into the process of social skills training, thereby providing leaders with information regarding the effects of skills training strategies on patients' social skill.

Despite the advantages of role-play tests, they have some disadvantages as well. The time required to standardize role-play situations and train raters makes formal role-play tests impractical for clinical use outside of the context of social skills training. Role-play tests have also been criticized as being artificial and superficial, for missing the nuances of normal social interactions, and for lacking sensitivity to the rules of different social subgroups and cultures. Despite these limitations, as will be discussed later on in this chapter, evidence supports the reliability and validity of role-play tests of social skill.

Naturalistic Observation

Naturalistic observation refers to observations made by staff members or significant others of the subject in his or her natural environment. Naturalistic observations are valuable because they can provide insight into the person's effectiveness in different social situations. Such observations may be useful not only for characterizing the skills and deficiencies of the patient, but also for gauging the response of the environment to the patient. For example, if the patient is living in a hostile, overly critical environment, even appropriately assertive behavior may result in a negative response. In such a situation, effective intervention may involve modifying both the patient's behavior as well as that of staff members or significant others.

Despite some of the advantages of naturalistic observation over role-play assessments, there are significant disadvantages. In particular, naturalistic observations are inconvenient and expensive to obtain, because they require highly trained observers who must conduct observations in a variety of different settings, and in many cases the observations themselves may be of low relevance (Bellack & Mueser, 1990). An additional disadvantage is that there are many situations in which naturalistic observations are difficult or impossible to conduct, such as situations involving interpersonal intimacy (e.g., asking someone for a date, discussing birth control). For these reasons, naturalistic observations are not generally relied on as the primary method for assessing social skills. However, such observations are frequently used to supplement role-play assessments.

Reports of Self and Significant Others

Self and other reports of social skill are useful for identifying general areas of social dysfunction, but not for pinpointing specific social skill deficits. Patients are frequently able to identify problem areas, such as conversational ability or assertiveness, which may benefit from social skills training. Similarly, relatives' and staff members' reports often complement those of patients in identifying areas for skills training. However, patients and significant others are not able to articulate skill deficits in sufficient detail to permit skills training for these deficits.

Comprehensive Assessment of Social Skill

Therefore, the comprehensive assessment of social skills requires a range of different strategies. Assessment usually begins at the most general level, obtaining reports from patients and significant others as to areas of social dysfunction. Following these reports, when possible, naturalistic observations may be conducted to better characterize the social difficulties the patient encounters. When this information has been obtained, role-play assessments of social skill can be conducted, tapping those situations in which the greatest social difficulties are encountered. Based on these role-play assessments, skills training interventions can be provided.

THEORIES OF SOCIAL SKILL

Two different theories have been advanced to account for the importance of social skills in schizophrenia and other psychiatric disorders, the *social skills model* and the *stress-vulnerability-coping skills model*. Although these two models are compatible with each other, they are based on different assumptions and differ somewhat in their implications for the rehabilitation of social functioning.

The Social Skills Model

The model posits that

1. Social competence is based on a set of component response skills.
2. These skills are learned or learnable.
3. Social dysfunction results when
   a. requisite behaviors are not in the person's repertoire;
   b. requisite behaviors are not used at the appropriate time; and
   c. the person performs socially inappropriate behaviors.
4. Social dysfunction can be rectified by skills training.

The most important features of the social skills model are that it hypothesizes that social skills are a necessary ingredient to effective social interactions, skills can be learned, and skills training may be an effective strategy for enhancing social skills. The social skills model does not assume that *all* social dysfunction is the result of poor social skills. Rather, social dysfunction can arise from a variety of nonskill factors as well as deficits in social skill. For example, neuroleptic side effects such as akathesia and akinesia, social mores, poor motivation, or a hostile or nonresponsive environment may all contribute to social dysfunction independent of social skills.

Stress-Vulnerability-Coping Skills Model

This model proposes that the outcome of schizophrenia, including the severity of symptoms, quality of social adjustment, and vulnerability to symptom relapses, is determined by the dynamic interplay of three constructs: biological vulnerability, environmental stress, and coping skills (Liberman et al., 1986; Nuechterlein & Dawson, 1984). *Biological vulnerability* is presumably determined at an early age by a combination of early environmental (e.g., subtle brain damage due to neurodevelopmental insults) and genetic influences. However, biological vulnerability can be decreased by regular use of neuroleptic medications and increased by substance abuse. The extent of biological vulnerability determines the overall severity of an individual's illness. *Environmental stressors,* such as life events and exposure to a tense, hostile familial environment, impinges on biological vulnerability so as to worsen symptom severity and increase vulnerability to relapses. The noxious impact of stressors on biological vulnerability is mediated by patient coping skill. *Coping skills* can be defined as abilities that enable an individual to either remove or reduce sources of stress or alternatively to minimize the negative effects of stress on vulnerability. Coping skills that are interpersonal in nature are social skills. Therefore, according to this model social skills are a subset of coping skills, which enable individuals to adjust more effectively to the effects of stress. This formulation suggests that effective social skills may protect individuals with schizophrenia from stress-induced relapses.

The social skills and stress-vulnerability-coping skills models have served as valuable heuristics in guiding research on social skills and the effects of social skills training in schizophrenia. In the next section we review research on social skill in patients with schizophrenia.

RESEARCH AT MEDICAL COLLEGE OF PENNSYLVANIA

We have confined our review of research on social skill in schizophrenia to studies conducted with well-defined cohorts of patients with diagnoses based on standardized instruments, such as the Structured Clinical Interview for DSM-III-R (SCID; Spitzer, Williams, Gibbon, & First, 1988). In addition, the focus of our review is on studies that have examined either the reliability or validity of social skills assessments in schizophrenia, or that evaluated the relationship of skills to other domains of functioning in schizophrenia. Specifically excluded from this review is any consideration of research on the effects of skills training in schizophrenia, or the prediction of skill acquisition in skills training.

We conducted many of the studies we describe in our review, in collaboration with other colleagues at the Medical College of Pennsylvania at Eastern Pennsylvania Psychiatric Institute (MCP/EPPI). Most of these studies employed role-play tests, used the same or similar instruments to establish diagnosis (SCID) and rate symptomatology (e.g., Brief Psychiatric Rating Scale [BPRS]; Overall & Gorham, 1962; Woerner, Mannuzza, & Kane, 1988), and used similar procedures for recruiting subjects into the study. In all studies, care was taken to ensure that all ratings demonstrated high interrater reliabilities. To facilitate reading our review of research on social skills, in Table 6.1 we have provided a summary of the methodological characteristics and key findings of the six studies we conducted on social skills in schizophrenia, using role-play tests, at MCP/EPPI between 1984 and 1994.

RELIABILITY AND VALIDITY OF SOCIAL SKILLS ASSESSMENTS

Reliability

Two types of reliability have been examined in research on social skills: interrater reliability and test–retest reliability. Satisfactory levels of interrater reliability of social skills ratings have been repeatedly demonstrated across numerous studies. In most studies, intraclass correlation coefficients for social skill ratings are reported in excess of .70, indicating a high level of agreement between raters. Although training is required to produce such high levels of agreement, this strong agreement indicates that highly reliable ratings of social skill can be obtained.

We examined the test-retest reliability of social skills assessments over 1 year (Mueser, Bellack, Douglas, & Wade, 1991). In this study, patients with schizophrenia or schizoaffective disorder participated in a role-play assessment of social skill several weeks following an acute symptom exacerbation, 6 months later when they were living in the community, and 1 year later when they were still living in the community. Both component skills and global social skill ratings were obtained based on videotapes of the role-play test.

Global ratings of social skill showed very high test–retest correlations, with $r = .61$ for the baseline to 6-month interval, $r = .78$ between 6 months and 1 year, and $r = .48$ between baseline and 1 year. Component ratings of social skill showed lower levels of test-retest reliability, which were nevertheless statistically significant for most components. For example, the 6-month to 1-year assessment test–retest reliabilities ranged from a low of $r = .13$ (not significant) for meshing (i.e., appropriateness of interactive turn-taking) to a high of $r = .55$ ($p < .01$) for duration of utterance. Furthermore, this study reported that in the absence of skills training interventions, social skills were relatively stable over the 1-year period. These results suggest that social skills are relatively stable over significant periods of time, and that global ratings of skill are more stable than ratings of individual skill components.

Validity

Several studies have examined the validity of role-play tests of social skill. Since role-play tests are generally considered the optimal measure of social skill, the validity of these tests has been evaluated by comparing performance on role-plays with either more naturalistic observations of patients' social behavior or ratings of social adjustment in patients' natural environment. Bellack, Morrison, Mueser, Wade, and Sayers (1990) examined the relationship between social skill performance on a brief role-play test, ratings of social adjustment based on the Social Adjustment Scale II (SAS-II; Schooler, Hogarty, & Weissman, 1978), and a more naturalistic interaction with a family member. The patients included a mixed cohort of patients with schizophrenia, schizoaffective disorder, and major affective disorder. All patients with major affective disorder had a chronicity of illness lasting at least 6 months to maximize their comparability to patients with schizophrenia. The results showed that performance on the role-play test was strongly related to both ratings on the SAS-II, as well as patient social skill during the family interaction. This study provided strong support that role-play assessments of social skill are related to skills in less contrived situations, as well as ratings of social functioning in the community.

Several other studies have also provided evidence that role-play assessments of social skill are related to other

Table 6.1. Summary of Social Skills Studies Conducted by Bellack, Mueser, and Colleagues at the Medical College of Pennsylvania at Eastern Pennsylvania Psychiatric Institute

STUDY	PUBLICATIONS	SUBJECTS[a]	ROLE-PLAY TEST[b]	OTHER MEASURES	MAIN FINDINGS[c]
Study 1	1. Bellack, Morrison, Mueser, Wade, & Sayers (1990) 2. Bellack, Morrison, Wixted, & Mueser (1990) 3. Mueser, Bellack, Douglas, & Morrison (1991) 4. Mueser, Bellack, Morrison, & Wade (1990) 5. Mueser, Bellack, Morrison, & Wixted (1990) 6. Mueser, Douglas, Bellack, & Morrison (1991)	57 Acute S 33 Acute A 20 NP	12 semistructured RPs assessing conversational skill, positive assertion, and negative assertion; repeated at 6 and 12 months for patient groups	For patients: Symptomatology Social Adjustment Quality of Life Family Problem Solving	• S < A < NP in SS • SS related to premorbid adjustment, negative symptoms, social adjustment, quality of life, and patient skill in family problem solving • Female S patients had better SS than male S patients • About 50% of S patients had stable SS deficits over 1 year • SS were fairly stable over time
Study 2	1. Mueser, Bellack, Douglas, & Wade (1991) 2. Mueser, Blanchard, & Bellack (1995)	45 Acute S 18 Acute A	6 semistructure RPs assessing expression of negative feelings and ability to compromise	Symptomatology Memory	• S < A in SS • SS not related to symptoms • SS related to memory for female S, but not male S, nor A patients
Study 3	1. Bellack, Mueser, Wade, Sayers, & Morrison (1992) 2. Mueser, Bellack, Wade, Sayers, Tierney, & Haas (1993)	34 Acute S 24 Acute A 19 NP	12 semistructured RPs assessing skill in situations involving benign or negative affect with a friend or relative	For patients: Symptomatology Social Perception Test (SPT) Relatives' Expressed Emotion (EE) Family Problem Solving	• S < A < NP in SS • All subjects had worse SS responding to negative than benign affect • Subjects, especially females, were more assertive in response to negative than benign affect • Subjects were more assertive with friends than relatives • S perceived negative affect as less unpleasant than A or NP on the SPT • For S, relative EE unrelated to SS • For S, SS in RPs was related to SS in Family Problem Solving Task
Study 4	1. Bellack, Sayers, Mueser, & Bennett (1994) 2. Sayers, Bellack, Wade, Bennett, & Fong (1995)	27 Acute S 19 Acute BP 17 NP	6 open-ended RPs assessing skill in initiating conversations, assertion, and compromise and negotiation	Social Problem Solving Measures For patients: Symptomatology Memory	• S, BP < NP in SS • SS related to other measures of social problem solving • SS related to memory

Study		Sample	Measures	Findings
Study 5	1. Bellack, Blanchard, & Mueser (1996) 2. Blanchard, Bellack, & Mueser (1994) 3. Mueser, Blanchard, & Bellack (1995)	35 Acute S 19 Acute BP 17 NP	6 semistructured RPs assessing skill in situations involving benign or negative affect Social Perception Test Memory Other cognitive measures Anhedonia (self-report scales) For patients: Symptomatology	• S < BP, NP in SS for males, but no differences for females • SS related to memory for female S, but not male S • Other cognitive measures not related to SS for S • Self-report anhedonia not related to SS for S or BP
Study 6	1. Mueser, Doonan, Penn, Blanchard, Bellack, Nishith, & deLeon (1996) 2. Penn, Mueser, Doonan, & Nishith (1995) 3. Penn, Mueser, & Doonan (1997)	28 Chronic S 15 NP	Two 3-minute open-ended Conversation Probes Facial and Emotion Recognition tests For patients: Symptomatology Social adjustment Physical attractiveness	• For S, SS related to facial and emotion recognition, and to social adjustment on the ward • For S, SS related to independent measures of physical attractiveness

[a] S = Schizophrenia or Schizoaffective Disorder; A = Major Affective Disorder; BP = Bipolar Disorder; NP = Nonpatient Controls
[b] RPs = Role plays
[c] SS = Social skill

measures of social behavior or social functioning. Mueser, Bellack, Wade et al. (1993) showed that social skill in role-plays involving conflict situations was significantly correlated with independent ratings of social skill during problem-solving interactions with a relative. For example, overall social skill on the role-play test was significantly correlated with patient ratings of quality of communication, quality of problem solving, negative valence, nonconstructive criticisms, and demands/commands during the family problem-solving task.

While the two studies by Bellack, Morrison, Mueser et al. (1990) and Mueser, Bellack, Wade et al. (1993) were conducted on acutely ill patients, there is also evidence that social skill ratings are related to other measures of social behavior in more chronic, long-stay patients with schizophrenia. Penn, Mueser, Doonan, and Nishith (1995) found that social skill assessed during an unstructured conversation probe was significantly correlated with independent ratings by staff members of the appropriateness of patients' social behavior on the ward. For example, fluency and clarity during the role-play were significantly correlated with social interactions on the ward, whereas overall social skill, the degree to which patients remained on topic, fluency, and clarity in the role-play were all significantly correlated with lower levels of inappropriate behavior on the ward. Finally, in a study of intermediate-stay patients with schizophrenia (inpatients participating in an 8-month rehabilitation program), Appelo et al. (1992) found that social skill on a role-play test was significantly correlated with independent global ratings of social competence made by staff members.

In conclusion, four different studies (Appelo et al., 1992; Bellack, Morrison, Mueser et al., 1990; Mueser, Bellack, Wade et al., 1993; Penn, Mueser, Doonan, & Nishith, 1995), including both acutely ill and chronic patients with schizophrenia, have found that ratings of social skill on role-play tests are related to independent measures of social behavior and role functioning. These studies do not prove that adequate social skills are necessary for good social functioning or appropriate social behavior, but they are consistent with this assumption.

RESEARCH ON SOCIAL SKILL IN SCHIZOPHRENIA

We next review research that examines the relationship between social skill in schizophrenia and other characteristics of the illness or subjects. Specifically, we will review studies that have examined social skill in schizo-

phrenia compared to other diagnoses, the prevalence of skills deficits in schizophrenia, social skill and symptomatology, social skill and cognitive functioning, social skill and social perception, social problem-solving skills, and interactions between social skill and gender.

Social Skill and Psychiatric Diagnosis

Impairment in social functioning is one of the core defining characteristics of schizophrenia. In contrast, although poor social functioning may be present in individuals with affective disorder, such impairments are not included as a diagnostic criterion for affective disorders. Therefore, to the extent that poor social functioning in schizophrenia may be mediated by social skills deficits, one would expect these patients to have poorer social skills than patients with affective disorders or nonpsychiatric controls. Several studies have examined the social skills performance of patients with schizophrenia compared to other diagnostic groups and nonpsychiatric controls.

In the first study, Bellack, Morrison, Wixted, and Mueser (1990) evaluated the social skills of a group of patients with schizophrenia, another group with major affective disorder, and a nonpsychiatric control group. Across a range of measures of social skill, including overall social skill, nonverbal and paralinguistic components, and appropriateness of verbal content, the patients with schizophrenia performed worse than the affective disorder patients, who, in turn, performed worse than the normal controls. When the schizophrenia group was subdivided into those with prominent negative symptoms versus those without prominent negative symptoms, based on Andreasen's (1982) criteria, the patients with negative symptoms had the worst social skills, but the nonnegative schizophrenia patients did not differ significantly from the affective disorder patients. This study suggests an association between negative symptoms and social skill deficits, a relationship we shall return to later in this chapter when we discuss research on symptoms and social skill.

Three other studies using different role-play scenarios have reported similar results. Bellack, Mueser, Wade, Sayers, and Morrison (1992) found that patients with schizophrenia were less skillful at managing conflict situations than either patients with a major affective disorder or nonpsychiatric controls, who did not differ. Similarly, Mueser, Bellack, Douglas, and Wade (1991) reported that patients with schizophrenia or schizoaffective disorder performed worse on a social skills test involving expressing negative feelings and compromising compared to patients with a major affective disorder. Finally, Mueser, Blanchard, and Bellack (1995) reported that patients with schizophrenia or affective disorder both demonstrated poorer overall skill at managing affectively charged conflict situations compared to nonpatient controls, whereas only the male patients with schizophrenia were less assertive than males with affective disorder or no psychiatric illness (see later section on Gender and Social Skill for more discussion of gender issues).

These four studies provide strong evidence that the social skills of patients with schizophrenia are more impaired than patients with major affective disorders or nonpatient controls. Of course, these studies do not address the origins of the social skills deficits. For example, it is possible that poor social skills are due to a generalized performance deficit characteristic of schizophrenia (Chapman & Chapman, 1978), and they are not specific to the social dysfunction present in the illness. On the other hand, the findings are consistent with the hypothesis that poor social skills contribute to social dysfunction in schizophrenia.

Prevalence of Social Skill Deficits

The three studies described in the preceding section indicate that as a group, patients with schizophrenia have more impaired social skills than other diagnostic groups or nonpatients. While this appears to be true, it is unclear what proportion of patients with schizophrenia have social skill deficits, or the nature of any deficits which may be present. To evaluate the prevalence of global and component social skills deficits in schizophrenia, Mueser, Bellack, Douglas, and Morrison (1991) compared the role-play performance of a group of patients with schizophrenia or schizoaffective disorder to a group of demographically matched nonpatient controls. The assessments used in the analysis included one conducted several weeks after hospitalization and another conducted 12 months later. Nonpatient controls were assessed just once. Social skill ratings across 12 role plays were made of overall social skill, nonverbal and paralinguistic components, and verbal content.

To estimate the prevalence of social skill deficits in the patients, an operational definition of *social skill deficit* needed to be created. A skills deficit was defined as skill performance (averaged across the 12 role-plays) that was worse than the performance of the *worst* nonpatient control. This definition avoided the difficulties inherent in de-

termining an arbitrary cutpoint for defining social skill deficits for the broader population of patients and nonpatients, because the nonpatient controls were de facto defined to be socially skilled. Consequently, this definition may have resulted in a conservative estimate of social skill deficits in schizophrenia. On the other hand, the definition is objective and has some intuitive appeal (i.e., patients whose social skills were observed to be worse than the skills of the nonpatient control group have the most conspicuous skill deficits).

Regarding overall social skill, approximately half the patients had consistent skills deficits at both assessments. In contrast, approximately 10% of the patients were rated consistently skilled at both assessments. The remaining patients showed variable levels of overall skill at the two assessments, sometimes being skilled and sometimes showing deficits in social skill.

Although many patients had deficits in overall social skill, focal deficits in specific component skills (e.g., gaze, appropriateness of verbal content) were rare. The only focal social skill deficit that was consistently present at both assessments for more than one patient was meshing (smoothness of conversational turn-taking). Meshing problems in schizophrenia are usually reflected by excessively long pauses before responding to another person's verbal statement. Fourteen percent of the patients had consistent deficits in meshing. These findings are intriguing in the light of the association between social skill and cognitive functioning, discussed below.

These results indicate that not all patients with schizophrenia had deficits of social skills, and that some patients were judged to be consistently skillful. However, only a narrow range of skills was assessed in the role-plays, including conversation initiation, negative assertiveness, and positive assertiveness. It is possible that if a wider range of more difficult skills was assessed a greater proportion of patients with schizophrenia would have been found to have deficits. On the other hand, there is no currently available evidence that indicates patients with schizophrenia have proportionally more problems handling more difficult situations than others. In the one study in which situational difficulty was experimentally manipulated (i.e., the role-play task involved responding to another person who acted in either a benign or a hostile fashion), all subjects performed worse in the more difficult situation, and there was no affect by diagnostic group interaction (Bellack, Mueser et al., 1992). A second conclusion from the Mueser, Bellack, Douglas, and Morrison study is that although the overall skill performance of most patients is impaired, the problems are not unique to one or two components of social skill, but rather are spread across many component skills. The absence of deficits in focal social skill in patients with schizophrenia suggests that the etiology of poor social skills in this disorder is heterogeneous, both within and across patients.

Symptomatology

The relationship between social skill and symptomatology in schizophrenia has been examined in a variety of studies, with most attention focused on the evaluation of positive and negative symptoms. Most studies that have assessed positive symptoms have found no significant relationship with social skill. For example, Bellack, Morrison, Wixted, and Mueser (1990) reported no significant association between thought disorder ratings on the BPRS and social skill ratings. Furthermore, when the patients of this study were divided into those with consistent positive symptoms across two assessments conducted one year apart and compared with patients who did not have consistently high levels of positive symptoms, there were no differences in social skill performance (Mueser, Douglas, Bellack, & Morrison, 1991). Several other studies have also found little association between the severity of positive symptoms and social skill performance in patients with schizophrenia (Mueser, Bellack, Douglas, & Wade, 1991; Penn, Mueser, Spaulding, Hope, & Reed, 1995; Jackson et al., 1989).

Only one study reported an association between severity of positive symptoms and social skills deficits in schizophrenia (Appelo et al., 1992). Interestingly, these authors also reported a high correlation between the severity of positive and negative symptoms ($r = .41$), in contrast to other studies which have usually reported low to moderate correlations between positive and negative symptoms (Mueser, Douglas, Bellack, & Morrison, 1991). The contradictory results of this study are difficult to explain because standardized measures of both social skill and symptomatology were employed. It may be of significance that the patients studied by Appelo et al. were all long-stay psychiatric inpatients participating in an 8-month rehabilitation program. Among the studies reporting no association between positive symptoms and social skill, only Penn, Mueser, Spaulding et al. (1995) found no relationship among patients participating in a long-stay rehabilitation program. Thus, positive and negative symptoms, as well as social skills, may be more strongly intercorrelated among more chronic patients.

In contrast to research on social skill and positive symptoms, several studies indicate that negative symptoms are related to social skill deficits. Bellack, Morrison, Wixted, and Mueser (1990) found strong correlations between social skill and ratings on the Scale for the Assessment of Negative Symptoms (SANS; Andreasen, 1982). For example, overall social skill was correlated significantly with all the SANS subscales, with correlations ranging from $r = .32$ for anhedonia/asociality and inattention to $r = .46$ for avolition-apathy. In an analysis of the same data, Mueser, Bellack, Morrison, and Wixted (1990) showed that negative symptoms were related to social skill, even after controlling for level of premorbid adjustment, which was also related to social skill. This finding is of theoretical significance because premorbid social functioning has been repeatedly linked to the later severity of negative symptoms after schizophrenia has developed (McGlashan & Fenton, 1992). In addition, the social skills model posits that skills are an important determinant of social functioning, either premorbidly or after the onset of schizophrenia. This finding suggests that the relationship between premorbid functioning and negative symptoms may be mediated in some way by poor social skill.

Appelo et al. (1992), Penn, Mueser, Spaulding et al. (1995), and Lysaker, Bell, Zito, and Bioty (1995) also reported an association between social skills and negative symptoms in schizophrenia. Similarly, using a cluster analysis Jackson et al. (1989) found that clusters of patients characterized by high negative symptoms also tended to have poor social skills. In a contradictory study, however, Mueser, Bellack, Douglas, and Wade (1991) reported no association between negative symptoms on the BPRS (the anergia subscale). It is noteworthy that in the Bellack, Morrison, Wixted, and Mueser (1990) study, social skills were strongly related to negative symptoms on the SANS, but not the anergia subscale of the BPRS. It is possible that the anergia subscale of the BPRS provides a more limited assessment of negative symptoms in schizophrenia, in comparison to the SANS, which provides a more comprehensive assessment of the symptoms. Finally Blanchard, Bellack, and Mueser (1994) found no association between anhedonia rated on the Chapman scales (Chapman, Chapman, & Raulin, 1976), and social skill in dealing with negatively charged conflict situations. This last study is somewhat difficult to interpret because no other studies have employed self-report scales of anhedonia and role-play measures of social skill. Another limitation is that this study only assessed skill in situations involving very negatively charged interactions, which may be of limited generalizability to other social situations.

Relatively few studies have examined the relationship between symptoms other than positive and negative symptoms and social skill, but the few studies that have do not suggest any consistent relationships. Bellack, Morrison, Wixted, and Mueser (1990) found no association between other symptoms (e.g., the anxiety-depression or activation subscales of the BPRS) and social skill, nor did Penn, Mueser, Spaulding et al. (1995). Mueser, Bellack, Douglas, and Wade (1991) reported that high levels of activation on the BPRS were related to poor social skill, but no other study has reported this relationship.

In summary, negative symptoms tend to be correlated with social skill, but positive symptoms are not. Although there is an overlap between some of the definitions of social skill and negative symptoms (e.g., paralinguistic features and blunted affect), the two constructs are not identical. The possibility that impairments in social skill represent a unique domain is consistent with speculations that relational impairment may be a feature of schizophrenia independent of other symptoms (Strauss, Carpenter, & Bartko, 1974). Furthermore, several factor analytic studies support the hypothesis that a dimension of relational impairment exists separate from negative and positive symptoms in schizophrenia (Minas, Klimidis, Stuart, Copolov, & Singh, 1994; Peralta, Cuesta, & deLeon, 1994).

Social Perception and Cognition

Theories of social skill and social competence have long hypothesized that effective communication requires accurate social perception, good cognitive functioning, and sufficient behavioral social skills (McFall, 1982; Morrison & Bellack, 1981; Trower, Bryant, & Argyle, 1978; Wallace et al., 1980). Social perception refers to the ability to recognize relevant social parameters in a situation that may limit the range of appropriate behaviors, such as facial expression, voice tone, or the level of familiarity with the other person. Despite the intuitive appeal of this theory of social behavior, until recently there were few data that examined the relationship between social skill and social perception or cognitive functioning. More recently, several studies have been conducted that bear on these relationships.

Several studies have examined the association between social skill and social perception in patients with schizophrenia. Appelo et al. (1992) examined the relationship between social skill and performance on the Picture Arrangement Task (PAT; Stinissen, Willems, Coetsier, & Hulsman, 1970). The authors reported that in multiple regressions predicting social skill from performance on the PAT and measures of symptomatology, social perception did not account for any unique variance in social skill. However, symptoms were strong predictors of social skill in this study, leaving relatively little variance that could be predicted by social skill. Data were not reported on the relationship between social skill and social perception independent of symptomatology.

Bellack, Mueser et al. (1992) examined the relationship between social perception and social skill in affectively charged or benign conflict situations. The measure of social perception involved ratings by subjects of brief videotaped conflict interactions, some involving high levels of negative affect and others with benign affect. For each vignette, subjects provided ratings along a number of different dimensions of affect (e.g., pleasantness, intensity). Ratings of affect, summed across a number of different dimensions, were significantly correlated with independent measures of social skill on the role-play test. Thus, consistent with theories of social competence, accurate social perception of affect was associated with higher levels of social skill in patients with schizophrenia.

Mueser, Doonan et al. (1996) examined the relationship between facial emotion perception on a task developed by Kerr and Neale (1993) and social skill in a group of long-term hospitalized patients with schizophrenia. Two 3-minute conversation probes, one with a male and one with a female confederate, were employed as the measure of social skill. Overall, there was a weak association between social skill and performance on the emotion perception task. Specifically, nonverbal–paralinguistic skills were related to emotion perception, but not global ratings of social skill or the appropriateness of the verbal content. Interestingly, measures of social functioning on the ward, based on the Social Behavior Schedule (Wykes & Sturt, 1986) were more strongly related to emotion recognition than social skill. Since social skills were also related to social adjustment on the ward in this sample (Penn, Mueser, Doonan et al., 1995), it is possible that the stronger association between emotion recognition and social adjustment is due to the fact that social adjustment on the ward was evaluated over a much longer period (the past month) than social skills, for which the ratings were based on only 6 minutes of interaction. This difference in the amount of information available to the raters may have contributed to greater stability in the ratings of social functioning on the ward than the social skill ratings.

In summary, there is evidence supporting an association between social perception and social skill, consistent with theories positing such a link (e.g., McFall, 1982; Morrison & Bellack, 1981). The strength of the association between social perception and social skill tends to be weak, perhaps reflecting the limitations of methods that have been used to assess each of these areas. For example, emotion recognition tests typically sample a very limited range of emotions, which are judged in a laboratory setting that is quite different from real-world encounters. Similarly, most role-play tests are relatively brief and do not tap social competence during more extended interactions or in the context of actual relationships.

Cognitive Functioning and Social Skill

More research has examined the relationship between cognitive functioning and social skill than between social perception and skill. The results of most of the studies are consistent with the hypothesis that poor cognitive functioning contributes to social skill impairments. Mueser, Bellack, Douglas, and Wade (1991) reported that social skills performance was strongly correlated with memory on the Wechsler Memory Scale (Wechsler, 1945) for patients with schizophrenia, but not patients with major affective disorders. Similarly, Bellack, Sayers, Mueser, and Bennett (1994) also found that social skill was related to both memory on the Wechsler Memory Scale-Revised (Weschler, 1987) and intelligence in patients with schizophrenia.

Several studies have found that other measures of cognitive functioning are also related to social skill. Bowen, Wallace, Glynn, Nuechterlein, Lutzker, and Kuehnel (1994) reported that social skill was related to performance on the Continuous Performance Task (Nuechterlein, Parasuraman, & Jiang, 1983), to a lesser extent with the Span of Apprehension Task (Asarnow & Nuechterlein, 1987), and not at all to the Digit Span Distractability Test (Oltmanns & Neale, 1975). Penn, Mueser, Spaulding et al. (1995) reported that social skill on a conversation probe was related to a variety of cognitive measures assessed with a computer-driven battery, Cognitive Laboratory (COGLAB) (Spaulding, Garbin, & Dras, 1989), including reaction time, a version of the Wisconsin Card Sorting Task, and a combined version of the Continuous Performance Task and the Span of Apprehension Task. Finally, in a study of a mixed sample of psychiatric patients, of whom 30% had schizophrenia spectrum disorders, the Allen Cognitive Level Test (Allen, 1990) was found to be significantly correlated with independent ratings of social skill (Penny, Mueser, & North, 1995).

These studies suggest that characteristic impairments in cognitive functioning in schizophrenia may contribute to poor social skills or that both are the result of a third factor (e.g., general deficits; Chapman & Chapman, 1978). However, several recent studies suggest that the relationship between cognitive functioning and social skill may differ between males and females. Mueser, Blanchard, and Bellack (1995) reported that despite the few differences between males and females in cognitive functioning, clinical measures, or social skill, social skill was related to poor memory for female but not male patients. Similarly, there was a weaker trend for other measures of cognitive functioning (e.g., the Test of Facial Recognition; Benton, Hamsher, Varney, & Spreen, 1983; the Speech Sounds Perception Test; Halstead, 1947) to be related to social skills for females, but not males. A reanalysis of the data previously reported in Mueser, Bellack, Douglas, and Wade (1991) also demonstrated that memory was correlated with social skills performance for female, but not male patients (Mueser, Blanchard, & Bellack, 1995). The similar results across these two studies are even more striking when one considers their methodological differences. The two studies employed different versions of the Wechsler Memory Scale, used different role-play tests of social skill (one employed audiotaped role-plays and the other employed videotaped role-plays), and were conducted approximately 4 years apart. The possibility that the association between cognitive functioning and social skill interacts with gender was given additional support in a reanalysis of data reported in Penn, Mueser, Spaulding et al. (1995). Penn, Mueser, and Spaulding (1996) found that performance on the cognitive measures included in COGLAB was significantly correlated with social skills on the conversation probe for female, but not male patients with schizophrenia. Of note, these patients were long-stay patients, compared to the patients studied in the Mueser, Blanchard, and Bellack (1995), who were acutely ill patients who had recently recovered from a relapse.

It is unclear what accounts for the differential association between cognitive functioning and social skill between male and female patients. It is possible that sampling procedures may have contributed to this effect. On average, women tend to have a more benign course of schizophrenia than men, characterized by spending less time in the hospital and better social functioning (Angermeyer & Kuhn, 1988; Goldstein, 1988). Thus hospitalized women are less representative of the population of women with schizophrenia than are hospitalized men. If cognitive factors mediate impairments in social skill for more severely ill patients, such a differential association might be found. Consistent with this, females in the Penn, Mueser, and Spaulding (1996) study had more severe positive symptoms than males. However, there were no gender differences in symptoms in the other two studies reported by Mueser, Blanchard, and Bellack (1995). Another possibility is that cognitive factors play a more important role in social skill for females than males, although this effect may not be limited to schizophrenia. Regardless of the interpretation, these studies underscore the importance of exploring gender interactions when examining the relationship between social skill and other areas of functioning, even when males and females score comparably on those measures.

In summary, social skills were related to cognitive functioning in most studies that examined these two domains. Similar to research examining the relationship between social perception and social skill, this area has been hampered by the use of different instruments across studies, making it difficult to compare and reconcile the results of different studies. Despite these limitations, the evidence is consistent with the hypothesized importance of cognitive functioning in social skills.

Social Problem Solving

Social problem solving is conceptualized as a complex social skill involving social perception or problem recognition, cognitive processing to generate and evaluate potential solutions, and behavioral skills to successfully implement a plan of action. Although a number of early studies of psychiatric patients were conducted evaluating cognitive models of problem solving (e.g., Platt & Spivack, 1972a, 1972b), these studies have been criticized for lacking an empirical basis for how individuals solve interpersonal problems, and the limited applicability of the model to many social situations (Bellack, Morrison, & Mueser, 1989).

Two more recent studies have examined more complex models of social problem solving. Donahoe et al. (1990) examined a model of problem solving that assumes the importance of three basic types of skills: *receiving skills* (i.e., social perception), *processing skills* (i.e., cognitive skills), and *sending skills* (i.e., social skills). To test their model, the authors compared a group of patients with schizophrenia to a group of nonpatient controls on a set of three tasks designed to assess each of the skill areas identified by the model. First, subjects were shown a brief vignette on videotape and were asked to state whether a problem was present and, if so, to describe the problem. Second, if the subject noted that a problem was present, the subject was asked how he or she would respond to the situation. These verbal descriptions were coded on several dimensions of appropriateness. Third, if a problem was noted, the subject was asked to demonstrate in a role-play how he or she would respond to the situation.

The patients with schizophrenia performed significantly worse on measures of receiving, processing, and sending skills than the nonpatient controls. In addition, examination of the intercorrelations and conditional probabilities between the different types of skill indicated strong associations, which the authors interpreted as supporting their model of social problem solving. Strengths of the study included the careful work that went into pilot testing the instrument, the refinement of different measures of skill hypothesized to be necessary for effective social problem solving, and an examination of their battery with a well-diagnosed group of patients. One limitation of the study is the absence of another psychiatric comparison group. Another limitation is the fact that subjects' processing and sending skills were not assessed for situations in which the subject judged that no problem was present. Instead, when subjects stated that no problem was present they were automatically coded as a "zero" for their processing and sending skills. This scoring strategy may have artificially increased the associations among the three types of skills. In addition, to the extent that patients with schizophrenia were less able to recognize interpersonal problems, it may have resulted in their achieving lower scores on the processing and sending skill measures than they otherwise might have earned.

The second study of social problem solving was conducted by Bellack, Sayers, Mueser, and Bennett (1994), who also based their study on a carefully developed, pilot-tested battery (Sayers, Bellack, Wade, Bennette, & Fong, 1995). The problem-solving battery assessed three types of skills hypothesized to be critical to successful problem solving: the ability to generate possible responses to a problem situation, the ability to evaluate the effectiveness of different possible responses, and social skills performance. Three groups of subjects were compared: patients with schizophrenia, patients with bipolar disorder, and nonpatient controls. All patients were currently receiving treatment for a recent acute exacerbation of their illness.

Overall, the results indicated that both patient groups performed significantly worse in their ability to generate good solutions to problem situations, their evaluation of the adequacy of different solutions, and their performance on the role-play test of social skills. However, the two patient groups did not differ on any of these measures. The sample size in this study was not large (total $n = 63$), and therefore power was low to detect between diagnostic group differences. However, the overall pattern of results suggests that while patients with schizophrenia have impairments in their social problem-solving skills, these impairments are not markedly worse than those present in patients with bipolar disorder. The authors suggested that different factors may have contributed to poor social problem solving in the two diagnostic groups: cognitive impairment for schizophrenia and acute symptoms for the bipolar patients. Some support for this hypothesis is provided by Penn et al. (1993), who reported stronger correlations between social cognitive problem solving on the means-ends problem-solving task (Platt & Spivack, 1975) and cognitive functioning on the COGLAB battery (Spaulding et al., 1989) for patients with schizophrenia than depressed patients. Another possible interpretation is that the study setting, a psychiatric hospital, may have resulted in a lower functioning cohort of bipolar patients, relative to the population of persons with bipolar disorder, compared to the cohort of schizophrenia patients, given the generally worse prognosis for schizophrenia than bipolar disorder. Additional work in this area is needed with patients with schizophrenia who are symptomatically stable and living in the community.

Gender and Social Skill

As briefly alluded to in the previous section, there is extensive research documenting gender differences in the onset and course of schizophrenia. For example, women tend to have a later age of onset of the disorder, are hospitalized at a later age, spend less time in the hospital over the course of their lives, are more likely to marry, and have better social functioning over the course of their illness than men with schizophrenia. The tendency for women to have a milder course of schizophrenia raises the intriguing question of whether males and females differ in their social skill, and whether such differences could mediate some of their differences in long-term outcome. A number of studies have examined gender differences in social skill in patients with schizophrenia.

In the only longitudinal study of social skill, Mueser, Bellack, Morrison, and Wade (1990) evaluated social skills in a sample of patients with schizophrenia following treatment of an acute exacerbation and one year later; patients with affective disorder and nonpatient controls were also assessed at baseline. An evaluation of skill difference between the diagnostic groups at baseline revealed a significant gender-by-diagnosis interaction, as well as a significant main effect for diagnosis. The interaction was due to the poor social skills of males with schizophrenia compared to bipolar or nonpatient controls, in contrast to females with schizophrenia who did not differ from the other two groups. A longitudinal analysis of gender differences in social skill in the patients with schizophrenia confirmed the superior performance of the females at both assessments. Although the male and female patients differed in social skill, there were no differences in other measures, including symptomatology, social adjustment, and quality of life. Despite the absence of gender differences in social functioning and quality of life, within-gender correlational analyses indicated that social skills were significantly related to both social adjustment and quality of life. Thus females tended to have better social skills than males, and these differences in social skill could not be attributed to differences in other domains of functioning.

Several other studies have also reported gender differences in social skill in patients with schizophrenia. Bellack, Mueser et al. (1992), studying social skills in affectively charged or benign conflict situations, reported a significant gender-by-affect interaction. Women tended to be more assertive when responding to negative affect situations than men, but this effect was present across the schizophrenia, affective disorder, and nonpatient control groups. No gender differences were present for overall social skills, however.

These findings were partially replicated in a subsequent study employing a role-play test of only the affectively charged conflict situations (Mueser, Blanchard, & Bellack, 1995). In this follow-up study, there were significant gender-by-diagnosis interactions for two of the three social skill variables studied. Women with schizophrenia tended to perform better than men in assertiveness and negative valence (the expression of negative feelings), but there were no gender differences for the affective disorder or nonpatient control groups. There was no gender-by-diagnostic group interaction for the third social skill variable, overall social skill. Thus, these two studies suggest that women with schizophrenia may respond to challenging, affectively charged social situations with more assertiveness than their male counterparts.

Finally, one other study indicated gender differences in social skill. Penny, Mueser, and North (1995) reported that female psychiatric patients had better social skills than males. The sample studied comprised a mixed group of psychiatric patients recently admitted to a psychiatric hospital for treatment of an acute exacerbation. Although gender differences within the sample of patients with schizophrenia were not examined separately, a diagnosis-by-gender interaction in social skill was not present. Methodologically, this study differs from other studies of social skill in that a role-play test was not employed to measure social skill. Rather, skills were rated following an interview at the administration of a cognitive test.

Several studies have failed to detect a difference in social skill between males and females with schizophrenia. Penn, Mueser, Spaulding, et al. (1995) found no relationship between gender and social skill on a conversation probe in long-stay patients with schizophrenia. Similarly, in another sample of chronic, hospitalized patients, Penn, Mueser, Doonan, et al. (1995) also found no association between gender and social skill in schizophrenia. Finally, the reanalysis of the data from Mueser, Bellack, Douglas, and Wade (1991; Mueser, Blanchard, & Bellack, 1995) found no association between gender and social skill on a role-play test in acute patients with schizophrenia.

Thus, there is some evidence suggesting that women with schizophrenia have better social skills than males. A total of four studies reported women had superior social skill (Bellack, Mueser et al., 1992; Mueser, Bellack, Morrison, & Wade, 1990; Mueser, Blanchard, & Bellack, 1995; Penny et al., 1995). Three studies reported no gender differences (Mueser, Bellack, Douglas, & Wade, 1991 reported in Mueser, Blanchard, & Bellack, 1995; Penn, Mueser, Doonan et al., 1995; Penn, Mueser, Spaulding et al., 1995). No studies reported that male patients with schizophrenia had better social skills. Three possible factors may account for the lack of gender differences in some studies of social skill. First, two of the three studies that reported no differences included chronic patients (Penn, Mueser, Doonan, et al., 1995; Penn, Mueser, Spaulding et al. 1995), whereas none of the studies reporting gender differences included chronic patients. It is possible that differences which are present in acutely ill patients are not apparent in more chronically ill patients. Second, the one study conducted on acute patients that failed to find gender differences used audiotaped role-play tests (Mueser, Bellack, Douglas, & Wade, 1991, re-

ported in Mueser, Blanchard, & Bellack, 1995), rather than videotaped tests, as in all the other studies. There is evidence indicating that nonpatient women are better nonverbal communicators than men (Buck, 1984; Hall, 1985), suggesting that audiotaped role-play tests might reduce any possible gender differences. Third, studies that failed to detect gender differences may have had low power to detect relatively small effect signs. Considering that the preponderance of data bearing on the better prognosis of female than male patients with schizophrenia is based on very large sample sizes, it seems quite feasible that any gender differences of social skill that exist might be relatively small in magnitude. Nevertheless, the available data provide some evidence that women with schizophrenia have better social skills than men, and that these skills may contribute to their better overall prognosis.

SUMMARY AND FUTURE DIRECTIONS

Recent research on social skill and schizophrenia supports the utility of this construct as a basis for psychosocial interventions. Over the last decade a series of studies have been completed on carefully diagnosed cohorts of patients employing standardized measures of social skill usually based on role-play tests. Across several studies there is ample support for the contention that patients with schizophrenia tend to have more deficits in their social skills, and that skills performance is correlated with other measures of social functioning in patients' natural environment. Furthermore, social skill does not appear to be an artifact of symptomatology. Most studies suggest low correlations between social skill and positive symptoms, and weak to moderate correlations between skills and negative symptoms. These studies are consistent with the viewpoint that interpersonal dysfunction is a semi-independent domain from symptomatology in schizophrenia (e.g., Peralta et al., 1994; Strauss et al., 1974), and supports the inclusion of social dysfunction as a necessary criterion for its diagnosis (e.g., DSM-IV; American Psychiatric Association, 1994).

Studies examining the association among social skills performance, cognitive functioning, and social perception indicate associations in the expected direction—patients with better social skills tend to also have better social perception and cognitive functioning. These data are consistent with the interpretation that adequate social behavior requires not only sufficient behavioral skills, but also effective cognitive or social perception skills. To the extent that poor social perception or cognitive functioning actually contribute to social skill impairments, effective interventions may need to address these areas such as by teaching social perception skills or strategies for compensating for cognitive limitations.

Finally, there is a need to develop new methods for assessing social skills, as well as relevant perceptual and cognitive skills, that tap into specific impression formation goals, as would be appropriate for situations such as work settings, job interviews, or impressing a potential love interest. The potential importance of such impression formation is illustrated by a study of the impact of social skill on ratings of physical attractiveness in inpatients with chronic schizophrenia (Penn, Mueser, & Doonan, 1997). Independent ratings of physical attractiveness were made based on either the first 2 seconds of a conversation probe or after viewing the entire 3-minute role play. The correlation between the two sets of attractiveness ratings was moderately strong ($r = .43$), but they only shared 18% of the variance. Independent ratings of social skill were correlated with the attractiveness ratings based on the entire role-play ($r = .48$), but not the ratings based on the first 2 seconds of the role-play ($r = .09$). Although both initial ratings of attractiveness and social skill were related to ratings of physical attractiveness after the role-play, together they accounted for less than half the variance in attractiveness. These findings suggest that impression formation (i.e., the physical attractiveness or social desirability projected by an individual during an interaction) may require perceptual, cognitive, and social skills that go beyond the component skills that have until now been the major focus of assessment.

REFERENCES

Allen, C. K. (1990). *Allen Cognitive Level Test Manual*. Colchester, CT: S & S Worldwide.

American Psychiatric Association (1984). *Diagnostic and Statistical Manual of Mental Disorders (Fourth edition)*. Washington, DC: Author

Andreasen, N. C. (1982). Negative symptoms in schizophrenia: Definition and reliability. *Archives General Psychiatry, 39*, 784–788.

Angermeyer, M. C., & Kuhn, L. (1988). Gender differences in age at onset of schizophrenia: An overview. *European Archives of Psychiatry and Neurological Science, 237*, 351–364.

Appelo, M. T., Woonings, F. M. J., van Nieuwenhuizen, C. J., Emmelkamp, P. M. G., Slooff, C. J., & Louwerens, J. W. (1992). Specific skills and social competence in schizophrenia. *Acta Psychiatrica Scandinavica, 85*, 419–422.

Asarnow, R. F., & Nuechterlein, K. H. (1987). UCLA computerized span of apprehension task: Version 1. (Computer program). Los Angeles: UCLA Department of Psychiatry and Biobehavioral Sciences.

Ayllon, T., & Azrin, N. H. (1968). *The Token Economy*. New York: Appleton-Century-Crofts.

Bellack, A. S. (1979). A critical appraisal of strategies for assessing social skill. *Behavior Assessment, 1*, 157–176.

Bellack, A. S. (1983). Current problems in the behavioral assessment of social skills. *Behavioral Research and Therapy, 21*, 29–42.

Bellack, A. S., Blanchard, J. J., & Mueser, K. T. (1996). Cue availability and affect perception in schizophrenia. *Schizophrenia Bulletin, 22*, 535–544.

Bellack, A. S., Morrison, R. L., & Mueser, K. T. (1989). Social problem solving in schizophrenia. *Schizophrenia Bulletin, 15*, 101–116.

Bellack, A. S., Morrison, R. L., Mueser, K. T., Wade, J. H., & Sayers, S. L. (1990). Role-play for assessing the social competence of psychiatric patients. *Psychological Assessment, 2*, 248–255.

Bellack, A. S., Morrison, R. L., Wixted, J. T. & Mueser, K. T. (1990). An analysis of social competence in schizophrenia. *British Journal of Psychiatry, 156*, 809–818.

Bellack, A. S., & Mueser, K. T. (1990). Schizophrenia. In A. S. Bellack, M. Hersen, & A. E. Kazdin (Eds.), *International Handbook of Behavior Modification* (2nd ed., pp. 353–369). New York: Plenum.

Bellack, A. S., Mueser, K. T., Wade, J. H., Sayers, S. L., & Morrison, R. L. (1992). The ability of schizophrenics to perceive and cope with negative affect. *British Journal of Psychiatry, 160*, 473–480.

Bellack, A. S., Sayers, M., Mueser, K. T., & Bennett, M. (1994). An evaluation of social problem solving in schizophrenia. *Journal of Abnormal Psychology, 103*, 371–378.

Benton, A. L., Hamsher, K., de S., Varney, N. R., & Spreen, O. (1983). *Contributions to neuropsychological assessment*. New York: Oxford University Press.

Blanchard. J. J., Bellack, A. S., & Mueser, K. T. (1994). Affective and social-behavioral correlates of physical and social anhedonia in schizophrenia. *Journal of Abnormal Psychology, 103*, 719–728.

Bowen, L., Wallace, C. J., Glynn, S. M., Nuechterlein, K. H., Lutzker, J. R., & Kuehnel, T. G. (1994). Schizophrenics' cognitive functioning and performance in interpersonal interactions and skills training procedures. *Journal of Psychiatric Research, 28*, 289–301.

Buck, R. (1984). *The communication of affect*. New York: Guilford.

Chapman, L. J.; & Chapman, J. P. (1978). The measurement of differential deficit. *Journal of Psychiatric Research, 14*, 303–311.

Donahoe, C. P., Carter, M. J., Bloem, W. D., Hirsch, G. L., Laasi, N., & Wallace, C. J. (1990). Assessment of interpersonal problem-solving skills. *Psychiatry, 53*, 329–339.

Goldstein, J. M. (1988). Gender differences in the course of schizophrenia. *American Journal of Psychiatry, 145,* 684–689.

Hall, J. A. (1985). *Nonverbal sex differences: Communication accuracy and expressive style.* Baltimore, MD: Johns Hopkins University Press.

Halstead, W. C. (1947). *Brain and intelligence.* Chicago: University of Chicago Press.

Hersen, M., & Bellack, A. S. (1976). Social skills training for chronic psychiatric patients: Rationale, research findings, and future directions. *Comprehensive Psychiatry, 17,* 559–580.

Hersen, M., & Bellack, A. S. (1977). Assessment of social skills. In A. R. Ciminero, K. S. Calhoun, & H. E. Adams (Eds.), *Handbook of Behavioral Assessment* (pp. 509–554). New York: Wiley.

Jackson, H. J., Minas, I. H., Burgess, P. M., Joshua, S. D., Charisiou, J., & Campbell, I. M. (1989). Is social skills performance a correlate of schizophrenia subtypes? *Schizophrenia Research, 2,* 301–309.

Kerr, S. L., & Neale, J. M. (1993). Emotion perception in schizophrenia: Specific deficit or further evidence of generalized poor performance? *Journal of Abnormal Psychology, 102,* 312–318.

Liberman, R. P. (1982). Assessment of social skills. *Schizophrenia Bulletin, 8,* 62–82.

Liberman, R. P., DeRisi, W. J., & Mueser, K. T. (1989). *Social skills training for psychiatric patients.* Needham Heights, MA: Allyn & Bacon.

Liberman, R. P., Mueser, K. T., Wallace, C. J., Jacobs, H. E., Eckman, T., & Massel, H. K. (1986). Training skills in the psychiatrically disabled: Learning coping and competence. *Schizophrenia Bulletin, 12,* 631–647.

Lysaker, P. H., Bell, M. D., Zito, W. S., & Bioty, S. M. (1995). Social skills at work: Deficits and predictors of improvement in schizophrenia. *Journal of Nervous and Mental Disease, 183,* 688–692.

McFall, R. M. (1982). A review and reformulation of social skills. *Behavior Assessment, 4,* 1–33.

McGlashan, T. H., & Fenton, W.S. (1992). The positive–negative distinction in schizophrenia: Review of natural history validators. *Archives General Psychiatry, 49,* 63–72.

Minas, I. H., Klimidis, S., Stuart, G. W., Copolov, D. L., & Singh, B. S. (1994). Positive and negative symptoms in the psychoses: Principal components analysis of items from the Scale for the Assessment of Positive Symptoms and the Scale for the Assessment of Negative Symptoms. *Comprehensive Psychiatry, 35,* 135–144.

Morrison, R. L., & Bellack, A. S. (1981). The role of social perception in social skill. *Behavior Therapy, 12,* 69–79.

Mueser, K. T., Bellack, A. S., Douglas, M. S., & Morrison, R. L. (1991). Prevalence and stability of social skill deficits in schizophrenia. *Schizophrenia Research, 5,* 167–176.

Mueser, K. T., Bellack, A. S., Douglas, M. S., & Wade, J. H. (1991). Prediction of social skill acquisition in schizophrenic

and major affective disorder patients from memory and symptomatology. *Psychiatry Research, 37,* 281–296.

Mueser, K. T., Bellack, A. S., Morrison, R. L., & Wade, J. H. (1990). Gender, social competence, and symptomatology in schizophrenia: A longitudinal analysis. *Journal of Abnormal Psychology, 99,* 138–147.

Mueser, K. T., Bellack, A. S., Morrison, R. L., & Wixted, J. T. (1990). Social competence in schizophrenia: Premorbid adjustment, social skill, and domains of functioning. *Journal of Psychiatric Research, 24,* 51–63.

Mueser, K. T., Bellack, A. S., Wade, J. H., Sayers, S. L., Tierney, A., & Haas, G. (1993). Expressed emotion, social skill, and response to negative affect in schizophrenia. *Journal of Abnormal Psychology, 102,* 339–351.

Mueser, K. T., Blanchard, J. J., & Bellack, A. S. (1995). Memory and social skill in schizophrenia: The role of gender. *Psychiatry Research, 57,* 141–153.

Mueser, K. T., Doonan, R., Penn, D. L., Blanchard, J. J., Bellack, A. S., Nishith, P., & deLeon, J. (1996). Emotion recognition and social competence in chronic schizophrenia. *Journal of Abnormal Psychology, 105,* 271–275.

Mueser, K. T., Douglas, M. S., Bellack, A. S., & Morrison, R. L. (1991). Assessment of enduring deficit and negative symptom subtypes in schizophrenia. *Schizophrenia Bulletin, 17,* 565–582.

Mueser, K. T., & Sayers, M. S. D. (1992). Social skills assessment. In D. J. Kavanagh (Ed.), *Schizophrenia: An overview and practical handbook* (pp. 182–205). London: Chapman and Hall.

Nuechterlein, K. H., & Dawson, M. E. (1984). A heuristic vulnerability/stress model of schizophrenic episodes. *Schizophrenia Bulletin, 10,* 300–312.

Nuechterlein, K. H., Parasuraman, R., & Jiang, Q. (1983). Visual sustained attention: Image degradation produces rapid sensitivity decrement over time. *Science, 220,* 327–329.

Oltmanns, T. F., & Neale, J. M. (1975). Schizophrenic performance when distractors are present: Attentional deficit or differential task difficulty? *Journal of Abnormal Psychology, 84,* 205–209.

Overall, J. E., & Gorham, D. R. (1962). The Brief Psychiatric Rating Scale. *Psychological Reports, 10,* 799–812.

Penn, D. L., van der Does, W., Spaulding, W. D., Garbin, C. P., Linszen, D., & Dingemans, P. (1993). Information processing and social cognitive problem solving in schizophrenia: Assessment of interrelationships over time. *Journal of Nervous and Mental Disease, 181,* 13–20.

Penn, D. L., Mueser, K. T., & Doonan, R. (1997). Physical attractiveness in schizophrenia: The mediating role of social skill. *Behavior Modification, 21,* 78–85.

Penn, D. L., Mueser, K. T., Doonan, R., & Nishith, P. (1995). Relations between social skills and ward behavior in chronic schizophrenia. *Schizophrenia Research, 16,* 225–232.

Penn, D. L., Mueser, K. T., & Spaulding, W. (1996). Information processing, social skill, and gender in schizophrenia. *Psychiatry Research.*

Penn, D. L., Mueser, K. T., Spaulding, W., Hope, D. A., & Reed, D. (1995). Information processing and social competence in chronic schizophrenia. *Schizophrenia Bulletin, 21,* 269–281.

Penny, N. H., Mueser, K. T., & North, C. T. (1995). The Allen Cognitive Level Test and social competence in adult psychiatric patients. *American Journal of Occupational Therapy, 49,* 420–427.

Peralta, V., Cuesta, M. J., & deLeon, J. (1994). An empirical analysis of latent structures underlying schizophrenic symptoms: A four-syndrome model. *Biological Psychiatry, 36,* 726–736.

Platt, J. P., & Spivack, G. (1972a). Problem-solving thinking of psychiatric patients. *Journal of Consulting and Clinical Psychology, 39,* 148–151.

Platt, J. J., & Spivack, G. (1972b). Social competence and effective problem-solving thinking in psychiatric patients. *Journal of Clinical Psychology, 28,* 3–5.

Platt, J. J., & Spivack, G. (1975). *Manual for the Means-Ends Problem Solving Procedure (MEPS): A measure of interpersonal cognitive problem-solving skills.* Philadelphia: Hahnemann Community Mental Health/Retardation Center.

Sayers, M. D., Bellack, A. S., Wade, J. H., Bennett, M. E., & Fong, P. (1995). An empirical method for assessing social problem solving in schizophrenia. *Behavior Modification, 19,* 267–289.

Schooler, N., Hogarty, G., & Weissman, M. (1978). Social Adjustment Scale II (SAS-II). In W. A. Hargreaves, C. C. Atkisson, & J. E. Sorenson (Eds.), *Resource materials for community mental health program evaluations.* Rockville, MD: National Institute of Mental Health, DHEW Publication No. (ADM)79–328.

Spaulding, W. D., Garbin, C. P., & Dras, S. R. (1989). Cognitive abnormalities in schizophrenic patients and schizotypal college students. *Journal of Nervous and Mental Disease, 177,* 717–728.

Spitzer, R. L., Williams, J. B. W., Gibbon, M., & First, M. B. (1988). *Structured Clinical Interview for DSM-III-R (SCID).* New York: State Psychiatric Institute Biometrics Department.

Stinissen, J., Willems, P. J., Coetsier, P., & Hulsman, W. L. L. (1970). Handleiding by de Nederlandse Bewerking van de Wechsler Adult Intelligence Scale (WAIS). Amsterdam: Swets en Zeitlinger.

Strauss, J. S., Carpenter, W. T. Jr., & Bartko, J. J. (1974). The diagnosis and understanding of schizophrenia, Part III: Speculations on the process that underlie schizophrenic symptoms and signs. *Schizophrenia Bulletin, 11,* 61–76.

Torgrud, L. J., & Holborn, S. W. (1992). Developing externally valid role-play for assessment of social skills: A behavior analytic perspective. *Behavior Assessment, 14,* 245–277.

Trower, P., Bryant, B., & Argyle, M. (1978). *Social skills and mental health.* Pittsburgh: University of Pittsburgh Press.

Wallace, C. J., Nelson, C. J., Liberman, R. P., Aitchison, R. A., Lukov, D., Elder, J. P., & Ferris, C. (1980). A review and critique of social skills training with schizophrenic patients. *Schizophrenia Bulletin, 6,* 42–63.

Wechsler, D. (1945). A standardized memory scale for clinical use. *Journal of Psychology, 19,* 87–95.

Wechsler, D. (1987). *Wechsler Memory Scale manual (rev. ed.).* San Antonio, TX: Psychological Corporation.

Woerner, M. G., Mannuzza, S., & Kane, J. M. (1988). Anchoring the BPRS: An aid to improved reliability. *Psychopharmacology Bulletin, 24,* 112–117.

Wykes, T., & Sturt, E. (1986). The measurement of social behavior in psychiatric patients: An assessment of the reliability and validity of the SBS Schedule. *British Journal of Psychiatry, 148,* 1–11.

CHAPTER 7

PHENOMENOLOGICAL PERSPECTIVES ON THE SOCIAL FUNCTIONING OF PEOPLE WITH SCHIZOPHRENIA

Larry Davidson
David Stayner
Karl E. Haglund

Dr. Anderson: "Ms. Gibbs, what are you doing sitting here in the Day Room all by yourself?"
Ms. Gibbs: (looking up, in her best Greta Garbo impersonation) "I vant . . . to be . . . alone."
Dr. Anderson: "Why is that?"
Ms. Gibbs: "Well, isn't that the stereotype for people with my condition?"

The above interaction took place in the deserted day room of a psychiatric unit in a general hospital. The patient was a middle-aged woman with a 35-year history of schizophrenia, admitted to the hospital following a suicide attempt in which she had slashed her wrists with a kitchen knife. Her presentation on the unit did, in fact, meet several of the essential requirements of the conventional picture of social functioning for people with schizophrenia: she mostly kept to herself and engaged only rarely in meaningful activities or social interactions; she spoke only in response to direct questions; she had blunted affect. Her life as a whole, however, presented a far more complicated picture. Ms. Gibbs was married, and had

been for over 30 years. At the time of her admission, she was raising two adolescent sons and had just sent one off to college. She had been functioning well enough as an outpatient that she and her psychiatrist had been tapering her dosage of antipsychotic medication. In her roles as wife and mother, as in her engaging and rather facetious response to Dr. Anderson's question, Ms. Gibbs could not be confined within the parameters of the schizophrenic stereotype she had learned of through her interactions with the mental health system and the culture at large. Despite the fact that her clinical presentation did fit the stereotypic picture in some ways, her life clearly consisted of more than that as well.

The aim of this chapter is to address the dilemma suggested by the life of Ms. Gibbs; that is, the dilemma of a possible discrepancy between the objective presentation of isolation and an underlying, subjective sense of sociality in people with schizophrenia. Through a review of the clinical literature and of patients' own accounts of their illnesses, of their struggles to recover, and of their lives more generally, we will explore both the ways in which people may come to embody the asocial, avolitional, an-ergic, apathetic, and anhedonic profile of "a schizo-phrenic," as well as the ways in which their lives may in-clude fuller and more satisfying relationships.

Our approach to this task will be "phenomenological" in the dual sense in which this term is currently used: ob-jective-descriptive and subjective. Within the objective-descriptive tradition of empiricism, the term *phenome-nology* first was brought to the forefront of psychiatric diagnosis and treatment with the third edition of the *Di-agnostic and Statistical Manual of Mental Disorders* (American Psychiatric Association, 1980). In this text, and in the objective-descriptive approach it has pro-moted, phenomenology is taken to refer precisely to those observable characteristics of disorders such as the specific signs and symptoms that constitute the objective presentation of a disease entity such as schizophrenia (Andreasen, 1991). A second use of the term *phenome-nology*, actually predating this first use, refers to the sys-tematic study of subjectivity. This subjective, experi-ence-based form of phenomenology draws its inspiration from the Continental philosophical tradition and focuses on the internal mental, emotional, and imaginal life of the person (Husserl, 1913/1983). To gain access to the subjective domain, this brand of phenomenological re-search immerses itself in first-person descriptions of the phenomena of interest and strives to achieve an under-standing of these experiences from the perspective of the individual subjects themselves (Davidson & Cosgrove, 1991; Giorgi, 1970).

Pursuit of either one of these phenomenological ap-proaches in isolation will not resolve discrepancies be-tween the objective presentation and subjective lives of people with schizophrenia. Rather, it will require a com-bination of both senses of phenomenology—an integra-tion of objective *and* subjective approaches—to overcome the limitations of each alone (Davidson, 1993, 1994; Davidson & Strauss, 1995; Davidson, Hoge, Godleski, Rakfeldt & Griffith 1996; Strauss, 1994). As in the exam-ple of Ms. Gibbs, it is important to know not only that she loves her husband and two children, but also that she sits alone in a deserted day room and appears isolative and ap-athetic in her interactions with others. In addition to un-derstanding the subjective experiences of patients from the perspective of these individuals themselves, it there-fore will be important to have as a context an objective de-scription of their social functioning from the perspective of others in their lives.

In this chapter, we begin with a brief overview of the application of both senses of phenomenology to research in psychopathology, paying particular attention to methodological issues. Next, we turn to an objective de-scription of social functioning in schizophrenia, offering a synthesis of the clinical research that supports the stereotype of schizophrenia to which Ms. Gibbs alluded. A bridging perspective, providing subjective data on the objective presentation of people with schizophrenia, is gleaned from reports of family members that describe how their loved ones are experienced in relationships in the course of illness and recovery. The patient's own point of view is then explored through a review of subjective, first-person accounts of living with schizophrenia. Use of these descriptions to provide an empathic entry into the inner lives of people with schizophrenia will afford us a glimpse *behind* the diagnosis to the person who often con-tinues, despite the disorder and its resulting disabilities, to desire and strive for meaningful social connections. In conclusion, we identify the contributions and limitations of each of these perspectives on the social functioning of people with schizophrenia and consider each perspective in dialogue with the others. By integrating the perspective of patients with those of family members and mental health professionals, we hope to achieve a three-dimen-sional view on this topic that would not be possible through the use of only one or two of these lenses alone (Miller, 1994).

PHENOMENOLOGY AND SCHIZOPHRENIA

The contemporary use of the term *phenomenology* to refer to a subjective, experience-based approach within the human and social sciences is derived primarily from the work of the German philosopher Edmund Husserl. Husserl (e.g., 1913/1983, 1952/1989, 1954/1970) devel-oped a reflective method for the systematic study of sub-jective experience, which quickly became adapted by Karl Jaspers (1912/1968, 1913/1963) for use within the clinical psychiatric and psychological communities of continental Europe. Jaspers and his colleagues argued that empathic understanding of the inner lives of people with psychiatric disorders should parallel and comple-ment the objective, quantitative approach of the natural sciences. Since that time, a considerable body of work has developed internationally within psychiatry, psychol-ogy, sociology, anthropology, pedagogy, and nursing demonstrating the value of qualitative explorations of the subjective lives of people experiencing a variety of conditions and life circumstances, including schizophre-nia, mania, depression, obsessions, phobias and anxiety, homelessness, rape and incest, and trauma (for a review of phenomenological work on schizophrenia, see Davidson, 1994).

Such qualitative studies have been important in delineating salient features of the lives of people experiencing extreme situations and in humanizing what might otherwise remain alien or foreign phenomena. However, the phenomenology of subjective experience is necessarily subjective in nature itself, in that it relies on self-report data and intuitive and inductive methods of data analysis. The involvement of subjectivity in all phases of the research process has raised methodological concerns regarding the reliability and validity of the interpretation of first-person descriptions, leaving qualitative research especially vulnerable to the influence of investigator bias and rendering its scientific status problematic. For example, some prior excursions into the phenomenology of serious mental illness (e.g., Laing, 1960, 1961; Van Den Berg, 1982) have been criticized for becoming immersed in the subjectivity of individuals with schizophrenia to the point of romanticizing their psychosis at the expense of a more realistic appreciation of the tragedy and paucity of their everyday lives (Davidson, 1994). Only recently have steps begun to be taken to address these concerns by paying careful attention to issues of sampling, reliability, validity, and generalizability in developing more rigorous empirical methods for qualitative research (Corin, 1990; Corin & Lauzon, 1992, 1994; Davidson, 1994; Giorgi, 1988; Kvale, 1989; Wertz, 1986).

These and other related concerns with the reliability of subjective approaches have contributed to the rise of the objective-descriptive form of phenomenology mentioned above. While this approach to phenomenology may also rely somewhat on patient self-reports to detect the presence of certain forms of symptomatology (e.g., hallucinations), it places more emphasis on the observable characteristics of disorders and on the use of structured and objective approaches to identifying and measuring such characteristics. This approach has been important in allowing for cross-person comparisons and the development of disease typologies based on shared and objective features. Its use has ushered in a considerable degree of nosological consensus to the psychiatric community. Criticisms of this approach have centered on its exclusive interest in surface appearances, its neglect of the personal dimensions of psychiatric disorders such as affect, intrapsychic conflicts and developmental issues, and its relative emptiness as a clinical paradigm due to its sacrifice of validity, salience, and meaningfulness in exchange for reliability and quantification (Strauss, 1994).

CLINICAL PERSPECTIVES

Delusions, hallucinations, and disorganized speech tend to occur early in the illness. As it progresses, these symptoms sometimes "burn out." The patient is then left only with prominent negative or defect symptoms. Looking at things superficially, one might think that a person is better off no longer hearing voices or feeling persecuted. . . . But the "burned-out" schizophrenic is an empty shell— [s/]he cannot think, feel, or act . . . [s/he] has lost the capacity both to suffer and to hope—and at present, medicine has no good remedy to offer for this loss. (Andreasen, 1984, p. 62–3).

As this passage suggests, the objective-descriptive approach to schizophrenia—in agreement with Ms. Gibbs' understanding—attributes a diminished capacity for socialization to people with this condition. So well established is this characteristic that it is included in the DSM-IV's diagnostic criteria for schizophrenia (American Psychiatric Association, 1994). According to the DSM-IV, people with schizophrenia are caught in a social undertow: most are unable to sustain a job or attain educational goals, a majority never marry, and most have only limited social contacts. When negative or defect symptoms predominate, the picture painted is that of profoundly asocial human beings: sitting dormant for long periods, uninterested in social participation, offering little or no eye contact, and exhibiting little verbal or nonverbal evidence of any mental or emotional activity. In this section, we will review the empirical support for this characterization provided in the objective-descriptive clinical research literature.

Observational studies of schizophrenic inpatients were some of the first to outline the asocial presentation of this population. A vast majority of schizophrenic inpatients, up to 80%, have been rated as to some degree withdrawn and asocial (Sylph, Ross, & Kedwarth, 1977). Even when placed in social situations in the hospital, such as a busy day room or gymnasium, they often fail to make an effort to interact with other patients (Rosen, 1980). While patients with affective disorders, for example, interact with the other inpatients and participate in activities, schizophrenic patients rarely even look around at the bustle occurring in their midst. They seem to be drawn into themselves or to be absent altogether and are unlikely to reciprocate even when given support by others (Gilliland & Sommer, 1961). It is no surprise, then, that most people with schizophrenia who enter a ward tend to end up with only a few friends, if any at all (Schooler & Spohn, 1960).

In the community, where a greater range of social opportunities is available, people with schizophrenia still appear to fail to become more socially connected. About half of a 1991 sample of people with schizophrenia living in the community reported having either no friends or only superficial social contacts (Breier, Schreiber, Dyer, & Pickar, 1991). Even when no residual symptoms are present such patients establish fewer social contacts than persons who have not experienced mental illness (Cohen & Sokolovsky, 1978). The number of persons with whom patients with schizophrenia have regular contact is about 6 to 12, significantly lower than the 30 to 40 persons reported for the general population (Wallace, 1984). Most distinctly absent from the social networks of people with schizophrenia are those people outside of the family on whom most people rely for friendship, recreation, intimacy, and support (Cohen & Kochanowicz, 1989; Tolsdorf, 1976). One study reported that 57% of schizophrenic subjects living in the community had no friends or relationships outside of the family (Hirschberg, 1985). An abnormally high proportion of nonkin relationships is based in only one context, such as religious, recreational, or economic; and, for the most part, people with schizophrenia receive much more support than they give back in these relationships (Cohen & Kochanowicz, 1989; Cohen & Sokolovsky, 1978; Tolsdorf, 1976). Consequently, family members remain the predominant elements of their networks and their primary sources of support, and tend, as a result, to feel overburdened by the needs of their schizophrenic relatives (Tolsdorf, 1976).

Empirical evidence garnered thus far has suggested four important contributors to this picture of restricted socialization in people with schizophrenia: (1) direct manifestations of the disease itself, especially negative symptoms, (2) indirect disease manifestations causing alienating behaviors and appearance, (3) a pervasive lack of basic social skills and judgment, and (4) undesired side effects of treatments, ranging from medication to hospitalization.

Symptoms

Both positive and negative symptoms have been correlated with decreased global (Breier et al., 1991) and social role functioning (Pogue-Geile & Harrow, 1984). However, negative symptoms are most *directly* related to social impoverishment (Hamilton, Ponzoha, Cutler, & Weigel, 1989) and dysfunction (Pogue-Geile & Harrow, 1984; Van der Does, Dingemans, Linszen, Nugter, Scholte, 1993) since, by definition, they directly manifest

as "deficits in interpersonal behavior relative to social expectations" (Pogue-Geile & Harrow, 1984, p. 372). The significance of this relationship is supported by the finding that levels of negative symptoms correlate significantly with the degree of disability in social and vocational role functioning (Van der Does et al., 1993). Furthermore, groups with the highest levels of negative symptoms have the poorest overall levels of social adjustment (Morrison, Bellack, Wixted, & Mueser, 1990) and the most impoverished networks (Hamilton et al., 1989). Such findings may result from the fact that patients with prominent negative symptoms appear to be poorly accepted by those in their potential social sphere, most markedly by those outside of the family (Hamilton et al., 1989). Because of their symptoms, people with negative symptoms may not provide the eye contact, body language, and degree of animation that offer social contacts a sense of interpersonal connection. Even in response to direct questions, such people may provide only minimal responses. In the face of this lack of interpersonal presence, often the only remaining components of social networks are relatives, perhaps largely out of a sense of loyalty (Hamilton et al., 1989).

Alienating Behaviors

Social isolation may also be brought about by the presence of behaviors that are bizarre and stigmatizing. Sylph and colleagues (1977) conducted a systematic study of maladaptive, disorganized behaviors of schizophrenic inpatients. They found that over half of their sample was unable to manage simple day-to-day living skills such as washing, bathing, and demonstrating appropriate table manners. If allowed to dress themselves, "many would attract unfavorable attention in the community" (p. 1391). At least a third of the sample exhibited antisocial behaviors such as outbursts of temper, rebellious behavior, or the use of profane language. Disordered sexual behavior may also be considered "common" in schizophrenia, according to Akhtar and Thomson (1980b, p. 166; 1980a). In their review of schizophrenic sexuality, they cite examples of aberrant behaviors ranging from celibacy and sexual anhedonia to hypersexuality, autoeroticism, incest, and rape. In one sample, 86% of schizophrenic inpatients exhibited some form of sexually deviant behavior (Lyketsos, Sakka & Mailis, 1983). Delusions or thought disorder may in some instances be at the root of bizarre behaviors, including sexually deviant behaviors (Akhtar & Thomson, 1980a, 1980b; Lyketsos et al., 1983). Persecutory delusions may cause the person with schizophrenia to be "difficult to deal with because s[/]he is suspicious, guarded, and irritable or angry" (Andreasen, 1984, p. 60). Thought disordered speech may confuse listeners due to semantic deviations and unclear references (Rosenberg & Tucker, 1979). There is also evidence to indicate that situations with close interpersonal contact (Seeman & Cole, 1977) or discussion of stressful topics (Docherty, Evans, Sledge, Seibyl, & Krystal, 1994) may further cloud schizophrenic speech. All of these behaviors may break social norms, reducing the "cultural predictability" of people with schizophrenia (Hammer, Makiesky-Barrow, & Gutwirth, 1978, p. 537), and ultimately contributing to their stigmatization and characterization as less socially acceptable (Beiser et al., 1987).

Social Skills and Judgment

Abilities to judge interpersonal situations accurately and to formulate appropriate responses are fundamental prerequisites to making connections with others. Yet, many persons with schizophrenia appear to lack these basic social skills. Lysaker and colleagues (1993) reported a lack of social skills as the limiting factor in schizophrenic subjects' vocational adjustment. Subjects were unsure of what constituted appropriate behavior for the workplace and were unsure of how to interpret the behavior of their coworkers. Several investigators have shown that, before acting, people with schizophrenia often fail to make use of abstract and subtle social cues in assessing social situations (Colussy & Zuroff, 1985; Corrigan & Green, 1993). They tend to judge situations in a black-and-white fashion rather than in subtler, more complex and accurate ways (Livesay, 1984). Corrigan and Green (1993) have hypothesized that the inability to make use of abstract cues in interpersonal interactions best explains the limited repertoire of social skills seen in people with schizophrenia.

In role-play tests of social skills, persons with schizophrenia consistently select more inappropriate responses to social problems and are rated as less skilled and more anxious than psychiatric and nonpsychiatric controls (Monti & Fingeret, 1987). Moreover, the performance of patients with schizophrenia worsens when they are confronted with negative affect (Mueser et al., 1993). Several investigators have proposed that their hypersensitivity to negative affect results in a "social cognitive deficit" that protects against recognizing signs of these unpleasant emotions in others (Mandal & Palchoudhury, 1985, p. 652; Morrison, Bellack, & Bashore, 1988). Although persons with schizophrenia can judge the social appropriateness of others accurately, they seem unable to identify their own social mistakes and, consequently, lack what might be helpful feedback to correct their own behavior (Carini & Nevid, 1992).

Treatment Side Effects

Finally, treatments for schizophrenia, both pharmacological and psychosocial, may have undesirable side effects that limit or alter social interactions. Many of the undesirable side effects of neuroleptics, such as akathisia and tardive dyskinesia, manifest themselves as unusual motor behaviors, calling attention to the persons exhibiting them, and resulting in limited social acceptance due to their disturbing appearance. Akinesia may mimic negative symptoms with its poverty of movement and speech, and, accordingly, may have the same effects on socialization as negative symptoms (Van Putten & Marder, 1987). Lindstrom (1994) has cited the "emotional and cognitive parkinsonism" induced by classical neuroleptics as the cause of low drive for social and vocational rehabilitation as well as decreased quality of life. Many people with schizophrenia, up to 63% in one sample (Lyketsos et al., 1983), also complain of sexual disorders due to neuroleptic side effects. For example, women complain of decreased sex drive and orgasmic difficulties, and men of dry orgasms and impotence (Ames, 1994).

Hospitalization and other interventions have also been shown to have detrimental effects on the social networks of schizophrenics. Holmes-Eber and Riger (1990) reported that as the number and frequency of hospitalizations increase the composition of social networks turns from friends and relatives to mental health professionals. The composition of networks can be similarly changed by community based programs designed to improve independence and living skills. For example, program participants who had greater numbers of professionals in their networks were found to have a greater need for support and to be less satisfied with the emotional support they did receive (Goering et al., 1992).

FAMILY PERSPECTIVES

The anguish is that this demon, schizophrenia, having completely deranged a brain and ravaged a life, has now released an empty shell of a person, as though shaking it like a rag doll and throwing it to the ground. (Smith, 1991, p. 690)

In this and the following section, we will offer phenomenological analyses of first-person accounts of living with schizophrenia, first from the perspective of family members and then from the perspective of patients themselves. To address the methodological concerns described earlier, representative samples of first-person accounts were selected from the larger pool of accounts published over the last 40 years (during the community-based era). All text that referred directly or indirectly to social relationships and functioning was then analysed independently by each of the authors according to an established phenomenological method (Davidson, 1994; Davidson, Hoge, Merrill, Rakfeldt, & Griffith 1995; Giorgi, 1970; Karlsson, 1993; Wertz, 1983). The three analyses were then compared and contrasted for areas of overlap and disagreement prior to the development of a consensus on the following findings.

Loss and Social Disability

A profound sense of loss pervades family accounts of schizophrenia. With the onset of the disease, a family member seems to disappear within a swirling fog of symptomatic behaviors, treatment regimens, and residential placements. Separated from this person and the familial relationships they knew before the illness, families are also cut off from possibilities and goals that they had shared and cherished for the future. They are left with what the family member quoted above describes as "an empty shell" of the person they knew before the ravages of the illness (Smith, 1991, p. 690). In accounting for these losses, family members describe the ways in which they see their loved ones disabled by schizophrenia, including grave difficulties in relating, social withdrawal, and isolation. One mother describes how "sustaining or contributing to a relationship of any kind [has become] beyond the realm of possibility" for her daughter (Smith, 1991, p. 690). The sister of another patient describes him as having "trouble engaging in any sustained conversations and frequently need[ing] to withdraw" (Brodoff, 1988, p. 113). Family members describe an excruciating vulnerability, hypersensitivity, and fear that they see their loved ones experiencing that interferes with the possibility of relating. This sister explains that her brother seems to see the world "through a magnifying glass," with a "sixth emotional sense," that can leave him transfixed by paralyzing fear and vulnerability, his eyes "vacant and haunted with the naked look of a frightened animal frozen by the beam of approaching head-lights" (Brodoff, 1988, pp. 114–115). Similarly, a mother describes her son's struggle to cope with his emotional vulnerability as a dy-

namic in which he seems to blunt his feelings in an effort to avoid psychosis, but then feels numb and dead and risks renewed psychosis in order to feel again. She writes: "At times, he appears to be trying to shield himself from the intensity of his emotions in order to avoid becoming acutely psychotic. At other times, he seems actually to seek a psychotic state as though to avoid slipping into an absence of feeling" (Bouricius, 1989, p. 207).

A Person Behind the Illness

Despite pervasive feelings of loss and perceptions of severe disability, families continue to sense that their loved one somehow remains, even if concealed or buried behind the illness. For instance, they describe the "thrill" that is felt during the rare or occasional periods of improvement or reconnection, when they see and hear the "real person" "break through the illness" (Moorman, 1988; Smith, 1991). Some family members also feel that they have an ability to make sense of some of the behaviors and speech of their loved ones that appear bizarre or disorganized and meaningless to others, affirming their sense that the person has continued to exist behind the scenes. They describe how their sense of loss is intensified when they see that the loved one with schizophrenia is also experiencing his/her own feelings of loss and empty longing. One mother, for instance, describes her daughter's painful yearning for a family life that "will never be a reality for her" (Smith, 1991, p. 690). Another mother tells of her son losing the girlfriend that he (and she herself) had cared for, and how he now "yearns for the touch of a young woman, affection and kisses and things like that"—while she herself fears that he will never again have such experiences due both to his illness and to the restrictions placed on him by the psychiatric facility in which he lives (Villamil, 1994, p. 56).

This last example illustrates another way in which family members remain invested in a person they perceive as continuing to exist behind the clouds of the disorder. They decry their resentment of a mental health system that houses and treats their loved ones with schizophrenia, but is unable or unwilling to comprehend and respond to the basic sexual needs and desires for human connectedness that these people continue to experience. At times, they are willing to take extraordinary steps and risks to circumvent the constraints of such a system. One father, for instance, describes his refusal to stop his son from leaving a treatment center against medical advice to go on a spontaneous trip to California with a girlfriend. After his son's return, the two shared a poignant scene in which they talked about the girlfriend leaving with another man—the kind of scene that is natural to the intense romantic adventures of teenage years: "Women! Is that what they're all like, Dad?" the son asked. "I don't know them all," the father replied, "but some are wonderful" (Weisburd, 1994, p. 2). A widowed mother describes her son's loss of his girlfriend and his yearning for sexual expression after the onset of his schizophrenia, something "strictly forbidden" by hospital staff even between consenting adult patients using protection. She set out to make it possible for him to be initiated into sexual expression in the same way that other young men of her culture have experienced for generations. With the help of an uncle she found a "decent" brothel, and in fear and trepidation told her story to the proprietor "who listened and understood"; then she met a young woman who was unafraid to be with her son, if he chose her. On her son's home pass, she slipped him some money, told of her visit to the brothel, and left him to decide if he wanted to go in. When he returned from his adventure, mother and son shared a deep, mostly silent sense of connection, release, and gratitude together—far from the disorganization and heightened psychotic symptoms that might have been expected. She writes:

> When I left the "house" I had the feeling that I was doing something extraordinary. And that it was good. Now, I know, you must be thinking I am an indecent person; a woman with no morals. You are right. No doubt about it. But this is from your perspective. Different cultures have different customs and rules we cannot understand. . . . You don't have to excuse me for what I did. But, perhaps you can understand. I cannot accept that the most elemental part of a man's life should be suppressed, denied, utterly obliterated. Don't you think that unnatural circumstance contributes to aggravating his illness? (Villamil, 1994, p. 57)

For the mental health system, these two young men were patients; but for their parents, they were sons who continued to experience the same basic, human needs for companionship and connection that others experience, whether or not they must contend with schizophrenia. Thus, while family members describe the impaired relating, social withdrawal and isolation, and apparent emotional vacancy of schizophrenia, they also continue to see, concealed within the effects of these negative symptoms, a lingering of the person they knew prior to the onset of the disorder. One mother, for instance, compares patients experiencing schizophrenia to poker players who may be experiencing emotions that they cannot or will not reveal. Concerned that mental health professionals would be misled by her son's appearance to assume that he no longer had feelings at all, she expresses a thin hope that "those who work with him will make every effort to find the emotions that may be hidden behind an expressionless face" (Bouricius, 1989, p. 207).

Need for Distance and Boundaries

In reaction to the distortions of the person brought on by the disorder and his/her own painful feelings of loss, family members describe a need they feel at times to distance themselves from the person experiencing schizophrenia. They report drawing "rigid boundaries" between themselves and the person with the illness in order to feel that they were not vulnerable to similar distortions, by "arming" themselves, for instance, "with evidence that we were nothing alike" (Brodoff, 1988, p. 115). Some attribute this need for distance to the chaos of the disease that confronted them in ways that threatened their own sense of ordered reality and sanity. A sister writes that her brother's "presence became a daily reminder that the carefully ordered world I had painstakingly created could easily topple down like an intricate sand castle washed away by a wave" (Brodoff, 1988, p. 115). Others tell how this need to distance oneself is exacerbated by feeling neglected, jealous, or resentful that so much familial attention is diverted to the person with schizophrenia. Family members also describe resenting and distancing themselves from the stigma of the label "schizophrenia," with all its second glances, unasked questions, and hushed explanations. They wish, and at times try, to reject the identity of "a schizophrenic's family" that had been forced on them by their loved one's illness.

Grief and/or Hope

At the center of many family members' descriptions is a wrenching tension between their need to distance themselves from the person with schizophrenia, to accept that their relationship has been irrevocably altered and diminished, and a lingering, at times fierce, desire and hope for the return of the person who has been lost to this disease. Hope is buoyed during periods of improvement, when they see incremental increases in responsiveness such as a person choosing his own clothes, sitting through a movie, smiling more, or asking about his sister for the first time in years (Najarian, 1995). Family members' expectancy can also be bolstered or rejuvenated when they hear of a new treatment or medication, and find themselves hoping yet again that this will be "the one" to bring about a cure (Moorman, 1988; Najarian, 1995). Yet they face what seems like an endlessly recurrent pattern of gradual improvements followed by setbacks—while a "chasm" continues to divide them from the person and the family life they knew before the onset of schizophrenia. Caught between yearning for the return of the person who has been lost to this disease and their need to accept and barricade themselves from its effects, families can experience a heart-rending tension. The pain associated with this tension can be even more difficult to bear than grief over a death, because it seems unending and unresolvable. A sister writes:

> Although grieving for someone who has died is painful, some sense of peace and acceptance is ultimately possible. However, mourning for a loved one who is alive—in your very presence and yet in vital ways inaccessible to you—has a lonely, unreal quality that is extraordinarily painful. (Brodoff, 1988, p. 116).

Though heard only rarely, family accounts of schizophrenia also suggest that some sense of resolution may be possible in accepting the loss of the person and familial relationships that family members knew in the past, while working to build a new family life on different terms— with relationships that are "as close as [the family member] can allow" (Smith, 1991, 690).

PATIENT PERSPECTIVES

> If I am to survive this maelstrom called schizophrenia, I must continuously try to gain the comprehension I need to withstand each plunge into darkness and find a way to share as much as I can in a way that will make me feel the least alone. (Ruocchio, 1991, p. 358).

The simple fact that there are ample data available for a phenomenological investigation of the subjective experience of schizophrenia—that people have provided autobiographical accounts, and in relatively large numbers when compared to individuals with other medical conditions (Sommer & Osmond, 1983), along with poetry and other artworks (e.g., Campbell, 1989)—suggests that at least some individuals with schizophrenia have a desire for personal expression and communication with others.

This impression is confirmed in the content and emotional tone of these accounts, which often speak directly to issues of isolation, loneliness, and the importance of social connection and relationships.

Loss, Loneliness, and the Desire for Love

The most pervasive themes articulated in these accounts are those of loss of interpersonal connections, loneliness, and isolation, at times to the point of despair. In the accounts of some individuals who had active and satisfying social lives prior to the onset of the illness, there are vivid recollections of traumatizing experiences of being rejected by loved ones at the first signs of illness, due either to stigmatizing attitudes on the part of mental health staff or the loved ones themselves, or to aspects of the illness itself (Kiley, 1994; North, 1987). Even in the accounts of the most seriously disabled, who appear to others to be withdrawn and at best indifferent to inter-personal interaction, one finds an undercurrent of profound feelings of alienation and estrangement, with painful yearnings for connection, companionship, and caring. For example, the diary of one young man with schizophrenia, who was rated independently by five clinicians as having pronounced negative symptoms, reveals excruciating experiences of desiring love yet feeling irrevocably disconnected from others. He writes: "I am a lonely nothing. . . . My afflictions fill the place that was meant for sharing love. I am crying in despair. . . . I have a dreadful fear of not loving" (quoted in Bouricius, 1989, pp. 202–205). This young man's sense of isolation was all the more stark in that it involved losses not only of previous relationships, but also of memories of those relationships and, with them, the possibility of imagining such relationships in the future:

> This feeling of loss seems to take away my smile, seems to be waiting for me when I awaken. It's there, cold and clear, this feeling that I have lost something. It's a feeling of all the things I've lost and can't remember, all the joys and good times that are not with me now. (quoted in Bouricius, 1989, p.207)

Whether they have access to painful memories of their earlier lives, or experience only a painful lack of access to such memories, patients report having strong desires for meaningful attachments to others, and at times intersperse their narratives with pleas for understanding and acceptance. Esso Leete has been a national spokesperson for the mental health consumer movement in the United States. Diagnosed with schizophrenia, she writes eloquently on the needs of individuals with this condition for relationships and a sense of belonging:

> What makes life valuable for those of us with mental illness? . . . Exactly what is necessary for other people. We need to feel wanted, accepted and loved. . . . We need support from friends and family and a sense of stability in our environment. We need to be accepted by and welcomed into our communities. We need to feel a part of the human race, to have friends. We need to give and receive love. (Leete, 1993, p. 127)

Such pleas derive from experiences patients appear to have frequently of not being accepted by and welcomed into their communities, of not having friends, and of not giving and receiving love on a consistent basis. The diary of the young man described above, who appeared according to objective criteria to lack interest in social involvements, contains passages that attest to his similar desire for connections and feelings of being thwarted in his efforts to give and receive love:

> I want to love. I envy those who can relate to each other. . . . When my heart burns away, will they pick up the ashes and say, ". . . He loved too much but he never knew how to show it so his heart burned away and here are the ashes"? . . . My desire burns to sorrow and freezes to ice. My cries hide in my heart. (quoted in Bouricius, 1989, pp. 204–205)

This last image, of cries hiding in the heart, suggests a sense of paralysis or incapacity in relation to social functioning on the part of some individuals with schizophrenia. It is reminiscent of Rilke's (1907–1938) panther (in the poem of that name) that has become so accustomed to coming into contact only with the bars of the cage itself, rather than with the world that lies beyond the cage, that it no longer even attempts to muster a response to the images that slip through the bars. It is as if patients have become so stunned and numbed by repetitive failures in connecting with others that they can no longer act on their desires for socialization. Opportunities for connection may initially arouse interest; but, as in Rilke's panther, the impulse to act reaches the person's heart only to die there very quickly thereafter.

If people with schizophrenia are so distressed by experiences of loss and rejection, and wish so fervently for love and relationships, why are they so isolated and lonely, at times to the point of despair? If they have such strong desires to give and receive love, what keeps them at such a social distance that they feel estranged and alienated from their communities? What factors do patients identify as contributing to their difficulties in relating, and how do they experience their own attempts, as well as those of others, to form and maintain attachments?

Barriers to Relating

Stigma

As mentioned above, patients identify stigmatizing attitudes on the part of mental health providers and loved ones as one of the primary contributors to their experiences of rejection and loss early in the course of illness. In a similar vein, they identify stigma as one of the main factors in their continued difficulty in developing relationships once they have been diagnosed. Stigma comes in many forms, from the doctor telling your boyfriend to forget about you and get on with his life because you will be spending the rest of yours in a state hospital (North, 1987), to more subtle instances of feeling formerly intimate and close relationships becoming incrementally more cold and distant (Kiley, 1994), and not going to church due to a creeping suspicion that people there will be able to tell that you are a mental patient who had been institutionalized, thereby excluding you from their community (cited in Davidson, Hoge, Merrill, Rakfeldt, & Griffith, 1995). Underlying all of these, and the many more examples patients give, is the devastating and demoralizing experience of being considered somehow less or other than human due to one's history of mental illness. Other people, regardless of whether it is the stranger on the street or one's own husband (Kiley, 1994), come to see the person only or primarily as a mental patient and no longer as an individual with his/her own unique blend of talents, frailties, and promise. This aspect of the life experiences of people with schizophrenia is also captured eloquently by Esso Leete:

> Life is hard with a diagnosis of schizophrenia. I can talk but I may not be heard. I can make suggestions, but they may not be taken seriously. I can report my thoughts, but they may be seen as delusions.

I can recite experiences, but they may be interpreted as fantasies. To be a patient or ex-client is to be discounted. Your label is a reality that never leaves you; it gradually shapes an identity that is hard to shed. (1989, p. 199)

Hypersensitivity

Of the various barriers that may be associated with the disorder itself, hypersensitivity to stimulation and affect appears in these reports as perhaps the most ubiquitous feature of the subjective experience of schizophrenia adversely impacting interpersonal relationships. This hypersensitivity has been described in a variety of ways, most often in relation to sensory stimulation, but also, and more importantly for our present interest, in relation to interpersonal interactions. On the perceptual level, patients describe this hypersensitivity as "a kind of added brightness or extra dimension to everyday things" (quoted in Hatfield & Lefley, 1993, p. 55). It is operative across sensory domains: "It's as if I am too wide awake—very, very alert"; "everything's brighter and louder and noisier"; "It's as if someone had turned up the volume" (quoted in McGhie & Chapman, 1961, pp. 104–105). Aware that the level of intensity of stimulation significantly increased with the onset of the disorder, one patient compares his premorbid state with being deaf in comparison to the heightened sensitivity resulting from the illness: "Have you ever had wax in your ears for a while and then had them syringed? That's what it's like now, as if I had been deaf before. Everything is much noisier and it excites me" (quoted in McGhie & Chapman, 1961, p. 105). Leete relates this heightened alterness and intensity in the perceptual domain to a parallel sensitivity within the social sphere, through which patients find themselves acutely attuned to subtle cues and other aspects of interpersonal interactions to which others may remain relatively deaf and blind. She writes:

> We must learn to go through life experiencing our surroundings with a greater intensity than others do. Sounds are louder, lights brighter, colors more vibrant. These stimuli are distracting and confusing for us, and we are unable to filter their impact to lessen their effect. In addition, I believe we are more sensitive in an interpersonal sense as well. I have noticed that others like myself are easily able to pick up emotional nonverbal cues and feelings that may be "hidden." (Leete, 1993, p. 119)

We will return to the issues of distraction, confusion, and difficulty filtering sensations in the next section. In addition to these consequences of hypersensitivity, "going through life" experiencing a "greater intensity than others do" can lead to a variety of problems in relating to others. For example, their heightened sensitivity to sensory stimulation can lead patients to become absorbed in, and preoccupied with, attending to their immediate perceptual environment, to the neglect of other people and the demands of the social milieu. Patients may also experience a heightened sense of vulnerability due to the constant bombardment of sensory impressions, leading them to develop sensory buffers out of necessity. These buffers may then overcompensate for their initial state of acute attunement, leaving them numb to their surroundings. In a related fashion, patients report becoming overwhelmed by the onslaught of sensations, finding that at times they simply "shut down" in the face of overstimulation. Reports one patient:

> It's like a temporary blackout—with my brain not working properly— . . . This happens when the tension starts to mount until it bursts in my brain. It has to do with what is going on around me—taking in too much of my surroundings—vital not to miss anything. I can't shut things out of my mind and everything closes in on me. It stops me thinking and then the mind goes blank and everything gets switched off. (quoted in Chapman, 1966, p. 231)

In the interpersonal domain, heightened sensitivity to subtle cues and "hidden" feelings may make it difficult for patients to tolerate some of the ordinary unpleasantness and intricacies of everyday interactions. With all aspects of an interaction, both implicit and explicit, assuming equal prominence, the formulation of a simple response may become exceptionally problematic. As one patient describes:

> I find emotions tremendously complex, and I am quite acutely aware of the many over and undertones of things people say and the way they say them. . . . I have difficulty handling social situations that require me to be artificial or too careful. (quoted in Hatfield & Lefley, 1993, p. 63)

Experiencing others' emotions in an intensified, larger-than-life form, patients also may find it difficult to respond to them in customary (e.g., "artificial" or "careful") ways that do not seem to do justice to their enormity in the patient's experience. This seems to be true particularly of what patients describe as the "negative" aspects of relationships: emotions and experiences such as anger, hostility, criticism, rejection, and disapproval. Suggests one patient: "The largest problem I face—I think the basic one—is the intensity and variety of my feelings, and my low threshold for handling other people's intense feelings, especially negative ones" (quoted in Hatfield & Lefley, 1993, p. 55). This contrast between the intensification of emotions experienced by patients and their relative paucity in ability to handle and respond to these emotions both in themselves and in the others with whom they interact is summarized in the following patient's account:

> Intimacy is an interesting problem in my life. In a way, I am capable of the deepest spiritual intimacy with people, yet, I am less capable than most people of handling the demands of relationships. I cannot share negative feelings other people have, because I am too sensitive to them: yet I can give a great deal of love and concern when I am protected against feelings like anger and cynicism. (quoted in Hatfield & Lefley, 1993, p. 63)

Experiencing everyday interpersonal interactions frequently as exceedingly complex, confusing, intense, and potentially overwhelming, patients may find themselves restricting their contacts with others despite their desires for connection and companionship. Particularly if they have felt inadequate in their attempts to overcome the problems described above, they may increasingly come to feel embarrassed and inept in their interactions with others and may withdraw from future occasions that seem to promise only more of the same failure and humiliation. In the extreme, such withdrawal may become an active avoidance and fear of others due to the impossible challenges they present to patients who have come to see themselves as incapable of responding to others. As one patient describes: "I began to be afraid of people, of my family and friends; not because of what they represented . . . but because of my own inability to cope with ordinary human contacts" (quoted in Hatfield & Lefley, 1993, p. 56).

Attention, Concentration,
and Communication Difficulties

Perhaps related to their hyper-sensitivity to stimulation, patients also report difficulty in focusing their attention, filtering out distracting and irrelevant details, and being able to concentrate on aspects of their environment or interactions that interest them. Describes one patient: "I am attending to everything at once and as a result I do not really attend to anything" (quoted in McGhie & Chapman, 1961, p. 104). Without being able to attend and concen-

trate, patients' ability to process and remember information then also becomes compromised. As another patient reports: "I seem to be always taking in too much at . . . one time and then I can't handle it and can't make sense of it" (quoted in McGhie & Chapman, 1961, p. 105).

One of the predominant ways patients experience an inability to filter out irrelevancies and otherwise control their focus of attention and concentration has been described by Freedman (1974) as "yielding to associative connections" (p. 335). This phrase refers to the experience of having one's perceptions, thoughts, and emotions constantly pulled in numerous directions in response to whatever stimuli happen to arise. In being so vulnerable to having one's thoughts redirected at the slightest breeze, people become unable to pursue a train of thought in any single direction for any substantial amount of time. This phenomenon has been referred to in the clinical literature accordingly as "derailment" and "loosening of associations." From the perspective of the patient, what seems most troubling about this experience is that it lies entirely outside of the person's control and does not appear to be changed as a result of any amount of effort on the person's part. In addition, patients may become acutely aware of how this difficulty affects their ability not only to think clearly, but also to communicate with others. Thus they may become aware that they make little to no sense to others when they talk, but may also be left feeling helpless and powerless to change this state of affairs, at least in the short term. As one patient describes:

> My thoughts get all jumbled up, I start thinking about something but I never get there. Instead I wander off in the wrong direction and get caught up with all sorts of things that might be connected with the things I want to say but in a way I can't explain. People listening to me get more lost than I do. (quoted in Torrey, 1983, p. 18)

In addition to making it difficult for patients to clarify and articulate their thoughts in conversations with others, impairments in attention and concentration make it difficult for them to attend to others in conversation, to follow their discourse, and to be able to process and remember the flow of the conversation. While this may be difficult enough in a dyadic context, it appears to make it virtually impossible for some patients to function within a group setting. Two patients describe the situation as follows:

> When people are talking I just get scraps of it. If it is just one person who is speaking that's not so bad, but if others join in, then I can't pick it up at all.

I just can't get into tune with that conversation. It makes me feel open—as if things are closing in on me and I have lost control."

If there are three or four people talking at one time I can't take it in. I would not be able to hear what they are saying properly and I would get the one mixed up with the other. To me it's just like a babble—a noise that goes right through me. (quoted in McGhie & Chapman, 1961, pp. 105–106)

The frustrations and failures involved in attempting to converse with others as a result of these difficulties discourage patients from pursuing or entering into relationships, at least through the verbal means central to patterns of relating in Western cultures. As we found in the discussion of hypersensitivity, repeated disappointments and embarrassments in this domain can work gradually to limit patients' spheres of interactions and lead to a withdrawal from, and active avoidance of, social contacts. One patient has described this eventuality in relation to his attempts to communicate his thoughts to others:

Often I have to go through two or three things in my head before I find the thought I want—words I don't want come out—not the correct words—not the words I wanted for the meaning I wanted to give. . . . People listening might hear something different from what I mean. Sometimes I do not say anything because of this. (quoted in Chapman, 1966, p. 236)

For another patient, memory problems and difficulties in participating in conversations led to the development of coping strategies intended to minimize her chances of getting lost in her own associations and maximizing her chances of coming up with a "sensible and appropriate" response. Despite her best efforts, she found keeping up with a conversation to entail hard work and be quite draining, and therefore curtailed her interactions with others significantly. She reports:

I can hear what they are saying all right, it's remembering what they have said in the next second that's difficult—it just goes out of my mind. . . . I am speaking but I'm not conscious of what I'm saying . . . so I don't know what I'm talking about. I've got a rigmarole in my mind now for checking what I say in advance so if somebody speaks to me I get on my guard straight away so that I can make a sensible answer. I try to say something sensible and appropriate but it is a strain because I'm not speaking automatically and when the conversation is going on. . . . I don't know what they are talking about or

what I was talking about. I keep talk to a minimum to prevent these attacks coming on. (quoted in Chapman, 1966, p. 237)

Bizarre Experiences and Behaviors

While not receiving prominent attention in patients' own accounts, it is worth noting the presence in their descriptions of experiences and behaviors that they themselves recognize as aberrant. Accounts include descriptions of conventional symptoms such as hallucinations and delusions, but also include less well articulated phenomena such as "loss of meaning," sudden paralysis, and behaviors that are driven either by hallucinatory or delusional content or in response to it. In her own analysis of first-person accounts, Freedman (1974) captured the phenomenon of "loss of meaning" as follows:

A number of [people] reported that they experienced a frightening, aphasic like, diffuse loss of meaning from common words, objects and people. This loss made their worlds seem unreal. In some cases, the patient could not remember who the people were, or what the relationships had meant to him. It was as if the function or importance of familiar objects had drained out of them, leaving them purposelessness, empty shells, to which the patient could not react. (p. 336)

Experiences of sudden paralysis seem to occur in the context of patients feeling overwhelmed by their heightened sensitivity and distractability—an external and motoric version of the mental "shut down" described above. Reports one patient:

I get stuck, almost as if I am paralysed at times. It may only last for a minute or two but it's a bit frightening. . . . Say I am walking across the floor and someone suddenly switches on the wireless, the music seems to stop me in my tracks and sometimes I freeze like that for a minute or two. (quoted in McGhie & Chapman, 1961, p. 106)

And another:

When I move quickly it's a strain on me. Things go too quick for my mind. They get blurred and it's like being blind. It's as if you were seeing a picture one moment and another picture the next. I just stop and watch my feet. Everything is alright if I stop, but if I start moving again I lose control. (quoted in McGhie & Chapman, 1961, p. 106)

Experiences of hallucinations and delusions range from the most severely damaging and torturous to more benign forms that provide companionship, coherence, and meaning for patients who have become increasingly distanced from the everyday consenual world (e.g., Freedman, 1974; Leete, 1987; Sherman, 1994). While they may experience themselves as different from others on the basis of such experiences, it is primarily in acting on, or in response to, these experiences that patients come to appear strange to others. Obvious examples are talking out loud to hallucinated voices and becoming reclusive and guarded in response to paranoid beliefs. A less obvious example is the patient who laughed in response to hallucinated jokes that others could not hear, giving him the appearance of "inappropriate affect" in relation to the somber content of the conversation going on around him. Any of these or similar behaviors potentially have the effect of keeping others at a safe distance.

Loss of Self and Fears of Engulfment

An especially distressing feature of the subjective experience of schizophrenia described by patients is the loss of their personal identity, specifically, and of the self as the agent or subject of experience, more broadly. While they identify a number of different sources that may contribute to this loss of identity, the more extreme situation in which a person feels the loss of any sense of agency whatsoever is most likely a consequence of the convergence of multiple processes. These include experiences of stigma in which one is treated by others like a nonperson, experiences of severe memory impairments in which any continuity between past, present, and future in terms of one's day-to-day life and identity is lost, and experiences of distractability and attentional impairment, in which the person loses any ability to control his/her attentional focus and the direction and stream of his/her own perceptions, emotions, and thoughts. Of these processes, it is most often the last that is associated directly by patients with their experiences of loss of self. Such a loss of mental control leads patients to feel that they no longer own their sensations, ideas, and emotions, and that they are no longer the subject or agent of their own experience. They either have become a nothing, or perhaps a machine; or these functions, if they continue to operate, have been taken over by forces external to the patient, which now control the content of his/her experience. Such beliefs can then form the basis for ideas of reference and delusions of control, in which the patient's mental life is controlled by

some specified others, such as the CIA, alien intelligence, computer chips implanted in the brain, or his/her neighbors (Davidson, in press). For the patient, the experience is one of becoming increasingly numb and deadened to the point of feeling more like an object than a subject. As one patient poignantly describes:

> Things just happen to me now and I have no control over them. I don't seem to have the same say in things anymore. At times, I can't even control what I want to think about. I am starting to feel pretty numb about everything because I am becoming an object and objects don't have feelings. (quoted in McGhie & Chapman, 1961, p. 109)

There are at least two ways in which the loss of self can pose a barrier to social functioning for people with schizophrenia. First, loss of self leaves patients feeling increasingly vulnerable, with highly permeable boundaries between themselves and others. Assuming that control is only exerted from outside, they perceive themselves as increasingly susceptible to the influence of others and may begin to feel that they no longer can be sure of where they leave off and others begin. Also, feeling that they no longer have an identity, they may begin to feel that they take on the identity of any others with whom they come in contact. One patient described: "When I look at somebody my own personality is in danger. I am undergoing a transformation and myself is beginning to disappear. . . . that's when I feel that I am the other person" (quoted in Chapman, 1966, p. 232). Experiences of merging with others, while in some ways desired by exceptionally lonely individuals, prove highly distressing and only serve to heighten preexisting feelings of vulnerability. Fears of becoming engulfed by others then become yet another powerful motivator for actively avoiding social contacts and relationships (Ruocchio, 1991).

A second outcome of the loss of self is that no one remains within the person who could be responsible for initiating and carrying out productive behaviors, including those required for developing and maintaining relationships with others. Either as another feature or as a result of this process, patients describe losing themselves to their psychosis: "giving in to death" (Ruocchio, 1991, p. 358), feeling that "the world collapses around you when the illness 'strikes'" (Weingarten, 1994, p. 374), leaving you "alone, abandoned, and adrift on a dead and silent sea" (Deegan, 1993, p. 8). Patients describe becoming inaccessible to themselves as well as to others; being pushed out to the margins of their own consciousness where they can be nothing more than a passive spectator of the chaos and storms that rage in their minds. Separated by a "wall of glass" (Ruocchio, 1991) from their own experiences, will, and ability to act, patients may feel that they have no choice but to resign themselves to the illness, and as a result, to identify with, to become, the illness itself. This feature of the loss of self to the disorder has been addressed by Patricia Deegan, another national spokesperson for the American mental health consumer movement, herself diagnosed with schizophrenia. She writes:

> Once a person comes to believe that he or she is an illness, there is no one left inside to take a stand toward the illness. Once you and the illness become one, then there is no one left inside of you to take on the work of recovering, of healing, of rebuilding the life you want to live. Once you come to believe that you are a mental illness, you give away all your power—and others take responsibility for you and for your life. (Deegan, 1993, p. 9)

Prior phenomenological investigation in this area has suggested that recovery from schizophrenia involves the discovery and reconstruction of an effective sense of self and agency, apart from the illness, that can then be responsible for initiating and carrying out the work Deegan describes (Davidson & Strauss, 1992). Prior to coming to imagine that such a functional sense of self is possible, however, patients are left feeling powerless to act on their own behalf. Perceiving themselves to be at the mercy and whim of the illness, they become passive and withdrawn, and increasingly come to act and present to others as they themselves feel inside: like a "nobody nowhere" (Weingarten, 1994, p. 374).

Poverty and Unemployment

The final barriers to relating that patients describe in their accounts derive more from their social and economic positions in life than from anything necessarily related to their disorder. While patients may end up unemployed and poor due to the consequences of their illness, the ramifications of poverty and unemployment that they describe in relation to social functioning could be experienced by other unemployed and poor people, regardless of the factors leading to their situation. Simply put, when you are not working you lose one of the primary sources for making new friends available to adults in contemporary Western cultures. Similarly, when you have no money in your

pockets or purse, your options for spending time in your local community recreating and socializing with others become severely restricted. In both cases there may also be significant damage to the self-esteem, confidence, and social status of the person required to feel comfortable taking risks in the social sphere. Describes one consumer advocate:

> Many of us have to learn to cope with little money, or no money from time to time. It almost always has an effect upon our relationships. If we lose a job . . . it is difficult to maintain self-respect and relationships with those we love, no matter what kind of relationship it is. (Seckinger, 1994, p. 20)

To Be or Not To Be Social

In the face of these considerable difficulties and obstacles to forming and cultivating attachments to others, people with schizophrenia are left with basically two options: either to persevere to the best of their abilities and continue to attempt to relate to others, or to give up. While undoubtedly a number of patients at least appear to have given up, it is more likely the case that most patients fall somewhere between these poles, alternately making efforts, succeeding in small ways or suffering additional failures and disappointments, and retreating for respite to lick their wounds and rest prior to trying again. It should be acknowledged, however, that this is one area where we have at least a potential bias in our data, in that people who truly have given up are extremely unlikely to go to the trouble of describing their experiences for the benefit of others. In the Discussion section, we will return to the question of whether or not it is possible for a human being to give up totally. In the present analysis, however, it will make most sense to describe the pathways patients traverse in their efforts, both successful and unsuccessful, to connect with others.

One of the primary strategies that patients employ in their attempts to preserve existing relationships and establish new ones is to find a way to articulate their experiences and share their internal struggles with others. It is in this sense that through relating their own stories in interviews and autobiographies, patients already have made efforts to communicate and connect with the larger community. The opening quotation of this section, from a patient describing her experiences in psychotherapy, speaks to this same issue on the interpersonal level. She reports that an important survival skill is finding a way to share as much as she could of her experience with her therapist in a way that allows her to feel "the least alone" (Ruocchio, 1991, p. 358).

While sharing all aspects of life experience with others is important in developing relationships, it seems to be those aspects of life most intimately associated with the disorder that may be both the most consuming and yet also the most difficult to put into words. This can be for several reasons in addition to those already described above. First, patients may be so confused and disoriented by what is happening to them that they would not know where to begin in describing their situation to others, nor would they know what to say about it. As one patient describes:

> It's just that I seem to be changing and I can't do anything about it. I feel I am losing myself more each day. That's bad enough but it's the vagueness of the whole thing that really troubles me. If the things that were happening were clearer so you could put them into words and tell somebody what it's like without sounding quite daft it wouldn't be so bad. (quoted in McGhie & Chapman, 1961, p. 110)

A second source of difficulty in articulating the experience of schizophrenia is the nature of some aspects of that experience itself; such aspects as the heightened intensity of sensation, the fragmentation of thought brought about by yielding to associative connections, and the loss of self that can take place at such a fundamental level that it borders on ineffable and can render the person immobile and speechless. Ruocchio (1991) describes her attempts as follows:

> My own inadequacy to use language to express what lies buried so deeply inside me, even when I am lucid, makes words a curse that blocks the proverbial light within the tunnel, and I am alone with my darkness. There are things that happen to me that I have never found words for, some lost now, some which I still search desperately to explain, as if time is running out and what I see and feel will be lost to the depths of chaos forever. With each uncommunicated experience the darkness grows. (1991, p. 358)

A last source of difficulty stems from stigma and fears that others will reject the speaker for talking about experiences that lie outside the realm of normal life and associate him/her with mental illness. Richard Weingarten, (1994), another advocate within the American mental health consumer movement, characterizes this process and its consequences of increased isolation, withdrawal, and passivity for people with schizophrenia:

> Aggravating matters more is the painful knowledge that you can't talk to anybody about these things. Not only are these things hard to talk about, but if you admit to having any of these kinds of problems you are likely to get puzzled looks or face immediate and often final rejection. Most people will put you in the category of "crazy" or "looney tunes" or "nutcase" or something similar. So to avoid this kind of abuse you are forced to hide or conceal your thoughts and feelings from others, and then ultimately from yourself, which only serves to worsen your situation. This is why persons with mental disorders are often passive, withdrawn, and avoid human contact. They are engaged in an inner struggle they can't express and which consumes them. . . . The invisibility of [this] struggle . . . and the isolation that results is what makes their situation so tragic. (p. 374)

As both of these passages suggest, failures to articulate and communicate experiences of the illness leave the person feeling increasingly alone and isolated. With each such failure, the person's sense of darkness and chaos deepens and grows, as does the chasm separating him/her from other people. We can imagine, too, that frustration and rage over the inability to connect with others, as well perhaps as a sense of despair and hopelessness over things ever improving, move more and more to the foreground, at times overshadowing desires for connection. At times such as these, patients report burying their feelings and thoughts, and sometimes their desires for relationships, so deeply inside of themselves that they risk becoming numb and dead inside. They may also fall back into an acute psychotic state or into some of the ongoing features of their illness, such as hallucinations or delusional ideation. Cut off from companionship in the real world, patients at these times may find that the only relationships available to them are with the phantoms and demons provided by their disorders. As one person somewhat cynically suggested in relation to his own delusional world inhabited by voices he heard on a daily basis: "You're never [really] alone when you're schizophrenic" (Sherman, 1994, p. 43). While patients who are in retreat may appear to others as the "nobody nowhere" they feel inside, their accounts suggest that this typically is not a static state of passivity, withdrawal, and resignation. It appears instead to involve a painful and dynamic struggle between the temptations of giving up and giving in to the familiarity of the illness and venturing out again into the social arena to risk yet another failure. Certainly there are times when patients feel that they simply cannot take any more such risks. But it seems that these times usually end, with new glimmers of hopefulness emerging to reawaken this tension. As Weingarten has suggested, however, this inner struggle may remain invisible to others, giving the patient an appearance of indifference while there is actually a lively internal debate raging. Such misperceptions only serve to increase the isolation the person already feels.

Not all efforts to relate are doomed to failure, however. Patients do find it possible, despite some or many of these obstacles, to communicate effectively with others and to develop relationships through verbal and other means. They do so by virtue of courage, perseverance, and creativity, which, again, may be aspects of their internal struggle that are not evident to others. As Leete (1989) comments: "These are the kinds of obstacles that confront individuals with a psychiatric disorder every day. Yet we are perceived as weak. On the contrary, I believe we are among the most courageous" (p. 199). In addition to the courage to keep trying and keep taking risks despite considerable difficulties and demoralization, patients describe a number of strategies they have developed to overcome or minimize these barriers to relating. Lessening distractions, withdrawing from stimulation, writing important information down and making lists, asking for clarification and examples of ambiguous or abstract speech, increasing daily organization and structure around particular tasks, and practicing self-care and self-soothing techniques (e.g., listening to music, taking a walk) when experiencing symptoms or stressors have all been described by patients as helpful in dealing with day-to-day life. Patients have also described learning self-discipline in not acting on hallucinatory or delusional content in public, finding ways to experience small successes that allow them to enhance their self-esteem and confidence, and coming to trust others to whom they could then look for "reality testing" in relation to their perceptions and fears. As Weingarten (1994) describes:

> Testing my perceptions of situations and relationships with my therapist and friends has also been helpful. Just realizing that a friend might be too busy with his own life to answer a letter from me is enough to eliminate the fear I had that something I did or wrote made him angry with me. (p. 373)

Each of these coping skills is related to the others, as a success in one area will provide the patient with a strength to build on in other areas. For example, increases in self-esteem seem to be associated with decreases in paranoia; as Weingarten (1989) describes: "The paranoia has lessened thanks to more positive feelings about myself. The more I can trust myself, the more I can trust others" (p. 638).

With success in coping with the disabilities associated with the disorder, patients are able to focus on the challenges entailed in developing and deepening relations with others. Ruocchio (1987) has suggested that the most difficult task for people with schizophrenia may be in this area, in "trying to find a niche among the many relationships that [s/]he has been so alien from for so many years" (p. 1224). Finding ways to share their struggles and pain with others can be an important step in building the trust and understanding that will be required for intimacy to develop. But coming to recognize and accept the limitations imposed by the illness can also be important in allowing for relationships to develop that may be somewhat different from the norm. For example, patients who continue to have severe difficulties in the verbal production and processing of language have been able to derive considerable comfort and companionship from relationships that revolve more around shared interests and activities (e.g., gardening), or involve quietly sharing time together, as opposed to talking in depth. In her ethnographic study of mentally ill homeless individuals in New York City, Lovell (1992) suggested that a different form of sociality exists on the street than within the mainstream culture; a sociality based on reciprocity of exchange of material resources and of time itself. In this culture, giving of one's time (e.g., visiting someone in the hospital) is considered a significant component of friendship, regardless of how that time is spent. A similar finding was obtained in an intensive study of a long-stay inpatient milieu, in which the exchange of goods was considered an "indicator of friendship to almost as great an extent as conversation" (Dunn, O'Driscoll, Dayson, Wills, & Leff, 1990, p. 847). As the investigators concluded: "It is conceivable that for patients with poor conversational skills and restricted expression of emotion, the exchange of goods and services creates as intimate a bond as the sharing of confidences" (Leff, O'Driscoll, Dayson, Wills, & Anderson, 1990, p. 851).

These studies suggest that a social "niche" for someone with schizophrenia may at least initially look different from what we may have come to expect for ourselves. Leete (1989), for example, writes: "I have come to realize my own diminished capacity for really close friendships, but also my need for many acquaintances" (p. 198). Weingarten (1989) also addresses the importance acquaintances can have in allowing people to develop a sense of belonging within their own community: "We should not underestimate those friendly 'hellos,' 'good mornings,' and small talk (at the drug store, bank, supermarket, etc.). They provide a sense of being, belonging, and acceptance in our lives" (p. 638). Creating a "secure, stable, friendly environment" reduces a person's paranoia and combats his/her sense of isolation and despair, offering a more solid base from which to then venture out in looking to deepen one's relationships (Weingarten, 1989). In a similar vein, Corin and Lauzon's (1992, 1994) phenomenological study of young men with schizophrenia in Montreal suggested that a position of "positive detachment" "at a distance" from the social world may be more adaptive than efforts to occupy more normative social roles. Becoming regular customers at such impersonal venues as shopping malls or MacDonald's, and relating primarily through shared interests such as short-wave radios or postal chess tournaments, may be necessary steps "toward renegotiation of an optimal link with others" (1992, p. 273).

Not all individuals with schizophrenia remain restricted to such relatively impersonal or distanced relationships, however, nor do they necessarily view these relationships as precursors to, or inferior to, verbally oriented relationships that would be considered more intimate by conventional standards. First-person accounts describe a range and variety of social interactions and relationships that approximate the full range and variety found in everyday life. Patients not only report that they experience the same basic needs as other people, such as needs for love, affection, and companionship, but also report some of the same pleasures, gratifications, and conflicts inherent to intimate, reciprocal relationships. Their descriptions suggest that caring comes in many forms, both for those with schizophrenia as well as for those without, and that the niche a person with schizophrenia may come to occupy can resemble, to varying degrees, those occupied by anyone else. Examples range from developing crushes from a distance (like a schoolboy for his teacher, or Dante for Beatrice, depending on how you view crushes) (Shove, 1994) and experimenting with promiscuous sex (Dolinsky, 1994), to sharing a candlelit dinner for two and being a spouse and parent (Kiley, 1994; Schraiber, 1994). The normal nature and tone of these relationships may be best captured in the words of a father writing about his experience of mental illness and the possibility of recovery. Referring to his relationship with his young son, he writes: "As for myself, I feel my prognosis is good whenever Joshua smiles or says, 'I love you, Daddy'" (Schraiber, 1994, p. 44).

Ways Others Help, and Ways They Hurt

While patients' own efforts are certainly essential to the development of relationships, such relationships are also made possible by virtue of the understanding, support, and efforts of caring others. Patients often identify the availability of supportive friends, family, and professionals to be an important factor in recovery, and specifically stress the need to feel that others are "there" for them, have faith in them, and care about them no matter what (Davidson & Strauss, 1992; Sullivan, 1994). Writes Leete: (1993): "It is clear to me now that a supportive, accepting, and loving relationship with others . . . has been the key element in my recovery" (p. 114). As another person describes, this is particularly valuable at low points in the course of the illness and recovery process, when "you need someone to believe in you 'cause you don't believe in yourself" (quoted in Hatfield & Lefley, 1993, p. 138). On a basic human level, the experience of giving and receiving love can act as both an impetus for, and a reward of, recovering. Deegan (1993) has gone so far as to suggest that it is this experience, more than any other, that makes recovery worthwhile. If others care about you, you also are more likely to care about yourself, to have more confidence and self-esteem, and thereby to have more resources to assist you in recovery. In addition, people describe how having someone to care about provides an important way to enhance their own self-esteem and inner resources through feeling useful to others. Describes one patient: "It [is] healing to get your mind off yourself and be able to love and help someone. It's really good therapy" (quoted in Sullivan, 1994, p. 23).

In addition to feeling cared about, what patients seem to need and value most in relationships are tolerance and acceptance of idiosyncracies and differences, understanding, compassion, clarity in communication and expectations, a focus on their strengths and competencies, and respect for them as individuals. In counteracting the sting of stigma, which discounts their experiences as "crazy" and dismisses them as "mental patients," patients also focus on the need to be and feel seen, heard, and validated for who they are in their entirety. Such experiences are not only valued in themselves as part and parcel of caring relationships, but are also often credited by patients with restorative powers. While mental health providers are at times included as some of the people who are capable of providing this kind of validation along with family members and friends, attitudes toward the mental health system as a whole are more complex. The role of psychotherapy provides a good example.

For some patients, psychotherapy, and in particular the relationship with their therapist, provided a crucial bridge back into the social world. As one patient describes: "My relationship with my therapist . . . was the first real relationship I had ever had; that is, the first I felt safe enough to invest myself in" (Anonymous, 1986, p. 69). Due perhaps to the safety of the therapeutic situation, and in some measure to the skill of the clinician, patients may find it possible to put their experiences into words and to feel understood and validated in therapy in ways that it would be hard to find elsewhere. This patient continues:

> I had drawn so far inside myself and so far away from the world, I had to be shown not only that the world was safe but also that I belonged to it, that I was in fact a person. This grew from years of our working together to develop mutual respect and acceptance and a forum of understanding, in which I believed that he had the capacity to comprehend what I said and that I had the potential to be understood. (Anonymous, 1986, p.70)

The fundamental affirmation that patients may find in such relationships can then serve as an example for them of the possibility of other relationships, with other people in the real world. Writes another patient: "The human connection I have developed with the therapist has helped me to reject the idea that I will never be able to relate to people or fit into society like a 'normal' person" (Anonymous, 1989, p. 345). This last comment highlights the dilemma patients may experience in psychotherapy, however; which is the need to experience as a fundamentally human connection a relationship that at least began on very different terms. What seems most essential to patients, particularly those accustomed to being treated as a nonperson, is that they be experienced as a *person* by another *person*. To the extent that they feel that they are being experienced as a *patient* by a *clinician,* the psychotherapeutic work, in paradoxical fashion, may not proceed. To be effective, then, the psychotherapeutic relationship must be able to transcend its own frame. A patient describes how essential this experience was in helping her to return to the world of human relationships:

> I often felt at odds with my therapist until I could see that he was a real person and he related to me and I to him, not only as patient and therapist, but as human beings. Eventually I began to feel that I too was a person, not just an outsider looking in on the

world. For a patient and therapist to work together so closely for so many years, they must establish a bond that is professional, certainly, but also based on the commonality of humanness that exists between two people. (Anonymous, 1986, pp. 69–70)

Outside of such individual, human relationships between two people, one of whom happened to be a mental health professional, most aspects of the mental health system are described by patients as posing additional obstacles to socialization. In addition to the presence of stigma within the mental health system itself, patients describe a variety of structural and attitudinal barriers they have encountered in mental health and social service programs that have discouraged rather than encouraged their relationships with others. Examples include entitlement regulations that provide disincentives for patients to live together, program policies that prohibit patients from dating or having sexual relations, and treatment models that consider the only commonalities between patients to be ones of deficit and disability (e.g., Schell, 1994). In her ethnographic study of patients in a PACT program, Estroff (1981) was struck by how the staff, even in a progressive, community setting, discouraged patients from confiding in or relying on each other, perhaps out of a belief (which the patients came to share) that patients could be of no real use to each other. An even more important finding of Estroff's seminal study, however, was the importance of the boundary that staff consistently maintained between themselves and patients in the program. In Estroff's terms, people were clearly divided up into the categories of "normals" and "crazies," with relationships between crazies and normals being asymmetrical. Patients came to believe that their only role in relation to normals was to be the recipients of services and care. There was no room within this framework for patients to have anything constructive or valuable to offer, for them to reciprocate within a relationship, or for them to be seen as an equal of the staff on any dimension of importance. Similar to a psychotherapeutic relationship in which the patient never transcends patient status to become another human being in the eyes of the clinician, patients in this program found it extremely difficult to be anything other than "crazy" in the eyes of the staff.

Such experiences are apparently not uncommon for patients in their interactions with the mental health system, however much they perpetuate the sense that patients have of being less or other than human. Patients thus often view mental health services as less than helpful in promoting social relationships and may feel that any relationships they do develop are in spite of, rather than due to, treatment. As one consumer advocate writes concerning her experiences of forming attachments with her peers within the confines of such dehumanizing settings, it is a sign of the resilience of the human spirit that she and others "will always find . . . friendships in friendless places" (Strimple-Padios, 1994, p. 19).

DISCUSSION

It just matters, being loved. (quoted in Sullivan, 1994)

We are now in a position to understand the dilemma posed by the life of Ms. Gibbs, which opened this chapter. The objective-descriptive perspective on the social functioning of people with schizophrenia reveals that a majority *do* tend to be isolative, to relate minimally to others, to have few friends outside of their families, and to be largely dependent on others—including mental health providers—with not much to offer in return. Family members also report losing their loved ones to the illness, with only lingering and occasional glimpses of the person they used to be, and with the vague sense that any relationship that will be possible with the person they have become will be different from what they had in the past. Both perspectives suggest that the person who existed prior to the illness has become largely inaccessible, and that what remains as a result of the disorder is for the most part an "empty shell." It may be somewhat surprising, then, to find that the patient's perspective provides such extensive and rich data on the experiences and struggles of the person who continues, despite and apart from the disorder, to desire and strive for connection. While patients describe becoming deadened and numbed through some of the sequelae of the disorder, they leave little doubt that the "shell" is in fact *not* empty. As in the image of Rilke's panther, their ability to act on their impulses, ideas, and desires may be compromised and, at times, completely immobilized by the disorder. Like clinicians and families, patients describe losing *themselves* to the disorder at times. But behind the bars of this cage, patients continue to wage hidden battles with the illness in order to regain their accessibility, first to themselves, and then to others. Like Ms. Gibbs, they often have more going on in their lives than the appearance of an empty shell would suggest, even if much of this takes place "behind the scenes."

A few examples drawn from our review may illustrate the need in cases such as these for integrating objective approaches that assess the observable characteristics of large numbers of people with subjective approaches that explore the inner lives of fewer people more intensively. All three perspectives concurred, for instance, that people with schizophrenia tend to be hyper-sensitive to stimulation, particularly to negative affect within interpersonal situations. A similar convergence of views can be found in regard to difficulties people with schizophrenia experience and exhibit in conversing with others. Patients agree with the clinical findings that suggest that they may get lost in the ambiguities and complexities of social situations, and they also describe how they become paralyzed in the face of overwhelming stimulation, needing to protect themselves from too much sensory input. Patient accounts shed useful light on the meaningful relationships that may exist between objectively identified factors that would otherwise remain separate and unrelated. First-person accounts help us to understand, for example, *how* hypersensitivity to stimulation can lead a person to withdraw and become isolative, or *how* having a thought disorder can make participating in conversations exceptionally difficult and humiliating. In these ways, objective and subjective approaches can confirm, complement, and enrich each other.

There are also examples in our findings, however, of how these perspectives may each be challenged and changed as a result of being brought into dialogue. These examples point out the limitations of each approach, and show how each requires the other for the development of a three-dimensional view that approximates patients' actual lives. A first example is provided by the role of stigma in limiting opportunities for relationships. Subjective accounts suggest that stigma is a primary source of rejection for people with schizophrenia, as well as a barrier to new relationships. If one were limited to subjective accounts alone, one might be led to conclude that the majority of people in the general community will reject patients once they discover their psychiatric history, and that patients are helpless victims of a social process to which they themselves make no contribution. But such conclusions lie outside the purview of subjective approaches. Just as objective approaches have little ability to tap the subjective domain, subjective approaches have little ability to identify causal relationships between events or to suggest explanations for the data they generate (Davidson, 1994). In the case of stigma, objective investigations have suggested that social rejection due to stigma is much less common than might be expected from these subjective accounts, and that it is internalized stigma, operating through the person's own self image, expectations, and projections, that most directly affects social behavior (Clausen, 1981; Kirk, 1974; Lally, 1989). In addition, the objective findings reviewed above suggest that people with schizophrenia are not good judges of their own presentation and its effect on social interactions. They may be unaware of some of the ways in which they alienate others through their lack of adherence to social norms concerning personal appearance and appropriate behavior in social situations. Such findings caution us not to take subjective data for more than they are; that is, accounts of how individuals experience and give meaning to their lives. While highly valuable in their own right, they should not be mistaken for complete accounts that can substitute for, or eliminate the need for, etiologic and causal explanations (Davidson, 1994).

An example of the limitations of the objective approach is provided by the picture it has painted of people with schizophrenia as "empty shells" who "cannot think, feel, or act," and have "lost the capacity both to suffer and to hope" (Andreasen, 1984, pp. 62–63). It should be obvious from the subjective data that even those people who are most likely to appear as "empty shells" in relation to others (i.e., those with prominent negative symptoms) still often retain a capacity to feel and think, and do in fact continue to suffer, at times to considerable depths of pain and anguish. From a third-person point of view, it is understandable how patients' inner struggles may remain invisible and how clinical investigators may be led to conclude, as Andreasen has, that the emptiness in patients' presentations "probably reflects an emptiness in their minds" (1984, p. 62). But the assumption that the person inside the patient has been taken over completely by the disorder oversteps the boundaries of the objective-descriptive approach. To the extent that the objective-descriptive approach documents that patients often appear *as if* they have been taken over by the disorder, it remains within its own paradigm. To the extent that this approach concludes on that basis that the person *is* no longer there, however, it purports to have access to, and credibility regarding, aspects of the subjective domain. We have seen in the subjective data reviewed above both how destructive to treatment as well as how inaccurate such an assumption is. One could respond that the patients who truly have "empty minds" have not been the ones to provide first-person accounts. But Deegan provides the following persuasive account of how giving up is experienced inside the person; it is hard to imagine that this does not cover those cases as well:

"The professionals called it apathy and lack of motivation. They blamed it on our illness. But they don't understand that giving up is a highly motivated and highly goal-directed behavior. For us giving up was a way of surviving. Giving up, refusing to hope, not trying, not caring: all of these were ways of trying to protect the last fragile traces of our spirit and our selfhood from undergoing another crushing. (Deegan, 1994, p. 19)

The difference between this account of giving up as a goal-directed strategy for surviving and Andreasen's description of "empty minds" provides another illustration of the problems that arise when one perspective is left to fill in data that should be provided by the other perspective. Had patients or family members been asked about what lies behind the appearance of emptiness associated with negative symptoms, they might have been able to prevent the kind of misunderstanding that Deegan describes. The same is also true in terms of the contributions that objective approaches make to conclusions regarding the role of stigma and other factors in leading to the social rejection of people with schizophrenia. An implication to be drawn from this review is that phenomena with multiple dimensions and multiple causes require multiple methods of inquiry to be understood in their complexity (Davidson, 1988, 1993; Estroff, 1994; Strauss, 1989; Strauss, Rakfeldt, Harding, & Lieberman, 1989).

Another implication to be drawn from this exercise concerns which perspective, if any, should be at the center of models for treatment and rehabilitation. All three perspectives concur that the person who lived prior to the onset of schizophrenia becomes inaccessible at times due to the impact of the disorder. The perspectives disagree, however, about how much of the person becomes inaccessible, for how much of the time, and the significance to be attributed to this loss. From the clinical perspective, this loss is seen primarily as a symptom of the disorder, and perhaps as a marker of treatment failure. From the perspective of family members, it is viewed as a tragedy for both the family and the patient, with the only hope for improvement often contained in a wish for the return of who the person was before the onset of the disorder. From the perspective of the patient, experiences of becoming inaccessible to one's self are viewed as temporary defeats by the illness. Both the illness and the ways in which it robs the person of his/her self are considered some of things the person is up against in life; things that s/he will have to learn to manage and overcome in order to have as full and satisfying a life as possible. To be most effective in supporting patients' efforts toward recovery, it seems advisable to place the patients' perspective and experience at the center of conceptualizations of treatment and rehabilitation. Clinicians and family members can be encouraged to join with the person remaining behind the clouds and chaos of the disorder, and to support his/her efforts to deal with the situation constructively, rather than to identify the person with the illness. As Deegan argued, identifying the person with the disorder leaves no one to take up a stand toward the disorder; no one to take up the work of recovery. In a similar fashion, conceptualizations of treatment that are rooted in the "empty shell" perspective of the objective paradigm will not be very effective in reaching and connecting with the person struggling with the disorder, but may lead instead to an abandonment of the patient and a further worsening of his/her condition (Corin & Lauzon, 1992; Estroff, 1989). It is thus essential that professionals and significant others not be misled by the "empty shell" appearance of some patients to adopt a pessimistic or dismissive attitude toward them and their prospects for recovery. While at times difficult to muster, acceptance and encouragement can be crucial in counteracting the devastation and demoralization patients already experience. As one consumer advocate suggests: "There is already enough negativity provided by the illness itself" (Orrin, 1994, p. 42).

REFERENCES

Akhtar, S., & Thomson, J. (1980a). Schizophrenia and sexuality, I: A review and a report of twelve unusual cases. *Journal of Clinical Psychiatry, 41,* 134–142.

Akhtar, S., & Thomson, J. (1980b). Schizophrenia and sexuality, II: A review and a report of twelve unusual cases. *Journal of Clinical Psychiatry, 41,* 166–174.

Ames, D. (1994). Anti-psychotic medication and sexual difficulties. *Journal of the California Alliance for the Mentally Ill, 5,* 66–69.

American Psychiatric Association. (1990). *Diagnostic and statistical manual of mental disorders, 3rd ed.*. Washington, DC: Author.

American Psychiatric Association. (1994). *Diagnostic and statistical manual of mental disorders, 4th ed.* Washington, DC: Author.

Andreasen, N. C. (1984). *The broken brain: The biological revolution in psychiatry.* New York: Harper & Row.

Andreasen, N. C. (1991). Reply to Phenomenology or physicalism? *Schizophrenia Bulletin, 17,* 187–189.

Anonymous. (1986). "Can we talk?": The schizophrenic patient in psychotherapy. *American Journal of Psychiatry, 143,* 68–70.

Anonymous. (1989). A delicate balance. *Schizophrenia Bulletin, 15,* 345–346.

Beiser, M., Waxler-Morrison, N., Iacono, W. G., Lin, T.-Y., Felming, J. A. E., & Husted, J. (1987). A measure of the "sick" label in psychiatric disorder and physical illness. *Social Science and Medicine, 25,* 251–261.

Bouricius, J. K. (1989). Negative symptoms and emotions in schizophrenia. *Schizophrenia Bulletin, 15,* 201–208.

Breier, A., Schreiber, J. L., Dyer, J., & Pickar, D. (1991). National institute of mental health longitudinal study of chronic schizophrenia. *Archives of General Psychiatry, 48,* 239–246.

Brodoff, A. S. (1988). Schizophrenia through a sister's eyes: The burden of invisible baggage. *Schizophrenia Bulletin, 14,* 113–116.

Campbell, J. (Ed.) (1989). *People say I'm crazy: An anthology of art, poetry, prose, photography and testimony by mental health clients throughout California.* Sacramento: California Department of Mental Health.

Carini, M. A., & Nevid, J. S. (1992). Social appropriateness and impaired perspective in schizophrenia. *Journal of Clinical Psychology, 48,* 170–177.

Chapman, J. (1966). The early symptoms of schizophrenia. *British Journal of Psychiatry, 112,* 225–251.

Clausen, J. (1981). Stigma and mental disorders: Phenomena and terminology. *Psychiatry, 44,* 287–296.

Cohen, C. I., & Kochanowicz, N. (1989). Schizophrenia and social network patterns: A survey of black inner-city outpatients. *Community Mental Health Journal, 25,* 197–207.

Cohen, C. I., & Sokolovsky, J. (1989). Schizophrenia and social networks: Ex-patients in the inner city. *Schizophrenia Bulletin, 4,* 546–560.

Colussy, S. A., & Zuroff, D. C. (1985). Schizophrenic and depressed inpatients' perceptions of congruent and incongruent communications. *Journal of Clinical Psychology, 1,* 331–337.

Corin, E., & Lauzon, G. (1992). Positive withdrawal and the quest for meaning: The reconstruction of experience among schizophrenics. *Psychiatry, 55,* 266–278.

Corin, E., & Lauzon, G. (1994). From symptoms to phenomena: The articulation of experience in schizophrenia. *Journal of Phenomenological Psychology, 25,* 3–50.

Corrigan, P. W., & Green, M. F. (1993). Schizophrenic patients' sensitivity to social cues: The role of abstraction. *American Journal of Psychiatry, 150,* 589–594.

Davidson, L. (1988). Psychologism in psychology: The case of schizophrenia. *Practice, 6,* 2–20.

Davidson, L. (1993). Story telling and schizophrenia: Using narrative structure in phenomenological research. *The Humanistic Psychologist, 21,* 200–220.

Davidson, L. (1994). Phenomenological research in schizophrenia: From philosophical anthropology to empirical science. *Journal of Phenomenological Psychology, 25,* 104–130.

Davidson, L. (in press). Intentionality and identity in schizophrenia: A phenomenological perspective. *Duquesne Studies in Phenomenological Psychology, 5.*

Davidson, L., & Cosgrove, L. (1991). Psychologism and phenomenological psychology revisited, Part I: The liberation from naturalism. *Journal of Phenomenological Psychology, 22,* 87–108.

Davidson, L., Hoge, M. A., Godleski, L., Rakfeldt, J., & Griffith, E. E. H. (1996). Hospital or community living? Examining consumer perspectives on deinstitutionalization. *Psychiatric Rehabilitation Journal, 19,* 49–58.

Davidson, L., Hoge, M. A., Merrill, M. E., Rakfeldt, J., & Griffith, E. E. H. (1995) The experiences of long-stay inpatients returning to the community. *Psychiatry, 58,* 122–132.

Davidson, L., & Strauss, J. S. (1992). Sense of self in recovery from severe mental illness. *British Journal of Medical Psychology, 65,* 131–145.

Davidson, L., & Strauss, J. S. (1995). Beyond the biopsychosocial model: Integrating disorder, health and recovery. *Psychiatry, 58,* 43–55.

Deegan, P. E. (1993). Recovering our sense of value after being labeled mentally ill. *Journal of Psychosocial Nursing, 31,* 7–11.

Deegan, P. E. (1994). "A letter to my friend who is giving up." *Journal of the California Alliance for the Mentally Ill, 5,* 18–20.

Docherty, N. M., Evans, I. M., Sledge, W. H., Seibyl, J. P., & Krystal, J. H. (1994). Affective reactivity of language in schizophrenia. *Journal of Nervous and Mental Disease, 182,* 98–102.

Dolinsky, P. (1994). Women come on to me. *Journal of the California Alliance for the Mentally Ill, 5,* 52.

Dunn, M., O'Driscoll, C., Dayson, D., Wills, W., & Leff, J. (1990). The TAPS project. 4: An observational study of the social life of long-stay patients. *British Journal of Psychiatry, 157,* 842–848.

Estroff, S. E. (1981). *Making it crazy: An ethnography of psychiatric clients in an American community.* Los Angeles: University of California Press.

Estroff, S. E. (1989). Self, identity, and subjective experiences of schizophrenia: In search of the subject. *Schizophrenia Bulletin, 15,* 189–196.

Estroff, S. E. (1994). Keeping things complicated: Undiscovered countries and the lives of persons with serious mental illness. *The Journal of the California Alliance for the Mentally Ill, 5,* 40–46.

Freedman, B. J. (1974). The subjective experience of perceptual and cognitive disturbances in schizophrenia: A review of autobiographical accounts. *Archives of General Psychiatry, 30,* 333–340.

Gilliland, G. W., & Sommer, R. (1960). A sociometric study of admission wards in a mental hospital. *Psychiatry, 24,* 367–372.

Giorgi, A. (1970). *Psychology as a human science: A phenomenologically based approach.* New York: Harper & Row.

Giorgi, A. (1988). Validity and reliability from a phenomenological perspective. In W. J. Baker, L. P. Mos, H. V. Rappard, &

H. J. Stamm (Eds.), *Recent trends in theoretical psychology.* (pp.167–176). New York: Springer-Verlag.

Goering, P., Durbin, J., Foster, R., Boyles, S., Babiak, T., & Lancee, B. (1992). Social networks of residents in supportive housing. *Community Mental Health Journal, 28,* 199–214.

Hamilton, N. G., Ponzoha, C. A., Cutler, D. L., & Weigel, R. M. (1989). Social networks and negative versus positive symptoms of schizophrenia. *Schizophrenia Bulletin, 15,* 625–633.

Hammer, M., Makiesky-Barrow, S., & Gutwirth, L. (1978). Social networks and schizophrenia. *Schizophrenia Bulletin, 4,* 522–545.

Hatfield, A. B., & Lefley, H. P. (1993). *Surviving mental illness: Stress, coping and adaptation.* New York: Guilford.

Hirschberg, W. (1985). Social isolation among schizophrenic outpatients. *Social Psychiatry, 20,* 171–178.

Holmes-Eber, P., & Riger, S. (1990). Hospitalization and the composition of mental patients' social networks. *Schizophrenia Bulletin, 16,* 157–164.

Husserl, E. (1970). *The crisis of European sciences and transcendental phenomenology* (D. Carr, Trans.). Evanston, IL: Northwestern University Press. (Original work published 1954)

Husserl, E. (1983). *Ideas pertaining to a pure phenomenology and to a phenomenological philosophy, First book: General introduction to a pure phenomenology* (F. Kersten, Trans.). The Hague: Martinus Nijhoff. (Original work published 1913)

Husserl, E. (1989). *Ideas pertaining to a pure phenomenology and to a phenomenological philosophy, Second book: Studies in the phenomenology of constitution* (R. Rojcewicz & A. Schuwer, Trans.). Boston: Kluwer Academic Publishers. (Original work published 1952)

Jaspers, K. (1963). *General psychopathology* (J. Hoenig & M. W. Hamilton, Trans.). Chicago: University of Chicago Press. (Original work published 1913)

Jaspers, K. (1968). The phenomenological approach in psychopathology. *British Journal of Psychiatry, 114,* 1313–1323. (Original work published 1912)

Karlsson, G. (1993). *Psychological qualitative research from a phenomenological perspective.* Göteborg, Sweden: Graphic Systems AB.

Kiley, N. (1994). It has taken a long time. *Journal of the California Alliance for the Mentally Ill, 5,* 40.

Kirk, S. A. (1974). The impact of labeling on rejection of the mentally ill: An experimental study. *Journal of Health and Social Behavior, 15,* 108–117.

Kvale, S. (1989). *Issues of validity in qualitative research.* Sweden: Chartwell Bratt.

Laing, R. D. (1960). *The divided self.* Great Britain: Tavistock Publications.

Laing, R. D. (1961). *Self and others.* Great Britain: Tavistock Publications.

Lally, S. J. (1989). Does being in here mean there is something wrong with me? *Schizophrenia Bulletin, 15,* 253–265.

Leete, E. (1987). The treatment of schizophrenia: A patient's perspective. *Hospital and Community Psychiatry, 38,* 486–491.

Leete, E. (1989). How I perceive and manage my illness. *Schizophrenia Bulletin, 15,* 197–200.

Leete, E. (1993). The interpersonal environment—A consumer's personal recollection. In A. B. Hatfield & H. P. Lefley (Eds.), *Surviving mental illness: Stress, coping and adaptation.* (pp. 114–128). New York: Guilford.

Leff, J., O'Driscoll, C., Dayson, D., Wills, W., & Anderson, J. (1990). The TAPS project. 5: The structure of social-network data obtained from long-stay patients. *British Journal of Psychiatry, 157,* 848–852.

Lindstrom, L. H. (1994). Long-term clinical and social outcome studies in schizophrenia in relation to the cognitive and emotional side effects of antipsychotic drugs. *Acta Psychiatrica Scandinavica, 89,* 74–76.

Livesay, J. R. (1984). Cognitive complexity-simplicity and inconsistent interpersonal judgment in thought-disordered schizophrenia. *Psychological Reports, 54,* 759–768.

Lovell, A. M. (1992). Seizing the moment: Power, contingency, and temporality in street life. In H. J. Rutz (Ed.), *The politics of time.* (pp. 86–107). American Anthropological Society Monograph Series No. 4. Washington, DC: American Anthropological Association.

Lyketsos, G. C., Sakka, P., & Mailis, A. (1983). The sexual adjustment of chronic schizophrenics: A preliminary study. *British Journal of Psychiatry, 143,* 376–382.

Lysaker, P., Bell, M., Milstein, R., Bryson, G., Shestopal, A., & Goulet, J. B. (1993). Work capacity in schizophrenia. *Hospital and Community Psychiatry, 4,* 278–280.

McGhie, A., & Chapman, J. (1961). Disorders of attention and perception in early schizophrenia. *British Journal of Medical Psychology, 34,* 103–116.

Mandal, M. K., & Palchoudhury, S. (1985). Decoding of facial affect in schizophrenia. *Psychological Reports, 56,* 651–652.

Miller, S. G. (1994). Borderline personality disorder from the patient s perspective. *Hospital and Community Psychiatry, 45,* 1215–1219.

Monti, P. M., & Fingeret, A. L. (1987). Social perception and communication skills among schizophrenics and nonschizophrenics. *Journal of Clinical Psychology, 43,* 197–205.

Moorman, M. (1988, September 11). A sister's need. *New York Times Magazine,* pp. 44 ff.

Morrison, R. L., Bellack, A. S., & Bashore, T. R. (1988). Perception of emotion among schizophrenic patients. *Journal of Psychopathology and Behavioral Assessment, 10,* 319–332.

Morrison, R. L., Bellack, A. S., Wixted, J. T., & Mueser, K. T. (1990). Positive and negative symptoms in schizophrenia: A cluster-analytic approach. *Journal of Nervous and Mental Disease, 178,* 377–384.

Mueser, K. T., Bellack, A. S., Wade, J. H., Sayers, S. L., Tierney, A., & Haas, G. (1993). Expressed emotion, social skill, and response to negative affect in schizophrenia. *Journal of Abnormal Psychology, 102,* 339–351.

Najarian, S. P. (1995). (1995). Family experience with positive client response to Clozapine. *Archives of Psychiatry Nursing, 9,* 11–21.

North, C. (1987). *Welcome silence: My triumph over schizophrenia.* New York: Simon & Schuster.

Orrin, D. (1994). Past the struggles of mental illness, toward the development of quality lives. *Innovations and Research, 3,* 41–45.

Pogue-Geile, M. F., & Harrow, M. (1984). Negative and positive symptoms in schizophrenia and depression: A followup. *Schizophrenia Bulletin, 10,* 371–387.

Rilke, R. M. (1938). *Translations from the poetry of Rainer Maria Rilke* (M. D. Herter Norton, Trans.). New York: W.W. Norton. (Original work published 1907)

Rosen, A. J., Tureff, S. E., Daruna, J. H., Johnson, P. B., Lyons, J. S., & Davis, J. M. (1980). Pharmacotherapy of schizophrenia and affective disorders: Behavioral correlates of diagnostic and demographic variables. *Journal of Abnormal Psychology, 89,* 378–389.

Rosenberg, S. D. & Tucker, G. J. (1979). Verbal behavior and schizophrenia: The semantic dimension. *Archives of General Psychiatry, 36,* 1331–1337.

Ruocchio, P. J. (1991). The schizophrenic inside. *Schizophrenia Bulletin, 17,* 357–359.

Ruocllio, P. J. (1987). Perils of social development for the schizophrenic patient. *Hospital and Community Psychiatry, 38,* 1223–1224.

Schell, B. H. (1994). The unmentionable. *Journal of the California Alliance for the Mentally Ill, 5,* 58–60.

Schooler, C., & Spohn H. E. (1960). Social interaction on a ward of chronic schizophrenics. *International Journal of Social Psychiatry, 6,* 115–119.

Schraiber, R. (1994). The 'C' word. *Journal of the California Alliance for the Mentally Ill, 5,* 44.

Seckinger, S. S. (1994). Relationships: Is 1–900 all there is? *Journal of the California Alliance for the Mentally Ill, 5,* 19–20.

Seeman, M. V., & Cole, H. J. (1977). The effect of increasing personal contact in schizophrenia. *Comprehensive Psychiatry, 18,* 283–293.

Sherman, W. (as told to Les Campbell) (1994). Never alone . . . *Journal of the California Alliance for the Mentally Ill, 5,* 42–43.

Shove, P. (1994). The lovers: Literature and my mental illness. *Journal of the California Alliance for the Mentally Ill, 5,* 46–47.

Smith, E. (1991). Living with schizophrenia. *Schizophrenia Bulletin, 17,* 689–691.

Sommer, R., & Osmond, H. (1983). A bibliography of mental patients autobiographies, 1960–1982. *American Journal of Psychiatry, 140,* 1051–1054.

Strauss, J. S. (1989). Subjective experiences of schizophrenia: Toward a new dynamic psychiatry II. *Schizophrenia Bulletin, 15,* 179–187.

Strauss, J. S. (1994). Is biological psychiatry building on an adequate base? Clinical realities and underlying processes in schizophrenic disorders. In N. Andreasen (Ed.), *Schizophrenia: From mind to molecule.* (pp. 31–44). Washington, DC: American Psychiatric Association.

Strauss, J. S., Rakfeldt, J., Harding, C. M., & Lieberman, P. (1989). Psychological and social aspects of negative symptoms. *British Journal of Psychiatry, 155,* 128–132.

Strimple-Padios, L. (1994). Friendships in friendless places in spite of madness. *The Journal of the California Alliance for the Mentally Ill, 5,* 18–19.

Sullivan, W. P. (1994). A long and winding road: The process of recovery. *Innovations and Research, 3,* 19–27.

Sylph, J. A., Ross, H. E., & Kedwarth, H. B. (1977). Social disability in chronic psychiatric patients. *American Journal of Psychiatry, 134,* 1391–1394.

Tolsdorf, C. C. (1976). Social networks, support, and coping: An exploratory study. *Family Process, 15,* 407–417.

Torrey, E. F. (1983). *Surviving schizophrenia: A family manual.* New York: Harper & Row.

Van den Berg, J. (1982). The schizophrenic patient: Anthropological considerations. In A. J. J. de Koning & F. A. Jenner (Eds.), *Phenomenology and psychiatry.* (pp. 155–164). London: Academic Press

Van der Does, A. J. W., Dingemans, P. M. A. J., Linszen, D. H., Nugter, M. A., & Scholte, W. F. (1993). Symptom dimensions and cognitive and social functioning in recent-onset schizophrenia. *Psychological Medicine, 23,* 745–753.

Van Putten, T., & Marder, S. R. (1987). Behavioral toxicity of antipsychotic drugs. *Journal of Clinical Psychiatry, 48,* 13–19.

Villamil, E. (1994). A young man s garden. *Journal of the California Alliance for the Mentally Ill, 5,* 56–57.

Wallace, C. J. (1984). Community and interpersonal functioning in the course of schizophrenic disorders. *Schizophrenia Bulletin, 10,* 233–257.

Weingarten, R. (1989). How I've managed chronic mental illness. *Schizophrenia Bulletin, 15,* 635–640.

Weingarten, R. (1994). The ongoing processes of recovery. *Psychiatry, 57,* 369–375.

Weisburd, D. E. (1994). Publisher's note. *Journal of the California Alliance for the Mentally Ill 5,* 1–2.

Wertz, F. J. (1983). From everyday to psychological description: Analyzing the moments of a qualitative data analysis. *Journal of Phenomenological Psychology, 14,* 197–241.

Wertz, F. J. (1986). The question of the reliability of psychological research. *Journal of Phenomenological Psychology, 17,* 181–205.

CHAPTER 8

DEVELOPMENTAL ORIGINS OF INTERPERSONAL DEFICITS IN SCHIZOPHRENIA

Craig S. Neumann
Elaine F. Walker

Impairment in social functioning is not only a defining feature of schizophrenia, but also a major impediment to rehabilitation. Social ambivalence and deficits in affective communication and cognitive functioning impede social interaction and make it difficult for patients to gain acceptance in familial and occupational settings (Bellack, Sayers, Mueser, & Bennett, 1994; Bowen et al., 1994; Brugha, Wing, Brewin, MacCarthy, & Lesage, 1993; Dworkin, 1992; Honeycutt & Belcher, 1991). The result is often social rejection. In addition, patients frequently manifest an aversion to social interaction that results in withdrawal from interpersonal contexts. Thus, many patients function in a social vacuum, with little or no support network and a failure to establish marital and family units (Sorensen, 1994; Thornicroft & Breakey, 1991; Thusholt, Jensen, Knop, Naylor, & Sogaard, 1993).

A central question concerns the origins of social impairment in schizophrenia. Is it a feature of the clinical disorder, such that deficits in interpersonal functioning emerge in conjunction with the positive psychotic symptoms of the illness? Alternatively, is social impairment a feature of vulnerability that predates the manifestation of the clinical syndrome labeled schizophrenia? For instance, long-standing interpersonal deficits, such as social withdrawal, might precede the interpersonal abnormalities observed in schizophrenia. In the present chapter, we explore the relative merits of these alternative conceptualizations by examining social behavior during the premorbid period in the life course of schizophrenia patients.

Based on our findings, and those of other investigators, we propose that impairment in social functioning is present in many patients long before the onset of clinical symptoms of psychiatric disorder. More specifically, we suggest that abnormalities in social expression, comprehension, and behavior characterize some patients in childhood, at times as early as infancy. Further, these deficits are a reflection of an underlying biological vulnerability that is expressed in the form of psychotic symptoms later in life, after central nervous system maturation activates the brain systems that subserve positive psychotic symptoms.

CHILDHOOD PRECURSORS
OF SCHIZOPHRENIA

Initially, research on the childhood precursors of schizophrenia drew on retrospective reports from parents and teachers. The findings indicated that social isolation characterized some, but not all, patients by middle childhood (for a review of this early work, see Offord and Cross, 1969). In addition, there was evidence of disruptive, aggressive behavior in some preschizophrenic children. Concerns about the reliability of retrospective reports led to a series of follow-back studies that used archival data sources, such as school and medical records. Again, the results suggested that both social isolation and behavioral disinhibition were present in preschizophrenic children, with some showing both types of adjustment problems simultaneously (Watt & Lubensky, 1976; Watt, 1978). However, these follow-back studies were limited with respect to the developmental periods they examined—data on preschool adjustment were not available.

The advent of prospective research on the biological offspring of schizophrenic parents provided the opportunity to study early childhood development in subjects at high risk for schizophrenia. Prospective high-risk research was aimed at identifying risk indicators in the 10 to 15% of schizophrenics' offspring who were expected to develop the illness themselves. The findings from studies of very young high-risk children indicated that behavioral abnormalities might extend back as far as infancy (Fish et al., 1992; Goodman, 1991; Hans & Marcus, 1991; Parnas et al., 1982; Sameroff, Seifer, Zax, & Barocas, 1987). However, only two of these studies with data on infancy also have information on adult psychiatric outcome. Fish et al. (1992) directly assessed a group of 12 high-risk infants and found that those with schizophrenia-spectrum outcomes showed greater abnormalities in neuromotor development. The Danish high-risk study (Parnas et al., 1982) was initiated when the subjects were, on average, in late childhood. Retrospective reports on early childhood behavior were obtained from parents, and those subjects with schizophrenic outcomes were described as more passive and less attentive infants. These results confirm the presence of behavioral abnormalities in preschizophrenic infants, including abnormalities in motor development, and they have important implications for our assumptions about etiology. First, consistent with the evidence from genetic research (Gottesman, 1991), they indicate that vulnerability is congenital in nature, for at least some patients. Second, they indicate that the premorbid deficits associated with schizophrenia are generalized to multiple domains.

The tremendous contributions of prospective high-risk research are well recognized; nonetheless, these studies have not provided systematic data on the socioemotional aspects of early child development. This is largely because most prospective high-risk studies were initiated when the subjects were in middle or late childhood. Of those that have directly assessed and followed subjects from infancy, only one has obtained follow-up data on psychiatric outcome (Fish, Marcus, Hans, Auerbach, & Perdue, 1992). However, the primary focus of the Fish study was early perceptual-motor development.

The Emory Study

In an effort to obtain a more detailed understanding of early development, we initiated an archival study of precursors that used childhood home movies of adult-onset patients as one source of information. The project was undertaken in 1989 and is ongoing. In the following, we describe the findings, to date, that bear on the issue of premorbid social behavior.

In a preliminary study aimed at determining the feasibility of our method, we asked a group of mental health experts, both psychiatrists and behavioral scientists, to view the childhood films of four sibships, each of which contained one preschizophrenic child (Walker & Lewine, 1990). The viewers were, of course, blind to the psychiatric outcome of the subjects. They were informed that one child in each sibship subsequently developed schizophrenia, and they were asked to offer their best judgment of which child this was. Viewers were also asked to record the behaviors they observed that influenced their judgments. The viewers predictions were significantly better than chance, indicating that they were able to detect behavioral indicators of vulnerability. Moreover, their predictions exceeded chance levels based only on observations within the first 8 years of the subjects' lives. Examination of the viewers aggregated comments revealed that their judgments were influenced by their perceptions of emotional nonresponsivity and motoric delays in the preschizophrenic children.

Following this feasibility study, we recruited a larger sample of subjects in order to obtain more systematic data. To date, we have used childhood films to study emotional expressions, neuromotor development, and activity level in preschizophrenic children and control subjects (Walker, Savoie , & Davis 1994; Walker, Grimes, Davis,

& Smith, 1993). In addition, we have obtained extensive developmental data, including comprehensive parental reports of childhood behavior (e.g., Baum & Walker, 1995; Neumann, Grimes, Walker, & Baum, 1995).

The methodological aspects of our study are described in detail elsewhere (Walker et al., 1993; Walker et al., 1994). For present purposes, the design of the study will be briefly described, followed by a review of some published findings. Then the results of recent analyses aimed at exploring the relations between premorbid emotional expressions and behavior problems will be presented. We also present some findings on the etiologic determinants of premorbid deficits in schizophrenia.

The Precursors Study

The subjects of the study are 32 young-adult-onset schizophrenia patients (7 females, 25 males). Their mean age at study entry was 33 years, with illnesses varying in length from 1 year to 20 years. As a group, the sample is typical of schizophrenia patients. None were diagnosed with a clinical disorder in childhood. All met DSM-III criteria for schizophrenia and have had at least one hospitalization. All are unmarried and dependent, at least in part, on parental support or public assistance. The main requirement for participation in the project was that childhood home movies of the patient be available for study. For 23 of the schizophrenia patients, films were made during the first 2 years of life, thus permitting the analysis of infant behavior.

For each patient, the nearest-in-age, healthy sibling was selected to serve as a comparison subject. Thus, the primary control group was comprised of individuals who came from the same familial contexts as the patients and who appeared in the same home movies. The preschizophrenic subjects and their healthy sibling controls are the focus of the studies reported here. Subsequently, three other comparison groups were added; a psychiatric comparison group of patients with major affective disorders (bipolar disorder and major depression), the nearest-in-age, healthy siblings of the affective patients, and a normal comparison group of subjects from families with no mental illness in first-degree relatives.

Participating family members provided all available home movies of the patient and siblings made from birth through 15 years of age. Films were then transferred in chronological order onto standard VHS videotapes, and a digital display of elapsed time was inscribed on the tapes in tenths of a second. At each age level, there were in-

stances of missing data (i.e., no film) for some subjects, so that the number of subjects varies by age. The average duration of total footage on subjects was 80 minutes (SD = 73.37). A preliminary study found no evidence of diagnostic group differences in the amount of footage of schizophrenic patients and their siblings or in the nature of the interpersonal contexts and events in which they appeared (Litter & Walker, 1993).

The Emotional Expressions of Preschizophrenic Children

Coding of facial expressions from the films was conducted using the Affect Expressions by Holistic Judgments (AFFEX) facial coding scheme (Izard, Dougherty, & Hembree, 1983). Coders were trained to reliability in the application of AFFEX and were blind to the psychiatric outcome of the subjects. Proportional scores were derived for positive ("joy") and negative emotion at four age periods; birth to 4 years, 4 to 8 years, 8 to 12 years and 12 to 16 years. To derive the emotion score, the total duration of the positive or negative emotion expressed during the age period was divided by the total duration of coded facial expressions for that period. (For further details on the emotion coding and findings, see Walker et al., 1993.)

Analyses of the facial expression data indicated that the preschizophrenic patients tended to show less joy and more negative expressions compared with their healthy siblings. However, the pattern of diagnostic group differences varied as a function of sex. When preschizophrenic females were compared with same-sex controls, there was a reduction in facial expressions of joy that was apparent as early as infancy and extended through adolescence. In contrast, the preschizophrenic males only showed a reduction in joy expressions during the first 4 months of life. For negative emotion, diagnostic group differences were consistent across sex. The preschizophrenic subjects of both sexes showed significantly more negative facial expressions than their same-sex siblings. (The positive and negative symptom ratings were only modestly negatively intercorrelated, so they do not represent the inverse of each other. Virtually all expressions that were not coded as positive or negative were classified in "interest" and "neutral" emotion categories.)

Some contemporary theorists view early emotional expressions as one manifestation of constitutionally based temperament (Goldsmith & Campos, 1986; Rothbart, 1994). This is based, in part, on the findings from studies of infant monozygotic and dizygotic twins (Cherny, Fulker, Corley, Plomin, & DeFries, 1994; Petrill & Thompson, 1993; Saudino & Eaton, 1991). Within this framework, our findings might be interpreted to indicate that preschizophrenic infants are predisposed to be more dysphoric and irritable.

Further, early emotional expressions are presumed to be more direct manifestations of internal state in contrast to later childhood and adult expressions, which are subject to greater influence by cognitive factors and conscience modulation (Lazarus, 1994; Rothbart, 1994). Thus, there is reason to believe that the processes determining the valence of the facial expressions displayed in social settings vary as a function of developmental level. In infancy and early childhood, biologically based irritability and consolability play primary roles in determining negative affect. In later childhood and adolescence, negative cognitions or deficits in social knowledge about display rules will be the primary determinants of negative affective displays.

Behavioral Problems of Preschizophrenic Children

In addition to the home movies, we also obtained data on childhood behavioral problems (Baum & Walker, 1995; Neumann et al., 1995; Neumann & Walker, 1995). We used a behavioral rating scale, which consisted of 104 items from the Child Behavior Checklist (CBCL; Achenbach, 1991). For our research, the CBCL questions were modified so that they were phrased in retrospective terms. Parents rated each of their children for four age periods: birth to 4 years, 4 to 8 years, 8 to 12 years, and 12 to 16 years. (Note: The elderly parents of three subjects were unable to complete the questionnaire because of debilitating illnesses.) The questionnaire items were combined to yield scores for the following behavior problem dimensions: Withdrawn, Anxious/Depressed, Social Problems, Thought Problems, Attention Problems, Delinquency, and Aggression. These dimensions are based on the factor analysis of population data obtained by the developers of the CBCL. Two of these behavior factors, Withdrawn and Social Problems, are particularly relevant to the subject's interpersonal capacities. The Withdrawn scale includes items such as "would rather be alone," "won't talk," and "shy." The Social Problems scale includes "doesn't get along with peers," "teased," "not liked by peers," and "prefers playing with younger children."

The findings suggested the following conclusions. First, the patients showed a broad range of childhood behavioral problems when compared with their healthy siblings. That is, both internalizing (i.e., Withdrawn, Social Problems, Anxious/Depressed) and externalizing (i.e., Aggression) behavior problems were significantly greater for the preschizophrenia subjects. The preschizophrenia subjects also showed more cognitive problems (i.e., Attention and Thought Problems).

Second, the problems manifested by the preschizophrenia subjects varied in their developmental course, with some types of problems showing a gradual but consistent increase across childhood and others showing more abrupt increases in adolescence. Specifically, at a very early age (birth to 4 years), the Attention Problems dimension significantly distinguished the patients from the siblings, and the patients continued to display a higher rate of Attention Problems for the remaining age periods. Group differences in problems with mood (Anxiety/Depression) and thought (Thought Problems) and social behavior (Social Problems) emerged in the 4-to-8-year age period. Withdrawn and Aggressive behavior became significantly greater among the patients during preadolescence—ages 8 to 12 years. There were no significant diagnostic group differences on the Delinquency factor at any age period.

These results suggest that, among the preschizophrenia children, early attentional problems were followed by abnormalities in mood, thought, and social behavior in the 4-to-8-year period, then later, in preadolescence, by behavioral problems involving interpersonal relations (e.g., withdrawal and aggression). Furthermore, once the patients' childhood behavior for a particular behavior dimension diverged from that of the siblings, they continued to show increased behavior problems for the respective dimension.

In summary, the findings from our studies of facial expressions and behavior problems indicate that deficits in social behavior characterize schizophrenia patients long before they manifest clinical symptoms of their illness. However, the group differences in facial expressions emerge earlier than the group differences in behavioral problems (although this might not be the case for Attention Problems). This raises the question of whether emotional expressions are linked with behavioral problems. In particular, are early childhood facial emotions a predictor of later behavior? Does greater negative and/or less positive emotion in early childhood portend more behavioral deficits as the child develops? If early emotion displays are an indicator of enduring temperamental characteristics, as some have suggested, then such relations would be predicted.

Relations between Childhood Emotional Expressions and Behavior Problems

To examine the association between affective expressions and behavior problems, the data for the preschizophrenia subjects and their siblings were combined. Table 8.1 shows the correlations, by age period, between the behavior dimensions and negative facial expressions. As can be seen, the ratings of negative expressions at the birth-to-4-years age period are significantly associated with Delinquent and Aggressive behavior at 4 to 8 years and onward. (It should be noted that the Delinquent Behavior factor includes items pertaining to guilt reactions, lying and swearing that are not uncommon in early childhood.) But there is relatively little association between negative emotion in the birth-to-4-year period and ratings of internalizing behavior problems (e.g., Withdrawn, Anxious/Depressed). Thus, the findings indicate that early negative emotion is primarily predictive of later externalizing behavior problems (i.e., Delinquency and Aggression). This suggests that the ratings of negative emotion in the birth-to-4-year period are tapping temperamental qualities, such as irritability or oppositionality, which increase the likelihood of *later* problems with behavioral control.

In contrast, Table 8.1 shows that the rate of negative expressions at the 8-to-12-year and the 12-to-16-year age periods are essentially correlated with internalizing behavior problems (i.e., Anxious/Depressed, Social Problems) and cognitive problems (Thought Problems, Attention Problems). Thus, negative emotional expressions in middle childhood and adolescence are related to problems in mood, cognition, and social interaction; however, they show no association with withdrawn or delinquent behavior at any age period. Further, the temporal ordering of the relations suggest that problems with mood (Anxious/Depressed) and interpersonal functioning (Social Problems) in early and middle childhood are increasing the likelihood of negative affect in adolescence.

There are some interesting exceptions to the general trends outlined above. For example, Anxious/Depressed problems are associated with negative expressions at the birth-to-4-year age period, as well as the 12-to-16-year age period. The Aggression dimension shows a similar pattern.

Briefly summarizing, negative expressions at one age period are not isomorphic with similar expressions at other age periods. That is, negative expressions at an early age period may be caused by more biologically driven, temperamental factors, whereas negative expressions at later age periods are influenced by more cognitively driven factors. This interpretation is consistent with developmental theories of the changing determinants of emotion as a function of age (Lazarus, 1994; Rothbart, 1994). Thus, the associations between behavior and affect (i.e., facial expressions) vary as a function of age. This does not, however, imply an absence of temporal continuity in affect; we find modest, positive intercorrelations among both the positive and the negative emotion rating across age periods (Walker et al., 1993). To some extent, therefore, our ratings of negative emotion are tapping a propensity that is long standing.

Turning to Table 8.2, the ratings of positive facial expressions show fewer significant associations with specific behavior problems. Most of the significant correlations are between positive emotion in the 4-to-8-year period and later problems. Higher rates of positive expressions during the 4-to-8-year period are associated with lower scores on the Anxious/Depressed, Thought, Attention, Delinquency, and Aggression behavior problem dimensions. Positive emotion, therefore, does not appear to be differentially associated with internalizing, cognitive, or externalizing behavior problems. It is not clear why ratings of positive emotion in the other age periods show relatively little association with behavior problems.

Taken together, the above results indicate that facial emotion is linked with overt behavior in childhood. Further, these relations are detected with data on emotions and behavior that were obtained from separate sources. Thus, the findings are not readily attributable to method artifact or parental report bias.

Associations between Childhood Emotional Expressions and the Rate of Change of Behavior Problems

In the previous analyses, we addressed the question of whether childhood emotional expressions are linked with the severity of behavior problems at the four age periods. In the following, we examine the relation between emotion and the *rate of developmental change* in behavior problems. Because the behavior ratings were obtained for all subjects at four age periods, it was possible to compute linear slope variables for each of the seven behavior dimensions. This type of analysis has been recommended for modeling development with longitudinal data, because it allows an examination of the slope or rate of change of a variable over time (e.g., Willett, 1988).

Table 8.3 shows the behavior-dimension slope means (standardized) for the preschizophrenia subjects and the

Table 8.1. Correlations between Negative Facial Expressions and Behavior Dimensions by Age Period: Preschizophrenics and Siblings

BEHAVIOR DIMENSIONS	NEGATIVE FACIAL EXPRESSIONS			
	BIRTH TO 4 (n = 45)	4 TO 8 (n = 50)	8 TO 12 (n = 40)	12 TO 16 (n = 35)
Withdrawn				
Birth to 4	−.08	.14	.17	.10
4 to 8	−.09	.06	.22	.12
8 to 12	−.01	.06	.17	.14
12 to 16	.02	.06	.14	.19
Anxious/Depressed				
Birth to 4	.25[a]	.09	.18	.33[a]
4 to 8	.22	.11	.18	.40[b]
8 to 12	.14	.12	.21	.56[b]
12 to 16	.12	.14	.21	.50[b]
Social Problems				
Birth to 4	.20	.21	.33[a]	.30[a]
4 to 8	.19	.09	.29[a]	.35[a]
8 to 12	.13	.04	.33[a]	.50[b]
12 to 16	.06	.14	.23	.37[a]
Thought Problems				
Birth to 4	−.15	.50[b]	.49[b]	.02
4 to 8	.27[a]	.29[a]	.43[a]	.09
8 to 12	−.06	−.11	.20	.54[b]
12 to 16	.01	.15	.13	.44[b]
Attention Problems				
Birth to 4	.22	−.07	.01	.09
4 to 8	.23	−.04	.14	.30[a]
8 to 12	.21	−.03	.17	.37[a]
12 to 16	.20	.11	.16	.43[b]
Delinquency				
Birth to 4	.24	−.19	−.02	−.13
4 to 8	.31[a]	−.24[a]	−.14	−.07
8 to 12	.41[b]	−.04	−.02	−.07
12 to 16	.52[b]	.14	.15	−.11
Aggression				
Birth to 4	.13	−.17	−.02	.01
4 to 8	.51[b]	.04	.22	.34[a]
8 to 12	.50[b]	.11	.21	.34[a]
12 to 16	.45[b]	.10	.07	.22

Note: One-tailed tests
[a] p < .05
[b] p < .01

sibling controls. One can see that the preschizophrenia subjects are typified by increases in behavior problems over time (i.e., positive slopes), whereas the siblings on average showed decreases in behavior problems over time (i.e., negative slopes). The group differences are significant for the following behavior dimensions: Withdrawn, $F(1,55) = 8.20$, $p<.01$; Anxious/Depressed, $F(1,55) = 9.91$, $p<.01$; Thought Problems, $F(1,55) = 6.27$, $p<.05$; Attention Problems, $F(1,55) = 4.53$, $p<.05$; and Aggression, $F(1,55) = 5.41$, $p<.05$.

Table 8.2. Correlations between Positive Facial Expressions and Behavior Dimensions by Age Period: Preschizophrenics and Siblings

BEHAVIOR DIMENSIONS	POSITIVE FACIAL EXPRESSIONS			
	BIRTH TO 4 (n = 45)	4 TO 8 (n = 50)	8 TO 12 (n = 40)	12 TO 16 (n = 35)
Withdrawn				
Birth to 4	.21	.03	−.08	.16
4 to 8	.17	−.20	−.18	.10
8 to 12	−.03	−.12	−.03	.08
12 to 16	−.07	−.19	−.04	.10
Anxious/Depressed				
Birth to 4	.01	−.02	−.17	.04
4 to 8	−.04	−.23	−.24	.03
8 to 12	−.22	−.27[a]	−.19	−.11
12 to 16	−.25[a]	−.27[a]	−.19	−.11
Social Problems				
Birth to 4	.15	−.05	−.10	−.06
4 to 8	.03	−.08	−.02	.02
8 to 12	−.08	−.17	−.12	−.05
12 to 16	−.12	−.18	−.06	−.12
Thought Problems				
Birth to 4	.07	−.02	−.10	−.10
4 to 8	−.06	−.35[b]	−.14	−.16
8 to 12	−.09	−.26[a]	−.24	−.29[a]
12 to 16	−.26[a]	−.13	−.04	−.20
Attention Problems				
Birth to 4	−.22	−.25[a]	−.09	.02
4 to 8	−.06	−.29[a]	−.19	−.09
8 to 12	−.07	−.29[a]	−.13	−.11
12 to 16	−.15	−.24[a]	−.19	−.13
Delinquency				
Birth to 4	.13	−.20	.27[a]	.07
4 to 8	.22	−.25[a]	.12	−.12
8 to 12	.02	−.42[b]	−.20	−.14
12 to 16	.09	−.26[a]	−.16	.12
Aggression				
Birth to 4	.10	−.22	−.07	−.22
4 to 8	−.05	−.35[b]	−.27[a]	−.20
8 to 12	−.07	−.36[b]	−.20	−.09
12 to 16	−.11	−.29[a]	−.21	−.02

Note: One-tailed tests
[a] $p < .05$
[b] $p < .01$

Tables 8.4 and 8.5 show the correlations between the behavior-dimension slope variables and the negative and positive facial expressions, respectively. An examination of Table 8.4 indicates a pattern of correlations similar to that seen in Table 8.1. That is, negative affective expres- sions in the birth-to-4-year range are significantly associ- ated with increases in externalizing behavior problems over time. Negative affect in the 12-to-16-year period is primarily associated with increases in internalizing be- havior problems (Anxious/Depressed) and cognitive

Table 8.3. Behavioral-Dimension Standardized Mean Slopes by Group

BEHAVIORAL SLOPE VARIABLE	PRESCHIZOPHRENICS ($n = 29$)	
	MEAN	SD
Withdrawn	.35	1.22
Anxious/Depressed	.38	1.25
Social Problems	.23	1.31
Thought Problems	.31	1.32
Attention Problems	.27	1.30
Delinquency	.23	1.23
Aggression	.29	1.24

BEHAVIORAL SLOPE VARIABLE	SIBLINGS ($n = 28$)	
	MEAN	SD
Withdrawn	−.36	0.52
Anxious/Depressed	−.39	0.35
Social Problems	−.24	0.44
Thought Problems	−.32	0.22
Attention Problems	−.28	0.40
Delinquency	−.24	0.62
Aggression	−.30	0.55

problems (Thought and Attention Problems) over time. Again, it appears that early negative affect is a precursor of later problems in behavioral inhibition, whereas later negative affect is preceded by increasing internalized behavior problems.

Turning to Table 8.5, one can see that lower rates of positive affective expressions in the birth-to-4-year period are generally associated with increases in internalizing behavior problems (Withdrawn, Anxious/Depressed, Social Problems) and in Thought Problems. Also, two of the behavior-dimension slope variables, Anxious/Depressed and Delinquency are inversely correlated with positive affect in the 4-to-8-year period. In interpreting these findings, it is of interest to note that home movies typically feature behavioral settings that draw for positive affect. Especially when children are young, parents and older siblings attempt to engage them in positive affective exchanges. Thus, a deficit in the display of positive emotion implies less responsivity to social cues aimed at eliciting positive affect. This interpretation is consistent with the observed correlation between positive emotion and the Withdrawn and Social Problems behavior slopes.

Note also that an individual's affective expressions may have an effect on the people with whom he or she interacts (see, for example, Mueser, Grau, Sussman, & Rosen, 1984). Thus deficits in the expression of positive affect could limit the subject's opportunities for social interaction because others avoid or reject the person.

Table 8.4. Correlations between Negative Facial Expressions and Behavior-Dimension Slopes by Age Period: Preschizophrenics and Siblings

BEHAVIORAL SLOPE VARIABLES	NEGATIVE EXPRESSIONS			
	BIRTH TO 4	4 TO 8	8 TO 12	12 TO 16
Withdrawn	.09	−.02	.06	.15
Anxious/Depressed	.04	.12	.16	.44[b]
Social Problems	−.11	−.03	.01	.22
Thought Problems	.00	−.01	−.02	.43[b]
Attention Problems	.14	.16	.21	.52[b]
Delinquency	.50[b]	.19	.16	−.08
Aggression	.42[b]	.20	.08	.21

Note: One-tailed tests
[a] $p < .05$
[b] $p < .01$

Table 8.5. Correlations between Positive Facial Expressions
and Behavior-Dimension Slopes by Age Period: Preschizophrenics and Siblings

BEHAVIORAL SLOPE VARIABLES	POSITIVE EXPRESSIONS			
	BIRTH TO 4	4 TO 8	8 TO 12	12 TO 16
Withdrawn	−.27[a]	−.21	.03	.02
Anxious/Depressed	−.29[a]	−.28[a]	−.13	−.15
Social Problems	−.30[a]	−.20	−.01	−.10
Thought Problems	−.26[a]	−.10	−.02	−.17
Attention Problems	−.09	−.19	−.18	−.18
Delinquency	.05	−.27[a]	−.26	.08
Aggression	−.16	−.21	−.15	.14

Note: One-tailed tests
[a] $p < .05$
[b] $p < .01$

It is not surprising that there are some differences between the pattern of relations obtained with the behavioral change scores *versus* the absolute level of the behavior scores at the separate age periods. For example, for Withdrawn behavior the rate of behavior change over time is related to lower levels of positive affect, but there are no significant relations between the emotion ratings and the absolute level of Withdrawn behavior at any age period. This lends support to the assumption that the predictors of developmental change in behavior can differ from the predictors of behavior within developmental periods.

Continuity between Childhood Behavior and Clinical Symptoms in Adulthood

In a recent paper, we reported on the relation between the ratings of childhood behavior problems and three dimensions of adult symptoms: cognitive disorganization, reality distortion, and psychomotor poverty (Baum & Walker, 1995). The results indicate that childhood social deficits, especially social withdrawal, are linked with the severity of psychomotor poverty symptoms in adulthood. The symptoms classified in this dimension include impairments in interpersonal behavior. In contrast, severity of symptoms in the Reality Distortion dimension, which includes hallucinations and delusions, was not linked with childhood behavior.

Other research has also shown an association between childhood premorbid functioning and adult psychomotor poverty (e.g., Goldberg et al., 1993; Mueser, Bellack, Morrison, & Wixted, 1990).

The Origins of Social Deficits in Schizophrenia

The findings presented above indicate (1) that preschizophrenic children show both affective abnormalities and behavior problems that distinguish them from their siblings with healthy outcomes, (2) that early abnormalities in affect regulation are linked with concurrent and subsequent behavioral dysfunction, and (3) that childhood behavior problems are associated with adult symptoms. Further support for the notion that deficits in interpersonal behavior are constitutionally based comes from our findings on the relation between childhood neuromotor abnormalities and behavioral problems (Neumann & Walker, 1995). Neuromotor abnormalities (e.g., motor overflow, choreiform movements) were associated with increased internalized behavior problems, cognitive problems and negative affective expressions in the 12-to-16-year period, and with decreased positive affective expressions in the birth-to-4-year period. As such, a presumed measure of central nervous system dysfunction (i.e., neuromotor abnormality) is related to problems in behavioral and affective functioning. These results are consistent with the assumption that the constitutional vulnerability for schizophrenia is expressed in "subclinical" deficits in interpersonal functioning long before it is expressed as a clinical syndrome.

However, arguing against this interpretation, Pogue-Geile (1991) and others have suggested that the constitutional liability for schizophrenia is not activated until late adolescence/early adulthood, at which point the clinical illness emerges. He, and others (Walker, Downey, & Nightingale, 1989), propose that childhood behavior problems may have independent origins, although they can increase the likelihood that the liability for schizophrenia will be expressed later in life. If it is the case that premorbid socioemotional deficits and the clinical disorder have different origins, then we would not expect any relation between indicators of genetic liability and the severity of premorbid impairment.

Genetic liability for schizophrenia is typically indexed by the presence of the disorder in biological relatives. The number of affected biological relatives is positively correlated with the individual's risk for developing the illness, as well as the severity of the illness (Gottesman, 1991). It appears that this positive relation also holds for measures of premorbid functioning. Several investigators have shown that the presence of a family history of schizophrenia is associated with an increased likelihood of premorbid behavioral problems in childhood (Foerster, Lewis, Owen, & Murray, 1991; Parnas, Schulsinger, Schulsinger, Mednick, & Teasdale, 1982). Similarly, using data from our precursors study, we have found that family history of schizophrenia (i. e., number of affected first- and second-degree relatives) is positively correlated with a global index of negative affect (averaged across age periods) in preschizophrenia subjects ($r = .44, p < .05$) and inversely correlated with the global index of positive affect ($r = -.43, p < .05$) (Walker & Neumann, 1995).

Numerous investigators have suggested that a congenital vulnerability to schizophrenia may be acquired through exposure to obstetrical complications (OCs) (e.g., McNeil, 1987). In this case, we might expect OCs to show a relation with premorbid behavior similar to that shown by indices of genetic liability. Consistent with this, we also find that OCs (summed frequency of prenatal and perinatal complications) are correlated with the rate of negative affect ($r = .45, p < .05$) for the preschizophrenia subjects. Significant relations between OCs and premorbid behavior are also reported by other investigators (McNeil, 1987; Parnas et al., 1982). Taken together, these findings indicate that both inherited and acquired constitutional factors contribute to the severity of premorbid behavioral deficits in schizophrenia.

Given the evidence that both inherited vulnerability and OCs have similar influences on premorbid functioning,

we examined the "fit" of a causal model that assumed that both have direct and mediated effects on premorbid behavioral problems. Specifically, a causal model was tested (using EQS; Bentler, 1990), which assumed that both genetic and acquired constitutional vulnerabilities lead to abnormalities in behavioral adjustment, and that some of these effects are mediated by abnormalities in affective regulation. The model included the following variables: family history of schizophrenia (FHS—number of first- and second-degree relatives with schizophrenia), obstetric complications (OCs—total number of prenatal and perinatal complications), premorbid positive emotion (POS—averaged proportion of positive emotion across age periods), premorbid negative emotion (NEG—averaged proportion of negative emotion across age periods), premorbid internalizing behavior problems (INT—summed scores for the Anxious/Depressed, Withdrawn, Social Problems dimensions) and externalizing problems (EXT—summed scores for the Delinquency and Aggression dimensions). Because a primary goal was to test the influence of the magnitude of the genetic liability on premorbid deficits, only the preschizophrenia subjects were included in the analysis.

The graphical representation of the model with standardized parameter estimates is presented in Figure 8.1. The direct effects (path coefficients) of FHS and OCs on the childhood emotion (POS and NEG) and behavior (INT and EXT) measures were tested for significance. In addi-

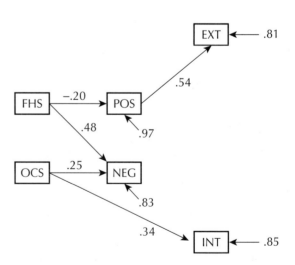

Figure 8.1. Mathematical model of the effects of family history of schizophrenia and obstetric complications on premorbid affective and behavioral functioning.

tion, the mediating effects of POS and NEG in the relation of FHS and OCs with behavior were tested. Only those path coefficients that were significant at $p < .05$ are included in the model. Because of the small sample ($n = 29$) on which this model is based, the results should be interpreted with caution and viewed only as a tentative representation of the relationships among these variables. Other weaknesses of the model include the use of indices of emotion and behavior that are aggregated across age periods, and the absence of some potentially relevant causal paths, such as that between internalizing and externalizing behavior problems. The model should be seen as a heuristic tool for generating hypotheses regarding the causes of premorbid social dysfunction. Nonetheless, the model resulted in good fit to the observed data. Specifically, there was a nonsignificant chi square (2.09, $p = 0.55$, $df = 3$), and the fit indices (Bentler-Bonett Fit Index = 0.96, Comparative Fit Index = 1.00) were quite good. More importantly, the model was able to reproduce the observed data with considerable precision (e.g., the average absolute standardized residual = 0.02).

Several aspects of the results are noteworthy. First, all of the significant effects of FHS on behavior problems are mediated by childhood affect. FHS is associated with less positive and greater negative emotion, and the latter variable, in turn, is linked with externalizing childhood behavior problems. In contrast, OCs are only predictive of increased negative emotion, but they also have a direct effect on the rate of childhood internalizing behavior problems.

In sum, the model results support the assumption that inherited vulnerability and obstetric complications contribute to deficits in premorbid functioning. Second, the model suggests that a family history of schizophrenia may contribute to problems in behavioral functioning indirectly by causing disturbances in affect regulation.

DISCUSSION

Taken together, our findings and those of other investigators indicate that behavioral deficits characterize some schizophrenic patients in early childhood and extends throughout the premorbid period. This conclusion has implications for our conceptualization of social impairment in schizophrenia. First, social dysfunction cannot be solely attributed to the clinical syndrome of schizophrenia. In other words, it does not arise solely as a consequence of the psychotic symptoms that are required for a clinical diagnosis of the disorder. Second, it seems rea-

sonable to assume that, for some patients, long-standing social deficits may have served to thwart their opportunities for exposure to the normative social experiences involved in the transition from childhood to adulthood. This assumption is consistent with the evidence that schizophrenia patients have sparse social networks and lower rates of marriage in the premorbid adult period.

Our findings, and those of other investigators, also suggest that premorbid behavioral abnormalities are, at least in part, a manifestation of the underlying vulnerability for schizophrenia. This contention is supported by the association between childhood behavior problems and adult symptoms, as well as by the relation between family history of psychopathology and childhood emotion abnormalities.

Of course, deficits in interpersonal behavior are not sufficient for a diagnosis of schizophrenia. The onset of psychotic symptoms marks a qualitative change in the overt behavior of individuals who succumb to the disorder. The fact that this onset is typically in late adolescence/early adulthood indicates that the expression of the diathesis is altered by maturational processes. In a recent paper, Walker (1994) offers some hypotheses about the manner in which central nervous system maturation might trigger the onset of psychotic symptoms. Specifically, it is proposed that the maturation of corticolimbic pathways that occurs during adolescence/early adulthood may set the stage for the "psychotic" expression of the congenital brain abnormality that underlies schizophrenia. This theoretical framework assumes a neurodevelopmental process in which the behavioral manifestation of vulnerability to schizophrenia changes with age; childhood behavioral deficits gradually increase, and typically culminate in psychotic symptoms in early adulthood.

A critical question that has been debated by researchers for years is whether this aberrant developmental process can be interrupted. In other words, can we prevent the onset of psychosis in vulnerable individuals? This question is particularly relevant to our discussion of premorbid behavioral deficits. Would the provision of an intervention aimed at enhancing interpersonal behavior modify the likelihood of psychotic symptoms? If so, what form might such an intervention take? If, as our findings suggest, premorbid behavioral problems stem from affective abnormalities, then preventive interventions might best be directed at the individual's capacity to self-regulate affective states. This might involve the use of cognitive-behavioral procedures to reduce negative affective arousal.

To date, few attempts at preventive intervention of schizophrenia have been undertaken. However, there have been a number of reports on intervention programs designed to reduce relapse in schizophrenia patients. These programs typically focus on the modification of overt behavior (e g., teaching social skills) and the remediation of deficits in attention. It may be fruitful to explore some experimental interventions that are designed to increase patients' capacity to self-regulate affective states. The enhancement of these capacities might have favorable implications for interpersonal behavior. If such interventions proved effective at enhancing interpersonal behavior, preventive intervention trials for children at risk for schizophrenia might be explored.

REFERENCES

Acherbach, T. (1991). Childhood Behavior Checklist. Department of Psychiatry, University of Vermont, 15 Prospect Street, Burlington, VT 05401.

Baum, K., & Walker, E. F. (1995). The relation between childhood behavior problems and clinical symptoms. *Schizophrenia Research, 16*, 111–120.

Bellack, A. S., Sayers, M., Mueser, K. T., & Bennett, M. (1994). Evaluation of social problem solving in schizophrenia. *Journal of Abnormal Psychology, 103*, 371–8.

Bentler, P. M. (1990). *EQS Program Manual.* Los Angeles, CA: BMDP Statistical Software.

Bowen, L., Wallace, C. J., Glynn, S. M., Nuechterlein, K. H., Lutzker, J. R., & Kuehnel, T. G. (1994). Schizophrenic individuals' cognitive functioning and performance in interpersonal interactions and skills training procedures. *Journal of Psychiatric Research, 28*, 289–301.

Brugha, T. S., Wing, J. K., Brewin, C. R., MacCarthy, B., & Lesage, A. (1993). The relationship of social network deficits with deficits in social functioning in long-term psychiatric disorders. *Social Psychiatry and Psychiatric Epidemiology, 28*, 218–224.

Cherny, S. S., Fulker, D. W., Corley, R. P., Plomin, R., & DeFries J. C. (1994). Continuity and change in infant shyness from 14 to 20 months. *Behavior Genetics, 24*, 365–379.

Dworkin, R. H. (1992). Affective deficits and social deficits in schizophrenia: What's what?. *Schizophrenia Bulletin, 18*, 59–64.

Fish, B., Marcus, J., Hans, L. H., Auerbach, J. G., & Perdue, S. (1992). Infants at risk for schizophrenia: Sequelae of a genetic neurointegrative defect. *Archives of General Psychiatry, 49*, 221–235.

Foerster, A., Lewis, S. W., Owen, M. J., & Murray, R. M. (1991). Low birth weight and a family history of schizophrenia predict poor premorbid functioning in psychosis. *Schizophrenia Research, 5*, 13–20.

Goldberg, T. E, Gold, J. M., Greenberg, R., Griffin, S., Schulz, S. C., Pickar, D., Kleinman, J. E., & Weinberger, D. R. (1993). Contrasts between patients with affective disorders and patients with schizophrenia on a neuropsychological test battery. *American Journal of Psychiatry, 150*, 1355–1362.

Goldsmith, H. H., & Campos, J. J. (1986). Fundamental issues in the study of early temperament: The Denver Twin Temperament Study. In M. E. Lamb, A. L. Brown, & B. Rogoff (Eds.), *Advances in developmental psychology* (pp. 231–283). Hillsdale, NJ: Lawrence Erlbaum.

Goodman, S. H. (1991). Early social and affective development in schizophrenic offspring. In E. Walker (Ed.), *Schizophrenia: A life-course developmental perspective.* New York: Academic Press.

Gottesman, I. (1991). *Schizophrenia genesis.* New York: Freeman.

Hans, S. L., & Marcus, J. (1991). Neurobehavioral development of infants at risk for schizophrenia: A review. In E. Walker (Ed.), *Schizophrenia: A life-course developmental perspective.* New York: Academic Press.

Honeycutt, N., & Belcher, J. R. (1991). Schizophrenia and social skills: An "identify and train" approach. *Community Mental Health Journal, 27*, 57–68.

Izard, C. E., Dougherty, L. M., & Hembree, E. A. (1983). A System for Identifying Affect Expressions by Holistic Judgments (AFFEX). Instructional Resources Center. University of Delaware.

Lazarus, R. (1994). Meaning and emotional development. In P. Ekman & R. J. Davidson (Eds.), *The nature of emotion: Fundamental questions,* (pp. 362–366). New York: Oxford University Press.

Litter, J., & Walker, E. (1993). Interpersonal behavior of preschizophrenic children. *Child Psychiatry and Human Development, 23*, 283–295.

McNeil, T. F. (1987). Perinatal influences in the development of schizophrenia. In: H. Helmchen & F. A. Henn (Eds.), *Biological perspectives of schizophrenia.* New York: Wiley.

Mueser, K. T., Bellack, A. S., Morrison, R. L., & Wixted, J. T. (1990). Social competence in schizophrenia: Premorbid adjustment, social skill, and domains of functioning. *Journal of Psychiatric Research, 24*, 51–63.

Mueser, K. T., Grau, B. W., Sussman, S., & Rosen, A. J. (1984). You're only as pretty as you feel: Facial expression as a determinant of physical attractiveness. *Journal of Personality and Social Psychology, 46*, 469–78.

Neumann, C. S, Grimes, K., Walker, E. F, & Baum, K. (1995). Developmental pathways to schizophrenia: Behavioral subtypes. *Journal of Abnormal Psychology, V, 104*, 558–566.

Neumann, C. S., & Walker, E. F. (1995). Childhood neuromotor soft signs, behavior problems, and adult psychopathology. In T. Ollendick & R. Prinz (Eds.), *Advances in clinical child psychology,* Vol. 18. (pp. 173–203). New York: Plenum.

Offord, D., & Cross, L. (1969). Behavioral antecedents of adult schizophrenia. *Archives of General Psychiatry, 21*, 267–283.

Parnas, J., Schulsinger, F., Schulsinger, H., Mednick, S. A., & Teasdale, M. A. (1982). Behavioral precursors of schizophrenia spectrum: A prospective study. *Archives of General Psychiatry, 38,* 658–663.

Parnas, J., Schulsinger, F., Teasdale, T. W., Schulsinger, H., Feldman, P. M., & Mednick, S. A. (1982). Perinatal complications and clinical outcome within the schizophrenic spectrum. *British Journal of Psychiatry, 140,* 416–420.

Petrill, S. A., & Thompson, L. A. (1993). The phenotypic and genetic relationships among measures of cognitive ability, temperament, and scholastic achievement. *Behavior Genetics, 23,* 511–518.

Pogue-Geile, M. (1991). The development of liability to schizophrenia: Early and late developmental models. In E. Walker (Ed.), *Schizophrenia: A developmental life-course perspective.* New York: Wiley.

Rothbart, M. K. (1994). Emotional development: Changes in reactivity and self-regulation. In P. Ekman & R. J. Davidson (Eds.), *The nature of emotion: Fundamental questions,* (pp. 369–372). New York: Oxford University Press.

Sameroff, A. J., Seifer, R., Zax, M., & Barocas, R. (1987). Early indicator of developmental risk: Rochester Longitudinal Study. *Schizophrenia Bulletin, 13,* 383–394.

Saudino, K. J., & Eaton, W. O. (1991). Infant temperament and genetics: An objective twin study of motor activity level. *Child Development, 62,* 1167–1174.

Sorensen, T. (1994). The intricacy of the ordinary. *British Journal of Psychiatry—Supplement, (23),* 108–114.

Thornicroft, G., & Breakey, W. R. (1991). The COSTAR programme. 1: Improving social networks of the long-term mentally ill. *British Journal of Psychiatry, 159,* 245–249.

Thusholt, F. J., Jensen, E. O., Knop, J., Naylor, A. S., Sogaard, U. (1993). [Use of psychiatric emergency clinics in Copenhagen and Frederiksberg by schizophrenic patients]. Skizofrene patienters brug af de psykiatriske skadestuer i Kobenhavn og Frederiksberg. *Ugeskrift for Laeger, 155,* 1459–1463.

Walker, E. F., Downey, G., & Nightingale, N. (1989). The nonorthogonal nature of risk factors. *Journal of Primary Prevention, 9,* 143–163.

Walker, E. F., Grimes, K., Davis, D., & Smith, T. (1993). Childhood precursors of schizophrenia: Facial expressions of emotion. *American Journal of Psychiatry, 150,* 1654–1660.

Walker, E. F., & Lewine, R. (1990). The prediction of adult-onset schizophrenia from childhood home movies. *American Journal of Psychiatry, 147,* 1052–1056.

Walker, E. F., & Neumann, C. S. (1995). Neurodevelopmental models of schizophrenia: The role of central nervous system maturation in the expression of neuropathology. In J. L. Waddington & P. F. Buckley (Eds.), *The neurodevelopmental hypothesis of schizophrenia.* Texas: R.G. Landes.

Walker E. F., Savoie, T., & Davis, D. (1994). Neuromotor precursors of schizophrenia. *Schizophrenia Bulletin, 20,* 441–452.

Walker, E. F. (1994). The developmentally moderated expression of the neuiopathology underlying schizophrenia. *Schizophrenia Bulletin, 20,* 453–480.

Watt, N. F. (1978). Patterns of childhood social development in adult schizophrenics. *Archives of General Psychiatry, 35,* 160–165.

Watt, N. F., & Lubensky, A. W. (1976). Childhood roots of schizophrenia. *Journal of Consulting and Clinical Psychology, 44,* 363–375.

Willett, S. B. (1988). Questions and answers in the measurement of change. In E. Z. Rothkopf, (Ed.), *Review of research in education.* Washington, DC: American Educational Research Association.

CHAPTER 9

LONG-TERM OUTCOME OF SOCIAL FUNCTIONING

Courtenay M. Harding
Andrew B. Keller

If social relatedness and functioning comprise much of the essence of human experience over the life span, these factors are no less the case for persons suffering with schizophrenia. A recent survey of treatment goals important to persons with schizophrenia placed social skills and relationships among those most valued (Coursey, Keller, & Farrell, 1995). While schizophrenia invariably has a negative impact on social functioning during the initial phase of the disorder (American Psychiatric Association [APA], 1994), there is a wide variability of social functioning over the longer term (Harding et al., 1987b). Further, schizophrenia manifests itself in a myriad of ways over its multiply determined course (E. Bleuler, 1911/1950; M. Bleuler, 1972/1978).

This chapter will review findings about social functioning from across the life course in persons who are suffering from schizophrenia. Examination of the results from seven recent long-term outcome studies will be presented. A discussion of the ever widening heterogeneity of function across catamnestic time will be presented. Suggestions of a few specific processes which may influ-

ence this variability will target (1) biological and genetic heterogeneity, (2) developmental factors, (3) sex-based differences, and (4) individual and environmental interactive catalysts. By addressing the potential impact on social functioning by such factors, we hope to demonstrate how such processes require a longitudinal perspective to be better understood (Ciompi, 1980b; Harding, Zubin, & Strauss, 1987 & 1992).

THE COURSE OF SCHIZOPHRENIA AND SOCIAL FUNCTIONING

In the schizophrenia literature, loss of social function has always played a crucial role in describing phases of the disorder. Social functioning has been variously described as consisting of many roles (e.g., coworker, housemate, spouse, friend, parent) and many conceptual models (e.g., degrees of interdependence, frequency of contact, quality of companionship, instrumental and affective supports, network size and density, individual–environment interaction, and level of activity). The periods marked by im-

Table 9.1. Long-Term Follow-Up Studies of Schizophrenia

INVESTIGATOR	YEAR OF STUDY	LOCATION OF STUDY	NUMBER IN COHORT	LENGTH OF FOLLOW-UP YEARS	% SIGNIFICANTLY IMPROVED/ RECOVERED	% SOCIALLY RECOVERED
M. Bleuler	1972	Switzerland	208	23	53–68[a]	46–59[a]
Huber et al.	1975	Germany	502	22	57	56
Ciompi & Müller	1976	Switzerland	289	37	53	57
Tsuang et al.	1979	Iowa/USA	186	37	46	21[b]
Harding et al.	1987	Vermont/USA	82[c]	32	62–68	68
Ogawa et al.	1987	Japan	105	24	56[d]	47
Desisto et al.	1995	Maine/USA	45[c]	36	42	49

[a] Multiple admissions vs. first admissions
[b] Marital status only recorded
[c] Live interviewed DSM III schizophrenia group—the hardest data
[d] Derived by adding 33% recovered, with a conservative 23% as significantly improved (from the 46% listed as improved)

paired social functioning have included lack of premorbid social competence (e.g., Cannon-Spoor, Potkin, & Wyatt, 1982; Gittleman-Klein & Klein, 1969; Phillips, 1953; Wittman, 1941); prodromal functioning (e.g., Green, 1996; Henrichs & Carpenter, 1985; Herz, Glazer, Mirza, Mostert, & Hafez, 1989; Hirsch & Jolley, 1989); onset characteristics (e.g., Docherty, van Kammen, Siris, & Marder, 1978); negative symptoms after onset (e.g., Andreasen, 1982; Strauss & Carpenter, 1974b); and short-term outcome (e.g., Bland & Orn, 1978; Gardos, Cole, & LaBrie, 1982; Strauss & Carpenter, 1974a).

While the criteria for a diagnosis for schizophrenia uniformly require a decline in social functioning (APA, 1994), in actuality, heterogeneity persists across all time epochs of the disorder (Bland & Orn, 1978; Bleuler, 1972/1978; Gardos et al., 1982; Harding, Zubin & Strauss, 1987; Strauss & Carpenter, 1974a; 1974b; World Health Organization [WHO], 1979). Prior to onset, some persons demonstrate early social withdrawal and isolation, while others appear to function well up until onset (Garmezy, 1970; Kant, 1944; Langfeldt, 1939). Onset usually occurs much later for females (Lewine, 1981; Seeman, & Lang, 1990), which allows females a more solid social developmental base on which to rely during the recovery process. Young males, however, tend to demonstrate the negative symptoms of schizophrenia (apathy, anhedonia, alogia, and blunted affect), all of which severely interrupt interpersonal relationships (Andreasen, 1982). These symptoms and other primary characteristics of the disorder, to the degree that

they occur, also tend to contribute to problematic social relating. Such characteristic symptoms include hallucinations and delusions, secondary depression, anxiety, suspiciousness, hostility, anger, cognitive impairment, odd uses of language, as well as stuporous or excited motor behaviors (APA, 1994). Overall, social function tends to be severely compromised during the early years of a person's efforts to cope with schizophrenia.

However, as time proceeds from acute phases into the early chronic phases (as early as the second through the fifth years of the disorder), heterogeneity increases (e.g., Strauss & Carpenter, 1974b & 1977). From that point onward, some investigators have found that the process continues to be one of ever widening variability (e.g., Ciompi, 1980a, 1980b; Harding, Brooks, Ashikaga, Strauss, & Breier, 1987b; Huber, Gross, Schüttler, & Lintz, 1980), while others have written that achievement in the first 5 years appears to be consistent thereafter (e.g., M. Bleuler, 1972/1978). The very long-term studies (over 2 to 3 decades) have all found substantial reconstitution of the ability to relate to others, and further development among a large percentage (46 to 68%) of the subjects studied (see Table 9.1).

SOCIAL SEQUELAE FROM SCHIZOPHRENIA

Across time, social sequelae to the disorder may be grouped into one of three outcomes. One group of patients adjusts social functioning to the disorder by withdrawing into a solitary, isolated existence. They conform their behavior and expectations to the limits imposed by the disorder. A second set of people with schizophrenia recover a marked degree of social functioning in spite of continued symptoms. They learn to titrate their social behavior or in some way transcend their symptoms in order to function well socially. A third group of people recover fully. They regain a level of psychological and social functioning comparable to that of persons who never had the disorder. Both the second and third groups eventually continue normal adult developmental tasks, such as achieving intimate relationships and interdependent friendships (Harding, Brooks, Ashikaga, Strauss, & Landerl, 1987c).

To understand the ways in which persons with schizophrenia progress to one of these three levels of social functioning, we must begin with the understanding that schizophrenia is probably a "group" of disorders, as suggested by E. Bleuler (1911/1950). These groups evolve over time in a variety of ways. After summarizing the research describing such heterogeneous long-term outcomes for the schizophrenias, we will explore some of the antecedents and modifiers of such courses.

DATA FROM THE LONG-TERM STUDIES OF SCHIZOPHRENIA

Table 9.1 displays the summary findings from seven worldwide studies completed in the last 2 decades that have followed cohorts of persons with schizophrenia for at least 20 years.

The Burghözli Study

Manfred Bleuler (1972/1978) conducted a prospective follow-along for 23 years of 208 patients. These patients were considered to be representative of 653 patients admitted sequentially to Burghölzli Hospital in Zurich, Switzerland, in 1942 and 1943. He used a more stringent criteria for schizophrenia than did his father, Eugen Bleuler, by combining both Bleulerian and Kraepelinian criteria (E. Bleuler, 1911/1950; Kraepelin, 1902). The combined diagnostic system has been considered to be narrower than DSM-II (APA, 1968) but wider than DSM-III (APA, 1980) (see Angst, 1988). M. Bleuler conducted personal but systematic interviews of all these cohort members. The findings revealed that 53% of all subjects and 66% of first admissions were felt to be recovered or significantly improved. Social functioning was rated as the capacity to earn a living as well as independence from

care and living in a nonsheltered residence. Forty-six percent of the cohort were rated as having no social impairment, while 59% of the first admission sample were so designated.

The Bonn Study

Gerd Huber and his colleagues (Huber, Gross, & Schüttler, 1975) used a triple combination of Kraepelinian/Bleulerian/Schneiderian criteria for the diagnosis of schizophrenia. The German team followed up 502 first and repeated admissions to the Bonn University Psychiatric Hospital for an average of 22 years. They used semistructured interviews and hospital records. Social outcome was defined as one of five levels targeting the ability to work. Social functioning was highly correlated with psychological health. Fifty-six percent of this cohort achieved social recovery (Huber et al., 1980).

The Lausanne Investigations

Ciompi and Müller (1976–1984) used the double combination Kraepelian/Bleuler criteria to diagnose and follow up 289 patients from the University Psychiatric Hospital who were first admitted before age 65 and who were over 65 by follow-up. They devised cross-sectional semistructured interviews and studied hospital records. The average length of follow-up was 37 years ranging up to 64 years after first admission. Fifty-seven percent were rated as "socially adapted" ("free of conflicts, calm, and peaceful" [Ciompi, 1980a]) but only a third were rated as performing well in functioning. This investigator wondered about the impact of advanced old age and whether those still classified as "dependent" were classified thusly due to the impact of having had a serious psychosis in their lives as opposed to continued psychopathology.

The Iowa 500 Study

The Iowa team (e.g., Tsuang & Winokur, 1975; and Tsuang, Woolson, & Fleming, 1979) selected a cohort from those admitted to the Iowa State Psychiatric Hospital in 1934 & 1944. Using the Feighner criteria (Feighner et al., 1972), this research team evaluated 3,800 records retrospectively. Two hundred patients were selected. They represented less than one-third of patients who once had been diagnosed with some form of schizophrenia. The patients, who were excluded, were those who did not meet this restrictive criteria and included those people who had episodic or short hospitalizations. These patients did not receive ECT, drugs, or outpatient treatment. Follow-up was conducted between 30 and 40 years ($\bar{x} = 35$ yrs) with a 95% found rate ($n = 186$). Outcome was rated on four dimensions: residential, work, symptoms, and marital status for each person. A comparison was made across other samples, including an affective disorder group as well as surgical controls. Findings revealed that 21% of the schizophrenic sample were married; 34% lived at home or with relatives; 35% were employed, retired, or a housewife; and 20% had no symptoms. Overall comparisons (54%) of the schizophrenic sample were rated as doing poorly compared with the affective and surgical controls who managed to do better.

The Japanese Long-Term Study

Ogawa et al., (1987) followed up 140 consecutively discharged patients diagnosed with ICD–9 schizophrenia (WHO, 1975) from the Department of Neuropsychiatry at Gunma University Hospital in Japan. From 1958 to 1962, this cohort had participated in a program of "neuroleptic drugs, the open-door system, and intensive aftercare" (p. 758). The rehabilitation strategy was known as "Seikatsu-rinsko." This program was described as "clinical work in a patient's everyday life" (p. 758) and was reported to be similar to a combination of case management and individual counseling.

The sample from Japan contained 81% of patients who were under the age of 30 years. Seventy-nine percent were experiencing their first admissions during the program. Using Eguma's Social Adjustment Scale (ESAS; Eguma, 1962; Ogawa et al., 1987), these investigators acquired multiple sources of information. At follow-up, 93% of the patients were assessed with 105 still living. The study findings across 21 to 27 years ($\bar{x} = 23.6$ years) follow-up revealed the following status: 57% achieved a favorable social outcome which included return to premorbid level of social functioning and independent social life without clinical interventions, as well as maintenance of a normal family life. "Semi-self supportive" ratings were given to an additional 19% of subjects, while 34% were considered to be "hospitalized and maladjusted cases." Those persons, who had achieved the highest ratings, were considered to be productive, mostly married, living in their own homes, and recovered psychologically.

This research team also conducted month-by-month longitudinal assessments of social functioning across time and generated patterns and trends for their cohort. The report emphasized early fluctuations in the course status for most patients with later differentiation between the "sta-ble, self-supporting" group and the chronically institutionalized group.

The Vermont Longitudinal Research Project

This project began in the 1950s with the introduction of a model demonstration psychosocial rehabilitation program and the new phenothiazines (Chittick, Brooks, Irons, & Deane, 1961). The program targeted 269 of the so-called hopeless cases from the back wards of Vermont State Hospital (from the residual 19%). These patients were carefully and slowly deinstitutionalized with the community treatment pieces put into place at a time long before the community mental health movement had begun. The mission of the program was one of rehabilitation, self-sufficiency, and community reintegration. Special aspects of the Vermont program included a strong client and clinician collaboration to design and implement the project, a semi-permeable membrane between the hospital and the community (meaning easy flow back and forth), continuity of care (hospital clinicians went with clients to the community and worked in both places), staff and client retraining for a more hopeful attitude, and comprehensive programming. The program components included activities of daily living, psychopharmacology, social skills training, vocational assessment, training, placement matched to skills and interests, and continued support; medication and symptom management, slow and careful deinstitutionalization; community components in place; linkages to primary care; case management (preferably building a client/clinician partnership); and integration into natural community support systems (e.g., bowling and baseball leagues, quilting bees, and church choirs) (Chittick et al., 1961).

Of the 118 patients who met DSM-III (APA, 1980) criteria for schizophrenia, 82 were alive at an average of 32 years after their first admission (Harding et al., 1987b). Ninety-seven percent of the original cohort ($n = 263$ of 269) were located in the overall study (Harding et al., 1987a).

Using rigorous methodology, the Vermont team assessed social functioning using a wide variety of standard instruments. There was blindness of their raters to record information as well as triangulated data, including two sets of prospectively written records abstracted by raters blind to field data. Further, they conducted corroborating interviews with family members, general practitioners, parish priests, or current mental health clinicians (Harding et al., 1987a). Good social outcome (meaning involved often with others and the development of meaningful relationships) was found in 62 to 68% of the cohort with DSM-III-schizophrenia (Harding et al., 1987b).

The Maine Longitudinal Research Project

This 36 year follow-up was recently completed as a matched comparison to the Vermont Study by DeSisto et al. (1995a, 1995b). Ninety-four percent of the Maine cohort ($n = 253$ of 269) were located. Each Vermont subject was matched to a patient at Augusta State Hospital in Maine on sex, diagnosis, age, and length of hospitalization. The hospitals, catchment areas, protocols, and treatment eras were also matched. The cardinal difference between the Vermont sample and the Maine sample was the rehabilitation program in Vermont and the standard custodial care in Maine. The Maine emphasis was on maintenance, stabilization, medications, and entitlements.

Findings from the Maine-Vermont Comparison indicated that the Mainers fared significantly less well than the Vermonters in work, symptoms, and global behaviors (DeSisto et al., 1995a). Nevertheless, for the entire cohort of mixed diagnoses or for the schizophrenia subset, the Mainers were not statistically significantly different in social functioning. This finding emerged after the effects of other variables on which the two samples were not matched were partialed out (e.g., education, acute/chronic onset, index year of discharge, or urban/rural origin). However, the quality of the Vermonters' lives was found to be significantly better across all contexts.

A Discussion of the Variability in the Findings

These seven studies described above have shed some light on the wide heterogeneity of outcome achieved across 2 to 3 decades by persons once suffering from schizophrenia. The projects found a range of social restoration from 21 to 68%. Although the Vermont subjects were the most chronic patients of those studied (Harding et al., 1987a, 1987b), they were also the only group to receive a very specific biopsychosocial rehabilitation intervention and were the group that achieved the highest social recovery rate (68%) (Harding et al., 1987b). Social functioning has shown even wider variability than restoration of psychological states (e.g., delusions or hallucinations). Several factors may be involved to explain the wide discrepancies between studies charting improvement and recovery.

There are many definitions of "recovery" and "improvement" in the worldwide literature, and these explanations often depend on the epistemology of the investigator or the zeitgeist of the times. In the narrow medical model, "recovery" means complete return to function, absence of any psychopathology, and no further use of medication. "Improvement" means significant amelioration of symptoms and return of most areas of function. Rehabilitation models often target "improvement" in specific areas of function (e.g., work, sociability, problem-solving, or medication management [e.g., Anthony, Cohen & Farkas, 1990; Liberman et al., 1993]). Consumers often describe "recovery" as the ability to get on with their lives despite persisting symptoms (Deegan, 1988; Lovejoy, 1982). Thus, reviewers and readers of outcome studies need to investigate such assumptions before drawing conclusions and clumping projects together.

Even though the diagnostic criteria are closer than ever before in follow-up studies, there is still a range of strictness. These studies all employed moderate to strict criteria for the diagnosis of schizophrenia (Kraepelin/Bleuler or Kraepelin/Bleuler/Schneider combinations, DSM-III, ICD 9, and Feighner). The Feighner criteria are the most restrictive, targeting single males with an established chronic course (Feighner et al., 1972). The European-combined diagnostic systems, while narrower than those of Eugen Bleuler (1911/1950), alone still included major depressive psychosis with mood incongruent features within the schizophrenia category, thus making its range greater. The Vermont-Maine studies used the DSM-III (APA, 1980), which was based on descriptive criteria and chronicity. Thus, the DSM-III lies somewhere in the middle of the continuum. Further, the DSM-III provided the potential for inter-rater reliability rather than simply a consensus of senior clinicians (as used in Iowa) and by clinical assignment (as used by the Europeans).

Further, one investigator used a clinical interview (Bleuler); others used semi-structured field interviews (Huber, Ciompi, Tsuang, and Ogawa); while the two New England studies used structured and reliable protocols. The later two investigations also used a wider variety of measures of social function than any of the other studies. The Iowa team only used marital status as the indicator of social outcome functioning but also used single status as secondary entry criteria for their Feighner criteria. This situation may have caused a tautology. In addition, it is not clear how much triangulated data were gathered by the Europeans in their outcome assessments as well.

Treatment differences across studies also ranged from custodial care and no drugs to an advanced psychosocial program similar in many ways to today's Wisconsin's PACT model (Test, 1992) and yesterday's program in Vermont. Social policy differences and implementation of programs to re-skill persons trying to reclaim a life may also have their impact (DeSisto et al., 1995a).

Sample selection differences were also significant. Vermont and Maine were focused on the back wards and the "bottom third" of the schizophrenia spectrum as well as the Iowa group. The European and Japanese samples were laced with short-stay first admissions. Thus, there exist significant differences across these studies with the exception of the Maine-Vermont, comparison, and clear consistent signals are difficult to detect about social functioning over the long-term.

Long-term social function appeared to be more complex and evolving than previously thought. For example, the Vermont Study revealed three groups of persons emerging over time with three different overall styles of social interaction: the "Loners," the "Self-Regulators," and the "Niche People."

As reported by Harding and her colleagues, (1987c), the "Loners" were people who were not recovered or even significantly improved over the study's 32 years. These persons were typically middle-aged males who lived by themselves in small rooms over stores in the middle of town. Still others were found living in board-and-care homes. When asked why they were not working, they tended to offer replies such as: "My family gave up on me, so I gave up on me." For these people, the illness and demoralization had taken its toll. Medication worked only minimally, family and friends were not present, and community integration was not achieved. Of the three groups, these people looked most like the conventional expectation for schizophrenia outcome which has dominated psychiatry over the past century (Kraepelin, 1902; APA, 1994).

The "Self-Regulators" were examples of successful adaptation and adjustment to the disorder. One such person was a 76-year-old woman who played the trumpet and in many ways appeared to have a lively social life as a member of a musical trio. On closer assessment, the raters discovered that she very carefully kept individual relationships at arm's length. Thus, she was able to only perform and in some way relate from the safety of the stage (Harding et al., 1987c). While not regaining social functioning in full, "Self-Regulators" had learned to regain a measure of social functioning through a process of careful regulation of their interactional distance behavior and life-style to cope with the requirements of illness sequelae or ongoing vulnerability (Zubin & Spring, 1977). An-

other example of a "Self-Regulator" appeared on the surface to be a "Loner," living by himself in an old fishing shack on the river. However, this man was known by nearly everyone in town as "the town character," was well-liked and friendly. He had several "drinking buddies." Nevertheless, he had no close friends or family.

Among those who flourished the most socially were called the "Niche People." This group came from the recovered portion of the sample. These people had been placed into living situations, often as part of their rehabilitation program. By luck or by design, these placements allowed them to grow and change as their illnesses lifted in what would be considered to be a good person-illness-environment fit. One subject was a shy withdrawn young woman who began her deinstitutionalization as a live-in chambermaid in a big inn. As she became stronger, her jobs became more socially interactive (or perhaps the requirements of the job helped her to become more healthy). At follow-up, she had become the Assistant Manager, a position which required significant social interaction all week. Another match occurred for an older woman who was placed as a boarder in a family home. At follow-up she had evolved into the respected grandmother of the house with all the rights and privileges that follow from such a position (Harding et al., 1987c).

Long-term studies have varied in their ability to depict the wide heterogeneity underlying schizophrenia's eventual outcomes. Many have employed a cross-sectional view and do not reveal the hidden complexity that only a longitudinal perspective yields. The various factors that contribute to outcome can be as paradoxically fortuitous as the example described by M. Bleuler (1972/1978) of patients who recovered after being suddenly required to care for another desperately ill member of their family. For other patients, the contributors to recovery were more straightforward, such as the Vermonters, who explained: "Someone told me that I had a chance of getting better," "Someone believed in me and my own persistence" (Harding & Zahniser, 1995).

THE SIGNIFICANT IMPACT OF ANTECEDENTS AND MODIFYING FACTORS ON LONG-TERM OUTCOME

Within each research sample or caseload, persons with schizophrenia differed on many factors, including good or poor premorbid function, school completed or not finished, job histories, coping or being overwhelmed, social supports or lack of them, ad infinitum (Harding, 1994).

Often this individual heterogeneity has been ignored, especially in research, and has been glossed over into a generalized homogeneity. In all probability, such strategies have missed important phenomena and subgroups. In the following section, we will review some important antecedents and modifiers which potentially contribute to the heterogeneity of outcome.

Biological Contributions

The authors assume a biopsychosocial interactive model. As such, we would be remiss if we did not include for the reader's consideration the following possible ingredients: the risk models of gene-environment interaction proposed by Kendler and Eaves (1986); the underlying vulnerability model suggested by Zubin and Spring (1977); the person-illness-environment interactive model advanced by Strauss and colleagues (Strauss, Hafez, Lieberman, & Harding, 1985); the addition of yet another neurological impairment in addition to the schizophrenia, the Deficit Syndrome (Kirkpatrick, Buchanan, McKenney, Alphs, & Carpenter, 1989); significant sex differences from conception to death, including symptom display and response to medications (Seeman & Lang 1995); and the organic sequelae of substance abuse to the already insulted brain.

Developmental Factors

Premorbid adjustment has been studied since the days of Kraepelin. He noted in the histories of his patients, especially in males, that they had exhibited "a quiet, shy, retiring position, made no friends, and lived only for themselves" (Kraepelin, 1919, p. 109). The problem was to determine whether the observations were targeting early morbidity or premorbidity (Cannon-Spoor et al., 1982) or a preschizophrenic vulnerability (Meyer, 1910). Little attention was focused on childhood asociality as a predictor of outcome (with Hoch, 1910, as the exception) until the late 1930s and 1940s, when Kant (1944) and Langfeldt (1939) attempted to split schizophrenia into two subgroups: one with a reactive extravert acute onset group and the other with a slow insidious introvert slow process group. The Process–Reactive Dichotomy, as it became known in the literature (e.g., Garmezy, 1970), appears to be more related to early relationships with etiology and short-term course (Bromet, Harrow, & Kasl, 1974), while the premorbid studies were related to early developmental task achievement (e.g., Childers & Harding, 1990; Gittleman-Klein & Klein, 1969; Phillips & Zigler, 1961).

The findings of both strategies appeared to have held up as predictors especially for males in many short-term studies (Gittleman-Klein & Klein, 1969; Lewine, 1981). However, both concepts were challenged in Vaillant's 10-year follow-up study in which he compared the outcome of patients divided into two groups (Vaillant, 1978). One group demonstrated good premorbid functioning, acute onsets, clear precipitants, affectivity to their symptoms, affective family history, clear sensorium, resolution of symptoms, and a return to baseline functioning, while the other group did not. At the 10-year follow-up, 61% of the good premorbid acute onset group were functioning well but 39% were not. The long-term studies discussed earlier (e.g., Bleuler, 1972/1978; Harding et al., 1987b) have also shown that it is possible for good premorbid subjects to cross over to poor outcome and for poor premorbid patients to enter the good outcome categories. While the trends in the data sets remain in the expected direction, their strength weakens decade by decade (Childers & Harding, 1990).

Having a very serious illness as an adolescent or young adult seriously disrupts normal developmental progression. However, the long-term studies have revealed that as the illness lifts, development as adults continues if patients are allowed to integrate the experience and are given opportunities to pursue continued developmental task completion (Strauss & Harding, 1990). These authors also contend that outcome is multifaceted (not just good or poor). Further, the adult developmental literature, itself, has revealed that normal adult development is not an orderly linear affair but one of "plasticity, resiliency, discontinuity, regression, advancement, and compensation " across time (p. 518 see also Harding, 1991). So it is also for patients reclaiming their lives as the example below illustrates.

The senior author (CMH) has related an experience with a Vermont subject who was 86 years of age. This story illustrates the fact that adult development does continue across the life course for both former patients and investigators. In the mid-1970s, the author was a younger woman frantically trying to balance career development and family commitments. She was interviewing the subject in the pilot study for the Vermont Longitudinal Research Study (Harding et al., 1987a). The older woman patted the younger one on the shoulder and said: "There, there, relax a little, dearie. I had my life interrupted by schizophrenia, but I have been able to accomplish all I set out to do. I just had to do it sequentially and so can you!"

The Yale Longitudinal Study team also charted the ways in which patients play active roles in their own reclamation projects (Strauss, Harding, Hafez, & Lieberman, 1987). The Yale group (Strauss et al., 1987) discussed the role of actively choosing compliance/noncompliance in treatment regimens, utilization of skills training, and the decision to be a collaborator and innovator (see Breier & Strauss, 1983). Further, Breier and Strauss (1984) also reported from the same study, the differential use of social supports depending on the phase of the recovery process. In the phase known as "convalescence," patients reported that they wanted ventilation, reality testing, social approval, integration, problem solving, and constancy. In the phase known as "rebuilding," the same patients described the shift to needing motivation, reciprocal relating, symptom monitoring, understanding, modeling, and insight as being more helpful. Reports of self-help activities have permeated the literature for decades (e.g., Bleuler, 1972/1978; Bockes, 1985; Brundage, 1983; Chamberlin, 1979; Deegan, 1988; Feder, 1982; Kaplan, 1964; Lovejoy, 1984; Strauss et al., 1987) as either single-case reports, autobiographical accounts, or the long-term studies referenced in this chapter. All of these strategies have been assessed or observed by the investigators in the long-term studies and thus appear to play a major role in the recovery process.

McCrory et al., (1980) have suggested that rehabilitation counselors as well as clinicians tend to step in the way of adult developmental growth by aiming toward maintenance and stabilization. Further, they have proposed a series of strategies designed to promote growth, which include role play, increased support, problem solving, and letting clients try their wings even at the risk of failure when they desire to try a developmental task such as going back to school, leaving their parent's home, getting a job, or asking someone out for a date. As a point of comparison, Olympic athletes, whose lives were seriously disrupted by extreme concentration on their athletic goals, need to be retrained in vocational as well as social skills once finished with their tasks by age 30. One primary difference between this disruption of development and that from the disorder of schizophrenia is that society judges them differently (Harding & Zahniser, 1995).

SEX-RELATED DIFFERENCES

Just as with persons in general, sex roles and beliefs shape the social functioning of persons with schizophrenia, and it is likely that these factors impinge on long-term social functioning as well. Men and women are imbedded within the culture and society in which they are raised and therefore carry all of that training into any illness which superimposes itself on them. Men with schizophrenia tend to endorse the same beliefs about masculinity as men in general (Keller, 1995). Just as other men (Spence & Sawin, 1985; Thompson & Pleck, 1987), men with schizophrenia tend to believe in the importance of controlling their emotions, limiting their expressiveness, and conforming in relationships to role expectations such as being a father, provider, or partner (Keller, 1995). For men in general, the masculine gender role has generally been seen as a limiting factor on social functioning (Eisler & Blalock, 1991; Fine, 1988; Kaufman, 1992; Rubin, 1986; Sattel, 1992; Skord & Schumacher, 1982; Thompson & Pleck, 1987; Wright, 1987). However, some have begun to question whether men are less able to function socially, proposing instead that men may have modes of relating that, while less emotionally expressive, nevertheless are quite functional and adaptive (Burda & Vaux, 1987; Heesacker & Prichard, 1992; Keller, 1995; Kelly & Hall, 1992).

Women also have recently been studied as to their special needs with severe and persistent mental illnesses (e.g., Bachrach & Nadelson, 1988; Holstein & Harding, 1992; Seeman, 1995). Socialization of women promotes behaviors to seek consensus, be emotionally expressive, play multiple roles (person, wife, mother, and worker), and seek medical help (Test & Berlin, 1981). All play important functions when these factors are disrupted by the symptoms and behaviors associated with schizophrenia. All of these sex-related differences should perform important functions in program design (Bachrach, 1988). Further, studies of the long-term outcome of social functioning in schizophrenia would require such measures of sensitivity in order not to miss the heterogeneity of social outcome related to sex roles.

Environmental Impact

Placing persons with schizophrenia back into their environmental context, instead of considering them in a vacuum, has been an important step in integrated understanding and treatment. Everyone lives within a social environment which interacts, second by second, with the person's sense of competency, self-esteem, safety, acceptableness, behaviors, and biological status (Bellack, Morrison, & Mueser, 1989). For psychiatric patients, the recent appreciation of this interaction began with Wing in 1945 (Wing & Brown, 1970), and was extended through the work of Brown, Birley, and Wing (1972), Goffman (1961), Hogarty et al. (1979), and Vaughn and Leff (1976). Their work has lead to the large social movement within the field to provide family supports and psychoeducation (Falloon, Boyd, McGill, Razani, Moss, & Gilderman, 1982; Goldstein, Hand, & Halweg, 1986; Tarrier & Barrowclough, 1990; Vaughn & Leff, 1976) and social skills training (Anthony et al., 1990; Liberman et al., 1993). These attempts at environmental re-engineering have resulted in significant reductions in the relapse rates for many patients (e.g., Goldstein et al., 1986; Vaughn & Leff, 1976).

Strauss, Rakfeldt, Harding, and Lieberman (1989), among others, have suggested that the dysfunctional social behaviors that often characterize schizophrenia, such as social withdrawal and loss of interest in social relatedness, tend to be labeled as negative symptoms (Strauss & Carpenter, 1974b). However, such behaviors may also be seen as efforts to cope with the overwhelming dysphoria and confusion caused by the illness' perceptual distortion, stimulus overload, and the often exacerbating effect of interpersonal stressors. By minimizing and controlling social interactions, stress is minimized and the person often is more able to cope with his or her symptoms. As such, the apparent social dysfunction of schizophrenia, especially in its early stages, can be seen as a type of social adaptation to the disorder. Such strategies are often viewed by clinicians as a permanent state when it is part of a phase for most patients.

The variability in outcome underlying the overall figures on the long-term outcome can be dramatically shown through a comparison of the social networks of recovered and unrecovered subjects from the Vermont Study. The social networks of psychiatric patients early in their careers have also been shown generally to be sparse (Hammer, 1981). As a result, the social supports experienced by these persons tend to be markedly reduced. This reduction is of particular importance since social supports have been shown to be of great value in the resilience toward and recovery from a variety of life-threatening disorders and stressors (Beels, 1981). Figures 9.1 and 9.2 depict the social networks of two female subjects with the same diagnosis, the same age range, and very different outcomes from the Vermont cohort. These figures illustrate the stark difference in social network composition between persons with recovered and unrecovered social function.

Studies that have examined the role of psychotherapy in the lives of persons with schizophrenia and other serious mental illnesses have repeatedly found the relationship with the therapist to be essential to improvement (Gunderson, 1978; Lamb, 1988; Neligh & Kinzie, 1983; McGlashan & Keats, 1989; Rogers, Gendlin, Kiesler, & Truax, 1967). A study of the attitudes of persons with schizophrenia in the residual phase of the disorder toward the therapeutic relationship found that over 70% saw

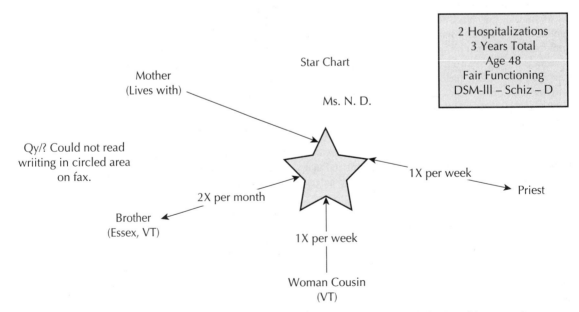

Figure 9.1. Wide network of person diagnosed with schizophrenia at index hospitalization with recovered social functioning at long-term outcome

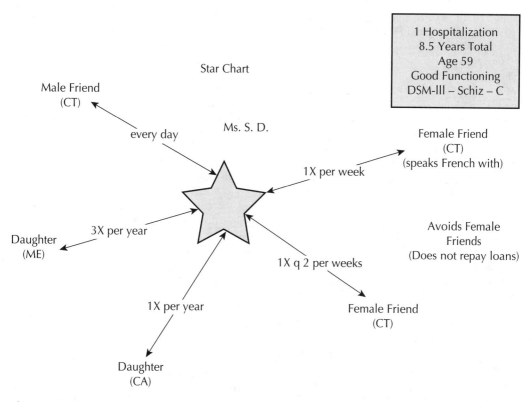

Figure 9.2.   Restricted network of person diagnosed with schizophrenia at index hospitalization with unrecovered social functioning at long-term outcome

friendliness as the most important characteristic in a therapist (Coursey et al., 1995). Given the ascendancy of biological interventions with schizophrenia, the role of psychotherapy has increasingly moved to an emphasis on psychosocial functioning, including social adaptation and relatedness (Coursey, 1989). The degree to which psychotherapy has served this role in the life of a person with schizophrenia should therefore effect social functioning over the long-term.

Clubhouse and residential settings offer social structure, through an informal social society that is structured and safe, in which people can titrate and practice social skills. The increasing use of clubhouse programs, such as those following the Fountain House model (Beard, Malamud, & Rossman, 1978), also offer an opportunity for persons with schizophrenia to practice social skills and begin new relationships within the context of a supportive community. Clubhouses, drop-in centers, and other member-run settings (Salem, Seidman, & Rappaport, 1988; Snow-

don, 1980) provide meaningful social roles for persons with schizophrenia, ranging from simply being a place to be with other people to work roles and leadership and advocacy opportunities. As such, clubhouses, drop-in centers, and some models of residential and day treatment facilitate social skill development by providing structured environments in which social interactions can be titrated and controlled in a way that facilitates skill acquisition.

Further, evidence has been accumulating from the UCLA training modules that social skills can be trained using behaviorally structured, problem-solving educational strategies (Chapter 19; Liberman et al., 1993). Building upon the success of cognitive interventions in treating other mental disorders, some have begun to apply cognitive theory to the treatment of schizophrenia in order to maximize the capacity to be rehabilitated (e.g., see Chapter 21). Ashbrook, Spaulding, and Cromwell, (1988) argue that many of the functional impairments that characterize schizophrenia, including problems in social functioning, stem from a continuum of cognitive impairments that impair performance, learning, memory, and executive functions (see also Nuechterlein & Dawson, 1984). Through cognitive interventions such as cognitive retraining in problem-solving skills integrated into a program of overall psychosocial intervention, the Nebraska team argued that social and other functioning can improve significantly. Brenner (1987) from Switzerland has also proposed correction of information-processing impairments associated with schizophrenia with daily interventions to retrain the brain much like the rehabilitation processes for stroke patients. Training in learning to better read and respond to social cues has also been proposed by Corrigan (1994).

While treatment can affect social functioning, so too can the administrative variables that affect the shape of treatment. Factors outside of the therapeutic and rehabilitative setting such as changes in benefit eligibility criteria, increased use of managed care techniques, and scarce resources for public sector mental health care can, therefore, also affect the course of social functioning. Such are the findings from the study of long-term outcome comparing two states, Vermont, which emphasized and funded psychosocial rehabilitation, and Maine, which did not. The study found significant differences in overall outcome associated with differences in mental health policy (DeSisto et al., 1995b). As changes in mental health care delivery systems proceed at a pace unrivaled in the history of mental health services, great care will need to be taken to ensure that such changes improve the quality of treatment outcomes as well as controlling the costs of treatment (Austin, Blum, & Murtaza, 1995; Brach, 1995; Hoge, Davidson, Griffith, Sledge, & Howenstine, 1994; Mechanic & Aiken, 1989; Schlesinger, 1989).

WHAT HAVE WE LEARNED FROM RESEARCH ABOUT SOCIAL FUNCTIONING?

Cross-sectional research or clinical snapshots do not take into account the processes that are inherently longitudinal in nature. Time is the construct that pulls it all together (Harding, 1995). What appears to be true at Time 1 may not be at all the case in Time 2, 3, or 4. The long-term studies have begun to capture the complexities, evolution, and wide heterogeneity in such processes.

Research needs to take into account the heretofore unacknowledged heterogeneity within each patient sample as well as changes across time. Triangulation of data across social contexts needs to be a consistent strategy. In-

strumentation, which has often been narrowly focused, needs to record and assess environmental opportunities and interactions available or not available to clients along their pathway. It is not clear that investigators clearly understand the "open-linked" character of the phenomena in social functioning. Past social functioning generally predicts future social functioning (but not always); sometimes past social functioning also predicts work functioning but, in general, past work predicts future work ability. Symptoms and length of hospitalizations, do not predict much of anything (Strauss & Carpenter, 1974a). We suggest that biopsychosocial etiologies that shape malfunction in social functioning have the mirror version of the same biopsychosocial ingredients which can help people restore their capacities and levels of function. Therefore, the whole person, the illness, and the environment must be measured simultaneously if we are to begin to understand these complex and interactive processes.

CONCLUSIONS

The social functioning of persons with schizophrenia tends, over the long-term, to adjust to the disorder, transcend continued symptoms, or improve as the person recovers. A multitude of factors interact to determine that eventual course such as genetic, biological, developmental, and sex-based differences. Such factors interact and restructure a wide variety of longitudinal evolutions of social functioning that are also variously impacted on and interactive with an array of environmental factors.

Building upon the broad-brush results of the long-term studies conducted in the last 25 years, current cross-sectional research has begun to describe indepth the underlying processes and structure of individual social functioning. The addition of longitudinal strategies in such investigations would promote better understanding of the pathways (Bellack, Sayers, Mueser, & Bennett, 1994; Strauss et al., 1985).

REFERENCES

American Psychiatric Association. (1968). *Diagnostic and statistical manual of mental disorders* (2nd Ed.). Washington, DC: Author.

American Psychiatric Association. (1980). *Diagnostic and statistical manual of mental disorders* (3rd Ed.). Washington, DC: Author.

American Psychiatric Association. (1994). *Diagnostic and statistical manual of mental disorders*. (4th Ed.). Washington, DC: Author.

Andreasen, N. C. (1982). Negative symptoms in schizophrenia: Definition and reliability. *Archives of General Psychiatry, 39,* 784–788.

Angst, J. (1988). European long-term follow-up studies of schizophrenia. *Schizophrenia Bulletin, 14,* 501–514.

Anthony, W., Cohen, M., & Farkas, M. (1990). *Psychiatric rehabilitation.* Boston: Center for Psychiatric Rehabilitation.

Ashbrook, R. M., Spaulding, W., & Cromwell, R. L. (1988). Computer-assisted cognition in psychiatric settings: An examination of the issues. In J. C. Mancuso & M. L. G. Shaw (Eds.), *Cognition and personal structure: Computer Access and Analyses,* (pp. 253–278). New York: Praeger.

Austin, M. J., Blum, S. R., & Murtaza, N. (1995). Local-state government relations and the development of public sector managed mental health care systems. *Administration and Policy in Mental Health, 22,* 203–216.

Bachrach, L. L. (1988). Chronically mentally ill women: emergence and legitimation of program issues. In L. L. Bachrach & C. C. Nadelson (Eds.), *Treating chronically mentally ill women* (pp. 75–96). Washington, DC: American Psychiatric Association.

Bachrach, L. L., Nadelson, C. C. (Eds.), (1988). *Treating chronically mentally ill women.* Washington, DC: American Psychiatric Association.

Beard, J. J., Malamud, T. J., & Rossman, E. (1978). Psychiatric rehabilitation and long-term rehospitalization rates: Findings from two studies. *Schizophrenia Bulletin, 4,* 622–635.

Beels, C. C. (1981). Social support and schizophrenia. *Schizophrenia Bulletin, 7,* 58–72,

Bellack, A. S., Morrison, R. L., & Mueser, K. T. (1989). Social problem solving in schizophrenia. *Schizophrenia Bulletin, 15,* 101–116.

Bellack, A. S., Sayers, M., Mueser, K. T., & Bennett, M. (1994). Evaluation of social problem-solving in schizophrenia. *Journal of Abnormal Psychology, 103,* 371–378.

Bland, R. C., & Orn, H. (1978). 14-year outcome in early schizophrenia. *Acta Psychiatrica Scandinavica, 58,* 327–338.

Bleuler, E. (1950). *Dementia praecox or the group of schizophrenias* (J. Zinkin, Trans.). New York: International Universities Press. (Original work published 1911).

Bleuler, M. (1978). *The schizophrenic disorders, long-term patient and family studies. (Die schizophrenen Geistesstörungen im Lichte langjähriger Kranken-und Familiengeschichten.)* Stuttgart: Georg Thieme. Translated (1978) by S. M. Clemens, New Haven, Yale University Press. (Original work published 1972).

Bockes, Z. (1985). Freedom means you have a choice. *Schizophrenia Bulletin, 11,* 487–489.

Brach, C. (1995). *Designing capitation projects for persons with serious mental illness: A policy guide for state and local officials.* Boston: Technical Assistance Collaborative, Inc.

Breier, A., & Strauss, J. S. (1983). Self-control of psychotic disorders. *Archives of General Psychiatry, 40,* 1141–1145.

Breier, A., & Strauss, J. S. (1994). Social relationships in the recovery from psychotic disorders. *American Journal of Psychiatry, 141,* 949–955.

Brenner, H. D. (1987). On the importance of cognitive disorders in treatment and rehabilitation. In J. S. Strauss, W. Böker, & H. D. Brenner (Eds.), *Psychosocial treatment of schizophrenia: Multidimensional concepts, psychological, family, and self-help perspectives* (pp. 136–151). Toronto: Hans Huber.

Bromet, E., Harrow, M., & Kasl, S. (1974). Premorbid functioning and outcome in schizophrenics and nonschizophrenics. *Archives of General Psychiatry, 30,* 203–207.

Brown, G. W., Birley, L. T., & Wing, J. K. (1972). Influence of family life on the course of schizophrenic disorders: A replication. *British Journal of Psychiatry, 121,* 241–258.

Brundage, B. E. (1983). First-person account: What I wanted to know but was afraid to ask. *Schizophrenia Bulletin, 9,* 583–585.

Burda, P. C., & Vaux, A. C. (1987). The social support process in men: Overcoming sex-role obstacles. *Human Relations, 40,* 31–44.

Cannon-Spoor, E., Potkin, S. G., & Wyatt, R. J. (1982). Measurement of premorbid adjustment in chronic schizophrenia. *Schizophrenia Bulletin, 8,* 470–484.

Chamberlin, J. (1979). *On our own.* New York: McGraw-Hill.

Childers, S. E., & Harding, C. M. (1990) Gender, premorbid social functioning, and long-term outcome in DSM-III schizophrenia. *Schizophrenia Bulletin, 16,* 309–318.

Chittick, R. A., Brooks, G. W., Irons, F. S., & Deane, W. N. (1961). *The Vermont Story.* Burlington, VT: Queen City Printers.

Ciompi, L. (1980a). Catamnestic long-term study on the course of life and aging schizophrenics. *Schizophrenia Bulletin, 6,* 606–618.

Ciompi, L. (1980b). Is chronic schizophrenia an artifact? Arguments and counterarguments. *Forschritte der Neurologie-Psychiatrie, 48,* 237–248.

Ciompi, L., & Müller, C. (1976–1984). *Lebensweg und Alter Schizophrenen. Eine katamnestische bis ins Alter.* Berlin, Springer Verlag. Translated (1984) by E. Forberg as *The life course and aging in schizophrenia: A catamnestic longitudinal study into advanced age.* for the Vermont Longitudinal Research Project. (Original work published 1976).

Corrigan, P. (1994). Social cue perception and intelligence in schizophrenia. *Schizophrenia Research, 13,* 73–79.

Coursey, R. D. (1989). Psychotherapy with persons suffering from schizophrenia: The need for a new agenda. *Schizophrenia Bulletin, 15,* 349–353.

Coursey, R. D., Keller, A. B., & Farrell, E. W. (1995). Individual psychotherapy and persons with serious mental illness: The client's perspective. *Schizophrenia Bulletin. 21,* 283–302.

Deegan, P. (1988). Recovery: The lived experience of rehabilitation. *Psychosocial Rehabilitation Journal, 11,* 167–170.

DeSisto, M. J., Harding, C. M., McCormick, R. V., Ashikaga, T., & Gautam, S. (1995a). The Maine-Vermont three decade studies of serious mental illness: Matched comparison of cross-sectional outcome. *British Journal of Psychiatry, 167,* 331–338.

DeSisto, M. J., Harding, C. M., McCormick, R. J., Ashikaga, T., & Brooks, G. W. (1995b). The Vermont-Maine three decade studies of serious mental illness: Longitudinal course comparisons. *British Journal of Psychiatry, 167,* 338–342.

Docherty, J. P., van Kammen, D. P., Siris, S. G., & Marder, S. R. (1978). Stages of onset of schizophrenic psychosis. *American Journal of Psychiatry, 135,* 420–426.

Eguma, Y. (1962). The prevention of failure in the rehabilitation of discharged schizophrenic patients. *Psychiatria et Neurologia Japonica, 64,* 921–927.

Eisler, J. M., & Blalock, J. A. (1991). Masculine gender role stress: Implications for the assessment of men. *Clinical Psychology Review, 11,* 45–60.

Falloon, I. R. H., Boyd, J. L., McGill, C. W., Razani, J., Moss, H. B., & Gilderman, A. M. (1982). Family management in the prevention of exacerbations of schizophrenia: A controlled study. *New England Journal of Medicine, 306,* 1437–1440.

Feder, R. (1982). Auditory hallucinations treated by radio headphones. *American Journal of Psychiatry, 139,* 1188–1190.

Feighner, J., Robins, E., Guze, S., Woodruff, R. Jr., Winokur, G., & Munoz, R. (1972). Diagnostic criteria for use in psychiatric research. *Archives of General Psychiatry, 26,* 57–63.

Fine, R. (1988). *Troubled men: The psychology, emotional conflicts, and therapy of men.* San Francisco: Jossey-Bass.

Gardos, G., Cole, J. O., & LaBrie, R. A. (1982). A 12-year follow-up study of chronic schizophrenics. *Hospital and Community Psychiatry, 33,* 983–984.

Garmezy, N. (1970). Process and reactive schizophrenia: Some conceptions and issues. *Schizophrenia Bulletin* (Experimental Issue #2), 30–74.

Gittleman-Klein, R., & Klein, D. K. (1969). Premorbid asocial adjustment and prognosis in schizophrenia. *Journal of Psychiatric Research, 7,* 35–53.

Goffman, E. (1961). *Asylums: Essays on the social situation of mental patients and other inmates.* New York: Doubleday Anchor.

Goldstein, M. J., Hand, I., & Halweg, K. (1986). *Treatment of schizophrenia: Family assessment and intervention.* Berlin: Springer-Verlag.

Green, M. F. (1996). What are the functional consequences of neurocognitive deficits in schizophrenia? *American Journal of Psychiatry, 153,* 321–330.

Gunderson, J. G. (1978). Patient-therapist matching: A research evaluation. *American Journal of Psychiatry, 135,* 1193–1197.

Hammer, M. (1981). Social supports, social networks, and schizophrenia. *Schizophrenia Bulletin, 7,* 45–57.

Harding, C. M. (1991). Aging and schizophrenia: Plasticity, reversibility, and/or compensation? In E. F. Walker, (Ed.), *Schizophrenia: A life course developmental perspective* (pp. 257–273). New York: Academic Press.

Harding, C. M. (1994). An examination of the complexities in the measurement of recovery in severe psychiatric disorders. In R. J. Ancill, S. Holliday, & J. Higenbottam (Eds.), *Schizophrenia: Exploring the spectrum of psychosis* (pp. 153–169). Chichester: Wiley.

Harding, C. M. (1995). The interaction of biopsychosocial factors, time, and course of schizophrenia: time is the critical covariate. In C. L. Shriqui & H. A. Nasrallah (Eds.), *Contemporary issues in the treatment of schizophrenia* (pp. 653–681). Washington, DC: American Psychiatric Press.

Harding, C. M., Brooks, G. W., Ashikaga, T., Strauss, J. S., & Breier, A. (1987a). The Vermont longitudinal study of persons with severe mental illness: I. Methodology, study sample, and overall status 32 years later. *American Journal of Psychiatry, 144,* 718–726.

Harding, C. M., Brooks, G. W., Ashikaga, T., Strauss, J. S., & Breier, A. (1987b). The Vermont longitudinal study: II. Long-term outcome of subjects who retrospectively met DSM-III criteria for schizophrenia. *American Journal of Psychiatry, 144,* 727–735.

Harding, C. M., Brooks, G. W., Ashikaga, T., Strauss, J. S., & Landerl, P. D. (1987c). Aging and social functioning in once-chronic schizophrenic patients 22–62 years after first admission: The Vermont Story. In N. Miller & G. D. Cohen (Eds.), *Schizophrenia and aging: Schizophrenia, paranoia, and schizophreniform disorders in later life* (pp. 160–166). New York: Guilford Press.

Harding, C. M., & Zahniser, J. (1995). Empirical correction of seven myths about schizophrenia. *Acta Psychiatrica Scandinavica. 90* (Suppl. 384), 140–146.

Harding, C. M., Zubin, J., & Strauss, J. S. (1987). Chronicity in schizophrenia: Fact, partial fact, or artifact? *Hospital and Community Psychiatry, 38,* 477–486.

Harding, C. M., Zubin, J., & Strauss, J. S. (1992). Chronicity in schizophrenia revisited. *British Journal of Psychiatry. 161* (Suppl. 18), 27–37.

Heesacker, M., & Prichard, S. (1992). In a different voice, revisited: Men, women, and emotion. *Journal of Mental Health Counseling, 14,* 274–290.

Heinrichs, D. W., & Carpenter, W. T. (1985). Prospective study of prodromal symptoms in schizophrenic relapse. *American Journal of Psychiatry, 142,* 371–373.

Herz, M. I., Glazer, W. M., Mirza, M., Mostert, M. A., & Hafez, H. (1989). Treating prodromal episodes to prevent relapse in schizophrenia. *British Journal of Psychiatry, 155* (Suppl. 5), 123–127.

Hirsch, S. R., & Jolley, A. G. (1989). The dysphoric syndrome in schizophrenia and its implications for relapse. *British Journal of Psychiatry, 155* (Suppl. 5), 46–50.

Hoch, A. (1910). Constitutional factors in the dementia praecox group. *Review of Neurological Psychiatry, 81,* 463–474.

Hogarty, G. E., Schooler, N. R., Ulrich, R., Mussare, F., Peregrino, F., & Herron, E. (1979). Fluphenazine and social therapy in the aftercare of schizophrenic patients. *Archives of General Psychiatry, 36,* 1283–1294.

Hoge, M. A., Davidson, L., Griffith, E. E. H., Sledge, W. H., &

Howenstine, R. A. (1994). Defining managed care in public-sector psychiatry. *Hospital and Community Psychiatry, 45,* 1085–1089.

Holstein, A. R., & Harding, C. M. (1992). Omissions in assessment of work roles: Implications for evaluating and social functioning in mental illness. *Journal of Orthopsychiatry, 62,* 469–474.

Huber, G., Gross, G., & Schüttler, R. (1975). A long-term follow-up study of schizophrenia: Psychiatric course of illness and prognosis. *Acta Psychiatrica Scandinavica, 50,* 49–57.

Huber, G., Gross, G., Schüttler, R., & Lintz, M. (1980). Longitudinal studies of schizophrenic patients. *Schizophrenia Bulletin, 6,* 592–605.

Kant, O. (1944). A comparative study of recovered and deteriorated schizophrenic patients. *Journal of Nervous and Mental Disease, 93,* 616–624.

Kaplan, B. (Ed.). (1964). *The inner world of mental illness.* New York: Harper & Row.

Kaufman, M. (1992). The construction of masculinity and the triad of men's violence. In M. S. Kimmel, & M. A. Messner, (Eds.), *Men's lives* (2nd ed., pp. 28–50). New York: Macmillan.

Keller, A. B. (1995). *Men with serious mental illness and their masculine beliefs.* Unpublished dissertation, University of Maryland, College Park, MD.

Kelly, K. R., & Hall, A. S. (1992). Toward a developmental model for counseling: Special mental health counseling for men. *Journal of Mental Health Counseling, 14,* 257–273.

Kendler, K., & Eaves, L. J. (1986). Models for joint effect of genotype and environment on liability to psychiatric illness, *American Journal of Psychiatry, 143,* 279–289.

Kirkpatrick, B., Buchanan, R., McKenney, P. D., Alphs, L. D., & Carpenter, W. T. (1989). The schedule for the deficit syndrome: An instrument for research in schizophrenia. *Psychiatry Research, 30,* 119–123.

Kraepelin, E. (1902). Dementia praecox. In A. R. Diefendorf (Trans.), *Clinical psychiatry: A textbook for students.* (6th ed.). New York: Macmillan.

Kraepelin, E. (1919). *Dementia praecox and paraphrenia.* Edinburgh: E. S. Livingston.

Lamb, H. R. (1988). One-to-one relationships with the long-term mentally ill: Issues in training professionals. *Community Mental Health Journal, 24,* 328 –337.

Langfeldt, G. (1939). *Schizophreniform states.* Copenhagen: E. Munksgaard.

Lewine, R. J. (1981). Sex differences in schizophrenia: Timing or subtypes. *Psychological Bulletin, 30,* 432–444.

Liberman, R. P., Wallace, C. J., Blackwell, G., Eckman, T. A., Vaccaro, J. V., & Kuehnel, T. G. (1993). Innovations in skills training for the seriously mentally ill: The UCLA social and independent living skills modules. *Innovations and Research, 2,* 43–59.

Lovejoy, M. (1982). Expectations and the recovery process. *Schizophrenia Bulletin, 8,* 605–609.

Lovejoy, M. (1984). Recovery from schizophrenia: A personal odyssey. *Hospital and Community Psychiatry, 35,* 809–812.

McCrory, D. J., Connolly, P. S., Mayer, T.P., Landolf, J. M., Barone, F. C., Blood, A. H., & Gilson, A. B. (1980). The rehabilitation crisis: The impact on growth. *Journal of Applied Rehabilitation Counseling, 11,* 136–139.

McGlashan, T. H., & Keats, C. J. (l989). *Schizophrenia: Treatment process and outcome.* Washington, DC: American Psychiatric Press.

Mechanic, D., & Aiken, L. H. (1989). Capitation in mental health: Potentials and cautions. *New Directions for Mental Health Services, 43,* 5–18.

Meyer, A. (1910). The dynamic interpretation of dementia praecox. *American Journal of Psychology, 21,* 385–403.

Neligh, G. L., & Kinzie, J. D. (1983). Therapeutic relationships with the chronic patient. In D. L. Cutler (Ed.)., Effective aftercare for the 1980s. *New directions for mental health services #19* (pp. 73–83). San Francisco: Jossey-Bass.

Nuechterlein, K. H., & Dawson, M. E. (1984). Information processing and attention functioning in the developmental course of schizophrenic disorders. *Schizophrenia Bulletin, 10,* 160–203.

Ogawa, K., Miya, M., Watari, A., Nakazawa, M., Yuasa, S., & Utena, H. (1987). A long-term follow-up study of schizophrenia in Japan—with special reference to the course of social adjustment. *British Journal of Psychiatry, 151,* 758–765.

Phillips, L. (1953). Case history data and prognosis in schizophrenia. *Journal of Nervous and Mental Disease, 117,* 515–525.

Phillips, L., & Zigler, E. (1961). Social competence and outcome in psychiatric disorder. *Journal of Abnormal and Social Psychology, 62,* 264–271.

Rogers, C. R., Gendlin, E. G., Kiesler, D. J., & Truax, C. B. (l967). *The therapeutic relationship and its impact: Study of psychotherapy with schizophrenics.* Madison: University of Wisconsin Press.

Rubin, L. B. (1986). On men and friendship. *Psychoanalytic Review, 73,* 165–181.

Salem, D. A., Seidman, E., & Rappaport, J. (1988). Community treatment of the mentally ill: The promise of mutual-help organizations. *Social Work, 33,* 403–408.

Sattel, J. W. (1992). The inexpressive male: Tragedy or sexual politics. In M. S. Kimmel, & M. A. Messner (Eds.), *Men's lives* (2nd. ed., pp. 350–358). New York: Macmillan.

Schlesinger, M. (1989). Striking a balance: Capitation, the mentally ill, and public policy. *New Directions for Mental Health Services, 43,* 97–115.

Seeman, M. (Ed.), (1995). *Gender and psychopathology.* Washington, DC: American Psychiatric Association.

Seeman, M., & Lang, M. (1985). The role of estrogens in schizophrenia gender differences. *Schizophrenia Bulletin, 16,* 185–194.

Spence, J. T., & Sawin, L. L. (1985). Images of masculinity and femininity: A reconceptualization. In V. O'Leary, R. Unger, &

B. Walston (Eds.), *Sex, gender and social psychology*. Hillsdale, NJ: Erlbaum.

Skord, K. G., & Schumacher, B. (1982). Masculinity as a handicapping condition. *Rehabilitation Literature, 43,* 284–289.

Snowdon, J. (1980). Self-help groups and schizophrenia. *Australian and New Zealand Journal of Psychiatry, 14,* 265–268.

Strauss, J. S., & Carpenter, W. T. (1974a). The prediction of outcome in schizophrenia II. Relationships between predictor and outcome variables. *Archives of General Psychiatry, 31,* 37–42.

Strauss, J. S., & Carpenter, W. T. (1974b). Characteristic symptoms and outcome of schizophrenia. *Archives of General Psychiatry, 30,* 429–434.

Strauss, J. S., & Carpenter, W. T. (1977). Prediction of outcome in schizophrenia III. Five-year outcome and its predictors. *Archives of General Psychiatry, 34,* 159–163.

Strauss, J. S., Hafez, H., Lieberman, P., & Harding, C. M. (1985). The course of psychiatric disorder: III. Longitudinal principles. *American Journal of Psychiatry, 142,* 289–296.

Strauss, J. S., & Harding, C. M. (1990). Relationships between adult development and the course of mental disorder. In J. Rolf, A. Master, D. Cicchetti, K. Nuechterlein, & S. Weintraub (Eds.), *Risk and protective factors in the development of psychopathology,* (pp. 514–525). New York: Cambridge University.

Strauss, J. S., Harding, C. M., Hafez, H., & Lieberman, P. (1987). The role of the patient in recovery from psychosis. In J. S. Strauss, W. Böker, & H. Brenner (Eds.), *Psychosocial management of schizophrenia* (pp. 160–166). Toronto: Hans Huber Publisher.

Strauss, J. S., Rakfeldt, J. H., Harding, C. M., & Lieberman, P. (1989). Psychological and social aspects of negative symptoms. *British Journal of Psychiatry, 155* (Suppl. 7), 128–132.

Tarrier, N., & Barrowclough, C. (1990). Social functioning in schizophrenic patients: I. The effects of expressed emotion and family interventions. *Social Psychiatry and Psychiatric Epidemiology, 25,* 125–129.

Test, M. A. (1992). Training in community living. In R. P. Liberman (Ed.), *Handbook of psychiatric rehabilitation* (pp. 153–170). New York: Macmillan.

Test, M. A., & Berlin, S. B. (1981). Issues of special concern to chronically mentally ill women. *Professional psychology, 12,* 136–145.

Thompson, E. H., & Pleck, J. H. (1987). The structure of male role norms. In M. S. Kimmel, (Ed.), *Changing men: New directions in research on men and masculinity* (pp. 25–36). Newbury Park, CA: Sage.

Tsuang, M., & Winokur, G. E. (1975). The Iowa 500: Field work in a 35-year follow-up of depression, mania, and schizophrenia. *Canadian Psychiatric Journal, 20,* 359–364.

Tsuang, M., Woolson, R. F., & Fleming, J. (1979). Long-term outcome of major psychoses, I. Schizophrenia and affective disorders compared with psychiatrically symptom-free surgical conditions. *Archives of General Psychiatry, 36,* 1295–1301.

Vaillant, G. E. (1978). A ten-year follow-up of remitting schizophrenics. *Schizophrenia Bulletin, 4,* 78–85.

Vaughn, C., & Leff, J. (1976). The influence of family and social factors on the course of psychiatric illness. *British Journal of Psychiatry, 129,* 125–137.

Wing, J. K., & Brown, G. W. (1970). *Institutionalism and schizophrenia*. London: Cambridge University Press.

Wittman, P. (1941). Scale for measuring prognosis in schizophrenia patients. *Elgin State Hospital Papers, 4,* 20–33.

World Health Organization. (1979). *Schizophrenia: An international follow-up study*. Chichester: Wiley.

World Health Organization. (1975). *International classification of diseases (ICD 9-CM), 9th revision, clinical modification*. Geneva: Author.

Wright, F. (1987). Men, shame and antisocial behavior: A psychodynamic perspective. *Group 11,* 238–246.

Zubin J., & Spring, B. (1977). Vulnerability: A new view of schizophrenia. *Journal of Abnormal Psychology, 86,* 103–126.

CHAPTER 10

GENDER DIFFERENCES IN SOCIAL FUNCTIONING

Gretchen L. Haas
Lorraine S. Garratt

Gender differences in the clinical course of schizophrenia have been reported in the clinical literature for nearly a century (Kraepelin, 1919), and yet they have become a focus of directed empirical investigation only over the past decade. Consistent with the early observations of Kraepelin, the empirical findings to date suggest that females experience a more benign course of illness in schizophrenia—characterized by a later age of onset, superior response to antipsychotic medication, better global outcome, fewer hospitalizations, and a lower risk of suicide (Seeman, 1982, 1985). This chapter is directed to the question, "Are there gender differences in social functioning in schizophrenia?" In addressing this question, we will review empirical data on sex-related variation in (1) psychosocial adjustment during the premorbid phase of development; (2) premorbid achievement in intellectual, academic, and occupational spheres; (3) short and long-term outcome on measures of social and occupational functioning; (4) pharmacologic and psychosocial treatment response as related to social functioning; and (5) lab-

oratory studies of social skills and response to social skills interventions. We will also attempt to address two questions regarding the essential nature of gender differences in social and occupational outcomes. The first question relates to whether gender differences in social functioning outcomes are governed by the competencies and deficits of the premorbid period of functioning. In other words, "Does premorbid social competency determine the range of functioning after the onset of the psychotic phase of illness?" A second important question has to do with the relationship between early age at onset and poor outcome: "Does an early onset of psychosis retard or foreclose development of social skills?" If so, does the tendency toward a later onset of illness offer the female some advantage in terms of social skill development? Gender differences in social functioning in schizophrenia will also be considered in the light of contemporary explanatory models of sex differences in schizophrenia. Finally, future directions for research on social and biologic determinants of sex-differentiated social functioning will be proposed.

GENDER DIFFERENCES IN PREMORBID ADJUSTMENT

Marital Status

Early interest in gender differences in premorbid social competence derived from observations that females with schizophrenia were more likely than males to marry—a finding that has been reported consistently over time and across cultures (e.g., Farina, Garmezy, & Barry, 1963; Walker, Bettes, Kain, & Harvey, 1985; Turner, Dopkeen, & Labreche, 1970). In fact, a higher rate of marriage among females is the most strikingly consistent sex difference in schizophrenia next to the finding of a later average age at onset among females. A majority of outcome studies report that among individuals with schizophrenia, females are more likely than males to be married or involved in heterosexual relationships (Salokangas, 1983; Riecher-Rössler, Fätkenheuer, Löffler, Maurer, & Häfner, 1992; Seeman, 1986; Gibbons, Horn, Powell, & Gibbons, 1984; Salokangas & Stengård, 1990; Goldstein, Tsuang, & Faraone, 1989), and/or to have children (Salokangas & Stengård, 1990).

Several studies have reported that among preschizophrenia individuals, females are more likely than males to be involved in heterosexual relationships—whether married or not—*before the onset of their illness* (Goldstein, Tsuang, & Faraone, 1989; Landis & Page, 1938; Raskin & Golob, 1966). In a study of 227 first contact schizophrenic patients, Salokangas and Stengård (1990) found that 75% of women, compared with only 52% of men, had established a heterosexual relationship by the time they reached the age of 23. In addition, 31% of the women were married at the time of first hospitalization, as compared with only 15.3% of the men. Riecher-Rössler et al. (1992) reported sex-specific age distributions at first admission for single versus married for a sample of 456 individuals with International Classification of Disease (ICD) criteria for schizophrenia; females were 3.6 times as likely as males to be married at the time of first admission to hospital.

Given the earlier age of marriage of females as compared with males in the general population, and the later age of illness onset among women with schizophrenia, it is of some interest whether the sex difference in rates of marriage is limited to the premorbid period—and thus whether females are more likely to marry prior to illness onset simply because they have more years of marriage eligibility prior to onset of illness. Although there are no

data that bear directly on this question, what data are available regarding the timing and frequency of marriage in schizophrenia suggest that males with schizophrenia are less likely to marry than are females at any point in the course of their lives. For example, in a follow-up study of 182 schizophrenic patients (at 18 months to 10 years following the index psychiatric treatment), Wattie and Kedward (1985) found that females were 2.5 times more likely than males to have established a conjugal relationship at some time in their lifetime; at the time of assessment, 50.7% of the women were married, compared with only 16.5% of the men. Overall, 69.9% of the women had been married at some point in their lives, whereas only 28.4% of the men had ever been married. When compared with marital status data for first-episode cases (e.g., Goldstein et al., 1989; Reicher-Rössler et al., 1992), these findings suggest that females are more likely than males to marry—even after onset of the active phase of schizophrenia. Consistent with this interpretation are the findings of Riecher-Rössler and colleagues (1992) who found in their sample of first-admissions with ICD–9 schizophrenia, that only 20% of the ever-married males and females married after the appearance of the earliest signs of psychiatric disorder. Of particular interest was the finding that 14% of the never-married females, as contrasted with 4% of the never-married males, married after the onset of the early symptoms.

Farina et al. (1963) observed that among individuals who experienced their first episode of schizophrenia *at any time* during adulthood (age 21 or later), marriage rates were lower than expected—based on age and sex-matched rates for the general population (a negative selection effect of illness on opportunity for marriage). These investigators also noted that this negative selection effect was greater for males than for females—within the early-onset (≤ age 30) cases. In summary, the cumulative findings suggest that in schizophrenia the negative impact of illness on marriage is observed over the full course of adulthood, but it has its the greatest impact on marriage among early-onset males.

Sociocultural Selection Hypothesis

Farina and his colleagues (Farina, Garmezy, & Barry, 1963; Farina, Garmezy, Zalusky, & Becker, 1962) proposed that sociocultural factors were likely to be at least partially responsible for the sex difference in marriage rates in schizophrenia. These investigators speculated that because males traditionally play the more active role in initiating heterosexual dating relationships and marriage, the social anhedonia and social withdrawal symptoms of schizophrenia may have a more dramatic negative impact on the heterosexual role functioning of males relative to females. Thus, because standards for adequate gender-specific role performances may be more demanding for males, one cannot be assured that the highly robust finding of a higher frequency of dating and marriage among females is evidence of greater social competence. On the other hand, although this sociocultural explanation for sex differences in marital status in schizophrenia is plausible, the bulk of the empirical data suggests that married women are no less socially skilled than are their married male counterparts. Also, Farina and colleagues (Farina et al., 1962) noted that they found no weaker a relationship between marital status and clinical outcome for females than for males—a finding that would tend to undermine the notion that a lower level of functioning is required for females to marry in our culture.

Marriage and Delay to Onset of Illness

Although females are more likely than males to marry—even after the onset of illness, more females marry prior to, rather than following, the onset of the psychotic symptoms of schizophrenia. Thus, it has been suggested that marriage may *protect* against, or delay, the onset of illness—a possible explanation for the later age at onset among females. The results of three epidemiologic studies provide some data that bear on this question. First, Farina, Garmezy, and Barry (1963) found that base rates of marriage among early-onset (ages 17 to 20) females admitted to hospital for their first episode of schizophrenia were substantially elevated above marriage rates for age and sex-matched community (U.S. Census) cohort. These data would suggest that at an early age, there may be a promoting influence rather than a protective influence of marriage on the timing of onset among females. Alternatively, one might conclude that there is a selection effect of illness on marriage, such that early onset of illness among females acts to increase the likelihood of marriage during the premorbid period (a less conceivable explanation).

A second set of relevant data come from a 7-year case register study of marital status among individuals experiencing their first hospitalization for schizophrenia. In this study, Eaton (1975) found no evidence to suggest any causal or promoting impact of marriage on the course of illness. Instead, Eaton's data yielded support for a nega-

tive selection effect of illness on marital status (i.e., a negative impact of the illness on the likelihood of marriage). Eaton also found that the so-called selection ratio (an age-corrected ratio of never married to widowed individuals with schizophrenia) was higher for males than for females and that the incidence of schizophrenia was higher among married females as compared with married males—which he interpreted as evidence that the premorbid social functioning of the male was more handicapping to the achievement of marriage than was the premorbid functioning of the female. A third, more recent study by Riecher-Rössler et al. (1992) tested the hypothesis that the later age of onset in women was "at least partly explained" by an earlier age of marriage. The authors noted that any causal relationship between age at onset and marital status could not be definitively determined because both marriage and morbid risk are age-dependent phenomena. They also reported that there was no evidence that marriage delayed hospitalization among those who had active symptoms.

Thus, the existing empirical data does not support the proposition that the later age at onset of psychosis among females is influenced by a protective effect of marriage. Instead, the converse may be true; that is, it may be that a later age at onset increases the opportunity for marriage during the premorbid phase of illness. Since, on average, females develop schizophrenia at a later age than males, it would be reasonable to expect that females would, on average, have more time to develop heterosexual relationships and to marry before the onset of illness. Also, in the general population, women tend to marry at an earlier age than men, thereby increasing the likelihood that among individuals with schizophrenia, females will more commonly marry than will males—particularly during the period prior to the onset of a schizophrenia disorder. Farina et al. (1963) found that the sex differential in marriage rates was restricted to early-onset cases (those for whom onset occurred before age 31)—a finding consistent with the notion that the female advantage of earlier maturation and earlier age at marriage is likely to have its greatest impact earlier on, rather than later, in the life course.

Relationship of Marital Status to Premorbid Functioning

In the early empirical research on premorbid adjustment, the search for demographic and clinical indicators of prognosis in schizophrenia targeted marital status as an indicator of premorbid competence and as a predictor of risk for psychiatric disorder (Malzberg, 1935), treatment response, and clinical course (Adler, 1953; Counts & Devlin, 1954). However, it was recognized that the prognostic value of marital status said little or nothing about the functional relationship between marital status and the course of illness in schizophrenia. Investigators acknowledged that it was unlikely that marital status *per se* influenced the course of illness (Farina et al., 1962; Gittelman-Klein & Klein, 1968), but rather that marital status served as a proxy for associated premorbid characteristics that directly influenced the course of illness. Citing lower rates of marriage among preschizophrenia males—as compared with rates for both preschizophrenia females and (U.S. census) rates for males in the general population—Farina, Garmezy, and Barry (1963) suggested that the lower rate of marriage among schizophrenic patients (and males, in particular) may be due to a more general deficiency in the development of interpersonal relationships.

Pursuing this question, Gittelman-Klein and Klein (1968, 1969) systematically evaluated the unique influence of marital status versus other aspects of premorbid adjustment on schizophrenia outcome. Their findings indicated that although marital status was empirically associated with outcome, marital status was an unlikely primary determinant of outcome. The results of multivariate analyses suggested that premorbid social factors other than marital status (e.g., social withdrawal and schizoid behaviors) were more direct (i.e. primary) contributors to the prediction of posthospital adjustment and, as suggested by Farina et al. (1962), were more likely to influence the evolution of intimate relationships and marriage. The investigators concluded that although marital status was an effective empirical indicator of prognosis, the association between marital status and outcome most likely represented the impact of a selection factor—in which a constellation of premarital psychosocial competencies "selected" certain individuals for marriage—simultaneously enhancing the prospects for a more competent accommodation to illness among those who were, and even those who had been, married. These findings would suggest that during the premorbid phase of schizophrenia, men and women come to marriage by way of developed social competencies and that deficiencies of premorbid socialized behaviors (e.g., a schizoid pattern of adjustment during childhood and adolescence) would mobilize against marriage. If premorbid social competency was less adequate among males, and if onset of schizophrenia tended to further retard heterosexual development and the achievement of conjugal partnering in these unmarried individuals, premorbid social deficits could, in effect, contribute to reduced rates of marriage among males. Thus, the possibility that, independent of premorbid marital status, males and females show differences in premorbid social adjustment and social skills will be examined in the next section.

Premorbid Psychosocial Adjustment

Patterns of Premorbid Deficit

Whereas marital status has been used as a univariate *index* of premorbid social achievement, multidimensional approaches to the measurement of premorbid adjustment reflect a psychosocial developmental perspective on the social and work functioning competencies or deficiencies that an individual manifests prior to the onset of the psychotic symptoms of schizophrenia. From the perspective of the psychosocial deficits or dysfunction that are considered a core feature of schizophrenia, early deficits in psychosocial adjustment and specifically, asociality and schizoid behavior (Gittelman-Klein & Klein, 1968, 1969), have been viewed as evidence of a *process* type of schizophrenia with insidious onset and its origins in early childhood or before (Zigler & Phillips, 1962). From this perspective, sex differences in successful adaptation to social role expectations and socially prescribed patterns of functioning (in family, school, peer relations, etc.) may be evident before the onset of the first psychotic symptoms of schizophrenia—and as early as childhood. Several early studies reported evidence consistent with the notion that an insidious onset or process form of schizophrenia is more common among males (Allon, 1971; Lane, 1968). This classical pattern of gradual onset and core psychotic symptoms of schizophrenia has been contrasted with an "atypical" pattern characterized by a precipitated acute onset, episodic course, and brief symptom duration—a pattern that is more common among females than males (Tsuang, Dempsey, & Rauscher, 1976). In a sample of 72 first-episode schizophrenia cases, Haas and Sweeney (1992) observed that males represented the majority of cases that manifested a premorbid pattern of insidious deterioration in social functioning over childhood and adolescence. Larsen, McGlashan, Johannessen, & Vibe-Hansen (1996) have observed a similar tendency for the premorbid adjustment of males to decline more steeply from childhood through adolescence until onset (up until 6 months prior to the onset of the first psychotic symptoms) of schizophrenia. Thus, examination of the premorbid phase of illness suggests that males are more likely to manifest prodromal indicators of illness, a nonacute or insidious onset of illness characterized by longer prodromal symptom duration, and a pattern of deterioration of social functioning prior to the onset of the psychotic phase of illness.

An innovative approach to the direct observational study of premorbid social behaviors in schizophrenia has been taken by Walker and her colleagues (Walker, Grimes, Davis, & Smith, 1993) in their research using home movies of preschizophrenia individuals and their well siblings as controls. Based on age-and sex-matched control comparisons, the preschizophrenia group, as a whole, manifested more frequent display of negative affect (as compared to the sibling controls) during the period of latency age development (5 to 7 years); preschizophrenia females showed a reduction in the expression of positive affects that began in infancy and continued through adolescence (Walker et al., 1993) and, among females (birth to 8 years of age) only, a higher ratio of positive affect (in relation to neutral and negative affect) displays was predictive of later age at onset of illness (Grimes & Walker, 1994). These direct observational data on the premorbid period of functioning suggest that there may be sex-specific deviations from normal developmental trajectories in the social behavior of individuals who go on to manifest schizophrenia. Moreover, evidence of sex differences in the prognostic significance of premorbid affect display suggest that males and females may manifest different developmental trajectories and likewise, different patterns of deviation from normative patterns in the development of social behavior. Such deviant trajectories are likely to become evident during the premorbid period and continue into the active phase of schizophrenia.

Psychosocial Adaptation and Competence

Premorbid psychosocial adjustment has been conceptualized and measured from several vantage points over the decades, as reflected by a few closely related concepts and assessment indicators, including (1) premorbid *psychosocial maturity,* as illustrated by the Phillips Scale (Phillips, 1953), which evaluates psychosexual maturity based on indicators of the achievement of sexual/conjugal relations; (2) premorbid *social competence* (i.e., demonstrated social skills) based on operational indicators of observable behavior within specified social settings (Lewine, Watt, Prentky, & Fryer, 1980); and (3) *psychosocial adaptation,* which is the achievement of social-

ized age-appropriate social role behaviors in accordance with the specific demands of various developmental stages—childhood, adolescence, and adulthood—and specific to the premorbid phase of illness, as measured using the Cannon-Spoor Premorbid Adjustment Scale (Cannon-Spoor, Potkin, & Wyatt, 1982).

Central to these approaches to the conceptualization and measurement of premorbid adjustment are various dimensions of social behavior and role functioning, including indices of adaptive role functioning and the achievement of specific developmental milestones in social, educational, and occupational spheres (Zigler & Phillips, 1960). Among the early studies that examined gender differences in the premorbid adjustment of individuals who have schizophrenia, several (Eaton, 1975; Farina et al., 1963; Forrest & Hay, 1972; Goldstein, 1978; Raskin & Golob, 1966; Rosen, Klein, & Gittleman-Klein, 1969; Salokangas, 1983; Schooler, 1963; Westermeyer & Harrow, 1984; Zigler & Levine, 1981) reported evidence of female superiority in premorbid social functioning. However, many of these studies used scales that included age at onset and marital status as constituent dimensions of premorbid adjustment. Unfortunately, the extent to which indicators of *social competence* (i.e., social skills) or *social adaptation* (i.e., the achievement of age-appropriate social roles and developmental milestones) independent of age and marital status differed between the sexes was rarely examined. Importantly, among those reports wherein premorbid adjustment measures did not rely on marital status and age at illness onset, the findings indicate a higher level of premorbid social competence among females (Beiser, Bean, Erickson, Zhang, Iacono, & Rector, 1994; Gittleman-Klein & Klein, 1969; Goldstein et al., 1989; Rosen et al., 1969). Likewise, findings from more recent studies using multidimensional measures that focus on occupational functioning (Childers & Harding, 1990; Dworkin, 1990; Foerster, Lewis, Owen, & Murray, 1991; Shtasel, Gur, Gallacher, Heimberg, & Gur, 1992) suggest that among individuals with schizophrenia, females have superior academic and vocational achievement, as well as more frequent marriage and/or involvement in heterosexual relationships during the premorbid phase of the disorder.

Educational Functioning

Premorbid educational performance indicators (e.g., grades), educational achievement (e.g., the highest grade completed or highest degree attained), and premorbid indices of intelligence (e.g., the intelligence quotient (IQ) test scores) tend to be higher among females as compared with males who have schizophrenia (Aylward, Walker, & Bettes, 1984; Offord, 1974; Salokangas & Stengård, 1990). In one of the earliest studies of gender differences in the academic performance of preschizophrenia children, Offord (1974) found that males had a significantly lower average IQ (88.2 versus 97.1), completed fewer grades (8.2 versus 10.1), and were more likely to repeat one or more grades (41% versus 25%), as contrasted with females. In addition, the investigators found that although preschizophrenia males fared significantly worse than healthy (nonpsychiatric) male control subjects from the community, there were no significant differences between preschizophrenia and control females.

FUNCTIONING OVER THE COURSE OF ILLNESS

One of the hallmarks of schizophrenia is a failure to achieve or to maintain expectable levels of social, educational, and occupational attainment, given the resources of the familial environment and the social and economic circumstances and upbringing of the individual. It is also recognized that there may be tremendous variability in functioning over the life course of the individual who has schizophrenia. Individuals who function at expected levels of social and occupational competence during the premorbid phase of illness may, after illness onset, regress to lower levels of functioning or fail to achieve age-appropriate levels beyond levels of functioning reached prior to the onset of illness.

Occupational Functioning

Methodologic Issues

There is considerable cross-study variability in the findings of gender differences in occupational functioning and achievement. This variability may be attributable to sociocultural definitions of what constitutes appropriate sex-differentiated role functioning and the attendant methodologic difficulties in measuring and comparing the occupational functioning of men and women. Some studies use objective quantitative indices of functioning (e.g., percentage of full-time employment); others rank-order the type of employment held in terms of *a priori* judgments of social status attributes of the job, such as using the Hollingshead scales of socioeconomic status (Holling-

shead, 1957), while still others attempt to give quantitative assessment to qualitative aspects of work and/or educational functioning in addition to the judged status level of the occupation.

Apart from these sources of methodologic heterogeneity, some aspects of the measurement of occupational functioning may introduce sources of potential gender bias into cross-sex comparisons. This is particularly true in the treatment of the "homemaker" role in the evaluation of instrumental (employment, housekeeping, and academic performance) role functioning. Whereas some researchers approach the evaluation of housekeeping functions by including the housekeeping/home management role in the evaluation of occupational functioning, others exclude homemakers from these analyses, whereas still others consider individuals whose primary role involves housekeeping/home management as unemployed workers. Since the majority of homemakers are women (and in some studies, the majority of women are homemakers), the treatment of the homemaker/home management role (e.g., including versus excluding homemakers from analyses of occupational role functioning) may have a significant impact on reported gender difference findings. Moreover, consistent with cultural dictates and historical trends, the proportion of women in the general population who work in competitive employment has also varied over time and across cultures, thereby magnifying the difficulties in interpreting and comparing findings across studies.

Given these sources of method variance, efforts to draw overall conclusions from the existing data on occupational role functioning in schizophrenia are, at best, complicated. The next section attempts to take these methodologic issues into account in a critical review of the literature which bears on the question of sex differences in occupational functioning.

Empirical Findings
on Occupational Functioning

Although there is considerable methodologic heterogeneity across studies, a majority of investigations that have found sex differences report better occupational functioning over follow-up for females (Affleck, Burns, & Forrest, 1976; Beiser et al., 1994; Bland, Parker, & Orn, 1976; Adler, 1953; Huber, Gross, Schuttler, & Linz, 1980; Schooler, Goldberg, Boothe, & Cole, 1967; Marneros, Steinmeyer, Deister, Rohde, & Jünemann, 1989; Mc-Glashan & Bardenstein, 1990; Nyman & Jonsson, 1983;

Raskin & Dyson, 1968; Salokangas, 1983; Salokangas & Stengård, 1990; Steinmeyer, Marneros, Deister, Rohde, & Jünemann, 1989; Goldstein et al., 1989; Bardenstein & McGlashan, 1990; Navarro, van Os, Jones, & Murray, 1996). An equivalent number of studies have found no sex differences (Gittelman-Klein & Klein, 1969; Munk-JØrgensen & Mortensen, 1992b; Kay & Lindenmayer, 1987; Bland & Orn, 1978; Bland et al., 1976; Mantonakis, Jemos, Christodoulou, & Lykouras, 1982; Giel, Wiersma, de Jong, & Slooff, 1984; Masterson, Jr., 1956; Lassenius, Ottosson, & Rapp, 1973; Westermeyer & Harrow, 1984; Vogel & Vliegen, 1975; Ciompi & Müller, 1976; Deister & Marneros, 1992; Müller, 1971), and, to our knowledge, only one study has found evidence of higher levels of employment status and/or occupational functioning among males (Hall, Smith, & Shimkunas, 1966; Schooler et al., 1967). Both of these reports derived from a single study conducted in the mid–1960s, an historical period when women, in general, tended not to seek steady employment outside of the home.

In the first of these reports, Hall et al. (1966) evaluated the posthospital occupational status of only those patients whose expected (i.e., prehospital) instrumental role was that of a wage earner, thus excluding from the analyses females who were homemakers. In addition, these investigators measured occupational achievement in terms of "success in returning to work." Whereas this approach can be successful in establishing a degree of homogeneity in the measurement of occupational status, it can be argued that it introduces a gender bias in using this outcome index in that there may have been fewer family, community, and financial pressures exerted on women (in contrast to men) to return to work after psychiatric hospitalization. This socially determined influence on sex differences in outcomes was commonly observed during an era when, in the general population, proportionately fewer women worked and many women were fully supported by their families. Thus, using what are often gender-correlated categorical indices is likely to yield higher percentages of males meeting criteria for "employed" status and success in returning to an employed status. Furthermore, the lack of healthy (i.e. nonpsychiatrically ill) community control samples or normative data to evaluate sex differences limits the interpretability of these findings.

To avoid gender bias in the definition and labeling of categorical indices of instrumental role functioning, Schooler et al. (1967) elected to evaluate occupational functioning in terms of two distinctive generic categories:

wage earners and homemakers. Thus, they approached the problem by excluding homemakers from the category of wage earners. In so doing, they found that a greater percentage of male (in contrast to female) wage earners were fully self-supporting. Again, one can argue that during this period of U.S. history, women experienced fewer demands to be fully self-supporting and that among those women who were employed outside of the home, their primary goal as wage earners was not necessarily full-time employment or self-support. Interestingly, although more males than females were fully self-supporting in the Schooler et al. (1967) analysis, the investigators found no significant differences between male and female wage earners in terms of (a) regularity of work, (b) job-skill requirements, or (c) number of jobs held since discharge from hospital.

Other elements of the Schooler et al. (1967) study illustrate a useful approach to the problem of equating homemakers and wage earners in an analysis of occupational role performance. Because level of functioning can vary according to the standard applied, the investigators determined that the pooling of homemakers and wage earners was an unsatisfactory approach to the analysis of role functioning competencies. By conducting independent analyses of homemakers and wage earners, Schooler and colleagues found that proportionately more homemakers than wage earners were successfully functioning in their instrumental role area. On the other hand, it was recognized that the standards of measurement varied with the occupation and that aspects of wage earner and homemaker roles could not be assumed to be comparable. For example, it was reported that homemakers were less compatible with their neighbors than wage earners were with their coworkers (Schooler et al., 1967), although it was acknowledged that interpersonal "compatibility" was likely to vary across these generic categories of occupational role function.

In contrast to the lack of sex differences in occupational functioning found in the NIMH study (Hall et al., 1966; Schooler et al., 1967), during the same period, Raskin and Dyson (1968) reported evidence that occupational functioning was superior among female, as compared with male, probands with schizophrenia. Unlike the earlier study, Raskin and Dyson (1968) combined homemakers with wage earners in their analyses. At one-year follow-up, they reported that 80% of females were able to fulfill instrumental role demands as compared with only 41% of males. However, this significant difference can be attributed, in part, to the classification of 35% of the females as homemakers fulfilling their instrumental role, whereas no males were classified as homemakers. Examination of their data for wage earners alone indicated that there was no significant difference in the percentage of females (48%) versus males (41%) who were working in competitive paid employment outside the home at follow-up.

Likewise, findings from other studies suggest that reported gender differences in occupational status are influenced by the homemaker status of many females. In a sample of patients who were living with significant others, Gibbons et al. (1984) reported that 27% of the men were working in full- or part-time paid employment, compared with only 12% of the women. However, it was noted that women were not necessarily without an occupational role; an additional 59% of the women had some recognized status and occupation as homemakers.

On review of studies reported since the 1960s, it is notable that the findings indicate either a higher level of occupational functioning among females (Affleck et al., 1976; Beiser et al., 1994; Huber et al., 1980; Nyman & Jonsson, 1983; Mantonakis et al., 1982; Salokangas, 1986; Steinmeyer et al., 1989; Wattie & Kedward, 1985; Navarro et al., 1996) or no significant differences between males and females (Bland & Orn, 1978; Bland et al., 1976; Giel et al., 1984; Kay & Lindenmayer, 1987; Lassenius et al., 1973; Loyd, Simpson, & Tsuang, 1985; Mantonakis et al., 1982; Müller, 1971; Bleuler, 1978; Möller, Werner-Eilert, Wüschner-Stockheim, & von Zerssen, 1982; Munk-Jørgensen & Mortensen, 1992a; Gittelman-Klein & Klein, 1969; Salokangas & Stengård, 1990) in terms of occupational status and functioning. However, several studies have limitations that make interpretation and cross-study comparison difficult. A majority of the studies that reported superior occupational functioning among women combined both homemakers and wage earners when evaluating occupational functioning (Affleck et al., 1976; Huber et al., 1980; Nyman & Jonsson, 1983; Salokangas, 1986; Wattie & Kedward, 1985; Mantonakis et al., 1982; Navarro et al., 1996), and most of these studies do not evaluate the influence that the subgroup of homemakers have on the findings, nor do they report the proportion of women classified as homemakers or attempt to control for occupational status by comparing female homemakers with female wage earners or by comparing male with female wage earners.

Examples of recent studies that allow for males and females to be compared on equivalent dimensions of instrumental role functioning have reported higher levels of occupational functioning for females (Haas, Glick, Clarkin, & Spencer, 1990; Beiser et al., 1994). Even when controlling for premorbid occupational competence, Beiser et al. (1994) found that sex contributed to the prediction of 18-month occupational outcomes (better occupational functioning among females) in a sample of 33 DSM-III first-episode schizophrenic patients; interestingly, this sex effect was not observed in a comparison sample of first-episode affective psychoses, suggesting that there may be some diagnostic specificity to the sex differences in occupational functioning.

A few caveats are in order before firmly concluding that schizophrenia takes a lesser toll on the instrumental role functioning of females. First, even when males and females are compared on the same dimensions (e.g., measures of functioning in competitive paid employment), the extent to which societal standards in competitive employment settings differ for males and females (e.g., standards for employment, occupational achievement, promotion, etc.) is difficult to evaluate. Therefore, it is impossible to rule out the influence of these social factors in the conceptualization and measurement of work performance as well as the extent to which such external factors influence motivation to perform and achieve competence in work roles. There may also be a gender-related self-selection bias in the measurement of wage earner function at follow-up, with only the highest functioning females returning to, or entering, competitive employment, and other females turning to unpaid domestic roles that maintain them in a noncompetitive work setting. In contrast, many more males with schizophrenia may be pressured by family or financial circumstances to earn wages, regardless of their level of functioning. Interestingly, Andia and Zisook (1991) have suggested that such cultural artifacts cannot fully account for sex differences in functioning in schizophrenia; these authors note that gender differences are more profound among the series of outcome studies published since 1945—the postwar era, which has been characterized by women's entry into competitive employment and thus less divergence of sex-role differentiated occupational functioning.

Another factor to be considered when interpreting the data on social and occupational functioning is the use of broad versus narrow diagnostic criteria. Studies based on relatively narrowly defined (Kraepelinian) schizophrenia tend to exclude more females than males from study samples (Lewine, Burbach, & Meltzer, 1984). Hence, the females and males who meet more restrictive criteria tend to be more homogeneous, and thus, less likely to show sex-related variance in functioning. An excellent example of this principle is reflected in a within-study comparison of DSM-III and DSM-II-defined schizophrenia cases (Westermeyer & Harrow, 1984). Within the DSM-II (broadly defined) schizophrenia sample, females showed superior outcomes on measures of occupational functioning, whereas among the DSM-III (more narrowly defined) schizophrenia sample, no sex differences on measures of occupational functioning were observed. Although these findings conflict with at least one other study, which showed better premorbid and follow-up occupational functioning among females within a sample of DSM-III schizophrenic patients, the general tendency for a narrowing of diagnostic boundaries to reduce the heterogeneity of schizophrenia, and in particular, sex-related dimensions of heterogeneity—in this case, evidence of a wider range and higher mean level of posthospital occupational functioning among women—is of importance in efforts to interpret the complicated and sometimes inconsistent pattern of findings on gender differences in schizophrenia.

Downward Social Drift

Whereas measures of *premorbid psychosocial adjustment* reference dimensions of social, educational, and occupational functioning or competence prior to the onset of illness, measures of *socioeconomic achievement* document the highest levels of lifetime achievement of educational and occupational roles. Operational definitions of *socioeconomic status* are based on sociologists' rankings of various levels of educational attainment and various occupational roles in the culture (Hollingshead, 1957; 1975). These two indices—premorbid social adjustment and highest level of lifetime socioeconomic status achieved—tend to covary. However, even in the general population, they may diverge considerably as, for example, in the case of an individual who had good peer relations and academic adjustment during childhood and adolescence (good premorbid adjustment) but had no ambition to pursue a college education or to seek other than an unskilled job (resulting in a relatively low level of occupational achievement and low socioeconomic status). Likewise, some individuals may have good premorbid adjustment, as indicated by a broad range of friends and varied social activities in childhood and adolescence, followed by an acute onset of schizophrenia during late adolescence that abruptly cuts short their education and opportunities for occupational training. In such cases, the onset of schizophrenia brings premature foreclosure on educational and occupational advancement.

Downward social drift refers to a characteristic pattern of lower socioeconomic status achieved by individuals with schizophrenia as contrasted with levels of socioeconomic (i.e., educational and occupational) status achieved by their parents (Grünfeld & Salvesen, 1968; Wiersma, Giel, De Long, & Slooff, 1983; Jones et al., 1993; Munk-JØrgensen & Mortensen, 1992b; Bland & Orn, 1981; Birtchnell, 1971). Because the phenomenon of downward social drift is based on measures of the highest level of *lifetime* achievement of educational and vocational status, it can reflect both primary premorbid deficits and/or post-onset dysfunction secondary to the impact of the active phase of the illness. Existing analyses of socioeconomic status data suggest that downward socioeconomic drift may be more common among males than females who have schizophrenia (Marneros et al., 1989; Wattie & Kedward, 1985). For example, Wattie and Kedward (1985) found that even though schizophrenic males and females came from similar social class backgrounds, at the time of followup, males had significantly lower economic status than females. Similarly, Marneros et al. (1989) found a correlation between gender and social drift in a combined sample of schizophrenic and schizoaffective disorder subjects and reported that males were less likely than females to fulfill expected levels of social and occupational achievement, as assessed by interviewers and based on available resources, education, and family status.

The question of whether the phenomenon of downward drift reflects failure to achieve expected premorbid levels of educational and occupational attainment or whether it reflects a secondary impact of the illness on later stages of adult development and achievement in these areas is an interesting, but rather complex, question. In an attempt to ascertain whether downward drift reflected premorbid underachievement or post-onset decline, Jones et al., (1993) examined indicators of premorbid and postonset occupational status of a series of patients with either schizophrenia disorder or affective disorder psychoses—using pairwise comparisons of patient status rankings with the occupational status rankings of their parents. Restricting their analyses to males, the investigators reported findings that suggested that premorbid occupational underachievement was specific to males with schizophrenia, whereas the decline in occupational status following the onset of psychosis was characteristic of males with either affective disorder or schizophrenia. Although the investigators indicated that the findings were no different when both sexes were included in the analyses, they were reluctant to compare the occupational status of males and females, acknowledging the possible impact of different sociocultural expectations for occupational role functioning across the two sexes.

In a comparison of first-episode and recurrent-episode schizophrenic disorder patients, Haas, Sweeney, Hien, Goldman, and Deck (1991a) found greater downward drift among males as compared with females on lifetime achievement indicators of both educational and occupational achievement. These findings were consistent for both first-episode and recurrent-episode groups—suggesting that evidence of a more profound downward social drift among males is not attributable solely to the post-onset phase of illness but is characteristic of the premorbid phase of development.

In summary, the limited available research on socioeconomic drift in schizophrenia suggests that downward drift during the premorbid period (i.e., failure to attain expectable levels of achievement) in occupational and educational roles may be specific to schizophrenia and that this intergenerational decline in social and instrumental role functioning may be more severe among males as compared with females who have this disorder.

Living Arrangements

Another interesting, although little noted, sex difference finding that relates to social functioning in schizophrenia is that independent of marital status, females are more likely than males to be living with relatives (Gibbons et al., 1984; Wattie & Kedward, 1985). Of those individuals with schizophrenia who live with relatives, males are more likely to live with parents (Gibbons et al., 1984; Salokangas, 1983; Salokangas & Stengård, 1990), whereas females are more likely to live with spouses, children, siblings, or other relatives (Gibbons et al., 1984). This difference is no doubt due, in part, to the greater tendency for females with schizophrenia to marry and/or to have children, as discussed above.

Researchers who have examined the nature and quality of living arrangements among individuals with schizophrenia have noted that it is more common for males than females to be living in institutional settings (e.g., hospitals, residential care and boarding homes, prisons). For example, Salokangas (1983) reported that in a follow-up sample of 175 former schizophrenia patients, men were more likely than women to be living in institutions or in temporary living quarters. Wattie and Kedward (1985) reported that males were more likely than females to be living in public residential settings (16.5% versus 4.1%),

whereas females were more likely than males to be living in private accommodations (95.8% versus 83.5%) at follow-up. Moreover, these investigators noted that of those who were living in noninstitutional residential accommodations, men were more likely to be living in one-room accommodations (e.g., single-room occupancy hotel or boardinghouse rooms), whereas women were more likely to be living in multiroom settings such as houses or apartments. Likewise, the investigators found that females with schizophrenia were living in households with higher mean levels of disposable income than were their male counterparts. Thus, in terms of the fairly detailed evaluation of household living arrangements in this study (Wattie & Kedward, 1985), females were in the position to benefit from a higher standard of living.

The implications of sex differences in living arrangements are unclear, although they raise the question of whether females are more likely to be situated in settings that are intrinsically more social in nature. Whether such a pattern reliably exists cannot be ascertained from the few studies that have evaluated living arrangement data. However, the existing data raises the question of whether females with schizophrenia do, in fact, tend to dwell in more social settings and whether some self-selection factor or other type of selection factors (e.g., family member tolerance for the problems of the relative with schizophrenia, or societal standards for remanding the psychiatric patient to institutional settings) operate to influence such a pattern.

Overall, women may have an advantage over men in terms of opportunities for interpersonal contact with others in their domicile. The origins or determinants of such differences in the residential living situation of males and females with schizophrenia are unknown. Whether such differences derive from self-selection processes (i.e., the selection of multiperson versus singleperson living arrangements on the basis of personal preference) or whether they derive from extraneous factors (the preferences of others) or an interaction of personal and other factors, has not, to our knowledge, been systematically examined. In fact, simple normative data on sex differences in living arrangements of individuals in the general population have not been provided in these studies. Thus, the extent to which sex differences in living arrangements among individuals with schizophrenia reflect sex differences in the general population, is not evident from the existing body of empirical research data. Further research is needed which aims to trace the longitudinal course of interpersonal relations and living arrangements among individuals with schizophrenia, in contrast to other psychiatric and non-psychiatric samples.

Negative Symptoms and Social Functioning

The prognostic value of negative symptoms in relation to social and occupational outcomes in schizophrenia has been recognized and reviewed over the past several decades (Dworkin, 1990; Dworkin, Lenzenweger, Moldin, Skillings, & Levick, 1988; Pogue-Geile & Harrow, 1985). Among contemporary investigators, there is a growing consensus that the negative symptoms that are stable over time represent "deficit symptoms" of schizophrenia (Carpenter, Heinrichs, & Wagman, 1988). However, there remains disagreement as to whether the specific dimensions of social anhedonia and social withdrawal fall within the domain of negative or deficit-type symptoms (e.g., Carpenter et al., 1988) or whether they represent an independent pathologic process with its own longitudinal course (Dworkin et al., 1988; Pogue-Geile & Harrow, 1985). In the early 1970s, Strauss, Carpenter, and Bartko (1974) suggested that the severe impairment in social functioning that is a hallmark of schizophrenia represents an independent component of schizophrenia with its own time course. They pointed out that "patterns of relating seem to be rather constant, ongoing functions relatively independent of, and preceding [the evolution of] psychiatric symptoms" (Strauss et al., 1974, p. 67).

Evaluating the hypothesis that there may be three independent pathologic processes in schizophrenia associated with positive symptoms, negative symptoms, and social withdrawal, respectively, Dworkin and colleagues (Dworkin, 1990; Dworkin et al., 1988) more recently presented evidence that social competence varies independently of the positive and negative symptoms of schizophrenia. Similarly, Bellack and colleagues (Bellack, Morrison, Mueser, & Wade, 1989; Bellack, Morrison, Wixted, & Mueser, 1990) have reported evidence that negative symptoms do not fully account for deficits in social skills and social functioning. These investigators concur that the direction of effect is not clear from correlations of negative symptoms with measures of social skill and indices of social competence. Nevertheless, they suggest that certain negative symptoms (e.g., affective flattening) are likely to impede social functioning, whereas some social skills deficits may contribute to the evolution of certain other negative symptoms (e.g., social withdrawal).

Dworkin (1990) has addressed the question of whether social anhedonia and social withdrawal vary independently from other negative symptoms of schizophrenia by examining sex differences in premorbid social and sexual adjustment, positive and negative symptoms, and specifically asociality and withdrawal in a sample of 151 schizophrenic probands. Results of this study indicated that males and females did not differ on measures of positive symptoms, paranoid symptoms, or negative symptoms (whether including asociality/withdrawal or not) as rated using a modified form of the Scale for the Assessment of Negative Symptoms (SANS; Andreasen, 1984). In contrast, a consistent pattern of sex differences (showing a female advantage) was observed specifically on measures of premorbid social competence, premorbid sexual adjustment, age at onset, and current symptoms of asociality-withdrawal.

Dworkin's aim in this study was not to explain the nature of the sex differences observed, but rather to provide further justification for viewing social anhedonia and withdrawal as characteristics of a dimension that varies independently of such negative symptoms as affective flattening, alogia, avolition-apathy, and attentional impairment. Nonetheless, this analytic approach and the resulting findings have obvious implications for the evaluation of sex differences in social functioning in schizophrenia, as they suggest that premorbid social deficits (which tend to show substantial cross-sex variance) may be related to the manifestation of social anhedonia and social withdrawal during the active phase of the disorder. From this perspective, the more severe premorbid social functioning deficits of males (as compared with females) would be expected to predict greater loss of interest in social relations and more severe social withdrawal among males during the active phase of the illness. Moreover, to be consistent with this developmental perspective, one would hypothesize that social anhedonia and withdrawal derived from developmental deficits in social functioning rather than a core deficit syndrome that encompassed primary deficit features. Thus, it would be expected that the features of social anhedonia and withdrawal would be more strongly correlated with premorbid social deficits than with other negative symptoms (e.g., alogia and flat affect) that also manifest sex-related patterns of variance (Carpenter et al., 1988; Haas, Sweeney, Hien, Goldman, & Deck, 1991a; Lewine, 1985; Ring, Tantam, Montague, & Newby, 1991) reflecting a pattern of greater severity among males. A competing explanation is that social functioning deficits derive, in part, from the influence of specific negative symptoms (e.g., flat affect, poor eye contact) on communication skills. This interpretation of the relationship between sex differences in social functioning, negative symptoms, and nonverbal social skill will be taken up in the next section.

SOCIAL SKILLS

Whereas the evaluation of premorbid social competence has generated substantial attention in research investigations of schizophrenia, virtually no studies prior to the 1980s attempted to directly measure the laboratory performance of social skills in schizophrenia. Only a handful have, thus far, reported on gender differences in social skills. As we will review, the bulk of the studies that have evaluated sex effects have investigated expressive communication skills (e.g., verbal, nonverbal, and paralinguistic characteristics of interpersonal speech), and a few have evaluated the social perceptual components of receptive communication skills.

Social Perception

Emotion Recognition and Receptive Communication Skills

The earliest studies of social perception skills in schizophrenia tested the ability to recognize specific emotional states reflected in photographs of human faces portraying specific affects through facial expression (Izard, 1959; Dougherty, Bartlett, & Izard, 1974). Several investigators have reported evidence that individuals with schizophrenia are less accurate than normals in identifying emotions depicted in such photographs (Morrison & Bellack, 1981; Muzekari & Bates, 1977; Walker, Marwit, & Emory, 1980). Whereas sex effects were not evaluated in these earlier studies, subsequent studies have found no effects of sex on emotion recognition (Muzekari & Bates, 1977; Walker et al., 1980; Heimberg, Gur, Erwin, Shtasel, & Gur, 1992). Individuals with schizophrenia were more deficient than affective disorder and normal control subjects; no sex differences were observed among the schizophrenic patients.

A few recent studies have examined receptive communication skills (e.g., the perception of affect and the perception of social cues) in schizophrenia. Corrigan and Green (1993) found no sex differences in sensitivity to abstract interpersonal cues (e.g., inferences about emotions or motivation, based on observed behavior) or concrete interpersonal cues (e.g., reporting of the observable aspects of an event: "I saw the man put down his baseball mitt" [Corrigan & Green, 1993, p. 589]) among schizophrenia patients during the viewing of videotaped interpersonal problem-solving interactions. Other studies of social perception skills did not specifically examine gender effects on social cue perception (Corrigan & Green, 1993; Corrigan, Green, & Toomey, 1994).

Expressive Communication Skills

Relationship to Negative Symptoms

Whereas social anhedonia and social withdrawal are considered by some to be negative symptoms (Barberger Gateau, Chaslerie, Dartigues, & Commenges, 1992) they are, by definition, negative symptom dimensions that are closely linked to aspects of social functioning in schizophrenia. The relationship between other negative symptoms (e.g., affective flattening and alogia) and social functioning has been little studied, but might also be presumed to influence social functioning in this disorder. In a study designed to evaluate the relationship between negative symptoms and social functioning, Bellack and colleagues (1990) found a strong relationship between negative symptoms, as measured on the SANS (Andreasen, 1984) and social role functioning, as indicated on the Social Adjustment Scale-II (SAS-II; Schooler, Hogarty, & Weissman, 1979) measures of family, social/leisure, work, and overall adjustment. The investigators found that a subgroup of subjects with prominent negative symptoms (what they termed *negative symptom schizophrenics*) demonstrated more severe deficits in social functioning than a subgroup of schizophrenic subjects without substantial negative symptoms (*nonnegative schizophrenics*). These investigators also observed that the nonnegative symptom schizophrenics demonstrated more severe social skills deficits and social adjustment deficits than did individuals with affective disorders or nonpatient control subjects. The investigators also reported that negative symptoms, especially SANS ratings of affective flattening, alogia, and anhedonia/asociality, were moderately correlated with laboratory measures of social skills on a simulated role-play test. Based on their cumulative findings, they concluded that impairment in social functioning was not simply a secondary effect of negative symptoms, but that social skills contributed substantially to social role performance in the community (i.e., that the deficiencies in role functioning of some schizophrenics may not result from negative symptoms *per se* but from specific social skills deficits).

With regard to sex differences in negative symptoms, several studies have now reported evidence of more severe negative symptoms, and in particular, affective flattening, among males as compared with females who have schizophrenia (Carpenter et al., 1988; Haas, Sweeney, Hien, Goldman, & Deck, 1991a; Lewine, 1985; Ring et al., 1991). Thus, it is reasonable to hypothesize that affective flattening may contribute to sex differences in expressive communication skills among individuals with this disorder. In one of the few laboratory studies that examined gender differences in social conversation skills, Mueser and colleagues (Mueser, Bellack, Morrison, & Wade, 1990) reported that females earned better affect ratings (reflecting a wider range of appropriate affects) as compared with males when tested on a series of simulated social interactions that varied from negative (e.g., confrontational) to more benign (e.g., calling for the expression of positive assertions).

In a subsequent study using a role play test involving conflict situations, Mueser, Blanchard, and Bellack (1995) observed that females earned higher ratings on a global measure of negative valence—a measure that included *both verbal and nonverbal components of negative affective expression* and related to the degree of negativity expressed, irrespective of the appropriateness of the expression of negative affect. Thus, the findings from studies that have included measurement of nonverbal as well as verbal affective display suggest that females may be more affectively expressive than males in social interaction. However, more systematic investigations of the various dimensions of affect expression across social situations are needed before any firm conclusions can be drawn regarding sex differences in this domain of social communication skill.

*Other Sex-Related
Dimensions of Expressive
Communication Skills*

Mueser and colleagues (Mueser, Bellack, Morrison, & Wade, 1990) conducted a series of analyses of gender effects on expressive communication skills in schizophrenia, using an interactive role-play test to measure certain behavioral components of social skill, both verbal and nonverbal, presumed to form the basis for effective communication. A sample of 57 schizophrenic patients, 33 affective disorder patients, and 20 nonpatient controls were tested

on a role-play test that involved test scenarios requiring a brief interaction of the subject with a confederate (research assistant). Gender of the confederate was counterbalanced across role-play scenarios; 12 test scenarios were of three types (four of each) involving (a) initiation of social interaction with peers, (b) positive assertion situations, and (c) negative assertion situations. Role plays were videotaped and rated on three major dimensions of social skill: nonverbal skills (gaze, length, meshing, affect), verbal content (expression of praise/appreciation for positive assertions, use of requests/compliance behaviors in negative assertion scenarios) and overall social skill. The investigators found that female schizophrenics had significantly better communication skills than male schizophrenics as measured by global ratings of overall communication skills, as well as ratings of verbal (request/compliance on the negative assertion task) and nonverbal (expression of affects) skills. No sex differences were found in terms of verbal behavior (praise/appreciation) on the positive assertion task, or on other dimensions of nonverbal behavior (gaze, length of verbalization, or meshing/coordination of communication with other speaker). The sex differences observed were stable over one year following symptom exacerbation and were not attributable to differences in symptom severity or chronicity. In contrast, no sex differences in social skills were found within the samples of affective disorder patients or nonpatient controls, suggesting that gender differences in social skills might be specific to schizophrenia.

In another report Mueser and colleagues (Mueser, Bellack, Morrison, & Wixted, 1990) examined the relationship between premorbid social adjustment and current social skill on the same schizophrenic and affective disorder samples, and adding a comparison sample of schizoaffective disorder (n = 16) patients. In this set of analyses, they found that laboratory-tested social skills (nonverbal and verbal content performance skills on the 12 role-play test scenarios) were influenced by sex of subject (males performed more poorly than females) as well as diagnosis (schizophrenic patients performed more poorly than schizoaffective and affective disorder patients). In addition, they found an interaction effect of sex and diagnosis—with schizophrenic and schizoaffective males showing a pattern of worse social skills as contrasted with females, whereas among the affective disorder patients the reverse pattern was observed (i.e., males performed better than females). These results suggest that sex differences in role-play performance skills in schizophrenia can be extended to include individuals with schizoaffective but not affective disorder, further confirming that this pattern appears to be characteristic of schizophrenia (broadly or narrowly defined).

In this second report, Mueser and colleagues also examined sex differences in premorbid adjustment and current social adjustment (Mueser, Bellack, Morrison, & Wixted, 1990). Results indicated that schizophrenics had lower levels of premorbid social adjustment than affective disorder subjects (whereas the premorbid social adjustment levels of the schizoaffective disorder patients fell in between the other two groups). In contrast to the diagnostic specificity of sex differences in social skills, the investigators found no interaction effect of sex and diagnosis on premorbid social adjustment—females had superior premorbid adjustment, irrespective of diagnosis. Moreover, measures of premorbid *sexual adjustment* were correlated with social skills measures among the schizophrenia and schizoaffective disorder patients but not the affective disorder patients; premorbid measures of (nonsexual) *social adjustment* were not correlated with social skills within any of the diagnostic groups. The authors noted that although it was presumed that the development of adequate social skills would be prerequisite to the achievement of premorbid social competencies, inferences regarding the functional relationship between premorbid adjustment and social skills in schizophrenia cannot be made from the correlations between current social skills measures and retrospective premorbid adjustment measures. Instead, they emphasized the fact that the pattern of superior social skills and premorbid psychosocial adjustment among female schizophrenic and schizoaffective disorder patients was consistent with the body of literature that shows superior premorbid adjustment among females.

In a third study that included a laboratory assessment of the interpersonal communication skills of schizophrenic patients and their relatives, Mueser, Bellack, Wade, Sayers, Tierney, and Haas (1993) found that on a more openended communication task—a family problem-solving communication task (Bellack, Haas, & Tierney, 1996)—female patients were rated as having more appropriate gaze and length of verbalizations than were male patients, although there were no differences between the two groups in terms of the frequency of other nonverbal or verbal communication behaviors (positive requests, constructive expression of negative feelings, nonconstructive criticism, demands or commands, and intrusive statements) or in terms of ratings of positive or negative affective expression, dominance, or global ratings of communication and problem-solving skills. Also, it was noted

that the relatives of females performed more poorly than did the relatives of males on measures of interpersonal communication and problem-solving skill. These findings would suggest that superior performance among females on some dimensions is unlikely to derive from greater performance adequacy of family members during the laboratory interaction task. Interestingly, no evidence was found for sex differences in verbal or nonverbal communication behaviors on the confederate simulated role-play task—described as above (although in this study, including 12 scenarios that focused exclusively on conflict situations). No sex differences were observed on social skills measures of social perception. The two groups showed no differences on measures of symptomatology or diagnosis that could account for gender differences in communication skills on the family problem-solving task.

Evaluation of Sex Differences in Social Role Performance

One of the curious findings to date is that although some dimensions of laboratory-measured social skills have been found to vary with sex of subject, social role functioning—global ratings of the adequacy of performance of social and instrumental roles—has not been found to vary by sex. Whether the lack of sex differences findings in the area of social role functioning is attributable to *method variance* (e.g., the use of retrospective report in contrast to behavioral observation) or to differences in the substantive nature of the functional domains evaluated (quantitative and qualitative aspects of the performance of social roles, in contrast to social skills) has not been examined. However, it is remarkable that social functioning, as evaluated on the basis of retrospective report using two of the most commonly used instruments for the evaluation of social functioning in schizophrenia—the Social Adjustment Scale-II (Schooler et al., 1979) and the Quality of Life Scale (Heinrichs, Hanlon, & Carpenter, Jr. 1984)—were not found to vary by sex of subject in the study by Mueser et al. (1990). These investigators observed that the clinical interview-based ratings of role performance in everyday social, family, leisure, and instrumental role functions were equivalent for females and males. This finding is somewhat surprising not only because sex differences have been observed on laboratory measures of social skills, but also because laboratory measures of social skills have correlated with social adjustment rather consistently across studies (Bellack et al., 1990; Halford & Hayes, 1995; Mueser, Bellack, Douglas,

& Wade, 1991; Mueser, Bellack, Morrison, & Wade, 1990). Thus, since females in this study were shown to have superior social skills compared with the males, one would also expect them to have demonstrated superior social role functioning.

One possible explanation for the lack of sex differences in these reports of social adjustment measures (Mueser et al., 1991; Mueser, Bellack, Morrison, & Wade, 1990) may be that sex differences are more likely to be revealed in laboratory observation studies than on clinical interview report measures of behavior in distal and/or naturalistic settings. Of note, several outcome studies (summarized below) have reported sex differences in social role performance in schizophrenia, with superior social adjustment among females as evaluated in terms of patient and other report of their roles in naturalistic settings. However, the bulk of these outcome studies rely on a relatively restricted set of objective indices (e.g., employed/unemployed status) that are, by their categorical nature, less likely to be influenced by self-report biases than are self-reported ratings calling for subtle gradations in the evaluation of role performance.

A second methodologic explanation for the lack of sex differences in measures of role functioning has been put forth by Mueser and colleagues (Mueser, Bellack, Morrison, & Wixted, 1990; Mueser, Bellack, Morrison, & Wade, 1990) who have noted a high degree of homogeneity in the sample with respect to chronicity and severity of symptomatology. In their 1990 report (Mueser, Bellack, Morrison, & Wade, 1990), Mueser and colleagues call attention to the fact that their schizophrenia samples included females who had a relatively early onset of illness and for whom the illness had been no less chronic or severe than for the male cohort. The investigators point out that the inclusion of what might be a relatively more severely ill sample of females may diminish contrasts between the sexes.

A third (also methodologic) explanation for a lack of sex differences in role functioning in these studies has to do with the statistical approach used to evaluate the role performance data in these reports—using multivariate analyses of variance (MANOVA) on a series of five role performance measures of questionable interrelatedness is vulnerable to Type II error. Indirect support for this explanation comes from the finding that the individual role performance scales showed variable patterns of relationship to social skills ratings. For example, social skills were associated with performance of work functions and household/family relations but not with performance of social and leisure activities or relations with members of the extended family. Thus, sex differences on one or more dimensions of role functioning could have been "washed out" by the lack of sex differences on the other dimensions. There is a need for further research on the relationship between social skills and specific dimensions of role functioning before one can conclude that there are no sex differences in role performance or that the sex differences in social skills observed in laboratory testing bear no relationship to role functioning in naturalistic settings.

Cognitive Functioning in Relation to Social Skills

A recent set of reports by Mueser and colleagues (Mueser et al., 1991; Mueser et al., 1995) evaluated the relationship between cognitive functioning and social skills in male and female schizophrenics who participated in a brief (2-week) social skills training group (Mueser et al., 1991). As in their previous reports, a series of laboratory role-play assessments were used to measure social skills and assertiveness in dealing with everyday interpersonal problems. These particular role plays simulated everyday interpersonal encounters and specifically called for the expression of negative feelings and/or negative assertion behaviors to promote compromise on interpersonal problems.

In the first of the two reports (Mueser et al., 1991), the investigators comment that sex differences in social functioning are not likely to be attributable to variance in cognitive functioning, because no sex differences were observed on a broad battery of cognitive measures. Although the investigators found no sex differences on measures of overall social skill or assertiveness across baseline (pretreatment) and one-month (posttreatment) postdischarge evaluations of the effects of a social skills training program, the investigators did observe a striking relationship between overall memory performance at baseline, as measured in terms of the Memory Quotient on the Wechsler Memory Scales (WMS; Rice, Rochberg, Endicott, Lavori, & Miller, 1992) and baseline, termination, and follow-up ratings of global assertiveness and other social skills (expressing negative feelings, compromise, and negotiation).

In a later reanalysis of these data (Mueser et al., 1995), the investigators found that specific (visual) and overall memory measures were associated with social skills measures among females only. Females had comparatively worse scores than males on Wechsler Memory Scale (WMS) measures of attention/concentration and verbal memory; however, these cognitive indices were not correlated with either of two global social skills dimensions (global assertiveness and global social skill). In the same publication (Mueser et al., 1995), a partial replication of several of these sex-specific correlational findings was reported with a second sample, which included 20 males and 18 females. As in the first sample, the investigators found *among females only,* correlations between assertiveness ratings and several indices of memory: visual memory (both WMS measures of immediate and delayed) as well as a general memory index (WMS Memory Quotient). In their discussion of these findings, Mueser and colleagues (Mueser, Bellack, Morrison, & Wade, 1990) offer that the sample of females may have been deviant (more severely ill) in relation to the larger population of females with schizophrenia, whereas the sample of males may have been more representative of the full range of schizophrenic males. The investigators point out that on purely statistical grounds, samples that include more severely affected cases and a broader range of scores are more likely to manifest correlations between deficits on one measure and deficits on another—in this case, a greater likelihood of manifesting evidence of an association between memory and social skills.

Penn, Mueser, and Spaulding (1996) used an open-ended role-play task that called for the subject to respond to relatively neutral prompts (e.g., "tell me about yourself" and "what are your hobbies?"). These investigators found no sex differences on nonverbal, paralinguistic, or overall (global) measures of social skills. The extent to which the unique constraints of the social prompts (eliciting responses to questions from the research assistant) in this study contributed to the failure to replicate sex differences in previous findings is unclear. However, consistent with the earlier study of Mueser et al. (1991), both male and female subjects included in this sample were relatively chronic with equivalent severity of negative, as well as positive, symptoms and equivalent levels of performance on cognitive testing. Also consistent with the earlier study, these investigators observed that cognitive skills were correlated with social skills for females, but not males. Penn and colleagues (in press) conclude from their findings that for females, cognition may govern key elements of social communication in interpersonal interaction situations, whereas among males, more global characteristics of the situation, such as the setting or role relationship between the participants, may drive communication behavior in the social interaction.

Before summarizing the findings in the area of social skills assessment, it is important to note that the nature of

role-play tasks varies across studies and, on review, it appears that studies that used a broad range of role-play situations, including benign or positive as well as negative or challenging social situations, were more likely to report sex differences in observer-rated social skills (Mueser, Bellack, Morrison, & Wade, 1990; Mueser et al., 1993) than on role-play tasks restricted to negative or challenging situations (Mueser et al., 1991; Mueser et al., 1995). In fact, the sex differences observed by Mueser and colleagues (Mueser, Bellack, Morrison, & Wade, 1990) on positive and negative assertion role-play tasks were restricted to the positive assertion role-play situations (Mueser, Bellack, Morrison, & Wade, 1990). Although the ramifications of these methodological variations are not clear, the pattern of findings suggest that sex differences in social skills may be specific to social situations that call for neutral or positive affects (i.e., other than negative or challenging circumstances).

In summary, although research findings are somewhat inconsistent with regard to sex differences in social skills in schizophrenia, on balance, it can be said that when sex differences have been found, they have favored females. Although the recent research in this area has taken important steps to rectify the methodologic weaknesses noted by Morrison and Bellack (1987) in their review of the first wave of research in this area, several aspects of the existing research limit conclusions regarding sex differences in social skills in schizophrenia. Few studies have yet been designed to prospectively examine sex differences in social skills. The few studies that report on sex differences have been conducted on relatively small samples or samples that fall short of representing the full range of females with schizophrenia. Also, the cross-study variance in the demand characteristics of the social interaction tasks is likely to contribute to inconsistencies in findings. Sex differences in communication skills are more likely to emerge in role-play situations that involve dialogue and that draw on a broad range of social skills, in particular, situations that call for positive assertive behaviors—which tend to elicit more skillful performance on both verbal and paralinguistic measures. A particularly promising area of research aims to identify the relationship between interpersonal communication skills and early information-processing and cognitive skills in schizophrenia. Such studies have suggested that higher cognitive processes (e.g., memory) may be more closely linked to verbal and nonverbal expressive communication skills in females than in males. However, the small sample size and relatively restricted range of patients sampled in these studies make these findings rather tentative at present. More conclusive findings will depend on a systematic approach for evaluating interpersonal social skills and continued careful attention to the role of symptomatology, cognition, and course of illness factors as they influence the social skills of males and females with schizophrenia.

SEX DIFFERENCES IN SHORT-TERM SOCIAL OUTCOMES

One of the earliest and largest empirical outcome studies to report on sex differences in short-term schizophrenia outcome came from the World Health Organization's (WHO) International Pilot Study of Schizophrenia (IPSS) (Sartorius, Jablensky, & Shapiro, 1977), which recruited 1,202 patients from nine collaborating study centers across several continents. The 2-year outcome data indicated that female gender was one of the best predictors of total time in remission from psychotic episodes. Leff, Sartorius, Jablensky, Korten, and Ernberg (1992) reported on the 5-year follow-up data for 807 of the original 1,202 patients and found that females continued to spend less time in psychotic episodes during the follow-up period. Several other short-term outcome studies have also found that men are at a greater risk for relapse and spend more time in the hospital over the follow-up period. For example, Hogarty et al. (Hogarty, Goldberg, & Schooler, 1974; Hogarty, 1974) reported that males relapsed at twice the rate of females during the first year of illness. British studies published by Brown, Birley, and Wing (1972) and Vaughn and Leff (1976) also report elevated rates of posthospital relapse among men with schizophrenia. Thus, in terms of postdischarge risk for relapse and rehospitalization, males appear to do more poorly in the short (less than two years) term.

A broader range of indicators also suggests a female advantage in short-term *social* outcome. In a report of 2-year outcome findings for a sample of 227 first-contact Finnish patients with DSM-III schizophrenia, Salokangas and Stenågrd (1990) describe a pattern of poorer social outcome among males. This pattern was characterized by less satisfactory heterosexual relationships, more negative symptoms, and poorer work functioning compared with females. Males were also more likely than females to be living with their parents over the follow-up period. In terms of heterosexual relationships, although both males and females experienced a decline in heterosexual contacts and an increase in divorce rates, men experienced a *greater* decrease in social contacts over the follow-up period. By the end of follow-up, only 16% of the males

and 42% of the females were involved in heterosexual relationships.

Consistent with the 2-year outcome findings of the Finnish sample, the 5-year follow-up data from the International Pilot Study of Schizophrenia also suggests superior short-term outcome for females (Leff et al., 1992). They reported that females showed less global social impairments as indicated by measures of occupational adjustment, relationships with friends, and the frequency of social contacts over follow-up.

Salokangas and Stengård (1990) found evidence that linked the poorer outcomes of males to poorer premorbid heterosexual development, negative symptoms, and less adequate involvement of males in posthospital outpatient treatments. Greater social withdrawal and a failure to establish heterosexual relationships during the premorbid period also distinguished the males from the females and suggested that a more schizoid pattern of adjustment may characterize the premorbid period among males. The investigators noted that the association between poor premorbid adjustment and poor outcome could not be attributed to an earlier age at onset because age at onset did not differ between males and females. Finally, and perhaps one of the most interesting findings in the study, was that the males, at the beginning of the follow-up period, conveyed a more pessimistic outlook with regard to their life situation over the next two years.

The extent to which family environment variables influence not only risk for relapse but short-term functional outcomes in schizophrenia has been understudied. In a random-assignment clinical trial of an inpatient family intervention added to a multimodal hospital treatment, Haas, Glick, Clarkin, Spencer, and Lewis (1990) found that at the time of patient admission to hospital, family members of female patients showed a trend for greater self-reported levels of family burden in caring for their ill relative as compared with the family of male patients—even though there were no differences between the sexes on baseline measures of role functioning or psychotic symptom severity. Among families who participated in the inpatient family treatment, the relatives of females showed a significant reduction in rejecting attitudes toward the patient over the course of inpatient treatment—a reduction that was maintained over 18-month follow-up. In contrast, the families of males showed no evidence of any reduction in these critical and rejecting attitudes. Given that female patients showed a better treatment response (in terms of both global clinical outcome and role functioning) than did males in association with the family intervention, the question arises as to whether family attitudes changed as a function of the clinical and functional status of the patients. However, in a follow-up report (Glick, Clarkin, Haas, Spencer, & Chen, 1991), the investigators determined that rejecting family attitudes (and support for treatment compliance) predicted symptomatology and role functioning at subsequent follow-up assessment points, suggesting that family attitudes may have been mediators of outcome, rather than simply reflective of the family's response to the clinical and social functioning outcomes of the patient. The results would also suggest that the reduction in rejecting attitudes toward female patient/relatives may have supported their more positive clinical and social functioning outcomes.

Findings of superior short-term outcomes for females are common, but by no means uniform throughout the literature. Angermeyer, Goldstein, and Kühn (1989) reviewed 50 studies reporting on gender and the posthospital clinical outcomes (e.g., rehospitalization rate, community tenure) associated with inpatient treatment for schizophrenia. Restricting the focus to those 23 studies that included short-term (what we are defining here as outcomes up to and including 5-year follow-up) clinical outcomes, 11 (48%) of the studies observed no sex differences on rehospitalization measures, 10 (43%) reported superior outcomes for females, and 2 (8.7%) reported superior outcome for males. Thus, although the sex-difference findings are not uniform with respect to short-term clinical outcome in schizophrenia, a large proportion of the published outcome studies report evidence of better short-term (≤ 5-year) clinical outcomes for females. Focusing specifically on indicators of social functioning, Angermeyer et al. (1989) reported that in terms of short-term (specifically defined as < 5-year) outcome, two of the six then published studies that evaluated sex differences in global *social adaptation* showed superior outcome for females, whereas four studies reported no gender differences.

The relative restrictiveness of selection criteria used to define study samples may explain the negative findings in a few of the reports. Outcome studies that include more homogeneous (restricted) samples are less likely to observe sex differences in outcome findings. As mentioned earlier in regard to occupational outcomes, the restrictiveness of the schizophrenia diagnosis not only can affect the proportion of females that are assigned the diagnosis, but can ultimately affect the outcomes reported for males and females. For example, in a study of short-term (2-to 3-year) outcome in 153 schizophrenic patients, Westermeyer and Harrow (1984) reported that sex was one of the most powerful predictors of overall outcome (as well as work outcome) among DSM-II-diagnosed schizophrenia patients. However, gender failed to predict outcome among those that met the more narrowly defined DSM-III criteria for schizophrenia. Many of the females with better outcomes did not meet the more restrictive DSM-III criteria and thus were *a priori* excluded from the more DSM-III category of schizophrenia. Similarly, another study with negative findings on sex differences in short-term (as well as long-term) outcomes selected subjects on the basis of the exceptionally narrowly defined (Feighner criteria) schizophrenia (Feighner, Robins, Guze, Woodruff, Winokur, & Munoz, 1972),

Several methodologic limitations preclude drawing more definitive conclusions on sex differences in short-term outcome. Foremost among these is the variability in outcome measures—the domains reported, the specific measures used, and the relative restrictiveness in the definition of schizophrenia (with sex differences least likely to be observed in studies that use relatively narrow definitions of schizophrenia, which tend to result in the *a priori* exclusion of with better outcomes). Unfortunately, as will become apparent in the discussion of long-term (what we have defined as less than 5-year follow-up) outcome studies, the evaluation of male–female differences in outcome becomes no less ambiguous over the long-term course of the illness.

SEX DIFFERENCES IN LONG-TERM SOCIAL OUTCOMES

Evidence of a higher rate of rehospitalization, longer hospital stay, and shorter community tenure for males comes from a tally of the findings reviewed by Angermeyer et al (1989) on the subset of long-term outcome studies that included gender comparisons of outcome. Of the 30 long-term (what we define as greater than 5-year) follow-up study samples, 17 (57%) reported the absence of any sex differences in outcome, 10 (33%) observed superior clinical outcomes for females, whereas 3 (10%) reported superior clinical outcomes for males.

Turning to midterm follow-up (5 to 10 years posthospital discharge), five out of the then seven published studies that evaluated sex differences in social adaptation reported superior global functioning among females, whereas two studies reported no significant gender differences in outcome. Three out of four studies reporting on sex differences in social integration (versus isolation/withdrawal) indicated better outcome for females (Körmendy & Schäfer, 1983; Nyman, 1978; Salokangas, 1983) whereas one study (Nyman & Jonsson, 1983), a later follow-up of the Nyman (1978) study, indicated that sex differences in the frequency of social contacts had diminished at 6 to 9 years after first hospitalization. Of the three studies that evaluated long-term (≥ 10-year) follow-up on social functioning indices, one of the studies reported superior outcomes for females and two of the studies reported no sex differences in social outcomes. One of the two studies that reported negative findings (Loyd et al., 1985) relied on narrowly defined (Feighner criteria) diagnoses of schizophrenia, which have been shown to be associated with a lack of sex differences in clinical status and outcome (Westermeyer & Harrow, 1984). Finally, a more recent study reporting sex effects on measures of social functioning showed males having greater downward drift in terms of both occupational and social functioning (Marneros et al., 1989).

By several reports, it appears that the female's advantage in terms of superior social functioning during the premorbid phase is a primary factor that helps drive and maintain better social outcomes for females over the long-term course of illness (Goldstein, 1988; Munk-JØrgensen & Mortensen, 1992a; Salokangas, 1983; Watt, Katz, & Shepherd, 1983). To some degree, the maintenance of adequate levels of functioning in social and occupational roles is also likely to be influenced by the individual's clinical status and course of illness (e.g., intermittent relapsing, chronic or infrequent relapse with good recovery of intermorbid functioning). Since men are hospitalized more often and for longer durations than women over the long-term course of schizophrenia (Leff et al., 1992; Salokangas, 1983; Salokangas & Stengård, 1990), it can be argued that men are more likely to have difficulty sustaining and/or reestablishing entry into social and occupational roles over follow-up. Thus, reported sex differences in social functioning may reflect the impact of a more complicated course of illness among males.

The extent to which sex differences in role functioning are secondary to sex-related variance in symptom severity or, in contrast, attributable to primary sex differences in core functional deficits, is not clear from existing data, nor is it easily evaluated. Controlled quantitative studies of sex differences in cognition, social skills, and their relationship to functional outcomes will be important in future efforts to address this question.

Finally, the extent to which gender differences in outcome are maintained over the course of the illness is a topic of contemporary debate. Bleuler (1978), Achte

(1967), and more recently Larsen, McGlashan, Johannsen, & Vibe-Hansen (1996) have remarked on a plateau-like pattern of stabilization occurring approximately 5 years into the psychotic phase of illness. Just as the influence of premorbid adjustment on long-term social outcome may diminish with time (Goldstein, 1988), the male–female differential may decrease with long-term (post 5-year) outcome (Angermeyer, Kühn, & Goldstein, 1990).

Unfortunately, some studies (Angermeyer et al., 1989; Angermeyer et al., 1990) report exclusively on clinical parameters (e.g., rehospitalization) and do not report on functional outcome parameters. Bleuler (Andreasen, Endicott, Spitzer, & Winokur, 1977), Kraepelin (Kraepelin, 1919), and others (Nyman & Jonsson, 1983; Brown, Bone, Dalison & Wing, 1966; Shepherd, 1959) have noted that the course of clinical outcomes can be independent of the course of functional outcomes in schizophrenia. Häfner and colleagues (1991) have presented longitudinal data on the independent patterns of clinical and psychosocial outcomes; their data suggest that in *both* domains, women's superior clinical and social outcomes may be restricted to the first 5 years of schizophrenia.

Other investigators (e.g., Nyman, 1978; Salokangas, 1983) have observed a significant difference in the patterns of long-term clinical and social functioning outcomes for males versus females. Consistent with Häfner et al. (1991), Salokangas and colleagues (Salokangas, 1983) have reported data from their 8-year follow-up study suggesting that the sex differential in clinical condition diminishes over the early course of schizophrenia. However, unlike the Häfner findings, they find a divergence of the trajectories of clinical and social outcomes with a continuation of better social, sexual, and work adjustment outcomes for females over the longer term. Other studies that report on both clinical and social outcomes during the first 6 to 10 years of illness report better mental health and work functioning, and higher rates of conjugal relationship among females, although no female advantage in terms of other types of social contacts, relapse rate, or treatment time (Nyman & Jonsson, 1983) and longer community tenure, better occupational functioning, and better social adjustment among women (Körmendy & Schäfer, 1983; Wattie & Kedward, 1985).

Among studies that have evaluated sex effects on 10-to 15-year outcomes in terms of dimensions of social and/or occupational functioning, those that find sex differences report better work functioning, lower morbidity, and lower rates of hospital admission among females (Affleck et al., 1976), and better social adjustment among females (Bland & Orn, 1978; Lo & Lo, 1977). The longest followup studies (extending 15 years or more beyond first hospitalization) report minimal sex differences favoring females on measures of *clinical outcome*: (1) level of clinical recovery at 23 years (Bleuler, 1978), (2) clinical remission at 23 years (Huber et al., 1980), (3) remission of symptoms at 37 years (Ciompi & Müller, 1976), (4) percentage of "good outcome" at 32 years after initial hospital admission (Childers & Harding, 1990) in the Vermont Longitudinal Research Project, and (5) percentage of follow-up time symptomatic (McGlashan & Bardenstein, 1990). Of those long-term (15 years or greater) follow-up studies that have reported on *social outcomes,* six (Bland et al., 1976; Bleuler, 1978; Childers & Harding, 1990; Ciompi & Müller, 1976; Loyd et al., 1985; Munk-JØrgensen & Mortensen, 1992a) report no difference of any magnitude and an equal number (Affleck et al., 1976; Bland & Orn, 1978; Deister & Marneros, 1992; Marneros et al., 1989; McGlashan & Bardenstein, 1990; Stephens, 1992) present evidence of superior social outcomes for females.

On overview, some evidence suggests that the female advantage in terms of clinical outcomes diminishes, whereas social functioning superiority is maintained, over the later course of illness. For example, Goldstein (Goldstein & Link, 1988; Goldstein, Faraone, Chen, & Tolomiczencko, 1990) and Childers and Harding (1990) have remarked on this possibility, suggesting that the attenuation of gender differences in clinical status (e.g., rates of rehospitalization and duration of hospital stay) may be due to any of a number of factors, including the loss of the protective effects of estrogen with menopause or the loss of a related advantage in terms of antipsychotic treatment response (Seeman & Lang, 1990). Interestingly, it does not appear that this trend applies to *social functioning outcomes.* Among the long-term studies that examine later-stage outcomes (15 years or more from first hospitalization), half of these studies report superior outcomes for females on indices of social and occupational outcome and half report no sex differences. As with any cross-study comparisons of follow-up data, variability in diagnoses, sample sizes, and outcome indices limit definitive conclusions. Nevertheless, on review of study findings that focus specifically on social and occupational outcomes, the proportion of positive findings with regard to sex differences in social functioning does not vary with the duration of the follow-up period and does not indicate any demonstrable time-related pattern of attenuation of

gender effects spanning the short-term (< 5-year) to the long-term (≥ 15-year) follow-up. This pattern of stability contrasts with what appears to be a reduction of the female advantage in terms of clinical course (rehospitalization rates and duration of hospitalization) and is consistent with the divergence of social and clinical outcomes observed by Bleuler (1978), Kraepelin (1919), and Strauss, Carpenter, and Bartko (1974). Whether the diminution of sex differences in clinical status reflects a deterioration in the clinical course for females, or rather a reduction in the frequency of symptom exacerbation among males, needs to be investigated. The latter possibility (a later-life reduction in the frequency of hospitalization among males) would not necessarily be inconsistent with findings of a continuation of the female advantage in domains of social and occupational functioning. Such differences in the longitudinal course of symptomatology and functioning have been proposed (Strauss et al., 1974).

CONCLUSIONS FROM THE EXISTING LITERATURE

Although there are some inconsistencies in the findings that limit one from drawing firm conclusions regarding sex differences in social functioning in schizophrenia, several general conclusions can be drawn from the existing literature that can be used to guide future research on sex differences in schizophrenia:

1. The bulk of the findings suggest that females manifest better social functioning and community adjustment during *both* the premorbid period *and* the active phase of schizophrenia. Findings in terms of vocational and occupational functioning are inconclusive, in part, due to the methodological complexities of comparing males and females in socially defined work roles (see comment 4 below).
2. Based on the findings of the limited number of investigations that have examined sex differences in social skills in schizophrenia, the existing data suggests that females demonstrate superior communication skills—on at least some dimensions (e.g., global communication skills, assertiveness, and affective expression). These sex differences are not found uniformly on all dimensions of communication skill. Further research is needed to confirm this pattern of findings and determine the relationship between communication skills and the social functioning outcomes that favor females.

3. Premorbid adjustment appears to have a significant impact on the long-term role performance of the individual with schizophrenia—irrespective of the sex of the individual. Thus, the tendency for females to achieve higher premorbid levels of social and occupational competence may account for superior outcomes among females in studies that compare males and females without controlling for premorbid functioning.

4. Comparative analyses of males and females with schizophrenia may be subject to inherent biases deriving from societal definitions of gender-related social and occupational roles, as well as gender-based social expectancies or standards for evaluation of role performances. As a result, direct comparisons of males and females in terms of social and occupational status, achievement, and functioning are difficult. Attempts to control for the confounding effects of social and cultural factors have been only partially successful, indicating equivocal findings in comparisons of males and females in similar roles, or in traditionally defined sex-differentiated occupational roles (e.g., homemaker versus wage earner). Further research would be strengthened by efforts to take into account such factors in the measurement of social and, in particular, occupational role functioning.

5. Progress in efforts to evaluate sex differences in social functioning will depend on the application of methods that take into account (a) the premorbid achievement and social adjustment of subjects, (b) age at onset of the psychotic phase of illness, (c) the specific nature of the roles that are being evaluated (e.g., whether domestic home management or competitive paid employment), (d) sex differences in the base rates of social and occupational roles and level of functioning in the nonpsychiatric (community) population, (e) the impact of sex differences in the clinical severity and course of illness, and (f) sex differences on measures of social skills to the extent that they may illuminate the nature of sex differences on measures of functional status and outcome.

EXPLANATIONS FOR GENDER DIFFERENCES IN SOCIAL FUNCTIONING

Ever since gender differences in the onset and clinical course of schizophrenia were noted by clinical investigators such as Kraepelin (1919), various theories have been posited to explain gender differences in schizophrenia. In the following section, we will give a brief overview of

how several of these explanatory theories can be applied to help understand gender differences in social functioning in schizophrenia. For a more comprehensive review of gender differences in schizophrenia, refer to reviews by Haas and Castle (1997) and Seeman (1985).

Women, in General, Have Superior Social Functioning

One view holds that gender differences in social functioning are not specific to schizophrenia, but rather, that women in all populations have superior social functioning as compared with men. Several studies of sex differences in schizophrenia have included diagnostic contrast groups (Foerster et al., 1991; Lewine et al., 1980; Mueser, Bellack, Morrison, & Wade, 1990; Mueser, Bellack, Morrison, & Wixted, 1990). The findings regarding premorbid adjustment have been mixed, with some studies (Foerster et al., 1991; Mueser, Bellack, Morrison, & Wade, 1990) reporting data suggesting that the female advantage in premorbid adjustment is specific to schizophrenia, and others (Lewine et al., 1980; Mueser, Bellack, Morrison, & Wixted, 1990) yielding results that suggest a generalized pattern of female superiority in premorbid functioning across disorders. To test the hypothesis that gender differences in the premorbid functioning of individuals with schizophrenia reflect sex differences characteristic of the general population, Lewine and colleagues (1980) calculated childhood premorbid social competence scores from the school records of 141 psychiatric patients and 141 nonpatient controls. As expected, the childhood social competence scores for subjects who subsequently developed schizophrenia were poorer than the social competence scores for future nonpatients as well as for those later diagnosed with personality disorders, psychotic depression, or neuroses. Also, preschizophrenia males had worse childhood (premorbid) social functioning as compared with preschizophrenia females. However, it was also found that males in the other psychiatric groups, as well as the nonpatient subgroup, had poorer childhood social competence scores than did the females in these groups, suggesting that gender differences in childhood social functioning may not be specific to schizophrenia.

Lewine et al. (1980) then calculated adult premorbid social competence scores based on data gathered from the hospital records of psychiatric patients. They found that both schizophrenics and personality-disordered patients had significantly lower social competence scores than psychotic depressives or neurotics. Consistent with their findings regarding childhood social competence scores, females as a whole were rated as having higher adulthood social competence scores than males. No significant interactions between sex and diagnosis were found on measures of adult social role performance, suggesting that higher levels of female functioning in adult social roles may not be specific to schizophrenia but rather characteristic of females in general.

In contrast to Lewine's findings, other researchers have reported evidence suggesting that gender differences in premorbid social functioning are specific to schizophrenia (Foerster et al., 1991; Mueser, Bellack, Morrison, & Wade, 1990). For example, Foerster et al., (1991) conducted premorbid history interviews, blind to diagnosis, with the mothers of 73 schizophrenia and affective disorder patients. Early (5 to 11 years) and late (12 to 16 years) childhood adjustment was poorer for preschizophrenia subjects than for affective disorder subjects; a significant interaction of sex and diagnosis indicated that the schizophrenic males had worse adjustment than did females during late childhood, whereas there was no sex effect for the affective disorder cases.

The question of the diagnostic specificity of sex differences has been extended to the evaluation of social skills. In the role-play study by Mueser et al. (1990), the investigators observed significant gender differences, favoring females, in the social skills of schizophrenia patients, but not affective disorder patients or nonpatient controls. Interestingly, whereas sex differences in social skills did appear to have some diagnostic specificity, sex differences in premorbid functioning were not specific to the schizophrenia sample, suggesting that sex-related variance in social skills is not likely to stem solely from sex differences in social adjustment during the premorbid period of functioning.

Social Roles and Expectations

A second view holds that gender differences in social functioning stem from sex differences in socialization. From this perspective, sex differences in ratings of social competence are dependent on the different social roles and social role demands placed on men and women in our society. Proponents of this view suggest that the specific symptoms of schizophrenia may differentially impede the social role performance of men and women—men being more drastically affected than women due to the unique role functions that are required of males. For example, Salokangas (1983) suggested that although many women

with schizophrenia continue to perform domestic tasks adequately well and thus function adequately as homemakers, these women would be less able to function effectively outside the home in competitive paid employment. Likewise, Seeman (1983a) suggested that certain symptoms of schizophrenia, such as bizarre behavior and eccentric dress, do not considerably interfere with the performance of domestic chores and the role of a homemaker, but can have a drastic impact on the interpersonal aspects of performance adequacy in paid jobs outside of the home. Salokangas (1983) has argued that even if the performance competencies of men and women alike are evaluated in positions of competitive paid employment outside of the home, the jobs traditionally held by men may require more skill and activity than the jobs most commonly held by women, thus making it more difficult for men to perform at the expected level of competence.

Family Tolerance of Illness

Rather than presume that the occupations of males are inherently more demanding than the those of females (an arguable assumption), another sociocultural explanation for sex differences in social functioning in schizophrenia is that society and/or families may be less tolerant of mental illness in males than females (Farina, 1981; Farina, Murray, & Groh, 1978; Seeman, 1983a; Tudor, Tudor, & Gove, 1977). Seeman (1983a) suggests that families are more willing to accept the educational and occupational limitations placed on a daughter with schizophrenia, but expect a son to achieve, regardless of the limitations that arise from his illness. As a result, men with schizophrenia may be judged more harshly and be expected to achieve more than women with schizophrenia.

Seeman and Hauser (1984) have also presented the argument that females with schizophrenia are likely to be less burdensome to their relatives than are males with this disorder; they suggest that females are "more calmly tolerated at home," and because females are more likely to have left home before the illness begins, relatives of females with schizophrenia are less likely to experience feelings of guilt and responsibility for the illness. Few studies have systematically evaluated whether family tolerance toward the patient and the illness may vary with the sex of the patient, and what few studies bear on this question offer mixed support for this hypothesis. Gibbons et al. (1984) observed that subjective distress of caretaker relatives did not differ with the sex of the schizophrenia patient living at home with them. Goldstein and Kreisman

(1988) investigated family attitudes toward male and female relatives with DSM-III schizophrenia; they found that although females were rated by parents as more psychotic than males, there was no significant difference in symptom tolerance across sons versus daughters (no investigation of differences in role functioning was included in this study). Fathers did feel more responsible for the care of female versus male offspring when faced with severe levels of psychotic symptoms, and the authors concluded that differences in the sense of responsibility for care of male versus female offspring may contribute to a greater tendency for males to be rehospitalized.

Finally, in the early research on expressed emotion (EE; Brown et al., 1972), Brown and colleagues observed that males had twice the risk of relapse, as compared with females, over short-term (less than one year) follow-up. Although Vaughn and Leff (1976) found no evidence that the EE findings varied with the sex of the patient, Hogarty (1985) has reported evidence from his intervention research that led him to conclude that expressed emotion predicts relapse among males but not females. What appear to be potentially important sex differences in the family environment of males and females with schizophrenia has been inadequately investigated in subsequent research, although at least one family treatment study has yielded evidence that suggests that positive changes in family attitudes toward the patient may be an important mediator of long-term clinical and social functioning outcomes (Haas et al., 1990).

Age at Onset

Many of the social skills and role competencies of adulthood are acquired during the later teens and refined during the early twenties—the same period during which the onset of the active phase of schizophrenia most commonly occurs among males (Loranger, 1984; Lewine, 1980; Häfner, Maurer, Löffler, & Riecher-Rösser, 1993). Multiple studies provide evidence of an earlier age at onset for females. For example, Häfner, Riecher-Rösser, Hambrecht, and Maurer (1992) found that 62% of males but only 47% of females experience the onset of schizophrenia prior to 25 years of age. Some researchers suggest that the delay of onset among women helps them acquire higher levels of social functioning compared with men (Goldstein, 1988; Häfner et al., 1992; Seeman, 1982; Strömgren, 1987). According to this hypothesis, females have more time to acquire social skills, to attain higher levels of occupational and educational achievement, and

to develop interpersonal and heterosexual relationships before the onset of illness.

A similar hypothesis suggests that there are distinct subtypes of schizophrenia differentiated in terms of the timing of onset—one characterized by an early (for example, prior to age 25) onset and the other defined in terms of onset later than this age. Some researchers have reported that greater psychosocial deficits at discharge from hospital are associated with early-onset, in contrast to what might be referred to as later-onset, cases of schizophrenia (Mayer, Kelterborn, & Naber, 1993). Murray and his colleagues (Castle & Murray, 1991; Lewis & Murray, 1987) have posited a model of very-late-onset ($\geq$ age 45) in schizophrenia, more common among females and characterized as a more benign and mainly affective disorder with few negative symptoms (Murray, O'Callaghan, Castle, & Lewis, 1992). Such sex differences in the clinical severity of the illness could, of course, account for sex differences in at least a portion of the schizophrenia spectrum. However, no study has yet adequately evaluated this hypothesis.

Häfner and colleagues (Häfner, Riecher-Rösser, Maurer, & Fätkenheuer, 1992) examined age and sex differences in social role functioning among first-episode patients in relation to the timing of the first sign of mental disorder, first psychotic symptom, and first hospitalization. After controlling age at onset, they found no sex differences in the sequence of social-role interruptions (e.g., loss of partner, or job, and of income) between males and females. However, the study also noted that there were differences in the average number of social roles performed prior to admission (i.e., professional qualification, employment, income and partnership) with women performing more roles prior to illness onset, and experiencing fewer posthospital interruptions in the performance of these roles, as contrasted with men (Häfner, Riecher-Rösser, Maurer, & Fätkenheuer, 1992). These findings tend to suggest that premorbid role achievement is associated with greater continuity in subsequent role performance among females as compared with males. However, as mentioned earlier, the more complicated clinical course of illness in males may contribute to greater discontinuities in role performance over time.

Estrogen Hypothesis

Another theory posited to explain gender differences in schizophrenia is that estrogen acts as a protective factor in females, delaying the onset of illness and perhaps reducing the severity of illness (Seeman, 1982; Häfner, Behrens, de Vry, & Gattaz, 1991). Because estrogen is known to have dopamine-blocking properties (e.g., Häfner, Riecher-Rössler, An Der Heiden, Maurer, Fätkenheuer, & Löffler, 1993) and because poor social functioning has been found to be associated with the overall severity of illness, the protective properties of estrogen may also directly (and/or indirectly) protect women from social functioning deficits during the pre-menopausal phase of life. Because estrogen levels are known to drop during peri- and postmenopausal phases, it would be expected that the protective properties of estrogen would recede during postmenopausal decades of life.

Medication Side Effects

A few researchers have suggested that sex differences in clinical and social outcomes are due, in part, to the side effects of antipsychotic medications that resemble negative symptoms (e.g., dystonias and dysphoria) and interfere with social functioning (Carpenter et al., 1988). Seeman (1983b, 1986) has cited evidence that females with schizophrenia require lower dosages of conventional antipsychotic medication than do males with schizophrenia. Whether this is the result of a less severe illness among females, the antipsychotic-like effects of estrogens, or a combination of these or other factors, is not yet resolved. Nevertheless, higher dosages of antipsychotics may introduce increased risk of side effects among males and thus contribute to and/or exacerbate deficits in social functioning.

In support of this theory, a recent study conducted by Faraone, Green, Brown, Yin, and Tsuang (1989) found that when dosages of antipsychotic medications were decreased in male subjects, those who did not relapse reported increased satisfaction with life, improvement in psychosocial skills, and an increase in social contacts. Although these findings suggest that medication dosage may play an important role contributing to sex differences in social functioning, further research is needed on sex differences in antipsychotic dose response; differences in metabolism may cause equivalent doses to have differential impact on individuals. One must further keep in mind that some deleterious medication effects may contribute to sex differences in posttreatment functioning, however, they would fail to account for premorbid sex differences in role functioning and level of premorbid social, educational, and occupational achievement.

Relationship of Negative Symptoms to Social Functioning Deficits

As discussed earlier, negative symptoms are associated with impairments in social functioning (Faraone et al., 1989; Mueser, Bellack, Morrison, & Wixted, 1990), and such findings have been reported among both females and males with schizophrenia (Chaves, Seeman, Mari, & Maluf, 1993; Breier, Schreiber, Dyer, & Pickar, 1991; Mignolli, Faccincani, & Platt, 1991). However, the relationship between negative symptoms and social functioning is complex. Because certain negative symptom parameters (e.g., social anhedonia and amotivation) are measured in terms of social functioning deficits, the relationship between negative symptoms and social functioning may be tautological rather than indicative of an association between core clinical features and distinct dimensions of social and occupational functioning.

There have been several reports of gender differences in symptom expression in schizophrenia—males presenting more severe negative symptoms and females presenting more severe psychotic and affective symptoms (Goldstein et al., 1990; Goldstein & Link, 1988; Haas, Sweeney, Hien, Goldman, & Deck, 1991; Haas, Sweeney, Hien, Waked, & Weiden, 1989; Lewine, 1980, 1981, 1985; Lewine et al., 1984; Pogue-Geile & Harrow, 1984; Ring et al., 1991). Men have also been reported to show more severe signs of apathy (than women) on admission to hospital (Mayer et al., 1993). Lewine (1985) has suggested that an "amotivational" pattern may be more characteristic of males than females. In one of the few systematic studies of a large sample of schizophrenia patients, Häfner et al. (1994) found the largest differences between males and females on measures of self-neglect, social withdrawal, social inattentiveness, low social adjustment, and other such behavioral items. Such findings have led some researchers to conclude that males are more prone to social functioning deficits compared with females because males tend to have more severe negative symptoms (Ring et al., 1991).

An alternative explanation is that there are certain dispositional factors that predate the onset of illness, causing poor premorbid social functioning, and eventually presenting as more severe negative symptoms during the active phase of illness (Keefe, Mohs, Losonczy, & Davidson, 1989). Bellack and colleagues (1990) suggest that whereas some negative symptoms (e.g., affective flattening) likely contribute to certain social skills deficits, social skills deficits could account for at least some of the negative symptoms (e.g., social withdrawal) of schizophrenia. From this perspective, less adequate social skills among males would be viewed as contributing to more severe degrees of social withdrawal and anhedonia. Yet other researchers have suggested that social functioning and negative symptoms are independent processes (Dworkin, 1990; Strauss et al., 1974) and that gender-based differences in social functioning are not caused by gender differences in negative symptoms (Dworkin, 1990) but instead represent an independent pathologic process with its own course and long-term outcome.

Neurodevelopmental Deficits

Over the past decade, there has been a substantial body of research suggesting that structural brain abnormalities may be more common among males than females with schizophrenia (Bogerts, Meertz, & Schonfeldt-Bausch, 1985; Brown et al., 1986; Falkai, Bogerts, Greve, & Pfeiffer, 1992; Lieberman et al., 1992; Pearlson, Garbacz, Moberg, Ahn, & DePaulo, 1985). This evidence is consistent with a hypothesis that males are more susceptible to a neurodevelopmental subtype of schizophrenia characterized by an early onset (Forrest & Hay, 1971; Murray et al., 1992), a history of obstetric complications (Forrest & Hay, 1971; O'Callaghan, Gibson, Colohan, Buckley, Walshe, & Larkin, 1992; Haas et al., 1991a), and most importantly for this discussion, developmental difficulties that result in poor premorbid adjustment (Foerster et al., 1991). Although it is still unclear why males may be more prone to a neurodevelopmental subtype of schizophrenia, this etiological theory would suggest that the poorer social functioning characteristic of at least some schizophrenic males may derive from a neurodevelopmental subtype of schizophrenia marked by early obstetric and perinatal complications, developmental deficits, and a pattern of poor premorbid functioning (Foerster et al., 1991).

CONCLUSIONS

Gender is one of the most salient and robust predictors of social adjustment and functioning in schizophrenia. Several studies document higher levels of premorbid psychosocial adjustment among females; females are more likely to marry, have children, and maintain social relationships both before and after the onset of schizophrenia. Whether such differences in social functioning are sec-

ondary effects of sex differences in the clinical severity or pathophysiology of the disorder or whether they reflect sex-related variance in the functional adaptation to the illness is not known.

Kraepelin's (1919) observation that the illness tends to manifest a more severe course in males is supported by the results of several outcome studies that indicate that females fare better than males on global indicators of clinical course and functioning (Angermeyer et al. 1989; Fenton & McGlashan, 1987; Watt et al., 1983; Bardenstein & McGlashan, 1990; Westermeyer & Harrow, 1984). Whether the female advantage in functioning is restricted to the premorbid and early active phases of illness, as suggested by some (e.g., Harding & Childers, 1990), or manifests over the long-term course is the subject of some debate. Evidence that male deficits in cognitive and social functioning may be restricted to the chronic/recurrent phase rather than the first episode of hospitalization (Haas et al., 1991a) suggests that males may experience greater deterioration in functioning over the early years of the active phase of illness.

Aside from the question of the timing of sex differences in cognitive and social functioning, there is substantial evidence that during the chronic phase of illness, females tend to have a less complicated course of illness in terms of time in hospital and frequency of relapse and rehospitalization (Hogarty et al., 1974; Hogarty et al., 1986; Goldstein, 1988; Huber, Gross, & Schuttler, 1975; Sartorius, Jablensky, & Shapiro, 1978). The underlying nature and etiology of these gender differences in the clinical course of illness are undetermined. One intriguing question is whether sex-related variance in age at onset or the clinical manifestations of the illness (e.g., symptom severity, clinical relapse, and exacerbation of symptoms) are primarily responsible for sex differences in long-term social adjustment and functioning, or whether these functional outcomes are largely determined by non-illness-related factors such as socioeconomic status or premorbid social competency and calls for more focused investigation.

From several vantage points, sex differences in social functioning represent an important focus of interest in contemporary research on schizophrenia. First, one of the most robust gender differences in schizophrenia—the later mean age at onset among females—points to differences in the timing of illness onset. Because females tend to have a later onset of the active phase of the illness, the social skills and social adjustment advantages of females may stem, at least in part, from the female's greater opportunity for achievement of social and other developmental milestones before the onset of psychosis.

Second, the last decade has yielded advances in recognition of cognitive deficits in schizophrenia, the specific functional and pathophysiologic nature of which is not yet understood. Efforts to identify linkages between cognitive deficits on laboratory measures and the core functional deficits that define the clinical syndrome are as yet in their infancy. Ultimately, the search for neurocognitive and pathophysiologic substrates of relatively robust gender differences in social skills, social adjustment, and role functioning may help to illuminate our understanding of the pathophysiology and functional impact of the disorder.

Third, evidence that the potentially powerful influence of social and family environment variables (e.g., expressed emotion) may have a more profound impact on the course of illness in males suggests a need to evaluate gender-linked mechanisms that mediate the response to environmental stressors. Such research offers promise in efforts to understand the modulating influence of environmental factors in the etiology and treatment of schizophrenia. The sex of the individual represents not only important biological determinants of outcome but gender-linked characteristics of social role and personal identity that influence adequacy of functioning in the social community. Thus, investigation into putative social and biologic origins of sex differences in social functioning may enhance our knowledge of the underlying pathophysiology of schizophrenia as well as our understanding of potentially important environmental and biologic modulators of treatment response, treatment outcome, and course of illness.

REFERENCES

Achte, K. A. (1967). On prognosis and rehabilitation in schizophrenic and paranoid psychoses. *Acta Psychiatrica Scandinavica, 43,* 5–217.

Adler, L. (1953). The relationship of marital status to incidence and recovery from mental disease. *Social Forces,* 185–194.

Affleck, J. W., Burns, J., & Forrest, A. D. (1976). Long-term follow-up of schizophrenic patients in Edinburgh. *Acta Psychiatrica Scandinavica, 53,* 227–237.

Allon, R. (1971). Sex, race, socioeconomic status, social mobility, and process-reactive ratings of schizophrenics. *Journal of Nervous and Mental Disease, 153,* 343–350.

Andia, A. M., & Zisook, S. (1991). Gender differences in schizophrenia: A literature review. *Annals of Clinical Psychiatry, 3,* 333–340.

Andreasen, N. C. (1984). *Modified scale for the assessment of negative symptoms (SANS).* Iowa City: University of Iowa.

Andreasen, N. C., Endicott, J., Spitzer, R. L., & Winokur, G. (1977). The family history method using diagnostic criteria: Reliability and validity. *Archives of General Psychiatry, 34,* 1229–1235.

Angermeyer, M. C., Goldstein, J. M., & Kühn, L. (1989). Gender differences in schizophrenia: Rehospitalization and community survival. *Psychological Medicine, 19,* 365–382.

Angermeyer, M. C., Kühn, L., & Goldstein, J. M. (1990). Gender and the course of schizophrenia: Differences in treated outcomes. *Schizophrenia Bulletin, 16,* 293–307.

Aylward, E., Walker, E., & Bettes, B. (1984). Intelligence in schizophrenia: Meta-analysis of the research. *Schizophrenia Bulletin, 10,* 430–459.

Barberger Gateau, P., Chaslerie, A., Dartigues, J. F., & Commenges, D. (1992). Health measures correlates in French elderly community population: The PAQUID study. *Journals of Gerontology, 47,* S88–S95.

Bardenstein, K. K., & McGlashan, T. H. (1990). Gender differences in affective, schizoaffective, and schizophrenic disorders: A review. *Schizophrenia Research, 3,* 159–172.

Beiser, M., Bean, G., Erickson, D., Zhang, J., Iacono, W. G., & Rector, N. A. (1994). Biological and psychosocial predictors of job performance following a first episode of psychosis. *American Journal of Psychiatry, 151,* 857–863.

Bellack, A. S., Haas, G. L., & Tierney, A. M. (1996). A strategy for assessing family interaction patterns in schizophrenia. *Psychological Assessment, 8,* 190–199.

Bellack, A. S., Morrison, R. L., Mueser, K. T., & Wade, J. (1989). Social competence in schizoaffective disorder, bipolar disorder, and negative and nonnegative schizophrenia. *Schizophrenia Research, 2,* 391–401.

Bellack, A. S., Morrison, R. L., Wixted, J. T., & Mueser, K. T. (1990). An analysis of social competence in schizophrenia. *British Journal of Psychiatry, 156,* 809–818.

Birtchnell, J. (1971). Social class, parental social class, and social mobility in psychiatric patients and general population controls. In J. A. Baldwin (Ed.), *Aspects of the epidemiology of mental illness: Studies in record linkage* (pp. 77–103). Boston: Little, Brown.

Bland, R. C., & Orn, H. (1978). 14-year outcome in early schizophrenia. *Acta Psychiatrica Scandinavica, 58,* 327–338.

Bland, R. C., & Orn, H. (1981). Schizophrenia: Sociocultural factors. *Canadian Journal of Psychiatry, 26,* 186–188.

Bland, R. C., Parker, J. H., & Orn, H. (1976). Prognosis in schizophrenia. A ten-year follow-up of first admissions. *Archives of General Psychiatry, 33,* 949–954.

Bleuler, M. (1978). *The schizophrenic disorders: Long-term patient and family studies* (S. M. Clemens, Trans.). New Haven: Yale University Press.

Bogerts, B., Meertz, E., & Schonfeldt-Bausch, R. (1985). Basal ganglia and limbic system pathology in schizophrenia: A morphometric study of brain volume and shrinkage. *Archives of General Psychiatry, 42,* 784–791.

Breier, A., Schreiber, J. L., Dyer, J., & Pickar, D. (1991). National Institute of Mental Health longitudinal study of chronic schizophrenia: Prognosis and predictors of outcome. *Archives of General Psychiatry, 48,* 239–246.

Brown, G. W., Birley, J. L. T., & Wing, J. K. (1972). Influence of family life on the course of schizophrenic illness. *British Journal of Psychiatry, 121,* 241–258.

Brown, G. W., Bone, M., Dalison, B., & Wing, J. K. (1966). Schizophrenia and social care. London: Oxford University Press.

Brown, R., Colter, N., Corsellis, J. A., Crow, T. J., Frith, C. D., Jagoe, R., Johnstone, E. C., & Marsh, L. (1986). Postmortem evidence of structural brain changes in schizophrenia: Differences in brain weight, temporal horn area, and parahippocampal gyrus compared with affective disorder. *Archives of General Psychiatry, 43,* 36–42.

Cannon-Spoor, H., Potkin, S. G., & Wyatt, R. J. (1982). Measurement of premorbid adjustment in chronic schizophrenia. *Schizophrenia Bulletin, 8,* 470–484.

Carpenter, W. T., Heinrichs, D. W., & Wagman, A. M. (1988). Deficit and nondeficit forms of schizophrenia: The concept. *American Journal of Psychiatry, 145,* 578–583.

Castle, D. J., & Murray, R. (1991). The neurodevelopmental basis of sex differences in schizophrenia. *Psychological Medicine, 21,* 565–575.

Chaves, A. C., Seeman, M. V., Mari, J. J., & Maluf, A. (1993). Schizophrenia: Impact of positive symptoms on gender social role. *Schizophrenia Research, 11,* 41–45.

Childers, S. E., & Harding, C. M. (1990). Gender, premorbid social functioning, and long-term outcome in DSM-III schizophrenia. *Schizophrenia Bulletin, 16,* 309–318.

Ciompi, L., & Müller, C. (1976). Lifestyle and age of schizophrenics. A catamnestic long-term study into old age. [German]. *Monographien aus dem Gesamtgebiete der Psychiatrie, 12,* 1–242.

Corrigan, P. W., & Green, M. F. (1993). Schizophrenic patients' sensitivity to social cues: The role of abstraction. *American Journal of Psychiatry, 150,* 589–594.

Corrigan, P. W., Green, M. F., & Toomey, R. (1994). Cognitive correlates to social cue perception in schizophrenia. *Psychiatry Research, 53,* 141–151.

Counts, R. M., & Devlin, J. P. (1954). Sexual experience as a prognostic factor in psychosis. *Journal of Nervous and Mental Disorders, 120,* 364–368.

Deister, A., & Marneros, A. (1992). Sex differences in functional psychoses—comparison between schizophrenic, schizoaffective and affective disorders. *Fortschritte der Neurologie Psychiatrie, 60,* 407–419.

DeLisi L. E., Dauphinais, I. D., & Hauser P. (1989). Gender differences in the brain: Are they relevant to the pathogenesis of schizophrenia? *Comprehensive Psychiatry, 30,* 197–208.

Dougherty, F., Bartlett, E., & Izard, C. (1974). Response of schizophrenics to expressions of the fundamental emotions. *Journal of Clinical Psychology, 30,* 243–246.

Dworkin, R. H. (1990). Patterns of sex differences in negative symptoms and social functioning consistent with separate dimensions of schizophrenic psychopathology. *American Journal of Psychiatry, 147,* 347–349.

Dworkin, R. H., Lenzenweger, M. J., Moldin, S. O., Skillings, G. F., & Levick, S. E. (1988). A multidimensional approach to the genetics of schizophrenia. *American Journal of Psychiatry, 145,* 1077–1083.

Eaton, W. W. (1975). Marital status and schizophrenia. *Acta Psychiatrica Scandinavica, 52,* 320–329.

Falkai, P., Bogerts, B., Greve, B., & Pfeiffer, U. (1992). Loss of sylvian fissure asymmetry in schizophrenia: A quantitative post mortem study. *Schizophrenia Research, 7,* 23–32.

Faraone, S. V., Green, A. I., Brown, W., Yin, P., & Tsuang, M. T. (1989). Neuroleptic dose reduction in persistently psychotic patients. *Hospital and Community Psychiatry, 40,* 1193–1195.

Farina, A. (1981). Are women nicer people than men? Sex and the stigma of mental disorders. *Clinical Psychology Review, 1,* 223–243.

Farina, A., Garmezy, N., & Barry, H. (1963). Relationship of marital status to incidence and prognosis of schizophrenia. *Journal of Consulting and Clinical Psychology, 67,* 624–630.

Farina, A., Garmezy, N., Zalusky, M., & Becker, J. (1962). Premorbid behavior and prognosis in female schizophrenic patients. *Journal of Consulting and Clinical Psychology, 26,* 56–60.

Farina, A., Murray, P. J., & Groh, T. (1978). Sex and worker acceptance of a former mental patient. *Journal of Consulting and Clinical Psychology, 46,* 887–891.

Feighner, J., Robins, E., Guze, S., Woodruff, R., Winokur, G., Munoz, R. (1972). Diagnostic criteria for use in psychiatric research. *Arch Gen Psychiatry, 26,* 57–63.

Fenton, W. S., & McGlashan, T. H. (1987). Prognostic scale for chronic schizophrenia. *Schizophrenia Bulletin, 13,* 277–286.

Foerster, A., Lewis, S., Owen, M., & Murray, R. (1991). Premorbid adjustment and personality in psychosis: Effects of sex and diagnosis. *British Journal of Psychiatry, 158,* 171–176.

Forrest, A. D., & Hay, A. J. (1971). Sex differences and the schizophrenic experience. *Acta Psychiatrica Scandinavica, 47,* 137–147.

Forrest, A. D., & Hay, A. J. (1972). The influence of sex on schizophrenia. *Acta Psychiatrica Scandinavica, 6,* 53–58.

Gibbons, J. S., Horn, S. H., Powell, J. M., & Gibbons, J. L. (1984). Schizophrenic patients and their families. A survey in a psychiatric service based on a DGH unit. *British Journal of Psychiatry, 144,* 70–77.

Giel, R., Wiersma, D., de Jong, P. A., & Slooff, C. (1984). Prognosis and outcome in a cohort of patients with non-affective functional psychosis. *European Archives of Psychiatry and Neurological Sciences, 234,* 97–101.

Gittelman-Klein, R., & Klein, D. F. (1968). Marital status as a prognostic indicator in schizophrenia. *Journal of Nervous and Mental Disease, 147,* 289–296.

Gittelman-Klein, R., & Klein, D. F. (1969). Premorbid asocial adjustment and prognosis in schizophrenia. *Journal of Psychiatric Research, 7,* 35–53.

Glick, I. D., Clarkin, J. F., Haas, G. L., Spencer, J. H., & Chen, C. L. (1991). A randomized clinical trial of inpatient family intervention: VI. Mediating variables and outcomes. *Family Process, Inc, 30,* 85–99.

Goldstein, J. M. (1988). Gender differences in the course of schizophrenia. *American Journal of Psychiatry, 145,* 684–689.

Goldstein, J. M., Faraone, S. V., Chen, W. J., & Tolomiczencko, G. S. (1990). Sex differences in the familial transmission of schizophrenia. *British Journal of Psychiatry, 156,* 819–826.

Goldstein, J. M., & Kreisman, D. (1988). Gender, family environment and schizophrenia. *Psychological Medicine, 18,* 861–872.

Goldstein, J. M., & Link, B. G. (1988). Gender and the expression of schizophrenia. *Journal of Psychiatric Research, 22,* 141–155.

Goldstein, J. M., Tsuang, M. T., & Faraone, S. V. (1989). Gender and schizophrenia: Implications for understanding the heterogeneity of the illness. *Psychiatry Research, 28,* 243–253.

Goldstein, M. J. (1978). Further data concerning the relation between premorbid adjustment and paranoid symptomatology. *Schizophrenia Bulletin, 4,* 236–243.

Grimes, K., & Walker, E. F. (1994). Childhood emotional expressions, educational attainment, and age at onset of illness in schizophrenia. *Journal of Abnormal Psychology, 103,* 784–790.

Grünfeld, B., & Salvesen, C. (1968). Functional psychoses and social status. *British Journal of Psychiatry, 114,* 733–737.

Haas, G. L., & Castle, D. J. (1997). Sex differences in schizophrenia. In M. S. Keshavan & R. M. Murray (Eds.) *Neurodevelopment and adult psychopathology* (pp. 155–177). New York: Cambridge University Press.

Haas, G. L., Glick, I. D., Clarkin, J. F., & Spencer, J. H. (1990). Gender and schizophrenia outcome: A clinical trial of an inpatient family intervention. *Schizophrenia Bulletin, 16,* 277–292.

Haas, G. L., & Sweeney, J. (1992). Premorbid and onset features of first-episode schizophrenia. *Schizophrenia Bulletin, 18,* 373–386.

Haas, G. L., Sweeney, J. A., Hien, D. A., Goldman, D., & Deck, M. (1991a, April). *Gender differences in schizophrenia.* Paper presented at the International Congress on Research in Schizophrenia, Tucson, AZ.

Haas, G. L., Sweeney, J., Hien, D., Goldman, D., & Deck, M. (1991b, August). *Neurocognition and sex differences in the course of schizophrenia.* Paper presented at the Annual Convention of the American Psychological Association, San Francisco.

Haas, G. L., Sweeney, J. A., Hien, D., Waked, W., & Weiden, P. (1989, May). *Sex differences in schizophrenia.* Poster presented at the Annual Meeting of the American Psychiatric Association, San Francisco.

Halford, W. K., & Hayes, R. L. (1995). Social skills in schizophrenia: Assessing the relationship between social skills, psychopathology and community functioning. *Social Psychiatry and Psychiatric Epidemiology, 30,* 14–19.

Hall, J. C., Smith, K., & Shimkunas, A. (1966). Employment problems of schizophrenic patients. *American Journal of Psychiatry, 123,* 536–540.

Häfner, H., Behrens, S., de Vry, J., & Gattaz, W. F. (1991). An animal model for the effects of estradiol on dopamine-mediated behavior: Implications for sex differences in schizophrenia. *Psychiatry Research, 38,* 125–134.

Häfner, H., Maurer, K., Löffler, W., & Riecher-Rösser, A. (1993). The influence of age and sex on the onset and early course of schizophrenia. *British Journal of Psychiatry, 162,* 80–86.

Häfner, H. Riecher-Rössler, A., Fätkenheuer, B., Hambrecht, M., Löffler, W., an der Heider, W., Maurer, K., Munk-Jørgensen, P., & Stromgren, E. Sex differences in schizophrenia, *Psychiatria Fennica,* 1991, 22:123–156.

Häfner, H., Riecher-Rössler, A., Hambrecht, M., & Maurer, K. (1992). IRAOS: An instrument for the assessment of onset and early course of schizophrenia. *Schizophrenia Research, 6,* 209–223.

Häfner, H., Riecher-Rössler, A., An Der Heiden, W., Maurer, K., Fätkenheuer, B., & Löffler, W. (1993). Generating and testing a causal explanation of the gender difference in age at first onset of schizophrenia. *Psychological Medicine, 23,* 925–940.

Häfner, H., Riecher-Rössler, A., Maurer, K., & Fätkenheuer, B. (1992). First onset and early symptomatology of schizophrenia: A chapter of epidemiological and neurobiological research into age and sex differences. *European Archives of Psychiatry and Clinical Neuroscience 24,* 109–118.

Heimberg, C., Gur, R. E., Erwin, R. J., Shtasel, D. L., & Gur, R. C. (1992). Facial emotion discrimination: III. Behavioral findings in schizophrenia. *Psychiatry Research, 42,* 253–265.

Heinrichs, D. W., Hanlon, T. E., & Carpenter, W. T., Jr. (1984). The Quality of Life Scale: An instrument for rating the schizophrenic deficit syndrome. *Schizophrenia Bulletin, 10,* 388–398.

Hogarty, G. E. (1974). Drug and sociotherapy in the aftercare of schizophrenic patients: III. Adjustment of nonrelapsed patients. *Archives of General Psychiatry, 31,* 609–618.

Hogarty, G. E. (1985). Expressed emotion and schizophrenic relapse: Implications from the Pittsburgh Study. In M. Alpert (Ed.), *Controversies in schizophrenia* (pp. 354–363). New York: Guilford.

Hogarty, G. E., Anderson, C. M., Reiss, D. J., Kornblith, S. J., Greenwald, D. P., Ulrich, R. F., & Carter, M. (1986). Family psychoeducation, social skills training, and maintenance chemotherapy in the aftercare treatment of schizophrenia: I. One-year effects of a controlled study on relapse and expressed emotion. *Archives of General Psychiatry, 43,* 633–642.

Hogarty, G. E., Goldberg, S., & Schooler, N. S. (1974). Drug and sociotherapy in the aftercare of schizophrenic patients: II. Two-year relapse rates. *Archives of General Psychiatry, 31,* 603–608.

Hollingshead, A. B. (1957). Two factor index of social position. New Haven: August B. Hollingshead.

Hollingshead, A. B. (1975). Four-factor index of social status. New Haven: Yale University.

Huber, G., Gross, G., & Schuttler, R. (1975). A long-term follow-up study of schizophrenia: Psychiatric course of illness and prognosis. *Acta Psychiatrica Scandinavica, 52,* 49–57.

Huber, G., Gross, G., Schuttler, R., & Linz, M. (1980). Longitudinal studies of schizophrenic patients. *Schizophrenia Bulletin, 6,* 592–605.

Izard, C. (1959). Paranoid schizophrenic and normal subjects' perception of photographs of human faces. *Journal of Consulting Psychology, 23,* 119–124.

Jones, P. B., Bebbington, P., Foerster, A., Lewis, S. W., Murray, R. M., Russell, A., Sham, P. C., Toone, B. K., & Wilkins, S. (1993). Premorbid social underachievement in schizophrenia: Results from the Camberwell Collaborative Psychosis Study. *British Journal of Psychiatry, 162,* 65–71.

Kay, S. R., & Lindenmayer, J. P. (1987). Outcome predictors in acute schizophrenia. Prospective significance of background and clinical dimensions. *Journal of Nervous and Mental Disease, 175,* 152–160.

Keefe, R. S., Mohs, R. C., Losonczy, M. F., & Davidson, M. (1989). Premorbid sociosexual functioning and long-term outcome in schizophrenia. *American Journal of Psychiatry, 146,* 206–211.

Körmendy, E., & Schäfer, E. (1983). Empirical course study of schizophrenic diseases in the area of a community psychiatric service. [German]. *Nervenarzt, 54,* 347–353.

Kraepelin, E. (1919). *Dementia praecox and paraphrenia.* Chicago: Chicago Medical Books.

Kreisman, D., & Blumenthal, R. (1985). *Social Adjustment Scale-Family Version.* New York: New York State Psychiatric Institute.

Kremen, W. S., Seidman, L. J., Pepple, J. R., Lyons, M. J., Tsuang, M. T., & Faraone, S. V. (1994). Neuropsychological risk indicators for schizophrenia: A review of family studies. *Schizophrenia Bulletin, 20,* 103–119.

Landis, C., & Page, J. D. (1938). *Modern society and mental disease.* New York: Farrar & Rhinehart.

Lane, E. A. (1968). The influence of sex and race on process-reactive ratings of schizophrenics. *Journal of Psychology, 68,* 15–20.

Larsen, T. K., McGlashan, T. H., Johannessen, J. O., & Vibe-Hansen, L. (1996). First-episode schizophrenia: II. Premorbid patterns by gender. *Schizophrenia Bulletin, 22, 257–269.*

Lassenius, B., Ottosson, J. O., & Rapp, W. (1973). Prognosis in schizophrenia. The need for institutionalized care. *Acta Psychiatrica Scandinavica, 49,* 295–305.

Leff, J., Sartorius, N., Jablensky, A., Korten, A., & Ernberg, G.

(1992). The International Pilot Study of Schizophrenia: Five-year follow-up findings. *Psychological Medicine, 22,* 131–145.

Lewine, R. R. (1980). Sex differences in age of symptom onset and first hospitalization in schizophrenia. *American Journal of Orthopsychiatry, 50,* 316–322.

Lewine, R. R. (1981). Sex differences in schizophrenia: Timing or subtypes? *Psychological Bulletin, 90,* 432–444.

Lewine, R. (1985). Schizophrenia: An amotivational syndrome in men. *Canadian Journal of Psychiatry, 30,* 316–318.

Lewine, R. R., Burbach, D., & Meltzer, H. Y. (1984). Effect of diagnostic criteria on the ratio of male to female schizophrenic patients. *American Journal of Psychiatry, 141,* 84–87.

Lewine, R. R., Watt, N. F., Prentky, R. A., & Fryer, J. H. (1980). Childhood social competence in functionally disordered psychiatric patients and in normals. *Journal of Abnormal Psychology, 89,* 132–138.

Lewis, S. W., & Murray, R. M. (1987). Obstetric complications, neurodevelopmental deviance, and risk of schizophrenia. *Journal of Psychiatric Research, 21,* 413–421.

Lieberman, J., Alvir, J., Woerner, M., Degreef, G., Bilder, R., Ashtari, M., Bogerts, B., Mayerhoff, D., Geisler, S., Loebel, A., Levy, D., Hinrichsen, G., Szymanski, S., Chakos, M., Koreen, A., Borenstein, M., & Kane, J. (1992). Prospective study of psychobiology in first-episode schizophrenia at Hillside Hospital. *Schizophrenia Bulletin, 18,* 351–371.

Litter, J., & Walker, E. (1993). Interpersonal behavior of preschizophrenic children: A study of home-movies. *Child Psychiatry and Human Development, 23,* 283–295.

Lo, W. H., & Lo, T. (1977). A ten year follow-up of Chinese schizophrenics in Hong Kong. *British Journal of Psychiatry, 13,* 63–66.

Loranger, A. W. (1984). Sex differences in age at onset of schizophrenia. *Archives of General Psychiatry, 41,* 157–161.

Loyd, D. W., Simpson, J. C., & Tsuang, M. T. (1985). Are there sex differences in the long-term outcome of schizophrenia? Comparisons with mania, depression, and surgical controls. *Journal of Nervous and Mental Disease, 173,* 643–649.

Malzberg, B. (1935). A statistical study of age in relation to mental disease. *Mental Hygiene, 19,* 449–476.

Mantonakis, J. E., Jemos, J. J., Christodoulou, G. N., & Lykouras, E. P. (1982). Short-term social prognosis of schizophrenia. *Acta Psychiatrica Scandinavica, 66,* 306–310.

Marneros, A., Steinmeyer, E. M., Deister, A., Rohde, A., & Jünemann, H. (1989). Long-term outcome of schizoaffective and schizophrenic disorders: A comparative study. III. Social consequences. *European Archives of Psychiatry and Neurological Science, 238,* 135–139.

Masterson, J. F., Jr. (1956). Prognosis in adolescent disorders. *Journal of Nervous and Mental Disease, 124,* 219–232.

Mayer, C., Kelterborn, G., & Naber, D. (1993). Age of onset in schizophrenia: Relations to psychopathology and gender. *British Journal of Psychiatry, 162,* 665–671.

McGlashan, T. H., & Bardenstein, K. K. (1990). Gender differences in affective, schizoaffective, and schizophrenic disorders. *Schizophrenia Bulletin, 2,* 319–329.

Mignolli, G., Faccincani, C., & Platt, S. (1991). Psychopathology and social performance in a cohort of patients with schizophrenic psychoses. A seven year follow-up study. *Psychological Medicine, 19,* 17–26.

Morrison, R. L., & Bellack, A. S. (1981). The role of social perception in social skill. *Behavior Therapy, 12,* 69–79.

Morrison, R. L., & Bellack, A. S. (1987). Social functioning of schizophrenic patients: Clinical and research issues. *Schizophrenia Bulletin, 13,* 715–725.

Möller, H. J., Werner-Eilert, K., Wüschner-Stockheim, M., & Zerssen, D. V. (1982). Relevante merkmale fur die 5-jahresprognose von patienten mit schizophrenen und verwandten paranoiden psychosen. [Relevant predictors of the 5 year outcome of patients with schizophrenic or similar paranoid psychoses]. *Archiv fur Psychiatrie und Nervenkrankheiten, 231,* 305–322.

Mueser, K. T., Bellack, A. S., Douglas, M. S., & Wade, J. H. (1991). Prediction of social skill acquisition in schizophrenic and major affective disorder patients from memory and symptomatology. *Psychiatry Research, 37,* 281–296.

Mueser, K. T., Bellack, A. S., Morrison, R. L., & Wade, J. H. (1990). Gender, social competence, and symptomatology in schizophrenia: A longitudinal analysis. *Journal of Abnormal Psychology, 99,* 138–147.

Mueser, K. T., Bellack, A. S., Morrison, R. L., & Wixted, J. T. (1990). Social competence in schizophrenia: Premorbid adjustment, social skill, and domains of functioning. *Journal of Psychiatric Research, 24,* 51–63.

Mueser, K. T., Bellack, A. S., Wade, J. H., Sayers, S. L., Tierney, A., & Haas, G. (1993). Expressed emotion, social skill and response to negative affect in schizophrenia. *Journal of Abnormal Psychology, 102,* 339–351.

Mueser, K. T., Blanchard, J. J., & Bellack, A. S. (1995). Memory and social skill in schizophrenia: The role of gender. *Psychiatry Research, 51(2),* 141–153.

Müller, H. W. (1971). Störungen des psychosozialen milieus und ihr einflß auf schizophrene Krankheitsverläufe. In H. Kranz & K. Heinrich (Eds.), *Schizophrenie und Umwelt* (pp. 58–72). Stuttgart: Thieme.

Munk-JØrgensen, P., & Mortensen, P. B. (1992a). Social outcome in schizophrenia: A 13-year follow-up. *Social Psychiatry and Psychiatric Epidemiology, 27,* 129–134.

Munk-JØrgensen, P., & Mortensen, P. B. (1992b). Incidence and other aspects of the epidemiology of schizophrenia in Denmark, 1971–87. *British Journal of Psychiatry, 161,* 489–495.

Murray, R. M., O'Callaghan, E., Castle, D. J., & Lewis, S. W. (1992). A neurodevelopmental approach to the classification of schizophrenia. *Schizophrenia Bulletin, 18,* 319–332.

Muzekari, L. H., & Bates, M. E. (1977). Judgment of emotion among chronic schizophrenics. *Journal of Clinical Psychology, 33,* 662–666.

Navarro, F., van Os, J., Jones, P., & Murray, R. (1996). Explaining sex differences in course and outcome in the functional psychoses. *Schizophrenia Research, 21,* 161–170.

Nyman, A. K. (1978). Non-regressive schizophrenia. Clinical course and outcome. *Acta Psychiatrica Scandinavica, Supplementum, 272,* 1–143.

Nyman, A. K., & Jonsson, H. (1983). Differential evaluation of outcome in schizophrenia. *Acta Psychiatrica Scandinavica, 68,* 458–475.

O'Callaghan, E., Gibson, T., Colohan, H. A., Buckley, P., Walshe, D. G., & Larkin, C. (1992). Risk of schizophrenia in adults born after obstetric complications and their association with early onset of illness: A controlled study. *British Medical Journal, 305,* 1256–1259.

Offord, D. R. (1974). School performance of adult schizophrenics, their siblings and age mates. *British Journal of Psychiatry, 125,* 12–19.

Pearlson, G. D., Garbacz, D. J., Moberg, P. J., Ahn, H. A., & DePaulo, J. R. (1985). Symptomatic, familial, perinatal, and social correlates of computerized axial tomography (CAT) changes in schizophrenics and bipolars. *Journal of Nervous and Mental Disease, 173,* 42–50.

Penn, D. L., Mueser, K. T., & Spaulding, W. (1996). Information processing, social skill, and gender in schizophrenia. *Psychiatry Research, 59,* 213–220.

Phillips, L. (1953). Case history data and prognosis in schizophrenia. *Journal of Nervous and Mental Disease, 117,* 515–525.

Pogue-Geile, M. F., & Harrow, M. (1984). Negative and positive symptoms in schizophrenia and depression: A follow-up. *Schizophrenia Bulletin, 10,* 371–387.

Pogue-Geile, M. F., & Harrow, M. (1985). Negative symptoms in schizophrenia: Their longitudinal courses and prognostic importance. *Schizophrenia Bulletin, 11,* 427–439.

Raskin, A., & Golob, R. (1966). Occurrence of sex and social class differences in premorbid competence, symptom and outcome measures in acute schizophrenics. *Psychological Reports, 18,* 11–22.

Raskin, M., & Dyson, W. L. (1968). Treatment problems leading to readmissions of schizophrenic patients. *Archives of General Psychiatry, 19,* 356–360.

Rice, J. P., Rochberg, N., Endicott, J., Lavori, P. W., & Miller, C. (1992). Stability of psychiatric diagnoses. An application to the affective disorders. *Archives of General Psychiatry, 49,* 824–830.

Riecher-Rössler, A., Fätkenheuer, B., Löffler, W., Maurer, K., & Häfner, H. (1992). Is age of onset in schizophrenia influenced by marital status? Some remarks on the difficulties and pitfalls in the systematic testing of a "simple" question. *Social Psychiatry and Psychiatric Epidemiology, 27,* 122–128.

Ring, N., Tantam, D., Montague, L., & Newby, D. (1991). Gender differences in the incidence of definite schizophrenia and atypical psychosis: Focus on negative symptoms of schizophrenia. *Acta Psychiatrica Scandinavica, 84,* 489–496.

Rosen, B., Klein, D. F., & Gittleman-Klein, R. (1969). Sex differences in the relationship between premorbid asociality and posthospital outcome. *Journal of Nervous and Mental Disease, 149,* 415–420.

Salokangas, R. K. (1983). Prognostic implications of the sex of schizophrenic patients. *British Journal of Psychiatry, 142,* 145–151.

Salokangas, R. (1986). Psychosocial outcome in schizophrenia and psychotherapeutic orientation. *Acta Psychiatrica Scandinavica, 74,* 497–506.

Salokangas, R. K., & Stengård, E. (1990). Gender and short-term outcome in schizophrenia. *Schizophrenia Research, 3,* 333–345.

Sartorius, N., Jablensky, A., & Shapiro, R. (1977). Two-year follow-up of the patients included in the WHO International Pilot Study of Schizophrenia. *Psychological Medicine, 7,* 529–541.

Sartorius, N., Jablensky, A., & Shapiro, R. (1978). Cross-cultural differences in the short-term prognosis of schizophrenic psychoses. *Schizophrenia Bulletin, 4,* 102–113.

Schooler, C. (1963). Affiliation among schizophrenics: Preferred characteristics of the other. *Journal of Nervous and Mental Disease, 137,* 438–446.

Schooler, N. R., Goldberg, S. C., Boothe, H., & Cole, J. O. (1967). One year after discharge: Community adjustment of schizophrenic patients. *American Journal of Psychiatry, 123,* 986–995.

Schooler, N. R., Hogarty, G. E., & Weissman, M. M. (1979). Social Adjustment Scale II (SAS II). In W. A. Hargreaves, C. C. Attkisson, & J. E. Sorenson (Eds.), *Resource materials for community mental health program evaluators.* (pp. 29–33). (No. ADM 79–328). Washington, DC: U.S. Government Printing Office.

Seeman, M. V. (1982). Gender differences in schizophrenia. *Canadian Journal of Psychiatry, 27,* 107–112.

Seeman, M. V. (1983a). Schizophrenic men and women require different treatment programs. *Journal of Psychiatric Treatment and Evaluation, 5,* 143–148.

Seeman, M. V. (1983b). Interaction of sex, age, and neuroleptic dose. *Comprehensive Psychiatry, 24,* 125–128.

Seeman, M. V. (1985). Sex and schizophrenia. *Canadian Journal of Psychiatry, 30,* 313–315.

Seeman, M. V. (1986). Current outcome in schizophrenia: Women vs. men. *Acta Psychiatrica Scandinavica, 73,* 609–617.

Seeman, M. V., & Hauser, P. (1984). Schizophrenia: The influence of gender on family environment. *International Journal of Family Psychiatry, 5,* 227–232.

Seeman, M. V., & Lang, M. (1990). The role of estrogens in schizophrenia gender differences. *Schizophrenia Bulletin, 16,* 185–194.

Shepherd, M. (1959). The social outcome of early schizophrenia. *Psychiatric Neurology, 137,* 224–229.

Shtasel, D. L., Gur, R. E., Gallacher, F., Heimberg, C., & Gur, R. C. (1992). Gender differences in the clinical expression of schizophrenia. *Schizophrenia Research, 7,* 225–231.

Steinmeyer, E. M., Marneros, A., Deister, A., Rohde, A., & Jünemann, H. (1989). Long-term outcome of schizoaffective and schizophrenic disorders: A comparative study. II. Causal-analytical investigations. *European Archives of Psychiatry and Neurological Sciences, 238,* 126–134.

Stephens, J. H. (1992). Long-term prognosis and follow-up in schizophrenia. *Schizophrenia Bulletin, 4,* 25–42.

Strauss, J. S., Carpenter, W. T., & Bartko, J. J. (1974). Part III. Speculations on the processes that underlie schizophrenic symptoms and signs. *Schizophrenia Bulletin, 11,* 61–69.

Strömgren, E. (1987). Changes in the incidence of schizophrenia. *British Journal of Psychiatry, 150,* 1–7.

Tsuang, M. T., Dempsey, G., & Rauscher, F. (1976). A study of "atypical schizophrenia": Comparison with schizophrenia and affective disorder by sex, age of admission, precipitant, outcome, and family history. *Archives of General Psychiatry, 33,* 1157–1160.

Tudor, W., Tudor, J. F., & Gove, W. R. (1977). The effect of sex role differences on the social control of mental illness. *Journal of Health and Social Behavior, 18,* 98–112.

Turner, R. J., Dopkeen, L. S., & Labreche, G. P. (1970). Marital status and schizophrenia: A study of incidence and outcome. *Journal of Abnormal Psychology, 76,* 110–116.

Vaughn, C., & Leff, J. (1976). The influence of family and social factors on the course of psychiatric illness: A comparison of schizophrenic and depressed neurotic patients. *British Journal of Psychiatry, 129,* 125–137.

Vogel, T., & Vliegen, J. (1975). Soziale auswirkungen der schizophrenie. *Nervenarzt, 46,* 569–575.

Walker, E., Bettes, B. A., Kain, E., & Harvey, P. (1985). Relationship of gender and marital status with symptomatology in psychotic patients. *Journal of Abnormal Psychology, 94,* 42–50.

Walker, E., Marwit, S. J., & Emory, E. (1980). A cross-sectional study of emotion recognition in schizophrenics. *Journal of Abnormal Psychology, 89,* 428–436.

Walker, E. F., Grimes, K. E., Davis, D. M., & Smith, A. J. (1993). Childhood precursors of schizophrenia: facial expressions of emotion. *American Journal of Psychiatry, 150,* 1654–1660.

Watt, D., Katz, K., & Shepherd, M. (1983). The natural history of schizophrenia: A 5-year prospective follow-up of a representative sample of schizophrenics by means of a standardized clinical and social assessment. *Psychological Medicine, 13,* 663–670.

Wattie, B., & Kedward, H. (1985). Gender differences in living conditions found among male and female schizophrenic patients on a follow-up study. *International Journal of Social Psychiatry, 31,* 205–216.

Westermeyer, J. F., & Harrow, M. (1984). Prognosis and outcome using broad (DSM-II) and narrow (DSM-III) concepts of schizophrenia. *Schizophrenia Bulletin, 10,* 624–637.

Wiersma, D., Giel, R., De Long, A., & Slooff, C. J. (1983). Social class and schizophrenia in a Dutch cohort. *Psychological Medicine, 13,* 141–150.

Zigler, E., & Levine, J. (1981). Premorbid competence in schizophrenia: What is being measured? *Journal of Consulting and Clinical Psychology, 49,* 96–105.

Zigler, E., & Phillips, L. (1960). Social effectiveness and symptomatic behaviors. *Journal of Abnormal and Social Psychology, 61,* 231–238.

Zigler, E., & Phillips, L. (1962). Social competence and the process-reactive distinction in psychopathology. *Journal of Abnormal Psychology, 65,* 215–222.

CHAPTER 11

AFFECT AND SOCIAL FUNCTIONING IN SCHIZOPHRENIA

Jack J. Blanchard
Catherine Panzarella

Changes in the experience and expression of affect have historically been described as key features of schizophrenia. Kraepelin (1919/1971) noted that "very striking and profound damage occurs as a rule in the emotional life of our patients" (p. 32). Similarly, Blueler (1911/1950) observed that "the fundamental affective symptoms often dominate the picture from the very start, in that the patients become increasingly indifferent and apathetic" (p. 254). Contemporary nosology continues to reflect this early significance ascribed to emotion in schizophrenia. Deficits in the expression of affect, affective flattening, are now indicated as one of the Criterion A characteristic symptoms in DSM-IV (American Psychiatric Association, [APA] 1994). Decreased capacity to experience pleasure, anhedonia, and displays of inappropriate affect (a defining feature of the Disorganized Type) are described as associated features of schizophrenia in DSM-IV. Affective deficits of anhedonia and affective flattening also figure prominently in subtypologies of symptoms as they are considered core negative (Andreasen, 1982) or deficit symptoms (Carpenter, Heinrichs, & Wagman, 1988).

In this chapter it will be argued that a full understanding of the social deficits of schizophrenia, as reviewed by other contributions to this volume, requires the study of affect. Specifically, it is the authors' thesis that affect and social functioning are inextricably linked, each giving rise to and resulting from the other. First, we will review evidence regarding affective experience and its association with social impairment. Specifically, this discussion will focus on (a) hedonic capacity and (b) the experience of anxiety, depression, and other affective symptoms in schizophrenia. The second major area to be reviewed will involve the negative symptom of affective flattening and how the diminished expression of emotion is related to both social functioning and affective experience.

AFFECTIVE EXPERIENCE

In reviewing affective experience in schizophrenia two domains will be discussed. First, the ability to experience pleasure, hedonic capacity, has been of historical and theoretical interest in particular with regard to the risk for the development of schizophrenia. Second, negative affective states such as anxiety and depression have been observed to be frequent clinical manifestations in schizophrenic patients. Each of these major domains will be discussed followed by an integrative summary.

Hedonic Capacity

Kraepelin (1919/1971) described a variety of emotional characteristics in schizophrenia including indifference involving the lack of joy or affection.

> The singular indifference of the patients towards their former emotional relations, the extinction of affection for relatives and friends, of satisfaction in their work and vocation, in recreation and pleasures, is not seldom the first and most striking symptom of the onset of the disease. The patients have no real joy in life, no human feelings ; to them nothing matters, everything is the same ; they feel no grief and no joy, their heart is not in what they say. (pp. 32–33)

Rado (1962) elevated the theoretical importance of this diminished pleasure, or anhedonia, beyond a mere symptom to the status of a central deficit of the disorder which was genetically based. Rado (1962) described anhedonia as being related to the weakening of a range of positive emotions including joy, affection, love, and pride. At the same time anhedonia was seen as being related to an increase in negative emotions such as fear and rage. Socially, Rado proposed that anhedonia disrupts sexual functioning and limits the schizotype's capacity for the appropriate enjoyment of his life activities, as well as for love and affectionate give and take in human relationships (Rado, 1962, p. 2).

Building on Rado s observations and theorizing, Meehl (1962) conjectured that anhedonia was a quasi-pathognomonic sign of schizophrenia. In this early model anhedonia was primary, leading to social withdrawal and isolation, increased aberrant interpersonal behavior, and ultimately cognitive deviance. Meehl (1990) subsequently revised his theory diminishing the role of anhedonia in schizophrenia to one of a dozen *normal range (nontaxonic) individual difference factors (dimensions)* that raise or lower the probability of decompensation (Meehl, 1990, p. 24, emphasis in original). Due to space limitations, the present review will only briefly address the status of anhedonia as a marker for the liability to develop schizophrenia; rather, the current discussion will focus on the relationship between anhedonia and social functioning in schizophrenia.

It is important to note that Meehl never construed anhedonia as a global deficit in the capacity to experience pleasure, but rather that the deficit appeared to be specific to the social-interpersonal realm. For example, Meehl (1962) originally observed that "schizoid anhedonia is mainly interpersonal, i.e., schizotypes seem to derive adequate pleasure from esthetic and cognitive rewards" (p. 833). Similarly, Meehl (1990), in explaining his preference for the term *hypohedonia,* indicated that even the most deteriorated schizophrenic can achieve pleasure from a few sources such as smoking or watching television.

Hedonic Capacity and Risk for Schizophrenia

Chapman, Chapman, and Raulin (1976) sought to examine the conjectures of Meehl and Rado. The Chapmans developed two true-false self-report questionnaires measuring anhedonia. The Physical Anhedonia Scale evaluates pleasure derived from sensory experiences such as listening to music or tasting food. The Social Anhedonia Scale measures pleasure obtained from interpersonal experiences such as talking and being with friends. The Chapmans speculated that the Physical Anhedonia Scale would appear more likely to reflect a biological defect such as that suggested by theorists of schizophrenic anhedonia (p. 381). The content of the Social Anhedonia Scale was thought to be more vulnerable to social influences on interpersonal behavior. (This original emphasis on physical anhedonia resulted in subsequent studies often using only the Physical Anhedonia Scale.) Chapman et al. (1976) found schizophrenic patients to have significantly greater physical and social anhedonia than did normal controls. Similar findings of increased anhedonia in schizophrenia compared with nonpsychiatric controls have been reported by other investigators (Berenbaum & Oltmanns, 1992; Clementz, Grove, Katsanis, & Iacono, 1991; Grove, Lebow, Clementz, Cerri, Medus, & Iacono, 1991; Schuck, Leventhal, Rothstein, & Irizarry, 1984).

To test the hypothesis that anhedonia is related to the genetic risk for the development of schizophrenia, studies have also examined anhedonia in the family members of schizophrenic patients. Berenbaum, Oltmanns, and Gottesman (1990) rated hedonic capacity from audiotaped interviews from the Gottesman and Shields twin study of schizophrenia (Gottesman & Shields, 1972). Berenbaum et. al. (1990) found intraclass correlations of .53 for monozygotic twins and −.38 for dizygotic twins, indicating a genetic influence on hedonic capacity. Grove et al. (1991) found that schizophrenic patients had higher physical anhedonia scores than did controls, and that schizophrenics' relatives also reported greater physical anhedonia than did controls. Similarly, Clementz et al. (1991) also found that schizophrenic patients and their relatives had higher physical anhedonia than did normal subjects. These data are consistent with the hypothesis that hedonic capacity is heritable and that low hedonic capacity may be an indicator of liability for the development of schizophrenia.

Although the above findings suggest support for Meehl's original conjectures there are other findings indicating that anhedonia may not be specific to schizophrenia. First, anhedonia is also part of the diagnostic criteria for depression (APA, 1994). Additionally, using the Chapman scales of anhedonia several studies have found no differences between schizophrenic patients and patients with depression (Berenbaum & Oltmanns, 1992; Schuck et al., 1984; Fawcett, Clark, Scheftner, & Gibbons, 1983). Bernstein and Riedel (1987) have proposed that, although anhedonia occurs in both schizophrenia and depression, the underlying causes of anhedonia may differ in these two populations. Specifically, anhedonia may be secondary to symptomatology in depression, which can be expected to wane with the remission of depression. Alternatively, it is proposed that anhedonia in schizophrenia is an enduring traitlike deficit that is independent of symptom status.

Consistent with this hypothesis Katsanis, Iacono, Beiser, and Lacey (1992) found that in psychotic affective disorders anhedonia was significantly correlated with symptomatology; however, there was no such relationship in schizophrenia. Additionally, anhedonia was related to premorbid functioning in schizophrenia but not in patients with psychotic affective disorder. Katsanis et al. (1992) concluded that these findings lend support to Bernstein and Ridel's hypothesis. In another examination of this hypothesis Blanchard, Bellack, and Mueser (1994) compared schizophrenic patients with bipolar affective disorder patients most recently in a manic phase. Thus, by using a comparison patient group not characterized by depression it was expected that schizophrenic patients would demonstrate greater anhedonia. Blanchard et al. (1994) did find that schizophrenia and schizoaffective disorder patients reported significantly greater physical and social anhedonia than did bipolar patients. Although these results are suggestive of a stronger role for anhedonia in schizophrenia than in affective disorders, they are not conclusive. A more definitive test of the hypothesized relationship between de-

pression and anhedonia in nonschizophrenic patients will require the longitudinal assessment of affective disorder patients to determine whether anhedonia does indeed covary with symptom status.

Another problem in concluding that anhedonia is unique to schizophrenia or uniquely predicts risk for this disorder comes from findings with relatives of psychiatric patients and studies of psychometrically identified individuals thought to be at risk for schizophrenia. First, Katsanis, Iacono, and Beiser (1990) found that physical and social anhedonia were elevated in both the relatives of schizophrenic patients and in the first-degree relatives of patients with psychotic affective disorders compared with nonpsychiatric controls. This failure to discriminate relatives of different psychotic probands clouds the interpretation presented by Katsanis et al. (1992) that anhedonia is secondary to affective symptomatology—why then is it elevated in probands family members? It is possible that anhedonia in family members was associated with affective symptomatology, but symptom data were apparently not collected on relatives of probands.

Second, the results of a 10-year longitudinal study conducted by the Chapmans (Chapman, Chapman, Kwapil, Eckblad, & Zinser, 1994) found that, in subjects high in magical ideation, social anhedonia from the baseline assessment was related to schizotypal dimensional personality scores and psychotic-like experiences at follow-up. No self-report scale predicted schizophrenia. Rather, the measures appeared to predict psychosis in general. Physical anhedonia was unrelated to psychosis or psychosis proneness. This later finding suggests that the original emphasis on physical anhedonia (Chapman et al., 1976) may have been misplaced. The findings of Katsanis et al. (1990) and Chapman et al. (1994) might be viewed as consistent with a unitary psychosis theory. That is, psychosis in schizophrenia and affective disorders share some aspects of phenomenology that may be expressions of a common etiology. Alternatively, current measures such as social anhedonia may simply be inadequate, by themselves, for the differential prediction of psychotic disorders.

Hedonic Capacity and Social Functioning

We will now address the relationship between anhedonia and social functioning. In their original study the Chapmans (Chapman et al., 1976) examined the hypothesis that anhedonia would be related to poor premorbid adjustment, reasoning that "one might speculate that anhedonia is the basis of such deficient activities because people very often tend to do what they enjoy" (p. 375). Results of dichotomizing schizophrenic patients into good and poor premorbid adjustment and those who were hedonic and anhedonic indicated that physically and socially anhedonic patients had poorer premorbid adjustment than did hedonic patients. As reviewed above, similar findings demonstrating a correlation between anhedonia and premorbid functioning were obtained by Katsanis et al. (1992).

Two studies have failed to find anhedonia to be uniquely related to premorbid adjustment in schizophrenic patients. Schuck et al. (1984) examined the association between physical anhedonia and premorbid adjustment in outpatients with schizophrenia, depression, and a psychiatric control group comprised mostly of patients with personality disorders as well as patients with bipolar affective disorders. Schizophrenic patients did not differ from other patients in physical anhedonia. Furthermore, physical anhedonia was found to be significantly correlated with premorbid adjustment in the schizophrenic patients as well as the combined psychiatric control group (depressives and other diagnoses). A difficulty with these findings is that Schuck et al. (1984) used a self-report scale to assess premorbid adjustment. Since this self-report questionnaire does not distinguish between recent or current functioning (no item explicitly refers to functioning prior to onset of the illness) the premorbid ratings in the Schuck et al. (1984) may be confounded by chronicity.

In a recent study Garnet, Glick, and Edell (1993) examined the association between physical anhedonia and premorbid competence in young nonpsychotic inpatients. Subjects, including those with nonpsychotic affective disorders, with greater physical anhedonia had lower premorbid adjustment ratings. However, concerns also arise regarding the interpretability of the interview ratings utilized by Garnet et al. (1993). Although these authors studied young patients, they apparently were not in their first episode. To the degree that this sample had early onset with multiple episodes of the illness, ratings of premorbid adjustment may be confounded by functioning postonset. Even though ratings were limited to childhood and early adolescence, Garnet et al. (1993) do not specifically indicate that competence ratings were only derived from the period preceding the illness. As noted by Lenzenweger and Dworkin (1987), if competence ratings are not limited to behavioral data from the premorbid period such ratings may be contaminated by the effects of chronicity and in-

stitutionalization. Thus, although the findings of Schuck et al. (1984) and Garnet et al. (1993) suggest that anhedonia's association with long-term (premorbid) characteristics is not unique to schizophrenia, these studies are characterized by potential methodological issues which should be considered in their interpretation.

In addition to examining the premorbid correlates of anhedonia it is important to determine anhedonia's relationship to current social functioning. If anhedonia underlies early social withdrawal and isolation, it may be associated with the failure to acquire and develop social skills. Although several studies have evaluated the association between anhedonia (specifically physical anhedonia) and social competence assessed with role-play measures (Beckfield, 1985; Haberman, Chapman, Numbers, & McFall, 1979; Numbers & Chapman, 1982) these have all been conducted with college students. One recent study (Blanchard et al., 1994) did evaluate the relationship between anhedonia as measured by the Chapman scales and social skill in a simulated social encounter (role play). Subjects included inpatients with schizophrenia and schizoaffective disorder, and inpatients with bipolar disorder. Neither physical or social anhedonia was related to role-play measures of social skill performance for any patient group.

As noted by Blanchard et al. (1994) an important consideration in the interpretation of these findings is the type of social interactions studied. Specifically, the role plays consisted of negatively valenced, conflictual encounters. It may be the case that anhedonic individuals can emit appropriate social behaviors in such negative encounters (e.g., assertiveness). However, anhedonia may be associated with decreased skillfulness in positively valenced, affiliative, social interactions. Such a possibility is currently being examined in an ongoing longitudinal study being conducted by the first author.

Anxiety, Depression, and Other Affective Symptoms

In addition to diminished hedonic capacity schizophrenia is also characterized by a range of affective symptoms such as anxiety and depression. Rado (1962) proposed that increased negative affectivity was the consequence of anhedonia: "Because of the absence of the buffering effect of the welfare emotions [based on the experience of pleasure], the emergency emotions, built on the anticipation of pain, are expanded. Thus, fear and rage may rise to exorbitant strengths" (pp. 66–67). Likewise, Meehl (1962) proposed that anhedonia resulted in what he termed *aversive drift*—the tendency to experience life as stressful. Evidence for heightened negative affect in schizophrenia comes from a variety of studies indicating that schizophrenia is often characterized by depression, anxiety, and hostility (Bartels, Drake, Wallach, & Freeman, 1991; DeLisi, 1986; Drake & Cotton, 1986; Knights & Hirsch, 1981; Williams & Dalby, 1989). These negative mood states have been found to presage relapse in retrospective (Herz & Melville, 1980) and prospective studies (Subotnik & Nuechterlein, 1988). Longitudinal studies have also found that negative mood is associated with poorer clinical course of the illness (Hogarty et al., 1979; Rajkumar & Thara, 1989), and is predictive of thought disturbance (Blanchard, Mueser, & Bellack, 1992) and suicide (Cohen, Test, & Brown, 1990). Although one might suspect that anxiety and depression occur secondary to psychotic symptoms, or the social and economic privations faced by individuals with schizophrenia, a number of studies indicate that negative affect precedes the onset of schizophrenia. Clinic follow-up studies and high-risk studies will be briefly reviewed with regard to premorbid affective and social characteristics (see Chapter 8 for a more detailed review of such studies).

Several clinic follow-up studies have found anxiety and social dysfunction to co-occur in children who later developed schizophrenia. In a follow-up of children seen at a child guidance clinic, O'Neal and Robins (1958) found that preschizophrenic children manifested more acting out (physical aggression, lying), had more anxiety symptoms, and tended to be more unhappy and overly dependent on their mothers than clinic children who did not develop a psychiatric disorder in adulthood. O'Neal and Robins did not report any gender differences in their findings. Similarly, Gardner (1967) followed up children who were seen at a child guidance clinic and found that anxiety characterized preschizophrenic boys but not girls. Mellsop (1973) also found that clinic referred children who ultimately developed schizophrenia were initially characterized by anxiety diagnoses, but not conduct disorder. Finally, in an analysis of school records Watt (1978) reported that preschizophrenic girls and boys evinced emotional and social problems with girls being characterized as unsociable and quiet, whereas boys were described as being unpleasant, uncooperative, and poorly behaved.

High-risk studies have also reported negative affective states as dominant in the offspring of schizophrenic patients. The Copenhagen longitudinal project (Cannon & Mednick, 1993; John, Mednick, & Schulsinger, 1982;

Mednick, Parnas, & Schulsinger, 1987) is one of the few studies to have published data on children at risk for schizophrenia following them from birth through the risk period. John et al. (1982) concluded that teacher reports of school behavior predicted schizophrenia and borderline schizophrenia successfully distinguishing these groups from each other as well as from other outcomes. Both the preschizophrenic patients and preborderline schizophrenics were more lonely, isolated, socially inept, tense, and anxious than children who later developed other disorders or who remained healthy. The preschizophrenics were distinguishable from the preborderline schizophrenics in that the former also showed poor inhibitory control (aggression). This was especially true for males. The latter is interesting in the light of follow-back studies, which indicate that preschizophrenic males are more aggressive (e.g., O'Neal & Robins, 1958; Watt, 1978).

In a study of genetically at-risk subjects and a comparison group followed from infancy to adulthood, Fish (1987) examined measures of emotional as well as social functioning. Children at the greatest risk of schizophrenia reported feelings of depression, loneliness, and rejection by peers. These same children also tended to have poor interpersonal relationships. In fact, Fish noted that by age three, half of the most disturbed schizophrenia risk subjects displayed blunted-detached affect and were isolated. They continued to show chronic disturbance throughout childhood; and, as adults, all six met criteria for schizophrenia-spectrum disorders according to Fish's nonblind diagnoses.

Recent findings from the Israeli high-risk project (Ingraham, Kugelmass, Frenkel, Nathan, & Mirsky, 1995; Kugelmass et al., 1995; Mirsky, Kugelmass, Ingraham, Frenkel, & Nathan, 1995) also point to the importance of anxiety. At ages 11 and 16, offspring of schizophrenic patients who later developed a schizophrenia-spectrum disorder (at age 25) had the highest levels of anxiety. Furthermore, offspring of schizophrenic patients who did not later receive a diagnosis also reported significantly greater anxiety than did the nondiagnosed control group.

Anxiety and social isolation also appear to be prevalent in the family members of schizophrenic patient probands. Kendler, McGuire, Gruenberg, and Walsh (1995) examined a range of schizotypal signs and symptoms in relatives of control probands and probands with schizophrenia, other nonaffective psychoses (e.g., schizoaffective, schizophreniform, or delusional disorder, or psychosis not otherwise specified), psychotic affective illness, and nonpsychotic affective illness. Factor derived scales of social dysfunction and avoidant symptoms (including items of social isolation, social anxiety, hypersensitivity, and anxiety) were found to be important predictors of whether a relative was related to a proband with schizophrenia versus a control proband. Furthermore, avoidant symptoms was the only factor that significantly discriminated between relatives of schizophrenics and relatives of both nonpsychotic and psychotic affective illness. Thus, social dysfunction and social anxiety are apparent in the relatives of schizophrenic patients, although the ultimate ability of these features to discriminate between the liability for the development of schizophrenia and other nonaffective psychotic disorders is unclear (Kendler et al., 1995).

Finally, a recent study based on a general population sample also reports findings relevant to negative affect, social functioning, and risk for schizophrenia (Jones, Rodgers, Murray, & Marmot, 1994). These investigators utilized data obtained from 5,326 people, followed for four decades, who were selected randomly from a British birth cohort in 1946. Jones et al. (1994) found that solitary play preference at ages 4 and 6 years, less self-rated social confidence at age 13, and anxiousness in social situations as rated by teachers at 15 years were associated with later schizophrenia.

In summary, evidence indicates that negative affective states such as anxiety, depression, and hostility are common features of the clinical presentation of schizophrenia. Studies also indicate that social anxiety and social isolation co-occur and predate the onset of the illness or are prevalent in individuals at risk for the development of schizophrenia. Findings regarding impulsive, undercontrolled, acting-act, or aggressive behavior in such studies have been less consistently replicated. Finally, some of these studies suggest that there may be gender differences in the type of affective manifestation evidenced with some indication that boys who are at risk for schizophrenia may be more likely to demonstrate acting-act or aggressive behavior.

Integration of Findings on Affective Experience

The preceding review suggests that schizophrenia is characterized by both decreased capacity to experience pleasure as well as increased negative affectivity (in particular social anxiety). Similarly, in a recent meta-analysis on personality and schizophrenia, Berenbaum and Fu-

jita (1994) found that schizophrenic patients were characterized by decreased extroversion and increased neuroticism. To the extent that extroversion and neuroticism reflect the affective dimensions of positive and negative affectivity (Tellegen, 1985; Tellegen & Waller, in press) this review suggests that schizophrenia is characterized by decreased trait positive affectivity and increased trait negative affectivity. Importantly, evidence to be reviewed below suggests that positive and negative affect are not merely opposites of a bipolar continuum but represent orthogonal dimensions of affective experience.

A number of studies have found two broad dimensions in self-report data of affect that are identified as positive affect and negative affect (e.g., Watson, 1988a; Watson & Clark, 1992a, 1992b; Watson & Tellegen, 1985; Tellegen, 1985; Tellegen & Waller, in press; Zevon & Tellegen, 1982). These dimensions of affect are viewed as largely independent dimensions that may have differential (not just opposite) correlations with other variables. For example, positive affect, but not negative affect, has been found to be associated with social activity (e.g., Watson, 1988b; Watson & Clark, in press; Watson, Clark, McIntyre, & Hamaker, 1992), exercise (Watson, 1988b; Watson & Clark, in press), and personality indices of extraversion (Costa & McCrae, 1980; Tellegen, 1985; Tellegen & Waller, in press; Watson et al., 1992). Alternatively, negative affect, but not positive affect, is related to physical problems (Clark & Watson, 1988) and personality markers of neuroticism (Costa & McCrae, 1980; Tellegen, 1985; Tellegen & Waller, in press; Watson et al., 1992).

One question that arises is how anhedonia is related to the dimensions of positive and negative affect. On the one hand, given the defining feature of this symptom as a deficit in pleasure one might hypothesize that anhedonia reflects low positive affect, with no relation to negative affect. Alternatively, both Rado and Meehl proposed that anhedonia was also associated with increased negative affect (Meehl's *aversive drift*). To examine the relationship between anhedonia and positive and negative affect, as well as social functioning, Blanchard, Mueser, and Bellack (in press) conducted a longitudinal study of schizophrenic patients in the community. This study also allowed for a test of the temporal stability of individual differences in affectivity. Outpatient schizophrenic patients and normal controls completed the Chapman anhedonia scales as well as trait scales of positive and negative affect and measures of social anxiety. Current social functioning was assessed in a clinical interview. Subjects were evaluated at a baseline assessment and again at approximately a 3-month follow-up. Putative trait measures of anhedonia and positive and negative affect were quite reliable over the follow-up period, indicating that these measures were tapping stable individual differences in affectivity. Group comparisons indicated that schizophrenic patients reported significantly greater anhedonia and less trait positive affectivity than did controls. Furthermore, schizophrenic patients reported significantly greater trait negative affectivity and social anxiety than did controls. These results indicate that schizophrenia is characterized by both a deficit in positive affectivity as well as an increased dispositional tendency to experience negative affect. These findings are also consistent with the literature finding decreased extraversion and increased neuroticism in schizophrenia (Berenbaum & Fujita, 1994).

Correlational analyses conducted by Blanchard et al. (in press) indicated that physical and social anhedonia were differentially correlated with trait dimensions of affectivity. Social anhedonia was negatively correlated with trait positive affect and was positively correlated with trait negative affect. Physical anhedonia was moderately, but not significantly correlated with trait positive affect and trait negative affect. Social anhedonia, but not physical anhedonia, was also significantly positively correlated with measures of social anxiety. Comparisons of the significance of differences between dependent correlations indicated that social anhedonia's correlations with indices of negative affect were significantly greater than those for physical anhedonia. These findings indicate that anhedonia in schizophrenia is associated with negative affect and this association appears to be particularly strong for social anhedonia.

Blanchard et al. (in press) found that physical and social anhedonia were both significantly correlated with social functioning in schizophrenic patients such that greater anhedonia was related to poorer current functioning. Consistent with these findings, trait positive affectivity was found to be robustly associated with social functioning in that high trait positive affect was associated with better social functioning. Finally, social anxiety was positively correlated with poorer social functioning. However, the results of partial correlations indicated that trait positive affectivity was a unique predictor of social functioning in schizophrenic patients—trait negative affect and social anxiety did not make any unique contribution to social functioning once trait positive affect was controlled. The results of

Blanchard et al. (in press) indicate that although schizophrenia is characterized by decreased trait positive affect and increased trait negative affect, each of these dimensions of affect may have differential (not just opposite) correlates with other dimensions of the illness. Specifically, low positive affect appears to be uniquely related to poor social functioning. To the extent that social anxiety and other markers of negative affect are related to poor social functioning it appears that this relationship is mediated by low positive affect (Blanchard et al., in press).

The link between social activity and hedonic experience is not unique to schizophrenia. Rather, several studies have demonstrated this relationship in nonpsychiatric populations. In a series of studies, Watson and Clark (Clark & Watson, 1988; Watson, 1988; Watson et al., 1992) have found positive affect to be significantly associated with social activity in both between-subjects and intraindividual analyses. Positive affect, but not negative affect, measured at the state level is consistently found to be elevated on those occasions involving social activity. Similarly, trait measures of positive affect are also positively related to social activity (Watson et al., 1992). Clearly, some forms of social activity are more strongly related to positive affect. Attending parties, going out to dinner or drinking, and physical activities were most strongly associated with increased positive affect, whereas sedentary activities, lessons, and club meetings were affectively neutral (Clark & Watson, 1988).

The direction of the observed findings is unclear. That is, does exposure to social activity result in elevated positive affect or does positive affect lead to social activity? Evidence indicates that social activity does result in elevations in positive mood. McIntyre, Watson, Clark, and Cross (1991) examined the effect of induced social interactions on affect. In two studies these authors found that two forms of experimentally induced social interaction resulted in elevations in positive affect. Negative affect was unaffected following these interactions. Thus, the findings of McIntyre et al. (1991) support the hypothesis that social activity can result in elevations in positive affect.

Alternatively, theories regarding anhedonia in schizophrenia clearly propose that the hedonic deficit is primary and that social withdrawal and isolation subsequently occurs (Rado, 1962; Meehl, 1962). Consistent with this conjecture, a number of laboratory mood induction studies with nonpsychiatric subjects indicate that elevations in positive mood may lead to preferences for social activities, interpersonal attraction, conversation initiation, and prosocial behavior. Strickland, Hale, and Anderson (1975) found that individuals in whom positive mood was induced reported enhanced preferences for social activities compared with depressed mood and neutral subjects. Positive mood induction has also been shown to enhance ratings of attraction for others (Gouaux, 1971; Griffit, 1970) and to enhance conversation initiation (Bateson, Coke, Chard, Smith, & Taliaferro, 1979; Isen, 1970). Finally, a large number of studies have demonstrated that positive mood induction results in prosocial helping behavior (for a review, see Isen, 1987).

Thus, the available evidence indicates that social activity and positive affect influence one another. Watson and Clark (in press) have proposed that such data reflect the expression of a system that underlies both positive affect and social behavior. A common neurobiological system may be involved in the initiation of behavior, incentive–reward motivation, and positive affect (Depue & Iacono, 1989).

One area of research that has been neglected in schizophrenia is understanding the mechanisms that may link anhedonia and poor social functioning. Initial conjectures take the form of behavioral descriptions such as, people very often tend to do what they enjoy (Chapman et al., 1976). However, it has been proposed that positive affect influences social behavior through several cognitive mechanisms (e.g. Isen, 1990). Affect may serve as information in self-assessment as well as in the assessment of others. Second, affect may direct attention toward different forms of information relevant to social behavior. Third, affect may produce mood congruent thought that serves to initiate and maintain social behaviors. Additionally, positive affect may selectively cue social material even when that material is affectively neutral (Isen, 1990). Thus, affect alters attention and recall, and through them, cognitions, which may influence social behaviors. This conceptualization of the influence of positive affect on social behavior suggests important cognitive factors that may mediate the connection between decreased hedonic capacity and social functioning in schizophrenia. It will be important to determine whether anhedonia is associated with alterations in attention and recall that are relevant to social behavior. Might it be the case that schizophrenics low in hedonic capacity fail to deploy attention to particular classes of social stimuli that have a positive valence? Can schizophrenic patients experience some positive affect in particular social interactions but subsequently fail to recall such hedonic experiences because lack of attention results in poor encoding? Or is properly encoded in-

formation difficult to later recall because of the typically low positive affective state of the individual?

AFFECTIVE FLATTENING AND SOCIAL FUNCTIONING

As indicated in the introduction, the negative symptom of affective flattening or blunting is another dimension of affect that has been shown to be related to social functioning. Negative symptoms including affective flattening, but not positive symptoms, have been shown to be related to both premorbid and current social impairment in schizophrenia (for reviews, see Pogue-Geile & Zubin, 1988; Walker & Lewine, 1988). Studies following these reviews have generally replicated earlier findings that negative symptoms are uniquely associated with poor premorbid functioning (Fenton & McGlashan, 1991; Kelley, Gilbertson, Mouton, & van Kammen, 1992; Mueser, Bellack, Morrison & Wixted, 1990) and poor current functioning (e.g., Bellack, Morrison, Mueser, & Wade, 1989; Bellack, Morrison, Wixted, & Mueser, 1990; Breier, Schreiber, Dyer, & Pickar, 1991; Van der Does, Dingemans, Linszen, Nugter, & Scholte, 1993). Similar findings relating negative symptoms and social impairment have been found in both interview-based measures of functioning and role-play assessments of social skill (Bellack et al., 1989; Bellack, et al., 1990). Studies employing Carpenter's more recent deficit syndrome distinction have found that schizophrenics with enduring negative symptoms demonstrate poor premorbid social functioning (Buchanan, Kirkpatrick, Heinrichs, & Carpenter, 1990) and poor current social functioning (Mueser, Douglas, Bellack, & Morrison, 1991).

Fewer studies have examined the social correlates of individual negative symptoms such as affective flattening. Fenton and McGlashan (1991) found flat affect to be negatively correlated with premorbid adjustment ($r = -.28$). Consistent with this finding, Kelly et al. (1992) reported affective flattening to be correlated with poorer premorbid adjustment during early ($r = .26$) and late ($r = .28$) adolescence as well as with an index of premorbid deterioration ($r = .24$). With regard to current functioning, Breier et al. (1991) found that affective flattening was significantly correlated with current social contacts ($r = -.55$), quantity of work ($r = -.52$), the ability to meet individual needs ($r = -.60$), and scores from the Global Assessment Scale ($r = -.68$). Bellack et al. (1990) reported that affective flattening was significantly correlated with poorer role-play ratings of nonverbal skill ($r = .55$) and overall skill ratings ($r = .36$). Furthermore, Bellack et al. (1990) found affective flattening to be negatively correlated with ratings of current interpersonal relations ($r = -.54$) and to be associated with poorer adjustment in a range of social domains (rs: household = .37; external family = .39; social/leisure = .52; overall adjustment = .47).

Although these findings suggest an important link between flat affect and premorbid and current social functioning, one should not conclude that other negative symptoms do not demonstrate such relations. For example, Fenton and McGlashan (1991) found that alogia, avolition, anhedonia, and impaired attention were all significantly correlated to premorbid adjustment (range of $rs = -.20$ to $-.31$). Similarly, Kelley et al. (1992) reported that alogia and attentional impairment were significantly correlated with poor premorbid adjustment in early and late adolescence (range of $rs = .28$ to .37). Finally, Bellack et al. (1990) found that each of the negative symptoms was variously correlated with ratings of social skill in a role-play test as well as current social functioning. Thus, negative symptoms other than affective flattening appear to be related to social dysfunction. Further investigation is required to determine whether affective flattening makes a unique contribution to social impairment or whether this potential relationship is the expression of some process that underlies the constellation of negative symptoms.

Although the correlational data presented thus far indicate that affective flattening (and other negative symptoms) is related to poor social functioning, other findings suggest that these phenomena may nonetheless be the expression of independent processes. Strauss, Carpenter, and Bartko (1974) proposed that three major types of processes may underlie the varied symptoms and signs of schizophrenia: positive symptoms, negative symptoms, and disorders in relating. This three-process model was evaluated by Lenzenweger, Dworkin, and Wethington (1991) using case histories of twin studies of schizophrenia. Case histories were rated for positive symptoms, negative symptoms, and premorbid adjustment. Confirmatory factor analysis indicated that a three-factor model based on Strauss et al. (1974) provided the best fit with the data. Although positive symptoms, negative symptoms, and premorbid functioning were found to result in three factors, findings also indicated that the latent variables underlying these factors were somewhat correlated: positive symptoms and negative symptoms ($r = .34$), negative symptoms and premorbid impairment ($r = .35$), however, consistent with the findings reviewed above, positive

symptoms and premorbid impairment were not significantly correlated ($r = -.02$).

Lenzenweger et al. (1991) found that postonset asociality-withdrawal was best classified with other negative symptoms rather than with premorbid impairment. Lenzenweger et al. proposed that this later finding suggests that current social functioning (i.e., following the onset of schizophrenia) and premorbid adjustment are not isomorphic and may have different correlates and different underlying processes—contrary to Strauss et al's (1974) view that patterns of relating are enduring over time. Findings discussed above that anhedonia is related to both premorbid (Chapman et al., 1976; Katsanis et al's, 1992; Schuck et al., 1984) and current (Blanchard et al., in press) social functioning in schizophrenia clearly indicate that there are also commonalities between premorbid and current functioning. Furthermore, the often replicated finding that premorbid adjustment predicts postonset functioning further suggests some continuity between pre- and postonset functioning (e.g., Zigler & Glick, 1986; Zigler & Phillips, 1961).

The findings of Lenzenweger et al. (1991) should be interpreted with some caution given the use of published clinical descriptions on which ratings were based. Method variance may have also contributed to the finding that the negative symptom of asociality-withdrawal loaded on a factor of other negative symptoms, rather than the pre- and postonset distinction. It will be important to replicate these findings with clinical ratings obtained from direct interviews and utilizing broader assessment of current and premorbid social functioning. Nonetheless, the findings of Lenzenweger et al. (1991) indicate that there may be dimensions of social dysfunction that only emerge after the clinical expression of schizophrenia, whereas other dimensions do show continuity across premorbid and postonset phases of the illness. The developmental trajectory of dimensions of social functioning will be important to evaluate in future studies.

In reviewing the relationship between affective flattening and social functioning, it becomes unclear what the symptom of affective flattening reflects. That is, does this paucity of emotional expression mirror impoverished emotional experience? If so, affective flattening may underlie social dysfunction, in part, because of a lack of emotional responding to social-affiliative cues (e.g., anhedonia). Alternatively, affective flattening may not be consistent with subjective experience but instead mask a range of emotional experience. This later situation is consistent with Kraepelin's (1919/1971) early description of a lack of congruence between the expression and experience of emotion in schizophrenia:

> Here and there it may be observed that the disposition of the patients is exactly *contrary to the actual state of affairs*. . . . Sometimes it is only a case of want of relationship between mood and expression—of paramimia. (p. 36, italics in original)

An accumulation of evidence indicates that affective flattening, as defined by existing measures such as the SANS, does not reflect a lack of emotional experience. Importantly, laboratory studies using affect-eliciting stimuli have found that although clinical ratings of affective flattening are related to a diminution of facial expression during exposure to eliciting stimuli, affective flattening it is not associated with a lack of emotional experience (Berenbaum & Oltmanns, 1992; Kring, Smith, Kerr, & Neale, 1993; Neale, Blanchard, Kerr, Kring, & Smith, in press). In these studies, patients with affective flattening were found to report levels of positive and negative affect equivalent to that experienced by nonflat schizophrenics and in some cases exceeded the reports of normal controls (Kring et al., 1993; Neale et al., in press). Psychophysiological data also indicate that the lack of expression is associated with higher than normal rates of nonspecific skin conductance responses (Neale et al., in press). Thus, it is incorrect to describe affective flattening as a generalized affective deficit. Rather affective flattening appears to reflect a disjunction among indicators of emotion in schizophrenia.

In considering the relationship between affective flattening and social functioning it might be important to consider the impact that flat affect has on those with whom the patient interacts. Given that the role of emotion expression is in part social communicative, one might predict that blunted affect would be related to social-interpersonal difficulties. If diminished expressivity of emotion is interpreted by an observer as reflecting a paucity of feelings, when in actuality such affective flattening is *unrelated* to the actual experience of emotion, disruption in social relations might occur. The lack of convergence between the outward expression of emotion and subjective experience might lead observers such as family members to make incorrect assumptions regarding a patient's emotional state. Thus, family members may misinterpret blunted affect as a true lack of emotional experience, as apathy, or insensitivity (i.e., make misattributions as a result of this symptom; see Hooley, Richters,

Weintraub, & Neale, 1987; Brewin, MacCarthy, Duda, & Vaughn, 1991).

To examine the hypothesis that affective flattening may result in errors in observers' perceptions of schizophrenic patients' subjective emotional experiences, preliminary data were collected during an investigation examining other features of social and emotional functioning in schizophrenia (Blanchard et al., 1994). Subjects were 22 inpatient schizophrenic patients. Trained clinical interviewers completed diagnostic interviews using the Structured Clinical Interview for DSM-III-R (SCID; Spitzer, Williams, Gibbon, & First, 1990) as well as assessments of symptomatology. Symptomatology during the one week prior to the assessment was evaluated with the Scale for the Assessment of Negative Symptoms (SANS; Andreasen, 1982) and an anchored version of the Brief Psychiatric Rating Scale (BPRS; Overall & Gorham, 1962, 1988; Woerner, Mannuzza, & Kane, 1988). The SANS generates five subscale scores: Affective Flattening or Blunting, Alogia, Avolition-Apathy, Anhedonia-Asociality, and Attention. Each of the 24 items of the SANS is rated on a 5-point scale (*not at all, mild, moderate, marked,* or *severe*). The five subscale scores were derived from the average of the scales' constituent items (in calculating this average the global ratings were not included as they are redundant). The BPRS consists of 18 items which are rated on a 7-point scale (*not reported* or *not observed, very mild, mild, moderate, moderately severe, severe,* and *very severe*). A total score for the BPRS was calculated based on the sum of the 18 items.

Patients with average Affective Flattening ratings from the SANS of 1.00 were coded as Nonflat ($n = 12$), and patients with average ratings greater than 1.00 were considered Flat ($n = 10$). The patient groups did not differ in age (Nonflat, $X = 34.00$, $SD = 11.55$; Flat, $X = 34.00$, $SD = 7.48$), education (Nonflat, $X = 11.58$, $SD = 0.90$; Flat, $X = 11.90$, $SD = 1.52$), $ps > .05$, or gender ($\chi^2 = 1.77$, ns). Symptom ratings for the two patient groups are listed in Table 11.1. As can be seen the groups differed significantly in ratings of Affective Flattening as well as Alogia; however, the groups did not differ significantly in any other negative symptom rating or in the total symptom score from the BPRS.

At the conclusion of the clinical interview (comprising the SCID, SANS, and BPRS), subjects' mood was measured by the patient and the clinician with a modified version of the Positive and Negative Affect Schedule (PANAS; Watson, Clark, & Tellegen, 1988). The PANAS is a 20-item self-report questionnaire designed to provide

Table 11.1. Symptom Ratings of Schizophrenics with and without Affective Flattening

	FLAT	NONFLAT	t
Affective Flattening	2.13 (0.88)	1.00 (0.00)	−4.44[a]
Alogia	1.75 (0.59)	1.13 (0.20)	−3.46[b]
Attention	1.89 (0.70)	1.67 (0.84)	−0.65
Apathy	4.37 (0.66)	4.17 (0.39)	−0.89
Asociality	2.58 (1.11)	2.29 (1.42)	−0.51
BPRS-Total	43.00 (4.37)	41.92 (6.46)	−0.45

[a] $p < .001$
[b] $p < .005$.

Table 11.2. Self- and Clinician-Rated Affect in Blunted on Nonblunted Schizophrenics

	BLUNTED		NONBLUNTED	
Positive Affect[a]				
Self-Rated	38.60	(8.88)	32.08	(11.05)
Clinician-Rated	29.30	(4.83)	31.42	(7.08)
Negative Affect[a]				
Self-Rated	24.90	(7.59)	26.58	(12.80)
Clinician-Rated	20.20	(5.45)	23.42	(5.87)

[a] Possible Range = 11 to 55

a quick, reliable, and valid measurement of positive affect (PA) and negative affect (NA). The PANAS PA scale includes the terms *active, alert, attentive, determined, enthusiastic, excited, inspired, interested, proud*, and *strong*. The PANAS NA scale consists of the terms *afraid, ashamed, distressed, guilty, hostile, irritable, jittery, nervous, scared*, and *upset*. For this study an additional adjective was added to the PA scale (*happy*) and the NA scale (*sad*) to enhance the scales' measurement of affect. Instructions were to rate on a 5-point scale (*very slightly or not at all, a little, moderately, quite a bit*, or *extremely*) the extent to which each of the 22 mood adjectives were experienced "*right now, that is, at the present moment*." Scores of PA and NA are the sums of responses to the 11 adjectives comprising each scale. Thus, self-ratings and clinician ratings of PA and NA were obtained. Clinicians were blind to the hypothesis being tested. Descriptive statistics for self- and clinician-rated PA and NA are presented in Table 11.2.

To examine group differences and differences in self- and clinician ratings, separate 2 (Group) by 2 (Method) repeated measures ANOVAs were conducted on ratings of positive and negative affect with the method of ratings (self, interviewer) treated as a within-subjects factor. For PA the main effect of group was not significant, $F(1,20)$ = .58. However, the main effect of method was significant, $F(1,20) = 5.50$, and the Method X Group interaction was marginally significant, $F(1,20) = 4.13, p < .06$. Paired comparisons indicated that self- and clinician-rated PA did not differ for nonflat subjects, $t(11) = 0.21, ns$. However, for Flat Affect patients self- and clinician ratings of positive affect were significantly different, $t(9) = 3.52, p < .01$. As can be seen in Table 11.2 clinician-rated PA was lower than self-reported PA for the Flat Affect pa-

tients. These findings indicate that clinicians significantly underestimated the PA experienced by schizophrenics with Flat Affect, but accurately rated PA of nonflat schizophrenic patients.

ANOVA results for NA indicated that the group effect was not significant, $F(1,20) = 0.55, ns$. The main effect of method was significant, $F(1,20) = 5.57, p < .05$, but the Group X Method interaction was not, $F(1,20) = 0.21, ns$. Inspection of the means for NA in Table 11.2 indicates that clinicians underestimated the negative affect experienced by both groups of schizophrenic patients.

In addition to group differences, it is informative to examine the correlates of affective flattening across all patients. Ratings of Affective Flattening were not significantly correlated with self-reported PA ($r = .11, ns$) or NA ($r = .19, ns$) or interview-rated NA ($r = −.01, ns$); however, Affective Flattening was significantly negatively correlated with interview-rated PA ($r = .42, p < .05$). This finding that higher ratings of Affective Flattening were correlated with lower interview ratings of PA is consistent with the group findings reported above. In examining the convergence between self- and interview ratings, correlational analyses indicated that self-rated NA and interview-rated NA were significantly correlated ($r = .71, p < .001$). Thus, although ANOVA results indicated that interview ratings of NA were somewhat lower than self-rated NA, there was generally good reliability between these methods of assessment. However, agreement between self- and interview-rated PA was low ($r = .26, ns$).

These results from a preliminary investigation replicate earlier findings that affective flattening in schizophrenia is not related to diminished self-reports of mood (Berenbaum & Oltmanns, 1992; Kring et al., 1993). The present results also indicate that affective flattening may have a significant impact on the perceptions that others have of a patient's emotional experience. In this study, clinical interviewers significantly underestimated the amount of positive affect that blunted schizophrenic patients were experiencing. Although affective flattening appeared to be uniquely related to observers' misperceptions of positive affect, this finding must be interpreted with caution. The clinical interviews focused on symptomatology and thus were largely concerned with the assessment of negative affective states such as depression, anxiety, and hostility. In this study positive affect was less of an explicit focus of the interview and may thus have been more dependent on the patients' spontaneous positive affective displays (verbal and nonverbal). Patients with affective flattening could be expected to demonstrate fewer such displays resulting in the underestimation of positive affect by interviewers. It is possible that negative and positive affective states may be equivalently vulnerable to errors in perceptions of the emotional experience of patients with affective flattening. The nature and focus of the interaction may ultimately determine whether positive or negative affective states are differentially vulnerable to observers' misperceptions related to affective flattening. This also suggests that misperceptions can be overcome by directed efforts at determining the emotional experience of schizophrenic patients with affective flattening, rather than relying on spontaneous expressions (e.g., asking specific questions about a patients' mood).

Factor analytic studies of negative symptoms may also support the distinction between expressive versus experiential deficits in emotion. Mueser, Sayers, Schooler, Mance, and Haas (1994) reported that a factor analysis of the SANS resulted in three factors corresponding to the Affective Flattening or Blunting subscale, the Avolition-Apathy and Anhedonia-Asociality subscales, and the Alogia and Inattention subscales. These results are consistent with three factor solutions obtained by Keefe et al. (1992) and have recently been replicated by Sayers, Curran, and Mueser (1996). Thus, although negative symptoms are intercorrelated they can be meaningfully clustered into factors representing expressive deficits and hedonic or social-motivational deficits (like the items comprising them, these factors are moderately correlated: e.g., $r = .56$ between the factors based on Affective Flattening and the factor corresponding to Avolition-Apathy and Anhedonia-Asociality; Sayers et al., 1996).

In examining findings regarding the correlates of negative symptoms, there are two measurement issues that pose interpretive difficulties. First, the pool of information on which ratings of negative symptoms are based can vary widely. Although Andreasen's (1982) original description of the SANS indicated that multiple sources of information should be used, including interview with the patient, discussion with other medical providers, and review of medical records, many studies only utilize a subset of such information. Furthermore, time-frames may vary between investigations. As suggested by Andreasen (1982), the time frame that investigators select should be based on their own study design. Thus, some studies utilize multiple sources of information and conduct assessments based on a month (or more) of functioning, whereas other studies only use the patient's report of recent functioning (e.g., the past week). For example, the multisite Treatment Strategies in Schizophrenia (Mueser et al., 1994) rated negative symptoms based only on interviews that focused on the patients' functioning in the past week.

When sources of information and time-frames are restricted, the stability and generalizability of SANS ratings may be limited. In a study conducted by Blanchard et al. (1994), data indicated that the correlation between interview-based ratings of anhedonia-asociality derived from the SANS were not significantly correlated with self-report trait questionnaire measures of social anhedonia ($r = .09$) or physical anhedonia ($r = -.04$). Blanchard et al. (1994) interpreted the lack of convergence between the two methods (self- and interview ratings) to be the result of the time-frame used for ratings of the SANS. The SANS Anhedonia-Asociality scale scores were based on a limited sample of behavior obtained within the restricted regime of hospital activities and thus may not have generalize. Such a limitation on the SANS might be expected to diminish its correlation with the Chapman scales, which presumably tap a larger domain of behavior and feelings. Of course, similar concerns apply to all negative symptom subscales, including that for Affective Flattening. The deficit syndrome, as defined by Carpenter et al. (1988), seeks to address this issue in differentiating between primary, enduring negative symptoms and negative symptoms that may be secondary to other aspects of the illness or its treatment.

The second difficulty in examining the relationship between affective flattening and social functioning concerns the measurement overlap that can occur when these constructs are studied. Dworkin (1992) has cautioned that affective flattening items such as eye contact, facial expression, and vocal intonation can be construed as indicators of an affective-expressive deficit; alternatively, such expressive deficits may occur because of poor social-interpersonal skill. Thus, observed correlations between affective flattening and social skill may be the result of shared item content of instruments used to measure these constructs rather than true relations existing between these constructs.

CONCLUSIONS

The foregoing review has sought to highlight the important affective features of schizophrenia and to review the potential links between these affective features and the social impairment of this disorder. Schizophrenia appears to be characterized by both a deficit in positive affect and increased negative affect. These two dimensions of affective experience were shown to have differential relations with social functioning. In particular, evidence was reviewed to indicate that low positive affect is uniquely associated with poor social functioning in schizophrenia.

There remains much that is not known about affective experience and social functioning in schizophrenia. It will be important to determine how trait dimensions of positive and negative affect are related to long-term functioning in schizophrenia. These two dimensions of affectivity may differentially predict outcome such that positive affect is associated with social functioning and negative affect is associated with symptomatology. Furthermore, the stability of these dimensions of affective experience across symptom status will need to be demonstrated. Given important gender differences in social functioning in schizophrenia (see Chapter 10), future investigations should examine the role of affective experience in these differences. Although much remains to be studied, the present evidence clearly indicates that a full understanding of social impairment in schizophrenia will require the study of affect.

ACKNOWLEDGMENTS

Preparation of this chapter was supported by National Institute of Mental Health grant MH51240 to Jack J. Blanchard.

REFERENCES

American Psychiatric Association. (1994). *Diagnostic and statistical manual of mental disorders* (4th ed.). Washington, DC: Author.

Andreasen, N. C. (1982). Negative symptoms in schizophrenia: Definition and reliability. *Archives of General Psychiatry, 39,* 784–788.

Batson, C. D., Coke, J. S., Chard, F., Smith, D., & Taliaferro, A. (1979). Generality of the "glow of goodwill": Effects of mood on helping and information acquisition. *Social Psychology Quarterly, 42,* 176–179.

Bartels, S. J., Drake, R. E., Wallach, M. A., & Freeman, D. H. (1991). Characteristic hostility in schizophrenic outpatients. *Schizophrenia Bulletin, 17,* 163–171.

Beckfield, D. F. (1985). Interpersonal competence among college men hypothesized to be at risk for schizophrenia. *Journal of Abnormal Psychology, 94,* 397–404.

Bellack, A. S., Morrison, R. L., Mueser, K. T., & Wade, J. (1989). Social competence in schizoaffective disorder, bipolar disorder, and negative and non-negative schizophrenia. *Schizophrenia Research, 2,* 391–401.

Bellack, A. S., Morrison, R. L., Wixted, J. T., & Mueser, K. T. (1990). An analysis of social competence in schizophrenia. *British Journal of Psychiatry, 156,* 809–818.

Berenbaum, H., & Fujita, F. (1994). Schizophrenia and personality: Exploring the boundaries and connections between vulnerability and outcome. *Journal of Abnormal Psychology, 103,* 148–158.

Berenbaum, H., & Oltmanns, T. F. (1992). Emotional experience and expression in schizophrenia and depression. *Journal of Abnormal Psychology, 101,* 37–44.

Berenbaum, H., Oltmanns, T. F., & Gottesman, I. I. (1990). Hedonic capacity in schizophrenics and their twins. *Psychological Medicine, 20,* 367–374.

Bernstein, A. S., & Riedel, J. A. (1987). Psychophysiological response patterns in college students with high physical anhedonia: Scores appear to reflect schizotype rather than depression. *Biological Psychiatry, 22,* 829–847.

Blanchard, J. J., Bellack, A. S., & Mueser, K. T. (1994). Affective and social-behavioral correlates of physical and social anhedonia in schizophrenia. *Journal of Abnormal Psychology, 103,* 719–728.

Blanchard, J. J., Mueser, K. T., & Bellack, A. S. (1992). Self- and interview-rated negative mood states in schizophrenia: Their convergence and prediction of thought disturbance. *Journal of Psychopathology and Behavioral Assessment, 14,* 277–291.

Blanchard, J. J., Mueser, K. T., & Bellack, A. S. (in press). Anhedonia, positive and negative affect, and social functioning in schizophrenia. *Schizophrenia Bulletin.*

Bleuler, E. (1950). *Dementia praecox or the group of schizophrenias* (J. Zinkin, Trans.). New York: International University Press. (Original work published in 1911).

Breier, A., Schreiber, J. L., Dyer, J., & Pickar, D. (1991). National Institute of Mental Health longitudinal study of chronic schizophrenia: Prognosis and predictors of outcome. *Archives of General Psychiatry, 48,* 239–246.

Brewin, C. R., MacCarthy, B., Duda, K., & Vaughn, C. E. (1991). Attribution and expressed emotion in the relatives of patients with schizophrenia. *Journal of Abnormal Psychology, 100,* 546–554.

Buchanan, R. W., Kirkpatrick, B., Heinrichs, D. W., & Carpenter, W. T. (1990). Clinical correlates of the deficit syndrome of schizophrenia. *American Journal of Psychiatry, 147,* 290–294.

Cannon, T. D., Mednick, S. A. (1993). The schizophrenia high-risk project in Copenhagen: Three decades of progress. *Acta Psychiatrica Scandinavica, Suppl 370,* 33–47.

Carpenter, W. T., Heinrichs, D. W., & Wagman, A. M. I. (1988). Deficit and nondeficit forms of schizophrenia: The concept. *American Journal of Psychiatry, 145,* 578–583.

Chapman, L. J., Chapman, J. P., Kwapil, T. R., Eckblad, M., & Zinser, M. C. (1994). Putatively psychosis-prone subjects ten years later. *Journal of Abnormal Psychology, 103,* 171–183.

Chapman, L. J., Chapman, J. P., & Raulin, M. L. (1976). Scales for physical and social anhedonia. *Journal of Abnormal Psychology, 85,* 374–382.

Clark, L. A., & Watson, D. (1988). Mood and the mundane: Relations between daily life events and self-reported mood. *Journal of Personality and Social Psychology, 54,* 296–308.

Clementz, B., Grove, W. M., Katsanis, J., & Iacono, W. G. (1991). Psychometric detection of schizotypy: Perceptual aberration and physical anhedonia in relatives of schizophrenics. *Journal of Abnormal Psychology, 100,* 607–612.

Cohen, L. J., Test, M. A., & Brown, R. L. (1990). Suicide and schizophrenia: Data from a prospective community treatment study. *American Journal of Psychiatry, 147,* 602–607.

Costa, P. T., & McCrae, R. R. (1980). Influence of extraversion and neuroticism on subjective wellbeing: Happy and unhappy people. *Journal of Personality and Social Psychology, 38,* 668–678.

DeLisi, L. E. (Ed.). (1986). *Depression in schizophrenia.* Washington, DC: American Psychiatric Press.

Depue, R. A., & Iacono, W. G. (1989). Neurobehavioral aspects of affective disorders. *Annual Review of Psychology, 40,* 457–492.

Drake, R. E., & Cotton, P. G. (1986). Depression, hopelessness and suicide in chronic schizophrenia. *British Journal of Psychiatry, 148,* 554–559.

Dworkin, R. H. (1992). Affective deficits and social deficits in schizophrenia: What s what? *Schizophrenia Bulletin, 18,* 59–64.

Fawcett, J., Clark, D. C., Scheftner, W. A., & Gibbons, R. D. (1983). Assessing anhedonia in psychiatric patients: The Pleasure Scale. *Archives of General Psychiatry, 40,* 79–84.

Fenton, W. S., & McGlashan, T. H. (1991). Natural history of schizophrenia subtypes. II. Positive and negative symptoms and long-term course. *Archives of General Psychiatry, 48,* 978–986.

Fish, B. (1987). Infant predictors of the longitudinal course of schizophrenic development. *Schizophrenia Bulletin, 13,* 395–409.

Gardner, G. G. (1967). The relationship between childhood neurotic symptomatology and later schizophrenia in males and females. *Journal of Nervous and Mental Disease, 144,* 97–100.

Garnet, K. E., Glick, M., & Edell, W. S. (1993). Anhedonia and premorbid competence in young, nonpsychotic psychiatric inpatients. *Journal of Abnormal Psychology, 102,* 580–583.

Gottesman, I. I., & Shields, J. (1972). *Schizophrenia and genetics: A twin study vantage point.* New York: Academic Press.

Gouaux, C. (1971). Induced affective states and interpersonal attraction. *Journal of Personality and Social Psychology, 20,* 37–43.

Griffitt, W. (1970). Environmental effects on interpersonal affective behavior: Ambient effective temperature and attraction. *Journal of Personality and Social Psychology, 15,* 240–244.

Grove, W. M., Lebow, B. S., Clementz, B. A., Cerri, A., Medus, C., & Iacono, W. G. (1991). Familial prevalence and coaggregation of schizotypy indicators: A multitrait family study. *Journal of Abnormal Psychology, 100,* 115–121.

Haberman, M. C., Chapman, L. J., Numbers, J. S., & McFall, R. M. (1979). Relation of social competence to scores on two scales of psychosis proneness. *Journal of Abnormal Psychology, 88,* 675–677.

Herz, M. I., & Melville, C. (1980). Relapse in schizophrenia. *American Journal of Psychiatry, 137,* 801–805.

Hogarty, G. E., Schooler, N. R., Ulrich, R., Mussare, F., Ferro, P., & Herron, E. (1979). Fluphenazine and social therapy in the aftercare of schizophrenic patients: Relapse analyses of a two-year controlled study of fluphenazine deanoate and fluphenazine hydrochloride. *Archives of General Psychiatry, 36,* 1283–1294.

Hooley, J. M., Richters, J. E., Weintraub, S., & Neale, J. M. (1987). Psychopathology and marital distress: The positive side of positive symptoms. *Journal of Abnormal Psychology, 96,* 27–33.

Ingraham, L. J., Kugelmass, S., Frenkel, E., Nathan, M., & Mirsky, A. F. (1995). Twenty-five-year follow-up of the Israeli high-risk study: Current and lifetime psychopathology. *Schizophrenia Bulletin, 21,* 183–192.

Isen, A. M. (1970). Success, failure, attention, and reaction to others: The warm glow of success. *Journal of Personality and Social Psychology, 15,* 294–301.

Isen, A. M. (1987). Positive affect, cognitive processes, and social behavior. In L. Berkowitz (Ed.), *Advances in experimental social psychology* (pp. 203–253). New York: Academic Press.

Isen, A. M. (1990). The influence of positive and negative affect on cognitive organization: Some implications for development. In N. L. Stein, B. Leventhal, & T. Trabasso (Eds.), *Psychological and biological approaches to emotion* (pp. 75–94). Hillsdale, NJ: Erlbaum.

John, R. S., Mednick, S. A., & Schulsinger, F. (1982). Teacher reports as predictor of schizophrenia and borderline schizophrenia: A Bayesian decision analysis. *Journal of Abnormal Psychology, 91,* 399–413.

Jones, P., Rodgers, B., Murray, R., & Marmot, M. (1994). Child developmental risk factors for adult schizophrenia in the British 1946 birth cohort. *The Lancet, 344,* 1398–1402.

Katsanis, J., Iacono, W. G., & Beiser, M. (1990). Anhedonia and perceptual aberration in first-episode psychotic patients and their relatives. *Journal of Abnormal Psychology, 99,* 202–206.

Katsanis, J., Iacono, W. G., Beiser, M., & Lacey, L. (1992). Clinical correlates of anhedonia and perceptual aberration in first-episode patients with schizophrenia and affective disorder. *Journal of Abnormal Psychology, 101,* 184–191.

Keefe, R. E., Harvey, P. D., Mohs, R. C., Lenzenweger, M. G., Davidson, M., Apter, S., Schmeidler, J., & Davis, K. L. (1992). Empirical assessment of the factorial structure of clinical symptoms in schizophrenia: Negative symptoms. *Psychiatry Research, 44,* 153–165.

Kelley, M. E., Gilbertson, M., Mouton, A., & van Kammen, D. P. (1992). Deterioration in premorbid functioning in schizophrenia: A developmental model of negative symptoms in drug-free patients. *American Journal of Psychiatry, 149,* 1543–1548.

Kendler, K. S., McGuire, M., Gruenberg, A. M., & Walsh, D. (1995). Schizotypal symptoms and signs in the Roscommon Family Study. *Archives of General Psychiatry, 52,* 296–303.

Knights, A., & Hirsch, S. R. (1981). Revealed depression and drug treatment for schizophrenia. *Archives of General Psychiatry, 38,* 806–811.

Kraepelin, E. (1971). *Dementia praecox and paraphrenia* (R. M. Barclay, Trans.). Huntington, NY: R. E. Krieger Publishing. (Original work published in 1919).

Kring, A., Smith, D. A., Kerr, S., & Neale, J. M. (1993). Flat affect in schizophrenia does not reflect diminished subjective experience of emotion. *Journal of Abnormal Psychology, 102,* 507–517.

Kugelmass, S., Faber, N., Ingraham, L. J., Frenkel, E., Nathan, M., Mirsky, A. F., & Shakhar, G. B. (1995). Reanalysis of SCOR and anxiety measures in the Israeli high-risk study. *Schizophrenia Bulletin, 21,* 205–217.

Lenzenweger, M. F., & Dworkin, R. H. (1987). Assessment of premorbid social competence in schizophrenia: A methodological note. *Journal of Abnormal Psychology, 96,* 367–369.

Lenzenweger, M. F., Dworkin, R. H., & Wethington, E. (1991). Examining the underlying structure of schizophrenic phenomenology: Evidence for a three-process model. *Schizophrenia Bulletin, 17,* 515–524.

McIntyre, C. W., Watson, D., Clark, L. A., & Cross, S. A. (1991). The effect of induced social interaction on positive and negative affect. *Bulletin of the Psychonomic Society, 29,* 67–70.

Mednick, S. A., Parnas, J., & Schulsinger, F. (1987). The Copenhagen high-risk project, 1962–1986. *Schizophrenia Bulletin, 13,* 485–495.

Meehl, P. E. (1962). Schizotaxia, schizotypy, schizophrenia. *American Psychologist, 17,* 827–838.

Meehl, P. E. (1990). Toward an integrated theory of schizotaxia, schizotypy, and schizophrenia. *Journal of Personality Disorders, 4,* 1–99.

Mellsop, G. (1973). Adult psychiatric patients on whom information was recorded during childhood. *British Journal of Psychiatry, 123,* 703–710.

Mirsky, A. F., Kugelmass, S., Ingraham, L. J., Frenkel, E., & Nathan, M. (1995). Overview and summary: Twenty-five-year followup of high-risk children. *Schizophrenia Bulletin, 21,* 227–239.

Mueser, K. T., Bellack, A. S., Morrison, R. L., & Wixted, J. T. (1990). Social competence in schizophrenia: Premorbid adjustment, social skill, and domains of functioning. *Journal of Psychiatry Research, 24,* 51–63.

Mueser, K. T., Douglas, M. S., Bellack, A. S., & Morrison, R. L. (1991). Assessment of enduring deficit and negative symptom subtypes in schizophrenia. *Schizophrenia Bulletin, 17,* 565–582.

Mueser, K. T., Sayers, S. L., Schooler, N. R., Mance, R. M., & Haas, G. L. (1994). A multisite investigation of the reliability of the scale for the assessment of negative symptoms. *American Journal of Psychiatry, 151,* 1453–1462.

Neale, J. M., Blanchard, J. J., Kerr, S., Kring, A. M., & Smith, D. A. (in press). Flat affect in schizophrenia. In W. F. Flack & J. D. Laird (Eds.), *Emotions in psychopathology: Theory and research.* (in press). New York: Oxford University Press.

Numbers, J. S., & Chapman, L. J. (1982). Social deficits in hypothetically psychosis-prone college women. *Journal of Abnormal Psychology, 91,* 255–260.

O'Neal, P., & Robins, L. N. (1958). Childhood patterns of adult schizophrenia: A 30-year follow-up study. *American Journal of Psychiatry, 115,* 385–391.

Overall, J. E., & Gorham, D. R. (1962). The Brief Psychiatric Rating Scale. *Psychological Reports, 18,* 799–812.

Overall, J. E., & Gorham, D. R. (1988). Brief Psychiatric Rating Scale. *Psychopharmacology Bulletin, 24,* 99.

Pogue-Geile, M. F., & Zubin, J. (1988). Negative symptomatology and schizophrenia: A conceptual and empirical review. *International Journal of Mental Health, 16,* 3–45.

Rado, S. (1962). *Psychoanalysis of behavior: The collected papers of Sandor Rado* (Vol. 2). New York: Grune & Stratton.

Rajkumar, S., & Thara, R. (1989). Factors affecting relapse in schizophrenia. *Schizophrenia Research, 2,* 403–409.

Sayers, S. L., Curran, P. J., & Mueser, K. T. (1996). Factor structure and construct validity of the scale for the Assessment of Negative Symptoms, *Psychological Assessment, 8,* 269–280.

Schuck, J., Leventhal, D., Rothstein, H., & Irizarry, V. (1984). Physical anhedonia and schizophrenia. *Journal of Abnormal Psychology, 93,* 342–344.

Spitzer, R. L., Williams, J. B. W., Gibbon, M., & First, M. B. (1990). *Structured Clinical Interview for DSM-III-R—Patient Edition.* Washington, DC: American Psychiatric Press.

Strauss, J. S., Carpenter, W. T., Bartko, J. J. (1974). The diagnosis and understanding of schizophrenia. Part III. Speculations on the processes that underlie schizophrenic symptoms and signs. *Schizophrenia Bulletin, 1* (Experimental Issue No. 11), 61–69.

Strickland, B. R., Hale, W. D., & Anderson, L. K. (1975). Effect of induced mood states on activity and self-reported affect. *Journal of Consulting and Clinical Psychology, 43,* 587.

Subotnik, K. L., & Nuechterlein, K. H. (1988). Prodromal signs and symptoms of schizophrenic relapse. *Journal of Abnormal Psychology, 97,* 405–412.

Tellegen, A. (1985). Structures of mood and personality and their relevance to assessing anxiety, with an emphasis on self-report. In A. H. Tuma & J. D. Maser (Eds.), *Anxiety and the anxiety disorders* (pp. 681–706). Hillsdale, NJ: Erlbaum.

Tellegen, A., & Waller, N. G. (in press). Exploring personality through test construction: Development of the Multidimensional Personality Questionnaire. In S. R. Briggs & J. M. Cheek (Eds.), *Personality measures: Development and evaluation* (vol. 1). Greenwich, CT: JAI Press.

Van der Does, A. J. W., Dingemans, P. M. A. J., Linszen, D. H., Nugter, M. A., & Scholte, W. F. (1993). Symptom dimensions and cognitive and social functioning in recent-onset schizophrenia. *Psychological Medicine, 23,* 745–753.

Walker, E., & Lewine, R. J. (1988). The positive/negative symptom distinction in schizophrenia: Validity and etiological relevance. *Schizophrenia Research, 1,* 315–328.

Watson, D. (1988). Intraindividual and interindividual analyses of positive and negative affect: Their relation to health complaints, perceived stress, and daily activities. *Journal of Personality and Social Psychology, 54,* 1020–1030.

Watson, D., & Clark, L. A. (1992a). Affects separable and inseparable: On the hierarchical arrangement of the negative affects. *Journal of Personality and Social Psychology, 62,* 489–505.

Watson, D., & Clark, L. A. (1992b). On traits and temperament: General and specific factors of emotional experience and their relation to the five-factor model. *Journal of Personality, 60,* 441–476

Watson, D., & Clark, L. A. (in press). Behavioral disinhibition versus constraint: A dispositional perspective. In D. M. Wegner & J. W. Pennebaker (Eds.), *Handbook of mental control.* New York: Prentice-Hall.

Watson, D., Clark, L. A., McIntyre, C. W., & Hamaker, S. (1992). Affect, personality, and social activity. *Journal of Personality and Social Psychology, 63,* 1011–1025.

Watson, D., Clark, L. A., & Tellegen, A. (1988). Development and validation of brief measures of Positive and Negative Affect: The PANAS Scales. *Journal of Personality and Social Psychology, 54,* 1063–1070.

Watson, D., & Tellegen, A. (1985). Toward a consensual structure of mood. *Psychological Bulletin, 98,* 219–235.

Watt, N. F. (1978). Patterns of childhood social development in adult schizophrenics. *Archives of General Psychiatry, 35,* 160–165.

Williams, R., & Dalby, J. T. (Eds.). (1989). *Depression in schizophrenics.* New York: Plenum Press.

Woerner, M., Mannuzza, S., & Kane, J. M. (1988). Anchoring the BPRS: An aid to improved reliability. *Psychopharmacology Bulletin, 24,* 112–117.

Zevon, M. A., & Tellegen, A. (1982). The structure of mood change: An idiographic/nomothetic analysis. *Journal of Personality and Social Psychology, 43,* 111–122.

Zigler, E., & Glick, M. (1986). *A developmental approach to adult psychopathology.* New York: Wiley.

Zigler, E., & Phillips, L. (1961). Social competence and outcome in psychiatric disorder. *Journal of Abnormal and Social Psychology, 63,* 264–271.

CHAPTER 12

AFFECT PERCEPTION AND SOCIAL KNOWLEDGE IN SCHIZOPHRENIA

Jonathan S. E. Hellewell
Jane F. Whittaker

Social impairments and deterioration in social functioning are key components of both major classificatory systems used in English-speaking psychiatry (Diagnostic and Statistical Manual, Fourth Edition, DMS IV, American Psychiatric Association, 1994; International Classification of Diseases and Health Related Problems-Tenth Revision, ICD-10, World Health Organization, 1992) and have been described as the hallmarks of schizophrenia (Bellack, Morrison, & Mueser, 1989).

Several modern neuropsychological and neurobiological theories of schizophrenia incorporate impairments of affect perception and social knowledge (e.g., Bentall, 1994; Kirkpatrick & Buchanan, 1990; Frith, 1992). However, it is still not clear how prevalent are the impairments of social knowledge and affect perception in schizophrenia. Schizophrenia is a heterogeneous disorder. It is still to be established that all patients with schizophrenia have these impairments, or indeed if schizophrenia is a single disorder.

Affect perception and social knowledge are difficult to define and still more difficult to measure, even in healthy subjects. Therefore, it is not surprising that there are difficulties in assessing these functions in clinical populations as diverse as patients suffering from schizophrenia.

In this chapter, for the sake of clarity, we will consider social knowledge and affect perception separately, while acknowledging the artificiality of this division.

We will start by examining definitions of social knowledge and affect perception. Next, we will place impairments in these functions in a developmental context. We will then consider other conditions in which abnormalities of affect perception and social knowledge are found. Finally, we will examine the evidence for these abnormalities in schizophrenia.

DEFINING SOCIAL KNOWLEDGE AND AFFECT PERCEPTION

Failing to accurately define what is meant by the concepts of affect perception and social knowledge is a major pitfall in research. Affect perception is a difficult term to define. Alpert and Rosen (1990) have provided a useful working definition of these terms. According to their discussion, *emotion* refers to an internal, subjective experience with a congruent physiological component (e.g., fear is accompanied by rapid heart rate, dry mouth, sweating palms, etc.).

In contrast, *affect* is a transient, internal, subjective experience with external signals and signs that are available to an observer. An observer of a broadly similar social group would recognize these signals as indicative of a specific emotional or feeling state. In particular, the internal state and the external signals would be congruent with each other and what is evaluated by the observer would be congruent with the subjective experience of the sender. Nevertheless, the terms *affect* and *emotion* are often used interchangeably.

Perception, in its most narrow definition, is the integration of external stimuli to create an internal representation. For this account, we adopt a broader definition that includes all cognitive processes starting from presentation of a stimulus to attribution of meaning to that stimulus.

Affect perception can be understood in terms of its function and the component processes that subserve it. Affect perception requires evaluation of the modular components of face affect expression, body gesture, and vocal prosody (the musicality of speech that gives emphasis and therefore meaning). Affect perception, therefore, depends on the integrity of a complex system that brings together information from these modalities.

There is a danger that a definition of social knowledge may become so broad a concept as to be meaningless (incorporating social perception, social cognition, social intelligence, social communication, and even theory of mind), or so narrow as to be beyond application to anything but the particular group under consideration. In this discussion, the term *social knowledge* will refer to the body of knowledge available to a person that allows that person to interact effectively with other members of a social group.

In comparison with affect perception, social knowledge is less easily defined in terms of modality and function. The accurate perception of social and affective signals from the environment is involved, but, in addition, there is a reliance on the appropriate application of prior knowledge. This information, which is organized in the form of social schemata, is acquired during development and by experience.

AFFECT PERCEPTION AND SOCIAL KNOWLEDGE IN A DEVELOPMENTAL CONTEXT

We have suggested that schizophrenia has a neurobiological basis. We would also suggest that affect perception and social knowledge have both a neurobiological basis and a developmental course. The acquisition of these skills is observable in children (Carey, 1992; Ellis, 1992). An apparent failure to develop these skills is most evident in autistic children (Hobson, 1995), but prospective studies have also identified impairments in language development, social interaction, and facial expressivity in children who later go on to develop schizophrenia (Walker, Grimes, Davis, & Smith 1993). Similarly, Hollis (1995), Parnas, Schulsinger, Schulsinger, Mednick, and Teasdale (1982), and Wolff, Wolff, Townshend, McGuire, and Weeks (1991) have also described maladaptive patterns of social interaction identifiable in childhood in those who go on to develop schizophrenia as adults. These findings suggest that, at least in a proportion of cases, schizophrenia has a neurodevelopmental basis, or, in other words, that the disorder we recognize as schizophrenia represents the culmination of a process of brain dysfunction that is evident many years before the development of psychosis.

AFFECT PERCEPTION, SOCIAL KNOWLEDGE, AND GENERAL PATHOLOGY

We have proceeded on the assumption that schizophrenia has a neurobiological basis. Patients with schizophrenia are found to have widespread abnormalities of brain structure and function (see Shapiro, 1993, for a recent review). To what extent abnormal brain function underlies the social dysfunction in schizophrenia has yet to be established. Impaired affect perception and social knowledge may represent secondary phenomena, occurring because of the disease process or its treatment. The classic study of Wing and Brown (1961) demonstrated a clear relationship between impairments of social functioning in schizophrenic patients and the quality of the social milieu of the institutions in which they lived. Patients in socially impoverished environments had more social impairments than those living in richer environments. Moreover, the expressed emotion of a patient's relatives, which can be thought of as indicative of the psychosocial environment of the patient's home, strongly influences relapse in schizophrenia. Therefore, there is little doubt that the quality of patients' social environment exerts a strong influence over the manifestation and prognosis of their illness.

We have suggested that abnormalities of biological mechanisms contribute to impairments in affect perception and social knowledge. Schizophrenia, however, would not be the only disorder in which social impairments result from neurobiological disturbance. Patients with acquired lesions of the right cerebral hemisphere of the brain are found to have impairments of receptive and expressive vocal prosody, impairments of face affect recognition and comprehension and interpretation of metaphor (Ross & Mesulam, 1979; Ross, 1981). Damage to the amygdala leads to impairment of face recognition (Young, Aggleton, Hellawell & Johnson, 1995).

The classic pattern of abnormalities in social and interpersonal behavior following frontal lobe damage has been recognized since 1868, when the case of Phineas Gage was first described (described in Kolb & Whishaw, 1990). More recently, Damasio, Tranel, and Damasio (1990) described a patient who, following surgical treatment for a brain lesion, had intact social knowledge on laboratory assessment, but was unable to use this knowledge in his dealings in the real world.

As we have shown, many neurological conditions cause impairments of the functions necessary for effective social and interpersonal functioning.

AFFECT PERCEPTION AND SCHIZOPHRENIA

General Points

We will now review experimental work investigating affect perception in schizophrenia. A key issue that must be considered first, however, is whether perception of any environmental stimulus is impaired in this disorder.

Visual Perception in Schizophrenia

Visual perception in schizophrenia has received considerable attention from investigators. Cutting (1985) reviewed studies of visual perception in schizophrenia and concluded that basic processes, such as sensitivity throughout the visual field, critical stimulus duration, and the ability to apprehend items in arrays of different sizes were normal in schizophrenia, although there may be some delay in processing this information.

At least two studies have suggested that schizophrenic patients are impaired on tests of perception and interpretation of ambiguous figures (Crookes & Hutt, 1970; Straube, 1975). This may be because patients use unconventional perceptual strategies (Bemporad, 1967; Schwartz, Place, & Gilmore, 1980; Reich & Cutting, 1982).

A number of studies have dealt with the perceptual aspects of face processing in general. Neufeld (1976) used a series of schematic faces, which varied in four dimensions (e.g., length of nose). He demonstrated abnormalities in judgment of intelligence between paranoid and nonparanoid schizophrenic patients compared with control subjects. However, the two groups of schizophrenic patients differed in the reason for the deficit. The paranoid patients were less systematic in the way that their judgments were related to the four dimensions, whereas the nonparanoid group assigned idiosyncratic weights to the four dimensions.

Levin and Benton (1977) showed that chronic schizophrenic patients, as a group, were worse than controls in a test of matching a presented face to a sample face. This suggests a perceptual impairment affecting the processing of faces, but it is not possible to conclude from this study whether patients have a specific face processing problem or a general difficulty interpreting any complex visuospatial stimulus.

Frith, Stevens, Johnstone, Owens, and Crow (1983) addressed the issue of specificity of deficit by giving 21 acute schizophrenic patients and 26 neurotic patients sets of schematic faces, nonsense objects, and geometrical forms. Each of the three sets of stimuli varied in five ways, and subjects had to sort them in various ways. The results showed that the neurotic patients were better at sorting faces than at sorting geometrical forms. By contrast, the schizophrenic patients were no better at sorting faces than geometric shapes. The authors concluded that schizophrenic patients, unlike normal subjects and nonschizophrenic psychiatric patients, do not form an integrated evaluation of a face and that, in schizophrenia, the "integrated gestalt of the face is not dominant over its components." (Frith, Stevens, Johnstone, Owens, & Crow 1983, p. 34.) This study provides evidence of a specific perceptual deficit affecting the processing of faces in schizophrenia.

To summarize, visuospatial impairments, particularly involving higher-order functions, are a feature of schizophrenia. However, McKenna (1994) suggests that these are not disproportionate to the general level of cognitive impairment found in the disorder.

Visual Affect Perception in Schizophrenia

Facial Affect Perception Studies in Schizophrenia

Abnormalities of face affect perception in patients with schizophrenia were reported over 30 years ago (e.g., Izard, 1959; Iscoe & Veldman, 1963; Levy, Orr, & Rosenzweig, 1960), although not all early studies found evidence of a deficit (Spiegel, Gerard, Grayson, & Gengerelli, 1962). Over the years, the field has been subjected to considerable scrutiny (e.g., Morrison, Bellack, & Mueser, 1988).

Two early studies of affect perception in schizophrenia are those of Dougherty, Bartlett, and Izard (1974) and Muzekari and Bates (1977). As these studies are often cited, they will be described in some detail.

Dougherty et al. (1974) used Izard's (1971) procedure for assessing facial affect recognition. Izard's task required subjects to identify the emotions depicted in 32 photographs, there being 4 photographs of each of 8 emotions (joy, anger, surprise, disgust, shame, fear, sadness, and interest). Subjects were tested on emotion perception using two tasks: (1) emotion labeling, in which patients were simply asked to describe the emotion depicted in the photograph, and (2) emotion recognition, which required the patient to sort the pictures of facial affect into the 8 predefined emotion categories. Subjects comprised 31 state hospital inpatients and 23 nonpsychiatric controls.

The schizophrenic subjects were impaired on both tasks. On the recognition task, the schizophrenic patients appeared to have particular difficulty with two categories of negative affect (disgust-contempt and shame-humiliation). However, the schizophrenic subjects had all been admitted to a hospital over 5 years previously, and therefore, it is possible that these results reflect chronicity of disorder, treatment effects or effects of prolonged institutionalization. There is no information given on diagnostic criteria either, so the patients may not be comparable with schizophrenic subjects used in other studies.

Muzekari and Bates (1977) showed subjects a series of posed photographs of the faces of actors simulating four emotions. Subjects were 32 inpatients with chronic schizophrenia, who were compared with 32 student controls. The students were better than the patients on both open-ended and multiple-choice questions on the affect portrayed.

Two other studies, which also produced similar results, were those of Walker, Marwitt, and Emory (1980) and Mandal and Palchoudhury (1985). Walker et al. (1980) assessed 48 state hospital inpatients suffering from schizophrenia. No standardized diagnostic criteria were employed, and the patients are likely to have had long inpatient admissions. These patients were compared with 48 nonpatient controls. Subjects completed Izard's (1971) tests of affect recognition. The schizophrenic subjects were significantly impaired relative to controls in identifying all of the affects shown.

In a simple study carried out in India, Mandal and Palchoudhury (1985) compared 12 schizophrenic patients, diagnosed by clinical judgment, with 12 nonpatient controls on two tasks using 48 locally produced posed photographs depicting six different facial emotions. The first task was to sort the photographs into groups showing similar affects, and the second was a multiple-choice affect identification task. Patients were worse than control subjects on both tasks, but performed relatively less well on the naming than the sorting task. The authors suggested that this may reflect greater impairment in the verbal reporting than in the perception of emotion.

In none of the four studies described above was there a control task of equivalent difficulty, but which did not involve affect processing. Consequently, we cannot be certain that the deficit identified is specific to facial affect processing. A further limitation is the absence of nonschizophrenic psychiatric comparison subjects, so we do not know whether any deficits are specific to schizophrenia.

One of the first studies to use nonpsychiatric comparison subjects was that of Pilowsky and Bassett (1980), who examined the reporting of judged facial emotion in patients with schizophrenia. They compared four groups of subjects: inpatients with schizophrenia and neurotic disorders, alcoholic patients, and nonpatient controls.

Subjects were asked to comment on the affects portrayed in photographs of facial affect from Ekman and Friesen's (1975) series. The schizophrenic patients were less likely to comment on affect and tended to comment on physical characteristics of the person pictured instead. Some years later similar results were reported by Cramer, Weegman, and O'Neill (1989) and Hellewell, Connell, and Deakin (1994) in studies using videotaped stimuli.

Nonschizophrenic psychiatric control subjects were also studied by Zuroff and Colussy (1986). They compared hospitalized schizophrenic patients with nonpatient controls and inpatients suffering from affective disorders. However, diagnoses were made on the basis of case note review and no information was given on length of illness or admission. Subjects completed Izard's test of recognition of emotion, as described above.

The schizophrenic patients were significantly less accurate in affect recognition than the nonpatients but not to a significantly greater extent than the depressed patients. No evidence was found to suggest that the patients were differentially inaccurate in identifying neutral, negative, or positive emotions.

This indicates that the deficits in affect recognition found in schizophrenia are not specific to the disorder and suggests that these are unlikely to be etiologically related to the development of the symptoms of schizophrenia.

One of the first studies to address the issue of specificity of deficit, by including both a control task and a nonschizophrenic psychiatric control group, was that of Cutting (1981). The performance of 4 groups (20 schizophrenic patients meeting Research Diagnostic criteria (RDS; Spitzer, Endicott, & Robins, 1975) with continuous inpatient stay of less than 6 months, 20 RDC schizophrenics with inpatient stay of greater than 6 months, 20 depressed patients, and 20 outpatients with diagnoses of personality or neurotic disorders) was compared on a task of judging which of two faces, shown in photographs, was the friendlier. The control task was to discriminate between two similar colors. The schizophrenic subjects with the shorter inpatient stay (the "acute" schizophrenic subjects in Cutting's terminology) were markedly impaired in judging friendliness, relative both to the other three groups and to their judgments about color.

In a second experiment, using a different control task, which required the judgment of age from faces, Cutting (1981) found that acute schizophrenic patients differed from both remitted psychotic patients and patients with psychotic depression in judgments of friendliness and meanness, but not in judgments of the age of the person portrayed.

A further attempt to address the issue of specificity of deficit was the study of Novic, Luchins, and Perline (1984). Long-stay schizophrenic inpatients were compared with a group of nonpatient controls on two tests of face processing. The test of facial affect recognition used the Izard photos, whereas the nonaffect control task was a test requiring the matching of faces. To control for the confounding effects of differential task difficulty, the authors first ensured that the two tasks were of comparable

discriminatory power and reliability, but unfortunately this process involved discarding all photographs showing positive emotions. Patients were worse than controls on the affect identification task, but this difference was removed when performance on the face-matching task was included in analyses as a covariate.

These results indicate that schizophrenic patients have extensive impairments in face processing, affecting both affect perception and identity processing. The authors suggested that earlier findings of a differential impairment in the identification of negative affect may reflect differential discriminatory power of positive and negative items.

Further evidence for a general deficit in face processing in schizophrenia emerged from the study of Pollard, Hellewell, and Deakin (1995), who tested 43 DSM-III-R schizophrenic subjects and 28 controls on Hobson's tests of matching emotion and identity (Hobson, Ouston, & Lee, 1988). The tasks were to match faces from Ekman and Friesen's (1975) series on the basis of emotion when identity is different and to match unfamiliar individuals despite variation in emotional expression (Hobson et al., 1988). Hobson had demonstrated a greater deficit in autistic children in matching by emotion than in matching by identity. The schizophrenic subjects, however, performed poorly on both tests and showed no evidence of a selective impairment of affect processing.

Contrasting findings emerged from the second study of Walker, McGuire, and Bettes (1984), in which the performance of 17 hospitalized RDC schizophrenic patients was compared with that of 14 affective disorder patients and 14 control subjects on four tests of face and affect processing. Stimuli for the affect identification tasks were drawn from Izard's series of face affect displays. Subjects completed tests of emotion discrimination (determining whether emotions depicted in pairs of photographs are the same or different), emotion labeling, and an emotion identification task using a multiple-choice question format. Pilot work confirmed that the tests were comparable and of adequate discriminatory power. The schizophrenic subjects were inferior to both the psychiatric and normal control groups on the affect discrimination task. In contrast, on the emotion recognition task the schizophrenic subjects were worse than the healthy controls but not different from the affective disorder patients. No group differences were seen, however, on the facial identity discrimination task, indicating, the authors suggested, a specific deficit in facial affect processing in schizophrenia that was independent of competence in processing facial identity.

Heimberg, Gur, Erwin, Shtasel, and Gur (1992) compared 20 DSM-III-R schizophrenic patients with matched nonpatient controls. Remarkably, 11 of the patients were drug-naive at the time of testing and 8 of the remaining 9 had not received neuroleptics for the preceding 2 weeks.

Stimuli comprised black-and-white photographs of actors with neutral, happy, and sad faces. Subjects were tested on emotion discrimination, which involved identifying which of a pair of photographs was either happy or sad, when each emotional face was shown paired with a neutral face, and on age discrimination, which involved identifying the older of two individuals, both pictured with neutral expression. The schizophrenic patients were impaired on both tasks, but poorer performance was observed on the test of emotion discrimination than on the test of age discrimination. Comparison of the performance of the schizophrenic patients with that of a group of depressed patients from an earlier study (Gur et al., 1992) indicated a greater deficit in schizophrenia than in depression. The authors noted that normal controls find the age discrimination test harder than the emotion judgment task and suggest, therefore, that the relatively poorer performance of the schizophrenic patients on emotion judgment cannot simply be attributed to greater task difficulty.

More detailed analysis of patterns of test performance indicated that the inaccuracy of schizophrenic subjects arose because of the attribution of affect to neutral faces, an observation that was also made by Zuroff and Colussy (1986) and that is consistent with the clinical impression that some schizophrenic patients perceive meaning in faces that are regarded as neutral by others.

Severity of schizophrenic symptoms, but not of nonspecific symptoms such as anxiety, was related to poor performance in emotion discrimination in the study of Heimberg et al. (1992). These results are consistent with those of Cutting (1981), who also observed relatively more impaired performance on affect discrimination in acutely ill than in chronically ill patients. Heimberg et al. suggested that impaired emotion processing may underlie some of the core features of schizophrenia and that the relatively short duration of illness, together with the lack of exposure to medication, made it unlikely that the deficits in the interpretation of emotion simply reflect the effects of institutionalization, understimulating environment, and medication.

Heimberg et al. (1992) also found no evidence for a greater deficit in the discrimination of negative rather than positive emotions, a finding in conflict with a number of earlier studies (e.g., Dougherty et al., 1974; Muzekari & Bates, 1977; Pilowsky & Bassett, 1980). There is evidence, however, that some negative emotional states may be more difficult to recognize than nonnegative states (Ekman, Friensen, & Ellsworth 1972; Zuckerman, Libets, Koivumaki, & Rosenthal, 1975) and, like Novic et al. (1984), Heimberg et al. (1992) suggested that findings of differential emotion identification abilities in earlier studies may reflect unequal task difficulty.

The issue of selectivity of impairment was also addressed by Feinberg, Rifkin, Schaffer, and Walker (1986). Twenty RDC schizophrenic patients were compared with 20 inpatients with major depressive disorder and 20 healthy volunteers on four tasks based on the facial affect photographs of Ekman. In the first two tasks, subjects had to judge whether two photographs of faces showing different emotions were of the same person. In one task the faces were inverted and in the other were the right way up. The third task involved judging whether two people were showing the same emotion. The fourth task, of emotion labeling, involved selection of an appropriate affect label from a list of seven.

The schizophrenic subjects were less accurate than the healthy controls on all four tasks, suggesting a general deficit in face processing. Performance of the depressed patients was worse than that of the healthy control subjects on the test of emotion labeling only, although the depressed patients were not as impaired as the schizophrenic patients.

Feinberg's study is notable, also, for its use of carefully controlled stimulus exposure times, as the inverted faces were shown for only 2 seconds and all other facial stimuli for only 500 msecs. Limited exposure times such as these may approximate more closely to the brief duration of facial expressions occurring in natural social interactions.

Another study to use limited stimulus exposure times was that of Borod, Martin, Alpert, Brozgold, and Welkowitz (1993), who compared 20 RDC schizophrenic patients with 21 normal controls and 19 patients with right hemisphere brain damage. Subjects were tested on two tasks of facial affect perception: (1) an emotion identification task and (2) an emotion discrimination task, using photographs from the Ekman series. In the discrimination task, subjects had to judge whether the emotions portrayed in two photographs of different individuals were the same. Limited stimulus exposure times of 3 seconds per photograph separated by a 1-second interval were used in the emotion discrimination task. No time limit was imposed in the emotion identification task, which involved the selection of the emotion portrayed from a list of seven emotions. Two control tasks involved matching to sample, the first using faces and the second abstract black-and-white patterns.

Both patient groups were inferior to controls on all four tests, which implies a general impairment in visuospatial perceptual processes. Significant differences remained between the schizophrenic and the normal control subjects on the affect identification task, but not the emotion discrimination task, once differences in performance on the control tasks had been accounted for. This suggests that schizophrenic patients may have a proportionately greater impairment in face affect processing than they do in perception generally.

Not all recent studies have found impairments in facial affect identification in schizophrenia. Haskins, Shutty, and Kellog (1995) compared 35 DSM-III-R schizophrenic patients and 12 schizoaffective patients with 51 nonpsychiatric controls on tests of facial affect identification and prosodic comprehension. Using a novel method, subjects were asked to select the quadrant showing a specified affect, when confronted with a photomontage of a single person's face, each quadrant showing a different emotion. The schizophrenic patients were no worse than controls on this task, despite poorer performance on the test of prosodic comprehension. Unfortunately, despite using operationally diagnosed patients, the inclusion of schizoaffective subjects and the use of the novel composite facial stimuli render the results of this study somewhat difficult to generalize.

A better designed study was that of Archer, Hay, and Young (1992), in which the performance of 12 DSM-III schizophrenic patients, 12 depressed patients, and 12 normal controls was compared on three tests of face processing. The tests were (1) a facial affect identification task, (2) a test of facial identity recognition (requiring the identification of a famous person) and (3) a test involving matching of unfamiliar faces. The schizophrenic patients were worse than the two control groups on all three tests, and there was no tendency for patients to be more impaired on the affect identification test.

Another study to find no evidence of a greater impairment in emotion judgment than in nonemotion judgment was that of Gessler, Cutting, Frith, and Weinman (1989).

Using tasks matched for difficulty and discriminating ability, 20 RDC acute schizophrenic patients were found to be as impaired on an age discrimination task as on a happy-sad discrimination task. This result again suggests a general impairment in face processing, rather than an impairment specific to face emotion processing. Interestingly, an impairment in emotion judgment was not seen in the 20 patients with chronic schizophrenia and the 20 subjects with remitted schizophrenia who were also included in this study, suggesting that this impairment does not form part of the chronic deficits that occur in schizophrenia.

Static Face Affect Displays—Summary

Taken together, the studies reviewed above show that schizophrenic patients are impaired in the identification of affect from static face images. To establish the extent of the deficit, a number of studies incorporated nonaffect face processing tasks, and patients have generally been impaired on these tasks, too. This suggests that deficits in face affect identification may form part of a broader impairment affecting many aspects of face processing.

Face Affect Processing—Dynamic Stimuli

As has been discussed in the preceding section, most studies examining the perception and interpretation of emotion in schizophrenia have used photographs of faces. A number of investigators (e.g., Joseph, Sturgeon, & Leff, 1992; Archer et al., 1992) have commented on the abstractions brought about by the use of this technique, as in real life people are likely to rely heavily on contextual information, on changes in expression over time, and on cues from posture and gesture when making judgments about emotion. The use of dynamic stimuli, such as videotaped affect and interaction displays, has been advocated as a strategy to overcome this problem.

One of the first studies to use videotaped material was that of Muzekari and Bates (1977), which is described more fully above. In addition to testing affect perception using posed photos, the 32 chronic schizophrenic patients and 32 controls were shown 8 silent videotapes, each of 2 minutes duration and depicting a different emotional state. The results showed that the schizophrenic subjects were less accurate than the normal controls in the identification of emotions portrayed on video, as they were with the posed photographs.

Contrasting results were reported by La Russo (1978), who showed a videotape of actors either anticipating or simulating the expectancy of receiving an electric shock. The 24 schizophrenic subjects were, as a group, significantly *more* accurate than a group of 24 controls in identifying the genuine emotions but were worse in the simulated instances.

Cramer et al. (1989) and Cramer, Bowen, and O'Neill (1992) showed a videotape of actors portraying various everyday social interactions to a group of 34 RDC schizophrenic patients and 15 normal controls. The videotapes had been produced so that the principal actor was addressing a second actor. Subjects were asked both to describe the emotion shown by the principal actor and to select 4 appropriate adjectives from a list of 17. On both measures, patients were less accurate than controls at identifying the emotion portrayed. The same videotape was used in a separate study by Joseph et al. (1992), which produced different results. Using an affect labeling task, 32 schizophrenic patients showed no impairment when compared with 10 normal controls. Joseph et al. commented that the major difference between the two studies was that all of Cramer's patients were in hospital and a high proportion were expressing psychotic symptoms, whereas all of the patients in their study had been in remission and on this basis suggested that the differences between the two studies may have reflected acute psychosis.

In an unrelated study, Hellewell et al. (1994) showed a videotape of actors portraying emotional states to a sample of 30 DSM-III-R schizophrenic patients and 20 healthy controls. Unlike the previous studies, the video showed only the face of a single actor, addressing the camera as if speaking directly to the viewer. To enforce reliance on facial expression, gesture, and prosody, the 8 video excerpts, each 30 seconds long, had been prepared and edited so that all references to situation, context, or antecedent events were absent and that the excerpt was capable of many interpretations. On a forced-choice adjective selection task, the patients used a wider range of adjectives and gave a greater proportion of first responses classified by an independent panel of raters as wholly inappropriate to the affect displayed. When asked to provide a commentary on the feelings of the character portrayed, the patients were more likely than controls to fail to comment on the emotion, commenting instead on the physical appearance of the actor, a finding also reported by Pilowsky and Basset (1980) and Cramer et al.

(1989). No associations were found, however, between test performance and symptoms at the time of testing.

A further study using videotaped stimuli was that of Berndl, von Cranach, and Grüsser (1986), in which a silent videotape was shown to 81 DSM-III schizophrenic patients and 78 normal control subjects. There were 13 scenes, each of 10 seconds duration, in which actors portrayed a range of emotions. After each scene subjects completed multiple-choice questions, some of which involved the interpretation of affect and some of which did not. The schizophrenic subjects showed a greater error rate on all of the tests, suggesting a general deficit. Closer examination of the pattern of performance on the various subtests indicated that the patients may have had particular difficulties with the excerpts involving gesture and facial expression rather than those involving speech. Despite the substantial sample size, no strong associations were found between test performance and symptoms.

Perhaps the most sophisticated study to use videotape stimuli was that of Archer, Hay, and Young (1994). Silent color videotapes were used to create dynamic face analogues of the unfamiliar face recognition, familiar face recognition, and facial emotion identification tasks used in their earlier study (Archer et al., 1992). In contrast to their earlier findings using static faces, which indicated that schizophrenic subjects have a generalized deficit in face processing, this study revealed no difference on the task requiring identification of familiar faces. The 10 schizophrenic patients, diagnosed according to DSM-III criteria, showed inferior performance to both 10 depressed inpatients and 10 normal controls on the tests of unfamiliar face recognition and emotion identification. In discussion of their results, the authors noted that, although it remained unclear whether or not schizophrenic patients have a generalized impairment in the processing of dynamic faces, the results underscore the importance of facial feature movement in the processing and interpretation of facial expression.

Dynamic Face Affect Displays—Summary

To date, the use of dynamic face images has allowed the development of new and imaginative methodologies to explore face affect processing. Unfortunately, these techniques have not greatly advanced our knowledge in this area. Although the majority of studies have demonstrated impairments in affect perception in schizophrenia, not all have done so.

The specificity of the deficit in affect perception remains unclear, and we cannot discount the possibility that this deficit is merely one part of a broader range of impairments affecting face processing in schizophrenia. The studies described above have not advanced our knowledge of the relationship of affect perception to clinical state.

Auditory Perception in Schizophrenia

The studies examining the basic processes of auditory perception in patients with schizophrenia give conflicting results: Rappaport, Hopkins, Silverman, and Hall (1972) and Gruzelier and Hammond (1979) reported impaired perception of tones; Balogh (Balogh, Schuck, & Leventhal, 1979; Balogh & Leventhal, 1982) reported impaired sound localization, but Bruder et al. (1975) found a normal auditory threshold for clicks. Hemsley and Zawada (1976) found no differences from depressed patients in speech perception. In a review of this area, Cutting (1990) concludes that any differences in the basic processes of speech perception in schizophrenia are likely to be minor.

Auditory Affect Perception in Schizophrenia

Two studies have examined the perception of emotion in music. Simon, Holzberg, Alessi, and Garrity (1951) asked schizophrenic patients, normal controls, and patients with affective disorders to identify the dominant mood of eight pieces of music. The results showed that the schizophrenic patients were worse than normal or depressed patients in their identification of sad music and were worse than normals, but equal to the affective disorders groups at identifying happy music. Conflicting results were obtained by Nielzen and Cesarec (1982), however, who found that schizophrenic subjects rated seven pieces of music as more cheerful and attractive than did depressed and normal control subjects.

There is more consistency in the studies of the ability of schizophrenic patients to perceive the prosodic quality of speech. Turner (1964) instructed a professional actor to read out 36 nonsense sentences in an emotive fashion and asked 6 other people to read them in a neutral fashion. Schizophrenic and normal subjects were then required to judge which of 6 emotions best described each of the emotional sentences and to identify the speaker of the neutral sentences. The two groups were equally proficient in identifying the speaker of a neutral sentence,

but the schizophrenic subjects, particularly those in the paranoid group, were less accurate in identifying the intended emotion.

Jonsson and Sjöstedt (1973) asked acute schizophrenics and neurotics to identify three types of intonation (friendly, threatening and neutral) in spoken words. They were then tested for perception of duration, loudness, and pitch. The schizophrenic subjects were significantly worse on all four tests, but the deficit in intonation perception still remained significant when performance on the other three had been taken into account.

Perhaps the most comprehensive study of the perception of emotion in speech by schizophrenic patients is that of Murphy and Cutting (1990). They compared the performance of schizophrenic patients, diagnosed according to Research Diagnostic Criteria, with patients with mania and major depression and normal controls on a series of tests of prosodic comprehension. Subjects listened to a series of sentences presented by audiotape and had to identify the word that had been emphasized (stress prosody) or the emotion that was being conveyed (emotional prosody). The schizophrenic subjects were impaired relative to the normal controls, but were no more impaired than the psychiatric comparison subjects on the comprehension of affective prosody. No group differences were seen on the test of stress prosody.

This suggests that, while impairments in perception of affective prosody may be seen in schizophrenia, these impairments are not specific to the disorder and may occur in other psychiatric disorders as well.

Whittaker, Connell, and Deakin (1994) were unable to replicate these findings. They compared the performance of 16 DSM-III-R schizophrenic patients with that of 11 normal controls on tests of the identification of stress and affective prosody in spoken sentences. In contrast to the earlier experiment, no differences were found in the identification of stress or affective prosody, although, in accordance with the studies described in the preceding section, the patients were impaired in their ability to identify, using a multiple-choice format, the emotion conveyed in posed photographs of faces.

Auditory Affect Perception—Summary

Although a number of studies have suggested that schizophrenic patients show impairments in the perception of emotion in speech, it remains unclear whether these impairments are specific for the disorder and whether the impairments are independent of deficits in the perception of speech more generally.

Summary of Affect Perception Impairments in Schizophrenia

We have reviewed many of the studies examining affect perception in schizophrenia. As we have seen, there has been great variation in experimental design, stimulus materials, and subjects studied. The first question that must be answered is whether there is an impairment in affect perception in schizophrenia. One conclusion that can safely be drawn from the above studies is that schizophrenic patients do have such a deficit, although by no means have all studies shown this. Many of the studies are open to methodological criticism, principally on the grounds of the omission of appropriate nonschizophrenic comparison subjects or control tasks.

Unresolved issues that remain are the basis and specificity of the deficit. One possibility is that affect perception impairments reflect the general cognitive dysfunction found in schizophrenia. One approach to this problem is the inclusion in a study of a control task that makes similar demands to the affect judgment task, but which does not involve affect judgment. Studies that have included such a control task have produced conflicting results, some implying a selective impairment in affect perception and others not. On the basis of the evidence available, we are not able to eliminate the possibility that impairments in face affect perception occur as part of a broader range of impairments involving facial or visuospatial processing.

Much of the work in this area has involved the use of facial stimuli, either static or dynamic. The studies showing impaired comprehension of affective tone in voice stimuli demonstrate that the impairment in affect perception is not confined to faces and the visual modality and indicates that patients may have a central impairment in the interpretation or reporting of affect, which is independent of modality of presentation. Unfortunately, few studies have examined the concordance between affect perception as measured using facial, vocal, and gestural stimuli.

There is conflicting evidence on the relationship of affect perception impairments to clinical state in schizophrenia. Some studies have suggested that impairments are greatest in those with negative symptoms and a chronic course, while in other studies, more acutely ill patients have been most impaired. There have been no stud-

ies examining the variation in affect perception impairments with time, and so we do not know whether affect perception impairments are variable or are a stable consequence of the schizophrenic illness. Similarly, we have only indirect information about the effects, either beneficial or detrimental, of medication on affect perception impairments. What can be said with certainty is that the heterogeneity of schizophrenia with regard to symptoms and cognitive dysfunction is true also of performance on tests of affect perception.

SOCIAL KNOWLEDGE AND SCHIZOPHRENIA

We will consider social knowledge in two ways. First, we will consider social knowledge as the information that we possess, without consciously recognizing it, that allows us to interact effectively with one another. There have been many studies examining social knowledge and social skills in healthy individuals and in patients with neurological impairments. The interested reader is referred to Baron and Bryne (1981) and Damasio et al. (1990).

Second, we will consider the relationship of social knowledge to real-world knowledge, as described by Cutting and Murphy (1990) and to semantic memory, as described by McKenna, Mortimer, and Hodges (1994).

Social Knowledge and Interaction in Schizophrenia

Corrigan and colleagues examined the ability of patients with schizophrenia to perceive and act on social cues and to abstract information about others from these cues. In the first study (Corrigan, Wallace, & Green, 1992), the relationship between social schemata and general, nonsocial information processing was examined. Corrigan et al. (1992) defined social schemata as "templates through which incoming social information is encoded and blueprints by which social behaviors are guided" (p. 129). He used two tests of social schemata: (1) a social recognition test, in which subjects had to distinguish appropriate from inappropriate responses in social situations, and (2) a social sequencing task, in which subjects were required to place a list of actions in the most appropriate sequence to permit a social interaction to be completed. Thirty schizophrenic patients and 15 healthy controls completed these tests and a neuropsychological test battery. No significant differences were found between patients and control subjects on any of the social schemata subtests. However, after the scores from the social schemata tests were combined, the patients with schizophrenia were found to have performed more poorly than the control subjects. Performance on the two social schemata tests was significantly correlated. Patient performance on a digit span test (a measure of working memory) significantly predicted social sequencing, whereas scores on a continuous performance test (a measure of the ability to sustain focused attention) significantly predicted social recognition.

In a second study Corrigan (Corrigan & Green, 1993) showed 24 patients with schizophrenia and 15 healthy controls videos of eight interpersonal situations. Patients were less sensitive to social cues from the videos than control subjects, and this was particularly so for abstract cues, rather than more concrete cues.

Both of these studies used imaginative means of assessing an individual's understanding of a social situation and ability to apply social knowledge to that situation. However, patients were not well matched with controls for educational level, and no measure of current or premorbid IQ was included in analyses. Consequently, we do not know from this study whether patients were impaired on measures of social knowledge simply because of educational disadvantage and illness-related intellectual decline.

Corrigan addressed the issue of the relationship between intellectual level and social knowledge in 1994 (Corrigan, 1994). Forty-three inpatients and outpatients suffering from schizophrenia and schizoaffective disorder completed the social cue recognition test described above, together with a measure of verbal intelligence. Verbal intelligence was not associated with accuracy in the recognition of social cues, but performance on the social cue test series as a whole did correlate with verbal intelligence. The performance of the patients was compared with that of control subjects from previous studies. Differences in social cue perception between schizophrenic patients and control subjects remained after controlling for current verbal IQ, suggesting that the impairments in this ability that are found in schizophrenia do not simply reflect general cognitive impairment.

Corrigan has developed his concept of social schema further and examined social understanding in patients with schizophrenia with respect to symptom profile and cognitive profile. In a recent study, Corrigan (1995) repeated his social sequencing tests on patients with schizophrenia and healthy controls. In addition, he developed short (easy) and long (complex) versions of this test. This

was to permit an examination of the effects of task complexity on social understanding. Symptoms were recorded using the Brief Psychiatric Rating Scale (BPRS), and these scores were factor analyzed to give composite factors approximating to clusters of positive symptoms ("thinking disturbance") and negative symptoms ("withdrawal/retardation").

Compared with controls, patients were relatively less impaired on the short version of the social sequencing task than on the long version, supporting the idea that complexity of task is important in schizophrenic patient performance. Patients scores on the social sequencing tasks correlated inversely with the withdrawal/retardation factor, but not with the thinking disturbance factor, which supports the view of Liddle (1987) and others that negative symptoms are particularly associated with social impairments in schizophrenia.

Penn et al. (1993) also studied the relationship between social cognitive information processing and cognitive function. Patients with schizophrenia were compared with both normal controls and importantly, nonschizophrenic psychiatric patients. Patients were assessed when acutely ill and 3 months later when their acute symptoms had partly resolved. Improvement in patients' symptoms was associated with an improvement in general information processing, but a corresponding improvement in social information processing was not found. In contrast, depressed patients showed improvements with recovery in both social and nonsocial information processing.

These results provide some evidence that, while the deficits in social cognitive information processing in depression show variability with clinical state, the corresponding deficits in schizophrenia may be relatively stable. The issue of stability of social cognitive deficits can only be resolved by further studies examining the relationship between social cognitive deficits and fluctuations in symptoms over time.

Carini and Nevid (1992) used role plays of appropriate and inappropriate social interactions, shown to 16 schizophrenic patients, 16 nonschizophrenic psychiatric controls, and 16 healthy controls. Patients with schizophrenia correctly recognized when the social behavior of others was not appropriate, but did not recognize when their own social behavior was inappropriate. Recently, Frith (1992) has described how many of the symptoms of schizophrenia can be understood as arising from deficits in the monitoring of one's own actions and in the adjustment of these actions in the light of new information. Carini's results, therefore, are consistent with this theory.

Corcoran and Frith (1994) studied the ability of schizophrenic patients to understand verbal hints, or indirect requests for action. Schizophrenic patients were found to be impaired in understanding the "real" intentions or wishes that the hints expressed, and the degree of this impairment was found to be related to the presence of schizophrenic symptoms. Essentially, patients with schizophrenia seemed to have lesser sensitivity to subtle social cues.

Of course, a major difficulty is that these experiments were performed under laboratory conditions and not in the real world. There may be little correspondence between the ability to function in a simulated, or imagined, social situation and the ability to participate in a real one.

The evidence reviewed above suggests that patients with schizophrenia are less effective as agents in social situations. Is this because of general cognitive impairments, or might social impairments represent key symptoms in their own right? Bellack et al. (1989) suggests that impaired social functioning is a cardinal symptom of schizophrenia, but that its relationship to general cognitive impairments is less clear.

How does this relate to social knowledge? Clearly, impaired social functioning will impinge on the ability to interact and therefore develop useful social schema. In social situations feedback from others may not be monitored or recognized and not reinforce what might otherwise have been a useful social strategy if effectively executed.

Laboratory conditions do not accurately reflect real life, and general cognitive factors may impinge on laboratory social situations more than real-life situations. Most studies address social knowledge by presenting subjects with vignettes or videos, essentially removing from the interaction many factors that might otherwise be involved (e.g., arousal). Finally, there is often a marked discrepancy between what people say they would do in a given social circumstance and what they actually do (Baron & Berne, 1981).

Social Knowledge, Real-World Knowledge,
and Semantic Memory

The concept of social knowledge can be expanded to include what might colloquially be referred to as commonsense. Cutting (1985) commented that patients with schizophrenia seem to lack or lose commonsense knowledge about their immediate social world or culture. Cutting and Murphy (1990) studied patients' knowledge about their culture and social world, referring to this concept as "real-world knowledge." Patients with schizophrenia were compared with patients with mania, depressed patients, and

healthy controls on a multiple-choice questionnaire, in which they were asked to select the most likely response to an event, (e.g., seeing a fight in the street). Patients with schizophrenia were significantly impaired relative to other psychiatric patients. In particular, schizophrenic patients were more impaired on this task than manic patients, indicating that the schizophrenic patients impairments were not due simply to nonspecific effects of psychosis.

How real-world knowledge relates to other aspects of cognitive functioning is not clear. If we conceptualize social schema as cognitive structures that guide our responses to social situations, we need to consider the conceptual cognitive store in which all these structures are organized—semantic memory. McKenna and colleagues (Tamlyn et al., 1992) have developed the episodic memory–semantic memory distinction described by Tulving (1972) and applied it to patients with schizophrenia. Tulving distinguished knowledge about oneself and autobiographical information (episodic memory) from knowledge about facts and the world (semantic memory). According to this group, semantic memory in schizophrenia is not only impaired, but also anomalous, which means that, in addition to the knowledge store itself being abnormal, it is used in an abnormal way.

This leads to the suggestion that loss of and anomalous use of the semantic store might underlie social knowledge deficits and perhaps subsequent impairments of social interaction. This is a hypothesis that merits testing.

This speculation takes our debate a step further and begs the question of how impairments of social knowledge might relate to symptom profile. Again, this has yet to be adequately examined. Deficits in social skills are a feature of many clinical rating scales. If the processes involved have been modeled correctly, then social impairments, as measured by clinical rating scales, should be reflected in impairments on laboratory measures of social knowledge and social skills. Penn's study, which has been described above, indicates that there is a stability of impairments in social knowledge over short periods of time, regardless of fluctuations in clinical state, but little is known about the relationship of these deficits to specific symptoms or their stability over longer periods of time.

Social Knowledge
and Schizophrenia—Summary

In summary, schizophrenic patients have been shown to have deficits in the deployment of social skills. To what extent this is a direct consequence of an overall impairment in cognitive functioning remains uncertain.

Many patients suffering from schizophrenia are impaired socially, and social impairments have been viewed as key elements of the disorder. The mechanisms by which impairments in the use of social knowledge contribute to the development of problems in social interaction and symptoms of schizophrenia have still to be defined. Many questions still need to be addressed, and these will be considered further in our conclusions.

CONCLUSIONS

Impairments of affect perception and social knowledge are found in patients suffering from schizophrenia. These impairments have been described in patients with acute, chronic, and remitted forms of the disorder. There is tentative evidence to suggest that similar impairments are also found in individuals who later go on to develop schizophrenia, before the emergence of overt psychosis.

Both positive and negative symptoms may be understood in terms of impairments of affect perception and the use of social knowledge. Dysfunction of affect perception, compounded by impairments in the use of social knowledge, may cause misreading of social and affective cues, leading to development and persistence of ideas of persecution. Impairments in these functions may lead to a patient being unable to recognize the social overtures of others and consequently failing to respond appropriately to them. In comparison with many alternative explanations of the development of the symptoms of schizophrenia, formulations of this sort have the advantage of being able to explain the coexistence of both positive and negative symptoms in the same patient. Unfortunately, however, these hypotheses have yet to be adequately tested, and we do not know whether social and affective impairments are causes of symptoms in schizophrenia or are themselves symptoms of the disorder.

Schizophrenia is a heterogeneous disorder, and we still cannot be sure whether schizophrenia is one disorder or several. Consequently, we have no reason to assume that these impairments, even if etiologically significant in the development of some symptoms, will be found in all patients. The relationship of these impairments to general cognitive functioning, symptom profile, and other factors such as duration of illness, medication, and other psychiatric disorders remains unclear.

Many of the studies reviewed have used imaginative methods to address impairments in social knowledge and affect perception in schizophrenia. In comparison with social knowledge, abnormalities of affect perception, especially face affect perception, have received relatively more attention. A problem with some of the research has been a failure to define precisely what is being measured. This means that tests may not be measuring what they are intended to measure. In addition, patients with schizophrenia are known to have impairments of general cognitive functioning, and it is not clear how to separate tasks measuring general, nonsocial cognitive processing from tests designed to measure social and affective information processing. Amotivation, inattention, and lethargy are commonly found in groups of schizophrenic patients and are therefore likely to impinge on test performance, regardless of study design.

The majority of studies reviewed above were conducted in the laboratory. The degree to which laboratory procedures model the real world is not clear. Furthermore, experimental material presented to subjects in studies is usually from a single modality and is static. A patient might be asked to comment on a photograph or a short vignette, whereas in real life social and affective interactions between people occur quickly and involve more than one modality.

Face and vocal stimulus material has usually been provided by actors generating affects or role players playing out social interactions. The correspondence between acted and genuine affects when used in experiments is not clear. Likewise, experiments in which patients are asked to role play social interactions may be assessing patients' ability to act rather than their behavior in a social situation.

Now that research has established that many patients with schizophrenia do have impairments of social knowledge and affect perception, new studies are needed to help us understand the relationship of these impairments to the symptoms, cognitive abilities, and social functioning of patients in the real world. First, well-characterized groups of patients should be compared on the basis of symptoms (e.g., positive and negative symptoms, delusions and amotivation) as well as diagnostic syndromes (schizophrenia, affective disorder).

Second, the effects on general cognitive function of antipsychotic and anticholinergic medications, which are used to treat most patients at some point during their illnesses, are not yet well understood (see Cassens et al., 1990 for a review). Even less is known about the effects of these medications on impairments of social knowledge and affect perception.

Third, long-term follow-up studies will allow an assessment of the progression of social and affective impairments over time, both in groups of patients and in patients individually. This would allow us to answer the crucial question of whether impairments of affect perception and social knowledge improve, either sponta-neously or as a result of therapy.

What are the implications of these deficits for the treat-ment of schizophrenia? If deficits in social knowledge and affect perception are fixed, core components of schizo-phrenia, then what are the implications for rehabilitation and therapy? Fixed deficits need not preclude the possi-bility of therapeutic intervention, for example, in attempt-ing to prevent the development of additional deficits that might compound the difficulties faced by the patient. Whether social and affect processing deficits are symp-toms or a cause of symptoms should not, in itself, influ-ence the provision of remedial therapy. The teaching of social skills, for example, is a form of therapy that does not rely on a distinction between symptom and etiological factor. However, we do not know how well social skills, if learned in a therapeutic environment, are generalized to the real world.

Until we have a better understanding of the cognitive dysfunction that underlies deficits of affect perception and social knowledge, it may be more worthwhile to concen-trate therapeutic effort on environmental manipulation, rather than attempting to induce changes within our pa-tients. A precedent for this approach is the reduction in re-lapse rates following manipulation of expressed emotion in a patient s home, even though the mechanisms by which high expressed emotion causes relapse are not clear.

The studies reviewed in this chapter represent a promis-ing beginning to understanding the relationship between social and affect impairments and the problems facing people with schizophrenia. Despite the volume of studies, there are still many unanswered questions. The goal of re-search in this area must be to fully appreciate the interac-tion of impairments in social knowledge, affect percep-tion, and general cognition, so as to better understand the symptoms and social difficulties of our patients.

REFERENCES

Alpert, M., & Rosen, A. (1990). A semantic analysis of the ways that the terms "affect", "emotion" and "mood" are used. *Journal of Communication Disorders, 23*, 237–246.

Archer J., Hay D. C., & Young, A. W. (1992). Face processing in psychiatric conditions. *British Journal of Clinical Psychol-ogy, 31*, 45–61.

Archer, J., Hay, D. C., & Young, A. W. (1994). Movement, face processing and schizophrenia: Evidence of a differential deficit in expression analysis. *British Journal of Clinical Psy-chology, 33*, 517–528.

Balogh, D. W., & Leventhal, D. B. (1982). The use of temporal and amplitude cues by schizophrenics, psychiatric controls and aged normals in auditory lateralization. *Journal of Nervous and Mental Diseases, 170*, 553–560.

Balogh, D. W., Schuck, J. R., & Leventhal, D. B. (1979). A study of schizophrenics' ability to localize the source of sound. *Jour-nal of Nervous and Mental Disease, 167*, 484–487.

Baron, R. A., & Byrne, D. (1981). *Social psychology: Under-standing human interaction*, 3rd ed. Boston: Allyn & Bacon.

Bellack, A. S., Morrison, R. L., & Mueser, K. T. (1989). Social problem solving in schizophrenia. *Schizophrenia Bulletin, 15*, 101–116.

Bemporad, J. R. (1967). Perceptual disorders in schizophrenia. *American Journal of Psychiatry, 123*, 971–976.

Bentall, R. P. (1994). Cognitive biases and abnormal beliefs: To-wards a model of persecutory delusions In A. S. David & J. C. Cutting (Eds.), *The neuropsychology of schizophrenia* (pp. 337–360). Hove, UK: Erlbaum.

Berndl, K., von Cranach, M., & Grüsser O.-J. (1986). Impairment of perception and recognition of faces, mimic expression and gestures in schizophrenic patients. *European Archives of Psy-chiatry and Neurological Science, 235*, 282–291.

Borod, J. C., Martin, C. C., Alpert, M., Brozgold, A., & Welkowitz, J. (1993). Perception of facial emotion in schizo-phrenic and right brain-damaged patients. *Journal of Nervous and Mental Disease, 181*, 494–502.

Bruder, G. E., Sutton, S., Babkoff, H., Gurland, B. J., Yozawitz, A., & Fleiss, J. L. (1975). Auditory signal detectability and fa-cilitation of simple reaction time in psychiatric patients and nonpatients. *Psychological Medicine, 5*, 260–272.

Carey, S. (1992). Becoming a face expert. *Philosophical Trans-actions of the Royal Society of London, Series B, 335*, 95–103.

Carini, M. A., & Nevid, J. S. (1992). Social inappropriateness and impaired perspectives in schizophrenia. *Journal of Clini-cal Psychology, 48*, 170–177.

Cassens, G., Inglis, A. K., Applebaum, P. S., & Gutheil, T. G. (1990). Neuroleptics: Effects on neuropsychological function in chronic schizophrenic patients. *Schizophrenia Bulletin, 16*, 477–494.

Corcoran, R., Frith, C. D. (1994). Theory of mind in schizo-phrenia. *Schizophrenia Research, 11(2) Special Issue*, 155–156.

Corrigan, P. W. & Addis, I. B. (1995). The effects of cognitive complexity on a social sequencing task in schizophrenia. *Schizophrenia Research, 16*, 137–144.

Corrigan, P. W. (1994). Social cue perception and intelligence in schizophrenia. *Schizophrenia Research, 13*, 73–79.

Corrigan, P. W., & Green, M. F. (1993). Schizophrenic patients' sensitivity to social cues: The role of abstraction. *American Journal of Psychiatry, 150*, 589–594.

Corrigan, P. W., Wallace, C. J., & Green, M. F. (1992). Deficits in social schemata in schizophrenia. *Schizophrenia Research, 8*, 129–135.

Cramer, P., Bowen, J., & O'Neill, M. (1992). Schizophrenics and social judgment. Why do schizophrenics get it wrong? *British Journal of Psychiatry, 160*, 481–487.

Cramer, P., Weegman, M., & O'Neill, M. (1989). Schizophrenia and the perception of emotions: How accurately do schizo-phrenics judge the emotional states of others? *British Journal of Psychiatry, 155,* 225–228.

Crookes, T. G., & Hutt, S. J. (1970). Perception of hidden figures by neurotic and schizophrenic patients. *British Journal of Psychiatry, 116,* 335–336.

Cutting, J. (1981). Judgment of emotional expression in schizo-phrenics. *British Journal of Psychiatry, 139,* 1–6.

Cutting, J. (1985). *The psychology of schizophrenia,* 1st ed. Edinburgh: Churchill Livingstone.

Cutting, J. (1990). *The right cerebral hemisphere and psychiatric disorders.* Oxford: Oxford University Press.

Cutting, J., & Murphy, D. (1990). Impaired ability of schizo-phrenics, relative to manics or depressives to appreciate social knowledge about their culture. *British Journal of Psychiatry, 157,* 335–338.

Damasio, A. R., Tranel, D., & Damasio, H. (1990). Individuals with sociopathic behavior caused by frontal damage fail to re-spond autonomically to social stimuli. *Behavioral Brain Research, 41,* 81–94.

Dougherty, F. E., Bartlett, E. S., & Izard, C. E. (1974). Responses of schizophrenics to expressions of the fundamental emotions. *Journal of Clinical Psychology, 30,* 243–246.

Ellis, H. D. (1992). The development of face processing skills. *Philosophical Transactions of the Royal Society of London, Series B, 335,* 105–111.

Ekman, P., & Friesen, W.V. (1975). *Unmasking the face.* Englewood Cliffs, NJ: Prentice Hall.

Ekman, P., Friesen, W. V., & Ellsworth, P. (1972). *Emotions in the human.* Elstead, NY: Pergamon Press.

Feinberg, T. E., Rifkin, A., Schaffer, C., & Walker, E. (1986). Facial discrimination and emotional recognition in schizo-phrenia and affective disorders. *Archives of General Psychiatry, 43,* 276–279.

Frith, C. D. (1992). *The cognitive neuropsychology of schizo-phrenia.* Hove, UK: Erlbaum.

Frith, C. D., Stevens, M., Johnstone, E. C., Owens, D. C., & Crow, T. J. (1983). Integration of schematic faces and other complex objects in schizophrenia. *Journal of Nervous and Mental Disease, 171,* 34–39.

Gessler, S., Cutting, J., Frith, C. D., & Weinman, J. (1989). Schizophrenic inability to judge emotion: A controlled study. *British Journal of Clinical Psychology, 28,* 19–29.

Gruzelier, J., & Hammond, N. (1979). Lateralized auditory pro-cessing in medicated and unmedicated schizophrenic patients. In J. Gruzelier, & P. Flor-Henry (Eds.), *Hemisphere asymme-tries of function in psychpathology,* (pp. 603–636). Amster-dam: Elsevier.

Gur, R. C., Erwin, R. J., Gur, R. E., Zwil, A. S., Heimberg, C., & Kraemer, H. C. (1992). Facial emotion discrimination: II. Be-havioral findings in depression. *Psychiatry Research, 42,* 241–251.

Haskins, B., Shutty, M. S., & Kellog, E. (1995). Affect process-ing in chronically psychotic patients: Development of a reli-able assessment tool. *Schizophrenia Research, 15,* 291–297.

Heimberg, C., Gur, R. E., Erwin, R. J., Shtasel, D. L., & Gur, R. C. (1992). Facial emotion discrimination: III. Behavioral findings in schizophrenia. *Psychiatry Research, 42,* 253–265.

Hellewell, J. S. E., Connell, J., & Deakin, J. F. W. (1994). Affect judgment and facial recognition memory in schizophrenia. *Psychopathology, 27,* 255–261.

Hemsley, D. R., & Zawada, S. L. (1976). Filtering and the cog-nitive deficit in schizophrenia. *British Journal of Psychiatry, 128,* 456–461.

Hobson, R. P. (1995). *Autism and the development of mind.* Hove, UK: Erlbaum.

Hobson, R. P., Ouston, J., & Lee, A. (1988). What's in a face? The case of autism. *British Journal of Psychology, 79,* 441–453.

Hollis, C. (1995). Childhood and adolescent (juvenile onset) schizophrenia: A case control study of premorbid develop-mental impairments. *British Journal of Psychiatry, 166,* 484–495.

Iscoe, I., & Veldman, D. J. (1963). Perception of an emotional continuum by schizophrenics, normal adults and children. *Journal of Clinical Psychology, 19,* 272–276.

Izard, C. (1959). Paranoid schizophrenic and normal subjects' perception of photographs of human faces. *Journal of Con-sulting Psychology, 23,* 119–124.

Izard, C. E. (1971). *The face of emotion.* New York: Appleton-Century-Crofts.

Jonsson, C.-O., & Sjöstedt, A. (1973). Auditory perception in schizophrenia: A second study of the intonation test. *Acta Psy-chiatrica Scandinavica, 49,* 588–600.

Joseph, P. L. A., Sturgeon, D. A., & Leff, J. (1992). The percep-tion of emotion by schizophrenic patients. *British Journal of Psychiatry, 161,* 603–609.

Kirkpatrick, B., & Buchanan, R. W. (1990). The neural basis of the deficit syndrome of schizophrenia. *Journal of Nervous and Mental Disease, 178,* 545–555.

Kolb, B., & Whishaw, I. (1990). *Fundamentals of human neu-ropsychology,* 3rd ed. New York: Freeman.

La Russo, L. (1978). Sensitivity of paranoid patients to nonver-bal cues. *Journal of Abnormal Psychology, 87,* 463–471.

Levin, H. S., & Benton, A. L. (1977). Facial recognition in "pseudoneurological" patients. *Journal of Nervous and Mental Disease, 164,* 135–138.

Levy, L., Orr, T. B., & Rosenzweig, S. (1960). Judgment of emo-tion from facial expressions by college students, mental retar-dates and mental hospital patients. *Journal of Personality, 28,* 342–349.

Liddle, P. F. (1987). Schizophrenic syndromes, cognitive perfor-mance and neurological dysfunction. *Psychological Medicine, 17,* 49–57.

Mandal, M. K., & Palchoudhury, S. (1985). Decoding of facial affect in schizophrenia. *Psychological Reports, 56,* 651–652.

McKenna, P. J., Mortimer, A. M., & Hodges, J. R. (1994). Se-mantic memory and schizophrenia. In A. S. David & J. C. Cut-ting (Eds.), *The neuropsychology of schizophrenia.* (pp. 163–178). Hove, UK: Erlbaum.

Morrison R. L., Bellack, A. S., & Mueser, K. T. (1988). Deficits in facial-affect recognition and schizophrenia. *Schizophrenia Bulletin, 14,* 67–83.

Murphy, D., & Cutting, J. (1990). Prosodic comprehension and expression in schizophrenia. *Journal of Neurology, Neurosurgery and Psychiatry, 53,* 727–730.

Muzekari, L. H., & Bates, M. E. (1977). Judgment of emotion among chronic schizophrenics. *Journal of Clinical Psychology, 33,* 662–666.

Neufeld, R. W. J. (1976). Relationship between conceptual judgments and stimulus dimensions among schizophrenics and normals. *British Journal of Social and Clinical Psychology, 15,* 85–91.

Nielzen, S., & Cesarec, Z. (1982). Emotional experience of music by psychiatric patients compared with normal subjects. *Acta Psychiatrica Scandinavica, 65,* 450–460.

Novic, J., Luchins, D. J., & Perline, R. (1984). Facial affect recognition in schizophrenia: Is there a differential deficit? *British Journal of Psychiatry, 144,* 533–537.

Parnas, J., Schulsinger, F., Schulsinger, H., Mednick, S. A., & Teasdale, T. W. (1982). Behavioral precursors of schizophrenia spectrum. *Archives of General Psychiatry, 39,* 658–664.

Penn, D. L., Van der Does, A. J. W., Spaulding, W. D. Garbin, C. P., Linszen, D., & Dingemans, P. (1993). Information processing and social cognitive problem solving in schizophrenia (assessment of interrelationships and changes over time). *Journal of Nervous and Mental Disease, 180,* 13–20.

Pilowsky, I., & Bassett, D. (1980). Schizophrenia and the response to facial emotions. *Comprehensive Psychiatry, 21,* 236–244.

Pollard, V. B., Hellewell, J. S. E., & Deakin, J. F. W. (1995). Performance of schizophrenic subjects on tests of recognition memory, perception and face processing. *Schizophrenia Research, 15,* 122.

Rappaport, M., Hopkins, H. K., Silverman, J., & Hall, K. (1972). Auditory signal detection in schizophrenics. *Psychopharmacologia, 24,* 6–28.

Reich, S. S., & Cutting, J. (1982). Picture perception and abstract thought in schizophrenia. *Psychological Medicine, 12,* 91–96.

Ross, E. D. (1981). The aprosodias: functional anatomic organization of the affective components of language in the right hemisphere. *Archives of Neurology, 38,* 561–569.

Ross, E. D., & Mesulam M. M. (1979). Dominant language functions of the right cerebral hemisphere, ? : Prosody and emotional gesturing. *Archives of Neurology, 38,* 144–148.

Schwartz, B. D., Place, E. J., & Gilmore, G. C. (1980). Perceptual organization in schizophrenia. *Journal of Abnormal Psychology, 89,* 409–418.

Shapiro, R. M. (1993). Regional neuropathology in schizophrenia: Where are we? Where are we going? *Schizophrenia Bulletin, 10,* 187–239.

Simon, B., Holzberg, J. D., Alessi, S. L., & Garrity, D. A. (1951).

The recognition and acceptance of mood in music by psychotic patients. *Journal of Nervous and Mental Disease, 114,* 66–78.

Spiegel, D. E., Gerard, R. M., Grayson, H. M., & Gengerelli, J. A. (1962). Reactions of chronic schizophrenic patients and college students to facial expressions and geometric forms. *Journal of Clinical Psychology, 18,* 396–402.

Spitzer, R., Endicott, J., & Robins, E. (1975). Research Diagnostic Criteria Instrument Number 58. New York State Psychiatric Institute, New York.

Straube, E. (1975). Experimente zur wahrnehmung schizophrener. *Archiv für Psychiatrie und Nervenkrankheiten, 220,* 139–158.

Tamlyn, D., McKenna, P. J., Mortimer, A. M., Lund, C. E., Hammond, S., & Baddeley, A. D. (1992). Memory impairment in schizophrenia: Its extent, affiliations and neuropsychological character. *Psychological Medicine, 22,* 187–239.

Tulving, E. (1972). Episodic and semantic memory. In E. Tulving and W. Donaldson (Eds.), *Organization of memory,* (pp. 381–403). New York: Academic Press.

Turner, J. B. (1964). Schizophrenics as judges of vocal expressions of emotional meaning. In J. R. Davis (Ed.), *The communication of emotional meaning,* (pp. 129–142). New York: McGraw-Hill.

Walker, E., Marwitt, S. J., & Emory, E. (1980). A cross-sectional study of emotion recognition in schizophrenics. *Journal of Abnormal Psychology, 89,* 428–436.

Walker, E., McGuire, M., & Bettes, B. (1984). Recognition and identification of facial stimuli by schizophrenics and patients with affective disorders. *British Journal of Psychiatry, 23,* 37–44.

Walker, E. F., Grimes, K. E., Davis, D. M., & Smith, A. J. (1993). Childhood precursors of schizophrenia: Facial expressions of emotion. *American Journal of Psychiatry, 150,* 1654–1660.

Whittaker, J. F., Connell, J., & Deakin, J. F. W. (1994). Receptive and expressive social communication in schizophrenia. *Psychopathology, 27,* 262–267.

Wing, J. K., & Brown, G. W. (1961). Social treatment of chronic schizophrenia: A comparative survey of three mental hospitals. *Journal of Mental Science, 107,* 847–861.

Wolff, S., Townshend, R., McGuire, R. J., & Weeks, D. J. (1991). Schizoid personality in childhood and adult life: II. the continuity with schizotypal personality disorder. *British Journal of Psychiatry, 154,* 620–624.

Young, A. W., Aggleton, J. P., Hellawell, D. J., & Johnson, M. (1995). Face processing impairments after anygdalotomy. *Brain, 118,* 15–24.

Zuckerman, M., Libets, M. S., Koivumaki, J. H., & Rosenthal, R. (1975). Encoding and decoding nonverbal cues of emotion. *Journal of Personality and Social Psychology, 32,* 1065–1076.

Zuroff, D. C., & Colussy, S. A. (1986). Emotion recognition in schizophrenic and depressed patients. *Journal of Clinical Psychology, 42,* 411–417.

CHAPTER 13

COGNITIVE FACTORS AND SOCIAL ADJUSTMENT IN SCHIZOPHRENIA

David L. Penn
Patrick W. Corrigan
J. Meg Racenstein

Individuals with schizophrenia have impairments in a number of areas of functioning, ranging from neurochemical imbalance to difficulties in role performance (Spaulding, 1986). Two areas in particular—cognitive factors and social adjustment—have been of great interest to clinical researchers and experimental psychopathologists. Interestingly, although volumes of research have been conducted on each area separately, it has only been in the last 5 years that the relationship between these two domains has been systematically addressed (Green, 1996).

Understanding the relationship between cognitive factors and adjustment has both theoretical and clinical value. A number of investigators have proposed models of social competence in schizophrenia that posit a critical role for cognitive factors (Liberman et al., 1986; Spaulding, Storms, Goodrich, & Sullivan, 1986; Trower, Bryant, & Argyle, 1978); social dysfunction is a result, in part, of deficits in the perception, processing, and representation of stimulus information. Furthermore, cognitive rehabilitation assumes that normalizing cognitive deficits will affect behavioral functioning (Brenner, Hodel, Roder, & Corrigan, 1992; Flesher, 1990; Stuve, Erickson, & Spaulding, 1991). Functional autonomy between cognition and social functioning may render cognitive rehabilitation a domain-specific intervention with limited implications for real-world behavior (Bellack, 1992; Hogarty & Flesher, 1992; Liberman & Green, 1992; Penn, 1991).

The purpose of this chapter is to summarize extant research regarding the role of cognitive factors in the social adjustment of individuals with schizophrenia. This chapter will focus on the relationship between performance on these laboratory-based information-processing tasks with various indices of social adjustment. The ensuing sections will describe the relationship of cognitive factors to social cognition/perception, social problem-solving skills, social skill, behavior in the treatment setting, and community functioning. Because other contributors to this volume have described the role of cognition in skills training/acquisition (Chapter 6) and in the development of behavioral problems among samples who later develop schizophrenia (Chapter 8), discussion of these areas will not be repeated here. The chapter concludes with clinical implications and future research directions.

SOCIAL PERCEPTION

Deficits in social perception have been posited to underlie social dysfunction in schizophrenia; patients who are unable to correctly interpret interpersonal situations will have significant difficulty interacting effectively in these situations (Liberman et al., 1986; Morrison & Bellack, 1981; Morrison, Bellack, & Mueser, 1988). Therefore, identifying cognitive correlates to social perception may have important implications for evincing change at the behavioral level (Corrigan, in press). Two studies have investigated the relationship between indices of social perception and various information-processing tasks. Corrigan, Wallace, and Green (1992) examined the cognitive factors that underlie "social schemata" in schizophrenia. Social schemata were conceptualized as cognitive templates that influence the interpretation and processing of social information (Argyle, Furnham, & Graham, 1981). Corrigan et al. (1992) based part of their assessment of social schemata on script theory (Schank & Abelson, 1977); social situations are comprised of stereotypical behavioral actions in a particular order. For example, the actions that comprise going on a date include meeting the person at his/her house, driving to a restaurant, etc.

Corrigan et al. assessed the relationship between two indices of social schemata (i.e., recognition of component actions and number of actions placed in the correct order [sequencing]) and measures of vigilance, verbal memory, and conceptual flexibility (i.e., Wisconsin Card Sorting Task [WCST]). Analyses revealed positive associations between schema recognition and measures of vigilance and verbal memory; schema sequencing was associated with verbal memory and conceptual flexibility. Thus, a schizophrenic individual's ability to negotiate social situations may be a function of his/her verbal memory and cognitive flexibility.

In a second study, Corrigan, Green, and Toomey (1994) investigated the relationship between social cue recognition and measures of information-processing (i.e., Continuous Performance Test, Span of Apprehension, WCST, and the Rey Auditory Verbal Learning Test). The social cue recognition test (SCRT; Corrigan & Green, 1993) consists of eight videotaped vignettes of two or three people talking. Following each vignette, the subject is instructed to answer 36 true-false questions regarding both concrete cues (e.g., what the person said in the vignette)

and abstract cues (e.g., what the person hoped to achieve in the vignette). Multiple regression analyses revealed that verbal recognition memory and vigilance performance independently predicted performance on the SCRT, accounting for about 65% of the variance. Symptomatology (i.e., BPRS Withdrawal/Retardation) added only 6% variance to the model. Corrigan and colleagues (1994) concluded that social cue perception may be a function of both simple and complex cognitive processes.

The results from Corrigan et al. (1992, 1994) converge on the role of verbal memory in the social perceptual skills of the person with schizophrenia. These findings suggest that adequate social perception is dependent on matching current stimulus input to information represented in verbal memory. Such a formulation is consistent with recent models of information-processing in schizophrenia (e.g., Cohen & Servan-Schreiber, 1993), which posit that intact working memory provides the context in which novel information is interpreted.

To date, only one study has examined the cognitive processes underlying deficits in facial affect recognition, the most widely investigated index of social perception in schizophrenia (reviewed by Morrison et al., 1988). Specifically, Schneider, Gur, Gur, and Shtasel (1995) found that performance on an emotion discrimination task was associated with abstraction and memory skills on a neuropsychological battery. Although a number of studies suggest that affect recognition deficits are part of a generalized cognitive deficit (i.e., affect recognition impairment was related to general, rather than specific cognitive impairment) (reviewed by Penn, Corrigan, Bentall, Racenstein, & Newman, 1997), these studies typically utilized only one cognitive measure (i.e., a facial recognition task). Therefore, whether facial-affect recognition is differentially related to measures of information-processing has yet to be conclusively determined. If differential correlations are observed, then the hypothesis that affect recognition reflects generalized cognitive impairment would be refuted.

SOCIAL PROBLEM SOLVING

Social problem solving has been hypothesized to be an important aspect of social adjustment (D'Zurilla & Goldfried, 1971; Spivack, Platt, & Shure, 1976). In general, individuals with schizophrenia demonstrate deficits in various aspects of social problem solving, including means-ends thinking (Platt & Spivack, 1972a; 1972b); receiving, processing, and sending skills (Donahoe et al., 1990); and alternative solution generation and evaluation

(Bellack, Sayers, Mueser, & Bennett, 1994). Social problem solving may be especially important in schizophrenia because successfully addressing interpersonal problems could prevent or delay the onset of future relapses.

Four studies have investigated the cognitive correlates to social problem solving-performance. Penn et al. (1993) examined the inter-relationships between an information-processing battery, (Cognitive Laboratory) (Spaulding, Garbin, & Crinean, 1989; Spaulding, Garbin, & Dras, 1989), and social–cognitive problem solving (SCPS) (i.e., means-ends thinking and generation of alternative solutions) among adolescent inpatients with schizophrenia. Subjects were tested within their first month of treatment and approximately 3 months later when symptoms had remitted. Their pattern of correlations was also compared with a sample of depressed patients enrolled in a day-treatment program, so as to determine if the correlational pattern is unique to schizophrenia or typical of psychopathology in general.

Pearson correlations were conducted on information-processing and social problem-solving variables both cross-sectionally and longitudinally. The results of the analyses revealed different correlational patterns for the two groups. For the depressed group, better SCPS at time 1 was associated with better performance on a backward-masking task (i.e., identification of two briefly presented digits immediately followed by a patterned mask [i.e., XX]). Interestingly, at time 2, when symptoms had remitted, none of the correlations were significant. This finding of relative orthogonality between cognition and SCPS was also found in the study's nonclinical control group (i.e., medical students), suggesting that as clinical status stabilizes, the predictive efficiency of information-processing approaches that of normal subjects. Longitudinally, changes in SCPS for depressed subjects were associated with changes in ability to disattend from distracting stimuli. Thus, it was hypothesized that the mechanisms underlying these relationships were sustained attention and effortful processes.

For the group with schizophrenia, better SCPS during symptom exacerbation and remission was associated with an increase in hits and false alarms during a vigilance task. In this task, subjects have to identify a briefly presented target digit (e.g., "4") across three conditions: (1) digits presented one at a time; (2) digits presented in an array of six; (3) digits presented in an array of six with a new target (i.e., the target is switched from "4" to "7"). The association between SCPS and vigilance performance became stronger as task demands increased (i.e., from condition 1 to condition 3). The relationship held during

the longitudinal analyses, with the additional cognitive variable of errors on a card-sorting task (analogous to the Wisconsin Card Sorting Task) being associated with changes in SCPS. Therefore, a liberal response style on a vigilance task (i.e., more likely to both correctly and incorrectly identify digits as the target) was the most consistent correlate of SCPS.

Penn and colleagues (1993) hypothesized that the liberal response style may result from patients compensating for information-processing deficits. For example, compensatory efforts may represent a cognitive barometer of readiness to improve functioning; individuals who have an awareness of their cognitive deficits are more likely to modify cognitive performance to changing task demands. This implicates the role of *metacognition* in the SCPS of individuals with schizophrenia; being able to monitor the match between cognitive performance and task demands may affect ability to generate solutions to interpersonal problems.

Bowen et al. (1994) investigated the cognitive correlates of a different measure of social problem solving, the Assessment of Interpersonal Problem-Solving Skills (AIPSS; Donahoe et al., 1990). The AIPSS is based on Wallace's (1982) sequential model of social problem solving as being comprised of receiving (i.e., identification and articulation of an interpersonal problem), processing (i.e., generation of alternative solutions), and sending skills (i.e., performance of appropriate/effective problem-solving behaviors). Therefore, the AIPSS includes both cognitive and behavioral indices of social problem-solving performance. Bowen et al. (1994) found performance on measures of vigilance (i.e., Span of Apprehension and Continuous Performance Test) to be significantly associated with social problem solving on the AIPPS.

Corrigan and Toomey (1995) extended on the work of Bowen et al. (1994) by assessing the relationship among the AIPSS, measures of vigilance, verbal memory, and cognitive flexibility, and a social cue perception task (Corrigan et al., 1994). Pearson correlational analyses revealed a surprising pattern: The most robust correlate of AIPSS performance was accuracy on social cue perception. The only cognitive variable significantly associated with the AIPSS was verbal memory; receiving and processing skills were both related to recognition memory. Furthermore, the correlation coefficients between AIPSS and social cue perception were significantly larger than the correlations between problem solving and cognitive measures for almost half the comparisons. Thus, social problem solving was more strongly related to social perception than to a range of cognitive measures.

Finally, Bellack et al. (1994) investigated the association between social problem solving during a role-play task with IQ and memory among schizophrenia patients in the latter stages of an acute hospitalization. The findings revealed that better social problem-solving skills were positively related to IQ and logical memory on the Wechsler Memory Scale.

It is difficult to compare the studies reviewed above as they largely differ in samples, studies, and measures utilized. This underscores the need for replication. Presently, research suggests that performance on memory and vigilance tasks is related to social problem-solving skills. At this point, however, it is too early to conclude whether any one type of cognitive process relates more strongly or consistently with social problem solving in schizophrenia than any other measure. Therefore, future work should assess the cognitive correlates (including vigilance, memory, and conceptual tasks) to a range of social problem-solving skills.

SOCIAL SKILL

Social skill is an important factor in the social adjustment of schizophrenia patients (Liberman, DeRisi, & Mueser, 1989). Specifically, social skills are related to global behavior on the ward (Appelo et al., 1992; Penn, Mueser, Doonan, & Nishith, 1995a) and role functioning in the community (Bellack, Morrison, Mueser, Wade, & Sayers, 1990; Bellack, Morrison, Wixted, & Mueser, 1990). Thus, understanding how cognitive variables relate to social skill may have important implications for prognosis.

Penn, Mueser, Spaulding, Hope, and Reed (1995) investigated how information processing correlates to social skill during a 3-minute unstructured role play. Role-play performance was coded for global social skill ("Global"), paralinguistic skills (e.g., speech fluency; "Paralinguistic"), and nonverbal skills (e.g., eye contact; "Nonverbal"). Pearson correlational analyses were conducted on COGLAB and social skill variables. Higher global social competence was associated with better performance on the Continuous Performance/Span of Apprehension (CP/SPAN; i.e., more hits, fewer false alarms) and reaction time tasks (i.e., faster reaction time). Better nonverbal skills were associated with fewer random errors (i.e., non-perseverative) on the card-sorting task. Finally, greater paralinguistic skills were associated with both faster reaction time and fewer random errors on the card-sorting task.

Backward multiple regression analyses revealed that global social skill was significantly predicted by fewer false alarms on the CP/SPAN task. Paralinguistic skill was significantly predicted by faster reaction time. Nonverbal skill was not significantly predicted by any of the COGLAB variables. Findings from the regression analyses remained stable after controlling for the mediating role of "third variables" (e.g., symptomatology). Thus, the associations between COGLAB and social skill could not be explained by demographic or symptom variables.

The findings suggest that better performance on the vigilance task (i.e., more hits, fewer false alarms) is associated with greater global social skill during a role play. Interestingly, the findings appear at odds with those reported by Penn et al. (1993), who found that a liberal response style (more hits and more false alarms) was associated with better social functioning. However, two factors may account for the apparent discrepant findings regarding vigilance false alarms. First, the schizophrenia patients in Penn, Mueser, Spaulding et al. (1995) were a chronic sample, whereas those in Penn et al. (1993) were acutely ill adolescents. Thus, the relationship between information-processing and social skill may be a function of illness chronicity and age of the subjects. Second, the index of social functioning differed across the two studies (i.e., social cognitive problem solving and social skill). Therefore, generative capacity (i.e., more false alarms) may be an important factor in social problem solving, whereas discriminative processing (i.e., more hits, fewer false alarms) may underlie appropriate social performance.

The other significant regression model involved the relationship between better paralinguistic skills and faster reaction time. Perhaps paralinguistic skills, such as frequent pauses, speech dysfluencies, and slow speech rate, are direct reflections of a longer latency to respond during a social encounter. Therefore, this relationship may be mediated by the ability to rapidly respond to stimuli in the environment.

In their discussion, Penn, Mueser, Spaulding et al. (1995) noted that the strength of association between COGLAB and social skill appeared stronger for female than male patients. This was noteworthy given that there were no multivariate gender differences in social skill or information-processing performance. Following more extensive data analysis (Penn, Mueser, & Spaulding, 1996), a differential pattern of correlations across gender was confirmed; COGLAB was related to social skill for female, but not male inpatients with schizophrenia.

This gender effect was also reported by Mueser, Blanchard, and Bellack (1995) who found a significant association between visual memory and social skill (e.g., assertiveness) for only female patients in two samples of subjects. The convergence of findings (i.e., Mueser et al., 1995 and Penn et al., 1996) is noteworthy given that the studies differed in a number of ways: Mueser assessed social skill with a structured role play, whereas Penn used an unstructured format; there was no overlap in the cognitive measures across the two studies (i.e., Mueser focused on memory, whereas Penn examined information-processing measures); the subjects in Mueser had recently experienced an acute exacerbation of symptoms, whereas those in Penn were stabilized, chronically ill inpatients. Thus, the gender finding appears to be quite robust and not a methodological or sample artifact.

Mueser et al. (1995) and Penn et al. (1996) suggest a number of explanations for the gender effects. Mueser raises the possibility that a sampling bias could have produced the differential pattern of correlations; since males have an earlier onset of schizophrenia (Lewine, 1981), the lack of differences between male and female patients in illness chronicity (reported in both studies) could have resulted in a more severely ill sample of female patients in the studies (i.e., relative to those in the general population of female schizophrenia patients). In other words, the issue is not severity of illness per se, but whether the continuum of illness severity differs across gender (i.e., the psychopathology of very ill females compared with less ill females is greater compared with their male cohorts). If gender differences exist in the range of illness severity, statistical equivalence in chronicity might reflect unrepresentative gender samples, thus limiting the generalizability of the findings.

Penn and colleagues raised an alternative interpretation; these findings reflect cognition-behavioral patterns also found in nonclinical samples. Females tend to have superior nonverbal, social perception skills relative to males (Hall, 1984) with these skills being associated with higher ratings of social competence (Costanzo & Archer, 1989). Therefore, the behavior of females, compared with males, may depend more on accurately perceiving and interpreting a given situation. This would require greater reliance on cognitive processes, such as memory (e.g., recalling previous interactions from similar contexts) and problem-solving skills (e.g., assessing whether a given behavioral strategy is received favorably). Thus, the greater role of cognitive processes in the social behavior of females relative to males should also be observed in schizophrenia patients.

The studies reviewed above indicate that cognitive processes are related to the social skills of female schizo-phrenia patients. In particular, vigilance accuracy and visual memory were positively associated with social skill. Once again, performance on vigilance and memory tasks appears to be tapping into significant aspects of social functioning. The gender effect, while theoretically interesting, may also have important implications for treatment. Specifically, cognitive rehabilitation may have a greater effect on social skill acquisition for females with schizophrenia than males. For males, treatment focused on molar skills and role performance may be especially appropriate.

BEHAVIOR IN THE TREATMENT SETTING AND FUNCTIONING IN THE COMMUNITY

The indices of social adjustment discussed thus far have been limited to performance on relatively contrived tasks (e.g., role plays). Performance on such tasks, while important, does not always correspond to naturally occurring behavior (Appelo et al., 1992; Penn, Mueser, Doonan et al., 1995). Therefore, the relationship between cognitive factors and social adjustment may change as assessment moves from the laboratory to natural environment. As a result, findings regarding the cognitive correlates of social skills may not parallel the cognitive correlates of behavior in the treatment setting or community.

The first systematic investigation of this issue was conducted by Spaulding (1978), who compared the performance on a variety of cognitive/perceptual measures (e.g., the Muller-Lyer Illusion; the Object Sorting Task) with ward behavior (the Inpatient Multidimensional Psychiatric Scale; IMPS) in 35 males with severe psychiatric disorders (i.e., 26/35 were diagnosed with schizophrenia). Correlational analyses revealed that the cognitive/perceptual measures were significantly associated with almost one-half of the ward behavior dimensions. Subsequent multiple regression analyses showed that the strongest predictor of hostile and paranoid behavior was perseverative errors on the Wisconsin Card Sorting Task. Spaulding (1978) concluded that the inability to modify conceptual set on a cognitive task may contribute to the clinical manifestation of paranoia. Relatedly, problems in modifying conceptual set, or cognitive flexibility, have been found to be associated with a combined index of ward behavior and symptoms among inpatients with schizophrenia (Dickerson, Ringel, & Boronow, 1991).

Two recent studies have investigated the cognitive correlates to ward behavior among inpatients with schizophrenia. Penn, Spaulding, Reed, and Sullivan (1996) assessed the cross-sectional relationship between COGLAB and social behavior on the ward as indexed by the Nurse's Observational Scale for Inpatient Evaluation (NOSIE–30) for 27 inpatients. This study, like Corrigan and Toomey's (1995) reported earlier, also included measures of social cognition (i.e., social-scripts, empathy, and affect perception task). Consistent with the findings of Corrigan and Toomey (1995), the social–cognitive variables had a more consistent association with ward behavior than the information–processing variables; total errors on a variation of the Wisconsin Card Sorting Task was the only information-processing variable to demonstrate a significant association with ward behavior.

In a more comprehensive study, Spaulding, Penn, and Garbin (in press) examined cross-sectional and longitudinal relationships between information-processing (i.e., COGLAB) and ratings on the NOSIE–30 among 112 chronic inpatients with schizophrenia. Information-processing and ward behavior were assessed on two occasions: during initial entry into psychiatric rehabilitation and approximately 6 months later. At time 1, higher functioning on the ward (i.e., more social competence and neatness, less irritability, psychoticism, and motor retardation) was best predicted by faster reaction time (RT); RT accounted for between 16 and 25% of the variance in the various regression models. At time 2, a similar pattern emerged with two changes: (1) nonperseverative errors on the computer version of the Wisconsin Card Sorting task entered the regression models for neatness and motor retardation; (2) cognitive variables (i.e., RT and nonperseverative errors) now accounted for between 8 and 36% of the variance in ward behavior, representing an increase in variance for 6/7 indices of ward behavior. Spaulding et al. (in press) interpreted the latter finding as being a reflection of patients' ability to respond to the greater cognitive demands associated with psychiatric rehabilitation at 6 months vis-à-vis the initial assessment; demands increase from maintaining personal hygiene and attending a few skill classes to being engaged in an active schedule, working within a token-economy system, and striving to graduate from skill classes.

Analyses of the changes in cognitive functioning with changes in ward behavior yielded a somewhat different picture than the cross-sectional analyses; improved vigilance performance on the vigilance task over 6 months was associated with improved social competence, neatness, and overall ward behavior. This finding is generally consistent with results reported by Penn, Mueser, Spaulding et al. (1995), who found a cross-sectional association between vigilance performance and social skill during an unstructured role play.

In summary, the results of Spaulding et al. (in press) indicate that ward behavior among inpatients with schizophrenia is most strongly predicted (cross-sectionally) by performance on a reaction time task. Reaction time reflects a number of processes, including response latency to stimuli in the environment (i.e., a motor component), sustained attention, and *anticipation* of stimulus onset. The latter process implicates the ability to maintain response "set," long considered an important deficit in schizophrenia (Shakow, 1963). Interestingly, Wykes, Katz, Sturt, and Hemsley (1992) have also found performance on a measure of reaction time to relate to social-behavior in psychiatric placements. Longitudinally, improvement in vigilance performance was associated with improved social-behavioral functioning on the ward. Taken together with findings from previous research (e.g., Penn, Mueser, Spaulding et al., 1995), this suggests that vigilance performance—the ability to accurately identify briefly presented stimuli—has implications for patients' ability to interact with others.

There have also been attempts to assess the relationship of cognitive processes and community functioning/outcome reviewed by Green (1996). Specifically, performance on the Wisconsin Card Sorting task was associated with general social adjustment (Breier, Schreiber, Dyer, & Pickar 1991; Jaeger & Douglas, 1992; Jaeger, Berns, & Douglas, 1992), and work performance (Lysaker, Bell, & Beam-Goulet, 1995). Reaction time predicted changes in dependence on psychiatric care (Wykes, 1994; Wykes Sturt, & Katz, 1990; Wykes et al., 1992), and verbal and visual memory predicted changes in general community functioning (Buchanan, Holstein, & Breier, 1994; Goldman et al., 1993). These findings lend strong support for the hypothesis that cognitive factors play a role, and in some cases, may be a predictive factor, in the community functioning of individuals with schizophrenia.

CONCLUSIONS AND FUTURE DIRECTIONS

This chapter reviewed the literature on the relationship between cognitive factors and social adjustment in schizophrenia. Although quite a few studies have been conducted in this area, there seems to be limited consensus across the findings. This is largely attributable to the differences in cognitive measures (e.g., information-processing versus memory) and indices of social functioning (e.g., social perception versus social skill) that were utilized across investigations. Therefore, the best that can be gleaned from the extant literature are general correlational patterns between cognition and social adjustment.

Table 13.1 summarizes the studies reviewed above. The findings converge on the role of four cognitive factors in the social adjustment of schizophrenia patients: performance on vigilance, verbal memory, reaction time, and conceptual tasks (e.g., Wisconsin Card Sorting Task). Less consistent relationships with social adjustment were found for performance on backward-masking, fluency, and visual memory tasks.

Given these findings, the next question is what processes underlie the observed correlational patterns? Recent models of information-processing suggest that performance on a number of cognitive tasks, such as the (Continuous Performance Test) and WCST, may be explained by working memory (Cohen & Servan-Schreiber, 1993; Goldman-Rakic, 1994). For example, inability to keep the correct concept in memory on the WCST may impair associative learning (i.e., learning the relationship between choosing a particular concept and the examiner's verbal feedback); as a result, fewer concepts are obtained and more response errors occur (Goldman-Rakic, 1994). Moreover, on vigilance tasks, if subjects cannot represent the target digit in memory, then accuracy will be compromised.

The hypothesized central role of working memory in cognitive tasks is consistent with the role of knowledge structures, such as social schemata, exemplars, scripts, and prototypes, in guiding behavior during social interactions (reviewed by Fiske & Taylor, 1991). These knowledge structures involve the representation of social information, the sequence of steps comprising social situations for scripts, and the list of trait attributes associated with certain individuals or groups for social schemata. Thus, individuals do not have to relearn certain behaviors each time they enter a novel social situation (e.g., an office party). Rather, similar situations are brought to mind (e.g., a friend's party) and behaviors, which are consistent across the class of situations, are applied to the novel interaction (e.g., smiling and being conversational). Deficits in the representation of social information may produce behavior that is either inappropriate to a given situation or that is data driven rather than conceptually driven (e.g., responding to certain behaviors in isolation, such as a momentary grimace, rather than a gestalt of the interaction—

the conversant was in a good mood, but had momentary indigestion).

The foregoing suggests that working memory guides our expectations about both cognitive and social information. It facilitates automatic processing of target stimuli, thus freeing up cognitive resources for other tasks. Therefore, behavior that is either overlearned or elicited in familiar situations (or situations that can be compared to those previously encountered) will be automatically demonstrated. Thus, one would expect that correlations between cognitive factors and social adjustment would be lower among individuals with intact working memory than those with memory impairment. Recent findings indicating some orthogonality between different levels of functioning among nonclinical control subjects is consistent with this hypothesis (Mueser et al., 1995; Penn et al., 1993; Toomey, Wallace, Corrigan, Schuldberg, & Green, in press). Interestingly, this leads to the prediction that as cognitive functioning stabilizes in schizophrenia, some functional autonomy between cognitive processes and social behavior may be expected. This hypothesis can be addressed in longitudinal research that includes subjects in both acute and remitted clinical states.

The foregoing suggests a number of future research directions. First, the greater role of cognitive factors in the social adjustment of female compared with male schizophrenia patients requires further investigation. For example, this issue has not been investigated in outpatients. Further, little is known beyond speculation about the causal mechanisms contributing to the gender effects. Second, the role of *social* cognition in social behavior warrants further study (Penn, Corrigan et al., 1997). There is growing evidence that impairments in social cognition have particular importance in understanding both the behavioral and clinical manifestations of schizophrenia (Bentall, Kinderman, & Kaney, 1994; Corrigan & Toomey, 1995; Penn, Spaulding et al., 1996). Specifically, persecutory delusions are associated with the recall of threatening rather than nonthreatening propositions (Kaney, Wolfenden, Dewey, & Bentall, 1992), whereas performance on various social–cognitive tasks (e.g., sequencing of social information, empathy) have a greater association with ward behavior than traditional information-processing measures (Penn, Spaulding et al., 1996). Thus, social–cognitive factors may add important information to cognitive factors in understanding the social adjustment of schizophrenia patients. Finally, most of the aforementioned studies utilized only one measure of social adjustment (e.g., social skill). Studies that include

Table 13.1. Summary of Studies Investigating the Relationships between Cognitive Factors and Social Adjustment in Schizophrenia

STUDY	COGNITIVE MEASURES	COGNITIVE CORRELATES[a]	INDEX OF SOCIAL FUNCTIONING
Bellack et al. (1994)	IQ; WMS	IQ+; Verbal Memory+	Social problem solving
Bowen et al. (1994)	O-CPT; DS-CPT; SPAN; DSDT	O-CPT+; DS-CPT+; SPAN+	Social problem solving
Brier et al. (1991)	WCST; Trails A and B; Verbal Fluency	Perseverative errors; Trails A and B; Verbal Fluency+	Social functioning in the Community
Buchanan et al. (1994)	WMS-R; WCST; Trails A and B; Stroop Test; Visuospatial tasks	WMS-R+	Community functioning
Corrigan et al. (1992)	DS-CPT; DSDT; RAVLT; WCST	Vigilance (Correct)+ Verbal Memory+	Schema recognition
		Verbal Memory+ WCST (Correct)+	Schema recall
Corrigan et al. (1994)	DS-CPT; SPAN; RAVLT; WCST; DSDT	Verbal Memory+ Vigilance (Correct)+	Social perception
Corrigan & Toomey (1995)	DS-CPT; DSDT; RAVLT; WCST	Verbal Memory+	Social problem-solving skill
Goldman et al. (1993)	Block Design; Trails A and B; V; BD; Selective Reminding Test	Selective Memory+	Community functioning
Jaeger et al. (1992)	WCST	WCST (PE)–	Role functioning
Lysaker et al. (1995)	WCST	WCST+	Work performance
Mueser et al.[b] (1995)	WMS and WMS-R	Visual Memory+	Assertiveness
Penn et al. (1993)	COGLAB	Cross-sectional: Vigilance FA+ Longitudinal: Vigilance FA+	SCPS
Penn et al.[b] (1995b)	COGLAB	Vigilance FA– WCST (Random Errors)– Reaction Time (RT)–	Social skill (SS) Nonverbal SS Paralinguistic SS
Penn et al. (1996b)	COGLAB	WCST (Total Errors)–	Ward behavior
Schneider et al. (1995)	Neuropsychological Battery	Abstraction + Memory + Language+ Spatial Organization +	Facial Emotion Discrimination
Spaulding (1978)	Muller-Lyer Object Sorting WCST Dogmatism Scale	Muller-Lyer– Object Sorting– WCST (PE)+ Dogmatism–	Ward behavior problems
Spaulding et al. (in press)	COGLAB	Cross-sectional: RT– Longitudinal: Vigilance FA–	Ward behavior
Wykes et al. (1990); Wykes (1994)	Reaction time	RT– (faster RT)	Movement to more independent psychiatric care
Wykes et al. (1992)	Reaction time	RT+	Social behavior problems

[a] Sign denotes direction of relationship
[b] Correlations were significantly higher for female compared to male subjects
WMS=Wechsler Memory Scale; O-CPT=Target digit "O", Continuous Performance Test; DS-CPT=Degraded Stimulus, Continuous Performance Test; DSDT=Digit Span Distractibilty Test; RAVLT=Rey Auditory Verbal Learning Test; WCST=Wisconsin Card Sorting Task; SPAN=Span of Apprehension; COGLAB=CPT, SPAN, WCST, Reaction Time, Size Estimation, Muller-Lyer; FA=False Alarms; SCPS-=Social Cognitive Problem Solving; PE=Perseverative Errors

comprehensive batteries of both cognition and social adjustment (e.g., social perception, social skill) may yield important information about the pattern of correlations across different levels of social functioning.

The most important direction for future research concerns treatment of social dysfunction in schizophrenia. As memory has been found to relate to both concurrent social adjustment and future social skill acquisition (Mueser, Bellack, Douglas, & Wade, 1991), then skills training may be enhanced by strategies that normalize memory functioning. A recent study has shown that remediation of memory deficits improves social perception among individuals with schizophrenia (Corrigan, Nugent-Hirschbeck, & Wolfe, in press). It seems likely that this kind of cognitive remediation will also lead to improved social adjustment.

Remediation of memory functioning may also affect *generalization* of social skills to novel situations, an oft-cited limitation of most behavioral approaches (reviewed in Mueser & Glynn, 1993). Thus, the next generation of social skills training research needs to determine whether remediation of cognitive deficits, especially those consistently related to social adjustment, augments treatment effectiveness, maintenance, and generalization.

REFERENCES

Appelo, M. T., Woonings, F. M. J., van Nieuwenhuizen, C. J., Emmelkamp, P. M. G., Sloof, C. J., & Louwerens, J. W. (1992). Specific skills and social competence in schizophrenia. *Acta Psychiatrica Scandinavia, 85,* 419–422.

Argyle, M., Furnham, A., & Graham, J. A. (1981). *Social situations.* Cambridge: Cambridge University Press.

Bellack, A. S. (1992). Cognitive rehabilitation for schizophrenia: Is it possible? Is it necessary? *Schizophrenia Bulletin, 18,* 43–50.

Bellack, A. S., Morrison, R. L., Mueser, K. T., Wade, J. H., & Sayers, S. L. (1990). Role play for assessing social competence of psychiatric patients. *Psychological Assessment: Journal of Consulting and Clinical Psychology, 2,* 248–255.

Bellack, A. S., Morrison, R. L., Wixted, J. T., & Mueser, K. T. (1990). An analysis of social competence in schizophrenia. *British Journal of Psychiatry, 156,* 809–818.

Bellack, A. S., Sayers, M., Mueser, K. T., & Bennett, M. (1994). Evaluation of social problem solving in schizophrenia. *Journal of Abnormal Psychology, 103,* 371–378.

Bentall, R. P., Kinderman, P., & Kaney, S. (1994). The self, attributional processes and abnormal beliefs: Towards a model of persecutory delusions. *Behavior Research and Therapy, 32,* 331–341.

Bowen, L., Wallace, C. J., Glynn, S. M., Nuechterlein, K. H.,

Lutzker, J. M., & Kuehnel, T. G. (1994). Schizophrenics' cognitive functioning and performance in interpersonal interactions and skills training procedures. *Journal of Psychiatric Research, 28,* 289–301.

Breier, A., Schreiber, J. L., Dyer, J., & Pickar, D. (1991). National Institute of Mental Health longitudinal study of chronic schizophrenia: Prognosis and predictors of outcome. *Archives of General Psychiatry, 48,* 239–246.

Brenner, H. D., Hodel, B., Roder, V., & Corrigan, P. (1992). Treatment of cognitive dysfunctions and behavioral deficits in schizophrenia. *Schizophrenia Bulletin, 18,* 21–26.

Buchanan, R. W., Holstein, C., & Breier, A. (1994). The comparative efficacy and long-term effect of clozapine treatment on neuropsychological test performance. *Biological Psychiatry, 36,* 717–725.

Cohen, J. D., & Servan-Schreiber, D. (1993). A theory of dopamine function and its role in cognitive deficits in schizophrenia. *Schizophrenia Bulletin, 19,* 85–104.

Corrigan, P. W. (in press). The social perceptual deficits in schizophrenia. Psychiatry.

Corrigan, P. W., & Green, M. F. (1993). Schizophrenic patients' sensitivity to social cues: The role of abstraction. *American Journal of Psychiatry, 150,* 589–594.

Corrigan, P. W., Green, M. F., & Toomey, R. (1994). Cognitive correlates to social cue perception in schizophrenia. *Psychiatry Research, 53,* 141–151.

Corrigan, P. W., Nugent-Hirschbeck, J., & Wolfe, M. (in press). Memory and vigilance training to improve social perception in schizophrenia. *Schizophrenia Research.*

Corrigan, P. W., & Toomey, R. (1995). Interpersonal problem solving and information-processing in schizophrenia. *Schizophrenia Bulletin, 21,* 395–403.

Corrigan, P. W., Wallace, C. J., & Green, M. F. (1992). Deficits in social schemata in schizophrenia. *Schizophrenia Research, 8,* 129–135.

Costanzo, M., & Archer, D. (1989). Interpreting the expressive behavior of others: The Interpersonal Perception Task. *Journal of Nonverbal Behavior, 13,* 225–245.

Dickerson, F. B., Ringel, N. B., Boronow, J. J. (1991). Neuropsychological deficits in chronic schizophrenics: Relationship with symptoms and behavior. *Journal of Nervous and Mental Disease, 179,* 744–749.

Donahoe, C. P., Carter, M. J., Bloem, W. D., Hirsch, G. L., Laasi, N., & Wallace, C. J. (1990). Assessment of interpersonal problem-solving skills. *Psychiatry, 53,* 329–339.

D'Zurilla, T. J., & Goldfried, M. R. (1971). Problem solving and behavior modification. *Journal of Abnormal Psychology, 78,* 107–126.

Fiske, S. T., & Taylor, S. (1991). *Social cognition.* New York: McGraw-Hill.

Flesher, S. (1990). Cognitive habilitation in schizophrenia: A theoretical review and model of treatment. *Neuropsychology Review, 1,* 223–246.

Goldman, R. S., Axelrod, B. N., Tandon, R., Ribeiro, S. C. M.,

Craig, K., & Berent, S. (1993). Neuropsychological prediction of treatment efficacy and one-year outcome in schizophrenia. *Psychopathology, 126,* 122–126.

Goldman-Rakic, P. S. (1994). Working memory dysfunction in schizophrenia. *Journal of Neuropsychiatry and Clinical Neurosciences, 6,* 348–357.

Green, M. F. (1996). What are the functional consequences of neurocognitive deficits in schizophrenia? *American Journal of Psychiatry, 153,* 321–330.

Hall, J. A. (1984). *Nonverbal sex differences: Communication accuracy and expressive style.* Baltimore, MD: Johns Hopkins University Press.

Hogarty, G. E., & Flesher, S. (1992). Cognitive remediation in schizophrenia: Proceed . . . with caution. *Schizophrenia Bulletin, 18,* 51–57.

Jaeger, J., Berns, S., & Douglas, E. (1992). Remediation of neuropsychological deficits in psychiatric populations: Rationale and methodological considerations. *Psychopharmacology Bulletin, 28,* 367–390.

Jaeger, J., & Douglas, E. (1992). Neuropsychiatric rehabilitation for persistent mental illness. *Psychiatric Quarterly, 63,* 71–94.

Kaney, S., Wolfenden, M., Dewey, M. E., & Bentall, R. P. (1992). Persecutory delusions and the recall of threatening and non-threatening propositions. *British Journal of Clinical Psychology, 31,* 85–87.

Lewine, R. R. J. (1981). Sex differences in schizophrenia: Timing or subtype? *Psychological Bulletin, 90,* 432–444.

Liberman, R. P., DeRisi, W. R., & Mueser, K. T. (1989). *Social skills training for psychiatric patients.* Needham Heights, MA: Allyn & Bacon.

Liberman, R. P., & Green, M. F. (1992). Whither cognitive-behavioral therapy for schizophrenia? *Schizophrenia Bulletin, 18,* 27–35.

Liberman, R. P., Mueser, K. T., Wallace, C. J., Jacobs, H. E., Eckman, T., & Massell, H. K. (1986). Training skills in the psychiatrically disabled: Learning coping and competence. *Schizophrenia Bulletin, 12,* 631–647.

Lysaker, P., Bell, M., & Beam-Goulet, J. (1995). Wisconsin card sorting test and work performance in schizophrenia. *Schizophrenia Research, 56,* 45–51.

Morrison, R. L., & Bellack, A. S. (1981). The role of social perception in social skill. *Behavior Therapy, 12,* 69–79.

Morrison, R. L., Bellack, A. S., & Mueser, K. T. (1988). Deficits in facial-affect recognition and schizophrenia. *Schizophrenia Bulletin, 14,* 67–84.

Mueser, K. T., Bellack, A. S., Douglas, M. S., & Wade, J. H. (1991). Prediction of social skill acquisition in schizophrenic and major affective disorder patients from memory and symptomatology. *Psychiatry Research, 37,* 281–296.

Mueser, K. T., Blanchard, J. J., & Bellack, A. S. (1995). Memory and social skill in schizophrenia: The role of gender. *Psychiatry Research, 57,* 141–153.

Mueser, K. T., & Glynn, S. M. (1993). Efficacy of psychotherapy for schizophrenia. In T. R. Giles (Ed.), *Handbook of effective psychotherapy.* (pp. 325–354). New York: Plenum Press.

Penn, D. L. (1991). Cognitive rehabilitation of social deficits in schizophrenia: A direction of promise or following a primrose path? *Psychosocial Rehabilitation Journal, 15,* 27–41.

Penn, D. L., Corrigan, P. W., Bentall, R. P., Racenstein, J. M., & Newman, L. (1997). Social cognition in schizophrenia. *Psychological Bulletin, 121,* 114–132.

Penn, D. L., Mueser, K. T., Doonan, R., & Nishith, P. (1995a). Relations between social skill and ward behavior in chronic schizophrenia. *Schizophrenia Research, 16,* 225–232.

Penn, D. L., Mueser, K. T., & Spaulding, W. D. (1996a). Information processing, social skill, and gender in schizophrenia. *Psychiatry Research, 59,* 213–220.

Penn, D. L., Mueser, K. T., Spaulding, W. D., Hope, D. A., & Reed, D. (1995b). Information-processing and social competence in chronic schizophrenia. *Schizophrenia Bulletin, 21,* 269–281.

Penn, D. L., Spaulding, W. D., Reed, D., & Sullivan, M. (1996b). The relationship of social cognition to ward behavior in chronic schizophrenia. *Schizophrenia Research, 20,* 327–335.

Penn, D. L., van der Does, A. J. W., Spaulding, W., D., Garbin, C. P., Linszen, D., & Dingemans, P. (1993). Information-processing and social-cognitive problem solving in schizophrenia: Assessment of interrelationships and changes over time. *Journal of Nervous and Mental Disease, 181,* 13–20.

Platt, J. J., & Spivack, G. (1972a). Problem-solving thinking of psychiatric patients. *Journal of Consulting and Clinical Psychology, 39,* 148–151.

Platt, J. J., & Spivack, G. (1972b). Social competence and effective problem-solving thinking in psychiatric patients. *Journal of Clinical Psychology, 28,* 3–5.

Schank, R. C., & Abelson, R. P. (1977). *Scripts, plans, goals, and understanding.* Hillsdale, NJ: Erlbaum.

Shakow, D. (1963). Psychological deficit in schizophrenia. *Behavior Science, 8,* 275–305.

Schneider, F., Gur, R. C., Gur, R. E., & Shtasel, D. L. (1995). Emotional processing in schizophrenia. Neurobehavioral probes in relation to psychopathology. *Schizophrenia Research, 17,* 67–75.

Spaulding, W. D. (1978). The relationships of some information-processing factors to severely disturbed behavior. *Journal of Nervous and Mental Disease, 166,* 417–428.

Spaulding, W. D. (1986). Assessment of adult-onset pervasive behavior disorders. In A. Ciminero, K. Calhoun, & H. Adams (Eds.), *Handbook of behavioral assessment* (2nd ed., (pp. 00). New York: Wiley.

Spaulding, W. D., Garbin, C. P., & Crinean, W. J. (1989). The logical and psychometric prerequisites for cognitive therapy for schizophrenia. *British Journal of Psychiatry, 155,* 69–73.

Spaulding, W. D., Garbin, C. P., & Dras, S. R. (1989). Cognitive abnormalities in schizophrenic patients and schizotypal college students. *Journal of Nervous and Mental Disease, 177,* 717–728.

Spaulding, W. D., Penn, D. L., & Garbin, C. (in press). Cognitive changes in the course of psychiatric rehabilitation. In H. Brenner, C. Perris, & M. Merlo (Eds.), *Cognitive rehabilitation of schizophrenia.* Toronto: Huber-Hogrefe.

Spaulding, W. D., Storms, L., Goodrich, V., & Sullivan, M. (1986). Applications of experimental psychopathology in psychiatric rehabilitation. *Schizophrenia Bulletin, 12,* 560–577.

Spivack, G., Platt, J. J., & Shure, M. B. (1976). *The problem-solving approach to adjustment.* San Francisco: Jossey-Bass.

Stuve, P., Erickson, R. C., & Spaulding, W. D. (1991). Cognitive rehabilitation: The next step in psychiatric rehabilitation. *Psychosocial Rehabilitation Journal, 15,* 9–26.

Toomey, R., Wallace, C. J., Corrigan, P. W., Schuldberg, D., & Green, M. F. (in press). Social processing correlates of nonverbal social perception in schizophrenia. Psychiatry.

Trower, B., Bryant, B., & Argyle, M. (1978). *Social skills and mental health.* Pittsburgh: University of Pittsburgh Press.

Wallace, C. J. (1982). The social skills training project of the mental health clinical research center for the study of schizophrenia. In J. P. Curran, & P. M. Monti (Eds.), *Social skills training: A practical handbook for assessment and treatment.* (pp. 57–89). New York: Guilford.

Wykes, T. (1994). Predicting symptomatic and behavioral outcomes of community care. *British Journal of Psychiatry, 165,* 486–492.

Wykes, T., Katz, R., Sturt, E., & Hemsley, D. (1992). Abnormalities of response processing in a chronic psychiatric group: A possible predictor of failure in rehabilitation programs? *British Journal of Psychiatry, 160,* 244–252.

Wykes, T., Sturt, E., & Katz, R. (1990). The prediction of rehabilitative success after three years: The use of social, symptom, and cognitive variables. *British Journal of Psychiatry, 157,* 865–870.

CHAPTER 14

SEXUALITY AND FAMILY PLANNING

John H. Coverdale
Henry Grunebaum

Unsafe sex, unwanted pregnancies, and sexually transmitted diseases are common among the mentally ill who both do not receive adequate gynecological care and have greater difficulties than other women in using contraception effectively. And both the birth rate and the rate of HIV infection among mentally ill women has risen substantially in the past few decades, because they are no longer confined to mental hospitals but reside in the community. Unfortunately the health care of mentally ill women, including offering them effective contraception, has, by and large, been ignored by the psychiatric profession, and mentally ill women have been ignored by family planning clinics.

Yet mentally ill patients, including those who are chronically psychotic, have sexual desires, have sexual intercourse, and find sexual partners. Even in the state mental hospitals patients found ways of having sexual intercourse (Barton, 1962). The AIDS epidemic, in particular, has caused psychiatric researchers to focus on the sexual risk behaviors of psychiatric patients. Nonetheless, the family planning needs of psychiatric patients remain a neglected topic in the psychiatric literature and in clinical practice as well.

The purpose of this chapter is to discuss population-based programs to enable mentally ill persons to live safe sexual lives. We will also discuss the problem and prevention of sexually transmitted diseases (STDs). Our goals are

1. to review the literature on the sexual behavior of chronic psychiatric patients, and schizophrenic patients in particular, and their attitudes toward pregnancy and contraceptive use;
2. to review the adverse consequences to both mother and child of unwanted pregnancies;
3. to describe the barriers that have been shown to prevent services from addressing patients' needs both for gynecological and contraceptive services;
4. to describe some programs that have successfully provided family planning counseling and gynecological care to the mentally ill; and
5. to discuss the ethical issues that arise in providing contraceptive care to mentally ill patients.

We must take seriously the fact that mental patients ask that family planning services be part of the psychiatric services they already receive. There are four major arguments favoring this integration. First, counseling mental patients requires an amount of time and special knowledge that standard community family planning programs cannot provide. Enabling mentally ill people to comprehend what they need to know to make informed and reasoned decisions about contraception is often not an easy task, particularly since informed consent is necessary. Second, the potential handicaps to both mother and child of unwanted pregnancies makes it ethically necessary to give mentally ill women the opportunity to make informed decisions. Third, these services are an integral part of primary prevention and thus belong in mental health services. In addition, it is our experience that mentally ill women do not receive adequate health care in general, including gynecological examinations. Fourth, it is difficult enough for mental patients to keep appointments at a psychiatric clinic and referral leading to a kept appointment at a family planning clinic is even more difficult, if not, as our experience would suggest, next to impossible. If we seek to have chronic mental patients use contraception, we must provide it.

There are important issues at the intersection of human sexuality and mental illness that we will not cover, because they are mainly important if one is counseling individual mentally ill clients. Among these are the inability of many mentally ill women and men to keep and parent their children and the feelings of loss and difference that this engenders, the effect of the menstrual cycle on mental illness, the effects of medication on the fetus, the problem of postpartum mental illness, and the tragedy, infrequent though it is, of infanticide. These topics are well covered in the recent book *Madness and the Loss of Motherhood* by Apfel and Handel (1993). This book, however, does not mention nor will this chapter discuss the effects of parental, particularly maternal, mental illness on the infant or child. Suffice it to say that there are a large number of studies of the offspring of the mentally ill that document that especially where there is family stress adverse consequences for the children of the mentally ill are more frequent.

SEXUAL BEHAVIOR AND CONTRACEPTIVE ATTITUDES OF MENTAL PATIENTS

Family Planning Studies

In the first study of the contraceptive practices of female mental inpatients, Grunebaum, Abernethy, Rofman, and Weirs (1971) found that these women had many unwanted pregnancies and unwanted children not surprisingly as they often had not used contraception. Abernethy and Grunebaum (1972) then went on to develop the first program that provided gynecological services including family planning counseling for mental patients.

A sample of 21 randomly selected women from the ward population of the Massachusetts Mental Health Center (Grunebaum et al., 1971), including seven schizophrenics as well as other patients with neurotic or other psychotic disorders, were interviewed. These women reported a high frequency of divorce, separation, and marital disharmony. A total of 26 unwanted pregnancies were reported by 13 of the sexually active women, which lead to 9 abortions and 17 unwanted children, many of which were given up to state care.

When the women were asked, "Do you use contraception?" most replied that they did, but, at another point in the interview, when asked to recollect the last time they had intercourse and whether they used contraception then, it turned out that most had not. In this sample, the reports of sexual desire, gratification, and orgasm did not seem significantly different from those of normal populations. However, their knowledge about sex and when pregnancy was most likely to occur was less. Without exception, these female mental patients thought that having family planning counseling available in the mental hospital would be advantageous.

Three personality traits seemed to be prominent in the women who had unwanted pregnancies. These characteristics appeared to be barriers to effective contraceptive use (Grunebaum et al., 1971). First, the women manifested excessive dependency needs that may have allowed them to abrogate responsibility to the man or to fate. They also appeared to desire a baby to whom they could give the nurturance they, themselves, needed. For example, one woman explained her promiscuity that led to two children by two different fathers on the grounds that she was "lonesome" and "wanted someone around." Second, unresolved passive–aggressive needs that often involve ambivalence toward men may have lead a woman to punish herself by getting pregnant or by tying her partner to an unwanted marriage. Such ambivalence may also have led to domestic strife and a lack of communication that often prevents adequate planning for effective contraception. A third prominent trait was an excessive use of the mechanism of denial, leading women to avoid acknowledging that they are having sexual relations or are likely to have them. The authors made no claim about the frequency of these traits in comparison with other samples, only that they appeared common in this sample.

The family planning needs of young adult mental patients was then investigated by Abernethy (1974). Sixty consecutive female inpatient admissions aged 13 to 28 to two state hospitals in Massachusetts were interviewed. Their diagnoses were distributed over all principal types of mental illness; many were diagnosed as having an "adolescent adjustment reaction," a common diagnosis at that time. More than two-thirds of the sample were sexually active. However, protection against pregnancy was infrequent and only 11 of 41 women who had sexual intercourse had used birth control at the time of last intercourse. At the same time, it was not clear how many of these women who had not used contraception had wanted to get pregnant. Of the 26 pregnancies to this group, 15 had resulted in a live birth but only 7 of the children were kept by their mothers and 8 were given up for adoption.

It is often difficult to be sure whether chronically ill women are actually having sex, as can be seen from a more recent study. Chronic mental patients were interviewed about their attitudes toward sex, pregnancy, and birth control. Despite being continuously hospitalized, 15 out of 23 chronic schizophrenic women reported having had intercourse during the previous 3 months, with a frequency ranging from once in the 3 months to once a day (McEvoy, Hatcher, Appelbaum, & Abernethy, 1983). It was difficult to ascertain whether the responses to questions were delusional or not. Six of the women reported that they would currently like to become pregnant, in some cases, urgently so. Mental health professionals thought that they were "incapable of caring for their own needs, much less the needs of children" and seemed "unable to identify themselves as impaired parents." Three women even indicated that there was no connection between having sex and becoming pregnant.

Of interest is that some women responded with bizarre or unusual associations when asked about the advantages of being pregnant. For example, one women responded by saying: "wearing white, yellow and orange clothes." Similarly, several patients responded with unusual associations to questions concerning birth control such as "you can go out to eat in restaurants" or "filling up your stomach."

These findings illustrate the challenge of identifying schizophrenic patients' family planning needs. Another example of this was demonstrated by the difficulty the authors had in obtaining accurate information from some of the women. Nearly all patients gave at least one response that was judged to be inaccurate; some gave obviously grossly inaccurate answers concerning the number of children they had. When asked if they were pregnant, five women indicated that they were when, in fact, this was not the case; three stated that they were carrying ten babies. One of the authors saw such a patient who neither knew that she was pregnant or that she had ever had intercourse much less with whom.

Long-term institutionalization is, of course, much less common. More and more patients are living in the community, with a consequent increase in the exposure of mental patients to the risk of pregnancy, and there is evidence for significant increases in their reproductive rates (Abernethy & Grunebaum, 1972). Indeed, one study reported an increased rate of pregnancy as state hospitals converted from locked to open wards (Abernethy, 1974). Bachrach (1985) has suggested that the needs of mentally ill women fully resident in the community would be much greater.

In fact, a study of the family planning needs of 80 female chronic mental patients fully resident in the community showed that a significant number were at risk of unwanted pregnancies (Coverdale & Aruffo, 1989). These patients, aged 18 to 40, were interviewed at a publicly funded county mental health clinic in Houston. Fifty percent had a DSM-III diagnosis of schizophrenia, another 11% were diagnosed with schizoaffective disorder, and most of the remainder had major affective disorders. Fifty-nine percent of the sample were white and 95% had a history of psychiatric hospitalization. Seventy-three percent of the patients indicated that they had sexual intercourse within the last year, with the majority of the group indicating that it had occurred within the last 3 months. Of the patients who had intercourse within the past year and had not wanted to become pregnant, 33% reported not having used contraception at the time of last intercourse. There was no relationship between diagnosis (schizophrenia or schizoaffective disorder versus other) and the use of birth control at time of intercourse.

Of the contraceptive methods used by this sample, tubal ligation, the intrauterine device, and the condom were the most frequently used contraceptive methods. Some also used methods such as cream, jelly or foam, the diaphragm, and the rhythm method. Several of the patients indicated that there had been times within the preceding year when a contraceptive method had not been used. It was not surprising then that unwanted pregnancies were common. In fact, 31% of the patients reported having had induced abortions, and of 75 children born to them, 60% were being reared by other people, most commonly the child's father or an adoptive family. These findings probably also reflect the difficulty some patients have in coping with the stress of parenthood. Two recent studies have confirmed that some female chronically ill psychiatric patients are at greater risk of unwanted pregnancies and are more likely to have a history of induced abortion and of children given up for others to raise than samples of non-psychiatrically ill patients (Miller & Finnerty, 1996; Coverdale et al., (1997).

In summary, many mentally ill women have intercourse especially if they are resident in the community, they are likely not to use contraception effectively or at all, and they frequently have unwanted pregnancies leading either to abortion or children placed with state agencies. In addition, clinical experience suggests that the men whom they have as partners are likely to be irresponsible and often alcoholic, psychopathic, or also mentally ill themselves. While it is beyond the scope of this chapter, there is ample evidence to demonstrate that the children of mentally ill women are at high risk for genetic and other difficulties including poor prenatal care and educational disadvantages. Finally, one may wonder how many adoptive parents would adopt the child of a psychotic mother if they knew about that heritage and what the effects of that knowledge might be on the rearing of the child.

AIDS-Risk Studies

Considerable light is shed on the contraceptive practices of mentally ill patients by recent studies of their risk behavior for AIDS. The prevalence of HIV seropositivity among the chronically mentally ill suggests that this is a population at high risk. In one study, a total of 7.1% of patients admitted to a voluntary psychiatric hospital in New York City were HIV positive (Sacks, Dermatis, Couser-OH, Burton, & Perry, 1992), and in a second study, 1 in every 18 (5.5%) of a predominantly psychotic patient population in New York City was found to be HIV positive (Cournos et al., 1991). In a third study of 352 patients admitted to a New York State psychiatric hospital, about one-half were found to be at high risk for HIV infection on the basis of application of a Risk Behaviors Questionnaire. Among the high-risk group HIV seroprevalence was 14% (Volavka et al., 1992).

Although chronic schizophrenia has been proposed as a risk factor for HIV (Seeman, Lang, & Rector, 1990), many of the studies delineating HIV-risk behaviors concern chronic mental patients independent of specific DSM diagnoses. It is clear that mental patients residing in the community are sexually active with rates ranging from 62% in the last year (Kelly et al., 1992) to 44% in the past

6 months. These chronic mental patients have multiple sexual partners with rates of 19% of the women and 42% of the men, and both men and women used condoms infrequently (Kelly et al., 1992). In another study the same investigators reported that multiple partners were reported by 29% of the women and 26% of the men (Kalichman, Kelly, Johnson, & Bulto, 1994).

Many of the sexual partners in this study had been met in bars or mental health clinics. The women (13%) sometimes had sex in exchange for money, drugs, or a place to stay. Coercion of the women was not uncommon, and 15 to 21% reported being pressured into unwanted sex. Another 10% had sex with a partner known for less than one day, and some patients indicated that they had met their partners on the street, in parks, or in public places.

Diagnosis was unrelated to HIV-risk measures in the above studies, and in addition Cournos, McKinnon, Meyer-Bahlburg, Guido, and Meyer (1993) also found no significant differences among those with schizophrenia, bipolar disorder, and other diagnoses including psychotic disorders in the rate of abstinence, number of sexual partners, and condom use. There are no significant differences found in risk behavior if the sample is confined to patients with a research diagnosis of schizophrenia alone (Cournos et al., 1994). Of interest is that sexual activity was associated with greater general psychopathology as measured by the general psychopathology scale of the Positive and Negative Syndrome Scale. However, there were no differences between the sexually active and abstinent patients in their overall level of functioning. Having multiple sexual partners was associated with younger age, a lower level of functioning, the presence of delusions, and more positive symptoms. Consistent with these findings previously described, 50% of the sexually active patients had exchanged sex for money or goods.

We have selected from studies on AIDS-risks those findings most pertinent to family planning. For example, many patients also have a history of intravenous drug abuse, which is an important risk factor for AIDS. These studies underline female patients' vulnerability and risk for contracting unwanted pregnancies.

Male Patients

We are aware of few studies specifically concerning male patients with schizophrenia or the needs of male chronic mental patients for contraception. As discussed above, studies on AIDS risk show that male patients are sexually active. It appears likely that among young adults with predominantly schizophrenic disorders, fewer men than women were reportedly sexually active (Test, Burke, & Wallisch, 1990). Even so, 41% of the males in the above study reported heterosexual experiences during each time period of the study. The lower rates in chronic male mental patients would be expectable since male schizophrenic patients are typically younger when they become ill and function less well socially.

Coverdale, Schotte, Ruiz, Pharies, and Bayer (1994) interviewed 35 male psychiatric patients, most of whom were diagnosed with schizophrenia, at the psychiatric outpatient clinic of a publicly funded county general hospital. Twenty (57%) indicated that they had had heterosexual intercourse within the last year. Seven of the 17 patients who were sexually active and who did not want children reported that they or their sexual partner had not used contraception. Others had used withdrawal by itself, which is relatively ineffective, or had not used contraception consistently. Furthermore, many of the children less than 16 years of age born to the fathers were not being reared by them, suggesting that they did not have the requisite personal skills and financial resources for rearing children. An interview study of 92 male chronically ill psychiatric patients established similar needs (Coverdale & Turbott, 1997).

A Few Representative Case Examples

One patient had one unwanted child who was living with the child's father. She was a 27-year-old white female with a history of brief reactive psychosis and polysubstance abuse who was sexually active and who did not want to get pregnant. Her primary method of contraception was the rhythm or calendar method. She mistakenly thought that she would be "completely safe" for 20 days after termination of menstruation although her menstrual cycle was regular and of about 4 weeks duration.

Another patient is interesting as she demonstrates the limitations of self-knowledge. She was a young Indian lady with a diagnosis of schizophrenia. She had one previous abortion and stated that she did not want to get pregnant again. She had just broken up with her boyfriend and had been using condoms and foam to prevent pregnancy. At the time of that interview, she was asked "If you found out you were pregnant and did not want to have a baby, would you have an abortion or continue on with the pregnancy?" She answered that she would continue on with the pregnancy. Four and a half months later, when pregnant, she was requesting an abortion.

A third patient was a single, 28-year-old woman diagnosed as chronic schizophrenia and polysubstance abuse.

Her previous pregnancies resulted in three live births all of whom were living with different parents. She was involved in just one relationship at the time of interview and was having sexual intercourse about once a week. She stated that they regularly used a condom as contraception. She denied wanting to get pregnant and said she would have an abortion if she found out she was pregnant. However, on direct questioning it transpired that she had missed three periods when previously they were regular. On being asked what this might mean she responded "something wrong—I don't know." She then said that she did not know if she would continue to have her period if pregnant. She would "just sit and wait" and not seek help or tell anyone, including the outpatient community mental health clinic staff. When asked how she could tell if she was pregnant, she responded that she would feel it inside. In her case, of course, there was a high possibility that she was pregnant and yet she was strongly denying this possibility. A phenomenon of denial of pregnancy sometimes occurs in chronic mental patients, although it is reportedly fairly uncommon (Miller, 1990). Women who deny their pregnancies tend to have a diagnosis of chronic schizophrenia, to have previously lost custody of children, and to anticipate separation from the baby they were carrying. Psychotic denial of pregnancy is associated with precipitous or unassisted delivery, fetal abuse, and neonaticide (Miller, 1990). Of course, its most usual effect is that the woman does not seek or receive prenatal care.

POSSIBLE ADVERSE CONSEQUENCES OF UNWANTED PREGNANCIES

Many patients with schizophrenia or chronic mental illness have normal pregnancies and deliveries and, of course, some have an induced abortion. There are, however, reasons to expect that these patients may be more likely to have adverse pregnancy outcomes than persons who do not have chronic mental illness.

The most common risk to mentally ill patients, especially those who are chronically ill, results from the fact that they are less likely to attend antenatal health appointments (Wrede, Mednick, HuHunen, & Nilsson, 1980) and to follow medical advice. To a considerable degree this is simply part of the general problem of the inadequate health care that mental patients receive. Certain risks arise from the fact that mental patients compared with the population tend to be less well educated, be less well off financially, have fewer support systems, and have greater social difficulties.

As stated earlier, psychotic denial of pregnancy, although uncommon, leads to inadequate prenatal care as well as to postpartum emotional disturbance in the mother and to precipitate an unassisted delivery (Miller, 1990). Risks to the pregnant patient with major mental disorder includes those when psychosis causes patients to endanger their health and the outcome of their pregnancy by acting on delusions or hallucinations (Rudolph, Larson, Swang, Hough, & Arororian, 1990).

Risks to the fetus include the effects of psychiatric medications and illicit drug use (Cohen, Heller, & Rosenbaum, 1989; Nurnberg, 1989; McCane-Katz, 1991; Packer, 1992). Results have been mixed, however, regarding the relationship between mental illness and obstetric outcome. In two controlled studies no relationship was found (Cohler, Gallant, Grunebaum, Weiss, & Gamer, 1975; McNeil, Persson-Blennow, & Kaij, 1974). But on the other hand, one prospective study found an increased incidence of fetal and neonatal deaths among offspring of schizophrenics when compared with a control group (Rieder, Rosenthal, Wender, & Blumenthal, 1975). More recent work found that prematurity, lower birth weight, and lower Apgar scores were related to the severity and chronicity of mental illness (Zax, Sameroff, & Babigan, 1977).

There are both genetic and environmental risks for children of mentally ill parents. The genetic risk is that of becoming afflicted with major mental disorders. The risk of schizophrenia, for example, approaches 45% if both parents are schizophrenic (Karno & Norquist, 1989), and if one parent is schizophrenic the risk is about 11%. Furthermore, mentally ill parents are impaired in their ability to respond to the needs of their children, and the children even if they do not become schizophrenic themselves are likely to be psychologically harmed (Goodman, 1989).[1]

The social costs of the children of mentally ill parents are considerable as they are at high risk for psychological, social, educational, and interpersonal difficulties. Many are reared in problematic situations by their mothers who often require and receive much support from many agencies. In our clinical experience it is usually the case that social agencies endeavor to keep the children with the mother and to return them to the mother after foster care. This pattern tends to persist far longer than would be the case if the child had an advocate. Some-

times the other parent cares for the child, but as stated earlier, it is frequent that they, too, suffer from various forms of psychopathology. Finally, when the children are adopted, they are still likely to have various forms of psychological difficulties as a result of their experiences before adoption.

WHAT ARE THE OBSTACLES TO EFFECTIVE FAMILY PLANNING FOR MENTALLY ILL PATIENTS?

Problems in the Delivery of Health Care to Mentally Ill Patients

The mentally ill receive abysmal health care in general. We have seen women who have not had a gynecological exam and a Pap smear in 20 years. Their failure to receive adequate family planning care is often part of the neglect of their general health. In addition, mental health professionals, family planning clinics, and patients have attitudes and act in ways that impede the provision of health care, which is generally regarded the right of every woman.

Mental health professionals (MHPs) often do not see it as their responsibility to address family planning issues with patients (as one senior psychiatric nurse based at an inpatient unit had commented to one of us), rather they believe that responsibility lies instead with family practitioners or family planning specialists. Second, family practitioners and family planning specialists do not believe that care of the mentally ill is their responsibility, nor do they feel qualified to care for them. Finally, patients, particularly mentally ill patients, are not reliable or often even able to keep appointments with either practitioners or family planning clinics.

Many clinicians may believe that patients who suffer from schizophrenia are invariably hyposexual (McEvoy et al., 1983). Other factors include that MHPs feel uncomfortable taking sexual histories, advising about contraceptive use, or discussing these issues, which they believe may be perceived as intrusive. Clearly, psychotherapists who believe in the neutrality of the psychoanalytic stance will find it difficult to take such proactive positions with their patients. Alternatively, some may view education about birth control as likely to be ineffective in preventing unwanted pregnancies (or STDs) in this population although our clinical experience suggests otherwise. In fact, a substantial proportion of mentally ill women continue to use contraception on follow-up. Another common barrier

---

[1]Many of the issues of risk to children of schizophrenic mothers are discussed in a recent issue of the *Schizophrenia Bulletin, 20(1)*, 1994.

is that MHPs may perceive that they, themselves, have insufficient knowledge or insufficient time to effectively address these issues.

In one study of 82 MHPs including psychiatrists based in community mental health clinics in Houston, Texas, 87% stated that they should provide information or programs on birth control (Coverdale & Aruffo, 1992). However, they also reported that they had raised the issue of birth control with only 25% of their patients. There was no significant difference found between different medical (nurses and psychiatrists) and nonmedical (caseworkers and psychologists) professionals; however, female professionals reported raising topics of birth control significantly more frequently than male professionals. MHPs were found to overestimate the patients' reported anxiety during sexual history-taking, which may well represent a discomfort they themselves experienced in taking sexual histories (Coverdale & Aruffo, 1992). Obviously, MHPs' failure to raise family planning issues with patients precludes estimating their risk for unwanted pregnancies and appropriate preventive interventions.

Difficulties of the Patient in Undertaking Family Planning

Patients with schizophrenia have difficulties in arriving at sound decisions about their health care, which includes reproductive decisions. The following six steps are normally involved in decision making about health care issues, and each is often impaired in schizophrenia (McCullough, Coverdale, Bayer, & Chervenak, 1992).

1. The patient must attend to the information that must be considered.
2. The patient must absorb, retain, and recall the necessary information offered in order to use it.
3. The patient must appreciate that this information has significance in his/her life and the lives of others. This step has been called "cognitive understanding" and requires that the patient appreciates that decisions about health care have consequences for the future and that present decisions have future possible consequences.
4. The patient must evaluate these consequences on the basis of his/her values and beliefs. This step has been called "evaluative understanding."
5. The patient must communicate both cognitive and evaluative understanding if other people are involved in either the decision or in taking action.
6. The patient must be able to act on his/her decision.

These steps must be completed sequentially and each depends on the successful completion of its predecessor.

Attention to the information disclosed and its absorption, retention, and recall may be impaired by auditory hallucinations, paranoia, or associated agitation. In addition, schizophrenia is associated with impaired ability to deploy and focus attention. Cognitive understanding may be impaired when patients deny the possibility of likelihood of engaging in sexual intercourse in the future. The reader will recall that the phenomenon of excessive use of denial was one trait prominent in patients in Grunebaum et al.'s (1971) original study.

Evaluative understanding can be impaired by paranoid or grandiose ideas or delusions. Several studies report that many of the patients have urgent desires to become pregnant and raise a family despite their being chronically institutionalized and incapable of caring for even their own needs (McEvoy et al., 1983; Schulz et al., 1982). Incoherence, circumstantiality, tangentiality, poverty of talk, and looseness of associations can disrupt the expression or communication of cognitive and evaluative understanding (McEvoy et al., 1983; Coverdale & Aruffo, 1989).

It is thus no wonder that patients with schizophrenia do have difficulty with reproductive decisions in particular. Drug or alcohol use in association with sexual activity may also increase risk as well as failure to follow a medication regimen (Kelly et al., 1992). Associated depression may also impair each of the six decision-making steps, particularly if there are associated symptoms such as hopelessness, helplessness, guilt, and worthlessness (Sullivan & Younger, 1994). This impairment may be, although is not always, a permanent feature of schizophrenia. Furthermore, this impairment may vary for each of the steps to differing degrees over time in the same patient dependent on the severity of psychosis, or the presence of stress, physical illness, or drug abuse. This clinical phenomena of ethical significance has been termed chronically and variably impaired autonomy (McCullough et al., 1992).

An important implication of chronically and variably impaired autonomy is that patients' ability to process information about contraceptive methods (and STDs) may fluctuate. While there are few studies specifically assessing patients' knowledge of contraception, McEvoy et al. (1983) showed, for example, that women's factual knowledge and understanding was quite limited and that they had many mistaken beliefs about birth control.

A further implication of chronically and variably impaired autonomy is that patients with schizophrenia are particularly vulnerable to coercion by their partners into behaviors that place them at risk for unwanted pregnancies (and STDs). Evidence to support this belief has already been referred to in studies concerning patients' AIDS risk (Seeman et al., 1990; Kelly et al., 1992), and there is evidence that coercive behavior by partners including physical assault and rape is prevalent (Jacobsen & Richardson, 1987; Jacobson, 1989). In one study, for example, of consecutive admissions over a 2-month period at a university-affiliated county hospital, 64% of the female patients had experienced physical and/or sexual assault as an adult and 38% reported a history of major sexual assault (Jacobson & Richardson, 1987).

ADMINISTRATIVE AND SERVICE ISSUES

That family planning issues are infrequently addressed with mental patients is not surprising given the heavy workloads, including excessive direct service demands common to community mental health centers, at least in the United States (Coverdale & Aruffo, 1992; Tucker, Turner, & Chapman, 1981). Furthermore, very few programs in the United States also integrate psychosocial treatments including cognitive-behavioral therapy and social skills training with biological treatments for the care of the chronically mentally ill. A significant technology gap exists between what research shows is optimal treatment for schizophrenia and what is practical in the field. This reflects in part a lack of funding and a staff-to-patient ratio that is too low to allow the provision of optimal care. A lack of funding and of staff in community mental health centers also has implications for the ability to provide comprehensive family planning programs.

Furthermore, there are few programs that have reported integrated family planning programs and sexually transmitted disease prevention services with outpatient or inpatient mental health services. Interagency referrals usually do not succeed in our experience when patients have to go to another location for family planning or STD services and have to find their own transportation.

Many outpatient services do not even make provision for medical care including physical exams. Psychiatrists may not routinely do these themselves or a physician assistant or other qualified health care professional may not be readily available. Often, community mental health centers lack physical examination rooms and functional examining equipment, and gynecological examinations for female chronic mental patients are often neglected (Han-

del, 1985). This lack of attention to the routine medical care that adults require is striking since the outpatient service often is the only medical care that mentally ill individuals receive.

PREVENTIVE INTERVENTIONS

Taking a Sexual History

It is necessary for mental health professionals to take a sexual history with every patient. This is sine qua non in the primary prevention of unwanted pregnancies and sexually transmitted diseases. Patients may be identified who are at risk of sexually transmitted diseases including AIDS by unsafe sexual practices such as promiscuous behavior. Benefits may also arise from identification of patients with sexual dysfunctions as well as those with a history of sexual abuse.

A secondary preventive function is served in that patients with an early pregnancy may be identified. In this way, medications that might harm the fetus can be avoided and referral made for easy obstetrical evaluation. Active inquiry is made more necessary by the finding that schizophrenic patients may deny their own pregnancy, as we saw in one of the earlier case examples.

Routine history forms should be provided in the medical chart for completing the sexual history. Such a form has been advocated for assessing risk for AIDS (Carmen & Brady, 1990). These forms have the advantage of ensuring that the relevant questions are asked in a consistent fashion. This method of structured interviewing of patients may also be fairly nonthreatening for patients. On the other hand, it can lead to an overly rigid style in history taking.

There are several general principles that apply to sexual history taking (McKinnon et al., 1993; Committee on Medical Education of the Group for the Advancement of Psychiatry, 1977). The attitude and manner of the interviewer is important in determining whether a valid picture of the patient's sexual situation is obtained. Any anxiety or discomfort on the interviewer's part may be conveyed to the patient. The interviewer should also ensure that his/her values are not imposed on the patient. The reason for the inquiry should be explained to the patient so that the patient understands its basis and does not inappropriately perceive the interviewer as being unduly curious about personal and sensitive matters. Patients may also find it easier to disclose information when less sensitive questions (for example, concerning a female patient's menstrual history) precede more sensitive questions.

One of the most important aspects of sexual history taking is the establishment of rapport between interviewer and patient (McKinnon et al., 1993). The interviewer should show genuine concern for the patient and demonstrate confidence and trust that provides a setting to enable the patient to freely express attitudes and feelings. Privacy and confidentiality should also be respected. Interviews are best conducted in a private, quiet area, and patients should be advised about the protection by confidentiality of information.

Questions concerning AIDS risk can also be asked in a fashion that achieves high reliability, and without exacerbation of psychiatric symptoms (McKinnon et al., 1993). Questions that have achieved high test–retest reliability include whether that patient is sexually active, the number of sexual partners, the number of sexual episodes, the proportion of episodes in which vaginal intercourse occurred, and the proportion of vaginal intercourse episodes in which condoms were used (McKinnon et al., 1993). Clearly questions concerning AIDS risk alone do not adequately assess family planning needs.

A complete sexual history should be obtained. In addition to a medical history, an obstetric history for female patients will include information about the number of previous pregnancies including those that ended in miscarriages, abortions, stillbirths, and live births, as well as birth outcomes and whether pregnancies were planned and/or wanted. The patient's children should be inquired about. Are they being reared by the patient, their father, other family members, or have they been given up for foster placement or adoption? Is the patient, perhaps, infertile due to a tubal ligation, a hysterectomy, or a history of pelvic inflammatory disease which might prevent them from getting pregnant. Patients should be asked about when they last had a pelvic examination. Inquiry should be made of the date of the last menstrual period, the number of days between periods, and their regularity.

It is also important to ask a patient whether she wants to get pregnant and about her values about contraception, pregnancy, and parenting. A sexual history should include questions about when a patient last had sexual intercourse, whether this was with a woman or man, the frequency of intercourse, and the number and gender of partners over a time period such as the last year. Patients should also be asked about whether birth control is used, the method of use, and their understanding of the various contraceptive methods. Patients should be asked to recollect the last

time they had sex and when that was. Asking whether they used contraception on that occasion also provides a better indication of the reliability of contraceptive use than a more general inquiry. Many sexually active individuals do not contracept faithfully, and mental patients are likely to be even more inconsistent users. The AIDS crisis also demands that we ask female patients about whether male sexual partners use condoms.

Contraceptive Methods with Particular Emphasis on Mental Patients

Since mental patients often have more difficulties than other people in using contraceptive methods that require forethought and making a sound decision at the time they have intercourse, the general principle is to encourage them to use methods that do not require these abilities. Here patients with regular partners differ from those with more casual partners. Patients with a regular partner often can use methods such as tubal ligation, the intrauterine device, long-acting hormones (Depo-provera), or the Pill. In our experience, the diaphragm is rarely a viable contraceptive method. The regular partners of mentally ill women are often reluctant to have more children and will ensure that family planning is faithfully used. They will often use a condom, themselves, to be sure.

Patients who have casual partners must be encouraged to carry condoms with them and to make sure that their partners use them. Here the prevention of AIDS is even more important than the prevention of pregnancy.

We have already shown how patients with schizophrenia may have difficulty in deciding about contraception, so it is particularly important in counseling them that informed consent is safeguarded. This may necessitate a very thorough and painstaking effort to impart information to patients. One must ensure that they understand the costs and benefits of the available options, including of not using contraception. This said, there are a number of considerations that may apply for patients with schizophrenia in their choice of contraception.

Sterilization is the least reversible of the available options and so should be approached with special caution. Published guidelines for voluntary sterilization for mentally ill women include that the decision should be independent of other major life events (such as an abortion); that the patient should fully participate in making the decision; and that if the patient is "not competent" to make the decision, it must be postponed. There should be a waiting time from the decision to the surgery in order to allow for a change of mind and exploration of the ambivalence (Apfel & Handel, 1993).

However, these guidelines do not take account of chronically and variably impaired autonomy since competency is often treated as an all-or-none phenomenon. Instead, patients with schizophrenia fall between the extremes of this dichotomy and must be treated as an ethically and clinically distinct group (McCullough et al., 1992). Furthermore, its irreversible nature may be problematic in patients who lack stable preferences. For instance, McEvoy et al. (1983) found that three women who had been surgically sterilized all said that they wanted to become pregnant and have more children.

Overshadowing these considerations is the need to protect against our making the patient do what we think is best for her. Safeguards proposed to protect against coercion include that the least reversible methods of sterilizations or vasectomies are not offered to patients in hospital settings (Grunebaum & Abernethy, 1977). This practice may also be reasonably adopted in outpatient settings as well. In many years of providing contraception to mental patients in Massachusetts, a state with a large Catholic population, there were only a few instances when sterilization seemed the appropriate method. In these instances we chose to forego this sterilization. Grunebaum et al. believed that doing it might jeopardize the whole program and thus did not arrange for any sterilizations. However, we were impressed that this choice was exceedingly rare.

Sterilization is now a less desirable alternative because of the availability of an effective, long-term, implantable, reversible contraceptive device (Norplant). This device must be implanted and removed by a surgical procedure, and it provides a reasonable option for this population (Goodman, 1989; Coverdale, Bayer, McCullough, & Chervenak, 1993).

The intrauterine device also provides a very useful contraceptive alternative for this population. It can be fairly readily inserted and removed. However, since some patients with schizophrenia have an increased threshold for pain, they may not respond as anticipated to early warning signs of pelvic inflammatory disease as a consequence of the intrauterine device (Sacks et al., 1992).

In choosing contraception, one must also consider the high degree of compliance needed for the oral contraceptive pill to be effective (Sacks et al., 1992). Patients often forget to take the Pill, for example, when acutely disturbed or at a time when they may be most at risk of an unwanted pregnancy. The diaphragm, cream, jelly, foam, and condoms must be used consistently and when sexual relations are imminent, and their partner must be willing to wait. These methods are usually not suitable for mentally ill women.

One implication of chronically and variably impaired autonomy is that female patients may have difficulty insisting that their male partner wear a condom, particularly when this is viewed as limiting spontaneity in sex or pleasure for the man (Coverdale, Bayer, McCullough, & Chervenak, in press). Thus, the provision of condoms to patients is not always effective as a preventive intervention. However, condoms can be provided cheaply and efficiently in both outpatient and inpatient settings and to both women and men—one emergency center in which one of us worked provided them routinely. Female condoms consisting of a polyurethane sheath that covers the cervix and vagina also require cooperation from the prospective male partner.

Other considerations in the choice of contraception include the need to protect against AIDS and other sexually transmitted diseases. HIV, genital herpes, and syphilis, unlike gonorrhea and chlamydia, may be transmitted by direct contact rather than by semen and may utilize vaginal or vulvar epithelium in addition to the cervix as a portal of entry (Stone & Peterson, 1992). Therefore, the diaphragm and cervical cap are unlikely to protect against these STDs. Latex condoms serve a double function by also protecting against STDs, and consistent use significantly decreases the risk of HIV seroconversion for couples discordant for HIV (Cates & Stone, 1992).

Other Interventions with Patients

Patient education is probably the single most important component of any family planning program for schizophrenic patients, since the vast majority of mentally ill patients freely desire family planning assistance (Coverdale, Aruffo, & Grunebaum, 1992). An intervention as simple as a poster or brochure indicating the receptiveness of staff to discuss family planning is viewed favorably by patients and will lead them to bring the subject up with mental health professionals.

The problem of initiating discussion of sexual behavior with mental patients is a very important obstacle to their receiving adequate contraceptive care. In one survey, however, only 10% of patients in a Houston community mental health center reported having discussed issues of family planning or STD prevention with staff (Coverdale & Aruffo, 1992). We believe this is largely because the staff does not initiate discussions. When possible a staff member should be specifically authorized to undertake the task of family planning counseling. This person can then initiate counseling with each patient who comes to the clinic. Alternatively, there can be a check list of topics that must be covered with each client. Often clinic records include such a list. If evaluation for family planning is on the list, it will then be routinely undertaken.

There are little published data that show that educational messages alone are effective in preventing unwanted pregnancies for this population. Lukoff, Gioia-Hasick, Sullivan, Golden, and Nuechterlein (1986) administered a sex education program for schizophrenic male outpatients. They used role playing, modeling, group exercises, and explicit sex therapy audiovisual material to improve patients' intimacy skills. The program was reportedly well received with patients asking a number of pertinent questions including about the relationship of medication to birth defects and about masturbation. There was also no evidence that the sex education program stimulated exacerbations or relapses.

However, Grunebaum and Barnum have hitherto unpublished data that demonstrates the effectiveness of counseling individual clients over a series of interviews. We endeavored to recontact discharged mental patients who had been counseled while in the hospital. This is a highly mobile population, and we were able to get in touch with approximately three-fourths of the original group. Of these patients, 80% were continuing to use the contraceptive method that they had decided to use in discussions with the counselor. Alternatively, patients may benefit by behavioral education that fosters assertiveness with partners so that they are not coerced into unwanted sex. Relevant strategies here include teaching communication skills and how to fit condoms.

Ethical Issues

We believe that an individual has a right to control his/her own fertility. From the patient's point of view, what is necessary is informed consent. This requires three major components: (1) adequate knowledge on which to base a decision, (2) competence to make a decision, and (3) absence of coercion in the decision-making process. It is often possible to provide the patient with the necessary information, although the process is likely to require more interviews than is usually the case. One important implication of being chronically and variably impaired is that

patients are never entirely devoid of decision-making capacities (McCullough et al., 1992).

The second problem is that of competence to make a decision. We have made two major assumptions: (1) that if the patient consents to medical treatment, that consent includes the provision of contraceptive care, and (2) that if a woman is competent to make the decision to have sexual relations, she is competent to decide to use contraception. We believe it would be illogical to maintain the reverse; namely, that one can decide to have sexual relations and take the risk of becoming pregnant and not be allowed to decide to avoid that risk. It might be maintained that a mentally ill woman is overcome by her impulses or coerced by the man involved. Here we would maintain that the decision to have safe sex is at least as rational as the decisions that lead to the sexual act.

Avoiding coercion in decision making is difficult. We cannot avoid the fact that mental patients are to some extent a captive population with diminished power. We have been very scrupulous in this area and have required that the patient actively give her consent. It must be acknowledged that a small proportion of women who probably should use contraception do not chose to do so. However, we have believed that attention to the rights of individuals to act other than in their best interests should prevail. Comprehensive ethically justified guidelines for family planning interventions to prevent pregnancy in this patient population have been published that introduce and take account of the concept of chronically and variably impaired autonomy (McCullough et al., 1992; Coverdale et al., 1993).

As we noted earlier, many patients with schizophrenia have normal pregnancies and deliveries; possible adverse risks include those to patients, to possible future children, and to society of unwanted pregnancies and children. Some risks are serious, such as when a patient decompensates during pregnancy and attempts to harm herself and the fetus. Also, risks to possible future children are significant due to their increased risk of contracting schizophrenia. Grounds for overriding a patient's autonomy are justifiable only when risks are serious, predictable with certainty, and irreversible. A risk of decompensation during pregnancy may be treatable or reversible, however, and the risk of a future possible child developing schizophrenia cannot be predicted with certainty. None of these risks, including social costs, have been shown to justify overriding patients' preferences, and this means that some, in our experience few, patients may decide to continue at risk of unwanted pregnancies.

Administration Issues

Staff training is a vital component of service provision. Mental health professionals are usually not educated to provide family planning advice, and inservice training is required for this purpose. This should include instruction on patients' needs, advantages and disadvantages of different contraceptive methods, and providing practice in sexual history taking. The latter is particularly important since often MHPs feel uncomfortable about discussing sexual matters making this is a barrier to their raising these matters with patients.

It is usually the case that family planning professionals are ill equipped to work with psychiatric patients. They are often afraid of psychiatric patients and are not familiar with the impairments in cognitive and evaluative understanding that these patients may manifest. The usual family planning clinic and its staff do not have the extra time and cannot offer the support mental patients may need in making contraceptive decisions.

In the light of the above, and the difficulty that many patients have in attending a clinic in a new and different location for family planning follow-up, we believe that family planning programs are best provided within the psychiatric services themselves (Coverdale et al., 1992). In an outpatient clinic, this can be achieved by employing a family planning counselor to counsel clients on a regular basis. Provision must also be made for physical and gynecological exams within the clinic itself, since this is likely to be the only setting where the patient receives any health care at all. In this way, patients may develop trust in a person who is seen as a regular member of the treatment team (although the counselor can also maintain some appropriate independence from the psychiatric team). Furthermore, through this process psychiatric staff can learn about family planning, and family planners can more readily learn about the special needs of psychiatric patients. Each clinic and hospital will have to develop a service structure that is suitable to its setting.[2]

We have shown that benefits accrue when family planning programs are integrated with services for preventing STDs, classes for improving parenting skills, and treatment for substance abuse (Coverdale et al., 1992). Female patients with chronic mental illness are particularly vulnerable to contracting STDs including AIDS (Coverdale et al., in press) and the provision of such services must be a high priority.

CONCLUSION

The theme of this chapter has been the need to provide mentally ill patients, including those with schizophrenia, assistance in their contraceptive choices. Indeed, a failure to provide comprehensive family planning services will violate patients' autonomy. Symptoms and conditions that underlie the variable nature of impaired autonomy should be treated to maximize patients' ability to attend to, absorb, retain, and recall information; to provide cognitive and evaluative understanding; and to communicate a decision based on such understanding. Patients' autonomy will also be enhanced by the implementation of our recommendations for the provision of comprehensive family planning services.

The goal is clear: to provide adequate gynecological and contraceptive services for a severely disadvantaged population at great risk for unwanted pregnancies and sexual transmitted disease, not the least of which is AIDS.

REFERENCES

Abernethy, V. (1974). Sexual knowledge, attitudes and practices of young female psychiatric patients. *Archives of General Psychiatry, 30*, 180–182.

Abernethy, V., & Grunebaum, H. U. (1972). Toward a family planning program in psychiatric hospitals. *American Journal of Public Health, 62*, 1638–1645.

Apfel, R. J., & Handel, M. H. (1993). *Madness and loss of motherhood: Sexuality, reproduction, and long-term mental illness.* Washington DC: American Psychiatric Press.

Bachrach, L. L. (1985). Chronic mentally ill women: Emergence and legitimation of program issues. *Hospital and Community Psychiatry, 36*, 1063–1069.

Barton, W. E., (1962). *Administration in psychiatry.* Springfield, IL: Charles C. Thomas.

Carmen, E., & Brady, S. M. (1990). AIDS risk and prevention for the chronic mentally ill. *Hospital and Community Psychiatry, 41*, 652–657.

Cates, W., & Stone, K. M. (1992). Family planning, sexually transmitted diseases, and contraceptive choice: A literature update—part I. *Family Planning Perspectives, 243*, 75–85.

Cohen, L. S., Heller, V. L., & Rosenbaum, J. F. (1989). Treatment guidelines for psychotropic drug use in pregnancy. *Psychosomatics, 30*, 25–32.

Cohler, B. J., Gallant, D.H., Grunebaum, H. N., Weiss, J. L., &

---

[2]Some years ago we developed a manual for family planning counselors working in a psychiatric setting, which would be updated were there sufficient interest.

Gamer, E. (1975). Pregnancy and birth complications among mentally ill and well mothers and their children. *Social Biology, 22,* 269–278.

Committee on Medical Education of the Group for the Advancement of Psychiatry. (1977). *Assessment of sexual function: A guide to interviewing.* New York: Mental Health Materials Center.

Cournos, F., Empfield, M., Horwath, E., McKinnon, K., Meyer, I., Shrage, H., Currie, C., & Agosin, B. (1991). HIV seroprevalence among patients admitted to two psychiatric hospitals. *American Journal of Psychiatry, 148,* 1225–1230.

Cournos, F., Guido, J. R., Coomaraswang, S., Meyer-Bahlburg, H., Sugden, R., & Horwath, E. (1994). Sexual activity and risk of HIV infection among patients with schizophrenia. *American Journal of Psychiatry, 151,* 228–232.

Cournos, F., McKinnon, K., Meyer-Bahlburg, H., Guido, J. R., & Meyer, I. (1993). HIV risk activity among persons with severe mental illness: Preliminary findings. *Hospital and Community Psychiatry, 44,* 1104–1106.

Coverdale, J. H., & Aruffo, J. (1989). Family planning needs of female chronic psychiatric outpatients. *American Journal of Psychiatry, 146,* 1489–1491.

Coverdale, J. H., & Aruffo, J. (1992). AIDS and family planning counseling of psychiatrically ill women in community mental health clinics. *Community Mental Health Journal, 28,* 13–20.

Coverdale, J. H., Aruffo, J., & Grunebaum, H. U. (1992). Developing family planning services for female chronic mentally ill outpatients. *Hospital and Community Psychiatry, 43,* 475–478.

Coverdale, J. H., Bayer, T. L., McCullough, L. B., & Chervenak, F. A. (1993). Respecting the autonomy of chronic mentally ill women in decisions about contraception. *Hospital and Community Psychiatry, 44,* 671–674.

Coverdale, J. H., & Turbott, S. H. (1997). Family planning outcomes of male chronically ill psychiatric outpatients. *Psychiatric Services, 48,* 1199–1200.

Coverdale, J. H., Turbott, S. H., & Roberts, H. (1997). Family planning needs and STD risk behaviors of female psychiatric outpatients. *British Journal of Psychiatry, 171,* 69–72.

Coverdale, J. H., Bayer, T. L., McCullough, L. B., & Chervenak, F. A. (in press). Sexually transmitted disease prevention services for female chronically mentally ill patients. *Community Mental Health Journal.*

Coverdale, J. H., Schotte, D., Ruiz, P., Pharres, S., & Bayer, T. (1994). Family planning needs of male chronic mental patients in the general hospital psychiatry clinic. *General Hospital Psychiatry, 16,* 38–41.

Goodman, S. H. (1989). Emory University project on children of disturbed parents. *Schizophrenia Bulletin, 13,* 411–423.

Grunebaum, H., & Abnernethy, V. (1977). Ethical issues in family planning for hospitalized psychiatric patients. *American Journal of Psychiatry, 132,* 236–240.

Grunebaum, H. U., Abernethy, V. D., Rofman, E. S., & Weirs, J. L. (1971). The family planning attitudes, practices and mo-

tivations of mental patients. *American Journal of Psychiatry, 128,* 96–99.

Handel, M. (1985). Deferred pelvic examinations: A purposeful omission in the care of mentally ill women. *Hospital and Community Psychiatry, 36,* 1070–1074.

Jacobsen, A., & Richardson, B. (1987). Assault experiences of 100 psychiatric inpatients: Evidence of the need for routine inquiry. *American Journal of Psychiatry, 144,* 908–913.

Jacobson, A. (1989). Physical and sexual assault histories among psychiatric outpatients. *American Journal of Psychiatry, 146,* 755–758.

Kalichman, S. L., Kelly, J. A. N., Johnson, J. R., & Bulto, M. (1994). Factors associated with risk for HIV infection among chronic mentally ill adults. *American Journal of Psychiatry, 151,* 221–227.

Karno, M., & Norquist, G. S. (1989). Schizophrenia: epidemiology, In H. I. Kaplan, & J. B. Sadock (Eds.), *Comprehensive textbook of psychiatry* (pp. 699–705). Baltimore: Williams and Wilkins.

Kelly, J. A. N., Murphy, D. A., Boccie, R., Brasfield, T. L., Davis, D. R., Hauth, A. C., Morgan, M. G., Stevenson, L. Y., & Eilers, M. K. (1992). AIDS/HIV risk behavior among the chronic mentally ill. *American Journal of Psychiatry, 149,* 886–889.

Lukoff, D., Gioia-Hasick, D., Sullivan, G., Golden, J. S., & Nuechterlein, K. H. (1986). Sex education and rehabilitation with schizophrenic male outpatients. *Schizophrenia Bulletin, 12,* 669–677.

McCane-Katz, E. F. (1991). The consequences of maternal substance abuse for the child exposed in utero. *Psychosomatics, 32,* 268–274.

McCullough, L. B., Coverdale, J., Bayer, T., & Chervenak, F. A. (1992). Ethically justified guidelines for family planning interventions to prevent pregnancy in female patients with chronic mental illness. *American Journal of Obstetrics and Gynecology, 167,* 19–25.

McEvoy, J. P., Hatcher, A., Appelbaum, P. S., & Abernethy, V. (1983). Chronic schizophrenic women's attitudes toward sex, pregnancy, birth control, and childrearing. *Hospital and Community Psychiatry, 34,* 536–539.

McKinnon, K., Cournos, F., Meyer-Bahlburg, H. F. L., Guido, J. R., Caraballo, L. R., Margoshes, E. S., Herman, R., Gruen, R. S., & Exner, T. M. (1993). Reliability of sexual risk behavior interviews with psychiatric patients. *American Journal of Psychiatry, 150,* 972–974.

McNeil, T. F., Persson-Blennow, I., & Kaij, L. (1974). Reproduction in female psychiatric patients: severity of mental disturbance near reproduction and rates of obstetric complications. *Acta Psyciatrica Scandinavia, 50,* 23–32.

Miller, L. J. (1990). Psychotic denial of pregnancy: phenomenology and clinical management. *Hospital and Community Psychiatry, 41,* 1233–1237.

Miller, L. J., & Finnerty, M. (1996). Sexuality, pregnancy and childrearing among women with schizophrenia-spectrum disorders. *Psychiatric Services, 47,* 502–506.

Nurnberg, H. G. (1989). An overview of somatic treatment of psychosis during pregnancy and postpartum. *General Hospital Psychiatry, 11,* 328–338.

Packer, S. (1992). Family planning for women with bipolar disorder. *Hospital and Community Psychiatry, 42,* 479–481.

Rieder, R. O., Rosenthal, D., Wender, P., & Blumenthal, H. (1975). The offspring of schizophrenics: Fetal and neonatal deaths. *Archives of General Psychiatry, 32,* 200–211.

Rudolph, B., Larson, G. L., Swang, S., Hough, E. E., & Arororian, K. (1990). Hospitalized pregnant psychotic women: Characteristics and treatment issues. *Hospital and Community Psychiatry, 41,* 159–163.

Sacks, M., Dermatis, H., Couser-OH, S., Burton, W., & Perry, S. (1992). Seroprevalence of HIV and risk factors for AIDS in psychiatric inpatients. *Hospital and Community Psychiatry, 43,* 736–737.

Schulz, P. M., Schulz, S. C., Dibble, E., Targum, S. D., van Kammen, D. P., & Gershon, E. S. (1982). Patient and family attitudes about schizophrenia: Implications for genetic counseling. *Schizophrenia Bulletin, 8,* 504–513,

Seeman, H. V., Lang, M., & Rector, N. (1990).Chronic schizophrenia: A risk factor for HIV? *Canadian Journal of Psychiatry, 35,* 765–768.

Stone, K. M., & Peterson, H. B. (1992). Spermicides, HIV, and the vaginal sponge. *Journal of the American Medical Association, 268,* 521–523.

Sullivan, M. D., & Younger, S. J. (1994). Depression, competence, and the right to refuse lifesaving medical treatment. *American Journal of Psychiatry, 151,* 971–978.

Test, M. A., Burke, S. S., & Wallisch, L. S. (1990). Gender differences of young adults with schizophrenic disorders in community care. *Schizophrenia Bulletin, 16,* 331–344.

Tucker, G. T., Turner, J., & Chapman, R. (1981). Problems in attracting and retaining psychiatrists in rural areas. *Hospital and Community Psychiatry, 32,* 118–120.

Volavka, J., Convit, A., O'Donnell, J., Denyon, R., Evangelista, C., & Czorbar, P. (1992). Assessment of risk behaviors for HIV infection among psychiatric inpatients. *Hospital Community Psychiatry, 43,* 482–485.

Wrede, G., Mednick, S. A., HuHunen, M. O., & Nilsson, C. G. (1980). Pregnancy and delivery complications in the birth of an unselected series of Finnish children with schizophrenic mothers. *Acta Psychiatric Scandinavia, 62,* 369–381.

Zax, M., Sameroff, A. H., & Babigan, H. M. (1977). Birth outcomes in the offspring of mentally disordered women. *American Journal of Orthopsychiatry, 47,* 218–229.

CHAPTER 15

SOCIAL NETWORKS AND SCHIZOPHRENIA

Eugenia T. Randolph

The assessment of social bonds as an important determinant in the course of schizophrenia has been a significant area of psychiatric research in recent years (Sorenson, 1994). Earlier findings suggesting that the prognosis for schizophrenia was more favorable in developing than in industrialized countries gave rise to speculation that the greater availability of social support in developing countries exerted a protective influence on the course of schizophrenia (World Health Organization [WHO]), 1979; Waxler-Morrison, 1979; Strauss & Carpenter, 1977). These findings led to considerable research aimed at understanding the role of social support in the course of schizophrenia. This chapter provides a general overview of the relationship between social networks and schizophrenia with emphasis on findings from key studies and their potential contribution to the clinical care of patients with schizophrenia (Beels, 1978; Breier & Strauss, 1984).

THE STRUCTURE AND FUNCTION OF SOCIAL NETWORKS

In the assessment of social networks, the personal network approach is the one most frequently used. The three components of personal networks are typically the kin-ship, friendship, and help-giving sectors (Erickson, 1975). This concept of networks is embedded in the broader notion of social support as having important effects on the outcome of mental illness (Sokolove & Trimble, 1986; Pattison & Pattison, 1981; Mosher & Keith, 1980; Kaplan, Cassel, & Gore, 1977; Brown, 1974). Social support is associated with emotional well-being (Cohen & Willis, 1985; Dean & Lin, 1977) and believed to mediate or buffer exposure to stress (Cassel, 1974; Turner & Marino, 1994).

Social networks are often discussed with reference to size, composition, and other key characteristics (Beels, Gutwirth, Berkeley, & Struening, 1984). Below, we provide a brief review of the structural characteristics of networks.

Size

Size refers to the number of network members enumerated in a network assessment. Network size has been found to be negatively associated with severity of psychopathology in several studies (Pattison, deFrancisco, Wood, Frazier, & Crowder, 1975; Cohen & Sokolovsky, 1978; Hammer, 1980, 1981). Smaller networks may be a predictor of hospitalization (Cohen & Sokolovsky, 1978) as well as a result of hospitalization and time spent away from the family and friends (Lipton, Cohen, Fischer, & Katz 1981). Large networks may provide a wider access to resources and help minimize the overburdening of some key network members. However, network size may not always have positive consequences. Networks dominated by overinvolved relatives or comprised of fragmented relationships may be a source of stress rather than comfort (Beels, 1981; Morin & Seidman, 1986).

Variations in size of reported networks may differ significantly based on the criteria used for defining network membership. Criteria may vary in a number of ways: (1) whether all members of the network are elicited or merely a representative group; (2) whether only individuals with a specified level of contact are listed or only those members the focal individual perceives as significant; (3) degree of frequency contact must occur for a member to be considered active (Mitchell & Trickett, 1980).

A sampling of criteria for social network membership include the following definitions:

- "All links within the preceding year with a frequency of at least one a month" (Cohen & Sokolovsky, 1978, p. 549).
- "Respondents list in matrix form up to 15 significant others with whom they were likely to interact at least once during any 2 week period" (Hirsch, 1979, p. 8).
- "We define the primary group as being made up of all kin, nominated friends, work associates, and neighbors" (Henderson et al., 1978, p. 77).

Density

Density is the degree of interconnectedness of network members. High density reflects a network in which most members know each other. Low density reflects a network in which few members know each other (Dozier, Harris, & Bergman, 1987). Some studies have shown high density to be associated with greater psychopathology (Stokes, 1983; Mueller, 1980). Dozier et al. (1987) found that networks of moderate density were associated with fewer days in the hospital in a sample of young psychotic patients.

Clusters

Clusters refer to the proportion of interconnections between the nuclear family network and the friend network (Estroff, Zimmer, Lachicotte, & Benoit, 1994; Morin &

Seidman, 1986). A cluster may be conceptualized as a group of people who share a common role (family members, coworkers, club members). When clusters are overly interconnected, the network may resemble one large cluster. The networks of nonpsychiatric populations usually have five or six clusters; the networks of psychiatric patients frequently have few clusters, creating an enmeshment that may reduce resources in times of stress (Hammer, 1981; Morin & Seidman, 1986).

Multiplexity

Multiplexity refers to the ability of a network member to fulfill more than one role (e.g., provide advice and emotional support). Multiplex relationships can be beneficial because they significantly increase available support (Morin & Seidman, 1986). For example, a friend may be unavailable for an outing but may lend money for bus fare and a movie. Multiplex relationships appear to decrease in the presence of severe psychopathology (Tolsdorf, 1976; Cohen & Sokolovsky, 1978). Hirsch (1979) reports that multiplexity of relationships is associated with overall satisfaction with one's network and perceived support.

In reviewing the research on social networks, Hammer, Makiesky-Barrow, and Gutwirth (1978) concluded that there is a good deal of consistency with respect to the structural characteristics of networks across cultural and social boundaries. The average person typically has a stable network of 25 to 30 persons with whom he or she has frequent and significant contact (Westermeyer & Pattison, 1981).

Open and Closed Networks

Functionally, qualities such as the capacity for activating connections to outside networks have led to the distinction between two broad types of networks (Escobar & Randolph, 1982). Open social networks are characterized by having a relatively large number of persons and connections whose ties are weak (low density). These networks often have a large number of nonrelatives (Phillips, 1981). Few of these persons may know or interact with other members of the network. These "weak" connections may act as bridges to other networks that considerably broaden available resources in time of need such as an emergency (Finlayson, 1976; McKinley, 1973).

Closed (close-knit) networks are distinguished by strong ties and a small number of members, usually close

relatives. Closed networks may promote strong maintenance of personal identity and provide stable emotional
support to its members (Walker, MacBride, & Vachon,
1977). However, the lack of connections to outside networks may be a detriment when additional resources are
required.

The Nature of Social Support

Henderson, Byrne, and Duncan-Jones (1981) enumerate six provisions of social relationships. Relying on the
work of Robert Weiss (1974), they list the following as
the key components of social support.

- *Attachment,* provided by close affectional relationships,
  which gives a sense of security and place
- *Social integration,* provided by membership of a network of persons having shared interests and values
- *Opportunity for nurturing others,* usually children,
  which gives some an incentive for continuing in the
  face of adversity
- *Reassurance of personal worth,* which promotes self-
  esteem and comes both from those at home and from
  friends and work associates
- *Reliable alliance,* which is obtained mainly from the
  more stable relationships with family members
- *Obtaining help and guidance,* typically from informal
  advisers when difficulties have to be resolved (Henderson et al., 1981, p. 31)

In a very real sense, these are the integral components of
the social bond that affectively integrate the individual
into the broader social context.

In reviewing the general functional aspects of an individual's network, research has shown that in most networks, relatives (kinship) are likely to provide long-term
assistance when needed. Neighbors are particularly useful
in "emergency" situations, given their geographical proximity. Friends seem more likely to provide help when it
concerns peer-related activities or personal problems (Litwak & Szclenyi, 1969).

STUDIES OF SOCIAL SUPPORT
AND SCHIZOPHRENIA

Hammer (1963–1964) was one of the first to examine
the effect of social networks on psychopathology and use
of services. In a sample of 55 males and females with clinical diagnoses of schizophrenia or manic–depressive ill-

ness, she found that a patient's position in the network
correlated with the decision to hospitalize. Subjects in positions critical to the family unit (primary wage earner,
homemaker) tended to be hospitalized more rapidly than
those in less essential positions.

In a study addressing specifically the content and function of social networks, Tolsdorf (1976) compared 10
schizophrenic patients with 10 medical patients. Schizophrenic patients reported fewer intimate relationships and
their networks were heavily dominated by family members. Schizophrenic patients also tended to have negative
orientations toward network members and exhibited a tendency to withdraw from networks or utilize networks only
superficially, thereby isolating themselves from potential
sources of support.

Sokolovsky, Cohen, Berger, and Geiger (1978) investigated the social networks of 43 SRO (single room occupancy) hotel residents with varying degrees of psychiatric
symptoms. They observed that residents with no psychiatric histories or minimal residual symptoms had significantly more network contacts and more functional network linkages. The high residual symptoms group formed
few instrumental linkages outside the hotel. The authors
concluded that, in the case of residents with few contacts
outside the hotel, failure to become integrated into the social organization of the hotel may be a critical factor contributing to rehospitalization. Individuals with small,
poorly connected networks were thought to constitute an
at-risk group requiring professional support if rehospitalization was to be prevented.

In a more broadly focused study, Pattison, Llamas, and
Hurd (1979) investigated the network characteristics of
normal, neurotic, and psychotic individuals. They reported that the networks of normal individuals had an average of 20 to 25 people (5 or 6 in each sector; e.g.,
friends, family, others). Network members typically rated
high on such variables as contact, positive feelings, and
reciprocity. Networks of neurotic individuals were composed of about 15 individuals and characterized by an increased reliance on nuclear family members. Interactions
were frequently weak and negative. The networks of psychotic individuals were considerably smaller and densely
interconnected. Interpersonal relationships tended to be
ambivalent or negative and highly asymmetric. The authors concluded that personal networks were important
mediators in stress management when they are normal but
tend to create or intensify stress when pathologic.

Lipton et al. (1981) compared the structure and function of the social networks of 15 single-admission and 15

multiple-admission schizophrenic patients. They reported that multiple-admission patients had smaller, less functional networks and fewer kin contacts. The authors concluded that schizophrenia creates a "network crisis." Acknowledging the limitations of a cross-sectional study, the authors hypothesized that changes in the network may follow the first hospitalization, and the breakdowns in the network may result from the patient's impaired social competence and the "antagonistic" reactions of those close to him or her.

Randolph and Escobar (1985) compared the social network characteristics of moderately and severely ill outpatients with schizophrenia with a nonpsychiatric control group with similar demographic characteristics. They found significant differences in network size for these groups: severely ill patients had a mean network size of 8.6 members; moderately ill patients had a mean network size of 10.7 members; controls had a mean network size of 13.5 members. The most notable difference between patients and controls related to the number of friends in the network. Patients had an average friendship sector ranging from 2.1 (severely ill) to 2.8 (moderately ill). Controls listed, on the average, 5.6 friends in their networks. Additionally, the authors found that as severity of illness increased, contacts with nonfamily members diminished and perception of available support declined significantly. Hypothesis relating to increased density and increased negativity in relationships for the more ill patients were not substantiated. However, social network size was not associated with rehospitalization for patients with schizophrenia in this sample (Escobar, Randolph, & Hill, 1988).

Dozier et al. (1987) examined the relationship of social network density, the extent to which network members know one another, and rehospitalization in a mixed sample of patients with schizophrenia, bipolar, and borderline personality disorders. They found that networks of moderate density were optimal for patients with frequent hospitalizations. Patients with networks of moderate density were hospitalized less than patients with low or high density networks.

Hamilton, Ponzoha, Cutler, and Weigel (1989) examined the degree to which positive symptoms of schizophrenia (hallucinations and delusions) and negative symptoms of schizophrenia (affective flattening, attentional impairment, anhedonia) were associated with social network characteristics in a sample of 39 chronic patients with schizophrenia. Patients with prominent negative symptoms reported significantly smaller social networks.

Positive symptoms did not correlated with network characteristics. The authors concluded that patients with limited emotional responsiveness had the most impoverished social networks.

In summary, these studies strongly suggest that persons with schizophrenia have fewer social resources and social ties than nonpsychiatric groups. Size of social networks is often correlated with severity of symptoms and rehospitalization. The social networks of schizophrenic patients are sometimes characterized by superficial and negative relationships.

FACTORS CONTRIBUTING TO DIMINISHED SOCIAL TIES

Sorensen (1994) provides an informative summary of factors that may contribute to the impoverishment of the social networks of schizophrenic patients. Below, his observations are used as the reference point for this section of the discussion.

1. *Psychopathology associated with schizophrenia.* Prominent symptoms of schizophrenia, such as hallucinations, delusions, bizarre behavior, and the sometimes attendant heightened suspiciousness and hostility, clearly disrupt normative expectations and reciprocity in social interaction. The high probability that symptoms first emerged in the transition from adolescence to early adulthood often precludes the development of adult social ties (Sorensen, 1994). Further, others have speculated that the negative symptoms of schizophrenia, such as avolition, anhedonia-asociability, affective flattening, alogia, and attentional impairment, may foster social isolation and avoidance behaviors. In a study of 39 schizophrenic patients, Hamilton et al. (1989) determined that patients with negative symptoms had significantly smaller and more dysfunctional networks. Positive symptoms did not correlate significantly with any network variables.

2. *Limited social skills.* Early age of onset, psychiatric hospitalizations, and recurrent exacerbations of psychotic symptoms may significantly impede the acquisition of social skills necessary for developing and maintaining social relationships. Patients with negative symptoms and a tendency toward isolation may have the most difficulty maintaining social relationships in the hospital and in the community (Hamilton et al., 1989; Sorenson, 1994). Both the nature and clinical course of schizophrenia present a number of

obstacles to fostering social ties, especially for patients vulnerable to frequent and prolonged symptomatic exacerbations. Prolonged hospitalizations, especially if the hospital is far from home, family, and the patient's community may further serve to weaken both family and friendship ties (Nelson, Hall, Squire, & Walsh-Bowers, 1992; Sorenson, 1994).

3. *Limited opportunities for "networking."* Chronic psychiatric patients often have ended their educational pursuits early and are frequently unemployed. Treatment settings are often their only opportunity and access to social ties (Sorenson, 1994). It is therefore not surprising that the social networks of chronic patients become increasingly inhabited only by other patients and treatment setting staff (Mitchell & Birley, 1983; Meeks & Murrell, 1994).

4. *Limited resources.* Most chronic psychiatric patients, even when disability compensation and other financial assistance is provided, have limited finances. Access to an automobile or a telephone, important tools for maintaining social relationships, is often limited if present at all (Sorenson, 1994). Similarly, diminished resources may limit participation in social activities and social organizations, further constricting the social orbit.

5. *Stigma.* Despite efforts to educate the public about mental illness, stereotypical attitudes toward psychiatric patients still prevail. Fear of unpredictable and possibly dangerous behavior may discourage social interaction (Sorenson, 1994). The stigma associated with mental illness, even in more enlightened communities, often embarrasses family members and leads, in a variety of ways, to diminished social ties and opportunity for social interaction.

SOCIAL NETWORKS AND THE COURSE OF SCHIZOPHRENIA

A critical question in investigations of social support and mental illness is the causal connection: Do the florid symptoms of schizophrenia lead to diminished social ties, or does increased social isolation render the individual more vulnerable to psychotic relapse? Few studies have attempted to address this question with an appropriate research design. A major problem is, of course, that the erosion of social relationships, even among severely disturbed individuals, may be a gradual and uneven process difficult to capture by the "window" provided in even the more ambitious prospective studies.

Isele, Merz, Malzacher, and Angst (1985) compared the premorbid social relations of a sample of 69 individuals with schizophrenia being hospitalized for the first time with a control sample of 60 individuals drawn at random from a rural community with no prior history of psychiatric treatment. The assessment interview made reference to the period 2 months prior to the onset of symptoms for the patients and 2 months prior to the interview for the controls. Compared with the controls, schizophrenic patients reported markedly diminished social networks characterized by a predominance of family links. Schizophrenic patients did not establish close relationships nor did they actively seek social interaction. Furthermore, they tended to withdraw from existing relationships, especially heterosexual relationships. While this study offers a useful insight with some premorbid social network characteristics, failure to control for severity of symptoms and the very narrow time frame for premorbid assessment limit the inference that may be drawn.

Erickson, Beiser, Iacono, Fleming, and Lin (1989) investigated the role of social relationships in the course of first-episode psychosis (schizophrenia and affective disorder) in comparison with a sample of community volunteers matched on gender and age. The Present State Examination (PSE; Wing, Cooper, & Sartorius, 1974) was administered at intake and at the 18-month follow-up to the schizophrenic and affective disorder patients. The Interview Schedule for Social Interaction (ISSI; Henderson et al., 1981) was used to enumerate the network of family and friends, availability of social resources, and perceived adequacy of social relationships.

Comparisons of size and composition of social networks at baseline revealed that schizophrenic patients identified the least number of friends (3.6, on average), affective disorder patients followed next (5.0), and normal volunteers the most (6.3). Differences in number of family members in the social networks of the three groups did not reach statistical significance. However, there was a trend showing that schizophrenic patients identified fewer family members within their social networks. Furthermore, schizophrenic subjects had fewer close relationships than affective psychosis and normal volunteer groups, but there were no group differences in the availability of acquaintances. There was a trend for schizophrenic patients to perceive social support from acquaintances as less adequate.

At the 18-month follow-up, availability and perceived adequacy of relationships with friends and acquaintances were positively associated with outcome. Greater involvement with and higher quality relationships yielded a better prognosis for schizophrenic patients. Interestingly, however, there was a negative relationship between number of family members and prognosis. A greater number of family members in their social network was associated with a less favorable prognosis for the schizophrenic sample.

CRITIQUE

Most of these studies of social networks and psychopathology are methodologically deficient in several areas. Study samples have been largely heterogeneous. First admissions, chronic patients, and diverse diagnostic categories have been grouped together. Diagnostic criteria have not been consistent. Controls for such important prognostic factors as premorbid history, marital status, family history of mental disorder, age of onset, and social class, among others, have not always been clearly delineated. Instruments utilized to identify and measure social networks have lacked consistency. For example, variables such as quantity and quality of social support have not been clearly defined or measured (Lin, Dean, & Ensel, 1981; McFarlane, Neale, Norman, Roy, & Streiner, 1981). Finally, most studies have been retrospective investigations. There is a need for longitudinal studies that may contribute information about the relationship of various network characteristics to clinical outcome. More specifically, we need to better understand the causal relationship between social networks and psychopathology. Existing studies, typically cross-sectional, tell us something about the association between psychopathology and the characteristics of social networks; however, we need to know more about the process by which mentally ill individuals fail to either develop or maintain an active social support network.

Many of these studies have addressed the *quantitative* aspects of social networks quite thoroughly. However, the more *qualitative* dimensions of social support have not been sufficiently addressed. Future studies need to investigate this dimension further. It is still not known whether the onset of psychiatric illness leads to diminished social ties or perceived lack of support exacerbates the vulnerability to psychiatric disorders. Longitudinal studies focusing on first-break schizophrenic patients would contribute greatly to the understanding of the causal directionality of the now well-replicated relationship between social networks and psychopathology.

CONCLUSION

Most studies indicate that the network linkages of schizophrenic patients are generally impoverished, especially in the friendship sector. These findings have two major clinical implications. First, since family linkages continue to exist even if somewhat strained, therapeutic interventions involving family members would be indicated. Assisting persons with schizophrenia to better relationships with family members, as well as assisting family members to better understand the nature of schizophrenic illness, might facilitate the development of stronger family ties.

Second, since severely ill patients report few friends in their networks, social skills training might encourage patients to develop ties outside their families and professional caregivers. There is considerable evidence that even severely disabled schizophrenic patients can significantly improve their social skills in well-structured training programs that utilize behavioral learning principles (Liberman, Mueser, & Wallace, 1986).

It has been suggested that individuals with schizophrenia are vulnerable to sensory overload and may attempt to limit contact as a means of dealing with social deficits (Heller & Swindle, 1983). Recent work on familial expressed emotion (EE), especially criticism and emotional overinvolvement, may help to shed some light on the social relationships of schizophrenic patients and their relatives. Leff and Vaughn (1984) reported that low EE relatives were more sensitive to the need for greater social support or increased social distance. On the other hand, high EE relatives were more likely to be intrusive, aggressively pursuing contact when patients were quiet or withdrawn, disregarding requests for privacy. Patients seldom avoided relatives who were low-keyed and nonintrusive. Even if they did not want to talk, they tended to stay in the same room and were unlikely to retreat from the relative's presence. But in high EE households, protective withdrawal was common. According to Leff and Vaughn, the link between a stressful stimulus (i.e., high levels of expressed emotion) and social withdrawal by the patient seemed quite clear.

Strachan et al.'s (1989) study of EE and patients' coping style provides further support for this view. Patient coping style, rated on the basis of a 20-minute family problem-solving task, was significantly related to EE. Schizophrenic patients interacting with high EE parents made an average of 4.8 criticisms during the 20-minute discussion, compared with an average of 1.7 made by patients interacting with low EE parents. Patients interacting with low EE parents made significantly more autonomous statements (clear self-motivated statements of intention or determination to achieve a goal or master a task), and significantly fewer critical statements (complaints directed at the relative to whom the person is speaking) compared with patients interacting with high EE parents. These observations and findings suggest that EE may be an important dimension in understanding the family network dynamics of schizophrenic patients. This relationship is important in understanding the conflicted nature of family relationships in individuals with schizophrenia.

COMMENT

It is noteworthy that most of the theoretical and empirical work on the relationship between social network and schizophrenia was carried out in the 1980s. In more recent years, only an occasional article appears in a peer review journal. Usually these articles have a relatively narrow focus. One might appropriately ask why, given the initial wave of interest and promise in this area, has there been such a decline of research on social networks and psychopathology? One might also ask why there has been so little clinical application of the information generated by these studies? Below, I would like to speculate on some of these issues.

First, it has been a research tradition lacking clear direction. We have had study after study showing that schizophrenic patients have fewer friends than other clinical groups or community controls. However, there has been little effort to translate these findings into clinical relevance. While most articles have the obligatory concluding comments about the importance of buffering the networks of schizophrenic patients, they have not generated interventions that specifically attempt to do so. Second, there has been no direct linkage between characterizing the social networks of schizophrenic patients and the development of effective techniques for helping schizophrenic patients enrich their social worlds. Social skills training is the notable exception to this. However, even in this area, there are limited data to indicate that social skills training in a laboratory setting can effectively generalize to actual behavior in the community.

There are important lessons to be learned from all of these studies, and there are important policy and clinical implications. First, it is the *perception* of social support that counts. One can list 10 friends and acquaintances and yet perceive that there is not one in that 10 that can truly be counted on in time of need. On the other hand, one can list one or two friends and feel well supported. Second, it may well be that while we have a good understanding of the negative effects of social isolation on the course of schizophrenia, or any illness for that matter, we do not know how to dramatically alter that. We may not be able to "teach" severely ill schizophrenic patients how to really expand their peer networks in the community. Furthermore, it is highly possible that many schizophrenic patients may not wish to seek out friends. For some patients, the very nature of social interaction and the attendant performance demands may feel too burdensome.

Perhaps the most salient observation that can be made from a review of this literature is that schizophrenic patients need some level of support in the community—especially instrumental support (i.e., ongoing help with meeting daily needs). Programs focusing on assertive case management (Stein & Test, 1980; Test, 1992) may be effective at providing that kind of support. In a very real sense these programs deliver the initial promise of the community mental movement. The core concept of assertive case management is to provide, through a mental health professional, the protective buffer and support required by most schizophrenic patients residing in the community.

REFERENCES

Beels, C. C. (1978). Social networks, the family, and the schizophrenic patient. *Schizophrenia Bulletin, 4*, 512–521.

Beels, C. C. (1981). Social support and schizophrenia. *Schizophrenia Bulletin, 7*, 58–72.

Beels, C. C., Gutwirth, L., Berkeley, J., & Struening, E. (1984). Measurements of social support in schizophrenia. *Schizophrenia Bulletin, 10*, 399–411.

Breier, A., & Strauss, J. S. (1984). The role of social relationships in the recovery from psychotic disorders. *American Journal of Psychiatry, 141*, 949–955.

Brown, G. W. (1974). Meaning, measurement and stress of life events. In B. S. Dohrenwend, & B. P. Dohrenwend (Eds.), *Stressful life events: Their nature and effects* (pp. 217–244). New York: Wiley.

Cassel, J. (1974). An epidemiological perspective of psychosocial factors in disease etiology. *American Journal of Public Health, 64*, 1040–1043.

Cohen, C. I., & Sokolovsky, J. (1978). Schizophrenia and social networks: Ex-patients in the inner city. *Schizophrenia Bulletin, 4*, 546–560.

Cohen, S., & Willis, T. A. (1985). Stress, social support, and the buffering hypothesis. *Psychological Bulletin, 98*, 31–57

Dean, A., & Lin, N. (1977). The stress-buffering role of social support: Problems and prospects for systematic investigation. *Journal of Nervous and Mental Disease, 165*, 403–417.

Dozier, M., Harris, M., & Bergman, H. (1987). Social network density and re-hospitalization among young adult patients. *Hospital and Community Psychiatry, 38*, 61–65.

Erickson, D. H., Beiser, M., Iacono, W. G., Fleming J. A. E., & Lin, T. (1989). The role of social relationships in the course of first-episode schizophrenia and affective psychosis. *American Journal of Psychiatry, 146*, 1456–1461.

Erickson, G. D. (1975). The concept of personal network in clinical practice. *Family Process, 14*, 487–498.

Escobar, J. I., & Randolph, E. T. (1982). The Hispanic and social networks, In R. M. Becerra, M. Karno, & J. I. Escobar (Eds.), *Mental health and Hispanic Americans, clinical perspectives* (pp. 41–57). New York: Grune and Stratton.

Escobar J. I., Randolph, E. T., & Hill, M. A. (1988). The cycle of schizophrenia: A sociocultural view. *VA Practitioner, 5*, 81–88.

Estroff, S. E., Zimmer, C., Lachicotte, W. S., & Benoit, J. (1994). The influence of social networks and social support on violence by persons with serious mental illness. *Hospital and Community Psychiatry, 45*, 669–679.

Finlayson, A. (1976). Social networks as coping resources. *Social Science and Medicine, 10*, 97–103.

Hamilton, N. G., Ponzoha, C. A., Cutler, D. L., & Weigel, R. M. (1989). Social networks and negative versus positive symptoms of schizophrenia. *Schizophrenia Bulletin, 15*, 625–633.

Hammer, M. (1963–1964). Influence of small social networks as factors on mental hospital admission. *Human Organization, 22*, 243–251.

Hammer, M. (1980). Predictability of social connections over time. *Social Networks, 2*, 165–180.

Hammer, M. (1981). Social support, social networks, and schizophrenia. *Schizophrenia Bulletin, 7*, 45–57.

Hammer, M., Makiesky-Barrow, S., & Gutwirth, L. (1978). Social networks and schizophrenia. *Schizophrenia Bulletin, 4*, 522–545.

Heller, K., & Swindle, R. W. (1983). Social networks, perceived social support, and coping with stress. In R. D. Felner, L. A. Jason, J. N. Moritsugee, & S. S. Farber (Eds.), *Prevention psychology: Theory, research, and practice* (pp. 87–103). New York: Pergamon Press.

Henderson, S., Byrne, D. G., & Duncan-Jones, P. (1981). *Neurosis and the social environment.* San Diego, CA: Academic Press.

Henderson, S., Duncan-Jones, P., McAuley, H., & Ritchie, K. (1978). The patient's primary group. *British Journal of Psychiatry, 132*, 74–86.

Hirsch, B. (1979). Psychological dimensions of social networks: A multimethod analysis. *American Journal of Community Psychology, 7*, 263–277.

Isele, R., Merz, J., Malzacher, M., & Angst, J. (1985). Social disability in schizophrenia: The controlled prospective Burgholzi study. *European Archives of Psychiatry and Neurological Science, 234*, 348–356.

Kaplan, B. H., Cassel, J. C., & Gore, S. (1977). Social support and health. *Medical Care, 15*, 47–58.

Leff, J., & Vaughn, C. (1984). *Expressed emotion in families: Its significance for mental illness.* New York: Guilford Press.

Lin, N., Dean, A., & Ensel, W. M. (1981). Social support scales: A methodological note. *Schizophrenia Bulletin 7*, 73–89.

Liberman, R. P., Mueser, K. T., & Wallace, C. J. (1986). Social skills training for schizophrenic individuals at risk for relapse. *American Journal of Psychiatry, 143*, 523–526.

Lipton, F. R., Cohen, C. I., Fischer, E., & Katz, S. E. (1981). Schizophrenia: A network crisis. *Schizophrenia Bulletin, 7*, 144–151.

Litwak, E., & Szclenyi, I. (1969). Primary group structures and their functions: Kin, neighbors, and friends. *American Sociological Review, 344*, 465–481.

McFarlane, A. H., Neale, K. A., Norman, G. R., Roy, R. G., & Streiner, D. L. (1981). Methodological issues in developing a scale to measure social support. *Schizophrenia Bulletin, 7*, 90–100.

McKinley, J. B. (1973). Social networks, lay consultation and health seeking behavior. *Social Forces, 52*, 274–292.

Meeks, S., & Murrell, S. A. (1994). Service providers in the social networks of clients with severe mental illness. *Schizophrenia Bulletin, 20*, 399–406.

Mitchell, R. E., & Trickett, E. J., (1980). Social networks as mediators of social support: An analysis of the effects and determinants of social networks. *Community Mental Health Journal, 16*, 27–45.

Mitchell, S. F., & Birley, J. L. (1983). The use of ward support by psychiatric patients in the community. *British Journal of Psychiatry, 142*, 9–15.

Morin R. C., & Seidman E. (1986). A social network approach and the revolving door patient. *Schizophrenia Bulletin, 12*, 262–273.

Mosher, L. R., & Keith, S. F. (1980). Psychosocial treatment: Individual, group, family and community approaches. *Schizophrenia Bulletin, 6*, 10–41.

Mueller, D. P. (1980). Social Networks: A promising direction for research on the relationship of the social environment to psychiatric disorder. *Social Science and Medicine, 14A*, 147–161.

Nelson, G., Hall, G. B., Squire, D., & Walsh-Bowers, R. T. (1992). Social network transactions of psychiatric patients. *Social Science and Medicine, 34*, 433–445.

Pattison, E. M., deFrancisco, D., Wood, P., Frazier, H., & Crowder, J. (1975). A psychosocial kinship model for family therapy. *American Journal of Psychiatry, 132*, 1246–1251.

Pattison, E. M., Llamas, R., & Hurd, G. (1979). Social network mediation of anxiety. *Psychiatric Annals, 9*, 56–57.

Pattison, E. M., & Pattison, M. L. (1981). Analysis of a schizophrenic psychosocial network. *Schizophrenia Bulletin, 7*, 135–143.

Phillips S. L. (1981). Network characteristics related to the well-being of normals: A comparative base. *Schizophrenia Bulletin, 7*, 117–124.

Randolph, E. T., & Escobar, J. I. (1985). *Social support, ethnicity, and schizophrenia.* Los Angeles, CA: Society for the Study of Psychiatry and Culture.

Sokolove, R. L., & Trimble, D. (1986). Assessing support and stress in the social networks of chronic patients. *Hospital and Community Psychiatry, 37*, 370–372.

Sokolovsky, J., Cohen, C., Berger, D., & Geiger, J. (1978). Personal networks of ex-mental patients in a Manhattan SRO hotel. *Human Organization, 37*, 5–15.

Sorenson, T. (1994). The intricacy of the ordinary. *British Journal of Psychiatry, 164*, 108–114.

Stein, L. I., & Test, M. A. (1980). Alternative to mental hospital treatment, I. Conceptual model, treatment program and clinical evaluation. *Archives of General Psychiatry, 37*, 392–397.

Stokes, J. D. (1983). Predicting satisfaction with social support form social network structure. *Journal of Community Psychology, 11*, 141–153.

Strachan, A. M., Feingold, D., Goldstein, M. H., & Miklowitz, D. J. (1989). Is expressed emotion an index of a transactional process? II. Patient's coping style. *Family Process, 28*, 169–181.

Strauss, J. S., & Carpenter, W. T., Jr. (1977). The prediction of outcome in schizophrenia: III. Five-year outcome and its predictors. *Archives of General Psychiatry, 34*, 159–163.

Test, M. A. (1992). Training in community living. In R. P. Liberman (Ed.), *Handbook of psychiatric rehabilitation* (pp. 153–170). New York: Macmillan.

Tolsdorf, C. C. (1976). Social networks, support, and coping: An exploratory study. *Family Process, 15*, 407–418.

Turner, R. J., & Marino, F. (1994). Social support and social structure: A descriptive epidemiology. *Journal of Health and Social Behavior, 35*, 193–212.

Walker, K. N., MacBride, A., & Vachon, M. L. S. (1977). Social support networks and the crisis of bereavement. *Social Science and Medicine, 11*, 35–41.

Waxler-Morrison, N. (1979). Is outcome for schizophrenia better in nonindustrial societies? *Journal of Nervous Mental Disorders, 167*, 144–158.

Westermeyer, J., & Pattison, M. E. (1981). Social networks and mental illness in a peasant society. *Schizophrenia Bulletin, 7*, 125–134.

Weiss, R. S. (1974). The provision of social relationships. In Rubin (Ed.). *Doing unto others* (pp. 128–143). Englewood Cliffs, NJ: Prentice Hall.

Wing, J. K., Cooper, J. E., & Sartorius, N. (1974). *Measurement and classification of psychiatric symptoms: An instruction manual for the PSE and Catego program.* Cambridge, England: Cambridge University.

World Health Organization. (1979). *Schizophrenia: An international follow-up study.* New York: Wiley.

CHAPTER 16

STIGMA

Amerigo Farina

How satisfying it would be to crisply begin this chapter by defining stigma and then presenting a clear overview of the nature of the phenomenon. The subject matter to which the term *stigma* refers is far too complicated for that. Its role in a wild variety of conditions has been examined. These conditions include ethnicity, skin color, obesity, deformities of the body, facial unattractiveness, criminality, and even pregnancy (Jones et al., 1984). Actually, many students of these matters believe that any significant departure, and possibly any noticeable departure, from societal ideals of pedigree, personal history, and appearance can be stigmatizing. Even if we confine ourselves to mental disorder, as in this chapter, between research and speculation we still find a sea of writings and we encounter irreconcilable disagreements. Some professionals even deny that the mentally disordered are in any way stigmatized (Crocetti, Spiro, & Ciassi, 1974) even as the bulk of them believe that those with mental problems are subjected to strong societal rejection and dislike.

It may be apparent, even for readers new to this area, that formulating a satisfactory and encompassing theory of the stigmatization process is a daunting task. To be sure, we can identify common elements that apply to a wide array of conditions. None of us would want stigmatizing characteristics either in ourselves or in our friends, and encountering someone with a striking blemish, and especially a visible blemish, makes us all feel uneasy. But the differences among degrading faults are quite apparent. Consider a convicted child rapist in comparison to a multiple amputee. It is difficult to imagine that anyone free of overwhelming problems would like to change places with either or would feel totally comfortable with them. But it is also true that most of us would have strong preferences as to which of the two we would least like living next door to us or for whom we would be more likely to do a favor. Blemishes differ in many ways and along numerous dimensions such as how dangerous the stigmatized person is perceived to be, to what extent the blemishes are visible, how much they interfere with the victim's functioning, and so forth.

Nevertheless, repeated attempts have been made to formulate a general and encompassing theory of stigma since such a theory could be enlightening and certainly practically useful (e.g., Goffman, 1963; Jones et al., 1984; Katz, 1981). And the results of these efforts do provide guidance and insights regarding the phenomenon of stigmatization. The works cited above have definitely influenced this chapter. However, unlike those efforts, I will not seek to construct central, encompassing theories. Even though the content, the subject matter of the chapter, will be largely restricted to mental disorder, there is a strategy that seems to hold more promise than seeking an overarching explanation for the stigmatization of those who have mental problems. Much research has been done with the stigma of mental disorder and pockets of pretty solid and clear information have emerged. For example, mental patients are characterized by certain peculiarities, such as tension, that arouse rejection and dislike from the public. We will examine these islands of knowledge that sometimes are not bridged or clearly connected to each other. Where theoretical ties seem helpful, I will strive to provide them. But an elegant, or even coherent, general theory seems premature and possibly misleading, and I will not attempt to concoct a grand scheme to tie everything together. Accordingly, this is the organization of what is to follow.

The present chapter will consist of the following three parts. First, we will return to a critical issue that has already been broached, that is, the question of whether there is a stigma of mental illness. Recall that disagreement exists regarding this matter. Second, those factors that are believed to play a causative role in that stigma will be identified and the evidence for this belief will be reviewed. An example of one such source of the social rejection of patients has already been described, namely, the tension and anxiety that is characteristic of those who are mentally disordered. Third, factors that are believed responsible for varying the level or intensity of stigma will then be identified and, here also, the evidence for this supposition will be reviewed. An example of such factors is the extent to which someone has interacted with mentally disordered people in the past. Individuals who have had few such interpersonal experiences appear to stigmatize those who are mentally ill more than individuals who have greater acquaintance with mental patients.

One additional issue needs brief consideration prior to entering into our subject matter. This book is about schizophrenia. Nevertheless, this particular chapter in the book will range over the entire continuum of adjustment and will not be limited to that specific type of mental disorder. There are two compelling and related reasons that, together, impel this broadening of the topic. First, if we did restrict ourselves to covering that which is known about the social stigmatizing of schizophrenic people exclusively, we would certainly have a very short chapter. There is little research that focuses on the stigma of schizophrenia per se, and even when such research is done, it is likely to be a study of societal responses to schizophrenics in comparison to other types of maladjustment. Second, the stigma literature makes it very clear that *all* forms of maladjustment elicit the same kinds of social responses. There is more rejection and degradation with increasingly severe disorders. However, we do not find qualitative changes but a continuum of responses, as will be seen from the research to be reviewed.

ARE MENTALLY DISORDERED PEOPLE STIGMATIZED?

As I have indicated, some mental health professionals have concluded that the stigma of mental disorders does not exist (Bentz & Edgerton, 1971; Crocetti & Lemkau, 1965; Crocetti et al., 1974). Others assert that, if it is still with us, it is retreating and we will soon be free of that social problem (Segal, 1978). However, the research that has been done convincingly shows that people who have experienced psychiatric problems are feared, disliked, and broadly rejected by society. The relevant literature has been summarized several times (e.g., Farina, 1981, 1982; Rabkin, 1972) and, in the aggregate, it makes the presence of stigmatization plain. Thus, one review concludes ". . . the nature of public attitudes toward mental disorders is quite clear. It toto the scores of studies indicate unequivocally that these attitudes are extremely negative" (Farina, 1982, p. 309). Here, I will not cover all of this literature. Rather, only the more recent studies and the studies most relevant to the purposes of the present chapter will be considered.

Contrary to some hopeful views, such as that cited above (Segal, 1978), numerous studies indicate that society is not becoming more tolerant and accepting of the mentally ill. Two studies will serve to support this assertion and to make it clearer. Olmsted and Durham (1976) in 1971 replicated a study done in 1962. They used a semantic differential to have students evaluate a series of concepts, including "most people," "mental patient," and "insane people." What was striking about their results was the *consistent negativity* of attitudes toward those with psychiatric problems over a decade. The correlations of the concept means over this period ranged between .95

and .99. In another study, Piner and Kahle (1984) carried out a conceptual replication of an experiment that was done about 20 years earlier (Farina & Ring, 1965). These experiments actually measured stigmatizing *behavior* toward those perceived as mentally disordered, and it was found that such behavior was as strongly present in the second study as it had been two decades earlier.

We should also consider a third experiment, this one by Brockman, D'Arcy, and Edmonds (1979), that also found social views toward psychiatrically troubled people are not becoming more benign. But these last researchers also have additional and possibly clarifying information for those who may have been puzzled by the inconsistency in studies of mental illness stigma. They arranged existing studies into two groups; those that report attitudes toward mental patients are improving and those that report they are not improving. They then proceeded to examine differences between these two groups, particularly in methodology used and in adequacy of training of the researchers. On the basis of the resulting data, they argue persuasively that the seeming improvement in attitudes is probably an artifact due to poor methods used by improperly trained investigators. The sounder studies, unfortunately, present a sadder picture of the fate facing victims of mental disorders in our society. While these findings would appear to resolve matters neatly, this area is very complex and requires caution and humility. There is certainly no reason to believe that the attitudes we are examining are immutable and some changes may be occurring.

However, there is little doubt that present attitudes are disparaging. One type of study that makes this starkly evident measures degree of favorability expressed by the public toward people with psychiatric problems in comparison to people beset with other kinds of stigmatizing conditions. Over the years, many categories of mental problems ranging in severity from "nervous person" to "mental patient," "psychotic person," or "insane person" have been compared to every imaginable other kind of condition causing social degradation. These blemishes have included alcoholism, amputation of limbs, being jailed for a felony, blindness, cancer, deafness, dwarfism, having heart disease, having a hunchback, leprosy, mental retardation, obesity, and tuberculosis (Brand & Clairborn, 1976; Colbert & Kalish, 1973; Drehmer, 1985; Lamy, 1966; Nunnally, 1961; Tringo, 1970). Favorability has been measured in numerous ways and in the context of various possible kinds of interactions such as having the target persons for neighbors or coworkers. In these many comparisons, it appears that people with severe mental problems are never viewed more favorably than someone with any of those other defaming marks. Rather, typically those with mental problems are regarded as the most abhorrent of social pariahs. Illustrative of how socially destructive problems of the mind can be is a study by Gussow and Tracy (1968) that showed people believe the two most horrible things that can befall someone are leprosy and insanity. Still, an "insane person" is regarded as more dangerous, bad, and foolish than a "leper" (Nunnally, 1961, pp. 270–272). And Lamy (1966) reports people believe a mother would choose to place her baby in the care of someone who had been jailed for committing a crime in preference to someone who had been a mental patient.

A lot of research on the stigmatization of mental patients has focused on their social reception in various facets of community living such as employment and housing. These facets can be considered individually, and the results are indeed revealing, particularly when the entire mosaic emerges. We will now examine the findings in several areas beginning with employment.

Work

Work is a cardinal determiner of someone's identification and worth as a person in Western society. It is perhaps of greater importance for a man than a woman, but the sexes are becoming similar in this regard. On meeting someone or hearing about him or her, a critical thing we seek to know is what is the person's occupation? Is he or she a salesperson, a lawyer, a janitor, or is he or she unemployed? Hugely different reactions can occur depending in which of these categories the person is revealed to be. But our occupational life affects more than the regard of others for us and our own self-respect, as significant as these are. The kind of work we do determines the kind of income we have and no work generally means virtually no income. So even our physical well-being is affected by our occupations or lack thereof. No wonder, then, that researchers have been concerned with the possible effects of stigma on the working life of people known to have been mental patients.

This area of research is very old, rich and varied, and, except for a few quirks, seemingly quite unequivocal. Some studies have utilized interviews and self-report questionnaires and the subjects have been both employers and former mental patients. In two studies (Olshansky, Grob, & Ekdahl, 1960; Olshansky, Grob, & Malamud, 1958), there being no extant laws against such discrimination at that time, 25% of the employers stated flatly that they would not hire a former mental patient. And 40% of those who would hire them would do so only if they could be placed in nondemanding, low-pressure jobs. More telling, only 26 of 200 employers had knowingly hired an ex-mental patient in the preceding 3 years and only 5 were prepared at that time to hire an ex-patient who was fully qualified for the job. Behavioral studies yield very similar results (Farina & Felner, 1973; Link, 1987; Link, Cullen, Mirotznik, & Struening, 1992. The first study listed is a particularly realistic one since an experimenter, in the guise of an unemployed worker, actually sought jobs from 32 business establishments. He gave identical work histories in each place but in 16 he also reported having had a psychiatric hospitalization while no such information was given to the other 16. The economy was depressed at the time of the study and not enough jobs were offered to test for differences between the two conditions, although four jobs were offered in the control in comparison to two jobs in the patient condition. Having expected such an outcome, the researchers also surreptitiously recorded the interview between the employment interviewer and the applicant. These tapes were then blindly rated for friendliness of the interviewer and for probability that the applicant would find a job there. The employment interviewers were found to be significantly less friendly and they indicated the probability of finding a job there was significantly poorer in the mental patient than the control condition.

The second study (Link, 1987; Link et al., 1992), although quite different, obtained results consistent with those of Farina and Felner. Former mental patients who expected society to reject people with a psychiatric history were, in fact, more likely to be unemployed than comparable individuals who did not anticipate stigmatization. For a control group free of mental problems, expectations that mental hospitalization would elicit rejection were not related to unemployment. It appears that, at least for ex-mental patients who are concerned about their employability, some noxious personal or interpersonal processes are generated that interfere with finding work.

Finding a job is not the only problem a man who has suffered from a psychiatric disorder may encounter if he seeks employment. If he is hired, he will find that difficulties engendered by his psychiatric history are by no means over. Please note that the preceding assertion refers to males. That is quite deliberate because research suggests that females may meet with a more generous reception in the workplace and rather clearly shows that women

are kinder to coworkers with a psychiatric history than are males (Farina, 1981). But male workers already on the job seem not to welcome someone as a coworker if that person has had a mental problem. In one relevant study (Farina, Felner, & Boudreau, 1973), male VA hospital workers were told that since they knew their own job best, management wanted them to meet a job applicant and evaluate how well he would do if hired to work with them. The "applicant" was actually a confederate who was presented as an ex-mental patient to half the workers and as an ex-surgical patient to the rest. The hospital workers expected to get along more poorly with those in the mental patient condition, they expected them not to do well on the job, they recommended them less strongly for the job, and they imbued them with stereotypic mental patient characteristics such as being unpredictable. That study was replicated with a female confederate who was presented to male workers as an ordinary applicant or as a former mental patient (Farina, Murray, & Groh, 1978). The workers again responded more negatively to the "applicant" in the mental patient condition, although the male confederate was more decisively rejected.

In the preceding research, for some of the studies the confederate was introduced as a presently hospitalized mental patient while in others he or she was described as discharged from the hospital. No differences in the way the workers responded to the applicant were noted between these two kinds of studies. This is relevant to the important issue broached early in this chapter, namely, the relation between the kind and severity of a mental disorder from which one suffers and the degree of social stigma the afflicted person encounters. We saw then that the public does make distinctions among disturbances but that all problems in adjustment elicit negative social reactions. Does the public respond differently to someone perceived as a *current* patient as compared to someone believed to be an *ex-patient*? The work just reviewed says no. However, this question is not settled and for the time being all we can say is that both categories of people are stigmatized.

To return to the present issue, in the analysis of the problems that a history of mental disorder can create in finding employment, the focus has been on society's prejudicial behavior. The ex-mental patient is not judged on his or her merits but is rejected just because of his or her history (i.e., he or she is stigmatized). That focus is in keeping with the purposes of this chapter. However, the population of ex-mental patients, both male and female, faces another kind of problem related to work, in addition to the kind of stigmatization that has been described. If the former patient has not fully achieved an adequate level of adjustment when returned to the community and in search of employment, that search is likely to be fruitless. While this difficulty is due to a different cause, it is opportune to consider it here since it also lowers an ex-patient's chances of finding work.

A pertinent study was done by Fischer et al. (1982). A sample of hospitalized women, all diagnosed as psychotic, underwent an employment interview that was videotaped. These tapes were later shown to employment interviewers in their own offices. The interviewers were informed that the women were psychiatric patients and they were asked to give a candid opinion as to each woman's chances of finding employment. The women were also independently rated for adequacy of interpersonal adjustment as manifested on the same tapes. Adjustment and employability were found to be highly and significantly correlated ($r = .63$). Patients who were rated as well-adjusted were judged most likely to be employed.

This finding is certainly consistent with intuition. What should be noted is that former psychiatric patients face another obstacle in finding work in addition to stigma, and it is an obstacle that we must distinguish from stigma. We should also note something that leads to less obvious and more pervasive consequences. People who become mental patients are not a random sample of the population, and one of the characteristics most clearly differentiating them from an average individual is poor interpersonal adjustment. This is true both before and after their hospitalization and this phenomenon will be discussed. The implication of these facts is that individuals with a history of mental disorder are handicapped by two burdens when seeking employment: social stigma and personal shortcomings in adjustment.

Housing

Both formal research and societal events convincingly indicate that ex-psychiatric patients encounter special obstacles in finding housing because of their history. A notorious incident occurred in Long Beach, New York, that was widely reported. By 1974 that seaside Long Island community was no longer attracting tourists, and many of its hotel rooms remained unoccupied. State mental hospitals began housing discharged patients in these hotels and the owners were eager to cooperate. The residents of the town were not so keen about this, however, and they passed a law barring anyone in need of continuous psy-

chiatric care and medication from living in those hotels. Quite obviously, this law was aimed at keeping former mental patients away from the community.

A carefully done study by Page (1977) strongly supports the conclusions prompted by the Long Beach incident. Advertisers wishing to rent furnished rooms or flats whose ads appeared in newspapers on a particular day were telephoned by a female researcher. She called a sample of 30 different advertisers in each of several conditions, in each case asking if the property was still available. She said nothing unusual about herself in the control condition, while for another condition she revealed that she was about to leave a mental hospital. In still another condition, she stated that she was inquiring for her brother who was about to be released from jail. Whereas she received 25 positive responses in the control condition, not more than 9 such responses were obtained in the other conditions. Both the jail and mental hospital conditions were significantly different from the control but were not different from each other. Twenty advertisers in either the mental hospital or jail condition who had reported their property to no longer be available were called a second time using the control procedure. On the second call, 18 of the 20 reported that the room or flat was available for rent. A recent replication of that study confirmed the earlier findings although the results were less striking (Page, 1995). An ex-patient seeking housing certainly faces a dismal situation and has good reason for not disclosing his or her troubled history to a potential landlord.

Neighbors

Why are landlords so cautious about renting to former mental patients? We might reasonably think they expect such individuals to have little money and they refuse them housing to avoid trouble trying to collect the rent. But we saw earlier that residents of Long Beach wanted to keep ex-patients out of their town when the payment of rent was not an issue. Most probably, the answer to the question of why people want to keep away from those who have had mental problems lies in the stigma society attaches to them. Unfortunately, that answer does not provide very much clarification. Stigma is a perplexing phenomenon that consists more of mystery than enlightenment, as I have indicated, and this chapter is an effort to bring some clarity to it. What the answer does suggest is that people who would become neighbors of former mental patients would not be happy to have ex-patients move near them. A surfeit of evidence makes the truth of the foregoing assertion amply clear. As in the case of housing, this evidence can be gleaned from societal events and can be found in the systematic research done by social scientists.

Some of the former kind of evidence has recently been conveniently gathered and published as a book (Fink & Tasman, 1992). The book is actually a report of part of the proceedings of the 1989 annual meeting of the American Psychiatric Association, the theme of which was "overcoming stigma." In one of the chapters of that book (Farina, Fisher, & Fischer, 1992), the authors cite newspaper reports that indicate deinstitutionalization is hampered by the resistance of people to having former patients move near them. A specific item cited by them appeared in the *Hartford Courant* and was based on a reporter's interview with Audrey M. Worrell who was then the Connecticut Mental Health Commissioner. According to Worrell, there were 14 group homes for deinstitutionalized mental patients in Connecticut at that time. In establishing them, community resistance had been encountered for 7 of the 14, in the form of "local zoning actions or regulatory delays." At least 8 proposed homes could not be opened because of local hostility. Also, 3 homes were under construction at that time and 2 of them had met with opposition.

The same chapter describes a notorious event that occurred in Greenwich, Connecticut, that vividly illustrates how unwelcome as neighbors people known to have mental problems are. A group home for psychiatric patients was opened in that town and residents on the same street asked the Greenwich Board of Tax Review to lower the amount at which their houses were evaluated for tax purposes. They argued that the presence of the shelter housing mental patients reduced the market value of their houses since potential buyers would not want to live near such an establishment. The Board evidently accepted the validity of this argument since the homeowners were granted reductions ranging from $2,960 to $10,270. This event is an unusual one and it was denounced by numerous officials. However, negative societal reactions to those with a history of mental disorder are far from unusual.

Some quite realistic but controlled studies also reveal this same objection that people have to living near ex-mental patients. Two of these studies are very similar and can be described simultaneously (Cutler, 1975; Farina, Thaw, Lovern, & Mangone, 1974). A male in his twenties went to people in their own homes and announced he was investigating the problem of finding a place to live faced by people who had been hospitalized for a prolonged period. Half the subjects were told the patients were hospitalized for medical reasons and the rest that they had been admitted for a nervous disorder. They were asked to listen to a tape-recorded interview between the alleged patient and the investigator in order to get a reasonable idea of what kind of person the patient was. Subjects in the two conditions actually heard the same recording. They were then asked a series of questions about how they and their neighbors would respond if that particular patient were to move into a house nearby.

The two studies show that the former mental patient is expected to have more trouble in finding a job, it is anticipated that the neighbors will not accept him, and he is expected to have greater difficulty in various areas of community functioning. Interestingly, respondents interviewed in the mental patient condition were significantly less willing to take part in similar future experiments than subjects in the medical patient condition. This finding may mean that people find it unpleasant to think about a former psychiatric patient moving into their neighborhood, even if they assert that they themselves—if not their neighbors—would welcome him.

What happens when the person afflicted with a mental disorder is a child? We do have some information regarding this and it is not very encouraging. Zultowsky and Farina (1989) did a relevant study and did it in much the same manner as the two studies just reviewed. In the Zultowsky and Farina study, also, researchers (two women in their twenties) went to homes, introduced themselves as students at a nearby university, and asked the resident for permission to interview them about children. It was then explained that children who once were routinely institutionalized were being returned to the community and the researchers wanted to know how they and their neighbors would feel if a home for such children were established near their houses. The home would house about 15 children but one-third of the subjects were told the children were orphans, one-third that they were emotionally disturbed, and remaining one-third that they were learning disabled. Following this, they were verbally given a questionnaire that asked for their reaction, as well as their belief about their neighbors' reactions, to such an event. The results showed that the response to establishing such a home was more negative in the retarded and disturbed conditions than in the orphan condition. The two former conditions did not differ from each other. The data also indicated that no group homes of any kind were wanted nearby.

The preceding study is consistent with other research in showing that mental problems are strongly stigmatized whether these afflict adults, children, or vice-presidential candidates. Like other studies, this one finds that the public rejects people with learning disabilities and those with emotional maladies equally, although quite aware of the difference between these conditions. A final point about this study should be noted. It is tempting to think people do not want mentally aberrant people nearby because they fear such people might run amuck and hurt available victims (i.e., the neighbors). This study suggests physical danger is not the only possible source of stigmatization since it does not seem likely that children constitute a physical threat for most people.

A study by Gillmore and Farina (1989), while not specifically focused on the behavior of neighbors, is concerned with children and is relevant to the reception they are likely to receive when their mental condition deviates from the expected. Fifth and eighth grade boys individually met at their school another boy of their own age. The boy they met was presented as a child who might be coming to their school. The "new boy" was actually one of six confederates, three of fifth and three of eighth grade age. Each subject was asked to tell the newcomer about the school, and he was also asked to judge how well the new boy would get along there. The confederate was presented to one-third of the subjects in each grade as an ordinary child, to another one-third as learning disabled, and to the final one-third as emotionally disturbed. The confederates were always blind to condition and, after the interaction, the subjects were questioned about the "new child" by an experimenter who was also blind to condition. Behavioral measures showed that subjects in the emotionally disturbed and retarded conditions were less friendly and more anxious than those in the control condition. They also wanted more social distance from the "retarded" and "disturbed" child and expected their peers to be more rejecting toward them relative to the control condition. Essentially the same results were obtained in the two grades and, as in the Zultowsky and Farina study, the subjects responded to the two mental problem conditions in the same way.

Stigma—A Pandemic Problem

And so, even though some mental health professionals disagree, there are compelling reasons for believing that people who have been afflicted by a mental disorder are strongly stigmatized. A question that now emerges is the following: is this phenomenon present in all societies or is it something unique to America? If it were a local occurrence, then we might begin to search for its causes in the peculiarities of our culture. If it is much more general than that, we might suspect the problem is generated by any kind of human interaction involving a mentally deviant person. Also, there might be cultures and subcultures that could provide a haven for people who suffer the misfortune of a mental disorder, a misfortune society magnified with its degradation. Or, conceivably, once the process is better understood, a social haven could even be constructed for afflicted individuals. Thus, there are both practical and theoretical reasons for being concerned with the generality of this phenomenon.

The clear answer to the question is that we, in the United States, are not the only ones plagued by these regrettable social events. For one thing, some of the research literature reviewed comes from other cultures such as Canada and England where psychological research has developed to a level comparable to our own. These studies report that social rejection of those with mental problems is the same as in the United States (e.g., Page, 1977). In addition, there are quite a number of reports that show stigmatization is present in cultures that are very different from ours. Thus, Davies and Morris (1990) found it present in Bengal and Thailand. Both Koizumi and Harris (1992) and Munakata (1989) report that the mentally disordered are stigmatized in Japan. Pearson and Phillips (1994) tell us that also happens in China, while Rodrigues (1992) finds that it is likewise present in Brazil. Whatever causes stigma seems not to be located in the immediate history of society and its social practices but, rather, deeply within the nature of human beings. Since the phenomenon appears to be a facet of basic human nature, we can expect a great deal of difficulty in eliminating or reducing it.

There are some encouraging findings in this rather dark picture, and I will end this section with a look at one of these reports. The study is costly but quite realistic (Farina, Hagelauer, & Holzberg, 1976). The authors noted that ex-mental patients complained of not being believed by physicians once their psychiatric history was known. Their symptoms tended to be dismissed as imaginary, they reported. To check this, appointments were made with 32 medical practitioners by a 23-year-old graduate student in the guise of someone suffering from some physical problems. His complaints in all cases were of stomach pains suggestive of ulcers. He reported having had a prior attack 9 months earlier. However, he told 16 of these doctors that he had been traveling abound the country at the time, while he told the other 16 that he had been in a mental hospital at the time.

The researcher had a small tape recorder hidden on his body, and the entire conversation between doctor and "patient" was recorded and later analyzed by raters blind to condition. Duration of conversation, time in the office, friendliness manifested by the doctor's voice, doctor's judged seriousness of the symptoms, and their expected duration were all compared across conditions, as were prescriptions, fees charged, and number of examining procedures used. The "ex-mental patient" was treated quite as well as the control. The only significant difference found was that more examinations not directly related to stomach pains (e.g., an eye examination) were done with the mental patient. This might mean that the report of a former psychiatric patient is not likely to be believed and doctors want to check things for themselves. But the important finding is that former mental patients seem likely to receive the same medical care as anyone else.

THE CAUSES OF STIGMA

In the preceding section we examined some of the voluminous evidence indicating that mentally troubled individuals are socially rejected and degraded. The question we will now attempt to answer is why this happens. The answer is neither simple nor unqualified. But factors can be identified that seem to be responsible for this social phenomenon.

Social Beliefs and Attitudes

Societal beliefs and attitudes may be the most critical elements in the devaluation and dehumanization of persons with mental afflictions. The terms *beliefs* and *attitudes* are abstractions whose origin we must also eventually understand, and they are immediate precursors of stigma. The two concepts are related but they differ in some ways and it is helpful to note some of these differences. Following Nunnally's (1961) distinction, beliefs refer to issues of fact such as the statement "Schizophrenics have glassy eyes." We can, potentially, determine the truth or falsity of such assertions, and personal feelings, such as whether we are fond of schizophrenics or dread them, need play no role in beliefs. Attitudes, on the other hand, deal with personal, subjective emotions that are

more vaguely connected to objective reality. "I don't like mental hospitals" expresses an attitude, and it is affect that is the important element, rather than truth or falsity.

For many reasons that we will consider, a host of beliefs that are unfavorable to mental patients, such as that they are unpredictable and potentially homicidal, have come to prevail in our society (and in virtually every other society). These beliefs, understandably, have generated negative affect toward mental patients. Obviously, if we believe that a class of people consists of potential killers, we will not feel very friendly toward a member of that class. Negative feelings probably are also created more directly by exposure to people who already harbor negative emotions toward the mentally disordered. We are likely to be influenced by the attitudes held by members of our group and probably come to share them.

One source of the present disparaging beliefs about the mentally ill are past events concerning mental disorders, and both actual and legendary occurrences play their part. Practically all the information that has come to us from the past indicates that insane individuals were regarded with fear and were imbued with nonhuman, demonic characteristics. Passages from the Bible, ancient Greek history and mythology, and writings from classical Roman times all portray the mentally ill as profoundly different from ordinary human beings (Deutsch, 1965; Farina, 1982; Zilboorg & Henry, 1941). According to these sources, they have become (or are possessed by) demons and can engage in unspeakable behaviors. Thus, Hercules, having become insane because a demon possessed him, killed his own children as well as the children of his brother. The popular name for mentally ill people in Roman times was *larvatus*, meaning full of phantoms. During the Middle Ages, a period marked by particularly strong superstitions, people who clearly would now be diagnosed as mentally ill were frequently thought to be witches or in league with the devil. Society considered it its duty to exorcise possessing demons, a procedure that often entailed killing the disordered person by burning him or her alive. The flavor of these beliefs from the past lingers with us and casts an unsavory aura on those who have adjustment problems in the present time. For example, the belief in demon possession is not entirely gone. Some religious denominations currently practice exorcism, which still seems to be of general interest to judge from the popularity of a mid-1970s movie (*The Exorcist*) about that rite.

Beliefs of more recent origin surely are also responsible for the social disfavor of mental patients. In colonial and postcolonial America, it was widely believed that the insane were not sensitive to heat or cold. We see here a view of them as creatures that are more reminiscent of snakes than of human beings. In keeping with this view, they were at times housed in quarters devoid of heat, even in cold climates. The discovery of that practice, in fact, influenced Dorothea Dix to devote herself to improving the life of mentally disturbed people. And the methods used over the years to treat mental disorders have no doubt had their deleterious effect on the esteem in which the public holds them. These treatments have included beatings and whippings, their head has been burned in order to cause "curative" blisters, and their fingers have been scarred, presumably also in the hope of improving their malady. Surgical procedures have been employed to remove parts of their intestines and to castrate men and remove the clitoris of women, the blood of animals has been transfused into their veins, and their own blood has been removed in prodigious quantities, although the last treatment was not confined to mental problems. And even very recently, the mentally ill were subjected to a variety of shock treatments using drugs and electricity to render them unconscious, with the latter procedure continuing to be used. Even more extreme was a variety of widely used operations that entailed penetrating the skull so that parts of their brains could be surgically destroyed. The institutions that provided for their care can still be seen at the edges of cities and towns, surrounded by walls, and looking very much like jails rather than places to heal people. Knowledge of these beliefs and practices is transmitted by various means across generations and, even if the totality is generally not known, the past still seems to convey an imagine if the mentally ill as fearful, mysterious, and satanic beings.

At this point we should ask why it is that these beliefs and attitudes have come to be. Is it a chance occurrence, with the mentally ill simply being unlucky to be selected for persecution and infamy over the centuries when any other identifiable group might have been chosen? That is improbable and does not seem to be the case. We will now review some facts that provide a partial explanation for their social repudiation, even if they do not justify it. We must here note that the mentally disordered population is not composed of randomly selected individuals. Rather, it is a group of people possessing an array of characteristics that brings social disapproval and rejection. It may seem cruel to point out the shortcomings of individuals who already are burdened with many problems. However, if we are to understand their social rejection and, conceivably, to improve their lot, there must be an objective and dis-

passionate examination of this matter. Let us now consider these unfortunate distinguishing features that bring social rejection to those who are mentally ill.

Lack of Interpersonal Skills

Psychiatric patients constitute a very heterogeneous population but a characteristic that, nevertheless, is common among them is a clear deficiency in social skills. One type of study that convincingly leads to this conclusion begins by identifying mental patients and then investigates the social history of those patients prior to the time that their disorder was apparent. These studies (Barthell & Holmes, 1968; Farina & Webb, 1956; Farina, Garmezy, Zalusky, & Becker, 1962; Farina, Garmezy, & Barry, 1963; Farina et al., 1992; Phillips, 1953) all show that those persons who where hospitalized because of mental problems had few and superficial relationships with others throughout their lives. The Barthell and Holmes study nicely illustrates these findings. The researchers identified a group of individuals who were diagnosed as mentally ill and a control group of comparable people for whom there was no evidence that they had ever experienced psychiatric problems. They then assessed the nature of their social relationships during their high school years by examining their high school yearbooks. Significantly fewer social activities were reported in the yearbooks for the mentally ill than the control group. Another typical finding reported by this kind of research is that the more severe the psychopathology someone develops (e.g., schizophrenia vs. neurosis), the more sparse and fleeting were that person's social relationships prior to the onset of the disorder.

Given these histories, we should expect that, as a group, maladjusted individuals would not develop a rich repertoire of interpersonal behaviors nor understand social relationships and comport themselves skillfully with others. And the research that has explored this matter reports just that—the more maladjusted the individual, the more marked is his or her interpersonal incompetence. While this concomitance may seem almost tautological, a brief examination of the specific findings will make clearer why mentally ill people are stigmatized by society. Farina, Holzberg, and Kimura (1966) studied the social relationships of four groups of women ranged along a continuum of maladjustment from very severely pathological to a control group. The results led them to conclude that the more poorly adjusted the subjects were, the more undifferentiated, amorphous, and meaningless were their relationships with other people. For example, friends and enemies were much the same to women with serious disorders whereas the better adjusted ones described large differences between them. Both Kelly, Farina, and Mosher (1971) and Rosenthal (1973) found that, for a group of female patients, the more severely disordered ones behaved in a less appropriate and skillful manner in responding to an interview. Many other studies, done in a variety of ways and even in different countries, indicate that a chronic and general deficit in social skills is a prominent feature of maladjustment (Sarason & Sarason, 1987, p. 11). Vandenberg (1962) and Walker, Marwit, and Emory (1980) found that schizophrenics were less accurate at identifying emotions displayed in photographs than comparable controls. Turner (1964) did an analogous study that required maladjusted men and control subjects to identify several emotions expressed vocally by an actor, and the maladjusted subjects were found to be less accurate than the controls.

These latter studies indicate that maladjusted individuals do not understand the feelings being experienced by other people very well. Since their ability to comport themselves in a socially appropriate manner is also poor, as the studies reviewed earlier show, we must expect their interpersonal behavior to be awkward and deviant, and it seems probable that others will find being with them unpleasant. Some researchers have investigated this possibility. In one of these studies, Greengrass (1974) used peer ratings to identify socially skilled and socially unskilled women and paired each subject with a randomly assigned woman. Each pair was required to discuss some interpersonal problems for about 10 minutes. At the end of that brief discussion, it was found that the socially competent subjects, in comparison to the less socially competent, were better liked and were preferred as friends. Jain and Greengrass (1975) repeated this study and found the same results. Moreover, they looked at the *partners* of the experimental subjects and found that those paired with socially incompetent women were rated as significantly more uncomfortable during the interaction than those assigned to socially skilled experimental subjects. Thus it appears that socializing with interpersonally inept individuals is stressful, and we can expect people will try to avoid relationships with such individuals. And in a longer-term study, Kelso (1978) measured how much students high or low in social competence were liked by their peers at two points in time. After being together in a dormitory for 2 weeks, there

was no difference between the groups. However, by the end of the semester the high-competence subjects were significantly better liked than those of low social skill. And so we see that interpersonal ineptitude is a characteristic of mental patients and that such a pattern of behavior is unpleasant and stressful to others. It is one of the reasons the mentally ill are stigmatized.

Alienating Behaviors

Another peculiarity of psychiatric patients that distinguishes them from nonpatients is symptoms of psychiatric disorders. The presence of these symptoms is presumably what leads to their identification as mentally disordered and, therefore, to their institutionalization. A list of psychiatric symptoms constitutes an array of behaviors that probably all of us find disagreeable, noxious, or offensive and that we strive to avoid. An old but still very useful study by Zigler and Phillips (1961) provides information about these symptoms and how commonly psychiatric patients display them. These researchers tabulated the signs of the disorder that the admitting or referring physician cited as the reason for the hospitalization for a total of 793 patients entering a state psychiatric hospital. The three most common symptoms, all shown by at least 35% of the patients, were depression, tension, and suspiciousness. Among the 15 most common symptoms were also hallucinations, assaultiveness, drinking, and withdrawal.

Evidence abounds that anyone who displays such behaviors will be disliked and shunned. Let us consider how society responds to those who are depressed and to those who show tension, the two most common of all psychiatric symptoms. Coyne (1976) did what is probably the first experiment on the effect that depressed individuals have on people around them. College students, without information about the person to whom they were talking, had a telephone conversation either with a depressed patient or with a control subject. Relative to those in the control group, students who talked to the depressed patients were themselves depressed, anxious, and hostile after the conversation and, moreover, they rejected and devalued the patient.

Although we do not have complete unanimity among researchers, the evidence very strongly suggests that depressed people are quite regularly rejected and that they arouse negative mood states in others, as Gurtman (1986) concluded after his review of the literature. Even quite differently done studies tell us that depressed individuals are disagreeable to those around them. For example, Hooley, Richters, and Weintraub (1987) found that wives of depressed psychiatric patients were more unhappy with their marriage than wives of nondepressed psychiatric patients even though the latter patients had seemingly more obtrusive and florid symptoms than the former. And Coyne, Kessler, and Tal (1987) assessed individuals living with a depressed patient who was experiencing a depressive episode at that time. These individuals were compared to similar subjects who also were living with a depressed patient but who was *not* then experiencing a depressive period. The former subjects were very much more distressed than the latter. Particularly disturbing to these individuals were the patient's lack of interest in socializing, fatigue, hopelessness, and worry.

The destructive effect of tension on social acceptance is even clearer. A series of five studies was carried out to determine how acceptable as a coworker an applicant who was tense and nervous would be to employees already on the job (Farina, Murray, & Groh, 1978). Samples of employees met a candidate who was supposedly applying for the same type of job they held but who was actually a confederate. The confederate behaved in a calm and relaxed manner for half the workers, and for the remainder he or she appeared tense and anxious. Tension was displayed in the same way in all five studies: to wit, the confederate seldom made eye contact, the head was kept down, occasionally the hands were wrung, and there was periodic swallowing as if due to a dry mouth. The experiment was done five times using five different confederates and new samples of employees for each replication. Three work settings were used. One was a large department store, another was a VA hospital, and the final setting was a plant maintenance division of a state university.

The effect of tension was unmistakable, strong, and virtually identical across the five studies. Whether male or female, and whether presented as an ex-mental patient or routine applicant, the tense individual was unequivocally rejected by workers of both sexes. They were regarded as poor prospects for the job and they were not wanted as coworkers. The consistency and strength of the findings are noteworthy in an area of research where inconsistency is common. It seems important for us to learn the reasons why this rejection occurs, and some inherently intriguing information might emerge from an inquiry into this matter. Whatever the future reveals, these results speak eloquently about the plight of mental patients. Those unfortunate individuals are devalued and spurned (i.e., stigmatized) if

they are tense. And, as we have seen, a goodly proportion of them *are* tense.

Physical Unattractiveness

A sizable literature concerned with the relation between physical attractiveness and adjustment has been accumulated and has been summarized several times (e.g., Burns & Farina, 1992). That literature reveals that at least three studies have found psychiatric patients to be less good looking than controls. Ten additional studies have looked for a comparable association using control subjects and nonhospitalized individuals suffering from a variety of maladjustments (see Farina et al., 1992). While at least one study in each category obtained negative results, the literature as a whole indicates that poorly adjusted individuals are less good looking than those whose mental health is good. Some evidence has been reported to the effect that it is unattractiveness that *causes* mental health problems because unattractive people are rebuffed and demeaned by society. Such experiences would be stressful and, moreover, being kept at arm's length, would interfere with the acquisition of the social skills required for good adjustment. Whatever the role of appearance in mental health, maladjusted individuals appear to be relatively unattractive. Certainly that is not to say that any given psychiatric patient is less good looking than anyone who has not experienced psychiatric problems. However, if that is true for the maladjusted segment of the population as a whole, then a great deal of research (e.g., Herman, Zanna, & Higgins, 1986) indicates that looks will be a factor leading to their stigmatization.

The attractiveness literature implies that hospitalized psychiatric patients being returned to the community will be welcomed there in keeping with how good looking they are. The more unattractive they are, the less cordial will be their social reception and, therefore, the more difficult will be their readjustment. This possibility was tested by Farina, Burns, Austad, Bugglin, and Fischer (1986) with a group of mental patients who were about to be discharged to the community.

The patients' looks were rated at the time they were discharged. Although all patients had presumably recovered enough to go home, it was found that the better looking the patient, the more successful was his or her readjustment to community living. In addition to this, the more disturbed and severely disordered individuals are, the less likely they are to take care of themselves and so the dirtier and the more disheveled will their appearance be (Farina, Arenberg, & Guskin, 1957). Hence, among the reasons maladjusted individuals are stigmatized by society are not only that they are unattractive physically, but also that they allow themselves to look disheveled and disreputable.

One might now ask if all the foregoing literature really tells us anything pertaining to *any* kind of stigma, be it of mental disorder or other. The research reviewed on the causes of stigmatization shows that when people deviate from social norms, either in behavior or appearance, as psychiatric patients do, they are rejected. This is perhaps regrettable. But where is the stigma in this societal phenomenon? If a mental patient were to look and to act in a completely "normal" fashion, would he or she still be spurned by people? The answer is a resounding *yes*. This pattern, generalization or stereotyping, is much broader than the area of mental illness and accounts for some of the problems experienced by ethnic and racial minorities. The studies that were cited earlier suggest the existence of this stigma, but there are others that show its presence more clearly. We will have a brief look at some of those other studies.

Farina and Ring (1965) asked pairs of male college students, who were strangers to each other, to write on a sheet of paper some personal and revealing information for the other person to read. The sheets were seemingly exchanged, but prepared handwritten sheets were substituted, one describing the writer as a typical student and another revealing that he had been in a mental hospital. These were randomly assigned college students, so there is no reason to expect those who received the mental hospital information differed in any way from those in the control group. Yet, relative to the control group, not only did the subjects want to avoid further contact with the supposed former patient, but they also saw him display behavioral inadequacies that, in fact, did not exist. Moreover, a jointly performed motor task was significantly affected by the belief that the partner had suffered a mental disorder. In an effort to learn more about the aforementioned behavioral effects of stigma, Farina, Holland, and Ring (1966) had a confederate present himself to a naive student either as an ordinary student or as a student who had been admitted to a mental hospital. The naive subject was required to teach the confederate a task by using electric shock to inform him that his solution was incorrect. While no electric shock was actually delivered, the intensities and durations of the shocks selected were recorded. The "subject" with the abnormal history was

given more painful shocks than the control and, as in the earlier study, his performance was seen as poorer than that of the control although the performances were identical. These studies tell us that the negative views and unfavorable treatment from society to which mentally troubled people are subjected are not totally due to aberrations on their part. Some are a result of stigma.

This demeaning of former and present mental patients occurs in a variety of contexts, and in many ways and it can appear *only because* their psychiatric history is known. What must be a distressing experience for them is that, among other affronts, their opinions tend to be disregarded by other people. A study showing this was done by Lawner (1966) who had students meet a confederate presented as another student. They were assigned a task requiring communication of information. The confederate was sent to another room where he ostensibly read about a measuring technique he would subsequently describe to the real subject. In describing the procedure, the confederate expressed a strongly favorably opinion of it and tried to convince the subject of its worth. The degree of influence he exerted was measured by how good the naive subject thought the technique was after he had listened to the confederate. The persuasive message was always delivered in the same way. However, half the subjects had earlier learned the confederate had been in a mental hospital, while the rest thought he was an ordinary student; this information was unknown to the confederate. Subjects in the mentally ill condition thought the technique was significantly less good than those in the control condition. Such experiences are demeaning and are a nicely illustrative sample of the fabric of stigma. And a study by Farina and Felner (1973) was previously cited that shows a kind of stigmatization that has broader and more practical consequences for those with a psychiatric history. The study showed that, all other things equal, someone with a psychiatric history has a more difficult time finding work than someone free of that blemish.

The literature, then, reveals that individuals with psychiatric problems are viewed negatively and treated badly both because of their personal aberrations, such as being tense, but also simply because the history of their mental problems is known. Some researchers have studied these two effects simultaneously. Harris, Milich, Corbitt, Hoover, and Brady (1992) had pairs of unacquainted third- to sixth-grade boys jointly perform some tasks. One of the boys, the perceiver, was always an average boy recruited from a school while the other boy, the target, was someone comparable to the perceiver for half of the pairs but was a psychiatrically disturbed child for the remainder. In addition, for each kind of pair, half the perceivers were told the other boy was psychiatrically disturbed while the remainder was given no such information. The *information* given to the perceiver about the target's mental condition, as well as the target's actual *psychiatric status*, had adverse effects on the perception and feelings of both boys. Their behavior during the interaction was also negatively affected. The most negative consequences occurred for pairs where the target actually had a mental problem and the perceiver was told that the problem existed. This finding is quite consistent with intuitions. There is another study, conceptually similar to the Harris et al. experiment, that supports those findings but also reports results that make important implications of such studies clear. Loman and Larkin (1976), by means of videotapes, also varied type of behavior displayed (disturbed or normal) and the label applied to a target person (paranoid or not labeled). While both the disturbed behavior and the label of paranoid had negative effects on how the target was perceived by subjects, the effect of the label was *stronger* than that of the behavior. This implies that the work of the mental hospital and the psychotherapist is unlikely to be totally successful since, if the patient's history is known, the community may respond negatively and strongly to the treated person even when that person is behaving in a perfectly normal way. Similarly, the discharged patient's plight seems like an unhappy one, in the light of these findings. He or she can be fully recovered, act in an exemplary fashion, realize this, and yet meet social rejection. This kind of experience is apt to be demoralizing, to make the former patient feel unfairly treated, and to lead to the conclusion that social acceptance is beyond reach.

A quite important matter is relevant to this discussion but, as it is also pertinent to a later section of this chapter, full consideration of it will be delayed until them. Namely, victims also play a role by making this social besmirchment a more serious problem for themselves as a result of their awareness that they are stigmatized. For now, a brief look at research done by Link and his colleagues will suffice to explain the process and to indicate the nature of the findings. Link's research is reported in a chapter presenting a lucid examination of some of the same matters herein considered (Link et al., 1992). The researchers measured how strongly stigmatized two groups of subjects believed mental illness to be. One group was composed of mental patients, while the second group consisted of comparable subjects without a history of mental problems. They found that for the patient group the more stigmatized they believed mental disorders to be, the more demoralized they were, the more income they lost, and the more likely they were to be unemployed. None of these associations were found for the control group. This appears to mean that individuals who fear being stigmatized are hampered by those concerns and bring negative consequences upon themselves.

As indicated, other and quite consistent findings will be reported. There is, however, one prominent inconsistency that requires mentioning at this point. While all of the foregoing is fully applicable to males, some of what has been said needs modification when females are considered. These surprising discrepancies between men and women will be presented and discussed in the final section of this chapter. Meantime, we will examine other factors that also play a role in the stigmatization of people whose adjustment is aberrant.

Stigmatization of the Mentally Ill by the Mass Media

It is widely believed among mental health workers that newspapers, movies, and TV contribute to the stigmatization of those with mental problems. Some of those professionals have assertively claimed that the media degrade the mentally ill by presenting them in a highly negative and inaccurate way (e.g., Hyler, Gabbard, & Schneider, 1989). Do the media cause mental patients to be socially stigmatized?

Nunnally, one of the earliest researchers to attempt to answer this question, carried out a series of relevant studies in the late 1950s (Nunnally, 1961). He systematically examined the way that psychiatric patients were pictured by the media. He reported that the mentally ill were portrayed as very different from ordinary people and in accordance with societal stereotypes of "crazy people." They were shown as unpredictable, dangerous, and, in the case of movies and TV, they even *looked* different. In some instances this differentiation appeared to be a dramatic technique for identifying a character's role but, for the most part, it was gratuitously demeaning. The kinds of stereotypes about mental patients that are perpetuated and enhanced by movies and television in their portrayal of them have been described by Hyler et al. (1989). These are the mental patient as *a rebellious free spirit*, a *homicidal maniac*, a *seductress,* and *enlightened citizen*, a *narcisstic parasite*, and a *zoo specimen.* The authors believe that these depictions contribute to the stigmatization of psychiatrically afflicted individuals in our society.

Investigators have gone beyond these suggestive but impressionistic examinations of the media's portrayals. They have looked for specific and quantifiable elements in the depictions of the mentally disordered, and they have also measured the volume of information about them that is presented to the public. Wahl and Roth (1982) selected the Washington, DC, area and examined prime time TV programs shown on each of five channels every day for an entire month. A total of 385 programs were viewed and 29% of them had contents involving mental illness. The mentally ill were predominantly males (the ratio was 2.5 males for each female), single, and the most frequent adjectives used by the raters in describing them were active, confused, aggressive, dangerous, and unpredictable. These authors also reviewed the literature and found that since 1900 mental disorder was a topic that appeared with increasing frequency in the mass media. As in their own study, other researchers reported that the afflicted were shown in a decidedly negative fashion, and, specifically, they were characterized as active, different, and dangerous. These findings are clearly supported by other researchers who also provide additional information. One of these researchers is Gerber (1980) who found, in his studies of the mass media, that the mentally ill were shown as unpredictable and dangerous. Prime time normal characters on TV were violent 40% of the time but the mentally ill were violent 73% of the time, nearly twice as often as normals. The mentally ill were also more likely to be victims of violence. A similar analysis of prime time TV programs by Signorielli (1989) also found that those afflicted by mental disorder were likely to commit violence and to be victimized. They were further demeaned by being shown as unemployed or as failures in their work. Day and Page (1986) analyzed news reports about the mentally ill printed in major Canadian newspapers. They contrasted this portrayal to an interesting sample of descriptions of psychiatric patients appearing in a journal and a newsletter, each concerned with mental health issues. In keeping with the complaints of mental health professionals, as well as the research reviewed, the newspaper accounts presented a much more negative picture of the mentally ill than the material written by mental health workers.

The foregoing literature, and a lot of additional information that is consistent with it, leave little doubt about the portrayal of mental patients in the mass media. They are pictured in a manner that is pejorative and debasing. But does that affect the esteem in which they are held by society? Does that portrayal stigmatize them? Yes, apparently it does. A very pertinent experiment was done by Wahl and Lefkowitz (1989). They showed a film to three groups of randomly assigned, and thus presumably comparable, subjects. One group saw a film made for TV in which a man who is hospitalized for mental illness comes home and kills his wife. A second group saw the same film but also saw a repudiation of an implied message of the film (i.e., that psychiatric patients are dangerous). The disclaimer asserted that mental patients are not dangerous, and it was presented three times, at the beginning, the middle, and the end of the film. The third group was shown a film that included a murder scene but did not involve mental illness. Attitudes toward the mentally ill and their care in the community were then measured for all three groups. These attitudes were significantly less favorable for the two groups that saw the mentally disordered person commit the crime in comparison to the group where the murderer was not a psychiatric patient. The message asserting that mental patients are not dangerous had no effect at all. These results are noteworthy and discouraging. It seems that exposure to unfavorable information about mental patients through the mass media *can* lead to their stigmatization. And, as we have seen, such information abounds. It also seems that such information gets indelibly written in the mind of the public and reassurances about the atypicality of what they have heard or seen are ineffective.

Patient-Created Social Rejection

In this section we will examine a surprising cause of the stigmatization of mental patients, one that appears contrary to intuitions. A part of the difficulties such individuals encounter in society is due to their fear that they will be stigmatized. This apprehension causes them to behave in ways that the public finds objectionable (e.g., they become tense). And so, by a self-fulfilling prophecy, they create the very outcome they wish to avoid. Let me try to make this process clearer by presenting a hypothetical clinical example.

A man has just returned to his community after a hospitalization for a mental disorder and meets an acquaintance who lives in the former patient's neighborhood. The acquaintance knows about the hospitalization, and the former patient is aware that he knows. Now our intuitions tell us that the ensuing interaction will be tense and unpleasant. In part, we expect this on the basis of the literature we have reviewed. That is, the "normal" person will contribute to this difficulty by his stereotypic and negative beliefs about mental patients. But the acquaintance is not the only member of the pair, and he may not be the only contributor to the ongoing interpersonal problems. It seems likely that the psychiatric hospitalization is more important and salient to the afflicted individual than to the observer, and the blemished person's feelings and behaviors may be affected by the stigma independently of how others behave. Such a conclusion was reached by John Clausen, a prominent researcher with many years of experience studying mental patients. In one of his publications he makes the following statement:

> It is my belief that the patient's fear of rejection, coupled with uncertainty about ability to function in everyday roles, is a far more significant barrier to social participation than is anything appropriately called stigma. (Clausen, 1981, pp. 293–294)

Research findings provide strong support for at least parts of this assertion, as will be shown.

Perhaps the first matter research should clarify for us is whether psychiatric patients are sensitive and responsive to being disliked and demeaned. Do they care what other people think of them and, if they care, how do they respond? Obviously, if they are immune to others' opinions of them and are not responsive to them, there is no reason to expect a self-fulfilling prophecy to occur. In several experiments, hospitalized psychiatric patients were led to believe that the person with whom they were interacting either had a favorable view of patients and expected them to behave competently or that he regarded them as deviant, incompetent, and vulnerable (Luppino, 1966; Rayne, 1969; Thaw, 1971). The results showed that patients are sensitive even to the *specific* views they think others have of them and respond in accordance with those views. They performed better when they believed they were held in high esteem and considered competent. They may have little incentive to do well when little is expected of them or they may not dare confront the other person with achievements of which he considers them incapable. What is made clear by these studies is that mental patients care and react to how they are regarded.

We now turn to research on the total process entailed by the self-fulfilling prophecy, and we find both correlational and experimental studies that are relevant. A relevant correlational study was done by Mansouri and Dowell (1989) whose subjects were recovering mental patients. These subjects were administered two measures, one assessed how severely stigmatized they felt because of their mental illness, and the other measured the degree of their psychological distress. The investigators found that the more the subjects felt socially degraded, the more psychologically distressed they were. This association might mean that the more sensitized and fearful of rejection the patients were, the more their social comportment was hampered, causing negative responses from others, and so creating greater personal stress. Clearly, other explanations are quite plausible, such as that feeling stigmatized simply contributes to tension and thus makes it greater. That would account for the correlation. A more convincing correlational study, already alluded to, was done by Link et al. (1992). He also measured the degree to which a subject expects mental patients to be rejected and correlated that score with three other measures obtained for that subject: extent of demoralization, income loss, and being unemployed. These measures were obtained for a group of mental patients and for a group of controls who had never had a mental problem. For the patients, the more they expected patients to be rejected, the more demoralized they were, the greater was their loss of income, and the more likely they were to be unemployed. These associations were not found for the controls. It seems probable that the patients' expectations of being socially degraded interfered with their functioning and so resulted in the negative consequences found. For the controls, even if they believed that mental disorders are strongly stigmatized, their comportment was not affected. *They* were not patients and so did not expect to be rejected.

Experimental studies that bear on the self-fulfilling hypothesis that is here being examined have also been done, and they generally provide a clearer, less contaminated answer than correlational studies. In one of these, male college students were asked to copy for transmission to another student either a description of themselves as someone who had suffered a mental disorder or some bland information (Farina, Allen, & Saul, 1968). In both conditions, the subject was told that what was copied would be read by the other student. Actually, the other student always received the same bland control statement regardless of what had been copied. In this way, for each pair, *only the belief* of one of the subjects about how he was perceived was varied. The results unambiguously showed that thinking he was stigmatized influenced that subject's own behavior and caused the other subject to reject him even though the other subject had *no* unfavorable information about him. Thus we see that social stigma adversely affects the stigmatized person's behavior independently of how others act. Because someone expects to be degraded and repulsed, he or she actually causes the rejection.

However, the subjects were not actually psychiatric patients but college students and so another study was done to see if patients also respond in that way. The study was done in a VA hospital that treats both psychiatric and medical-surgical patients (Farina, Gliha, Boudreau, Allen, & Sherman, 1971). Former psychiatric patients who had been discharged from that hospital were asked to participate in a study that, allegedly, was to find out whether employers discriminate against former mental patients in their hiring practices. They were told they would meet one of a group of employment interviewers brought to the hospital to evaluate the potential of patients as workers. It was also explained that to determine if bias existed, some of the interviewers would know that the subjects were former psychiatric patients, but others would be informed that their subjects were ex-*medical* patients. Half the subjects were then informed that their interviewer knew they had been mental patients, while the rest were assured the interviewer thought they had been medical patients. In fact, all subjects met the same confederate who did not know in which group they were. All subjects were required to do a task, to explain it to the "employment interviewer," and to complete a questionnaire that measured their feelings and perceptions. Also, the former patient's behavior was rated by the confederate.

A consistent and clear pattern of results emerged. When the subjects believed they were viewed as former mental patients, they felt less appreciated, they found the task more difficult, and they performed more poorly than did subjects in the other condition. The confederate also rated them as more tense, anxious, and poorly adjusted than the subjects in the medical patient group. These studies, experimental and correlational together, indicate that both the feelings and the behaviors of former mental patients are negatively affected because they believe others know about their mental disorder. What would happen if these ex-patients were uncertain as to whether others were aware of their psychiatric history? If the reasoning inherent in this section is correct, a likely possibility would be that the self-destructive effects of stigma would be less severe since the victims could console themselves with the thought that they might be regarded as normal. Farina and Burns (1984) did research to answer just this question. They compared the impact of stigma on subjects who were led to believe they were definitely viewed as mental patients in comparison to a

group who were unsure if they were being viewed in such a way. The results suggested that the subjects in the former condition *were* more adversely affected than those in the latter. And so it appears that the existence of stigma, and the sensitivity to it on the part of those who are degraded, actually produces stigmatization.

The processes observable for mental illness should not be unique to that social stain alone. If the foregoing analysis is valid, other conditions deemed unsavory should have similar consequences. The perception of homosexuality in our society is rapidly changing and becoming more positive, but it was negative in the past and it is a condition whose stigmatizing effects were also studied. Farina, Allen, and Saul (1968) induced male subjects to believe they were viewed as homosexuals, and they showed both subjective and behavioral changes as a result. Those subjects were not truly homosexuals, thus making for some difficulty in the interpretation of the results. However, in a later study (Pollack, Huntley, Allen, & Schwartz, 1976), the subjects *were* all homosexuals, and they were asked to do a cognitive task and to report on their mood after being randomly assigned to one of two conditions. In one of these, they thought their homosexuality had been revealed to the examiner, whereas in the other they believed he was unaware of it. Actually, the examiner was always ignorant about the subjects' sexual orientation. Both the mood and task performance of the subjects was significantly affected by believing their sexual orientation was known. A study was also done with stupidity as the degrading condition (Farina, Thaw, & Boudreau, 1970) and, again, feeling and behaviors were affected. However, the interpersonal effects of homosexuality and stupidity were not identical to those of mental illness. Although differences as a function of the particular blemish studied should be expected, more research is required before we will know the effects of the many debasing conditions that exist and in what ways these effects are similar and in what ways different.

Contamination as a Cause of Stigma

Many years ago, Erving Goffman (1963) wrote a poetic and compelling treatise on stigma. In that work, he called attention to the phenomenon of contamination, which he named "courtesy stigma" (p. 30). Goffman was likening that type of stigmatization to the privileges (courtesy) extended by private clubs to relatives of a member. Being related to a member results in receiving treatment like the member just as being related to a blemished person results in stigmatization for the relative like that inflicted on the blemished person. What happens in this process is that socially degrading conditions rub off on or stigmatize friends, relatives, and acquaintances of people who possess that condition. A nice overview of this phenomenon has been provided by Posner (1976):

> [I]n our society it is not only the deviant who is stigmatized but also those who are associated or acquainted with the deviant. . . . Even an innocuous or casual walk down the street with a stigmatized other tends to stigmatize a person who accompanies such an individual. (p. 27)

It appears, then, that fear of contamination is another source of the stigma of mental illness. People realize that contamination occurs and, to avoid social repudiation, they distance themselves from those who are marked by blemishes. And so the blemished are spurned. Social degradation *is* transmitted in this way, as the literature supporting these assertions (to be reviewed) will indicate. But why this happens is perhaps more amenable to comprehension by intuition than by logical analysis. Jones et al. (1984) offer some speculations regarding this. One of the suggestions they make is that maybe a "birds of a feather" assumption prevails in our society, and when someone accompanies a cripple or a blind person it is assumed the two are acquainted because both have the same problem. Another is that perhaps the apparent "normal" of the pair is dislikable and unpleasant and, consequently, so devoid of friends that he or she must be satisfied with the company of marginal individuals. Here, we must note another possible facet of this process. Fear of contamination could mean the mentally ill are hit by a double-barreled blast. The stigmatized are aware that contagion exists and so will recognize that those who maintain a friendly relationship with them incur social penalties. They might wonder why these friends choose to suffer the penalties and understandably conclude that it is because of pity. If so, the relationship will certainly become more awkward and the blemished might themselves decide to terminate it.

This process is clearly not confined to mental blemishes, like so much that makes up the phenomenon of stigma. Considerable research has been done that shows a wide variety of stains can infect people associated with the aggrieved. Alcoholism in a family member has been found to degrade other members, even though those members did not drink. Burk and Sher (1990) report that both high school students and mental health professionals negatively stereotyped adolescents who had an alcoholic fam-

ily member. And Stafford and Petway (1977) found that the spouses of alcoholics were themselves degraded. Another social stain, being imprisoned, causes the family members of the convict to be stigmatized (Sack, Seidler, & Thomas, 1976). Handicapped children, either because of physical problems (Voysey, 1972) or because of a learning disability (Birenbaum, 1970), caused their parents to face awkward, embarrassing, and difficult social situations. Also, and surprising in the present-day "enlightened" time, homosexuality was found to powerfully stigmatize a friend of homosexual individuals (Neuberg, Smith, Hoffman, & Russell, 1994).

Mental illness as a contaminating mark has also received considerable attention, as was indicated. The plight of the family of the affected individual has been of particular interest to both practitioners and researchers, and there is broad agreement that family members are severely stigmatized. No doubt, one reason for this is that the family has been regarded as being partly responsible for causing this particular degrading condition. An extensive literature on this topic exists but it consists primarily of reports based on practice and clinical observation and, while that kind of information can be highly valuable, the conclusions it permits are, at best, tentative. We begin with a brief overview of the clinical literature and then turn to the small number of systematic studies that have been done to date.

A prolific writer who has often reviewed the literature on the social demeaning of mental patients' families is Harriet Lefley. She argues persuasively that this stigmatization places a heavy burden on the family, a burden that has two components, an objective and a subjective part (Lefley, 1992). The objective burden consists of hurtful behaviors by neighbors such as holding the family responsible for aberrant acts on the part of the patient and condemning and ostracizing individual family members. Children might be teased by peers and neighbors may curtail relationships to the point of isolating the family. Subjectively, the family (particularly the parents) perceives itself blamed for having caused the problem and feels resentful and angry at what they see as unfair treatment and blame. All this comes on top of distressing experiences, including expected negative changes in family life, due to the disabling condition of the afflicted member. Lefley believes that one kind of severe damage that is done by the negative reaction of society is to the family members' self-esteem. Another report describes a practice, common among Mexican Americans (Jenkins, 1988), that is regarded as a clue to the degradation that families expect when a member becomes mentally ill. Instead of using the common terms *mentally ill* or *schizophrenic* when referring to their afflicted relative, they employ a folk explanation of the condition. That explanation is called *nervios* and apparently it is intended to ward off the disgrace associated with mental illness.

More systematic questionnaire and experimental studies also provide a picture of the mental patient's relatives as beset by problems in relating to others and bothered by negative feelings and emotions. Wahl and Harman (1989) administered a questionnaire to 487 subjects from families that had a mentally ill member. The questionnaire was intended to reveal how social stigma affected them. A majority of the respondents, 56%, reported that stigma had a large negative impact on the individuals within the family and, specifically, damage to the self-esteem was often cited. An interesting study, involving an experimental manipulation, was done by Weyand (1983). Undergraduate male students were told the university was trying a new way to help incoming freshman adapt to college life and was seeking help from people like them who had just gone through the experience. They were given some fictitious biographical information about a prospective student and his family, and they heard a recording of the student being interviewed. A randomly selected third of the subjects learned the incoming student's father had a mental problem, another third that he had a problem with alcohol, and the final third received none of that information. All other information about the son and the family was identical. The subjects were then given a questionnaire measuring how well or poorly they thought the prospective student would get along at the university, and they were also asked to tape-record a message to the student that would warn him of possible problems and ease his way into college life. Relative to the control group, sons of the stigmatized fathers were expected to have an inordinate number of problems, and they were advised not to disclose their father's condition to other people.

A similar experiment, but one involving more potentially stigmatizing paternal conditions, was carried out by Mehta and Farina (1988). Male and female college students were asked to imagine they had a roommate (of the same sex) whom they had not known for long and the roommate now disclosed something new about his or her father. Subjects, divided in groups of equal size, heard that the father had one of these six conditions: he was chronically depressed, he was in jail for tax fraud, he was an alcoholic, he was 70 years old, he had a job that took him away from home for two weeks of every month, or he

had only one leg. They were then asked how much trouble they expected the roommate to have in four domains of living: school, family, career, and friends. Highly significant differences were found in the difficulties the roommate was expected to have as a function of the kind of problem that afflicted his or her father. The magnitude of the expected problems decreased in the order in which the paternal conditions are listed above. The most severe problems were expected to beset the offspring of the mentally troubled father while the least severe were expected to be encountered by the student whose father had only one leg. The researchers had included the amputee condition as a lesser stigma while the "away from home" condition was intended to be the unstigmatized control group. They suggest the outcome indicates the complex nature of stigma. It elicits sympathy as well as rejection.

All of the tested areas of an offspring's life, the findings suggest, would be disrupted by a stigmatized father. When people become mentally ill (or acquire some other degrading condition) not only they but their family members are negatively influenced in many ways, including in finding work. The magnitude of the contagion effect was found to be in the order listed above, the most problems being engendered for life in school and the least with friends. The findings also indicated that the severity of contamination varies *both* as a function of the stigmatizing condition and the area of life considered. Thus school was most disrupted by psychiatric problems while alcoholism would be most destructive of family life. Returning to the central point of this section, contagion as a source of the social stigma that plagues mental patients, it seems inhumane to suggest that family members would degrade their own kin because they have themselves been humiliated and possibly materially damaged by him or her. In most cases it seems probable that family members would resist showing overt signs of resentment but resentment would typically be there, particularly if the patient's condition was annoying, as it often is. And if the formal family ties are not close, or if the afflicted is a friend, the aggravation might be openly displayed.

These researchers also offer hypotheses as to why this contamination occurs. Two of these are essentially the same as those offered by Jones et al. (1984) that were previously cited: (1) people who appear together are seen as alike, and (2) if someone associates with a marginal person, he or she can't be worth very much. A third possibility suggested is that the stain may be regarded by society as transmissible from one generation to another, either through the genes or because of a shared pathogenic environment. So people think that a psychopathological parent is likely to have a similarly afflicted child and, in consequence, the apparently healthy relative is transformed into a deviant. Mehta and Farina also suggest that fear of entanglements may play a role in stigmatizing relatives and friends of mentally ill persons. People may worry because such individuals are in an emergency situation and are urgently seeking help. They may be distressed at what has happened to someone important to them and starving for companionship and support. But if such support is offered today, can it be denied tomorrow? Fear of a "tar baby" trap may impel people to avoid individuals in such a plight. Concerns about financial needs, rides to the hospital, and caring for children and pets could have a similar repelling effect.

FACTORS THAT CHANGE THE STRENGTH OF STIGMA

We have seen that the mentally ill are stigmatized, and we have examined some of the causes of the phenomenon. In this section we ask, Are there factors (variables, conditions) that change the potency of stigmatization so as to make rejection and degradation very strong or relatively benign? Such variables could be aspects of the target or marked person or of the "normal" stigmtizer, it could be situational conditions, and it could be a combination or interaction involving these elements. Obviously, the possible factors that could influence the strength of stigmatization are many. But if our task is to understand the social degradation of psychiatrically afflicted people, we need not be concerned with all of these possible variables. Some are more important than others, on both practical and theoretical grounds. Furthermore, the fact is that relatively few variables have been investigated so that we know only some of those that potentially exist. And so, our task is much simplified. Those factors that the literature indicates are capable of modifying the virulence of stigmatization will now be examined.

Differences Between Men and Women

A very large number of studies have been done that indicate whether males and females respond differently to mentally ill individuals or whether afflicted men are viewed or treated differently from comparably afflicted women. Clearly, then, this raises two questions and here we will consider them one at a time. In addition to this distinction between the sex of the stigmatized versus the sex of the observer, another differentiation is necessary. Some studies measure stigma by means of questionnaires or interviews (i.e., they obtain *verbal* measures of stigmatization from their subjects, such as whether they would marry someone who has had a psychiatric hospitalization). Other studies rely on *behavioral* measures, such as the painfulness of a shock subjects are required to administer to a former mental patient. These two kinds of measures do not yield the same results. This discrepancy itself raises some very provocative questions that will be considered. However, for the present task of organizing a review of the literature, it means that each question posed will be divided into two: studies using verbal measures and studies using behavioral measures. Following is an overview of the results for each of these four kinds of studies.

Sex Differences Among Observers—Verbal Studies

The literature on each of these four questions was reviewed in 1981 (Farina, 1981), and I have found only four additional studies since that time. The new information does not change the conclusions of the earlier review and so this review will be general and brief. The reader is invited to look at the earlier work if detailed information is desired.

The largest number of studies relevant to sex differences in stigmatization falls in this category. There are 27 of them, including three of the four not included in the earlier review (Link, 1987; Link & Cullen, 1986; Link, Cullen, Frank, & Wozniak, 1987). Fourteen of these investigations find no differences between men and women. Six other studies obtain results that are not the same for males and females, but these differences are not clearly related to stigmatization. An example of such a study is one where cross-cultural differences were found for females but not males. Sex differences were found in the remaining seven reports but, while females were found to be more stigmatizing in four of these, it was males who expressed more disfavor toward the mentally ill in the other three studies. Judging by these numbers, we must conclude that men and women express equal disfavor toward people with mental disorder. Of course, just counting studies is not the only way to arrive at conclusions from this literature. However, I have also critically examined the research and find no reason to alter the conclusions the numerical pattern prompts. Men and women respond very similarly when asked to express their feelings toward people afflicted with a mental disorder.

Effects of the Sex of the Mentally Disordered—Verbal Studies

A total of 22 pertinent studies fall into this category, including the last of the studies not previously reviewed (Grunt, 1973). The largest number, nine, reports that sex of the victim does affect the response of subjects but does not bring greater favorability to one sex than to the other. For example, subjects perceive certain kinds of stressors to be associated with greater pathology in men than women while the opposite is true for other stressors. Of the remaining studies, four find that males and females are comparably regarded, six that females are favored over males, and the remaining three report that males are liked better than females. It seems that the patient's sex plays a small role in what people say about their liking for that patient, but the role is a function of other factors such as type of symptom displayed. The research also hints that mentally ill women are regarded more favorably than comparable men and that depression, in particular, is more acceptable when displayed by a female than a male.

Sex Differences Among Observers—Behavioral Studies

The research that is based on behavioral measures of stigmatization is far less extensive than that relying on verbal reports. Probably that is a simple reflection of the greater difficulty encountered in actually observing negative behaviors taking place as compared to asking people what they would do. This literature, in its entirety, seems to consist of five articles reporting the results of nine studies plus a book by Chesler (1972) that is based on her review of research and her personal observations and experiences. To begin with the book, the author concludes assertively and unequivocally that men, and not women, have behaved in a harmful and even inhuman way toward female mental patients. She actually holds men responsible for causing some of the mental problems afflicting her sex by making women helpless and unhappy and then interpreting their well-justified complaints as symptoms of madness.

Three of the four remaining articles report five separate studies that are very similar and that can most coherently and economically be reviewed together. These were cited in another context (Farina, Felner, & Boudreau, 1973; Fa-

rina & Hagelauer, 1975; Farina, Murray, & Groh, 1978). The studies were actually partial replications that varied the sex of the subjects and the sex of a confederate who was presented as a mental patient. Here we will look at the impact of the *subject's* sex. The subjects were all employees at one of three sites who were told by their supervisor that management was interested in using workers to hire new people. It was explained that because they knew their own job and its requirements, they would help decide if new applicants should be hired to work with them. They were also told that management was trying to hire some disadvantaged persons, ex-mental patients, and some employees would evaluate former patients while others would evaluate ordinary job seekers. Half the workers were then told they would meet an ex-patient while the rest were informed they were assigned to an ordinary applicant. All employees actually met one of five confederates, a different confederate being used for each of the five studies. The confederates were never aware of what the worker had been told, but they were instructed to behave normally for half the subjects in each condition and to act in a nervous and tense fashion with the rest. The studies were all conducted at the subjects' workplace during their regular working hours.

Two of the studies were done with female subjects and female "applicants" and the remainder involved all possible combinations of sex of confederate and sex of subject. The results were clear and unequivocal. Relative to the control group, the males strongly rejected the "applicant" with the history of psychiatric problems, indicating that he or she would do poor work and that others would not get along with him or her, and they recommended that he or she not be hired. In striking contrast, female subjects who were in the "mental patient" condition were as accepting of the "applicant" as were those who evaluated an ordinary job seeker. In terms of *behavior*, at least, it seems that women are less stigmatizing and more accepting of former mental patients than men.

The studies just examined were all carried out in the context of work, and the sex differences found might be a result of those special circumstances. While the picture may be changing, paid work traditionally has been a more central part of the male than the female role. If work is more important to men than women, perhaps men are more critical about the people with whom they work and so reject those they see as tainted whereas women are less involved and less discriminating. However, the last article in this group refutes that possibility (Farina, Thaw, Felner, & Hust, 1976). The aspects of the four studies reported in that article that are relevant here are these: Four independent groups of college students, two composed of males and two of females, were recruited to be subjects in a study. The study was described to them as intending to find out what kind of volunteer worked best with residents of a state institution. The subjects were taken to the institution and some were told they were going to work with a college student volunteer (the control group) while others were told they would be working with someone who had suffered a psychiatric disorder. Their task was explained as teaching the resident a series of button presses which they would know but the learner would not know. They would communicate by means of electrically connected panels located in different rooms. At first, the resident would need to guess the correct sequence in which he or she was to press the buttons. But, the subjects were told, they could inform the learner if the guess was wrong by administering an electric shock that could be varied in length and so guide the learner to the correct solution. They were assured that the resident had agreed to these arrangements and that the shocks were not really painful. No shocks were actually given, of course, but the durations the subjects *thought* they were delivering were measured and constituted the main dependent measure of the study. Clearly, how much pain is inflicted on someone is good index of favorability of treatment.

Each of the four groups of subjects met a different confederate who was uninformed about what the subjects had been told. The confederates were males for the two groups of male subjects and females for the two female groups. The results were significant and clear. Both samples of males shocked the confederate longer in the mentally ill than the control condition whereas for the females that was not true in either sample. In fact, females shocked the confederate *less* in the mentally disordered than in the control condition. It appears that men's disposition to be less favorable than women toward those with psychiatric problems is not limited to employment situations. And it is in deeds, and not in words, that females show greater acceptance of mental patients than males.

Effects of the Sex of the Mentally Disordered—Behavioral Studies

Here, as in research on effects of the observer's sex, we find a sharp disagreement between expressed attitudes and actual behaviors. Female sufferers are treated better than comparable males, in spite of the fact that both men and women express the same degree of liking for a person with mental problems regardless of that person's sex. There are many possible explanations for the inconsistency, but these are beyond the scope of this chapter's purposes. Unfortunately for the mentally ill, the more negative index is probably also the more significant one. A total of five studies consistently lead to the foregoing conclusion, although they utilize quite different dependent measures.

Two of the pertinent studies devised indices to measure degree of rejection by the community and used these indices to compare males with psychiatric problems to similar females. In one of these studies, Linsky (1970) computed a ratio of voluntary to committed patients from a given area. He reasoned that the more rejecting the attitudes are toward a given class of individuals, the more of them would be hospitalized against their wishes (i.e., committed) relative to a kind of base rate of psychopathology provided by voluntary admission rates. Based on that index, he concluded that males with mental problems are more rejected than comparable females. A similar study was done by Tudor, Tudor, and Gove (1977), and they obtained the same results. Males with mental problems were treated less tolerantly and more harshly by the community than similarly afflicted females. An aspect of the study by Farina, Murray, and Groh (1978), which was briefly discussed, is relevant here. That study found that male workers rejected a female applicant with a history of mental disorder more than one without such a history. But the rejection was much more limited and milder than that accorded a comparable male applicant by another group of male workers (Farina et al., 1973). Findings reported by Clausen (1980) also seem to be a reflection of this same phenomenon. He found that discharged male psychiatric patients whose adjustment was poor were more likely to be divorced by their wives than ex-patients who were better adjusted. However, discharged wives who were poorly adjusted were no more likely to be divorced than wives whose adjustment was good. It may be that disturbed females are better tolerated than disturbed males.

Why should disturbed men be less socially acceptable than equally disturbed women? A ready explanation is that for deviant and unpredictable individuals, as mental patients are commonly perceived to be, the stronger and more aggressive they are, the more dangerous they are. And men are stronger and more aggressive than women. But a review of the research literature on childhood psychopathology by Eme (1979) suggests that more than this is involved in these differences between men and women.

Eme summarizes the studies by saying that both teachers and mothers "are more likely to view the same disturbance as more pathological in the male than in the female" (p. 576). These findings with children are consistent with what the literature indicates about adults, but they suggest that danger may not be the reason why male mental patients are more rejected and badly treated than comparable females. While a man may be more dangerous than a woman, a boy and a girl do not seem to differ much in the danger they pose for society.

Sex does seem to be a factor determining the severity of rejection and denigration of mental patients. Women appear to be more even-handed than men in their *treatment* of such individuals, and so men may be mainly responsible for the bad deeds done to those with psychiatric woes, if not the bad words. As if in repayment for good works, women who become mentally disordered are themselves treated better than comparable men. This is the conclusion also reached by Rabkin (1980) who, having minutely examined this literature, states that "males are more likely to be stigmatized than females" (p. 22). Although females who have suffered a mental disorder are generally favored over comparable men, we should not assume that they are always so fortunate. One can imagine settings and roles where females might be at a disadvantage. One such role is suggested by Nunnally's (1961) finding that when an afflicted woman is described as a mother, she elicits a virulent negative reaction from people (pp. 141–142).

Personal Experience with the Mentally Ill

The issue addressed in this section is this: Will exposure to people suffering from psychiatric problems change attitudes and behaviors toward such people and, if there is change, is this change favorable or unfavorable? These are theoretically significant questions and questions that have enormous practical importance. The success of the wholesale deinstitutionalization of mental patients that has taken place in this and other countries is greatly affected by this issue. Patients have been removed from large, insulated psychiatric hospitals to many locations within the community where it is far more likely that residents will be exposed to them. If such encounters have a positive effect on the residents' feelings and comportment, this augurs well for deinstitutionalization. But if the changes are unfavorable, we must expect a growing rejection of mental patients and increasing resistance to

their living in the community. Negative changes would also imply that families would grow less and less tolerant of their stricken member, and they might eventually refuse to accept him or her.

Not surprising, in view of the importance of this matter, a lot of research has been done. Fortunately for those who have suffered psychiatric problems, this research consistently indicates that familiarity with mental patients reduces the extent to which they are stigmatized. In what follows, this literature is briefly reviewed. It is organized in accordance with the nature of the research done, from the casual and anecdotal, and therefore not always persuasive, to the disciplined and systematic, and hence more compelling.

Casual, Opportunistic, and Correlational Research

Phillips (1967) used a simple technique to check on the effect of exposure to mental patients on the stigmatization of such patients. He measured the attitudes toward mental patients of two groups of subjects, one of the groups reporting they had never known such an individual, while all members of the other group had personal experience with them. Those who had personal contact were less rejecting of someone who was suffering from a mental disorder. Researchers have sought out subjects known to have interacted with psychiatric patients, such as members of families having a psychiatric casualty and hospital workers whose job entails interacting with mental patients. Serrano (1985) measured propensity to derogate the mentally disordered by members of families with an afflicted relative and by control family members. The former subjects expressed more benign attitudes, presumably as a result of the ameliorative effects of contact with the stricken relative.

Many investigations have utilized subjects associated with mental hospitals. Wright and Klein (1965) compared two groups of non professional hospital workers: those who had little contact with mental patients, such as laundry workers, and those who regularly interacted with patients, such as nursing assistants. Those who had more exposure to patients also had more favorable attitudes toward them. A similar study was done by Smith (1969), who compared the feelings toward the mentally disordered of individuals who had experience with them to control subjects. The former were hospital employees, student nurses, and the patients themselves. The feelings of all three groups who had interacted with patients were more favorable than those of the controls. And finally, a rather strange study that may support the same underlying processes as the preceding investigations, was done by Harrow, Fox, and Detre (1969). The subjects were a group of psychiatric patients and the patients' spouses. Favorability of perception of the self and of the marital partner was measured one week following hospitalization, and it was found that the afflicted partner was viewed less favorably than the unaffected partner by each member of the pair. A second measurement taken 7 weeks later showed that while the unaffected person's views of the partner were still derogatory, the hospitalized partner's self-concept had become significantly more favorable. This change may have resulted from the beneficial effects of interacting with other patients.

Several investigators have taken advantage of a program called "companion program" that was commonly found in American colleges and universities prior to deinstitutionalization. The program seems virtually designed to answer the questions posed in this section. College student volunteers agreed to spend time with a particular patient who was in a nearby mental hospital. The students interacted with the patients in a friendly and supportive manner and on a regular basis. The hospitals hoped to improve the patients' mental condition but, as a result, the students had extensive exposure to those patients. Using such volunteers as subjects are two studies that, although done independently, are remarkably similar (Chinsky & Rappaport, 1970; Holzberg & Knapp, 1965). Both studies found that the experience led to significant increases in favorability of attitudes toward psychiatric patients. The students were more approving and accepting of patients and viewed them as being more like ordinary people after having served as companions. A very good, albeit still a correlational study, was done by Link and Cullen (1986). Samples from the general population provided an index of favorability toward the mentally ill by describing how dangerous they thought these individuals were. Reasonably, the authors assumed that the more dangerous the subjects regarded the mentally ill to be, the less favorable their attitudes were. The subjects also reported the degree of personal contact they had with patients. Link and Cullen found that the greater the degree of contact with patients, the less dangerous they were regarded to be. These findings are consistent with what the other studies imply (i.e., that acquaintance with patients improves attitudes toward them). But because of the study's methodology, there is a possibility the correlation means only that people who think patients are not dangerous will spend more time with them

than people who think they are a threat. Therefore, the authors selected subjects whose contact with mentally disordered people was not voluntary, such as those who were acquainted with the victim prior to morbidity. They found the contact–dangerousness relation to be the same for that sample as for those whose contact might have been fully voluntary. This suggests that it is indeed contact that causes favorability, rather than the reverse.

Research Using Experimental Procedures

We now come to studies using the preferred methodology, experimentation, in attempting to determine what effect contact with mental patients has on feelings and behaviors toward them. An early such study was done by Nunnally in 1961 and reported in his seminal book, *Popular Conceptions of Mental Health* (Nunnally, 1961). Nunnally had a speaker talk to groups of subjects. To vary the degree to which the subjects had been exposed to mental patients, some were later informed that the speaker had been mentally ill, while others were given no such information. Thus, subjectively, the former subjects had one more exposure to a mental patient than the latter, and it was a recent one. After three days, attitudes toward the mentally ill were measured, and it was found that those who had heard the "ex-mental patient" were more favorable than the controls. Two studies by Gelfand and Ullmann yielded results very much in keeping with Nunnally's findings. One of the studies entailed measuring 36 nursing students' views of psychiatric patients both before and after exposure to patients in one of their rotations in the hospital (Gelfand & Ullmann, 1961a). Another group of 23 students, not exposed to mental patients, also had their attitudes measured twice over a comparable period. Relative to the control group, the attitudes of the students exposed to patients became more accepting and benign. The second study replicated the first but, this time, the subjects were medical students (Gelfand & Ullmann, 1961b). Again, they found that the subjects who interacted with the mental patients expressed more favorable feelings toward mental disorders than did a control group of medical students. A very similar study to Gelfand and Ullmann's 1961a study was done by Altrocchi (1960), and he also found that contact changed the views of the nursing students in a more favorable direction.

Will all personal encounters with psychiatric patients increase the liking for such patients for the person that meets them? Probably not. If the experience with the patient is unpleasant, it seems intuitively likely that attitudes will become more negative rather than more positive. In fact, there is a study that indicates that is what happens. Schwartz, Myers, and Astrachan (1974) measured the adjustment of patients being discharged to their families and subsequently assessed the attitudes of the patients' relatives toward mental disorder in general. They found that the poorer the patient's adjustment when going home, the more negative were the relative's attitudes toward mental disorders. It seems probable that it was the more disturbed patients who displayed the most disagreeable and upsetting behavior and, hence, caused their relatives to view all mentally disordered people negatively. Overall, however, the very consistent research findings indicate that most encounters with patients improve attitudes and make people like patients better. And so, exposure to mental patients is a factor that affects how strongly stigmatized patients will be. These findings also have some obvious practical implications, one of which is that deinstitutionalization may help to reduce the degradation of people with mental disorders.

Conceptions of Psychopathology

Understanding the basic nature of mental disorders has apparently been a central interest for those concerned with it since human beings have been aware of the phenomenon. A wide variety of conceptions have been held, radically different and sometimes incompatible. As alluded to earlier, mental disorders have been viewed as outward manifestations of the inner presence of demons, as bodily diseases like any other disease, as genetically caused, and as the products of experience in somatically sound people. These conceptions have been accompanied by striking differences in the social status accorded the afflicted and in the kinds of treatments that have been employed to cure them. When demons were the problem, theology was the agency concerned with their care and cure. When the belief that the genes were the culprit predominated, eugenics, the removal of the faulty gene from the genetic pool of the population, was accepted as the only effective remedy. Several states, such as Virginia and North Carolina, passed laws permitting the sterilization of some classes of patients and these laws were at times enforced.

At the present time, there are two salient and important views that, in their extreme form, are at opposite ends of a continuum of conceptions about the nature of mental disorders. One of these views is that psychopathology is a bodily disorder, like diabetes or pneumonia, that causes the deviant behavior as inescapably as pneumonia causes fever. This conception has been strongly promoted. No one who has lived in our society for long can be unaware of the massive effort to try to convince us that mental illness is a disease like any other disease. The main purpose of that effort, likely, is to lead society to regard the afflicted not as blameworthy, bad, or evil persons but, rather, as innocent people like ourselves who have been victimized by misfortune. Clearly, this effort bears very strongly on the main concern of this chapter. Does the strategy work? Research has been done to find an answer to this question and we will review it. At the other extreme of the continuum is the conception of the mentally ill as people who have learned behaviors that are maladaptive, that do not provide personal satisfaction, and/or who have endured traumatizing experiences. In any case, they are considered physically healthy individuals and not sick. This is not to say that the two views are clearly and specifically understood by everybody. But it is fair to say that people concerned with mental illness certainly recognize these conceptions and the continuum they anchor.

Unlike other variables that affect the vehemence of stigma, for the issue of what *is* the basic nature of mental disorders, we have advocates and champions of each position and, as we might expect, there is disagreement among them. It appears that the larger number supports the illness conception, although they do not all do it in the same way. Mechanic, McAlpine, Rosenfield, and Davis (1994), for example, report that the well-being of the afflicted is greatly improved if they regard their condition as a "physical, medical, or biological" problem. Specifically, they report that those who viewed their disorder in that way felt less stigmatized and had better social relationships than those who did not. Dowbiggin (1988), on the other hand, asserts that portraying mental disorders as bodily diseases has not reduced social stigmatization, in spite of claims to the contrary. In fact, he accuses the French psychiatrists who, in 1870, took the lead in medicalizing psychopathology, of feathering their own nest by converting behavioral problems into conditions that made them, as physicians, the experts.

The Public's Beliefs About Mental Disorders and Their Effect on Stigma

Persuasive messages are clearly effective in changing the beliefs of targets about the nature of psychopathology, as will be seen. It is also clear that those changes can alter stigmatization. However, it seems that the consequences can be favorable for the mentally ill or they can be harmful to them. Moreover, while the target of the communication may be the general population, special components of society are also likely to receive it, and they may be influenced in a different and possibly unwanted way. In what follows, the relevant literature will be reviewed separately for the public, for the mental health professionals, and for the mentally ill. For each of these population segments, the aim will be to understand the effect on stigmatization of these persuasive messages. An explanation about the aim of determining if messages to mental patients will change their degradation of other mental patients is needed here. That aim may seem peripheral to this chapter's purposes, if not strange. But if the messages alter patients' views of mental disorders, there might be changes in their behavior and that could affect their social acceptability. More probable, the victims' self-esteem may be changed by these communications and that warrants a slight detour.

People's beliefs about the nature of psychopathology can be changed very easily, as Nunnally (1961) demonstrated a long time ago. Attending a class, receiving psychiatric treatments, being exposed to the ideas of others, or merely reading a few phrases embedded in a different message have all been shown to alter beliefs about what mental disorders are (Farina & Fisher, 1982). The earliest research to determine what consequences follow these changes in beliefs appears to be that of Rothaus, Hanson, Cleveland, and Johnson, reported in 1963. Their subjects were hospitalized psychiatric patients. They were coached to present the cause of their hospitalization in two different ways and each patient was then interviewed twice. For one interviewer, they reported that their hospitalization was caused by an *illness*. They used such terms as *nervous breakdown* and their treatment was described as consisting of tranquilizers and other drugs. For a different interviewer, *social problems* were cited as having caused the hospitalization. On that occasion patients described their own particular personality problems (e.g., being shy) and stated their treatments were designed to help them solve their interpersonal difficulties. Otherwise, the patients behaved comparably in the two conditions. The interviewers judged the patients in the social problems condition as more likely to be given a job than the same patients in the illness condition. So the study suggests that medicalizing mental disorders makes the sufferer *less* socially acceptable, rather than more.

Another study using very different procedures and done in Norway supports the findings of Rothaus et al. Ommundsen and Ekeland (1978) told their student subjects that the study in which they were participating was researching traffic accidents. The subjects were then randomly divided into three groups and were given the same description of a driver losing control of a car and running into a tree. One of the groups was told that the driver had been hospitalized for appendectomy while the other two groups learned that the driver had been in a psychiatric hospital. In addition, for one of the two latter groups the psychiatric condition was presented as an *illness* by quoting the ex-patient as saying that he had gotten sick, had trouble with his nerves, but that medicine helped him. For the final group, the condition was presented as an *interpersonal problem* by reporting the ex-patient as saying he had trouble on the job, economic problems, and he could not cope with the stress. The subjects were then asked to indicate which of 16 factors, some placing the blame on the driver, others on conditions, were responsible for the accident. When the psychiatric disorder was presented as an illness, the driver was blamed for the accident significantly more than the control (appendectomy) driver. There was no significant difference in blame assigned between the control driver and the ex-patient driver when his psychiatric disorder was presented as an interpersonal problem. The difference between the two psychiatric conditions was also unreliable.

Three separate studies were done by Farina, Fisher, Getter, and Fischer (1978) and Fisher and Farina (1979), all having the same aim, to wit, to induce changes in the subjects' beliefs about mental illness and to examine the effect of the changes on stigmatization. Two of the studies were done identically using college students as subjects. The beliefs were significantly altered as intended by means of a message describing the student mental health clinic. Half the subjects were informed that mental health problems were social and the remainder that they were medical in nature. The manipulation was radically different in the third study and, since the technique used was successful, the study has engaging implications. The subjects were students enrolled in two abnormal psychology classes and the beliefs about mental disorders of the members of the two classes were comparable at the beginning of the course. But one of the classes was taught by someone who described mental problems as almost exclusively due to social learning, while the other instructor assigned an important role to genetic and somatic factors. As indicated, at the end of the course the beliefs of the students differed significantly and in the expected direction. In all three of the studies, subjects were asked how degrading they believed mental disorders to be. In none of the three was there a significant difference between those subjects who believed mental disorders were illnesses and those who viewed them as interpersonal problems. Actually, there were directional differences in all three experiments with the social learning groups describing mental disorders as *less* degrading than the illness groups. An additional finding obtained in all the experiments was that subjects in the social learning groups, relative to subjects in the other condition, believed that people suffering from mental problems had better control over their condition. The meaning of this finding will be considered.

The foregoing studies have *manipulated* conceptions of mental disorders and found that viewing them as illnesses neither reduced stigmatization nor improved the perception of the afflicted. Yet, as indicated, that seems to be the cardinal reason for the shower of messages directed at society. That hypothesis could be checked in another way, utilizing individuals whose conceptions of psychopathology inherently lean toward an illness or a learned direction. Some research bearing on this question has been done. Golding, Becker, Sherman, and Rappaport (1975) constructed a scale measuring a dimension quite similar to the learning-to-illness dimension. Subjects holding an illness conception rated mental patients as more disturbed and expressed more reluctance to become friends with them than did subjects holding learning conceptions. In a second study, the researchers showed a videotape of moderately disturbed patients to learning-view and illness-view subjects. The latter subjects saw the patients as more deviant and expected greater deviance in social interaction with them than subjects who believed mental illness to be learned. Here we see evidence again that a disease conception of psychopathology does not decrease stigmatization. It seems to do just the opposite.

Mental Health Workers Beliefs About Mental Disorders and Their Effect on Stigma

Quite clearly, what mental health workers (aides, nurses, professionals) think is wrong with their charges can make a large difference in how the afflicted are treated. Those workers typically have considerable power over patients and, if these beliefs affect behavior, the beliefs of the caretakers may be important. And some research focusing on the social learning–illness dimension indicates that beliefs that psychopathology is a learned condition lead to more favorable perception and treatment of patients than a disease view. Cohen and Struening (1964) carried out a major study of this issue. They first devised a questionnaire to measure the degree to which a respondent regards mental disorders as illnesses as compared to learned patterns of behavior. These questionnaires were then admin-

istered to representative samples of mental health workers at each of 12 mental hospitals. The measure of favorability of behavior toward patients that they used was number of days the patients spent in the community during their first year of hospitalization: a measure more reasonable in those days (early 1960s) of many involuntary hospitalizations than it would be now. The researchers found that, for hospitals where staff beliefs were toward the disease end of the continuum, patients spent fewer days in the community than patients from hospitals staffed by workers with more of a social learning view.

Langer and Abelson (1974) were also specifically interested in beliefs that psychiatric problems are learned or are manifestations of a disease. Their subjects were two groups of mental health professionals, one group believing mental disorders were exclusively learned while the other group thought biological factors played an important role. All subjects were shown the same videotaped interview but half the subjects in each group were told the interviewee was a job applicant while the rest were informed that he was a mental patient. The learning-oriented professionals described the interviewee comparably in the two conditions, but those with an illness view described the "patient" as significantly more disturbed than the "job applicant." We saw earlier that degree of disturbance and severity of stigmatization are positively correlated. Hence, we see once again that a disease conception of mental disorders appears to have an unfavorable effect on the esteem and treatment of psychiatric patients. In this case, the disease-oriented mental health professionals, perceiving nonexistent disturbed behavior, may cause the institution of unneeded treatments and restrictions of freedom.

Patients' Beliefs About Mental Disorders and Their Effect

While the main target of the messages that mental disorders are illnesses is the general public, the patients are also certain to hear them. How are they affected? At this time, we know that they *are* influenced, but as to whether this influence is good or bad, the situation is not yet clear.

Mechanic et al. (1994) divided schizophrenic patients into two groups on the basis of what they thought to be the nature of their affliction. One group leaned toward blaming their condition on a disease or biological process, while the second group was not disposed to attribute it to medical factors. This distinction is quite comparable to the social learning–illness continuum that has been our focus. The researchers report that the illness group, relative to the other group, reported better social relations and a higher quality of life. This was presumably due to feeling less stigmatized and having higher self-esteem. And so it would seem that the illness conception should be promoted among mental patients.

However, reports from other studies raise serious questions about this conclusion. Morrison, Bushell, Hanson, Fentiman, and Holdridge-Crane (1977) observed that the more outpatients believed psychiatric conditions were illness, the more dependent they felt on mental health professionals. That is worrisome since patients who acquire a somatic view may do less to improve their interpersonal functioning and so may become socially isolated, chronic cases. This interpretation is supported by a study (Morrison, 1976) in which a group of psychiatric outpatients had their views of mental disorders shifted in a social learning direction while another group served as a control. Six months after the manipulation, psychiatric hospitalization had occurred less frequently for the experimental group than for the control. Especially relevant is a study by Farina, Fisher, Getter, and Fischer (1978). Female college students were recruited to receive a psychotherapy session which, they were told, was intended to help them with their own personal problems. Half of them were then induced to view mental disorders as illnesses and the rest to view them as interpersonal problems. Following the therapy, they were asked to make a note in a journal during the subsequent week each time they thought about a personal problem such as was discussed in therapy. The social learning group thought about personal problems significantly more frequently than the disease group. Evidently people with an illness conception of mental disorders not only believe there is little they can do about their problems in adjustment, but actually do little to cope with their difficulties. Thus, the conception patients have of their condition, whether as illness or learned, seems to have good and bad components. When they view their condition as an illness, patients may be more comfortable with themselves and may be more pleasant companions. However, they may also torpidly accept their own defective social behavior, depending on the experts to "cure" it.

Talking Openly About the Mental Disorder

Another variable thought to affect strength of stigmatization that has been studied is the strategy of having the blemished person grant people permission to openly discuss the affliction. We have seen that someone in interaction with a severely blemished individual, and aware of the blemish, feels uncomfortable and unsure about how to behave. Intuitively it seems plausible that the stigmatized individual could ease the awkwardness of the interaction by openly acknowledging what both parties know, thus permitting discussion of the stain and, at once, indicating that it is not personally devastating. Most of the research has been done with physical aberrations.

In an early study of this issue, college student subjects were paired with a confederate posing as another subject (Farina, Sherman, & Allen, 1968). The confederate appeared as either mildly disabled (wearing a built-up shoe and limping) or as severely disabled (in a wheelchair and with a leg seemingly amputated below the knee). They were told that experiment was to understand communication, which entailed having one subject deliver electric shocks to the other. First, they held a discussion during which the confederate either talked about his blemish, reporting it created some problems in college, or else said nothing about it. The confederate, seemingly by chance, was always chosen to receive the shocks. In this way, both pain inflicted on the confederate and the impression he made on the subject could be measured. The only significant finding that emerged was that subjects administered shorter shocks when the confederate seemed more severely disabled. Making the affliction an allowable topic had essentially no effect. On the basis of this study, it would appear that the strategy tested has no effect.

A later set of experiments by Hastorf, Wildfogel, and Cassman (1979) paints quite a different picture, however. Their studies also focused on physical disabilities. Subjects were told the researchers wanted to learn about communicating with handicapped individuals. They would be shown a videotape of two paraplegic students being interviewed, and they would then choose one of them as a partner for a subsequent interaction. The videotapes of the paraplegics were then shown to the subjects, they were asked questions about them, and they were told to make their choice regarding with which of the two they wished to interact. The giving or withholding of permission to talk about the handicap was varied by having one of the students describe his affliction as a problem in college while the other denied having problems. (These roles were appropriately counterbalanced.) The acknowledging student was preferred to the one who did not, even when additional experiments were done to test alternatives to the explanation that acknowledgment eases social interactions. To paraphrase the authors, acknowledging the handicap appears to be effective in reducing social rejection, at least for some kinds of blemishes.

Bugglin (1986, 1987) has cleverly explored the acknowledgment strategy for non-physical blemishes, including psychological problems. In one experiment (1986), female subjects (students) agreed to have some degrading information revealed to a similar other subject. The information could be either about herself (caught shoplifting) or about the family (alcoholic father). One finding that raises questions about the benefits of the strategy was that acknowledgment negatively affected the revealing subject, making her tense and nervous. However, the effect on the other subject was positive since she was less stigmatizing when she learned the debasing information from the blemished person herself rather than from the experimenter. In the second study (Bugglin, 1987), the stain was having been a patient in a psychiatric hospital. Revealing the information had the expected negative effect on the subject who learned it (tense, awkward behavior). But the most interesting result of the study was the effect of the disclosure on the blemished subject. When she revealed the negative information herself, she was more comfortable and she liked her partner better than when it was disclosed by the experimenter. This finding indicates that acknowledgment may have a smoothing effect on the interaction by influencing both parties involved. The "normal" likes the acknowledging stigmatized person better than the one who does not, as Hastorf et al's (1979) study demonstrates. And the disclosing blemished person also benefits by her disclosure, as indicated by the Bugglin experiment.

CONCLUSIONS

The present chapter focused on the stigmatization of mentally disordered people. Stigma, the social rejection of an individual because he or she bears a degrading mark, is a pandemic problem that plays a particularly virulent role in psychopathology. The literature on the topic is such that the chapter could not reasonably be restricted to schizophrenia, the subject of this book, but ranges over mental disorders in general. An important goal guiding this effort was to present the most well-established and clear information about stigmatization and not to attempt the formulation of a general, encompassing theory since that seems premature. To do that, the chapter was organized into three main sections: (1) does the stigma of mental illness exist? (2) what causes it?, and (3) can the strength of that stigmatization be changed?

While there is disagreement regarding the existence of the phenomenon, I believe the available research convincingly shows that people who have suffered mental problems are unfavorably viewed and rejected by society. A multitude of studies, done both in the laboratory and in the field, show the existence of this pattern of social behavior. Such individuals find it difficult to obtain work and, if employed, are likely to encounter an unfriendly reception from their coworkers. Finding housing and lodging has been clearly shown to be a harder task for them than for otherwise comparable people. Former patients who would like to move to a particular neighborhood are unwanted by residents of that neighborhood. Sometimes their rejection is displayed in a particularly open and crass manner. Moreover, this stigmatization does not seem peculiar to our society and to societies similar to ours but appears to be much broader and possibly universal.

What causes stigma? An important reason for the social degradation of the mentally disordered is that members of society believe many unfavorable things about them and have believed such things for a very long time. These beliefs include that mental patients are unpredictable, that they are dangerous, and that they possess alien, strange, and offensive characteristics. Given these beliefs, it is not surprising that the mentally disordered are rejected. But why does society believe these disparaging things? A partial answer to this question is provided when we examine the characteristics of the mentally troubled population. That population consists of people who, in the aggregate, lack interpersonal skills, display alienating behaviors, and even seem to be relatively unattractive in appearance. Of course, this is not to say that those characteristics justify the rejection. The mass media also seem to play a part in engendering stigma. Events involving mental patients are sensationalized and the patients are demonized, possibly to enhance the newsworthiness of those reports. And the fear of social rejection on the part of the afflicted may create a self-fulfilling prophecy since their fear causes them to be tense and to behave in a disagreeable manner thus eliciting rejection. Finally, another factor that may play a role in this stigma is fear of contamination. To some degree, we are judged by the company we keep and by the character of our relatives, and we are aware of being thusly judged. Consequently, association with stigmatized people, such as the mentally ill, brings us disapproval and so those afflicted with mental problems may be rejected for that reason.

Many variables have been shown to modify the virulence of the degradation that psychiatrically disordered individuals encounter. The sex of both the afflicted and of the observer affects stigmatization. Women tend to behave in a kinder and more accepting manner toward the mentally ill than men. In turn, female victims of such disorders tend to be better treated and more favorably viewed by both sexes than male victims. An encouraging finding is that personal experience with the victims of mental disorders reduces the level of disfavor in which they are held and the badness of their treatment. The implication is that the unfavorable beliefs held about mental patients are both excessively negative and amenable to corrective experience. Much research has been done on the effects of stigma of viewing mental disorders as diseases as compared to regarding them as learned patterns of behavior. This is probably due to the many mental health groups who believe that stigma would disappear if mental disorders were "recognized" as diseases and that "recognition" is what these groups advocate. However, it seems that both the public and mental health professionals are less stigmatizing if they view such conditions as learned. The patients' conception of their own problem has a clear effect on them, but it can be favorable or unfavorable, depending on circumstances. A readily usable strategy that might modify social rejection is for a blemished person, whose stain is known, to acknowledge the problem to those with whom he or she is interacting. Tension might, thereby, be reduced because the stain would not be a forbidden topic that must be carefully skirted and the blemished person would be seen as able to deal with the problem. There is some evidence that acknowledgment does ease social interaction for physical blemishes. For mental problems, the research available suggests that the strategy affects both the afflicted and the observer and that it may also ease interpersonal interaction.

In conclusion, stigma is an important factor in psychopathology and is an inextricable part of its fabric. It has significance for virtually every facet of mental disorders. We saw its importance for such basic day-to-day matters impinging on the afflicted as finding work and housing. It also has an effect on the laws governing mental disorders and the facilities and support structures that society provides for the afflicted. Less obvious, but particularly interesting, stigma is responsible for some of the concrete and specific behaviors viewed as symptoms of psychopathology. Consider two individuals who are observing the same person behaving in exactly the same way, but the first observer thinks the person is a mental patient while the second thinks he is "normal." The research we have reviewed tells us the two observers

will see different behaviors being displayed. The first will perceive tension and unpredictable behaviors that he sees *only* because of his beliefs. Similarly, when a mental patient believes his mental problems are known, he will actually *behave* in a more tense way than when he believes he is viewed as normal. These types of behavior, which are commonly thought to be the essence of psychopathology, are actually the product of stigma, a social phenomenon.

REFERENCES

Altrocchi, J. (1960). Changes in favorableness of attitudes toward concepts of mental illness. *American Psychologist, 15*, 461.

Barthell, C. N., & Holmes, D. S. (1968). High school yearbooks: A nonreactive measure of social isolation in graduates who later became schizophrenics. *Journal of Abnormal Psychology, 73*, 313–316.

Bentz, W. K., & Edgerton, J. W. (1971). The consequences of labeling a person mentally ill. *Social Psychiatry, 6*, 29–33.

Birenbaum, A. (1970). On managing courtesy stigma. *Journal of Health and Social Behavior, 11*, 196–206.

Brand, R. C., & Clairborn, W. L. (1976). Two studies of comparative stigma: Employer attitudes and practices toward rehabilitated convicts, mental, and tuberculosis patients. *Community Mental Health Journal, 12*, 168–175.

Brockman, J., D'Arcy, C., & Edmonds, L. (1979). Facts or artifacts?: Changing public attitudes toward the mentally ill. *Social Science and Medicine, 13*, 673–682.

Bugglin, C. S. (1986). *Managing stigma in dyadic interactions.* Unpublished master's thesis, University of Connecticut, Storrs, CT.

Bugglin, C. S. (1987). *The impact on others of disclosing a past psychiatric hospitalization.* Unpublished doctoral dissertation, University of Connecticut, Storrs, CT.

Burk, J. P., & Sher, K. J. (1990). Labeling the child of an alcoholic: Negative stereotyping by mental health professionals and peers. *Journal of Studies on Alcohol, 51*, 156–163.

Burns, G. L., & Farina, A. (1992). The role of physical attractiveness in adjustment. *Genetic, Social, & General Psychology Monographs, 118*, 157–194.

Chesler, P. (1972). *Women and madness.* New York: Doubleday.

Chinsky, J. M., & Rappaport, J. (1970). Attitude change in college students and chronic patients: A dual perspective. *Journal of Consulting and Clinical Psychology, 35*, 388–394.

Clausen, J. A. (1980). The family, stigma, and help-seeking in severe mental disorder. In J. G. Rabkin, L. Gelb, & J. B. Lazar (Eds.), *Attitudes towards the mentally ill: Research perspectives. Report of an NIMH workshop, January 24–25, 1980* (DHHS Publication No. ADM 80–1031). Washington, DC: U.S. Government Printing Office.

Clausen, J. A. (1981). Stigma and mental disorder: Phenomena and terminology. *Psychiatry, 44*, 287–296.

Cohen, J., & Struening, E. L. (1964). Opinions about mental illness: Hospital social atmosphere profiles and their relevance to effectiveness. *Journal of Consulting Psychology, 28*, 292–298.

Colbert, J. N., & Kalish, R. A. (1973). Two psychological portals of entry for disadvantaged groups. *Rehabilitation Literature, 34*, 194–202.

Coyne, J. C. (1976). Depression and response of others. *Journal of Abnormal Psychology, 85*, 186–193.

Coyne, J. C., Kessler, R. C., & Tal, M. (1987). Living with a depressed person. *Journal of Consulting and Clinical Psychology, 55*, 347–352.

Crocetti, G. M., & Lemkau, P. V. (1965). On rejection of the mentally ill. *American Sociological Review, 30*, 577–588.

Crocetti, G. M., Spiro, H. R., & Siassi, I. (1974). *Contemporary attitudes toward mental illness.* Pittsburgh, PA: University of Pittsburgh Press.

Cutler, W. D., (1975). *The relationship of subjects' sex to attitudes and behaviors toward male mental patients.* Unpublished doctoral dissertation, University of Connecticut.

Davies, T. W., & Morris, A. (1990). A comparative quantification of stigma. *Social Work and Social Sciences Review, 1*, 109–122.

Day, D. M., & Page, S. (1986). Portrayal of mental illness in Canadian newspapers. *Canadian Journal of Psychiatry, 31*, 813–817.

Deutsch, A. (1965). *The mentally ill in America* (2nd ed.). New York: Columbia University Press.

Dowbiggin, I. R. (1988). French psychiatric attitudes towards the dangers posed by the insane circa 1870. *Research in Law, Deviance, and Social Control, 9*, 87–111.

Drehmer, D. E. (1985). Hiring decisions for disabled workers: The hidden bias. *Rehabilitation Psychology, 30*, 157–164.

Eme, R. F. (1979). Sex differences in childhood psychopathology: A review. *Psychological Bulletin, 86*, 374–395.

Farina, A. (1981). Are women nicer people than men?: Sex and stigma of mental disorders. *Clinical Psychology Review, 1*, 223–243.

Farina, A. (1982). The stigma of mental disorders. In A. G. Miller (Ed.), *In the eye of the beholder* (pp. 305–363). New York: Praeger.

Farina, A., Allen, J. G., & Saul, B. B. B. (1968). The role of the stigmatized person in affecting social relationships. *Journal of Personality, 36*, 169–182.

Farina, A., Arenberg, D., & Guskin, S. (1957). A scale for measuring minimal social behavior. *Journal of Consulting Psychology, 21*, 265–268.

Farina, A., & Burns, G. L. (1984). The effect of uncertainty as to whether others believe that we have had a mental disorder. *Journal of Social and Clinical Psychology, 2*, 244–257.

Farina, A., Burns, G. L., Austad, C., Bugglin, C., & Fischer, E. H. (1986). The role of physical attractiveness in the readjustment of discharged psychiatric patients. *Journal of Abnormal Psychology, 95*, 139–143.

Farina, A., & Felner, R. D. (1973). Employment interviewer reactions to former mental patients. *Journal of Abnormal Psychology, 82*, 268–272.

Farina, A., Felner, R. D., & Bourdreau, L. A. (1973). Reactions of workers to male and female mental patient job applicants. *Journal of Consulting and Clinical Psychology, 41*, 363–372.

Farina, A., & Fisher, J. D. (1982). Beliefs about mental disorders: Findings and implications. In G. Weary & H. Mirels (Eds.), *Integrations of clinical and social psychology* (pp. 48–71). New York: Oxford University Press.

Farina, A., Fisher, J. D., & Fischer, E. H. (1992). Societal factors in the problems faced by deinstitutionalized psychiatric patients. In P. J. Fink, & A. Tasman (Eds.), *Stigma and mental illness* (pp. 167–184). Washington: American Psychiatric Press.

Farina, A., Fisher, J. D., Getter, H., & Fischer, E. H. (1978). Some consequences of changing people's views regarding the nature of mental illness. *Journal of Abnormal Psychology, 87*, 272–279.

Farina, A., Garmezy, N., & Barry III, H. (1963). The relationship of marital status to incidence and prognosis of schizophrenia. *Journal of Abnormal and Social Psychology, 67*, 624–630.

Farina, A., Garmezy, N., Zalusky, N., & Becker, J. (1962). Premorbid behavior and prognosis in female schizophrenic patients. *Journal of Consulting Psychology, 26*, 56–60.

Farina, A., Gliha, D., Boudreau, L. A., Allen, J. G., & Sherman, M. (1971). Mental illness and the impact of believing others know about it. *Journal of Abnormal Psychology, 77*, 1–5.

Farina, A., & Hagelauer, H. D. (1975). Sex and mental illness: The generosity of females. *Journal of Consulting and Clinical Psychology, 43*, 122.

Farina, A., Hagelauer, H. D., & Holzberg, J. D. (1976). The influence of psychiatric history on physicians' response to a new patient. *Journal of Consulting and Clinical Psychology, 44*, 449.

Farina, A., Holland, C. H., & Ring, K. (1966). The role of stigma and set in interpersonal interaction. *Journal of Abnormal Psychology, 71*, 421–428.

Farina, A., Holzberg, J. D., & Kimura, D. S. (1966). A study of interpersonal relationships of female schizophrenic patients. *Journal of Nervous and Mental Disease, 142*, 441–444.

Farina, A., Murray, P. J., & Groh, T. (1978). Sex and worker acceptance of a former mental patient. *Journal of Consulting and Clinical Psychology, 46*, 887–891.

Farina, A., & Ring, K. (1965). The influence of perceived mental illness on interpersonal relations. *Journal of Abnormal Psychology, 70*, 47–51.

Farina, A., Sherman, M., & Allen, J. G. (1968). The role of physical abnormalities in interpersonal perception and behavior. *Journal of Abnormal Psychology, 73*, 590–593.

Farina, A., Thaw, J., & Boudreau, L. A. (1970). *People's reaction to being viewed as blemished and degraded.* Unpublished manuscript, University of Connecticut, Storrs, CT.

Farina, A., Thaw, J., Felner, R. D., & Hust, B. E. (1976). Some interpersonal consequences of being mentally ill or mentally retarded. *Journal of Mental Deficiency, 80*, 414–422.

Farina, A., Thaw, J., Lovern, J. D., & Mangone, D. (1974). People's reactions to a former mental patient moving to their neighborhood. *Journal of Community Psychology, 2*, 108–112.

Farina, A., & Webb, W. W. (1956). Premorbid adjustment and subsequent discharge. *Journal of Nervous and Mental Disease, 124*, 612–614.

Fink, P. J., & Tasman, A. (Eds.). (1992). *Stigma and mental illness.* Washington, DC: American Psychiatric Press.

Fischer, E. H., Farina, A., Council, J. R., Pitts, H., Eastman, A., & Millard, R. (1982). The influence of adjustment and physical attractiveness on the employability of schizophrenic women. *Journal of Consulting and Clinical Psychology, 50*, 530–534.

Fisher, J. D., & Farina, A. (1979). Consequences of beliefs about the nature of mental disorders. *Journal of Abnormal Psychology, 88*, 320–327.

Gelfand, S., & Ullmann, L. P. (1961a). Attitude changes associated with psychiatric affiliation. *Nursing Research, 10*, 200–204.

Gelfand, S., & Ullmann, L. P. (1961b). Changes in attitudes about mental illness associated with psychiatric clerkship. *International Journal of Social Psychiatry, 8*, 292–298.

Gerber, G. (1980). Stigma: Social functions of the portrayal of mental illness in the mass media. In J. G. Rabkin, L. Gelb, & J. B. Lazar (Eds.), *Attitudes towards the mentally ill: Research perspectives. Report of an NIMH Workshop, January 24–25, 1980* (DHHS Publication No. ADM 80–1031). Washington, DC: U.S. Government Printing Office.

Gilmore, J. L., & Farina, A. (1989). The social reception of mainstreamed children in the regular classroom. *Journal of Mental Deficiency Research, 33*, 301–311.

Goffman, E. (1963). *Stigma: Notes on the management of spoiled identity.* Englewood Cliffs, NJ: Prentice-Hall.

Golding, S. L., Becker, E., Sherman, S., & Rappaport, J. (1975). The behavioral expectations scale: Assessment of expectations for interaction with the mentally ill. *Journal of Consulting and Clinical Psychology, 43*, 109.

Grunt, M. (1973). Aspects of informal labeling and sanctions for mentally deviant behavior. *Kolner Zeitschrift fur Sociologie und Socialpsychologie, 25*, 363–385.

Gurtman, M. B. (1986). Depression and the response of others: reevaluating the reevaluation. *Journal of Abnormal Psychology, 95*, 99–101.

Gussow, Z., & Tracy, G. S. (1968). Status, ideology, and adaptation to stigmatized illness: A study of leprosy. *Human Organization, 27*, 316–325.

Greengrass, M. J. (1974). *Interpersonal behavior of people selected as socially skilled and unskilled.* Unpublished master's thesis, University of Connecticut, Storrs, CT.

Harris, M. J., Milich, R., Corbitt, E. M., Hoover, D. W., & Brady, M. (1992). Self-fulfilling effects of stigmatizing information on children's social interactions. *Journal of Personality and Social Psychology, 63*, 41–50.

Harrow, M., Fox, D. A., & Detre, T. (1969). Self-concept of the married psychiatric patient and his mate's perception of him. *Journal of Consulting and Clinical Psychology, 33*, 235–239.

Hastorf, A. H., Wildfogel, J., & Cassman, T. (1979). Acknowledgment of handicap as a tactic in social interaction. *Journal of Personality and Social Psychology, 37*, 1790–1797.

Herman, C. P., Zanna, M. P., & Higgins, E. T. (Eds.). (1986). *Physical appearance, stigma, and social behavior: The Ontario Symposium, Volume 3.* Hillsdale, NJ: Lawrence Erlbaum.

Holzberg, J. D., & Knapp, R. H. (1965). The social interaction of college students and chronically ill mental patients. *American Journal of Orthopsychiatry, 35*, 487–492.

Hooley, J. M., Richters, J. E., & Weintraub, S. (1987). Psychopathology and marital distress: The positive side of positive symptoms. *Journal of Abnormal Psychology, 96*, 27–33.

Hyler, S. E., Gabbard, G. O., & Schneider, I. (1989). *Homicidal maniacs and narcissistic parasites: Stigmatization of mentally ill persons in the movies.* Paper presented at the annual meeting of the American Psychiatric Association, San Francisco, CA.

Jain, S. & Greengrass, M. J. (1975). *Development and validation of an empirically derived scale of social competence.* Unpublished manuscript, University of Connecticut.

Jenkins, J. H. (1988). Ethnopsychiatric interpretations of schizophrenic illness: The problem of nervios within Mexican-American families. *Culture, Medicine, and Psychiatry, 12*, 301–329.

Jones, E. E., Farina, A., Hostorf, A. H., Marcus, H., Miller, D. T., & Scott, R. A. (1984). *Social stigma: The psychology of marked relationships.* New York: W. H. Freeman.

Katz, I. (1981). *Stigma: A social psychological analysis.* Hillside, NJ: Erlbaum.

Kelly, F. S., Farina, A., & Mosher, D. L. (1971). The ability of schizophrenic women to create a favorable or unfavorable impression on an interviewer. *Journal of Consulting and Clinical Psychology, 36*, 404–409.

Kelso, F. W. (1978). *The role of physical attractiveness and other variables in determining how much a person is initially and subsequently liked.* Unpublished master's thesis, University of Connecticut, Storrs, CT.

Koizumi, K., & Harris, P. (1992). Mental healthcare in Japan. *Hospital and Community Psychiatry, 43*, 1100–1103.

Lamy, R. E. (1966). Social consequences of mental illness. *Journal of Consulting and Clinical Psychology, 30*, 450–454.

Langer, E. J., & Abelson, R. P. (1974). A patient by any other name . . . : Clinician group difference in labeling bias. *Journal of Consulting and Clinical Psychology, 42*, 4–9.

Lawner, P. (1966). *Unfavorable attitudes and behavior toward those bearing mental illness stigmas.* Unpublished master's thesis, University of Connecticut, Storrs, CT.

Lefley, H. P. (1992). The stigmatized family. In P. J. Fink, & A. Tasman (Eds.), *Stigma and mental illness* (pp. 127–138). Washington, DC: American Psychiatric Press.

Link, B. G. (1987). Understanding labeling effects in the area of mental disorders: An assessment of the effects of expectations of rejection. *American Sociological Review, 52*, 96–112.

Link, B. G., & Cullen, F. T. (1986). Contact with the mentally ill and perceptions of how dangerous they are. *Journal of Health and Social Behavior, 27*, 289–303.

Link, B. G., Cullen, F. T., Frank, J., & Wozniak, J. F. (1987). The social rejection of former mental patients: Understanding why labels matter. *American Journal of Sociology, 92*, 1461–1500.

Link, B. G., Cullen, F. T., Mirotznik, J., & Struening, E. (1992). Consequences of stigma for persons with mental illness: Evidence from social sciences. In P. J. Fink, & A. Tasman (Eds.), *Stigma and mental illness* (pp. 87–96). Washington, DC: American Psychiatric Press.

Linsky, A. R. (1970). Who shall be excluded: The influence of personal attitudes in community reaction to the mentally ill. *Social Psychiatry, 5*, 166–171.

Loman, L. A., & Larkin, W. E. (1976). Rejection of the mentally ill: An experiment in labeling. *Sociological Quarterly, 17*, 555–560.

Luppino, A. V. (1966). *The nature of chronic schizophrenia: Implications derived from the effects of social reinforcement on performance*. Unpublished doctoral dissertation, University of Connecticut, Storrs, CT.

Mansouri, L., & Dowell, D. A. (1989). Perceptions of stigma among the long-term mentally ill. *Psychological Rehabilitation Journal, 13*, 79–91.

Mechanic, D., McAlpine, D., Rosenfield, S., & Davis, D. (1994). Effects of illness attribution and depression on the quality of life among persons with serious mental illness. *Social Science and Medicine, 39*, 155–164.

Mehta, S., & Farina, A. (1988). Associative stigma: Perceptions of the difficulties of college-aged children of stigmatized fathers. *Journal of Social and Clinical Psychology, 7*, 192–202.

Morrison, J. K. (1976). Demythologizing mental patients' attitudes toward mental illness: An empirical study. *Journal of Community Psychology, 4*, 181–185.

Morrison, J. K., Bushell, J. D., Hanson, G. D., Fentiman, J. R., & Holdridge-Crane, S. (1977). Relationship between psychiatric patients' attitudes toward mental illness and attitudes of dependence. *Psychological Reports, 41*, 1194.

Munakata, T. (1989). The socio-cultural significance of the diagnostic label "neurosthenia" in Japan's mental health care system. *Culture, Medicine, and Psychiatry, 13*, 203–213.

Neuberg, S. L., Smith, D. M., Hoffman, J. C., & Russell, F. J. (1994). When we observe stigmatized and "normal" individuals interacting: Stigma-by-association. *Personality and Social Psychology Bulletin, 20*, 196–209.

Nunnally, J. C. (1961). *Popular conceptions of mental health*. New York: Holt, Rhinehart, & Winston.

Omsted, D. W., & Durham, K. (1976). Stability of attitudes: A semantic differential study. *Journal of Health and Social Behavior, 17*, 35–44.

Olshansky, S., Grob, S., & Ekdahl, M. (1960). Survey of employment experience of patients discharged from three mental hospitals during the period 1951–1953. *Mental Hygiene, 44*, 510–521.

Olshansky, S., Grob, S., & Malamud, I. T. (1958). Employer's attitudes and practices in hiring of ex-mental patients. *Mental Hygiene, 42*, 391–401.

Ommundsen, R., & Ekeland, T. J. (1978). Psychiatric labeling and social perception. *Scandinavian Journal of Psychology, 19*, 193–199.

Page, S. (1977). Effects of the mental illness label in attempts to obtain accommodation. *Canadian Journal of Behavioral Science, 9*, 84–90.

Page, S. (1995). Effects of the mental illness label in 1993: Acceptance and rejection in the community. *Journal of Health and Social Policy, 7*, 61–68.

Pearson, V., & Phillips, M. (1994). Psychiatric social work and socialism: problems and potential in China. *Social Work, 39*, 280–287.

Phillips, D. L. (1967). Education, psychiatric sophistication, and rejection of mentally ill help-seekers. *Sociological Quarterly, 8*, 122–132.

Phillips, L. (1953). Case history data and prognosis in schizophrenia. *Journal of Nervous and Mental Disease, 117*, 515–525.

Piner, K. E., & Kahle, L. R. (1984). Adapting to the stigmatizing label of mental illness: Forgone but not forgotten. *Journal of Personality and Social Psychology, 47*, 805–811.

Pollack, S., Huntley, D., Allen, J. G., & Schwartz, S. (1976). The dimensions of stigma: The social situation of the mentally ill person and the male homosexual. *Journal of Abnormal Psychology, 85*, 105–112.

Posner, J. (1976). Death as a courtesy stigma. *Essence, 1*, 26–33.

Rabkin, J. (1972). Opinions about mental illness: A review of the literature. *Psychological Bulletin, 77*, 153–171.

Rabkin, J. G. (1980). Determinants of public attitudes about mental illness: Summary of the research literature. In J. G. Rabkin, L. Gelb, & J. B. Lazar (Eds.), *Attitudes towards the mentally ill: Research perspectives. Report of an NIMH Workshop, January 24–25, 1980.* (DHHS Publication No. ADM 80–1031). Washington, DC: U.S. Government Printing Office.

Rayne, J. T. (1969). *The effect of perceived attitudes on expectancy for punishment by psychiatric patients*. Unpublished doctoral dissertation, University of Connecticut, Storrs, CT.

Rodrigues, C. R. (1992). Comparacion de actitudes de estudiantes de medicina brasilenos y espanoles hacia la enfermedad mental. *Actas Luso Espanolas de Neurologia Psiquiatrica y Ciencias, 20*, 30–41.

Rosenthal, B. S. (1973). *Schizophrenics' reaction to social roles as a function of social skills*. Unpublished master's thesis, University of Connecticut, Storrs, CT.

Rothaus, P. & Hanson, P. G., Cleveland, S. E., & Johnson, D. L. (1963). Describing psychiatric hospitalization: A dilemma. *American Psychologist, 18,* 85–89.

Sack, W. H., Seidler, J., & Thomas, S. (1976). The children of imprisoned parents: A psychological exploration. *American Journal of Orthopsychiatry, 46,* 616–628.

Sarason, I. G., & Sarason, B. R. (1987). *Abnormal psychology.* Englewood Cliffs, NJ: Prentice-Hall.

Schwartz, C. C., Myers, J. K., & Astrachan, B. M. (1974). Psychiatric labeling and the rehabilitation of the mental patient. *Archives of General Psychiatry, 31,* 329–334.

Segal, S. P. (1978). Attitudes toward the mentally ill: A review. *Social Work, 23,* 211–217.

Serrano, P. F. (1985). Actitudes hacia la enfermedad mental de los familiares del esquizofrenico. (Attitudes toward mental illness in families of schizophrenic patients.) *Actas Luso Espanolas de Neurologia, Psiquiatria y Ciencias Ofines, 13,* 387–396.

Signorielli, N. (1989). The stigma of mental illness on television. *Journal of Broadcasting and Electronic Media, 33,* 321–325.

Smith, J. J. (1969). Psychiatric hospital experience and attitudes toward mental illness. *Journal of Consulting and Clinical Psychology, 33,* 302–306.

Stafford, R. A., & Petway, J. M. (1977). Stigmatization of men and women problem drinkers and their spouses. *Journal of Studies on Alcohol, 38,* 2109–2121.

Thaw, J. (1971). *The reactions of schizophrenic patients to being patronized and to believing they are unfavorably viewed.* Unpublished doctoral dissertation. University of Connecticut, Storrs, CT.

Tringo, J. L. (1970). The hierarchy of preference toward disability groups. *Journal of Special Education, 4,* 295–306.

Tudor, W., Tudor, J. F., & Gove, W. R. (1977). The effect of sex role differences on the social control of mental illness. *Journal of Health and Social Behavior, 18,* 98–112.

Turner, J. B. (1964). Schizophrenics as judges of vocal expressions of emotional meaning. In J. R. Davitz (Ed.), *The communication of emotional meaning* (pp. 129–142). New York: McGraw-Hill.

Vandenberg, S. G. (1962). La mesure de la deterioration de la comprehension sociale dans la schizophrenie. *Revue de Psychologie Appliquee, 12,* 189–199.

Voysey, M. (1972). Impression management by parents with disabled children. *Journal of Health and Social Behavior, 13,* 80–89.

Wahl, O. F., & Harman, C. R. (1989). Family views of stigma. *Schizophrenia Bulletin, 15,* 131–139.

Wahl, O. F., & Lefkowitz, J. Y. (1989). Impact of a television film on attitudes toward mental illness. *American Journal of Community Psychology, 17,* 521–528.

Wahl, O. F., & Roth, R. (1982). Television images of mental illness: Results of the metropolitan Washington Media Watch. *Job, 26,* 599–605.

Walker, E., Marwit, S. J., & Emory, E. (1980). A cross-sectional study of emotion recognition in schizophrenics. *Journal of Abnormal Psychology, 89,* 428–436.

Weyand, C. A. (1983). *The associative stigma: Social degradation of a son because of his stigmatized father.* Unpublished doctoral dissertation, University of Connecticut, Storrs, CT.

Wright, F. H., & Klein, R. A. (1965). *Attitudes of various hospital personnel categories and the community regarding mental illness.* Unpublished manuscript, Biloxi, MS: VA Center.

Zigler, E., & Phillips, L. (1961). Psychiatric diagnosis and symptomatology. *Journal of Abnormal and Social Psychology, 63,* 69–75.

Zilboorg, S., & Henry, G. W. (1941). *A history of medical psychology.* New York: Norton.

Zultowsky, D., & Farina, A. (1989). *Community acceptance of mentally retarded and emotionally disturbed children.* Unpublished manuscript, University of Connecticut, Storrs, CT.

CHAPTER 17

SUBSTANCE USE DISORDERS AND SOCIAL FUNCTIONING IN SCHIZOPHRENIA

Robert E. Drake
Mary F. Brunette
Kim T. Mueser

The negative impact of substance abuse on social functioning is a defining feature of substance use disorders. Aspects of both social competence and social networks are central to understanding addictive behavior. Indeed, the current biopsychosocial model of addiction specifies that environmental influences and social coping behaviors, as well as other factors, are involved in developing and maintaining substance-abusing behaviors (Donovan, 1988; Moos, Finney, & Cronkite, 1990). Within the general addictions field, social factors are critical to understanding treatment and recovery (Higgins et al., 1991; Moos et al., 1990; Vaillant & Milofsky, 1982). Extra treatment factors, such as social skills, social supports, and family environment, are related to recovery from substance abuse, with some causal influence probably occurring in both directions (Billings & Moos, 1983). Little of this research has, however, been replicated with persons with schizophrenia or the broader population of severe mental illness.

The purpose of this chapter is to review the literature on relationships between social factors and substance use disorders in schizophrenia. We will consider research on two aspects of social functioning: (a) social competence, which refers to an individual's ability to satisfy affiliative needs (e.g., friendship) and to use relationships with others to solve problems and achieve goals, and (b) social networks, which refers to an individual's social support system. After considering the available research, we will address implications for treatment and suggest future avenues for research.

LITERATURE REVIEW

Relationships between social factors and substance use in schizophrenia can be viewed in several ways. In what follows, we will review studies that address (1) premorbid social adjustment, (2) subjective experiences regarding the subjective effects of substance use on social life, (3) self-reported reasons for use that involve social functioning, (4) assessments of social competence, (5) assessments of social networks, (6) treatment interventions, and (7) longitudinal changes in social adjustment and substance use.

Premorbid Adjustment

Several studies have examined premorbid social functioning among schizophrenic patients who abuse alcohol and other drugs. Historical data indicate that persons with schizophrenia and co-occurring substance use disorder are different premorbidly from those who have schizophrenia alone. Specifically, dually disordered individuals tend to have better social competence and more social contacts than those with schizophrenia without comorbid substance disorder.

Four studies have found that those with dual disorders had better premorbid social functioning than those with schizophrenia alone; one study found that those with dual disorders were more antisocial; and one study found no differences. Arndt, Tyrrell, Flaum, and Andreasen (1992) examined 131 schizophrenic patients and found that those with substance abuse comorbidity were better on five of seven measures of premorbid functioning, including social withdrawal and peer relationships. Alcohol use was most consistently related to better premorbid social functioning. Marijuana use was also related to premorbid adjustment, but use of other drugs was not.

Breakey, Goodell, Lorenz, and McHugh (1974) examined 103 schizophrenic patients and found that those who used drugs had better premorbid functioning than those who did not in areas such as sexual interest and number of friends. Dixon, Haas, Weiden, Sweeney, and Frances (1991) interviewed 83 inpatients with schizophrenia-spectrum disorders and found that the drug-abusing patients reported better sexual adjustment during adolescence. Tsuang, Simpson, and Kronfol (1982) compared 72 drug abusers with psychoses and 43 schizophrenic patients without drug abuse. The schizophrenic patients were more likely to have schizoid or paranoid premorbid histories, suggesting worse premorbid social adjustment.

In contrast to the studies of Arndt et al. (1992), Breakey et al., (1974), Dixon et al. (1991), and Tsuang et al. (1982), Sevy, Kay, Opler, and Van Praag (1990) found no differences in premorbid adjustment related to cocaine abuse in 51 inpatients with schizophrenia. Andreasson, Allebeck, and Rydberg (1989) examined 21 patients with schizophrenia and found that those with co-occurring cannabis abuse had more antisocial backgrounds, including problems with police and in school. This last finding is interesting in the light of several studies that have shown that patients with schizophrenia and antisocial personality disorder (which requires childhood conduct disorder), who engage in a pattern of antisocial behaviors

(e.g., felonies, truancies, runaways, out-of-wedlock pregnancies), are more likely to have substance use disorders than patients without antisocial personality disorder (Caton, Shrout, Eagle et al., 1994; Caton, Shrout, Dominguez et al., 1995; Mueser et al., in press; Westermeyer & Walzer, 1975).

Interpreting these findings is somewhat complicated by their retrospective nature and by the diagnostic heterogeneity in the Tsuang et al. study. When schizophrenic patients are mixed with other psychiatric patients, diagnosis and premorbid adjustment are inevitably confounded because schizophrenic patients generally have worse premorbid adjustment. Furthermore, greater premorbid antisocial behavior among those with dual disorders in the Andreasson et al. (1989) study could be due to the effects of early substance abuse, which often begins several years prior to the onset of overt schizophrenic illness (Mueser, Nishith, Tracy, DeGirolamo, & Molinaro, 1995; Test, Wallish, Allness, & Ripp, 1989). Despite these problems, the weight of the evidence indicates that patients with schizophrenia who are more socially competent and socially active premorbidly are at increased risk of developing substance use disorders. Considering the social context of much substance use behavior, the higher rate of substance use disorders for patients with good premorbid functioning may be due to their increased exposure to substances through social relationships.

Subjective Experiences

A number of studies attempt to identify why people with schizophrenia use alcohol and other drugs, either indirectly by asking about their subjective response to substances or directly by asking patients to identify reasons for their use. We will review studies of subjective effects first. Most of the studies in this area focus on internal experiences rather than interactive or social experiences. One consistent finding regarding symptoms is that many people with schizophrenia identify relief of anxiety and depression, rather than amelioration of psychotic symptoms, as a positive effect of substances. (They also typically report some negative effects, such as exacerbation of psychosis.) Relief of anxiety may refer to social anxiety, but is not always identified as such.

In at least six studies, schizophrenic patients reported that alcohol or drugs such as cannabis relieve anxiety (Bergman & Harris, 1985; Baigent, Holme, & Hafner, 1995; Dixon et al., 1991; Noordsy et al., 1991; Test et al., 1989; Warner et al., 1994). Two of these studies identified social anxiety. Bergman and Harris (1985) interviewed 23 patients with severe mental illness and found that they commonly reported that alcohol relieved social anxiety. Noordsy et al. (1991) interviewed 75 schizophrenic patients regarding subjective responses to alcohol using an extensive symptom list. Relief of social anxiety was the most commonly reported effect (by 70%), but patients also reported improvements in interpersonal rapport (42%), shyness (39%), social withdrawal (38%), and sexual anxiety (24%).

Similar to the effects of substances on anxiety, several studies indicated that schizophrenic patients report beneficial effects of alcohol, cannabis, and cocaine on depression or dysphoria. Pristach and Smith (1996) found that among 41 schizophrenic patients recently admitted to the hospital, 34% stated that their primary reason for using alcohol before admission was to relieve depression. Among schizophrenic outpatients, Noordsy et al. (1991) found that 62% of schizophrenic patients with alcohol abuse reported positive effects of alcohol use on dysphoric mood. Extending these findings, other researchers have found that in addition to alcohol, cannabis and cocaine use are associated with improvements in depression (Baigent et al., 1995; Dixon et al., 1991; Warner et al., 1994).

These studies show a clear finding that schizophrenic patients perceive that alcohol use decreases anxiety and, to a lesser extent, facilitates social interactions. The results are consistent with the well-known anxiolytic and disinhibiting effects of alcohol and with findings in the general population (Brown, Christiansen, & Goldman, 1987; Cooper, Russell, Skinner, Frone, & Mudar, 1992). The studies suggest that alcohol, cannabis, and cocaine are all perceived by patients to have positive effects on a variety of mood problems, including anxiety, tension, dysphoria, apathy, anhedonia, and social isolation associated with schizophrenia. The findings are consistent with the tendency of patients to report using substances in order to cope with unpleasant feelings (Mueser, Nishith et al., 1995).

Reasons for Use

In several studies, schizophrenic patients have been asked directly why they use alcohol and other drugs. Responses may represent reasons for initial use or post hoc rationalizations for use rather than reasons for persistence. Nevertheless, patients' self-reports are remarkable for their consistent focus on social factors.

In 10 studies patients reported that they used alcohol and other drugs to enhance social life. Bergman and Harris (1985) interviewed 23 patients with severe mental illness and found that two-thirds of the cannabis users attributed their use to peer group and social pressure. Dixon et al. (1991) interviewed 83 schizophrenic inpatients, and 55% reported using substances to get along socially. Hekimian and Gershon (1968), based on interviews with 112 inpatients who had used drugs prior to admission, found that friends and environment were the most important reasons for marijuana use. Knudsen and Vilmar (1984) found that 3 of 10 cannabis-using schizophrenic patients reported that they used to promote social contacts and lifestyle. Mueser, Nishith et al. (1995) used standardized measures of motives and expectancies with 70 schizophrenic patients and found that abusers were more likely than nonabusers to report using alcohol and drugs for enhancing socialization.

Test et al. (1989) interviewed 27 schizophrenic patients who abused alcohol or other drugs. The three most commonly reported reasons for use were to relieve boredom (63%), to do something with friends (44%), and to relieve anxiety (44%). Pristach and Smith (1996) found that 56% of schizophrenic patients recently admitted to the hospital stated their primary reason for using alcohol before the current admission was "to be more sociable." Treffert (1978) reported that two of four schizophrenic patients used cannabis to improve social relationships. Warner et al. (1994) found that, among 79 outpatients with severe mental illness (two-thirds with schizophrenia), activity with friends was the most commonly reported reason for substance use (73%). Finally, Baigent et al. (1995) reported that "group attachment" was an important motivating factor for substance use among 53 inpatients with schizophrenia and substance use disorders.

One clear implication of these findings is that schizophrenic patients use alcohol and drugs in social situations and with peer groups of other substance abusers. The causal attribution may not be as important as the consistent finding regarding the perceived relationship between having a group of friends and using substances. Indeed, in the Pristach and Smith (1996) study, 66% of schizophrenic patients indicated that their primary reason for using alcohol before their first psychiatric admission was to be more sociable. Combining the findings regarding premorbid adjustment with studies of subjective effects and reasons for use, it appears that patients with greater premorbid social competence are exposed to alcohol and drugs, perhaps because of their social activity. They then use substances, at least initially, to feel less social anxiety and to pursue social contacts.

Social Competence

The studies cited thus far indicate that dually disordered patients tend to be more socially competent and more involved with substance-abusing peer networks than patients with schizophrenia alone. Several studies have examined these issues more directly by assessing current social competence and current social networks. We first consider studies of social competence.

Many years ago, Cohen and Klein (1970) observed that chronically impaired psychiatric patients appeared to lack the social skills to sustain heavy drug use. The few available studies on this topic offer mixed support. Mueser et al. (1990) found that, among 149 schizophrenic patients, those with a history of cannabis abuse were less likely to be asocial than nonabusers. This study, however, found few differences in social functioning between schizophrenic patients with present or past substance abuse and those with no history of substance abuse. Sevy et al. (1990) compared 16 cocaine-abusing schizophrenic patients and 35 nonabusing schizophrenic patients in the hospital. The cocaine-abusing patients were rated by nurses as less social, perhaps because they were more depressed immediately after discontinuing cocaine. Among 187 outpatients with severe mental disorders, Drake and Wallach (1989) found no associations between substance abuse and relationships with nonprofessionals or with mental health staff, as rated by case managers. Carey and Carey (1990) examined problem-solving skills among 25 dually diagnosed patients, 19 patients with severe mental illness only, and 21 non-mentally-ill controls. The dually diagnosed patients were similar to the other psychiatric patients, and both groups had worse skills than controls.

In an ethnographic study of psychiatric patients, Schwab and Alverson (1992) found that dually diagnosed patients were more socially active than their nonabusing peers. Their relationships with other substance abusers were complex, involving bargaining, reciprocities, and negotiations around resources such as money and transportation, and sleeping quarters. When they became extremely disabled by their substance abuse, however, they tended to become less socially competent and more isolated.

In general, the literature supports the view that dually diagnosed patients, at least before they become disabled by severe drug dependence, are socially competent, particularly in comparison with schizophrenic patients who

are often isolated, paranoid, or asocial. There appears to be a reciprocal relationship between social functioning and substance abuse in schizophrenia. More socially active patients with schizophrenia use substances, and substance use in turn promotes greater social activity by virtue of the social context in which substances are used.

The relationship between substance abuse and antisocial behavior in schizophrenia has not been well studied, although it is probably complex and involves the interactions between predisposing factors and the effects of substance use. As with other substance abusers (Vaillant, 1983), schizophrenic patients who abuse substances may become more antisocial in the context of participating in illegal activities and substance-abusing cultures (Westermeyer & Walzer, 1975). However, substance abuse is not the only cause of antisocial behavior in patients with schizophrenia. There is ample evidence that conduct disorder, or similar behavior problems in childhood such as aggression and delinquency, has been linked to the later development of schizophrenia (Nuechterlein, 1986; Offord & Cross, 1969; Parnas, Schulsinger, Schulsinger, Mednick, & Teasdale, 1982; Robins, 1966). Conduct disorder, and the antisocial personality disorder that often follows, may increase the propensity of patients who later develop schizophrenia to abuse substances just as these disorders are related to substance abuse in persons who do not have schizophrenia (Dolan & Coid, 1993; Kazdin, 1995). Thus, conduct disorder and antisocial personality disorder may lead to substance abuse in some patients with schizophrenia, whereas in some other patients antisocial behavior may be the consequence of substance abuse.

Social Networks

In most diagnostic schemes, impairment in social functioning stands as a central criterion for making a diagnosis of substance use disorder (American Psychiatric Association [APA], 1987). In studies of schizophrenic patients using the Michigan Alcoholism Screening Test (Selzer, 1971), which primarily assesses consequences of drinking, complaints by family are commonly identified (McHugo, Paskus, & Drake, 1992). Studies of networks and family relationships also identify clear problems. Westermeyer and Walzer (1975) found that among 100 young psychiatric inpatients, those with dual disorders had diminished social resources. Patients with heavy drug abuse were more likely to be divorced or separated. In an ethnographic study of 25 dually diagnosed adults,

Schwab, Clark, and Drake (1991) found that over half had lost custody of children. Blankertz and Cnaan (1994) also found that 54% of 176 homeless, dually diagnosed adults had lost custody of their children. Test et al. (1989) found that 15% of patients with schizophrenia and substance use disorders reported loss of significant relationships due to substance use.

Dixon, McNary, and Lehman (1995) compared 101 psychiatric inpatients with severe mental illness and concurrent substance use disorder with 78 patients with severe mental illness only. Patients with concurrent substance abuse reported significantly lower family satisfaction and a desire for family treatment, although there were no differences in objective indicators of family contact. Kashner et al. (1991) reported on the families of 121 schizophrenic patients discharged from a VA facility, based on reviews of records by a social worker. Substance-abusing patients were more likely to have family relationships characterized by severe problems such as hopelessness and conflict. Teague, Drake, McHugo, and Vowinkle, (1994), in a statewide survey of patients with severe mental illness, found that comorbid substance abuse was associated with living apart from family. Clark and Drake (1994), based on interviews with 169 families of dually diagnosed patients in New Hampshire, found that almost 90% of these families provided some direct care during the previous month. Three-fourths of the patients did not live with their families, but those with more severe substance dependence had returned to live with their families.

The evidence suggests that early in the course of dual diagnosis, familial relationships become severely strained and may be severed altogether. As these family relationships deteriorate, they appear to become supplanted by an alternative social network of substance-abusing peers. These new social networks may grow and sustain ongoing substance use behavior.

In an ethnographic study of dually diagnosed patients, Schwab and Alverson (1992) found that more than half of the day treatment patients participated in a rather large substance-abusing culture of more than 50 patients. Furthermore, the network also facilitated contacts with non-mentally-ill substance abusers outside of the mental health system. The extensive and interlocking network provided them with social contacts, supports of certain kinds, and substances of abuse. It was also clear that the network maintained substance abuse, since communications, activities, and support revolved around using alcohol and drugs. Part of the norms of the culture involved relative alienation from non-drug users, including families and professionals. Because of the multiple interlocking relationships, it was difficult for patients to give up substances without also giving up the network, their primary source of social support and friendship. However, when dually diagnosed patients became overwhelmed by substance abuse and began to sell their possessions and sex in an increasingly desperate effort to support their addictions, they were perceived to be undesirable and unacceptable by their substance-abusing peers because they were no longer able to participate in the reciprocities of the network.

Through leading focus groups and therapy groups with homeless, dually diagnosed women, Harris (1996) also observed this thorough loss of control and slide into self-destructiveness. Blankertz and Cnaan (1994) found that 176 homeless, dually diagnosed patients reported high levels of conflict with their families and small networks of friends. Only 49% reported having any close friends, and 37% of these had only one friend. Based on interviews and participant observation, Toth (1993) documented the self-destructiveness and isolation of the dually diagnosed people who lived underground in the abandoned tunnels of New York City. They were often unable or unwilling to control their substance abuse and mental illness sufficiently to live in regular housing, homeless shelters, or even underground social groups.

In sum, research supports the view that early in the course of substance abuse dually diagnosed patients experience a deterioration or loss of familial relationships, but they are nevertheless socially active within a relatively large substance-abusing network of peers. Consistent with their involvement with substance-abusing peers, dually diagnosed patients often report that their substance use is socially motivated and socially reinforced. When substance abuse progresses to severe addiction, however, it can destroy the social competence and social networks that initially facilitated substance use. These same patients often become self-absorbed and self-destructive. At this point, dually diagnosed patients often lose their peer networks and sometimes return to live with families.

Interventions Addressing Social Functioning

Treatments for schizophrenia often address social functioning, as do treatments for substance disorder. In both areas a variety of treatments have been developed that focus on either social competence (e.g., social skills training) or social network issues (e.g., family psychoeducation or treatment in peer groups). Nevertheless, few studies have addressed these interventions with dually diagnosed patients.

Carey, Carey, and Meisler (1990) studied 29 dually diagnosed patients in day treatment who were randomly assigned to a problem-solving skills training group or usual day treatment. The experimental group received 12 sessions of structured problem-solving training. Skills were evaluated before training, immediately afterward, and one month following training. The results showed no enhancement of skills at either follow-up evaluation.

Noordsy, Schwab, Fox, and Drake (1996) examined participation by dually diagnosed patients in peer-oriented substance abuse treatment groups. Across several studies, patients with schizophrenia were unlikely to sustain long-term involvement with self-help groups in the community such as Alcoholics Anonymous. However, they often participated actively in special dual-disorder groups that were conducted in mental health centers.

Bebout and colleagues (Bebout, 1993) devised a social network intervention specifically for homeless, dually diagnosed patients. The intervention attempted to reconstruct networks so that patients developed new peer networks with nonabusers and repaired relationships with their families. The results of this study indicated that the patients who received the social network treatment improved more in substance abuse outcomes (especially alcohol abuse) than the patients who received the comparison treatment, which consisted of treatment as usual (Drake, Yovetich, Bebout, Harris, & McHugo, 1997).

The issues of whether and how dually diagnosed patients learn social skills and at what stage of recovery from substance abuse this occurs optimally are obviously critical. The acquisition of social skills during social skills training tends to be slower in patients with schizophrenia who have cognitive impairments such as poor memory, verbal learning, or vigilance (Bowen et al., 1994; Kern, Green, & Satz, 1992; Mueser, Bellack, Douglas, & Wade, 1991). These problems may be exacerbated in schizophrenic patients who abuse alcohol or drugs because of the effects of these substances on a wide range of cognitive functions (Grant, 1987; Herning, Glover, Koeppl, Weddington, & Jaffe, 1990; O'Malley & Gawin, 1990; Parsons, Schaeffer, & Glynn, 1990). However, since the available evidence suggests that cognitive impairments slow the rate of skill acquisition in schizophrenic patients, but do not interfere with the maintenance of newly acquired skills (Mueser et al., 1991), there is a need for sys-

tematic evaluations of social skills training for dually diagnosed patients.

Similarly, the role of peer groups and families in the treatment of dual diagnosis is a central question for treatment studies. It appears that these patients have a difficult time participating in the existing self-help system for substance abusers in the community but that many are willing to participate in peer groups that are specifically designed for people with dual disorders. Social networking and family interventions also appear to be obvious strategies for treatment. At this time, however, there are few outcome data on any of these interventions that either target social functioning or assess it as an outcome measure.

Longitudinal Changes

One might expect that social networks would be involved in the process of changing substance-abusing behaviors, both as cause and effect. That is, abstinence may both require and facilitate social contacts with healthier, nonabusing network members, including professionals, families, and peers. The empirical evidence on these issues is thus far meager.

In an ethnography of 10 dually diagnosed persons, Schwab and Alverson (1992) found that patients were intricately linked with a substance-abusing peer group and grappled with the issues of loss of supports and loneliness when they considered giving up substance abuse. Few of these patients changed their social networks substantially during one year of observation.

In a separate ethnographic study of psychiatric patients participating in supported employment, Alverson, Becker, and Drake (1995) found that 9 of 13 patients who were former substance abusers reported that they had changed their social networks, with great difficulty, in order to maintain abstinence. Changes included severely limiting or severing ties with former substance-abusing peers.

Jerrell and Ridgely (1995) evaluated 147 patients with dual-disorders who participated in specialized dual-disorder treatment over 12 to 18 months. Patient self-report ratings showed no change on social adjustment, only marginal improvement in family relationships, and no improvement in satisfaction with social life. However, interviewers rated these same patients as significantly improved in terms of social contacts. The reason for the discrepancy between self-report and interviewer ratings is unclear; it could be due to differences in raters' perspectives (e.g., clients' perspectives could change over time while researchers maintained a constant standard), lack of correction for multiple tests, or the limits of some measures.

Between 1987 and 1990, the National Institute of Mental Health sponsored 13 demonstration projects on young persons with severe mental illness and substance abuse. Most of these studies did not concentrate on social functioning and have not been published, but they were recently reviewed (Mercer-McFadden, Drake, Brown, & Fox, 1997). Two of the projects did show improvements in interpersonal relationships over approximately one year of dual-diagnosis treatment, while three studies showed no change in various aspects of social functioning, including levels of social contacts and social supports. A significant limitation of these studies was the brief (usually one year) follow-up. Results from the skills training literature (Mueser, Wallace, & Liberman, 1995) and longitudinal research on dual diagnosis (Drake, Mueser, Clark, & Wallach, 1996) would argue that longer interventions are necessary to achieve positive outcomes in schizophrenia.

In sum, the research data on changes in social functioning over time offer only minimal support for the notion that social competence and social networks change along with substance-abusing behavior in a reciprocal fashion. To a large extent, these essentially negative findings reflect the absence of data on this topic rather than the existence of contradictory data or many studies suggesting no relationships between social functioning and substance abuse.

CONCLUSIONS

The data reviewed here support the view that substance use and social functioning are intricately related in schizophrenia. Substance-abusing patients with schizophrenia compared to their peers with schizophrenia who never use substances, tend to be more socially active premorbidly, and their substance abuse, at least before it results in severe addiction, tends to promote active social participation in relatively large social networks that require some social competence. Indeed, their social needs and skills appear to be strong underlying factors in initiating and maintaining substance abuse. These findings indicating higher levels of social participation for schizophrenic patients who abuse substances contrast with the lower rates of social interaction characteristic of schizophrenia (APA, 1994).

At the same time that schizophrenic patients' substance abuse expands their social functioning in certain ways, it appears to damage and restrict social functioning in other areas. Relationships with families, in particular, often suffer as the dually diagnosed person becomes part of a network of other alcohol and drug abusers. The dually diagnosed person's behavior takes more of an antisocial tone as they become part of a network involved in illicit behaviors. And there is also the realistic danger that milder forms of substance abuse, which are associated with active social participation, often become transformed into severe addiction that seriously compromises the capacity for social functioning. When this happens, the individual is prone to become isolated, homeless, and institutionalized. Some patients return to live with families at this point.

Because of the social nature of substance abuse, many interventions for primary substance abusers focus on social functioning. These include self-help groups, peer-oriented group therapies, marital and family therapies (Steinglass, Bennett, Wolin, & Reiss, 1987), social skills training interventions (Monti, Abrams, Kadden, & Cooney, 1989), and community reinforcement approaches (Hester & Miller, 1989). Many proposed dual-diagnosis treatment interventions also include attempts to increase social skills (Carey, 1996; Drake, Bartels, Teague, Noordsy, & Clark, 1993; Mueser, Fox, Kenison, & Geltz, 1995; Noordsy & Fox, 1991) and to intervene with peers (Harris, Bergman, & Bachrach, 1986; Noordsy & Fox, 1991), families (Clark & Drake, 1994; Ryglewicz, 1991), and broader social networks (Bebout, 1993). Unfortunately, these interventions have not often been evaluated. In fact, despite the social nature of substance abuse among the dually diagnosed, few studies have focused on social functioning. The findings reviewed above in most cases were culled from secondary or accessory data in studies that focused on other issues.

When investigators have assessed social functioning, there is no consensus on measures and on how to assess the substance-abusing character of the network. Since substance abuse, particularly when it involves illicit drugs, is to a large extent a secretive phenomenon, accurate assessment may be difficult. It may also be the case that changes are qualitative rather than quantitative. For example, dually diagnosed patients may change the individuals in their networks over time as they recover from substance abuse but the network size may not change substantially. Qualitative studies and family studies should be particularly informative in this regard.

Research on intervening at the level of social competence and social networks might pursue several strategies.

These include (1) social skills training to resist drug over-tures and to initiate contacts with nonabusers, (2) training patients in skills for coping with anxiety, dysphoria, and other experiences associated with substance abuse, (3) teaching strategies for developing new relationships and increasing recreational activities that are not related to drug use, (4) offering substance abuse treatments in peer-oriented groups, (5) addressing substance abuse in indi-vidual family sessions and multiple family groups, and (6) intervening at the level of social networks with more com-prehensive approaches that involve major restructuring of networks. Much work remains to be done in understand-ing the relationships between substance abuse and social functioning in schizophrenia, and in the development of more effective interventions that target these areas in du-ally diagnosed patients. However, we have now reached the point where we are able to articulate the relevant ques-tions to guide our inquiry in this area.

REFERENCES

Alverson, M., Becker, D. R., & Drake, R. E. (1995). An ethno-graphic study of supported employment. *Psychosocial Reha-bilitation Journal, 18,* 115–128.

American Psychiatric Association. (1987). *Diagnostic and statis-tical manual of mental disorders (3rd ed., rev.).* Washington, DC: Author.

American Psychiatric Association. (1994). *Diagnostic and statis-tical manual of mental disorders (4th ed.)* Washington, DC: Author.

Andreasson, S., Allebeck, P., & Rydberg, U. (1989). Schizo-phrenia in users and nonusers of cannabis: A longitudinal study in Stockholm County. *Acta Psychiatrica Scandinavica, 79,* 505–510.

Arndt, S., Tyrrell, G., Flaum, M., & Andreasen, N. C. (1992). Co-morbidity of substance abuse and schizophrenia: The role of pre-morbid adjustment. *Psychological Medicine, 22,* 379–388.

Baigent, M., Holme, G., & Hafner, R. J. (1995). Self reports of the interaction between substance abuse and schizophrenia. *Australian and New Zealand Journal of Psychiatry, 29,* 69–74.

Bebout, R. R. (1993). Contextual case management: Restructur-ing the social support networks of seriously mentally ill adults. In M. Harris & H. C. Bergman (Eds.), *Case management for mentally ill patients: Theory and practice* (pp. 59–82). Lang-horne, PA: Harwood Academic Publishers.

Bergman, H. C., & Harris, M. (1985). Substance use among young adult chronic patients. *Psychosocial Rehabilitation Journal, 9,* 49–54.

Billings, A. G., & Moos, R. H. (1983). Psychosocial processes of recovery among alcoholics and their families: Implications for clinicians and program evaluators. *Addictive Behaviors, 8,* 205–218.

Blankertz, L. E., & Cnaan, R. A. (1994). Assessing the impact of two residential programs for dually diagnosed homeless indi-viduals. *Social Service Review, 68,* 536–560.

Bowen, L., Wallace, C. J., Glynn, S. M., Nuechterlein, K. H., Lutzker, J. R., & Kuehnel, T. G. (1994). Schizophrenic indi-viduals' cognitive functioning and performance in interper-sonal interactions and skills training procedures. *Journal of Psychiatric Research, 28,* 289–301.

Breakey, W. R., Goodell, H., Lorenz, P. C., & McHugh, P. R. (1974). Hallucinogenic drugs as precipitants of schizophrenia. *Psychological Medicine, 4,* 255–261.

Brown, S. A., Christiansen, B. A., & Goldman, M. S. (1987). The Alcohol Expectancy Questionnaire: An instrument for the as-sessment of adolescent and adult expectancies. *Journal of Studies on Alcohol, 48,* 483–491.

Carey, K. B. (1996). Substance use reduction in the context of outpatient psychiatric treatment: A collaborative, motiva-tional, harm reduction approach. *Community Mental Health Journal, 32,* 291–306.

Carey, K. B., & Carey, M. P. (1990). Social problem-solving in dual diagnosis patients. *Journal of Psychopathology and Be-havioral Assessment, 12,* 247–254.

Carey, M. P., Carey, K. B., & Meisler, A. W. (1990). Training mentally ill chemical abusers in social problem solving. *Be-havior Therapy, 21,* 511–518.

Caton, C. L. M., Shrout, P. E., Dominguez, B., Eagle, P. F., Opler, L. A., & Cournos, F. (1995). Risk factors for homeless-ness among women with schizophrenia. *American Journal of Public Health, 85,* 1153–1156.

Caton, C. L. M., Shrout, P. E., Eagle, P. F., Opler, L. A., Felix, A. F., & Dominguez, B. (1994). Risk factors for homelessness among women with schizophrenia. *American Journal of Pub-lic Health, 84,* 265–270.

Clark, R. E., & Drake, R. E. (1994). Expenditures of time and money by families of people with severe mental illness and substance use disorder. *Community Mental Health Journal, 30,* 145–163.

Cohen, M., & Klein, D. F. (1970). Drug abuse in a young psy-chiatric population. *American Journal of Orthopsychiatry, 40,* 448–455.

Cooper, M. L., Russell, M., Skinner, J. B., Frone, M. R., & Mudar, P. (1992). Stress and alcohol use: Moderating effects of gender, coping, and alcohol expectancies. *Journal of Ab-normal Psychology, 101,* 139–152.

Dixon, L., McNary, S., & Lehman, A. (1995). Substance abuse and family relationships of persons with severe mental illness. *American Journal of Psychiatry, 152,* 456–458.

Dixon, L., Haas, G., Weiden, P. J., Sweeney, J., & Frances, A. J. (1991). Drug abuse in schizophrenic patients: Clinical corre-lates and reasons for use. *American Journal of Psychiatry, 148,* 224–230.

Dolan, B., & Coid, J. (1993). *Psychopathic and antisocial per-sonality disorders: Treatment and research issues.* London, England: Gaskell.

Donovan, D. M. (1988). Assessment of addictive behaviors: Implications of an emerging biopsychosocial model. In D. M. Donovan & G. A. Marlatt (Eds.), *Assessment of addictive behaviors* (pp. 3–48). New York: Guilford Press.

Drake, R. E., Bartels, S. J., Teague, G. B., Noordsy, D. L., & Clark, R. E. (1993). Treatment of substance use disorders in severely mentally ill patients. *Journal of Nervous and Mental Disease, 181,* 606–611.

Drake, R. E., Mueser, K. T., Clark, R. E., & Wallach, M. A. (1996). The course, treatment, and outcome of substance disorder in persons with severe mental illness. *American Journal of Orthopsychiatry, 66,* 42–51.

Drake, R. E., & Wallach, M. A. (1989). Substance abuse among the chronic mentally ill. *Hospital and Community Psychiatry, 40,* 1041–1046.

Drake, R. E., Yovetich, M. A., Bebout, R. R., Harris, M., & McHugo, G. J. (1997). Integrated treatment for dually diagnosed homeless adults. *Journal of Nervous and Mental Disease, 185,* 298–305.

Grant, I. (1987). Alcohol and the brain: Neuropsychological correlates. *Journal of Consulting and Clinical Psychology, 55,* 310–324.

Harris, M. (1996). Treating sexual-abuse trauma with dually diagnosed women. *Community Mental Health Journal, 32,* 371–385.

Harris, M., Bergman, H. C., & Bachrach, L. L. (1986). Individualized network planning for chronic psychiatric patients. *Psychiatric Quarterly, 58,* 51–56.

Hekimian, L. J., & Gershon, S. (1968). Characteristics of drug abusers admitted to a psychiatric hospital. *Journal of the American Medical Association, 205,* 125–130.

Herning, R. I., Glover, B. J., Koeppl, B., Weddington, W., & Jaffe, J. H. (1990). Cognitive deficits in abstaining cocaine abusers. In J. W. Spence & J. J. Boren (Eds.), *Residual effects of abused drugs on behavior* (pp. 167–178). [National Institute of Drug Abuse Research Monograph 101] Washington, DC: National Institute of Drug Abuse.

Hester, R. K., & Miller, W. R. (Eds.). (1989). *Handbook of alcoholism treatment approaches: Effective alternatives.* Boston: Allyn and Bacon.

Higgins, S. T., Delaney, D. D., Budney, A. J., Bickel, W. K., Hughes, J. R., Foerg, F., & Fenwick, J. W. (1991). A behavioral approach to achieving initial cocaine abstinence. *American Journal of Psychiatry, 148,* 1218–1224.

Jerrell, J. M., & Ridgely, M. S. (1995). Evaluating changes in symptoms and functioning of dually diagnosed clients in specialized treatment. *Psychiatric Services, 46,* 233–238.

Kashner, M. T., Rader, L. E., Rodell, D. E., Beck, C. M., Rodell, L. R., & Muller, K. (1991). Family characteristics, substance abuse, and hospitalization patterns of patients with schizophrenia. *Hospital and Community Psychiatry, 42,* 195–197.

Kazdin, A. E. (1995). *Conduct disorders in childhood and adolescence (2nd. ed.).* Developmental Clinical Psychology and

Psychiatry Series, Vol 9. Thousand Oaks, CA: Sage Publications.

Kern, R. S., Green, M. F., & Satz, P. (1992). Neuropsychological predictors of skills training for chronic psychiatric patients. *Psychiatry Research, 43,* 223–230.

Knudsen, P., & Vilmar, T. (1984). Cannabis and neuroleptic agents in schizophrenia. *Acta Psychiatrica Scandinavica, 69,* 162–174.

McHugo, G. J., Paskus, T. S., & Drake, R. E. (1992). Detection of alcoholism in schizophrenic patients using the MAST. *Alcoholism: Clinical and Experimental Research, 17,* 187–191.

Mercer-McFadden, C., Drake, R. E., Brown, N. B., & Fox, R. S. (1997). The community support program demonstrations of services for young adults with severe mental illness and substance use disorders. *Psychiatric Rehabilitation Journal, 20,* 13–24.

Monti, P. M., Abrams, D. B., Kadden, R. M., & Cooney, N. L. (1989). *Treating alcohol dependence.* New York: Guilford Press.

Moos, R. H., Finney, J. W., & Cronkite, R. C. (1990). *Alcoholism treatment: Context, process and outcome.* New York: Oxford University Press.

Mueser, K. T., Bellack, A. S., Douglas, M. S., & Wade, J. H. (1991). Prediction of social skill acquisition in schizophrenic and major affective disorder patients from memory and symptomatology. *Psychiatry Research, 37,* 281–296.

Mueser, K. T., Fox, M., Kenison, L. B., & Geltz, B. L. (1995). *The better living skills group.* Concord, NH: The New Hampshire-Dartmouth Psychiatric Research Center.

Mueser, K. T., Nishith, P., Tracy, J. I., DeGirolamo, J., & Molinaro, M. (1995). Expectations and motives for substance use in schizophrenia. *Schizophrenia Bulletin, 21,* 367–378.

Mueser, K. T., Rosenberg, S. D., Drake, R. E., Miles, K. M., Wolford, G., Vidaver, R., & Carrieri, K. (in press). Conduct disorder, antisocial personality disorder, and substance use disorders in schizophrenia and major affective disorder. *Journal of Studies on Alcohol.*

Mueser, K. T., Wallace, C. J., & Liberman, R. P. (1995). New developments in social skills training. *Behavior Change, 12,* 31–40.

Mueser, K. T., Yarnold, P. R., Levinson, D. F., Singh, H., Bellack, A. S., Kee, K., Morrison, R. L., & Yadalam, K. G. (1990). Prevalence of substance abuse in schizophrenia: Demographic and clinical correlates. *Schizophrenia Bulletin, 16,* 31–56.

Noordsy, D. L., Drake, R. E., Teague, G. B., Osher, F. C., Hurlbut, S. C., Beaudett, M. S., & Paskus, T. S. (1991). Subjective experiences related to alcohol use among schizophrenics. *Journal of Nervous and Mental Disease, 179,* 410–414.

Noordsy, D. L., & Fox, L. (1991). Group intervention techniques for people with dual disorders. *Psychosocial Rehabilitation Journal, 15,* 67–78.

Noordsy, D. L., Schwab, B., Fox, L., & Drake, R. E. (1996). The role of self-help programs in the rehabilitation of persons with mental illness and substance use disorders. *Community Mental Health Journal, 32,* 71–81.

Nuechterlein, K. H. (1986). Childhood precursors of adult schizophrenia. *Journal of Child Psychology and Psychiatry, 27,* 133–144.

Offord, D. R., & Cross, L. A. (1969). Behavioral antecedents of adult schizophrenia: A review. *Archives of General Psychiatry, 21,* 267–283.

O'Malley, S. S., & Gawin, F. H. (1990). Abstinence symptomatology and neuropsychological impairment in cocaine abusers. In J. W. Spence & J. J. Boren (Eds.), *Residual effects of abused drugs on behavior* (pp. 179–190). [National Institute of Drug Abuse Research Monograph 101] Washington, DC: National Institute of Drug Abuse.

Parnas, J., Schulsinger, F., Schulsinger, H., Mednick, S. A., & Teasdale, T. W. (1982). Behavioral precursors of schizophrenia spectrum: A prospective study. *Archives of General Psychiatry, 39,* 658–664.

Parsons, O., Schaeffer, K., & Glynn, S. (1990). Does neuropsychological test performance predict resumption of drinking in posttreatment alcoholics? *Addiction Behavior, 15,* 297–307.

Pristach, C. A., & Smith, C. M. (1996). Self-reported effects of alcohol use on symptoms of schizophrenia. *Psychiatric Services, 47,* 421–423.

Robins, L. N. (1966). *Deviant children grown up.* Huntington, NY: Robert E. Krieger Publishing.

Ryglewicz, H. (1991). Psychoeducation for clients and families: A way in, out, and through in working with people with dual disorders. *Psychosocial Rehabilitation Journal, 15,* 79–89.

Schwab, B., & Alverson, M. (1992). *An ethographic study of people with dual disorders.* Unpublished paper.

Schwab, B., Clark, R. E., & Drake, R. E. (1991). An ethnographic note on clients as parents. *Psychosocial Rehabilitation Journal, 15,* 95–99.

Selzer, M. L. (1971). The Michigan Alcoholism Screening Test: The quest for a new diagnostic instrument. *American Journal of Psychiatry, 127,* 1653–1658.

Sevy, S., Kay, S. R., Opler, L. A., & Van Praag, H. M. (1990). Significance of cocaine history in schizophrenia. *Journal of Nervous and Mental Disease, 178,* 642–648.

Steinglass, P., Bennett, L. A., Wolin, S. J., & Reiss, D. (1987). *The alcoholic family.* New York: Basic Books.

Teague, G. B., Drake, R. E., McHugo, G. J., & Vowinkle, S. (1994). *Alcohol and substance abuse, housing, and vocational status in a statewide survey of seriously mentally ill clients.* Final Report to the National Institutes on Alcohol Abuse and Alcoholism.

Test, M. A., Wallish, L., Allness, D., & Ripp, K. (1989). Substance use in young adults with schizophrenic disorders. *Schizophrenia Bulletin, 15,* 465–476.

Toth, J. (1993). *The mole people.* Chicago: Chicago Review Press.

Treffert, D. A. (1978). Marijuana use in schizophrenia: A clear hazard. *American Journal of Psychiatry, 135,* 1213–1215.

Tsuang, M. T., Simpson, J. C., & Kronfol, Z. (1982). Subtypes of drug abuse with psychosis: Demographic characteristics, clinical features, and family history. *Archives of General Psychiatry, 39,* 141–147.

Vaillant, G. E. (1983). Natural history of male alcoholism V: Is alcoholism the cart or the horse to sociopathy? *British Journal of Addiction, 78,* 317–326.

Vaillant, G. E., & Milofsky, E. S. (1982). The natural history of alcoholism: IV. Paths to recovery. *Archives of General Psychiatry, 39,* 127–133.

Warner, R., Taylor, D., Wright, J., Sloat, A., Springett, G., Arnold, S., & Weinberg, H. (1994). Substance use among the mentally ill: Prevalence, reasons for use, and effects on illness. *American Journal of Orthopsychiatry, 64,* 30–39.

Westermeyer, J., & Walzer, V. (1975). Sociopathy and drug use in a young psychiatric population. *Diseases of the Nervous System, 36,* 673–677.

CHAPTER 18

ECONOMICS OF SOCIAL DYSFUNCTION

Massimo Moscarelli

The comprehensive evaluation of schizophrenia is probably one of the most challenging tasks that exists in medicine. It must take into account the changes of the psychic lives of patients, their behavior, the repercussions of these on their families, and on their social and working abilities and responsibilities. Patients affected by schizophrenia cope with their own expectations of life (according to their frequently idiosyncratic point of view) and with the expectations of their families, worksite, friends, spouse, children, health care providers, and society; each of them with a different point of view, responsibility, assertive capacity, and executive power. Moreover, the stigma frequently related to the condition can influence negatively the attitudes of patients and others in coping with the illness.

Awareness of the multiple points of view in the evaluation of illnesses seems particularly important, because each party gives its particular value to patients' clinical and social condition and sets some priorities for their therapeutic change, including the patients themselves. Each of these points of view needs to be informed about what is relevant for patients' own interests and decisions.

The evaluation of the consequences of illnesses requires an interdisciplinary collaboration to properly consider the relationships among the clinical consequences of illnesses, the social consequences, and the values given to each of them, including the economic one.

ILLNESS CONSEQUENCES AND ECONOMIC ANALYSIS

The study of the course and outcome of schizophrenia for their use in economic analysis should not be limited to the clinical syndrome but must also consider the complex nature of the patient's social relationships.

A tripartite division for the description of the consequences of illness was proposed (ICDH, 1980) and a draft revision is in progress (Cooper, 1993). Cooper states that one of the major problems was that the terms *impairment, disability,* and *handicap* have been used interchangeably

290

in both physical and social contexts, and the sequence of disease, impairment, disability, and handicap would be aimed at clarifying the potential contribution of medical services, rehabilitation facilities, and social welfare, respectively. *Impairment* is defined as any loss or abnormality of psychological, physiological, or anatomical structure or function. *Disability* refers to any restriction or lack of ability to perform an activity in the manner or within the range considered normal for an human being, resulting from impairment. A *handicap* is a disadvantage resulting from an impairment or disability that limits or prevents the fulfillment of a "normal" social role (Cooper, 1993).

The social and occupational disabilities related to schizophrenia and their improvement in rehabilitation needs to be evaluated independent of the severity of characteristic symptoms (Jong et al., 1991). In DSM-IV (American Psychiatric Association) [APA], 1994), while retaining the unified Global Assessment of Functioning (GAF) scale reported on Axis V, it is also proposed in some settings that the Social and Occupational Functioning Assessment Scale (SOFAS) be used to measure the level of personal, social, occupational, and school functioning on a continuum from excellent functioning to grossly impaired functioning, which is not directly influenced by the overall severity of the individual's psychological symptoms. The SOFAS includes impairments in functioning due to physical limitations, as well as those due to mental impairments. To be considered, impairment must be a direct consequence of mental and physical health problems; the effects of lack of opportunity and other environmental limitations are not to be considered (Table 18.1). The problems of the reliability of social and occupational scales in the different settings are considered in Goldman, Skodol, and Lave (1992).

Some of the major social roles affected by schizophrenia, relevant for a comprehensive social and economic evaluation of the burden of the disease, include the following:

1. *Work.* The issues related to work in schizophrenia are of great importance. The World Health Organization (WHO, 1988) collaborative study on the assessment and reduction of psychiatric disabilities found work performance as the most impaired role in schizophrenic patients at initial evaluation. The reliable comparison of the different work situations (sheltered/ competitive, supported/independent, full/part-time, permanent/tran-

Table 18.1. Social and Occupational Functioning Assessment Scale

(Note: Use intermediate codes when appropriate)

100	Superior functioning in a wide range of activities
90	Good functioning in all areas, occupationally and socially effective
80	No more than a slight impairment in social, occupational, or school functioning (e.g., infrequent interpersonal conflict, temporarily falling behind in schoolwork)
70	Some difficulty in social, occupational, or school functioning, but generally functioning well, has some meaningful interpersonal relationships
60	Moderate difficulty in social, occupational, or school functioning (e.g., few friends, conflicts with peers and coworkers)
50	Serious impairment in social, occupational, or school functioning (e.g., no friends, unable to keep a job)
40	Major impairment in several areas, such as work or school, family relations (e.g., depressed man avoids friends, neglects family, and is unable to work; child frequently beats up younger children, is defiant at home, and is failing at school)
30	Inability to function in almost all areas (e.g., stays in bed all day; no job, home, or friends)
20	Occasionally fails to maintain minimal personal hygiene; unable to function independently
10	Persistent inability to maintain minimal personal hygiene; unable to function without harming self or others or without considerable external support (e.g., nursing care and supervision)

American Psychiatric Association: SOFAS, DSM-IV, 1994.

sitional) is difficult because these situations vary significantly from the United States to Europe, from one European country to another, or even among different settings in a single country. International comparison is hindered also by varying factors related to the labor market, such as the rate of women at work, school attendance, age of retirement, sociodemographic trends, and the rate of unemployment. The unemployment rates differ greatly from the United States to European countries; in the latter, unemployment is frequently above 10%. Regulations on disability insurance and protection for the handicapped vary greatly as well (Salvador & Velasquez, 1996). According to Morgan

(1975), unemployment rates above the 2% may seriously hamper access to competitive work, while unemployment rates above 6% may render competitive jobs almost inaccessible for the mentally ill. The employer is the individual who is going to hire, so it is important to know what the employer is looking for, what his or her expectations, awareness, and knowledge about mental illness are, what the factors contributing to hiring are, the employer's retention criteria, and the incentives for hiring, tax credits, and support services (Kiernan & Rowland, 1989; Wesoleck & McFarlane, 1991).

2. *Student.* In schizophrenia, the age of illness onset is frequently between about 16 and 25. The social disability related to the role of the student will involve a segment of the general population with possibly different rehabilitation aims.

3. *Self-care and independence skills.* Schizophrenia can result in an inability to perform everyday skills, with family care or other intervention necessary to compensate the deficits.

4. *Parental and spouse role.* The inability to perform the role of spouse and parent will require social support for family and children.

The social and work dysfunction is not only responsible for the decrease in quality of life of patients and their families, but also causes a severe economic burden to individuals and society, due to the inability of patients to participate in the social production of richness and in the social expenditures related to support their social dysfunctions.

QUALITY OF LIFE

There is an increased attention to the development of measures of patient quality of life (Baker & Intagliata, 1982, Lehman, 1983). The new National Institute of Mental Health (NIMH) research plan identifies quality of life as one of the mayor outcome areas to be assessed in new research efforts, because of a prevailing concern that outcome assessments should include the patient's perspective (Attkinson et al., 1992). The measures for evaluating subjective and objective quality of life in schizophrenia are discussed in Chapter 1. These measures are specific and developed in a clinical background. They differ from the economic measures of quality of life, such as Quality Adjusted Life Years (QALY), because these last refer to the evaluation of utilities and preferences between health states and interventions; they are general, universal indices and are proposed for setting priorities between interventions according to their cost/QALY results and for comparing interventions for different illnesses.

COURSE AND OUTCOMES OF ILLNESS AND ECONOMIC ANALYSIS

Course

The course of schizophrenia from a longitudinal perspective can be divided into a premorbid period; a prodromal period; an early illness onset period with the onset of positive symptoms, deficit symptoms, and functional disabilities that lead to the diagnosis of schizophrenia; a middle illness epoch; and a late course epoch. These periods are frequently characterized by large variations in services use: the majority of inpatient hospitalization costs accrue over the first 5 to 10 years of manifest illness, and treatment needs and costs plateau at different levels during the middle to late illness epochs, and significant family burden is expected to happen during the prodromal phase. Substantial variability in illness cost across individual patients should be anticipated. Data from longitudinal studies suggest that variation in illness severity and/or subtype may be the major source of variance in long-term disabilities. Over the long term, cost variance associated with differences in illness severity may exceed variance attributable to any specific therapeutic intervention or service delivery configuration (Fenton, 1996).

Particular attention should be given to the onset period. The age of the earliest signs of mental disturbance (depression and anxiety), first psychotic symptom, beginning of index episode, and index admission are, respectively, 24.3, 26.5, 27.8, and 28.5 in males, and 27.5, 30.6, 31.7, and 32.4 in females (Hafner Richier-Rossler, Maurer, Fatkenheuer, & Loffler, 1992). It suggests the importance already revealed of this period (Crow, McMillan, Johnson & Johnstone, 1986; Keith & Matthews, 1991; Moscarelli, Capri, & Neri, 1991) in the evaluation of its repercussions on the disability, services use, and costs during the course of schizophrenia and the possible savings by an early detection and intervention (Falloon, 1992).

Research on the economic aspects of the health and social course of illness will enable more informed and refined financing programs, tailored on the different social and clinical services needed for the different degrees of severity, the different periods of the illness, and individual variability.

Health and Social Outcomes

There is no consensus about which specific indicators should be used to evaluate outcome of health care interventions (Sartorius, 1995). The research on the evaluation of short-, medium-, and long-term health outcomes should consider different domains and different priorities. They are related to the persistence and severity of specific and non-specific symptoms; acute and long-term side effects of antipsychotic medication; cognitive, attentional, and memory functioning; physical health status consequences of illness; and social disabilities in the different domains (work, housing, family roles, friends, etc). It should consider also quality of life measures.

Since the burden of the illness falls frequently on the family, measuring of quality of life, anxiety, depression, demoralization, and discouragement in the "key" relative as well as the changes in performing his or her social roles due to taking care of the patient should be also considered.

Prediction of Course and Outcome

The heterogeneity of the spectrum of disorders of schizophrenia suggests that even the very narrow construct of schizophrenia created by DSM-III or DSM-IV is clearly heterogeneous and does not lend itself to "one size fits all" guidelines about treatment management. The use of specific diagnoses to prescribe treatment or anticipate expected outcome of the treatment is not sufficient (Andreasen & Schultz, 1996). The debate on the exemption for psychiatric illness in the United States from the reimbursement of hospitalization according to Diagnoses-Related Groups (DRG; English, 1988) reveals the repercussions on financing systems of the current difficulties in predicting resources utilization, course, and outcome in mental disorders.

To develop research on the identification of predictors should allow the development of prospective cost models based on severity case mix data in order to enable more precise health and economic planning for groups or individuals. In schizophrenia, poor premorbid social functioning is considered the best predictor of poor social functioning at outcome, while preillness unemployment is

the best predictor of work disability at follow-up. The best method for prospectively estimating hospital utilization over a 2-year period would be examination of hospitalization history over the preceding 2 years. Illness severity and subtype may be better predictors of course over a period of decades (Carpenter & Strauss, 1991; Fenton, 1996; Fenton & McGlashan, 1991).

BURDEN OF DISEASE

Disability was chosen for measuring the burden of diseases. This approach is based on incidence perspective and was developed for providing an estimate that combined the number of years of life lost due to premature death and the number of years of life lived with a disability arising from new cases of diseases or injury. An economic measure was developed, named Disability Adjusted Life Years (DALYs), that considers the combination of these two components. It provides a measure for comparing the social burden of different illnesses due to either mortality or morbidity. The results of this approach were first utilized in the World Development Report: Investing in Health (World Bank, 1993).

The duration of time lost due to premature death is measured with the standard expected years of life lost. The nonfatal health outcomes are evaluated relying on International Classification of Impairments, Disabilities, and Handicaps (ICIDH), in which a linear progression from disease to pathology to manifestation to impairment to disability to handicap is proposed. *Impairment* is a level of organ system (e.g., loss of finger). *Disability* is the impact on the performance of the individual (e.g., loss of fine motor function). *Handicap* is the overall consequences that depend on the social environment (e.g., violin player or bank teller).

To evaluate the severity of the conditions, a universal index was developed. Six disability classes have been defined between perfect health and death in order to capture the multiple dimensions of human function. Each class represents a greater loss of welfare or increased severity than the class before, and the weights for each class (Table 18.2) were calculated on the basis of independent experts in order to reach the comparability both between the utility of time lived in six disability classes and the utility of time lost due to premature mortality (Murray, 1994a).

This weighing procedure is taken from the "preference" or "utility" economic framework. It seems useful to summarize briefly the background of these procedures.

Table 18.2   DALY: Definitions of Disability Weighting

	DESCRIPTION	WEIGHTS
Class 1	Limited ability to perform at least one activity in one of the following areas: recreation, education, procreation, and occupation	0.096
Class 2	Limited ability to perform most activities in one of the following areas: recreation, education, procreation, and occupation	0.220
Class 3	Limited ability to perform activities in two or more of the following areas: recreation, education, procreation, and occupation	0.400
Class 4	Limited ability to perform most activities in all of the following areas: recreation, education, procreation, and occupation	0.600
Class 5	Needs assistance with instrumental activities of daily living such as meal preparation, shopping, or housework	0.810
Class 6	Needs assistance with activities of daily living such as eating, personal hygiene, or toilet use	0.920

C. J. L. Murray, Bulletin of the World Health Organization, 1994.

Clinicians are accustomed to the clinical rating scales for the evaluation of illness-specific health states, such as symptoms, disabilities, and quality of life, or global measures of mental health state or functioning (GAS, GAF, etc). Economic measures such as Quality Adjusted Life Years (QALY) and Disability Adjusted Life Years (DALY) are related to the concept of *preference* between health states (or disabilities): they raise the problem of the different perspectives on the social and individual value given to the different health states.

PREFERENCES

The role of the economist is to evaluate therapeutic options so as to identify the *value* of what is given up to provide care (the cost) and the *value* of what is gained in terms of improved health status (Maynard, 1993).

The difference between measures of health status and measures of utility value given to different health states and the principal methods are described by Drummond, Stoddart, and Torrance (1987). They state that *utility* refers to the value or worth of a specific level of health status (or improvement in health status) and can be measured by the *preferences* of individuals or society for any particular set of health outcomes. To explain that the utility of an outcome, effect, or level of health status is different from the outcome, effect, or level of health status itself, they present the following example: Suppose that twins, identical in all respects except occupation (one being a sign painter and the other a translator), both broke their right arm. While they would be equally disabled (or conversely, equally healthy), if we asked them to rank "having a broken arm" on a scale of 0 (dead) to 1 (perfect health) their rankings might differ considerably because of the significance each one attaches to arm movement, in this case due to occupation. Consequently, their assessments of the utility of treatment (e.g., the degree to which treatment of the fractures improved the quality of their lives) would also differ. The attempts made by the clinician to measure in a valid and reliable way the detailed picture of the condition refer to the patient's health state, whereas the economic evaluation of preferences or utilities attempts to ascertain how much better the quality of life is in one health situation or "state" compared with another. Several techniques are available for making the comparison in order to produce an adjustment factor with which to increase or decrease the value of time spent in health situations or "states," resulting from the alternative in question relative to some baseline.

Following are some main procedures to measure the utility of the health states.

1. *Rating scale*: A typical rating scale consists of a line on a page with clearly defined endpoints. The most preferred health state is placed at one end of the line and the least preferred at the other end. The remaining health states are placed on the line between these two, in order of their preference, and such that intervals or spacing between the placements correspond to the differences in preference as perceived by the subject.

2. *Standard gamble*: It is the classical method for measuring cardinal preferences. The subject is offered two alternatives:

   Alternative 1: A treatment with two possible outcomes (a return to normal health and living a certain number of additional years or immediate death).

   Alternative 2: The certain outcome of chronic state for life.

3. *Time trade-off*: The individual is offered two alternatives:

Alternative 1: Life expectancy of an individual with the chronic condition followed by death.

Alternative 2: Healthy for shorter time followed by death. Time is varied until the respondent is indifferent between the two alternatives.

The standard gamble and time trade-off methods determine the subject's "indifference" point. These definitions show clearly how the aims and methods of these measures used by health economists for measuring preferences differ from the clinical rating scales of common use in psychiatry for measuring health states. A fundamental aim of economists is to provide measures for the value given to the health states to be used for informing priority setting.

PRINCIPAL APPROACHES OF ECONOMIC ANALYSIS

Two main approaches are used in economic analysis: the human capital approach and the willingness-to-pay approach.

Human Capital Approach

The method was developed by Becker (1964) and refined by Rice (1966). It is rooted in labor economics. Its basic assumption is that an individual's value to society is his or her production potential. Mortality and morbidity associated with a specific disease reduces the production potential of an individual by causing premature death, reducing time spent in productive work, or forcing the individual to leave the labor force completely. The cost of illness studies based on the human capital approach distinguish direct and indirect costs. The *direct costs* are the resources used for treatment (e.g., services use), and the *indirect costs* are those for which resources are lost (e.g., earning losses). Housekeepers' hours are valued on the basis of relevant market wages.

The main disadvantages of the human capital approach are that because it values life using market earnings, it yields very low values for children and the retired elderly. In addition, psychosocial costs, such as pain and suffering, referred to as *intangibles*, are components of the burden of illness omitted from the human capital computation of indirect costs. Cost of illness studies based on the human capital approach clearly represent a societal perspective: the method reflects the loss of national income due to reduced or lost productivity (Rupp & Keith, 1993)

Willingness-to-Pay Approach

This approach, suggested by Shelling (1968), values life according to what individuals are willing to pay for a change that reduces the probability of illness or death. The intangible factors of schizophrenia for the individuals and the family include pain, suffering, isolation, vulnerability, stigma, and major disruption of family life. This approach was applied to several illnesses. A review by Robinson (1986) claims that it is subjective and suffers from circularity because the values placed by individuals on government health programs are clearly influenced by those policies. Applications of this approach to schizophrenia, however, would provide further insights into the impact of these illnesses on human life. This approach can be linked to economic measures of quality of life and may assess how patients and families value their health status improvements or avoidance of health status deterioration. This approach represents an individual perspective and could provide a consumer measure of treatment benefits (Rupp & Keith, 1993).

Prevalence versus Incidence Costs

Prevalence-based costs estimate the direct and indirect economic burden incurred in a period of time (the base period usually one year, as a result of the prevalence of disease). Included are the costs of the base year or any time prior to the base year. Prevalence-based costs measure the value of resources used or lost during a specified period of time, regardless of the time of disease onset. Incidence-based costs represent the lifetime costs resulting from a disease or illness (Rice, Kelman, & Miller, 1992). The approach used depends on the purpose of the analysis. If the results are to be used for cost control, then prevalence-based costing is appropriate; it identifies the major components of current expenditures and forgone resources and identifies possible targets for economy. If the analysis is aimed at making a decision about which treatment or research strategy to implement, then the incidence-based approach is more appropriate because it provides the basis for predictions about the likely savings from programs that reduce incidence or improve outcomes (Andrews et al., 1985).

Disability and Transfer Payments

A controversial matter is how to evaluate the financial initiatives to help individuals cope with the disabling consequences of the illness (unemployment, inability to perform the parental role, food and housing inadequacy, etc.). Welfare, disability payments, and other benefit payments under public and private programs constitute a reallocation of resources, named *transfers*, and the net cost to society is zero. Inclusion of transfer payments would result in double counting and are not included in the cost estimates (Rice et al., 1992).

According to Rupp and Keith (1993), no consistent information exists today on public expenditures for health and mental health care, rehabilitation, disability-related cash assistance, food stamps, housing subsidies, and many other publicly funded programs that serve people with severe mental illness. In the late 1980s, there were about 1.2 million people in the United States receiving disability benefits on the basis of mental impairments (about 24% of all disabled beneficiaries), and approximately 10% of the totally and permanently disabled population is composed of people suffering from schizophrenia. Their conclusion is that the exclusion of disability payments from cost of illness studies seems to ignore that if illness does not occur, transfer payments can be used for other purposes

In the case of schizophrenia, disability benefits can last for decades, the patient frequently never being in the workplace. The adequacy of services for vocational evaluation for matching the patient's social disability with a range of possibly suitable work (in particular when the patient has never been in the labor force), the development of rehabilitation programs for market-based employment, and the availability in the worksite of a number of initiatives for enabling different work opportunities that take into account some particular aspects of the illness are activities that require financial interventions, and it seems that the current separation of budgets for services provision and disability benefits does not encourage the financing from one budget if the benefits will fall on another budget.

Services Use Expenditures

Treating schizophrenia is extremely costly and requires an extensive array of services, ranging from mental health and medical care to social and legal services to informal family assistance (Hargreaves, Shumway, & Hu, 1996; Hu, Shumway, & Hargreaves, 1996; Allen & Beecham, 1993). It is important also to categorize health expenditures according to both financing and provision of services by government, parastatal agencies (social security and social insurance programs of the government), and private sector.

ECONOMIC EVALUATIONS IN SCHIZOPHRENIA

Cost of Illness Studies

There is an increasing interest in evaluating the social burden of individual illnesses, in particular chronic, long-lasting illnesses with high social costs. The quality of these studies depends on the reliability of epidemiological studies that estimate incidence and prevalence of psychiatric disorders, the availability of detailed inpatient and outpatient services use, employment data, and disability data that are related to diagnosis. A number of cost of illness studies in schizophrenia have been performed in different countries (Gunderson & Mosher, 1975; Andrews et al., 1985; Andrews, 1991; Rice & Kelman, 1992 (this last relied for the economic analysis on data from the NIMH ECA study); Davies & Drummond 1991, 1994; Lund, 1994; Wyatt, Henter, Leary, & Taylor, 1995; Kavanagh, 1994; Evers & Ament, 1995). These studies have generally used the human capital approach, measured direct and indirect costs, and in many cases described, with costs, the related services utilization data. The direct costs of the global health expenditures of schizophrenia ranged from 1.6% in the United Kingdom (Davies & Drummond, 1991) to 2.5% in the United States. The evaluation of indirect costs was quite sensitive to the different evaluation methods; for example, while the direct costs of schizophrenia evaluated by Rice et al. (1992) and Wyatt et al. (1995) in the United States were quite similar (respectively about 17 (1990$) and 19 (1991$) billion dollars, the indirect costs were about 12 (1990$) and 46 (1991$) billion dollars, respectively. Further research is needed in considering different components of the indirect costs in schizophrenia. Issues relating to the evaluation of capital costs (e.g., health services buildings, McGuire, 1991), the economic burden on families (Franks, 1990), and the costs incurred on the criminal justice system (Rice et al., 1992) have also been considered. It is expected that the standardization of methods and measures of direct and indirect costs will, in the future, improve international comparisons.

Expenditures and Consequences

There are an increasing number of studies that include economic variables in the evaluations of the effects of individual interventions, coordination of interventions, financing procedures, and so forth. This approach is relatively new; it was introduced in the 1960s and was based on methods developed to analyze military investments (Klarman, Francis, & Rosenthal, 1968). Health economists have developed four main ways of evaluating this relationship that can be summarized according to the relationships between expenditures and consequences. *Cost minimization* is used when health consequences are considered identical in the two programs (e.g., minor surgery for adults) and the only aim is to evaluate the efficiency component in order to choose the less costly alternative. The *cost–benefit analysis* attempts to value the consequences of programs in monetary terms, so as to be commensurate with the costs. Practically both by the numerator and by the denominator the measure is easily comparable, being expressed only in money terms. The method says nothing about the effects on the patient's health: different programs can show different results on health (differently from cost minimization, where the health consequences must be identical), but they are not considered if they cannot be given a monetary value. *Cost-effectiveness analysis* values the consequences of the financial resources related to programs. The denominator measures health-related units such as "years of life gained." In this technique, a general unit such as "years of life" is implicitly introduced, that is, considered "objectively" worthy of being gained. Nothing in this analysis refers to the evaluation of the values of disability–quality of life states. *Cost–utility analysis* measures the time units adjusted by health utility weights related to the consequences of interventions or coordination of interventions. It can enable the assessment of the quality-of-life adjusted years gained. It is considered particularly useful for those health treatments or programs that extend life only at the expense of side effects (e.g., chemotherapy for certain types of cancer) or treatments with the same mortality rates but different quality of life (such as kidney transplantation versus hemodialysis) and produce reduction in morbidity rather than mortality.

According to these definitions, the low mortality, chronic, long-standing illnesses (such as schizophrenia) seem to require further research on the methods of measuring and integrating costs, health outcomes, and utilities (e.g., to consider measures of the value of disability, the evaluation of quality of life for decision making in the few

years of survival of some tumors has necessarily a different meaning compared to the possible of 50 years of life the schizophrenic patient is expected to survive) on the basis of the interdisciplinary collaboration among the epidemiologist, clinician, health economist, health policy researcher, and so forth.

A number of studies have tried to relate expenditures and health consequences in schizophrenia (for reviews, see Frank, 1985; Knapp & Kavanagh, 1992; Goldberg, 1994). The terms *cost-benefit* and *cost-effectiveness* have been frequently used in a way that is not consistent with the definitions given previously: they are used generally when the economic and clinical-social (symptoms, disabilities, etc.) results are measured and matched. The first attempts at measuring clinical and economic variables were natural studies (Hafner & an der Heiden, 1989; Moscarelli, Capri & Neri, 1991; Santos et al., 1993; Wiersma, 1988, 1991, 1995), randomized controlled trials comparing hospital and community psychiatric treatment or different community programs (Weisbrod, Test, & Stein, 1980; Bond, 1984; Fenton, 1984; Jackson, 1993; Burns, Raftery, Beadsmore, McGuigan, & Dickson, 1993; Marks et al., 1994; Knapp et al., 1994; McCrone, Beecham, & Knapp, 1994), community based treatment and case management approach (Hu & Jerrell, 1991), and outcomes and costs evaluations of different financing strategies (Cole, Reed, Babigian, Brown, & Fray, 1994; Reed, Hennessy, Mitchell, & Babigian, 1994; Wells, 1995).

A number of economic studies were also performed on the cost-effectiveness of drug treatment in schizophrenia, in particular clozapine (Revicki, Luce, Weschler, Brown, & Adler, 1990; Davies & Drummond, 1993; Meltzer et al., 1993). Economic evaluations of drugs are required (e.g., Australia) or encouraged in a number of countries for securing adequate prices and reimbursement status.

Reporting that the development of a new drug in the United States requires a large financial investment, between about $194 million and $231 million, Frankenburg (1993) claims that in past decades the development of antipsychotic drugs were particularly stagnant. If we assume that the drug companies themselves need to follow allocative efficiency (a dollar in research and development of a new drug must be spent on other illnesses if a higher return is expected, such as illnesses with an higher prevalence in the population), the necessity of encouraging the development of new effective drugs for low-prevalence illnesses with high social costs such as schizophrenia seems to require more effective rules for pricing, repricing, and reimbursement future new drugs that can change the health and economic burden of an illness in individuals and society.

The use of the economic research studies being strictly related to decisions in financial allocation by decision makers (e.g., to buy a new drug or prefer the reimbursement of one drug instead of another) raised the problem of potential biases in the conduct and reporting of economic evaluations (Drummond, 1992) and the concern of scientific journals in reviewing articles for publication when the economic evaluation was performed by private, for-profit companies financed by drug companies that can have an interest in presenting favorable results (Kassirer & Angell, 1994).

In general the health and social outcomes in these pioneering cost-effectiveness studies were evaluated according to global data on functioning, symptoms, social disability, satisfaction with care of patients and relatives, quality of life, living arrangements, work functioning, and so forth. Greater attention should be given in the future to evaluating individual items that are particularly disturbing or disabling and/or are responsible for higher services use and costs, and which of the different items are given a priority value by each of the different participants in the health care systems (e.g., patients, clinicians, families, society, drug companies). If only global data are reported, information that can enable sensitive and tailored decisions is hidden.

Two studies were performed in schizophrenia using cost–utility measures. Wilkinson, Williams, Krekorian, McLees, and Falloon (1992) adopted a single value outcome: the utility measure Quality Adjusted Life Year (QALY), calculated using the Chairing Cross health indicator (CH-X; Rosser & Watts, 1972). They suggested that the use of QALY methodology in comparing medical and mental health programs may require the adoption of multidimensional measures of health in order to fulfill its proposed role in priority setting. Cowley and Wyatt (1993) calculated the cost per Disability Adjusted Life Year (DALY) in schizophrenia in order to compare this value to that of other medical illnesses (e.g., coronary artery bypass surgery, cancer treatment programs) for the establishment of financing priorities in developing countries.

A number of prospective clinical studies with economic data are expected in future years, considering individual interventions, coordination of interventions, systems of financing, as well as variations between results of theoretical *efficacy* in randomized clinical trials and results in the practical *effectiveness* of the everyday settings.

In planning these studies, the clinician and the health economist should consider together the aims of the study and which variables need to be measured in order to enable decision makers to use the data properly. Such consideration is essential in order to obtain a comprehensive evaluation of the illness and of its consequences that is relevant and significant not only on the epidemiological-clinical side but also on the economic one.

SETTING PRIORITIES

Using limited resources means, by definition, giving up the opportunity to use them in some other way; providing benefits means forgoing them elsewhere. "Purchasers have to make difficult choices and, in so doing, determine who will die and who will live in what degree of pain and discomfort" (Maynard, 1993, p. 732).

Priority setting means developing analyses and procedures to ensure that the policies that get priorities are those that provide the greatest benefits per additional dollar spent: If the dollars could have been better spent elsewhere, then they should have been spent elsewhere (Mooney & Creese, 1993).

Some analyses have compared costs and effects of a wide range of health interventions in order to inform resource allocations across the entire health care sector. The Oregon Health Services Commission (Kitzhaber, 1993) examined 714 condition–treatment pairs (e.g., appendectomy for acute appendicitis, bone marrow transplant for leukemia) using the QALY (a general utility measure) and calculated the cost per QALY gained. Mental health illnesses and treatments were not considered (Dixon & Welch, 1991). The ranked list of interventions chosen by this process is aimed at selecting the interventions that Medicaid will finance in the state, which plans to fund (in order of the rank list) each intervention maximally until the budget runs out.

In the Health Sector Priorities Review undertaken by the World Bank from 1987 to 1993, 26 major health problems of developing countries were reviewed by teams of economists, public health specialists, and epidemiologists. The cost-effectiveness of more than 50 interventions were evaluated using a standard methodology for costs and benefits. These databases provide information on cost-effectiveness that could help to determine resource allocations across the entire health sector. Cowley and Wyatt (1993) presented a model based on best-case scenario for providing estimates of the cost and cost-effectiveness of a case management program in schizophrenia to be implemented in developing countries. The cost-effectiveness of this model showed a value of $223 per DALY gained, less expensive than most of the adult chronic disease interventions, such as coronary artery bypass and cancer treatment programs.

Building largely on the Health Sector Priorities Review, the World Bank has promoted the *World Development Report—Investing in Health*, in which estimates of the current burden of diseases are combined with a cost-effectiveness rank list of interventions. This combination is aimed at deriving packages of services that, for a given budget, will purchase the largest improvement in health as measured by DALY. In this case, the choice for funding will consider the illnesses that represent a higher burden *and* those for which there are cost-effective interventions. Murray, Kreuser, and Whang (1994) claim that with the use of general health measures (QALY or DALY) comparisons of the cost-effectiveness of interventions targeting different health problems have become possible, and the ranking or "league table" of the cost-effectiveness, the cost per life-year or cost per quality-adjusted life-year gained of different interventions are a natural consequence.

Providing information to the decision maker on priority setting refers fundamentally to a purpose of *equity*. Murray, Loez, and Jamison (1994) state that a major issue in the use of general, universal indices was that when health planners or decision makers are faced with a multitude of health problems and priorities for action, some diseases will have the most influential advocates, whereas some others will continue to be ignored. They claim that a process through which every disease or health problem would be evaluated in an *objective* fashion provides a framework for *objectively* identifying epidemiological priorities, which together with information on cost-effectiveness of interventions can help when decisions on the allocation of resources have to be made.

If the effort made by the World Bank in mapping illness consequences, separating disability severity and duration, and evaluating the burden of individual illnesses on society in the different countries seems relevant, the proposal of general, universal utility measures to objectively evaluate and individually measure disability, death, and their value requires an interdisciplinary methodological discussion. The use of general, universal indices of value for decision making has limitations (Harris, 1987; La Puma & Lawlor, 1990; Eddy, 1991; Spiegelhalter et al., 1992; Salvador, in press).

In sociology the universal values have been considered *values of persuasion* because the universal agreement is only on their vagueness; the more precise they become,

the more they are in conformity with the aspirations of particular groups and the less they are shared by the entire group (Perelman & Olbrechts-Tyteca, 1958). Prost and Jancloes (1993) state that attempts to impose epidemiology as an indisputable tool for decision making, in view of the neutral character of the scientific analysis, are perceived as a limitation to the freedom of judgment, and as a technique to impose targets and objectives that meet the concern of donors rather than the needs of beneficiaries. They warn that any attempt from the payers and from the deciders to impose policy decisions on the basis of an epidemiological rationality will be rejected.

An ethical need seems to require a clear separation between *health states* measures, in which the items to be collected can be chosen by the different parties in health care system but that remain clinical measures (such as symptoms, disabilities, functions, quality of life, side effects) and the measures of the *value given to the different health states* by different parties according to the utility value given by each of them (patients, relatives, clinicians, decision makers, society) to health, impairment, disability, handicap, or quality of life. Consensus is needed among all actors in the health sector (such as providers, users, advocate groups, payers, and policymakers) on the items of interest to be collected and on the value to give to them.

The risk of using current measures such as DALY for priority-setting issues is that when joining two different dimensions into a single universal indicator, the first related to the health state and the second to the value or utility of the health state, this latter is given a hierarchically superior function and the objectivity of the disability as a state is confused with the subjectivity of disability as a value of the state. It does not seem to encourage the long and difficult process of groups of patients with the same illness, in particular for severe illnesses, of developing and establishing their particular perspectives, utilities, and preferences according to their own interests and negotiating for them with the decision makers of the other interest groups in society, with a bottom-up direction.

These issues were considered also by the National Advisory Mental Health Council (1993). It produced a report on the cost of insurance coverage for medical treatment for severe mental illnesses commensurate with the coverage for other illnesses and an assessment of the efficacy of treatment for severe mental disorders in comparison with other medical illnesses. The severity criteria were defined in the domains of recent treatment, symptoms, and social/occupational/school functioning and the Global Assessment Scale rating 50 or less. Simulations of mental health service utilization and costs under various benefit packages commensurate to other medical specialties have been performed using the human capital approach. Further $6.5 billion would be required for providing commensurate coverage for adults and children with severe mental disorders. The annual savings in indirect costs and general medical services are expected to amount to approximately $8.7 billion. A comparison of the burden of illness across different diseases leads to questions of the relative efficiency of using resources to deal with different illnesses. In this study, schizophrenia has been compared with severe diabetes. In 1990 the total cost of severe diabetes was $25 billion (61% direct), and the cost of schizophrenia was $32.5 billion (55% direct). The total direct cost of treating each person with schizophrenia was $7,158, whereas the direct costs of treating each person with severe diabetes was $7,725. This means that per patient, severe diabetes imposes more costs for treatment than does schizophrenia. It also means that the potential gains in terms of reducing morbidity and mortality costs through treatment are greater for schizophrenia (National Advisory Mental Health Council, 1993).

INFORMATION AND CHOICE

In recent years, there has been an impetus for giving to the patients, their families or their agents a more active role in the choice of interventions and professionals. A number of issues are involved: the need for information on the risk (for self, offspring, parents) during life to be affected by severe illnesses, on the available insurance options, on the available preventive and care options and their theorical efficacy, on the different practical effectiveness variability during time of the carers particularly when an illness requires a long-lasting coordination of treatments, and on the expected long-term costs. These attempts are aimed at stimulating competition between carers on the basis of the information to purchasers on their comparable health and economic results.

These changes in the field of medicine must consider how schizophrenic patients, their relatives, and their agents can use these opportunities to actively intervene according to their interests, considering that only a few decades ago the principal interest of society was custody (Clausen, 1989). The voluntary admission to mental hospitals in the United Kingdom was introduced on the basis that the 1930 Mental Health Treatment Act aimed at gradually replacing custody with treatment. The reforms introduced by the 1990 National Health System and the Community Care Act try to encourage patients and users

to put greater emphasis on bottom-up, needs-led decision making (Knapp, 1996b).

The concept of need for medical care, or potential need, where a problem of social disability associated with psychiatric disorder exist irrespective of whether an effective and acceptable solution has been demonstrated (Wing, 1990) can be considered a function of the perspective of who uses the term. Perceived need for services may involve persons who are directly distressed by the symptoms (e.g., pain for physiological problems). From the relative's point of view, perceived need may be influenced by the extent to which a person is suicidal, aggressive, incontinent, or delusional. Health care professionals' points of view tend to define need in terms of whether they think the condition the patient is experiencing should and can be appropriately and effectively treated by the services under consideration. The definition of need by an epidemiologist is more likely to consider needs in terms of some objective definition of disease that can be consistently operationalized. The patient, relative, community member, and health planner may still hold quite divergent concepts of what constitutes need (Cleary, 1989).

The views of mental health consumers on their unmet needs were analyzed in collaboration with the National Alliance for the Mentally Ill (NAMI). The highest levels of unmet need were reported in the areas of keeping busy, recognizing and controlling symptoms, maintaining friendships and intimate relationships, and controlling anger. The factor *role restoration*—consisting of four items related to keeping busy, maintaining friendships, maintaining intimate relationships, and employment— was the strongest factor, constituting a scale with adequate reliability. When considering quality of life, there was a clear link between meeting role restoration needs and achieving an improved quality of life (Uttaro & Mechanic, 1994).

The demand for mental health services also is a relative concept, with the additional issue of the social stigma related to the overt manifestation of psychiatric health problems. It was said that because of stigma many patients do not accept or admit to their difficulties, understand or accept their illness, and actively learn how to cope with their symptoms and disabilities (Leete, 1987). This can overwhelm the weak ability of the patient pushed by distressing experiences to demand help, and push the relatives into asking for obligatory treatment when the situation has become unmanageable. Frequently, this process is experienced by the patient more as "normalization" than as demand for care.

The schizophrenic patients' evaluation of the effects of the care they have received or they expect to receive has a repercussion on their *compliance*. "As obvious as it may appear, it needs to be said that no matter how comprehensive and how good our service system is, it is of no value to those schizophrenics who are unwilling to use it" (Lamb, 1986). The high rate of treatment noncompliance among schizophrenics suggests that the utility patients attribute to interventions must be taken into account (Finn, Bailey, Schultz, & Faber, 1990). In situations with conflicting trade-offs among effects, it may be satisfactory to examine directly the subjective preferences of the consumers or stakeholders and evaluate which outcome patients, family members, clinicians, and taxpayers would prefer. The problem of constructing appropriate utility functions in such complex situations, especially when the stakeholder values may vary according to the stakeholder's position, has not been solved and might be a useful subject for methodological research (Hargreaves & Shumway, 1989). The value given by the patients' relatives to family interventions is also important for their compliance (Tarrier, 1991). In any case, the values given by patients and relatives, however idiosyncratic they might be, are unavoidable, and further research in this field should be developed.

The difficulty for these patients to effectively advocate for themselves and their need for an agent for helping or making the choices is addressed by Frank (1989). He states that in the United States in the 1950s, virtually all decision making in mental health was controlled by professional judgment, subject to budgets set by state legislatures. The greater reliance in recent years on patients behaving as self-interested consumers and on providers as sellers of services must take into account that a large proportion of mental health services that are used by individuals who may be so seriously ill that their decision-making capacity is significantly limited. This leads to the direction of agency relationships that try to make efficient choices for consumers who have their choice capacity more or less impaired in a number of ways.

There is increased attention in providing proper, ready-to-use information to different people involved in decision making, from the individual patient to his or her agent, relatives, providers of services, purchasers, and policymakers. Two important problems related to the provision of information need to be considered. Traditionally, disability has been assessed in a cross-sectional fashion, which defines the prevalence by age and sex of disabling conditions in a population. The retrospective assessment of the underlying cause of disabilities; the

prospective information on the nature, timing, and severity of subsequent complications and associated morbidities; and the impact of interventions need the establishment of *prospective monitoring systems* that can identify new disabilities and then follow the evolution of these disabilities (Murray & Lopez, 1994b). In the meantime, a consensus needs to develop among all actors in the health care system—providers, users, payers, and policymakers—on the information of interest to be collected.

POLICY ETHICS

A major program is performed by the World Bank for improving governmental policies in the management of illnesses and their consequences. Policies are considered successful if they lead to increased welfare through better outcomes, greater equity, more consumer satisfaction, or lower total costs than would occur in the absence of public action. The governmental intervention through the regulation of the competition among providers—including between the public and private sectors, as well as among private providers, whether profit or nonprofit—is considered useful for reaching these purposes. A number of difficulties to the introduction of competition in the health care system are recognized by the World Bank. Sometimes governments themselves artificially stifle competition, interfering unduly with the operation of private health care providers (e.g., protecting domestic producers of drugs and vaccines). Governments may be vulnerable to special interests both within and outside the health system (e.g., protecting domestic industries) and "may not have the capacity to administer or implement policies well . . . may suffer from corruption and from sheer incompetence." The economy of scale in production—which occurs when a single large producer is much more efficient than many small ones—also leads to noncompetitive situations (World Bank, 1993, p. 59).

Another ethical issue to consider is whether the concept of limited available resources or scarcity, which pushes decision makers to choose priorities, should refer only to the health care sector annual budget or should refer to the gross national product as a whole. The proposal by the World Bank of establishing on the basis of equity in different developing countries priorities between "essential" and "discretary" packages of health services to be financed ("discretary" includes, for low-income developing countries, the neuropsychiatric disorders) may give rise to some paradoxical effects in relation to preferences given by societies to the different sources of national expenditures. For example, a low-income developing country had in 1990 a health expenditure (World Bank, 1993) of $12 per capita ($6 public and $6 private). The World Bank report suggested that in low-income developing countries the financing of a number of public health and essential clinical packages, for a spending of $12, could be obtained by shifting financial resources from nonessential or discretionary expenditures. The financing of "discretary" health services for illnesses such as neuropsychiatric disorders should be shifted to other "essential" health services for other illnesses. If we consider this problem of priority in a larger framework, we see that in the same country (World Bank, 1993) there is a total external debt of about $200 per capita, and the 27.9% of central government expenditure is allocated to defense against the 1% to health and the 1.6% to education. It is expected that, in the interest of the development of the world population health, the World Bank will not limit the debate on priorities to the health sector but will also evaluate the setting of priorities between the different sources of expenditures in the different countries.

In front of the government policies for establishing rules for the competition among providers of health services, providers of health technologies, and providers of insurance products, encouragement must be given to the purchasers of these products in order to develop their own technology related to the production and use of the information they need to make choices.

The World Bank suggests a number of government activities for generating the information necessary to guide health policies and public spending and provide certain types of information about provider performance that would be too costly for consumers to collect. The government could then possibly synthesize and publicize this information to aid consumers in making informed choices about health care (World Bank, 1993).

CONCLUSION

Assessing the health situation in populations has traditionally been carried out on the basis of mortality data, and most discussions of international public health priorities ignore issues of disability. This lack of social information on low mortality, chronic, long-standing, disabling illnesses has probably obscured the burden of neuropsychiatric disorders that appear as major problems when using a disability measure (Blue & Harpham, 1994).

A great research effort is needed for improving measures that will enable one to comprehensively evaluate and monitor over time the clinical, social, and economic consequences of severe illnesses. The integration of this interdisciplinary evaluation is expected to determine the value of these losses and the utility of interventions in order to help the individual, the providers, and the purchasers establish their priorities, improve their choices, and develop their policies taking into account the particular aspects of each illness (Moscarelli, 1994).

A great effort is also needed in evaluating individual interventions, coordinations of interventions, comprehensive management systems, as well as the results of health policies themselves to develop a fruitful feedback between health research and practice and policy.

We should at last consider if the current fragmentation of interventions is dependent on the fact that the "real" outcomes of severe mental illnesses are not measured on a large scale and nobody is charged with the responsibility for the health and social outcomes variations of these populations of patients over the years. If the two main goals are the comprehensive, coordinated provision of clinical and social interventions for each individual patient and his or her family from the early phases onwards and the provision of the outcomes information needed by the consumers, agents, and purchasers to make choices, it seems that research into the costs and benefits of few comprehensive care provision systems, focused on individual severe illnesses, acting at a national or international level, and combined with large-scale outcomes information collection should be encouraged.

Research is also needed to evaluate how economy of scale and competition could be addressed together. If health care providers for quite homogeneous populations may act on a large scale, and if their results are measured over time and ready-to-use by purchasers' choices, this could give to the until now socially "invisible" health care product related to the severe chronic illnesses a better chance to compete with the other easily visible and comparable products that are advertised on the market, according to the preferences given by purchasers.

An increasing number of epidemiologists, clinicians, health economists, and health policy researchers are currently involved in the mental health field, and it is hoped that the development of a continuous, interactive relationship between researchers and the decision making in mental health at national and international levels will enable the development of this interdisciplinary field.

REFERENCES

Allen, C., & Beecham, J. (1993). Costing services: Ideals and reality. In A. Netten & J. Beecham (Eds.), *Costing community care*. Cambridge: University Press.

American Psychiatric Association. (1994). *Diagnostic and statistical manual of mental disorders* (4th ed.). Washington, DC: Author.

Andreasen, N. C., & Schultz, S. K. (1996). Assessing the symptoms of schizophrenia. In M. Moscarelli, A. Rupp, & N. Sartorius (Eds.), *Handbook of mental health economics and health policy: 1. Schizophrenia* (pp. 15–22). Chichester: Wiley.

Andrews, G. (1991). The cost of schizophrenia revisited. *Schizophrenia Bulletin, 17,* 389–394.

Andrews, G., Hall, W., Goldstein, G., Lapsley, H., Bartels, R., & Silove, D. (1985). The economic costs of schizophrenia: Implications for public policy. *Archives of General Psychiatry, 42,* 537–543.

Attkinson, C., Cook, J., Karno, M., Lehman A., McGlashan, T. H., Meltzer, H. Y., O'Connor, M., Richardson, D., Rosenblatt, A., Wells, K., Williams, J., & Hohman, A. A. (1992). Clinical services research. *Schizophrenia Bulletin, 18,* 561– 626.

Baker, F., & Intagliata, J. (1982). Quality of life in the evaluation of community support systems. *Evaluation and Program Planning, 5,* 69–79.

Becker, G. (1964). *Human capital.* New York: National Bureau of Economic Research.

Blue, I. & Harpham, T. (1994). The World Bank World Development Report 1993: Investing in health (Reveals the burden of common mental disorders, but ignores its implications): *British Journal of Psychiatry, 165,* 9–12.

Bond, G. R. (1984). An economic analysis of psychosocial rehabilitation. *Hospital and Community Psychiatry, 35,* 356–362.

Burns, T., Raftery, J., Beadsmore, A., McGuigan, S., & Dickson, M. A. (1993). A controlled trial of home-based psychiatric services. 2. Treatment patterns and costs. *British Journal of Psychiatry, 163,* 55–61.

Carpenter, W. T., & Strauss, J. S. (1991). The prediction of outcome in schizophrenia IV: Eleven year follow-up of the Washington follow-up cohort. *Journal of Nervous and Mental Disease, 179,* 517–525.

Clausen, J. A. (1989). Commentary. In C. A. Taube, D. Mechanic, and A. A. Hohmann (Eds.), *The future of mental health services research* (DHHS Publication No. ADM 89–1600, pp. 199–200). Washington, DC: U.S. Government Printing Office.

Cleary, P. D. (1989). The need and demand for mental health services, In: C. A. Taube (Eds.), *The future of mental health services research* (DHHS Publication No. ADM 89–1600, pp. 161–184). Washington, DC: U.S. Government Printing Office.

Cole, R. E., Reed, S., Babigian, H. M., Brown, S., & Fray, J. (1994). A mental health capitation program: I.Patient outcomes. *Hospital and Community Psychiatry, 45, 1090–1096.*

Cooper, J. E. (1993). Draft Paper of ICDH–93. Unpublished manuscript. Geneva: World Health Organization.

Cowley, P., & Wyatt, R. (1993). Schizophrenia and manic-depressive illness. In D. T. Jamison, W. H. Mosley, A. R. Measham, & J. L. Bobadilla (Eds.), *Disease control priorities in developing countries* (pp. 661–670). Oxford: Oxford University Press.

Crow, T. J., McMillan, J. F., Johnson, A. L., & Johnstone, E. C. (1986). The Nortwich Park study of first episodes of schizophrenia. II A randomized controlled trial of prophilactic neuroleptic treatment. *British Journal of Psychiatry, 148,* 120–127.

Davies, L. M., & Drummond, M. F. (1991). The economic cost of schizophrenia. *Psychiatric Bulletin, 14,* 522–525.

Davies, L. M., & Drummond, M. F. (1993). Assessment of costs and benefits of drug therapy for treatment-resistant schizophrenia in the United Kingdom. *British Journal of Psychiatry, 162,* 38–42.

Davies, L. M., & Drummond, M. F. (1994). Economics of schizophrenia: The real cost. *British Journal of Psychiatry, 165* (Suppl. 25), 18–21.

Dixon, J., & Welch, G. H. (1991). Priority setting: Lessons from Oregon. *The Lancet, 337,* 891–894.

Drummond, M. F. (1992). Economic evaluation of pharmaceuticals. Science or marketing? *Pharmacoeconomics, 1,* 8–13.

Drummond, M. F., Stoddart, G. L., & Torrance, G. W. (1987). *Methods for the economic evaluation of health care programms.* Oxford: Oxford University Press.

Eddy, D. M. (1991). Oregon's methods. Did cost-effectiveness analysis fail? *Journal of the American Medical Association, 266,* 2135–2141.

Evers, S. M. M. A., & Ament, A. J. H. A. (1995). Cost of schizophrenia in the Netherlands. *Schizophrenia Bulletin, 21,* 141–153.

Falloon, I. R. H. (1992). Early intervention for first episodes of schizophrenia: A preliminary exploration. *Psychiatry, 55,* 4–15.

Fenton, W. (1996). Longitudinal course and outcome of schizophrenia. In M. Moscarelli, A. Rupp, & N. Sartorius (Eds.), *Handbook of mental health economics and health policy: 1. Schizophrenia* (pp. 79–91). Chichester: Wiley.

Fenton, W. S., & McGlashan, T. H. (1991). Natural history of schizophrenia subtypes. *Archives of General Psychiatry, 48,* 969–986.

Fenton, F. R., Tessier, L. Struening, E. L., Smith, F. A., Bendit, C., Contandriopoulos, A. P., & Nguyen, H. (1984). A two-year follow-up of a comparative trial of the cost-effectiveness of home and hospital psychiatric treatment. *Canadian Journal of Psychiatry, 29,* 205–211.

Finn, S. E., Bailey, J. M., Schultz, R. T., & Faber, R. (1990). Subjective utility ratings of neuroleptics in treating schizophrenia. *Psychological Medicine, 20,* 843–848.

Frank, R. G. (1981). Cost-benefit analysis in mental health services. A review of the literature. *Administration in Mental Health, 8,* 161–175.

Frank, R. G. (1989). Regulatory responses to information deficiencies in the market for mental health services. In C. A. Taube, D. Mechanic, & A. A. Hohmann (Eds.), *The future of mental health services research* (DHHS Publication No. ADM 89–1600, pp. 113–137). Washington, DC: U.S. Government Printing Office.

Frankenburg, F. R. (1993). Is Clozapine worth its cost? *Pharmacoeconomics, 4,* 311–314.

Franks, D. D. (1990). Economic contribution of families caring for persons with severe and persistent mental illness. *Administration and Policy in Mental Health, 18,* 9–18.

Goldberg, D. (1994). Cost-effectiveness in the treatment of patients with schizophrenia. *Acta Psychiatrica Scandinavica, 89* (Suppl. 382), 89–92.

Goldman, H. H., Skodol, A. E., & Lave, T. R. (1992). Revising axis V for DSM-IV: A review of measures of social functioning. *American Journal of Psychiatry, 149,* 1148–1156.

Gunderson, J. G., & Mosher, L. R. (1975). The cost of schizophrenia. *American Journal of Psychiatry, 132,* 901–906.

Hafner, H., & an der Heiden, W. (1989). Effectiveness and cost of community care for schizophrenic patients. *Hospital and Community Psychiatry, 40,* 1, 59–63.

Hafner, H., Richier-Rossler, A., Maurer, K., Fatkenheuer, B., & Loffler, W. (1992). First onset and early symptomatology of schizophrenia. *European Archives of Clinical Neuroscience, 242,* 109–118.

Hargreaves, W. A., & Shumway, M. (1989). Effectiveness of mental health services for the severely mentally ill. In C. A. Taube (Eds.), *The future of mental health services research* (DHHS Publication No. ADM 89–1600, pp. 253–284). Washington, DC: U.S. Government Printing Office.

Hargreaves, W. A., Shumway, M., & Hu, T.-W. (1996). Measuring services use and delivery. In M. Moscarelli, A. Rupp, & N. Sartorius (Eds.), *Handbook of mental health economics and health policy: 1. Schizophrenia* (pp. 347–358). Chichester: Wiley.

Harris, J. (1987). QALYfying the value of human life. *Journal of Medical Ethics, 13,* 117–123.

Hu, T.-W., & Jerrell, J. (1991). Cost-effectiveness of alternative approaches in treating severely mentally ill in California. *Schizophrenia Bulletin, 17,* 461–468.

Hu, T.-W., Shumway, M., & Hargreaves, W. A. (1996). Estimating costs of schizophrenia and its treatment. In M. Moscarelli, A. Rupp, & N. Sartorius (Eds.), *Handbook of mental health economics and health policy: 1. Schizophrenia* (pp. 359–372). Chichester: Wiley.

Jong, A. de, van der Lubbe, P. M., & Wiersma, D. (1996). Social dysfunctioning in rehabilitation: Classification and assessment. In M. Moscarelli, A. Rupp, & N. Sartorius (Eds.), *Handbook of mental health economics and health policy: 1. Schizophrenia* (pp. 27–38). Chichester: Wiley.

Kassirer, J. P., & Angell, M. (1994). The Journal's policy on cost-effectiveness analysis. *New England Journal of Medicine, 331,* 669–670.

Kavanagh, S., Knapp, M. R. J., Beecham, J. K., & Opit, L. (1994). *The cost of schizophrenia care in England: Preliminary estimates* (Discussion Paper 920). Personal Services Research Unit, University of Kent at Canterbury.

Keith, S. J., & Mattews, S. M. (1991). The diagnosis of schizophrenia: A review of onset and duration issues. *Schizophrenia Bulletin, 17,* 51–67.

Kiernan, W. E., & Rowland, S. (1989). Factors contributing to success and failure in the work environment. In W. E. Kiernan & R. L. Schalock (Eds.), *Economics, industry and disability* (pp. 333–349). Baltimore: Paul H. Brookes.

Kitzhaber, J. A. (1993). Prioritizing health services in an era of limits: The Oregon experience. *British Medical Journal, 307,* 373–377.

Klarman, H. E., Francis, J. O. S., & Rosenthal, G. (1968). Cost-effectiveness analysis applied to the treatment of chronic renal disease. *Medical Care, 6,* 48–54.

Knapp, M. (1996a). The health economics of schizophrenia treatment. In M. Moscarelli, A. Rupp, & N. Sartorius (Eds.), *Handbook of mental health economics and health policy: 1. Schizophrenia* (pp. 385–398). Chichester: Wiley.

Knapp, M. (1996b). From psychiatric hospital to community care: Reflections of English experience. In M. Moscarelli, A. Rupp, & N. Sartorius (Eds.), *Handbook of mental health economics and health policy: 1. Schizophrenia* (pp. 475–484). Chichester: Wiley.

Knapp, M., Beecham, J., Koutsogeorgopoulou, V., Hallam, A., Fenyo, A., Marks, I. M., Connolly, J., Audini, B., & Muijen, M. (1994). Service use and costs of home-based versus hospital-based care for people with serious mental illness. *British Journal of Psychiatry, 165,* 195–203.

Knapp, M., & Kavanagh, S. (1992). Health economics relevant to development in community psychiatry. *Current Opinion in Psychiatry, 5,* 314–319.

Lamb, H. R. (1986). Some reflections on treating schizophrenics. *Archives of General Psychiatry, 43,* 1007–1011.

La Puma, J., & Lawlor, E. F. (1990). Quality-adjusted-life-years. Ethical implications for physicians and policymakers. *Journal of the American Medical Association, 263,* 2917–2921.

Leete, E. (1987). The treatment of schizophrenia: The patient's perspective. *Hospital and Community Psychiatry, 38, 405,* 486–491.

Lehman, A. F. (1983). The well-being of chronic mental patients: Assessing their quality of life. *Archives of General Psychiatry, 40,* 369–373.

Lund, T. (1994, October). *Calculation of the costs of schizophrenia in Denmark.* Paper presented at the Third Workshop on Costs and Assessment in Psychiatry, Venice.

Marks, I. M., Connolly, J., Muijen, M., Audini, B., McNamee, G., & Lawrence, R. E. (1994). Home-based versus hospital-based care for people with serious mental illness. *British Journal of Psychiatry, 165,* 179–194.

Maynard, A. (1993). Cost management: The economist's viewpoint. *British Journal of Psychiatry, 163* (Suppl. 20), 7–13.

McCrone, P., Beecham, J., & Knapp, M. (1994). Community psychiatric nurse teams: Cost/effectiveness of intensive support versus generic care. *British Journal of Psychiatry, 165,* 218–221.

McGuire, T. (1991). Measuring the economic cost of schizophrenia. *Schizophrenia Bulletin, 17,* 375–388.

Meltzer, H. Y., Cola, P., Way, L., Thompson, P. A., Bastani, B., Davies, M. A., & Snitz, B. (1993). Cost-effectiveness of Clozapine in neuroleptic-resistant schizophrenia. *American Journal of Psychiatry, 150,* 1630–1638.

Mooney, G., & Creese, A. (1993). Priority setting for health service efficiency: The role of measurement of burden of illness. In D. T. Jamison, W. H. Mosley, A. R. Measham, & J. L. Bobadilla (Eds.), *Disease control priorities in developing countries* (pp. 731–740). Oxford: Oxford University Press.

Morgan, R., & Creadie, A. J. (1975). Unemployment impeded resettlement. *Social Psychiatry, 10,* 63–67.

Moscarelli, M. (1994). Health and economic evaluation in schizophrenia. Implications for health policies. *Acta Psychiatrica Scandinavica, 89* (Suppl. 382), 84–88.

Moscarelli, M., Capri, S., & Neri, L. (1991). Cost evaluation of chronic schizophrenic patients during the first 3 years after first contact. *Schizophrenia Bulletin, 17,* 421–426.

Murray, C. J. L. (1994a). Quantifying the burden of disease: The technical basis for disability-adjusted life years. *Bulletin of the World Health Organization, 72,* 429–445.

Murray, C. J. L., Kreuser, J., & Whang, W. (1994). Cost-effectiveness analysis and policy choices: Investing in health systems. *Bulletin of the World Health Organization, 72,* 663–674.

Murray, C. J. L., & Lopez, A. D. (1994). Quantifying disability: Data, methods and results. *Bulletin of the World Health Organization, 72,* 481–494.

Murray, C. J. L., Lopez, A. D., & Jamison, D. T. (1994). The global burden of disease in 1990: Summary results, sensitivity analysis and future directions. *Bulletin of the World Health Organization, 72,* 495–589.

National Advisory Mental Health Council (1993). Health care reform for Americans with severe mental illnesses. *American Journal of Psychiatry, 150,* 1447–1465.

National Institute of Mental Health (1991). *Caring for people with mental disorders: A national plan of research to improve services.* (DHHS Publications No. ADM 91–1762).

Perelman, C., & Olbrechts-Tyteca, (1958). *Traité de l'Argumentation. La Novelle Rhetorique,* Presses, Universitaires de France.

Prost, A., & Jancloes, M. (1993). Rationale for choice in public health: The role of epidemiology. In D. T. Jamison, W. H. Mosley, A. R. Measham, & J. L. Bobadilla (Eds.), *Disease control priorities in developing countries* (pp. 661–670). Oxford: Oxford University Press.

Reed, S. K., Hennessy, K. D., Mitchell, O. S., & Babigian, H. M. (1994). A mental health capitation program. II. Cost-benefit analysis. *Hospital and Community Psychiatry, 45,* 1097–1103.

Revicki, D. A., Luce, B. R., Weschler, J. M., Brown, R. E., & Adler, M. A. (1990). Cost-effectiveness of Clozapine for treatment-resistant schizophrenic patients. *Hospital and Community Psychiatry, 41,* 850–854.

Rice, D. P. (1966). *Estimating the cost of illness.* Health Economics Series, No. 6 (DHEW Publication No. PHS 947–6, U.S.).

Rice, D. P., Kelman, S., & Miller, L. (1992, September). *The economic burden of schizophrenia.* Paper presented in the Sixth Biennial Research Conference on the Economics of Mental Health, Bethesda, MD.

Robinson, J. C. (1986). Phylosophical origins of the economic value of life. *Millbank Memorial Fund Quarterly, 64,* 133–135.

Rosser, R. M., & Watts, V. C. (1972). The measurement of hospital output. *International Journal of Epidemiology, 1,* 361–368.

Rupp, A., & Keith, S. J. (1993). The cost of schizophrenia. Assessing the burden. *Psychiatric Clinics of North America, 16,* 413–423.

Salvador-Carulla, L. (1997). Measuring quality of life in economic analysis: Controversies and use in mental health. In H. Katschning, H. Freeman, & N. Sartorius (Eds.), *Quality of life in mental disorders.* Chichester: Wiley.

Salvador-Carulla, L., & Velasquez, R. (1996). Vocational assessment in schizophrenia. In M. Moscarelli, A. Rupp, & N. Sartorius (Eds.), *Handbook of mental health economics and health policy: 1. Schizophrenia* (pp. 51–64). Chichester: Wiley.

Santos, A. B., Hawikins, G. D., Julius, B., Deci, P. A., Hiers, T. H., & Burns, B. J. (1993). A pilot study of assertive community treatment for patients with chronic psychotic disorders. *American Journal of Psychiatry, 150,* 501–504.

Sartorius, N. (1995). Economics of anxiety and depression—forward. *The British Journal of Psychiatry, 166,* Suppl. 27.

Schelling, T. C. (1968). The life you save may be your own. In S. B. Chase (Ed.), *Problems in public expenditure analysis.* Washington: The Brookings Institute.

Spigehalter, D. J., Gore, S. M., Fitzpatrick, R., Fletcher, A. E., Jones, D. R., & Cow, D. R. (1992). Quality of life measures in health care. III. Resources allocation. *British Medical Journal, 305,* 1205–1209.

Tarrier, N. (1991). Some aspects of family interventions in schizophrenia. I. Adherence to interventions programs. *British Journal of Psychiatry, 159,* 475–480.

Uttaro, T., & Mechanic, D. (1994). The NAMI consumer survey analysis of unmet needs. *Hospital and Community Psychiatry, 45,* 372–374.

Weisbrod, B., Test, M., & Stein, I. (1980). An alternative to mental hospital treatment. 2. Economic cost benefit analysis. *Archives of General Psychiatry, 37,* 400–405.

Wells, K. B. (1995). Cost containment and mental health outcomes: Experiences from U.S. studies. *British Journal of Psychiatry, 166* (Suppl. 27), 43–51.

Wesoleck, J. S., & McFarlane, F. R. (1991). Current developments in vocational assessment and evaluation in the USA. In *Vocational assessment and evaluation: Report of the seminar of the vocational commission* (pp. 18–32). Hoehnsbroeck, Holland: Rehabilitation International.

Wiersma, D., Giel, R., de Jong, A., & Sloof, C. J. (1988). Schizophrenia: Results of a cohort study with respect to cost-accounting problems of patterns of mental health care in relation to course of illness. In D. Schwefel, H. Zollner, & P. Potthoff. (Eds.), *Costs and effects of managing chronic psychotic patients* (pp. 115–125). Berlin: Springer Verlag.

Wiersma, D., Kluiter, H., Nienhuis, F., Ruphan, M., & Giel, R.

(1991). Costs and benefits of a day treatment with community care for schizophrenic patients. *Schizophrenia Bulletin, 17,* 411–419.

Wiersma, D., Kluiter, H., Nienhuis, F. J., Ruphan, M., & Giel, R. (1995). Costs and benefits of hospital and day treatment with community care of affective and schizophrenic disorders. *British Journal of Psychiatry, 166* (Suppl. 27), 52–59.

Wilkinson, G., Williams, B., Krekorian, H., McLees, S., & Falloon, I. (1992). QALY in mental health: A case study. *Psychological Medicine, 22,* 725–731.

Wing, J. K. (1990). Meeting the needs of people with psychiatric disorders. *Social Psychiatry and Psychiatric Epidemiology, 25,* 2–8.

World Bank. (1993). *World development report 1993—Investing in health.* New York: Oxford University Press.

World Health Organization. (1980). *International classification of impairment, disabilities and handicaps (ICIDH).* Geneva: Author.

World Health Organization. (1980). *International classification of impairments, disabilities and handicaps.* Geneva, WHO.

World Health Organization. (1988). *WHO psychiatric disability assessment schedule (WHO-DAS).* Geneva: Author.

Wyatt, R. J., Henter, I., Leary, M. C., & Taylor, E. (1995). An economic evaluation of schizophrenia—1991. *Social Psychiatry and Psychiatric Epidemiology, 30,* 196–205.

CHAPTER 19

SOCIAL SKILLS TRAINING

Alex Kopelowicz
Patrick W. Corrigan
Mark Schade
Robert Paul Liberman

Schizophrenia can no longer be viewed as a chronic, inexorably deteriorating disorder with little chance for rehabilitation or recovery. Outcome studies from the United States, Europe, and Japan have repeatedly demonstrated that when people with even severe forms of schizophrenia are evaluated 20 to 40 years after the most disabling period of their illness, more than half are functioning in a reasonably normal way (Harding, Brooks, Ashikaga, & Strauss, 1987; Ciompi, 1980; Bleuler, 1968). However, these felicitous outcomes are achieved only if treatment and rehabilitative services are continuously provided to individuals and their families (Harding, Zubin, & Strauss, 1992).

This hopeful viewpoint has contributed to a paradigm shift in the treatment for schizophrenia. Practitioners are no longer content to rely solely on a biomedical model of treatment that reduces the disorder to the biological correlates of psychotic symptoms. Instead, a biopsychosocial perspective, which emphasizes the interaction among the brain, behavior, and the environment (Engel, 1977, 1980),

serves as the foundation for the rapidly growing field of psychiatric rehabilitation. Psychiatric rehabilitation has arisen specifically to develop, evaluate, and disseminate those techniques which improve the social functioning of people with serious mental illnesses such as schizophrenia.

In this chapter, we will focus on one of the most well-studied and widely utilized rehabilitation modalities, social skills training. We will provide a brief historical background of social skills training with an overview of variations in training formats. We will review the research literature vis-à-vis schizophrenia, with particular emphasis on social functioning. This will lead to a discussion of the limitations of social skills training for this population and to descriptions of some of the newer technologies designed to overcome these limitations. Finally, we will consider the variety of social and cultural norms that define effective social functioning and address how these norms may influence the maintenance and generalization of social skills.

VULNERABILITY-STRESS-PROTECTIVE FACTORS MODEL OF SCHIZOPHRENIA

Models of social skills training for schizophrenia have been influenced by two scientific disciplines: experimental psychopathology and behavior therapy. Experimental psychopathologists have developed a vulnerability-stress

model to describe the relationships among socioenvironmental stressors that act on the biochemical vulnerabilities underlying schizophrenia, producing its characteristic symptoms and debilitating social dysfunctions (Goldstein, 1987; Zubin & Spring, 1977). According to this model, people who develop schizophrenia are born with enduring, subtle psychobiological vulnerabilities which may become manifest neurodevelopmentally as attentional and

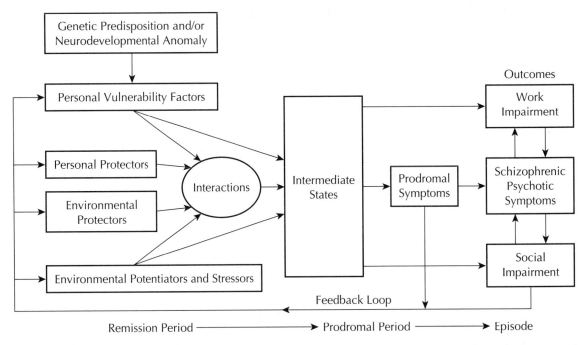

Figure 19.1. This diagram is a heuristic framework for possible vulnerability, stress, and protective factors in the course of schizophrenic disorders. Vulnerabilty factors are relatively enduring abnormalities of individuals at risk for schizophrenia that are present before, during, and after psychotic episodes. Given that 60 to 70% of the liability to develop schizophrenia is likely due to genetic factors, we hypothesize that some personal vulnerability factors will reflect a specific *genetic predisposition* to schizophrenia. In some cases of schizophrenia, however, a *neurodevelopmental anomaly caused by environmental factors* (e.g., exposure of the biological mother to influenza virus during the second trimester) may create similar neurobiological vulnerability without specific genetic predisposition. *Potentiators* are biological and psychosocial environmental factors during an individual's development that raise the likelihood that vulnerability to schizophrenia will be activated into schizophrenic symptomatology under a given level of stress. *Precipitating stressors* are transient events that demand adaptive changes from the individual, challenge the individual's current coping abilities, and sometimes serve as triggers for psychotic episodes. *Personal and environmental protective factors* allow a vulnerable individual to reduce the deleterious effects of environmental potentiators and stressors, resulting in decreased likelihood that a psychotic episode will occur.

According to this framework, vulnerability factors in the individual interact with environmental potentiators and stressors to produce *transient intermediate states* that precede the development of prodromal symptoms, particularly if personal and environmental protective factors are not sufficient buffers. The transient intermediate states reflect subclinical processes that often lead to *clinically observable prodromal symptoms* unless an intervention occurs. Prodromal symptoms, in turn, proceed to a schizophrenic psychotic episode through continued interaction of vulnerability and stress factors. Prodromal symptoms may contribute to stressors in the natural environment by disrupting supportive social relationships that would usually serve as protective factors. The development of symptoms is viewed as continuing, unless successfully interrupted by increases in protective factors, until an individual's threshold for the development of psychotic symptoms is reached. The outcomes of these processes are shown as *schizophrenic psychotic symptoms, work impairment,* and *social impairment.*

schizotypal abnormalities. When under stress, an individual who has these vulnerabilities may develop prodromal symptoms during adolescence, which may then emerge as psychotic symptoms at the onset of the disorder. Stressors may take the form of major life events that everyone experiences as they progress through various life stages (e.g., leaving home for college or military service, developing sexual relationships).

The combination of prodromal symptoms and cognitive vulnerabilities are thought to thwart the acquisition of social and coping skills during key periods of adolescence and young adulthood by individuals destined to develop schizophrenia. As a result, many patients with schizophrenia show an impoverished repertoire of social and independent living skills, especially those who have an early onset of the disorder before passing social maturational milestones. Individuals with few social and coping skills, and with bizarre and unpredictable symptoms and behavior, can become alienated from their family and friends; consequently, their support network can become severely depleted (Holmes-Eber & Riger, 1990; Meeks & Murrell, 1994). It is no accident that upwards of one-third of all those who homelessly roam the streets of our inner cities are suffering from schizophrenia (Koegel, 1991). In this developmental cascade of diminished interpersonal skills and social support, individuals who have the vulnerability to schizophrenia have a low threshold to life stressors (Ventura, Nuechterlein, Hardesty, & Gitlin, 1992).

More recently, the vulnerability-stress model has been expanded to include protective factors, schematically outlined in Figure 19.1. The vulnerability-stress-protective factors model is useful because it suggests how psychiatric interventions may be designed to have a positive impact on schizophrenia (Nuechterlein & Dawson, 1984; Anthony & Liberman, 1992). Therapeutic interventions can be targeted at reducing stress (as through avoiding challenging situations), enhancing protective factors (as in building coping skills and social support through family education), and mitigating brain vulnerability (as through antipsychotic drugs). For example, antipsychotic medications likely ameliorate acute symptoms and moderate hyperaroused states through blocking certain neurotransmitter receptors, thereby buffering the underlying, biological vulnerability to psychosis. Social skills training can help individuals who suffer from schizophrenia learn various interpersonal and coping skills and therefore become more resilient to stressors. Thus, an enhanced repertoire of social skills can diminish the likelihood of stress-induced relapses (Liberman, Vaccaro, & Corrigan, 1995).

BEHAVIORAL MODELS OF SKILLS TRAINING

Behavior therapy has led to development of the technology that drives social skills training. Three models of social skills training can be differentiated by their distinctive targets for training of social behavior: response topography, content-related behavior, and cognitive problem-solving skills (Corrigan, Schade, & Liberman, 1992; Morrison & Bellack, 1984; Wallace et al., 1980). Topographical models focus on the specific nonverbal and paralingusitic behaviors that comprise interpersonal behaviors such as voice volume, fluency, eye contact, and hand gestures. This model contrasts with skills training which targets content-related behaviors, such as expressing appreciation, making a positive statement, and requesting information. In both topographic and content-related models (Bellack, Morrison, & Mueser, 1989; Trower, 1982), participants in skills training learn the expressive components of social skills, which they might later call upon to address interpersonal and instrumental needs; for example, participants in a training program for conversation skills learn how to introduce themselves: "Hi. My name is Mary. What's yours?" Unfortunately, these expressive components do not help an individual to flexibly develop responses needed for novel situations. For example, what does one say to the reply, "Why do you want to know my name?"

Patients who learn cognitive problem solving may acquire a more flexible repertoire of social skills. Rather than learning mechanical formulas, or "sending skills," to react to specific cues, patients learn to accurately perceive and interpret social situations and interactions, to generate alternatives for coping with a problem situation, and to use appropriate verbal and nonverbal skills to put into effect one of the alternatives. In short, problem solving enables individuals to learn social norms or behavioral rules that help them negotiate interpersonal situations.

The seven steps of interpersonal problem solving, summarized in Table 19.1, help patients overcome obstacles that block attaining interpersonal goals (D'Zurilla, 1986; Platt & Spivack, 1972a, 1972b). For example, encouraging patients to list *all* possible solutions to a problem overcomes the tendency to rely on the first idea that occurs to an individual. By discouraging "premature closure," skills trainers may facilitate the successful resolution of the identified problem. Effective problem-solving skills have been shown to correlate positively with social competence and inversely with severe psychopathology (D'Zurilla, 1986; Phillips, 1978). In comprehensive skills training

Table 19.1.   Seven Steps of Problem Solving

1. Stop and think: How do you problem solve?
2. What is the problem?
3. What are the different ways the problem can be solved?
4. Evaluate the alternatives.
5. Choose and plan to implement one or more of the alternatives.
6. What resources will you need?
7. Set a time to implement your chosen solution and DO IT!

programs, patients learn to mix topographic, content-related, and problem-solving behaviors and the fundamentals of independent living skills in mastering rules that can be used to mold these fundamentals into individually meaningful responses.

FOCUS AND FORMAT OF SOCIAL SKILLS TRAINING

Skills trainers share the conviction that a structured, learning-oriented approach is an important component of psychiatric rehabilitation for the many people with schizophrenia or other disabling mental illnesses. The process of psychiatric rehabilitation begins with a comprehensive assessment of individuals' personal goals for role functioning in social, occupational, residential, and recreational domains of life. This overall perspective "frames" the functional and symptom assessment process which identifies the individuals' assets, symptoms, deficits, unacceptable and deviant behaviors, motivating reinforcers, and environmental supports and resources. The results of the assessment are used to formulate realistic and incremental goals that specify improvements in functioning to be achieved with interventions included in the rehabilitation plan. The interventions are based on a biopsychosocial approach to treatment: maintenance psychopharmacotherapy ("bio") combined with training in social and independent living skills, supplemented with the supportive services that sustain individuals' use of these skills in their living environments ("psychosocial").

In general, skills training increases coping and competence by promoting the acquisition of skills specific to the individual and the demands of his or her environments. For severely disabled psychiatric patients, rehabilitation goals may include acquisition of a daunting range of cognitive and behavioral skills, such as medica-

tion self-administration, negotiating with mental health providers, responding appropriately to supervision in the workplace, self-monitoring of ongoing psychiatric symptoms, independently completing basic self-care behaviors such as grooming and appearance, talking to others without stigmatizing oneself, stress management, and self-control of anger and hostility. The acquisition of these and other relevant skills assist individuals recovering from psychiatric disability by increasing their competence in a greater variety of challenging situations, thus reducing their risk of succumbing to stress-induced, psychotic relapses.

Quality of life is also enhanced by skills training. From the patients' perspective, they are provided with a sense of personal effectiveness and a wider range of realistic choices among social, vocational, recreational, and community living situations which they can adequately cope with and enjoy. Thus, skills training clearly belongs within the broad framework of psychiatric rehabilitation with severely disabled individuals (Anthony & Liberman, 1992).

Skills trainers select from an arsenal of behavioral teaching methods which utilize operant and social learning principles derived from applied behavior analysis. These techniques, which include shaping, modeling, reinforcement, instructions, and prompts, have been found to be effective with cognitively and behaviorally disabled psychiatric patients (Corrigan et al., 1992; Paul & Menditto, 1992; Wallace et al., 1980). The choice of which basic methods to use in a skills training program depends on the current functioning of the patient and the focus of training. For example, a patient with relatively intact conversational skills and a relatively good level of functioning who wishes to practice job interviewing skills may need only a few sessions of role playing with a trainer modeling the appropriate behavior. In contrast, a patient who has lived most of his life in a state hospital, has significant positive and negative symptoms, and has never developed even rudimentary verbal skills will need a more in-depth program which may use a shaping, prompting, and generalization protocol to build and reinforce appropriate behaviors (Massell, Corrigan, Liberman, & Milan, 1991). Thus, skills training formats may differ on such dimensions as the relative emphasis placed on specific techniques; the frequency, standardization, and duration of the interventions; and the level and complexity of the targeted social deficits. Three different skills training programs will be described in sufficient detail to illustrate this variety.

Individualized Social Skills Training

The most flexible and widely applicable form of skills training tailors the training goals to the individualized needs and preferences of the patient (Liberman, King, DeRisi, & McCann, 1975; Liberman, DeRisi, & Mueser, 1989). The initial challenge to the practitioner is to help the patient articulate and identify his/her long-term personal goals—in the domains of family life, friendships, work, education, recreation, and instrumental role functioning. This may require specific and structured questioning such as, "How would you like your life to change for the better?" or "What kinds of activities and relationships would you like to have a year from now?" Examples of overall, personal goals include *having at least two friends with whom I can do things and go places, holding a job, completing a course in a community college,* and *having a positive relationship with my family.*

Reaching the long-term, personal goals requires a stepwise approach with many intermediate steps or subgoals, each of which is practiced in the training sessions and attained in real-life, homework assignments. For example, one patient whose schizophrenic symptoms were in remission had as his personal, overall goals (1) increasing his involvement and success in music; (2) improving the supportiveness and reciprocity in his family relations; (3) increasing the scope of his work assignments at his volunteer job; and (4) increasing his social network. For the first goal, numerous intermediate steps were rehearsed in the skills training group, including:

- Making contact with his brother, who was in the music business, and asking him to arrange a test recording with Capitol Records.
- Calling Capitol Records and making a positive request for a recording date.
- Interacting with the staff at Capitol Records when making the recording.
- Asking a hospital employee if he might teach her daughter how to play the keyboard or piano for a modest fee.
- Following up with this person to confirm a date and time for the initial lesson.
- Calling his brother and asking about additional opportunities for him to play his music.

It is clear that a shaping approach is utilized in this individualized form of skills training, with the key elements being repeated practice in the training sessions, abundant praise and social reinforcement for progress, and successful homework assignments. The latter sometimes requires

having a staff person accompany the individual into the natural environment and demonstrate or model the interaction that needs to be used by the patient.

During training, the patient engages in a role play of a desired interaction that would be a step toward achieving his/her personal, long-term goals. Alternatively, the patient might select a problem situation that has occurred recently or is likely to occur again in the near future, often using other group members to participate in relevant roles. For the first role play or "dry run" of each problem situation, the patient is instructed to act as if he or she were in the actual situation. Assets, deficits, and excesses in performance are noted, and the individual is praised for appropriate behaviors and efforts. Other group members are encouraged to offer positive feedback. Feedback may initially be immediate in practice situations, but is increasingly delayed over time, while instructor assistance is faded.

In subsequent role plays, the trainer demonstrates the target behaviors, prompts the patient to perform specific responses, and reinforces successive approximations to the desired goal. Component behaviors are added one by one. As one component skill (e.g., eye contact) is mastered, others (e.g., facial expression, vocal tone, loudness, posture, speech content) are sequentially introduced. After each role play, appropriate elements of the individual's performance are praised and corrective feedback is provided. Generalization of the newly learned behavior to real-life situations is promoted by giving homework assignments to practice the skills in the natural environment and providing positive feedback for successful performance. Transfer of skills may be further facilitated by repeated practice and overlearning, fading the amount of structure and frequency of training over time, and enlisting the help of friends, family members, psychiatric staff, and others to ensure that the natural environment is socially responsive and reinforcing to the patient's performance of competent behavior. This approach also allows techniques for remediating attentional and information processing deficits to be incorporated into the training protocols (Liberman, Mueser, Wallace, Jocobs, Eckman, & Massel, 1986; Wallace, 1982; Wallace et al., 1980).

Social Skills Training Modules: Structured Curricula

Structured curricula focus on a specific group of skills which represent a domain of integrated behaviors (such as conversational skills, symptom monitoring, and job skills) that are of functional utility for a large number of individuals with schizophrenia. In these curricula, patients proceed through a series of skill-building exercises in a structured, standardized format that follows a preset sequence. These exercises include the full range of shaping and teaching techniques adapted for patient groups who are able to sustain their attention and process verbal information for at least 45-minute sessions (Corrigan et al., 1992; Sprafkin, Gershaw, & Goldstein, 1993). The targeted skills are broken into manageable steps, but represent a functional grouping of integrated behaviors needed to perceive situations accurately, select appropriate responses, accurately perform the behaviors required, and adapt to problematic or unexpected situations.

Investigators at the UCLA Clinical Research Center for Schizophrenia and Psychiatric Rehabilitation have designed step-by-step multimedia curricula for training social and independent living skills to people with severe mental illness. Several user-friendly modules are now available, including Basic Conversation, Recreation for Leisure, Community Re-Entry, Symptom Self-Management, and Medication Self-Management (Psychiatric Rehabilitation Consultants, 1994). Together, the modules form a comprehensive rehabilitation program, but they also can be used selectively in combination with existing programs in a wide variety of hospital and community settings.

Each module includes a Trainer's Manual with stepwise instructions, a Patient's Workbook with exercises and homework assignments, and a videocassette to be shown to patients, demonstrating the skills to be learned. The techniques described in the Trainer's Manual for each component include all of the behavioral learning principles known to help people with schizophrenia overcome their learning disabilities: behavioral rehearsal, repetition and overlearning, coaching, shaping and fading, modeling, video feedback, and positive reinforcement. Each module is divided into separate skill areas that have specific educational objectives. The patients proceed through each skill area by employing eight learning activities (see Table 19.2).

The Medication Self-Management module has five skill areas: obtaining information about antipsychotic medication; correctly self-administering and evaluating the medication's effects and side effects; identifying the side effects of the medication and distinguishing between benign and serious side effects; negotiating medication issues with health care providers; and understanding the

Table 19.2. Learning Activities for Each Skill Area

LEARNING ACTIVITY	TRAINER'S TASKS
1. Introduction to Skill Area	Tell participants the skills that will be taught and the benefits of learning them.
2. Videotape and Questions/Answers	Show participants a videotaped demonstration of the skills and ask questions to be sure the material is understood.
3. Role Play	Help participants practice the skills.
4. Resource Management	Teach participants to identify the resources needed to perform the skills and methods of obtaining these resources.
5. Outcome Problems	Teach participants to solve problems that might occur when the skills are used in new situations.
6. In Vivo Exercises	Supervise participants as they perform the skills in new situations.
7. Homework Assignments	Encourage participants to perform the skills independently in new situations.
8. Booster Sessions	Provide participants with "refresher" courses on an as-needed basis.

value and benefit of using long-acting neuroleptics. In the Symptom Self-Management module, patients learn how to identify the warning signs of relapse; how to intervene early to prevent relapse once these signs appear; how to cope with the persistent psychotic symptoms that continue despite medications; and how to avoid alcohol and other drugs of abuse. Each skill area can be further divided into target behaviors. For example, in the skill area "Identifying Warning Signs of Relapse," patients learn how to discuss warning signs with their relatives and physician so that there is agreement on the symptoms that predict relapse (e.g., insomnia, irritability, social withdrawal, ideas of reference). Patients are also taught to keep a checklist of warning signs for monitoring themselves over time. This is designed to help patients understand the benefits of early intervention and realize when to request help.

These modules were designed to compensate for the cognitive and symptomatic obstacles to learning that are regularly experienced by many patients with schizophrenia. The results of a controlled clinical trial of these two skills training modules documented their efficacy in a carefully selected group of schizophrenic patients who were studied in a research clinic at the UCLA-affiliated West Los Angeles VA Medical Center (Eckman et al., 1992). Eighty outpatients with DSM-III-R schizophrenia who were receiving standardized maintenance neuroleptic therapy were randomly assigned to group therapy or to structured, modularized skills training. After the 6-month training period, patients who received skills training made significant gains in each of the areas taught, whereas those in group therapy did not. These skills were retained one year after training was completed.

The significant effect of module training on skill acquisition was particularly impressive, because it occurred in spite of patients' varied levels of baseline psychopathology and was documented by research staff members interacting with patients outside of the module training sessions. Statistical analyses revealed that patients who were high in negative or positive symptoms (or both) were able to master and retain skills, although greater effort was required of trainers in teaching more symptomatic patients. Furthermore, after patients had completed the module training, research nurses and case managers rated patients' use of the specific medication and symptom management skills in their everyday life; in all areas that were rated, subjects who participated in the modules were rated as using significantly more of the designated skills than comparison group subjects. These findings indicated that the modules were useful for schizophrenic patients with severe psychopathology, and that module skills were utilized outside of the formal classes that were held in a research clinic.

In a separate publication, the authors noted that nearly all of the patients who participated in skills training regularly monitored their warning signs throughout the training period, reflecting an increase in the collaborative relationship with the prescribing clinician (Wirshing, Eckman, Liberman, & Marder, 1991). Other results suggest that these skills may help patients cope better with prodromes, thereby surviving longer in the community (Wirshing et al., 1991).

A second goal of the study was to evaluate the effect of skills training on social adjustment. Subjects who were randomly assigned to skills training (versus supportive group therapy) showed significantly improved participation in social and recreational activities, greater social intimacy and independence, significantly more employment, and significantly better subjective quality of life. Furthermore, the skills learned in the modules appeared to complement the protective effects of antipsychotic medication against relapse since subjects assigned to skills training plus placebo supplementation at times of incipient relapse had significantly fewer relapses than their counterparts who received supportive group therapy plus placebo (Marder et al., 1996).

More recently, studies using the training modules from the UCLA Social and Independent Living Skills Program on outpatient populations have demonstrated that the training of interpersonal problem-solving skills generates improved social adjustment in the community and that 6 months of 12 hours per week of training, in conjunction with clinical case management aimed to generalize the skills into the patients' natural living environments, produced better social functioning, lower relapse rates, and higher subjective quality of life than a contrast program using traditional, psychosocial occupational therapy (Liberman et al., 1993).

Comprehensive Social Learning Program

The Social Learning Program (Paul & Lentz, 1977) is a highly structured, comprehensive learning environment for severely disabled, treatment refractory, institutionalized psychiatric patients. The program uses the full range of behavioral teaching strategies to promote acquisition of skills for independent, community living and self-control of problem behaviors. The program combines ongoing observation of behavior with a variety of structured teaching situations to provide a continuous training environment during all waking hours. In addition, an elaborate token economy system promotes patient participation. Patients monitor their own progress through a level system of gradually increasing responsibilities and privileges, in which they are weaned from staff supervision and the token economy, and are increasingly exposed to community settings. The Social Learning Program has been demonstrated to be the psychiatric rehabilitation treatment of choice for this patient population (Glynn & Mueser, 1992; Paul & Menditto, 1992).

EFFICACY OF SOCIAL SKILLS TRAINING

There are a number of considerations in evaluating the effectiveness and usefulness of social skills training. First, it is essential to determine whether the training results in the acquisition of the desired skills. Second, the acquired skills must be durable; that is, patients should be able to perform the skills at adequate levels long after the completion of the initial skills training. "Booster sessions" may be required on a periodic basis to refresh a patient's memory and to reinforce the skills that have been learned. Finally, for patients to receive the maximum benefit from skills training, they must be able to generalize and apply the skills to a variety of real-life situations outside the treatment setting. Like any transfer of learning, successful generalization is dependent on a responsive social environment that gives opportunities, encouragement, and reinforcement for using the skills learned during training sessions.

In the past few years, a number of reviews have been published on skills training for schizophrenia which have summarized most of the research conducted prior to 1990 (Donahoe & Driesenga, 1988; Benton & Schroeder; 1990; Corrigan, 1991; Halford & Hayes, 1991). More recently, a review of the literature and review of the reviews was conducted by the Schizophrenia Patient Outcomes Research Team (PORT) (Lehman & Steinwachs, 1994). This section will focus on the results of these reviews and data from more recent studies.

Acquisition

The acquisition of targeted skills immediately after training has been measured using naturalistic observation, role-play tests, and self-report. Although naturalistic observation has been argued to be a more reliable and valid measure of skill acquisition than role play (Bellack, Hersen, & Turner, 1978), researchers most commonly evaluate the success of training by constructing role-play situations specific to the content of the social skills training intervention tested in their investigation. Role-play tests have been shown to be reliable and valid as evidenced by high interrater agreement and significant correlations between role-play tests and more direct measures of social competence (Bellack, Morrison, Mueser, Wade, & Sayers, 1990). Self-report measures such as the Social Adjustment Scale II (Weissman & Bothwell, 1976), are relatively easy to collect, but are not very sensitive to the effects of focal social skills training (Corrigan, 1991).

The results of a meta-analysis evaluating all three data collection methods indicated that social skills training strongly and consistently enhanced acquisition of skills in a psychotic (predominantly schizophrenic) population (Corrigan, 1991). Other reviews mentioned above echo

the conclusion that individuals with schizophrenia are capable of learning new skills through skills training (Lehman & Steinwachs, 1994). Although acquisition is the necessary first step in the skills training endeavor, the strength of these findings has led researchers to focus more recent studies of social skills training on the maintenance and generalization of skills training, as well as on reductions in positive and negative symptoms, quality of life, and relapse and rehospitalization rates (Wong et al., 1993; Dobson, McDougall, Busheikin, & Aldous, 1993; Matousek, Edwards, Jackson, Rudd, & McMurray, 1992; Hayes, Halford, & Varghese, 1994).

Maintenance

After a patient has acquired a skill in a behavioral program, it is important that the skill become a relatively permanent element in his or her behavioral repertoire. If the skill is either forgotten after the patient leaves the skills training program, or if the skill is not used in natural situations, the training will make little difference on any outcome measure of practical interest. To properly test the maintenance of skills, assessment should be done using measures in conditions similar to those used to assess skill acquisition. Almost all the studies reviewed in the meta-analyses that assessed maintenance of skills found positive results regardless of the follow-up period. Although it was rare that a study employed "booster" training sessions to promote skill maintenance (e.g., van Dam-Baagen & Kraaimaat, 1986), patients were able to retain the skills learned for up to 2 years (Longin & Rooney, 1975).

These maintenance results are quite striking, yet clinical experience cautions us to be wary of assuming that once a schizophrenic patient acquires a skill, he or she will remember it and use it indefinitely. Several biases against negative results may be operating, including less likelihood to publish negative results, attrition of lower functioning patients who relapse, or failure to include patients who are lost to follow-up assessments and may be less likely to exhibit long-term skill maintenance.

Generalization

Although it has been generally accepted that social skills training can help people with schizophrenia learn and maintain a variety of skills and competencies, it is important to demonstrate that these skills can be used effectively in patients' daily lives. The most common method to test skill generalization has been to test trained subjects with role-play situations similar to the ones used in training. For example, it is common to use a subset of scenes from a role-play test during skills training, and to test for generalization of skill by administering other scenes from that assessment instrument after training is complete. Studies employing this kind of strategy almost invariably have found positive results (Donahoe & Driesenga, 1988).

However, for this assessment strategy of generalization to be meaningful, patients' responses to situations in the role-play assessment must be predictive of how they will perform in similar naturalistic situations. There has been conflicting evidence supporting the predictive validity of role-play instruments such as the Behavioral Assessment Test-Revised Version (Eisler, Hersen, Miller, & Blanchard, 1975; Bellack et al., 1978); however, more recent evidence has documented the reliability and validity of role plays (Bellack, Morrison, Mueser, Wade, Sayers 1990). There is some evidence regarding the validity of judgments of competence of molar skills when the criterion is a judgment made by an observer of the patient's behavior in a natural setting (Wessberg et al., 1981).

Some studies have taken these factors into account. Social competence was found to improve using a simulated real-life behavior test in which subjects were prompted to initiate a conversation with a stranger (confederate), ask the stranger to lunch, and terminate the conversation after 10 minutes (Liberman et al., 1984; Wallace & Liberman, 1985). Other studies have found generalization of skills to job interviews (Furman, Geller, Simon, & Kelly, 1979) and actual job settings (Mueser, Foy, & Carter, 1986). In some cases, generalization has also been found in unprompted situations. For example, subjects taught verbal skills in an office setting were monitored covertly in the ward dayroom and courtyard and found to successfully utilize the conversational skills they had learned (Wong et al., 1993).

One meta-analysis of 27 controlled studies of social skills training in schizophrenia concluded that the modality, in contrast with control conditions, has significant effectiveness in yielding skills acquisition, durability, and generalization as well as significant reductions in rates of relapse and hospitalization (Benton & Schroeder, 1990). However, other reviews concluded that evidence is lacking on whether changes in treatment settings generalize to community settings (Halford & Hayes, 1991), or on the effects of skills training in reducing the psychopathology of schizophrenia (Lehman & Steinwachs, 1994).

It is likely that the lack of consensus on the generality of social skills training stems from differences in the extent and duration of the training sessions as well as the degree to which the individual's natural environment prompts and reinforces the skills acquired in training sessions. For example, in a controlled study that offered twice weekly training sessions for a year, followed by once weekly "booster" sessions for another 6 months, evidence was obtained attesting to the significantly greater utilization of social skills in the natural environment and the better social adjustment of individuals who received skills training versus those who received equivalent amounts of supportive group therapy (Eckman et al., 1992; Marder et al., 1996). In this study, a comprehensive array of skills were taught, including medication and symptom self-management, interpersonal problem solving, and achieving individualized and personalized life goals.

In another comprehensive, one year, skills training program that included personalized goals and strengthening the family's ability to cope with the burdens of a mentally disabled member, social adjustment was significantly improved and relapse rates were reduced to nil (Hogarty et al., 1986). Many of the earlier studies of social skills training provided limited amounts of training and were designed more to meet the convenience of the investigator (e.g., completion of a doctoral dissertation) than the needs of the patients.

Information Processing and Social Skills Training

Although there is a difference of opinion on the overall effectiveness of social skills training, there is consensus that the subtle cognitive deficits which may impede individuals with schizophrenia from acquiring basic social and coping skills during adolescence and young adulthood are also likely to undermine their ability to learn independent living skills during training sessions. This has led to the development of a model of skills training which focuses on the cognitive processes mediating interpersonal effectiveness from input of social information to socially competent responses (Corrigan et al., 1992). From this perspective, the application of social skills depends in part on the individual's ability to *receive* information (that is, read the social environment and its norms and expectations accurately), *process* information (interpret the information, generate options, and select a response that matches the situation), and *send* information (appropriately implement the selected response). The deficits in social perception, processing, and sending skills demonstrated by schizophrenic patients with social disabilities appear to be related to impaired social competence (Bellack & Hersen, 1978; Livesay, 1981; Morrison & Bellack, 1981; Morrison, Bellack, & Mueser, 1988; Nuechterlein & Dawson, 1984; Trower, Bryant, & Argyle, 1978; Wallace, 1982; Wallace et al., 1980; Liberman et al., 1986).

One study has examined whether the individual components of the receiving-processing-sending model of social interactions can be trained (Liberman, Mueser, & Wallace, 1986; Wallace, 1982; Wallace & Liberman, 1985). Twenty-eight schizophrenic patients were randomly assigned to information-processing training or to "holistic health therapy" for a 9-week period. A comprehensive assessment of outcome found that patients in the skills training program improved significantly on the components of social skills, overall social skills, and social adjustment measures with the effects maintained at 24-month follow-up. These findings suggested that the division of social skills into receiving, processing, and sending skills and the incorporation of these components in the training process may be a fruitful strategy for developing social rehabilitation.

Neurocognitive Predictors of Learning Social Skills

Clinical investigators have examined the brain information-processing correlates of social functioning in general and skill learning in particular. The cognitive deficits that appear to function as "rate limiting" factors, or barriers, to learning social and instrumental skills include verbal memory, sustained attention, and span of apprehension (Corrigan, Wallace, Schade, & Green, 1994; Bowen et al., 1994). Findings from this research suggest that specific cognitive deficits in visual vigilance, verbal memory, and conceptual flexibility may need to be ameliorated to optimize patients' participation and success in social skills training.

Researchers have long recognized that early information-processing functions, such as auditory and visual sustained attention, may be the determinants of social disability in schizophrenia (Silverman, 1964; Venables, 1964). Extrapolating from this theory, one would expect deficits in attentional capacities to be highly related to social skill learning. In fact, research findings have been mixed regarding the relationship between visual vigilance and social skill learning. Some authors have found a significant relationship (Bowen et al., 1994), while others have not (Corrigan et al., 1994). In explaining this discrepancy, it may be conjectured that the strength of the relationship between vigilance and skill learning depends

on the complexity of the skills being taught, with higher levels of vigilance being required for more elaborate sequences of social skills. An alternative explanation views the relationship between attentional capacity and skills acquisition as categorical. That is, patients whose attentional abilities fall below a hypothetical threshold may have significant difficulty with skills training tasks while the remainder do not. A longitudinal, prospective study of individuals in the early stages of schizophrenia found a robust predictive relationship between attentional capacity at entry into treatment and social and vocational functioning one year later (Nuechterlein, Dawson, & Green, 1994).

In another domain of cognition, a significant relationship has consistently been found between verbal memory and skill learning (Corrigan et al., 1994; Kern, Green, & Satz, 1992; Mueser, Bellack, Douglas, & Wade, 1991). This is readily understandable since much of social interaction depends on the accurate reception, processing, and sending of verbal information. While the limited research on the subject has not shown a significant association between information-processing functions of a higher order, such as conceptual flexibility, and social skills learning (Corrigan et al., 1994), this may be a function of the low level of complexity of the targeted skills that were assessed.

Behavior Therapy of Cognitive Deficits

Various behavioral interventions have been developed to remediate the information-processing deficits of schizophrenia. A review of the literature in this area is available in Chapter 21. Although promising, the cognitive remediation strategies described in these studies have been criticized because they do not seem to readily generalize to more ecologically valid experiences (Corrigan & Storzbach, 1993; Ellis, 1986) or demonstrate any clinical impact. Few studies have shown that improvement in attention to single digits flashing on a computer screen generalizes to better participation in skills training programs. In part, this is a shortfall in methodology; generalizability and clinical utility of the effects of cognitive remediation has been largely ignored by researchers. Alternatively, the limitations in generalizability may be a function of the qualitatively different stimuli that are processed in the real world of social cognition versus those stimuli used in isolated, laboratory tests of information-processing (Holyoak & Gordon, 1984; Ostrom, 1984). Therefore, strategies need to be developed that address the information-processing deficits that directly mediate and influence the social functioning of individuals with schizophrenia.

Can a combination of social skills training and cognitive remediation help patients circumvent their information-processing deficits en route to improving interpersonal functioning? For example, Interpersonal Psychological Therapy (IPT) is a comprehensive rehabilitation program designed to ameliorate both cognitive and social dysfunctions (Brenner, Hodel, Roder, & Corrigan, 1992; Brenner et al., 1994). IPT comprises discrete training modules that target primary processing deficits, intermediate social cognitive deficits, and molar social skills. Preliminary research has suggested that patients who participated in IPT showed greater improvements in both social and cognitive functioning than matched controls (Brenner et al., 1994). However, the field of cognitive training is in its infancy and much research remains to be accomplished before its clinical value will be known (Liberman & Green, 1992; Green, 1993).

Social Skills Training for Remediation of Negative Symptoms

Another potential limitation to the effective learning of social skills is the presence of negative symptoms. Negative symptoms are deficiencies in domains of functioning such as motivation, social initiative, energy, the experiencing of pleasure, the desire for socialization, and the expression of emotion. One perspective holds that negative symptoms represent a basic neurobiological impairment which results in the social disability so prevalent in schizophrenia. Thus, negative symptoms may impede the requisite participation in social skills training leading to the development of the skills necessary for social competence. For example, a lack of social interest or motivation will limit an individual's opportunities to practice social skills and even attendance at training sessions. Furthermore, a failure to experience pleasure or to desire social contact may significantly reduce social reinforcement of skills that are adequately performed.

An alternative view of social disability posits that the lack of social skills may be due to inadequate learning, the intrusion of positive symptoms, social anxiety, or assumption of the "sick role." Consistent with this view is the finding from one study that persistent negative symptoms do not preclude patients from acquiring or maintaining social skills, whereas patients with persistent positive symptoms were less likely to retain learned social skills at one month follow-up (Mueser, Kosmidis, & Sayers, 1992). However, it is difficult to tease apart the contribu-

tions of negative symptoms and other causes of social skill deficits to social dysfunctions, since alogia and asociality are defined as negative symptoms as well as deficits in social skills.

Still another perspective on negative symptoms and social disability emphasizes the need to distinguish primary from secondary negative symptoms, where primary negative symptoms are part of the deficit syndrome (Carpenter, Heinrichs, & Wagman, 1988). The primary or deficit syndrome represents basic and enduring aspects of the illness characterized by an increased frequency of structural brain impairments and decreased cognitive functioning (Buchanan, Kirkpatrick, Heinrichs, & Carpenter, 1990), while secondary negative symptoms are the result of other factors; for example, medication side effects (e.g., akinesia), inadequate social stimulation, unrecognized depression, and the intrusion of positive symptoms of psychosis. The importance of this distinction lies in the treatable nature of secondary negative symptoms through the identification of their causes and subsequent pharmacological and/or psychosocial interventions.

The negative symptoms and social deficits of the seriously mentally ill have been the rationale for and therapeutic target of social skills training techniques. Patients with negative symptoms have been found to be significantly more impaired with respect to social functioning than those with nonnegative schizophrenia (Mueser, Bellack, Morrison, & Wixted, 1990). That patients with negative symptoms have an impaired capacity to benefit from social skills training has been suggested (Bellack, Turner, Hersen, & Luber, 1984) and tested (Matousek et al., 1992). The latter study employed a multiple-baseline design across behaviors with three patients who had prominent negative symptoms. The subjects received nonverbal skills training along with the Stacking the Deck social skills game (Foxx & McMorrow, 1983) every day for 2 weeks. Social skills were assessed via the Simulated Social Interaction Test (Curran, 1982), while negative symptoms were monitored using the Scale for the Assessment of Negative Symptoms (Andreasen, 1983). Modest improvements in social skills and negative symptoms were achieved at first, but then waned at 3-month follow-up. The authors speculated that longer periods of treatment may be necessary to sustain clinical improvement and that secondary factors (e.g., levels of social interaction, depression, and extrapyramidal side effects) may have contributed to the failure to observe long-term benefits.

However, this research failed to adequately differentiate between primary and secondary negative symptoms. It is conceivable that the deficit syndrome prohibits, while secondary negative symptoms only inhibit, the acquisition, durability, and generalizability of social skills. To investigate this question, we recently completed a pilot study on six patients comparing the efficacy of social skills training for individuals with schizophrenia who did or did not have the deficit syndrome (Kopelowicz, Liberman, Mintz, & Zarate, 1997). Consistent with our hypothesis, the patients who did not have the deficit syndrome demonstrated significantly better social skills and lower negative symptoms both after training and at followup than patients with the deficit syndrome.

An Integrated Biobehavioral Approach Promotes Improved Social Functioning

Although elimination or optimal control and stabilization of psychotic symptoms remains a high priority in the biobehavioral treatment and rehabilitation of persons suffering from schizophrenia, the preceding sections have illustrated how information-processing deficits and negative symptoms frequently present a more formidable impediment to recovery. Effective pharmacotherapy may improve cognitive functioning and make afflicted individuals more responsive to learning from their environments (Liberman, Corrigan, & Schade, 1989). Conversely, the substantial minority of individuals who are refractory to antipsychotic drug treatment alone show improvements in their social functioning when focused social skills training is added to the concurrent administration of antipsychotic medications (Kuehnel, Liberman, Marshall, & Bowen, 1992; Liberman, Kopelowicz, & Young, 1994).

Unfortunately, antipsychotic medication may also hamper the information-processing functions of schizophrenic patients. Although low to moderate doses of antipsychotic medication seem to improve the attentional capacities of schizophrenic patients (Orzack, Kornetsky, & Freeman, 1967; Spohn, Lacoursiere, Thompson, & Coyne, 1977; Strauss, Lew, Coyle, & Tune, 1985; Wahba, Donlon, & Meadow, 1981), and have little effect on memory functioning (Corrigan & Penn, 1995), high doses have been found to diminish patients' vigilance (Pearl, 1962; Spohn et al., 1985; Sweeney et al., 1991). Moreover, anticholinergic medication, prescribed to manage some of the side effects of antipsychotic medication, has been shown to cause significant decrements in verbal memory (Baker, Cheng, & Amara, 1983; Hitri, Craft, Fallon, Sethi, & Sinha, 1987; Perlick, Stastny, Katz, Mayer, & Mattis,

1986; Van Putten et al., 1987). Concommitant use of these agents might impair instrumental role functioning, even while reducing psychotic symptoms and neurological side effects (Mintz, Mintz, & Phipps, 1992).

The advent of a new generation of antipsychotic agents, with clozapine as the prototype (Baldessarini & Frankenburg, 1991), may yield additive benefits to individuals receiving biobehavioral treatments. Both clozapine and risperidone, the first two drugs with combined antagonism of serotonin and dopamine receptors, have demonstrated greater efficacy on negative symptoms with less or no extrapyramidal side effects than conventional neuroleptics that are solely dopamine antagonists (Kane & Mayerhoff, 1989; Choiunard et al., 1993). Moreover, a number of studies have demonstrated the efficacy of clozapine in schizophrenic patients previously refractory to antipsychotic medications (Kane et al., 1988; Pickar et al., 1992; Meltzer, 1992).

Of special interest is the possibility that the improved efficacy of these novel agents is in part due to their remediating the cognitive deficits that inhibit learning of social skills in schizophrenia. Although one study found no change in a variety of measures of cognitive capacities in a sample of 15 patients after an average of 15 months on clozapine (Goldberg et al., 1993), a more comprehensive investigation of 36 patients with treatment refractory schizophrenia revealed significant improvements in tests of executive functioning, attention, and recall and retrieval from reference memory 6 months after beginning clozapine (Hagger et al., 1993). In another study, the effect of clozapine on some tests of attention and verbal fluency was significantly greater than that of typical neuroleptic treatment in non-treatment-resistant schizophrenia (Lee, Thompson, & Meltzer, 1994).

Because of its limited time on the market (FDA approval was granted in January 1994), there have been few studies of the cognitive benefits of treatment with risperidone. In a direct comparison with clozapine, patients taking risperidone performed better on visual memory tasks for designs and on the Wisconsin Card Sorting Test of conceptual flexibility (Daniel, 1994). In another study comparing patients with treatment-resistant schizophrenia receiving haloperidol to patients receiving risperidone, subjects on risperidone demonstrated superior performance on verbal memory (Green et al., 1997).

Some investigators have hypothesized that the combination of skills training with atypical antipsychotic agents would lead to greater improvements in instrumental role functioning (Liberman, Kopelowicz, & Young, 1994). A project of the UCLA Clinical Research Center, "Management of Risk of Relapse in Schizophrenia," has focused on the development of innovative psychosocial and pharmacological treatments for patients with chronic schizophrenia living in the community. The present phase of the study is comparing haloperidol with a novel antipsychotic, namely risperidone, which possesses fewer side effects and is designed to mitigate schizophrenic apathy, isolation, and withdrawal in an effort to maximize the benefits of social skills training.

The social skills training component of the study is comparing 15 months of clinic-based skills training that employs the modules in the UCLA Social and Independent Living Skills Program (Psychiatric Rehabilitation Consultants, 1994) with a program of the same duration that augments the modules with in vivo coaching by a case manager. The case manager "runs interference" for the patient, influencing the patient's living and working environments to accommodate to the patient's deficits and reinforce the application in real life of newly learned social skills. The investigators hypothesize that the combination of risperidone plus *in vivo amplified skills training* will yield the best clinical outcomes.

Social Roles and Social Skills Training

The rapidly expanding knowledge base of the neurobiological and neuropharmacological substrates of the pathophysiology of schizophrenia promises innovative drug therapies with greater therapeutic effects. However, to avoid a reductionistic biological approach to psychiatric treatment and rehabilitation, a broader biopsychosocial conceptualization of treatment is needed. After all, no medication will ever teach a socially disabled individual with schizophrenia how to cope with the interpersonal challenges of everyday life in the community. Optimal employment of social skills training requires the consideration of social and cultural norms. The appropriateness and impact of social behavior are defined by cultural standards for behavior expected in situational context. Thus, social competence depends on how accurately an individual discriminates the normative demands and expectations of a wide variety of people and settings.

The ability to process information correctly may underly accurate social perception. Social perception, in turn, may be related to *social schemas,* which are cognitive representations of normatively constrained *behavior settings.* Behavior settings are situationally specific interactions between people and environments which include setting-specific cues, social roles, and rules or "scripts"

for expected and acceptable behavior (Barker & Wright, 1955; Wicker, 1987; Willems, 1976).

Social schemas may distort interpretation of social information when individuals make faulty attributions—a process which may be exaggerated in psychiatric patients. For example, severely depressed individuals have been shown to possess schemas that distort incoming information to conform to a highly negative view of self, others, and the future (Beck, 1967; Ingram & Hollon, 1986). Social schemas may also influence social skills by guiding the specific behavioral elements that make up an interaction—the "scripts" which describe the expected sequence of skilled behaviors and social interactions. For example, a paranoid individual may misconstrue a friendly greeting from a new neighbor as a suspicious overture and select a "respond-to-hostile-intruder" script as a basis for reacting. Another person with conceptual disorganization may not be able to comprehend the friendly introduction at all. In the latter case, no script is selected and the individual withdraws or responds inappropriately.

Severely disabled psychiatric patients, unfamiliar with the routines and scripts prescribed in a social interaction, will find themselves unable to respond rapidly to social cues with appropriate reactions. For example, a socially withdrawn and inexperienced individual who attends a party may be unaware that an introductory statement made by a guest should be returned with a response at a similar level of self-disclosure. When the guest asks him how he's feeling, he might go overboard with excessive self-disclosure saying, "I'm not doing too well today because my voices are bothering me." In another example, an individual may not understand that receipt of his change after payment of the bill at a restaurant is typically followed by saying thanks for the service and leaving a tip. In both situations, the person may unintentionally appear rude from lack of knowledge of social expectancies.

Patients disabled by schizophrenia have been found to have an inadequate number of templates with which to interpret social situations and too few scripts or routines with which to respond to these interpretations (Endler, 1973; Mariotto, 1978; Mariotto & Paul, 1975). Thus, treatment programs based on the social schema model have been designed to expand the number of adaptive responses patients can enlist to confront difficult situations. One such program yielded improvements in self-report measures, an interpersonal role-play test, and a naturalistic interpersonal interaction test (Goldsmith & McFall, 1975). In another program, patients were taught minute increments of scripts until an appropriate social role was learned as a unit (Magaro, Johnson, & Boring, 1986). This approach was tested with a group of schizophrenic patients by teaching them the sequential components of conversational skills. As the specific skills of the patients increased, their schizophrenic symptoms diminished (Magaro & West, 1983).

One important determinant of social role is the cultural and ethnic background of the individual. Different cultures may vary in the social norms and expectations they prescribe for situationally determined behavior. For example, the Protestant ethic ideals prevalent in Anglo-American culture, which emphasize work functioning, assertiveness, and independent living, may not correspond to other cultures' views of a successful living situation. A Mexican American individual with schizophrenia may not be expected to live independently, but rather encouraged by his/her family to function in a limited way within the home environment. Similarly, an Asian American patient may not wish to display assertiveness with his/her elders, as this behavior may be in conflict with the deferential attitude which is highly valued by the members of this culture. Sensitivity to these cultural factors may enable practitioners to make culturally appropriate modifications to the skills training endeavor and thus increase the relevance and effectiveness for minority ethnic groups.

Self-Control

One limitation of many social skills training programs is their inflexibility in prefabricated scripts or social routines which can result in a failure of the learned behavior to generalize to novel situations. Self-control techniques can help individuals with schizophrenia to increase their flexibility in fitting their social behavior to the varied expectations of the full range of situations. Using cognitive-behavioral principles, the self-control model aims to promote self-directed initiation of responses that increase the probability of desired social interactions and outcomes. Self-control methods have also been utilized by schizophrenic patients in coping with and managing the intrusive symptoms of their disorder (Falloon & Talbott, 1981; Breier & Strauss, 1982; Rund, 1990). Self-control approaches improve the individual's ability to manage his or her own behavior by building skills of self-monitoring, self-evaluation, and self-reinforcement (Kanfer, 1975; Kanfer & Karoly, 1972; Rehm, 1982, 1984).

Self-monitoring refers to the process of observing one's own behavior, the situations in which it occurs, and the consequences that follow it. Observable behaviors, such

as "crazy talk," as well as internal events, such as social anxiety, may be monitored. Self-evaluation occurs when a individual's estimate of his or her performance, based on self-monitoring, is compared to internal or external criteria for appropriate behavior. It is important that performance criteria be realistically attainable, and that the initiation of appropriate social behavior be attributed to internal, rather than external, causes (Rehm, 1984). Furthermore, patients' self-monitoring of internal states and their evaluation of such states have been found to be prerequisites for effective self-control of symptoms (Breier & Strauss, 1982; McCandless-Glimcher et al., 1986).

Self-reinforcement refers to the self-administration of overt or covert rewards or punishments contingent upon the outcome of the self-evaluation process. Self-reinforcement supplements external reinforcement in strengthening appropriate social behavior and serves to maintain appropriate functioning when external reinforcers are delayed or unavailable (Rehm, 1977). The utility of these approaches has provided an impetus for including self-control techniques in skills training programs for psychiatrically disabled clients and has contributed to the durability of the learned skills (Becker, Heimberg, & Bellack, 1987; Meichenbaum, 1969; Meichenbaum & Cameron, 1973; Miller, Norman, & Keitner, 1989; Hersen & Bellack, 1976; Hersen, Bellack, & Himmelhoch, 1982; Van Dam-Baggen & Kraaimaat, 1986).

CONCLUSIONS

The increasing pace of research on social skills training for persons with schizophrenia has documented its efficacy and brought it to the fore as a psychosocial treatment of choice in schizophrenia (Liberman, 1994). Some forms of training—for example, the modules in the UCLA Social and Independent Living Skills Program—have been widely disseminated to practitioners and even translated and validated in studies from Germany, Switzerland, Quebec, Japan, Sweden, Finland, Norway, and Poland. However, many questions remain about the effectiveness of skills training in terms of application on a routine basis by practitioners. One limitation of the technique relates to the cognitive impairments of patients with schizophrenia. We have reviewed studies that document the relationship of such cognitive functions as sustained attention and verbal memory to the acquisition of social skills. Individuals who have substantial cognitive deficits and who show high levels of thought disorder and conceptual disorganization are poor candidates for most of the social skills training formats that have been developed. This may exclude many acutely psychotic patients as well as about 15% who have chronic and persisting thought disorder.

The effectiveness of social skills training versus its efficacy must be demonstrated in large-scale, services research projects. While the efficacy of antipsychotic drugs was established in the early 1960s, the effectiveness of these agents was for many years inhibited by inappropriate use by psychiatrists in the field. Only in the 1980s, a generation after they were widely disseminated, were the polypharmacy and overdosing patterns of use of antipsychotic drugs recognized and corrected with practice guidelines. Similar attention will have to be paid to the fidelity with which social skills training is carried out. Already, one services research project has documented a failure of skills training to have an effect when the trainer deleted several key learning activities (Wallace, Liberman, MacKain, Blackwell, & Eckman, 1992).

The challenge to promote generalization and durability of the skills learned in training sessions will stimulate innovative ways to advance the utilization of the skills in the patients' natural environments. One strategy that will be tested involves the use of cognitive remediation to normalize or improve the cognitive deficits of persons with schizophrenia. While laboratory studies have been successful in this endeavor, it remains to be seen whether the improvements obtained in the lab will generalize to the clinic. A variant of cognitive remediation that should be tested in the coming years is the teaching of social schemas and scripts to patients. This may improve their awareness of the expectations and consequences of their social behavior and equip them with social responses that are appropriate to the situational context.

Another avenue to enhanced generalization and durability of skills, already being explored, is the involvement of professional or natural "aides" who can influence the patients' social environments to become more accommodating to the patients' efforts at using the skills learned during training sessions. For example, one study at the UCLA Clinical Research Center for Schizophrenia is employing friends and relatives who are designated by the schizophrenic patients to become *partners in autonomous living*. This entails assisting the patients to apply their social and independent living skills, making opportunities and encouragement available to use the skills, and ensuring that the patients' fledgling efforts are greeted with abundant positive reinforcement. A similar approach has been described with the use of a case manager to provide *in vivo amplified skills training*. Certainly, it will be nec-

essary for skills trainers to become culturally competent in the setting of goals and being sensitive to the cultural and ethnic nuances of verbal and nonverbal social skills.

The well-replicated efficacy of *behavioral family management* or *psychoeducation family interventions* suggests that the family environment can be favorably influenced by education and training. This reliably leads to a more equitable family emotional climate, better coping by patient and family members, and reduced relapse. The two studies that have combined family intervention with social skills training found favorable results (Wallace & Liberman, 1985; Hogarty et al., 1986).

Perhaps the most promising future direction of social skills training comes from combining it with the novel antipsychotics that appear to have greater impact on negative symptoms and cognitive deficits. Clozapine and risperidone are just the first two of what is expected to be a parade of new antipsychotic drugs designed to have optimal therapeutic effects on positive and negative symptoms while producing minimal side effects. Side effects of antipsychotic drugs have impeded the learning of social skills, as in the intrusive and deleterious effects of sedation, tremor, memory impairments, and akathisia. With improved benefit–risk ratios, the novel antipsychotic drugs should minimize cognitive dysfunctions and intrusive psychotic symptoms, setting the stage for enhanced learning, durability, and generality of social skills training.

REFERENCES

Andreasen, N.C. (1983). *Scale for the assessment of negative symptoms.* Iowa City: University of Iowa.

Anthony, W. A., & Liberman, R. P. (1992). Principles and practice of psychiatric rehabilitation. In R. P. Liberman (Ed.), *Handbook of psychiatric rehabilitation* (pp. 1–29). New York: Macmillan.

Baker, L. A., Cheng, L. Y., & Amara, I. B. (1983). The withdrawal of benztropine mesylate in chronic schizophrenic patients. *British Journal of Psychiatry, 143,* 584–590.

Baldessarini, R. J., & Frankenburg, F.R. (1991). Clozapine: A novel antipsychotic agent. *New England Journal of Medicine, 324,* 746–754.

Barker, R. G., & Wright, H. T. (1955). *Midwest and its children: The psychological ecology of an American town.* Evanston, IL: Row Peterson.

Beck, A. T. (1967). *Depression: Clinical, experimental, and theoretical aspects.* New York: Harper.

Becker, R. E., Heimberg, R. G., & Bellack, A. S. (1987). *Social skills training treatment for depression.* Elmsford, NY: Pergamon Press.

Bellack, A. S., & Hersen, M. (1978). Chronic psychiatric patients: Social skills training. In M. Hersen & A. S. Bellack (Eds.), *Behavior therapy in the psychiatric setting* (pp. 169–195). Baltimore: Williams & Wilkins.

Bellack, A. S., Hersen, M., & Turner, S. M. (1978). Role play tests for assessing social skills: Are they valid? *Behavior Therapy, 9,* 448–461.

Bellack, A. S., Turner, S. M., Hersen, M., & Luber, R. F. (1984). An examination of the efficacy of social skills training for chronic schizophrenic patients. *Hospital and Community Psychiatry, 35,* 1023–1028.

Bellack, A. S., Morrison, R. L., & Mueser, K. T. (1989). Social problem solving in schizophrenia. *Schizophrenia Bulletin, 15,* 101–116.

Bellack, A. S., Morrison, R. L., Mueser, K. T., Wade, J. H., & Sayers, S. L. (1990). Role play for assessing the social competence of psychiatric patients. *Psychological Assessment, 2,* 248–255.

Benton, M. K., & Schroeder, H. E. (1990). Social skills training with schizophrenics: A meta-analytic evaluation. *Journal of Consulting and Clinical Psychology, 58,* 741–747.

Bleuler, M. (1968). A 23-year longitudinal study of 208 schizophrenics and impressions in regard to the nature of schizophrenia. In: D. Rosenthal & S. S. Kety (Eds.), *The transmission of schizophrenia.* Oxford: Pergamon.

Bowen, L., Wallace, C. J., Glynn, S. M., Nuechterlein, K. H., Lutzger, J. R., & Kuehnel, T. G. (1994). Schizophrenics' cognitive functioning and performance in interpersonal interactions and skills training procedures. *Journal of Psychiatric Research, 28,* 289–301.

Breier, A., & Strauss, J. S. (1982). Self-control in psychotic disorders. *Archives of General Psychiatry, 40,* 1141–1145.

Brenner, H., Hodel, B., Roder, V., & Corrigan, P. W. (1992). Treatment of cognitive dysfunctions and behavioral deficits in schizophrenia. *Schizophrenia Bulletin, 18,* 21–26.

Brenner, H.D., Roder, V., Hodel, B., Kienzle, N., Reed, D., & Liberman, R. P. (1994). *Integrated psychological therapy for schizophrenic patients.* Toronto: Hogrefe & Huber.

Buchanan, R. W., Kirkpatrick, B., Heinrichs, D. W., & Carpenter, W. T. (1990). Clinical correlates of the deficit syndrome of schizophrenia. *American Journal of Psychiatry, 147,* 290–294.

Carpenter, W. T., Heinrichs, D. W., & Wagman, A. M. I. (1988). Deficit and nondeficit forms of schizophrenia: The concept. *American Journal of Psychiatry, 145,* 578–583.

Chouinard, G., Jones, B., Remington, G., Chouinard, G., Jones, B., Remington, G., Bloom, D., Addington, D., MacEwan, G. W., Labelle, A., Beauclair, L., & Arnott, W. (1993). A Canadian multicenter placebo-controlled study of fixed doses of risperidone and haloperidol in the treatment of chronic schizophrenic patients. *Journal of Clinical Psychopharmacology, 13,* 25–40.

Ciompi, L. (1980). Catamnestic long-term study of life and aging of schizophrenics. *Schizophrenia Bulletin, 6,* 606–618.

Corrigan, P. W. (1991). Social skills training in adult psychiatric populations: A meta-analysis. *Journal of Behavior Therapy and Experimental Psychiatry, 22,* 203–210.

Corrigan, P. W., Penn, D. L. (1995). The effects of antipsychotic and antiparkinsonian medication on psychosocial skill learning. *Clinical Psychology: Science and Practice, 2,* 251–262.

Corrigan, P. W., Schade, M. L., & Liberman R. P. (1992). Social skills training. In R. P. Liberman (Ed.), *Handbook of psychiatric rehabilitation* (pp. 95–126). New York: Macmillan.

Corrigan, P. W., & Storzbach, D. (1993). The ecological validity of cognitive rehabilitation for schizophrenia. *The Journal of Cognitive Rehabilitation,* May, June.

Corrigan, P. W., Wallace, C. J., Schade, M. L., & Green, M. F. (1994). Learning medication self-management skills in schizophrenia: Relationships with cognitive deficits and psychiatric symptoms. *Behavior Therapy, 25,* 5–15.

Curran, J. P. (1982). A procedure for the assessment of social skills: The Simulated Social Situation Interaction Test. In J. P. Curran & Monti, P. M. (Eds.), *Social skills training: A practical handbook for assessment and treatment* (pp. 348–373). New York: Guilford.

Daniel, D. G. (1994). Comparison of risperidone and clozapine on clinical and cognitive functions in psychotic disorders [abstract]. *Biological Psychiatry, 35,* 667.

Dobson, D. J. G., McDougall, G., Busheikin, J., & Aldous, J. (1993). *Social skills training and symptomatology in schizophrenia.* Paper presented at the Twenty-seventh Annual Convention of the Association for the Advancement of Behavior Therapy, Atlanta, Georgia.

Donahoe, C. P., & Driesenga, S. A. (1988). A review of social skills training with chronic mental patients. In M. Hersen, R. M. Eisler, & P. M. Miller. (Eds.), *Progress in Behavioral modification* (Vol. 23, pp. 131–164). Newbury Park, CA: Sage Publications.

D'Zurilla, T. J. (1986). *Problem solving therapy: A social competence approach to clinical intervention.* New York: Springer.

Eckman, T. A., Wirshing, W. C., Marder, S. R., Liberman, R. P., Johnston-Cronk, K., Zimmerman, K., & Mintz, J. (1992). Technique for training schizophrenic patients in illness self-management: A controlled trial. *American Journal of Psychiatry, 149,* 1549–1555.

Eisler, R. M., Hersen, M., Miller, P. M., & Blanchard, E. B. (1975). Situational determinants of assertive behavior. *Journal of Consulting and Clinical Psychology, 43,* 330–340.

Ellis, E. S. (1986). The role of motivation and pedagogy on the generalization of cognitive strategy training. *Journal of Learning Disabilities, 19,* 667–670.

Endler, N. (1973). The person versus the situation a pseudo issue? A response to Alker. *Journal of Personality, 41,* 287–303.

Engel, G. L. (1977). The need for a new medical model: A challenge for biomedicine. *Science, 196,* 129–136.

Engel, G. L. (1980). The clinical application of the biopsychosocial model. *American Journal of Psychiatry, 137,* 535–544.

Falloon, I. R. H., & Talbott, R. E. (1981). Persistent auditory hallucinations: Coping mechanisms and implications for management. *Psychological Medicine, 11,* 329–339.

Foxx, R. M., & McMorrow, M. J. (1983). *Stacking the deck: A social skills game for retarded adults.* Champaign, IL: Research Press.

Furman, W., Geller, M., Simon, S. J., & Kelly, J. A. (1979). The use of a behavioral rehearsal procedure for teaching job-interviewing skills to psychiatric patients. *Behavior Therapy, 10,* 157–167.

Glynn, S. M., & Mueser, K. T. (1992). Social-learning programs. In R. P. Liberman (Ed.), *Handbook of psychiatric rehabilitation* (pp. 127–152). New York: Macmillan.

Goldberg, T. E., Greenberg, R. D., Griffin, S. J., Gold, J. M., Kleinman, J. E., Pickar, D., Schulz, S. C., & Weinberger, D. R. (1993). The effect of clozapine on cognition and psychiatric symptoms in patients with schizophrenia. *British Journal of Psychiatry, 162,* 43–48.

Goldsmith, J. B., & McFall, R. M. (1975). Development and evaluation of an interpersonal skills training program for psychiatric inpatients. *Journal of Abnormal Psychology, 84,* 51–58.

Goldstein, M. J. (1987). Psychosocial issues. *Schizophrenia Bulletin, 13,* 157–171.

Green, M. F. (1993). Cognitive remediation in schizophrenia: Is it time yet? *American Journal of Psychiatry, 150,* 178–187.

Green, M. F., Marshall, B. D., Wirshing, W. C., Ames, D., Marder, S. R., McGurk, K., Kern, R. S., & Mintz, J. (1997). Does Risperidone improve verbal working memory in treatment-resistent schizophrenia? *American Jounral of Psychiatry, 154,* 799–804.

Hagger, C., Buckley, P., Kenny, J. T., Friedman, L., Ubogy, D., & Meltzer, H. Y. (1993). Improvement in cognitive functions and psychiatric symptoms in treatment-refractory schizophrenic patients receiving clozapine. *Biological Psychiatry, 34,* 702–712.

Halford, W. K., & Hayes, R. (1991). Psychological rehabilitation of chronic schizophrenic patients: Recent findings on social skills and family psychoeducation. *Clinical Psychology Review, 23,* 23–44.

Harding, C. M., Brooks, G. W., Ashikaga, T., & Strauss, J. S. (1987). The Vermont longitudinal study of persons with severe mental illness. *American Journal of Psychiatry, 144,* 718–735.

Harding, C. M., Zubin, J., & Strauss, J. S. (1992). Chronicity in schizophrenia: Revisited. *British Journal of Psychiatry, 165* (Suppl. 18), 27–37.

Hayes, R. L., Halford, W. K., & Vargese, F. T. (1994). *Social skills training with chronic schizophrenic patients: Effects on negative symptoms and community functioning.* Unpublished manuscript.

Hersen, M., & Bellack, A. S. (1976). Social skills training for chronic psychiatric patients: Rationale, research findings, and future directions. *Comprehensive Psychiatry, 17,* 559–580.

Hersen, M., Bellack, A. S., & Himmelhoch, J. M. (1982). Skills training with unipolar depressed women. In J. P Curran & P. M. Monti (Eds.), *Social skills training: A practical handbook for assessment and treatment* (pp. 159–184). New York: Guilford Press.

Hitri, A., Craft, R. B., Fallon, J., Sethi, R., & Sinha, D. (1987). Serum neuroleptic and anticholinergic activity in relationship to cognitive toxicity of antiparkinsonian agents in schizophrenic patients. *Psychopharmacology Bulletin, 23,* 33–37.

Hogarty, G. E., Anderson, C. M., Reiss, D. J., Kornblith, S. J., Greenwald, D. P., Javana, C. D., & Madonia, M. J. (1986). Family psycho-education, social skills training and maintenance chemotherapy in the aftercare treatment of schizophrenia. Part I: One year effects of a controlled study on relapse and expressed emotion. *Archives of General Psychiatry, 31,* 633–642.

Holmes-Eber, P., & Riger, S. (1990). Hospitalization and the composition of mental patients' social networks. *Schizophrenia Bulletin, 16,* 157–164.

Holyoak, K. J., & Gordon, P. C. (1984). Information processing and social cognition. In R. S. Wyer & T. K. Srull (Eds.), *Handbook of social cognition* (Vol. 1; pp. 39–70). Hillsdale, NJ: Erlbaum.

Ingram, R. E., & Hollon, S. D. (1986). Cognitive therapy of depression from an information processing perspective. In R. E. Ingram (Ed.), *Information processing approaches to clinical psychology* (pp. 261–284). New York: Academic Press.

Kane, J., Honigfeld, G., Singer, J., Kane, J., Honigfeld, G., Singer, J., & Meltzner, H. (1988). Clozapine for the treatment-resistant schizophrenic: A double-blind comparison with chlorpromazine. *Archives of General Psychiatry, 45,* 789–796.

Kane, J., & Mayerhoff, D. (1989). Do negative symptoms respond to pharmacological treatment? *British Journal of Psychiatry, 155* (Suppl. #7), 115–118.

Kanfer, F. H. (1975). Self-management methods. In F. H. Kanfer & A. P. Goldstein (Eds.), *Helping people change: A textbook of methods,* (pp. 309–355). Elmsford, NY: Pergamon Press.

Kanfer, F. H., & Karoly, P. (1972). Self-control: A behavioristic excursion into the lion's den. *Behavior Therapy, 3,* 398–416.

Kern, R. S., Green, M.F., & Satz, P. (1992). Neuropsychological predictors of skills training for chronic psychiatric patients. *Psychiatry Research, 43,* 223–230.

Koegel, P. (1991) Understanding homelessness: An ethnographic approach. In R. Jahiel (Ed.), *Homelessness: A prevention oriented approach.* Baltimore: Johns Hopkins University Press, pp. 127–138.

Kopelowicz, A., Liberman, R. P., Mintz, J., & Zarate, R. (1997). Comparison of efficacy of social skills training for deficit and nondeficit negative symptoms in schizophrenia. *American Journal of Psychiatry, 154,* 424–425.

Kuehnel, T. G., Liberman, R. P., Marshall, B. D., & Bowen, L. (1992). Optimal drug and behavior therapy for treatment refractory institutional schizophrenics. *Effective Psychiatric Rehabilitation.* Special Issue of *New Directions in Mental Health Services,* San Francisco: Jossey-Bass, pp. 67–68.

Lee, M. A., Thompson, P. A., & Meltzer, H. Y. (1994). Effects of clozapine on cognitive function in schizophrenia. *Journal of Clinical Psychiatry, 55* (Suppl. B), 82–87.

Lehman, A. F., & Steinwachs, D. M. (1994). *Literature review: treatment approaches for schizophrenia.* Schizophrenia Patient Outcomes Research Team (PORT), University of Maryland, Baltimore, MD.

Liberman, R. P. (1994). Psychosocial treatments for schizophrenia. *Psychiatry, 57,* 104–114.

Liberman, R. P., Corrigan, P. W., & Schade, M. L. (1989). Drug and psychosocial treatment interactions in schizophrenia. *International Review of Psychiatry, 1,* 283–294.

Liberman, R. P., DeRisi, W. J., & Mueser, K. T. (1989). *Social skills training for psychiatric patients.* New York: Pergamon.

Liberman, R. P., & Green, M. F. (1992). Whither cognitive therapy for schizophrenia? *Schizophrenia Bulletin, 18,* 27–35.

Liberman, R. P., King, L. W., DeRisi, W. J., & McCann, M. (1975). *Personal effectiveness: Guiding people to assert their feelings and improve their social skills.* Champaign, IL: Research Press.

Liberman, R.P., Kopelowicz, A., & Young, A. S. (1994). Biobehavioral therapy and rehabilitation of schizophrenia. *Behavior Therapy, 25,* 89–107.

Liberman, R. P., Lillie, F., Falloon, I. R. H., Harpin, R. E., Hutchinson, W., & Stoute, B. (1984). Social skills training with relapsing schizophrenics: An experimental analysis. *Behavior Modification, 8,* 155–179.

Liberman, R. P., Mueser, K. T., & Wallace, C. J. (1986). Social skills training for schizophrenic individuals at risk for relapse. *American Journal of Psychiatry, 143,* 523–526.

Liberman, R. P., Mueser, K. T., Wallace, C. J., Jacobs, H. E., Eckman ,T., & Massel, H. K. (1986). Training skills in the psychiatrically disabled: Learning coping and competence. *Schizophrenia Bulletin, 12,* 631–647.

Liberman, R. P., Vaccaro, J. V., & Corrigan, P. W. (1995). Psychiatric rehabilitation. In H. Kaplan, & B. J. Sadock (Eds.), *Comprehensive textbook of psychiatry* (6th ed. pp. 2696–2727). Baltimore: Williams & Wilkins.

Liberman, R. P., Wallace, C. J., Blackwell, G., Eckman, T. A., Vaccaro, J. V., & Kuehnel, T. G. (1993). Innovations in skills training for the seriously mentally ill: The UCLA Social and Independent Living Skills Modules. *Innovations and Research, 2,* 43–60.

Livesay, J. R. (1981). Inconsistent interpersonal judgment in thought-disordered schizophrenia. *Psychological Reports, 49,* 179–181.

Longin, H. E., & Rooney, W. M. (1975). Training denial assertion to chronic hospitalized patients. *Journal of Behavior Therapy and Experimental Psychiatry, 6,* 219–222.

Magaro, P. A., Johnson, M. H., & Boring, R. (1986). Information processing approaches to schizophrenia. In R. E. Ingram (Ed.), *Information processing approaches to clinical psychology,* pp. 283–304. New York: Academic Press.

Magaro, P. A., & West, A. N. (1983). Structured learning therapy: A study with chronic psychiatric patients and level of pathology. *Behavior Modification, 7,* 29–40.

Marder, S. R., Wirshing, W. C., Mintz, J., McKenzie, J., Johnston-Cronk. K., Eckman, T. A., Lebell, M., & Liberman, R. P. (1996). Two-year outcome of social skills training and group psychotherapy for outpatients with schizophrenia *American Journal of Psychiatry, 153,* 1585–1592.

Mariotto, M. J. (1978). Interaction of person and situation effects for chronic mental patients: A two-year follow-up. *Journal of Abnormal Psychology, 87,* 676–679.

Mariotto, M. J., & Paul, G. L. (1975). Person versus situations in real-life functioning of chronically institutionalized mental patients. *Journal of Abnormal Psychology, 84,* 483–493.

Massel, H. K., Corrigan, P. W., Liberman, R. P., & Milan, M. (1991). Conversation skills training in thought-disordered schizophrenics through attention focusing. *Psychiatry Research, 38,* 51–61.

Matousek, N., Edwards, J., Jackson, H. J., Rudd, R. P., & McMurray, N. E. (1992). Social skills training and negative symptoms. *Behavior Modification, 16,* 39–63.

McCandless-Glimcher, L., McKnight, S., Hamera, E., Smith, B. L., Peterson, K. A., & Plumlee, A. A. (1986). Use of symptoms by schizophrenics to monitor and regulate their illness. *Hospital and Community Psychiatry, 37,* 929–933.

Meeks, S., & Murrell, S. A. (1994). Service providers in the social networks of clients with severe mental illness. *Schizophrenia Bulletin, 20,* 399–406.

Meichenbaum, D. H. (1969). The effects of instructions and reinforcement on thinking and language behavior of schizophrenics. *Behaviour Research and Therapy, 7,* 101–114.

Meichenbaum, D. H., & Cameron, R. (1973). Training schizophrenics to talk to themselves: A means of developing attentional controls. *Behavior Therapy, 4,* 515–534.

Meltzer, H. Y. (1992). Dimensions of outcome with clozapine. *British Journal of Psychiatry, 160* (Suppl. 17), 46–53.

Miller, I. W., Norman, W. H., & Keitner, G. I. (1989). Cognitive-behavioral treatment of depressed inpatients. *Behavior Therapy, 20,* 25–47.

Mintz, J., Mintz, L. I., & Phipps, C. C. (1992). Treatments of mental disorders and the functional capacity to work. In R. P. Liberman (Ed.), *Handbook of psychiatric rehabilitation* (pp. 290–316). New York: Macmillan.

Morrison, R. L., & Bellack, A. S. (1981). The role of social perception in social skill. *Behavior Therapy, 12,* 69–79.

Morrison, R. L., & Bellack, A. S. (1984). Social skills training. In A. S. Bellack (Ed.), *Schizophrenia: Treatment, management, and rehabilitation* (pp. 247–279). Orlando, FL: Grune & Statton.

Morrison, R. L., Bellack, A. S., & Mueser, K. T. (1988). Deficits in facial affect recognition and schizophrenia. *Schizophrenia Bulletin, 14,* 67–83.

Mueser, K. T., Bellack, A. S., Douglas, M. S., & Wade, J. H. (1991). Prediction of social skill acquisition in schizophrenic and major affective disorder patients from memory and symptomatology. *Psychiatry Research, 37,* 281–296.

Mueser, K. T., Bellack, A. S., Morrison, R. L., & Wixted, J. T. (1990). Social competence in schizophrenia: Premorbid adjustment, social skill, and domains of functioning. *Journal of Psychiatric Research, 24,* 51–63.

Mueser, K. T., Foy, D. W., Carter, M. J. (1986). Social skills training for job maintenance in a psychiatric patient. *Journal of Counseling Psychology, 47,* 189–191.

Mueser, K. T., Kosmidis, M. H., & Sayers, M. D. (1992). Symptomatology and the prediction of social skills acquisition in schizophrenia. *Schizophrenia Research, 8,* 59–68.

Nuechterlein, K. H., & Dawson, M. E. (1984). Information-processing and attentional functioning in the developmental course of schizophrenic disorders. *Schizophrenia Bulletin, 10,* 160–203.

Nuechterlein, K. H., Dawson, M. E., & Green, M. F. (1994). Information-processing abnormalities as neuropsychological vulnerability indicators for schizophrenia. *Acta Psychiatrica Scandinavica, 90,* 71–79.

Orzack, M. H., Kornetsky, C., & Freeman, H. (1967). The effects of daily administration of carphenazine on attention in the schizophrenic patient. *Psychopharmacologia, 11,* 31–38.

Ostrom, T. M. (1984). The sovereignty of social cognition. In R. S. Wyer & T. K. Srull (Eds.), *Handbook of social cognition* (Vol. 1; pp. 1–37). Hillsdale, NJ: Erlbaum.

Paul, G. L., & Lentz, R. J. (1977). *Psychosocial treatment of chronic mental patients: Milieu versus social-learning programs.* Cambridge: Harvard University Press.

Paul, G. L., & Menditto, A. A. (1992). Effectiveness of inpatient treatment programs for mentally ill adults in public psychiatric facilities. *Applied and Preventive Psychology, 1,* 41–63.

Pearl, D. (1962). Phenothiazine effects in chronic schizophrenia. *Journal of Clinical Psychology, 18,* 86–89.

Perlick, D., Stastny, P., Katz, I., Mayer, M., & Mattis, S. (1986). Memory deficits and anticholinergic levels in chronic schizophrenia. *American Journal of Psychiatry, 143,* 230–232.

Phillips, E. L. (1978). *The social skills basis of psychopathology: Alternatives to abnormal psychology and psychiatry.* New York: Grune & Stratton.

Pickar, D., Owen, R. R., Litman, R. E., Konicki, P. E., Gutierrez, R., & Rapaport, M. H. (1992). Clinical and biologic response to clozapine in patients with schizophrenia: Crossover comparison with fluphenazine. *Archives of General Psychiatry, 49,* 345–353.

Platt, J. J., & Spivack, G. (1972a). Problem-solving thinking of psychiatric patients. *Journal of Consulting and Clinical Psychology, 39,* 148–151.

Platt, J. J., & Spivack, G. (1972b). Social competence and effective problem-solving thinking in psychiatric patients. *Journal of Clinical Psychology, 28,* 3–5.

Psychiatric Rehabilitation Consultants. (1994). *Modules in the UCLA Social and Independent Living Skills Series.* (Available from Psychiatric Rehabilitation Consultants, PO Box 6620, Camarillo, CA 93011–6620).

Rehm, L. P. (1977). A self-control model of depression. *Behavior Therapy, 8,* 787–804.

Rehm, L. P. (1982). Self-management in depression. In P. Karoly & F. H. Kanfer (Eds.), *The psychology of self-management: From theory to practice.* Elmsford, NY: Pergamon Press.

Rehm, L. P. (1984). Self-management therapy for depression. *Advances in Behavioral Research and Therapy, 6,* 83–94.

Rund, B. R. (1990). Fully recovered schizophrenics: A retrospective study of some premorbid and treatment factors. *Psychiatry, 53,* 127–139.

Silverman J. (1964). The problem of attention in research and theory in schizophrenia. *Psychological Review, 71,* 352–379.

Spohn, H. E., Coyne, L., Lacousiere, R., Mazur, D., & Hayes, K. (1985). Relation of neuroleptic dose and tardive dyskinesia to attention, information-processing, and psychophysiology in medicated schizophrenics. *Archives of General Psychiatry, 42,* 849–859.

Spohn, H. E., Lacoursiere, R. B., Thompson, R., & Coyne L. (1977). Phenothiazine effects on psychological and psychophysiological dysfunction in chronic schizophrenics. *Archives of General Psychiatry, 34,* 633–644.

Sprafkin, R. P., Gershaw, N. J., & Goldstein, A. P. (1993). *Social skills for mental health: A structured learning approach.* Boston: Allyn & Bacon.

Strauss, M. E., Lew, M. F., Coyle, J. T., & Tune, L. E. (1985). Psychopharmacologic and clinical correlates of attention in chronic schizophrenia. *American Journal of Psychiatry, 142,* 497–499.

Sweeney, J. A., Keilp, J. G., Haas, G. L., Hill, J., & Weiden, P. J. (1991). Relationships between medication treatments and neuropsychological test performance in schizophrenia. *Psychiatry Research, 37,* 297–308.

Trower, P. (1982). Toward a generative model of social skills: A critique and synthesis. In J. P. Curran & P. M. Monti (Eds.), *Social skills training: A practical handbook for assessment and treatment* (pp. 399–427). New York: Guilford Press.

Trower, P., Bryant, B., & Argyle, M. (1978). *Social skills and mental health.* London: Methuen.

Van Dam-Baggen, R., & Kraaimaat, F. (1986). A group social skills training program with psychiatric patients: Outcome, dropout rate, and prediction. *Behavior Research and Therapy, 34,* 161–169.

Van Putten, T., Gelenberg, A. J., Lavori, P. W., Falk, W. E., Marder, S. R., Spring, B., Mohs, R. C., & Brotman, A. W. (1987). Anticholinergic effects on memory: Benztropine vs. amantadine. *Psychopharmacology Bulletin, 23,* 26–29.

Venables, P. H. (1964). Input dysfunction in schizophrenia.

In B. A. Maher (Ed.), *Progress in experimental personality research* (Vol. 1; pp. 417–441). New York: Academic Press.

Ventura, J., Nuechterlein, K. H., Hardesty, J., & Gitlin, M. J. (1992). Life events and schizophrenic relapse during medication withdrawal. *British Journal of Psychiatry, 161,* 615–620.

Wahba, M., Donlon, P. T., & Meadow, A. (1981). Cognitive changes in acute schizophrenia with brief neuroleptic treatment. *American Journal of Psychiatry, 138,* 1307–1310.

Wallace, C. J. (1982). The Social Skills Training Project of the Mental Health Clinical Research Center for the Study of Schizophrenia. In J. P. Curran & P. M. Monti (Eds.), *Social skills training: A practical handbook for assessment and treatment* (pp. 57–89). New York: Guilford Press.

Wallace, C. J., & Liberman, R. P. (1985). Social skills training for schizophrenics: A controlled clinical trial. *Psychiatry Research, 15,* 239–247.

Wallace, C. J., Liberman, R. P., MacKain, S. J., Blackwell, G., & Eckman, T. A. (1992). Effectiveness and replicability of modules for teaching social and instrumental skills to the severely mentally ill. *American Journal of Psychiatry, 149,* 654–658.

Wallace, C. J., Nelson, C. J., Liberman, R. P., Aitchison, R. A., Lukoff, D., Elder, J. P., & Ferris C. (1980). A review and critique of social skills training with schizophrenic patients. *Schizophrenia Bulletin, 6,* 42–63.

Weissman, M. M., & Bothwell, S. (1976). Assessment of social adjustment by patient self-report. *Archives of General Psychiatry, 35,* 1111–1115.

Wessburg, H. W., Curran, J. P., Monti, P. M., Corriveau, D. P., Coyne, N. A., & Dziadosz, T. H. (1981). Evidence for the external validity of a social simulation measure of social skills. *Journal of Behavioral Assessment, 3,* 209–220.

Wicker, A. W. (1987). Behavior settings reconsidered: Temporal stages, resources, internal dynamics, context. In D. Stokols & I. Altman (Eds.), *Handbook of environmental psychology* (Vol. 1; pp. 613–653). New York: Wiley.

Willems, E. P. (1976). Behavioral ecology, health status, and health care: Applications to the rehabilitation setting. In I. Altman & J. F. Wohlwill (Eds.), *Human behavior and environment* (pp. 211–263). New York: Plenum Press.

Wirshing, W., Eckman, T. A., Liberman, R. P., & Marder, S. R. (1991). Management of risk of relapse through skills training of chronic schizophrenics. In C. Tamminga & S. C. Schulz (Eds.), *Schizophrenia research* (pp. 255–267). New York: Raven Press.

Wong, S. E., Martinez-Diaz, J. A., Massel, H. K., Edelstein, B. A., Weingand, W., Bowen, L., & Liberman, R. P. (1993). Conversational skills training with schizophrenic inpatients: A study of generalization across settings and conversants. *Behavior Therapy, 24,* 285–304.

Zubin, J., & Spring, B. (1977). Vulnerability—A new view of schizophrenia. *Journal of Abnormal Psychology, 86,* 103–126.

CHAPTER 20

SOCIAL FUNCTIONING AND FAMILY INTERVENTIONS

Christine Barrowclough
Nicholas Tarrier

Since the early 1980s a number of studies of psychosocial interventions with families of schizophrenia patients have been published. There have been several detailed reviews of these studies (Barrowclough & Tarrier, 1984; Lam, 1991; Kavanagh, 1992; Mari & Streiner, 1994), which have set out the achievements and limitations of the work to date. While outlining details of controlled studies of family interventions, this chapter will provide a narrower focus than previous reviews, primarily attending to issues associated with the patient's social functioning in the context of family interventions. We will aim to look at the role of the patient in the family studies; examine evidence of benefits to patient functioning associated with family interventions; look at possible mechanisms for family interventions improving social functioning; and make recommendations for future studies.

BACKGROUND TO THE FAMILY INTERVENTIONS

We have suggested that there were a number of reasons for the development of interventions with the families of schizophrenia sufferers (Tarrier & Barrowclough, 1990).

These included the recognition that neuroleptic treatments provided only limited protection to illness recurrence with 30 to 50% of drug-compliant patients relapsing in the first year after discharge (Falloon, Watt, & Shepherd, 1978; Hogarty et al., 1979) and the influence of psychobiological vulnerability-stress models in formulating models of relapse mechanisms (Zubin & Spring, 1977). The principle of this vulnerability-stress formulation, that psychological and social stressors and mediators can influence the course of schizophrenia, provided a rationale to management strategies aimed at modifying these factors with the goal of producing positive change in the course of the disorder. However, undoubtedly the greatest impetus to the family intervention work was the development of the concept of expressed emotion (EE).

In the early 1950s a series of research studies carried out by Brown and his colleagues at the Medical Research Council (MRC) Social Psychiatry Unit in London investigated the outcome of patients discharged from psychiatric hospitals (Brown, 1985; Leff & Vaughn, 1985). The initial finding that patients diagnosed as suffering from schizophrenia who returned to live with their parents and close family did worse than those who lived alone or in hostel accommodations (Brown, Carstairs, & Topping, 1958) stimulated an attempt to investigate the nature of the home environment (Brown, 1985). This resulted in the development of the measure of EE. Although what EE actually represents is still the subject of much debate (see, for example, Kavanagh, 1992), it was initially formulated as an index of the emotional climate within the home environment and an attempt to assess the quality of the relationship between patient and relative. The nature of this emotional climate was viewed as potentially important in the development of the course of schizophrenia. The initial studies of Brown and colleagues (Brown, Monck, Carstairs, & Wing, 1962; Birley & Wing, 1972) and the later study of Vaughn and Leff (1976) demonstrated an association between EE and relapse. In these studies, patients were recruited during hospitalization for an acute episode of schizophrenia, and their relatives' EE status was assessed. A significant link was established between the EE status of the relatives and the relapse rates of the patients in a 9-month follow-up period. Many replications have followed with largely similar results. Kavanagh (1992) reviewed 23 prospective studies examining the relationship between EE and relapse. Twenty studies showed a higher relapse rate in patients returning to live in high EE households, and 17 of these associations were significant. Bebbington and Kuipers's (1994) recent aggregate analysis of 25 studies from around the world gave a relapse rate of 50% for patients from high EE households and 21% for low EE families. Because EE was a reliable predictor of relapse in patients who had experienced episodes of illness, it was suggested that high EE was not simply a risk factor but an explanatory variable in relapse. A number of intervention studies were driven by the rationale that change in the EE status of the relatives from low to high would reduce relapse rates.

CONTROLLED STUDIES OF FAMILY INTERVENTIONS IN HIGH EE HOUSEHOLD

In these controlled studies, sometimes EE has been used as an index of high risk of relapse, as in the studies of Falloon and colleagues and Hogarty and colleagues (Falloon et al., 1982, 1985, Hogarty et al., 1986, 1991); or EE has been an important focus of the intervention whereby there has been an explicit attempt to change relatives' EE status from high to low in the intervention families, as in the studies of Leff and colleagues and Tarrier and colleagues (Leff, Kuipers, Berkowitz, Eberlein-Fries, & Sturgeon, 1982; Leff, Kuipers, Berkowitz, & Sturgeon,

1985; Tarrier et al., 1988, 1989; Tarrier, Barrowclough, Porceddu, & Fitzpatrick, 1994). Patients from high EE households are randomly assigned to treatments and a comparison is made either with routine care alone (treatment as usual) or other psychosocial interventions. The main outcome evaluated is relapse rate (see Table 20.1 for a summary). There is considerable variation in the rationales and content of these family intervention packages. This variation is partly attributable to our inadequate knowledge about psychosocial relapse mechanisms. Although the link between EE and patient relapse is well established, our knowledge of how the EE measure translates into behaviors capable of triggering relapse is unclear. Certainly we have no understanding of what are the most damaging or stressful aspects of high EE relatives' behavior. Hence, interventions are at best driven by clearly stated assumptions about targeted areas for change, and usually the techniques for change are derived from the particular background and experience of the researchers. One aspect of the variation in content of interventions is the degree of involvement of the patient in the family intervention studies. While the main target of intervention in all the studies has been the relatives, all except one study, that of Vaughan et al. (1992) in Sydney, have included some degree of direct intervention with the patient.

Three trials of family intervention with high EE families have taken place in the United Kingdom, and two of these have been carried out by Julian Leff and colleagues at the Institute of Psychiatry in London. The first trial evaluated a family intervention consisting of education for relatives about schizophrenia, relatives' groups, and individual family therapy sessions in the home (Leff et al., 1982, 1985). Their therapeutic approach is best described as eclectic and included systemic techniques. The relatives' groups aimed to provide support and some alternative strategies for dealing with problems, and low EE relatives were encouraged to attend the groups for the purpose of modeling appropriate behaviors. Patients attended an initial joint session with the relatives, but improving the patient's functioning was not an explicit aim of the intervention and they did not attend the groups. They were sometimes included in the home family therapy sessions. These sessions were not initially planned, and the original intervention consisted of education sessions and relatives' groups only (Berkowitz, Kuipers, Eberlein-Fries, & Leff, 1981). The researchers found that some relatives did not attend groups, and certain issues could not be dealt with in group context, so home visits were arranged which varied in frequency according to the therapist's judgment of the family's needs

Table 20.1. Relapse Rates (in percentages) for Family Intervention Studies

STUDIES	9–12 MONTHS	18–24 MONTHS	60 MONTHS	90 MONTHS
Comparisons with no treatment				
LONDON STUDY 1 (Leff et al., 1982, 1985)				
Family Intervention*	8%	20%		
Routine Treatment*	50%	78%		
CALIFORNIA STUDY 1 (Falloon et al., 1982; 1985)				
Family Intervention*	8%	33%		
Individual Intervention*	17%	36%		
HAMBURG STUDY (Kottgen et al., 1984)				
Psychodynamic Groups*	33%			
Control Group*	43%			
PITTSBURGH STUDY (Hogarty et al., 1986, 1991)				
Family Intervention*	23 (19)%	(33%)		
Social Skills Training*	30 (20)%	(43%)		
Combined FI & SST*	9 (0)%	(25%)		
Control Group*	41%	66%		
SALFORD STUDY (Tarrier et al., 1988, 1989, 1994)				
Family Intervention*	12 (5)%	33 (24)%	62%	67%
Routine Treatment*	48%	59%	83%	88%
SYDNEY STUDY (Vaughan et al., 1992)				
Relatives' Counseling*	41%			
Control Group*	65%			
CALIFORNIA STUDY 2 (Randolph et al., 1994)				
Family Intervention	14.3%			
Customary Care	55%			
AMSTERDAM STUDY (Linszen et al., 1996)				
Family Intervention & ST	16%			
Standard Treatment (ST)	15%			
SHASI CITY (CHINA) STUDY (Xiong et al., 1994)				
Family Intervention	12%	12.5%		
Control Group	33%	44%		
Comparison of different forms of family intervention				
LONDON STUDY 2 (Leff et al., 1989, 1990)				
Family Therapy*	8%	33%		
Relatives' Groups*	17%	36%		
NEW YORK STATE (6-SITE STUDY) (McFarlane et al., 1995)				
Family Groups	16 (14)%	28 (30)%		
Individual Family Treatment	28 (31)%	42 (48)%		
NIMH (5-CENTER STUDY) (Schooler et al., 1997)				
Intensive Family Intervention	28%	34%		
Supportive Family Intervention	26%	35%		

Percentages in parentheses represent treatment takers only and exclude those who did not complete the intervention program.
Studies marked * recruited patients from high EE households, those without * are mixed.
In the Amsterdam study, ST consisted of inpatient work with families and considerable outpatient intervention.

(there was a range of 1 to 25 visits with a median of 4.7). Leff and colleagues' first intervention lasted 9 months and was compared to routine care carried out by the local National Health Service (NHS) mental health services. Their second trial attempted to examine which of the components of their intervention package were effective. Accordingly, a comparison was made between education plus relatives' groups and education plus individual family therapy. The authors describe the approaches to be similar to those in the earlier study (Leff et al., 1989, 1990). Thus patients would have usually taken part in at least some of the individual therapy sessions but not the relatives' groups. Attendance at the relatives' groups, however, was poor with only 50% of the families attending one or more of the sessions.

The third U.K. study was carried out by Tarrier and Barrowclough and colleagues in Salford (Tarrier et al., 1988, 1989, 1994). Although like Leff's group they were guided by the EE concept, this group was strongly influenced by the behavior therapy movement. Unlike Leff, they explicitly targeted the patient as well as the relative for intervention. Three types of intervention for high EE families were compared with NHS routine care: a short, two-session education program which provided relatives with information about schizophrenia and general advice on how best to manage the patient at home and two extended, 9-month interventions which consisted of the short education program, four sessions on stress management, and nine sessions on goal setting to increase patient functioning. The latter two experimental conditions were described as symbolic and enactive, both being identical in content, but the symbolic was carried out through discussion and verbal advice (symbolic level) and the enactive used behavioral rehearsal and other interventions at the enactive level. Patients living with low EE families were also recruited into the study and a comparison of outcomes was made between the education program and routine care with these families. The family intervention had two principal aims. The first was to decrease EE from high to low in the intervention groups, and the second was to encourage an increase in the patient's level of functioning, through a systematic identification of needs and planning of goals to meet those needs. Hence, with most families there was considerable involvement of the patient in the intervention.

Two studies targeting high EE families have been completed in the United States. The first by Falloon and colleagues was carried out in California (Falloon et al., 1982, 1985). Falloon and his colleagues were influenced by the EE research and also by their prior work on social skills training (Wallace et al., 1980), which they now applied to the family setting using behavioral methods to improve communication within the family and a problem-solving format to enhance the use of these communication skills. Their trial tested the efficacy of a family intervention package consisting of an education program for relatives, communication training, and problem solving. The control group received an identical program carried out with the individual patient rather than the family. Patients in Falloon's study had greater involvement than in any of the other controlled trials, since it was felt that improvement of both the relatives' and the patients' problem-solving ability to deal with stressors was necessary to achieve good patient outcomes. They saw the restoration of the patient to a level of effective psychosocial functioning as an even more important goal than relapse prevention.

The second North American study was carried out by Hogarty and colleagues in Pittsburgh (Hogarty et al., 1986, 1991). This group had a research tradition of intervention studies with schizophrenia, having published the results of two large trials which evaluated the effectiveness of maintenance neuroleptic medication (active versus placebo) and "sociotherapy" (intensive individual social casework) (Hogarty, Hogarty, Goldberg, & the Collaborative Group, 1973); and depot versus oral medication and "social therapy" (individual plus family casework) (Hogarty et al., 1979). Hogarty and his colleagues then progressed to a large study examining the efficacy of family intervention (FI), social skills training (SST), a combination of both FI and SST, and medication alone with patients living with high EE relatives. The FI was termed Psychoeducation and consisted of four phases: Connecting—involving forming a therapeutic alliance with the relatives; Survival Skills' Workshop—a day-long, multiple-family workshop designed to give relatives information about the illness and to establish the themes of the rest of the program; Reentry and Application of Survival Skills Themes to Individual Families these—family sessions included the patient with biweekly sessions over a minimum of 6 months and included communication training and problem solving; and Continued Treatment or Disengagement—giving families the option to move to family therapy or continued support. The majority of the family intervention sessions were attended by the patient. The SST involved the patient alone but focused on the patient's interaction skills in dealing with his or her family and later in the wider community setting.

One study was carried out in Hamburg, Germany, and differs from the others in that it was largely psychodynamic in content and consisted of separate groups for relatives and patients (Kottgen, Soinnichsen, Mollenhauer, & Jurth, 1984; Dulz & Hand, 1986). Although the patients were directly involved in therapeutic sessions, they were always seen separately from the relatives. They describe their intervention method as "indirect family therapy" (Dulz & Hand, 1986, p. 61), derived from an eclectic-psychodynamic basis which appears quite different from the direct and problem-oriented methods of most of the other family intervention studies. The frequency and content of the sessions varied for different groups of relatives and patients; and attendance of both relatives and patients was poor with only 38% of relatives and 31% of patients attending regularly (Kottgen et al., 1984). The results suggest little benefit from this type of intervention. The study is also unusual in that a low EE control group had much higher relapse rates (65%) than high EE groups.

A further study which failed to reduce relapse from family intervention was carried out in Sydney, Australia, by Vaughan and colleagues (Vaughan et al., 1992). These workers had a behavioral tradition and adapted their intervention from the work of Hogarty and colleagues. This intervention was of much shorter duration than the others, being of 10 sessions over 3 months instead of extending over 9 to 12 months as in the other controlled trials. It aimed to reduce relatives' levels of EE and was carried out solely with the relatives. The research intervention team had no contact with the patient. Because the behavior and characteristics of the relatives were viewed of paramount importance to patient relapse risk, the research team did not liaise at all with the clinical team that was caring for the patient.

As we have noted, these controlled studies differed in the content and orientation of their family interventions. However, they are all characterized by the recruitment of patients whose relative(s) are assessed as high EE status while the patient has been suffering an acute psychotic episode, the vast majority of patients being hospitalized at the time of recruitment. The intervention commenced on their discharge and the patient was followed up usually after 9 or 12 months. Except in the Sydney study the intervention took place over this follow-up period.

CONTROLLED STUDIES OF INTERVENTIONS FOR BOTH LOW AND HIGH EE PATIENTS

Two studies have evaluated family interventions for patients drawn from samples of low as well as high EE family constellations (see Table 20.1 for relapse rates). A recently published trial carried out by Randolph and colleagues (1994) compared the Falloon version of behavioral family management with customary care. Whereas the original trial of Falloon and coworkers had involved intervention being delivered to the family's home, Randolph et al.'s intervention was clinic based, and

patients allocated to intervention and control conditions were from both high (58%) and low (42%) EE families. Significant benefits were again reported for family intervention over the control treatment. It was further reported that family intervention conferred advantage to both high EE and low EE families.

The Amsterdam study (Linszen et al., 1996) compared an inpatient and outpatient intensive individual therapy (standard treatment, ST) with the same program plus a Falloon-style family intervention (ST + FI), which commenced on discharge. As with the Falloon group's intervention, all the family intervention work took place in conjoint sessions attended by relatives and patients. In both ST alone and ST + FI, relatives attended one or two sessions with the patient's treatment staff to establish a collaborative alliance and participated in two sessions of psychoeducation groups during the inpatient treatment. Furthermore, in ST patients received intensive individual therapy. Patients were assigned to the conditions in proportion to their EE status in the sample as a whole (37% low, 63% high). The family intervention did not add any further benefit to ST as measured by relapse rates. However, relapse rates in both groups were low. Unlike the Randolph study, patients from low EE families who received FI appeared to do worse that those from low EE families who did not. Linszen mixed family involvement across both his treatment groups during the inpatient phase although only the combined ST + FI group received family aftercare on an outpatient basis. Although there appeared to be no advantage in family care on an outpatient basis, it remains questionable whether the inpatient family involvement mediate reduced relapse rates 9 months after discharge in the standard treatment group. Or did the individual treatment account for all patient gains?

FURTHER CONTROLLED STUDIES OF FAMILY INTERVENTION

Four further controlled studies have been reported where the EE status of patients' families has not been assessed. In an evaluation of family intervention versus standard care carried out in China (Xiong et al., 1994), relapse and rehospitalization rates were significantly reduced at 12 and 18 months in the intervention group. The authors remark that many of the assumptions made in Western family intervention work could not be made in China. They note that the complex family relationships in Chinese culture make such goals as independence for the patient untenable, and family intervention goals and practice had to be modified to accommodate these issues. In a study carried out in Munich (Hahlweg et al., 1995), two groups receiving family intervention had different drug protocols, one the standard continuous prophylactic dose of neuroleptics and the other targeted medication. Although the relapse rates for the former group were lower at 9 and 18 months than the targeted medication group, the relapse rates of the latter were still low compared to those found in the control groups of other studies. Despite there being considerable focus on the improvement of the patient in these two studies, little is known about social functioning outcomes.

The results of two multisite family intervention studies are now available. McFarlane et al. (1995) compared outcomes in psychoeducational multiple-family group treatment versus psychoeducational single-family treatment. They report that the style and content of the interventions were derived from those developed by Anderson et al. (as used in the Hogarty study) and by Falloon. Six sites in New York State participated, with a total sample of 172 patients. Contrary to the study of Leff et al. (1989), the multiple-family group format was more effective than its single-family treatment counterpart in terms of relapse outcomes and appeared to be most advantageous with patients who were more symptomatic at hospital discharge. In the National Institute of Mental Health study (Schooler et al., 1997), five centers across the United States participated in a trial investigating dose reduction of antipsychotic medication in interaction with family treatments. Two levels of family intervention were compared: Supportive Family Management, consisting of monthly group meetings, and Applied Family Management, with weekly intensive home-based sessions following the approach of Falloon. The results indicated that there were no differential effects of the two family treatment conditions.

RELAPSE OUTCOMES

The percentage relapse rates for all the reported controlled studies are presented in Table 20.1 All studies present relapse rates of 9 to 12 months. A total of 9 studies compared family intervention with routine care, and it can be seen from Table 20.1 that 6 (Leff et al., 1982; Falloon et al., 1982; Hogarty et al., 1986; Tarrier et al., 1988; Randolph et al., 1994, Xiong et al., 1994) demonstrate significant reductions in relapse rates for families receiving the family intervention at 9 to 12 months; and in studies where different forms of family interventions were compared (Leff et al., 1989; McFarlane et al., 1995; Schooler

et al., 1997), the rates for all forms of interventions are lower than the rates for routine care alone in the earlier studies. Three studies, the Hamburg study (Kottgen et al., 1984) the Sydney study (Vaughan et al., 1992), and the Amsterdam study (Linszen et al., 1996), were unable to demonstrate significant benefits of their interventions although as noted above, relapse rates for the latter study were very low across groups and there was some family involvement and individual treatment in the standard care. However, the relapse rates for the former two studies were high and demonstrated significant benefits of their interventions. It should be noted that both these studies used interventions which differed markedly from those implemented by the successful trials. Significantly, the Sydney study excluded the patient from all sessions; and the Hamburg study separated the patients from the relatives while using therapy techniques (psychodynamic) which were different from all the other interventions. Four studies (Leff et al., 1989; Tarrier et at, 1988; McFarlane et al., 1995; Schooler et al., 1997) compared different forms of family interventions. With the exception of the McFarlane and colleagues' study, differences in neither the format nor the quantity of intervention resulted in significant differences in relapse rates.The second study of Leff and colleagues compared two parts of the original intervention package but was not able to show a superiority of relatives' groups over individual family session; Tarrier and colleagues were unable to demonstrate a superiority of their Enactive intervention over their Symbolic intervention as they had predicted (Tarrier & Barrowclough, 1995); neither was their short Education program found to be significantly better than routine care. Schooler et al.'s multisite study found no superiority of weekly individual family sessions over monthly group meetings. McFarlane and coworkers found reduced relapse rates in the multiple-family group over single-family group condition and attribute the superiority of the group format to its expansion of the patient's and family's social network. Hogarty and colleagues found that at 12 months family intervention and social skills training were approximately equivalent, but in combination the intervention prevented relapses in families who completed treatment. Relapses were fewer in the family intervention group compared to the SST group if treatment dropouts were included.

Nine studies have included a 2-year follow-up which demonstrated that although relapses increase in the second year a significant benefit is still maintained from family intervention. Schizophrenia is a disorder which frequently starts in late adolescence or early adulthood and continues for the rest of the patient's life, hence, 2 years as a follow-up period is a very short time. Tarrier and colleagues (Tarrier, Barrowclough, Porceddu, & Fitzpatrick, 1994) have followed up their patient cohort through examination of the psychiatric notes for a longer period, assessing relapse at both 5 years and 8 years. Because of the earlier results which did not demonstrate a difference between Enactive and Symbolic treatments or between Education and routine care, the groups have been collapsed into three groups: family intervention, high EE control, and low EE control.

These results indicate that although there is an accumulating increase in the number of patients who relapse over the extended follow-up period the difference between the family intervention group and the high EE control group is maintained for up to 8 years. However, over two-thirds of patients who received family intervention with their families do eventually relapse.

SOCIAL FUNCTIONING OUTCOMES

Two of the studies included improvement in patient functioning as an explicit family intervention goal (Falloon, Boyd, & McGill, 1984; Barrowclough & Tarrier, 1990), and accordingly they systematically measured social functioning in the patient before and after intervention. In Leff et al.'s (1989) study of individual family therapy versus relatives' groups, they looked at the effects of the interventions on patients' social and occupational activities by using data from the time budget of the Camberwell Family Interview and from the therapists' reports. Information was collected under the headings of living group, sexual relationship, friends, and occupation. For the 22 patients included in the analysis, 2 patients moved to independent living, 3 patients showed small improvement in social activity, and there was a small net loss in sexual relationships. Two of the 3 employed patients lost their jobs, while 5 patients began day care. One is struck by the very limited social progress of this group and the continued social impairment that such lack of progress implies. Leff's group suggests that progress in social functioning depends on the amelioration of the negative symptoms of schizophrenia, and that this occurs more slowly than improvement in positive symptoms, hence one cannot expect much change over a 9-month follow-up. However, the deficits in interpersonal functioning of schizophrenic patients are more than a consequence of positive and negative symptoms, and patients exhibit so-

cial skills deficits even in remission and in the absence of a manifest negative syndrome (Halford & Hayes, 1991).

Both the Falloon and Tarrier studies were more encouraging as regards the potential of family interventions to improve social functioning. They found that patients in the family intervention group showed significant improvements in social functioning, although the improvements were small. In the Salford study the patients' social functioning was assessed using Birchwood, Smith, Cochrane, Wetton, and Copestake's (1990) Social Functioning Scale (SFS). The scale consists of seven subscales: withdrawal, interpersonal functioning, prosocial activities, recreation, independence (competence), independence (performance), and employment, and a total score. The scales were completed by the relative who had most contact with the patient at several assessment points, including index admission and 9 months after discharge. For the high EE intervention group, there were significant improvements between admission and 9 months on withdrawal, interpersonal functioning, prosocial activities, and total score. The high EE control group had significant improvement on only one subscale (interpersonal functioning) and no significant change in total score. Patients with low EE relatives showed improvement on the total score and two subscales (interpersonal functioning and independence-performance). The changes in the total score are represented in Figure 20.1, again groups have been collapsed into family intervention group and high EE control group. As can be seen the changes although significant are quite small. If the changes in the patients' social functioning are graphed by dividing patients into those whose

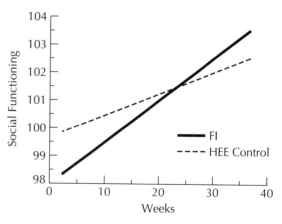

Figure 20.1. Changes in social functioning with family intervention

relatives remained high EE at 9-month follow-up and into those whose relatives changed from high to low EE at follow-up the difference is quite dramatic (see Figure 20.2). In Figure 20.2 it can be seen that there is a considerable increase in patients' level of social functioning when the patients' relatives change from high to low EE, whereas where relatives remain high EE the patients' level of social functioning remains static.

Falloon et al. (1984) assessed the social functioning of the patients in three ways: clinical reports of the patient's work, study, and leisure activities; patient's self-report of his or her work, leisure, interpersonal, and family functioning using the Social Adjustment Scales (SAS; Weissman, Prusoff, Thompson, Harding, & Myers, 1978); and the report of a family informant on the patient's social performance and behavioral disturbance using the Social Behavior Assessment Schedule (SBAS; Platt, Weyman, Hirsch, & Hewitt, 1980). As regards clinical impressions, the authors report (Falloon et al., 1984) that family treatment appeared to enhance work and educational activities, whereas there was no increase in the activity levels of the individually treated patients. For self-reports of social functioning, "small but significant gains in social adjustment occurred in patients receiving family intervention, whereas the group receiving individual treatment showed no overall improvement" (p. 842).

However, Falloon's group reports that several patients had difficulty completing the SAS questionnaire in a valid manner. The primary measure of social functioning was derived from the SBAS. For both behavioral disturbance and social performance, there were significant gains in the

family treated patients over those receiving individual help. As with Barrowclough and Tarrier's (1990) findings, these gains were by and large small. Most improvement was shown in the social impairments associated with schizophrenia, such as withdrawal, bizarre behavior, and neglect. There was less change in areas associated with affective disturbance (e.g., sleep disturbance) and at least 50% of the family treated patients remained impaired in the areas of household tasks, leisure activities, and work or study. In Barrowclough and Tarrier's study, there was no significant improvement in these areas as assessed on the SFS. In Falloon et al.'s study, however, relatives of family treated patients reported substantially less distress than relatives of individually treated patients concerning the impaired social performance at 9-month follow-up. Falloon et al. suggest that family therapy may have contributed to a reduction in the level of expectations for relatives of unimpaired social functioning in their sons and daughters.

The fact that the interventions to date have only demonstrated modest gains in the functioning of patients may help explain the findings of Glick et al. (1990). In an 18-month follow-up of a randomized clinical trial of inpatient family intervention, they found that the family intervention was more efficacious for poorer functioning patients in terms of their global functioning, symptomatology and role functioning, and also relatives of such patients showed more positive attitudes. The authors suggest that their "poorer functioning" group were similar to patients in outpatient family intervention studies: a tentative conclusion is that to date, the interventions have not addressed how to improve patient functioning beyond a very basic level.

Although Hogarty et al.'s study contained a social skills training (SST) component, relapse rates are the only form of outcome report. Hence, we are unable to assess whether this study confirms Falloon's finding that social skills training has a superior effect on social functioning when it takes place within rather than outside of the family context, or whether the social skills training had a specific or nonspecific effect on outcome. However, we do know from Hogarty's study that intervention with the patient alone can have a significant effect on clinical outcome, and that this effect matches that of family intervention at least during the first year's follow-up. At 2-year follow-up, the effect of the SST component was no longer observed, and hence there was no combined additive effect of family therapy and social skills training by 2 years. However, survival analysis indicates that the SST alone

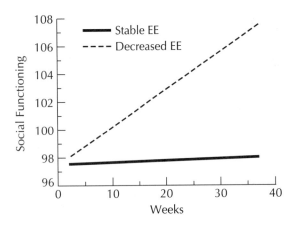

Figure 20.2. Patients' social functioning and changes in relatives' EE

effect was lost only late in the second year. Hogarty et al. (1991) suggest that this decay in SST effect might be accounted for by the "preparation for termination" process in the latter part of year 2. While there were options for continuing family therapy, there was no option for continued SST after termination of the study. "This awareness might have contributed to the destabilization of some SST recipients late in the second year" (p. 345).

TRAINING PROGRAMS

A set of studies has examined the dissemination of family intervention work into clinical practice by evaluating training programs in which professional staff, mainly community psychiatric nurses (CPNs), were instructed on how to carry out family interventions and are then supervised in its practice. In these studies patients and their families were recruited from the nurses' caseloads; hence, recruitment was made during community tenure rather than during an acute episode and hospitalization. One measure of the effectiveness of the training program was an assessment of patient outcomes, including social functioning as measured by the Social Functioning Scale (SFS; Birchwood et al., 1990) completed by the patients' relatives. In the first study, Brooker, Tarrier, Barrowclough, Butterworth, and Goldberg (1992), using a quasi-experimental design, allocated nine CPNs to training in family intervention methods with the aim of treating three families each. A similar number of control CPNs, matched for age, sex, training, and experience aimed to recruit three families each to act as controls. The CPNs were trained in family intervention methods used in the Salford Family Intervention Project (Barrowclough & Tarrier, 1992). This would have provided a total of 54 patients and their families in the study. Initially 87% ($n = 47$) of the target sample was achieved; however, 17 families dropped out and 30 families (64% of the target sample) completed the trial. Social functioning significantly improved in the treatment group over the 6-month treatment period and over the 6-month follow-up. No significant changes were observed in the patients cared for by the untrained control nurses. There were also indications that relatives' satisfaction with the patients' performance significantly increased in the treatment group but not in the control group.

In a second evaluation of family management training also carried out in Manchester by Brooker et al. (1994), 10 CPNs were recruited for training and 48 of their patients and families were selected for the project. Patients were randomly allocated either to receive family intervention or to a wait list control group from which they would be offered family intervention at the end of the study. Forty-one patients were eventually recruited, of which 34 remained in the study for 12 months. On this occasion training was carried out by the Falloon group. In the group of patients who received intervention, there was a significant improvement in positive and negative symptoms of schizophrenia and in the scores on the Social Functioning Scale.

Partially in response to the studies of Brooker and his colleagues and partially in response to a general demand to disseminate more widely the research findings on psychosocial intervention, the Thorn Nurse Training project was established. The project, funded by the Sir Jules Thorn Charitable Trust, established two training centers, one at Manchester and one at the Institute of Psychiatry, London, who were mandated to offer to CPNs problem-oriented training in the psychosocial management of schizophrenia. The training course consisted of part-time study for one academic year in three modules: case management, family intervention, and psychological treatment of schizophrenia. As in previous studies, the evaluation of the training program incorporated measurement of patient outcomes including social functioning, but in this evaluation the SFS was completed by the patient with the help of the nurse. Although the study has yet to be completed, the initial results indicate that significant increases in social functioning are demonstrated in patients under the care of Thorn-trained nurses (Lancashire et al., 1997). Figure 20.3 displays the changes in scores on the

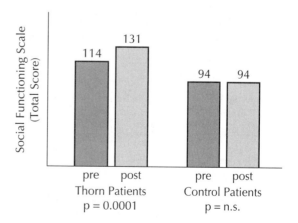

Figure 20.3. Changes in social functioning of patients cared for by Thorn trainees

total score of the Social Functioning Scale of two cohorts of Thorn trainees from the Manchester course and includes the results of the control patients from Brooker et al.'s (1994) study for comparison.

These training evaluation studies differ from the family intervention studies in that they do not recruit patients during a hospital admission for an acute episode, they do not select high EE families, and they do not focus on relapse as the principle outcome measure. The training studies use a broader range of outcomes, including social functioning, with which to test their main hypothesis. These studies are, however, evaluations of training programs for which patient outcomes are being used as an evaluation measure, and they are not evaluations of treatment efficacy using functioning as their principle outcome measure. Some caution must therefore be used in their interpretation.

SOCIAL FUNCTIONING AND FAMILY INTERVENTION PROGRAMS

The outcomes of the controlled family intervention studies raise some important questions concerning social functioning in patients. First, can individual social skills training improve clinical outcome in patients living with families, or is family intervention superior? Second, what are the mechanisms for family intervention achieving improved social functioning in patients? Third, what influences external to the training program will effect social functioning outcomes? Finally, how might future interventions be designed so that they achieve improvements in patient functioning as well as reductions in positive symptoms?

Individual Treatment Versus Family Intervention

While the Hogarty group's individual SST had a significant effect on relapse rates, at least in the short term, the Falloon group's individual treatment had no significant effect on clinical outcomes. Linszen and colleagues' study outcome is more difficult to interpret since individually treated patients had family involvement during the inpatient phase.

Is it then possible to achieve a decrease in symptomatic exacerbations of the illness without involving the patients' family, even when the relatives are high EE? What mechanisms might have operated in the Hogarty or Lin-

szen study that were not working in Falloon's individual treatment group? As noted above, without measures of social adjustment we are unable to assess specific treatment effects in Hogarty's individually treated group. However, it is notable that the emphasis of the SST in Hogarty's group was on behaviors and strategies that were designed to reduce conflict in a high EE household, and on social perception training in appropriate relationships including those within the family. Thus whereas in Falloon's study only the patient's behavior is targeted, in Hogarty's study, although the patient is individually treated both they and through their changed responses, the relatives are the targets for change. A second explanation for the efficacy of Hogarty's SST is that this intervention changed the patients' perceptions of their relatives and that this contributed to a decrease in their relapse risk. Hooley and Teasdale (1989) assessed perceived criticism by the spouse of hospitalized depressed patients. The rating predicted relapse over the next 9 months and adding EE to the classification did not significantly improve prediction. Similar findings were shown in a study by Labell et al. (1993). Patients' perceptions of their relatives' attitudes toward them was a predictor of risk of psychotic exacerbation in a 1-year follow-up, and patients in frequent contact with a positively perceived relative had significantly better survival rates without psychotic exacerbation. The patient–relative interaction studies have given evidence for the patient contributing to the escalation of communication difficulties in families: Hahlweg et al. (1989) demonstrated a greater conditional probability of reciprocation of verbal negativity between patient and relative in high EE families. Thus negative communication in high EE families is not a one-way process, hence changing the negative response of the patient would improve the communication pattern and hence be hypothesized to improve relapse risk. Evidence suggests that simple improvement in the patient's social functioning is insufficient to change their relatives' response. An uncontrolled study of Tomaras, Vlachonikolis, Stefanis, and Madianes (1988) looking at the effect of individual psychosocial treatment on the family atmosphere of schizophrenic patients demonstrated that improvement in the patients' social functioning had no immediate effect on family attitudes. Although we have insufficient information about the process of change in the intervention studies, on the available evidence it is difficult to argue that there is a straightforward relationship between patient functioning and relatives' attitudes or that improvement in patient functioning will be accompanied by changed family attitudes with a subsequent drop in the high-risk status of the patients.

Aside from the work of the Hogarty and Falloon groups, there are few other studies which have evaluated the effect of individual treatment on relapse outcomes. One other controlled study has looked at the effect of social skills training in outpatient schizophrenic patients on clinical outcomes. In Bellack, Turner, Hersen, and Luber's (1984) study, two forms of social skills training were compared with day hospital treatment only, and no superiority of the SST was found. The day hospital group were found to have improved on positive schizophrenic symptomatology to an approximately equal extent to the social skills training group, and the number of rehospitalizations over the next year were comparable between groups (approximately 50%). A further study by Wallace and Liberman (1985) randomly assigned schizophrenic inpatients to either behavioral SST or holistic health therapy (HHT) in the context of family treatment and medication. The SST group was significantly more improved than the HHT group on social adjustment measures at 9- and 12-month follow-ups, and during the 2-year follow-up the HHT patients were rehospitalized almost twice as many times as the SST group, although with only 28 patients the study had insufficient power to demonstrate a statistically significant difference. A tentative conclusion from all these studies is that individual social skills training with patients (at least those residing with relatives) only improves relapse risk when directed at improving patients' communication with and perception of high EE relatives.

Mechanisms for Family Intervention

Falloon et al. (1984) suggest that the superiority of the family treated group on measures of social functioning was due to several reasons. These included the longer periods spent in symptomatic exacerbation of the individually treated patients, which prevented them from engaging in prosocial activities. However, as noted above, a decrease in positive symptomatology does not automatically lead to improvement in social functioning. Their suggestion that family therapy led to the relatives facilitating the patients with practical matters important to obtaining and sustaining social activity "motivating them to participate in household activities and social functions, practicing jobseeking skills . . . and helping to solve difficulties associated with these activities" (p. 342) would be supported by our experience in the Salford study. In our

study, the goal-setting component of the intervention targeted aspects of the patient's low functioning for systematic intervention. However, due to the lack of process measures, we are unable to assess whether improvements in social functioning were the outcome of such specific intervention effects. Halford and Hayes (1991) suggest that the superiority for family intervention maintaining patients' functioning could be looked at in terms of operant conditioning. One of the biggest problems in social skills training with schizophrenic patients is the transfer of skills learned in treatment to the living environment. Halford and Hayes report that generalization and maintenance of socially skilled behavior may be enhanced by *behavioral traps*, social environments which provide prompts and reinforcers salient to individual patients and thereby maintain socially skilled behavior. These authors comment that in family intervention where both the patient's responses and the patient's social environment (the behavior of the family) are targeted, changes in the family's response to the patient can be seen as an example of an effective behavioral trap to maintain patient functioning.

Finally, another possibility not ruled out of the studies of both Falloon's group and Tarrier's group (and the Brooker training program research which followed from these studies) is that family management may result in a global improvement in the relatives' perceptions of the patient. Given that the main outcome measures for social functioning in both studies were completed by the relatives who had taken part in the intervention, there is good reason to suspect a confounding of relatives' attitude change with reported patient behavior change. In Birchwood et al.'s (1990) original description of the SFS it was indicated that there was a strong relationship between the relative's report of the patient's social functioning and the patient's self-report of their own functioning when the SFS was administered to each independently. There is some evidence, however, that low and high EE relatives appraise schizophrenia illness characteristics differently, with low EE relatives underestimating the patient's problems and symptoms. A study by Minz, Nuechterlein, Goldstein, Mint, and Snyder (1989) looked at differences in relatives' perceptions of duration of schizophrenic illness prior to hospital admission. They found that although high EE relatives' estimates of preadmission illness were longer than those of low EE relatives, the best estimates, based on a compilation from all sources, indicated that low EE relatives significantly underestimated the prehospitalization duration of illness. Barrowclough, Johnson, and Tarrier (1994) found that low EE relatives gave less causal attributions about patient behavior and symptoms than did high EE, a result they interpreted as suggesting that low EE relatives appraised the illness as less negative or threatening than did high EE. Falloon group's finding that relatives reported significantly less distress concerning the patient's functioning following intervention is consistent with the idea that one of the main outcomes of the intervention was a change in relatives' appraisal of the problems associated with the illness, possibly as a result of more realistic expectations, feeling less threatened or challenged by the illness, or increased optimism for the future. An objective measurement of the extent of real improvements in patients' functioning following family management would require assessments to be performed by assessors who were independent and blind to the patient's treatment condition.

External Influences on Social Functioning

It should be borne in mind that measures of social functioning usually reflect both the capability and the performance of various skills. The ability to function in an appropriate manner across a range of situations will depend on the availability of those situations and also of various resources. For example, to be in employment requires the availability of appropriate jobs; to engage in various leisure, recreational, sporting, or cultural activities and pursuits requires the appropriate facilities. All these factors will probably be strongly influence by the economic standing of the community and locality and most probably by the economic condition and policies of the nation. For various reasons the social outcomes of people with schizophrenia will be strongly influenced by economic and political factors as well as by the availability of various treatments.

Designing Interventions to Improve Patient Functioning

The use of reduction in positive symptomatology as the main outcome measure in the family intervention studies has been criticized in recent reviews (for example Mari & Streiner, 1994). It has been suggested that this emphasis on relapse fails to take into account broader quality of life issues for patients: in some circumstances reduced relapse risk may be associated with limited social functioning and thus be of little subjective value to patients or their fam-

ily. Conversely, patients and relatives may prefer to suffer the consequences of increased relapses if the quality of life for the patient is better. The above review cites a study by Kreisman, Blumenthal, Borenstein, Woerner, Kane, Rifkin and Reardon (1988) which assessed the effects of lowered doses of neuroleptics on outpatient schizophrenic patients. Although the findings of the study are limited by the low completion rate, the study found that despite the higher relapse rate among the low-dose group, families were more satisfied with this group who had more romantic encounters and were more able to take care of their own needs.

It is important to keep in mind the fact that the main aim of the family intervention was to reduce relapse risk, and the principle target for change was the relative. If included at all, patients generally had a limited role in treatment, and improvement in social functioning was a secondary aim of the researchers. Although two studies have demonstrated that improvement in social functioning was associated with decreased relapse risk, these improvements were generally modest, and for the majority of schizophrenic patients serious impairment in all areas of social adjustment is the long-term consequence of the illness. Changing outcome measures to focus on wider issues of patient functioning will not automatically lead to better outcomes without a reassessment of the goals and rationales of family interventions. Certainly we will need to substantially revise the content of the intervention programs to evaluate if further improvement in the well-being of patients is a realistic goal. Recent developments in cognitive behavioral treatment (CBT) with individual patients (see Kingdon, Turkington, & John, 1994; Sellwood, Haddock, Tarrier, & Yusupoff, 1994 for reviews) have produced significant benefits in the frequency of positive symptoms and the distress associated with them. Social functioning again has been of secondary consideration and improvements if achieved at all have been modest (Tarrier, Beckett, Harwood, Baker, Yusupoff, 1993; Kuipers, Fowler, Chamberlain, & Dunn, 1994), although there are some indications that when CBT is focused on improving social functioning gains are possible. These treatments have been developed separately from the family interventions, and the combined effects of family interventions and CBT have yet to be carefully evaluated. The provisional evidence from the Thorn study in which nurses are trained in both family intervention and individual CBT treatment has been more encouraging and suggests that these two approaches may well complement each other and result in aggregated benefits (Lancashire et al., 1997). The various psychological and psychosocial interventions need to be marshaled together with a clear focus on promoting improvements in social functioning and quality of life. A thorough development and an evaluation of this type of approach has yet to be done.

REFERENCES

Barrowclough, C., & Tarrier, N. (1984). Psychosocial interventions with families and their effects on the course of treatment. *Psychological Medicine, 14,* 629–642.

Barrowclough, C., & Tarrier, N. (1990). Social functioning in schizophrenic patients. I: The effects of expressed emotion and family intervention. *Social Psychiatry and Psychiatric Epidemiology, 25,* 125–129.

Barrowclough, C., & Tarrier, N. (1992). *Families of schizophrenic patients: Cognitive behavioral intervention.* London: Chapman & Hall.

Barrowclough, C., Johnston, M., & Tarrier, N. (1994). Attributions, expressed emotion and patient relapse: An attributional model of relatives' response to schizophrenic illness. *Behavior Therapy, 25,* 67–88.

Bebbington, P., & Kuipers, L. (1995). The predictive utility of expressed emotion in schizophrenia: An aggregate analysis. *Psychological Medicine, 24,* 579–599.

Bellack, A. S., Turner, S. M., Hersen, M., & Luber, R. F. (1984). An examination of the efficacy of social skills training for chronic schizophrenic patients. *Hospital and Community Psychiatry, 35,* 1023–1028.

Berkowitz, R., Kuipers, L., Eberlein-Fries, R., & Leff, J. (1981). Lowering expressed emotion in the relatives of schizophrenics. In M. J. Goldstein, (Ed.), *New developments in interventions with families of schizophrenics* (pp. 27–48). San Fransisco: Jossey-Bass.

Birchwood, M., Smith, J., Cochrane, R., Wetton, S., & Copestake, S. (1990). The Social Functioning Scale: The development and validation of a scale of social adjustment for use in family intervention programs with schizophrenic patients. *British Journal of Psychiatry, 157,* 853–859.

Brooker, C., Tarrier, N., Barrowclough, C., Butterworth, A., & Goldberg, D. (1992). Training community psychiatric nurses for psychosocial intervention: Report of a pilot study. *British Journal of Psychiatry, 160,* 836–844.

Brooker, C., Falloon, I. R. H., Butterworth, A., Goldberg, D., Graham-Hole, V., & Hillier, V. (1994). The outcome of training community psychiatric nurses to deliver psychosocial intervention. *British Journal of Psychiatry, 165,* 222–230.

Brown, G. W. (1985). The discovery of expressed emotion: Induction or deduction. In J. P. Leff & C. E. Vaughn (Eds.), *Expressed emotion in families* (pp. 7–25). New York: Guilford.

Brown, G. W., Carstairs, G. M., & Topping, G. (1958). Posthospital adjustment of chronic mental patients. *Lancet, ii,* 685–689.

Brown, G. W., Monck, E. M., Carstairs, G. M., & Wing, J. K. (1962). Influence of family life on the course of schizophrenia. *British Journal of Preventative and Social Medicine, 16,* 55–68.

Brown, G. W., Birley, J. T. L., & Wing, J. K. (1972). Influence of family life on the course of schizophrenia: A replication. *British Journal of Psychiatry, 121,* 241–258.

Dulz, B., & Hand, I. (1986). Short-term relapse in young schizophrenics: Can it be predicted and affected by family (CFI), patient and treatment variables? An experimental study. In M. J. Goldstein, I. Hand, & K. Hahlweg (Eds.), *Treatment of schizophrenia: Family assessment and intervention* (pp. 59–75). Berlin: Springer-Verlag.

Falloon, I. R. H., Watt, D. C., & Shepherd, M. (1978). A comparative controlled trial of pimozide and fluphenazine decanoate in the continuation therapy of schizophrenia. *Psychological Medicine, 7,* 59–70.

Falloon, I. R. H., Boyd, J. L., & McGill, C. W. (1984). *Family care of schizophrenia.* New York: Guilford Press.

Falloon, I. R. H., Boyd, J. L., McGill, C. W., Razani, J., Moss, H. B., & Gilderman, A. M. (1982). Family management in the prevention of exacerbations of schizophrenia. *New England Journal of Medicine, 306,* 1437–1440.

Falloon, I. R. H., Boyd, J. L., McGill, C. W., Williamson, M., Razani, J., Moss, H. B., Gilderman, A. M., & Simson, G. M. (1985). Family management in the prevention of morbidity of schizophrenia: Clinical outcome of a two year longitudinal study. *Archives of General Psychiatry, 42,* 887–896.

Garety, P. A., Kuipers, L., Fowler, D., Chamberlain, F. & Dunn, G. (1994). Cognitive behavioral therapy for drug resistant psychosis. *British Journal of Medical Psychology, 67,* 259–271.

Garety P., Fowler, D., Kuipers, E., Freeman, D., Dunn, G., Bebbington, P., Hadley, C., Jones S. (1997). London-East Anglia randomised controlled trial of cognitive-behavioural therapy for psychosis: II. Predictors of outcome. *British Journal of Psychiatry, 171,* 420–426.

Glick, I. D., Spencer, J. H., Clarkin, J. F., Haas, G. L., Lewis, A. B., Peyser, J., DeMane, N., Good-Ellis, M., Harris, E., & Lestelle, V. (1990). A randomized clinical trial of inpatient family intervention. IV. Follow-up results for subjects with schizophrenia. *Schizophrenia Research, 3,* 187–200.

Goldberg, D., & Williams, P. (1988). *A user's guide to the General Health Questionnaire.* Windsor: NFER Nelson.

Hahlweg, K., Goldstein, M. J., Nuechterlein, K. H., Doane, J. A., Miklowitz, D. J., & Snyder, K. S. (1989). Expressed emotion and patient–relative interaction in families of recent onset schizophrenia. *Journal of Consulting and Clinical Psychology, 57,* 11–18.

Hahlweg, K., Wiedemann, G., Muller, U., Feinstein, E., Hank, G., & Dose, M. (1995). *Effectiveness of behavioral family management in combination with standard dose or targeted medication to delay relapse in schizophrenia.* Unpublished manuscript.

Halford, W. K., & Hayes, R. (1991). Psychological rehabilitation of chronic schizophrenic patients: Recent findings on social skills training and family psychoeducation. *Clinical Psychology Review, 11*, 23–45.

Hogarty, G. E., Goldberg, S. C., and the Collaborative Study Group (1973). Drug and sociotherapy in the aftercare of schizophrenic patients: One year relapse rates. *Archives of General Psychiatry, 28*, 54–64.

Hogarty, G. E., Schooler, N. R., Ulrich, R. F., Mussare, F., Ferro, P., & Herron, E. (1979). Fluphenazine and social therapy in the aftercare of schizophrenic patients. *Archives of General Psychiatry, 36*, 1283–1294.

Hogarty, G. E., Anderson, C. M., Reiss, D. J., Kornblith, S. J., Greenwald, D. P., Javan, C. D., & Madonia, M. (1986). Family psychoeducation, social skills training and maintenance chemotherapy in the aftercare treatment of schizophrenia.1: One year effects of a controlled study on relapse and expressed emotion. *Archives of General Psychiatry, 43*, 633–642.

Hogarty, G. E., Anderson, C. M., Reiss, D. J., Kornblith, S. J., Greenwald, D. P., Ulrich, R. F., & Carter, M. (1991). Family psychoeducation, social skills training, and maintenance chemotherapy in the aftercare treatment of schizophrenia. II: Two year effects of a controlled study on relapse and adjustment. *Archives of General Psychiatry, 48*, 340–347.

Hooley, J. M., & Teasdale, J. D., (1989). Predictors of relapse in unipolar depressives: Expressed emotion, marital distress and perceived criticism. *Journal of Abnormal Psychology, 94*, 229–235.

Kavanagh, D. (1992). Recent developments in expressed emotion and schizophrenia. *British Journal of Psychiatry, 160*, 601–620.

Kingdon, D., Turkington, D., & John, C. (1994). Cognitive behavior therapy of schizophrenia. *British Journal of Psychiatry, 164*, 581–587.

Kottgen, C., Soinnichsen, I., Mollenhauer, K., & Jurth, R. (1984). Results of the Hamburg Camberwell Family Interview study, I–III. *International Journal of Family Psychiatry, 5*, 61–94.

Kreisman, D., Blumenthal, R., Borenstein, M., Woerner, M., Kane, J., Rifkin, A., & Reardon, G. (1988). Family attitudes and patient social adjustment in a longitudinal study of outpatient schizophrenics receiving low dose neuroleptics: The family's view. *Psychiatry, 51*, 3–13.

Kuipers, E., Garety P., Fowler, D., Dunn, G., Bebbington, P., Freeman, D., Hadley, C. (1997). London-East Anglia randomised controlled trial of cognitive-behavioural therapy for psychosis: I. Effects of the treatment phase. *British Journal of Psychiatry, 171*, 319–327.

Lam, D. (1991). Psychosocial family interventions in schizophrenia: Review of empirical studies. *Psychological Medicine, 21*, 423–441.

Lancashire, S., Haddock, G., Tarrier, N. Baguley, I., Butterworth, A., & Brooker, C. (1997). The impact of training community psychiatric nurses to use psychosocial interventions with people who have serious mental health problems: The Thorn Nurse Training Project. *Psychiatric Services, 48*, 39–42.

Lebell, M. B., Marder, S. R., Mintz, J., Mintz, L. I., Tompson, M., Wirshing, W., Johnston-Cronk, J., & McKenzie, J. (1993). Patients' perceptions of family emotional climate and outcome in schizophrenia. *British Journal of Psychiatry, 162*, 751–754.

Leff, J. P., & Vaughn, C. E. (1985). *Expressed emotion in families.* New York: Guilford Press.

Leff, J. P., Kuipers, L., Berkowitz, R., Eberlein-Fries, R., & Sturgeon, D. (1982). A controlled trial of intervention with families of schizophrenic patients. *British Journal of Psychiatry, 141*, 121–134.

Leff, J. P., Kuipers, L., Berkowitz, R., & Sturgeon, D. (1985). A controlled trial of social intervention in the families of schizophrenic patients. *British Journal of Psychiatry, 146*, 594–600.

Leff, J. P., Berkowitz, R., Shavit, A., Strachan, A., Glass, I., & Vaughn, C. E. (1989). A trial of family therapy v. relatives' groups for schizophrenia. *British Journal of Psychiatry, 154*, 58–66.

Leff, J. P., Berkowitz, R., Shavit, A., Strachan, A., Glass, I., & Vaughn, C. E. (1990). A trial of family therapy v. relatives' groups for schizophrenia: Two year follow up. *British Journal of Psychiatry, 157*, 571–577.

Linszen, D., Dingemans, P. M., Van der Does, A. J. W., Nigter, M. A., Scholte, W. F., & Lenior, M. E. (1996). Treatment, expressed emotion and relapse in recent onset schizophrenia and related disorders. *Psychological Medicine, vol. 26*, 333–342.

Mari, Jair de Jesus, & Streiner, D. L. (1994). An overview of family inteventions and relapse on schizophrenia: Meta-analysis of research findings. *Psychological Medicine, 24*, 565–578.

McFarlane, W. R., Lukens, E., Link, B., Dushay, R., Deakins, S., Newmark, M., Dunne, E. J., Horen, B., & Toran, J. (1995). Multiple family groups and psychoeducation in the treatment of schizophrenia. *Archives of General Psychiatry, 52*, 679–687.

Miklowitz, D. J., Goldstein, M. J., Falloon, I. R. H., & Doane, J. A. (1984). Interactional correlates of expressed emotion in families of schizophrenics. *British Journal of Psychiatry, 144*, 482–487.

Mintz, L. I., Nuechterlein, K. N., Goldstein, M. J., Mintz, J., & Snyder, S. (1989). The initial onset of schizophrenia and family expressed emotion: Some methodological considerations. *British Journal of Psychiatry, 154*, 212–217.

Randolph, E. T., Eth, S., Glynn, S. M., Psaz, G. G., Leong, G. B., Shaner, A. L., Strachan, A., van Vort, W., Escobar, J. L., & Liberman, R. P. (1994). Behavioral family management in schizophrenia outcome of a clinic based intervention. *British Journal of Psychiatry, 164*, 501–506.

Platt, S., Weyman, A., Hirsch, S., & Hewitt, S. (1980). The Social Behavior Assessment Schedule (SBAS): Rationale, contents, scoring and reliability of a new intervention schedule. *Social Psychiatry, 15*, 380–387.

Schooler, N. R., Keith, S. J., Severe, J. B., Matthews, S. M., Bellack, A. S., Glick, I. D., Hargreaves, W. A., Kane, J. M., Ninan, P. T., Frances, A., Jacobs, M., Lieberman, J. A., Mance, R., Simpson, G. M., & Woerner, M. G. (1997). Relapse and rehospitalization during maintenance treatment of schizophrenia: The effects of dose reduction and family treatment. *Archives of General Psychiatry, 54,* 453–463.

Sellwood, W., Haddock, G., Tarrier, N., & Yusupoff, L. (1994). Advances in the psychological management of positive symptoms of schizophrenia. *International Review of Psychiatry, 6,* 201–215.

Stratton, P., Heard, D., Hanks, H. G. I., Stratton, P., Heard, D., Hanks, H. G. I., Munton, A. G., Brewin, C. R., & Davidson, C. (1986). Coding causal beliefs in natural discourse. *British Journal of Social Psychology, 25,* 299–313.

Tarrier, N., & Barrowclough, C. (1990). Family intervention for schizophrenia. *Behavior Modification, 14,* 408–440.

Tarrier, N., Beckett, R., Harwood, S., Baker, A., Yusupoff, L. & Ugarteburu, I. (1993). A trial of two cognitive-behavioral methods of treating drug-resistant psychotic symptoms in schizophrenia. *British Journal of Psychiatry, 162,* 524–532.

Tarrier, N., & Barrowclough, C. (1995). Family interventions in schizophrenia and their long term outcomes. *International Journal of Mental Health, 24,* 38–53.

Tarrier, N., Barrowclough, C., Vaughn, C. E., Bamrah, J. S., Porceddu, K., Watts, S., & Freeman, H. (1988). The community management of schizophrenia: A controlled trial of a behavioral intervention with families to reduce relapse. *British Journal of Psychiatry, 153,* 532–542

Tarrier, N., Barrowclough, C., Vaughn, C. E., Bamrah, J. S., Porceddu, K., Watts, S., & Freeman, H. (1989). The community management of schizophrenia: A controlled trial of a behavioral intervention with families to reduce relapse: A two year follow-up. *British Journal of Psychiatry, 154,* 625–628.

Tarrier, N., Barrowclough, C., Porceddu, K., & Fitzpatrick, E. (1994). The Salford Family Intervention Project for schizophrenic relapse prevention: Five and eight year accumulating relapses. *British Journal of Psychiatry, 165,* 829–832.

Tomarus, V., Vlachonikolis, I. G., Stefanis, C. N., & Madianes, M. (1988). The effect of individual psychosocial treatment on the family atmosphere of schizophrenic patients. *Social Psychiatry and Psychiatric Epidemiology, 23,* 256–261.

Valone, K., Norton, J. P., Goldstein, M. J., & Doane, J. A., (1983). Parental expressed emotion and affective style in an adolescent sample at risk for schizophrenia spectrum disorders. *Journal of Abnormal Psychology, 92,* 399–407.

Vaughan, K., Doyle, M., McConaghy, N., Blaszczynski, A., Fox, A., & Tarrier, N., (1992). The Sydney intervention trial: A controlled trial of relatives' counseling to reduce schizophrenic relapse. *Social Psychiatry and Psychiatric Epidemiology, 27,* 16–21.

Vaughn, C. E. (1986). Patterns of emotional response in the families of schizophrenic patients. In M. J. Goldstein, I. Hand, & K. Hahlweg, (Eds.), *Treatment of schizophrenia: Family assessment and intervention* (pp. 76–78). Berlin: Springer-Verlag.

Vaughn, C. E., & Leff, J. P., (1976). The influence of family and social factors on the course of psychiatric illness: A comparison of schizophrenic and depressed neurotic patients. *British Journal of Psychiatry, 129,* 125–137.

Wallace, C. J., & Liberman, C. J. (1985). Social skills training for patients with schizophrenia: A controlled clinical trial. *Psychiatry Research, 15,* 239–247.

Wallace, C. J., Nelson, C. J., Liberman, R. P., Aitchison, R. A., Lukoff, D., Elder, J., & Ferris, C. (1980). A review and critique of social skills training with schizophrenic patients. *Schizophrenia Bulletin, 6,* 42–64.

Weissman, M. M., Prusoff, B. A., Thompson, W. D., Harding, P. S., & Myers, J. K. (1978). Social adjustment by self-report in a community sample and psychiatric outpatients. *Journal of Nervous and Mental Disease, 166,* 317–326.

White, E. (1990). *The third national quinquennial survey of community psychiatric services.* Leeds: CPNA Publications.

Wooff, K., Goldberg, D., & Fryers, T. (1988). The practice of community psychiatric nursing and mental health social work in Salford. *British Journal of Psychiatry, 152,* 783–792.

Xiong, W., Phillips, M. R., Hu, X., Wang, R., Dai, Q., Kleinman, J., & Kleinman, A. (1994). Family-based intervention for schizophrenic patients in China. *British Journal of Psychiatry, 165,* 239–247.

Zubin, J., & Spring, B. (1977). Vulnerability: A new view of schizophrenia. *Journal of Abnormal Psychology, 86,* 103–126.

CHAPTER 21

COGNITIVE REMEDIATION IN SCHIZOPHRENIA

Robert S. Kern
Michael F. Green

Studies of schizophrenia have led to the identification of deficits in a number of cognitive domains including attention, memory, executive functioning, perception, language processing, and motor speed (Goldberg, Weinberger, Berman, Pliskin, & Podd, 1987; King, 1991; Maher, 1991; Spring, Weinstein, Freeman, & Thompson, 1991; Saykin et al., 1991). It now appears highly likely that certain cognitive deficits impede or restrict psychiatric patients' ability to acquire new skills (e.g., basic conversational skills). The limitations imposed by cognitive deficits may explain why many, but not all, psychiatric patients benefit from comprehensive skills training programs. Perhaps, targeting particular cognitive deficits directly for remediation may add to the number of patients who already benefit from such programs (Erickson, 1988; Erickson & Binder, 1986; Erickson & Burton, 1986; Stuve, Erickson, & Spaulding, 1991).

Over the past decade, studies of cognitive remediation in schizophrenia have appeared with greater frequency in the literature, and the sophistication of the interventions used in these studies appears to be advancing as well. A number of the early investigations tested the feasibility of modifying discrete cognitive functions. Other, more ambitious studies have attempted to modify a range of cognitive, social, and occupational deficits. This chapter will review both types of studies and examine the correspondence between them. The primary focus will be to determine whether findings from focused feasibility studies can influence the comprehensive, clinically based programs. Most of the findings presented in this chapter were collected from studies that have been limited to schizophrenia patients; however, it is believed that the effects of cognitive remediation may apply to psychotic patients in general.

Specifically, this chapter will (a) review selected feasibility studies, including studies that have targeted deficits in verbal memory, early visual processing, and prefrontal functioning as evidenced by performance on the Wisconsin Card Sorting Test, (b) review selected comprehensive, clinically based programs of cognitive remediation, and (c) present preliminary conclusions about cognitive remediation in psychiatric rehabilitation.

FEASIBILITY STUDIES OF COGNITIVE REMEDIATION: MODIFICATION OF DISCRETE COGNITIVE PROBES

Typically, feasibility studies have attempted to test the malleability of certain deficits by attempting to modify performance on a single measure. Performance measures of interest have included (a) measures of verbal memory; (b) measures of early stage deficits; and (c) the Wisconsin Card Sorting Test (WCST), a measure of prefrontal functioning.

Modification of Verbal Memory Deficits

Rate-limiting factors (Green, 1993), when used in reference to cognitive remediation, refer to those cognitive deficits that limit or restrict the acquisition of new skills and abilities, such as those required to improve social or occupational functioning. As in chemistry, in which a particular compound may restrict the flow of a chemical reaction, it seems highly likely that certain cognitive deficits may restrict the acquisition of new skills and abilities in schizophrenia patients. Rate-limiting factors are typically examined in terms of their influence on more clinically meaningful behaviors (e.g., social behavior).

A number of studies have examined the relationship between selected cognitive factors and performance in skills training programs. These studies have consistently identified the significance of verbal memory, among others, in skill acquisition and competence. Corrigan, Wallace, Schade, and Green (1994) reported that performance on the Rey Auditory Verbal Learning Test (a list learning measure) predicted skill acquisition. Kern, Green, and Satz (1992) found that verbal memory was associated with pretraining skill competence, but not posttraining performance 8 months later. In a short-term follow-up study, Mueser, Bellack, Douglas, and Wade (1991) found that memory ability as measured by the Wechsler Memory Scale significantly correlated with social skill improvement in a sample of schizophrenia and schizoaffective disorder patients.

Interestingly, despite the reported importance of verbal memory to skill competence and acquisition, very few feasibility studies have attempted to remediate this particular area of cognition in schizophrenia patients over the past 20 years. This neglect is particularly surprising given the focus that memory deficits have received in cognitive rehabilitation programs for the braininjured. Although the following studies are somewhat dated, they keenly illustrate the value of discrete interventions to modifying verbal memory deficits.

A series of studies were conducted in the 1970s that tested the malleability of performance deficits by schizophrenia patients on tests of list learning. Initially, Bauman (1971a) attempted to improve the serial recall of a group of acute schizophrenia inpatients (the majority had been hospitalized less than one year). The sample was divided into two groups of 12 patients each. Ten trigrams were presented on a memory drum to both groups, and recall was assessed after each of three learning trials. The two groups differed by the type of instruction they received prior to administration of the trigrams. One group received information about the trigram list (i.e., each trigram begins with a different letter of the alphabet) and specific instructions to "think of the first letter" of each trigram (an alphabetical encoding strategy). Patients in the other group were simply told to try their best. The study failed to show any significant group or interaction (i.e., group × trial) effects, despite the fact that one group received specific instructions that should have enhanced encoding and subsequent recall of the list items. However, no procedures were used to ensure that the schizophrenia patients were actually using the instructions to help them remember the items.

In a separate follow-up study, Bauman (1971b) was able to demonstrate that schizophrenia patients' recall of list items could be improved. The patients were presented a word list that contained exemplars of selected taxonomic categories under separate conditions. In one condition, they were presented a list of words in a prearranged format, sequentially ordered by taxonomic category, and in the other condition the words were randomly ordered. Recall of the words in the prearranged condition was superior to recall in the random order condition. Although these findings demonstrated within-subject improvement, the patients' performance on the prearranged condition was still inferior to that of normal controls.

Koh and his colleagues summarized the findings of a series of list learning studies, stating that schizophrenia patients were inferior to normal controls at serial recall of unrelated (Koh & Kayton, 1974; Koh, Kayton, & Berry, 1973), categorically related (Koh, Kayton, & Berry, 1973), and affectively loaded words (Kayton & Koh, 1975). A series of planned investigations followed. Koh and colleagues hypothesized that the performance deficits of schizophrenia patients in the recall of word lists was due to inefficient encoding of the to-be-learned material.

It was speculated that semantic elaboration of verbal material would enhance recall. Although semantic elaboration is a function performed routinely by most normal individuals, it apparently is not utilized by schizophrenia patients.

Koh, Kayton, and Peterson (1976) manipulated the processing of word list items. The study included a group of schizophrenia patients, nonschizophrenia psychiatric patients, and normal controls who received measures of recall under incidental and intentional recall conditions. In incidental recall, the subject is unaware that memory is being assessed. For example, the subject may be asked to rate a series of words on the basis of some arbitrarily selected characteristic (e.g., frequency of usage), and then unbeknownst to the subject tested for recall of the presented words later. In contrast, in intentional recall, the subject is explicitly informed of the nature of the task. In the Koh et al. experiment, subjects rated a series of words according to their degree of pleasantness-unpleasantness. Then, without warning, the subjects were tested for their recall of the presented words. Word list recall of the schizophrenia and psychiatric patients was comparable to that of the normal controls. One week later, all subjects were tested for recall of a different set of words under intentional recall conditions. All subjects rated the new list of words according to pleasantness-unpleasantness as used previously the week before. Even under intentional recall conditions, no significant differences were found between the patient groups and the normal control group.

In summary, these findings suggest that when schizophrenia patients use a mnemonic encoding strategy (e.g., rating words by degree of pleasantness-unpleasantness), list learning can be improved to a level of performance comparable to normal controls. It is important to note that in the Koh et al. studies (a) the intervention was under the direct control of the experimenter, (b) it could be assessed whether or not the intervention was being used by the subject (e.g., by examining the ratings), and (c) it required little conscious effort on the part of the patient. These early studies did not test the efficacy of any of the well-known mnemonic strategies currently used in rehabilitation programs for the brain injured. The employment of mnemonic techniques such as visual imagery (e.g., method of loci), verbal chaining or linking (used for word lists), and peg word strategies (i.e., associating images of concrete objects with to-be-remembered words) have been utilized in both clinical and nonclinical populations successfully. At this time, we are unaware whether such techniques would be effective with schizophrenia patients.

In conclusion, these early studies demonstrated the feasibility of modifying list learning deficits in schizophrenia patients. Recall was enhanced by manipulating the semantic encoding of the to-be-remembered material. These results suggest that at least one putative rate-limiting factor (i.e., memory functioning) is subject to modifiability.

Remediation of Early Visual Processing Deficits

The term *vulnerability indicator* of schizophrenia is used in reference to a performance disturbance that meets two criteria: (a) The disturbance is present in both schizophrenia patients and their at-risk first-degree relatives, but not in healthy individuals or nonschizophrenic psychiatric patients, and (b) the disturbance persists both before and after acute psychotic episodes (Cromwell & Spaulding, 1978; Zubin & Spring, 1977). Evidence in support of the span of apprehension as a vulnerability indicator of schizophrenia is based largely on the findings from a few well-controlled studies that have found significant differences between remitted schizophrenia patients and at-risk individuals compared to normal controls, as well as those reports that have found the performance disturbance present both during and between psychotic episodes (Asarnow & MacCrimmon, 1978, 1981; Asarnow, Steffy, MacCrimmon, & Cleghorn, 1977).

Two recent studies have tested the modifiability of performance on a version of the span of apprehension task, a putative vulnerability marker to schizophrenia. Both studies used the same version of the span of apprehension task, a partial report procedure in which subjects are required to identify one of two target letters (presented for 70 ms) from array sizes of 3 or 12 letters (Estes & Taylor, 1966). However, the studies reported discrepant findings.

In a study from our lab (Kern, Green, & Goldstein, 1995), chronic schizophrenia inpatients were sequentially assigned to one of four groups (Groups A through D). Each group received four administrations of the span of apprehension task: (a) at baseline, (b) during the intervention, (c) at immediate posttest, and (d) at a one-week follow-up. The methodological procedures for the four groups differed only by the type of intervention received at the second administration. All other administrations of the span followed traditional testing procedures. At the time of the intervention, Group A received repeat administration of the span of apprehension task, Group B received monetary reinforcement in the form of 2 cents for each correct response, Group C received verbal and visual prompts designed to alert the subject about necessary task components, and Group D received a combination of monetary reinforcement plus the prompts described for Group C above. The results revealed superior gains in performance in the group that received the combination of reinforcement plus instruction (Group D). As illustrated in Figure 21.1, Group D showed a substantial improvement in percent accuracy at the time of the intervention which was maintained on two subsequent follow-up administrations (immediate follow-up and one week later). Of clinical significance, the level of performance attained by this group of chronic inpatients approached levels typically observed in normals on this version of the span of apprehension task.

Another study failed to find significant effects of training for remediating performance deficits on the span (Benedict et al., 1994). The sample included 33 outpatients with chronic histories of schizophrenia who were randomly assigned to an experimental group ($n = 16$) and a control group ($n = 17$). The experimental group received approximately 14 to 15 50-minute sessions (three to five times per week) of computer-based attention training in addition to participation in a multidisciplinary day-treatment program. The control group received no attention training, but participated in the same day treatment program as the experimental group. Attentional training consisted of guided practice on six computerized tasks that

included reaction time, vigilance, visuomotor tracking, immediate verbal memory, speed reading, and a paced auditory serial addition task. Although the patients in the experimental group showed improvement on the computerized tasks, these gains failed to generalize to other outcome measures that included the span of apprehension. However, cognitive retraining in this study was conducted using a computerized program that did not include training procedures specific to span performance deficits. Rather, the training tasks consisted of exercises designed to improve attentional skills in general. On the other hand, the computer-based training did include selected components that hypothetically appear related to span performance.

In summary, two studies tested the modifiability of early visual processing deficits on the span and achieved somewhat discrepant findings. The study that found the deficit modifiable used an intervention that combined incentive and readiness prompts. The discrepancy between these studies' findings could be due to certain methodological differences in the approach to remediation. The study by Kern et al. attempted to remediate span deficits by applying an intervention directly to performance on the span. In contrast, the Benedict et al. study used a training procedure designed to enhance other cognitive functions, and then examined the generalizability of training to span performance. Further replication studies using these and

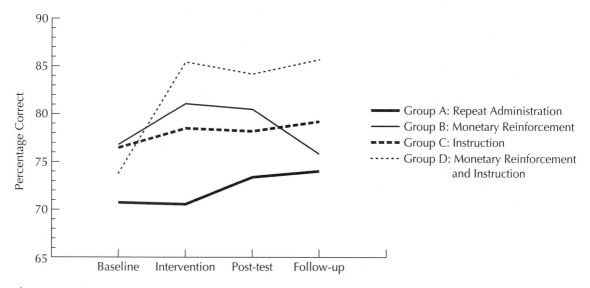

Figure 21.1. Schizophrenia patients' mean number correct and mean perseverative errors on the Wisconsin Card Sorting Test under four administration conditions

other techniques with similar populations appear necessary at this time. The findings of the Kern et al. study are promising in that they suggest that it is possible to modify early visual processing deficits, even ones that place limited demands on higher cognitive processes. Hence, even basic perceptual processes can potentially be successful targets of remediation.

Cognitive Remediation Interventions for the Wisconsin Card Sorting Test

Perhaps, no single measure has received as much attention in the cognitive remediation literature in psychopathology as the Wisconsin Card Sorting Test (WCST). Interventions have included the use of explicit instruction, contingency reinforcement, and more recently, errorless learning.

Goldberg et al. (1987) initially tested the modifiability of performance deficits on the WCST by using explicit instruction. The study included three groups of schizophrenia inpatients that received five serial administrations of an abbreviated version of the WCST on the same day, and a follow-up administration 2 weeks later. One group ($n = 15$) served as a control and received the WCST according to standard administration procedures (Heaton, 1981). The other two groups served as experimental groups and received the WCST under differing administration conditions in which they received information about the possible sorting categories, information about the required shifting of set, and detailed step-by-step instruction at different times. The performance of the experimental groups was superior to the control group only under the condition in which they were provided detailed step-by-step instruction. The improvement in performance was not maintained on subsequent follow-up administrations when instruction was not provided. A later study conducted by Goldman, Axelrod, and Tompkins (1992) found somewhat different results in terms of the amount of information needed to improve performance. Providing only instructional cues about possible sorting categories and shifting of set at the outset and then at three subsequent intervals (i.e., after every 32 cards over a total administration of 128 cards) improved the performance in both schizophrenic and mood disorder patients. However, two factors are likely relevant to interpretation of these data: (a) the sample in the Goldman et al. study was less chronic than the Goldberg et al. sample, and (b) the durability of the performance gains was not tested beyond the period of instruction.

Other investigators have also tested other types or combinations of interventions for their efficacy in remediating the performance deficits of schizophrenia patients on the WCST. Green, Staz, Ganzell, and Vaclav (1992) and Bellack, Mueser, Morrison, Tierney, and Podell (1990) examined the effects of contingent monetary reinforcement with and without instruction on WCST performance. In the Green et al. study two groups of subjects (a schizophrenia group [$n = 46$] and a mixed psychotic disorder group [$n = 20$]) received four serial administrations of a computerized version of the WCST. At baseline, both groups were administered the WCST under traditional administration procedures. During the second administration, both groups received contingent monetary reinforcement (i.e., 2 cents for every correct response). For the third administration, both groups received detailed step-by-step instruction plus contingent monetary reinforcement. For the fourth administration, both groups received contingent reinforcement only. As illustrated in Figure 21.2, both groups showed significant improvement from baseline at the third administration (combined instruction plus reinforcement), which was somewhat maintained at the fourth administration when instruction was not provided, but contingent monetary reinforcement was maintained. This study failed to support the effectiveness of contingent monetary reinforcement alone (comparison of first and second administrations).

Bellack et al. (1990), like Green et al. (1992), examined the effects of monetary reinforcement with and without instruction on WCST performance in a sample of schizophrenia patients. The Bellack et al. study included a less chronic group of schizophrenia patients than Green et al. or Goldberg et al. The effects of reinforcement on WCST performance were tested first. A small group of schizophrenia inpatients ($n = 16$) were assigned to two groups (contingent versus noncontingent monetary reinforcement) to test the effects of differing schedules of reinforcement on WCST performance. The results failed to support the effectiveness of either schedule of reinforcement on WCST performance. Next, another intervention was tested, one that combined explicit verbal instruction plus contingent monetary reinforcement. A separate group of subjects ($n = 12$) received general information about the test, specific detail about possible matching categories and shifting of set, as well as 5 cents for each correct response. This group performed significantly better than a comparison group that received contingent monetary reinforcement only. The improvement in performance was maintained on an immediate and 24-hour follow-up. The

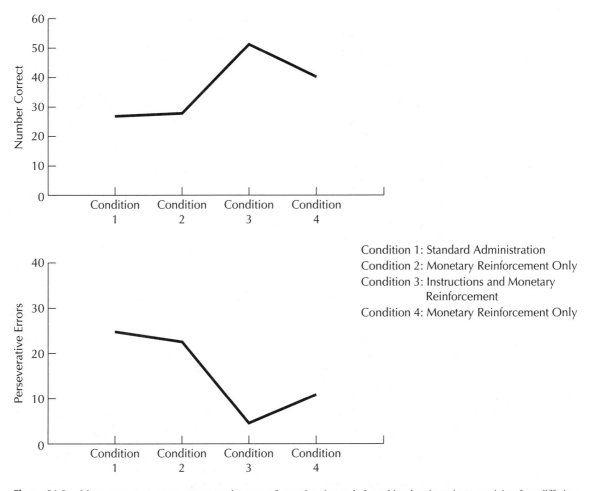

Condition 1: Standard Administration
Condition 2: Monetary Reinforcement Only
Condition 3: Instructions and Monetary
          Reinforcement
Condition 4: Monetary Reinforcement Only

Figure 21.2. Mean percent accuracy scores on the span of apprehension task for schizophrenia patients receiving four differing interventions

findings from this study failed to support the effectiveness of reinforcement alone, but did support the effectiveness of the combined intervention of contingent reinforcement plus verbal instruction.

One study yielded positive results for the effects of contingency interventions alone. Summerfelt et al. (1991) tested a small group of schizophrenia and schizoaffective disorder inpatients and outpatients using an experimental design that included a two-period crossover in which two administration conditions were counterbalanced over two periods of testing (approximately one week apart). In the one condition, subjects received the WCST under

traditional administration procedures. In the second condition, subjects were initially provided a stake of $7.50 and earned 10 cents for every correct response, but lost 5 cents for every incorrect response. The results showed that patients who were administered the WCST under conditions that included monetary reinforcement, and response cost made fewer perseverative errors than a control group which received the test according to traditional administration.

These studies examined the efficacy of reinforcement and explicit verbal instruction either alone or in combination at remediating WCST deficits in schizophrenia patients. The findings for the efficacy of verbal instructional cues administered alone are mixed (one study reported negative results, one study reported positive results). When combined with contingent reinforcement, however, two studies found short-term durability of performance gains. With respect to benefits of reinforcement alone, two studies failed to find significant effects; however, positive results were found in a study that used a combination of monetary reinforcement plus response cost (a procedure not employed in the other two studies). A cautious interpretation of these findings might be that the most effective form of training is one that combines explicit verbal instruction with some form of incentive (contingent monetary reinforcement). There is limited support for the value of reinforcement alone in remediating WCST deficits.

In these studies, the durability of training effectiveness was (a) not addressed (Green et al., 1992), (b) done so in a limited fashion (Bellack et al., 1990—one day, Summerfelt et al., 1991—one week), or (c) not substantiated (Goldberg et al., 1987). One approach that offers promise for producing more durable training effects is errorless learning. Versions of errorless discrimination training, initially proposed by Terrace (1963), have been successfully employed with developmentally disabled individuals with profound cognitive deficits. Under errorless learning training conditions, autistic children have been shown to be able to repeatedly make simple visual discriminations, and subsequently maintain high levels of performance for extended periods of time (Touchette, 1968). Our lab recently developed a training procedure for the WCST that is an adaptation of errorless learning principles (Kern, Wallace, Hellman, Womack, & Green, 1996). Errorless learning is essentially founded on two basic principles. First, training begins on simple, elementary tasks where there is a high likelihood of successful performance. Second, training progresses to more complex tasks with increasing task demands through a series of training stages where new or more difficult task demands are gradually introduced, so as to maintain the high levels of performance achieved at earlier stages. Our WCST training procedures began with training on basic elements of the test (e.g., stimulus feature identification) and progressed through a series of training phases that included increasing task demands (e.g., shifting set). Performance criteria were established for each stage, and subjects advanced to more difficult levels only after criterion for mastery at earlier stages were achieved. The level of difficulty was purposely manipulated so as to maximize successful performance. The results from our recent study support both the effectiveness and durability of these training procedures in a group of chronic psychotic inpatients, most with schizophrenia-spectrum diagnoses. Of clinical note, the patients' scores on the WCST were highly comparable to published norms for persons of similar education, and these levels of performance were maintained up to 4 weeks posttraining without further intervention.

COMPREHENSIVE PROGRAMS OF COGNITIVE REMEDIATION

The studies surveyed thus far have found several techniques to be useful at improving deficits on discrete cognitive probes. To what extent are these interventions being used by larger scale, clinically based, comprehensive programs of cognitive rehabilitation?

Comprehensive programs of cognitive rehabilitation for psychiatric patients are beginning to emerge with greater frequency in the United States and Europe. Although these programs typically include interventions designed to remediate discrete cognitive deficits, the primary goal is broader (i.e., to improve functional independence). For example, aspects of social and occupational behavior may be targeted for treatment intervention. The implicit hypothesis for these programs is that remediation of discrete cognitive deficits generalizes to more complex behaviors (a kind of upward generalization). In the United States, Spaulding and Sullivan (1991), Yozawitz (1986), Heinssen and Victor (1994), and Jaeger, Berns, Tigner, and Douglas (1992) have made contributions in this area. In Europe, Brenner's Integrated Psychological Therapy (IPT; Brenner, Hodel, Roder, & Corrigan, 1992) and van der Gaag's cognitive retraining program (van der Gaag, 1992) are two examples of such programs.

To structure this section, we will divide the comprehensive programs into two groups: (a) idiographic-based programs and (b) nomothetic-based programs. In the United States, the cognitive rehabilitation approaches of Yozawitz and Spaulding, best fit an idiographic approach (Spaulding, however, has also investigated the efficacy of group cognitive rehabilitation programming). Specific interventions are developed for the purposes of remediating the individual's own areas of cognitive dysfunction. For example, if a patient presents with relatively isolated disturbances in memory, then a set of procedures may be devised to ameliorate that particular deficit. An emphasis of such programs is on the initial assessment of cognitive functioning. In contrast, the rehabilitation programs described by Heinssen and Victor (1994), Jaeger et al. (1992), Brenner et al. (1992), and van der Gaag (1992) use a nomothetic model. In these programs, rehabilitation is conducted on groups of patients through a planned series of hierarchically scaled interventions. Although individual differences are acknowledged, the predicted group deficits serve as the foundation for developing the components of training. In these programs, the primary emphasis is on training and not the identification of the cognitive deficit profile of individual members. Let us now direct our attention to those programs that use an idiographic model.

Yozawitz (1986) proposed a multidisciplinary program for cognitive rehabilitation that began with an initial screening conducted by an interdisciplinary team staffed by a psychiatrist, neurologist, neuropsychologist, and internist. The results of the screening are used to selectively refer patients for medical treatment, psychiatric treatment, or cognitive rehabilitation. Those patients referred for cognitive rehabilitation receive a more comprehensive neuropsychological evaluation to assess conceptual, language, visuospatial, and motor abilities. A selective deficit in any of these four areas would indicate the need for specialized intensive training in that area. For example, an individual with deficits in conceptual abilities might receive training in verbal reasoning, sustained attention, visual reasoning, planning, and orienting. Training may be complemented by using the selective strengths of the patient to compensate for deficits in other areas. Progress in training is continually assessed and proceeds through a series of increasingly advanced exercises until competency is attained within each of the four basic areas of cognitive training. Rehabilitation then transitions to a different series of skills, focusing on academic skill development (i.e., reading, spelling, and arithmetic). On successful completion of academic skill training, patients may then proceed to training in community-based activities (e.g., occupational skills). Follow-up counseling and assessment continue after discharge, with patients being followed every 6 months to assess progress and maintenance of independent functioning. Little information is available about the specific training interventions used in this program; however, the methods appear to be task driven. Patients advance through the training program by completing a series of basic cognitive exercises. It appears that performance gains on particular tasks are achieved primarily through repetition.

Another example of an idiographic approach by Spaulding and colleagues (Spaulding & Sullivan, 1991)

uses a traditional neuropsychological model of cognitive remediation for psychiatric patients. In this approach, cognitive rehabilitation is based on an individual's cognitive deficit profile. The focus of training is dictated by the results of a comprehensive neuropsychological assessment that includes psychophysiological, attentional, cognitive, and social-behavioral measures. The aim of assessment is to identify the individual's areas of dysfunction. Once the key cognitive disturbances are identified, training begins with those particular areas. If the patient shows no striking areas of cognitive dysfunction, cognitive remediation is not required, and training begins directly with more complex behaviors (e.g., social skills training). Let's consider a case example from Spaulding and Sullivan (1991). A patient with selective deficits in executive functioning based on the WCST behaved in a socially inappropriate manner in the community. It was hypothesized that executive deficits were interfering with his ability to function socially. A training intervention was devised to increase his ability to reconceptualize social situations rapidly. Training consisted of 10 therapy sessions in which the patient was requested to generate alternative percepts to a series of inkblots and then similarly generate alternative stories to a series of Thematic Apperception Test cards. Training was complemented with counseling about how to develop conceptual flexibility, particularly in social situations. After treatment, the patient was retested with the same assessment battery that had been administered prior to training. Previously noted deficits on the WCST had improved and follow-up reports of this patient revealed improvements in irritability and attitude.

It is unclear whether the idiographic approaches to cognitive rehabilitation proposed by Yozawitz and Spaulding utilize the specific interventions that have been found to be effective for remediating performance deficits on discrete cognitive probes. The critical focus of such programs is on evaluation, and less emphasis is placed on the specific methods of intervention. Typically, the interventions used in such programs are tailored to fit the processing needs of the individual patient.

Recently, a number of researchers have developed cognitive rehabilitation programs that use a nomothetic approach. Heinssen and Victor (1994) reported the findings from a project designed to train a group of chronic schizophrenia patients to develop a set of particular vocational skills (e.g., gardening). In developing the training components, certain basic cognitive and psychiatric deficits common to many patients were considered. These included low motivation, high distractibility, limited concentration, poor memory, poor decision making, and inadequate socialization skills.

Initially, training began in a small section of a greenhouse on the hospital grounds; one free from distraction. Posters were displayed about the training area that conveyed key information about plant care (e.g., planting, watering, spraying, and pruning). Skill acquisition for produce care was accomplished through a series of training steps. For example, for watering, patients were trained to attend to relevant perceptual information (e.g., check out the soil), make accurate discriminations (e.g., is the soil light or dark?), retain the relevant information, and execute an appropriate response. Training began with exercises that included simpler, more elementary task demands and proceeded to increasingly more difficult ones. The training procedures were modeled after those used in the well-established social and independent living skills programs and included explicit instruction, modeling, rehearsal and corrective feedback, and contingent reinforcement (Bellack & Hersen, 1979).

Specifically, training of gardening skills began with procedures designed to orient the subject to the task and then to attend to the relevant stimulus features (e.g., the soil). Training then proceeded to teaching how to make correct visual and tactile discriminations. The instructor modeled correct discriminations by sorting pots and placing them under the appropriate corresponding signs (e.g., light vs. dark). Patients practiced sorting pots according to whether they were light or dark and then later wet or dry, verbalizing their responses while sorting. The instructor highlighted correct choices with verbal feedback. Training on pot sorting continued until criterion for mastery was attained (i.e., 90% accuracy) on two consecutive trials. Decision-making skills were trained last. Training in this phase relied heavily on algorithms displayed on posters illustrating the correct decisions to be followed given certain discrimination information. For example, the poster read: "Is the soil light or dark? It looks light. Is the soil wet or dry? It feels dry. It's light and dry. So the correct decision is to water the plant." Following successful mastery of decision-making skills, training moved to within the greenhouse (the actual worksite).

In the greenhouse, patients practiced the skills acquired during the previous training phase. The instructor modeled appropriate water techniques, and patients practiced watering skills and discrimination decisions on the plants in the greenhouse. Following successful mastery of gardening skills in the greenhouse, direct supervision was re-

duced and provided on an intermittent basis. The program included four training sessions per week over 29 weeks.

The efficacy of the program at improving vocational interest and job attainment was examined in 10 patients who participated in the program and 10 control subjects matched for gender, age, and diagnosis, who were being treated at the hospital. Patients in the control group received traditional milieu therapy in place of vocational training. Both groups had similar number of patients with hospital jobs prior to the study. Eight of the 10 patients in the work training group had hospital jobs 6 months later compared to only 2 in the control group. A one-year follow-up showed that the work group continued to maintain vocational interest, with four continuing employment in the hospital work program and four gaining community placements.

Jaeger and Douglas (1992) have proposed the use of a hierarchically based cognitive retraining program with psychiatric patients. Training begins on elementary cognitive functions of attentional processes (i.e., sustained, selective, shifting and divided attention), then transitions to more complex cognitive processes associated with memory and executive functioning. The program is based on a cognitive rehabilitation model proposed by Sohlberg and Mateer (1989). The model consists of six fundamental rehabilitation principles: (1) The conceptualization of cognitive functioning is model driven, with each cognitive domain characterized by distinct subcomponents. (2) Cognitive retraining is accomplished by administering selected cognitive tasks repeatedly that target components of selected cognitive domains. (3) The goals and objectives of each task are hierarchically organized according to levels of task difficulty. (4) Evaluation of performance is data based. Performance is assessed and evaluated at each level of task difficulty, and when set criteria are reached, training proceeds to tasks with greater task demands. For example, training of sustained attention might initially require the patient to push a buzzer every time a certain number is presented (e.g., 4). More advanced exercises would require increasing task demands, such as pushing the buzzer every time the number 4 is followed by a 7. (5) Generalization probes allow the measurement of treatment success. (6) Ultimate success is measured by improvements in vocational ability and independent living.

This model suggests that cognitive functions can be arranged according to a hierarchically ordered schema, such that certain domains of cognitive functioning are more basic or elementary than others. In addition, such a model proposes that certain higher order cognitive processes may be adversely affected by deficits in more basic cognitive processes. For example, deficits in memory functioning (a higher order function) may be partially affected by attentional disturbances (a lower order function). According to such a model, retraining of attentional disturbances would be necessary before proceeding to retraining of memory functioning. No data are presently available on the efficacy of this training program with psychiatric patients. Similar to the cognitive rehabilitation proposed by Yozawitz, the procedures outlined above appear to be task driven rather than intervention driven. That is, cognitive retraining is accomplished by having the patient execute a series of repetitive cognitive tasks that vary in their level of difficulty. It is unclear whether formal training procedures are used to maximize performance within any given task by means of intervention.

Cognitive rehabilitation for psychiatric patients has also received notable contributions from Europe. One such program, Brenner's Integrated Psychological Therapy (IPT; Brenner et al., 1992), is a systematic training program designed to improve a broad spectrum of functioning, ranging from cognitive processes associated with concept formation to more complex aspects of social behavior. The rehabilitation program consists of training in five subprograms that include cognitive differentiation, social perception, verbal communication, social skills, and problem-solving skills. The subprograms are arranged hierarchically, such that early interventions target simpler cognitive operations involved in cognitive differentiation and proceed stepwise thereafter concluding with training on social problem solving. Treatment is conducted in a group format with 60- to 75-minute session held five times per week over approximately 3 months. Similar to the procedures described by Sohlberg and Mateer (1989), training involves repeated administration of distinct cognitive tasks. However, unlike the former program, the pace of the program is not traditionally determined by the performance of individual group members. Instead, a series of hierarchically ordered lesson plans are sequentially followed and training concludes with the completion of the last scheduled lesson. Cognitive remediation is theoretically accomplished through the repeated practice of instructor guided exercises. The training exercises at the higher level subprograms closely follow the strategies used in the skills training literature for the development of problem-solving skills.

Another European contributor to cognitive rehabilitation, van der Gaag's (1992) cognitive retraining program

also proceeds in steps from fairly elementary to complex cognitive exercises. In the efficacy study, three main strategies were applied in training: self-instruction, mnemonics, and inductive reasoning. Subjects participated in 22 training sessions over about a 3-month period. Sessions lasted 15 to 25 minutes and were conducted two times per week. Sessions 1 through 12 included training on visual, auditory, tactile, and proprioceptive perception tasks; sessions 13 through 15 included training on tasks that integrated perceptual and language processing; and sessions 16 through 22 included training on more complex exercises of social perception. The results indicated that the experimental group performed significantly better than an attention-placebo group on measures of social perception and memory, but not attention or problem-solving ability. Given the amount of training devoted to improving perceptual processing, it may be that memory was improved through the activation of perceptual processes that facilitated the encoding of the to-be-remembered material. Social perception may have been affected more directly through the training exercises. Like Brenner's IPT, training is conducted over a series of prescribed training sessions, rather than being dictated by the patients' achievement of specified goals.

CONCLUSIONS

Our review of selected laboratory-based feasibility studies of cognitive remediation indicates that certain procedures have been effective at ameliorating cognitive deficits in schizophrenia. Specifically, semantic encoding, explicit instruction, contingent reinforcement, and errorless learning have all shown some degree of success at improving various areas of cognitive functioning in psychiatric patients.

One aim of this chapter was to assess the degree of correspondence between the findings of laboratory-based feasibility studies and those methods/interventions used in clinic-based comprehensive rehabilitation programs. The structured approach to training in the comprehensive programs is consistent with traditional neuropsychological approaches to cognitive rehabilitation in that training typically begins on simpler, more elementary task components and advances to more complex tasks that are inherently more difficult. Based on this selected review of comprehensive programs, it would appear that the methods used by the majority of the clinic-based comprehensive programs to ameliorate cognitive deficits follow a general stimulation approach and consist of repetitive administration of various cognitive tasks, and specific interventions to improve performance on tasks within a given cognitive domain are typically not employed.

The general stimulation approach was widely used in the neuropsychological rehabilitation programs for brain-injured individuals in the 1970s and 1980s (Hanlon, 1991). It requires the patient to perform repetitive drills and exercises in an attempt to ameliorate the deficit. Typically, the measure used to identify the deficit serves as the task used for the repetitive drills and exercises. Although the approach is a practical one, there has been little empirical support for its efficacy, at least outside of the laboratory (Wilson, 1982; Prigatono et al., 1984). In general, repetitive practice is probably a necessary component to facilitating improvement in function; however, practice alone appears insufficient to produce significant changes in cognitive functioning.

Aside from the program described by Heinssen and Victor (1994), the remainder of the comprehensive programs that we reviewed do not appear to be using many of the specific interventions that have been found to be effective in ameliorating cognitive deficits in schizophrenia patients. Specific procedures such as self-talk, visual and verbal prompts, semantic encoding, monetary reinforcement, and errorless learning are conspicuously absent. It is possible that selected comprehensive programs may in fact be using these procedures, but simply have not described their use in published reports. In addition, some of these procedures have only recently appeared in the psychopathology cognitive remediation literature.

Selected programs, such as Brenner's IPT, have utilized procedures from the skills training programs. Although these programs are not specifically designed for cognitive remediation, selected procedures used in skills training modules (many of which are behaviorally based) have been found to be effective in remediating certain cognitive deficits (e.g., performance deficits on the WCST). The primary method of instruction within the subprograms of IPT typically involves the use of instructor generated open-ended questions. That is, the instructor asks the group a question about some aspect of the to-be-learned material (e.g., concept formation) and a member of the group attempts to provide the correct answer. Inaccurate responses are gently corrected. This approach is markedly different from errorless learning in that the former is geared toward eliciting and then correcting erroneous responses. In contrast, errorless learning reduces the opportunity or possibility of committing errors.

The training methods used in the majority of the comprehensive programs to improve performance on selected tasks are borrowed from cognitive rehabilitation programs for the brain injured. Although this may be a logical starting point for developing such programs, the characteristic cognitive deficits and psychiatric symptoms found in schizophrenia have a number of important differences from the types of disturbances found in brain-injured groups. In schizophrenia, the brain disorder is generally believed to be diffuse or multifocal, and the magnitude of cognitive dysfunction is often less severe than that seen in acute brain-injured groups. In addition, the constellation of negative symptoms (e.g., amotivation, anhedonia) may pose significant constraints to successful rehabilitation in working with schizophrenia patients. Hence, psychiatric rehabilitation programs for remediation of cognitive deficits need to take such differences into account. At the very least, the interventions that have been found effective at remediating the cognitive deficits in schizophrenia should be carefully considered for use in the clinically based comprehensive programs.

Perhaps future comprehensive programs of cognitive rehabilitation in psychiatric patients will use the results from the feasibility studies of discrete cognitive probes to complement existing methods. At this time, it appears that the comprehensive programs' reliance on task repetition to achieve functional gains could pose a major stumbling block to successful rehabilitation. The results from the feasibility studies provide a possible means to improve task performance within selected cognitive domains.

REFERENCES

Asarnow, R. F., & MacCrimmon, D. J. (1978). Residual performance deficit in clinically remitted schizophrenics: A marker of schizophrenia? *Journal of Abnormal of Psychology, 87,* 597–608.

Asarnow, R. F., & MacCrimmon, D. J. (1981). Span of apprehension deficits during the postpsychotic stages of schizophrenia: A replication and extension. *Archives of General Psychiatry, 38,* 1006–1011.

Asarnow, R. F., Steffy, R. A., MacCrimmon, D. J., & Cleghorn, J. M. (1977). An attentional assessment of foster children at risk for schizophrenia. *Journal of Abnormal Psychology, 86,* 267–275.

Bauman, E. (1971a). Schizophrenic short-term memory: A deficit in subjective organization. *Canadian Journal of Behavioral Science, 3,* 55–65.

Bauman, E. (1971b). Schizophrenic short-term memory: The role of organizational input. *Journal of Consulting and Clinical Psychology, 36,* 14–19.

Bellack, A. S., & Hersen, M. (1979). *Research and practice in social skills training.* New York: Plenum.

Bellack, A. S., Mueser, K. T., Morrison, R. L., Tierney, A., & Podell, K. (1990). Remediation of cognitive deficits in schizophrenia. *American Journal of Psychiatry, 147,* 1650–1655.

Benedict, R. H. B., Harris, A. E., Markow, T., McCormick, J. A., Nuechterlein, K. H., & Asarnow, R. F. (1994). Effects of attention training on information processing in schizophrenia. *Schizophrenia Bulletin, 20,* 537–546.

Brenner, H. D., Hodel, B., Roder, V., & Corrigan, P. (1992). Treatment of cognitive dysfunctions and behavioral deficits in schizophrenia: Integrated psychological therapy. *Schizophrenia Bulletin, 18,* 21–26.

Corrigan, P. W., Wallace, C. J., Schade, M. L., & Green, M. F. (1994). Cognitive dysfunctions and psychosocial skill learning in schizophrenia. *Behavior Therapy, 25,* 5–15.

Cromwell, R. L., & Spaulding, W. (1978). How schizophrenics handle information. In W. E. Fann, I. Karacan, A. D. Pokorny, & R. L. Williams (Eds.), *Phenomenology and treatment of schizophrenia* (pp. 127–162). New York: Spectrum Press.

Erickson, R. A. (1988). Neuropsychological assessment and the rehabilitation of persons with severe psychiatric disabilities. *Rehabilitation Psychology, 33,* 15–25.

Erickson, R. A., & Binder, L. M. (1986). Cognitive deficits among functionally psychotic patients: A rehabilitative perspective. *Journal of Clinical and Experimental Neuropsychology, 8,* 257–274.

Erickson, R. A., & Burton, M. (1986). Working with psychiatric patients with cognitive deficits. *Cognitive Rehabilitation, 4,* 26–31.

Estes, W. K., & Taylor, H. A. (1966). Visual detection in relation to display size and redundancy of critical elements. *Perception and Psychophysics, 1,* 9–16.

Gaag, M. van der (1992). *The results of cognitive training in schizophrenic patients.* Oegstgeest: Eburon Delft.

Goldberg, T. E., Weinberger, D. R., Berman, K. F., Pliskin, N. H., & Podd, M. H. (1987). Further evidence for dementia of the prefrontal type in schizophrenia? A controlled study of teaching the Wisconsin Card Sorting Test. *Archives of General Psychiatry, 44,* 1008–1014.

Goldman, R. S., Axelrod, B. N., & Tompkins, L. M. (1992). Effect of instructional cues on schizophrenic patients' performance on the Wisconsin Card Sorting Test. *American Journal of Psychiatry, 149,* 1718–1722.

Green, M. F. (1993). Cognitive remediation in schizophrenia: Is it time yet? *American Journal of Psychiatry, 150,* 178–187.

Green, M. F., Satz., P., Ganzell, S., & Vaclav, J. F. (1992). Wisconsin Card Sorting Test performance in schizophrenia: Remediation of a stubborn deficit. *American Journal of Psychiatry, 149,* 62–67.

Hanlon, R. E. (1991). Neuromotor activation in the facilitation of language production: Rehabilitation applications. In R. E. Hanlon & J. W. Brown (Eds.), *Cognitive microgenesis: A neuropsychological perspective* (pp. 180–196). New York: Springer-Verlag.

Heaton, R. K. (1981). *Wisconsin Card Sorting Test manual.* Odessa, FL: Psychological Assessment Resources.

Heinssen, R. K., & Victor, B. J. (1994). Cognitive-behavioral treatments for schizophrenia: Evolving rehabilitation techniques. In W. D. Spaulding (Ed.), *Cognitive technology in psychiatric rehabilitation* (pp. 159–181). Lincoln: University of Nebraska Press.

Jaeger, J., Berns, S., Tigner, A., & Douglas, E. (1992). Remediation of neuropsychological deficits in psychiatric populations: Rationale and methodological considerations. *Psychopharmacology Bulletin, 28,* 367–390.

Jaeger, J., & Douglas, E. (1992). Adjunctive neuropsychological remediation in psychiatric rehabilitation: Program description and preliminary data. *Schizophrenia Research, 4,* 304–305.

Kayton, L., & Koh, S. D. (1975). Hypohedonia in schizophrenia. *Journal of Nervous and Mental Disorder, 161,* 412–420.

Kern, R. S., Green, M. F., & Goldstein, M. J. (1995). Modification of performance on the span of apprehension, a putative marker of vulnerability to schizophrenia. *Journal of Abnormal Psychology, 104,* 385–389.

Kern, R. S., Green, M. F., & Satz, P. (1992). Neuropsychological predictors of skills training for chronic psychiatric patients. *Psychiatry Research, 43,* 223–230.

Kern, R. S., Wallace, C. J., Hellman, S. G., Womack, L. M., & Green, M. F. (1996). A training procedure for remediating WCST deficits in chronic psychotic patients: An adaptation of errorless learning principles. *Journal of Psychiatric Research, 30,* 283–294.

King, H. E. (1991). Psychomotor dysfunction in schizophrenia. In S. R. Steinhauer, J. H. Gruzelier, & J. Zubin (Eds.), *Handbook of schizophrenia, Vol. 5: Neuropsychology, psychophysiology and information processing* (pp. 273–301). Amsterdam: Elsevier Science Publishers.

Koh, S. D., & Kayton, L. (1974). Memorization of "unrelated" word strings by young nonpsychotic schizophrenics. *Journal of Abnormal Psychology, 33,* 14–22.

Koh, S. D., Kayton, L., & Berry, R. (1973). Mnemonic organization in young nonpsychotic schizophrenics. *Journal of Abnormal Psychology, 81,* 299–310.

Koh, S. D., Kayton, L., & Peterson, R. A. (1976). Affective encoding and consequent remembering in schizophrenic young adults. *Journal of Abnormal Psychology, 85,* 156–166.

Maher, B. A. (1991). Language and schizophrenia. In S. R. Steinhauer, J. H. Gruzelier, & J. Zubin (Eds.), *Handbook of schizophrenia, Vol. 5: Neuropsychology, psychophysiology and information processing* (pp. 437–464). Amsterdam: Elsevier Science Publishers.

Mueser, K. T., Bellack, A. S., Douglas, M. S., & Wade, J. H. (1991). Prediction of social skill acquisition in schizophrenic and major affective disorder patients from memory and symptomatology. *Psychiatry Research, 37,* 281–296.

Prigatano, G. P., Fordyce, D. J., Zeiner, H. K., Roueche, J. R., Pepping, M., & Wood, B. C. (1984). Neuropsychological rehabilitation after closed head injury. *Journal of Neurology, Neurosurgery, and Psychiatry, 47,* 505–513.

Saykin, A. J., Gur, R. C., Gur, R. E., Mozley, P. D., Mozley, L. H., Resnick, S. M., Kester, D. B., & Stafiniak, P. (1991).

Neuropsychological function in schizophrenia: Selective impairment in memory and learning. *Archives of General Psychiatry, 48,* 618–624.

Sohlberg, M. M., & Mateer, C. A. (1989). *Introduction to cognitive rehabilitation.* New York: Guilford Press.

Spaulding, W. D., & Sullivan, M. (1991). From the laboratory to the clinic: Psychological methods and principles in psychiatric rehabilitation. In R. P. Liberman (Ed.), *Handbook of psychiatric rehabilitation* (pp. 30–55). Elmsford, NY: Pergamon Press.

Spring, B., Weinstein, L., Freeman, R., & Thompson, S. (1991). Selective attention in schizophrenia. In S. R. Steinhauer, J. H. Gruzelier, & J. Zubin (Eds.), *Handbook of schizophrenia, Vol. 5: Neuropsychology, psychophysiology and information processing* (pp. 335–370). Amsterdam: Elsevier Science Publishers.

Stuve, P., Erickson, R. C., & Spaulding, W. (1991). Cognitive rehabilitation: The next step in psychiatric rehabilitation. *Psychosocial Rehabilitation Journal, 15,* 9–26.

Summerfelt, A. T., Alphs, L. D., Wagman, A. M. I., Funderburk, F. R., Hierholzer, R. M., & Strauss, M. E. (1991). Reduction of perseverative errors in patients with schizophrenia using monetary feedback. *Journal of Abnormal Psychology, 100,* 613–616.

Terrace, H. S. (1963). Discrimination learning with and without errors. *Journal of the Experimental Analysis of Behavior, 6,* 1–27.

Touchette, P. E. (1968). The effects of graduated stimulus change on the acquisition of a simple discrimination in severely retarded boys. *Journal of the Experimental Analysis of Behavior, 11,* 39–48.

Wilson, B. (1982). Success and failure in memory training following a cerebral vascular accident. *Cortex, 18,* 581–594.

Yozawitz, A. (1986). Applied neuropsychology in a psychiatric center. In I. Grant & K. M. Adams (Eds.), *Neuropsychological assessment of neuropsychiatric disorders* (pp. 121–146). New York: Oxford University Press.

Zubin, J., & Spring, B. (1977). Vulnerability—A new view of schizophrenia. *Journal of Abnormal Psychology, 86,* 103–126.

CHAPTER 22

MODELS OF CASE MANAGEMENT AND THEIR IMPACT ON SOCIAL OUTCOMES OF SEVERE MENTAL ILLNESS

Tom K. J. Craig

This chapter provides an overview of approaches aimed at improving the coordination and delivery of community-based services for people suffering from severe mental illness. It summarizes the main findings from evaluative research and illustrates the principles with reference to case examples taken from the everyday work of an assertive community treatment team based in South London.

BACKGROUND

Many severe mental illnesses, and schizophrenia in particular, are prone to a chronic course with profound impact on social-adaptive processes. Although florid symptoms and associated behavioral disturbance may be controlled by medication, many patients continue to experience difficulties in social interaction, employment, and everyday self-care. These difficulties may arise as a direct consequence of residual delusions (e.g., the grandiose patient who refuses offers of sheltered work as he believes he is a multimillionaire) or of negative symptoms (e.g., profound volitional impairments that result in

shabby grooming and poor personal hygiene) or even because the illness began before the patient had completed basic education or had developed mature social skills. Regardless of their origin, such impairments are the main obstacle to survival outside institutional settings. It is now widely accepted that social outcomes are just as important as symptomatic remission; that effective rehabilitation must include interventions to improve patients' social, vocational, and personal competence; and that these interventions are most effective when carried out in the community settings in which we expect our patients to live.

Such community care of people suffering from severe mental illness (SMI) has a long and respectable history in Britain. Every resident of the population is entitled (and expected) to be registered with a general practitioner who provides continuing supervision of chronic health problems. Community psychiatric nurses (CPNs), first introduced over three decades ago and now numbering well over 5,000, supplement this supervision by regular contacts with patients in their own homes (White, 1991). The state welfare system provides assistance with shelter, transport, and the essentials of daily living through a broad range of statutory benefits at a level which still far outstrips that available in many other countries, and there is a well-established system of social care to ensure that patients have access to the majority if not all essentials of daily living. Modern community services have established multidisciplinary professional teams based in mental health centers, providing comprehensive care from settings that are free of the stigma of the old hospital asylums (Patmore & Weaver, 1991).

With this range of provision, one might imagine that there is very little chance of patients' needs going unrecognized or of their falling out of care. And yet, here as in North America, it is clear that this system has largely failed the severely mentally ill with a pronounced mismatch between levels of need and actual service uptake— the least needy consuming the greater amount of service (Goering, Wasylenki, Lancee, & Freeman, 1984; Melzer, Hale, Malik, Hogman, & Wood, 1991; Wasylenki, Goering, Lancee, Fischer, & Freeman, 1985). In one such study, the local service included two community mental health centers which were considered models of their kind in the United Kingdom. One had been set up to deal with the needs of severely mentally ill people and employed staff with contracts dedicated to caring for this population. In this Center, a study of the referral pathways and of the clinical activity of team members showed a clear drift away from the ideals established when the center first opened. While the districtwide number of referrals of patients suffering from psychoses remained relatively constant across the 5 years of the evaluation, there was a marked rise in the numbers of cases with minor neuroses, and within 2 years of opening, the majority of face-to-face clinical activity was geared to dealing with these referrals. Not only was the amount of time spent with psychotic patients eroded under this pressure, but the numbers of SMI people registered at the center steadily declined, with the majority being managed by the traditional outpatient services that the center was to have replaced. An earlier apparent reduction in hospitalization for psychosis was entirely lost (Sayce, Craig, & Boardman, 1991).

A similar story can be related about many day hospitals. Originally established to provide more intensive treatment and care than could be delivered by outpatients to SMI patients, many were found to be running at around 60% occupancy, largely comprising chronic attenders with very little turnover and considerable difficulty holding on to new referrals. Interventions often took the form of block treatments to which patients were expected to conform rather than individualized interventions.

These depressing observations echoed contemporaneous reports from North American psychiatrists who reported widespread neglect of community provision for the housing, social, and occupational needs of SMI people and resulting increases in the numbers of mentally ill in prisons, homeless, or perpetually revolving round a fragmented and disorganized service (Goering et al., 1984; Lamb, 1984, 1987).

Perhaps the single most important explanation for the shortfall of community care lies in a conflict between the requirement of throughput of cases and the need for continued treatment and supervision. Throughput models emphasize the importance of vigorous, effective treatment of acute episodes with the expectation that most patients can be safely passed back to primary health care for ongoing monitoring until the next, if any, acute episode. It is a model that works fairly well across most of medicine and is defended in terms of rationing expert resources to the times where these are most needed and in discouraging dependency of institutionalization. A continuing care model, on the other hand, emphasizes the importance of sufficiently intense levels of ongoing intervention to maintain the benefits of acute treatment and minimize relapse or deterioration.

The throughput model has dominated psychiatry for much of the last three decades. Studies have shown that brief hospitalization with intensive treatment can achieve just as much (in terms of symptom reduction) as longer hospital stays, while at the same time there, has been criticism of asylum care on the grounds that this fosters dependency and actually increases social disabilities of inmates. Together, these contributed to an impression that rehabilitation services consisted of long-stay wards of the old mental hospital to which patients were sent when psychiatry had nothing else to offer. A psychiatrist, psychologist, or mental health nurse could complete his or her training with minimal exposure to the nuts and bolts of rehabilitation and with the barest grasp of how to implement let alone supervise problem-focused interventions to tackle core deficits in daily living skills such as budgeting, shopping, and household chores or persistent difficulties in self-care and social relationships. Without an emphasis on the importance of these mundane interventions, a patient's repeated failure to sort out his or her finances, to persist in unhygenic habits, and to forget to pay the rent were all too likely to be mislabeled as indicative of "personality disorder"—that time-honored professional excuse for disengagement. Over half of the patients suffering from schizophrenia seen by specialist teams for homeless mentally ill people in London had been discharged from the caseload of a CPN because they had repeatedly failed to keep appointments and were deemed uncooperative with treatment (Craig, Bayliss, Klein, Manning, & Reader, 1995).

Another important reason for the failure of community services was the lack of effective administrative structures for coordinating and delivering the complex array of services that are required for effective continuing care. In the institutional settings from which all community services originated, therapeutic roles were divided between professional groups—the doctor prescribed medication, the nurse administered it; the occupational therapist conducted assessments of daily living skills and provided training or diversional activities, while the psychologist advised on specific behavioral interventions. Patients were dispatched from the ward to occupational therapy departments, medications administered on fixed schedules, and treatments given in a way that minimized the disruption to staff routines. The hospital itself provided an institutional framework for the provision of shelter, day-to-day finances, meals, and clothing. But away from the institution, these services fell to separate organizations. Mental health professionals still provided care but now were seldom to be found together on one site, and basic needs of shelter, finance, and social activity were met by entirely separate organizations, each with their own priorities and rules regarding access.

Case Management: A System for Delivering Coordinated Community Care

Case management is a shorthand term that encompasses a range of strategies aimed at minimizing these problems of poor coordination and service fragmentation with a shift in emphases toward a continuing care model of service delivery. The essential focus is the attempt to ensure the orderly, uninterrupted movement of clients across diverse elements of a complex service system. This, in turn, relies on the presence of a long-term relationship between clients and their main professional carers, a flexible and individualized approach to arranging services, and good communication between clients and service providers in order to minimize obstacles to access (Bachrach, 1981). Under most current systems, clients are allocated to a named "case manager" (confusingly sometimes also referred to as a "key worker" or "care manager") who has the job of ensuring that needs have been assessed and that these needs are addressed by whatever agency is best placed to provide the required service.

While all case management models recognize the importance of long-term delivery of coordinated community care, there are considerable variations in the way this is achieved. Actual implementations range along a continuum from brokerage approaches, which provide few services directly but act as a central point for the coordination of other agencies, through full clinical models, in which the case management team is seen as the main provider of the most essential elements of treatment and care. In practice, there is a growing agreement that both brokerage and direct services are required to meet the complex needs of SMI clients and a corresponding shift toward more clinically orientated approaches.

But despite this apparent convergence toward clinical case management, there is still a wide variation in how this is structured and in the underlying assumptions that guide the model. Four basic models have been described (Robinson, Bergman, & Scallet, 1989). The *expanded broker model* stresses the importance of linkage and coordination. It assumes that the specific treatments are best provided by experts in the field and that it is system chaos and inflexibility that lies at the root of the problem with community care. The main function of case mangers is to facilitate contacts with the right services in the belief that the natural inclination of services to care and patients to respond will do the rest. Closely related is the *personal strengths model* based largely on an advocacy–mentor approach. Here, the primary focus is on enhancing the abilities and strengths of individual clients, empowering choice, and recognizing the right of clients to take control of their lives and treatment. Interventions are aimed at facilitating "healthy" behaviors, enhancing positive self-esteem, and aiding personal growth. The underlying assumption is that people have a will to improve their lot in life and can be most helped by removing barriers to achievement. The *rehabilitation approach* focuses on improving living skills and is based firmly on the theory and practice of psychiatric rehabilitation. Individualized rehabilitation plans are based on skill acquisition including in vivo training, explicit goal setting, and the importance of the working relationship between therapist and client. The therapist–client relationship contains many of the attributes of supportive psychotherapy—most notably the notion of empathic listening where the therapist attempts to gain insight into the problems of clients by placing themselves "inside" their clients' experiences (Schwaber, 1981). Finally, the full support model, also known as *assertive community treatment* (ACT), encompasses the rehabilitation framework but takes a more paternalistic, directive approach. Interventions are vigorous, often led by the therapist, and typically explicitly behaviorally orientated. Full support models can include specific treatments such as family psychoeducation interventions, and the case management team is often the main provider of both medical and social care.

Case management services can also be organized on individual or team models. In the individual model, each patient has a relationship to a single, named case manager. This is the most common arrangement and emphasizes the importance of the individual relationship as the cornerstone to achieving long-term alliance between patient and services (Harris, 1988). However, it has the disadvantage of disruptions when case managers move on and can be burdensome on staff when more seriously behaviorally disturbed patients comprise the majority of an individual case manager's caseload. A team-based approach aims to share the care of patients between two or more case managers who work collectively as part of a (multidisciplinary) team. This is said by some proponents to reduce staff burnout and to improve long-term care for complex cases (Bond, Miller, Krumwied, & Ward, 1988).

Finally, the implementation of case management also depends to a great extent on the wider organization of social and medical care services. In Britain, the National Health Service (NHS) and Community Care Act (1990) and attendant guidances to health providers (Department of Health, 1989) introduced the concept of care management under which local authorities have the responsibility for ensuring that the social care and housing needs of vulnerable people (including those suffering from SMI) are comprehensively assessed and explicitly linked to the development of individualized care plans. Care managers are empowered to arrange or purchase whatever services may be required to meet these needs (including domicillary services or residential care). The care manager provides an overseeing role monitoring the delivery of these services. A similar system is recommended for providers of health care. Under this Care Program Approach (CPA; Department of Health, 1989), mental health services are required to ensure that all psychiatric patients have a comprehensive assessment of health needs, a documented community care plan developed in collaboration with the patient and his or her main carers, and a nominated key worker to oversee this plan and coordinate its implementation. Within this broad framework, certain patient groups are further highlighted as requiring special attention, notably those who have been compulsorily admitted to hospital, and those who are assessed as being of significant risk of self-harm or a danger to others. For these patients, there is an additional requirement that their names should be held on a central supervision register and that they should receive priority for continuing care in the community. In an ideal world, therefore, SMI patients would have all their needs assessed and addressed by experts through care plans collaboratively developed between health and social services. Although not explicitly set out, there is the assumption that some negotiation would occur as to the specific roles of the key worker (health) and care manager (social care) but that the net result would be that the complex mix of health and care provision would be well planned, executed, and coordinated across the lifetime of the patient. Unfortunately, this ideal is still seldom realized as there have been minimal increases in resources to deliver services and the availability of two potential coordinators of care continues to be a recipe for confusion. In most centers, service providers have adopted an informal hierarchy, largely dependent on availability of staff in which the latter two groups (i.e., compulsorily hospitalized or placed on a supervision register) are given priority allocation to the care management/CPA system with the majority of SMI clients in the community getting very little more than they did prior to the introduction of the new legislation.

Table 22.1 summarizes the main differences between typical British implementations of each of these approaches.

The Research Evidence

Despite the rapid growth of case management approaches to the care of SMI people, there is a surprising dearth of evidence for its effectiveness, particularly concerning the relative strengths of alternative models. By far the best evidence in support of case management comes from a small number of studies that have evaluated assertive community treatment models, and it is these studies which have largely driven international interest in case management as a means for delivering community care. It is not the purpose of this chapter to comprehensively review all these studies. Rather I shall select a small number of well-designed and well-executed investigations that throw some light on what may be the essential ingredients of effective care (for comprehensive reviews of the more important studies, see Burns & Santos, 1995; Taube, Morlock, Burns, & Santos, 1990).

The published research evidence for the efficacy of case management falls into three broad groups: studies that have recruited SMI patients during an acute episode

Table 22.1. Comparison of Typical Assertive Community Treatment (ACT), Care Management (CM), and Care Program Approach (CPA) Services in Britain

CHARACTERISTIC	ACT SERVICE	CM SERVICE	CPA SERVICE
Client mix	Predominantly SMI	Predominantly SMI	Mixed SMI/minor morbidity
Staff–client ratio	1:10 to 1:15	1:20 to 1:30	1:30 to 1:50
Frequency of contact	Daily	Weekly to fortnightly	Fortnightly or longer
Team structure	Multidisciplinary—team based; staff provide most of the social and medical care	Individual worker (often social work staff) oversees a range of care components provided by different agencies	Individual worker (often CPN) provides some direct care and monitors implementation of wider care plan
Emergency and out-of-hours service	Provided by team	Provided by hospital services	Provided by hospital services
Treatment base	Community	Mainly clinic/office	Mainly community
Hospital admission	Controlled by team	Little/no direct control	Hospital controlled
Treatment orientation	Practical problem solving plus a range of specialized family and cognitive-behavioral therapies	Emphasis on assessment of need and advocacy rather than direct treatment; care provided by different agencies depending on needs assessment	Mainly supervising medication and some practical help; few have specialist training in specific interventions for SMI patients and rely on other professionals
Outcome evaluation	Explicit component of model, outcome goals negotiated with patient	Limited evaluation of outcome of interventions delivered by provider agencies	Goal-oriented methods seldom employed as routine
Social care (housing, occupation, social activities)	Responsibility of team; seen as being as important medical treatment goals	Responsibility of case manager to arrange/monitor; main focus tends to depend on profession of case manager	Tends to be seen as responsibility of social services

with the intention to prevent immediate hospitalization; studies that have targeted more chronic disorders on discharge from hospital or already in the community; and studies aimed at testing these models in specific client groups such as the homeless or dually diagnosed.

Case Management as a Means of Reducing the Need for Acute Hospitalization

The earliest and most widely known study was designed by Stein and Test (1980) in Madison, Wisconsin. They randomly allocated 130 patients at the point of admission to hospital to an intensive community-based service or to hospital followed by traditional outpatient care. Approximately half of the patients had a diagnosis of schizophrenia. Case management was provided by a multidisciplinary team who worked intensively with patients in the community helping them secure food, shelter, and clothing; providing in vivo rehabilitation focused on the activities of daily living; and supervising or administering medication. On average, each case manager cared for 10 patients. The team set no time-limit to their involvement and provided a 24-hours-per-day, 7-days-a-week service. During the subsequent year, the team managed all admissions to hospital, serving as the main gatekeepers of inpatient care, coordinating and working with inpatient staff when hospitalization was necessary. At the end of 12 months, compared to the standard service, subjects in the experimental service had spent significantly less time in hospital and had superior clinical and social outcomes.

Close replications of this approach have been evaluated in Sydney, Australia, and London, England. In Sydney, Hoult et al. (1983) described an intervention targeted on consecutive referrals of patients requiring hospitalization. These referrals were randomly allocated to standard hospital care or to the experimental community treatment program. Patients allocated to community treatment received a comprehensive assessment including a clear definition of the presenting problem, physical and mental state examination, the quality of interpersonal relationships in the family, and immediate social supports and needs. As part of the initial assessment, care plans were developed collaboratively with the patients and their relatives, information was given about the illness and its expected course, and acute disturbance dealt with by rapid tranquilization if necessary. The team then returned the patients to their homes, or if the situation at home appeared untenable, they took the patients to alternative accommodation such as a boarding house. Patients and their families were offered intensive daily support during the initial phase of the illness. Staff could stay with patients for many hours, monitoring medication and side effects and reassuring the patients and their families. Patients, carers, and proprietors were encouraged to call the team at any time with a guaranteed response within 30 minutes. The team visited frequently during the first few days and took the patients out with them to give relief to the families. Patients were encouraged to take responsibility for their actions and to return to normal functioning as quickly as possible. Staff provided in vivo training in daily living skills to improve and maintain adequate hygiene, self-care, and use of community transport, shops, day centers, and workshops. A small number of patients required hospitalization during this acute phase of treatment and were supervised in hospital by the community team. On discharge they were offered the same treatment as those who were not hospitalized.

Assessments of psychiatric and social functioning and of relatives' and patients' satisfaction were carried out by independent researchers at baseline, 1, 4, 8, and 12 months. At baseline, there were no statistically significant differences between experimental and comparison group patients on any of the demographic, clinical, or social factors measured. Three-quarters of the patients had previous admissions, and a similar proportion had a diagnosis of functional psychosis (half were schizophrenic). Over half were involuntary patients at referral. At 12 months, the experimental group had experienced significantly fewer and shorter admissions to hospital. Community treatment also achieved a superior clinical outcome with significantly lower symptom scores. Both patients and relatives considered community treatment to be more satisfactory than hospital treatment and standard aftercare. Community treatment did not result in any more legal offenses or police contacts but was somewhat less effective in reducing the number of suicide threats and attempts though no patients committed suicide (Hoult, 1986; Hoult et al., 1983).

In the London study (Marks et al., 1994; Muijen, Marks, Connolly, & Audini, 1992), 189 patients who faced an emergency admission to hospital were randomized to the Daily Living Program (home-based care) or hospitalization followed by standard out-patient care. The DLP provided 24-hour, 7-days-per-week access to services. DLP staff liaised with relatives, friends, and neighbors as well as the full range of statutory and voluntary services. Each patient was allocated to a case manager though the service was team-based and the case manager did not necessarily carry out all interventions. Case managers visited as often as necessary, which in a crisis could often be several times daily for hours at a time. Each patient's problems was formulated in negotiation with the patient and recorded as a simple written problem statement and care plan goal. Interventions included nutrition, budgeting, housing, and recreation as well as clinical treatments aimed at symptom reduction or improvements in daily living skills. Outcome measures included the number and length of subsequent hospitalizations, mental state, social function, and satisfaction of patients and relatives at baseline, 8, 12, and 18 months follow-up. The DLP care resulted in a marked reduction in the number of days in hospital during the follow-up though the absolute number of admissions was similar in the experimental and comparison group. Patients' symptoms improved slightly more than those of controls as did social adjustment. Patient's and relatives' satisfaction were markedly greater for DLP patients than controls. However, the clinical and social gains of these patients were modest and the numbers unemployed actually rose during the study. Furthermore, over a 15-month withdrawal phase which succeeded the study, the benefits of the DLP largely disappeared (Audini, Marks, Lawrence, Connolly, & Watts, 1994).

All three studies shared a common philosophy of team-based, problem-oriented clinical case management in which explicit goals for intervention were negotiated with patients and monitored by the case manager throughout the intervention. Patients were recruited at a crisis point in their illness. The disorders suffered by patients in these studies appear similar with over three quarters suffering from a psychotic illness (about half suffering from schizophrenia). A somewhat greater proportion of cases were first admissions in the London study. All three studies achieved savings of up to 80% in hospital days. Madison reported the lowest rate of admissions (18%) and London the highest (84%). The difference between case management and control treatments in terms of clinical and social outcomes only achieve statistical significance in the Madison study though there are trends in Sydney and

London. All three centers demonstrated superior patients' and relatives' satisfaction with control services throughout the follow-up and probably reflects the parallel falloff in outpatient contact that characterizes most standard outpatient care.

Not all such programs have resulted in a sustained reduction in hospital use. (Mulder, 1985) in Kent County, Michigan, assessed a case management program that closely followed the Stein and Test model. Staff from Madison trained the Harbinger clinicians, and the model service included assertive community treatment with a 24-hour availability. Patients were randomly assigned at the time of voluntary admission to intensive case management or to hospitalization. After 30 months in treatment, patients in the control group had been hospitalized almost five times more often than patients in case management, and the patients in the latter service were found to be functioning at higher levels than controls on a number of measures. However by 66 months, experimental patients had used significantly more crisis intervention services and were more likely to be in residential care. There were also no significant differences between groups in terms of global or occupational function and control patients were more likely to have social contacts. This pattern of an initial but unsustained improvement may be related to attrition of better functioning patients from the Harbinger program or to a general waning of enthusiasm and high turnover of staff as the program proceeded.

Case Management as a Means of Caring for Chronic Mentally Ill Patients

All four studies recruited patients at a time of crisis, diverting them from emergency clinics to home care. Other studies have attempted to evaluate assertive community treatments as a means of providing aftercare aimed at preventing relapse and readmission. Very few of these have adopted an assertive treatment model and report interventions based on combination of rehabilitation and strengths approaches—possibly reflecting a more chronic target population.

Expanded Brokerage Models

American studies of brokerage models of case management, even when these include a significant clinical component, have seldom established a major reduction in the use of inpatient treatment. For example, in one study, 435 patients discharged from psychiatric hospital in Harlem,

New York, were assigned to one of three types of service: intensive clinical case management, less intensive case management, or routine aftercare with no case management services. Patients who received intensive case management had twice as many psychiatric hospitalizations as patients who received routine aftercare and about the same number as patients receiving less intensive case management. Although the nature of "intensive" case management is not fully described, it is clear that the approach placed greater reliance on the coordination of external treatment agencies than that typical of the assertive treatment approach (Curtis, Millman, & Struening, 1992).

These findings were echoed by an investigation involving 2,152 patients served by case managers at 16 different sites in the United States. Patients' overall functional levels bore very little relation to the amount of service they received, and case managers spent most of their time providing initial assessments, monitoring (rather than delivering) treatment, and arranging transportation (Clark & Landis, 1990).

In Britain, the CPA, Supervision Registers, and Care Management are all examples of bureaucratic solutions to the problem of coordinating aftercare. None prescribe any specific form of treatment or set out the manner in which this care is to be delivered and monitored. Since no assumptions are made of the nature of care, they provide good models for study of what can be achieved in terms of patient outcome through average mental health services given attention to improving coordination but with little special training or specific therapeutic requirements.

The only randomized controlled trial of Care Management in Britain failed to demonstrate any statistically significant differences in numbers of needs, quality of life, employment status, quality of accommodation, social behavior, or psychiatric symptoms over a 14-month treatment period, though there was a significant reduction in deviant behavior on a standardized behavior rating scale. As the authors conclude, it is unfortunate that such social services–led case management was not evaluated in advance of its implementation as the cornerstone of community care in the United Kingdom (Marshall, Lockwood, & Gath, 1995).

In s similar study, but involving health care staff, Muijen, Cooney, Strathdee, Bell, and Judson (1994) compared the effectiveness of a community support team (CST) offering case management services with that of a generic CPN team. The CST comprised four nurses who provided a case management/advocacy service for 8 to 11 patients. These patients were referred exclusively from specialist psychiatric services and all suffered from a long-term mental illness. The team dealt with social as well as clinical aspects of care. They managed welfare benefits, housing problems, and leisure pursuits as well as provided more clinical interventions such as the administration and monitoring of medication. Six generic CPNs comprised the comparison service. These nurses worked independently, with considerably larger caseloads which also included non-SMI patients referred directly to them from general practitioners in the local area. For the study, 82 patients with schizophrenia or affective psychoses lasting more than 2 years and having at least two previous hospital admissions in the last 2 years were randomly allocated to the CST or generic CPN service. The two groups were compared at 6, 12, and 18 months on multiple measures of mental state, social functioning, and service utilization. There was a striking difference in service use between the groups at all follow-up points with the case managed group having higher rates of contact with the service and greater uptake of a number of social benefits and help with practical problems of housing, finance, and legal problems. Despite the consistent evidence for greater service utilization by case managed patients, there were no significant differences on any measure of clinical or social functioning and no reduction in the number or length of hospitalizations across the follow-up (Muijen et al., 1994). A parallel cost-effectiveness analysis found that the CST did not confer cost-effectiveness advantages over standard CPN care (McCrone, Beecham, & Knapp, 1994).

In a more recent audit of local services, Pierides et al. (1996) examined the clinical and social outcomes of 80 schizophrenic patients following an acute episode of illness requiring hospitalization. Thirty one patients received community aftercare according to CPA guidelines and 49 received standard care. The CPA guidelines stipulated that each patient should be allocated to a named key worker prior to discharge from hospital and that this key worker would have responsibility for ensuring that there was a comprehensive community care plan involving all the agencies involved in providing services to the individual client. The CPA key worker ensured that all these staff met regularly to discuss and update the care plan and worked with the client to ensure uptake of these services. Following discharge from hospital, the CPA group were less likely to lose their accommodation in the community, or become homeless; less likely to be readmitted in crisis or to be compulsorily detained under the Mental Health Act; and substantially more likely to be in receipt of a range of community care services. They had more regular outpatient contacts, were more likely to be registered with

a general practitioner, and had higher attendance rates at structural day activities. However, there was no difference in the frequency or duration of rehospitalization, and there were no significant differences in clinical state or social disability. By 3 years all advantages for CPA and been lost though this was partially because the CPA had, by then, been widely implemented and many of the comparison subjects had been allocated key workers. It was also apparent that this expansion of CPA services had greatly stretched the clinical team. Caseloads had risen from 1:10 for the original CPA group to 1:30; rates of contact had dropped off for the original group of patients, and crisis hospitalization, imprisonment, and homelessness were now at levels not far from those seen in the comparison series earlier in the study.

Strengths/Rehabilitation Models

In Spokane, Washington, 72 chronically ill patients were allocated to a case management program comprising eight case managers, one supervising nurse coordinator, and one psychiatrist. The program emphasized a strengths model in which staff were expected "to have an overall nurturent affection and to be comfortable with an approach of limited directiveness toward patients" (Borland, McRae, & Lycan, 1989 p. 371). The service, available 24 hours daily, provided coordinated aftercare for patients' housing, welfare, occupational, and medical management. The study used a pre–post design in which patients were their own controls. Over the 5-year study period, hospital admissions were reduced by 70% compared to a 2-year prestudy baseline, and patients' days in hospital were reduced by 75%. There were similar dramatic decreases in the use of emergency services and after-hours on-call facilities. However, these reductions were offset by a massive (190%) increase in the use of residential care in the community (nursing home and staffed hostels). Patients' level of functioning as rated by the Global Assessment Scale, medication compliance, and substance abuse remained essentially unchanged across the 5 years (Borland, McRae, & Lycan, 1989).

Another program based firmly on the strengths model and aimed at patients with a chronic SMI has recently been reported from London, England. In this study, Ford et al. (1995) randomly allocated 77 patients to case management team or standard outpatient care. Outcome measures over a 2-year period included service uptake, mental state, social functioning, and quality of life. Case managers in the experimental arm of the study received training in the principles of care coordination, with an emphasis on techniques to improve patients' engagement with services. Specialist interventions (e.g., family work, specific rehabilitation interventions, cognitive therapy) were provided by the wider psychiatric service, and the case managers' job was envisaged as getting their patients into such services rather than providing these directly. At the end of the 2 years, case management was superior to standard care in terms of most aspects of service uptake. Significantly fewer clients were lost to care, there were improvements in outpatient contacts, and an uptake of statutory social security benefits. However, these interventions did not reduce hospitalization (which actually exceeded that in the control group, possibly as a result of uncovering previously unmet needs), nor were they superior to the comparison service in terms of the patients' clinical state, social functioning, or quality of life (Ford et al., 1995).

Interventions employing rehabilitation models appear to be somewhat more successful in terms of social and occupational outcomes. In one such study, 82 patients who suffered from chronic illness, poor employment history, social isolation, and residential instability were allocated to a team of eight case managers and matched to a similar number of patients who had been discharged from the same inpatient facility before the case management program was established. A rehabilitation model was chosen, which emphasized the practitioner's ability to serve the patients' functional needs through empathic counseling, in vivo training in daily living skills, and linking individual patients to specific community resources. Caseloads averaged between 15 and 20 patients per case manager throughout the study. Outcome was assessed at 6 and 24 months for case managed and matching control patients. At 6 months, the case managed group had used significantly more services but did not differ on other outcome measures. At 2 years, case managed clients did significantly better in terms of occupational functioning, time living independently, and social involvement, but there were no differences in the number of readmissions or length of stay despite the case managed patients consuming more services (Goering, Wasylenki, & Farkas, 1988).

Hornstra, Bruce-Wolfe, Sagduyu, and Riffle (1993) also report a comparison of a rehabilitation model of intensive case management and a traditional outpatient service. One hundred twelve schizophrenic patients were enrolled in the intensive case management service and matched by age, number of previous hospitalizations, and days in hospital with 112 schizophrenics receiving standard outpatient care. Patients in the intensive case management program used significantly more services during the study period compared with patients in the control group. Both groups showed an increase in the number of hospitalizations over the study period compared with the average over the previous 6 years. Although the experimental group had fewer hospitalizations and shorter admissions than the control group, these differences were not statistically significant (Hornstra et al., 1993).

ACT-like Interventions

Based on an earlier successful demonstration program in Chicago, Gary Bond and his colleagues (1988) randomly allocated 167 patients to standard services or to standard services plus case management. All patients in the study suffered from psychotic disorders and were at risk of rehospitalization or had been hospitalized between one and four times during the previous 2 years. The case management model was that successfully developed in the earlier Thresholds Bridge demonstration project (Witheridge & Dincin, 1985). This included the extensive use of in vivo interventions, attention to the practical problems of daily living, assertive outreach, and manageable caseload sizes. The experimental intervention differed from the full support model in that referrals to outside agencies played a more significant part in patients' care plans and there was greater separation between the case management team and hospital staff, who continued to control inpatient admissions. At 6 months, case managed patients had significantly shorter rehospitalizations, but no differences were found between groups in quality of life, medication compliance, involvement in therapy programs, or contacts with the legal system. One of the three centers performed significantly less well than the others, a finding which may be explained by the fact that this center experienced difficulties implementing the case management model with staff expressing confusion about roles and providing less direct service to clients than in any other center. Their orientation remained "less pragmatic and more insight oriented than with the other teams" (Bond, Miller, Krumwied, & Ward, 1988 p. 417).

More recently, this research team has reported on the 18-month outcomes of patients managed by assertive community treatment (ACT) teams at six community metal health centers in Indiana (McGrew, Bond, Dietzen, McKasson, & Miller, 1995). In this study, 212 patients with SMI were studied using a within-subjects, pre–post design. Improvement of clients was examined by a linear trend analysis of variance. Data on previous hospitalizations were obtained for the 2 years prior to enrollment, and baseline data were collected when patients were admitted to the program. Four criteria were used for admission to the program: aged 18 or over, suffering from a chronic mental illness, were poor users of existing services, and were judged to be at significant risk of rehospitalization. Outcomes were assessed in terms of rehospitalization rates, and a number of independent measures of social functioning, physical and mental health, housing, and subjective quality of life. Significant improvements in client outcomes were found at five of the six sites. Hospitalization rates and number of days in hospital were reduced at four of the sites. There was a progressive improvement in clients' quality of life (on both subjective and objective measures) with better family and social support, increased self-reliance, and improved daily living skills. However, clients also reported more legal problems and were no more likely to be employed at any follow-up point (around 10% of clients were in any form of employment at baseline and at 18 months).

Finally, Rosenheck, Neale, Leaf, Milstein, and Frisman (1995) have recently reported preliminary findings from a national Veterans Affairs evaluation of case management based on an assertive community treatment model. This randomized study covered 10 separate sites in the United States, involving 873 frequent users of inpatient services. Subjects were randomized on discharge from hospital to assertive community treatment or standard aftercare and followed up for 2 years. Patients in the ACT arm of the study used an average of a third fewer inpatient days over the 2-year period following randomization and service costs for the experimental group were up to a fifth less than that for standard care. Cost savings were greatest for patients with chronic disorders and those with a high previous level of service (inpatient) use, while the strongest evidence for clinical benefit was found in patients with more acute illness. As in the Chicago studies (Bond et al., 1988), there was some variation in the fidelity of implementation of the assertive treatment model between sites with the greatest efficacy (in terms of rehospitalization) being linked to centers that were most faithful to the assertive treatment model.

Case Management for Special Groups

There have been several recent attempts to modify the ACT model of case management to target specific patient groups. Morse, Calsyn, Allen, Tempelhoff, and Smith (1992) randomly assigned 178 homeless mentally ill people to three treatment conditions: a drop-in center, outpatient treatment, and an assertive community treatment team. At 12-month follow-up, 42% of cases were lost to follow-up but the ACT group had the least dropouts. Improvements in symptoms, income, social adjustment, and self-esteem were observed across all groups, but the assertive community treatment group also showed a significant increase in the use of community facilities, fewer days homeless, and greater satisfaction with the service (Morse et al., 1992). Preliminary results of further trials of assertive community treatment for homeless mentally ill people have recently been reported though as, yet, no definitive outcome data have been published (Dixon, Krauss, Kernan, Lehman, & DeForge, 1995).

Assertive community treatment has also been used as the basis for interventions for people with comorbid major mental illness and substance abuse (Drake, McHugo, & Noordsy, 1993; Drake, Teague, & Warren, 1990; Martin & Scarpitti, 1993; Teague, Drake, & Ackerson, 1995). Drake et al. (1993), for example, report data from a pilot study of patients with a diagnosis of schizophrenia and alcohol dependence. In this study, more than half the patients achieved a stable remission from alcoholism at 4 years with a mean duration of abstinence of 26.5 months.

Finally, there have also been some attempts to study the efficacy of combining ACT with other psychosocial interventions. For example, McFarlane, Stastny, and Deakins (1992) randomly assigned 72 patients to assertive community treatment alone or combined with family psychoeducation. After 12 months, patients in the experimental condition had a lower rate of relapse (22% versus 40%) and a higher rate of employment (37% versus 15%). There was no difference between groups in terms of hospital use (McFarlane et al., 1992).

MAIN THEMES EMERGING FROM THE RESEARCH

The review of community treatment programs of varying levels of intensity and with a varied emphasis on the content of care leads to the following conclusions:

1. In virtually all these studies, patients receiving any form of case management were more likely to remain in contact with services, to be in receipt of increased amounts of medical and social care, and to be more compliant with a wider range of services and medication than patients managed conventionally. The fol-

lowing attributes of these interventions are the likely explanations for these improvements:

a. The involvement of both the patients and their informal carers in treatment plans and the willingness of staff to provide information, advice, guidance, and support.

b. Consistent care by a single team, or at least, continued contact with a named member of staff who stays with the patients throughout their contact with treatment agencies.

c. Assertive outreach with a clear remit to maintain contact with the patients even when this is met with reluctance or hostility.

d. In vivo skills training and support in the activities of daily living. These interventions not only ensured that patients obtained essential supplies of food, clothing, and shelter during acute episodes of illness but helped to establish routines that continued throughout the recovery phase of the illness.

2. While all these studies have demonstrated benefits in terms of service uptake, only a few have achieved marked reductions in hospitalization. This appears to be largely confined to programs based on assertive community treatment, is mainly a reduction in the length rather than the number of hospitalizations, and almost never attained in studies of brokerage models (Hoult et al., 1983; Marks et al., 1994; Rosenheck et al., 1995; Stein & Test, 1980).

3. Clinical benefit in terms of symptomatic relief appears to be confined to assertive community treatment and rehabilitation models (Goering et al., 1988; Hoult et al., 1983; Marks et al., 1994; McFarlane et al., 1992; McGrew et al., 1995; Stein & Test, 1980).

4. Improvements in social functioning have been reported by some studies across all models of case management though even here, results are not entirely consistent. For example, early reports of employment gains have not been substantiated in later research and improvement in independent living without a parallel increase in the use of sheltered accommodation has been reported in just three studies (Morse et al., 1992; Rosenheck et al., 1995; Stein & Test, 1980). The main gains appear to be reductions in social isolation, better recreational functioning, and improved personal care (Goering et al., 1988; McGrew et al., 1995; Muijen et al., 1992; Stein & Test, 1980; Wasylenki, Goering, Lemire, Lindsey, & Lancee, 1993). There is some suggestion that gains in social function may not emerge for many months or even years (Goering et al., 1988),

and it is possible that the absence of a convincing effect on functional outcomes reflects the low statistical power in many studies, difficulties measuring social impairments, or the limited gains that can be achieved by SMI patients within the relatively short time span of most experimental studies (Burns & Santos, 1995).

5. The most successful interventions in terms of reduced hospitalization have, in addition to the factors outlined earlier, provided:

a. The full support (assertive community treatment) model with intensive community-based care at the point of first contact with the psychiatric service for that episode of illness. The Madison, Sydney, and London (DLP) interventions all recruited patients in an acute episode of illness and provided particularly intensive care at this point. Patients were returned to their homes and both patients and carers learned, for the first time, that effective problem solving was possible even when things seemed to be at their worst. The staff team, too, learnt that such care was possible and carried no special risk that could not be managed by intensive care in the patient's home. This almost certainly influenced behavior in subsequent relapses and thus maintained the advantage (in terms of hospitalization) gained by diverting the initial admission. At least two other studies, not primarily concerned with case management but offering intensive home treatment at the point of acute illness have demonstrated overall reductions in hospital use and significantly greater patient satisfaction (Dean, Phillips, Gadd, Joseph, & England, 1993; Merson, Tyrer, & Onyett, 1992).

b. A 24-hour, rapid-response service with the domiciliary use of acute tranquilization and intensive nursing care is an essential component of any strategy that aims to intervene in an acute episode of illness.

c. A focus on specific problems with clearly specified care plans to address these and agreed outcome goals which are shared by therapist, patient, and relatives.

6. Linked to reductions in hospital use, some services have demonstrated cost effectiveness (Hoult et al., 1983; Knapp et al., 1994; Stein & Test, 1980). These findings are most clearly established for the few studies that have used random assignment to experimental and control groups and where interventions have begun at the point of referral for admission to hospital.

In these studies there appear to be both cost savings from the reduction in hospitalization and benefits in terms of improved social functioning. Only one study found that case management was effective in improving patients' chances of employment (e.g., Stein & Test, 1980).

7. The most impressive results have been obtained by the handful of studies that employed an approach in which the major components of treatment were provided by the case management team. These teams also adopt a rather aggressive if not paternalistic approach to treatment. Unfortunately there are no studies which explicitly contrast services based on alternative treatment models, and it is not possible to say with any certainty whether the better results obtained by full support interventions are a reflection of the model of case management or have more to do with the timing of the intervention (i.e., initially at a time of crisis) or the client population (less chronic disorders).

8. In most studies that have examined the issue, clients and their relatives express greater satisfaction with these services than standard care. This probably reflects a deterioration in satisfaction with standard aftercare as this is mainly apparent later on in the course of the study.

GUIDELINES FOR SETTING UP AN ASSERTIVE COMMUNITY TREATMENT TEAM

Case management has gained widespread popularity in North America, Australia, Britain, and elsewhere in Europe. Yet it is clear from the published literature that there is a wide variation in implementation, target populations, and models of service, ranging from approaches where the clinical team attempts to provide virtually all the interventions to those where case managers perform a largely brokerage function. Partially to serve the needs of consistency in research evaluation but also driven by the growing evidence for the effectiveness of the assertive treatment model in reducing expensive hospitalization, there have been a number of attempts to develop "fidelity" guidelines (McGrew, Bond, & Dietzen, 1994). Studies examining the efficacy of programs against these guidelines suggest that more successful programs involve direct provision rather than brokerage, staff–patient ratios of around 1:15, daily delivery of medications if needed, a psychiatrist as a member of a multidisciplinary team, and possibly a shared team approach to the care of more difficult

clients. To this can be added a general philosophy of providing care and training in living skills in vivo rather than relying on clinic-based interventions, assertive outreach (including the use of legal powers to enforce compliance when these are available) to engage and maintain clients in treatment, and perhaps most crucially in terms of reduced hospital use, a 24-hour responsibility for a discrete group of clients with the case management team serving as the main gatekeeper to inpatient services.

CASE STUDIES IN ASSERTIVE COMMUNITY TREATMENT

Lewin Road community mental health center is situated in South London, providing frontline assessment and treatment services to all ambulatory referrals from a population of 80,000 adults. In 1991, in response to the results of a local survey of the treatment needs of SMI patients in the district (Melzer et al., 1991), a case management team based on the assertive community treatment model was established at the center. The team of seven case managers and full-time psychiatrist targets 130 patients with a diagnosis of SMI who have histories of multiple hospitalizations, poor compliance with medication, or complex care needs. A specialized training program was developed to teach staff structured assessments of mental state, social functioning, medication side-effect profiles, and to implement a problem-oriented approach to psychosocial interventions which include in vivo training in the activities of daily living, individualized cognitive-behavioral interventions for residual psychotic symptoms, and family psychosocial education. The service is closely linked to inpatient wards and the case managers act as gatekeepers to inpatient services for their clients. Clients are allocated to a single case manager though the approach is team based so that all staff know something of all clients and more difficult cases are always coworked. The service currently operates 12 hours daily from Monday through Saturday with a 24-hour telephone help line.

Frequent assessments of the clinical and social functioning of patients together with an evaluation of treatment compliance and risk of harm to self or others governs the level of intensity of supervision provided by the service. Patients whose medical condition is stable and who are willing to attend the center are supervised through outpatient/depot medication clinics and receive a comprehensive care plan review at approximately 6-month intervals. At the other extreme are patients who are in an acute episode of illness or who are persistently noncompliant with treatment and require daily visiting, domicillary administration of medication, and urgent attention to crises in finance, shelter, or nutrition. These patients form the core clients of the case management service. Each has care plans which can be revised at either of two daily team meetings during which priorities are set, work allocated, and short-term changes monitored. Between these extremes are a group who may be intermittently compliant but who have continuing needs for in vivo rehabilitation and who may still require frequent home visits to supervise medication. The important point to emphasize is that all these patients are managed by a single team, who use a standardized set of assessment tools and are managed proactively by interventions which have prespecified outcome targets. Some idea of the style of interventions provided may be gleaned from a couple of case examples.

Example 1

Philip is a 28-year-old, single man with a 10-year history of schizophrenia. He has been admitted to hospital on average once each year, typically following public outbursts of aggression. His referral to the team followed an incident when he threw a brick through the window of a local police station where be believed a "laser machine" had been placed to monitor his movements. He believed this machine was able to watch him 24 hours daily and was the explanation for burning sensations in his legs whenever he left his flat. As a result of the pains in his legs, he seldom went out, had not collected his benefits, and was in arrears for his rent. As be believed the laser rays had something to do with electricity, he had discontinued his electricity supply and did all his cooking on a camping stove in his spartan sitting room. In all of his previous admissions, his symptoms subsided rapidly with neuroleptic medication, but returned on discharge as he refused to accept medication once out of hospital.

Initially, three overlapping problem statements and associated targets were negotiated between Philip and his case manager:

Problem 1: I am worried about my debts. If I cannot make arrangements to reduce my arrears, I may be evicted from my flat. Problem rated as marked by Philip and his case manager (CM).

Desired outcome: To make arrangements with housing to pay off my debts by an affordable amount each week. This means that I will also have to go to the post office each week to collect my GIRO (benefits).

Plan steps to achieve outcome: (1) CM to help Philip write a letter to housing seeking arrangements to settle arrears. (2) CM to accompany Philip to post office to collect and cash GIRO. (3) CM to help Philip work out a weekly budget for food and other bills. (4) Philip to open a building society account to save any spare money.

This practical problem, although caused by his mental illness, was both the most serious in terms of immediate threat and also judged to be the most amenable to intervention by the case manager. It was believed that if his worries about money could be alleviated, this would contribute to building trust between Philip and the CM as well as provide a way into tackling his fears about leaving his flat.

Problem 2: I get pains in my legs which I believed are caused by a laser. Because of these pains I am afraid to leave my flat, and as a result I cannot manage my shopping or attend the day center. Problem rated maximal by Philip and as marked by CM.

Desired outcome: To be less afraid of the laser and to be able to do my weekly shopping and attend the day center.

Plan steps: (1) CM to arrange for Philip to see his GP to see if there are physical explanations for the pains in his legs. (2) CM to accompany Philip to local shops once per week to buy essential food items. (3) CM to explore ways in which Philip copes with his fears of the laser.

This problem statement is a first attempt at tackling the core problem of Philip's tactile hallucinations. Philip believes his pains are caused by a laser, but it is possible that they have another explanation. The plan to consult the GP is something of a double-edged sword. On the one hand, this may rule out a treatable physical cause for his painful legs, but on the other, a negative result may serve to reinforce Phillips belief in the laser. The second plan step has a practical outcome in that it partly tackles the problem of his inadequate nutrition (though he still has to be persuaded to put back on his electricity in order to do any cooking). The third plan step is really a further assessment, looking at practical and psychological coping strategies which may be helpful.

Problem 3: I do not believe the hospital has given me truthful information about these drugs, and I worry about side effects that they might have. Problem rated some by Philip but marked by CM.

Desired outcome: Philip to have a full explanation about medication and to be able to make an informed choice about taking the prescribed drugs.

Plan steps: (1) Give Philip information sheets on medication. (2) Discuss benefits of regular medication with Philip. (3) Discuss ways in which we can monitor side effects.

His erratic compliance is a source of major concern to the CM though Philip is only worried about one aspect. Rather than attempting to tackle his compliance directly, the CM has used his expressed concern about side effects and offered to provide education in the form of written booklets and an open sharing of other information.

These plans were put into place over several months. Philip and his CM reviewed progress on these problems and scored the problem severity and progress made at regular intervals. Within 8 weeks, the first problem had been satisfactorily resolved. Arrangements had been made for Philip to pay an additional £5 rent per week and for this to be deducted at source from his benefits. He had managed to collect his GIRO, had opened his building society account, and had a weekly agreed budget plan. His CM had also negotiated a community care grant supplement which Philip had lodged to his building society account. Philip had agreed to collect his GIRO on his own and had managed this without problems over the next month. The third problem had also been tackled. He had read the information leaflet and attended a session with Dr. P in which he agreed to complete side-effect monitoring charts though he was not convinced that medication was necessary and still refused to consider depot medication.

The second problem, as predicted, proved less amenable to change. His GP had confirmed there was no physical explanation for his painful legs, and though Philip was able to do his weekly shopping, he continued to express some fears about the laser and to experience discomfort when away from his flat on his own. However, he commented that the laster was probably less powerful now as he was able to go to the post office and the supermarket and agreed that he might go out more often given that nothing terrible had happened so far. He agreed to attend the day center and an evening social club.

Example 2

Sheila is a 56-year-old woman with a history of schizophrenia going back at least 20 years. She is well known in the neighborhood, but at the time of referral to the team,

had been banned from the local cafe for persistent abusive behavior. The priest at her local church was also at his wits end as she had taken to calling him up at night and frequently disrupting services. There were concerns that she was particularly vulnerable to abuse from the public, and there was alarm when it was discovered that she was carrying a kitchen knife for protection. Several attempts were made to arrange emergency assessments with a view to compulsory hospitalization, but for various reasons, these had failed to be carried through. At the point of referral, she was refusing contact with her psychiatrist and would not attend any treatment facility.

Initial problem statements had to be formulated by the CM without Sheila's involvement. The most important of these was as follows.

Problem 1: Because of her behavior, Sheila has alarmed and alienated most of the people who support her in the community and is about to be rejected by them.

Desired outcome: Reassure carers and keep Sheila in contact with her main supports in the community.

Plan steps: Meet with carers and attempt reassurance. See whether they will accept her continued attendance if the service can guarantee a rapid response and hospitalization if necessary. Persuade them to give this plan a couple of weeks if things do not get any worse.

Contact was initially made with the local church. The CM spent several days visiting Sheila's usual haunts, speaking to the manager of the local cafe, to the staff in the local benefits office, and to the priest who was her main support. Through the priest's intervention, Sheila agreed to meet the CM and to allow the CM to accompany her to the cafe and benefits office. Although clearly psychotic and refusing medication, it soon became apparent that the service involvement had greatly reduced the anxiety of the people around her, and as they relaxed, Sheila's behavior also improved. By the end of the week it was clear that hospitalization was not needed as an emergency, and it became possible to work out a few simple problem statements with Sheila herself.

One of these problems was her inadequate nutrition. On the basis of a delusional belief that she was going to have a baby, she was spending all her shopping money on tinned baby food. She agreed that this meant she was not eating properly herself.

Problem 2: I have lost a lot of weight recently because I have not been eating properly.

Desired outcome: To put back on the weight I have lost without endangering the baby.

Plan steps: To go shopping with CM and let her help me get good food for myself and my baby.

This is an interesting intervention as the CM does not attempt to challenge the delusional belief directly but works around it. Sheila worked well with this plan and soon decided that she did not need to hoard the baby food anyway. The problem has not recurred in the last year, and the delusion itself seems to have faded. This is not to say that her psychotic illness has greatly improved. She continues to display a very complex number of grandiose and persecutory delusions. Although she has remained out of hospital for the last year and continues to enjoy the local support, she is still only intermittently compliant with medication and compulsory hospitalization is again being actively considered.

CONCLUSIONS

A number of models of case management have been described in this review. These range from approaches which emphasize coordination through others which are based on assertive community treatments provided by a multidisciplinary team, 24-hours daily, 7 days per week. While there is some evidence that these all improve patients' contact with services, increase service utilization, and reduce the numbers defaulting from care, approaches limited to coordination (e.g., care management) are least effective in terms of clinical and social outcomes and have little impact on hospitalization. It also seems that the better results obtained by ACT-based interventions are not simply a matter of intensity of contact or small caseloads, as these interventions achieve lower hospitalization rates even when compared to high-quality clinical case management (Essock & Kontos, 1995). On present evidence, it appears that ACT achieves superior outcomes through the provision of a range of therapeutic interventions by a team of professionals who also have direct control of inpatient facilities as well.

Apart from this broad conclusion, a number of important questions remain unanswered. Which patients most need these intensive services? What are the critical components? How long do patients have to spend under the supervision of the ACT team? How can the model be adapted to dovetail with wider community care provision? The research so far has concentrated on a fairly narrow group of patients when viewed from the perspective of a busy district service. By and large, these studies have excluded patients whose illness are complicated by substance abuse or severe personality disorder or where organic etiologies are suspected. Patients with particularly challenging behaviors involving danger to themselves or others may never be comfortably managed in community settings and ACT may not be cost-effective for patients with chronic though stable illness conditions. We also know very little about which aspects of ACT are essential for its success. For example, it may not be necessary to provide 24-hour service if there is already a good crisis program in place. Similarly, the direct provision of social care may be less important in British settings where there is a well-established system for monitoring patients' welfare and where social and health services are well-integrated with social work staff already based with psychiatric teams. It is not at all clear whether the majority of SMI patients need to remain in ACT for many years if not indefinitely. Studies which have followed patients through a withdrawal phase show a fairly rapid loss of any advantage in the experimental group once ACT teams are disbanded and patients return to standard care. And yet, it is unlikely that there will ever be enough human or material resources to provide ACT for all the patients who might benefit for as long as is needed. It may be that the solution lies in having a range of community provision that includes both ACT and high-quality clinical case management to which patients can be safely transferred once their condition has stabilized.

While these and other questions remain unanswered, there can be no doubt that ACT has already had a huge influence on the practice of community psychiatry. Virtually no other psychosocial intervention has received so much scientific scrutiny or been so widely implemented in such a short period of time.

REFERENCES

Audini, B., Marks, I. M., Lawrence, R. E., Connolly, J., & Watts, V. (1994). Home-based versus out-patient/inpatient care for people with serious mental illness. Phase II of a controlled study. *British Journal of Psychiatry, 165*, 204–210.

Bachrach, L. L. (1981). Continuity of care for chronic mental patients: A conceptual analysis. *American Journal of Psychiatry, 138*, 1449–1455.

Bond, G. R., Miller, L. D., Krumwied, R. D., & Ward, R. S. (1988). Assertive case management in three CMHCs: A controlled study. *Hospital and Community Psychiatry, 39*, 411–418.

Borland, A., McRae, J., & Lycan, C. (1989). Outcomes of five years continuous intensive case management. *Hospital and Community Psychiatry, 40*, 369–376.

Burns, B. J., & Santos, A. B. (1995). Assertive Community Treatment: An update of randomized trials. *Psychiatric Services, 46*, 669–675.

Clark, K. A., & Landis, D. (1990). The relationship of client characteristics to case management service provision. *Evaluation and Program Planning, 13*, 221–229.

Craig, T. K. J., Bayliss, E., Klein, O., Manning, P., & Reader, L. (1995). *The Homeless Mentally Ill Initiative: An evaluation of four clinical teams.* London: Department of Health.

Curtis, J. L., Millman, E. J., & Struening, E. (1992). Effect of case management on rehospitalization and utilization of ambulatory care services. *Hospital and Community Psychiatry, 43*, 895–899.

Dean, C., Phillips, J., Gadd, E. M., Joseph, M., & England, S. (1993). Comparison of community based service with hospital based service for people with acute, severe psychiatric illness. *British Medical Journal, 307*, 473–476.

Department of Health. (1989). *Discharge of patients from hospital* (Vol. Health Circular, HC(89) 5). London, England: HMSO.

Dixon, L. B., Krauss, N., Kernan, E., Lehman, A. F., & DeForge, B. R. (1995). Modifying the PACT model to serve homeless persons with severe mental illness. *Psychiatric Services, 46*, 684–688.

Drake, R. E., McHugo, G. J., & Noordsy, D. L. (1993). Treatment of alcoholism among schizophrenic outpatients: 4-year outcomes. *American Journal of Psychiatry, 150*, 689–695.

Drake, R. E., Teague, G. B., & Warren, R. S. (1990). New Hampshire's dual diagnosis program for people with severe mental illness and substance abuse. *Addiction and Recovery, 10*, 35–39.

Essock, S. M., & Kontos, N. (1995). Implementing Assertive Community Treatment teams. *Psychiatric Services, 46*, 679–683.

Ford, R., Beardsmore, A., Ryan, P., Repper, J., Craig, T., & Muijen, M. (1995). Providing the safety net: Case management for people with a serious mental illness. *Journal of Mental Health, 4*, 91–97.

Goering, P., Wasylenki, D., & Farkas, M. (1988). What difference does case management make? *Hospital and Community Psychiatry, 39*, 272–276.

Goering, P., Wasylenki, D., Lancee, W., & Freeman, S. J. J. (1984). From hospital to community: Six month and two year outcomes for 505 patients. *Journal of Nervous and Mental Disease, 172*, 667–673.

Harris, M. (1988). New directions for clinical case management. In M. Harris & L. L. Bachrach (Eds.), *Clinical case management, New directions for mental health services.* San Francisco: Jossey-Bass.

Hornstra, R. K., Bruce-Wolfe, V., Sagduyu, K., & Fiffle, D. W.

(1993). The effects of intensive case management on hospitalization of patients with schizophrenia. *Hospital and Community Psychiatry, 44*, 844–847.

Hoult, J. (1986). Community care of the acutely mentally ill. *British Journal of Psychiatry, 149*, 137–144.

Hoult, J., Reynolds, I., Charbonneau-Powis, M., Weekes, P., & Briggs, J. (1983). Psychiatric hospital versus community treatment: The results of a randomized trial. *Australian and New Zealand Journal of Psychiatry, 17*, 160–167.

Knapp, M., Beecham, J., Koutsogeorgopoulou, V., Hallam, A., Fenyo, A., Marks, I. M., Connolly, J., Audini, B., & Muijen, M. (1994). Service use and costs of home-based versus hospital-based care for people with serious mental illness. *British Journal of Psychiatry, 165*, 195–203.

Lamb, H. R. (1984). Deinstitutionalization and the homeless mentally ill. *Hospital and Community Psychiatry, 35*, 899–907.

Lamb, H. R. (1987). Young adult chronic patients: The new drifters. *Hospital and Community Psychiatry, 33*, 465–468.

Marks, I. M., Connolly, J., Muijen, M., Audini, B., McNamee, G., & Lawrence, R. E. (1994). Home-based versus hospital-based care for people with serious mental illness. *British Journal of Psychiatry, 165*, 179–194.

Marshall, M., Lockwood, A., & Gath, D. (1995). Social service case management for long-term mental disorders: A randomized controlled trial. *Lancet, 345*, 409–412.

Martin, S. M., & Scarpitti, F. R. (1993). An intensive case management approach for paroled IV drug users. *Journal of Drug Issues, 23*, 43–59.

McCrone, P., Beecham, J., & Knapp, M. (1994). Community psychiatric nurse teams: Cost effectiveness of intensive support versus generic care. *British Journal of Psychiatry, 165*, 218–221.

McFarlane, W. R., Stastny, P., & Deakins, S. (1992). Family aided assertive community treatment: A comprehensive rehabilitation and intensive case management approach for persons with schizophrenic disorders. *New Directions for Mental Health Services, 53*, 43–54.

McGrew, J. H., Bond, G. R., & Dietzen, L. (1994). Measuring the fidelity of implementation of a metal health program model. *Journal of Consulting and Clinical Psychology, 62*, 670–678.

McGrew, J. H., Bond, G. R., Dietzen, L., McKasson, M., & Miller, L. D. (1995). A multisite study of client outcomes in assertive community treatment. *Psychiatric Services, 46*, 696–701.

Melzer, D., Hale, A. S., Malik, S. J., Hogman, G., & Wood, S. (1991). Community care for patients with schizophrenia one year after hospital discharge. *British Medical Journal, 303*, 1023–1026.

Merson, S., Tyrer, P., & Onyett, S. (1992). Early intervention in psychiatric emergencies: A controlled clinical trial. *Lancet, 339*, 1311–1314.

Morse, G. A., Calsyn, R. J., Allen, G., Tempelhoff, B., & Smith,

R. (1992). Experimental comparison of the effects of three treatment programs for homeless mentally ill people. *Hospital and Community Psychiatry, 43*, 1005–1010.

Muijen, M., Cooney, M., Strathdee, G., Bell, R., & Hudson, A. (1994). Community psychiatric nurse teams: Intensive support versus generic care. *British Journal of Psychiatry, 165*, 211–217.

Muijen, M., Marks, I., Connolly, J., & Audini, B. (1992). Home-based care and standard hospital care for patients with severe mental illness: A randomized controlled trial. *British Medical Journal, 304*, 749–754.

Mulder, R. (1985). *Evaluation of the Harbinger Program, 1982–1985.* Lansing, MI: Department of Mental Health.

National Health Service and Community Care Act. (1990). London, England: HMSO.

Patmore, C., & Weaver, T. (1991). *Community mental health teams: Lessons for planners and managers.* London: Good Practices in Mental Health.

Pigrides, M., Dudley, A., & Roy, D. (1996). *Evaluating the care programme approach for patients with schizophrenia.* Unpublished manuscript.

Robinson, G. K., Bergman, G. T., & Scallet, L. J. (1989). *Choices in case management: A review of current knowledge and practice for mental health programs.* Rockville, MD: National Institute of Mental Health.

Rosenheck, R., Neale, M., Leaf, P., Milstein, R., & Frisman, L. (1995). Multisite experimental cost study of intensive community care. *Schizophrenia Bulletin, 21*, 129–140.

Sayce, L., Craig, T. K. J., & Boardman, A. P. (1991). The development of community mental health centers in the UK. *Social Psychiatry and Psychiatric Epidemiology, 26*, 14–20.

Schwaber, E. (1981). Narcissism, self-psychology and the listening perspective. *Annual of Psychoanalysis, 9*, 115–131.

Stein, L. J., & Test, M. A. (1980). Alternative to mental hospital treatment. 1. Conceptual model, treatment program and clinical evaluation. *Archives of General Psychiatry, 37*, 392–397.

Taube, C. A., Morlock, L., Burns, B. J., & Santos, A. B. (1990). New directions in research on assertive community treatment. *Hospital and Community Psychiatry, 41*, 642–647.

Teague, G. B., Drake, R. E., & Ackerson, T. H. (1995). Evaluating use of continuous treatment teams for persons with mental illness and substance abuse. *Psychiatric Services, 46*, 689–695.

Wasylenki, D., Goering, P., Lancee, W., Fischer, L., & Freeman, S. J. J. (1985). Psychiatric aftercare in a metropolitan setting. *Canadian Journal of Psychiatry, 30*, 329–336.

Wasylenki, D. A., Goering, P. A., Lemire, D., Lindsey, S., & Lancee, W. (1993). The hostel outreach program: Assertive case management for homeless mentally ill persons. *Hospital and Community Psychiatry, 44*, 848–853.

White, E. (1991). *The 3rd Quinquinnel National Community Psychiatric Nursing Survey.* Manchester: University of Manchester.

Witheridge, T. F., & Dincin, J. (1985). The Bridge: An assertive outreach program in an urban setting. *New Directions for Mental Health Services, 26*, 65–76.

CHAPTER 23

THE ROLE OF SOCIAL FUNCTIONING IN VOCATIONAL REHABILITATION

Gary R. Bond
Robert E. Drake
Deborah R. Becker

Social and vocational functioning are the primary indicators of adult status in this country and much of the world (Parsons, 1951). As such, these two areas of functioning have been the central interests of rehabilitation and research on rehabilitation for persons with severe mental illness (SMI). In this chapter we explore the nature of relationships between the two domains. Specifically, we examine the following issues: (1) the conceptual relationship between social and vocational functioning, (2) the empirical relationship, (3) the effects of interventions across the two domains, and (4) the predictive relationship between social functioning measured during the course of an intervention program and later vocational functioning. We assume, for the sake of this discussion, that social and vocational functioning refer to performance behaviors and that social supports/social networks refer to environmental influences.

By *vocational functioning,* we are referring to a person's success in holding a competitive job. Other experiences that involve similar behaviors in sheltered or non-

integrated settings or that are not compensated by competitive wages are considered here to be prevocational activities. A related concept, used in many research studies (e.g., Goering, Wasylenki, Farkas, Lancee, & Ballantyne, 1988; Hogarty et al., 1974; Test, 1992), is "instrumental role functioning," typically defined as performance in one's primary role, as worker, student, or housewife. Much of the treatment outcome literature uses this latter construct (Mintz, Bond, & Mintz, in press). We define vocational functioning in terms of actual behaviors, and not simply *capacity to work,* recognizing that many exogenous factors influence whether an individual is employed.

Social functioning has been defined as "one's capacity to interact appropriately and communicate effectively with other individuals both at work and in one's personal life" (Goldman, Rosenberg, & Manderschied, 1988, p. 30). Mueser, Bellack, Morrison, and Wixted (1990, p. 52) distinguish three related concepts: *social competence,* which is "the overall ability of the patient to impact favorably on his or her social environment," *social adjust-*

ment, which is "the actual meeting of instrumental and affiliative needs that is the natural consequence of social competence," and *social skills,* which "refer to a specific set of abilities, including cognition, verbal and nonverbal behaviors that are needed for effective interpersonal performance." In the literature, there is no standardized use of any of these terms. We will use the term *social functioning* broadly to include a wide variety of behaviors and abilities, including social skills, social judgment, ability to present oneself appropriately in public, and capacity to form relationships.

A *social support system* has been defined as "the enduring pattern of continuous or intermittent ties that functions to augment a person's strengths to facilitate his mastery of his environment" (Caplan, 1974, p. 7). House (1981) distinguished four different types of support: emotional, instrumental, informational, and evaluative. Emotional support includes such activities as providing empathy and reassurance and acting as a confidant. Instrumental support includes tangible help, such as money and transportation. Examples of informational support would be referrals, job leads, and information about different careers. Evaluative support includes assistance in appraising and making choices among alternatives. Most of the research on persons with SMI has not distinguished among these different functions. The most common distinction has been between supports provided by professionals and "natural supports," which include coworkers, family members, and friends (Marrone, Balzell, & Gold, 1995).

CONCEPTUAL RELATIONSHIP BETWEEN SOCIAL AND VOCATIONAL FUNCTIONING

It is hard to imagine any form of employment that does not involve interpersonal relationships and contacts. These include contacts with supervisors, coworkers, and customers. Employment also involves social functioning outside the job, including the impact of work on relationships with friends and with family. Obviously, interpersonal demands vary widely, with some jobs requiring a high level of social interaction, and others involving very little.

The employment process includes at least two distinct phases—acquiring a job and then keeping it. The challenges in each phase differ (Braitman et al., 1995); each has a somewhat different set of interpersonal demands.

The job acquisition process includes locating available jobs (sometimes through contacting others), successfully interviewing for a job, and acclimating to an unfamiliar setting. Job retention, on the other hand, in addition to requiring that one perform the task requirements of the job, also requires skills in getting along with others for an extended period of time.

It is also apparent that the nature of the contact varies greatly among jobs, with some work settings being highly supportive environments, whereas others are highly stressful. Coworkers can be supportive and a positive aspect of employment, but they also can be sources of stress (Watts, 1983).

Not only is social competence essential to achieving success in employment, but also employment has a reciprocal influence, having both positive and negative effects on social functioning and social networks. On the positive side, community employment may increase integration and assimilation into society. Social expectations in the workplace are a powerful impetus for developing appropriate social interactions. Through working, one may develop new friendships. On the negative side, employment may increase social isolation by reducing the time and energy available to socialize. Feelings of rejection and alienation can be heightened when workers do not "fit in." On the other hand, *not* working has a potent effect on one's social functioning and networks as well, typically reducing the opportunity for social contacts.

Deficits in Social Functioning for People with SMI

Despite extensive theoretical writings on the deficits in social functioning among people with schizophrenia and other forms of SMI, there is yet a surprising lack of clarity about what the core deficits are and how they affect vocational functioning. Many observers have noted a range of poor social skills present in people with schizophrenia, including such specific skills as making eye contact, carrying on a conversation, and expressing appropriate affect (Mueser, Bellack, Douglas, & Morrison, 1991). Some of these features overlap with (but are not identical with) the negative symptoms of schizophrenia, which include flat affect, poverty of speech, apathy, and avolition (McGlashan & Fenton, 1992). However, the problems with interpersonal relationships found in schizophrenia extend beyond negative symptoms; Strauss and Carpenter (1974) argue that schizophrenia includes a "disorder of relating" distinct from negative symptoms. Distrustfulness and fearfulness, found in many people with SMI, often precipitate interpersonal problems.

Another aspect of schizophrenia is that it is an "environmentally sensitive" disorder (Hogarty, 1995). Extrapolating from the expressed emotion literature on families (Brown, Birley, & Wing, 1972), we may speculate that the social stimulation of high pressure work environments can lead to exacerbation of psychiatric symptoms.

One current theory is that neuropsychological deficits lie at the root of problems in social functioning. Brenner, Hodel, Roder, and Corrigan (1992) have described the relationship between cognitive deficits and social dysfunction as a "vicious cycle" in which cognitive deficits prevent acquisition of appropriate social skills, which in turn leads patients to become more exposed to social stressors and subsequently to diminished cognitive capacity. Hogarty (1995) views social dysfunction in schizophrenia as deriving from cognitive impairments relating to the difficulty in taking the viewpoint of another person ("second person perspective taking"), reading social cues, and interpreting the informal rules of conduct.

No summary of the interpersonal problems encountered by people with SMI would be complete without noting the way they are characteristically viewed by others. Among the general public, mental illness carries a substantially greater stigma than physical disability (Harris & Associates, 1993). Employer attitudes mirror these societal attitudes (Berven & Driscoll, 1981). Thus, the negative stereotypes held by employers and coworkers toward psychiatric disability may adversely affect the employability of people with SMI (Link, 1982; 1987; Link, Cullen, Frank, & Wozniak, 1987; Link, Cullen, Struening, Shrout, & Dohrenwind, 1989). For example, Olshansky and his colleagues concluded that disclosing a psychiatric hospitalization during a job interview leads to lower rates of job offers (Olshansky, Grob, & Ekdahl, 1960; Olshansky, Grob, & Malamud, 1958). Analog studies using experimental designs have also suggested the existence of discrimination against persons with psychiatric disabilities (Berven & Driscoll, 1981; Bottrill, 1994; Farina & Felner, 1973; Farina, Felner, & Boudreau, 1973).

As we gain a better understanding of the prevalence and manifestations of these social deficits, it may be possible to make more precise predictions about the nature of the problems people with SMI are likely to encounter in the vocational domain. For example, lack of initiative, lack of

assertiveness, and poor eye contact lead to a poor presentation in a job interview.

Summary

Clearly, there is conceptual overlap between the social and work domains. It is also apparent that the influence between social and vocational functioning is bidirectional, such that good social skills and supportive social networks contribute to success in employment, while work experiences have the potential to broaden one's social network and to enhance social functioning.

This brief review of the theoretical relationship between the social and vocational domains also reveals a complex set of issues that are not well understood. Undoubtedly part of the ambiguity is a function of individual differences among people with SMI. Unfortunately, these conceptual issues have rarely been incorporated into research studies. Very little research, for example, differentiates between different types of social dysfunction, or between different phases of the employment process. Moreover, vocational functioning is often defined in terms of actuarial indicators, such as employment status, job tenure, and hours of employment. These indicators do not measure actual performance on the job, but merely the fact that a person has been present at the job during a time period. Within the rehabilitation literature, there have been efforts to measure work performance through observation of behavior, often in prevocational work settings (Rogers, Sciarappa, & Anthony, 1991). However, measuring work performance in this fashion has been problematic insofar as such measures use brief samples in artificial settings. The measurement of social functioning is even more problematic than of vocational functioning, with a lack of consensus about the most critical dimensions (Mintz et al., in press). The same could be said about social support.

SOCIAL AND VOCATIONAL FUNCTIONING: EMPIRICAL RELATIONSHIPS

Cross-sectional Studies

Scattered throughout the literature are many studies examining cross-sectional associations between social and vocational functioning. Most of these studies have involved follow-up interviews with patients after discharge from a psychiatric hospital (Ellsworth, Foster, Childers,

Arthur, & Kroeker, 1968; Freeman & Simmons, 1963; Strauss & Carpenter, 1972; Breier, Schreiber, Dyer, & Pickar, 1991; Moller, von Zerssen, Werner-Eilert, & Wüschner-Stockheim, 1982; Faulkner, McFarland, Larch, Harris, & Yohe, 1986; Jonsson & Nyman, 1991). In these studies, the correlation between social and vocational functioning ranged from .35 to .63, with a mean correlation of .52. Using community samples, Arns and Linney (1995), Bellack, Morrison, Wixted, and Mueser (1990), and Turner (1977) also found substantial correlations between social and vocational functioning.

Not all cross-sectional studies have found a strong relationship, however. Four studies found very small correlations, ranging from .07 to .16 (Tessler & Manderscheid, 1982; Summers & Hersh, 1983; Ciardiello, Klein, & Sobkowski, 1988; Brekke, Levin, Wolkon, & Slade, 1993). The common denominator of these studies is that they sampled individuals enrolled in day treatment or other community treatment programs, thereby undersampling people with good vocational outcomes and leading to a potential restriction of range problem.

Longitudinal Studies

The best-known work examining the longitudinal relationships between different domains of functioning is that of Strauss and Carpenter (1974, 1977), who concluded that the best predictors in each domain is premorbid functioning in that same domain. So, for example, they found that social adjustment at an initial interview was a better predictor of future social functioning than any other measure.

Premorbid social functioning is modestly predictive of later vocational outcomes, with mean correlation of .34 in four studies reviewed by Stoffelmayr, Hunter, and Dillavou (1983). We found a mean correlation of .24 (range = .06 to .44) in five studies (Sturm & Lipton, 1967; Lorei & Gurel, 1972; Strauss & Carpenter, 1974; Harrow, Westermeyer, Silverstein, Strauss, & Cohler, 1986; Strauss & Carpenter, 1977), with two other studies noting nonsignificant correlations (Jonsson & Nyman, 1991; Cook, Solomon, & Mock, 1989).

We found few studies examining premorbid vocational functioning as a predictor of social functioning. Three studies found vocational functioning to strongly predict subsequent social adjustment (Strauss & Carpenter, 1977; Moller et al., 1982; Shepherd, Watt, Falloon, & Smeeton, 1989).

Retrospective Interviews

As part of a longitudinal study Westermeyer and Harrow (1987) asked former inpatients to identify factors interfering with their working. A majority mentioned at least one factor related to interpersonal contacts (distrust of people, difficulties relating to other people, fear of social relationships). Thus, from the client's perspective, social demands are but one of several types of barriers to employment. Westermeyer (1992) found that "distrust of other people" and "fear of social relationships" were negatively correlated with work outcome among people with schizophrenia.

Summary

Overall, the empirical relationship between social and vocational functioning is well established, when these comparisons are made at a single point in time and when a broad cross-section of subjects is used. Though not as strong, the longitudinal studies are also mildly supportive of the importance of social functioning for work functioning.

It is surprising that there are relatively few published studies examining the social-vocational relationship in the large-scale prospective longitudinal studies. McGlashan (1988) identified 10 large-scale prospective studies of the longitudinal course of schizophrenia. Because these studies all measured social and vocational functioning, they are the logical databases in which to examine the predictive questions. However, most of these investigators have focused primarily on the prediction of overall functioning at follow-up, rather than prediction in particular areas of role functioning. These databases may represent an untapped resource for examining the social-vocational relationship.

Despite the fair number of studies reporting correlational findings, this literature is not satisfying. For example, Avison and Speechley's (1987) major review concluded that little theoretical or methodological progress had been made in identifying the social-psychological correlates of role performance. Contributing factors have been the lack of a guiding framework and of standardized measures.

What this correlational literature does not explain are the mechanisms by which social and vocational functioning influence each other. Questions include: How influential are social competence, supportive networks, and the social context in finding and obtaining jobs? What role does social functioning play in actual work performance? How influential are social skills and social networks for retaining employment?

TRADITIONAL APPROACHES TO PREPARING PEOPLE FOR EMPLOYMENT

In practice, the dominant approach to vocational rehabilitation (VR) in the United States and elsewhere is what might be labeled the "mental health treatment and referral" model. The paradigm is that mental health clients must first achieve adequate symptom management before employment goals are considered. The dominant service configuration for most clients with SMI consists of case management services combined with medication management. In some cases, clients receive residential services. In addition, partial hospitalization programs are popular in many places, with over a thousand such programs in the United States (Parker & Knoll, 1990).

In the strongest version of the treatment and referral model, group therapy or skills training are used to help improve social functioning and address problems of everyday living. Paradigmatically, once these objectives are achieved, a referral to a separate agency for VR services is the next step. The implicit assumption in this approach is that independent employment is at the end of a chain of developmental tasks that include as prerequisites such milestones as symptom stability, housing stability, drug and alcohol abstinence, and acquisition of appropriate social skills.

The research evidence regarding the effectiveness of this paradigm for achieving competitive employment is mostly indirect, but it is also overwhelmingly negative. Clients receiving usual mental health services plus referral to VR typically show no change whatsoever in their employment rates (Chandler, Meisel, Hu, McGowen, & Madison, in press; McFarlane, Dushay, Deakins, & Stastny, 1995). An explanation for this lack of impact on employment is that the last link in the chain—referral to VR services—is often inadequate in actual practice. Many reasons have been advanced for the inadequacy of the vocational approaches involving this referral process (Drake, Becker, Xie, & Anthony, 1995). Surveys have suggested that only about 5% of mental health clients actually have access to employment services (Tashjian, Hayward, Stoddard, & Kraus, 1989). Clients who are referred to VR services often fail to achieve eligibility (Mar-

shak, Bostick, & Turton, 1990), it may be speculated, partly because of their lack of assertiveness (i.e., their lack of an important set of social skills). At least we know that people with SMI are less adroit in navigating the VR service system than people with other disabilities.

While the referral component of this model appears to be a major stumbling block, a second assumption is also suspect. This second assumption is that providing excellent mental health services will prepare clients for employment by removing the personal barriers. For example, Mueser, Bond, Drake, and Resnick (in press) found little evidence that excellent case management programs had any effect on employment, unless they had an explicit employment focus. Similarly, in their review of individual and group therapies (which excluded the skills training studies), Mosher and Keith (1980) found that psychotherapy did little to improve any aspect of role functioning, including vocational. The theory that day treatment or psychotherapy intended to improve social functioning subsequently will result in better employment outcomes has not been supported (Gunderson et al., 1984; Vitale & Steinbach, 1965; Summers, 1981; Wilder, Levin, & Zwerling, 1966). One study found that closing a day treatment program and replacing it with a direct placement employment program led to both higher employment rates and more integration of clients in the surrounding community (e.g., by clients spending more time at restaurants, health clubs, and community businesses) (Drake et al., 1994).

There is no evidence that clients improve their chances at employment after completing social skills training (Dilk & Bond, 1996). One experimental study comparing two supported employment programs, one incorporating skills training and the other using direct placement in employment, found that the approach using skills training had poorer employment outcomes (Drake, McHugo, Becker, Anthony, & Clark, 1996).

Within the psychosocial literature, however, a few studies do suggest that psychosocial interventions not specifically targeted to vocational functioning may generalize to improve instrumental functioning (Goering et al., 1988; Hogarty et al., 1974; Hogarty et al., 1995). Unfortunately, these studies do not provide detailed information on vocational functioning, and significant findings appear to be limited to the broader measure of instrumental functioning.

One other type of psychosocial intervention—family therapy—should be mentioned. An implicit assumption in family approaches is that by helping develop or maintain a strong support system and by reducing stress in nonvocational environments, clients will be more able to benefit from rehabilitation, including vocational interventions. Although Mintz, Mintz, and Phipps (1992) concluded the evidence was at best weak regarding the impact of family-oriented approaches on vocational outcomes, more recent family treatment research is more encouraging. Four controlled clinical trials have reported employment outcomes favoring clients in the family treatment condition (Falloon, McGill, Boyd, & Pederson, 1987; McFarlane, Lukens, Toran, & Dunne, 1991; Hogarty et al., 1991; Xiong et al., 1994), whereas one found no differences (Barrowclough & Tarrier, 1990). Although these studies generally have neither targeted employment as a major goal of their interventions nor evaluated employment outcomes in adequate detail to ensure confidence in the findings, the pattern of results suggests that family treatment warrants further investigation.

Within the general rehabilitation literature, studies have found that family support in seeking work is correlated with employment (Bolton, 1983) and that most jobs are found through family, friends, and direct contact to employers (Zadny & James, 1978). Three studies suggest that families are important to job retention (Alverson, Becker, & Drake, 1995; Gervey, 1995; Neff, 1958), although three studies found no relationship (Cook, Solomon, & Mock, 1989; Mowbray, Bybee, Harris, & McCrohan, 1996; Trotter, Minkoff, Harrison, & Hoops, 1988).

Summary

Despite the research showing a significant association between social and vocational functioning, the literature on broad psychosocial interventions for people with SMI provides little evidence that programs that aim at improving social functioning will help improve vocational functioning. This conclusion is consistent with the well known principle, especially applicable to people with SMI, that learning is situationally specific and that there is relatively little transfer of training across domains (Stein & Test, 1980).

VOCATIONAL REHABILITATION APPROACHES

Examination of the full range of vocational rehabilitation approaches for people with SMI lies beyond the scope of this chapter (see Bond, 1992; Clark & Bond,

1996; Lehman, 1995). Instead, we examine exemplars representing four of the most popular approaches. In practice, most programs are hybrids of these exemplars, but for the purpose of conceptual clarity, we have presented these as pure types. In each case, we describe the approach, present the implicit or explicit philosophy regarding the role of social adjustment and social support in the employment process, and summarize the research on its effectiveness in increasing employment and in improving social functioning.

Surprisingly, despite the social deficits associated with mental illness and the widespread acknowledgment that social functioning should affect work functioning, intervention approaches do not always take into account the specific nature of mental illness in the design of programs. Rather, most vocational programs are pragmatic, basing their organization on commonsense beliefs and borrowing from approaches developed for other disability populations.

Job Club

The job club is a structured behavioral approach to helping unemployed persons find jobs (Azrin & Besalel, 1980). It is the best-known of a number of related "self-directed job placement" approaches, which provide systematic guidance in developing job leads, making telephone and in-person contacts, and obtaining jobs (Wesolowski, 1981). Methods have been refined for teaching skills for interviewing for a job (Furman, Geller, Simon, & Kelly, 1979; Kelly, Laughlin, & Clairborne, 1979). In addition, job clubs use peer support as a way to encourage clients to continue the search process. In many applications, the job club is a stand-alone program, with the assumption that providing support and teaching skills will enable clients to find jobs on their own. An implicit assumption in some versions of this model is that it helps participants avoid becoming dependent on professionals.

The job club and related approaches have had encouraging rates of job acquisition with some groups of clients with SMI (Azrin & Philip, 1979; Eisenberg & Cole, 1986; Jacobs, Kardashian, Kreinbring, Ponder, & Simpson, 1984; Jacobs, Wissusik, Collier, Stackman, & Burkeman, 1992; Keith, Engelkes, & Winborn, 1977). However, dismal results have been reported in other studies (Kramer & Beidel, 1982; Deacon, Dunning, & Dease, 1974).

Jacobs et al. (1984) concluded that for persons with SMI, the job club needed to be adapted to provide more direction, interpersonal support, and encouragement from counselors than in the standard approach. It also appears that job clubs are most suitable for people who already have adequate social skills, especially interviewing skills (Jacobs et al., 1992). No studies have reported the impact of job clubs on social functioning outcomes.

Conclusions about this approach are limited by the fact that no experimental studies of the job club targeted for people with SMI have been reported in the literature. However, from an analysis of the social deficits in SMI, the job club does not appear to be a good match for this population. One common problem is a high dropout rate (Jacobs et al., 1992; Kramer & Beidel, 1982). Negative symptoms of schizophrenia, as manifested in lack of initiative and the tendency to give up easily, are personal characteristics that would be expected to lead to early termination. In addition, the peer group format is ill-suited for shy, withdrawn, distrustful individuals. One main weakness of the job club model, therefore, is that it is least suited for people with low initiative or who are not comfortable in groups.

A second weakness is the assumption that obtaining work is the primary barrier to employment. In its original formulation, the job club provides no mechanism for retaining jobs once a client begins working, even though some researchers have concluded that, for people with SMI, job retention is more of a problem than job acquisition (Becker, Drake, Bond et al., in press; Cook, 1994). It is not surprising, therefore, that studies have yielded poor job retention rates (Jacobs et al., 1992; Kramer & Beidel, 1982).

A third weakness is that the job club essentially ignores the problem of stigma. As noted above, an extensive literature suggests that employers are less likely to hire someone they believe to be mentally ill. For people who, because of odd mannerisms, cannot "pass" as normal, the job interview may be a formidable barrier to employment.

Prevocational Training

A variety of prevocational training approaches have been developed to prepare people to work in community jobs. The underlying rationale for prevocational training (or "work adjustment training") is that clients can become more "work ready" by working in a low-pressure work setting. Work readiness includes a constellation of behaviors and attitudes, such as attendance, punctuality, good hygiene, ability to take instructions, cooperativeness, and getting along with supervisors (Bond & Friedmeyer, 1987). Another feature of prevocational training is that it

permits rehabilitation staff to observe clients in work settings to assess their readiness and to give feedback to improve their performance.

Social functioning may be an especially important aspect of this prevocational training. Anthony and Jansen (1984) suggested that adequate performance on the job included three main elements: getting along, doing the job, and being dependable. Of these, they hypothesized that the interpersonal dimension was the most important for psychiatric disabilities.

Prevocational training occurs in noncompetitive work settings, including sheltered workshops, hospital programs, and mental health centers, with the intent of increasing clients' work skills and habits to enable them to succeed in community jobs. Sheltered workshops provide paid employment opportunities (usually paying subminimum wage) in protected settings, either on jobs subcontracted from industry, or manufacturing goods for sale (Black, 1988). Hospital-based programs, now offered mainly in Veterans Administration hospitals, typically consist of a variety of work stations throughout a medical center, sometimes in paid positions, sometimes in volunteer jobs (Lysaker & Bell, 1995). One common assumption is that these settings are less threatening and less demanding, and that clients therefore can cope more easily with the workplace demands.

Prevocational training has not proved to be an effective means for improving competitive employment outcomes (Bond, 1992). The evidence is inconsistent for a more limited hypothesis, that prevocational training improves work performance within the sheltered setting. Four studies found no improvement over time in work performance (Smith, 1969; Soloff & Bolton, 1969; Schultheis & Bond, 1993; Watts, 1978) compared to two studies that did find improvement (Anthony, Rogers, Cohen, & Davies, 1995; Cook, 1985). Clients who work in sheltered settings may be less motivated to work than those who work in community settings (Bond & Friedmeyer, 1987; Schultheis & Bond, 1993).

One hospital-based program combining work adjustment and transitional placements found that clients significantly improved vocational performance, but with no change in social functioning (Bell & Ryan, 1984). The authors concluded that "rehabilitation helped patients function better, but without improving the underlying disorder" (Bell & Stiens, 1991, p. 97). In a later study, Lysaker and Bell (1995) followed patients with schizophrenia placed in employment sites within the hospital. Participants' social skills improved significantly over the period, but work motivation and task orientation did not. The authors hypothesized three active agents of change: the intrinsic reward of being a productive worker, expectations of normal interactions by others at the work site, and the role of support groups sponsored by the rehabilitation program.

Meltzoff and Blumenthal (1966) evaluated employment outcomes for clients randomly assigned to a day-treatment program with a sheltered workshop or to a psychotherapy control group. Regardless of condition, clients who were competitively employed at follow-up were rated as being better adjusted socially than those who were not. The authors concluded that the initially better adjusted patients were more successful in achieving employment.

Some observers have concluded that the impact of segregated programs on social networks and social functioning is generally negative. One disadvantage is the lack of integration with normal society. As a result, sheltered workshop clients may have difficulty making friends outside the workshop (Walker, Adamson, Alexander, & Stoffelmayr, 1973). Some observers have noted that people with SMI often view sheltered workshops as demeaning and stigmatizing (Estroff, 1981; Warner & Polak, 1995), although workshops vary widely in their management, social environment, and types of work opportunities, and some workshops do not have this impact.

A number of studies have shown that prevocational approaches are ineffective for helping people achieve competitive employment. The impact of prevocational work settings on social adjustment has not been widely studied, but it does isolate clients from normal society.

Clubhouse

The clubhouse model dates its history from the founding of Fountain House in New York in 1948 (Beard, Propst, & Malamud, 1982). The clubhouse designation originates in the fact that its activities revolve around a central meeting place for "members" to socialize and recreate. Its philosophy emphasizes the importance of voluntary participation, "member" status of participants (rather than "client"), and member involvement on all aspects of the clubhouse governance. A central activity in the clubhouse is participation in work units (e.g., meal preparation) as part of the "work-ordered day" (Macias, Kinney, & Rodican, 1995). Beard et al. (1982) hypothesized that members benefited from participation in the clubhouse, because they felt *needed* for its successful functioning. Thus, a cohesive and supportive group is a crucial feature of the clubhouse model.

Fountain House also pioneered transitional employment (TE) as a way for members to try out paid employment in community settings. TE positions are temporary, part-time community jobs that employ clubhouse members in order to expose them to the world of work, increase their self-confidence, and help them build up their résumés. Clubhouse staff workers negotiate with community employers for these TE positions, which are typically entry-level positions. Members are paid prevailing wages and are considered employees of the community employer, although the positions are not permanent (Beard et al., 1982). While working on a TE, members may receive on-site support at the work site from clubhouse staff and, when on group TE placements, peer support from other members assigned to the same work site (Bond & Dincin, 1986). Moreover, TE workers are expected to continue involvement in clubhouse activities, thereby benefiting from those supportive activities.

Despite its popularity, there has been little research on the clubhouse model. Uncontrolled studies have reported competitive employment rates exceeding 40% (Malamud & McCrory, 1988; Noble, 1991; Ruffner, 1986), but the sole experimental studies of clubhouse approaches found no impact on employment (Beard, Pitt, Fisher, & Goertzel, 1963; Dincin & Witheridge, 1982). A recent large-scale evaluation of a transitional employment program yielded a competitive employment rate of 26% (Cook & Razzano, 1995). In addition, it appears that some clubhouses devote most of their attention to the prevocational units, with only modest attention to community employment (Bond et al., 1995; Connors, Graham, & Pulso, 1987; Turkat & Buzzell, 1982).

The impact of clubhouses on social functioning has not been studied extensively. Surveys of clubhouses indicate that members do value group membership and recreational opportunities (Bond et al., 1995; McCall, 1994). However, participation in a clubhouse does not appear to improve social functioning (Dincin & Witheridge, 1982; Noble, 1991). Rosenfield and Neese-Todd (1993) examined the relationship between involvement in clubhouse programs and subjective ratings of quality of life. Members who had more social contacts in the program were more satisfied with their social relations, and participation in transitional employment was associated with greater satisfaction with finances. There was some evidence that social integration was a compensatory mechanism for those who were *not* working; help in increasing social contacts was related to more positive feelings about being unemployed. In a study of social networks of clubhouse members, Beard (1992) found that away from the clubhouse, most members affiliated mainly with their family and with other members. Only 25% spent time with neighbors, members of their church, friends, or coworkers. Beard concluded that clubhouses may be isolating.

The rationale for the clubhouse is that the supportive social structure of the clubhouse provides the home base from which clients can develop. It provides a low-risk opportunity to try out community jobs. These features are a good fit with the social deficits associated with mental illness. Transitional employment is well-suited for individuals who are fearful of working and who do poorly on job interviews.

One question about clubhouse programs is the extent of self-selection (Stroul, 1986). The clubhouse environment may foster a "clique" atmosphere in which it is difficult for new members to join (Bond et al., 1995). In addition, not everyone subscribes to (or benefits from) the basic clubhouse value of affiliating with others with similar problems (Sheehan, 1982). Another question is whether the supportive environment of prevocational work units creates a dependency inhibiting movement into competitive employment (Bond & Dincin, 1986). Finally, the modest evidence for competitive employment among clubhouse members raises questions about "transfer of training" from the work units and transitional employment to competitive employment.

Supported Employment

Supported employment (SE) is a direct placement approach involving ongoing support from a professional known as an "employment specialist." Although there are many different models, the following components appear to be common across many SE programs: permanent competitive employment is the goal, with minimal screening for employability, avoidance of prevocational training, individualized placement (i.e., not enclaves or mobile work crews), time-unlimited support, and consideration of client preferences (Bond, Drake, Mueser, & Becker, 1997).

Supported employment has a series of explicit assumptions about the social context of employment. Employment specialists often act as an intermediary between the client and the employer, in some instances locating a job for a client without requiring the client to initiate a job interview. Job matching is another feature of the SE approach. The job matching strategy seeks jobs that correspond to clients' preferences (Becker, Drake, Farabaugh, & Bond, 1996) and minimize conditions that are stressors for the client.

SE assumes that clients need ongoing support, perhaps on a time-unlimited basis. For people with SMI, this support is typically off site, and the nature of this support is often in the form of reassurance (Cook & Razzano, 1992). Employment specialists also assist the client in active problem solving (Becker & Drake, 1994). In the SE literature there has been frequent reference to "natural supports" as a long-term alternative to professional support, but the research documenting the viability of natural supports is still rudimentary (Dauwalder & Hoffman, 1992; Marrone et al., 1995; Nisbet & Hagner, 1988).

Another element of the SE philosophy is an emphasis on environmental modification, or "reasonable accommodations," to use the terminology of the Americans with Disabilities Act, which has codified this process. Most SE programs have little or no focus on training social skills, but rather concentrate in focusing on finding a good job match and on making job accommodations to minimize the interference of psychiatric disability, which often include social deficits. Given the nature of the deficits for people with SMI, accommodations are typically in response to low stamina (leading to work schedule accommodations) or modifications on how the interpersonal environment is constructed. So, for example, instructions on how to do a task may be written, rather than verbally given. For persons with SMI who have difficulty with intense personal contact, they may be placed in a work area away from interpersonal contact (Fabian, Edelman, & Leedy, 1993).

An emerging literature is examining the types of accommodations made for persons with SMI (Carling, 1995; Fabian, Waterworth, & Ripke, 1993; Mancuso, 1990; Office of Technology Assessment [OTA], 1994; West & Parent, 1995). By looking at the prevalence of accommodations made for interpersonal limitations, we might infer the centrality of social issues in the work domain for this population. Implicit in these accommodations is the modification of the social environment to be more understanding and flexible in the light of the psychiatric disability.

Six experimental evaluations of SE for people with SMI have suggested significantly better competitive employment rates for SE participants (Bond et al., 1997). However, the critical features of the SE model responsible for the better outcomes have not been clarified. It could be one of the features relating to support and/or modification of the social environment that may account for the success of SE, but the research has not systematically examined this question.

By contrast, program evaluations of SE have not found improvement in social functioning, social relations, or satisfaction with social support as a result of participation in SE programs (Danley, Rogers, MacDonald-Wilson, & Anthony, 1994; Drake et al., 1996; Fabian, 1992; Noble, Conley, Banerjee, & Goodman, 1991). Although these studies have been relatively short term, it is not clear whether even an extended follow-up period in an SE program would reveal improved social functioning (Test, 1995).

The employment outcomes from SE are encouraging. However, the hypothesis that the vocational gains generalize to overall better social functioning has not been shown in the few studies that have examined this question. The diversity of work environments and individual reactions to employment probably contribute to this apparent lack of impact.

PROCESS STUDIES

Some research has examined the predictive relationship between social functioning measured during the course of an intervention program and later vocational functioning. These include studies of provision of support services, studies of prevocational work assessments, and studies of job terminations.

Studies Examining Correlations between Professional Support and Outcome

Cook and Rosenberg (1993) found that clients who received continuous follow-along support after termination from a psychiatric rehabilitation program were significantly more likely to be working than those who received either intermittent support or stopped receiving support altogether. However, the correlation between receiving support after closing and employment at follow-up was modest ($r = .18$). Surprisingly, we found no other studies examining this relationship.

Studies of Prevocational Work Assessments

Numerous studies have examined staff ratings of work behaviors in prevocational settings as predictors of future employment, typically in an effort to determine work readiness. Most of these studies include subscales con-

sisting of interpersonal behaviors (e.g., getting along with coworkers, responding appropriately to supervisors, and general interpersonal appropriateness). Various reviews have concluded that staff ratings of work performance in general (including interpersonal behavior) are predictive of future employment (Anthony & Jansen, 1984; Griffiths, 1974; Van Allen & Loeber, 1972; Watts, 1983).

Seven hospital studies support the contention that social functioning is predictive of vocational success, although the conclusion that social functioning is the single best predictor is more tenuous (Cheadle, Cushing, Drew, & Morgan, 1967; Cheadle & Morgan, 1972; Ethridge, 1968; Distefano & Pryer, 1970; Griffiths, 1973, 1977; Watts, 1978). Studies conducted in nonhospital settings have had mixed results, however. Two studies in community rehabilitation settings found that staff ratings of work performance predicted subsequent success in community jobs, though, as found in most hospital studies, ratings of interpersonal behavior in work settings did not emerge as the uniquely best predictor (Bond & Friedmeyer, 1987; Stauffer, 1986). By contrast, two other studies failed to find significant correlations between situational assessment ratings and future employment (Black, Carpenter, & Robinson, 1986; Rogers et al., 1991). Rogers et al. (1991) attributed their lack of findings to the restriction of range in their sample to already motivated clients, unlike early hospital studies.

Only a few studies have examined whether social skills prior to entering a prevocational program might predict social functioning and work performance in such programs. Hoffmann and Kupper (1996) found that social competence, measured by means of a role-play test, predicted work performance in a prevocational program. Lysaker et al. (1993) found that poorer quality of social contacts reported during an admission interview predicted poor social skills in job placements. Quality of social contacts was not predictive of other aspects of work performance, leading the authors to speculate that studies linking prior social functioning to work performance might actually be due to a more specific relationship between prior social functioning and social skills at work. In a second study, a measure of hostility at admission was associated with difficulties in work motivation and conforming to rules and regulations on the job (Lysaker & Bell, in press).

Studies of Job Terminations

Given that job tenure is often short and that job terminations are often unsatisfactory, many different factors have been identified as contributing to the difficulties, including lack of work experience and poor social skills (Anthony & Jansen, 1984), inadequate supports (Cook, 1992), and stressful work environment (Bond, 1994). Interactions among these factors have also been suggested (Dawis, 1976). A modest literature has begun to be developed around retrospective explanations for termination from employment. Studies agree that unsatisfactory job terminations are common for persons with psychiatric disabilities, but they are inconsistent regarding the reasons (Cook, 1992; Lagomarcino, 1990; MacDonald-Wilson, Revell, Nguyen, & Peterson, 1991). Several studies of job endings, however, do hint at an important role for interpersonal stresses in the decision for termination. Becker, Drake, Bond et al. (in press) found that interpersonal problems on the job were noted in 58% of unsatisfactory job endings, as compared to only 10% of satisfactory job endings. According to retrospective reports by case managers and employment specialists, interpersonal problems was the single most frequently mentioned problem in unsatisfactory jobs, more frequent, for example, than poor job performance. Pitsch (1981) surveyed former supervisors of clients with SMI who failed in job placements. Social isolation and odd behaviors were mentioned as contributing factors. Wallner and Clark (1989) found that rehabilitation counselor ratings of effective interaction with employers and coworkers were correlated with job tenure for clients with SMI placed in community jobs.

Another issue that has not been adequately examined is the extent to which people with SMI differ from other workers. For example, Mueller (1988) notes that in the general population, employers are more likely to terminate employees from entry-level jobs for social reasons rather than nonsocial reasons. Two studies were found comparing work performance of employees with psychiatric disabilities to their nondisabled counterparts. Howard (1975) found no differences between ex-patients and nondisabled workers on a range of supervisor ratings of job performance, including measures of interpersonal functioning. However, Shupe, Cole, and Allison (1966) found that employees with SMI were rated as poorer workers than matched controls, notably on several interpersonal items.

DISCUSSION

This review of the literature reveals that we know far less about the relationship between social and vocational functioning than might have been imagined. For the most part, the correlational literature supports the view that these two domains, which seem so closely linked conceptually, are in fact moderately associated. Longitudinal studies, while showing weaker associations, are still somewhat supportive. These findings are relatively robust, despite the fact that a wide range of methods, samples, and research designs have been used to examine these associations.

Turning to the intervention literature, the picture is far more confusing. There is practically no evidence that helping people with SMI improve their social functioning actually improves their vocational functioning. At first blush, this finding is puzzling. If adequate social functioning is so integral to success in the workplace, why is it, then, that programs that aim at betterment of social skills have had such a dismal track record in improving employment? We have alluded to several lines of reasoning that might explain these nonfindings—stigma, systems barriers, and the failure to differentiate between different phases of the employment process. Another line of reasoning is that the mechanisms for change in social functioning are poorly understood and the principles incorrectly applied. One example is the common practice of teaching social skills with contrived role-playing exercises in office settings, rather than addressing dilemmas in the settings in which they occur. Teaching skills relating to specific interpersonal problems encountered on a job may make the training more meaningful and applicable (Mueser, Foy, & Carter, 1986). Another viewpoint is offered by Hogarty (1995), who has hypothesized that skills training is often too narrow and specific. He argues that we need to train people with SMI in broader coping skills if they are to meet the demands of the workplace and other complex environments. Still another viewpoint is that the answer lies not in training in social skills or problem solving, but in selecting and creating more benign social environments (Bellack, 1992). Whatever the reasons, it is fair to conclude that our theories of functioning in people with SMI have not led to fruitful psychosocial intervention strategies with regard to employment.

Evaluations of vocational programs have also failed to support the hypothesis that improvements in vocational functioning should have a more general effect on social functioning. Again, we can offer post hoc explanations for these nonfindings—the multiple and contradictory effects of employment (providing new friends, causing isolation and withdrawal, creating stress, etc.), individual differences among people with SMI and among jobs—but the lack of a demonstrable impact on social functioning points to a failure of theory. The impact of vocational experiences on social functioning is assuredly complex and poorly documented in the empirical literature.

Given the disappointing state of the research literature, we devote the remainder of this chapter to identifying directions for future research, following the outline as in the body of the chapter.

Conceptual Relationship between Social and Vocational Functioning

A more comprehensive theory is needed, incorporating the specific social deficits found in schizophrenia and other forms of SMI; the types of social support systems and how they influence employment; the social environments of the workplace; and the interactions between these factors. Work in each of these areas is at present incomplete. This is no simple undertaking. It may require borrowing from other fields, such as industrial-organizational psychology.

Empirical Relationship between Social and Vocational Functioning

The concurrent association between social and vocational functioning for people with SMI is well established. However, because of the diversity of measures used and the global quality to measures used in many of these studies, research showing this relationship does not offer much insight about the nature of the social functioning and how it affects work functioning. Also, these studies do not allow for inferences about the direction of causality, or whether a third cause—for example, cognitive functioning—might explain both social and vocational outcomes. For these reasons, we believe that there is little reason to pursue any further correlational studies using global measures of social and vocational functioning. Instead, we propose more attention to qualitative methods, neuropsychological assessment strategies, analysis of the social requirements of jobs, and process studies.

Qualitative methods also may help generate more grounded hypotheses, for example, in understanding the role of social networks (Alverson et al., 1995) and the time course of vocational functioning in the context of other life events (Strauss, Hafez, Lieberman, & Harding, 1985). Neuropsychological approaches to assessing social functioning may ultimately prove to yield more specific measures of social dysfunction that will permit predictions of work capacity.

We also need a clearer articulation and empirical study of the social requirements of different occupations and work environments. Intuitively, it would seem obvious that social skills are required to function in most jobs. But what are the social demands which are most salient or cause the most difficulty for persons with SMI? Given the wide variability in jobs, is it possible to make any generalizations?

Surprisingly, very little research has examined in detail the social demands of different types of jobs. McConaughy, Stowitschek, Salzberg, and Peatross (1989) found that supervisors rated the following items as most important in entry-level jobs: following instructions, getting necessary information, providing job-related information to others, offering to help someone else, and using social amenities. According to this survey, the skills supervisors seek in entry-level workers include basic interpersonal skills. Also, a large body of research suggests that high contact with the public fosters worker burnout (Lee & Ashforth, 1996).

It is plausible that certain types of occupations and/or work settings are better suited to people with SMI. A quiet, undemanding, somewhat isolated social experience may contribute to a better adjustment for people with schizophrenia (Liberman, 1982). Clients with SMI who are more detached, less sociable, and less agreeable may be more productive in certain types of work environments (Walker et al., 1973). Wilson and Rasch (1982) found that jobs held longest by clients with SMI involved working with things rather than people or data. In a similar vein, Muntaner, Pulver, McGrath, and Eaton (1993) reasoned that the vulnerability of persons with schizophrenia to high-arousal environments would lead to "occupational self-selection." They found that people with schizophrenia, as compared to patients with other psychotic disorders, were more likely to work in low-complexity jobs (e.g., janitors, construction laborers, gardeners, and food preparers), whereas people with bipolar disorders were more likely to hold jobs requiring high levels of interpersonal contact (e.g., sales workers, cashiers, general office clerks, secretaries, and waiters). Undoubtedly, cognitive complexity, degree of social interaction, and many other factors figure in the job fit.

At best, however, occupational stereotyping by diagnosis accounts for only a small portion of the variance in predicting vocational success. To extrapolate from the more effective rehabilitation models, individualized approaches to placement that find jobs for clients matching their occupational preferences, personality styles, capacities and preferences for social interaction, and social supports are most likely to lead to successful employment (Becker, Drake, Farabaugh et al., 1996). We are a long way from translating these complexities into testable hypotheses, nor is it certain that we will ever be able to fully quantify the intuitive clinical strategies for locating suitable matches. Certainly, paper-and-pencil tests have not been useful in determining these job matches (Bond & Dietzen, 1993).

Research is especially needed to understand what types of support are helpful for obtaining and maintaining employment. Although supportive social networks are widely assumed to have a positive effect on employment, little research can be cited to show this is true. With regard to the converse question—whether employment increases social networks—what little research and anecdotal reports available bearing on this question suggest that employment probably does not have this general effect.

The evidence suggesting that ongoing professional support positively influences vocational success is largely circumstantial. Because of the centrality of this assumption in the SE model, there is a need for this assumption to be tested experimentally.

Psychosocial and Vocational Interventions

Most of the current models of psychosocial interventions and of vocational rehabilitation have only loosely articulated theories about the relationships of social functioning and social networks to vocational outcomes.

The lack of findings regarding the impact of vocational programs on social functioning does not imply that clients' social skills at entry into a vocational program do not influence their subsequent success. More socially adept individuals appear more likely to benefit from the job club approach. It is less clear whether social skills play a role in the success in other vocational approaches, because the research has not examined this question extensively.

It is also reasonable to hypothesize that individuals with psychiatric disabilities can compensate in their search for employment by "hiding" their social deficits or finding work in which their social deficits are not a major barrier. Individualized placement approaches (e.g., Becker & Drake, 1994) seek to do just that by their selection of occupations and job sites that maximize the clients' ability to succeed.

The research suggests that family interventions can improve the social functioning of a relative with schizophre-

nia. Several of these studies found modest improvement in vocational functioning, despite the fact that the treatment approaches in these studies apparently lacked an explicit vocational component. It is a puzzle that a relatively indirect approach—working with families—should apparently have more of an effect on employment than some more direct interventions. One hypothesis is that family approaches, because they are among the most potent of psychosocial interventions for schizophrenia reported in the psychiatric literature, may have a global effect on functioning that generalizes to vocational functioning. There is also some evidence that families are a critical source of support for clients once they are employed.

Process Studies

The understanding of the social-vocational relationship will progress faster through the design and implementation of process studies. These studies seek to pinpoint the specific mechanisms by which social skills and networks influence the vocational process, and vice versa. At a practical level, these studies can offer concrete guidance to the design of rehabilitation programs. Process studies of the type envisioned would generate testable hypotheses, which could be examined by devising interventions that would be predicted to result in particular outcomes. For example, Gervey's (1995) observational study, which suggests that clients who have employment specialists accompany them to the job interview have more job offers could be examined experimentally, supplementing the main outcome measure (job offers) with interviews with employers to uncover reasons for the differences (e.g., stigma, clients' interviewing skills, support of rehabilitation program).

The current popularity of supported employment is based partly on the assumption that time-unlimited support is necessary for people with SMI to stay competitively employed. This assumption is largely untested. Nor are the kinds of support necessary for maintaining employment well specified. Evidence is likewise lacking for the popular belief that natural supports are a desirable element in an employment program.

CONCLUSION

The development of a comprehensive theory about the relationships between social and vocational functioning is not simply an academic exercise but potentially an important guide to the design of vocational programs. A better understanding will be possible only if our theories move beyond the global level to examine specific processes involved in getting and keeping a job.

REFERENCES

Alverson, M., Becker, D. R., & Drake, R. E. (1995). An ethnographic study of coping strategies used by people with severe mental illness participating in supported employment. *Psychosocial Rehabilitation Journal, 18,* 115–128.

Anthony, W. A., & Jansen, M. A. (1984). Predicting the vocational capacity of the chronically mentally ill: Research and implications. *American Psychologist, 39,* 537–544.

Anthony, W. A., Rogers, E. S., Cohen, M., & Davies, R. R. (1995). Relationship between psychiatric symptomatology, work skills, and future vocational performance. *Psychiatric Services, 46,* 353–358.

Arns, P. G., & Linney, J. A. (1995). Relating functional skills of severely mentally ill clients to subjective and societal benefits. *Psychiatric Services, 46,* 260–265.

Avison, W. R., & Speechley, K. N. (1987). The discharged psychiatric patient: A review of social, social-psychological, and psychiatric correlates of outcome. *American Journal of Psychiatry, 144,* 10–18.

Azrin, N. H., & Besalel, V. A. (1980). *The job club counselor's manual: A behavioral approach to vocational counseling.* Baltimore: University Park Press.

Azrin, N. H., & Philip, R. A. (1979). The job club method for the job handicapped: A comparative outcome study. *Rehabilitation Counseling Bulletin, 23,* 144–155.

Barrowclough, C., & Tarrier, N. (1990). Social functioning in schizophrenic patients. I. The effects of expressed emotion and family intervention. *Social Psychiatry and Psychiatric Epidemiology, 25,* 125–129.

Beard, J. H., Pitt, R. B., Fisher, S. H., & Goertzel, V. (1963). Evaluating the effectiveness of a psychiatric rehabilitation program. *American Journal of Orthopsychiatry, 33,* 701–712.

Beard, J. H., Propst, R. N., & Malamud, T. J. (1982). The Fountain House model of rehabilitation. *Psychosocial Rehabilitation Journal, 5,* 47–53.

Beard, M. L. (1992). Social networks. *Psychosocial Rehabilitation Journal, 16,* 111–123.

Becker, D. R., & Drake, R. E. (1994). Individual placement and support: A community mental health center approach to vocational rehabilitation. *Community Mental Health Journal, 30,* 193–206.

Becker, D. R., Drake, R. E., Bond, G. R., Xie, H., Dain, B. J., & Harrison, K. (in press). *Job terminations among persons with severe mental illness participating in supported employment. Community Mental Health Journal.*

Becker, D. R., Drake, R. E., Farabaugh, A., & Bond, G. R. (1996). Job preferences among people with severe psychiatric disorders participating in supported employment. *Psychiatric Services, 47,* 1223–1226.

Bell, M. D., & Ryan, E. (1984). Integrating rehabilitation into hospital psychiatry. *Hospital and Community Psychiatry, 35,* 1017–1022.

Bell, M. D., & Stiens, R.E. (1991). Ego function change through rehabilitation: A pilot study. *Psychosocial Rehabilitation Journal, 14,* 97–101.

Bellack, A. S. (1992). Cognitive rehabilitation for schizophrenia: Is it possible? Is it necessary? *Schizophrenia Bulletin, 18,* 43–50.

Bellack, A. S., Morrison, R. L., Wixted, J. T., & Mueser, K. T. (1990). An analysis of social competence in schizophrenia. *British Journal of Psychiatry, 156,* 809–818.

Berven, N. L., & Driscoll, J. H. (1981). The effects of past psychiatric disability on employer evaluation of a job applicant. *Journal of Applied Rehabilitation Counseling, 12,* 50–55.

Black, B. J. (1988). *Work and mental illness: Transitions to employment.* Baltimore: Johns Hopkins Press.

Black, B. J., Carpenter, M. D., & Robinson, P. E. (1986). *Using manpower training programs in the vocational rehabilitation of the mentally restored.* Altro Institute for Rehabilitation Studies, Professional Monograph Series, Vol. 2. New York: Altro Health and Rehabilitation Services.

Bolton, B. (1983). Psychosocial factors affecting the employment of former vocational rehabilitation clients. *Rehabilitation Psychology, 28,* 35–44.

Bond, G. R. (1992). Vocational rehabilitation. In R. P. Liberman (Ed.), *Handbook of psychiatric rehabilitation* (pp. 244–275). New York: Macmillan.

Bond, G. R. (1994). Applying psychiatric rehabilitation principles to employment: Recent findings. In R. J. Ancill, S. Holliday, & J. Higenbottam (Eds.), *Schizophrenia: Exploring the spectrum of psychosis* (pp. 49–65). Chichester, England: Wiley.

Bond, G. R., & Dietzen, L. (1993). Predictive validity and vocational assessment: Reframing the question. In R. L. Glueckauf, L. B. Sechrest, G. R. Bond, & E. C. McDonel (Eds.), *Improving assessment in rehabilitation and health* (pp. 61–86). Newbury Park, CA: Sage.

Bond, G. R., Dietzen, L. L., Vogler, K., Katuin, C., McGrew, J. H., & Miller, L. D. (1995). Toward a framework for evaluating costs and benefits of psychiatric rehabilitation: Three case examples. *Journal of Vocational Rehabilitation, 5,* 75–88.

Bond, G. R., & Dincin, J. (1986). Accelerating entry into transitional employment in a psychosocial rehabilitation agency. *Rehabilitation Psychology, 31,* 143–155.

Bond, G. R., Drake, R. E., Mueser, K. T., & Becker, D. R. (1997). An update on supported employment for people with severe mental illness: A review. *Psychiatric Services, 48,* 335–346.

Bond, G. R., & Friedmeyer, M. H. (1987). Predictive validity of situational assessment at a psychiatric rehabilitation center. *Rehabilitation Psychology, 32,* 99–112.

Bottrill, K. (1994). *Effects of disability type and seeking reasonable accommodation on pre-employment evaluations.* Unpublished masters thesis, Indiana University-Purdue University at Indianapolis.

Braitman, A., Counts, P., Davenport, R., Zurlinden, B., Rogers, M., Clauss, J., Kulkarni, A., Kymla, J., & Montgomery, L. (1995). Comparison of barriers to employment for unemployed and employed clients in a case management program: An exploratory study. *Psychiatric Rehabilitation Journal, 19*, 3–8.

Breier, A., Schreiber, J. L., Dyer, J., & Pickar, D. (1991). National Institute of Mental Health Longitudinal Study of Chronic Schizophrenia. *Archives of General Psychiatry, 48*, 239–246.

Brekke, J. S., Levin, S., Wolkon, G. H., & Slade, E. (1993). Psychosocial functioning and subjective experience in schizophrenia. *Schizophrenia Bulletin, 19*, 599–608.

Brenner, H. D., Hodel, B., Roder, V., & Corrigan, P. (1992). Treatment of cognitive dysfunctions and behavioral deficits in schizophrenia. *Schizophrenia Bulletin, 18*, 21–26.

Brown, G. W., Birley, J. L., & Wing, J. K. (1972). Influence of family life on the course of schizophrenic disorders: A replication. *British Journal of Psychiatry, 121*, 241–258.

Caplan, G. (1974). *Support systems and community mental health: Lectures on concept development.* New York: Behavioral Publications.

Carling, P. J. (1995). *Return to community: Building support systems for people with psychiatric disabilities.* New York: Guilford Press.

Chandler, D., Meisel, J., Hu, T., McGowen, M., & Madison, K. (in press). A capitated model for a cross-section of severely mentally ill clients: Employment outcomes. *Community Mental Health Journal.*

Cheadle, A. J., Cushing, D., Drew, C. D., & Morgan, R. (1967). The measurement of the work performance of psychiatric patients. *British Journal of Psychiatry, 113*, 841–846.

Cheadle, A. J., & Morgan, R. (1972). The measurement of work performance of psychiatric patients: A reappraisal. *British Journal of Psychiatry, 120*, 437–441.

Ciardiello, J. A., Klein, M. E., & Sobkowski, S. (1988). Ego functioning and vocational rehabilitation. In J. A. Ciardiello & M. D. Bell (Eds.), *Vocational rehabilitation of persons with prolonged mental illness* (pp. 196–207). Baltimore, MD: Johns Hopkins Press.

Clark, R. E., & Bond, G. R. (1996). Costs and benefits of vocational programs for people with serious mental illness. In M. Moscarelli, A. Rupp, & N. Sartorius (Eds.), *Schizophrenia* (pp. 219–237). Sussex, England: Wiley.

Cook, J. A. (1985). *Using crew evaluations to predict subsequent work performance among Thresholds members.* Unpublished paper. Chicago: Thresholds Research and Training Center.

Cook, J. A. (1992). Job ending among youth and adults with severe mental illness. *Journal of Mental Health Administration, 19*, 158–169.

Cook, J. A. (1994). Recent trends in vocational rehabilitation for people with psychiatric disability. *American Rehabilitation, 20(4)*, 2–12.

Cook, J. A., & Razzano, L. (1992). Natural vocational supports for persons with severe mental illness: Thresholds supported

competitive employment program. *New Directions for Mental Health Services, 56*, 23–41.

Cook, J. A., & Razzano, L. (1995). Discriminant function analysis of competitive employment in a transitional employment program for persons with severe mental illness. *Journal of Vocational Rehabilitation, 5*, 127–139.

Cook, J. A., & Rosenberg, H. (1993). Predicting community employment among persons with psychiatric disability: A logistic regression analysis. *Journal of Rehabilitation Administration, 18*, 6–22.

Cook, J. A., Solomon, M. L., & Mock, L. O. (1989). What happens after the first job placement: Vocational transitioning among severely emotionally disturbed and behavior disordered adolescents. In S. L. Braaten, R. B. Rutherford, T. F. Reilly, & S. A. DiGamgi (Eds.), *Programming for adolescents with behavioral disorders* (pp. 71–93). Reston, VA: Council for Children with Behavioral Disorders.

Connors, K. A., Graham, R. S., & Pulso, R. (1987). Playing the store: Where is the vocational in psychiatric rehabilitation? *Psychosocial Rehabilitation Journal, 10*, 21–33.

Danley, K. S., Rogers, E. S., MacDonald-Wilson, K., & Anthony, W. A. (1994). Supported employment for adults with psychiatric disability: Results of an innovative demonstration project. *Rehabilitation Psychology, 39*, 269–276.

Dauwalder, J. P., & Hoffman, H. (1992). Ecological vocational rehabilitation. *New Directions for Mental Health Services, 53*, 79–86.

Dawis, R. V. (1976). The Minnesota Theory of Work Adjustment. In B. Bolton (Ed.), *Handbook of measurement and evaluation* (pp. 227–248). Baltimore: University Park Press.

Deacon, S., Dunning, R. E., & Dease, R. (1974). A job clinic for psychotic clients in remission. *American Journal of Occupational Therapy, 28*, 144–147.

Dilk, M. N., & Bond, G. R. (1996). Meta-analytic evaluation of skills training research for persons with severe mental illness. *Journal of Consulting and Clinical Psychology, 64*, 1337–1346.

Dincin, J., & Witheridge, T. F. (1982). Psychiatric rehabilitation as a deterrent to recidivism. *Hospital and Community Psychiatry, 33*, 645–650.

Distefano, M. K., & Pryer, M. W. (1970). Vocational evaluation and successful placement of psychiatric clients in a vocational rehabilitation program. *American Journal of Occupational Therapy, 24*, 205–207.

Drake, R. E., Becker, D. R., Biesanz, J. C., Torrey, W. C., McHugo, G. J., & Wyzik, P. F. (1994). Rehabilitation day treatment vs. supported employment: I. Vocational outcomes. *Community Mental Health Journal, 30*, 519–532.

Drake, R. E., Becker, D. R., Xie, H., & Anthony, W. A. (1995). Barriers in the brokered model of supported employment for persons with psychiatric disabilities. *Journal of Vocational Rehabilitation, 5*, 141–149.

Drake, R. E., McHugo, G. J., Becker, D. R., Anthony, W. A., & Clark, R. E. (1996). The New Hampshire study of supported employment for people with severe mental illness: Vocational outcomes. *Journal of Consulting and Clinical Psychology, 64,* 390–398.

Eisenberg, M. G., & Cole, H. W. (1986). A behavioral approach to job seeking for psychiatrically impaired persons. *Journal of Rehabilitation, 52,* 46–49.

Ellsworth, R. B., Foster, L., Childers, B., Arthur, G., & Kroeker, D. (1968). Hospital and community adjustment as perceived by psychiatric patients, their families, and staff. *Journal of Consulting and Clinical Psychology, 32* (5, part 2), 1–41.

Estroff, S. E. (1981). *Making it crazy.* Berkeley: University of California Press.

Ethridge, D. A. (1968). Pre-vocational assessment of rehabilitation potential of psychiatric patients. *American Journal of Occupational Therapy, 22,* 161–167.

Fabian, E. S. (1992). Supported employment and the quality of life: Does a job make a difference? *Rehabilitation Counseling Bulletin, 36,* 84–97.

Fabian, E. S., Edelman, A., & Leedy, M. (1993). Linking workers with severe disabilities to social supports in the workplace: Strategies for addressing barriers. *Journal of Rehabilitation, 59,* 29–34.

Fabian, E. S., Waterworth, A., & Ripke, B. (1993). Reasonable accommodations for workers with serious mental illness: Type, frequency, and associated outcomes. *Psychosocial Rehabilitation Journal, 17,* 163–172.

Falloon, I. R. H., McGill, C. W., Boyd, J. L., & Pederson, J. (1987). Family management in the prevention of morbidity of schizophrenia: Social outcome of a two-year longitudinal study. *Psychological Medicine, 17,* 59–66.

Farina, A., & Felner, R. D. (1973). Employment interviewer reactions to former mental patients. *Journal of Abnormal Psychology, 82(2), 268–272.*

Farina, A., Felner, R. D., & Boudreau, L. A. (1973). Reactions of workers to male and female mental patient job applicants. *Journal of Consulting and Clinical Psychology, 41,* 363–372.

Faulkner, L. R., McFarland, B. H., Larch, B. B., Harris, W. J., & Yohe, C. D. (1986). Small group work therapy for the chronic mentally ill. *Hospital and Community Psychiatry, 37,* 273–279.

Freeman, H. E., & Simmons, O. G. (1963). *The mental patient comes home.* New York: Wiley.

Furman, W., Geller, M., Simon, S. J., & Kelly, J. A. (1979). The use of a behavioral rehearsal procedure for teaching job interviewing skills to psychiatric patients. *Behavior Therapy, 10,* 157–167.

Gervey, R. (1995, February). *To disclose or not to disclose.* Presentation at the New Hampshire-Dartmouth Psychiatric Research Center, Lebanon, NH.

Goering, P. N., Wasylenki, D. A., Farkas, M. D., Lancee, W. J., & Ballantyne, R. (1988). What difference does case management make? *Hospital and Community Psychiatry, 39,* 272–276.

Goldman, H. H., Rosenberg, J., & Manderscheid, R. W. (1988).

Defining the target population for vocational rehabilitation. In J. A. Ciardiello & M. D. Bell (Eds.), *Vocational rehabilitation of persons with prolonged mental illness* (pp. 19–34). Baltimore, MD: Johns Hopkins Press.

Griffiths, R. D. (1973). A standardized assessment of the work behavior of psychiatric patients. *British Journal of Psychiatry, 123,* 403–408.

Griffiths, R. D. (1974). Rehabilitation of chronic psychotic patients. *Psychological Medicine, 4,* 316–325.

Griffiths, R. D. (1977). The prediction of psychiatric patients' work adjustment in the community. *British Journal of Social and Clinical Psychology, 16,* 165–173.

Gunderson, J. G., Frank, A. F., Katz, H. M., Vannicelli, M. L., Frosch, J. P., & Knapp, P. H. (1984). Effects of psychotherapy in schizophrenia: II. Comparative outcome of two forms of treatment. *Schizophrenia Bulletin, 10,* 564–596.

Harris, L., & Associates. (1993). *Attitudes of disabled people on politics and other issues.* New York Lou Harris and Associates.

Harrow, M., Westermeyer, J. F., Silverstein, M., Strauss, B. S., & Cohler, B. J. (1986). Predictors of outcome in schizophrenia: The process-reactive dimension. *Schizophrenia Bulletin, 12,* 195–206.

Hoffmann, H., & Kupper, Z. (1996, April). *Relationships between social competence, psychopathology, and work performance and their predictive value for vocational rehabilitation of schizophrenic patients.* Presentation at the Fifth Congress of the World Association of Psychosocial Rehabilitation, Rotterdam, The Netherlands.

Hogarty, G. E. (1995). Schizophrenia and modern mental health services. *Decade of the Brain, 7,* 3–6.

Hogarty, G. E., Anderson, C. M., Reiss, D. J., Kornblith, S. J., Greenwald, D. P., Ulrich, R. F., Carter, M. & the EPICS Research Group. (1991). Family psychoeducation, social skills training, and maintenance chemotherapy in the aftercare treatment of schizophrenia. *Archives of General Psychiatry, 48,* 340–347.

Hogarty G. E., Goldberg, S. C., Schooler, N. R., & Collaborative Study Group. (1974). Drug and sociotherapy in the aftercare of schizophrenic patients: III: Adjustment of nonrelapsed patients. *Archives of General Psychiatry, 31,* 609–618.

Hogarty, G. E., Kornblith, S. J., Greenwald, D., DiBarry, A. L., Cooley, S., Flesher, S., Reiss, D., Carter, M., & Ulrich, R. (1995). Personal therapy: A disorder-relevant psychotherapy for schizophrenia. *Schizophrenia Bulletin, 21,* 379–393.

House, J. S. (1981). *Work stress and social support.* Reading, MA: Addison-Wesley.

Howard, G. (1975). The ex-mental patient as an employee: An on-the-job evaluation. *American Journal of Orthopsychiatry, 43,* 479–483.

Jacobs, H. E., Kardashian, S., Kreinbring, R. K., Ponder, R., & Simpson, A. S. (1984). A skills-oriented model for facilitating employment among psychiatrically disabled persons. *Rehabilitation Counseling Bulletin, 28,* 87–96.

Jacobs, H. E., Wissusik, D., Collier, R., Stackman, D., & Burke-man, D. (1992). Correlations between psychiatric disabilities and vocational outcome. *Hospital and Community Psychiatry, 43,* 365–369.

Jonsson, H., & Nyman, A. K. (1991). Predicting long-term outcome in schizophrenia. *Acta Psychiatrica Scandinavica, 83,* 342–346.

Keith, R. D., Engelkes, J. R., & Winborn, B. B. (1977). Employment-seeking preparation and activity: An experimental job-placement training model for rehabilitation clients. *Rehabilitation Counseling Bulletin, 21,* 159–165.

Kelly, J. A., Laughlin, C., & Clairborne, M. (1979). A group procedure for teaching job interviewing skills to formerly hospitalized psychiatric patients. *Behavior Therapy, 10,* 299–310.

Kramer, L. W., & Beidel, D. C. (1982). Job-seeking skill groups: Review and application to a chronic psychiatric population. *Occupational Therapy in Mental Health, 2,* 37–44.

Lagomarcino, T. R. (1990). Job separation issues in supported employment. In F. R. Rusch (Ed.), *Supported employment: Models, methods, and stress* (pp. 301–316). Sycamore, IL: Sycamore Publishing.

Lee, R. T., & Ashforth, B. E. (1996). A meta-analytic examination of the correlates of the three dimensions of burnout. *Journal of Applied Psychology, 81,* 123–133.

Lehman, A. F. (1995). Vocational rehabilitation in schizophrenia. *Schizophrenia Bulletin, 21,* 645–656.

Liberman, R. P. (1982). Social factors in schizophrenia. In L. Greenspoon, (Ed.), *American Psychiatric Association annual review* (pp. 97–111). Washington, DC: American Psychiatric Association Press.

Link, B. G. (1982). Mental patient status, work, and income: An examination of the effects of a psychiatric label. *American Sociological Review, 47,* 202–215.

Link, B. G. (1987). Understanding labeling effects in the area of mental disorders: An assessment of the effects of expectations of rejection. *American Sociological Review, 52,* 96–112.

Link, B. G., Cullen, F. T., Frank, J., & Wozniak, J. F. (1987). The social rejection of former mental patients: Understanding why labels matter. *American Journal of Sociology, 92,* 1461–1500.

Link, B. G., Cullen, F. T., Struening, E., Shrout, P. T., & Dohren-wind, B. P. (1989). A modified labeling theory approach to mental disorders: An empirical assessment. *American Sociological Review, 54,* 400–423.

Lorei, T. W., & Gurel, L. (1972). Use of a biographical inventory to predict schizophrenics' posthospital employment and readmission. *Journal of Consulting and Clinical Psychology, 38,* 238–243.

Lysaker, P., & Bell, M. (in press). Negative symptoms and vocational impairment in schizophrenia: Repeated measurements of work performance over six months. *Acta Psychiatrica Scandinavica.*

Lysaker, P., & Bell, M. (1995). Work performance over time for people with schizophrenia. *Psychosocial Rehabilitation Journal, 18,* 141–145.

Lysaker, P., Bell, M., Milstein, R., Bryson, G., Shestopal, A., & Goulet, J. B. (1993). Work capacity in schizophrenia. *Hospital and Community Psychiatry, 44,* 278–280.

MacDonald-Wilson, K. L., Revell, W. G., Nguyen, N., & Peterson, M. E. (1991). Supported employment outcomes for people with psychiatric disability: A comparative analysis. *Journal of Vocational Rehabilitation, 1,* 30–44.

Macias, C., Kinney, R., & Rodican, C. (1995). Transitional employment: An evaluative description of Fountain House practice. *Journal of Vocational Rehabilitation 5,* 151–158.

Malamud, T. J., & McCrory, D. J. (1988). Transitional employment and psychosocial rehabilitation. In J. A. Ciardiello & M. D. Bell (Eds.), *Vocational rehabilitation of persons with prolonged mental illness* (pp. 150–162). Baltimore: Johns Hopkins Press.

Mancuso, L. L. (1990). Reasonable accommodation for workers with psychiatric disabilities. *Psychosocial Rehabilitation Journal, 14,* 3–19.

Marrone, J., Balzell, A., & Gold, M. (1995). Employment support for people with mental illness. *Psychiatric Services, 46,* 707–711.

Marshak, L. E., Bostick, D., & Turton, L. J. (1990). Closure outcomes for clients with psychiatric disabilities served by the vocational rehabilitation system. *Rehabilitation Counseling Bulletin, 33,* 247–250.

McCall, B. (1994, June). Survey of psychosocial rehabilitation programs. *Research notes.* Richmond, VA: VA Department of Mental Health, Mental Retardation, & Substance Abuse Services.

McConaughy, E. K., Stowitschek, J. J., Salzberg, C. L., & Peatross, D. K. (1989). Work supervisors' ratings of social behaviors related to employment success. *Rehabilitation Psychology, 34,* 3–15.

McFarlane, W. R., Dushay, R., Deakins, S. A., & Stastny, P. (1995, October). *Employment outcomes in Family-aided Assertive Community Treatment (FACT).* Presentation at the American Psychiatric Association Institute on Psychiatric Services, Boston, MA.

McFarlane, W. R., Lukens, E., Toran, J., & Donne, E. (1991). *Executive summary: Outcome results from the Family Psychoeducation in Schizophrenia Project.* Unpublished paper, Biosocial Treatment Research Division, New York State Psychiatric Institute.

McGlashan, T. H. (1988). A selective review of recent North American long-term follow-up studies of schizophrenia. *Schizophrenia Bulletin, 14,* 515–542.

McGlashan, T. H., & Fenton, W. S. (1992). The positive-negative distinction in schizophrenia. *Archives of General Psychiatry, 49,* 63–72.

Meltzoff, J., & Blumenthal, R. L. (1966). *The day treatment center: Principles, application, and evaluation.* Springfield, IL: Charles C. Thomas.

Mintz, J., Bond, G. R., & Mintz, L. I. (in press). Assessment of work function in mental health research. *Cost effectiveness of psychotherapy.* Rockville, MD: National Institute of Mental Health.

Mintz, J., Mintz, L. I., & Phipps, C. C. (1992). Treatments of mental disorders and the functional capacity to work. In R. P. Liberman (Ed.), *Handbook of psychiatric rehabilitation* (pp. 290–316). New York: Macmillan.

Moller, H., von Zerssen, D., Werner-Eilert, K., & Wüschner-Stockheim, M. (1982). Outcome in schizophrenic and similar paranoid psychoses. *Schizophrenia Bulletin, 8,* 99–108.

Mosher, L. R., & Keith, S. J. (1980). Psychosocial treatment: Individual, group, family, and community support approaches. *Schizophrenia Bulletin, 6,* 127–158.

Mowbray, C. T., Bybee, D., Harris, S. N., & McCrohan, N. (1996). *Predictors of work status and future work orientation in persons with a psychiatric disability.* Manuscript submitted for publication.

Mueller, H. H. (1988). Employers' reasons for terminating the employment of workers in entry-level jobs: Implications for workers with mental disabilities. *Canadian Journal of Rehabilitation, 1,* 233–240.

Mueser, K. T., Bellack, A. S., Douglas, M. S., & Morrison, R. L. (1991). Prevalence and stability of social skill deficits in schizophrenia. *Schizophrenia Research, 5,* 167–176.

Mueser, K. T., Bellack, A. S., Morrison, R. L., & Wixted, J. T. (1990). Social competence in schizophrenia: Premorbid adjustment, social skill, and domains of functioning. *Journal of Psychiatric Research, 24,* 51–63.

Mueser, K. T., Bond, G. R., Drake, R. E., & Resick, S. G. (in press). Models of community care for severe mental illness: A review of research on case management. *Schizophrenia Bulletin.*

Mueser, K. T., Foy, D. W., & Carter, M. J. (1986). Social skills training for job maintenance in a psychiatric patient. *Journal of Counseling Psychology, 33,* 360–362.

Muntaner, C., Pulver, A. E., McGrath, J., & Eaton, W. W. (1993). Work environment and schizophrenia: An extension of the arousal hypothesis to occupational self-selection. *Social Psychiatry and Psychiatric Epidemiology, 28,* 231–238.

Neff, W. S. (1958). The success of program: A follow-up study. *Monograph #3.* Chicago, IL: Jewish Vocational Service.

Nisbet, J., & Hagner, D. (1988). Natural supports in the workplace: A re-examination of supported employment. *Journal of the Association for Persons with Severe Handicaps, 13,* 260–267.

Noble, J. H. (1991). *The benefits and costs of supported employment for people with mental illness and with traumatic brain injury in New York state.* Final Report No. C–0023180, Amherst, NY: Research Foundation of the State University of New York.

Noble, J. H., Conley, R. W., Banerjee, S., & Goodman, S. (1991). Supported employment in New York state: A comparison of benefits and costs. *Journal of Disability Policy Studies, 1,* 39–73.

Office of Technology Assessment. (1994). *Psychiatric disabili-ties, employment, and the Americans with Disabilities Act.* OTA-BP–124. Washington, DC: U.S. Government Printing Office.

Olshansky, S., Grob, S., & Ekdahl, M. (1960). Survey of employment experience of patients discharged from three mental hospitals during the period 1951–1953. *Mental Hygiene, 44,* 510–521.

Olshansky, S., Grob, S., & Malamud, I. T. (1958). Employer attitudes and practices in hiring ex-mental patients. *Mental Hygiene, 42,* 391–401.

Parker, S., & Knoll, J. L. (1990). Partial hospitalization: An update. *American Journal of Psychiatry, 147,* 156–160.

Parsons, T. (1951). *The social system.* New York: Free Press.

Pitsch, R. (1981). Attempts at reintegrating psychically ill persons into working life. *International Journal of Rehabilitation Research, 4,* 88–90.

Rogers, E. S., Sciarappa, K., & Anthony, W. A. (1991). Development and evaluation of situational assessment instruments and procedures for persons with psychiatric disability. *Vocational Evaluation and Work Adjustment Bulletin, 24,* 61–67.

Rosenfield, S., & Neese-Todd, S. (1993). Elements of a psychosocial rehabilitation program associated with a satisfying quality of life. *Hospital and Community Psychiatry, 44,* 76–78.

Ruffner, R. H. (1986). The last frontier: Jobs and mentally ill persons. *Psychosocial Rehabilitation Journal, 9,* 35–42.

Schultheis, A. M., & Bond, G. R. (1993). Situational assessment ratings of work behaviors: Changes across time and between settings. *Psychosocial Rehabilitation Journal, 17, 107–119.*

Sheehan, S. (1982). *Is there no place on earth for me?* New York: Vintage Books.

Shepherd, M., Watt, D., Falloon, I., & Smeeton, N. (1989). The natural history of schizophrenia: A five-year follow-up study of outcome and prediction in a representative sample of schizophrenics. *Psychological Medicine, S15,* 1–46.

Shupe, D. R., Cole, N. J., & Allison, R. B. (1966). II. Specific characteristics of work performance related to psychiatric diagnosis. *Hospital and Community Psychiatry, 17,* 48–50.

Smith, M. M. (1969). *The reliability of work evaluation ratings made after one day compared to ratings made after thirty days.* Materials Development Center, University of Wisconsin-Stout, Menonomie, WI.

Soloff A., & Bolton, B. F. (1969). The validity of the CJVS Scale of Employability for older clients in a vocational adjustment workshop. *Educational and Psychological Measurement, 29,* 993–998.

Stauffer, D. L. (1986). Predicting successful employment in the community for people with a history of chronic mental illness. *Occupational Therapy in Mental Health, 6,* 31–49.

Stein, L. I., & Test, M. A. (1980). An alternative to mental hospital treatment. I: Conceptual model, treatment program, and clinical evaluation. *Archives of General Psychiatry, 37,* 392–397.

Stoffelmayr, B. E., Hunter, J. E., & Dillavou, D. (1983). Premorbid functioning and outcome in schizophrenia: A cumulative analysis. *Journal of Consulting and Clinical Psychology, 51*, 338–352.

Strauss, J. S., & Carpenter, W. T. (1972). The prediction of outcome in schizophrenia. I. Characteristics of outcome. *Archives of General Psychiatry, 27*, 739–746.

Strauss, J. S., & Carpenter, W. T. (1974). Prediction of outcome in schizophrenia. II. Relationships between predictor and outcome variables. *Archives of General Psychiatry, 31*, 37–42.

Strauss, J. S., & Carpenter, W. T. (1977). Prediction of outcome in schizophrenia. III. Five-year outcomes and its predictors. *Archives of General Psychiatry, 34*, 159–163.

Strauss, J. S., Hafez, H., Lieberman, P., & Harding, C. M. (1985). The course of psychiatric disorder. III: Longitudinal principles. *American Journal of Psychiatry, 142*, 289–296.

Stroul, B. A. (1986). *Models of community support services: Approaches to helping persons with long-term mental illness.* Boston: Center for Psychiatric Rehabilitation, Boston University.

Sturm, I. E., & Lipton, H. (1967). Some social and vocational predictors of psychiatric hospitalization outcome. *Journal of Clinical Psychology, 23*, 301–307.

Summers, F. (1981). The post-acute functioning of the schizophrenic. *Journal of Clinical Psychology, 23*, 301–307.

Summers, F., & Hersh, S. (1983). Psychiatric chronicity and diagnosis. *Schizophrenia Bulletin, 9*, 122–133.

Tashjian, M. D., Hayward, B. J., Stoddard, S., & Kraus, L. (1989). *Best practice study of vocational rehabilitation services to severely mentally ill persons.* Washington, DC: Policy Study Associates.

Tessler, R. C., & Manderscheid, R. W. (1982). Factors affecting adjustment to community living. *Hospital and Community Psychiatry, 33*, 203–207.

Test, M. A. (1992). Training in community living. In R. P. Liberman (Ed.), *Handbook of psychiatric rehabilitation* (pp. 153–170). New York: Macmillan.

Test, M. A. (1995, October). *Impact of seven years of assertive community treatment.* Presentation at the American Psychiatric Association Institute on Psychiatric Services, Boston, MA.

Trotter, S., Minkoff, K., Harrison, K., & Hoops, J. (1988). Supported work: An innovative approach to the vocational rehabilitation of persons who are psychiatrically disabled. *Rehabilitation Psychology, 33*, 27–36.

Turkat, D., & Buzzell, V. (1982). Psychosocial rehabilitation: A process evaluation. *Hospital and Community Psychiatry, 33*, 848–850.

Turner, R. J. (1977). Jobs and schizophrenia. *Social Policy, 14*, 32–40.

Van Allen, R., & Loeber, R. (1972). Work assessment of psychiatric patients: A critical review of published scales. *Canadian Journal of Behavioral Science, 4*, 101–117.

Vitale, J. H., & Steinbach, M. (1965). The prevention of relapse of chronic mental patients. *International Journal of Social Psychiatry, 11*, 85–95.

Walker, L. G., Adamson, F. A., Alexander, D. A., & Stoffelmayr, B. E. (1973). A negative correlation between improved production in psychiatric rehabilitation and social behavior outside. *British Journal of Psychiatry, 123*, 409–412.

Wallner, R. J., & Clark, D. W. (1989). The functional assessment inventory and job tenure for persons with severe and persistent mental health problems. *Journal of Applied Rehabilitation Counseling, 20(4)*, 13–15.

Warner, R., & Polak, P. (1995). The economic advancement of the mentally ill in the community: 2. Economic choices and disincentives. *Community Mental Health Journal, 31*, 477–492.

Watts, F. N. (1978). A study of work behavior in a psychiatric rehabilitation unit. *British Journal of Social and Clinical Psychology, 17*, 85–92.

Watts, F. (1983). Employment. In F. N. Watts & D. H. Bennett (Eds.), *Theory and practice of psychiatric rehabilitation* (pp. 215–240). New York: Wiley.

Wesolowski, M. D. (1981). Self-directed job placement in rehabilitation: A comparative review. *Rehabilitation Counseling Bulletin, 25*, 80–89.

West, M. D., & Parent, W. S. (1995). Community and workplace supports for individuals with severe mental illness in supported employment. *Psychosocial Rehabilitation Journal, 18(4)*, 13–24.

Westermeyer, J. F. (1992). *Work and social disruption among schizophrenics, schizoaffectives, manics and depressives.* Unpublished paper.

Westermeyer, J., & Harrow, M. (1987). Factors associated with work impairments in schizophrenic and nonschizophrenic patients. In R. R. Grinker (Ed.), *Clinical research in schizophrenia: A multidimensional approach* (pp. 280–298). Springfield, IL: Charles C. Thomas.

Wilder, J. F., Levin, G., & Zwerling, I. (1966). A two-year follow-up evaluation of acute psychotic patients treated in a day hospital. *American Journal of Psychiatry, 122*, 1095–1111.

Wilson, R. J., & Rasch, J. D. (1982). The relationship of job characteristics to successful placements for psychiatrically handicapped individuals. *Journal of Applied Rehabilitation Counseling, 13*, 30–33.

Xiong, W., Philips, M. R., Hu, X., Wang, R., Dai, Q., Kleinman, J., & Kleinman, A. (1994). Family-based intervention for schizophrenic patients in China: A randomized controlled trial. *British Journal of Psychiatry, 165*, 239–247.

Zadny, J. J., & James, L. F. (1978). A survey of job-search patterns among state vocational-rehabilitation clients. *Rehabilitation Counseling Bulletin, 22*, 60–65.

CHAPTER 24

PHARMACOLOGICAL TREATMENTS IN SCHIZOPHRENIA

Eve C. Johnstone
Robert Sandler

HISTORICAL BACKGROUND

Since antiquity, the administration of medicines and the use of other physical techniques have been recommended for the treatment of psychiatric disorders (Adams, 1856), and the widespread use of physical treatments of psychiatric conditions over 300 years ago in this country has been clearly documented (MacDonald, 1981). The treatments that are now in general use have all become available in the last 50 years. They have been widely employed and extensively studied during that time.

There are two main reasons for the interest shown in these treatments. First, there is no doubt that physical treatments are effective in relieving and controlling psychiatric disease. Second, the pathological basis of most psychiatric disorders remains obscure, but the fact that methods of treatment which have measurable modes of action in physiological terms do have effects on psychiatric illnesses is strong evidence that these disorders must have a basis in physiological dysfunction and provides the possibility that understanding of the mode of action of ef-

fective treatment will give information about the biological basis of the condition that it relieves.

A number of terms have been used to describe the main group of drugs used to treat schizophrenia, principally *major tranquillizers, neuroleptics,* and the simple descriptive term *antipsychotics.* Included in this class are phenothiazines, butyrophenones, thioxanthenes, and others. Methylene blue, synthesized in the last century, is the first phenothiazine derivative for which effects in the central nervous system have been described. It possesses a mild hypnotic effect and prolongs the action of barbiturates (Konzett, 1938). The discovery of these properties led to further work on phenothiazines, and in the late 1940s promethazine was produced. Because of its strong sedative properties it was tried on patients with schizophrenia, but was found to be no more effective than barbiturates. It was used by a French surgeon, Henri Laborit, who was investigating preoperative medications, and he incorporated promethazine into his so-called lytic cocktail designed to reduce postoperative shock by reducing anxiety, decreasing the amount of general anaesthetic required, and speeding up postoperative recovery. In 1950 the chemist Paul Charpentier synthesized a new phenothiazine, chlorpromazine. This drug was less antihistaminic than promethazine but produced a greater reduction in autonomic activity. It was particularly suitable for incorporation in the preoperative lytic cocktail of Henri Laborit, who noted that it produced an unusual calm, unemotional indifference to the environment, which he described as "l'hibernation artificielle" (Laborit & Huguenard, 1951, 1952). This simple, direct clinical observation led him to suggest that it might be useful to psychiatrists. A suggestion from a surgeon was not initially particularly warmly received by psychiatrists, but they did try it, and in 1952 Jean Delay and Paul Deniker of L'Hopital St. Anne in Paris reported its use in schizophrenia at the Centennial of the Society Medico Psychologique (Delay & Deniker, 1952). Although Delay and Deniker believed that chlorpromazine was actively antipsychotic, this idea was not initially widely accepted. Over the next 10 years, however, several large-scale trials, particularly in the United States, demonstrated the antipsychotic and not merely sedative efficacy of antipsychotics such as chlorpromazine, thioridazine and haloperidol in the treatment of acute schizophrenia (Hollister, Traub, & Prusmack, 1960; National Institute of Mental Health, [NIMH], 1964).

MODE OF ACTION

A great deal of research effort has been devoted to understanding how new phenothiazines and related antipsychotics act on the brain. Initially their mode of action was obscure but a number of pieces of evidence pointed to the relevance of dopaminergic mechanisms. This evidence included their ability to induce parkinsonian features (Flugel, 1953), which the work of Hornykiewicz (1973) had related to depletion of dopamine from the basal ganglia, the selective effects of antipsychotic drugs on central dopamine turnover (Carlsson & Lindqvist, 1963), and the fact that the drugs are able to reverse amphetamine-induced abnormal behaviors that are dependent on central dopamine release (Randrup & Munkvad, 1965). A major advance in this field of study was the development of in vitro systems which assess the ability to block dopamine receptors. The first of these was the detection in striatal tissue of dopamine-sensitive adenylate cyclase (Kebabian, Petzold, & Greengard, 1972), and potency in inhibiting this system correlates well with the therapeutic effect of phenothiazines and thioxanthenes (Clement-Cormier, Kebabian, Petzold, & Greengard, 1974; Miller,

Horn, & Iversen, 1974), although butyrophenones did not fit this model. The adenylate cyclase linked receptor is referred to as the D_1 receptor. The second assay system depends on the use of potent butyrophenones such as spiperone as radioligands. Binding in this system is inhibited by all classes of typical antipsychotics, and the correlation with antipsychotic potency is high (Seeman, Lee, Chau-Wong, & Wong, 1976; Burt, Creese, & Snyder, 1977; Peroutka & Snyder, 1980). These receptors are known as D_2 receptors, and it is considered that they represent the key site of action of typical antipsychotic drugs. Much of the work on mode of action of antipsychotic agents is laboratory-based, but the facts that dopamine may act as the primary prolactin inhibiting factor (PIF) (Ben-Jonathan, Oliver, Weiner, Mical, & Porter, 1977) and that the administration of neuroleptics leads to a reproducible and dose-dependent elevation in individual subjects (Langer, Sachar, Gruen, & Halpern, 1977) have allowed clinical studies relating antipsychotic effect to a measure of dopaminergic blockade. There is, however, considerable interindividual variation in the magnitude of the response. Some studies have established a positive relationship between antipsychotic effect and prolactin elevation (Meltzer & Fang, 1976; Siris, van Kammen, & de Fraiters, 1978), but there are others in which such a relationship is not found (Kolakowska, Wiles, McNeilly, & Gelder, 1975; Johnstone et al., 1983). The relationship between prolactin level and antipsychotic effect is generally not sufficiently strong for prolactin level to be used as a predictor of clinical response in the individual case.

Apart from the studies relating antipsychotic properties to elevation of prolactin levels, most of the extensive work testing aspects of the dopamine hypothesis of antipsychotic effect was laboratory based (Miller et al., 1974; Seeman et al., 1976; Burt et al., 1977). Using the dopamine-sensitive adenylate cyclase assay, Miller et al. (1974) demonstrated that certain thioxanthene compounds exhibit stereo isomerism, the blockade of dopamine receptors being selectively associated with one of the two isomers. An example of this is flupenthixol, of which the standard oral preparation consists of a racemic mixture of two isomers, cis and trans. Only the cis-isomer possesses significant activity in blocking dopamine receptors (Miller et al., 1974; Enna, Bennett, Burt, Cresse, & Snyder, 1976).

Based on these observations, Johnstone, Crow, Frith, Carney, and Price (1978) conducted a study which addressed the dopamine hypothesis as it concerned living patients who suffered from schizophrenia. This entailed a clinical trial of the two isomers. The study blindly compared three groups of patients with acute schizophrenia, one receiving cis-flupenthixol, one trans-flupenthixol, and one inactive placebo. In this study all patients showed a significant ($p < 0.05$) tendency to improve, but this was significantly greater in the patients on cis-flupenthixol, the results in the placebo and trans flupenthixol groups being closely similar. The result is consistent with the hypothesis that antipsychotic efficacy is dependent on dopamine-receptor blockade and excludes various alternative mechanisms, but it does not rule out serotonin-receptor antagonism as being of at least some relevance (the cis-isomer being significantly more effective as a serotonin antagonist).

CLINICAL EFFICACY

Neuroleptic drugs were initially used in schizophrenia for the purpose of treating the positive symptoms of acute episodes. The efficacy of typical neuroleptics in this situation is well established (NIMH, 1964), but about 30% of patients show only limited improvement in acute treatment trials (Davis, 1976) and about 7% of cases do not appear to show any response at all, even to prolonged treatment (Tuma & May, 1979; Macmillan, Crow, Johnson, & Johnstone, 1986). Numerous studies have focused on the role of neuroleptics in reducing schizophrenic relapse. Benefits of both oral (Leff & Wing, 1971) and parenteral medication (Hirsch, Gaind, Rohde, Stevens, & Wing, 1973) have been demonstrated. In a review of 24 controlled studies, Davis (1975) concluded that the evidence for efficacy of maintenance neuroleptic treatment is overwhelming. Neuroleptics, however, do not abolish susceptibility to relapse. Hogarty, Goldberg, Schooler, and Ulrich (1974) followed up patients treated with neuroleptics or placebo for 2 years and found a substantial effect for medication. For patients on placebo, the relapse rate over 2 years was 80%; for those on neuroleptics, it was 48%. To exclude the possibility that this substantial relapse rate in patients prescribed neuroleptics was due to failure of compliance, Hogarty et al. (1979) conducted a later study comparing relapse rate in patients on oral neuroleptics with that in patients on depot neuroleptics, whose compliance was assured. There was no difference between the two groups, and the 2-year relapse rate remained substantial.

The productive symptoms of acute schizophrenic episodes are often very distressing, and the recurrent relapses present considerable problems for many sufferers. It is, however, not difficult to make the case that it is the slow steady development of the defect state characterized by negative symptoms of apathy, loss of will, and inability to respond emotionally or to relate to others which is the greatest disability suffered by schizophrenic patients. There is no drug treatment which can be reliably recommended as relieving negative symptoms in the same way that typical neuroleptics relieve positive symptoms. The effect of typical neuroleptics is uncertain. At present, controlled trials have yielded evidence that neuroleptic medications may improve (Goldberg, Klerman, & Cole, 1965; Meltzer, 1985), have no effect on (Johnstone et al., 1978; Angrist, Rotrossen, & Gershon, 1980), or exacerbate (Marder et al., 1984; Kane & Rifkin, 1985; Hogarty, McEvoy, & Munetz, 1988) negative symptoms. To some extent these inconsistencies may relate to the relative difficulties in rating negative symptoms (Johnstone, 1989), but it is fair to conclude as Pogue-Geile and Zubin (1988) have done on the basis of this evidence that negative symptoms are probably not overwhelmingly affected by current pharmacological methods, and that this is an area which requires further research.

DISADVANTAGES OF TYPICAL NEUROLEPTICS

Apart from the fact that the benefits of typical neuroleptics are limited in the above ways, the administration of these drugs is also associated with certain disadvantages. Neuroleptics affect a wide range of neurotransmitter and systemic organ systems. Adverse effects are therefore common, and indeed experienced in some degree by almost all patients. Failure to acknowledge this fact helps no one. Side effects may be simply classified as nonneurological or neurological.

Nonneurological Effects

The main effects are general, cardiovascular, or endocrine.

General

Most are associated with dryness of the mouth, blurring of vision, and urinary problems. It is likely that these are principally anticholinergic effects, although antiadrenergic actions may also be involved. Such mixed effects are probably the basis of the widespread sexual difficulties (usually anorgasmia in females and erectile impotence and ejaculatory dysfunction in males) that occur. Many patients do not like to complain about such effects and their frequency is generally underestimated.

Cardiovascular

Most antipsychotics increase heart rate, although this does not usually produce symptoms, but the significant hypotension which may occur, especially with low potency phenothiazines with marked anticholinergic effects (e.g., thioridazine) can cause distressing dizziness and unsteadiness, particularly in older patients. The question of sudden death occurring in patients on antipsychotics is a cause of appropriate concern. Such deaths are generally thought to result from ventricular arrhythmias (Committee on Safety of Medicines, 1990). Reports generally involve young, fit patients being treated with relatively high doses of antipsychotics for prominent positive symptoms. It is impossible to say what part autonomic activity as a direct consequence of profound mental state disturbances may play in such situations, and to what extent these deaths may appropriately be considered to be direct drug effects. These deaths are exceedingly rare, but the fact that they occur at all underlines the need to adjust drug doses carefully, avoid very high doses and sudden changes, and monitor the cardiovascular state in severely psychotic patients who may be receiving high doses of neuroleptics.

Endocrine

All typical antipsychotic agents produce a marked rise in serum prolactin as a result of tubero-infundibular dopaminergic blockade. This is usually clinically insignificant, but may be associated with galactorrhea and may contribute to the amenorrhea which occurs frequently in psychotic patients. High prolactin levels can contribute to false positive pregnancy tests. Patients on antipsychotics frequently complain of weight gain and this may be considerable. The causes are ill understood, but probably involve endocrine change including fluid retention and interference with hypothalamic 5-HT systems regulating appetite.

Allergic and toxic reactions may occur with antipsychotics as with any other drug. Such reactions include skin rashes, photosensitivity, and liver problems, which are usually benign.

The term *neuroleptic malignant syndrome* is used to describe the sudden development of hyperpyrexia, rigidity, confusion, and autonomic instability in patients on antipsychotics. Serum creatinine phosphokinase (CPK) lev-

els are often dramatically raised, and a fatal outcome or permanent neurological damage may ensue. The nature of this syndrome is uncertain. Similar states (including the fatal outcome) have certainly occurred in psychotic patients for over a century, well before antipsychotic drugs were introduced (Mann et al., 1986). Furthermore, critical assessment of published cases (Levinson & Simpson, 1986) suggests that known medical factors could possibly or definitely account for the hyperpyrexia and other features in more than half of the cases. Thus, although it is probable that antipsychotics are a major causative factor in some cases of this syndrome, this is not the only possibility, and other causes must not be overlooked. Neuroleptic malignant syndrome can be successfully treated without permanent sequelae (Levinson & Simpson, 1986). In its unequivocal form it is very rare and it is worth pointing out that many psychiatrists in a working lifetime see no cases of this condition or of sudden deaths in patients on antipsychotics.

Neurological Effects

The extrapyramidal side effects of antipsychotics are well established (Baldessarini et al., 1980) and are the most important adverse effects associated with their use. They are most simply classified as early (occurring within hours or days of introduction of drugs), intermediate (occurring within days or weeks to months), and late (occurring within months or years of introduction of drugs).

Early

The early effects are acute dystonias—involuntary movements which are sustained for a variable period at the point of maximum contraction (Owens, 1990). Any muscle group can be involved, the neck and tongue being most often affected. These symptoms are extremely distressing and may be regarded as hysterical by the ill informed. They can be rapidly relieved by the slow intravenous injection of an anticholinergic agent such as procyclidine 10 mg I.V.

Intermediate

The principal intermediate neurological side effect is parkinsonism, of which the core features are bradykinesia, rigidity, and tremor. Minor clinically insignificant degrees of this, such as reduced arm swing, can be elicited in many patients on antipsychotic agents but treatment with anti-parkinsonian drugs is best avoided unless clinically significant symptoms appear. Parkinsonism results from blockade of nigrostriatal dopamine receptors.

Late

The principal late extrapyramidal effect is tardive dyskinesia—a syndrome of chronic, spontaneous, involuntary movements of a complex nature which may occur in any muscle group but which most commonly affect oro-facial, neck, and upper limb muscles. The prevalence is probably around 20% (Jeste & Wyatt, 1981; Kane & Smith, 1982), but is higher if mild disorder is included. This condition is not easy to treat and may be irreversible. The pathophysiology is probably not fully understood, but it is conventionally considered that it involves supersensitivity of dopamine receptors resulting from dopaminergic blockade. Normal motor function may be seen as a result of a balance between cholinergic and dopaminergic systems in the striatum. Reduction in dopaminergic activity results in cholinergic dominance and hence motor poverty as in parkinsonism. Anticholinergics act to restore the balance. Supersensitivity is seen as tipping the balance on to the dopaminergic side, resulting in hyperkinesis. Hence tardive dyskinesia may be seen as the pathophysiological opposite of parkinsonism, with anticholinergics predisposing to and exacerbating hyperkinesis.

Other Problems

In addition to the clear-cut physical effects described above, many patients on antipsychotics complain of tiredness, and there is evidence that, at least to some extent, their impaired performance on some psychological tests may be related to medication rather than to severity of illness (Hoff et al., 1990). Furthermore, later follow-up of the patients who entered the Northwick Park First Episodes of Schizophrenia Study (Johnstone, Macmillan, Frith, Benne, & Crow, 1990) showed that in spite of significant associations between relapse and poor outcome, and between relapse and placebo medication in those patients with a shorter pretreatment duration of illness, those on placebo had a significantly better outcome with regard to the work that they were able to do. This finding suggests the disquieting conclusion that the benefits of antipsychotics in reducing relapse may exert a price in occupational terms. This is one of the relatively few placebo-controlled neuroleptic treatment trials which has directly considered a measure of social functioning other

than relapse of symptoms. Most such treatment trials are conducted on inpatients with severe positive symptoms over relatively short periods of time. In these circumstances measures of social function are not applicable. In general terms positive psychotic symptoms are associated with profound impairments of social function. While there are a few patients whose social presentation can be maintained and who can continue to work in the face of delusions or even hallucinations, this is very unusual, occurring in about 2 to 3% of cases (Johnstone, 1994). In general patients' social function is likely to improve with the reduction in their positive symptoms produced by neuroleptic drugs. However, social functioning is impaired by negative symptoms as well as by positive symptoms. Since negative symptoms are little affected by any pharmacological treatment, the resolution of positive symptoms is not always associated with as much improvement in social functioning as might be anticipated.

The tiredness of which patients complain on neuroleptics may reduce their activity generally, and it is usually advisable to chose a less sedative regime for patients who are in remission and wish to work or resume their domestic responsibilities. There is no consistent evidence to suggest that any mode of administration is better than any other as far as social functioning is concerned, and any apparent differences between different typical neuroleptics or different regimes are probably dosage effects. It is important to try to minimize all types of side effects in order to maximize patients' chances of achieving good social function. Sedative effects should be kept to a minimum. Untreated, drug-induced parkinsonism may have an adverse effect on the nonverbal aspects of social communication. While some patients do not seem to be greatly distressed by abnormalities of movement, this is no reason not to attempt to treat a problem which other patients admit to finding distressing and embarrassing.

ATYPICAL NEUROLEPTICS

The association of antipsychotic effects with extrapyramidal effects of the neuroleptic drugs led to the notion that action on the extrapyramidal system was a necessary effect of a drug that had antipsychotic properties. Both effects were thought to be mediated by blockade of the dopamine D_2 receptor, and in the 1970s and early 1980s the psychopharmacology of acute schizophrenia was dominated by this idea. Indeed, the efforts of the pharmaceutical industry were directed toward synthesizing more specific dopamine-blocking agents and eliminating other actions. One of the paradigms adopted in the preclinical testing of an antipsychotic drug was the assessment of the efficacy of the drug in producing motor effects in experimental animals that were comparable to extrapyramidal side effects in humans. However, some effective antipsychotic drugs, such as thioridazine, sulpiride, and clozapine, did not cause major extrapyramidal effects. As time progressed, it also became increasingly clear that dopamine D_2 receptor blockade was not necessarily associated with improvement in clinical features. Certainly in some studies there were patients who showed substantial rises in prolactin levels in response to antipsychotic drugs (reflecting blockade of dopamine D_2 receptors), but who remained severely psychotic (Johnstone et al., 1978; Johnstone et al., 1983).

Differing concepts of atypicality have been used. Antipsychotic efficacy without production of extrapyramidal symptoms becomes one of the defining characteristics (Johnstone, 1992). Kerwin (1994) defines the atypical antipsychotic as a drug that has a wide therapeutic ratio for its antipsychotic effects and extrapyramidal side effects such that the latter are not seen at clinically effective doses. Commonly accepted defining characteristics consist of criteria to be met in preclinical and clinical testing (Lieberman, 1993):

Pre-clinical Criteria

1. Efficacy in standard antipsychotic screening paradigms (e.g., antagonism of dopamine agonist induced stereotypies, conditioned avoidance response)
2. No induction of catalepsy
3. No up-regulation of dopamine D_2 receptors
4. No development of tolerance to increased dopamine turnover or depolarization block of A_9 dopamine neurones with chronic treatment

Clinical Criteria

1. Antipsychotic efficacy
2. No or markedly reduced induction of acute extrapyramidal side effects and tardive dyskinesia
3. No elevation of prolactin

These criteria have not always been rigorously applied in the reporting of new compounds, leading to some claims of atypicality when it is not warranted (Lieberman, 1993).

There are currently two atypical antipsychotic compounds in clinical usage, clozapine and risperidone.

Clozapine

Clozapine is a dibenzodiazepine first synthesised in 1960. It was introduced as an antipsychotic agent in the 1970s, and it was shown to be effective in schizophrenic patients, particularly the more severely ill (Fischer-Cornelssen & Ferner, 1976). The administration of this drug was, however, found to be associated with agranulocytosis in a small percentage of cases (Idänpään-Heikkilä, Alhava, & Olkinvora, 1977), and it was withdrawn from use in Great Britain, the United States, and much of continental Europe. The resurgence of interest in its use followed the study by Kane, Honigfeld, Singer, and Meltzer (1988) showing that clozapine had significantly greater benefits than a standard neuroleptic regime in treatment-resistant cases.

Pharmacology

Clozapine has effects on a number of neurotransmitter systems. It is not known whether clozapine's antipsychotic properties are due to its effect on a single neurotransmitter receptor type or a particular combination of receptors of different types. Clozapine is less potent than most other antipsychotic compounds in blocking dopamine D_2 receptors (Peroutka & Snyder, 1980; Lieberman, 1993). It has greater affinity for dopamine D_1 and D_4 receptor subtypes. In addition it is more potent than typical neuroleptics in blocking muscarinic acetylcholine receptors as well as histamine, serotonin (5-HT), and noradrenergic receptors (Lieberman, 1993). Hypotheses regarding clozapine's mechanism of antipsychotic action include:

1. The blockade of a combination of dopamine D_2 and $5\text{-}HT_2$ receptors
2. The blockade of dopamine D_1 and/or D_4 receptors

Evidence of Efficacy

Acute treatment studies. Early acute treatment studies of clozapine were of an open-label design and were often uncontrolled. These studies gave generally favorable results, including a relative lack of extrapyramidal side effects (Safferman, Lieberman, Kane, Szymanski, & Kinon, 1991). Subsequent double-blind studies showed that clozapine was comparable to other antipsychotic agents in patients with acute schizophrenia (Van Praag, Korf, & Dols, 1976; Shopsin, Klein, Aaronsom, & Collora, 1979).

Efficacy in treatment-refractory patients. Following initial reports of agranulocytosis associated with clozapine, clinical use was generally restricted (Idänpään-Heikkilä, Alhava, Olkinuora, & Palva, 1975; Idänpään-Heikkilä et al., 1977). However the drug continued to be used in Europe where experience suggested that deaths associated with clozapine-induced agranulocytosis could be prevented by weekly blood count monitoring (Safferman et al., 1991). The results of the early studies had indicated that clozapine may be of value in patients with schizophrenia who were refractory to other antipsychotic agents. In a double-blind controlled trial involving 268 patients who had failed to respond to typical antipsychotics, clozapine was compared to chlorpromazine over a 6-week period of treatment (Kane et al., 1988). Thirty percent of the clozapine-treated patients were judged to respond, compared to only 4% in those receiving chlorpromazine.

Long-term studies. After 2 years of follow-up of 96 patients designated as either treatment refractory (85%) or neuroleptic intolerant (15%), 62 were still on clozapine (Lindström, 1988). Forty-three percent were significantly improved and 38% moderately improved. In a study following 216 patients for 12 years, therapeutic benefit was reported in 30 to 50% (Povlsen, Noring, Fog, & Gerlach, 1985).

Effects on negative symptoms. Though only a limited number of studies have specifically addressed the efficacy of clozapine in relieving negative schizophrenic symptoms, the results show that clozapine is more efficacious than haloperidol in this regard (Opler, Albert, & Ramirez, 1994). Reduction of negative symptoms probably takes longer to achieve than reduction of positive symptoms and may only be fully appreciated with long-term follow-up studies.

Effects on tardive dyskinesia. Clozapine has a low propensity to cause tardive dyskinesia and some studies have shown a beneficial effect on preexisting tardive dyskinesia (Caine, Polinsky, Kartzinel, & Ebert, 1979; Small, Milstein, Marhenke, Hall, & Kellams, 1987; Lieberman, Saltz, Johns, Pollack, & Kane, 1989) though studies have been small and uncontrolled.

Clinical Usage

Indications. Clozapine should be reserved for severely ill schizophrenic patients who have failed to respond adequately to treatment with appropriate courses of standard antipsychotic drugs. The lack of response may be because of insufficient effectiveness or the inability to achieve an effective dose due to intolerable adverse effects of the typical antipsychotic drugs. At present there are no well-validated criteria for defining refractory illness although operational criteria (Kane et al., 1988) and a system of levels of responsivity/resistance have been used (May, Denker, Hubbard, Midha, & Liberman, 1988).

Dosage. Clozapine is commenced at a dose of 12.5 mg once or twice on the first day then 25 to 50 mg on the second day. The dose is slowly increased in steps of 25 to 50 mg. If well tolerated, the dose will be up to 300 mg after 14 to 21 days. If necessary the dose may be further increased in steps of 50 to 100 mg weekly. The usual antipsychotic dose is 200 to 450 mg per day taken in divided doses. The maximum daily dose is 900 mg per day (British National Formulary, 1994).

White Blood Cell (WBC) count monitoring. WBC and differential counts must be normal before treatment. Patients with a WBC count below 3,500/mm^3 should not be started on clozapine. WBC and differential counts must be monitored weekly for the first 18 weeks, then at least fortnightly. Clozapine must be stopped if the leukocyte count falls below 3000/mm^3 or absolute neutrophil count below 1500/mm^3 (British National Formulary, 1994).

Advantages

Clozapine has been shown to have greater efficacy than typical antipsychotics in the treatment of severely ill, neuroleptic-refractory schizophrenic patients. Clozapine's low propensity to cause extrapyramidal side effects makes it more tolerable in this regard than typical antipsychotics, a factor likely to improve compliance. Clozapine may be an effective treatment for tardive dyskinesia in some patients. The absence of sustained hyperprolactinaemia with secondary effects of oligomenorrhea or amenorrhea may enhance compliance.

Adverse Effects

Agranulocytosis. Agranulocytosis is the most serious adverse effect of clozapine. Sixteen cases of agranulocytosis (out of an estimated 2,500 to 3,200 patients) were reported in Finland in the first 6 months of 1975 (Idänpään-Keikkilä et al., 1975; 1977; Amsler, Leerenhovi, Barth, Harjula, & Vuopio, 1977). This led to the withdrawal of clozapine from the market in some countries and its restriction in others to use in treatment-refractory patients in whom regular WBC monitoring was performed. The greatest risk of clozapine-induced agranulocytosis appears to be between 4 and 18 weeks of starting treatment (Krupp & Barnes, 1992) with a rate of agranulocytosis in patients treated for 1 year of 2%. A more recent study of 11,555 patients treated with clozapine determined a 0.8% cumulative incidence of agranulocytosis after one year of treatment (Alvir, Lieberman, Safferman, Schwimmer, & Schaaf, 1993). Mortality rate is significantly reduced if there is regular WBC monitoring and if clozapine is immediately withdrawn when agranulocytosis occurs. Any fever or sign of infection is an indication for a WBC, especially within the first 18 weeks of treatment. Drugs that have a high likelihood of causing agranulocytosis or leukopenia, such as co-trimoxazole or carbamazepine, should not be administered with clozapine.

Seizures. Clozapine causes EEG changes, predisposing to seizures in a dose-related manner with a 5% incidence of seizures with doses over 600 mg per day (Safferman et al., 1991). Combination with anticonvulsants can significantly alter the blood levels of each drug, and carbamazepine should be avoided because of the risk of agranulocytosis.

Sedation. Sedation is a common side effect with a reported incidence of 39% (Safferman et al., 1991). It is most prominent early in treatment but tolerance develops over the first few days or weeks (Lindström, 1988; Lieberman, Kane, & Johns, 1989)

Other Central Nervous System (CNS) effects. Other effects reported include dizziness (19%), syncope (6%), and confusion or delirium (3%) (Safferman et al., 1991).

Hypersalivation. Sialorrhea occurs early in the course of treatment in 31% of patients (Safferman et al., 1991). Though some tolerance occurs, the effect is often persistent.

Cardiovascular effects. The most frequent cardiovascular side effects are tachycardia (25%) and hypotension (9%) (Safferman et al., 1991). The tachycardia often persists until the dose is reduced though tolerance to hypotension usually develops with time. ECG changes are comparable to those seen with other antipsychotics.

Gastrointestinal effects. The most common gastrointestinal side effect is constipation (14%).

Genitourinary effects. Reported effects include enuresis, frequency, urgency, hesitancy, urinary retention, and impotence.

Thermoregulation. Mild hypothermia is observed in the majority of patients on clozapine (87%). Benign hyperthermia occurs in 5%. It is a mild elevation of temperature which usually occurs in the first few weeks of treatment and resolves over a few days. More severe elevation of temperature may be indicative of drug fever, intercurrent infection, infection secondary to agranulocytosis, dehydration, heat stroke, and possible neuroleptic malignant syndrome.

Weight gain. Weight gain has been reported in 4% of patients on clozapine (Polvsen et al., 1985). This propensity may be more than typical antipsychotics (Lieberman, Kane, et al., 1989).

Extrapyramidal system. A low incidence of acute extrapyramidal side effects is reported and no confirmed cases of tardive dyskinesia have been attributed to clozapine (Safferman et al., 1991).

Neuroleptic malignant syndrome. There have been no reports of neuroleptic malignant syndrome occurring when clozapine was the sole agent, though it has been reported when clozapine has been combined with lithium or carbamazepine (Safferman et al., 1991).

Most side effects can be minimized by a gradual dose titration and by using the lowest effective dose. The requirement for weekly venipuncture to check the WBC may deter some patients from its use.

Risperidone

Risperidone is an antipsychotic compound first tested clinically in the late 1980s. It has a limited propensity to cause extrapyramidal side effects.

Pharmacology

Risperidone is a benzisoxazole derivative that combines potent $5HT_2$ antagonism with dopamine D_2 antagonism. The development of a compound with this profile of pharmacological activity was based on the observation that the addition of a $5HT_2$ antagonist to the regimen of schizophrenic patients treated with haloperidol improved the negative symptoms, ameliorated depression and anxiety, and reduced movement disorder (Livingston, 1994). Risperidone also has affinity for α_1 and α_2 noradrenergic receptors and is antihistaminic. Although these actions are associated with side effects, they are not thought to be relevant to the antipsychotic actions of the compound.

Evidence of Efficacy

Several double-blind studies have demonstrated the antipsychotic efficacy of risperidone (Chouinard & Arnott, 1993; Marder & Meibach, 1994). Some studies have also reported an improvement in negative symptoms (Marder & Meibach 1994). There is as yet insufficient evidence to indicate whether risperidone is effective in treatment-refractory or poorly responsive cases, though early studies are encouraging (Remington, 1993).

Clinical Usage

At present the indications for risperidone are prominent negative symptoms or intolerable movement disorder (Livingston, 1994). Its therapeutic efficacy and limited extrapyramidal side-effect profile suggest that it may be used as a first-line treatment for schizophrenia in the future, but its high cost precludes this at present.

Treatment should be initiated gradually to avoid postural hypotension—1 mg twice daily on day one, 2 mg twice daily on day two, and 3 mg twice daily on day three. The 6 mg per day dose should be maintained for several weeks to await an antipsychotic response (Livingston, 1994). Thereafter the dose may be increased gradually if required but initial studies have tended to find that 6 mg per day is an optimal dose (Chouinard & Arnott, 1993; Marder & Meibach, 1994). There is likely to be little overall clinical advantage above 10 mg per day.

Advantages

The major advantages of risperidone are its low extrapyramidal side-effect profile and its possible beneficial effect in the treatment of negative symptoms.

Limitations

Risperidone produces postural hypotension due to its α_1 adrenergic blocking effect, but the effect is mild. An important side effect is weight gain. As with other dopamine D_2 blocking drugs, risperidone causes a dose-related rise in prolactin which may result in amenorrhea, galactorrhea, gynaecomastia, and decreased libido (Livingston, 1994).

DOSE REGIMES AND COMPLIANCE

As noted above, it is with regard to the control of the florid symptoms of acute schizophrenic episodes and as prophylactic agents against relapse that the value of typical neuroleptics in the treatment of schizophrenia is best established. Their place in the management of negative symptoms is much less certain. Their effects on social functioning depend on a balance among the benefits of their effect in reducing positive symptoms, the disability from negative symptoms which may become more evident once the positive symptoms have abated, and the possibility that drug-induced tiredness and lethargy may enhance social difficulties.

The dose regimes appropriate for acute episodes depend in part on the presence or absence of behavioral disturbance. In all cases the need is to provide a drug regime which the patient can tolerate without distress, which controls nonspecific symptoms such has anxiety and sleeplessness, and which is flexible enough to take account of the fact that acute psychotic states fluctuate a good deal. In this situation depot medication does not really have the flexibility required. Where the patient is behaviorally disturbed or where there is a possibility of behavioral disturbance, a low-potency drug which is relatively sedative is a wise choice—chlorpromazine or thioridazine in a dose of 300 to 600 mg per day, increasing to 800 mg if required is appropriate. Equivalent doses of sulpiride are equally suitable. Dosage adjustment every 1 to 2 days, taking account of amount of distress, level of sedation, and the presence of side effects is likely to be required. It will be about 14 days before antipsychotic effects become apparent in the average case (Johnstone et al., 1978), and improvements before this are likely to be nonspecific or due to sedation. It is wise to have an initial regime of perhaps chlorpromazine 75 mg B.D. and 200 mg at night, with additional dosages of 50 mg chlorpromazine to be given up to four times per day at the nurse's discretion. The requirement for this will provide a guide to changes in the baseline regime.

In patients where behavioral disturbance is not an issue, the sedative effects of low-potency neuroleptics are not helpful, and such patients will be better pleased with a high-potency drug such as trifluoperazine or haloperidol.

While all typical neuroleptics share the property of D_2 receptor blockade, their additional actions relating to anticholinergic effects, alpha-adrenergic blockade, and sedation vary a great deal, and the profile of side effects suffered by individual patients can be a useful guide to choice of neuroleptic. If patients develop dystonic symptoms or marked parkinsonian features in an acute episode, anticholinergic drugs should be prescribed, but they should not be given routinely. While benzodiazepines do not have antipsychotic effects, they can be very valuable in relieving anxiety and can aid sedative neuroleptics in providing adequate sleep. On an intravenous basis they provide rapid control of acute behavioral disturbance.

It is important to appreciate the time that will be required to stabilize an acute psychotic episode. Patients are generally improving after 2 to 3 weeks and stabilized within 4 to 6 weeks, but there are often fluctuations on the road to recovery, and it is important not to reduce the regime required to control the symptoms too quickly. In the 1970s there was a fashion for rapid neuroleptization. This involved frequent dosages (sometimes hourly) and very high intake within the first few days of hospitalization. Sometimes doses were very high (e.g., 3 grams chlorpromazine/day: haloperidol 160 mg/day), but controlled studies did not demonstrate any benefits for these rapid high-dose regimes (Neborsky, Janowsky, Munson, & Depry, 1981). Once the patient has achieved stability on his or her acute treatment regime and the florid symptoms are under control, it is appropriate to begin to consider changes to a maintenance regime. Once he/she is more well, the patient will have less tolerance of relatively high neuroleptic doses, and the sedation which was a benefit when the illness was acute and distressing will cause problems for a patient who is trying to regain his or her capacity to concentrate and organize day-to-day activities. The aim will be to achieve a simple plan with the minimum necessary number of drugs and a once or twice daily regime if possible. It is worth thinking about changing to depot, injectable neuroleptics at this stage, and certainly if compliance is known to be a problem this is advisable. It is probably wise to maintain neuroleptics for longer than 6 to 12 months and unless their illness has been very difficult to treat, a planned withdrawal of neuroleptics at a time when few life events would be anticipated and when a minor relapse would be less troublesome than it might be at some other times, is appropriate. In patients who have had previous episodes, evidence concerning the value of maintenance medication should be discussed with them.

There is evidence (Hoge et al., 1990) that poor compliance in patients with schizophrenia is often associated with a lack of understanding of the nature of the illness and of the purpose of maintenance medication, and that improved understanding is associated with better compliance. Nevertheless it is often difficult to persuade patients to continue on neuroleptics, and alternative strategies of maintenance medication have received attention. These principally consist of (a) continuous low-dose regimes and (b) targeted or intermittent regimes. A number of low dose versus standard dose studies have been conducted (Kane et al., 1983; Marder et al., 1987; Johnson, Ludlow, Street, & Taylor, 1987; Hogarty et al., 1988). Essentially all showed that the low dose was associated with more relapses and more minor exacerbations but dose reduction was also associated with decreased extrapyramidal side effects, fewer symptoms of anxiety, and fewer negative symptoms. For patients who could tolerate dose reduction there were benefits, but overall there was an increased risk of psychotic exacerbation. The above studies continued for at least a year, involved depot medication to ensure compliance and did not include a placebo group. A brief early study by Caffey, Diamond, and Frank (1964) compared standard dose, low dose, and placebo. They found 5%, 15%, and 45% relapse rates in these groups over a 4-month period, suggesting the possibility that the low dose had some advantage over placebo.

The principle of targeted or intermittent treatment is to withdraw neuroleptics and to monitor the patient closely for prodromal symptoms of psychosis. When these are evident, antipsychotics are reintroduced. Such regimes have been compared with continuous maintenance treatment by Carpenter et al. (1990), Jolley, Hirsch, McRink, and Manchanda (1989), Jolley, Hirsch, and Morrison (1990), Herz et al., (1991). The targeted treatment program was shown to be feasible in all studies, but the likelihood of relapse was greater, and this did not seem to be offset by substantial improvements in functioning. Such regimes are superior to intervention only when a relapse has occurred and may be worthwhile in patients who are unwilling to take maintenance antipsychotics but will accept monitoring when medication-free (Schooler, 1993).

One of the difficulties of advocating prophylactic maintenance antipsychotic medication for patients with schizophrenia is that while the benefits of this for groups of patients are undoubted (Davis, 1975), there are some patients who will remain well without such treatment (Crow, Macmillan, Johnson, & Johnstone, 1986). Unfortunately it is difficult to identify these individuals. It was considered that patients who recovered from a functional psychotic illness (principally schizophrenic in nature) on placebo medication (Johnstone, Crow, Frith, & Owens, 1988) might well be those who would not require antipsychotics on a maintenance basis. Follow-up over 2 years did not support this hypothesis (Johnstone, Crow, Owens, & Frith, 1991), and it was concluded that recovery from an acute episode of psychosis did not identify a group of patients who could be predicted to do well without maintenance antipsychotics.

ADJUNCTIVE MEDICATION

Antipsychotic agents are the cornerstone of psychopharmacological management of schizophrenia, and their continued use unquestionably reduces the risk of psychotic relapse. Patients are not, however, entirely well and in many substantial functional impairment and subjective distress persist even though florid psychosis is controlled. The addition of other medications designed to relieve some aspect of symptomatology associated with schizophrenia or its treatment can be valuable. The main groups of such adjunctive medication are

- anti-parkinsonian agents
- benzodiazepines
- propranolol
- antidepressants
- mood stabilizers

Anti-parkinsonian Agents

Anticholinergics

The addition of anti-parkinsonian medication during acute episodes will reduce the frequency of dystonic reactions and parkinsonian symptoms. Avoidance of serious symptoms of this kind will aid future compliance and the value of this adjunctive medication is generally recognized (Lavin & Rifkin, 1991). The value of additional anticholinergics to extended maintenance antipsychotic programs is less well established, and it has been difficult to achieve adequate methodology in the prolonged studies that would be required to evaluate this issue appropriately (Siris, 1993). The dry mouth and blurred vision associated with anticholinergic agents can be irritating for patients, but the memory problems associated with anticholinergic use in some patients (Fayen, Goldman, & Maulthrop, 1988) can add to the functional impairments that they

have. There are case reports (Wells et al., 1989) of abuse of anticholinergic antiparkinsonian agents. The prevalence of this remains unclear, but it is an issue which should be borne in mind. During long-term maintenance treatment it is easy to miss neuroleptic-induced akinesia, which can resemble the features of a schizophrenic defect state (Rifkin, Quitlin, & Klein, 1975). If there is any doubt, a full test dose trial of anticholinergic anti-parkinsonian medication should be tried.

There is evidence that anticholinergics may have an adverse effect on positive schizophrenic symptoms (Johnstone et al., 1983; Tandon, DeQuardo, Goodson, Mann, & Greden, 1992) though they may also reduce negative symptoms (Tandon et al., 1992). Many antipsychotic and antidepressant drugs have pronounced anticholinergic properties and combinations of these drugs together with an anticholinergic drug may lead to anticholinergic toxicity. There is a danger that this may be interpreted as a worsening of psychotic symptoms leading to the use of increasing doses of the neuroleptic. The combination of anticholinergics with drugs such as clozapine, which is a potent anticholinergic, may have the potential to precipitate the neuroleptic malignant syndrome (Nemecek, Rastogi-Cruz, & Csernansky, 1993).

Dopamine Agonists

Dopamine agonists such as L-dopa and bromocriptine may induce psychotic symptoms and are not used as anti-parkinsonian agents in patients with schizophrenia. However, current theories that propose a cortical dopamine deficiency in schizophrenia have led to pilot studies of these agents in combination with antipsychotics. Though the studies are small, there is evidence of reduction of positive symptoms (Wolf, Diener, Lajeunesse, & Shirqui, 1992; Owens, Harrison-Read, & Johnstone, 1994) and improvement in cognitive function (de Beaurepaire, de Beaurepaire, Cleau, & Bornstein, 1993).

Benzodiazepines

The use of benzodiazepines for sedation will allow very high doses of antipsychotics to be avoided. In addition benzodiazepines may be useful in the management of antipsychotic-induced akathisia (Fleischhacker, Roth, & Kane, 1990). These benefits have to be set against the known problems of long-term benzodiazepine use, and doses should be kept to the minimum necessary and sustained use avoided if possible.

Propranolol

Propranolol is sometimes advocated as an adjunct to conventional neuroleptic agents to enhance antipsychotic effect in schizophrenics who are not responding well (Lader, 1988), but the value of this treatment is controversial (Siris, 1993). Propranolol has been shown to be valuable in the management of akathisia (Adler et al., 1986). This symptom can be very distressing and it is often difficult to relieve.

Antidepressants

The occurrence of depressive symptoms in schizophrenic patients when they are not actively psychotic has been increasingly reported (McGlashan & Carpenter, 1976; Hirsch et al., 1989; Siris, 1991). The value of adjunctive antidepressants has been clearly demonstrated (Siris, Morgan, Fagerstrom, Rifkin, & Cooper, 1987), and a recent trial has shown that maintenance imipramine treatment is of benefit in patients who have shown a good initial response to tricyclics (Siris, Bermanzohn, Mason, & Shuwall, 1994).

Mood Stabilizers

Some investigations have shown a benefit in terms of control of psychotic symptoms for the addition of lithium to maintenance regimes (Small, Kellams, Milstein, & Moore, 1975; Delva & Letemendia, 1982), although not all studies have shown positive results (Johnstone et al., 1991).

Carbamazepine has not been shown to be of value as a maintenance treatment for schizophrenia (Carpenter et al., 1991), but in the acute situation its addition to neuroleptic regimes has sometimes been shown to be helpful (Christison, Kirch, & Wyatt, 1991), especially in disturbed, excited patients (Klein, Bental, Lerer, & Belmaker, 1984).

CONCLUSION

Despite the limitations in understanding and the problems associated with antipsychotic drugs, pharmacological treatments have had a major impact on the management of patients with schizophrenia. Alleviation of symptoms by pharmacological means has paved the way for the discharge of patients who were previously managed by long-term custodial care and catalysed the movement toward community care. This has in turn presented the challenge of understanding social functioning in patients with schizophrenia and how best to deal with disabilities and problems that are less amenable to pharmacological treatment.

At the present time new antipsychotic drugs are being introduced at a rapid rate. Since this chapter was written a number of additional antipsychotic agents have been introduced. These may all be classed as atypical drugs. They include sertindole, olanzapine, zotepine, quetiapine (Fleischhacker & Hummer, 1997) and ziprasidone (Tamminga & Lahti, 1996). In general they all have an affinity for a range of receptors including dopamine D_2 and $5HT_{2a}$ receptors. The clinical potential of these drugs is yet to be fully established. Their introduction does not materially change the situation described in the chapter.

REFERENCES

Adams, F. (Ed. and Trans.). (1856). *Aretaeus, the Cappadocian. The extant works.* Boston: Mulford House.

Adler, L., Angrist, B., Peselow, E., Corwin, J., Maslansky, R., & Rotrosen, J. (1986). A controlled assessment of propranolol in the treatment of neuroleptic induced akathisia. *British Journal of Psychiatry, 149,* 42–45.

Alvir, J. J., Lieberman, J. A., Safferman, A. Z., Schwimmer, J. L., & Schaaf, J. A. (1993), Clozapine induced agranulocytosis. Incidence and risk factors in the United States. *New England Journal of Medicine, 329,* 162–167.

Amsler, H., Leerenhovi, L., Barth, E., Harjula, K., & Vuopio, P. (1977). Agranulocytosis in patients treated with clozapine: A study of the Finnish epidemic. *Acta Psychiatrica Scandinavica, 56,* 241–248.

Angrist, B., Rotrosen, J., & Gershon, S. (1980). Differential effects of amphetamine and neuroleptics on negative vs. positive symptoms in schizophrenia. *Psychopharmacology, 72,* 17–19.

Baldessarini, R. J., Cole, J. O., Davis, J. M., Gardos, G., Preskom, S. H., Simpson, G. M., & Tansy, D. (1980). *Tardive dyskinesia: A task force report.* Washington, DC: American Psychiatric Press.

Ben-Jonathan, N., Oliver, C., Weiner, H. J., Mical, R. S., & Porter, J. C. (1977). Dopamine in hypophyseal portal plasma of the rat during the oestrus cycle and throughout pregnancy. *Endocrinology, 100,* 452–458.

British National Formulary No. 28. (1994). London: British Medical Association.

Burt, D. R., Creese, I., & Snyder, S. H. (1977). Antischizophrenic drugs: Chronic treatment elevates dopamine receptor binding in the brain. *Science, 196,* 326–328.

Caffey, E. M., Diamond, L. S., & Frank, T. V. (1964). Discontinuation or reduction of chemotherapy in chronic schizophrenics. *Journal of Chronic Disease, 17,* 347–358.

Caine, E. D., Polinsky, R. J., Kartzinel, R., & Ebert, M. H. (1979). The trial use of clozapine for abnormal involuntary movement disorders. *American Journal of Psychiatry, 136,* 317–320.

Carlsson, A., & Lindqvist, M. (1963). Effect of chlorpromazine and haloperidol on formation of 3-methoxy-tyramine and normetanephrine in mouse brain. *Acta Pharamcologica Toxicologica, 20,* 140–144.

Carpenter, W. T., Harlon, T. E., Heinrichs, D. W., Summerfelt, A. T., Kirkpatrick, B., Levine, J., & Buchanan, R. W. (1990). Continuous vs. targeted medication in schizophrenic outpatients: Outcome results. *American Journal of Psychiatry, 147,* 1138–1148.

Carpenter, W. T., Kurz, R., Kirkpatrick, B., Hanlon, T. E., Summerfelt, A. T., Buchanan, R. W., Waltrip, R. W., & Breier, A. (1991). Carbamazepine maintenance treatment in outpatient schizophrenics. *Archives of General Psychiatry, 48,* 69–72.

Chouinard, G., & Arnott, W. (1993). Clinical review of risperidone. *Canadian Journal of Psychiatry, 38* (Suppl. 3), S89-S95.

Christison, G. W., Kirch, D. G., & Wyatt, R. J. (1991). When symptoms persist: Choosing among alternative somatic treatments for schizophrenia. *Schizophrenia Bulletin, 17,* 217–240.

Clement-Cormier, Y. C., Kebabian, J. W., Petzold, G. L., & Greengard, P. (1974). Dopamine sensitive adenylate cyclase in mammalian brain: A possible site of action of antipsychotic drugs. *Proceedings of the National Academy of Sciences, U.S.A., 71,* 1113–1117.

Committee on the Safety of Medicines (1990). Cardiotoxic effects of pimozide. *Current Problems in Pharmacovigilance, 29,* Medicinea Control Agency.

Crow, T. J., Macmillan, J. F., Johnson, A. L., & Johnstone, E. C. (1986). The Northwick Park study of first episodes of schizophrenia. II. A randomized controlled trial of prophylactic neuroleptic treatment. *British Journal of Psychiatry, 148,* 120–127.

Davis, J. M. (1975). Overview: Maintenance therapy in psychiatry I. Schizophrenia. *American Journal of Psychiatry, 132,* 1237–1245.

Davis, J. M. (1976). Recent developments in the drug treatment of schizophrenia. *American Journal of Psychiatry, 133,* 208–214.

de Beaurepaire, C., de Beaurepaire, R., Cleau, M., & Bornstein, P. (1993). Bromocriptine improves digit symbol substitution test scores in neuroleptictreated chronic schizophrenic patients. *European Psychiatry, 8,* 89–93.

Delay, J., & Deniker, P. (1952). Le traitment des psychoses par une methode neurolyptique derive de l'hibernotherapie. In P. Cossa (Ed.), *Neurologistes de France, Paris & Luxembourg* (pp. 497–502). Masson et cie, Editeurs, Libraires de L'Academie de medecine.

Delva, J. J., & Letemendia, F. J. J. (1982). Lithium treatment in schizophrenia and schizoaffective psychosis. *British Journal of Psychiatry, 141,* 387–400.

Enna, S. J., Bennett, J. P., Burt, D. R., Cresse, I., & Snyder, S. H. (1976). Stereospecificity of interaction of neuroleptic drugs with neurotransmitters and correlation with clinical potency. *Nature (London), 263,* 338–347.

Fayen, M., Goldman, M. B., & Moulthrop, M. A. (1988). Differential memory function with dopaminergic and cholinergic treatment of drug-induced extrapyramidal effects. *American Journal of Psychiatry, 145,* 483–486.

Fischer-Cornelssen, K. A., & Ferner, U. J. (1976). An example of European multicenter trials: Multispecial analysis of clozapine. *Psychopharmacology Bulletin, 12,* 34–39.

Fleischhacker, W. W., Roth, S. D., & Kane, J. M. (1990). The pharmacologic treatment of neuroleptic induced akathisia. *Journal of Clinical Psychopharmacology, 10,* 12–15.

Fleischhacken, W. W., & Hummer, M. (1997). Drug treatments of schizophrenia in the 1990s. *Drugs, 53,* 915–929.

Flugel, F. (1953). Therapeutique par medication neuroleptique obtenue en realisant systematiquement des etats parkinsoniformes. *L'Encephale, 45,* 1090–1092.

Goldberg, S. C., Klerman, G. L., & Cole, J. O. (1965). Changes in schizophrenic psychopathology and ward behavior as a function of phenothiazine treatment. *British Journal of Psychiatry, 111,* 120–133.

Herz, M. I., Glazer, W. M., Mosteret, M. A., Sheard, M. A., Szymanski, H. V., Hafez, H., Mirza, M., & Vana, J. (1991). Intermittent vs. maintenance medication in schizophrenia. *Archives of General Psychiatry, 48,* 333–339.

Hirsch, S. R., Gaind, R., Rohde, P. D., Stevens, B. C., & Wing, J. K. (1973). Outpatient maintenance of chronic schizophrenic patients with long acting fluphenazine: Double blind placebo trial. *British Medical Journal, 1,* 633–637.

Hirsch, S. R., Jolley, A. G., Barnes, T. R. E., Liddle, P. F., Curson, D. A., Patel, A., York, A., Bercu, S., & Patel, M., (1989). Dysphoric and depressive symptoms in chronic schizophrenia. *Schizophrenia Research, 2,* 259–264.

Hoff, A. L., Shukla, S., Aronson, T., Cook, B., Ollo, C., Baruch, S., Jandorf, L., & Schwartz, J. (1990). Failure to differentiate bipolar disorder from schizophrenia on measures of neuropsychological function. *Schizophrenia Research, 3,* 253–360.

Hogarty, G. E., Goldberg, S. C., Schooler, S., & Ulrich, R. F. (1974). Collaborative study group. Drugs and Sociotherapy in the aftercare of schizophrenic patients. II. Two year relapse rates. *Archives of General Psychiatry, 31,* 603–608.

Hogarty, G. E., McEvoy, J. P., & Munetz, M., (1988). Dose of fluphenazine, familial expressed emotion and outcome in schizophrenia. *Archives of General Psychiatry, 45,* 797–805.

Hogarty, G. E., Schooler, N. R., Ulrich, T., Mussare, F., Ferro, P., & Herron, E. (1979). Fluphenazine and social therapy in the aftercare of schizophrenic patients. *Archives of General Psychiatry, 36,* 1283–1294.

Hoge, S. K., Appelbaum, P. S., Lawlor, T., Beck, J. C., Litman, R., Greer, A., Gutheil, T. G., & Kaplan, E., (1990). A prospective multicenter study of patients' refusal of antipsychotic medication. *Archives of General Psychiatry, 47,* 949–956.

Hollister, L. E., Traub, L., & Prusmack, J. J., (1960). Use of thioridazine for intensive treatment of schizophrenics refractory to other tranquillizing drugs. *Journal of Neuropsychiatry, 1,* 200–204.

Hornykiewicz, O., (1973). Dopamine in the basal ganglia. Its role and therapeutic implications. *British Medical Bulletin, 29*, 172–178.

Idänpään-Heikkilä, J., Alhava, E., & Olkinvora, M. (1977). Agranulocytosis during treatment with clozapine. *European Journal of Clinical Pharmacology, 11*, 193–198.

Idänpään-Heikkilä, J., Alhava, E., Olkinuora, M., & Palva, I. P. (1975). Clozapine and agranulocytosis. *Lancet, ii*, 611.

Jeste, D. V., & Wyatt, R. J. (1981). Changing epidemiology of tardive dyskinesia: An overview. *American Journal of Psychiatry, 138*, 297–309.

Johnson, D. A. W., Ludlow, J. M., Street, K., & Taylor, R. D. W. (1987). Double-blind comparison of half dose and standard flupenthixol decanoate in the maintenance treatment of stabilized outpatients with schizophrenia. *British Journal of Psychiatry, 151*, 634–638.

Johnstone, E. C. (1989). The assessment of negative and positive features in schizophrenia. *British Journal of Psychiatry, 155* (Suppl. 7), 41–44.

Johnstone, E. C., (1992). Atypical treatments for schizophrenia. *Lancet, 339*, 276–277.

Johnstone, E. C., (1994). *Searching for the causes of schizophrenia.* Oxford: Oxford University Press.

Johnstone, E. C., Crow, T. J., Ferrier, I. N., Frith, C. D., Owens, D. G. C., Bourne, R. C., & Gamble, S. J. (1983). Adverse effects of anticholinergic medication on positive schizophrenic symptoms. *Psychological Medicine, 13*, 513–527.

Johnstone, E. C., Crow, T. J., Frith, C. D., Carney, M. W. P., & Price, J. S., (1978). Mechanism of the antipsychotic effect in the treatment of acute schizophrenia. *Lancet, i*, 848–851.

Johnstone, E. C., Crow, T. J., Frith, C. D., & Owens, D. G. C. (1988). The Northwick Park 'functional' psychosis study: Diagnosis and treatment response. *Lancet, ii*, 119–126.

Johnstone, E. C., Crow, T. J., Owens, D. G. C., & Frith, C. D., (1991). The Northwick Park 'functional' psychosis study. Phase 2: Maintenance treatment. *Journal of Psychopharmacology, 5*, 388–395.

Johnstone, E. C., Macmillan, J. F., Frith, C. D., Benn, D. K., & Crow, T. J., (1990). Further investigation of the predictors of outcome following first schizophrenic episodes. *British Journal of Psychiatry, 157*, 182–189.

Jolley, A. G., Hirsch, S. R., McRink, A., & Manchanda, R. (1989). Trial of brief intermittent prophylaxis for selected schizophrenic outpatients: Clinical outcome at one year. *British Medical Journal, 298*, 985–990.

Jolley, A. G., Hirsch, S. R., & Morrison, E. (1990). Trial of brief intermittent neuroleptic prophylaxis for selected schizophrenic outpatients—Clinical and social outcome. *British Medical Journal, 301*, 837–842.

Kane, J., Honigfeld, G., Singer, J., & Meltzer, H. (1988). Clozapine for the treatment-resistant schizophrenic: A double blind comparison versus chlorpromazine/benztropine. *Archives of General Psychiatry, 45*, 789–796.

Kane, J. M., & Rifkin, A. (1985). High dose vs. low dose strate-

gies in the treatment of schizophrenia. *Psychopharmacology Bulletin, 21*, 533.

Kane, J. M., Rifkin, A., Woerner, M., Reardon, G., Sarantakos, S., Schiebel, D., & Ramos-Lokenzi, J. (1983). Low-dose neuroleptic treatment of outpatient schizophrenics. *Archives of General Psychiatry, 40*, 893–896.

Kane, J. M., & Smith, J. M., (1982). Tardive dyskinesia: Prevalence and risk factors 1959–1979. *Archives of General Psychiatry, 39*, 473–481.

Kebabian, J. W., Petzold, G. L., & Greengard, P. (1972). Dopamine-sensitive adenylate cyclase in caudate nucleus and its similarity to the dopamine receptor. *Proceedings of the National Academy of Sciences, U.S.A., 79*, 2145–2149.

Kerwin, R. W. (1994). The new atypical antipsychotics. A lack of extrapyramidal side effects and new routes in schizophrenia research. *British Journal of Psychiatry, 164*, 141–148.

Klein, E., Bental, E., Lerer, B., & Belmaker, R. H. (1984). Carbamazepine and haloperidol v. placebo and haloperidol in excited psychoses: A controlled study. *Archives of General Psychiatry, 41*, 165–170.

Kolakowska, T., Wiles, D. H., McNeilly, A. S., & Gelder, M. G. (1975). Correlation between plasma levels of prolactin and chlorpromazine in psychiatric patients. *Psychological Medicine, 5*, 214–216.

Konzett, H. (1938). Forderung von schlor und narkose dur farbstoffe. *Naunyn-schmiedeberg. Archiv Für Experimentelle Pathologie und Pharmacologie, 188*, 349–359.

Krupp, P., & Barnes, P. (1992). Clozapine-associated agranulocytosis: Risk and aetiology. *British Journal of Psychiatry, 160* (Suppl. 17), 38–40.

Laborit, H., & Huguenard, P. (1951). L'hibernation artificielle par moyens pharmacodynamics et physique. *Presse Medicale, 59*, 1329.

Laborit, H., & Huguenard, P. (1952). Technique actuelle de l'hibernation artificielle. *Presse Medicale, 60*, 1455–1456.

Lader, M. (1988). Beta-adrenoceptor antagonists in neuropsychiatry: An update. *Journal of Clinical Psychiatry, 49*, 213–223.

Langer, G., Sachar, E. J., Gruen, P. H., & Halpern, F. S. (1977). Human prolactin responses to neuroleptic drugs correlate with antischizophrenic potency. *Nature, 266*, 639–640.

Lavin, M. R., & Rifkin, A. (1991). Prophylactic antiparkinsonian drug use. I. Initial prophylaxis and prevention of extrapyramidal side effects. *Journal of Clinical Pharmacology, 31*, 763–768.

Leff, J. P., & Wing, L. K. (1971). Trial of maintenance therapy in schizophrenia. *British Medical Journal, 3*, 599–604.

Levinson, D. F., & Simpson, G. M. (1986). Neuroleptic induced extrapyramidal symptoms with fever. *Archives of General Psychiatry, 43*, 839–848.

Lieberman, J. A. (1993). Understanding the mechanism of action of atypical antipsychotic drugs. A review of compounds in use and development. *British Journal of Psychiatry, 163* (Suppl. 22), 7–18.

Lieberman, J., Kane, J., & Johns, C. (1989). Clozapine: Guidelines for clinical management. *Journal of Clinical Psychiatry, 50*, 329–338.

Lieberman. J. A., Saltz, B. L., Johns, C. A., Pollack, S., & Kane, J. (1989). Clozapine effects on tardive dyskinesia. *Psychopharmacology Bulletin, 25*, 57–62.

Lindström, L. H. (1988). The effect of long term treatment of clozapine in schizophrenia: A retrospective study of 96 patients treated with clozapine for up to 13 years. *Acta Psychiatrica Scandinavica, 77*, 524–529.

Livingston, M. G. (1994). Risperidone. *Lancet, 343*, 457–460.

MacDonald, M. (1981). Mystical bedlam: Madness, anxiety and healing in seventeenth century England. Cambridge: Cambridge University Press.

Macmillan, J. F., Crow, T. J., Johnson, A. L., & Johnstone, E. C. (1986). The Northwick Park study of first episodes of schizophrenia. II. Short-term outcome in trial entrants and trial eligible patients. *British Journal of Psychiatry, 148*, 128–133.

Mann, S. C., Caroff, S. N., Bleier, H. R., Welz, W. K. R., Kling, M. A., & Hayashida, M. (1986). Lethal catatonia. *American Journal of Psychiatry, 143*, 1374–1381.

Marder, S. R., & Meibach, R. C. (1994). Risperidone in the treatment of schizophrenia. *American Journal of Psychiatry, 151*, 825–835.

Marder, S. R., Van Putten, T., Mintz, J., Labell, M., McKenzie, J., & May P. R. A. (1987). Low and conventional dose maintenance therapy with fluphenazine decanoate: Two year outcome. *Archives of General Psychiatry, 44, 518–521.*

Marder, S. R., Van Putten, T., Mintz, J., McKenzie, J., Lebell, M., Faltico, G., & May, P. R. A., (1984). Costs and benefits of two doses of fluphenazine. *Archives of General Psychiatry, 41*, 1025–1029.

May, P. R. A., Dencker, S. J., Hubbard, J. W., Midha, K. K., & Lieberman, R. P. (1988). A systematic approach to treatment resistance in schizophrenic disorders. In S. J. Denker & F. Kulharek (Eds.), *Treatment resistance in schizophrenia* (pp. 22–23). Vieweg. Weisbaden: Braunschweig.

McGlashan, T. H., & Carpenter, W. T. (1976). Post psychotic depression in schizophrenia. *Archives of General Psychiatry, 33*, 231–239.

Meltzer, H. Y. (1985). Dopamine and negative symptoms in schizophrenia: Critique of the Type I-II hypothesis. In: *Controversies in schizophrenia. Changes and constancies* (pp. 110–136). New York: Guilford. M. Alpert (Ed.).

Meltzer, H. Y., & Fang, V. S. (1976). The effect of neuroleptics on serum prolactin in schizophrenic subjects. *Archives of General Psychiatry, 33*, 279–284.

Miller, R. J., Horn, A. S., & Iversen, L. L. (1974). The action of neuroleptic drugs on dopamine stimulated adenosine cyclic 3'5' monophosphate production in neostriatum and limbic forebrain. *Molecular Pharmacology, 10*, 759–766.

National Institute of Mental Health (1964). Phenothiazine treatment of acute schizophrenia. *Archives of General Psychiatry, 10*, 246–261.

Neborsky, R., Janowsky, D., Munson, E., & Depry, D. (1981). Rapid treatment of acute psychotic symptoms with high and low dose haloperidol. *Archives of General Psychiatry, 38*, 195–199.

Nemecek, D, Rastogi-Cruz, D., & Csernansky, J. G. (1993). Atropinism may precipitate neuroleptic malignant syndrome during treatment with clozapine. *American Journal of Psychiatry, 150*, 1561.

Opler, L. A., Albert, D., & Ramirez, P. M. (1994). Psychopharmacologic treatment of negative schizophrenic symptoms. *Comprehensive Psychiatry, 35*, 16–28.

Owens, D. G. C. (1990). Dystonia-A potential psychiatric pitfall. *British Journal of Psychiatry, 156*, 620–634.

Owens, D. G. C., Harrison-Read, P. E., & Johnstone, E. C. (1994). L-dopa helps positive but not negative features of neuroleptic-insensitive chronic schizophrenia. *Journal of Psychopharmacology, 8*, 204–212.

Peroutka, S. J., & Snyder, S. H. (1980). Relationship of neuroleptic drug effects at brain dopamine serotonin adrenergic and histamine receptors to clinical potency. *American Journal of Psychiatry, 137*, 1518–1522.

Pogue-Geile, M. F., & Zubin, J. (1988). Negative symptomatology and schizophrenia. A conceptual and empirical review. *International Journal of Mental Health, 16*, 3–45.

Povlsen, U. J., Noring, U., Fog, R., & Gerlach, J. (1985). Tolerability and therapeutic effect of clozapine: A retrospective investigation of 216 patients treated with clozapine for up to twelve years. *Acta Psychiatrica Scandinavica, 71*, 176–185.

Randrup, A., & Munkvad, I. (1965). Special antagonism of amphetamine-induced abnormal behaviors. *Psychopharmacologia, 7*, 416–422.

Remington, G. J. (1993). Clinical considerations in the use of risperidone. *Canadian Journal of Psychiatry, 38* (Suppl. 3), S96-S100.

Rifkin, A., Quitkin, F., & Klein, D. F. (1975). Akinesia. *Archives of General Psychiatry 32, 672–674.*

Safferman, A., Lieberman, J. A., Kane, J. M., Szymanski, S., & Kinon, B. (1991). Update on the clinical efficacy and side effects of clozapine. *Schizophrenia Bulletin, 17*, 247–261.

Schooler, N. R. (1993). Reducing dosage in maintenance treatment of schizophrenia. *British Journal of Psychiatry, 163* (Suppl. 22), 58–65.

Seeman, P., Lee, T., Chau-Wong, M., & Wong, K. (1976). Antipsychotic drug doses and neuroleptic/dopamine receptors. *Nature (London), 216*, 717–719.

Shopsin, B., Klein, H., Aaronsom, M., & Collora, M. (1979). Clozapine, chlorpromazine and placebo in newly hospitalized acutely schizophrenic patients: A controlled double-blind comparison. *Archives of General Psychiatry, 36*, 657–664.

Siris, S. G. (1993). Adjunctive medication in the maintenance treatment of schizophrenia and its conceptual implications. *British Journal of Psychiatry, 163* (Suppl. 22) 66–78.

Siris, S. G., Bermanzohn, P. C., Mason, S. E., & Shuwall M.A. (1994). Maintenance imipramine therapy for secondary depression in schizophrenia. *Archives of General Psychiatry, 51*, 109–115.

Siris, S. G., Morgan, V., Fagerstrom, R., Rifkin, A., & Cooper, T. B. (1987). Adjunctive imipramine in the treatment of post-psychotic depression: A controlled trial. *Archives of General Psychiatry, 44*, 533–539.

Siris, S. S., van Kammen, D. P., & de Fraites, E. G. (1978). Serum prolactin and antipsychotic responses to pimozide in schizophrenia. *Psychopharmacology Bulletin, 14,* 8–9.

Small, J. G., Kellams, J. J., Milstein, V., & Moore, J. (1975). A placebo controlled study of lithium combined with neuroleptics in chronic schizophrenic patients. *American Journal of Psychiatry, 132,* 1315–1317.

Small, J. G., Milstein, V., Marhenke, J. D., Hall, D. D., & Kellams, J. J. (1987). Treatment outcome with clozapine in tardive dyskinesia, neuroleptic sensitivity and treatment-resistant psychosis. *Journal of Clinical Psychiatry, 48*, 263–267.

Tamminga, C. A., & Lahti, A. C. (1996). The new generation of antipsychotic drugs. *International Clinical Psychopharmacology, 11*, (Suppl. 2), 73–76.

Tandon, R. DeQuardo, J. R., Goodson, J., Mann, N. A., & Greden, J. F. (1992). Effect of anticholinergics on positive and negative symptoms in schizophrenia. *Psychopharmacology Bulletin, 28*, 297–302.

Tuma, A. H., & May, P. R. A. (1979). And if that doesn't work what next? A study of treatment failures in schizophrenia. *Journal of Nervous and Mental Disease, 167*, 566–571.

Van Praag, H. M., Korf, J., & Dols, L. C. W. (1976). Clozapine versus perphenazine: The value of the biochemical mode of action of neuroleptics in predicting their therapeutic activity. *British Journal of Psychiatry, 129*, 547–555.

Wells, B. G., Marken, P. A., Richman, L. A., Brown, C., Hamann, G., & Grimmig, J. (1989). Characterizing anticholinergic abuse in community mental health. *Journal of Clinical Psychopharmacology, 9*, 431–435.

Wolf, M., Diener, J., Lajeunesse, C., & Shriqui, C. L. (1992). Low-dose bromocriptine in neuroleptic-resistant schizophrenia: A pilot study. *Biological Psychiatry, 31*, 1166–1168.

CHAPTER 25

SOCIAL FUNCTIONING AND CHALLENGING BEHAVIOR

Geoff Shepherd

This chapter is concerned with the nature of so-called challenging behavior and its relationship to social functioning in the context of the care of people with schizophrenia. We will consider what is meant by challenging behavior and exactly what kinds of challenges are presented to services and to individual. We will examine the impact of challenging behavior on the lives of those who experience it and the options that are available to mental health services in terms of treatment and management. Finally, we will address the questions of risk assessment and the management of risk, which lie at the heart of an effective clinical response to these problems. This is a difficult topic. It is often poorly defined and fraught with both theoretical and practical problems. It also contains some of the central ethical dilemmas in psychiatry. It is certainly not an area where there are many easy answers.

WHAT IS CHALLENGING BEHAVIOR?

Challenging behavior is often a euphemism for aggression. However, defining challenging behavior simply in terms of aggressive or violent acts would provide a very narrow basis for understanding the problem or for formulating an adequate response. Within mental health services there are certainly individuals who show levels of aggression and violence which pose very serious threats to personal and public safety, but they are relatively rare and are usually dealt with by specialized services (special hospitals, medium secure units, forensic teams, etc.). Many will also be cared for outside the mental health services, in the criminal justice system. Their problems are qualitatively, as well as quantitatively, different from those in mainstream mental health services who, from time to time, show outbursts of anger or violence and/or episodes of self-harm, or extreme self-neglect, but who for the most part can be looked after in open services, without special security arrangements. It is this group that will be our main focus.

The term *challenging behavior* will therefore be interpreted as referring to people who are clearly suffering from a serious mental illness, usually (but not exclusively) schizophrenia, and who, in addition to severe and intractable symptomatology, also show a range of behavioral problems, such as aggression (verbal or physical), violence (destruction of property, etc.), repeated self-harm (cutting, overdosing), extreme self-neglect (sufficient to endanger physical health or the safety of others), fire setting, or inappropriate sexual behavior. They present a challenge to services, not just in the sense of their encounters with individual practitioners, but also because they expose the inadequacies of the current range of services aimed at providing comprehensive care. In the past, they might have gravitated toward a long-stay ward in a mental hospital; now they are increasingly found in acute units, often in general hospitals, where they remain by default simply because there is no other option. Otherwise they may be caught in the revolving door of inpatient admissions, interspersed with brief periods in the community, and sometimes also in prison. In the United Kingdom, these patients are at the center of the controversies surrounding the closure of mental hospital beds and the current perceived shortage of acute admission beds. What do we know in detail about their characteristics?

In the United Kingdom, many people with the label *challenging behavior* form the group also referred to as "new" long-stay inpatients. This term was first coined almost 20 years ago by Mann and Cree (1976) to refer to patients who had then been in hospital continuously for more than 1, but less than 5, years. ("More than 1 year" to discriminate them from the majority of short-term admissions, and "less than 5 years" to discriminate them from the old, institutionalized, long-stay patients.) Mann and Cree reported on a national survey of such patients and described a population with multiple disabilities, 60% of whom had a diagnosis of psychotic disorder (mostly schizophrenia). They showed severe positive and negative symptoms which were generally highly resistant to treatment. They were also socially unskilled, with poor work records, few family ties, and poor physical health. Many exhibited a range of other behavioral problems (e.g., violence, self-harm, extreme antisocial behavior), which made them difficult to look after outside the hospital. Nevertheless, about a third were judged to be capable of living in the community if highly supervised hostel placements were available, about a third were deemed to require further treatment in hospital, and the remainder were so multiply handicapped that it was difficult to see where they might be placed.

Has this picture changed in recent years? In 1994, the Royal College of Psychiatrists' research unit reported on a national audit of patients who had been in hospital continuously more than 6 months, but less than 3 years (Lelliot, Wing, & Clifford, 1994; Lelliot & Wing, 1994). Despite these slightly different criteria, they showed many of the same characteristics as the original Mann and Cree

sample. However, the proportion with a diagnosis of schizophrenia had increased from 44% to 62% and the proportion compulsorily detained had almost tripled (from 9% to 29%). The number with more than five admissions had also increased from 30% to 50%. Thus, the group seemed more disturbed and had more of a history of revolving-door contact with services. These changes probably reflect the reduced availability of suitable, highly supervised accommodation (because of the loss of long-stay hospital beds) and the increasing tendency toward early discharge and subsequent readmission. An increased pressure on acute beds may also have raised the threshold for admission, hence increasing the use of compulsory detention.

The interplay of these clinical, behavioral, and system factors illustrates the difficulties of defining this population using criteria based solely on their patterns of admission (e.g., more than 6 months, or more than 12 months, continuously in hospital). Thus, the factors that make someone "new long stay," or "challenging" and "difficult to place" in one area may be different from those in another area because of differences regarding the availability of beds or other residential alternatives. However, despite these local differences in services, a group of basic clinical problems do seem to remain common.

This is confirmed by examining studies in the United States of comparable populations. For example, Okin, Pearsall, and Athearn (1990) and Salit and Marcos (1991) have documented the growth of new long-stay patients and note how they have started to accumulate in general hospital units as state hospital provisions have reduced and specialized residential alternatives in the community have been slow to develop. Regarding their clinical characteristics, the classic paper of Sheets, Prevost, and Reihman (1982) hypothesized three subgroups among these new young chronics. They described one group characterized as low energy/low demand with long histories of contact with services, passivity, low motivation, poor personal hygiene, and treatment-resistant symptomatology. They appeared to be burned out and accepting of their status as chronic patients, despite their relative youth. Second, there was a group of high energy/high demand individuals, characterized by low frustration tolerance, mobility, rapidly fluctuating levels of functioning and symptoms, acting-out behavior, aggression, and contact with the law. They were very demanding, uncooperative, and difficult to manage. Finally, there was a high functioning/high aspiration group, characterized by relatively good premorbid history, coming from the middle class, having high ambitions, but unable to realize them. They often also had significant problems with drug or alcohol abuse. This group also rejected their status as chronic patients, but accepted help from mental health services insofar as it would enable them to lead relatively normal, unstigmatized lives. This classification has provided a useful set of archetypes to illustrate the needs of this group; however, it has never been subject to any rigorous evaluation. Thus, it is not clear whether these categories can be defined reliably or whether they have any discriminant or predictive validity.

Gudeman and Shore (1984) also described the characteristics of patients in their service in Boston who had proved very difficult to look after in conventional community accommodation. They consisted of a mixture of elderly, demented people with behavioral disturbance (20%), mentally retarded persons with concomitant psychiatric illness and aggressive behavior (20%), people with acquired brain damage and loss of impulse control (10%), and two groups of predominantly schizophrenic patients, one with unremitting assaultive or suicidal behavior (17%) and the other, while not being a frank danger to themselves or others, with such unacceptable social behavior (e.g., disrobing in public, eating garbage, continually vomiting food at meal times) that they would not be tolerated in an ordinary community setting (33%). Similarly, Bigelow, Cutler, Moore, McComb, and Leung (1988) studied a group nominated as "hard to place" by staff in a state hospital. Almost three quarters (70%) had a primary diagnosis of schizophrenia, often in association with drug and alcohol problems, and there were relatively high levels of violent and assaultive behavior (present in 62% of their sample). They also note the high prevalence of poor self-care, leisure, and social skills.

Thus, a consistent picture emerges, across very different settings and local conditions, of the type of person who is likely to be challenging or difficult to place. First, there is a group of young men, almost all of whom have a primary diagnosis of schizophrenia, who show severe and intractable positive and negative symptoms and a variety of behavioral problems. They may also have concomitant drug or alcohol misuse. (Not surprisingly, this is more common in the United States than in the United Kingdom.) This is the largest group and, depending on local circumstances, is likely to account for between two thirds and three quarters of the total. Second, there is a group of older persons, primarily women, who are more likely to have treatment-resistant affective psychoses (depressed type of rapid cycling bipolar conditions) and who present a significant risk to themselves and may show extreme self-neglect when they are acutely depressed. They are

likely to account for a further 20%. Third, there is an heterogeneous group, usually having organic brain syndromes (e.g., acquired brain damage, presenile dementia, low IQ, alcoholism) again, often with other associated behavioral problems, sometimes also showing comorbidity with psychosis. They usually account for about 10%. Psychosis, particularly schizophrenia, is thus prominent in all three groups.

Estimating numbers is difficult because of the local differences already highlighted; however, Wykes and Wing (1991) using case register data from 1988 found an actual prevalence of beds occupied for more than 1, but less than 5, years in England and Wales of around 12 per 100,000 of the population. The more recent study by Lelliot and Wing (1994) found that beds occupied continuously for more than 6 months, but less than 3 years, amounted to just over 6 per 100,000. Even taking into account the different criteria used (and the large local variations), this would seem to reflect a significant change in bed use. Assuming that the actual numbers of such individuals has not changed much, it suggests that many more are now in the community and many less are in hospitals. It is also possible that a higher number are now in secure, or semisecure, provisions.

Of course, current prevalence may, or may not, accurately reflect *need*. Wing (1992) suggests that what may be *needed* in terms of specialized residential care for this group is between 10 and 30 places per 100,000, and this is consistent with Gudeman and Shore's (1984) estimate of 12 per 100,000 (excluding provision for the elderly). The majority of these individuals will have a diagnosis of schizophrenia. In the United Kingdom, therefore, at a minimum, we probably only have about half as many specialized residential places as we currently need, and in many areas (e.g., inner cities where the availability of alternative housing is most scarce and where the reduction of long-stay hospital beds has been greatest) the shortfall is probably much greater. As mentioned earlier, such potential consequences as inappropriate placements on acute wards, "bed blocking," or premature discharges, already seem to be evident.

SOCIAL CONSEQUENCES OF CHALLENGING BEHAVIOR

The social consequences of these problems may be profound. In extreme cases, they may lead to premature death, whether by accident or design, and in less extreme cases, the individuals are likely to be incarcerated in hospital (or in prison) for long periods. Even under the best circumstances, they are likely to drift out of contact with services—if they do not actively seek to avoid them—and may remain untreated for long periods. They are then likely to take longer to stabilize (Wyatt, 1991) and, as a result, may be even more difficult to discharge. Providing good-quality, well-coordinated, long-term care in the community is extremely difficult.

The risk of premature death among people with schizophrenia is now well established. McGlashan (1988) estimates that survival rates may be shortened by as much as 10 years in males and 9 years in females, most of this being attributable to suicide. Similarly, Caldwell and Gottesman (1990) note that the risk of suicide in people with schizophrenia is as much as 50 times greater than the general population (500/100,000 versus 10/100,000) and approaches the level of risk for people with major affective disorders. While suicidal behavior is difficult to predict with any accuracy, the profile of the at-risk individual—young, socially isolated, repeated relapses, previous history of self-harm, hopeless about the future—fits many of those with challenging behavior all too well.

People with challenging behavior may also be assumed to be difficult to place and therefore likely to accumulate in institutions. This is generally true; however, one of the remarkable features of the literature on the new long stay is that, even without special facilities, a substantial proportion do seem to manage to return to the community and cope in some way. For example, McCreadie and McCannell (1989) followed up a group of inpatients with current lengths of stay of between 1 and 6 years and found that 28% were actually discharged within 5 years. Just under a quarter had died and the remainder were still inpatients. Similarly, O'Driscoll, Marshall, and Reed (1990) found that after 2 years, almost half of their original cohort of new long stays had been discharged either to nursing homes or to other kinds of sheltered accommodation in the community and a few were living with relatives. On the basis of data collected over a 2.5 year period on over 1,000 patients in five hospitals, Clifford, Charman, Webb, and Best (1991) suggest there may be a "fast" and a "slow" stream among the new long stay. The fast stream has a relatively good chance of being discharged within 2 to 3 years; however, once this threshold is passed the likelihood of discharge then becomes increasingly remote. Even in Bigelow et al.'s (1988) study, almost half of those identified by staff as difficult to place were, in fact, discharged 6 months later.

Thus, despite having apparently exhausted all possibilities for living outside hospital, a substantial proportion of those regarded as most difficult and challenging may eventually return to the community. Again, this highlights the dangers of using service-related definitions and also demonstrates the power and resourcefulness of individuals, their families, and local services. If people really *want* to manage outside hospital, remarkable feats may be achieved. Outcomes are certainly not easily predictable—particularly on an individual basis.

Of course, once in the community, this does not necessarily mean that the person is functioning well, or that they are particularly satisfied with their lives. We have already noted that one of the characteristics of those with challenging behavior and schizophrenia is their difficulties with social relationships and their tendency to remain socially isolated. The implication of this in terms of their community tenure and their risk of readmission is very important. Thus, because they are likely already to have experienced several admissions, of increasing duration, they are also likely to have relatively fewer relatives and friends in their social networks and have to rely more on mental health professionals and other service users (Homes-Eber & Riger, 1990). This is not only likely to lead to lowered satisfaction (Goering, Durbin, & Foster 1992) but may also create networks which are relatively poor at providing support in a crisis, since they are diffuse and lack the dense interconnections necessary to mobilize support in an emergency (Dozier, Harris, & Bergman, 1987). The impact of challenging behavior on social supports is therefore to create the conditions for a cycle of repeated admissions, further weakening of social networks, and increasing despair (Dayson, Gooch, & Thornicroft, 1992). If they then fall out of follow-up and remain in the community in an untreated psychotic state, the consequences may be very serious.

This has been a common thread running through some of the worst failures of community care in the United Kingdom in recent years, such as the case of Christopher Clunis who stabbed an innocent member of the public to death in a London subway (Ritchie, Dick, & Lingham, 1994). Clunis had a well-documented history of violence, especially when he was floridly psychotic, and the inquiry report into his case demonstrated clearly that what went wrong was not so much a failure of resources, but a failure of communication and insufficiently assertive follow-up. As a result, one person died and the patient remains in a secure hospital from which he is unlikely to be released for a very long time. It is somewhat disturbing to note that when the inquiry team visited Clunis in hospital they found him "intelligent, easy going, articulate, with a good sense of humour" (Ritchie et al., 1994, p. 103), and this accords with descriptions of him before he became ill (Mental Health Foundation, 1994, p. 21). While he clearly remains a substantial risk to the public because of his dangerousness when acutely psychotic, appropriately medicated he is clearly a very different man. Services therefore clearly failed him, rather than the other way around. To what extent someone like Christopher Clunis can be managed safely on a community basis will be discussed later.

Apart from these very obvious and dramatic social consequences—perhaps underlying them—is the problem of stigma and rejection of those with challenging behavior by services and by professionals themselves. Most life-threatening conditions attract a degree of sympathy, and extra resources may even be made available to try to prevent premature death or the accumulation of unnecessary disabilities. But chronic schizophrenia, especially when it is associated with disturbed or aggressive behavior, tends to attract neither sympathy nor resources. On the contrary, it is more likely to provoke blame, censure, and a wish to punish, not least from the professionals who are most directly involved with the care of these people. Perhaps this is not surprising. Challenging behavior, especially aggression, tends to provoke very strong reactions in carers—fear, distrust, anger, even hatred—and these feelings can easily interfere with the process of treatment and management. In the extreme case, they may even lead to acts of violence directed toward patients; in less extreme instances, they may simply undermine the determination to provide humane, sympathetic, good quality care.

To counteract these negative feelings requires a high level of clinical skills and high-quality supervision and support for staff. This support and training must address the feelings which are an inevitable reaction to having to deal with unpleasant and frightening behavior. Staff must be helped to examine to what extent they are affected and whether their anger with the patient is part of their own frustration and inability to help. The central challenge of challenging behavior is therefore how to help staff continue to work with these very difficult people in a humane and supportive way. Understandably, staff may seek to minimize their contact and, if they are faced with close and repeated encounters, they may develop distancing defenses to protect themselves from the pain and despair which is so often very close to the surface in these individuals. Staff must be helped not to turn away, or to dehumanize their contacts, but to develop understanding attitudes and somehow to remain optimistic, while at the same time being objective and realistic. This is not easy. As the English criminologist Hershel Prins has so clearly put it, these patients are "the unloved, the unlovely and the unlovable" (Prins, 1993, p. 4). Socially, perhaps this is their biggest handicap of all.

TREATMENT AND MANAGEMENT OPTIONS

The treatment and management options for such people essentially fall under two broad headings: (a) specialized residential care, and (b) specialized community teams. These will now be discussed and the advantages and limitations of each considered.

Residential Care

For some time now, the Department of Health in the United Kingdom has been encouraging health authorities to establish specialized residential provisions for this group along the lines of a "hospital hostel" or "ward-in-a-house" (Bennett, 1980; Wykes, 1982). This attempts to combine the best features of high-quality hospital care (e.g., high staffing levels, intensive professional input, highly individualized programs) with a setting that is both home and domestic in scale and operation (e.g., located in an ordinary house, with good access to community facilities, normal expectations of participation in cooking, cleaning, housework). Most of these units have been relatively small—12 to 15 residents or less—and are often located in ex-staff housing near to existing hospital sites. Their general mode of operation has been described in a Department of Health publication by Young (1991) and in detail by Shepherd (1995a).

Historically, they bear many similarities to the York "Retreat," which provided the model for institutional care in the early nineteenth century (Digby, 1985). The Retreat prided itself on its homey atmosphere and the quality of the surroundings (in marked contrast to the dirt and squalor of early Victorian cities) and was, of course, the founder and pioneer of the "moral treatment" approach which placed a central importance on the relationship and quality of interaction between staff and residents. The staff (attendants) were selected with special attention to their personal characteristics, and these are clearly described in the regulations of 1847: "they should take pains to acquire a knowledge of the character of the patients, and to obtain their confidence by friendly treatment, and by actively promoting their comfort and real enjoyment.

Their requests should be complied with, within reasonable bounds; but no promises should be made, or expectations given to them, which cannot be performed. Kind and respectful, not domineering, language should be used to the patients; they should be asked, not commanded, to do whatever may be desired of them" (cited in Digby, 1985, p. 148).

Attendants were therefore trained in the use of positive methods of behavioral control (e.g., praise, encouragement) rather than physical punishment and restraint, which were the more common methods for managing the insane at the time. While the moral treatment approach has received some criticism for its covert rigidity and control aspects (e.g., Scull, 1982) nevertheless, there is still much that we could learn from it today.

The modern ward-in-a-house is based on the four key principles shown in Table 25.1. First, each person is regarded as an individual with a unique set of needs and abilities. No one is given care that he or she does not need and, conversely, no one is denied help because of general rules or expectations regarding levels of functioning or performance. Each person has a careful individualized assessment over the first few weeks in which all staff collaborate to build up a picture of the individual's strengths and difficulties. Staff use their everyday observations of working with the residents in a variety of community settings (e.g., shops, public transport, eating houses) to make direct assessments of their skills and deficits. For example, they may go on a shopping trip to buy food for the house and use this as an opportunity to observe task skills, social skills, and how the person copes with residual symptoms.

Table 25.1. Principles of Care in a Hospital Hostel (Ward-in-a-House)

1. *Individualized care*—care programs based on in vivo assessment and training, negotiated and agreed with resident wherever possible.

2. *Focus on functional abilities not psychopathology*—emphasis on the practical problems of living and working together, rather than symptomatic treatment.

3. *Importance of quality as well as quantity of staff–resident interactions*—regular and consistent staff training in an attempt to create and maintain a low EE atmosphere.

4. *Teamwork and continuity*—high face-to-face contact, regular reviews, group training, and support to improve and maintain consistent team approach.

All these assessments are carried out in vivo and little use is made of artificial tasks or simulated practice.

Once these initial assessments have been made, the observations are collated in a multidisciplinary team meeting, strengths and weaknesses are identified, and the first care plan is drawn up. Specific goals may be suggested (e.g., being up by a certain time, participation in household tasks, bathing/washing routines, attendance at day programs), and strategies for dealing with specific problem behaviors (e.g., violence, verbal abuse, absconding) are formulated. Goals are set so as to represent only a small improvement over baseline functioning (e.g., being up by 11:30 A.M., rather than 12:00 midday; bathing regularly once a week, instead of erratically) and are usually negotiated in a one-on-one meeting with the resident concerned. If there is disagreement, a compromise is sought. The care plan provides the basic structure for the interactions between staff and residents and is monitored every day. Most residents also review their care plans at least weekly with their key worker. Most of the units do not use formal token economies, although individualized incentive schemes are sometimes employed. The major aim is to create an active, information rich environment in which staff use their relationships with residents, in the context of collaboration over everyday activities, to shape behavior. Clear goals and expectations are set and there is clear—and mainly positive—feedback.

The second principle of care concerns the focus on practical tasks and daily living skills and the deemphasis of pathology. This is not to say that problems and emotional difficulties are ignored or not acknowledged, but almost by definition, these residents will have exhausted most conventional therapeutic approaches. The central question regarding symptoms is therefore not how can we remove them, but to what extent do they interfere with the person's ability to *function* in everyday life? A range of social, psychological, and physical treatments, (e.g., skills training, psychoeducation, counselling, cognitive behavioral techniques) may be used, but the emphasis is on improving and maintaining functioning, not simply on symptomatic improvement. Medication can play an important role in this, and some of the new atypical neuroleptics (e.g., clozapine) have been particularly useful in providing symptomatic relief for individuals who are otherwise highly treatment resistant (Meltzer, 1992). However, even if symptoms do improve, this does not necessarily mean that functioning will also automatically improve.

This emphasis on functioning rather than symptoms gives a clear normalizing message to residents and contributes to the maintenance of a normal household atmosphere. The environment is thus very unlike a "disturbed" ward in a hospital, although that is actually where many of the residents might well otherwise find themselves, and every attempt is made to convey an attitude that "this is a house, and like any other house, it has to be kept reasonably clean and tidy, food has to be bought and prepared, people have to agree on basic rules of conduct, etc." This distinction between a house and a ward is fundamental to the success of these projects and is sometimes difficult to sustain. The hospital has to be persuaded not to provide meals or cleaners or gardeners and not to appoint staff who will automatically make the beds and tidy the rooms. These tasks are carried out by staff and residents working *together*, and this sense of common purpose helps to highlight what they have in common, rather than what divides them. In this way, it also helps reduce the distance between the groups and bridge the empathic gap discussed earlier.

Of course, a clear structure and a practical orientation are not sufficient to guarantee a good quality of care, and the third principle concerns the importance of the *quality* of interactions between staff and residents. Quality in this context means not only a respect for the individual and his/her uniqueness, but also the establishment of a style of interaction that conveys clear expectations about performance in a way that is not domineering or dictatorial and tries to minimize criticism and censure. It is now well established that there is a strong relationship between high expressed emotion (EE) in families—particularly criticism and hostility—and the probability of symptomatic relapse (Kuipers & Bebbington, 1988). Similar evidence is also beginning to emerge that these processes may apply to interactions between nonfamily carers (i.e., staff) and residents (Ball, Moore, & Kuipers, 1992; Moore, Kuipers, & Ball, 1992). If this proves to be the case, then the model for family intervention developed by the EE researchers may also have utility as a tool for training care staff and for organizing care. For example, it is a common clinical observation that staff often make the same blame attributions for negative symptoms which seem to underlie the responses of high EE relatives (Brewin, MacCarthy, Duda, & Vaughn, 1991; Barrowclough, Johnston, & Tarrier, 1994) and therefore the same kinds of educational and skills-based programs that have been developed for families (e.g., psychoeducation, problem solving, communication training) may be equally relevant for staff (Ranz, Horen, McFarlane, & Zito, 1991).

In the Cambridge service, we paid particular attention to regular staff training and support sessions. These sessions were conducted weekly and focused on both the practical difficulties in implementing care plans and the nature of good and bad interactions. We used materials adapted from working with families to help staff identify negative symptoms and to explore how best to understand and to manage them. A style of low EE interaction was therefore encouraged, emphasizing the importance of voice tone and nonverbal cues in communicating affect. Staff were made aware that *how* they communicated was just as important as *what* they said. Time was also allocated in these staff support groups to discussing the daily hassles of work (e.g., bureaucracy, staff shortages, difficulties with managers), as these can affect the general atmosphere of the house and lower the threshold for critical, irritable behavior on that part of carers.

The final principle of care concerns the attempt to maintain consistency and continuity through good teamwork and communication. It is a truism to state that consistency and teamwork are important, but nevertheless it bears repeating. Creating and maintaining a permanent therapeutic environment is perhaps the most difficult task of all in psychiatry and, if we have learned any lesson at all from the history of the last 200 years, it is that high-minded, therapeutic principles have a tendency to disappear under the pressure of institutional change and bureaucracy. To counteract this teams have to be strong, they have to know *what* they are doing and *why*, and they have to develop something of a special culture to reinforce their sense of self-belief and to protect themselves from being drawn into the institutional pressures of the organization. This idea of a separate elite culture obviously has its dangers and must not be allowed to lead to staff becoming too isolated as there is then an increased risk of abuse and neglect (Martin, 1984). However, it is important for morale in such units that staff do have some sense of being "special." They need to meet regularly and to have the opportunity continually to review their work with senior colleagues. Regular daily and weekly meetings are therefore the main vehicles for developing a consistent approach to which everyone is committed. From time to time, these may need to be supplemented with crisis meetings if particularly dangerous or violent incidents occur, and residents may also be involved in these to emphasize the joint approach. A lot of time and effort therefore needs to go into maintaining and "feeding" the team. Teams are fragile, delicate structures, and they need constant attention to keep them functioning at their highest level. It is not a task that is ever completed once and for all.

A final area which is particularly important for the long-term success of these ventures is the recruitment and selection of staff. Staff should be employed to work specifically in the houses and not shifted around without consultation. This is particularly important for the senior nurses staff who become the "culture carriers" and are crucial in inducting new staff and ensuring that the traditions of care are passed on from one to another.

What is the evidence for the effectiveness of these units? This has been previously reviewed by Shepherd (1991) and is summarized, together with the most recent studies, in Table 25.2. These data suggest that such units may be effective in improving the functioning of up to 40% of those referred sufficiently such that they are able to be resettled in less highly supervised accommodation in the community. It should be borne in mind that this is being achieved with a group who, by definition, have already proved themselves to be very difficult to resettle and support successfully in the community. This process seems to take on average 2 to 3 years, although it can take a lot longer. The notion that there is a tendency for most improvement to occur within the first 2 to 3 years is consistent with the other evidence regarding the rates of change in this population without specialized intervention (e.g., Clifford et al., 1991). In comparative terms, residents in these specialized units make more progress than controls regarding their social functioning and they show increased contact with the community and higher levels of satisfaction. This latter finding is not surprising given the lack of privacy and increased disruption which people living in traditional ward settings routinely experience. For those who are not resettled, the units are effective in maintaining their functioning, but they do not produce sufficiently stable changes to allow for resettlement. Costs are generally less than in general hospital acute units, but higher than in long-stay wards in mental hospitals. The increased costs are mainly attributable to increased staffing ratios and higher direct-care costs, as opposed to indirect, hostel expenses—meals, cleaning, pottering, etc.—many of which activities are actually performed by staff and residents in the houses themselves (Hyde et al., 1987).

Although such units are effective for the majority of referrals, there is a sizable minority (up to a third) who do not improve and are too difficult to manage in the physical space of a domestic environment. They are often transferred and sometimes require further care in a more secure setting (e.g., a locked ward) before moving to somewhere which is socially less demanding. These individuals tend to show the highest levels of dangerous and acting-out behavior. The remainder of the referrals are simply ongoing. For them, the hostel ward provides an alternative to the traditional long-stay ward of a mental hospital.

King and Shepherd (1994) attempted to analyze the differences between these three outcome groups (resettled, transferred, and ongoing) and, although the numbers were small, found some interesting features. First, it was not possible to identify any variables on entry which were predictive of later outcome. This suggests that one should approach the rehabilitation of this group with an entirely open mind. All have a potential to be resettled (or to be transferred) and the likely outcomes will only gradually emerge after a prolonged period of careful monitoring. Because all residents also commonly show a pattern of initial improvement, irrespective of their later progress, it is certainly unwise to begin to formulate any judgment until after a minimum of 6 months. The overlap in lengths of stay between the groups, and the range of lengths of stay in the discharged group, indicate that successful resettlement can still take place after many months (or even years) of slow progress. What one should be looking for in the group most likely to be resettled is consistent evidence of improvement and an absence of deterioration and long-term fluctuations in functioning.

The group likely to do least well are those who show clear evidence of deterioration—albeit after a period of initial improvement—often culminating in a series of aggressive or violent incidents. It is interesting that this group do not show a raised level of aggressive or violent behavior for the whole of their admission, but only in the period leading up to transfer. They are also not generally characterized by a reluctance to be in the unit, or a lack of motivation to be resettled—quite the contrary sometimes—instead, they seem to find the demands of living and working with a group of other people (residents and staff) in the close confines of an ordinary house just too stressful. They often function better in a setting with less demanding patterns of social interaction and more opportunities for social withdrawal (e.g., a traditional long-stay ward). However, there were also instances where they did well living relatively independently (e.g., in a "bed sit" or small flat) as long as they continued to receive fairly intensive support. Providing they are not overstressed by social and interpersonal demands, they could function quite well. The challenge for this group is how to create settings which allow a degree of social withdrawal and the avoidance of overstimulation, while at the same time offering intensive support when it is required. Individual flatlets,

Table 25.2. Summary of Outcome Studies from Hostel-Ward (HW) Projects

AUTHORS	LOCATION	DESIGN OF STUDY	OUTCOMES
Wykes (1982)	111 Denmark Hill (Maudsley)	Controlled trial $n = 10$ (HW) vs. $n = 15$ in traditional long-stay wards over approx. 2.5 years	• HW residents improved more than controls • Most change in first 6 months • Some problems with occupation • Patients and careers generally positive
Gibbons (1986)	Cranbury Terrace (Southampton)	Controlled trial $n = 20$ (HW) vs. $n = 8$ district general hospital ward over 18 months	• HW residents improved more in social functioning • Increased time spent in work, education, and leisure • More contact with community
Hyde et al. (1987)	Douglas House (Manchester)	Random controlled trial ($n = 11$ matched controls) + cost benefit analysis over 2 years	• HW residents improved socially and showed less psychotic deterioration compared with controls • HW cost *less* than acute ward, particularly re nondirect care staff, but more than traditional ward
Garety et al. (1988)	111 Denmark Hill (Maudsley)	10-year follow-up of all admissions ($n = 33$) 1977–1987	• 57% discharged • 7% died • Of those discharged, 58% not readmitted • Average length of stay for successfully resettled group 3 years (range 6 months to 6.5 years) • Unplanned discharge and diagnosis of schizophrenia associated with poorer outcome
Creighton et al. (1991)	Douglas House (Manchester)	7-year follow-up of all admissions ($n = 24$) 1982–1990	• 38% discharged, 25% transferred • Of those discharged, 66% not readmitted • Average length of stay for successfully resettled group 2.5 years • Unplanned discharge and organic syndromes associated with poor outcomes
Shepherd, King, & Fowler (1994)	Cedars & No. 1 The Drive (Cambridge)	Follow-up study of $n = 70$ admissions to 2 hostel wards 1986–1989	• 40% successfully resettled with mean length of stay of 17 months (range 3–55) • 31% transferred with mean length of stay 18 months (range 1–44) • Remainder ongoing with mean length of stay 18 months (range 2–89)
Reid & Garety (1994)	111 Denmark Hill (Maudsley)	16-year follow-up study of all admissions ($n = 47$) 1977–1993 [N.B. Includes patients from Garety et al., 1988]	• 42% discharged successfully • 11% died • O those discharged, 61% not readmitted • Average length of stay for successfully resettled group 4 years (range 1.5–6 years) • Decreasing lengths of stay over time

with intensive support from a central house on a core-and-cluster model, is one possible arrangement.

Although the ongoing group were the most disabled, they actually showed the highest number of improving trends. This could be understood as indicating a "still improving" pattern of change, in contrast to the "improved" pattern (i.e., a stable plateau) shown by the discharged group. The other feature which appeared characteristic of the ongoing group was the higher number of oscillatory fluctuations in their functioning. This raises some intriguing questions. Since the ratings were made by different staff at different times, and reflect changes over such relatively long periods, it seems unlikely that they were measurement artifacts. They seem to be genuine phenomena, but what they are related to is unclear. It is also puzzling how such long-term fluctuations in functioning influenced the clinical decision-making process, given the relatively rapid rate of staff turnover. However, most senior staff (psychiatrist, psychologist, charge nurse) had worked in the unit since it first opened and knew the residents (and their families) very well. It is therefore possible that they used their knowledge of fluctuations in residents' functioning to prevent staff from proceeding with plans for resettlement when improvements occurred which, they knew from experience, were likely to be unstable. If such a process was occurring, staff were not consciously aware of it.

To illustrate these different patterns of change, data from the REHAB total behavior scores (Baker & Hall, 1983) for individuals from each of the three different outcome groups are shown in Figures 25.1, 25.2, and 25.3.

Figure 25.1 is an example of a resident showing consistent and stable improvement which eventually led to successful resettlement in the community. Figure 25.2 is an individual from the transferred group who shows a pattern of initial improvement followed by a period of gradual deterioration, culminating in a major aggressive outburst and transfer from the unit. Finally, Figure 25.3 is of an ongoing resident who, again shows initial improve-

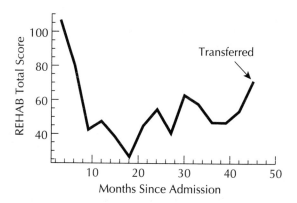

Figure 25.2. Example of transferred individual showing gradual deterioration

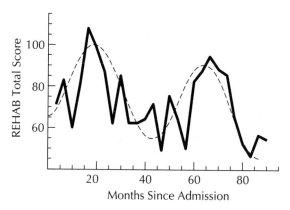

Figure 25.3. Example of ongoing resident showing oscillations in functioning with Fourier transformation superimposed

ment, but then whose functioning is characterized by fluctuations or unstable improvement.

To summarize, hospital hostels or ward-in-a-house facilities may provide an effective solution for the majority of new long-stay or difficult to place patients, many of whom also show some degree of aggressive or violent behavior. However, such units are neither cheap nor easy to run. They are also not a panacea, and they do experience difficulties with those individuals who show the greatest tendency to repeatedly act out in a violent or aggressive manner. (Of course, they may not necessarily be judged the most dangerous.) These individuals are difficult to identify a priori, but they show more evidence of deterioration (and less improvement) over time. They may need a higher level of security (e.g., a regional secure or

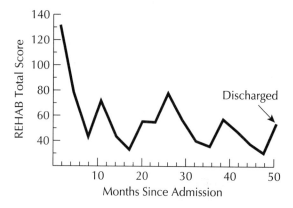

Figure 25.1. Example of successfully resettled individual showing improvement over time

medium secure unit) but may also function well in a less intensive and less socially demanding environment.

Intensive Community Support

The second option for this group is not to use any kind of institutional facility, but to attempt to care for them in ordinary residential settings in the community by delivering intensive, flexible, domiciliary-based support. As indicated, this may be a particularly useful option for those who find the demands of living in close proximity with other patients (and staff) too stressful. It may also be more consistent with the expressed wishes of many service users who do not want to be labeled as mental patients and who do not want to live with a group of other people with mental health problems whom they do not know and have not chosen to be with (Carling, 1993; Tanzman, 1993). These are legitimate wishes and we should strive to take them seriously, if for no other reason than in doing so we may help to build a good relationship and thereby facilitate compliance with other aspects of care (e.g., medication). However, to be successful in supporting such a difficult group in ordinary community settings, the quality of the community care has to be quite extraordinarily good. The literature on using assertive case management approaches to support people with severe and disabling conditions is now quite impressive (e.g., Stein & Test, 1980; Olfson, 1990; Thompson, Griffith, & Leaf, 1990; Chapter 22), and there is little doubt that such interventions can maintain contact and reduce numbers and lengths of admissions for a significant number of the most severely disabled people. This can be achieved with higher levels of consumer satisfaction and no disadvantage in terms of symptomatic improvement, providing that the community teams have access to good medical and psychiatric care. The impact on improved social functioning is more doubtful and certainly takes longer to become evident. The effectiveness of these kinds of approaches with the group with whom we are concerned with here is less well researched, but there is now beginning to be some interest, particularly in those with forensic histories (Shepherd, 1993; Cooke, Ford, Thompson, Wharne, & Haines, 1994). We shall now focus on some of the practical problems for community teams in working with this population.

First, they need to be very clear about their aims and objectives. Many community mental health teams attempt to provide a mixture of extended outpatient support (mainly for people with neurotic disorders), treatment of acute crises (acting as an alternative to inpatient admission where this is feasible), and intensive support for a more disabled population whose needs are primarily social but who may, from time to time, go through periods of acute destabilization. Teams cannot perform all these functions simultaneously and well. Therefore, they need to be clear about their priorities and to have ways of monitoring their workloads so that they ensure they remain targeted on a particular client group.

Depending on their objectives, they will then need a particular skill mix within the team. If they are primarily concerned with symptomatic treatment (whether dealing with neurotic disorders or acute psychosis), they will need a highly professionalized team with very good medical and psychological input. However, if they are more concerned with delivering social care—as is often the case with the kinds of people we are concerned with today—then they may benefit from the input of nonprofessionally trained care assistants or support workers who can attend to the patients' practical needs (e.g., shopping, cooking, going to the Post Office). Of course, such workers will still need good professional supervision, and there are dangers in deprofessionalizing the service. However, there is also a balance to be struck between professional and nonprofessional involvement, and this can only be resolved by being clear about exactly what range of functions we wish teams to perform. It terms of professional skills, there is a strong argument for a collaboration between forensic specialists (e.g., psychiatrists, nurses, psychologists) and mainstream mental health professionals. The expertise of forensic colleagues in the ongoing assessment of risk and the management of noncompliance is of particular value.

Regarding the methods of operation of the team, they must be able to deliver at least daily visits and operate on an extended-hours basis (i.e., provide a service at evenings and weekends) preferably with some kind of on-call arrangement for 24-hour cover. To achieve this, they need to be adequately resourced, and team members should, ideally, have a more or less full-time commitment so that they can be restored to provide the after-hours cover. Teams also need to have limited and protected caseloads. The literature suggests that we should aim for caseloads of less than 20, preferably less than 10 (Ryan, Ford, & Clifford, 1991). Staff must also be prepared to practice assertive outreach and develop a different attitude to working with unmotivated clients. This may challenge some fundamental assumptions about the balance between the rights of the individual and the need to exert a degree of control and social pressure.

At the heart of effective teamworking lie the issues of communication and accountability. Teams need to be clear about not only what they are supposed to be doing, but also *who* is supposed to be doing it. To achieve this, they need to be effectively managed and, at least in the United Kingdom, this is probably the area that requires most attention (Onyett, Pillinger, & Muijen, 1995; Shepherd, 1995b). Effective team management requires weakening of professional line management structures and a strengthening of operational, clinical management. We also have to reconcile the apparent conflict between operational management of the team as a whole and the *individual* accountability of specific members. Within an effective team, each person remains responsible for his/her own actions within his/her sphere of professional or personal competence, and no one professional therefore carries ultimate responsibility for the actions of the team. Although certain individuals may have important statutory or legal responsibilities, the concept of ultimate clinical responsibility is therefore neither legally accurate nor conceptually clear. There is only the collection of individual responsibilities which go to make up the work of the team.

To maintain continuity, and because of the likelihood that individuals will be absent from time to time (e.g., on holiday, sick, on a training course), teams must also not adhere too strictly to a model of individual responsibility. They must share responsibilities and carry a team accountability for the transmission of information and the performance of certain actions. Hence, we need clear *individual* accountability within the framework of a well functioning *team* (Test, 1979). This is very difficult to achieve.

One of the key areas of individual responsibility (which also cannot be delegated) is to pass on clinically important information regarding the mental state or behavior of the patient to colleagues in the team or to outside agencies. Team members need to reconcile the conflict between the need to preserve confidentiality between themselves and the client, and the need for other professionals—and other agencies—to be aware of certain key information. In the case of Christopher Clunis, which was cited earlier, the greatest weaknesses in his care actually revolved around failures on the part of professional staff to pass on information concerning his mental state and behavior to relevant others. Similarly, in another recent horrific incident in which a young occupational therapist was murdered by a man suffering from schizophrenia (Andrew Robinson) who was, at the

time, detained in an acute inpatient unit, it was clear that there had been failures to communicate accurately regarding crucial information about previous violent incidents in his past. This information might have led staff to take a very different view of his dangerousness and therefore his appropriate management (Blom-Cooper, Hally, & Murphy, 1995). These are difficult decisions; clearly one doesn't want to argue for broadcasting personal information in an irresponsible way, but on the other hand, professionals cannot hide behind confidentiality as an excuse for poor or sloppy communication.

Last, teams need effective mechanisms of review, both in terms of their operational procedures and in terms of clinical matters. Teams are not fixed objects; they are continually changing and therefore they have to be continually reviewed. Similarly, clients are continually changing and it is the essence of good practice to ensure that their care is constantly monitored and adjusted in the light of changing needs and circumstances. This may be done on an individual or group basis. The content of such supervision must pay particular attention to the dangers of high EE and the staff frustrations discussed earlier. One must also be on guard for the development of overinvolved relationships between staff and patients. There is often an implicit challenge to succeed where others have failed, and this can blind staff to the realities—and the dangers—of where their relationships are leading.

Again, to refer to the case of Andrew Robinson (Blom-Cooper et al., 1995), for some time prior to the inpatient admission during which the murder took place he was maintained in the community by a single psychiatrist working more or less alone. They developed a close relationship and the psychiatrist came to believe that Robinson had been misdiagnosed and was actually suffering from a personality disorder, rather than schizophrenia. This led to an underestimation of the seriousness of his previous history of violence (he had attempted to murder a female fellow student with a shotgun), and this distorted picture was then transmitted to the professionals who were subsequently involved in his care. The inquiry team made it clear that, in their view, this contributed significantly to the final tragedy. They refer to the dangers of staff working alone and not being subject to regular peer review and regard this as a serious flaw. This clearly has implications for the process of risk assessment and management which is to be discussed next.

It has to be acknowledged that getting teams to work effectively together is difficult, but unfortunately there is no other way forward. The care of individuals with serious mental illness, particularly those with a potential for serious violence or self-harm, is simply too complicated to be carried out by any one individual. Effective teamwork is thus the *only* means whereby the range of necessary skills to address the problems can be brought together. Similarly, good teamwork is the only way that crucial information can be shared, and made available in a crisis, and that some semblance of continuity of care can be achieved. To be successful, teams have to use *all* the resources available, including the general practitioner, the family, and independent advocates acting on behalf of users, if they are available. Teams will also always be restricted by the social conditions and the infrastructure in which they operate. If the person is living in poor housing, with no money, nothing to do, hostile neighbors, and no social support, then it will be difficult for a team—no matter how good—to achieve very much. Effective teams are at the heart of good services, but they cannot be expected to plug the gaps left by a deficiency of basic provisions.

RISK ASSESSMENT AND MANAGEMENT

As we have seen time and again in this chapter, whether in residential settings or in the community, the central problem in the management of those with difficult and challenging behavior lies in the accurate assessment and management of their risk in terms of self-harm and/or harm to others. There is a considerable literature on the prediction of both violent and suicidal behavior (e.g., Monahan, 1988; Goldstein, Black, Nastullah, & Winokur, 1991; Crichton, 1995), and the somewhat depressing conclusion is that it is not possible to predict either, with any degree of accuracy, in the individual case. This is *not* to say that we know nothing about the kinds of factors that are associated with an increased risk of violence or self-harm, nor that we can do nothing to minimize and better manage risk in those who are vulnerable. However, despite understandable demands, both from the general public and the legal system, regrettably we cannot predict precisely who is likely to be a danger, nor when. The risk of misses and both false positives and false negatives is simply too high.

This has led to a shift in thinking away from the question of *predicting* behavior, toward making more informed, intelligent decisions regarding the degree of *risk* posed by an individual at a particular point in time. Thus, risk is no longer seen as a fixed characteristic of the person, but as dynamic entity which will change according to circumstances. Certain factors (e.g., a previous history of violence) will always be important, but need to be interpreted in the light of the present circumstances (e.g., receiving regular medication versus not receiving regular medication; in a similar relationship versus not in a similar relationship). This may be characterized as risk management (Pollock, McBain, & Webster, 1989), and as the English forensic psychiatrist Adrian Grounds has put it, "The test is not one of accuracy, but how defensible the decision is in terms of social realities and current scientific knowledge" (Grounds, 1995, p. 49). So, what are the risk factors that we should be looking for?

Both with regard to violence and self-harm, many of the factors that are most important in indicating an increased risk in psychiatric populations are the same as those indicating an increased risk in the general population. For example, with regard to violence, the best predictors are age (young), gender (male), social class (IV & V), and current substance abuse (Crichton, 1995). Similarly, for successful suicide, the best predictors are gender (male), social class (IV & V), unemployment, social isolation, and depressed mood, together with a sense of hopelessness and despair about the future (Caldwell & Gottesman, 1990; Williams & Pollock, 1993). Regarding both violence *and* self-harm, by far the most important single factor is *history*. This is why the communication of information concerning past history is so vital to effective management (see pp. 420, and also Ritchie et al., 1994; Blom-Cooper et al., 1995).

In terms of predicting violent behavior, Monahan (1981) has provided a brief list of questions based on the available research, and these are reproduced in Table 25.3. It is evident that the focus of these questions is on making a judgment as to what extent the person's current situation resembles situations in the past in which violence has occurred. Again, the crucial importance of clinicians being aware of the *details* of the index offense is underlined. There is also a recognition of cognitive and emotional factors which predispose the individual to cope in a violent or nonviolent way. This highlights the importance of the presence of acute symptoms, and it is clear that active psychotic symptoms significantly increase the risk of violent behavior (Swanson, Holzer, Ganju, & Jono, 1990; Link, Andrews, & Culle, 1992). Both Christopher Clunis and Andrew Robinson had clear histories of violent behavior when psychotic. The threshold for violent behavior is also lowered by drug or alcohol misuse (Soyka, 1994).

Table 25.3. Checklist for Predicting Violent Behavior

1. What are the person's relevant demographic characteristics?

2. What is the person's history of violent behavior?

3. What is the base rate of violent behavior among individuals of this person's background?

4. What are the sources of stress in the person's current environment?

5. What cognitive and emotional factors indicate that the person may be predisposed to cope with stress in a violent manner?

6. What cognitive and emotional factors indicate that the person may be predisposed to cope with stress in a *non*violent manner?

7. How similar are the contexts in which the person has used violent coping mechanisms in the past to the contexts in which the person is likely to function in the future?

8. In particular, who are the likely victims of the person's violent behavior and how available are they now?

9. What means does the person possess to commit violence?

Source: Adapted from Monahan (1981).

A detailed study of the events preceding violent incidents in hospital has recently been reported by Powell, Caan, and Crowe (1994). They studied over 1,000 incidents ranging from those in which the victim suffered actual injury (18%) to less severe incidents of verbal threat. The three most common antecedents were (1) patient showing a general raised level of agitation of disturbance, (2) patient being subject to clinical or legal restrictions, and (3) provocation by other patients, relatives, or visitors. It was rare for staff behavior to contribute directly to the incidents. They also noted that 8% ($n = 21$) of the individuals contributed to over 40% of the incidents (each responsible for 10 or more) and that these incidents were *less* likely to have the common antecedents (restrictions, provocation) and more likely to have serious incidents themselves (e.g., self-harm, absconding, arson) as antecedents. There was also an association between discharge diagnosis of paranoid schizophrenia and the severity of the incident. The authors discuss their results in terms of strategies for risk reduction and suggest that improving communication (to reduce misunderstandings, anxiety, etc.), reviewing certain aspects of the hospital regime (e.g., policies concerning restriction of move-

ments, how medication is administered), and intervening in certain interactions between patients, and with some visitors, might be of value. There are also some individuals who are clearly at greater risk than others, and their behavior clearly justifies particularly close monitoring.

Regarding the risk factors for suicide in schizophrenia, Table 25.4 provides a checklist based on Caldwell and Gottesman's (1990) excellent review.

Historical factors are again of central importance, but so too are psychological factors concerned with how well patients are coping with the impact of the disorder on their life and their hopes for the future. This raises the possibility that psychological interventions might have something to offer—at least in the ongoing management of these feelings of despair and hopelessness—and there is, indeed, a little evidence that specialized cognitive behavioral treatments may have some effect (Williams & Pollock, 1993).

However, for both suicide and violence, our ability to effectively intervene and change these patterns of behavior, even if we could predict them, is probably very limited. We therefore need to concentrate on the *management* of risk and how to minimize patients' and staff's exposure to risky conditions. As Grounds (1995) points out, it is also important to distinguish between "worry" and "risk."

Table 25.4. Checklist for Predicting Suicide in Schizophrenia

1. Is the person young (under 40) and male?

2. Do they have a past history of suicide attempts?

3. Have they experienced long-term problems with numerous relapses?

4. Are they currently unemployed?

5. Have they recently been discharged from inpatient treatment?

6. Are they currently unmarried and/or socially isolated?

7. Are they currently reporting depressed mood and/or suicidal ideation?

8. Do they have a realistic awareness of the deteriorating course of their condition and nondelusional pessimistic ideas about the future (particularly in association with good premorbid functioning)?

9. Do they show *either* (a) excessive dependence on treatment or (b) a loss of faith in treatment?

Source: Adapted from Caldwell & Gottesman (1990).

Unfortunately, there is often a poor correlation between the people who are most at risk and the people who staff are most worried about. We are all susceptible to trusting our own judgment of a situation, rather than relying on actuarial predictions of probability, but actuarial predictions are usually much more accurate. Staff must be aware of these predictive factors, based on a careful analysis of the individual case. Only then can effective risk management become a reality.

CONCLUSIONS

We have seen in this chapter that challenging behavior is challenging in more ways than one. It may not only challenge us physically, but also challenge services to respond in ways that are both humane and effective. At the center of the problems of caring for this group, there is a fundamental dilemma of where to draw the line between concerns for the liberties and civil rights of the individual and concerns for the safety of the public who must be protected from random acts of aggression or violence. If we are to succeed in resolving these dilemma, it will depend not only on good clinical care, but also on adequate resources and facilities and on the quality of the staff and the organization and training that we give them. If we fail to provide adequate care for this most vulnerable and difficult group, then not only will they jeopardize the rest of mainstream mental health services and the safety of the public, but also a number of unfortunate individuals will find themselves living in more restrictive conditions than perhaps is necessary.

We have mentioned the case of Christopher Clunis several times in this chapter and how the inquiry team found him in hospital, an "easy going man, articulate and with a good sense of humour." They go on to describe how, "He recalls being muddled, hallucinated and finding that he could not look after himself. His subsequent memory of admissions to hospitals or hostels and of the care he received, is of needing help, but not knowing how to ask for it; of lack of explanation as to what he was suffering from; of frustration that he was not involved in the decisions that were being made for him; and an absence of planned help towards settling down in a home of his own. He thought that some of the people who had sought to help him had tried very hard, but seemed not to understand his needs. He wanted to return to North London, but said he had no choice in the matter. 'A person in my position has not got the availability of choice' " (Ritchie et al., 1994, p. 103). This quote captures some of the muddle and confusion

surrounding the care of people with these kinds of problems. At their center is the muddle and confusion in the mind of the individual him or herself. Their needs are often very simple—a roof over their heads, food, money, suitable treatment for their symptoms, someone to talk to, and something meaningful to do. How to ensure that they receive these and also retain the availability of choice is, indeed, a considerable challenge.

REFERENCES

Baker, R., & Hall, J. N. (1983). *REHAB (Rehabilitation Evaluation Hall and Baker)*. Aberdeen: Vine Publishing.

Ball, R., Moore, E., & Kuipers, L. (1992). Expressed emotion in community care staff. *Social Psychiatry and Psychiatric Epidemiology, 27*, 35–39.

Barrowclough, C., Johnston, M., & Tarrier, N. (1994). Attributions, expressed emotion, and patient relapse: An attributional model of relatives' responses to schizophrenic illness. *Behaviour Therapy, 25*, 67–88.

Bennett, D. H. (1980). The chronic psychiatric patient today. *Journal of the Royal Society of Medicine, 73*, 301–303.

Bigelow, D. A., Cutler, D. J., Moore, L. J., McComb, P., & Leung, P. (1988). Characteristics of state hospital patients who are hard to place. *Hospital and Community Psychiatry, 39*, 181–185.

Blom-Cooper, L., Hally, H., & Murphy, E. (1995). *The falling shadow*. London: Duckworth.

Brewin, C. R., MacCarthy, B., Duda, K., & Vaughn, C. E. (1991). Attribution and expressed emotion in the relatives of patients with schizophrenia. *Journal of Abnormal Psychology, 100*, 546–554.

Caldwell, C., & Gottesman, I. (1990). Schizophrenics kill themselves too: A review of risk factors for suicide. *Schizophrenia Bulletin, 16*, 571–589.

Carling, P. (1993). Housing and supports for persons with mental illness: Emerging approaches to research and practice. *Hospital and Community Psychiatry, 44*, 439–449.

Clifford, P., Charman, A., Webb, Y., & Best, S. (1991). Planning for community care: Long-stay populations of hospitals scheduled for rundown or closure. *British Journal of Psychiatry, 158*, 190–196.

Cooke, A., Ford, R., Thompson, T., Wharne, S., & Haines, P. (1994). "Something to lose": Case management for mentally disordered offenders. *Journal of Mental Health, 3*, 59–67.

Creighton, F. J., Hyde, C. E., & Farragher, B. C. (1991). Douglas House: 7 year's experience of a community hostel ward. *British Journal of Psychiatry, 159*, 500–504.

Crichton, J. (1995). The prediction of psychiatric patient violence. In J. Crichton (Ed.), *Psychiatric patient violence: Risk and response* (pp. 27–33). London: Duckworth.

Dayson, D., Gooch, C., & Thornicroft, G. (1992). The TAPS project 16 difficult to place long-term psychiatric patients: Risk factors for failure to resettle long stay patients in community facilities. *British Medical Journal, 305*, 993–995.

Digby, A. (1985). *Madness, morality and medicine: A study of the York Retreat, 1796–1914.* Cambridge: Cambridge University Press.

Dozier, M., Harris, M., & Bergman, A. (1987). Social network density and rehospitalization among young adult patients. *Hospital and Community Psychiatry, 38*, 61–65.

Garety, P. A., Afele, H. K., & Isaacs, D. A. (1988). A hostel-ward for new long-stay psychiatric patients: The careers of the first 10 years residents. *Bulletin of the Royal College of Psychiatrists, 12*, 183–186.

Gibbons, J. S. (1986). Care of "new" long-stay patients in a District General Psychiatric Unit. *Acta Psychiatrica Scandinavica, 73*, 582–588.

Goering, P., Durbin, J., Foster, R., Bayles, S., Babiak, T. & Lancee, B. (1992). Social networks of residents in supported housing. *Community Mental Health Journal, 28*, 199–213.

Goldstein, R. B., Black, D. W., Nastullah, A., & Winokur, G. (1991). The prediction of suicide. *Archives of General Psychiatry, 48*, 418–422.

Gudeman, J. E., & Shore, M. F. (1984). Beyond deinstitutionalization: A new class of facilities for the mentally ill. *New England Journal of Medicine, 311*, 832–836.

Grounds, A. (1995). Risk assessment and management in a clinical context. In J. Crichton (Ed.), *Psychiatric patient violence: Risk and response* (pp. 43–59). London: Duckworth.

Holmes-Eber, P., & Riger, S. (1990). Hospitalization and the composition of mental patients' social networks. *Schizophrenia Bulletin, 16*, 157–164.

Hyde, C., Bridges, K., Goldberg, D., Lowson, K., Sterling, C., & Faragher, B. (1987). The evaluation of a hostel ward: A controlled study using modified cost-benefit analysis. *British Journal of Psychiatry, 151*, 805–812.

King, C., & Shepherd, G. (1994). *Outcomes in hospital hostels: A preliminary search for predictors.* Paper presented at the Ninth Annual TAPS Conference, Royal Free Hospital, London.

Kuipers, L., & Bebbington, P. (1988). Expressed emotion research in schizophrenia: Theoretical and clinical implications. *Psychological Medicine, 18*, 893–909.

Lelliot, P., & Wing, J. K. (1994). A national audit of new long-stay psychiatric patients. II: Impact on services. *British Journal of Psychiatry, 165*, 170–178.

Lelliot, P., Wing, J. K., & Clifford, P. (1994). A national audit of new long-stay psychiatric patients. I: Method and description of the cohort. *British Journal of Psychiatry, 165*, 160–169.

Link, B., Andrews, H., & Cullen, F. (1992). The violent and illegal behavior of mental patients reconsidered. *American Sociological Review, 57*, 275–292.

Mann, S., & Cree, W. (1976). "New" long stay psychiatric patients: A national sample survey of fifteen mental hospitals in England and Wales 1972–73. *Psychological Medicine, 6*, 603–616.

Martin, J. P. (1984). *Hospitals in trouble.* Oxford: Blackwells.

McCreadie, R. G., & McCannell, E. (1989). The Scottish survey of new chronic in-patients: Five-year follow-up. *British Journal of Psychiatry. 155*, 348–351.

McGlashan, T. H. (1988). A selective review of recent North American long-term follow-up studies of schizophrenia. *Schizophrenia Bulletin, 14*, 515–542.

Meltzer, H. Y. (1992). Treatment of the neuroleptic-nonresponsive schizophrenic patient. *Schizophrenia Bulletin, 18*, 515–542.

Mental Health Foundation. (1994). *Creating community care: A report of the Mental Health Foundation inquiry into community care for people with severe mental illness.* London: Author.

Monahan, J. (1981). *The clinical prediction of violent behavior.* U.S. Department of Health and Human Services.

Monahan, J. (1988). Risk assessment of violence among the mentally disordered: Generating useful knowledge. *International Journal of Law and Psychiatry, 11*, 249–257.

Moore, E., Kuipers, E., & Ball, R. (1992). Staff–patient relationships in the care of the long-term mentally ill. *Social Psychiatry and Psychiatric Epidemiology, 27*, 28–34.

O'Driscoll, C., Marshall, J., & Reed, J. (1990). Chronically ill patients in a district general hospital unit; A survey and two-year follow-up in an inner-London health district. *British Journal of Psychiatry, 157*, 694–702.

Okin, R. L., Pearsall, D., & Athearn, T. (1990). Predictions about new long-stay patients: Were they valid? *American Journal of Psychiatry, 147*, 1596–601.

Olfson, M. (1990). Assertive community treatment: An evaluation of the experimental evidence. *Hospital and Community Psychiatry, 41*, 634–641.

Onyett, S., Pillinger, T., & Muijen, M. (1995). *Making community mental health teams work.* London: Sainsbury Center for Mental Health.

Pollock, N., McBain, I., & Webster, C. D. (1989). Clinical decision making and the assessment of dangerousness. In K. Howells & C. R. Hollin (Eds.), *Clinical approaches to violence* (pp. 23–38). Oxford: Wiley.

Powell, G., Caan, W., & Crowe, M. (1994). What events precede violent incidents in psychiatric hospitals? *British Journal of Psychiatry, 165*, 107–112.

Prins, H. (1993). Offender-patients: The people nobody owns. In W. Watson and A. Grounds (Eds.), *The mentally disordered offender in an era of community care: New directions in provision* (pp. 7–19). Cambridge: Cambridge University Press.

Ranz, J. M., Horen, B. T., McFarlane, W. R., & Zito, J. M. (1991). Creating a supportive environment using staff psychoeducation in a supervised residence. *Hospital and Community Psychiatry, 42*, 1154–1159.

Reid, Y., & Garety, P. (1994). *A Hostel ward for "new" long stay patients: Sixteen years progress.* Unpublished manuscript. Department of Psychology, Institute of Psychiatry, London.

Ritchie, J. H., Dick, D., & Lingham, R. (1994). *The report of the inquiry into the care and treatment of Christopher Clunis.* London: HMSO.

Ryan, P., Ford, R., & Clifford, P. (1991). *Case management and community care.* London: RDP Publications.

Salit, S. A., & Marcos, L. R. (1991). Have general hospitals become chronic care institutions for the mentally ill? *American Journal of Psychiatry, 148,* 892–897.

Scull, A. T. (1982). *Museums of madness.* London: Penguin Books.

Sheets, J., Prevost, J., & Reihman, J. (1982). Young adult chronic patients: Three hypothesized subgroups. *Hospital and Community Psychiatry, 33,* 197–203.

Shepherd, G. (1991). Psychiatric rehabilitation for the 1990s. In F. N. Watts & D. H. Bennett (Eds.), *Theory and practice of psychiatric rehabilitation.* Chichester: Wiley.

Shepherd, G. (1993). Case management. In W. Watson & A. Grounds (Eds.), *The mentally disordered offender in an era of community care: New directions in provision* (pp. 106–121). Cambridge: Cambridge University Press.

Shepherd, G. (1995a). The "ward-in-a-house"—Residential care for the severely disabled. *Journal of Mental Health, 31,* 53–69.

Shepherd, G. (1995b). Care and control in the community. In J. Crichton (Ed.), *Psychiatric patient violence: Risk and response* (pp. 111–126). London: Duckworth.

Shepherd, G., King, C., & Gowler, D. G. (1994). Outcomes in hospital hostels. *Psychiatric Bulletin, 18,* 619–612.

Soyka, M. (1994). Substance abuse and dependency as a risk factor for delinquency and violent behavior in schizophrenic patients. *Journal of Clinical Forensic Medicine, 1,* 3–7.

Stein, L. I., & Test, M. A. (1980). Alternatives to mental health treatment: I. Conceptual model, treatment program and clinical evaluation. *Archives of General Psychiatry, 37,* 392–397.

Swanson, J., Holzer, C., Ganju, V., & Jono, R. (1990). Violence and psychiatric disorder in the community: Evidence from the epidemiologic catchment area surveys. *Hospital and Community Psychiatry, 41,* 761–770.

Tanzman, M. (1993). An overview of surveys of mental health consumers' preferences for housing and support services. *Hospital and Community Psychiatry, 5,* 450–455.

Test, M. A. (1979). Continuity of care. In L. I. Stein (Ed.), *Community support systems for the long term patient.* San Francisco: Jossey Bass.

Thompson, K., Griffiths, E., & Leaf, P. (1990). A historical review of the Madison model of community care. *Hospital and Community Psychiatry, 41,* 625–633.

Williams, J. M. G., & Pollock, L. (1993). Factors mediating suicidal behavior: Their utility in primary and secondary prevention. *Journal of Mental Health, 2,* 3–26.

Wing, J. (1992). *Epidemiologically-based mental health needs assessments.* London: Royal College of Psychiatrists.

Wyatt, R. J. (1991). Neuroleptics and the natural course of schizophrenia. *Schizophrenia Bulletin, 17,* 325–351.

Wykes, T. (1982). A hostel-ward for "new" long-stay patients: An evaluative study of a "ward-in-a-house." In J. K. Wing (Ed.), *Long term community care: Experience in a London borough* (pp. 59–97). Psychological Medicine Monograph Supplement 2. Cambridge: Cambridge University Press.

Wykes, T., & Wing, J. K. (1991). "New" long-stay patients: The nature and size of the problem. In R. Young (Ed.), *Residential needs of severely disabled psychiatric patients—The case for hospital hostels.* London: HMSO.

Young, R. (1991). *Residential needs of severely disabled psychiatric patients—The case for hospital hostels.* London: HMSO.

AUTHOR INDEX

SUBJECT INDEX